W9-CDU-737

History of the Theatre

HISTORY
of the
THEATRE

THIRD EDITION

Oscar G. Brockett
Indiana University

Allyn and Bacon, Inc.   ***Boston / London / Sydney / Toronto***

Copyright © 1977, 1974, and 1968 by Allyn and Bacon, Inc.,
470 Atlantic Avenue, Boston, Massachusetts 02210

All rights reserved. Printed in the United States of America. No
part of the material protected by this copyright notice may be
reproduced or utilized in any form or by any means, electronic
or mechanical, including photocopying, recording, or by any
information storage and retrieval system, without written permission from the copyright owner.

Library of Congress Cataloging in Publication Data

Brockett, Oscar Gross, 1923–
 History of the theatre.

 Bibliography: p.
 Includes index.
 1. Theater—History. 2. Drama—History and
criticism. I. Title.
PN2101.B68 1977   792'.09   76-52379

ISBN 0-205-05774-8

Second printing . . . November, 1977

CONTENTS

PREFACE

The first edition of this book was published in 1968, the second in 1974. Through this third edition I seek to update my account of the theatre's past. I shall be grateful if its reception equals that given the first two editions.

I have made many minor changes throughout the book in an effort to sharpen points, reinterpret data, and correct errors. I have also made a number of major changes. First, I have added one new chapter (chapter 4) in which I treat the Byzantine theatre, the rise of Islam, the early theatre of India and China, and major developments in western Europe between the fall of Rome and the high Middle Ages. Second, I have relocated the chapter on Oriental theatre in an attempt to place it more accurately within the chronological framework I have used throughout the book; I have also revised considerably many sections of my earlier account and have provided much new information about Eastern theatre and drama. Third, within each chapter I have added new sections about the intellectual, social, and political forces or events that place the theatre within the context of its own time. Fourth, I have introduced some new features. Each chapter now ends with a section, "Looking at Theatre History," in which I discuss problems relating to historical study and writing and in which I reprint excerpts from source materials. My motives in including this feature are to assist readers in understanding the problems posed by historical research, to familiarize them with some of the methods used by historians, and to develop in them a critical perspective on history and historiography. Toward these ends, I have also reprinted (see the Appendix) an essay on the nature, scope, materials, and methods of historical study. Fifth, the number

of illustrations has been considerably increased, and the overall quality of the illustrations has been greatly improved. Sixth, the format of the book has been wholly redesigned.

In this edition I have attempted to trace the development of the theatre from its beginnings until 1976, when I completed the manuscript. I have placed special emphasis on Europe and America and have treated the Oriental theatre much less extensively.

The theatre is an extremely complex institution, since it encompasses playwriting, directing, acting, costume, makeup, scenery, lighting, properties, theatre architecture, machinery, special effects, management, audiences, and criticism. I have touched on all of these subjects, although the space devoted to each varies. For example, because drama is treated as one element in the total theatrical context, only the basic outlines of its development have been traced, for it would require a book of equal or greater scope to do it justice. My objective has been to provide a chronological narrative of the theatre's history as an institution rather than an exhaustive treatment of any one part. Furthermore, since the theatre cannot be divorced from the many forces that have shaped it, I have sought not only to show how the theatre has developed but also to suggest whenever possible why it took particular paths. Although I have included facts in abundance, my major concern has been for those practices that give each era its distinctive flavor and those trends that were to influence succeeding eras.

While history aims at recapturing the past, it is seldom a purely factual study. The evidence, whether slight or copious, must always be interpreted. Thus, the scholarly reconstructions of theatrical practices in any period often vary widely. I have tried to alert readers to important differences of opinion and to encourage them to read several accounts before accepting any as definitive.

A book of this scope obviously depends heavily on the work of many scholars. It has been impossible for me to acknowledge each debt within the text, for to do so would double the length of the book. Instead I have included bibliographies arranged according to chapters, both as an indication of the principal sources used and as a guide to further reading. Since the theatre can at times be best understood through a study of visual materials, I have also supplied many illustrations in each chapter both to clarify the text and to give a flavor of the theatre in that period.

I acknowledge the assistance of many persons in the preparation of this book. In addition to the published works of established scholars, I am also indebted to countless students who have contributed to my knowledge in classes and seminars. For their assistance with illustrations, I wish to thank John Brokaw, William Elwood, John Hu, Wu-chi Liu, Robert Garfias, Rod Bladel, Allan Jackson, Anthony Latham, Nancy Murphy, and Craig Hamilton. For their assistance with translations, I am grateful to Barbara Spear and Lenyth Brockett. For their comments on my manuscript, suggestions for improvements, or for calling attention to errors in past editions, I thank John Brokaw, Wendell Cole, Herb Felsenfeld, Craven Mackie, John Hu, Stephen Archer, Abraham Grossman, David Copelin, Ed Kasky, and others whose names I may have failed to record here. For their editorial assistance, I wish to thank Frank Ruggirello, Nancy Farrell, and Nancy Murphy of Allyn and Bacon, Inc. My indebtedness to individuals, publishers, libraries, and collections for permission to reprint materials is acknowledged in the credits accompanying the illustrations and source materials.

History of the Theatre

1

The Origins of the Theatre

Theatrical and dramatic elements are present in every society, no matter how unsophisticated or complex it is. The elements are as evident in the dances and ceremonies of primitive peoples as they are in our own political campaigns, parades, sports events, religious services, and children's make-believe. Nevertheless, most participants do not consider such activities to be primarily theatrical, even when they make use of spectacle, dialogue, and conflict. Consequently, it is usual to acknowledge a distinction between *the theatre as a form of art* and *the incidental use of theatrical elements in other activities.* This distinction is especially important here, for it would be impossible to construct a coherent history of all the theatrical devices found in humanity's diverse undertakings through the ages. Therefore, this book is primarily about the theatre as an institution—its origin and subsequent development.

In seeking to describe the origin of the theatre, the historian must rely heavily upon theory, since reliable evidence is lacking. To answer the question "How did the theatre come into existence?" he must try to imagine a time before there were theatrical elements, and then theorize about how they may have been discovered, how they were refined, and how they were consolidated eventually into that autonomous activity labeled "theatre." But since much of this process occurred before the dawn of recorded history, it can be reconstructed by the historian only through guesswork. Therefore, it is not surprising that many theories about the origin of the theatre have been advanced and that none can be verified. But the most persistent of these theories declares that theatre developed from myth and ritual.

THE THEORY OF RITUAL ORIGIN

Interest in the origin of the theatre has increased steadily since the late nineteenth century, when anthropologists began to be fascinated by the problem. Since that time anthropological opinion has gone through at least three major phases.

During the first phase, extending from about 1875 to about 1915, anthropologists, led by Sir James Frazer, argued that all cultures go through the same evolutionary stages; consequently, those primitive societies still in existence supply reliable evidence about the origin of the theatre thousands of years ago. ("Primitive" is used throughout this chapter in the technical sense employed by anthropologists to designate a society that has not yet developed a written language.)

The process perceived by these early anthropologists may be summarized briefly. In the beginning, people gradually become aware of forces that appear to control their food supply and the other determinants of existence. Having no clear understanding of natural causes, they attribute them to supernatural or magical forces. Next, they begin to search for means to win the favor of these powers. Over a period of time, they perceive an apparent connection between certain of the devices they have used and the outcome they have sought to bring about. These devices are then repeated, refined, and formalized until they become rituals. At this stage, the entire group usually performs the rites, while the "audience" is the supernatural force.

Stories or myths usually grow up around the rites to explain, illustrate, or idealize them. Often these myths contain elements based on real events or persons, although they are usually considerably transformed in the stories. Frequently the myths include representatives of those supernatural forces which the rites celebrate or hope to influence. Performers may then impersonate the mythical characters or supernatural forces in the rituals or in accompanying celebrations. This impersonation is one sign of a developing dramatic sense.

As a people become more sophisticated, their conceptions of supernatural forces and causal relationships change. As a result, they abandon or modify some rites. But the myths that have grown up around the rites may be retained as a part of the group's oral tradition, and in some instances stories based on myth may be acted out in a simple drama divorced from all ceremonial concerns. When this occurs, the first significant step has been taken toward theatre as a specialized activity, and thereafter the aesthetic gradually comes to replace the utilitarian or religious aims of ritual. This, in summary, is the late nineteenth-century view of how the theatre developed out of ritual.

A few points should be made about these early anthropologists. First, they begin with two unstated assumptions: that they themselves are enlightened and objective scholars, whereas those about whom they are writing are superstitious and subjective savages; and that modern technological society is superior to all primitive cultures. Second, they approach the past through "cultural Darwinism"; that is, they apply Darwin's theory about the evolution of biological species to cultural phenomena—and as a result they argue that all human institutions have evolved through an inevitable process in which there is an orderly accretion of parts which lead from simple to complex forms. Consequently, their accounts convey an air of condescension about primitive peoples and conclude that in all societies cultural institutions go through similar developmental patterns.

A second phase of thought began around 1915 when another school of anthropologists (led by Bronislaw Malinowski) rejected Frazer's deductive method for an inductive approach. They concentrated on in-depth, on-the-spot studies of how specific societies function from day to day. Thus, they are often called "functionalists." They also viewed each culture as highly individual and cast considerable doubt on the earlier belief that evidence drawn from modern primitive groups can be used to explain the origin of institutions in antiquity. They suggest instead that cultural institutions originate and develop through processes which differ from one society to another.

After World War II a third phase was initiated by still other anthropologists, called structuralists, led by Claude Lévi-Strauss. (Most of today's anthropologists, nevertheless, continue to be functionalists.) Like the functionalists, Lévi-Strauss rejects cultural Darwinism and believes that each society develops along individual lines. On the other hand, like Frazer, he is concerned with universal patterns, although ones quite unlike those sought by Frazer. Lévi-Strauss is interested above all in how the mind functions and seeks the answer through an analysis of myth, which he considers a form of logic different from but no less complex than the logic used by advanced societies in scientific inquiry. He concludes that there are at least two ways of thinking—scientific and mythical/magical—that approach problems from different but equally valid perspectives. The "savage mind" (as Lévi-Strauss labels the mythical/magical) works primarily with signs rather than concepts. A society's modes of logic and thought can be found in these signs or images (embedded in myths and such visual embodiments as masks and rituals). In the "savage mind" they are in an integrated form, as opposed to the fragmented approach of societies in which knowledge and thought have been subdivided into fields such as science, history, and philosophy.

During the past century, then, anthropologists have written a great deal about the relationship of myth and ritual to cultural institutions and thought. Despite changes in approach, they agree on a fundamental point: that ritual and myth are important elements in all societies. Together, they support the belief that theatre emerged out of primitive ritual. Thus, today most critics and historians agree that ritual is one source of theatre, although not necessarily the only one. On the other hand, most scholars now reject the idea that theatre has followed a similar evolutionary pattern in all societies. Furthermore, they no longer view primitive societies condescendingly; they recognize that advanced societies may benefit from specialized knowledge and technology but are often deficient in the cohesiveness characteristic of less advanced groups.

USES AND MEANS IN RITUAL

Although the rituals of still-existing primitive societies are no longer considered entirely reliable evidence about the theatre's origin in antiquity, they continue to be helpful in other ways. For example, they can tell us much about the use to which ritual has been put in primitive societies (although not all such groups use ritual for all of the purposes we can perceive). A brief summary of these uses can be revealing.

First, ritual is a form of knowledge. Myth and ritual embody a society's understanding of the universe, for they represent attempts to define people and their relationship to the world.

Second, ritual may be didactic. Since the distinguishing mark of a primitive society is the absence of a written language, ritual may serve as a means of passing on traditions and knowledge. Many primitive tribes perform initiation rites, some occupying only a few days but others extending over years, to acquaint the young with sacred beliefs, taboos, mores, and history. Such rites are still common among Australian and African peoples and were once traditional among American Indians.

Third, ritual may be intended to influence or control events. One of the fundamental premises of many rituals is that a desired effect—such as success in battle, adequate rainfall, or the favor of some supernatural power—can be achieved by acting it out. For example, numerous rituals are related to seasonal changes, since some primitive peoples have not perceived that the years recur in a fixed pattern and have thought it essential to enact rites to insure the return of spring and the continuance of fertility. At times they have resorted to sexual orgies to induce fertility in the earth, or they have staged ritual combats between representatives of Winter/Death and Spring/Life, ending with the triumph of the latter.

Fourth, ritual is often used to glorify—a supernatural power, a victory in hunt or war, the society's past, a hero, or a totem (that is, an animal, plant, or natural element with which the group thinks itself closely related).

Fifth, ritual may entertain and give pleasure. Even the most serious ceremony provides pleasure through spectacle, the repetition of formal patterns, or the skill of the performers.

FIGURE 1.1 Bull Dance of the Mandan tribe of North America. Note the figures at center front wearing buffalo headdresses and skins. Painting by George Catlin (1796–1872). Courtesy National Collection of Fine Arts, Smithsonian Institution, Washington.

In seeking to synthesize types of myth and ritual, Joseph Campbell argues that most of them are related to one of three concerns: pleasure (food, shelter, sex, and parenthood); power (the urge to conquer, consume, or aggrandize self or tribe); and duty (to the gods, the tribe, or the mores and values of the society). These concerns work together to assure an abundance of food and children, power over enemies, and the integration of the individual into society (including acceptance of its world view).

It should be clear that most of these functions may be served, in varying degrees and ways, by theatre. Thus, primitive ritual and theatre as we know it are clearly related.

Similarly, ritual and theatre may employ the same basic elements: music, dance, speech, masks, costumes, performers, audience, and stage. For example, the majority of primitive rituals use pantomimic dance and rhythmical musical accompaniment as primary means. Vocal sound is also common but speech and dialogue are used less frequently. Masks and costumes are typical

FIGURE 1.2 Costume and mask made of bark cloth and used for a jaguar dance. From the Amazon River region of Brazil. Courtesy American Museum of Natural History, New York.

accessories. Many groups believe that a spirit is attracted by and enters into its likeness. Masks and costumes, therefore, are means of attracting or embodying the spirit to be controlled, consulted, or propitiated. They may also be used to represent an animal to be killed or as aids in bringing about desired events.

Makeup—in the form of paint, ashes, or juices—may supplement masks and costumes by covering parts of the body. There must also be "actors," highly skilled and disciplined ones when no deviations in the ritual are permitted. Once rites have become fixed, initiates, elders, or priests may exercise strict control over the performance and serve a function comparable to that of a theatrical director. An "acting area" and, if there are

spectators, an "auditorium" are also utilized. The spatial arrangements for rituals vary widely. A circular area surrounded by spectators is common, but in some instances, as in certain Australian ceremonies which use painted bark or cloth panels as a background, the audience sits or stands on three sides of the performers. Some groups employ a number of different performance sites or a continuous space, as when the participants move from the village to the sea and back again. Thus, the basic elements found in ritual are those used in our own theatre.

Is there then, no significant difference between ritual and theatre? Some scholars have made a sharp distinction, while others have argued that the differences are so minor that most ritual should be considered a part of theatrical history. This controversy cannot be resolved, but perhaps the grounds of disagreement can be lessened by considering some fundamental premises. First, the human mind cannot tolerate chaos; therefore, it is forever seeking order and in the process raising questions about the causes of things (how the world came into being; why natural phenomena occur or recur; why people act and react as they do). Out of this search, people in each age formulate ideas about their relationship to the gods, the universe, society, and themselves. Second, people shape their religion, science, social and political institutions, and art from these perceptions. Third, the theatre in each period reflects current beliefs about people and their place in the universe and in society. Thus, as peoples' view of causality and their place in the scheme of things alters, so too does the theatre, since it cannot help but reflect prevailing notions about truth and reality.

If we accept these premises, then it seems likely that, in the beginning, "theatrical" activity existed primarily within ritual, which at that time was humanity's primary means of formalizing views about itself and the world. Since primitive man tended to believe that supernatural powers were the major determinants of well-being, it is only logical that his formulations should be more nearly religious than secular. Later, as man's confidence in his own powers increased, so did the secular element in his theatre and drama, and, as specialized fields developed, theatre as an activity in its own right came to be separated from ritual, which still continued to serve religious purposes. Thus, the history of the theatre is in part a record of humanity's changing views of itself and the world. At times, ritual and theatre have merged, but in advanced societies, each usually serves distinct functions, even if the boundaries between them are not always sharply defined.

OTHER THEORIES OF ORIGIN

Although origin in ritual is the most popular, it is by no means the only theory about how the theatre came into being. A number of scholars have sought its source in storytelling. They declare that to relate and listen to stories are fundamental human traits. Consequently, they suggest a pattern of development in which the telling of tales (about the hunt, war, or other feats) is gradually elaborated, at first through the use by the narrator of impersonation, action, and dialogue and then through the assumption of each of the roles by a different person. According to this theory, then, drama and theatre originate in the narrative instinct. A closely related theory sees theatre as having gradually evolved out of dances that are primarily rhythmical and gymnastic or from imitations of animal movements and sounds. In each, it is in large part the virtuosity and grace of the performers that is valued, and supposedly these qualities are encouraged until they are elaborated into fully realized theatrical performances. Both of these theories depict the theatre as developing quite independently of ritual.

In addition to exploring the possible antecedents of theatre, scholars have also theorized about the motives that led men to develop the art we call theatre. Why did theatre develop and why was it valued after it ceased to fulfill ritualistic functions? Most answers fall back on theories about the human mind or about human needs.

In the fourth century B.C., Aristotle argued that man is by nature an imitative creature—that he takes pleasure in imitating persons, things, and actions and in seeing such imitations. In the twentieth century, a number of psychologists have suggested that man has a gift for fantasy, through which he seeks to reshape reality into more satisfying forms than those encountered in daily life. Thus, fiction (of which drama is one form) permits people to objectify their anxieties and fears so that they may confront them or to fulfill their hopes and dreams. In this sense, then, the theatre is one tool whereby people define and understand their world or one whereby they escape from unpleasant realities.

But neither the human imitative instinct nor penchant for fantasy invariably leads to an independent theatre. Therefore, additional explanations are required. One necessary condition seems to be a conception of the world sufficiently sophisticated to permit a detached and objective view of human problems. For example, one sign of this conception is the appearance of the comic vision, for it requires sufficient objectivity to view deviations from norms as ridiculous rather than as serious threats to the welfare of the whole group. Another sign is the development of an aesthetic sense. For example, as a people's conceptions of their world change, they often cease to consider certain rites and myths essential to their well-being. Nevertheless, they often retain the myths for some time as part of their traditional lore. Eventually they come to value these stories for their aesthetic qualities rather than for their religious or societal usefulness. Two other conditions related to the aesthetic sense are also important: the appearance of people who can organize theatrical elements into experiences of a high order, and a society that can recognize the value of theatre as an independent, specialized activity.

Another concept which helps to place the history of theatre in perspective is the theory of static and dynamic societies. In every society some forces seek to maintain existing conditions, while others promote change. Usually one tendency is dominant in a given society or during a particular period. A society also may be dynamic for a time and then become static. Those societies normally called primitive are ones that have become static at an early stage of development. But some advanced societies, such as those of Ancient Egypt or of Japan in the seventeenth and eighteenth centuries, also have become relatively static and have devoted their energies to maintaining an existing way of life and to suppressing forces that promote change. Still other societies have emphasized progress and have viewed stasis as a prelude to decay and dissolution.

Joseph Campbell's analysis of the differences between Western and Eastern thought throws some light on these contrasting conditions. In Western myths, the major concern is the relationship between two types of beings—gods and humans—and the distinctive qualities of Western thought may be attributed in part to the tension between those roles assigned the human and the divine. These roles are not fixed but vary considerably from one period to another and from one society to another. Sometimes major emphasis has been placed on the

FIGURE 1.3 Masked dancers at an Owuru Festival in Nigeria. Originally seven performers were used in this dance, but the number has now dwindled to two. Photo made in 1971. Courtesy of Phil Peek.

supreme power of god, with people relegated to a position of total dependence (this, in essence, is the religious view); at others, primary stress has been given to man's ability as a rational being to manage his own affairs (the humanistic view). Primitive, ancient Near Eastern and Egyptian, and Medieval man tended to emphasize the religious view and to see the world as controlled by divine will emanating from some eternal, unchanging realm. It was the Greeks who enlarged the human role and established the dominant strain in Western thought, in which man (sometimes as an agent of god but often quite independent) is assigned a major share in action and control. Since the Renaissance the humanistic vision has been increasingly accepted and the notion of divine interference has steadily decreased. Thus, in Western thought the world has come to be seen primarily from the human point of view—that is, as a place of conflict, change, and progress—with mankind as the principal agent both for good (through rationality) and evil (through selfishness).

On the other hand, the dominant strain in Eastern thought recognizes no basic dichotomy between god and man. In Eastern myths, man seeks to transcend temporal limitations and achieve oneness with the mystery of being, in which all divisions—including human and divine—disappear. Although on the surface everything in this world may seem tempestuous and ever-changing, behind this apparent flux lies a harmony so complete as to defy all attempts to define it. The Eastern view encourages a conception of world order in which all duties, roles, and possibilities are fixed; it does not see reality as a series of constantly changing relationships (as does the West) but as a fixed state of being. Man cannot influence this being; he can only try to become one with it. Consequently, to the Eastern mind change and progress are illusions, whereas to the Western mind they are the essence of truth and reality.

Perhaps this helps to explain why the theatrical traditions of Asia and Africa have been most attuned to tradition and stasis, those of Europe to progress and change. This book will trace the "progressive" European tradition. Before taking up that history, however, it is necessary to look briefly at developments in Egypt and the Near East, where civilization is usually thought to have begun.

RITUAL IN ANCIENT EGYPT AND THE NEAR EAST

Recent studies of artifacts from the Ice Age have suggested that people may already have been performing rituals some 30,000 years ago. Several centuries later (about 20,000 years ago) man left a record in the form of paintings on the walls of caves in France and Spain that suggest rituals related to hunting. But our ideas about these early artifacts remain vague because we lack information that would clarify them.

The picture becomes somewhat clearer when we reach the period in which humans began to develop the skills and habits that made civilization possible: the domestication of animals (by *c.* 9000 B.C.); the cultivation of grain (by *c.* 7000); the invention of pottery (by *c.* 6500); and the abandonment of a nomadic existence as hunter and food-gatherer to become fixed residents raising animals and food. The earliest permanent settlements seem to have been established in that part of the Near East called Mesopotamia sometime around 8000 B.C. Evidence surviving from that time shows that fertility rites were already common.

By 3500 to 3000 B.C., cities had grown up in both Mesopotamia and Egypt, and by 3000 Egypt had formed an effective central government. For 2,500 years thereafter, Egypt and the Near East were to be the major centers of civilization. Forms of writing were devised and elaborate monuments and buildings were constructed. Although Egypt and the Near East developed more or less simultaneously, in the brief overview that follows Egypt will be given primary emphasis, since it was more stable than the Near East where numerous empires (Sumerian, Babylonian, Hittite, Assyrian, Chaldean, Canaanite, and Persian) flourished and declined.

Most of our information about ancient Egypt is based on the hieroglyphics, decorations, and artifacts preserved in the great pyramids built as tombs for the pharoahs and in the temples of the numerous Egyptian gods. Many of these remains relate in some way to Egyptian myths whose most typical feature is the recurrence of birth, maturity, death, and resurrection—the pattern of the seasons and of life. This pattern is embodied in

stories of gods who engage each other in battles, are killed, and resurrected. These stories of the gods, in turn, are also associated with the pharoah, who himself was usually considered to be a god. Thus, though one pharoah may die, another takes his place, just as one season follows another. Consequently, the myths reveal the triumph of order and continuity over chaos and disruption in both the universe and the state.

The Egyptian myths formed the basis for numerous rituals. It is difficult to assess to what degree these rituals were dramatic, since scholars disagree about what many of the surviving texts represent. For example, hieroglyphics and scenes, depicting the trials through which the spirit must pass before being admitted to an honorable place in afterlife, appear on the walls of many pyramids. The more than fifty surviving "Pyramid Texts" date from around 2800 to 2400 B.C.; although

FIGURE 1.4 Horned god (or a man disguised as an animal). Drawing from a prehistoric cave in the Volp River region of France. The figure has been redrawn by the Abbé H. Breuil. From Henri Begouen and l'Abbé H. Breuil, *Les Cavernes du Volp* (1958). Courtesy Arts et Métiers Graphiques, Paris.

FIGURE 1.5 Egyptian acrobatic dancers. Note how the hair is weighted and how the figures at left seem to be providing a clapping accompaniment. Relief sculpture from a tomb at Saqqara.

Another ritual, sometimes called the Memphite Drama, appears to have been performed each year on the first day of spring. It dates from about 2500 B.C. and tells of the death and resurrection of Osiris and the coronation of Horus. Some historians interpret this as a drama in which Horus, symbolizing the regenerated year spirit, was impersonated by the pharoah.

But the most important of Egyptian rituals was the so-called Abydos Passion Play, which treated the

certain passages were probably traditional by that time and may have originated a thousand years earlier. Some scholars have argued that they are dramas which were enacted by priests at regular intervals to insure the well-being of the dead pharoah and to show the continuity of life and power. This view that the works are dramatic is based principally on the presence of occasional passages of dialogue and indications of action. But there is no definitive evidence that they were intended to be acted out or that they were ever performed. Consequently, equally reputable scholars have denied any connection between the Pyramid Texts and dramatic representation, pointing out that such nondramatic works as epic poems and the Bible also contain passages in dialogue and indications of action.

Other contested texts relate to the coronation of pharoahs. One of the few remaining fragments has been interpreted by some scholars as a series of ritualistic scenes performed at various places in Egypt, with the new ruler symbolically taking possession of his kingdom in this way. In this text, the pharoah is associated with Horus, who in mythology succeeded his father, Osiris, as king.

FIGURE 1.6 A Near Eastern wall panel from the palace of Ashur-nasir-apal II, King of Assyria, ninth century B.C. Depicted is an eagle-headed, winged-being pollinating a sacred tree. This appears to be connected with fertility rites and the cycle of life. Courtesy Metropolitan Museum of Art, Gift of John D. Rockefeller, Jr., 1932.

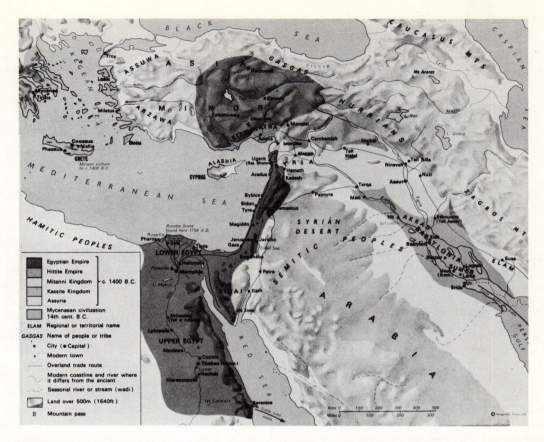

FIGURE 1.7 **Map showing the empires of the Middle East and Eastern Mediterranean,** *c.* **1400 B.C.
From** *Pergamon General Historical Atlas* **(1970). Reprinted by permission of the Pergamon Press, Inc.**

death and resurrection of the god Osiris. According to Egyptian mythology, Osiris, son of Geb (the earth) and Nut (the sky), succeeded his father as ruler and married his sister Isis. His brother, Set, jealous of Osiris' power, eventually killed him and buried parts of the body at various spots in Egypt. Isis gathered the pieces of the body and, with the aid of Anubis, later the god of embalming, revived Osiris. Unable to remain on earth, Osiris, after his body was buried at Abydos, went to dwell in the underworld, where he became the judge of souls. Horus, the son of Osiris, fought with Set and won back his father's kingdom. This was the most revered of all Egyptian myths.

At Abydos, the most sacred spot in Egypt, a ritual relating to Osiris (the Abydos Passion Play) was performed annually from about 2500 until about 550 B.C. In spite of this long history, no part of the text remains.

What we know of it is deduced primarily from an account left by Ikhernofret, a participant sometime between 1887 and 1849 B.C., in which he tells what he did during one of the celebrations. Again, however, scholars disagree markedly in their interpretations of Ikhernofret's account. Some have argued that the major events of Osiris' life were reenacted with much spectacle (including battles, processions, and burial ceremonies), the principal roles being taken by priests and the crowds portrayed by the people. Furthermore, they suggest that each section of the play was performed in a different location, and perhaps over several weeks or months. According to them, this ritual was one of the most elaborate dramatic spectacles ever staged. Contrarily, other historians have vigorously objected to the designation of this ritual as a "passion play" and have denied that the life or death of Osiris was reenacted. Rather, they see the ritual as

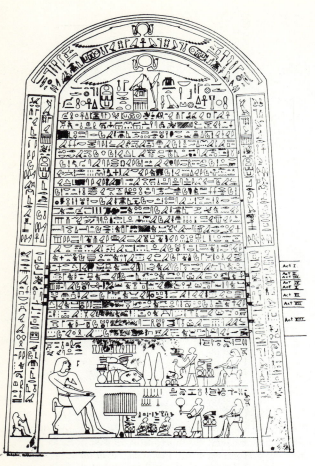

FIGURE 1.8. The Ikhernofret stone (dated about 1868 B.C.), the primary evidence concerning the so-called Abydos Passion Play. At right, the events have been divided into acts by a modern scholar. From Schaefer, *Untersuchungen zur Geschichte und Altertumskunde Aegyptens,* IV (1904).

commemorating all the dead pharoahs, each of whom is symbolized in Osiris. They argue that the basic premise of the ritual was that Osiris is dead and that consequently the ceremony had the characteristics of a royal funeral.

In addition to Egyptian rituals, others from the Near East—Sumerian, Babylonian, Hittite, Canaanite, and so on—date from *c.* 2500 B.C. onward and show that the number of gods worshipped by the people of that region was enormous. Their rituals were for the most part concerned with the seasonal pattern of birth, growth, maturity, death, and rebirth. (Translations and discussions of selected Near Eastern and Egyptian texts can be found in Theodor Gaster's *Thespis.*)

As this brief survey should suggest, the difficulty in studying these early years lies not in establishing that numerous rituals were enacted but in determining how they were enacted. Present-day religious services certainly do little to help us envision them. In Egypt and the Near East a temple was usually considered to be the private residence of the god, to which admission was granted no one other than those (priests) appointed by the ruler to act as the god's servants. These priests dressed the god's image daily, served him food, and treated him as they might the king himself (who was often considered to be a god or god's representative on earth). Through most of the year, then, the ordinary people participated in major religious rites only at second hand through the ruler and his priest-assistants. But on a few occasions each year, the god's image was taken from the temple in a procession over some prescribed route where at certain stations rites were performed in the presence of (and sometimes with limited participation by) the general populace. Thus, the common people were allowed only occasional glimpses of their earthly and heavenly rulers. It seems likely that the rites, both those performed within the temples and out-of-doors, were elaborate, lavish, and precise, for nothing less would have been thought suitable to beings greater even than the king himself.

Some historians have suggested a direct influence from Egypt and the Near East on the development of Greek theatre and drama. The most important evidence in support of this view is found in an account by the Greek historian Herodotus (*c.* 484–*c.* 425 B.C.). After visiting Egypt about 450 he noted two performances there and suggested that Dionysus, the god in whose honor plays were presented in Greece, was another version of Osiris. But although Herodotus points out interesting parallels, no direct connection has yet been established between the Egyptian and Greek theatrical traditions. Even if direct influence could be verified, an important difference between Egypt and Greece would remain. The Egyptians maintained an advanced civilization for about 3,000 years (a period longer than the one that separates us from the beginnings of Greek drama) and never developed theatrically beyond ritual. Theirs was a relatively static society which resisted changes that might have led to an autonomous theatre. The Greeks, on the other hand, took steps that established the theatre as an independent institution. Thus, it is in Greece that one must seek the beginnings of the European tradition in theatre and drama.

LOOKING AT THEATRE HISTORY

The difficulties encountered by a present-day historian seeking to deal with Egyptian texts can be seen in this translation of Ikhernofret's account of his participation in the ceremonies at Abydos:

I celebrated the (feast of) "Going Forth" of Upwawet, when he proceeded to champion his father. I repelled the foe from the sacred barque, I overthrew the enemies of Osiris. I celebrated the "Great-Going-Forth," following the god at his going. I sailed the divine boat of Thoth upon ——. I equipped the barque (called) "Shining-in-Truth" of the lord of Abydos, with a chapel. (I) put on his regalia when he went forth to —— Peker; I led the way of the god to his tomb before Peker; I championed Wennofer at "That Day of the Great Conflict"; I slew all the enemies upon the flats of Nedyt. I conveyed him into the barque (called) "The Great," when it bore his beauty; I gladdened the heart of the eastern highlands; I ——ed the rejoicing in the western highlands. When they saw the beauty of the sacred barge, as it landed at Abydos, they brought [Osiris, First of the Westerners, lord] of Abydos to his palace, and I followed the god into his house, to attend to his ——, when he resumed his seat. I loosed the knot in the midst of his attendants, among his courtiers.

Translation from JAMES HENRY BREASTED, *Ancient Records of Egypt,* vol. I (Chicago: University of Chicago Press, 1906), p. 300.

Roger Shattuck suggests another approach to historical study. Shattuck tells of his visit to Egypt, his inability to understand the ruins, and his puzzlement over why, even after studying translations, Egyptian inscriptions "seemed so uninteresting, so completely devoid of profound thought, of anything but the most superficial ritual of religion, of any convincing description of human actions and feelings." Then Alexandre Varille, an Egyptologist working in Egypt, explained to Shattuck his belief that the Egyptians expressed their knowledge through a form of total symbolism which requires that all elements of a building (including the inscriptions) be considered as a whole; that to isolate an inscription in order to "translate" it robs it of its meaning. Varille declared:

No one in our day has grasped the whole message. The inscriptions, read alone, come out as dry descriptions of ceremonial or lists of royal exploits. . . . A literary translation, no matter how well it is done, will never serve. The Egyptians had no literature as we know it. . . . This [temples and monuments] is their writing. . . . How do you translate a temple unless you can stand someone inside it and walk around it and . . . talk about it? There is a way. . . . A film. Or rather hundreds of films. In a film I can show a general view of a building, its plan, an overlay of successive plans alternated with details of the structure, inscriptions . . . , and the fall of the sunlight and moonlight, which often picks out the text appropriate to a particular season.

Shattuck concludes:

So great a distance intervenes between us and Egypt, the premises of their thinking in religion, politics, philosophy, and morality are so remote from ours, that . . . the first task of translation will be to find a suitable form. . . . The only language we know that can begin to express three millenia of dressed stone architecture and divine kingship lies in our most complex and sensitive art form, the moving picture. . . . The film director has yet to claim his role as translator of certain domains of expression still barely explored.

ROGER SHATTUCK, "Artificial Horizon: Translator as Navigator," *The Craft and Context of Translation,* a symposium edited by William Arrowsmith and Roger Shattuck (Austin: University of Texas Press, 1961). The material summarized above appears on pages 142–145.

2

Theatre and Drama in Ancient Greece

While the civilizations of the Near East and Egypt were flourishing, others were evolving in neighboring areas. For our purposes, the most important were the Aegean forerunners of the Greeks. The Minoan culture flourished on the island of Crete from about 2500 until 1400 B.C., when it was destroyed by an earthquake or fire in a catastrophe still little understood. After this time, interest shifts to the mainland of Greece, especially Mycenae, where an Helladic culture, partly influenced by Crete, flourished from around 1600 to 1100 B.C. Another major center was Troy, a city in Asia Minor near the entrance to the Hellespont, a civilization destroyed by the Greeks in the Trojan War around 1184–1174 B.C. Shortly afterwards, Mycenean civilization was overrun by invaders from the north and a "dark age" followed which lasted from *c.* 1100 to 800 B.C. These early Aegean civilizations had little to do directly with the development of the theatre, but their indirect influence was enormous, for their gods, heroes, and history supplied the material for Homer's (eighth century B.C.) *Iliad* and *Odyssey* and for most Greek drama. Thus, these civilizations are in many ways the fountainhead of Western literature.

The Greek civilization that was to produce the first great era of the theatre gradually took shape between the eighth and sixth centuries. The major political unit came to be the *polis* (or city-state, composed of a town and its surrounding countryside). The most important of these city-states were Attica (Athens), Sparta, Corinth,

Thebes, Megara, and Argos, but there were others on the coast of Asia Minor and on the Aegean islands; in addition, after 750 B.C., numerous colonies were founded in places ranging from the Black Sea in Asia to the coasts of Africa, Spain, and France, although the most important were those in Sicily and southern Italy. All of these Greeks acknowledged their kinship and considered all non-Greeks to be barbarians, but they also insisted on differences among themselves based primarily on dialect. The primary divisions were Dorian (with Sparta and Corinth as the major cities) and Ionian (represented by Athens and the cities of Asia Minor). Most of these states depended on control of the seas (as the major avenue of trade) for their wealth, power, and well-being. Consequently, rivalries for dominance motivated them to form leagues or to wage war with each other or with non-Greek states.

In the beginning, the city-states were ruled by kings, but after 800 B.C. nobles were able to assume considerable power. The more ambitious nobles soon learned they could win support through promises of improved rights for tradesmen and farmers, who had few privileges. A number of "tyrants" won control of states through such means between 650 and 500 B.C. Many of these tyrants did much to improve social conditions and to promote the arts. For example, Peisistratus, who dominated Athens from 560 to 510, redistributed land, promoted farming and foreign trade, made Athens the leading center of the arts, and established or enlarged

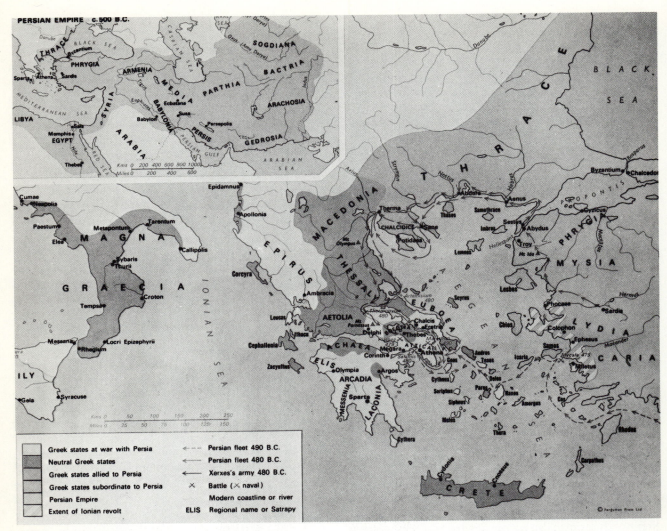

FIGURE 2.1 Map showing Greek territories, *c.* 480 B.C. From *Pergamon General Historical Atlas* (1970). Courtesy Pergamon Press, Inc.

numerous festivals (including the City Dionysia, which was to be the major home of drama). But by the late sixth century Greeks were weary of tyrants and found means to prevent them from assuming power. Athens' solution was to found the world's first democracy (in 508).

Although by 500 B.C. Athens was the artistic center of Greece, Sparta was the major power and the head of an alliance that encompassed most of the city-states, including Athens. But war with Persia soon altered this arrangement. At the beginning of the fifth century, Persia, already the most extensive empire in the world, sought to expand into Europe. In 490 the Greeks de-

feated the Persians at Marathon, and in 480–479 the Athenian fleet dealt the Persians a mortal blow. Because of troubles at home, in 477 Sparta withdrew from further involvement in the conflict (which continued for many years as Greek cities in Asia Minor rebelled against Persia). Consequently, Athens rapidly became the major force in the Mediterranean, and in return for protecting others it exacted payments and gained other rights which brought it great wealth and power. In effect, Athens ruled an empire during the remainder of the fifth century. Under the leadership of Pericles (*c.* 460–430 B.C.), Athens built numerous temples and public buildings (among them the Parthenon and portions of the Theatre of Dionysus). Athens' political power was broken in 404, when it was defeated in the Peloponnesian War, but throughout the fifth century it enjoyed a privileged place both politically and artistically.

No doubt the Athenians' confidence in their strength and worth did much to motivate artistic expression during the fifth century. Equally important, however, was the Greek view of man and the gods, never a wholly coherent view since it was composed of diverse elements (some derived from the earlier Helladic civilization, some from more recent times, and others from adjacent societies). For the most part, the Greeks conceived of their gods in human terms. Zeus presided over a number of other deities who were as unpredictable as their earthly counterparts. If wooed with prayers and sacrifices, the gods might help men, but they were just as apt to take offense and hold grudges. Furthermore, they often differed among themselves, and some assisted and others opposed the same men or undertakings. In addition, the gods themselves were not immune to Fate, which lurked behind all Greek thought and made all destiny, both human and divine, uncertain.

Perhaps the most important aspect of Greek culture, unlike that of any people who preceded them, was its central concern with man. The Greeks were the inventors of philosophy, and they systematically raised and sought answers to almost all issues, including the nature of the gods and the universe. As time went by, they became increasingly skeptical about Greek myths, and before the end of the fifth century Protagoras had proclaimed, "Man is the measure of all things."

Nevertheless, the Greeks never ceased to set limits on what man can know, and they always acknowledged the unpredictability of fate. Thus Greek thought is characterized by a tension between belief in human rationality and recognition of irrational and unknowable elements. That the Greeks established democracy tells much about their faith in man, although even here they were not wholly consistent, for they did not hesitate to enslave others. Overall, in Greek thought man was elevated to a place of great prominence, but happiness still depended on a conjunction of human and superhuman forces; when the two were in harmony, life could be peaceful, but the truce was always fragile and could be broken without warning. Such a view promoted a drama that centers on human struggles, but one in which the supernatural element always reminds us that we have not left the era of ritual behind altogether.

THE ORIGIN OF TRAGEDY

As in all emerging societies, records relating to the origin of theatre and drama in Greece are scarce. The Greeks learned to write sometime after 700 B.C., when they borrowed the Phoenician alphabet and adapted it to their own use. Thereafter, written records increase, but those relating to the theatre continued to be rare until the Athenian government accorded official sanction and financial support to drama. This connection between theatre and state began in 534 B.C. when Athens instituted a contest for the best tragedy presented at the City Dionysia, a major religious festival.

Although tradition credits Thespis (winner in 534 of the first contest) with the invention of drama, some ancient accounts place him as late as sixteenth in the line of tragic poets. This disparity is probably due to impreciseness in the original meaning of *tragedy* (literally "goat song"), a term now thought to date from a time when the chorus danced either for a goat as a prize or around a goat which was then sacrificed. Unfortunately, none of the theories about how the term tragedy originated (and there are many) provides important clues as to how the dramatic form we call tragedy evolved.

The earliest still-extant account of how Greek drama originated—a chapter in Aristotle's *Poetics* (c. 335–323 B.C.)—states that tragedy developed out of improvizations by the leaders of dithyrambs. Consequently, it may be helpful to look briefly at the dithyrambic form, a hymn sung and danced in honor of Dionysus, the Greek god of wine and fertility. Originally the dithyramb probably consisted of an improvised story (sung by a choral leader) and a traditional refrain (sung by the chorus). It was later transformed into a literary composition by Arion (c. 625–585 B.C.), allegedly the first to write dithyrambs on well-defined, heroic subjects and to give them titles. Arion is sometimes associated with the beginnings of tragedy because his performers were called *tragoidoi* and their songs *tragikon drama*. Furthermore, Arion lived at Corinth, a major center of the Dorian Greeks, who later claimed to have invented tragedy. Although this claim is unjustified (insofar as a dramatic form is concerned), the Dorians did develop to a high degree certain elements in the dithyramb—lyric poetry, choral singing and dancing, and mythological subjects—which were later emphasized in dramatic tragedy. That the Dorians considered Arion's compositions to be tragedy probably explains why some ancient writers placed Thespis so late in the line of tragic writers.

FIGURE 2.2 Men dressed in bird costumes, probably for some ritual. Note the flute player at the extreme left. A Greek vase of the late sixth or early fifth century B.C. Courtesy British Museum.

Exactly how dithyramb may have evolved into tragedy or over how long a period is unclear, but the final step is now usually attributed to Thespis. His innovation probably involved the addition of a prologue and lines (spoken by an actor impersonating characters) to what had previously been a wholly narrative work sung and danced by a chorus and its leader. This change did not come about by enlarging the role of the chorus leader (the *coryphaios*), for he continued his original function after the introduction of an actor (the Greek term for which was *hypokrites* or "answerer"). Virtually nothing is known of Thespis. It is possible that as early as 560 B.C. he was performing in Icaria, a subdivision of Attica. Horace, writing some 500 years later, declares that Thespis traveled about on a cart with plays. If that is true, Thespis probably performed in several Greek towns other than Athens.

Not all scholars believe that Greek drama developed out of dithyramb. Alternate theories are numerous and too complex to summarize here. One declares that drama evolved from rites performed at the tombs of heroes, and almost all depict drama as having gradually emerged from rituals of one kind or another. In a quite different vein, Gerald Else has advanced the theory that drama was a deliberate rather than a gradual creation. As he sees it, for some time prior to 534 religious festivals had featured oral readers (or rhapsodes) in recitations of passages from such epic poems as the *Iliad* and *Odyssey*. He believes that these readings had become increasingly dramatic and that when the City Dionysia was reorganized in 534 the crucial step of joining dramatized narrative and chorus was taken. Else more or less reverses the dithyrambic theory, for he believes that the individual performer (the rhapsode) linked his work to a chorus rather than emerged from it.

But all of the theories must remain conjectural, for evidence to substantiate any of them is missing. Whatever its origin, the major step toward drama had been taken by 534 B.C., when it was accorded official recognition. At this time an association with Dionysus was also established, one which was to continue, for thereafter all state-sponsored dramatic productions in Athens were given at festivals in honor of that god.

THE CITY DIONYSIA IN THE SIXTH CENTURY

The worship of Dionysus probably originated in the Near East and was imported into Greece perhaps as early as the thirteenth century B.C. At first the cult met considerable resistance because of its ecstatic nature: its celebrations often involved intoxication, sexual orgy, and the rending and devouring of sacrificial victims (frequently human). In spite of all resistance, however, worship of Dionysus was gradually accepted throughout Greece. In some places he displaced other gods whose attributes were then assigned to him. Gradually the orgiastic aspects of the Dionysian rites abated and by the sixth century they had largely disappeared.

According to myth, Dionysus was the son of Zeus (the greatest of Greek gods) and Semele (a mortal). Reared by satyrs (who are often associated with him in dithyramb, drama, and art), he was killed, dismembered, and resurrected. As a god, he was associated with fertility, wine, and revelry, while the events of his life linked him with the year-spirit found in other early religions—that is, the cycle of the seasons and the recurring pattern of birth, maturity, death, and rebirth. Through their rites, Dionysian worshippers sought a mystical union with the primal creative urge. On a more practical level, they sought to promote fertility: to guarantee the return of spring, the productivity of both human beings and the land, and ample harvests.

The Greeks honored each of their gods through one or more annual festivals. In Attica, where Athens was the principal town, four festivals were held each year in honor of Dionysus, and it was at one of these—the City Dionysia—that drama was first presented. Although the City Dionysia was the last of the four festivals to be inaugurated, it rapidly became the most important after it was reorganized in 534, the year in which tragedy was recognized.

From time to time the events that made up the City Dionysia were altered to meet changing conditions. In 508 the Athenian democracy was created and, in order to break up the family loyalties which had been at the root of past rivalries, all the inhabitants of Attica were divided into ten tribes. It may have been out of the desire to stimulate loyalty to the recently created tribes that about this time a new contest—for dithyrambic performances—was inaugurated at the City Dionysia. Thereafter, each tribe, in competition with the other nine, presented one dithyramb each year. Around 501 another innovation in the City Dionysia added a contest for satyr plays. After this time, each dramatist was required to present three tragedies and a satyr play each time he entered the competition. Thus, by 500 the City Dionysia had become relatively complex.

Other than Thespis, only three dramatists of the sixth century are known to us: Choerilus, Pratinas, and Phrynichus. Choerilus, who began competing between 523 and 520 and continued into the fifth century, is said to have written 160 plays, to have won 13 contests and to have made unspecified innovations in costumes and masks. Pratinas, who wrote about 50 dramas, was especially noted for satyr plays, a form he is sometimes said to have invented. Phrynichus (*fl.* 511–476), the first author known to have written on contemporary subjects, is also credited with introducing female characters into drama. He was noted for the beauty of his choral lyrics and for inventing new varieties of choral dance.

No drama from the sixth century has survived. The scraps of information that have come down to us suggest that in these early years experimentation with dramatic forms and conventions was common, that the lyrical and choral elements were dominant and highly developed, that all characters were played by a single actor (who used masks and costumes to effect changes in role), and that subject matter was drawn primarily from mythology or occasionally from recent history.

TRAGEDY IN THE FIFTH CENTURY

Our knowledge of Greek tragedy is based almost entirely on the work of three playwrights of the fifth century: Aeschylus, Sophocles, and Euripides. Historians usually assume that the surviving plays are representative, but it is perhaps well to remember that only 31 tragedies by three authors remain from the more than 1,000 that were written by numerous playwrights between 500 and 400 B.C.

A number of recurring structural features can be perceived in the surviving plays. Most of the tragedies begin with a *prologue* which provides information about events that have occurred prior to the opening of the play. Next comes the *parodos*, or entrance of the chorus; if there is no prologue, the *parodos* begins the play. The *parodoi* of extant plays vary in length from 20 to 200 lines; they introduce the chorus, give exposition, and establish the proper mood. Following the *parodos*, a series of episodes, varying in number from three to six and separated by choral songs (or *stasima*), develop the main action. The *exodus*, or concluding scene, includes the departure of all the characters and the chorus.

The point of attack in the plays is late—that is, the story is usually taken up just prior to the climactic moment, and only the final part is dramatized. Thus considerable exposition of earlier events is required. Most of the tragedies (but not all of them, for example, Sophocles' *Ajax* is an exception) place scenes of death and physical violence offstage; this convention requires the frequent use of messengers to relate what has occurred elsewhere. In most of the plays, the time of the action is continuous, but there are notable exceptions, as in Aeschylus' *Eumenides*. Similarly, most of the tragedies occur in a single place, but again some works, among them *Ajax*, deviate from the usual pattern.

All extant Greek tragedies are based on myth or history. Each writer was free, however, to alter the stories and to invent motivations (which are seldom provided in myth) for characters and events. Thus, though dramatists might begin with the same basic story, they ended with widely differing interpretations of it. Agathon, writing at the end of the fifth century, was the first to invent stories for tragedy, but his example was never widely followed and none of his plays has survived.

Greek dramatists were very economical in the number of events and character traits they included, preferring a few broad strokes to multiplicity of detail. They paid little attention to the physical and sociological aspects of characterization, concentrating instead on the psychological and ethical attributes of their personages.

The oldest surviving Greek plays are by Aeschylus (523–456), who began competing at the City Dionysia about 499. Although about eighty titles are known, only seven of his plays have survived: *The Persians* (472), *Seven Against Thebes* (467), the *Oresteia*, a trilogy of plays made up of *Agamemnon, Libation Bearers,* and *Eumenides* (458), *The Suppliants,* and *Prometheus Bound* (exact dates unknown but probably after 468). The major innovation attributed to Aeschylus is the introduction of the second actor. It is usually assumed that this occurred early in his career, but no date can be fixed for it. After about 468, when Sophocles introduced the third actor, Aeschylus made use of this additional performer.

All of Aeschylus' extant plays, with the exception of *The Persians,* formed parts of trilogies (three plays based on a single story or common theme). That Aeschylus often needed three plays to encompass his tragic idea indicates his interests and method. For example, the *Oresteia* (the only surviving Greek trilogy) shows the evolution of the concept of justice, with the impersonal power of the state eventually replacing personal revenge, which up to the final play creates an endless chain of private guilt and punishment. In this trilogy, Aeschylus dramatizes conflicting ideals of justice as they are embodied in human affairs, but, because he is able to reconcile them in an all-encompassing principle, the action can be resolved happily. This developmental pattern, found in several of his works, indicates that Aeschylus was interested in a kind of tragedy different from that of Sophocles and Euripides.

Because Aeschylus' characters embody cosmic conflicts, they are sometimes said to be superhuman. They usually have a limited number of traits, but these are incisive, powerful, and entirely appropriate to the action. Although Aeschylus is essentially a philosophical and religious dramatist, he is also the most theatrical of the Greek tragedians, for he makes great demands on the theatre's resources. His plays often call for spectacle on a monumental scale: second choruses and numerous at-

tendants; chariots drawn by horses; picturesque and sometimes frightening mythological characters; and so on. He also makes considerable use of visual symbolism, unusual choral dances, and lavish costumes. If Aeschylus was somewhat primitive in his dramatic technique, the grandeur of his conceptions has seldom been surpassed.

Sophocles (*c.* 496–406) is thought to have written more than 120 plays, but only 7 have survived: *Ajax* (between 450 and 440), *Antigone* (*c.* 441), *Oedipus Rex* (*c.* 430–425), *Electra* (*c.* 418–410), *Trachiniae* (*c.* 413), *Philoctetes* (409), and *Oedipus at Colonus* (406). A substantial portion of one satyr play, *The Trackers,* is also extant. Sophocles won twenty-four contests, the first in 468 when he defeated Aeschylus, and he never placed lower than second. He is credited with the introduction of the third actor, with fixing the size of the chorus at fifteen members, and with the first use of scene painting.

In comparison with Aeschylus, Sophocles placed increased emphasis on individual characters and reduced the role of the chorus. His personages are complex and psychologically well motivated. The protagonists, noble but not faultless, are usually subjected to a terrible crisis that leads to suffering and self-recognition, including the perception of a higher than human law behind events.

Sophocles is the most skillful of Greek dramatists in mastery of dramatic structure: his *Oedipus Rex* is often called the most perfect of Greek tragedies. In his plays, exposition is carefully motivated; scenes are built through suspense to a climax; the action is clear and logical throughout. His poetry has been universally admired for its beauty and clarity of expression. There are no elaborate visual effects; the impact derives almost entirely from the force of the dramatic action itself.

Euripides (*c.* 480–*c.* 406) wrote about ninety plays, of which eighteen have survived: *Alcestis* (438), *Medea* (431), *Hippolytus* (428), *The Children of Heracles, Andromache, Hecuba, Heracles, The Suppliants, Ion* (dates unknown, but probably between 430 and 415), *The Trojan Women* (415), *Electra, Iphigenia in Tauris* (dates unknown, but probably between 417 and 408), *Helen* (412), *The Phoenician Women* (*c.* 409), *Orestes* (408), *The Bacchae, Iphigenia in Aulis* (produced after Euripides' death), and *Cyclops,* a satyr play (date unknown). The relatively large number of extant plays by Euripides is explained by his enormous popularity in later Greek times, although he was little appreciated during his lifetime.

There are at least two reasons for the adverse judgment made on Euripides by his contemporaries.

FIGURE 2.3   Vase painting from the late fifth century B.C. showing actors of a satyr play. Note the masks and various kinds of garments. From Baumeister, *Denkmaler des Klassichens Altertums* (1888).

First, he often introduced subjects thought unsuited to the stage, and he questioned traditional values. His use of Phaedra's love for her stepson, Medea's murder of her children, and Pasiphae's passion for a bull were denounced for their abnormality, and his realistic exploration of psychological motivations was sometimes thought too undignified for tragedy. Euripides' characters often questioned the gods' sense of justice, since they seemed sources of misery more than of happiness. At times Euripides suggested that chance rules the world, and that human beings are more concerned with moral values than are the gods—at least as depicted in myths. Second, his dramatic method was not always clear. The unifying element in most of Euripides' plays is thought, and since his basic themes are not always readily grasped, the significance of the dramatic action is sometimes obscure. His techniques, growing out of this concern for thought, often seem inadequate when compared with those of Sophocles. For example, many of his plays begin with a monologue-prologue baldly summarizing past events; the episodes are not always causally related and some may even appear superfluous; speeches often resemble forensic addresses; choral passages are at times only tenuously related to the dramatic action; and gods are frequently used to resolve conflicts and to foretell the future. Thus, Euripides was thought dangerous because of his ideas and artistically inferior because of his dramatic techniques. But, if Euripides' techniques call attention to themselves, they are counterbalanced by realistic strokes in characterization, dialogue, and costuming.

Euripides began many dramatic practices that were developed more fully in the fourth century. He often turned to minor myths for his subjects or severely altered the major ones. Such works as *Ion, Helen,* and *Iphigenia in Aulis,* which pass over into tragicomedy and melodrama, are often cited as signs that late fifth-century Greek tragedy was already abandoning profundity for intrigue and startling reversals. As Euripides' popularity rose in succeeding centuries, it was the sentimental and melodramatic aspects of his work that were most often imitated.

THE SATYR PLAY

The tragic dramatist of the fifth century also had to master one kind of comic writing since he was required to supply a satyr play each time he competed at the City Dionysia. As with tragedy, little is known of the origin of the satyr play. Some historians have argued that it was the first form of drama and that gradually both tragedy and comedy emerged from it. But critical consensus credits Pratinas with having invented this form sometime between 534 and 500 B.C.

Out of the hundreds of satyr plays written, the only complete example that has survived is Euripides' *Cyclops.* It is based on an episode from the *Odyssey* in which Odysseus meets the Cyclops and a captive band of satyrs led by Silenus. In addition, a large part of Sopho-

SAINT PETER'S COLLEGE LIBRARY
JERSEY CITY, NEW JERSEY 07306

cles' *The Trackers* is extant. It tells of Apollo's attempt to find a herd of cattle stolen by Hermes, the god of thieves. Because of the limited evidence available to us, it is difficult to generalize about the form. But we know enough to speculate about the typical structure of satyr plays.

The satyr play takes its name from the chorus, which was made up of the half-beast, half-human companions of Dionysus. The leader of the chorus was Silenus, the father of the satyrs. Sometimes the story of a satyr play connected it in theme or subject with the tragedies it accompanied, but more often it was entirely independent. Essentially a burlesque treatment of mythology (often ridiculing gods or heroes and their adventures), the boisterous action occurred in a rural setting and included vigorous dancing and indecent language and gesture. In structure, the plays resembled tragedy, since the action was divided into a series of episodes separated by choral odes. Language and meter deviated from what was typical of tragedy by tending toward the everyday and colloquial. Serving as afterpieces to the tragedies, the satyr plays provided a kind of comic relief from serious plays that had gone before.

FIGURE 2.4 Old man wearing a wreath and phallus. Statuette of a comic actor, *c.* 400 B.C., probably in Old Comedy, and probably from Athens. Courtesy Museum of Fine Arts, Boston.

GREEK COMEDY IN THE FIFTH CENTURY

Comedy was the last of the major dramatic forms to receive official recognition in Greece, not being admitted to the City Dionysia until 487–486 B.C. Its history prior to that time is largely conjectural.

Aristotle says that comedy grew out of the improvisations of the leaders of phallic songs, but since there were many phallic rites it is not clear which he had in mind. Some of the pre-dramatic ceremonies were performed by a dancing chorus who at times masqueraded as animals, rode on animals, or carried an animal as a representative; there were also choruses of fat men, satyrs, and men on stilts. The rites often included a procession with a chorus who sang and danced as they carried large phallic symbols aloft on poles. These ceremonies provided opportunity for considerable byplay and mockery between participants and spectators. All of these elements have their parallels in early comic drama.

None of the phallic rites was dramatic, however, and the process by which they achieved comic form is uncertain. As with tragedy, the Dorians claimed to have invented comedy; Aristotle associates the decisive step with Epicharmus, who lived at Syracuse, a Dorian colony on the island of Sicily. Little is known about Epicharmus except that he was certainly writing plays between 485 and 467 B.C. The extant fragments of his works show these characteristics: some scenes have as many as three speakers, but there is no evidence of a chorus; elaborate word play, parody, "patter" speeches, and farcical situations abound. The relationship of these plays to the comedies performed in Athens is unclear, however, since comedy had been recognized at the City Dionysia before the first known work of Epicharmus was written. A direct influence might have been exerted, nevertheless, since Epicharmus may have been writing long before our records of his work begin, and the first Athenian comedies, the nature of which is unknown, may have been patterned after those of Epicharmus.

Another possible source of Dorian influence on Athenian comedy is the mime, which supposedly first appeared in Megara (a city some twenty-five to thirty miles from Athens) shortly after 581 B.C. No mimes from this early period survive, but later ones are short satirical treatments of everyday domestic situations or are burlesqued versions of myths. It is possible that the

FIGURE 2.5 Laughing girl. Statuette of actor, supposedly from Old Comedy. Courtesy Museum of Fine Arts, Boston.

of which eleven survive: *Acharnians* (425), *Knights* (424), *Clouds* (423), *Wasps* (422), *Peace* (421), *Birds* (414), *Lysistrata* (411), *Thesmophoriazusae* (411), *Frogs* (405), *Ecclesiazusae* (392/391), and *Plutus* (388). Although it is usual to treat Aristophanes' compositions as typical of Old Comedy (as the plays of this period are called), it is unclear how his works compare with those of his predecessors and contemporaries. Nevertheless, generalizations about Old Comedy are necessarily based on Aristophanes' practice.

Probably the most noteworthy characteristic of Aristophanic comedy is its commentary on contemporary society, politics, literature, and above all the Peloponnesian war. The plays are organized around a ruling theme, embodied in a rather farfetched "happy idea" (such as a private peace with a warring power or a sex strike to bring an end to war). Although the events of most Old Comedies could not occur in everyday life, parallels with real events are abundantly clear, the fantastic exaggerations serving to point up the absurdity of their real-life

Athenians borrowed mimic scenes and combined them with their own phallic choruses. Some of the dances in Athenian comedy—such as the *kordax* and *mothon*—also were Dorian in origin.

Regardless of its origin and early history, comedy was sufficiently developed by 487–486 to be accorded a place at the City Dionysia. (It had probably been performed earlier without official sanction or financial aid.) The names of a few early comic dramatists have been recorded: Chionides, who supposedly won the prize at the first contest; Magnes, who won eleven victories with such plays as *Birds, Fig-flies,* and *Frogs;* Ecphantides, who is said to have written a more refined comedy than that of his predecessors; Cratinus (*fl.* 450–422), credited with twenty-one plays and thought to have been the first truly outstanding comic writer; Crates (*fl.* 449–425), who dropped personal satire, which had previously been typical of comedy, in favor of more general subjects; and Eupolis (*fl.* 429–411), Aristophanes' chief rival, noted for his witty satire and inventiveness.

All of the extant comedies of the fifth century, however, are by a single author, Aristophanes (*c.* 448–*c.* 380). He is thought to have written about forty plays,

FIGURE 2.6 Terracotta statuette representing an actor from Old or Middle Comedy. Old woman holding a child. One of seven statuettes found in an Athenian tomb. It probably dates from the fourth century. Courtesy Metropolitan Museum of Art, Rogers Fund, 1913.

counterparts. In addition to fantasy, farcical situations are typical, and considerable emphasis is placed on the pleasures of eating, drinking, sex, wealth, and leisure. Coupled with the comic elements are some of the most beautiful lyrics and some of the most obscene passages in Greek literature.

Although there are many variants, the basic structural pattern of Aristophanic comedy is simple. A prologue establishes the mood and sets forth the "happy idea"; the chorus enters, and there follows a debate (or *agon*) over the merits of the idea and a decision is made to try the scheme. A *parabasis* (or choral ode in which the audience is addressed directly) divides the play into two parts. In the *parabasis*, some social or political problem is often discussed and a line of action advocated. At times, however, the *parabasis* is used to praise the author of the play, to plead for the audience's favor, or for similar purposes. The second part of the play shows, in a series of loosely connected scenes, the results of adopting the happy idea. The final scene (or *komos*) usually concludes with the reconciliation of all the characters and their exit to a feast or revels. These features of comic structure are sometimes rearranged but are almost always present.

After 404, when Athens was defeated in the Peloponnesian War, political and social satire gradually disappeared from comedy and new types evolved. The quality of tragedy also declined after this time. Thus the world's first great age of dramatic writing was largely over by 400 B.C.

THE DRAMATIC FESTIVALS OF THE FIFTH CENTURY

Although in Athens four annual festivals were held in honor of Dionysus, plays were presented only at one—the City Dionysia—prior to 442, almost 100 years after the first dramatic contests were introduced. At one festival, the Anthesteria, plays were never produced. But by the late fifth century drama was important at the Lenaia and the Rural Dionysia as well as at the City Dionysia, although the latter continued to command the greatest prestige. Drama was never a part of the festivals held in honor of other gods.

The City Dionysia, which commemorated the coming of Dionysus to Athens, was held each year at the end of March and extended over several days. Both a civic and religious festival, it was open to the whole Greek world and served as a showcase for Athenian wealth and culture. It was under the general supervision of the *archon eponymous,* the principal civil magistrate of Athens.

A few days before the festival began, each dramatist appeared with his actors at a *proagon* and announced the subject of his plays. After another preliminary event (the reenactment of Dionysus' coming to Athens), there was a procession, which included public officials, the *choregoi* (sponsors of the plays), and many others, who carried gifts or escorted sacrificial animals for the god. This procession wound through much of Athens, stopped for dances at various altars, and ended with the presentation of offerings and the sacrifice of a bull at the altar of Dionysus.

Next came the dithyrambic contests. During the fifth century, ten 50-member choruses, one from each tribe, competed annually. Then came the plays. Each of three dramatists presented three tragedies and one satyr play, the works of one playwright consuming a whole day. After 487–486, each of five comic writers presented a single play (except during the Peloponnesian War, when the number of comedies was reduced to three). The comedies were probably all given on the day preceding the tragedies, but the precise arrangement is unclear. Until 449, prizes were offered only for plays; after that time prizes were also given to actors. Two days after the festival ended, an assembly was convened to consider the conduct of the officials in charge of it and to receive complaints about misconduct by citizens during the festival.

The Lenaia was celebrated near the end of January under the supervision of the *archon basileus,* the principal religious official of Athens. It has been suggested that originally the Lenaia was identical with the Rural Dionysia, and that its date and nature were changed only after Athens lost its rural character. No deme (or subdivision) of Attica celebrated both the Lenaia and the Rural Dionysia, and the Lenaia was observed only in the city. As the seas were considered unsafe in January, the Lenaia was primarily a local festival. Consequently, more freedom of expression was permitted, and the Lenaia came to be associated especially with comedy, in which Athenian officials and political affairs were often severely ridiculed.

Dramatic activities were not officially recognized at the Lenaia until about 442, although plays may have been presented there on an informal basis before that date. By the late fifth century the plays were being performed in the Theatre of Dionysus (Athens' major theatrical structure, but when they were first given there is unclear. Originally the Lenaia may have been held elsewhere, for Dionysus was worshipped under a number of guises, and each cult had its own sacred area, just as Christian sects do today. The City Dionysia was presented in honor of Dionysus Eleutherios and the Theatre of Dionysus was erected within his sacred precinct, whereas the Lenaia was held in honor of Dionysus Lenaios, whose sanctuary's location is now unknown. Today, many scholars assume that originally there was a performance area in the Agora (or principal marketplace) and that the Lenaia plays were at first performed there. Some historians have suggested that the plays continued to be presented in the Agora until they were given official sanction in 442 and at that time they were transferred to the Theatre of Dionysus.

Contests at the Lenaia were at first only for comic dramatists and actors, but in 432 other competitions were added for tragic playwrights and actors. As at the City Dionysia, five comic writers competed each year (except during the Peloponnesian War), but only two tragic dramatists (who offered two plays each) participated. Satyr plays and dithyrambs were never presented.

The Rural Dionysia was celebrated in December, although not necessarily on the same day in all demes. It was under the supervision of the *demarchos* (principal magistrate) of each deme. The principal feature of the festival was a procession in which a giant phallus was carried aloft on a pole, apparently with the purpose of reviving fertility at a time when the sun was at its weakest. It is unclear when dramatic performances became a part of this festival. It is unlikely that all of the more than 100 demes included plays in their celebrations, but drama may have appeared in some of them before it was recognized at the Lenaia. It is certain that plays were being performed in a number of demes before the end of the fifth century, and the custom seems to have been widely adopted during the fourth century. Plato (*c.* 427–347 B.C.) wrote that in his time the Rural Dionysia was held on different days in different demes so that people might travel from one to the other to see plays presented by troupes of traveling actors. The demes in which dramatic production was most important were Piraeus (where Euripides is said to have presented at least one play), Icaria, Salamis, and Eleusis. Many of the rural demes built their own permanent theatres.

Most of our information about the Rural Dionysia

dates from the fourth century or later. By that time actors were reviving works already produced elsewhere, but the source of plays presented in the fifth century is unknown. The Rural Dionysia may have served as a tryout theatre, or as an outlet for plays not accepted for the City Dionysia or Lenaia, or as a place where works already seen in the city were revived. While the Rural Dionysia probably had little effect on the development of Greek drama, its activities suggest how intense the interest in drama was and show that the theatre was not confined to Athens.

PLAY SELECTION AND FINANCING

Each author wishing to have his plays produced at a festival had to apply to the *archon* for a chorus. It is not known how this official chose the plays to be presented, but it has been suggested that each dramatist recited parts of his work before a committee. The choices of the next year's plays were made approximately one month after the end of each festival. Although this would have left about eleven months until performance, it is unknown how much of this time was actually used for rehearsals.

After about 501, a large share of the expense of play production was borne by the *choregoi*, chosen by the *archon* from wealthy citizens who performed this duty in rotation as a part of their civic and religious responsibilities. The *choregus* (one was appointed for each author and for each dithyrambic chorus) underwrote the training and costuming of the chorus and probably paid the musicians. In addition, he may have supplied properties and supernumerary actors and may have met other demands (such as a second chorus required by some plays) not provided by the state. The responsibility of the state seems to have been restricted to the theatre building, prizes (for authors, *choregoi*, and actors), and payments to actors and, possibly, to dramatists. Because he bore the major financial burden, a *choregus* could do much to help or hinder the playwright. Most *choregoi* seem to have been liberal, perhaps because prizes for plays were awarded to them and the author jointly.

Nearly all tragic dramatists directed their own works, but it was not unusual for comic playwrights to turn this task over to someone else. In Aeschylus' time, the author acted in his plays, trained the chorus, invented the music and dances, and supervised every aspect of production. Thus the primary source of unity was the playwright-director, whose task was as complex as that of any director today. The playwright's key role in the early years is indicated by the term applied to him, *didaskalos* (teacher), for he was considered to be the instructor of both the performers (during the process of play production) and the audience (through the finished product).

ACTORS AND ACTING

Originally the actor and the dramatist were one. Separation of the two roles did not begin until early in the fifth century when Aeschylus introduced a second actor. Playwrights continued to act in their own plays, however, until the time of Sophocles, who abandoned this practice about 468 and introduced a third actor. It seems likely that when the contest for tragic actors was inaugurated (around 449) the separation of actor from playwright was complete. Nevertheless, in the fifth century actors were at best semi-professionals, for there was as yet no demand for full-time performers and they must have supplemented their income through other activities.

After about 468, the number of actors available to each tragic playwright was fixed at three, although these few performers might impersonate any number of characters. The "three-actor rule" was softened somewhat by allowing supernumeraries to assume nonspeaking roles or to speak a very limited number of lines. Still, Sophocles' *Oedipus at Colonus* could have been performed by three actors only if the same character were played by different actors in successive scenes. The difficulties presented by this three-actor convention (at least by modern standards) has led many scholars to question whether such a rule ever existed. Nevertheless, there seems to be sufficient evidence to verify that it was observed.

Comedy was subject to fewer restrictions. Most scenes in the extant plays could have been acted by three actors, but several require four and at least one would have required five. Since restrictions were probably established in order to make the contests fair, those at the Lenaia may have differed from those at the City Dionysia, since other conditions differed at the two festivals.

Before about 449 (that is, up until the inauguration of contests for actors), each playwright probably selected his own cast, but after that time the leading actors were assigned by lot to the competing dramatists. This procedure was probably adopted to insure that no writer had an unfair advantage over his rivals. The other two actors allotted to each dramatist were probably selected jointly by the playwright and his leading actor. Although all of the actors were paid by the state, only the leading actor could compete for the prize, which could be awarded for a performance in a non-prize-winning play.

The Greeks seem to have placed considerable emphasis upon the voice, for they judged actors above all by beauty of vocal tone and ability to adapt manner of speaking to mood and character. Nevertheless, the actor's delivery was probably more declamatory than realistic, for he did not attempt to reproduce the attributes of age or sex so much as to project the appropriate emotional tone. Furthermore, the plays demanded three kinds of delivery: speech, recitative, and song. As the primary means of expression, the voice was trained and exercised by the actor much as it might be by an opera singer today. While the best actors attained high standards of vocal excellence, others apparently ranted and roared.

Facial expression was of no importance to the Greek actor, since he was always masked. In tragedy, gesture and movement appear to have been simplified and broadened; in comedy, everyday actions—running the gamut from the commonplace to the bizarre—were exaggerated in the direction of the farcical and ludicrous. It is sometimes suggested that movement tended toward a set of conventionalized, stylized, or symbolic gestures like those used in mimetic dance.

Although it is now impossible to describe accurately the style of acting seen in fifth century Greece, several of its attributes, all leading away from realism, can be listed. First, the same actor usually had to play more than one role in a play. Second, men played all roles, including those of women. Third, the liberal use of song, recitative, choral passages, dance, and masks led to considerable stylization. On the other hand, the extreme stylization which characterized acting in late Greece was probably not typical of the fifth century. Both tragic and comic acting undoubtedly departed from the everyday—tragedy in the direction of idealization, comedy in the direction of burlesque—but they remained sufficiently recognizable to link the dramatic events to the spectator's own world.

Several additional elements influenced style: the chorus, music and dance, costumes and masks, and theatre architecture. An examination of these elements should help to define the total impression created by productions in the fifth century.

THE CHORUS

In the early tragedies the chorus was dominant, since there was only one actor, who left the stage often to change roles. In Aeschylus' plays, although a second actor was available, the chorus was still given as many as one-half of the lines. Furthermore, in *The Suppliants* the chorus serves as protagonist, while in *The Eumenides* it is the antagonist. After Aeschylus' time the role of the chorus diminished progressively until in the plays of Euripides it is often only tenuously related to the dramatic action.

Historians disagree about the size of the tragic chorus. The traditional view holds that the number was originally fifty, but that it was reduced to twelve during the career of Aeschylus and was then raised to fifteen by Sophocles. There is no clear evidence to support any of these figures. The arguments for a fifty-member chorus are deduced primarily from two sources. First, there is Aristotle's statement that tragedy developed out of improvisations by leaders of dithyrambic choruses. With this can be grouped the assertions of later classical writers who fix the size of the early tragic chorus at fifty largely because that was the size of the dithyrambic chorus. Although this early testimony must be respected, it cannot be verified, for we do not know how large the dithyrambic chorus was before its size was fixed at fifty, probably around 508 B.C., and thus after tragedy was well established. The second major source of evidence for a fifty-member chorus is Aeschylus' *The Suppliants,* in which the chorus is composed of the Daughters of Danaus, who in mythology numbered fifty. Aeschylus does not state how many daughters there are in his play. Furthermore, recently discovered evidence has redated this play (formerly thought to have been written *c.* 490) as having been produced after Sophocles began to compete (that is, after 468) and thus within the period when some scholars maintain that the chorus numbered only twelve or fifteen. Thus, there is much testimony that the chorus originally numbered fifty, but there is also much skepticism about this testimony.

The evidence to support the idea of a twelve-member chorus is based primarily on a twelve-line choral passage in the *Agamemnon,* which, according to some critics, was divided among the individual members of the chorus. That the lines were assigned to individuals, however, is pure conjecture. Those who support the theory of a twelve-member chorus usually argue that at some time during Aeschylus' career the chorus was divided to assign an approximately equal number of the original fifty to each of the four plays an author presented when he competed. The reason given for this change is usually economic—that is, to reduce the expenses of production.

The evidence for a chorus of fifteen is found in the commentaries of authors writing several centuries after Sophocles' lifetime. They cite no authority for their statements. Nevertheless, it has long been accepted that the probable size of the chorus was fifteen in all the extant plays of Sophocles and Euripides. In later times, the chorus diminished in size, sometimes having no more than three members.

Some Greek tragedies require a second chorus, essentially mute though sometimes provided with a few lines. Aeschylus' *The Suppliants* includes a chorus of attendants on the Daughters of Danaus, while Euripides' *Hippolytus* has two quite distinct choruses.

As a rule, the chorus entered with a stately march, but occasionally members came in singly or in small groups from various directions. Most choral passages were sung and danced in unison, but at times the chorus was divided into two groups who performed in turn. Sometimes the chorus exchanged spoken dialogue with a character, and, in rare instances, individual members may have spoken single lines. As for acting, it is assumed that all members responded appropriately to the situations, but it is unknown how they were grouped or placed during episodes or how their formations changed during choral odes.

Since satyr plays were presented in conjunction with tragedy, the satyr chorus was probably governed by the same basic conventions as those used for the tragic chorus. Because it was less serious than tragedy, the satyr play permitted many deviations toward the comic.

The chorus of Old Comedy was composed of twenty-four members. Sometimes it was divided into two semi-choruses, as in *Lysistrata* where the two are of opposite sexes. Comedy seems to have enjoyed much more freedom than tragedy and consequently the entrances, dances, and uses of the chorus were more varied. The texts of the plays suggest that the chorus was extremely active throughout the performance of the play.

In each dramatic form, the chorus normally made

its entrance after the prologue and remained until the end of the play. In a few instances, however, it was present at the opening and occasionally it left and returned during the action.

The chorus serves several functions in Greek drama. First, it is an agent in the play; it gives advice, expresses opinions, asks questions, and sometimes takes an active part in the action. Second, it often establishes the ethical or social framework of the events and sets up a standard against which the action may be judged. Third, it frequently serves as an ideal spectator, reacting to the events and characters as the dramatist might hope the audience would. Fourth, the chorus helps to set the overall mood of the play and of individual scenes and to heighten dramatic effects. Fifth, it adds movement, spectacle, song and dance, and thus contributes much to theatrical effectiveness. Sixth, it serves an important rhythmical function, creating pauses or retardations during which the audience may reflect upon what has happened and what is to come.

In the fifth century, the members of the chorus were amateurs. Nevertheless, they probably were not inexperienced, since choral dancing was so common in Greece and since there were at least 500 participants each year in the dithyrambic contests at the City Dionysia. Since choruses were usually awarded to playwrights approximately eleven months prior to performance, training was probably spread over a long period. In the beginning, the playwright choreographed and trained the chorus, but these tasks were later taken over by professionals. Most of the information that has survived about choral training concerns dithyrambs, but historians usually assume that the same practices were used with drama. We are told that training was long and arduous, involving diet, exercise, and disciplined practice under the watchful supervision of several persons. We are also told that choruses were often pampered and given special treatment. Training and outfitting the chorus were the most important and expensive parts of the choregus' duties.

MUSIC AND DANCE

Music was an integral part of Greek drama. It accompanied the passages of recitative and was an inseparable part of the choral odes. Only rarely was it used apart from words, and then only for special effects. In the beginning, the musical accompaniment was probably subordinated to insure that the words would be understood. By the time of Euripides, however, the accompaniment had become more elaborate, and lengthy trills prolonged single syllables in many words. As a result, some verbal passages were rendered unintelligible. Some critics suggest that this may be one reason for the decline in importance of choral odes.

The musical accompaniment for drama was played on a single flute resembling a modern oboe or clarinet in tone. Other instruments, including the lyre, the trumpet, and various forms of percussion, were used occasionally for special effects. The flute player preceded the chorus into the orchestra, but his placement thereafter is uncertain. Some historians maintain that he wore a wooden shoe with which he marked the beat. Occasionally an actor used the lyre to accompany his own recitative or song.

It is unclear who composed the music. At times the playwright may have done so, but ordinarily this was probably the responsibility of the flute player.

So little Greek music has survived that no accurate reconstruction of it is possible. The Greeks believed that music had ethical qualities. This suggests that they associated particular kinds of music with particular emotions or ideas. They recognized a large number of *modes,* which differed from each other in tonality and in sequence of intervals. The tones of the various modes were not always equal in value, however, some of the intervals being as small as quarter-tones. In quality, Greek music probably resembled Oriental more than modern Western music. The principal modes were the Dorian, Ionian, Phrygian, Aeolian, and Lydian, but there were many variations on these, such as Hypodorian or Myxolydian. Each had qualities which associated it with a particular range of feeling. Consequently, some modes were thought suitable to tragedy, others to comedy, and some unsuited to any form of drama.

Like music, dance was considered to have ethical qualities. The Greeks defined dance as any expressive rhythmical movement; thus dance did not necessarily mean patterns created by the feet, for gestures or pantomime, if rhythmical, might qualify as dance. Most Greek dance was mimetic (expressive of a particular kind of character or situation). In theatrical performances, dance seems to have been closely related to the words through a set of moment-by-moment symbolic gestures *(or cheironomia).*

By the fourth century the dances of tragedy had

come to be called *emmeleia* (a term that signifies harmony, grace, and dignity). This classification obviously was broad, for the choral passages range from religious processions, wedding dances, ecstatic frenzies, to many other types.

The dances of comedy were less dignified than those of tragedy. Many were intentionally ridiculous. Often at the end of plays the chorus exited dancing wildly. Comic choral dances were derived from many sources: animal movements, religious ceremonies, victory celebrations, and various other activities and rites. The individual actors performed dances which involved kicking the buttocks, slapping the chest or thighs, leaping, performing high kicks, spinning like a top, or beating other actors. The most common term for the comic dances is *kordax.*

The basic dance of the satyr play was the *sikinnis,* which probably involved vigorous leaping, horseplay, and lewd pantomime. Often it burlesqued the tragic dances.

COSTUMES AND MASKS

The overall visual style of a Greek theatrical production was greatly influenced by costumes and masks. Several historians have argued that the standard costume for all tragic actors was a sleeved, highly decorated tunic, usually full-length, although sometimes shorter. This garment is said either to have been derived from the robes of the Dionysian priests (thus indicating the actor's sacred and ceremonial function) or to have been invented by Aeschylus early in the fifth century. That the actor wore a standardized garment, however, is far from certain. Its presumed appearance is derived almost entirely from figures depicted on vase paintings. But this evidence is open to doubt for several reasons: (1) most of the vases are from a period later than the fifth century; (2) the relation of the paintings to actual theatrical practice is unclear; (3) most important, other vase paintings, usually ignored by those who argue for a standardized garment, show actors in quite different costumes, and even those vases showing the presumed standard often depict deviations from it, including complete nudity. Other evidence cited for a conventionalized garment is the statement of several ancient commentators (writing long after the fifth century) that robes designed by Aeschylus for his actors were later adopted by the priests at Eleusis.

FIGURE 2.7 The so-called Andromeda vase, dating from the late fifth century B.C. The figure at center and those in the upper corners are often cited as examples of tragic costuming, although there is no evidence to connect this vase with theatrical performance. Note also that some figures are nude. From Engelmann, *Archaeologische Studien zu den Tragikern* (1900).

Aristophanes' *Frogs,* on the other hand, merely credits Aeschylus with clothing tragic actors in garments more dignified than those worn by ordinary persons. Thus, though the sleeved, decorated tunic may have been used, there are many reasons for questioning whether it was standardized and worn by all actors.

The plays surviving from this period contain few references to costume. Some indicate that the characters are in mourning, for which black was the usual color in Greek daily life. In Euripides' *Alcestis,* Death is said to

FIGURE 2.8 Fragments of a vase from about 470 B.C. showing an actor's mask. This is the oldest extant visual evidence concerning theatrical masks. Note the garment on the right, supposedly used in the theatre. At left, note the foot covering. Courtesy American School of Classical Studies, Athens.

be clothed in a black and "terrifying" garment. Several of Euripides' characters wear rags, and the protagonists of Sophocles' *Oedipus at Colonus* and *Philoctetes* refer to their torn clothing. Although these lines may merely be included to justify departures from standard practice, they suggest that costume was not rigidly prescribed. It has also been suggested that costumes may at first have been highly formal and that they became more realistic toward the end of the fifth century.

The plays also give some information about the dress of the chorus. In Aeschylus' *The Suppliants* the chorus is said to be wearing non-Greek garments, while in Sophocles' *Philoctetes* the opposite point is made. An oft-repeated account of the first performance of Aeschylus' *Eumenides* states that the chorus of Furies was so frightening in appearance that several women in the audience miscarried. Other textual evidence suggests a wide variety of costumes for the chorus. As a result, historians, even those who argue for a standardized costume for actors, have suggested that the dress of the chorus was determined by relatively realistic criteria (such as sex, age, nationality, and social status). Did, then, one principle govern the costume of the chorus and a quite different one that of the actors? Although this seems unlikely, it is not impossible, since the state or the performers presumably supplied the actors' costumes while the *choregoi* supplied those for the choruses. A uniform principle would seem more logical, nevertheless, and it is possible that such characters as foreigners, gods, and other supernatural beings wore the sleeved, decorated tunic, for which there was no precedent in native Greek dress, while the more familiar personages wore some variation on Greek garments.

In addition to the tunic (or *chiton*), both actors and chorus might wear a short cloak *(chlamys)* or a long one *(himation)*. The identity of both might be established in part by symbolic properties: the king by his scepter, the warrior by his spear, the suppliant by his branch, the herald by his wreath, and so on.

Footwear in tragedy varied. The usual foot covering seems to have been a soft shoe or boot, often reaching to the calf. In later times this was called a *cothornus* and was given a thick sole, but neither the name nor the elevation seems to have been used in the fifth century. In vase paintings, figures are shown in a wide variety of footwear, or even as barefoot.

Fortunately, there is more agreement among scholars about comic costuming, although the available evidence is no more reliable than that for tragedy. Most

FIGURE 2.9 Statuette representing a figure from Old Comedy. From Robert, *Die Masken der Neueren Attischen Komoedie* (1911).

agree that costumes were adapted from those worn in everyday Greek life. For theatrical purposes, the *chiton* was frequently made too short and too tight to emphasize comic nudity. It was worn over flesh-colored tights, which were often padded. Male characters, but not the chorus, wore the *phallus*.

This costume, shown in much of the extant pictorial evidence, was probably that of the comic slaves and ridiculous old men. But it was not likely to have been the universal costume, for the plays also include many young men who are ridiculed only slightly. Probably the comically grotesque costume was considerably modified toward typical daily dress for these characters. Similarly, there is a wide range of female characters, for whom there was less attempt than with male characters to emphasize sexual attributes through costume. Since some comedies parodied scenes from well-known tragedies, it may be that tragic costume was sometimes adapted and ridiculed.

Relatively little attention has been paid by historians to the costuming of satyr plays. The satyrs are thought to have worn goatskin loincloths, to which were attached the phallus in front and a horse-like tail in the rear; other parts of the body appeared to be nude, but in the theatre this probably meant some kind of flesh-colored garment. Silenus, the leader of the chorus, is usually depicted as wearing shaggy or fleecy tights under an animal-skin cloak. Since the characters in satyr plays are usually mythological personages, the costumes probably were somewhat ridiculous variations on tragic costumes.

All performers during the fifth century, with the possible exception of flute-players, wore masks. This practice seems to have evolved during the sixth century, for in the rituals which predate tragedy masks were sometimes but not always worn. Consequently, Thespis had two traditions to draw upon and, according to ancient commentators, he experimented with several types of disguise for the face—such as smearing it with wine dregs and dangling leaves in front of it—before adopting the mask. Tradition has it that Phrynichus was the first to introduce female masks and that Aeschylus was the first to use painted masks. No masks used by actors have survived since they were made of perishable linen, cork, or lightweight wood. Although in later periods the masks seem to have been considerably larger than the face and to have had exaggerated features, in the fifth century neither the size nor the expression seems to have been unduly enlarged. Masks covered the entire head and thus included the appropriate hairstyle, beard, ornaments, and other features.

It is impossible to determine whether masks for tragedy were restricted to a few conventionalized types during the fifth century. Some historians have argued that they were, but others have suggested that experimentation was encouraged. The masks for the characters of a single play must have been sufficiently differentiated to make the frequent change of roles readily apparent. On the other hand, chorus members in tragedy were always identical in appearance.

The masks for comedy were extremely varied. The choruses often represented birds, animals, or insects, all of which were identified by appropriate, though not necessarily realistic masks. The masks of human characters often exaggerated those attributes, such as baldness or ugliness, considered to be ridiculous. Although all of

the members of some choruses wore identical masks, others were individualized. When actors portrayed well-known Athenians, such as Socrates in *The Clouds*, "portrait masks" were used.

Members of the satyr chorus are usually depicted as snub-nosed, with dark, unkempt hair and beards, and pointed, horse-like ears. Sometimes they are shown as partially bald and at others they are given horns. Silenus is portrayed as having grey hair and beard. It is assumed that the actors wore masks similar to those used in tragedy.

The great importance of costumes and masks in the Greek theatre means that the costumer and mask-

FIGURE 2.10 **Fragment of a vase from Tarentum showing a tragic actor holding a mask. Note the short fringed tunic and the tasseled boots. This fragment probably dates from the fourth century** B.C. **Courtesy Martin von Wagner Museum of the University of Wurzburg.**

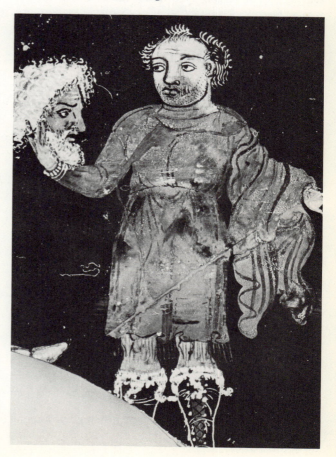

maker were crucial. Nevertheless, virtually nothing is known about them or their working methods.

THEATRE ARCHITECTURE

In Greece, places of performance were usually connected with the sacred precincts of the gods. Before dramatic contests were established there were many of these places. Excavations in the Minoan palaces of Crete have uncovered "theatral areas" with stone seats on two sides of a rectangle approximately 40 by 35 feet in size. These areas were probably used for dances, ceremonies, and bull-leaping. Some scholars believe that the earliest theatrical spaces on the Greek mainland also were square or rectangular. Recent excavations of Isthmia (near Corinth) tend to support this view, as does the theatre at Thorikos (perhaps the oldest in Attica), which is partially rectangular. Whatever its original form, Greek theatres were primarily circular by the fifth century. Furthermore, although there were several other theatres in Greece, historical interest centers on the Theatre of Dionysus in Athens, for all the surviving Greek plays were first presented there.

The earliest feature of the Theatre of Dionysus (located on the precinct of Dionysus Eleutherios on the

FIGURE 2.12 **The Theatre of Dionysus as it may have looked in the late sixth century B.C. From Fiechter, *Antike Griechische Theaterbauten.* Courtesy Verlag W. Kohlhammer GmbH, Stuttgart and Dr. Charlotte Fiechter.**

slope of the hill below the Acropolis) was the *orchestra* (or dancing place). Originally it was probably the only essential feature, since the audience sat or stood on the hillside to watch the choral performances which predated tragedy. Sometime during the sixth century a terrace was formed at the foot of the hill and on it a circular orchestra, about 66 feet in diameter, was laid out. An altar, or *thymele,* was placed in the center. With minor exceptions, the orchestra remained essentially unchanged until the Christian era.

The scene building, or *skene,* is probably of later origin than the orchestra. Since *skene* means "hut" or "tent," the scene house probably developed out of some temporary structure intended originally as a dressing room but later incorporated into the action by some imaginative playwright. In seeking to date the *skene* as a scenic structure, most scholars turn to the extant plays, of which Aeschylus' *Oresteia* (produced in 458 B.C.) is the first clearly to require a building as a background. Since virtually all parts of the early scene house have long since vanished, its appearance cannot be determined. Some of the many possible arrangements are shown in the accompanying illustrations (see Figures 2.13 and 2.21).

Extensive changes were made in the Theatre of Dionysus when Pericles built the Odeion (or music hall) adjoining it, probably in the 440s. At this time, the old curved retaining wall of the orchestra terrace was replaced with a straight one. Ten grooves were cut on the

FIGURE 2.11 **Plan of the theatre at Thorikos, at least part of which dates from the sixth century B.C. Note the modified rectangular shape. From Dörpfeld, *Greichische Theater* (1896).**

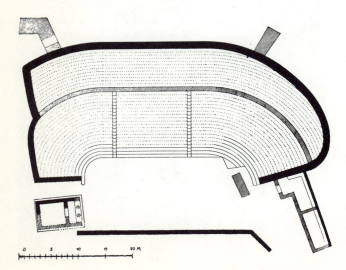

FIGURE 2.13 Three reconstructions showing possible appearances of the stage house of the Theatre of Dionysus in the fifth century B.C. From Fiechter, *Das Dionysostheater in Athen.* Courtesy Verlag W. Kohlhammer GmbH, Stuttgart and Dr. Charlotte Fiechter.

scene building had been built by the late fifth century, most date the permanent *skene* from the fourth century and thus after the era of great drama was over.

Questions relating to the *skene* are closely bound up with others about scenery. Was the background for all plays the scene house's conventionalized facade, or was some type of scenery used to suggest locale more specifically? Although these questions cannot be answered definitively, they can be illuminated.

It is important to distinguish between scenic practices before and after the scene building was introduced, for they probably changed when the *skene* became the background for the action. The challenges posed in the period before a *skene* was clearly available are well illustrated by Aeschylus' *Prometheus Bound* in which a rugged mountainous locale is supposedly engulfed in an earthquake during the final scene. Some commentators have argued that for this play a set-piece representing a mountain cliff was erected at the edge of the orchestra terrace and that during the supposed earthquake it was tipped over the embankment. Others have countered that the whole performance was highly conventionalized and that the idea of an earthquake was conveyed entirely by the lines. Still others have insisted that a fully developed stage house was already in use and that for this play it was disguised to represent the mountainous terrain. None of these theories can be verified, but they illustrate some possible approaches to staging in the early period.

inner face of this wall (that facing the auditorium). Most historians believe that these cuts were designed to hold the heavy wooden posts used to support the scene house. In addition, a stone-surfaced area or terrace jutted from the wall toward the orchestra. Although the purpose of this area is unknown, it may have served as a foundation for theatrical machinery. These sketchy physical remnants are all that now remain from the fifth century structure.

Historians usually assume that in the fifth century a temporary scene house was erected for each festival, that its framework consisted of heavy timbers (some of which were inserted in the grooves found in the retaining wall), and that the scene house extended forward from the retaining wall toward the audience. The facilities required by the extant plays are simple: one or more doors (opening onto an acting area) and an upper level (either the roof or a platform on a second level) used primarily for the appearance of gods or to represent high places. Although some scholars have argued that a stone

FIGURE 2.14 Plan showing changes made in the Theatre of Dionysus in the 440s. W—the new retaining wall with slots for timbers; OW—original retaining wall; T—stone terrace at orchestra level; H—the hall later built below the retaining wall. Drawing by Douglas Hubbell.

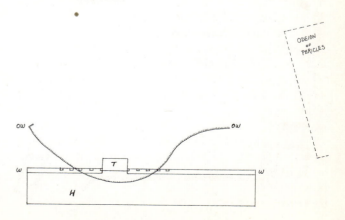

It is usually assumed that after 458 all plays used the *skene* as a background (an assumption that may be incorrect if the building was temporary). The *skene* could easily meet the demands of most plays since the majority are set before a temple, palace, or some other type of building. But what of those works set before caves (as are *Philoctetes* and numerous satyr plays), in groves of trees *(Oedipus at Colonus)*, or in army camps *(Ajax)*? Answers to this question have varied. Some historians have argued that a few stock sets, designed to meet the range of possible locales, were used. Others have argued that a few symbolic properties (such as shields to identify an army camp, or shells and rocks to indicate a seashore, or a single tree to suggest a grove) were merely added to the otherwise undisguised scene house. Still others have suggested that the spoken lines provided the necessary indications of locale and that the facade of the *skene* served as a conventionalized background for all plays.

This controversy is closely allied with another concerning scene painting. Aristotle (writing in the late fourth century) credits Sophocles with inventing scene painting, while Vitruvius (first century B.C.) states that it originated in the time of Aeschylus. In seeking to reconcile these two statements, some historians have placed the beginnings of painted scenery sometime between 468 and 456 (that is, during the years when the careers of Aeschylus and Sophocles overlapped). Vitruvius' description of the first scene painting suggests that it was an architectural design on a flat surface; this has been interpreted variously to mean that an attempt was made to create the illusion of real architectural details or, conversely, that a previously undecorated surface was now given some schematic but nonillusionistic pattern.

The issue of conventionalization versus illusionism is an important one, for, if illusion was attempted, then a single background could not have met the demands of all plays without changes of some kind. Consequently, those who have argued for a degree of representationalism have also had to suggest means whereby the appearance of the *skene* could have been altered. Two major devices have been proposed: *pinakes* (or painted panels similar to modern flats), and *periaktoi* (or triangular prisms with a different scene painted on each of their three sides). *Pinakes* supposedly could be attached to the scene building and changed as needed. But, though the use of *pinakes* in the fifth century is well documented, the practice of changing them for different plays is not. It is possible that painted panels were used to create the visible exterior of the temporary *skene*. In later periods, *periaktoi* were mounted on a central pivot and revolved to show the appropriate side, but the use of this device during the fifth century has not been definitely established.

Most Greek tragedies occur in a single locale, but the successive plays offered on the same day were often set in different locales. Thus, if scene changes were attempted, they could have been made between plays in most instances. On the other hand, some tragedies (such as Aeschylus' *Eumenides* and Sophocles' *Ajax*) and numerous comedies change place during the action. How could these changes have been handled? In addition to the possibilities already enumerated *(pinakes* and *periaktoi)*, several others have been suggested. In some instances, the actors and chorus may have left the scene and then returned, thus indicating a change in the place of the action. In some comedies, a trip around the orchestra probably accomplished the same result. It also seems likely that in comedy individual doors or sections of the *skene* were sometimes used to represent widely separated places; it is possible that this convention was also used in tragedy.

Enough has been said to demonstrate that the evidence concerning scenic practices in the fifth century is inconclusive. Nevertheless, it appears unlikely that illusionism was ever attempted to any marked degree. The use of a few symbolic properties or set pieces would not have been out of keeping with other Greek artistic conventions of the period, but the eventual erection of a permanent stone *skene* suggests that conventionalization predominated over illusionism.

Inconclusive evidence has also led to disagreement over whether the Theatre of Dionysus had a stage during the fifth century. Those who believe that there was none argue: (1) that the extant plays require the free mingling of actors and chorus, which a raised stage would have prevented; (2) that no extant plays require a stage; (3) that the choral performances that preceded the invention of drama did not use a stage and thus would have provided no precedents for one; (4) that during the fifth century there was no Greek word for stage, the term *logeion* dating from a later time after the stage was introduced; and (5) that there are no archeological remains of a stage from this period. On the other hand, those who favor a stage argue: (1) that all ancient commentators, though they admittedly lived much later, unanimously believed that there was a raised stage in the fifth century; (2) that since every other innovation, such as the introduction of the second and third actors and of scene painting, was recorded, so drastic a change as the introduction of a stage would scarcely have gone unnoted; (3) that a number of extant plays indicate that actors are on a higher level than the orchestra; and (4) that the intermingling of actors and chorus is not often required and that a low raised stage with steps to the orchestra would have accommodated these scenes.

The evidence cited on both sides is subject to opposing interpretations, but on closer examination the gulf between the two views is not so great as might appear at first. A. W. Pickard-Cambridge, the most influential recent opponent of the raised stage, is concerned primarily with refuting the idea of a high platform, and he admits that broad steps may have led up to the *skene* or that there may have been a stage one or two feet in height. Peter Arnott, the chief recent defender of the stage, suggests that the platform was about four feet high and connected to the orchestra by steps. A reading of the plays clearly suggests the need for some raised areas, but whether these were temporary set pieces or a permanent platform is unclear. If a permanent platform was used, it lay between the *skene* and the orchestra, and presumably would have extended the full width of the stage house.

In the fifth century, a limited amount of machinery was available for special effects. The most important devices were the *ekkyklema* and the *mechane* or *machina*. The *ekkyklema* (a device for revealing tableaux, most often the bodies of characters killed offstage) was probably a platform that could be rolled out through the central doorway of the *skene*. On the other hand some ancient accounts state that it was revolved or turned, while others associate it with the upper story of the scene house or with the side doors. The *mechane*, or crane, was used to show characters in flight or suspended above the earth. Occasionally characters are said to be in chariots or on the backs of birds, insects, or animals, while at other times the actor seems to have been suspended by a harness. The crane was probably situated so that an actor could be attached to it out of sight of the audience (behind either the scene house or some part of an upper level) and then raised in the air and swung out over the acting area. The crane was most often used for the appearance of gods, but certain human characters in tragedy might require it (for example, Perseus on his flying horse). In comedy, it was often used to parody tragedy or to ridicule human pretensions. It is difficult to establish the use of the crane prior to about 430, but it may have been available much earlier. Its overuse in

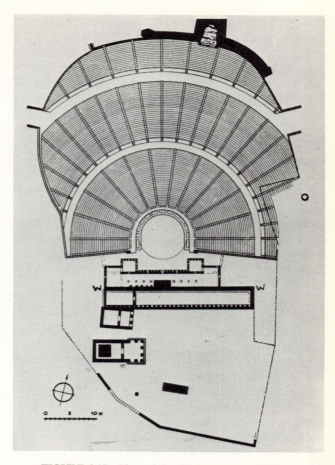

FIGURE 2.15 Plan of the Theatre of Dionysus as it probably appeared when completed in the late fourth century, B.C. The wall erected during the 440s is indicated by W-W. The square notches at the wall's front edge represent the slots allegedly used to hold the timbers of the temporary stage house. Below the wall is the hall, perhaps used for storage, and touching the wall at its left corner is the old temple of Dionysus; the new temple and the sacrificial altar are shown in the lower part of the picture. The *skene* and *paraskenia* are shown immediately forward of W-W. The upper crosswalk of the auditorium incorporated a public road. At the extreme top, a monument is set into the supporting walls of the Acropolis. O indicates the location of the Odeion. From Dörpfeld, *Griechische Theatre* (1896).

the last part of the century (especially by Euripides, who often employed gods to resolve his plots), led to the term *deus ex machina,* god from the machine, to describe any contrived ending.

Although stage properties were not numerous, they were essential elements of the productions. In many plays, characters sacrifice to a god or take refuge at an altar. Some scholars have argued that the altar in the center of the orchestra was used at these times; others have argued that since this altar was dedicated to Dionysus its use as a stage property would have been considered sacrilegious. Arnott suggests that there was a low structure in front of the central doorway that could be used either as altar or tomb. Other essential properties included chariots drawn by horses, biers for dead bodies, statues of various gods, and torches and lamps to indicate night scenes. Furniture was rarely required in tragedy and was restricted to couches for persons too ill or weak to stand. On the other hand, both furniture and other common domestic articles were numerous in comedy. In neither comedy nor tragedy were properties used to create the illusion of reality; they served instead to make some dramatic point.

AUDITORIUM AND AUDIENCE

Thus far, only those elements relating to the acting areas and performers have been considered. But the auditorium and audience were also important ingredients of a performance. In Greek theatres, the auditorium and scene house were always separate architectural units. Between them lay the orchestra and the *parodoi* (or entrances into the orchestra at either end of the stage house). The *parodoi* were used primarily by the chorus, although actors might enter there as well. The *parodoi* were also used by the audience as entrances to or exits from the auditorium.

The first *theatron* (or "seeing place," as the auditorium was termed by the Greeks) of the Theatre of Dionysus was the hillside which sloped down from the Acropolis. Originally, spectators probably stood to watch performances, but stadium-like seating may have been erected during the late sixth century, for the first major remodeling of the auditorium, undertaken shortly after 500, was probably caused by the collapse of wooden seats. At this time, the hillside was regraded to change the slope, and a series of terraces, on which rested wooden benches, were probably laid out. When the Odeion was built in the 440s, the slope was changed again and a number of supporting walls were added. The seats seem to have remained temporary, for Aristophanes refers to them as *ikria*, a term normally reserved for wooden benches. Stone seats may have been introduced gradually, but the stone auditorium was not completed

until some time between 338 and 326 B.C. (A plan of the first stone theatre is shown on p. 35.)

It is estimated that the completed stone auditorium seated 14,000 to 17,000 persons. Nevertheless, only a small portion of the population could have attended the theatre at any one time, since in the second half of the fifth century Attica had about 150,000 to 200,000 residents. Thus, while the theatre may have been open to all, only about one-tenth could have attended any given performance. This may explain the introduction of tickets and an admission fee around the middle of the fifth century (although it is possible that admission was charged from the very beginning). To equalize the opportunity to attend, Pericles established a "theoric fund" around 450 to provide tickets for the poor. He also may have specified the price to be charged, but there is no definite record of admission costs until the late fourth century, when all seats not reserved by the state were sold at a uniform charge (the nominal sum of two obols). This money seems to have gone to the man who leased the theatre and was responsible for its upkeep.

Tickets admitted holders to a section of the theatre rather than to specific seats. It has been suggested that each tribe had its own section and that within these areas one part was set aside for women. The central seat in the front row was reserved for the priest of Dionysus. Seats were also reserved for other priests and priestesses, for certain state officials, visiting ambassadors, and persons the state wished to honor. The audience was composed of women, men, boys, and slaves. Officials were responsible for keeping order and for checking tickets to see that their holders sat in the correct section. Violence in the theatre was punishable by death.

It is usually assumed that performances lasted all day, since a number of plays were presented in sequence. If so, there must have been much coming and going and considerable eating and drinking in the theatre. The audience expressed its opinions noisily and at times hissed actors off the stage; tradition has it that Aeschylus once had to take refuge on the altar to escape the wrath of the spectators. Some ancient writers damned the audience as debased, but others praised it as discriminating. Probably the spectators represented a cross-section of tastes as well as of society.

One of the high points of each festival was the awarding of prizes. Although not all of the details are clear, these are the probable procedures: at some time prior to the festival, a list of potential judges (one list for each of the ten tribes) was drawn up; all of the names from the same tribe were placed in a single urn; the ten urns were then sealed and placed under guard until the beginning of the contest, when they were brought into the theatre, where the *archon* drew one name from each urn; these men then served as judges for the contest. Each judge placed his vote in an urn, from which the *archon* drew five. On the basis of these five votes, the winner was declared.

The nature of the prizes is unclear, but they may have included money. Certainly the honor was great, and victorious *choregoi* often erected monuments to commemorate victories. State records were kept of the awards, and many ancient commentators drew upon them in writing their accounts.

Although there are many unresolved questions about the theatre in the fifth century, we can be reasonably sure that it was a vigorous institution, in high repute with the general populace and with the civil and religious authorities. Drama was the most prized form of literature and the theatre the most popular of the arts.

GREEK DRAMA AFTER THE FIFTH CENTURY

Following the Peloponnesian War, economic prosperity returned and the old forms of government continued for a time, but loyalty to the *polis* had been severely undermined and internal dissensions greatly increased thereafter. Sparta's domination of Greece passed to Thebes in 371 and then in 338 to Macedonia (a semi-barbaric kingdom in the Balkans), which made the Greek city-states dependencies. Nevertheless, the outward changes in Greek life were not extreme, and Athens actually gained in reputation as a cultural center. Thus, it is usual to consider the first three quarters of the fourth century a continuation of the classical age. Records indicate that in quantity artistic activity in the fourth century exceeded that in the fifth. Unfortunately, so few dramatic works have survived that we are unable to judge them fairly.

After 400 B.C. tragic output continued unabated. Many writers who are no longer remembered, such as Theodectes, Astydamas, and Chaeremon, ranked at the forefront of dramatists in their day. Of their later tragedies, only one—*Rhesus*, once attributed to Euripides— has survived. Based on the tenth book of the *Iliad*, it is noteworthy primarily for its simulation of night, during which the entire action occurs.

FIGURE 2.16 Terracotta statuette of an old woman from New Comedy, Courtesy British Museum.

During the fourth century, writers began to turn to the lesser myths, especially those of a slightly sensational nature, and to employ forensic elements and melodramatic devices with increasing frequency. Some of these changes may have come about because of Euripides' growing influence. Many of the earlier dramatists were admired, and after about 341 B.C. at least one old tragedy was presented each year at the City Dionysia. But if tragedy degenerated into imitations of earlier works, new plays continued to be written until the second century A.D.

Little is known of the satyr play after the fifth century. It must have declined in popularity, however, for beginning around 341 only one satyr play was produced each year during the City Dionysia.

On the other hand, comedy increased in popularity after the fifth century. Later commentators divided Greek comic writing into three periods: Old, dating from the beginning of the form until the end of the Peloponnesian War in 404; Middle, from 404 until 336 (when

FIGURE 2.17   Terracotta statuette of a Greek actor in the role of a running slave. From the Hellenistic period. Courtesy Museum of Fine Arts, Boston.

financial worries, and family relationships. New Comedy eventually became repetitious both in terms of situation and dramatic devices (especially concealed identity, coincidence, and recognition). Often the plots revolve around a young man who, against the bitter opposition of his father, seeks to marry a girl, frequently a slave about to be forced into prostitution; after many comically unsuccessful attempts to circumvent the father's wrath, the son achieves his goal when it is discovered that the girl is the long-lost daughter of some wealthy Athenian. Thus, the entire action is based upon a misunderstanding, which, when cleared up, removes the basis of conflict. New Comedy was not restricted to this kind of plot, however, for many plays were essentially character studies and others were based on myth.

The structure of New Comedy (a prologue followed by a series of episodes separated by choral passages) was borrowed from tragedy, a change from Old Comedy which some critics have attributed to the influ-

FIGURE 2.18 Statuette of a slave from New Comedy. From Robert, *Die Masken der Neueren Attischen Komoedie* (1911).

Alexander the Great came to power); and New, after 336. Middle Comedy is essentially a transitional type, moving away from personal invective and political and social satire toward events based on contemporary life and manners or alternatively on mythological burlesque. Although we know the names of about fifty writers and have a number of fragments of Middle Comedy, the only complete plays that have survived are Aristophanes' *Ecclesiazusae* (392–391) and *Plutus* (388). Both lack the political satire and the parabasis of Old Comedy, and the role of the chorus has been markedly reduced. Other than Aristophanes, the most famous writers of this form were Antiphanes, Alexis, Anaxandrides, and Eubulus.

New Comedy differs markedly from Old Comedy. Although writers still drew upon mythological subjects occasionally, they typically treated the domestic affairs of the Athenian middle-class citizenry. Unlike Old Comedy, New Comedy ignored social and political problems in favor of a more generalized concern for love,

FIGURE 2.19 A bas-relief from Naples of a scene from New Comedy: two old men at the left, the flute player in the center, and a youth and slave at the right. From Robert, *Die Masken der Neueren Attischen Komoedie* (1911).

291 B.C.), who wrote more than one hundred plays after 321, is by far the most important author of New Comedy. In addition to *The Grouch*, a comedy of character about an irascible old man, Menander's works are now known from lengthy fragments of *The Arbitration*, *The Girl from Samos*, and *The Shorn Girl*, and lesser fragments of about eighty-five other plays. In the ancient world, Menander was celebrated for his varied and sympathetic characterizations, his easy, natural style, his ability to adapt sentiment to character, and his ingenuity in constructing plots. In Rome, where his plays were frequently adapted, Menander's reputation was higher than that of any Greek author except Homer. Other important writers of New Comedy include Diphilus, Philemon, and Apollodorus.

After the third century B.C., comedy began to decline, just as tragedy had a century earlier. New Comedy was the last vital expression of drama in ancient Greece.

ence of Euripides, who is also credited with creating popularity for such story elements as long-lost children and scenes of recognition. The choral passages in New Comedy usually had little connection with the incidents and in many of the plays the chorus appeared onstage only during the interludes between episodes. In others, however, the chorus was present throughout and played a more organic part in the plot. New Comedy was also mixed in tone, for in many plays pathetic and moral elements injected a serious note. Others, however, were primarily farcical. The language reflected everyday usage but was not extremely colloquial, for dialogue was still cast in verse.

Characters were gradually conventionalized into a restricted number of types. Pollux (a Greek lexicographer of the second century A.D.) gives the following list of character types in New Comedy: nine old men, four young men, seven slaves, five young women, and various soldiers, parasites, and other types. Pollux's description shows that each subtype within these broad groupings was differentiated by some distinctive quality reflected in his mask and costume.

Although the names of sixty-four writers of New Comedy are known and about 1,400 plays of this type were probably produced, only one complete work—*The Grouch* by Menander—has survived. Menander (342-

THE ATHENIAN THEATRE IN THE FOURTH CENTURY

Athens continued to be the major theatrical center of Greece through the fourth century B.C. But during this century many changes were made in the dramatic festivals. At the City Dionysia, contests for the production of old plays were instituted in the last part of the century, a practice seemingly never permitted at the Lenaia. The increased popularity of comedy was reflected in the institution of a contest for comic actors at the City Dionysia. A decline in personal wealth among Athenians led (some time between 317 and 307) to the discontinuance of the practice of appointing *choregoi*. After this time an elected official, the *agonothetes*, was given a state appropriation out of which to finance all theatrical productions.

The fourth century also brought an increase in professionalism. By about 350, professional singer-dancers, who appeared in both comic and tragic choruses, were replacing amateurs used in earlier times, and they were being rehearsed by professional trainers. Acting also grew in importance and came to overshadow playwriting. Probably as a result, around 350 the rules governing tragic performers at the City Dionysia were changed to require each of the three leading actors to appear in one play by each of the competing dramatists. Many actors might rightfully be termed stars, for the fame of Polus,

FIGURE 2.20   Marble relief sculpture of Menander with three masks. In his hand, Menander holds the mask of a youth; on the table are masks of a young woman and a man. Courtesy the Art Museum, Princeton University.

Theodorus, Thettalus, Neoptolemus, Athenodorus, Aristodemus, and others spread throughout the Greek world. By 300, such well-known actors were touring almost everywhere. By this time they had also gained such ascendancy over dramatists that they changed texts to suit their talents and often indulged in elaborate displays of vocal virtuosity.

It is ironic that the Theatre of Dionysus was not given its permanent stone form until about 325, by which time the Athenian theatre was already losing its privileged position. This permanent structure is important, nevertheless, for its archeological remains have served as the primary basis for most conjectures about theatre architecture in the fifth century. (It is often assumed that the stone theatre was merely a more permanent version of an earlier temporary structure.) After 300, Athens was no longer in the forefront of developments, and its theatre building was soon considered old-fashioned.

During the fourth century, Greek thought became increasingly secularized. Although religious worship and festivals continued, belief in their efficacy was seriously undermined by the intellectual scrutiny to which the

gods and myths were subjected during this great age of Greek philosophy, epitomized above all by the work of Plato (*c.* 429–347) and Aristotle (384–322). During this time philosophers inquired into every aspect of Greek life, including the theatre. Plato argued for censorship and strict state control over drama, whose powerful influence he feared. Aristotle referred to the theatre in several of his works, but his major ideas are set forth in the *Poetics* (*c.* 335–323), the first systematic treatise ever written on drama. In addition to its discussion of tragedy, the *Poetics* contains in its early chapters the oldest surviving history of dramatic forms. While preparing to write this work, Aristotle is said to have compiled a record of the plays and winners at all the festivals, a major source of information for subsequent historians of Greece and Rome.

Aristotle's influence has been especially great on critical theory, for his *Poetics* has been crucial in practically all discussions of tragedy since the sixteenth century, when it first became widely known. Because many of Aristotle's ideas are stated cryptically, however, the *Poetics* has been interpreted variously. It must be read with great care if it is to be helpful.

Aristotle states in the *Poetics,* that every drama has six parts: plot, character, thought, diction, music, and spectacle. He discusses unity of action, probability, the requirements of plot, characteristics of the tragic hero, problems of diction, and many other topics. His conclusions continue to be sources of inspiration and controversy.

THE HELLENISTIC THEATRE

Historians usually make a distinction between the classical (*c.* 500–336) and the Hellenistic (beginning with the reign of Alexander the Great) ages. Between 336 and his death in 323, Alexander conquered the Persian empire and extended his realm into present-day India and Egypt. Wherever he went he built new cities and promoted Greek culture and learning. As a result, the entire eastern Mediterranean was Hellenized. Athens continued to be a major cultural center, but its preeminence was challenged in the third century by Pergamum (in Asia Minor) and especially by Alexandria (in Egypt), which became the literary capital of the Greek world because of its library and institute for literary research.

Alexander's empire disintegrated after his death, but major parts of it were maintained by others until

FIGURE 2.21 **A reconstruction of the Theatre of Dionysus as it appeared when completed by Lycurgus in the late fourth century B.C. From Frickenhaus,** *Die Altgriechische Bühne* **(1917).**

Rome took it over. Mainland Greece regained a somewhat precarious independence, but it was so lacking in unity that it could put up no effective resistance to Rome and became a Roman province in 146 B.C.

The Hellenistic age saw many changes in the theatre. One was initiated by the victory festivals held by Alexander, at one of which he is said to have assembled 3,000 performers from all over the Greek world. Thereafter, the occasions on which plays might be presented were numerous, especially since rulers began to encourage worship of themselves as gods and to establish festivals in their own honor. Consequently, plays were no longer performed exclusively at Dionysian festivals.

The rapid expansion in the number of festivals created a demand for qualified performers, and perhaps as a result the theatre of the Hellenistic period became almost totally professionalized. A major step in that direction was taken with the formation of a guild of performers, sometimes called the Artists of Dionysus. Although the date of this guild's formation is uncertain, it was clearly in existence by 277 B.C., for it was given official sanction in a decree of that year. It continued to be active into the Christian era.

The Artists of Dionysus included among its members poets (dramatic, epic, and lyric), actors (tragic, comic, and satyric), oral readers, members of the chorus, trainers, musicians, and costumers—all the personnel needed to produce plays and to give recitations at festivals. Popular entertainers of other kinds were never admitted to this guild.

As the name of the guild suggests, the performers retained their connection with Dionysus, even though they produced plays and acted at some non-Dionysian festivals. The head of the organization was usually a priest of Dionysus. The guild had a number of subdivisions, each with its own headquarters. Of the three major branches, the Athenian was probably the oldest and was long the most respected. A second branch, the Nemean and Isthmian guild, had its headquarters at Corinth, and the third major branch, the Ionian and Hellespontine guild, was based at Teos in Asia Minor. There may have been a fourth branch at Alexandria. As the theatre grew, each major branch created its own subdivisions to serve the areas under its jurisdiction.

When planning a festival, a city apparently negotiated a contract with the nearest guild. The obligations of each party were clearly specified in the agreements. Because of the importance of the festivals and because following the death of Alexander the Hellenic world had broken up into a number of states, international agreements were reached under which the safety of the guild's members was guaranteed; in some instances performers

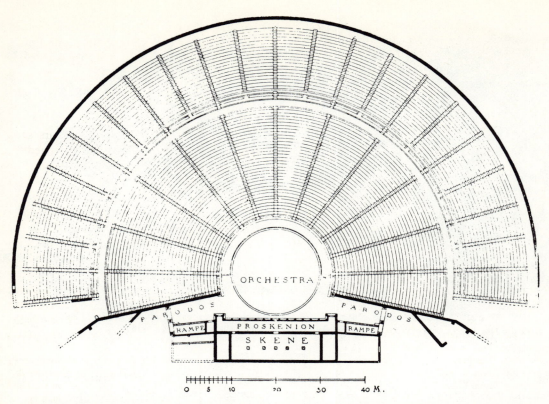

ORCHESTRA

PARODOS

PARODOS

RAMPE

RAMPE

PROSKENION

SKENE

0   5   10   20   30   40 M.

FIGURE 2.22   Plan of the Theatre at Epidaurus. It shows the high raised stage, reached by ramps, and a fully circular orchestra, unusual for a Hellenistic theatre. From Dörpfeld, *Griechische Theater* (1896).

were made immune from arrest and military service. Because they could move about freely, actors occasionally served as ambassadors between states. But, though actors enjoyed greater professional security than in earlier years, they were already being looked upon as somehow suspect. Even in the fourth century Aristotle had asked why actors are usually "disreputable" and "incontinent," and such questions subsequently became more common.

Theatre architecture also underwent considerable change in this period. Between the middle of the fourth century and the first century B.C., a theatre structure quite unlike that of the Theatre of Dionysus evolved. Normally called Hellenistic (to distinguish it from the Athenian type), important examples were built at Priene, Oropus, Ephesus, Delos, Epidaurus, Oeniadae, Sicyon, Pergamum, Corinth, and Alexandria.

Although the basic features of the Hellenistic theatre are reasonably well established, the date and place of their origin are disputed. Some scholars argue that drastic alterations in the Athenian plan were made

as early as the fourth century, but others date them from the second century B.C. The theatres at Priene, Epidaurus, and Alexandria have each been cited as the first of the new type. The evidence is hopelessly confused, primarily because archeologists cannot agree upon the dates when the original structures were built or when they underwent the various remodelings to which all were subjected. The details of this controversy are unimportant here; it is sufficient to note that the basic structural features of the Hellenistic theatre may have been present as early as 300 B.C. or may have evolved gradually over a period of 150 years. Almost all scholars agree that the Hellenistic theatre building was fully developed by about 150 B.C.

Probably the most important Hellenistic innovation was the high raised stage. Varying from 8 to 13 feet in height, it was sometimes as long as 140 feet, although it was only from 6½ to 14 feet deep. Since *paraskenia* (or side wings of the scene house) were eliminated, this long, narrow platform was open at both ends. In some theatres, ramps parallel to the *parodoi* led up to the stage;

FIGURE 2.23   The remains of the Hellenistic theatre at Epidauraus. This is the best preserved of all the ancient Greek theatres. For festivals, a temporary stage house is erected over the foundations seen at left. Courtesy Royal Greek Embassy.

orchestra merely a vestigial structural feature which no longer served any necessary function? Both affirmative and negative answers have been advanced for each of these questions, none of which can be accepted with certainty.

Many problems also arise in relation to scenic practices. For example, in the early Hellenistic theatre the *proskenion* was composed of pillars spaced several feet apart; often these pillars were notched so as to hold *pinakes* (painted panels). In many theatres dating from later than the second century B.C., however, the pillars are no longer notched. On this basis, some historians have argued that as long as performances occurred in the orchestra a scenic background had to be provided; whereas later, when all action was transferred to the stage, the *proskenion* became merely an open colonnade, since *pinakes* were no longer needed at the orchestra level.

As time passed, the facade of the second story also underwent a number of changes. During the second century B.C., the *episkenion*, which originally had been fitted with from one to three doors, was converted into a

FIGURE 2.24   The Hellenistic theatre at Eretria. The upper view shows an early phase in the stage building's development, while the lower shows fully developed *thyromata*. From Fiechter, *Antike Griechische Theaterbauten.*

in others, steps to the orchestra were provided at the ends of the stage; in still others, the stage could be entered only from the scene house. The front edge of the stage was supported by the *proskenion* (or facade of the lower story), while the *episkenion* (or facade of the second story) rose at the back of the raised stage. Often the two facades were approximately equal in height. In some theatres, the *proskenion* overlapped the outer rim of the orchestra circle by a few feet, although in others the full circle of the orchestra remained entirely visible. The auditoriums underwent no significant changes, but they varied widely in seating capacity, ranging from 3,000 at Oropus to 25,000 at Ephesus.

The alterations in the *skene* raise many questions about staging. Was the orchestra used by all performers when old plays requiring a large chorus were revived, and was the raised stage reserved for those newer plays in which the chorus was small or incidental? Did the actors use the stage and the chorus the orchestra? Was the upper stage at first used only for gods and special scenes and only later transformed into the usual active area for all scenes? Was the orchestra used only for nondramatic performances (such as dithyrambic choruses)? Was the

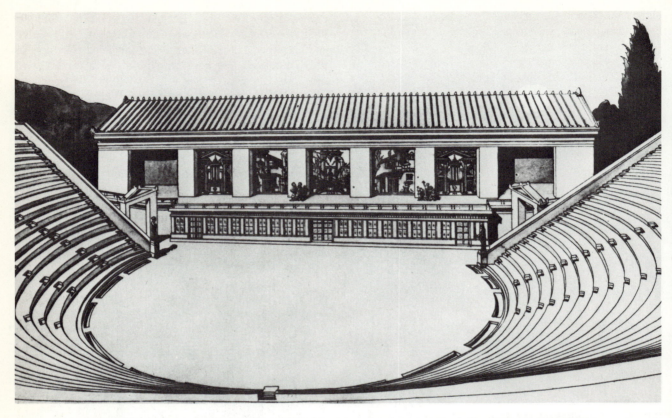

FIGURE 2.25 Reconstruction of the Hellensitic theatre at Ephesus. Note the thyromata treated as though each were a miniature proscenium stage. From Frickenhaus, *Die Altgriechische Bühne* (1917).

series of sizable openings (or *thyromata*) varying in number from one to seven. These *thyromata*, averaging about 10 to 12 feet in width and extending upward as high as the roof would permit, were separated from each other by narrow upright supports. Thus, on the upper level there was now a long shallow forestage backed by a rear stage equally as deep or deeper.

This change is usually associated with the decline of the chorus and the increased use of the high platform for the action. Some scholars have also assumed that *thyromata* were created to permit greater scenic illusion, and they have suggested that each opening served as a miniature proscenium arch behind which individual settings could be erected. This theory (as well as all others about the *thyromata*) is entirely conjectural.

Vitruvius, writing in the first century B.C. of the Greek theatre, describes the facade as providing spaces for *periaktoi*. Possibly *periaktoi* were set up in *thryomata*.

Vitruvius also says that there were three kinds of backgrounds: one each for tragedy, comedy, and satyr plays. Though some historians have interpreted this passage to mean that illusionistic scenery was used, others have argued that it merely suggests some type of conventionalized background.

Tragic costumes and masks changed considerably after the fifth century. Although the progressive changes cannot be dated, it is reasonably clear that by the first century B.C. the tragic actor was padded, wore thick-soled boots *(cothornoi)*, and a high headdress *(onkos)*, all intended to increase his apparent size. The facial features of the masks were also enlarged and exaggerated. In other words, the tragic actor was now made larger than life and his overall appearance was distorted and conventionalized. Pollux (writing in the second century A.D.) lists twenty-eight basic masks, supposedly covering the categories of tragic characters: six old men, eight young men, eight women, and six servants. In addition, he lists several unusual masks, such as one for Argos (who according to myth had many eyes).

In New Comedy, costume, although somewhat conventionalized, was based on the dress of ordinary life. The typical garment was the *exomis* (a plain white tunic, unseamed on the left side). Over this, old men wore a long white cloak *(himation),* young men of good family a red or purple *himation,* and parasites a black or gray *himation.* Slaves wore a short white cloak over the *exomis.* Old women were dressed in green or light blue; priestesses wore white, as did young women.

Pollux lists forty-four masks for New Comedy; nine for old men, four for young men, seven for slaves, three for old women, five for young women, seven for courtesans, two for maidservants, one for rustics, two for soldiers, one for flatterers, and three for parasites. Thus, it would appear that the character types of comedy were considerably more extensive than those of tragedy. Although most masks apparently were realistic, some, such as those for slaves and certain old men and ridiculous characters, were caricatured. Hair color was also somewhat conventionalized. For example, most slaves had red hair, while courtesans usually had yellow.

Although the Greek theatre continued until after 500 A.D., its vitality declined rapidly after the first century B.C. Beginning in the second century B.C., the Romans gradually gained power over all the Eastern Mediterranean and, though Greek ideals persisted for a time, Roman standards eventually superseded them. After the first century A.D., most of the theatres were remodeled to conform more nearly to the Roman ideal of theatre architecture. These remodeled structures are usually called Greco-Roman, since they have some features characteristic of each type. Many purely Roman theatres were also erected in Greek territories.

The theatre in Athens was not immune to these changes, although it long resisted them. The Theatre of Dionysus retained its classical form until sometime between the third and first centuries B.C. when it was remodeled along more fashionable Hellenistic lines. Other extensive changes were made in the first century A.D., when the stage was extended forward over part of the orchestra to make it conform more nearly to the Roman ideal. After this time, gladiatorial contests were sometimes staged in the orchestra (which was by then fenced in with a stone barricade); about the fourth century A.D. the orchestra was sealed so that water spectacles could be given in it.

It is not clear when the Athenian dramatic contests ceased. The records of the City Dionysia continue until the first century A.D., while those of the Lenaia can be traced only until about 150 B.C. Nevertheless, the contests may have gone on for some time after our records cease. The Theatre of Dionysus was used for various kinds of spectacles until at least the fourth century A.D. and perhaps longer. Thus ended a truly remarkable history, for few other theatres can boast 1,000 years of continuous usage.

GREEK MIMES

It is now customary to study the Greek theatre almost wholly in terms of comic and tragic performances at

FIGURE 2.26 The "golden courtesan" of New Comedy. From Robert, *Die Masken der Neueren Attischen Komoedie* (1911).

official festivals. But it is clear that from the beginning there was extensive theatrical activity of a less ambitious sort. We know little about it because it was not a part of the state-supported festivals; so, few records relating to it were kept.

All types of entertainment are often grouped under the heading of "mime," a term applied indiscriminately both to scripts and performers. Mime ranged through short playlets, mimetic dance, imitations of animals and birds, singing, acrobatics, juggling, and so on. Small troupes of mimes may have performed at banquets and on other occasions as early as the fifth century. Thus, mimes were probably the first professional entertainers; they certainly were the first to include women among their ranks.

Short mime playlets seem to have originated in Megara in the sixth century B.C. The Greek colonies of southern Italy and Sicily favored them during the fifth century, but not until Hellenistic times did they flourish throughout Eastern Mediterranean areas. After

300 B.C., mime performers appeared increasingly at festivals, although they were never admitted to membership in the Artists of Dionysus. The increased vogue for mimes is reflected in the rise of a school of "literary mime" writers at Alexandria and in southern Italy around 300–250 B.C. Eight playlets by Herodas, who lived in Alexandria in the first half of the third century, still survive. They are short (most no more than 100 lines), relatively subtle and realistic scenes of daily life.

In southern Italy, mimes were called *phlyakes*. Rhinthon, who lived at Tarentum in the first half of the third century, is said to have formalized this type. Of the thirty-eight plays attributed to him, most are *hilarotragodiai*, or burlesques of tragedy. Only a few fragments survive. Although mimes were popular throughout the Hellenic world, *phlyakes* have received the most attention because a series of vases from southern Italy were once thought to depict scenes from this form. These vases have now been redated to 400–325 B.C., about a century before any known *phlyax* plays were written, but they are

FIGURE 2.27 Scene from a *phlyax* vase of the fourth century B.C. Note the portico, steps, raised stage, and costumes. From Baumeister, *Denkmaler des Klassischen Altertums* (1889).

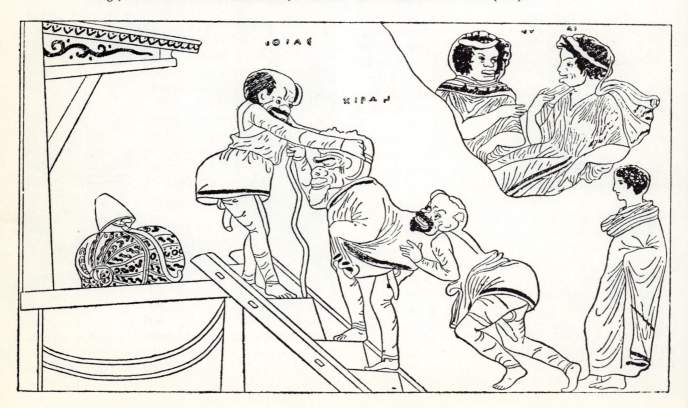

still called *phlyax* vases, even though their connection with mime performances is uncertain. (The scenes they depict may be based on Old or Middle Comedy.) The characters wear padded tights, short chitons, and the phallus. The subjects range from mythological burlesque (the adventures of Heracles is a favorite) to daily life. Lovemaking, gluttony, beatings, thievery, and trickery are popular motifs.

Probably of greatest interest is the representation of the stage. The paintings show a raised platform, varying in height and resting on posts or decorative columns, between which are draperies or painted panels. Steps, often being used by actors, lead up from the ground level to the stage. The facade at the back of the stage varies: sometimes it is composed of a portico and door, at others there are columns and decorative motifs, sometimes there is a window or gallery on an upper level. Trees, altars, thrones, chests, and tables appear among the properties. Some scholars have interpreted the paintings as evidence that mime performers used a temporary stage which could be erected as needed by traveling troupes; others have suggested that the vases show the stages of permanent theatres but depicted in a simplified manner because of the limited space available to the vase painters.

Regardless of how the vases are interpreted, it is clear that the theatre flourished in southern Italy. It was there, in the third century B.C., that the Romans first encountered Greek culture. After this time, historical interest shifts to Rome, where Greek forms and practices were adopted and transformed. From Rome they were transmitted to other areas and to later times, although it should not be forgotten that the Greek theatre continued throughout the Roman era.

LOOKING AT THEATRE HISTORY

One of the primary ways of approaching the Greek theatre is through archeology, the systematic study of such material remains as architecture, inscriptions, sculpture, vase-paintings, and other forms of decorative art. About the contributions of archeology to our knowledge of ancient civilizations, it has been said: "The recovery of these long-forgotten episodes in human history has been an astonishing performance—as remarkable . . . as . . . reaching the moon. As a result . . . our own generation is aware of more aspects of the distant past than were dreamed of by our great-grandfathers."

Serious on-site excavations began in Greece around 1870, but W. Dörpfeld did not begin the first extensive study of the Theatre of Dionysus until 1886. Since that time many other theatres have been uncovered. These excavations have revealed much that was previously unknown, especially about the dimensions and layout of theatres. Nevertheless, they still do not permit us to describe the precise appearance of the *skene* (illustrations printed in books are conjectural reconstructions), for many pieces are irrevocably lost because the buildings in later periods became sources of stone for other projects and what remains is usually broken and scattered. That most of the buildings were remodeled many times has created great problems in dating both the parts and the successive versions. Despite these drawbacks, archeology has provided the most precise information we have about the theatre structures of ancient Greece. (The best summary in English of what is known about the Theatre of Dionysus is A. W. Pickard-Cambridge's *The Theatre of Dionysus in Athens*.) But, if they have told us much, archeologists have not completed their work and many sites have scarcely been touched.

Perhaps the most controversial use of archeological evidence in theatre history is vase paintings, thousands of which have survived from ancient Greece. (Most of those used by theatre scholars are reproduced in Margarete Bieber's *The History of the Greek and Roman Theater*.) Depicting scenes from mythology and daily life, the vases are the most graphic pictorical evidence we have. But they are also easy to misinterpret. Some scholars have considered any vase that depicts a subject treated in a surviving drama or any scene showing masks, flute players, or ceremonials to be valid evidence of theatrical practice. This is a highly questionable assumption, since the Greeks made widespread use of masks, dances, and music outside the theatre and since the myths on which dramatists drew were known to everyone, including vase painters, who might well depict the same subjects as dramatists without being indebted to them. Those vases showing scenes unquestionably theatrical are few, but very useful.

Perhaps most of all, Greek artifacts can help us understand prevailing styles in visual expression and how they changed, a not inconsiderable aid in trying to envision theatrical performances as they might have appeared originally.

One of the tasks always faced by historians is to assess the reliability of the available evidence. They must develop the habit of systematic doubt and ask such questions as: What was the relationship of the author to the event he is reporting? Was he an eyewitness? If so, what was his role (had he any reason to alter details so as to escape blame or to take credit)? If not, on what did he base his account? How much time had elapsed between the event and the record of it (time has a way of altering perception and memory)? Is the account either verified or contradicted by other sources?

Assessing the reliability of the extant written evidence about the Greek theatre is difficult indeed. By far the majority of material was compiled several hundred years after the events occurred. Sometimes these compilers mention sources, but often we do not know how accurately the sources have been used or on what they themselves were based. In the absence of material nearer in time to the events, however, historians have been forced to rely on such evidence, and they are grateful to have it, since so few accounts of any kind have survived. Historical treatment of the Greek theatre is something like assembling a jigsaw puzzle with many pieces missing: the historian arranges what he has and seeks to reconstruct (as logically as possible) what has been lost. As a result, though the broad outlines of Greek theatre history are reasonably clear, many of the details cannot be established with absolute certainty.

One good example of the type of evidence available to historians is *The Deipnosophists*, compiled by Athenaeus in Egypt around 200 A.D. In the following passages, he writes about events in Greece some 600 years earlier. Much of what he says is consistent with other reports, and his testimony has been repeated so often that it has been accorded the status of fact, but its reliability cannot be firmly established. It is amusing to note that his final statement is almost never quoted, although it is difficult to see why Chamaeleon should be considered an unreliable witness on this point if he is to be believed on others.

Sophocles, in addition to being eminent for personal beauty, was very accomplished in music and dancing, having been instructed in those arts while a boy by Lamprus . . . ; and when he exhibited his Thamyris he himself played the harp; and he also played at ball with great skill when he exhibited his Nausicaa. . . .

But Aeschylus was not only the inventor of becoming and dignified dress, which the hierophants and torch-bearers of the sacred festivals imitated; but he also invented many figures in dancing, and taught them to the dancers of the chorus. And Chamaeleon states that he first arranged the choruses, not using the ordinary dancing-masters, but himself arranging the figures of the dancers for the chorus; and altogether that he took the whole arrangement of his tragedies on himself. And he himself acted in his own plays very fairly. . . . But Aeschylus was often drunk when he wrote his tragedies, if we may trust Chamaeleon: and accordingly Sophocles reproached him, saying, that even when he did what was right he did not know that he was doing so.

ATHENAEUS, *The Deipnosophists, or Banquet of the Learned*, trans. C. D. Yonge, 3 vols. (London: H. G. Bohn, 1854), Bk. I, chs. 37 and 39.

3

Roman Theatre and Drama

According to tradition, Rome was founded in 753 B.C. (about the time the Greeks were colonizing southern Italy and Sicily). It remained an insignificant town under the domination of neighboring Etruria, the home of several of its early rulers, until it expelled its last Etruscan king and founded a republic in 509 (just as Athens was becoming a democracy). During the fourth century, Rome began to expand and by 265 controlled the entire Italian peninsula, including the Etruscan areas to the north and the Greek territories to the south. Next, following the first Punic War with Carthage (264–241), Rome acquired Sicily. As a result of its expansion between 270 and 240, Rome took over several Greek territories in which the theatre had long flourished. By 240, a sufficiently large number of Romans were familiar with Greek art and theatre that regular drama (either translations or imitations of Greek plays) was introduced into Rome. Consequently, the year 240 B.C. is often said to mark the beginning of Roman theatre.

But while this date may establish when regular Roman drama began, it does not mark the beginning of Rome's theatrical activity, which can be traced back more than a century prior to that time. If we are to understand Roman theatre, it is essential to recognize from the outset that drama in the Greek sense played only a small role in it, since it was always dominated by variety entertainment. We can probably grasp the essence of Roman theatre more readily by comparing it with American television programming, for it encompassed acrobatics,

trained animals, jugglers, athletic events, music and dance, dramatic skits, short farces, and full-length dramas. The Roman public was as fickle as our own: like channel-switchers, they frequently left one event for another and demanded diversions capable of withstanding all competion. From time to time, new forms of entertainment were introduced to Rome; some of these were retained for several centuries, whereas others lost their popularity more quickly and were either discarded or relegated to a minor role. Regular drama must be included among the forms that flourished for a time and then declined.

ETRUSCAN INFLUENCE

In the period prior to 240 B.C., Etruria was the dominant influence on Roman theatrical activities, although it is difficult to assess the culture's contributions fully since so few written records have survived from Etruscan civilization. Nevertheless, it was probably from Etruria that Rome inherited many features of its religious festivals (the occasions on which theatrical performances were given in Rome). Sacred festivals in Etruria included acting, dancing, flute playing, juggling, prizefighting, horseracing, acrobatics, and competitive sports. The Etruscans also believed that the religious portions of its festivals must be performed precisely and without error,

FIGURE 3.1 Etruscan musician playing the double flute. From the tomb of the Leopards, Tarquinii. From *Jahrbuch des deutschen archäologischen Instituts,* Vol. 31 (1916).

a belief which the Romans shared and which often led them to repeat entire festivals when mistakes were made. Some Etruscan festivals were held in conjunction with fairs to which people came from faraway places. All these attributes help to explain the nature of Roman festivals, which mingled diverse activities in an atmosphere partly religious, partly secular, even carnival-like. Other Etruscan practices also probably influenced Roman theatre. Among these was the use of music, dance, and masks in almost all Etruscan ceremonies; music was especially important, for it accompanied activities ranging from sacrifices to boxing matches to daily work. The Etruscans also originated gladiatorial contests, although as funeral ceremonies rather than the form of entertainment they became under the Romans.

The influence of Etruria on Roman theatre is attested to by many ancient sources. The Roman poet Horace (65–8 B.C.) states that Latin drama originated in the Fescennine Verses (a name thought by some to be derived from Fescennium, a town on the Etruscan border), compositions consisting of improvised, abusive, and often obscene dialogue exchanged between masked clowns at harvest and wedding celebrations. On the other hand, Livy (59 B.C.–17 A.D.), the Roman historian, dates the first theatrical performances in Rome at 364 B.C.,

when musical and dancing performers were imported from Etruria in an effort to appease the gods when plague was ravishing the city. Rome derived its term for actors *(histriones)* from these professional performers (called *ister* by the Etruscans). Subsequently, according to Livy, improvised dialogue was added to the music and dance to create a new form, performed at first by amateurs but later by professionals. It was also an Etruscan ruler of Rome, the elder Tarquin (616–579 B.C.), who established the *ludi Romani* (the festival at which Greek drama was later first presented) with its chariot races, boxing contests, and other entertainments. Since Etruscan tomb paintings show grandstands for spectators at festivals, stadium-like seating was probably used in Rome long before the Greek theatre was known there.

In addition to Etruria, southern Italy contributed to Rome's early theatre. The primary influence came from the Atellan farce *(fabula Atellana),* which takes its name from the Oscan town of Atella (near what is now Naples). It was probably imported to Rome during the first half of the third century, for by 275 B.C. the Romans had become undisputed masters of the Oscan region. Little is known of the early Atellan farce. Some scholars argue that it was probably derived from the *phlyakes* or other mimes of southern Italy. It was probably short, largely improvised, and based on domestic situations or mythological burlesque. Type characters, each with its own fixed costume and mask, seem also to have been characteristic.

Thus, by 240, when Greek drama was imported into Rome, various kinds of entertainments (music, dance, farce, chariot races, and boxing) were already well established at Roman festivals. Regular drama was merely added to them.

THE ROMAN CONTEXT

By 146 B.C., Rome had conquered Greece and thereafter it gradually absorbed the entire Hellenic world. In turn, Rome was heavily influenced by Greek culture. From the third century onward, Greek tutors were in demand in Rome and many Romans went to study in Greece. Furthermore, most Roman art and literature after 240 B.C. was based on Greek models.

As a people, the Romans are noted for adopting the ideas and practices of others. But they were neither indiscriminate nor unintelligent borrowers, for of all the

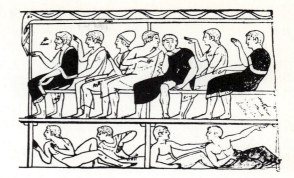

FIGURE 3.2   Stands for audience at an Etruscan entertainment. Wall painting from a tomb at Corneto. From *Jahrbuch des deutschen archäologischen Instituts,* Vol. 31 (1916).

people who came into contact with the Greeks only the Romans embraced Greek artistic forms. Nevertheless, Romans should not be viewed as mere extensions of the Greeks, for their own character made them reject much that was distinctively Greek.

The Romans were almost wholly devoid of the philosophical bent so characteristic of the Greeks. A practical people, they were for the most part uninterested in theoretical questions. Though they were among the greatest engineers, military tacticians, and administrators the world has known, they did not speculate about these subjects or seek to reduce them to principles. They were content to discover how things worked without asking why. These traits also affected their art, which tended to be grandiose, sentimental, or diversionary rather than, as with the Greeks, a serious exploration of the human condition.

Rome's history can best be understood by dividing it into two phases: the republic (509–27 B.C.) and the empire (27 B.C.–c. 476 A.D.). It was the republican "virtues"—discipline, economy, endurance, military precision, and loyalty to family and state—that made it possible for Rome to become a world power. Until the first century B.C., Romans were noted for their incorruptibility, their sense of duty to the republic, and their faith in law and order. Conservative Romans always considered Greek influence to be a sign of weakness and decadence.

By the first century B.C., Rome ruled a vast territory that poured wealth into the capitol. Roman citizens were receiving grain free of charge, the army had become professionalized, and the government was bureaucratized. By 27 B.C., power had passed from representative bodies to the emperor. Thereafter, the virtues that had built

Rome gradually disappeared. The basic problem became how to maintain and administer Rome's far-flung territories. That the empire endured so long is a testament to the Roman genius for organization.

Elements of the same change can be noted in the theatre. Under the rule of the republic regular drama prospered: tragedy's appeal probably lay in its echo of republican sentiments about virtue, honor, and loyalty, whereas comedy's was in the light-hearted treatment of familiar complications that were always resolved happily. Neither form seems to have reflected any philosophical concerns or to have questioned Roman values. Under the empire, regular drama was largely abandoned in favor of variety entertainment; the theatre became increasingly diversionary, with novelties of all kinds demanded and offered—new types of entertainments, ever-increasing lavishness and elaborateness of spectacle, thrills of all sorts (nudity, sex, violence, and bloodshed among them).

Nevertheless, it should not be forgotten that the theatre in Rome almost always was associated with festivals, most of them religious. Thus, theatrical offerings (regardless of content) were thought to be pleasing to (or capable of propitiating) the gods. Not only were Roman counterparts of the Greek gods worshipped, but household spirits and animistic forces were lauded as well; as Rome expanded, new gods were continually added to the list, for the Romans were a superstitious people fearful of offending any supernatural power. The Romans seem to have placed as much or more emphasis on the form as on the substance of religious ceremonies. Perhaps this explains why at the festivals honoring the gods the content of theatrical entertainments mattered less than the fact that the entertainments were routinely offered.

Overall, it seems clear that Roman drama did not reach a level comparable to that of fifth-century Greece. But it is equally true that in Rome the theatre was far more highly developed, varied, and extensive than in any earlier culture.

ROMAN FESTIVALS

Most state-sponsored theatrical performances in Rome were given at official religious festivals, or *ludi*, honoring various gods. A number of other festivals were given on special occasions (such as after major victories in war, at the dedication of public buildings or monuments, at the funerals of important personages, or when a private individual wished to curry favor).

The oldest of the official festivals was the *ludi Romani*, given in honor of Jupiter each September. Established in the sixth century B.C., it included theatrical performances beginning in 364 and regular comedy and tragedy beginning in 240 B.C. Eventually five other festivals also were of special importance for theatrical entertainment: the *ludi Florales* (given in April in honor of Flora), instituted in 238 and made annual in 173; the *ludi Plebeii* (given in November in honor of Jupiter) inaugurated not later than 220 B.C. and with plays introduced not later than 200; the *ludi Apollinares* (held in July in honor of Apollo), begun in 212 and with theatrical performances inaugurated about 179; the *ludi Megalenses* (given in April in honor of the Great Mother), instituted in 204 and with theatrical productions added by 194; and the *ludi Cereales* (given in honor of Ceres), established by 202 B.C. In addition, several other festivals included theatrical entertainments from time to time.

It is difficult to estimate how many days the Romans devoted to performances annually, since the number of official festival days differed from year to year and special celebrations were often permitted. Furthermore, festivals were sometimes repeated, since whenever any irregularity in the rituals occurred the entire festival, including the plays, had to be repeated. (Such repetition was labelled *instauratio*.) That *instauratio* was not uncommon is shown by the repetition of the *ludi Romani* in eleven of the years between 214 and 200 and of the *ludi Plebeii* seven times in one year.

Although the precise number of performances in any given year cannot be determined, they increased steadily after 240 B.C. Probably only one day was set aside for theatrical productions in the beginning, but by 200 B.C. the number had grown to between four and eleven, by 190 to between seven and seventeen, by 150 to about twenty-five, and by the beginning of the Christian era to about forty. Under the empire, the number of performances was greatly inflated, for this was the period especially noted for offering the people "bread and circuses." In 354 A.D., 100 days were devoted to theatrical entertainments and another 75 to such events as chariot races and gladiatorial contests. After 400 A.D., as the empire began to disintegrate, the number seems to have varied considerably from one reign to another, but performances continued into the sixth century. In addition to the state festivals, there probably were privately arranged indoor performances and even some public performances given for paying audiences by traveling troupes.

DRAMA UNDER THE ROMANS

By the time Rome ceased to be a republic in 27 B.C., regular drama had already declined markedly and the minor forms had become dominant. Of the more than 900 years over which the history of Roman theatre extends, only about 200 are of much importance for drama since it was during this time that most of the plays intended for performance were written.

Roman literature is usually said to have begun with Livius Andronicus (*fl.* 240–204 B.C.), for the comedies and tragedies that he wrote, translated, or adapted (beginning in 240) were the first important literary works in Latin. Little is known of Andronicus. Some scholars believe that he was a slave, while others suggest that he was expressly imported from Tarentum (located in the Greek territories of southern Italy) to produce plays. The first native-born dramatist was Gnaeus Naevius (*c.* 270–*c.* 201 B.C.), who began writing about 235. He excelled at comedy, although like Andronicus, who was best at tragedy, he wrote both types. Naevius did much to naturalize the drama by introducing many Roman allusions into the Greek originals and by writing plays on Roman stories. By the time Andronicus and Naevius died, drama was well established in Rome. Since each of their successors tended to specialize in a single form, the development of tragedy and comedy followed separate paths thereafter.

FIGURE 3.3   A scene from Roman tragedy. A wall painting in Pompeii of the first century A.D. or earlier. From Dieterich, *Pulcinella* (1897).

Perhaps because comedy was more popular than tragedy in Rome, the names of many comic writers have come down to us. Two of these—Plautus and Terence—are of principal interest since they are the authors of the only surviving Roman comedies. Titus Maccius Plautus (*c.* 254–*c.* 184 B.C.) was the first important successor to Livius Andronicus and Naevius in comedy. His popularity was so great that after his death as many as 130 plays came to be attributed to him. In seeking to resolve the question of authorship, the Roman scholar Varro (116–27 B.C.) divided the plays into those which were certainly by Plautus, those which were of doubtful authorship, and those which were clearly not by Plautus. In the first group he placed twenty-one works, all of which have survived and are still credited to Plautus: *The Comedy of Asses, The Merchant, The Braggart Warrior, The Casket, Pot of Gold, Stichus, Pseudolus, Curculio, The Two Bacchides, Casina, Amphitryon, The Captives, Epidicus, The Menaechmi, The Haunted House, The Persian, The Carthaginian, The Rope, Trinummus, The Churl,* and *Vidularia.* Few of the plays can be dated with certainty, although all were probably written between 205 and 184.

All are based on New Comedies but, since none of the Greek plays on which he drew survive, it is impossible to estimate the extent of Plautus' originality. He added many Roman allusions and was much admired for his Latin dialogue, his varied poetic meters, and his witty jokes. Although his plays show a wide range of comic powers, Plautus is best known for his farce.

Publius Terentius Afer (195 or 185–159 B.C.) is said to have been born in Carthage, brought to Rome as a slave when a boy, educated, and freed. He wrote six plays, all of which have survived: *Andria* (166), *Mother-in-Law* (165), *Self-Tormentor* (163), *Eunuch* (161), *Phormio* (161), and *The Brothers* (160). Terence's plots are more complex than those of his predecessors, for he combined stories from more than one Greek original, a practice for which he was often denounced. The chief interest in his works, however, does not lie in intrigue but in character and the double plots that provided him with opportunities for showing contrasts in human behavior. His sympathetic treatment of characters moves his plays toward romantic or sentimental comedy. Since he strove for consistency, he avoided inserting Roman

FIGURE 3.4 **Wall painting from the Casa di Casca in Herculaneum showing a comic scene. At left a priestess and in the background an altar. First century A.D. From Baumeister,** *Denkmaler des Klassischen Altertums* **(1889).**

allusions into the Greek plots upon which he drew. His language, that of everyday polite conversation, lacks the great metrical variety found in Plautus' plays. Terence was much more conscious of artistic principles than was Plautus, but he never equalled the latter's popularity.

Of the other comic writers, the most important was Caecilius Statius (*c.* 219–168 B.C.), the principal dramatist in the years between Plautus and Terence and considered by many Roman critics the greatest of all comic authors. Unfortunately, none of his plays survive. His work is thought to have combined characteristics of both Plautus' and Terence's plays and to form a transition between them. Other comic writers were Marcus Atilius, Aquilius, Lucius Lanuvinus, and Sextus Turpilius. Turpilius (d. 103 B.C.) is the last known writer of *fabula palliata* (comedy based on Greek originals), although the works by these authors continued to be produced for some time.

It is customary to distinguish comedies based on Greek subjects (*fabula palliata*) from those based on Roman materials (*fabula togata*). No plays of the latter type have survived, and only three authors—Titinius, Afrianus, and Atta—are known to have written this form.

Except in subject matter, the *fabula togata* seems to have differed in no important respect from the *fabula palliata;* it never attained the popularity accorded the *palliata*.

Comedy ceased to be a vital form after about 100 B.C., but the works of Plautus and Terence survived, even after the decline of Rome, perhaps because they were valued as models of spoken Latin. Since later critics turned to them as the foremost examples of comic drama, the plays of Plautus and Terence exerted enormous influence on Renaissance comedy. All of the extant Roman comedies are adaptations of Greek plays. It is usually assumed (though on no solid evidence) that Plautus and Terence departed little from the structure of the originals and that whatever changes they made were minor. One of the principal deviations is the elimination of the chorus, with the result that the plays are not divided into episodes. (The division into acts found in most present-day editions of the plays was made by later editors.) An important addition is the musical accompaniment of dialogue, a feature probably derived from the Etruscan heritage. In Plautus' plays about two-thirds and in Terence's about one-half of the lines were accompanied by music. In subject matter, plot devices, and characterization, Roman comedy seems to have differed little from Greek New Comedy. (For a discussion of New Comedy, and thus indirectly of Roman comedy, see pp. 37–39.) All of the action takes place in the street, with the result that many offstage events must be narrated, and scenes that logically would occur inside are placed out of doors. Eavesdropping is common and many complications turn on overheard conversations.

Although Roman tragedy is treated condescendingly today, it was highly regarded by critics and audiences of the time. Nevertheless, the names of only three tragic writers between 200 and 75 B.C. are now known: Quintus Ennius (239–169), Marcus Pacuvius (*c.* 220– *c.* 130), and Lucius Accius (170–*c.* 86). It is difficult to generalize about this early tragedy, since no plays survive. Judging from fragments, titles, and contemporary comments, however, the majority of the plays were adapted from Greek originals (a type labeled *fabula crepidata*), while a smaller number were based on Roman subjects (called *fabula praetexta*). They probably did not depart structurally in any important way from Greek tragedies, but they seem to have emphasized bolder effects (such as extremes of virtue, vice, horror and noble deeds, melodramatic plots, and rhetorical and spectacular display).

Although tragedy was regularly performed into the Christian era, no new plays seem to have been written with production in mind after 29 B.C. when *Thyestes* by

FIGURE 3.5 A bas-relief allegedly showing a scene from Roman comedy. From Dörpfeld, *Griechische Theatre* (1896).

Varius Rufus was seen at a festival celebrating the victory at Actium.

Historians speculate that public taste coarsened to such an extent under the empire that tragedy could no longer hold its own and that complete plays ceased to be performed at the festivals, although excerpts or shortened versions continued to be presented. Nevertheless, closet dramas were written, such as *Medea* by Ovid (43 B.C.– *c.* 17 A.D.). It is possible that scenes from these later plays were recited at banquets.

The only Roman tragedies that have survived are from this later period. Of these, all but one are by Lucius Annaeus Seneca (5 or 4 B.C.–65 A.D.). Born in Spain and educated in Rome, Seneca was famous for his works on rhetoric and philosophy and became one of the most influential men in Rome after his pupil Nero was named emperor in 54 A.D. He subsequently declined in favor and committed suicide in 65.

Nine of Seneca's plays survive: *The Trojan Women, Medea, Oedipus, Phaedra, Thyestes, Hercules on Oeta, The Mad Hercules, The Phoenician Women,* and *Agamemnon.* All are adapted from Greek originals. Although it is unlikely that Seneca's plays were presented in Rome's public theatres, they were destined to become major influences in the Renaissance. Since they helped shape tragedy in the age of Shakespeare, their characteristics are important.

First, Seneca's plays are divided into five episodes by choral interludes only loosely related to the action. In the Renaissance, the five-act form was to become standard, while the chorus, though reduced to a single character, often commented on the action. Second, Seneca's elaborate speeches, often resembling forensic addresses, were imitated by later writers. Third, Seneca's interest in morality, reflected through sensational deeds that illustrate the evils of unrestrained emotion and in *sententiae* (or pithy, proverbial generalizations about the human condition), is paralleled in Renaissance drama by the use of horrifying examples of evil behavior and in moralizing ruminations on humanity. Fourth, Seneca's scenes of violence and horror (for example, in *Oedipus* Jocasta rips open her womb and in *Thyestes* the bodies of children are served at a banquet) were imitated by later writers. Fifth, Seneca's preoccupation with magic, death, and the interpenetration of the human and superhuman worlds paralleled a major interest of the Renaissance. Sixth, Seneca's creation of characters who are dominated by a single obsessive passion (such as revenge) that drives them to their doom provided Renaissance dramatists valuable lessons in establishing psychological motivations and in creating unified characters. Seventh, many of Seneca's technical devices, such as soliloquies, asides, and confidantes, were taken over by later authors. Thus, even though he is now thought to be an inferior dramatist, Seneca exerted enormous influence in later times.

Octavia, sometimes mistakenly attributed to Seneca, is the sole surviving example of *fabula praetexta*, or tragedy on Roman themes. Of little merit, it deals with the death of Nero's wife, and Seneca appears in it as a character.

If regular comedy and tragedy had lost their popularity on the public stages by the first century A.D., this was certainly not true with the minor forms that dominated the Roman repertory from the first century B.C., onward. The Atellan farce and mime were chief among these minor forms. Both had been presented at the festivals since the third century B.C. , although little is known of their early history, since they remained nonliterary types until the first century B.C. It was not until the major forms began to decline that the *fabula Atellana* and the mime were first written down.

Pomponius and Novius (writing between 100 and 75 B.C.) are credited with making the Atellan farce literary. At this time, the *fabulae Atellanae* seem to have been short, perhaps 300–400 lines, and to have served as *exodia*, or afterpieces, to regular drama. The Atellana emphasized rural settings, characters, and speech, while its subject matter most often involved cheating, gluttony, fighting, or sexual exploits. Its rustic atmosphere and its use as an afterpiece led many Romans to associate it with the satyr play, and Roman references to the latter form may in actuality be to the Atellan farce.

Four stock characters appeared in the *fabula Atellana*: Bucco, a vivacious, boisterous braggart; Pappus, a comic old man; Maccus, a gluttonous fool; and Dossenus, a hunchback of frightening appearance. Standardized costumes were probably worn by these figures. Consequently, many historians have traced the similar conventions of the *commedia dell'arte* of sixteenth-century Italy back to the Atellan farce. The peak of popularity for the *fabula Atellana* was reached during the first century B.C., after which its place was increasingly usurped by the mime.

The first clear reference to the mime, or *fabula riciniata*, is found in Rome in 211 B.C., although it probably had been performed there much earlier. Under the republic it was associated especially with the *ludi Florales*, a festival honoring one of the fertility goddesses and

FIGURE 3.6 Dossenus of the *fabula Atellana*, a mimic fool, or a grotesque actor of farce. Graeco-Roman bronze statuette found in southern Italy. It has been dated 300–100 B.C. Courtesy Metropolitan Museum of Art, Rogers Fund, 1912.

noted for its license. This festival was especially popular with the common people. Like the Atellana, mime was transformed into a literary type in the first century B.C. Decimus Laberius (106–43 B.C.) and his contemporary, Publius Syrus, are usually credited with this development. Under the empire, the mime appears to have reverted to a nonliterary type, although its popularity increased until it virtually drove all other forms from the stage. The term *mime* seems also to have been used in this period to designate almost any kind of entertainment offered in the theatre. Basically, however, the mime was a dramatic form, usually short, but sometimes quite an elaborate and complex spectacle with large casts. It might treat almost any subject and could be either serious or comic, but usually it dealt with some aspect of everyday life seen from a comic or satiric point of view. Modern scholars have tended to discuss these mimes almost wholly in terms of obscene and violent examples, although it is far from certain that these were typical. There seems little reason to doubt that extramarital affairs were frequent subjects, but some historians have assumed that because one of Rome's more depraved emperors, Heliogabalus (ruled 218–222 A.D.) ordered sexual acts to be performed realistically this was typical throughout the empire. It is true that the mimes reflected the taste of the period, as can be seen from the numerous beatings, fights, deaths and other forms of violence included in them. But many of the examples often cited to illustrate the depravity of the theatre actually occurred in the amphitheatres, which were always more bloodthirsty than the theatres.

The mimes were especially disliked by the Christians, whose sacraments and beliefs were often ridiculed on stage. Overall, there seems sufficient evidence to show that the mimes were artistically inferior, but we should remember that much of the testimony about their depravity and excesses comes from Christian writers seeking to undermine the theatre's appeal.

In addition to dramatic pieces, mime troupes also presented a wide range of incidental entertainment, including various feats performed on tightropes and trapezes, firespitting, sword swallowing, juggling with balls, daggers, and other objects, stilt walking, trained animals (who sometimes performed in dramatic pieces), singing (sometimes approaching the operatic), dancing, and so on. Audiences seem to have constantly demanded what was new and unusual, so the range of mimic offerings was extremely wide.

Under the empire, pantomime (or *fabula saltica*) was also popular. Roman pantomime was a forerunner of modern ballet for it was essentially a story-telling dance. As a form, it was known in Greece as early as the fifth century, although there it usually involved two or more dancers. In Rome, it was essentially a solo dance, although there might be an assistant who was kept very much subordinate. Pantomimic plots were usually taken from mythology or history. The action was accompanied by a chorus (who sang an explanatory libretto) and an orchestra of flutes, pipes, and cymbals. This form of pantomime seems to have been introduced at Rome in 22 B.C. by Pylades and Bathyllus. Characteristically, it was serious, but occasionally it was comic (a type in which Bathyllus excelled). Although the comic mode soon declined in popularity, the serious form of pantomime gradually usurped the position formerly held by tragedy and came to be especially admired by sophisticated audiences. The emperors and nobles often kept

FIGURE 3.7 Terracotta plaque showing a charioteer about to round one end of the race track in a Roman circus. Courtesy British Museum.

their own pantomime performers and intense rivalries developed over the relative merits of dancers. Pantomime was also long a favorite with the common people, although after the second century A.D. it was increasingly subordinated to mime.

OTHER ENTERTAINMENTS

The theatre had to compete with several other kinds of entertainments. The oldest and most popular of these was chariot racing, supposedly introduced by the Etruscan king, the elder Tarquin (616–578 B.C.). These races were included among the events of several religious festivals during both the republic and the empire. Their popularity was enormous during the empire, when four main factions (or bands of supporters) grew up and engendered bitter rivalries. This pastime was favored by the Romans and continued until at least 549 A.D. Several other entertainments were given in the circuses built to accommodate chariot races. These included horseracing (sometimes with trick riding), mock cavalry battles, footraces, acrobatics, prizefighting, wrestling, exhibitions of wild and trained animals, and fights between animals or between animals and men.

Gladiatorial contests provided another kind of popular entertainment. Introduced into Rome in 264 B.C. as funeral games given by private individuals, they did not become a part of official state festivals until 105 B.C., when (it is said) they were inaugurated to counteract Greek culture that some Romans found too effete. Before the end of the first century A.D. the contests were established throughout the empire. The number of combatants steadily increased, and in 109 A.D. 5,000 pairs were said to have appeared at one festival following a military victory. It was primarily as a place for gladiatorial contests that amphitheatres were built, the first constructed in 46 B.C. and others built eventually throughout the empire. As time went by, the contests became more and more elaborate; often they were accompanied by mood music and sound effects and even appropriate costuming and scenic elements. Special schools trained the gladiators, most of whom were slaves. As in the mimes, novelty was demanded and captives from faraway Britain fought others from Africa or Asia. Various types of weapons and battle techniques were employed. Romans seem to have taken special delight in this game of life and death in which at least one member of each pair was always doomed unless he won the crowd's favor.

The *venationes,* or wild animal fights, were closely related to the gladiatorial contests and were also staged in amphitheatres. Wild animals seem to have been exhibited first at the Circus Maximus in 186 B.C., and soon afterwards they were being used to fight each other or men. By the middle of the first century B.C., *venationes* had become very elaborate. Still, such entertainments were not frequent until the Colosseum was opened in 80 A.D. Some 9,000 animals were killed during the 100–day celebration of this event. Many of the animals seen in the arena were trained beasts who performed but did not fight. Most, however, were used in one of two ways: in wild beast hunts, during which armed bands were allowed to track down and kill animals in the arena; or as man-killers who stalked human prey. The best known example is one in which Christians were put into the arena with lions as a form of persecution. As with other entertainments during the empire, the desire for novelty led to the importation of animals from all over the world; in addition, the arenas were often fitted out with trees, hillocks, and other scenic elements to simulate some environment and the victims were often costumed accordingly. Above all other forms of entertainment these gladiatorial contests and *venationes* earned late Rome its reputation for bloodthirstiness.

Perhaps the most spectacular of all the entertainments were the *naumachiae,* or seabattles. The first was given in 46 B.C. by Julius Caesar on a lake dug for the occasion; it featured a battle involving 2,000 marines and 6,000 oarsmen. Later the amphitheatres were sometimes flooded for such events. By far the most ambitious of all

FIGURE 3.8   A reconstruction made in the Renaissance of a *naumachia* of the reign of Domitian (late first century, A.D.). From Laumann, *La Machinerie au Théâtre* (1897).

the *naumachiae* was given in 52 A.D. on the Fucine Lake east of Rome to celebrate the completion of a water conduit. On that occasion, 19,000 participants fought and many perished.

Occasionally, pale imitations of such entertainments were given in theatres, where the orchestra was sometimes flooded for miniature seabattles or water ballets, or where a few gladiators fought in the orchestra or on stage. But the theatre was ill equipped to compete with the vast arenas available in most cities. On the other hand, theatrical spectacle seems to have been imported increasingly into amphitheatres, where machinery for raising and lowering scenic elements and performers became highly developed. Furthermore, the gladiatorial contests and *venationes* seem to have been given novelty occasionally by the inclusion of entertainments approximating modern ballets with large casts and elaborate scenic effects.

Although many of the entertainments described here were not technically theatrical, they cannot be ignored in a study of the Roman theatre. Such spectacles frequently were presented in festivals alongside plays, and actors often had to compete with them. Thus it is often said that the necessity of holding an audience's attention under such circumstances led to the general coarsening of theatrical fare during the empire. That the theatre was partially successful in this contest is shown by the fact that as late as the mid-fourth century A.D. 100 days were devoted to theatrical fare as compared to 75 days for all other types of entertainments (although it should be remembered that all the theatres in Rome combined did not hold as many spectators as the Circus Maximus alone).

PRODUCTION ARRANGEMENTS

The state festivals at which entertainments were given were under the management of magistrates, who received a grant to cover expenses. The magistrates themselves frequently supplied additional funds, since a well-received festival reflected honor on them. For the *ludi scaenici* (or theatrical portions of the festivals), the magistrates contracted with the managers (*domini*) of acting troupes (*grex*) to produce the plays. The leader of each troupe probably bought plays directly from authors and arranged for music, properties, and costumes. The plays may have been performed before the magistrates prior to public viewing, both for purposes of censorship and to insure a high quality of performance. It is not clear whether any public notice of plays was given under the republic, but during the empire posters listed the various attractions.

Several companies normally presented plays at a festival. Each received a basic fee, but additional prizes or payments were made to companies, individual actors, and authors who especially pleased the audience. Occasional references are found to claques and attempted bribery of audiences and officials in awarding favors. During the empire, rulers exerted considerable power over the plays, and often granted or withheld favors to actors. Ordinarily, however, it was the popular audience who most influenced theatrical performances. Each play was given without intermissions. Even the intervals between plays were usually filled with incidental entertainment or short mimes; consequently, performances were continuous throughout each day devoted to *ludi scaenici*.

Admission to state-supported performances was always free and all classes attended. Plautus refers to nurses and children, slaves, prostitutes, magistrates' attendants, and women, and he indicates that there was considerable jostling for places. In some periods, special seats in the orchestra were reserved for the Senators. Some tickets dating from the empire have survived, but it is not clear whether these were for the privileged few for whom seats were reserved, or whether they were required of everyone to prevent overcrowding in the the-

atre. It seems likely that, for the most part, seats were occupied on the "first come, first served" basis.

The theatres seated thousands of persons. The capacity of the early temporary structures is unknown, but the first permanent theatre held approximately 10,000 persons. Obviously, only a fraction of Rome's population could be accommodated in the theatre at a given time, for Rome grew in size from about 215,000 persons in 200 B.C. to about 1,000,000 during the empire. Ordinarily, all of the plays for a festival were presented in the same theatre, but for one elaborate celebration in 17 B.C., three different theatres were used continuously for three consecutive days and nights.

Spectators were interested primarily in entertainment, and though special officials maintained order, the audience was free to come and go during a performance. Furthermore, other attractions competed for the audience's favor. The first two productions of Terence's *Mother-in-Law* were failures because at the first the audience left to see a rope dancer and at the second to watch gladiators. Spectators might also leave to buy food and drink, which were sold just outside the theatre.

The audience seems to have been quick to express praise or condemnation, and, since its response determined whether a troupe received additional payments, its favor was constantly sought. Many commentators have blamed the decline of the Roman theatre on catering to the increasingly debased taste of the common people.

THE ROMAN THEATRE STRUCTURE

The first permanent theatre building in Rome was not constructed until 55 B.C., almost 200 years after the introduction of regular drama, and over 100 years after the last surviving comedy was written. Consequently, as in Greece, the permanent structures date from a considerably later time than the period of significant dramatic writing.

In the third century B.C. there were several architectural precedents upon which the Romans could have drawn: (1) the Etruscan, (2) the Atellan, and (3) the Greek. Which of these, if any, they chose is unknown. It seems likely that Livius Andronicus would have adapted the Hellenistic structure for his plays, since he was most familiar with it. On the other hand, since many types of entertainment were given and a new temporary structure was supposedly erected for each festival, considerable experimentation would have been possible.

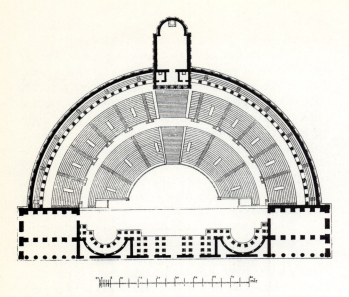

FIGURE 3.9 Plan (made in late Roman times) of the Theatre of Pompey. Note the temple of Venus at top and the elaborate *scena frons* at bottom. From Streit, *Das Theater* (1903).

The problem is complicated by the relationship between theatrical performances and religious rites. Unlike the early Greeks, the Romans presented plays in honor of many gods, each of whom had his or her own sacred precinct in which it was considered unsuitable to dedicate offerings to any other god. Hanson, in *Roman Theater-Temples,* concludes that "all sites for *ludi scaenici* which can be located with certainty or probability before the erection of a permanent theatre in Rome are not only connected with a temple but are further specified as in front of a temple." He also suggests that performances were always given "in sight of the god" to whom they were dedicated, and that consequently the stage was erected facing the temple, where the image of the god was set up to view the performances.

The first permanent theatre in Rome had a temple dedicated to Venus at the top of the auditorium. Many historians have seen this as a sly trick to overcome the objections of the Senate to building a permanent theatre. Although this interpretation may be correct, it is equally possible that Pompey (the official in charge) was following a tradition. On the other hand, there was always a group in Rome who objected to theatrical performances on grounds of decadence and expense. Some historians believe that it was as a concession to this group that no

permanent theatres were erected prior to 55 B.C. Again, however, it may be that before this time the Senate thought it unwise to build a theatre dedicated to one god unless they were to honor equally the other gods to whom plays were dedicated, and that it was too costly to build so many theatres. In any case, the permanent theatres which were begun in 179, 174, and 155 B.C. were abandoned. Perhaps under the empire the claims of many gods could be met by placing altars dedicated to them in the theatre, and by bringing the effigy of the one being honored into the theatre during his festival. Regardless of the reasons for the change from temporary to permanent structures, the distinctions between them should be noted.

If we assume that there were at least five festivals each year, and that a temporary structure was erected and dismantled for each, then well over 500 would have been required prior to 55 B.C. It seems improbable that they were uniform in size or design. Their general characteristics are at best conjectural, and scholars who have attempted to reconstruct the temporary stages have usually made them merely flimsier and somewhat simpler versions of the later stone theatres. Disagreements among historians about the details of the temporary theatres center around such matters as the elaborateness of the stage background, the size of the stage, and the extent

FIGURE 3.10 Plan of the theatre at Orange. From Durm, *Handbuch der Architecktur* (1905).

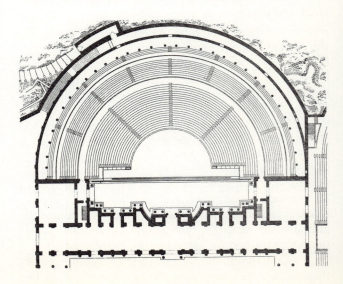

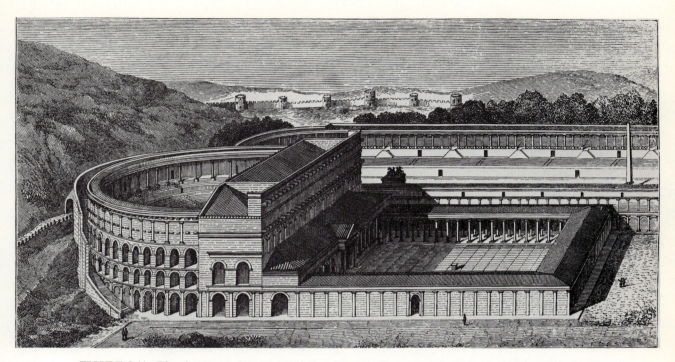

FIGURE 3.11 **The theatre at Orange. Note the elaborate forecourt adjoining the stage house. Note also that this theatre is built into a hillside and takes advantage of it for some entrances. Alongside the theatre the circus can be seen. From Caristie,** *Monuments Antiques à Orange* **(1856). Courtesy Boston Public Library.**

to which seating was provided for the audience, none of which can be resolved.

The structures appear to have become progressively more sumptuous and detailed. In 99 B.C. Claudius Pulcher is said to have erected a theatre with such realistically painted details that birds tried to perch on them. Pliny (23–79 A.D.) states that Marcus Aemilius Scaurus built a theatre in 58 B.C. with a stage of three stories, the first of marble, the second of glass, and the third of gilded wood, the whole being decorated with 360 columns and 3000 bronze statues; the auditorium supposedly accommodated 80,000 people. Pliny also states that in 50 B.C., Gaius Scribonius Curio built two theatres back to back, each on a pivot; while the audience remained seated, the two parts were supposedly revolved to form an amphitheatre. Although modern historians seriously question their reliability, Pliny's accounts are indicative of structures sufficiently unusual and sumptuous to have become legendary by Pliny's time.

Considering the elaborateness of these temporary theatres, it is not surprising that Pompey was allowed to erect a permanent theatre in 55 B.C. Before the end of the century, two others had been built in Rome: the theatre of Balbus in 13 B.C. (seating approximately 8,000), and the theatre of Marcellus in 11 B.C. (seating approximately 14,000). No other permanent theatres were ever built in Rome, although temporary structures continued to be used there and elsewhere for some time. The temporary structures throughout the empire were gradually replaced with permanent buildings.

The theatres of the empire are sufficiently similar in design to allow generalizations about their basic characteristics. Typically they were built on level ground, rather than on a slope as the Greek theatres were. Corridors and stairways around and beneath the auditorium allowed an efficient flow of traffic. When theatres utilized natural slopes, corridors were cut into the hillsides. A number of vertical aisles divided the auditorium (or *cavea*) into sections, while at least one broad aisle about half-way up the slope and a covered portico at the top permitted horizontal movement. It is perhaps worth noting that it was the Roman exploitation of the arch but most were very large by modern standards, being from 20 to 40 feet in depth and from 100 to more than 300 feet in length. There were from three to five doors in the rear wall, and at least one door in the wings (or *versurae*) which enclosed the ends of the stage.

The facade (or *scaena frons*) of the stage house was decorated with columns, niches, porticos, and statues, and was often painted or gilded. The stage was covered by a roof which probably improved acoustics and protected the elaborate *scaenae frons*. Most of the early permanent theatres probably had straight facades; but after the second century A.D., curved niches, forming deep vestibules and alcoves, were usual. This later arrangement cut into the backstage space until little more than a corridor remained. Dressing rooms and other work space were housed in the side wings. Trap doors in the stage floor were common, and in some theatres a peephole vantage point was provided at one side of the stage probably for the stage manager's use.

The Romans were concerned with the comfort of audiences. Under the empire they perfected a system of cooling based on air blowing over streams of water. To protect the audience from the sun, awnings (or *vela*) were introduced around 78 B.C. Attached to masts set in two rows of corbels (or supporting projections) around the top edge of the auditorium, the awnings were brightly colored and occasionally had a scene painted on the visible surfaces. (For example, Nero had himself depicted on an awning as the Sun God driving a chariot.)

Under the Roman Empire about 125 permanent theatres were built. Among the most important were those at Ostia (in Italy), built between 30 and 12 B.C.; Arles (in France), perhaps as early as 46 B.C.; Orange (in France), first or second century A.D.; Merida (in Spain), 18 B.C.; Timgad, Djemila, Dugga (all in North Africa), between 138 and 192 A.D.; Sabratha (North Africa), *c.* 200 A.D.; Aspendus (in southern Asia Minor), 161–180 A.D.; and Athens, 161 A.D.

A few purely Roman theatres were built in Greek areas of the empire, but the usual practice was to remodel the existing Greek structures along Roman lines. In some, the *thyromata* were replaced by a Roman *scaenae frons;* many retained the high stage, but in others it was lowered to five feet. To increase the depth, the Greek stage was often extended forward into the orchestra as much as 20 feet. Since many of the Greek structures had no side wings, an extra door was often placed in the rear facade at the extreme ends to give a total of five to seven doors.

FIGURE 3.12 Reconstruction of the Roman theatre at Ostia, built between 30 and 12 B.C. and remodeled *c.* 200 A.D. From d'Espouy, *Fragments d'Architecture Antique,* Vol. 2 (1901).

that permitted far more massive structures than had been possible in Greece, where post-and-lintel construction was standard. Thus, the Romans did not have to seek out hillsides to support seating.

The stage house (or *scaena*) and the auditorium were joined to form a single architectural unit the same height all the way round. The passages corresponding to the *parodoi* were roofed over to provide corridors (or *vomitoria*) into the orchestra and auditorium. Over each there was sometimes a box reserved for the magistrates who had supervised the festival, or for the Emperor and other important persons. The orchestra, an exact half-circle, was usually used for seating privileged groups, although at times it accommodated dancing, animal fights, gladiatorial contests, or water ballets.

The stage (or *pulpitum*) was raised about 5 feet, and its front placed on the diameter of the orchestra circle. In theatres built before 100 A.D., a slot was provided for the curtain near the front edge of the stage; after the second century, when other means of handling the curtain were developed, the slots were filled in. The size of the stage was determined by that of the theatre,

OTHER STRUCTURES FOR ENTERTAINMENTS

In addition to theatres, structures were erected in Rome and elsewhere to meet the demands of other types of entertainment. The Circus Maximus, designed for chariot races, was the oldest and largest of these structures. Laid out originally around 600 B.C., it was approximately 2,000 feet long by 650 feet wide. At the beginning of the empire, its stadium seating accommodated some 60,000 spectators, but it was later enlarged. Its primary feature was the track that permitted twelve chariots to race at the same time. But, though designed for chariots, the Circus Maximus also housed other circus games *(ludi circenses)* such as horseracing, prizefighting, wrestling, wild animals, and so on. Eventually three other smaller circuses were built in Rome, the last in 309 A.D.

The other principal type of structure was the amphitheatre, designed primarily to house gladiatorial contests and *venationes,* although occasionally *naumachiae* were held there. The first amphitheatre was built in 46 B.C., but this and its two successors were temporary structures. Then, in 80 A.D., the Flavian amphitheatre (now called the Colosseum) was completed. Originally three stories tall, it was increased to four in the third century A.D. It was then 157 feet tall, 620 feet long, and 513 feet wide and seated approximately 50,000 persons. The arena measured 287 by 180 feet. The space beneath the arena is of special interest: it housed elevators capable of raising scenic elements, wild beasts, and combatants to the arena level.

SCENERY

The basic scenic background in the Roman theatre was the *scaenae frons.* In comedy, this facade was treated as a series of houses opening onto a city street, represented by the stage. In tragedy, the facade normally represented a palace or temple. Although some plays are set in the country or other open places devoid of buildings, there was probably little attempt to change the visual appearance of the stage from one play to another. As the Prologue of *The Menaechmi* says: "This city is Epidamnus during the performance of this play; when another play is performed it will become another city." The audience probably depended primarily upon the dramatists' words to locate the action.

There are, notwithstanding, a number of problems relating to the scenic background. One concerns the amount and kind of three-dimensional detail required by the plays of Plautus and Terence. Some scholars argue that there were numerous porticos, alcoves, or similar architectural features, while others maintain that all details were painted on the back wall of the stage facade. The question has arisen largely because of the many scenes in comedies involving eavesdropping or the failure of one character to see others who are on stage at the same time. One group of historians has insisted that three-dimensional structures would have been necessary to stage the scenes convincingly, while another insists that the conventions of the Roman stage permitted characters to see each other or not as the dramatic situation dictated.

Closely connected with this problem is another involving interiors. Since a few scenes in the comedies depict banquets or other actions which would ordinarily occur indoors, some scholars have argued that such scenes were staged in porches or vestibules in front of doors to give a more convincing sense of an interior. Others have insisted that none of these scenes occur indoors, and that it is only the influence of modern realism that has led historians to such conjectures. Neither

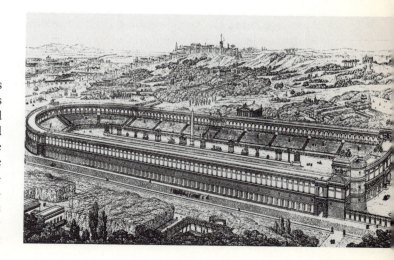

FIGURE 3.13 **Reconstruction of the Roman circus of Caligula and Nero, built in the first century A.D. From Durm,** *Handbuch der Architecktur* **(1905).**

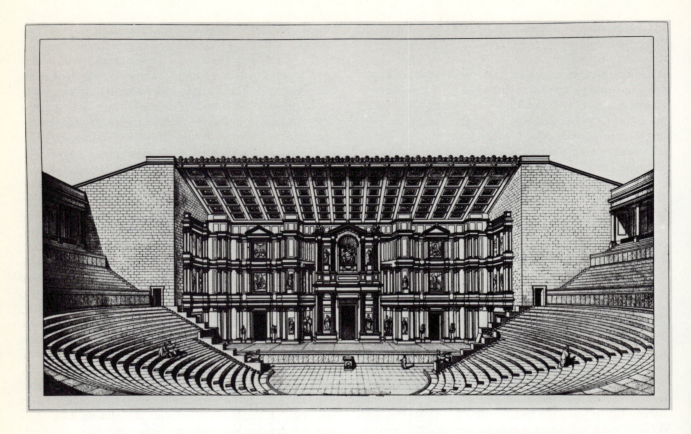

FIGURE 3.14 *Scaenae frons* **and interior of the theatre at Orange; a reconstruction of what the theatre supposedly looked like in its original state. From Caristie,** *Monuments Antiques à Orange* **(1856). Courtesy Boston Public Library**

of these arguments can be resolved, although it seems likely that convention was stronger than realism in the time of Plautus and Terence.

The doors of the *scaenae frons* are of considerable scenic importance, since each may represent a different house, and since they are referred to so frequently by the characters. In the comedies, doors attract the attention of the actors by squeaking; characters beat on them and lock or unlock them. In tragedy, all of the doors in the *scaenae frons* were probably treated as entrances to the same building; some ancient commentators state that the central doorway was reserved for the principal personage, while the side doors were used by the lesser characters. If so, staging must have been highly conventionalized. The doors leading into the *versurae* may also have had conventionalized uses, for many ancient writers declare

that one was understood to lead to the forum and the other to the harbor or country.

For the most part, *periaktoi* seem to have been the chief means of differentiating place. Vitruvius, writing about 15 B.C., states: "The *scaena* itself displays the following scheme. In the center are double doors decorated like those of a royal palace. At the right and left are the doors of the guest chambers. Beyond are the spaces provided for the decoration—places that the Greeks call *periaktoi,* because in these places are triangular pieces of machinery which revolve, each having three decorated faces." As to what was painted on the *periaktoi,* Vitruvius adds: "There are three kinds of scenes, one called the tragic, second, the comic, third, the satyric. Their decorations are different and unlike each other in scheme. Tragic scenes are delineated with columns, pediments,

66

statues, and other objects suited to kings; comic scenes exhibit private dwellings, with balconies and views representing rows of windows, after the manner of ordinary dwellings; satyric scenes are decorated with trees, caverns, mountains, and other rustic objects delineated in landscape style." The meaning of this passage has been the subject of endless debate. The most sensible interpretation seems to be that the decoration for each type of play was conventionalized and painted on *periaktoi* placed near each end of the stage. In any case, the *periaktoi* could not have covered more than a very small portion of the vast *scaenae frons,* most of which would have remained visible.

Most discussions of the stage background concentrate on the requirements of regular drama, but the permanent theatres were built after the rise to prominence of the minor dramatic forms, some of which placed considerable emphasis on spectacle. Nevertheless, we know little of the scenic conventions of these lesser types. Perhaps some clues are offered by the uses made of two types of curtains: the *auleum,* or front curtain; and the *siparium,* or background curtain. The *auleum* may have been introduced as early as 133 B.C. and was certainly in use by 56 B.C. Originally, it was lowered into a slot at the front of the stage by means of a series of telescoped poles. Extending the poles upward to their full height raised the curtain, while the reverse process lowered it. After the second century A.D., the curtain was suspended from overhead and raised by ropes. The front curtain was important to spectacle, for it permitted the sudden revelation of a scene or the rapid concealment of a striking tableau. Before its introduction, all characters had to be brought on and gotten offstage in full view of the audience. After its introduction, producers seem to have capitalized on the surprises and striking effects it made possible.

The *siparium* probably came into the theatre with the mime. Originally a small curtain, it may have been hung at the rear of an improvised platform to serve both as background for the action and as masking for the offstage space. Entrances were probably made through slits cut in it. As the mime grew in importance, the *siparium* increased in size and was often hung against the *scaenae frons* in the manner of a backdrop. Nothing is known, however, of the scenes painted on these curtains or precisely how they were related to the facade. There appear to have been simultaneous and contradictory trends toward more elaborate curtains and more elaborate permanent facades.

Many spectacular effects were achieved through the use of large numbers of supernumeraries in dances, battles, and processions. This trend toward mass effects had begun as early as the first century B.C., for Cicero states that at the dedication of the Theatre of Pompey in 52 B.C. 600 mules crossed the stage in one play and that 3,000 bowls were displayed in another. Such excesses increased under the empire, when realism of spectacle and sensationalism seem to have been among the primary goals of the theatre.

Although intricate machinery is seldom mentioned in ancient accounts, the Romans knew how to achieve mechanical scenic marvels. This machinery seems to have been developed in the amphitheatres, especially in the Colosseum, during the first century A.D., to lift the animals from subterranean spaces to the arena level. Soon this machinery was being used for scenic purposes, and a building was erected nearby to house scenic elements and properties. These props and scenic elements were transported as needed to the Colosseum's basement, which extended some twenty-one feet beneath the arena. Martial (*c.* 40–*c.* 102 A.D.) speaks of intricate spectacles in the Colosseum, including "sliding cliffs and a miraculous and moving wood." On another occasion, the ground repeatedly opened and a magic wood with fountains appeared and was immediately filled with exotic animals from foreign places.

Sometimes plays or pantomimes were acted out in the arena. In one instance, a criminal impersonating Orpheus appeared from below the arena level as if coming from Hades. He played music which enchanted rocks and trees so that they moved to greet him and animals crouched at his feet; then, at the end of this display, he was torn to pieces by a bear.

In the eastern part of the empire, where spectacles were less bloody, more emphasis was placed on Pyrrhic dances (or ballet-like performances). Apuleius (second century A.D.), in his novel *Metamorphoses,* describes such a performance in the amphitheatre at Corinth in Greece. The scenery seems to have been three-dimensional and practicable, for it represented a towering mountain on which were shrubs, trees, a stream, grazing goats, and a shepherd. An entertainment based on the story of Paris' judgment on the beauty of Hera, Athena, and Aphrodite was enacted on the mountain. At the end, a fountain of wine sprang out of the mountain's top and the entire structure sank out of sight.

Although these accounts concern amphitheatres, they make it clear that Roman engineers had developed scenic devices as complex as any that would be introduced into the theatre prior to modern times.

ACTORS AND ACTING

The usual term for actors in Rome was *histriones*, although *cantores* (or declaimers) was also used. At first a clear distinction was made between the actors of regular dramas and the performer of mimes (the *mimus* or *saltator*), the latter being considered inferior. In late Rome, however, the term *histriones* came to be applied to all actors. The majority of performers were male, for only in mimes did women appear on stage.

The social status of the Roman actor has been much disputed. Some historians have suggested that all actors were slaves owned by company managers. While this arrangement may have been used in some cases, it was by no means universal. Roscius, the most famous of Roman actors, was certainly never a slave and was eventually raised to the nobility. Similarly, Aesopus, a contemporary of Roscius, was a member of the Optimate, a group which exercised considerable control over public affairs because of its wealth, influence, and ability. In the early years many actors were also members of the *collegium poetarum*, an association of writers and actors founded in 207 B.C. Records show honors being paid to members of this association which could be given only to men with full civil rights. On the other hand, mime actors appear always to have been considered inferior, and many of them probably were slaves. It seems likely, therefore, that the social status of the actor varied considerably, although the majority always ranked low in public esteem.

Little is known about the professional performers in Rome prior to the introduction of comedy and tragedy in 240 B.C. by Livius Andronicus, who acted in his own plays. Succeeding dramatists, however, seldom followed his practice and instead left production entirely to the professional managers. Thus, in Rome there was not the intimate connection between playwriting and performance found in early Greece.

Although there apparently were no restrictions on the number of actors that could be used on the Roman stage, the extant plays could have been performed by a company of five or six actors, if doubling was practiced and supernumeraries used occasionally. Troupes may have been much larger, however, for no information

FIGURE 3.15 Two Roman comic actors. Bronze figures on the cover of a third century B.C. box or chest found in Praeneste, near Rome. Courtesy British Museum.

about their size during the Republic has survived. The names of only a few actors from the early period are known. Plautus refers to Pellio as an actor in one of his plays, and Lucius Ambivius Turpio was the actor-manager for all of Terence's plays.

In the first century B.C., as the regular drama declined, emphasis shifted to the "star" performer, and a series of scenes designed to display the talents of an actor began to be substituted for entire plays. Similarly, pantomime featured a single dancer, and in the mime one performer was almost always starred, even though a large number of supernumeraries might be used for spectacular effects. Many stars amassed fortunes, and under the empire they had followings not unlike those of a modern movie star. In the sixth century A.D. Theodora, a mime actress, married Justinian, Emperor of the Eastern Roman Empire. In late Rome, many of the most popular performers were tightrope walkers, trapeze artists, jugglers, sword-swallowers, fire-eaters, and dancers.

Acting style probably varied according to the dramatic form. In comedy and tragedy, acting seems to have followed conventions already developed by the Greeks. For example, in the regular forms all the actors were male, wore masks, and probably doubled in roles. In tragedy, delivery seems to have been slow, stately, and declamatory; in comedy, it was more rapid and conversational. Most roles required proficiency in speaking, singing, and dancing. Contemporary writers also make it clear that expressive gesture and pantomime (perhaps heavily dependent on stock attitudes and poses) were prominent ingredients in every performance. In tragedy, movement seems to have been slow and dignified, but in comedy it was more lively, for running, beatings, and farcical horseplay of all sorts were common. Judging from contemporary accounts, many Roman actors received extensive technical training about the angle of the head, placement of the feet, use of the hands, and vocal intonations appropriate to each emotion and type of situation. Since the theatres sometimes seated as many as 14,000 persons, the actors' gestures and movements probably were also considerably enlarged. All of these factors would indicate extensive stylization. On the other hand, Roman teachers of oratory often suggested actors as suitable models for imitation by public speakers. Consequently, it would appear that typical human movement, gesture, and intonation were reduced to their essentials and then exaggerated and conventionalized for stage use.

For the most part, actors seem to have specialized in one type of drama, although Andronicus and Roscius departed from the usual practice by performing in both comedy and tragedy. It is often stated that Andronicus separated singing and speaking and that after his time musical passages were sung by one performer while another mimed the scene. This idea seems to be based on an anecdote about a single occasion upon which Andronicus lost his voice as a result of giving several encores. Most scholars now reject the notion that this practice ever was typical and point to the close connection between musical and spoken passages in the plays of Plautus and Terence where it would be difficult indeed to separate the work of actor and singer. That the actor often gave encores of well-received passages, however, tells much about the Roman approach to acting.

In the mimes, masks usually were not worn and consequently facial expression was important. Through much of its history, mime was in part improvised, and therefore it required a talent for the invention of dialogue, business, and movement. Mime actors seem to have been selected either for their physical beauty or comic ugliness, for the plots most typically revolved around sexual desirability or some grotesquerie. In the second century B.C., the companies were probably very small, with perhaps no more than three or four members; but under the empire they included as many as sixty entertainers, although some of these were tightrope dancers, tumblers, and jugglers. Many supernumeraries were added for the great spectacles.

In pantomime, the emphasis was upon the solo performer. Noted for their handsomeness and athletic qualities, these actors depended entirely upon gesture and movement to portray a series of characters and situations. Many were renowned for the subtlety and complexity of their portrayals at a time when the mimes were becoming increasingly obvious and exaggerated.

FIGURE 3.16   Female mime performer performing a dance. In her hands she holds clappers and on her left foot she wears a footclapper (scarabellum). Bells are attached to her cap, skirt, and ankle. Bronze statuette, *c.* 200 A.D. Courtesy Art Museum, Princeton University.

FIGURE 3.17   Masks for Terence's *Andria*. From a ninth century A.D. manuscript now in the Vatican Library. Courtesy Biblioteca Vaticana.

In addition to the public performers, there may have been a number of private troupes in late Rome. These were probably composed of slaves kept by rich men to provide entertainment for their households and friends.

MASKS AND COSTUMES

Until recently, historians accepted as true a statement by a writer of the fourth century A.D. that Roscius, seeking to hide his squint, introduced the mask into the Roman theatre in the first century B.C. Newer studies, however, have noted many references to masks long before Roscius' time and have concluded that masks were used from the beginning of the Roman theatre. There is much evidence to support this conclusion. All of the areas of major influence on Rome—Etruria, Greece, southern Italy—had used masks in their entertainments, and it seems unlikely that the Romans would have rejected a standard part of Greek comedy and tragedy, of the Atellan farce, and of Etruscan dances. The use of masks would also have made the doubling of roles much easier and have simplified the problem of casting characters of identical appearance, as in Plautus' *Menaechmi* and *Amphitryon.*

Masks were made of linen and, with the attached wig, formed a complete covering for the head. Since it is usually assumed that Roman masks resembled those used in the Hellenistic theatre, Pollux' list of masks (see chapter 2) has served as the basis for most discussions. Other sources are illustrated manuscripts, dating from the fourth or fifth century A.D., of Terence's plays, which depict the masks for each production (see Figure 3.17).

The masks for pantomime had closed mouths. Writing in the second century A.D., Lucian describes them as being much more natural than those for tragedy, which were by then much exaggerated. Quintilian, writing in the first century A.D., refers to masks with one cheerful and one serious side, apparently an attempt to indicate a change of emotion without a change of mask. Mime actors did not usually wear masks, and, as mime increased in popularity under the empire, the use of masks in the theatre became less common.

Costumes varied with the type of play. Comedy based on Greek life (the *fabula palliata*) followed the costuming conventions of New Comedy (see chapter 2), for which everyday Athenian dress was adapted. Similar principles probably governed the costumes for comedies based on Roman life (the *fabula togata*), in which Roman garments were substituted for Greek. In this case, the Roman tunic was the usual garment over which the cloak, or *toga,* was worn.

The costume for tragedy was also based upon Greek practice. The *fabula crepidata* (or tragedies on Greek themes) probably followed the conventions of the Hellenistic theatre (described in chapter 2), although some scholars have suggested that it was Roman influence which led to the extreme stylization of dress in late Greek tragedy. Regardless of the direction of influence, it seems likely that Greek and Roman tragic costumes were similar. For the *fabula praetexta* (or tragedies on Roman materials), costumes probably followed the conventions of the *fabula crepidata,* except that Roman garments were used as a basis. The toga with a purple border (the *toga praetexta*) was sufficiently typical that the dramatic form took its name from it.

It is usually assumed that each of the four stock characters of the *fabula Atellana* had his own standardized mask and costume and that these remained the same from one play to another. Since most of the other characters were rustics, their costumes were probably exaggerated versions of country dress. Some of the

FIGURE 3.18 **Ivory statuette showing a tragic actor** *c.* **second century A.D. Note the distorted mask, high headdress, and thick-soled boots. Some scholars believe it represents a Greek actor of the Hellenistic period, but it is more likely Roman. From Baumeister,** *Denkmaler des Klassischen Altertums* **(1889).**

known titles of Atellan farces refer to doctors, musicians, painters, fortune tellers, and fishermen, each of whom may have been indicated by costume.

The pantomime performer wore a long tunic and cloak that allowed freedom of movement. As a subtle variation on tragedy, pantomime probably used a less exaggerated version of tragic dress. Nothing is known of the costume for comic pantomime, the popularity of which was short-lived.

Mime actors wore the tunic as a basic garment, but their most distinctive accessory was the *ricinium*, or hood, frequently used for purposes of disguise. Some mime characters, probably the fools, wore the *centunu-*

culus, or patchwork jacket, and had shaven heads. Others represented fashionable and sophisticated men and women, and, like modern film stars, were dressed lavishly in the latest fashions.

MUSIC

Although music was not highly valued by the Romans, it was used, perhaps because of Etruscan influence, more extensively in Latin than in Greek plays. Up to two-thirds of the lines of Plautus' plays were accompanied by music, and it figured only slightly less prominently in the works of other authors.

As with Greek music, we know little of the Roman modes. The accompaniment used in the theatre seems to have been composed by each troupe's own flute player, although probably he merely played suitable mood music. One reference from the first century B.C. suggests that the accompaniment was so conventionalized that the audience could tell what kind of character was to appear by listening to the music. Thus, it may have resembled the more trite musical scores of our motion pictures. That the musician was valued, however, is indicated by

FIGURE 3.19 **Musicians shown on a mosaic of a villa in Pompeii. Some scholars interpret it as representing a choral interlude in Greek New Comedy but it is as likely an entertainment of some other type. The musicians perform on double flute and percussion instruments. From Fiechter,** *Die Baugeschichte des Antike Theaters* **(1917).**

records which list his name immediately after that of the principal actor.

The music for plays was performed on a "flute" with two pipes, each about 20 inches long, that was bound to the performer's head to leave his hands free to work the stops. The flute player was on stage throughout the performances and supposedly moved about to accompany first one character and then another.

The musical element in pantomime was more elaborate than that for regular drama, for it required an orchestra of flutes, pipes, cymbals, and other percussion instruments. It is also likely that the music for mimes became more extensive during the late empire as the performances became more spectacular and ornate.

THE DECLINE OF THE THEATRE

In terms of numbers of performances, theatres, and spectacular display, the Roman theatre reached its height during the fourth century A.D. Although it continued as a publicly supported institution for another two hundred years, it had already encountered difficulties that were eventually to overwhelm it.

One source of opposition was the rising Christian church. At first the new sect was very weak, and, as it came to popular attention, met considerable opposition on political as well as religious grounds. Its adherents refused to place allegiance to the state above the dictates of religious teachings, and they insisted that other gods were false despite the Roman tradition of accepting all gods out of a desire to offend none. Consequently, the Romans were willing to accept the Hebrew god as another deity but were unwilling to abandon others. The intractability of the Christians resulted in the decision of the emperor to stamp out the new religion as a subversive element in the state.

In spite of persecution, the power of Christianity gradually increased. Constantine (emperor, 324–337) first made Christianity lawful, while in 393 Theodosius I made the profession of any religion other than Christianity unlawful. After about 400 A.D., therefore, some of the excesses of the theatre abated and state festivals ceased to be given in honor of the pagan gods, but by that time the Roman populace considered theatrical entertainments one of its fundamental rights and thereby insured their continuance. Gladiatorial contests were abolished in 404, however, and *venationes* in 523 A.D.

The theatre was a favorite target of the Christians for at least three reasons. First, it was associated with the festivals of pagan gods. Second, the licentiousness of the mimes offended the moral sense of the church leaders. Third, the mimes often ridiculed such Christian practices as baptism and the sacrament of bread and wine. As a result, the break between church and theatre was inevitable. Tertullian (*c.* 150–*c.* 220 A.D.), the North African theologian, denounced the theatre in his *De Spectaculis,* arguing that Christians forswore the theatre when they were baptized. From about 300 A.D. on, church councils sought to dissuade Christians from attending performances, and in 398 the Council of Carthage decreed excommunication for anyone who went to the theatre rather than to church on holy days. Actors were forbidden the sacraments of the church unless they forswore their profession, a decree not rescinded in many places until the eighteenth century.

But church opposition seems to have had no decisive effect on the Roman theatre. Alone, the Christians perhaps would not have succeeded in prohibiting performances. But two other forces were at work: the decay of the Roman Empire from within, and pressures from barbarian tribes from without. The sense of loyalty to the state which had been the strength of the republic was increasingly undermined after the second century A.D. as military and governmental bureaucracies took over all functions and made citizen concern irrelevant. Furthermore, the soldiers and bureaucrats were increasingly recruited from remote provinces that had little interest in the capital city. To simplify administering its vast territories, the empire was also divided into two parts which by 400 A.D. were almost completely independent of each other; Rome remained the capital in the west, but Constantinople had become even more powerful as the center of the eastern empire, which was more stable and wealthier than the west.

The internal weakness of the west made it difficult to withstand invasions by barbarian tribes there, and by 410 A.D. the Visigoths had sacked Rome itself. When the capital was taken again in 476, Rome's last native emperor was deposed and thereafter it was ruled by barbarians. Consequently, some historians use 476 to mark the end of the western empire, although the barbarians sought to continue it, for they were not so much interested in destroying as controlling it. Nevertheless, the Roman Empire rapidly disintegrated and by the sixth century A.D. its western half had lost all semblance of unity.

During the fifth and sixth centuries, however, the barbarian rulers, like their predecessors, found it expedient to support the theatre, and after each upheaval theatrical performances were resumed. Theodoric (the Ostrogoth who ruled Italy from 493 to 526) even restored the Theatre of Pompey. But during the sixth century order crumbled. The last definite record of a performance in Rome is found in a letter written in 533. The theatre may have persisted, but it does not seem to have survived the Lombard invasion of 568, after which state recognition and support of theatrical performances definitely ceased. Thereafter, the theatre in the western territories returned to that obscurity out of which it had slowly emerged some 900 years earlier.

LOOKING AT THEATRE HISTORY

Since the interests or prejudices of writers inevitably influence their view of events, students of history should learn to pinpoint the slant of works used as evidence about the past. The theatre during the Roman era, more so than in most periods, has been especially subject to prejudicial views, partially because since the early nineteenth century there has been a tendency to praise the Greeks at the expense of the Romans. Thus, the Greeks are almost always treated reverently and seldom are their shortcomings acknowledged; on the other hand, the Romans are almost always treated condescendingly and their strengths are acknowledged only grudgingly. Such attitudes are so deeply ingrained in modern thought that it is difficult to obtain a balanced view of Roman theatre from works written during the past century. This problem is not confined to treatments of Greece and Rome, for there is a widespread tendency to take some aspect (often the sensational or what is so out of the ordinary as to stand out) and convert it into the typical. In this way the best or most unusual or most shocking is often treated as standard or representative.

The following excerpts are from two accounts written about the Roman theatre of the second century A.D. In the first the author is seeking to persuade Christians to avoid the theatre, and he makes all that he dislikes typical. In the second, the author is concerned with showing the superiority of pantomime as a theatrical form, and he makes all that he likes typical. Both eventually acknowledge that there is another side but treat the deviations either as minor or insidious.

. . . demons, . . . with the purpose of attracting man away from his Lord and binding him to their own service, achieved their purpose by granting him the artistic talents required by the shows. . . .

. . . Christians are forbidden the theatre . . . where . . . the best path to its god's favor is the vileness of the Atellan gestures or the buffoon in woman's clothing. . . . in His law it is stated that the man is cursed who attires himself in female garments; what then must be his judgment on the pantomime, who is trained up to play the woman! . . . Granted you have in the theatre pleasant things both agreeable and innocent in themselves, even some excellent things . . . , [for to accomplish his purposes] the devil puts into his deadly draught things most pleasant and acceptable stolen from God. . . .

From Tertullian, *On the Spectacles, c.* 200 A.D. A complete translation of this section can be found in *The Writings of Septimus Florens Tertullianus,* trans. S. Thelwell (Edinburgh, 1869).

Other entertainments of eye or ear are but manifestations of a single art. . . . The pantomime is all-embracing. . . . The performer's art is as much intellectual as physical: there is meaning in his movements; every gesture has its significance. . . . he must be a critic of poetry and song, capable of discerning good music and rejecting bad. . . . So potent is his art that the licentious spectator is cured of his infirmity by seeing the evil effects of passion, and he who enters the theatre in sorrow leaves it serenely. . . . Pantomimes cannot all be artists; there are ignorant performers who badly bungle their work.

From *The Works of Lucian Samosta, c.* 125–180 A.D. A complete translation of Lucian's comments on pantomime can be found in *The Works of Lucian of Samosta,* vol. III, trans. H. W. Fowler and F. G. Fowler (Oxford, 1905), pp. 249–263.

One of the difficulties facing anyone today seeking to envision a performance in a Roman or Greek theatre is that of scale. For the most part, we are used to relatively small theatres and tend to place considerable value on intimacy between actor and audience. But to get some sense of a Greek or Roman performance we would do well to think of the performance space in terms of a baseball stadium or sports arena rather than the indoor theatres we know. Even a very large indoor theatre in our time usually holds no more than 4,000 people, whereas a Greek or Roman theatre might be five times as large. This difference in scale is crucial, since it cannot help but affect matters of style and presentation.

4

East and West: Cross-Currents of a Thousand Years

By the fifth century A.D. the western Roman Empire had disintegrated. But the eastern part remained and flourished. Thus, after the fall of Rome the center of civilization shifted once more to the Hellenized areas of the eastern Mediterranean. In actuality, these areas had always been the most sophisticated parts of the empire, for though Rome was the center of power, the Hellenic territories were more advanced in terms of culture, manufacture and trade, and Rome depended much on the east for its learning, luxuries, and crafts.

THE BYZANTINE EMPIRE

The east began to assume a dominant role politically in the early fourth century A.D. after Diocletian divided the empire into two parts to simplify its administration. In 330, the Emperor Constantine moved the capital of the entire empire to a city he had built on the Bosporus, Constantinople. After 395 the division of the empire into east and west became permanent. Consequently, the Byzantine Empire (as the eastern part came to be called) is considered by many historians to date from this time. It was to continue for more than 1,000 years, until 1453, when it was overrun by the Turks.

The rulers of the Byzantine Empire thought of themselves as Romans and considered their government a continuation of the Roman Empire. They viewed the territories in the west as temporarily lost to invaders or usurpers, and from time to time sought to regain them. Under Justinian (527–565) much of the west was retaken, but Byzantium became and remained primarily an eastern Mediterranean power. Justinian was also the last of the emperors to speak Latin, and thereafter the official language of the empire was Greek.

Between the time of Constantine and Justinian the empire was converted into a Christian state. In Byzantium the emperor assumed leadership in religious as well as secular affairs and came to be considered God's regent on earth. He appointed all major church officials and took an active part in settling doctrinal differences, which were numerous and intense. This subordination of church to state, along with disputes over the authority of the Bishop of Rome (the Pope), became a source of controversy so great that after 1054 the church permanently broke into two parts: Roman Catholic and Eastern Orthodox. The latter prevailed in most of eastern Europe, Russia, and Asia Minor, and the former in the rest of Europe. To this schism can be attributed many of the differences in outlook and culture between eastern and western Europe down to the present time.

The Byzantines considered themselves the defenders of Christian territories from the encroachment of others. With Islam's rise and territorial expansion from the seventh century onward, their empire came under increasing pressure. Eventually it appealed to western Christians to aid in holding or recapturing the holy lands

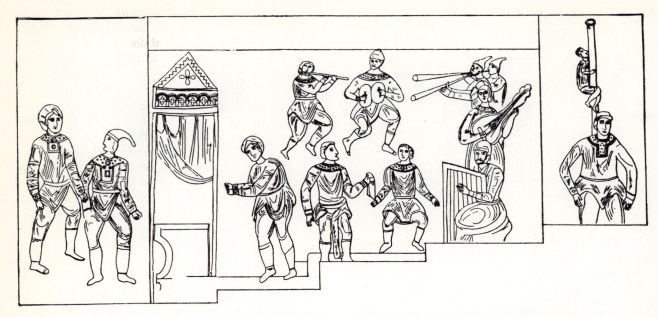

FIGURE 4.1   Eastern mimes of the eleventh century. Fresco in St. Sophia at Kiev (Russia). Redrawn and published in *Sapeski Emperatorskago Archaeologishago Obshchestva,* **N.s. vol. 3 (1903).**

of the eastern Mediterranean. To meet this challenge, the west launched six "crusades" between 1096 and 1229. Unfortunately, the westerners respected Byzantine Christians no more than they did Mohammedans, and in 1204 they took Constantinople itself and divided its territories. Although the empire was reestablished in 1261, it never regained its former strength, and in 1453 it fell to the Turks, who refashioned Constantinople into their own capital, Istanbul.

THE BYZANTINE THEATRE

Byzantium was merely another phase in a continuous history reaching back through the Romans and Alexander the Great to the world of Classical Greece. Although it was self-consciously Christian, the Byzantine Empire was also proud of its Greek heritage, which it sought to preserve even as it denied the pagan gods and myths that had shaped it. The results were a paradoxical mixture of cultures, for though Christianity was intertwined with almost every aspect of religious and civic life, Byzantine popular entertainments resembled those of late Rome. In turn, Byzantine scholars scorned the popular theatre and devoted their attention to the drama of classical Greece. Thus, Byzantine theatre has three main aspects: popular, religious, and scholarly.

It is difficult to assess the extent and nature of Byzantine theatre because the surviving evidence is so slight and historians cannot agree on how the evidence should be interpreted. Nevertheless, it is probable that theatrical performances continued throughout the Byzantine period.

Originally, Constantinople is said to have had two theatres of the Roman type, and at least one survived into late Byzantine times. The empire also included most of those eastern Mediterranean territories in which Hellenistic and Graeco-Roman theatres had been built. Unfortunately, we know little about what went on in these theatres. According to one account, the comedies of Menander were still being performed at Antioch (in Syria) as late as the fifth century A.D. Almost all other records, however, suggest that the fare resembled that of late Rome: mime, pantomime, scenes or recitations from tragedies and comedies, dances, and variety entertainment of all sorts. It is not always clear if the performances being referred to took place in theatres or in circuses or amphitheatres.

The center of secular entertainment in Constantinople was the Hippodrome, modeled after the Circus Maximus in Rome and designed primarily for chariot races. Two factions much like modern political parties grew up around the races there. Perhaps this explains why the Hippodrome was also used as a forum, for the emperor often addressed the people and issued proclamations there. It was, in effect, the city's chief place of assembly. Entrance to the Hippodrome was open to all male inhabitants regardless of class or occupation; a token was required for entrance but no charge was made. Estimates of the Hippodrome's capacity range from 40,000 to 80,000. In addition to chariot races, *venationes* were also held there, and sometimes political prisoners were tortured, executed, or forced to fight in gladiatorial contests. Religious processions, such as the major one on Palm Sunday, also made use of the Hippodrome. Theatrical entertainments can be added to these activities, for the intervals between chariot races were filled with performances by mimes, acrobats, dancers, and miscellaneous acts of all sorts. Some festivals were devoted entirely to team sports intermingled with variety performers.

Entertainments were also given in places other than the Hippodrome or theatre. Mimes, acrobats, and ceremonial dancers appeared at banquets given by the emperor on state occasions; revels of various sorts were features of urban festivals; and wandering performers played at rural festivals and wine harvests. Foreign visitors to Byzantium often reported their amazement and delight at the variety and skill of its entertainments, which exceeded anything then known in western Europe.

But though actors may have been plentiful, they seem to have been considered disreputable. Churchmen often denounced them, and in 692 the Trullan Synod sought to have all mimes and theatrical performances banned. According to ecclesiastical rules, both professional entertainers and anyone who married them were to be expelled from the church. The state also denied actors many civil rights. Clearly there were exceptions, however, for Justinian took a mime actress, Theodora, as his empress. The ambivalent attitude toward the theatre is perhaps best summed up by noting that, despite all reservations, performances were included in state festivals and that the emperor, who was head both of state and church, blessed the participants with the sign of the cross from his box in the Hippodrome. After a time, the church seems to have ceased trying to abolish theatrical entertainments and contented itself with prohibiting them on Saturdays and Sundays and denying performers the church's sacraments.

Some have suggested that the theatrical impulse in Byzantium was satisfied by the numerous church ceremonies with their rich vestments and accessories. Celebrations were especially elaborate during the Easter season, when the events of Christ's last days were recalled in processions that wound through the streets from one church to another to the accompaniment of responsive singing.

FIGURE 4.2 Ivory diptych *c.* 517 A.D. showing Byzantine entertainments. At left can be seen trained horses (above) and mime scenes (below); at right are scenes of animal baitings. Courtesy Bibliothèque National, Paris.

FIGURE 4.3 Miniatures from the Byzantine *Homilies of the Monk John* depicting Mary and Joseph before the Sanhedrin. Courtesy Bibliothèque Nationale, Paris.

Where scholarly opinion divides, however, is on the question as to whether the Byzantines developed a liturgical drama. The view that there was drama is based on a number of surviving homilies (or sermons) with dialogue sections (always involving episodes from the life of Christ or the Virgin Mary). It is argued that some of these dialogues were so long (about thirty lines) that it would have been difficult for one person to deliver them effectively and that they must either have been acted or chanted responsively by others. Since they date from the period prior to the ninth century, some scholars think these homilies exerted direct influence on western liturgical drama, which emerged in the tenth century. Such views remain theories, however, for there is no evidence that shows how or if the dialogues were performed or that they influenced western practices.

In addition to homilies, a few other pieces of evidence relating to religious drama have survived. One is a play, the *Christus Paschon*, formerly thought to date from the fourth century A.D. but now assigned to the eleventh or twelfth century. Most scholars agree that it is a closet drama not intended for performance. Mingling material about Christ's death with classical elements, it begins: "Now in the manner of Euripides, I will the Passion tell which saved the world." About one-third of the 2,640 lines are paraphrased from Euripides' tragedies. Overall, the play is perhaps most interesting as a demonstration of the Byzantine desire to reconcile Christianity with the classical heritage.

Another drama from the east, a passion play in ten scenes or episodes, has also survived. Estimates of when it was written range from the tenth to the fourteenth century. There seems little doubt that it was staged, but the manuscript comes from Cyprus during the period when it was governed by westerners, and therefore many scholars argue that it was imported from Europe, where religious drama was by then flourishing.

Still another argument that religious plays were staged in Byzantium is based on a tenth-century account by Luidprand of Cremona, a bishop sent by the German ruler Otto as an ambassador to the Byzantines. In his report, Luidprand tells of performances he saw in Constantinople. It is often stated that he describes a play in which the prophet Elijah was flown up to heaven, thus proving that religious drama was highly developed in Constantinople. But other scholars now argue that Luidprand's account has been misinterpreted and that he was objecting to the performance of mimes during a religious festival honoring the ascent of Elijah to heaven. On the basis of such evidence, it is impossible to know whether the Byzantines had a religious drama.

Regardless of what one concludes about Byzantine performances, Constantinople is important in theatre history for another reason: its preservation of classical Greek manuscripts. Byzantine scholars were interested in classical drama especially during the final centuries of the empire, and when Constantinople fell in 1453, many fled to the west taking with them the manuscripts on which our texts of the Greek plays are based. Without the efforts of these scholars, many Greek plays would have been lost forever.

To sum up, then, it seems clear that theatrical entertainments persisted throughout the 1,000-year history of the Byzantine Empire. Nevertheless, no indisputedly Byzantine plays intended for performance have survived, and our records concerning entertainments are so sparse that they render suspect any firm conclusions about the nature and extent of Byzantine theatre. Still, from what remains we gain glimpses that suggest a rich theatrical life and even more intriguing possibilities that Byzantine practices may have played a significant role in the revival of western drama. That it would have been possible for Byzantium to influence western Europe is clear, for communication and trade between the two never completely ceased. Without question, Byzantine art influenced western church architecture and motifs in the early ninth century. The Crusades also increased contacts between East and West beginning in the eleventh century. But despite the obvious opportunities, it is impossible to prove direct influence on Western theatre. Nevertheless, Byzantium probably kept alive a theatrical tradition, and some parts of it may have affected later artists.

THE RISE OF ISLAM

The Byzantine Empire finally succumbed to the forces of Islam (the Moslems or Mohammedans). The Moslem world had expanded rapidly after the teachings of Mohammed (570–632 A.D.) began to be accepted around 622. In the century following his death, Mohammed's followers took all of north Africa and penetrated into Europe through Spain as far as France before they were finally halted in a battle at Tours in 732. They also spread eastward into Persia and India, and eventually as far as present-day Indonesia and the Philippines. Until the nineteenth century, they were to remain one of the major political forces of the world.

The early Moslems had great respect for learning: they founded many universities; they preserved and transmitted much of the heritage from Greece, Persia, and Egypt to succeeding generations; and they made many contributions of their own to medicine, philosophy, mathematics, and geography. Because of their far-flung territories, they were the medium through which many oriental inventions—such as paper and the magnetic compass—reached the West. They created a brilliant and graceful civilization beside which western Europe in the eighth and ninth centuries seemed barbarous and even Byzantium appeared backward.

In a history of theatre, however, Islam is largely a negative force. It forbade artists to make images of living things because Allah was said to be the only creator of life and to compete with him was considered a mortal sin. Thus, Islamic art remained primarily decorative rather than representational. The prohibitions extended to the theatre, and consequently in those areas where Islam became dominant advanced theatrical forms were stifled. Storytelling survived almost everywhere and in some places a crude folk drama persisted. In other areas, especially India, Indonesia, Turkey, and Greece, shadow puppets became popular. But these puppets were kept as nonrepresentational as possible. They were two-dimensional cut-outs made of translucent leather and worked with sticks. Furthermore, usually only their shadows—projected on a cloth by the light of lanterns or torches—were actually seen. In several countries shadow puppetry became a highly developed art, though one considerably removed from the craft of the live actor.

In Turkey, shadow puppets seem to have been introduced around the fourteenth century. After the fall of Byzantium, they became the principal theatrical form in areas that had formerly seen performances in the great classical, Hellenistic, and Graeco-Roman theatres. In these areas, the puppet plays revolved around Karagoz and his farcical adventures (which could be pointedly satirical and topical). Eventually these entertainments came to be called Karagoz, and have survived under that name to the present day.

In other areas, still other means were found to circumvent the prohibitions, but all tended to avoid direct representationalism. Thus, while the Moslems did not obliterate theatrical activities in their territories, they did discourage them and in most instances succeeded in confining them to minor forms.

INDIA

It is still further east—to India—that one must look to find the most highly developed and sophisticated drama of the first millennium of the Christian era. Civilization in India can be traced back almost as far as in Egypt and the Middle East. But our knowledge of it is slight until the Aryans arrived from central Asia around 1500 B.C. In the centuries that followed, those features that were to be most significant in Indian life and art emerged. Perhaps the most important of these influences on drama were to be Hinduism, the caste system, and Sanskrit literature.

FIGURE 4.4 Turkish Shadow puppets. Courtesy Puppentheatersammlung, Munich Stadtmuseum.

Hinduism teaches that the essence of all things is spirit or soul and that the ultimate goal is to achieve union with the Supreme World-Soul, or Brahman, who is infinite, eternal, indescribable, and perfect. In all creation, only Brahman is unchanging, and since only what is permanent is real, he is also the ultimate reality from which all else emanates and to which all else seeks to return. Although it emphasizes oneness of spirit, Hinduism sanctions the worship of hundreds of gods or spirits, since all are merely aspects of Brahman. Nevertheless, Hindus tend to honor three principal gods who personify different aspects of Brahman: Brahma, the creator; Siva, the destroyer; and Vishnu, the preserver. Hindus also believe it is impossible to achieve spiritual perfection during one lifetime and posit the necessity of successive reincarnations.

The early Hindus encouraged the representation of living beings in literature, drama, and art as manifestations of spirit. Thus, Hinduism was almost the opposite of Mohammedanism, which denied all gods except Allah and forbade the representation of living beings in art. Hinduism was as hospitable to theatre as Islam was antipathetic.

Before the beginning of the Christian era, India had evolved a caste system based partly on social, economic, and racial concepts but also on notions of spiritual development. Although the number of castes eventually became numerous, there are four traditional ones: Brahmins, the priests and intellectuals; Kshatriyas, the warriors and rulers; Vaisyas, the artisans and farmers; and Sudras, the unskilled laborers. These castes were considered to be hereditary and binding, and each was assigned specific duties, rites, tasks, and diets.

The language of Indian drama was primarily Sanskrit. Originally, Sanskrit was the commonly spoken language, but by the early Christian era it was primarily a medium of written expression, and most people spoke one of the Prakrits, or dialects.

A Sanskrit literature began to emerge in India sometime between 1500 and 1000 B.C. The *Rigveda*, a collection of prayers or hymns, is usually considered the oldest literary piece in any Indo-European language. It was followed by other religious works. But more important for drama are two great epics, *Mahabharata* and *Ramayana*, which may have begun as early as 1000 B.C. but did not assume their final form until about 250 A.D. These two epics are to Sanskrit literature what the *Iliad* and *Odyssey* are to Greek. They were to be the major sources of material for Sanskrit dramatists. As Hinduism spread throughout southeast Asia, they also inspired much drama in those areas.

Both the *Mahabharata* and *Ramayana* are compounds of history, legend, and myth. The former deals primarily with the struggle between various members of two ruling families, but imbedded in it are tales of love, war, and adventure involving numerous gods and heroes. The *Ramayana* tells of the expulsion of Prince Rama and his wife Sita from their kingdom because of the machinations of Rama's stepmother, their wandering during a period of fourteen years, Sita's abduction by a demon king, her rescue through the help of a monkey king, and their triumphant return to their kingdom. These epics, Hinduism, and the society summed up in the caste system form the basis for most Indian drama.

A "golden age" of Indian culture began around 120 A.D. and lasted until about 500. It reached its peak during the fourth and fifth centuries when the Gupta Empire of northern India was a major center of art, learning, and medicine. Beautiful cities arose there, universities were founded, and a great and graceful civilization flourished. Another high point came during the first half of the seventh century under the rule of King Harsha, who was also the major playwright of that time. During Harsha's reign India's influence spread throughout southeast Asia, laying the basis for future developments in drama in those areas.

SANSKRIT DRAMA

It is difficult to determine when drama first appeared in India. Rituals and entertainments of various sorts seem to have been common from the earliest times. They must have been highly formalized by the beginning of the Christian era, for our major source of information about Sanskrit theatre, *Natyasastra*, written some time between 200 B.C. and 200 A.D., codifies practices in dance, drama, acting, costume, and makeup. *Natyasastra (The Science of Dramaturgy)* is the work of the sage Bharata, who claimed to have been taught the art of drama by Brahma, who himself had created the art. Nevertheless, the beginnings of Sanskrit drama remain vague, in part because of Indian indifference to chronology and record-keeping. As a result, modern scholars have assigned a wide range of dates to surviving dramas. Most agree,

however, that the earliest fragments date from approximately 100 A.D. About twenty-five plays have survived, some perhaps as late as the ninth century, although the best come from the fourth and fifth centuries A.D.

Instead of concentrating on character development or philosophical issues, Sanskrit drama was organized around rasas (fundamental moods), to which all other dramatic elements were subordinated. Thus Sanskrit plays are not categorized as comedy, tragedy, or melodrama, but according to one of nine *rasas*: erotic, comic, pathetic, furious, heroic, terrible, odious, marvelous, or peaceful. While a single work may employ many moods, incompatible ones are avoided, and since the final aim is to induce a sense of composure and harmony, all plays end happily. Death and violence are banished from the stage, and right and wrong are clearly differentiated. Joy and sorrow may be mingled, but all must be resolved into happiness in an ending that shows good triumphant over evil.

The plays are complex, nevertheless, because of their many elements. The heroic and the domestic, the exalted and the commonplace exist side by side. The mixture is exemplified in the typical practice of making the hero's confidant a bald, dwarfish, gluttonous clown, who provides considerable comic relief from a basically serious story. The diversity may also be seen in the dialogue, a mixture of verse (used for heightened expression in scenes of intense emotion) and prose (used for more ordinary scenes) and of Sanskrit (the learned language, spoken by gods, kings, ministers, generals, and sages) and Prakrit (the everyday dialect, used for women, children, servants, peasants, and persons of low birth). Considerable variety is also achieved by grouping several subsidiary plots, ranging from the farcical to the serious, around the main story.

Sanskrit plays vary in length from one to ten acts. According to the accepted rules, the events of a single act must be confined to a 24-hour period, while no more than one year may elapse between successive acts. In technique, the Sanskrit drama resembles the epic poem, for it employs narrative to set the scene and to describe events occurring between acts, since the action shifts freely among various locales, including both heaven and earth. Bharata describes ten major kinds of plays, including monologues, farces, operatic works, social plays, and, most important, heroic drama (based upon mythology or history, in which an exemplary hero defends a righteous cause). In the heroic play, there is usually a love story in which the lovers are kept apart by some evil force until the end of the play.

Thirteen plays by Bhasa (second or third century A.D.) are the oldest surviving complete Sanskrit dramas. The best known of these is *Charudatta,* perhaps because it is based on the same story as King Shudraka's *The Little Clay Cart* (*c.* fourth century), one of the most famous of all Sanskrit dramas. A social play, according to the traditional Hindu classifications, *The Little Clay Cart* tells of the love of a Brahmin for a courtesan. Written in ten acts, it has a number of subplots which come together in the resolution in which the true prince, previously aided by the courtesan, recaptures his throne and unites the courtesan and Brahmin, who have narrowly escaped death at the hands of the evil prince.

Kalidasa's (late fourth–early fifth–centuries) *Shakuntala,* a heroic drama in seven acts, is generally considered the finest of all Sanskrit dramas. It tells of King Dushyanta's meeting with Shakuntala (the foster daughter of a hermit), their love and separation (prolonged by a curse pronounced by a rejected suitor), and their eventual reunion. Renowned in part for its beautiful descriptive passages evoking the forest, stream, and other natural phenomena, it moves freely between heaven and earth, forest and court, from the serious and romantic to the comic. The lyrical and the fantastic mingle with the everyday as the play moves through a wide range of human experience.

Other Sanskrit dramatists include King Harsha (seventh century A.D.), with *The Pearl Necklace, The Lost Princess,* and *Nagananda;* Bhavabhuti (late seventh century), with *The Story of the Great Hero, The Later Story of Rama,* and *The Stolen Marriage;* and Vishakhadatta (seventh century?), with *The Signet Ring of Rakshasa.*

In *Natyasastra,* Bharata also lists eighteen kinds of "lower" drama. What these were is not entirely clear. There is evidence that farce was being performed in the seventh century A.D., but lesser types of drama must have existed before that time. The shadow puppet play is among the oldest of these, for it was probably invented by the Indians several centuries before the Christian era began. It seems to have spread both east and west from India to become a popular entertainment in many areas that had few other types of theatrical entertainment.

Beginning in the late seventh century India was subjected to political upheaval, and the lack of stability probably contributed to the rapid decline of Sanskrit drama. After the assumption of power by Moslems in the twelfth and thirteenth centuries, dramatic entertainments were probably reduced to shadow plays, folk drama and ceremonies, dance, and incidental entertainments.

Since Hindu drama was concerned ultimately with the internal and spiritual rather than the external and material, it turned away from realistic production techniques. Its spiritual inspiration was always recognized in an elaborate ritualistic ceremony performed before each play to propitiate the gods and prepare performers and spectators for the drama. The performances were given only on special occasions, such as a religious festival, a marriage, coronation, victory, or state visit, and lasted four or five hours.

Little is known about the playhouses of ancient India. Bharata states that most performances occur in palaces or temples but that when theatres are set up they should adhere to the following rules: the theatre should be 96 feet long by 48 feet wide and divided into two equal parts (auditorium and stage). Four pillars (white, red, yellow, and blue) indicate where members of the social castes are to sit (although in most instances the audience was probably restricted to the upper two). The total seating capacity was only about 400. A curtain divided the stage area into two equal parts, the front half to be used for the dramatic action and the rear half as dressing rooms and off-stage space. The stage may have had two levels, the lower for the majority of the action and the upper for the less frequent scenes set in heaven, in a tower or other high place.

No scenery was used (but the stage was decorated with paintings and carvings as a decorative background). At the beginning of the play, a prologue established the time, place, and situation. In each scene, descriptive passages and pantomime evoked place as needed. The actors used stylized movement and gestures to suggest such actions as climbing a hill, picking flowers, crossing a stream, riding a horse, or driving a chariot. A walk around the stage indicated a long journey. Because scenery was not used, place could shift rapidly as one scene flowed into the next.

The primary emphasis in performance was placed on the actor, who was said to have four basic resources at his disposal: movement and gesture; speech and song; costume and makeup; and psychological insight. Movement and gesture, although based upon natural behavior, were limited to rigidly prescribed signs as described by Bharata and other Hindu writers. Classified according to the parts of the body and inner feelings, gestures were

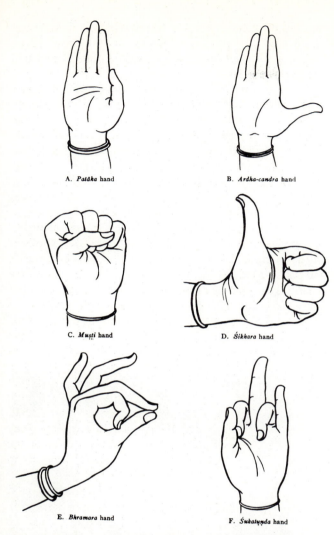

A. *Patāka* hand

B. *Ardha-candra* hand

C. *Muṣṭi* hand

D. *Śikhara* hand

E. *Bhramara* hand

F. *Śukatuṇḍa* hand

FIGURE 4.5 Hand positions used in Sanskrit drama and dance. From *The Mirror of Gesture* (1917).

codified into thirteen movements of the head, six of the nose, six of the cheek, seven of the eyebrows, nine of the neck, seven of the chin, five of the chest, thirty-six of the eyes, thirty-two of the feet, and twenty-four of the single hand. These were combined (according to character type, mood, and situation) to create a sign language as complex as speech.

There was a similar classification of verbal speech and music in which elaborate patterns of intonation, pitch, and tempo were mingled according to the emotion, character, and situation. Each play was accompanied throughout by music played on the drum and stringed instruments. The drum was considered most essential, for it followed the dialogue closely and enhanced rhythmic effects. Singing was also used extensively. The musicians provided information about the situation or characters through entrance or exit songs, while other songs indicated changes in mood or bridged gaps in the action.

Costume and makeup for each character were also strictly prescribed. The makeup indicated the character's caste, social position, and place of birth, as well as the historical period. Color was used symbolically: the Sun and Brahma were golden, lesser gods orange, high caste characters red, low caste characters blue, and so on. Ornaments such as earrings, bracelets, belts, necklaces, and headgear differentiated characters within categories. Properties were used symbolically: as examples, the presence of an elephant was indicated by the use of a goad, a horse by a bit, and a chariot by a whip.

Characters were divided into clearly differentiated categories. For example, there were four basic types of hero: the sublime, the impetuous, the gallant, and the quiet. There were nine classifications of emotions: love, laughter, pathos, anger, energy, fear, disgust, wonder, and quietude. The actor, then, sought to weld conventionalized gestures and movements, speech and intonation, costume and makeup, emotion and character type into a performance capable of arousing the appropriate *rasa*.

By the thirteenth century, Sanskrit drama had retreated to a few temples, where its traditions were to survive into modern times. Hindu dance had a similar history. Dance is undoubtedly even more ancient than drama and was obviously well developed by the time Bharata wrote his *Natyasastra*, for in it he codified 108 dance poses. Like drama, Hindu dance probably reached its peak during the fourth and fifth centuries A.D., although treatises analyzing its subtleties continued to be written until the fifteenth century. With the coming of the Mohammedan invaders, the dance retreated southward to the state of Madras, where it was preserved by temple dancers. Several centuries were to pass before it once more came into prominence.

THEATRE IN CHINA

During the years when India's drama was flourishing, the theatre in China also began to take shape, especially in the area around Peking, which like Egypt and the Middle East is one of the cradles of civilization. Our records, however, are scant until about 1500 B.C. when the Shang Dynasty assumed power. From the beginning, dance, music, and ritual (relating to fertility, success in war, and the prevention of disease or disaster) played an important role in Chinese life, and some early rulers considered them crucial to a harmonious state. By the eighth century B.C. some temples may have had performers associated with them. Historians have sought to draw a parallel between such practices and the dithyrambic choruses of Greece.

After 1000 B.C. there are references to secular entertainments at court banquets, where dwarfs, buffoons, and court jesters performed mimes, dances, and songs. There is also at least one reference to a raised stage.

By 210 B.C. a large portion of China was united under a single ruler who had built the Great Wall to keep out invaders. By this time we also hear of emperors who kept thousands of entertainers at court, and often the accounts associate such practices with debauchery and license.

The first great period of Chinese art and literature came under the Han Dynasty (206 B.C.–221 A.D.), during which China came to equal the Roman Empire in size. All sorts of entertainments seem to have flourished, so many in fact that they came to be called the "hundred plays." They included tightrope walking, pole climbing, athletic displays, conjuring, juggling, sword and fire swallowing, music, dance, and mime. Many of these entertainments were presented at fairs and markets as well as at court. The Han emperors actively encouraged the arts and in 104 B.C. established the Imperial Office of Music to organize entertainments and to promote music and dance. Many of the instruments still used in Chinese theatre orchestras date from this period. The Chinese also trace the origin of the shadow play to about 121 B.C.

FIGURE 4.6 Chinese shadow puppets made of skin. They are manipulated by rods attached to the back. Courtesy the Performing Arts Program of the Asia Society, New York.

when it was first used by wizards to materialize departed souls or gods. Not until later did it become a form of entertainment. (Most historians credit the Hindus with originating this form.)

The Han Dynasty was followed by some 400 years of conflict and unrest. But entertainments seem to have continued. We hear of marionettes between 265 and 420 A.D. and of impersonations of historical personages in the fourth century. After China was reunified under the Hui Dynasty (589–614 A.D.), the forms of entertainment were conglomerations of native traditions with elements imported from India and central Asia. The emperor Yang-ti became so interested in this new version of the "hundred plays" that he set up a training school to encourage its development. Before his reign ended in 614 he is said to have staged a festival involving 18,000 to 30,000 performers in an area extending over four miles.

During the succeeding T'ang Dynasty (618–904) great progress was made toward a distinctive theatrical form incorporating music, dance, dialogue, and acrobatics. In 714 Emperor Hsuan Tsung established a school to train singers, dancers, and other court entertainers. It differed from earlier schools in its stress on popular and innovative (rather than traditional) forms and in its scope (at one time it included 11,409 students and entertainers). This school underwent several changes but it is usually known as "The Pear Garden." To the present day all Chinese actors trace their descent from this school. "Students of the Pear Garden" has roughly the same meaning in China as "Thespians" does in the West. Stories of considerable length that would form a repository for future dramatists also began to appear in abundance in this era.

The T'ang Dynasty was followed by a period of unrest before the Sung Dynasty (960–1279) brought China another of its great cultural eras. Not only did the arts flourish during this time, but its scientists produced such inventions as the magnetic compass, gunpowder, and movable type. Story-telling also reached a new peak. Two of the most famous Chinese novels, *Romance of the Three Kingdoms* and *The Water's Edge,* both of which evolved over many centuries, took definite shape. These and other tales were narrated by professional storytellers at teahouses and were dramatized for puppet and shadow play theatres, two of the most popular entertainments of the common people.

At this time innovations were made in poetry that were to affect drama thereafter. Previously, Chinese verse had used an identical number of written symbols in each

FIGURE 4.7 A Chinese theatre used for a festival of the twelfth century at Kaifeng, the northern capital of the Sung Dynasty. A silk scroll of the twelfth century, recopied in the eighteenth century. Courtesy of John Hu and the Taipei Museum.

line; but when these were sung they often did not fit many of the melodies that had been imported from other countries. Efforts to eliminate these incongruities led to a new type of poetry in which the number of symbols differed in each line. By 1000, this new form had been combined with dance and pantomime, and subsequently a number of different verses were grouped to tell a sustained story. The form remained more nearly narrative than dramatic, however.

A fully developed drama did begin to emerge during the Sung Dynasty. Our knowledge of these works was very slight until 1920 when three plays were discovered. Since then more than 150 titles and several play fragments have been recovered. *Chang Hsieh, The Doctor of Letters* is the most important of the surviving plays since it is considered the oldest extant Chinese drama. Like the others, it includes a prologue (which summarizes the action) and a main story told through dialogue and songs.

During the Sung Dynasty the best performers were recruited for the court where elaborate celebrations were given on such occasions as the emperor's birthday. Other performers played wherever they could. They banded together into troupes of five to seven members and played in villages or cities, in teahouses, or improvised theatres. In the cities, playhouses were situated in special areas called "tile districts." There are said to have been fifty or more theatres in Kaifeng, the northern Sung capital. In Hangchow, there were seventeen "tile districts." According to contemporary accounts, these theatres were fenced enclosures, above which flags and banners flew; the stage was a roofed platform open on three sides; at ground level there was a large area where people might stand, and around this there might be raised stands or balconies.

By the thirteenth century, then, entertainments of various sorts were a common feature of Chinese life. But there was no literary drama until after the Mongols gained control of China in 1279. The major developments in the Chinese theatre still lay ahead.

WESTERN EUROPE

While eastern cultures were flourishing, western Europe was declining. Beginning in the fourth century A.D. general disorder increased and gradually towns and industry decayed and long-distance trade diminished to a trickle. Wars, famine, and disease depopulated many areas and much tilled land returned to forest.

As civil authority decreased, the church began to fill the gap with its own hierarchically organized bureaucracy. From the fourth century onward, the Bishop of Rome, claiming to be the successor to St. Peter, asserted his precedence over all other church officials, and gradually Rome's primacy was acknowledged both in church governance and in doctrinal matters. But during the sixth and seventh centuries the church's power decayed considerably as education declined and as formerly pagan groups (who clung to their superstitions and rites) were incorporated into it. By this time, European society consisted primarily of three groups: a great mass of peasants who tilled the soil, and over them two kinds of lords, secular and ecclesiastical.

The arts held a precarious foothold in this insecure world. Building in stone almost ceased, and art objects were intentionally small so they might be transported easily in times of upheaval. Illuminated manuscripts, containers to hold the remains of saints or other sacred objects, articles used in church ceremonies, and various kinds of jewelry were the principal outlets for artistic expression. The writings of the period were primarily hymns, sermons, and similar theologically oriented works. Latin became merely a literary medium and

was replaced in everyday life by local dialects, the forerunners of the modern European languages.

The major preservers of learning in this period were the monasteries. From the beginning of Christianity, those seeking to lead especially holy lives had abandoned society to live under the simplest possible conditions. In Europe such people often banded together, and eventually buildings (or monasteries) were constructed for them. Because they were looked upon as especially holy places, monasteries were relatively immune from the violence of the times. As oases in a turbulent world, they became the primary repositories of manuscripts and learning. For several centuries the monastic schools were the only ones of consequence in western Europe.

In the eighth century Europe returned to greater stability under the Carolingian kings. The progenitor of this line, Charles Martel, defeated the Arabs at Tours in 732, primarily through his innovative use of armored horsemen as the principal military force (thus initiating what would develop into the tradition of knighthood). But the most important ruler from this line was Charlemagne (reigned 768–814), who extended his realm eastward into Slavic territories (forcibly converting non-Christians on the way) and southward to Spain and into Italy. In Rome on Christmas Day in 800, Charlemagne was crowned by the Pope, who pronounced him the legitimate successor to Constantine. This was the first attempt to establish what would later (from 962 to 1806) be called the Holy Roman Empire, ostensibly the continuation of the original Roman Empire. As the one who bestowed the crown, the Pope also asserted his precedence over all secular princes.

The arts revived somewhat under the reign of Charlemagne. He promoted learning and sought to increase literacy among the clergy. His palace school was the first major center of learning outside of monasteries. While in Italy, Charlemagne visited the Byzantine churches that had been built by Justinian at Ravenna, and upon his return to Aachen (Aix-la-Chapelle) erected a chapel modeled on one of them. This was one of the first important stone structures built in western Europe after the fall of Rome. It also opened a period of Byzantine influence on Western religious art.

Unfortunately, Charlemagne's empire rapidly disintegrated following his death in 814. Not only did his descendants fight among themselves, but they were unable to withstand a new menace from the north: the still-pagan Vikings. Just as the Arabs had come to control the Mediterranean, the Vikings controlled the northern seas, from which they launched devastating raids. Once more Europe broke into small units isolated from each other and the world at large. But gradually a system took shape that is usually called feudalism, the set of societal patterns that underlay medieval culture.

Historians usually divide the Middle Ages into stages. In the earliest of these (*c. 900–c. 1050*) life was still relatively simple, for towns and industry had not yet revived. During these years feudalistic patterns were first fully established.

Under feudalism, the basic unit was the *manor* (or large estate) headed by a nobleman who assumed absolute authority over the serfs or peasants who worked his land collectively. In turn, the lords of manors were the *vassals* (or subjects) of some greater lord, and he in his turn was the vassal of a king or ruler of a state. Vassals were bound to supply their lords a specified number of knights upon demand and the lords in return were bound to protect their vassals. This arrangement was the source of the various ranks and titles of nobility, many of which have persisted to the present day.

FIGURE 4.8 Miniature showing a trained horse. From *Li Romans d'Alixandre,* a manuscript from *c.* 1340. Courtesy the Curators of the Bodleian Library, Oxford.

THE THEATRE, 500 to 900 A.D.

The theatre also began to revive during the early Middle Ages. Following the disintegration of the Roman Empire, organized theatrical activities had virtually disappeared in western Europe as conditions returned to a stage similar to the period that preceded the emergence of drama in the sixth century B.C. But theatrical elements survived in at least four different kinds of activities: the remnants of the Roman mimes; Teutonic minstrelsy; popular festivals and pagan rites; and Christian ceremonies. The theatre was to emerge again from these wellsprings during the early Middle Ages.

After the western Roman Empire crumbled and the state ceased to finance performances, the mime troupes had broken up. Small nomadic bands seem to have traveled about thereafter, performing wherever they could find an audience. For the most part they were probably storytellers, jesters, tumblers, jugglers, rope dancers, and exhibitors of trained animals. None of the surviving records indicate that they were giving dramatic pieces, although it is possible that they presented crude sketches. Such performers were most common in southern Europe, which had been most fully Romanized. From

the beginning they were denounced by the church, which branded them infamous and sought to make them outcasts. But by the ninth century they seem to have been especially active, for the number of church edicts against *mimi, histriones,* and *ioculatores*—terms used interchangeably for all secular performers—are most numerous at that time.

In northern Europe (in Germanic or Teutonic territories) where Roman influence had been slight, another type of performer—the *scop*—flourished from the fifth to the seventh or eighth centuries. The *scop* was a singer and teller of tales about the deeds of Teutonic heroes. As the principal preserver of the tribe's history and chronology, he was prized and awarded a place of honor in society. His songs and stories were major features of feasts and other great occasions. After the Teutonic tribes were converted to Christianity during the seventh and eighth centuries, however, the *scop* was denounced by the church. From the eighth century onward, the once honored *scop* was classed with mimes and like them was branded infamous.

There were also numerous festivals throughout western Europe. Itinerant entertainers often came to these celebrations and took their place among other events. But most of these festivals were outgrowths of centuries-old pagan rites. The church made slow headway against such festivals, for many of the people were

FIGURE 4.9 **Figures wearing animal masks suggestive of rituals or entertainments of the early middle ages. Miniature from *Li Romans d'Alixandre, c.* 1340. Courtesy the Curators of the Bodleian Library, Oxford.**

only nominally Christian, having been forcibly converted or merely enrolled as Christians when their rulers were converted. Not surprisingly, many pagan rites persisted and some of their elements found their way into Christian ceremonies.

A large proportion of the pagan rites were related to the mid-winter solstice and sought to revive the year spirit or the waning sun by bringing evergreens indoors, by lighting bonfires or torches, or by wild, ecstatic dancing (often involving costumed demon figures who were routed). Perhaps even more common were the spring fertility rites. They might involve dancing around the phallic maypole or going about fields with ceremonial carts carrying fertility symbols, statues of gods, or young men and women crowned with flowers. Many of the ceremonies symbolized the struggle between life and death or summer and winter, and often took the form of fights with swords or staffs, wrestling, racing, or other athletic

events. Overall, there was a large number of festivals and many of them were strongly entrenched.

It is often argued that the church, in seeking to convert western Europe to Christianity, usurped many of the existing festivals. For example, the date of Christ's birth was not fixed as December 25 until the fourth century. Some historians argue that this date was chosen to displace the pagan festivals that had grown up around that time of the year. Similarly, Easter is said to have been located to replace the spring fertility festivals. Other festivals may have been created to replace those honoring local pagan deities; often a festival was assigned by the church to that area's patron saint and a church honoring him was built on a site previously dedicated to some pagan god. Thus, existing festivals were permitted to continue but were reoriented. Nevertheless, some pagan rites survived and some eventually became entertainments after their religious signficance was forgotten. For example, the sword dance and the Morris dance, popular entertainments in the sixteenth and seventeenth centuries, appear to be secularizations of rituals relating to the year spirit.

As time went by, the rites of the Christian church also became more elaborate, and drama was ultimately to emerge out of these elaborations—and within the church itself—during the tenth century. This final step, however, was merely a culmination of innovations that can be traced back into preceding centuries.

THE LITURGICAL DRAMA

By the early Middle Ages the church had two kinds of services: the Mass and Hours. The Mass was divided into two parts: the introduction and the sacrament of bread and wine. The introduction was largely devotional and included readings from the Bible, prayers, sermons, and psalms; it varied from day to day according to the church calendar. The second part, the sacrament, varied little, for it was the central and unchanging focus of worship. The importance of the Mass discouraged innovations; consequently, few dramatic episodes were ever attached to it. (It is perhaps worth noting, however, that some scholars have argued that the Mass itself is a drama.) The services of the Hours were far more significant in the revival of drama, for they included no indispensable act. Since they were variable in content from day to day, the Hours could accommodate drama more easily than the Mass, and most church playlets eventually were performed at these services. By the tenth century there were eight Hours services each day: Matins, Lauds, Prime, Terce, Sext, Nones, Vespers, and Compline. Since lay Christians could not attend nine church services daily, the Hours were associated primarily with monasteries.

The church calendar also provided an incentive toward dramatization because it commemorated particular Biblical events on specific days of the year. By the tenth century a number of theatrical elements had been incorporated into these annual celebrations in an attempt to vivify them. For example, Palm Sunday was usually observed with an elaborate procession (which included a figure representing Christ riding on an ass) from outside the city to the church. On Good Friday a cross was often wrapped in burial clothes and placed in a symbolic tomb, from which it was raised on Easter Sunday. Similar ceremonies commemorated other events of the Christian year.

Symbolic objects and actions—church vestments, altars, censers, and the pantomime of the priests—constantly recalled the events which lie behind Christian ritual. Certain emblems had also come to be associated with specific Biblical characters (such as "the keys of the kingdom" with Saint Peter and the dove with the Virgin Mary), making it easy to identify these characters and also providing a basis for costumes in the plays.

In addition, a type of dialogue existed in the church's antiphonal songs, whose responses were divided between two groups or between an individual and a group. By the end of the sixth century these choral portions of the services had been arranged in Pope Gregory the Great's *Antiphonarium* according to their appropriateness for specific days of the church calendar.

By the ninth century, the musical portion of church services had become extremely complex and had motivated the introduction of tropes or interpolations into an existing text. These first took the form of lengthened musical passages, originally of the final syllable of Alleluia. Eventually this extended melody became so elaborate that words were added, one syllable for each note, as an aid to memory. Although the origin of this practice is obscure, it was perfected at the monastery at St. Gall (in Switzerland) under Notker Balbulus (c. 840-912). By the early tenth century tropes were being used in most choral passages of the Mass.

Liturgical drama is most often traced to a trope written for an Easter service. The oldest extant Easter trope dates from about 925. It reads in its entirety:

ANGELS: *Whom seek ye in the tomb, O Christians?*

THE THREE MARYS: *Jesus of Nazareth, the crucified, O Heavenly Beings.*

ANGELS: *He is not here, he is risen as he foretold. Go and announce that he is risen from the tomb.*

This text, found in the introductory portion of the Easter Mass, was probably merely antiphonal (that is, sung responsively by two groups) and probably did not involve actors impersonating the characters.

But the step into drama was soon taken. The earliest extant playlet, complete with directions for its performance, is found in the *Regularis Concordia* (or *Monastic Agreement*) compiled between 965 and 975 by Ethelwold, Bishop of Winchester (England). Although it has usually been assumed that Ethelwold was merely adopting practices already established on the continent, this is by no means certain. At this time, monasteries

FIGURE 4.10 The three Marys encounter the angel at the tomb. From the *Benedictional* (c. 965–975) of Ethelwold, Bishop of Winchester. Courtesy Trustees of the British Museum.

she was drawn to Terence because of his style, but fearing the adverse influence of these pagan works she set out to provide a suitable alternative. It seems unlikely that her plays—*Paphnutius, Dulcitius, Gallicanus, Callimachus, Abraham,* and *Sapientia*—were produced at this time. They remained unknown until they were published in 1501. Historians have differed widely on the significance of Hrosvitha's plays, some seeing in them the first important step toward a full-fledged medieval drama, others considering them interesting but irrelevant to subsequent trends.

Without question it was the emerging liturgical drama that set the tone for what was to follow. In the beginning, liturgical plays were performed almost entirely in the Benedictine monasteries. They flourished especially at Limoges and Fleury (in France), St. Gall (in Switzerland), Richenau (in Germany), and Ripoll (in Spain).

The full development of liturgical drama, however, did not occur until the second phase of medieval civilization (c. 1050–c. 1300). By the middle of the eleventh century the Vikings had been converted to Christianity and had ceased their plundering. Conditions had become sufficiently stable that town life began to revive and industry and trade were able to flourish. This revival was rapid and felt throughout Europe. Sizeable cities arose, many of them independently governed, and as they gained power manorial feudalism declined. Contacts with the Byzantines and Arabs greatly increased because of trade and the six crusades that were launched between 1096 and 1229. These contacts greatly enlarged political, intellectual, and artistic horizons.

As confidence grew, monumentally scaled buildings increased in number. Earlier, fortified castles had begun to be built, and a few sizeable churches had been erected. But large-scale buildings did not become common until the eleventh century and later. Churches erected prior to about 1150 were in the Romanesque style, using the Roman arch as the primary form. Perhaps the most famous church of this type was at Cluny, completed around 1100 and measuring 415 feet by 119 feet. In the middle of the twelfth century the Gothic mode, with its pointed arches and buttressed walls, came into being, first with the church of St. Denis, just outside Paris, in 1144. Thereafter the Gothic style rapidly replaced the Romanesque, and by 1300 monumental churches, richly decorated with statuary, carvings and stained glass, has been built throughout western Europe.

Schools grew up around these cathedrals and

were being revived in England after a long period of civil disorders, and the *Regularis Concordia* was designed to establish uniform practices and to encourage a sense of purpose and order in England's monasteries. It may well be, therefore, that Ethelwold introduced liturgical drama as a device to stimulate and educate the monks. During this monastic revival, the arts and various forms of learning flourished in England and came to exert considerable influence throughout Europe. Consequently, plays may have been among England's exports. Regardless of where liturgical drama originated, however, it had become widespread before the end of the tenth century.

In addition to liturgical dramas, one set of non-liturgical plays has survived from this period. At about the time when liturgical drama was coming into being, Hrosvitha, a nun at Gandersheim in northern Germany, wrote six plays modeled after Terence's comedies but using religious subjects. According to her own account, universities began to evolve out of them in the twelfth century to displace the monastic schools as the primary seats of learning. After these cathedrals were built, liturgical drama also began to be performed in them and thus they became more accessible to laymen. Religious drama continued to be performed exclusively within churches—whether cathedrals or monasteries—until after 1200, when occasionally it began to be presented out of doors. Even after that time, however, plays remained a part of religious ceremonies in many churches until the sixteenth century.

Liturgical drama spread as far east as Russia and from Scandinavia to Italy. The most prolific areas were France and Germany. In Italy, the plays were few in number, perhaps because the papacy opposed them. In Spain (except in the northeastern part which had been liberated about 800) the Moorish occupation hampered the spread of drama. Because the total number of liturgical plays is so great, it is sometimes forgotten that a single church usually performed no more than one or two each year. Therefore, though a dramatic revival was underway, plays remained rarities almost everywhere.

The length and complexity of liturgical plays differed considerably from one area to another. Some of the simplest extant works date from the fifteenth century, while some of the most elaborate had been written by the eleventh century. Consequently, no clear pattern of development can be traced. Although it is frequently assumed that the plays grew by the gradual addition of new episodes, this is not necessarily true, for complex plays may have been written as soon as the desirability of dramatization was accepted.

The oldest and most numerous of existing plays deal with the visit of the three Marys to the tomb of Christ; more than 400 have been discovered. The most elaborate Easter dramas date from the thirteenth century. One of these, found at Klosterneuberg in Germany, includes the following episodes: after the burial of Christ, Jewish high priests ask Pilate to set a watch over the tomb; Pilate agrees and the priests lead Roman soldiers to the tomb and give them money; while the soldiers are keeping guard, an Angel appears and strikes them to the ground; the Marys stop at a perfume seller's stall to purchase ointments and then proceed to the tomb, where they discover that Christ has risen; the soldiers revive and report the news to the priests, who bribe them to declare that the body has been stolen; Mary Magdalen reports the news to Peter and John, who rush to the tomb; Mary Magdalen meets Christ disguised as a gardener;

COMQVARTA ABRAHAM ET MARI

FIGURE 4.11 Hrosvitha's *Abraham and Maria*. From the first published edition of her plays (1501).

Christ is led by two Angels to the gates of Hell, which he forces open to free the imprisoned souls; the Marys and apostles proclaim the resurrection of Christ. In spite of the numerous events, there are only about 200 lines of dialogue. It is a long play, nevertheless, in comparison with most liturgical dramas.

The crucifixion was rarely dramatized. Only three plays on this subject have survived, and two of these are contained in the *Carmina Burana*, a thirteenth century manuscript-collection of plays and poems discovered at the monastery of Benediktbeuern in Germany. The longest treats several events in the life of Christ and ends following the crucifixion, the point at which most Easter plays begin.

Augustine throughout the Middle Ages) that sought to convict the Jews of error in their dealing with Christ by summoning their own prophets. The witnesses were called one by one, each speaking his prophecy concerning Christ. In the extant plays of this type, the number of characters vary from two to twenty-eight, and in some plays such pagan figures as Virgil and the Sybil appear. Most of the plays of the Christmas season were short and associated with particular days of the church calendar. Only one surviving work, found in the *Carmina Burana*, unites all of the episodes of the Christmas story into a single drama.

Although Easter and Christmas plays are by far the most numerous, others dramatized a wide range of Biblical materials: the Raising of Lazarus, the Conversion of St. Paul, the Wise and Foolish Virgins, Pentecost, Isaac and Rebecca, Joseph and his Brethren, Daniel in the Lion's Den, and various events in the life of the Virgin Mary. The most elaborate play of all is the *Antichrist,* dating from the twelfth century. Based upon the prediction that before the second coming of Christ a deceiver will appear and attempt to subvert Christ's mission, its scenes are set at places ranging over the known world, and its battles and other complex episodes are so numerous that some scholars have doubted that it was ever performed.

THE STAGING OF LITURGICAL DRAMA

A number of staging conventions that evolved in the church continued in use throughout the Middle Ages. The playing area had two basic components: small scenic structures (variously called mansions, *sedes, loci,* or *domi*) and a generalized acting area (the *platea,* playne, or place). The mansions served to locate the scene and to house any properties required. But since the action could not be performed in the limited area of the typically small mansions, the actors appropriated as much of the adjacent space (the *platea*) as they needed, so that the same area was often used for several different scenes. Mansions were arranged around this neutral playing space, and the performers moved from one area to another as the action demanded.

The earliest liturgical plays required only one mansion, but more complex plays used many mansions dispersed about the church. The individual mansions varied considerably in size and complexity. For example,

FIGURE 4.12   Interior of St. Zeno's, a Romanesque church built in Verona (Italy) in the twelfth century. Note the raised apse and the crypt beneath it. This picture was made around 1910. From *Romanesque Art in Italy* (1913).

Next to Easter, the Christmas season prompted the greatest number of dramas. Few, however, treat the nativity itself; those which do are simple. On the other hand, there are many plays about the Three Kings (performed on January 6), some of which include Herod's rage and his massacre of the children. A few separate plays also dramatize the "slaughter of the Innocents," commemorated on December 28.

Another popular drama of the Christmas season was the Prophets Play. Unlike other liturgical plays, it was derived from a non-Biblical source, a sermon of the fifth or sixth century (inaccurately attributed to St.

a simple altar sometimes represented the tomb of Christ, but in some of the great cathedrals imitations of the "true sepulchre" in Jerusalem, large enough for several persons to enter at once, were used. A few mansions housed elaborate and numerous properties (especially those for the Last Supper, Nebuchadnezzar's fiery furnace, Daniel's lion den, and Isaac and Rebecca's kitchen) and some had curtains so that characters or objects might be revealed at the right moment or concealed at the end of an episode. The choir loft was sometimes used to represent high places or Heaven, while the crypt (usually located beneath the main floor) often served for low places or Hell. Elementary flying machinery was also used at times to pull the star ahead of the Three Kings, to raise a figure representing Christ on Ascension Day, or to lower a dove for the Annunciation or flames for Pentecost.

The costumes for these dramas were usually church vestments, to which might be added realistic or symbolic accessories. Female characters usually wore dalmatics (a type of enveloping robe) with the hoods pulled up to cover their heads. Angels were signified by wings added to church vestments. The prophets and the Three Kings were sometimes given elaborate nonclerical garments, and symbolic properties were often used to identify personages.

In most cases, the actors were members of the clergy or choir boys, although in the thirteenth century some roles may have been taken by wandering scholars or schoolboys. Much of our knowledge about the staging of plays comes from the rather detailed prescriptions contained in the church manuals of the period. More space in these manuals is often taken up with stage directions, especially those concerning movement, panto-

FIGURE 4.13   Conjectural reconstruction of a medieval church interior with mansions set up between supporting pillars and in the nave. In this reconstruction the choir and apse of the church are not used at all, the mansion at the right being fitted into the transept just forward of the choir. From Richard Leacroft, *The Development of the English Playhouse* (1973). Courtesy Eyre Methuen and the Cornell University Press.

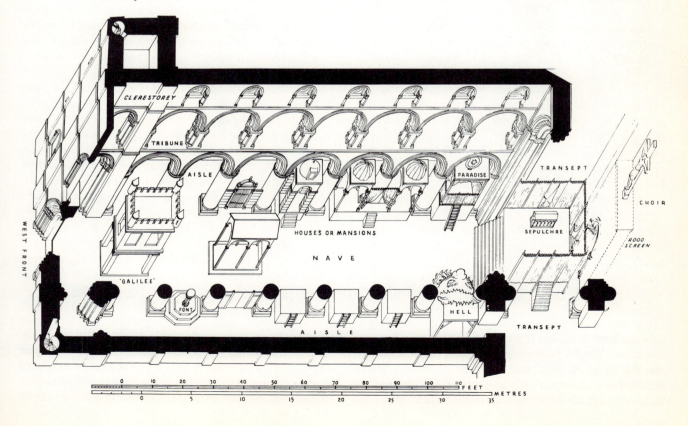

mime, and tone of voice, than with lines of dialogue. As long as the plays were performed in the church, the majority of lines were chanted rather than spoken, and the acting in general was probably more schematic than realistic.

THE FEAST OF FOOLS

Although most of the performances in the church were probably serious and devotional, an element of buffoonery may have crept into some plays associated with Christmas. During this season a number of days were assigned to the minor clergy, who conducted the church services, staged processions through the town, and often collected gifts or exacted payments. St. Stephen's Day (December 26) was given over to the deacons; the Feast of the Holy Innocents (December 28) to the choir boys; and the Feast of the Circumcision (January 1) or alternatively January 6 or 13 to the subdeacons.

One of these festivals—the subdeacons' revelries, commonly called the Feast of Fools—was especially important in the development of comedy. The festival's appeal was in the inversion of status that allowed the lesser clergy to ridicule their superiors and the routine of church life. Much of this is reminiscent of the earlier pagan festivals and many scholars have linked the Feast of Fools with them. Although such practices may not have been typical, at times during this feast the celebrants rang the church bells improperly, sang out of tune, wore strange garments and masks, and used puddings, sausages, and old shoes as censers. The Feast of Fools was presided over by a "bishop fool" who assumed ecclesiastical authority during the time of the festival. It is not clear when this celebration began, but it was well established by the end of the twelfth century and efforts to suppress it were not successful until the sixteenth century. The festivities were accompanied by much revelry, some of which passed over into licentiousness. Sometimes plays were staged as a part of the occasion and a certain amount of burlesque and comedy probably crept into the liturgical plays in this manner. Extensive development of comic episodes had to await the separation of drama from the liturgy. But the Feast of Fools undoubtedly influenced the development of comedy both in religious and secular plays.

The choir boys' celebrations, commonly known as the Feast of the Boy Bishop, included some of the same inversion of status found in the Feast of Fools, but it was much more sedate and restrained. Perhaps for that reason, it encountered little opposition. On the other hand, it probably had little influence on the development of drama.

By 1300 liturgical drama seemingly had developed as far as it could within the confines of the church and consequently plays began to be given out of doors. Although liturgical plays would continue to be presented within the church for another 300 years, they would undergo no significant change. Therefore, innovation and growth were to come from nonliturgical drama. By the thirteenth century, drama also had begun to regain respectability—ironically, because of the church that had denounced it since Roman times—and the time was ripe for a secular resurgence.

This resurgence was not to be confined to western Europe. Throughout the world during the 1000 years prior to 1300 the theatre had been restricted primarily to minor dramatic forms and incidental entertainments. Only India, where Sanskrit drama had flourished for a time, can be counted an exception to this rule. But by 1300, theatre in the East and the West was on the threshold of new developments that would bring it to a new peak in succeeding centuries.

LOOKING AT THEATRE HISTORY

The student can learn a great deal about how scholars investigate theatre history by examining some of the primary sources on which an historical account is based. When he does he often finds that the interpretation given the source by historians is questionable indeed. One good example of how such material can be distorted is the following portion of a single sentence which has been used by some scholars as proof that dramas were staged in Byzantine churches with machinery so elaborate that Elijah could be flown up to the dome. In actuality, from this passage one can conclude no more than that on Elijah's feast day plays were performed somewhere, but neither the place nor the nature of the plays is evident from this passage:

Also on the twentieth [of July] on which day the capricious Greeks celebrate the ascension of the Prophet Elijah with scenic plays, he ordered me to come to him. . . .

> From *Legatio Luidprandi ad Nice-phorum Phocam,* trans. Barbara Spear. (The date referred to by Luidprand is 968 A.D.)

A more precise description of a Byzantine entertainment (this one at a court banquet) is given by Liudprand in his account of another visit to Constantinople in 949 A.D.:

Someone came in bearing on his head, without using his hands, a wooden pole 24 or more feet in length, which a cubit lower than the top had a crossbar 2 cubits long. Also two boys were led in naked except for girded-up loin cloths; they climbed the pole while it remained as steady as if it were rooted in earth: then after one came down, the other who remained and performed alone left me astonished.

> From *Rerum Gestarum ab Europae Imperatoribus et Regibus,* Liber VI, cap. iv., trans. Barbara Spear.

We are inclined to dismiss as unimportant or incomprehensible things from unfamiliar cultures. To many students the Oriental theatre seems remote because its conventions are so different from those they know. But when the visual language of the Oriental theatre is comprehended performances become far more precise than those in the West. Thus, close study of the theatrical conventions of other societies can be extremely rewarding, although they are very difficult to master. The complexity of such a "language" as it relates to Sanskrit dance and drama can be seen if the following descriptions are read in relation to the drawings of hand gestures shown on page 85. Note that each gesture has several possible meanings; the specific meaning at any given time depends on the context and how it is related to other elements in the performance:

Pataka (flag): the thumb bent to touch the fingers, and the fingers extended. Usage: beginning a dance, cloud, forest, forbidding things, bosom, night, river, world of the gods, horse, cutting, wind, reclining, walking, prowess, graciousness, moonlight, strong sunlight, knocking . . . entering a

street, equality . . . , taking an oath, silence, benediction. . . .

Ardha-candra (half-moon): the thumb of the Pataka hand is stretched out. Usage: the moon on the eighth day of the dark fortnight, a hand seizing the throat, a spear, consecrating an image, origin, waist, anxiety, meditation, prayer, touching, greeting common people. . . .

Musti (fist): the four fingers are bent into the palm, and the thumb set on them. Usage: steadiness, grasping the hair, holding things, wrestling.

Sikhara (spire): in the same hand, the thumb is raised. Usage: the God of Love, bow, pillar, silence, husband, tooth, entering, questioning, the body, saying no, recollection, untying the girdle, lover, sound of a bell, pounding. . . .

Bhramara (bee): the second finger and thumb touching, the forefinger bent, the rest extended. Usage: bee, parrot, crane, cuckoo, union.

Sukatundaka (parrot's beak): the third finger of the Arala hand is also bent. Usage: shooting an arrow, throwing a spear, mystery, ferocity.

> From *The Mirror of Gesture,* trans. Ananda Coomaraswamy and Gopala Kristnayya Duggirala (Cambridge, Mass., 1917), pp. 26–35.

The instructions included in church manuals when dramatic episodes began to be performed in the churches of the West are very precise. In fact, by using them one can reconstruct many liturgical performances more fully than one can any earlier theatrical forms. The following is an excerpt from the oldest surviving instructions for presenting a liturgical play:

While the third lesson is being read, four brethren shall dress, one of whom, wearing an alb as if for some other reason, shall enter and go secretly to the site of the sepulchre, and holding a palm in his hand shall sit there quietly. And while the third respond is being pronounced, the remaining three shall follow, all wearing hoods and bearing censers with incense in hand, step by step as though looking for something, shall come to the sepulchre. These things are done in imitation of the angel sitting on the tomb, and of the women coming with perfumes to anoint the body of Jesus. When, therefore, the one seated shall see the three approach as if wandering and seeking something, he shall begin to sing in a sweet modulated voice Quem Quaeritis? *With this sung to its end, the three shall answer, with one voice,* Ihesum Nazarenum. *The former shall respond:* Non est hic. Surrexit sicut praedixerat. Ite, nuntiate quia surrexit a mortuis. *At this command the three shall turn to the choir saying,* Alleluia. Resurrexit Dominus. *With this sung, the one seated, as if calling the others back, shall say the antiphon* Venite et videte locum. *Then he shall rise and raise the veil and show them the place, empty of the cross but with the linen in which the cross was wrapped; at this sight they shall set down their censers in that same sepulchre, and shall take up the linen and hold it before the clergy and, as if showing that the Lord had risen and was no longer wrapped in it, they shall sing this antiphon:* Surrexit Dominus de sepulcro, *and shall then place the linen on the altar.*

> From Ethelwold, Bishop of Winchester, *The Monastic Agreement of the Monks and Nuns of the English Nation*, trans. Barbara Spear. The complete work can be read in a translation made by Dom Thomas Symons and published by Oxford University Press in 1953.

Definition is crucial in historical study, for we must be able to establish the limits of a subject before we can determine what materials constitute legitimate evidence. At times definitions are relatively easy to arrive at, but at others they involve fundamental conflicts. Nowhere is this more evident than in the study of liturgical drama. Where does ritual end and drama begin? Following are two major scholarly points of view. One rules out the Mass as a form of drama, the other insists that it is an archetypal play. Obviously, the second view, if accepted, requires the inclusion of a much larger body of evidence than does the first, and the resultant historical accounts may differ markedly.

By some criterion we must be able to discriminate between what is merely dramatic *or* theatrical, *because of its simi-*

larity to things familiar upon the stage, and what is authentically a play. No one can have failed to observe that in its external resemblances to stage-performances the Roman liturgy is abundantly dramatic. . . . Dramatic externalities of this kind, however, must not be mistaken for genuine drama itself, in which the essential element is not forms of speech and movement, but impersonation. *. . . (pp. 79–80) The Mass, then, has never been a drama, nor did it ever directly give rise to drama. The dramatic features of this service, . . . may have contributed suggestions as to the possibility of inventing drama, and may, indirectly, have encouraged it; but the liturgy itself, in its ordinary observances, remained always merely worship. (p. 85)*

> KARL YOUNG, *The Drama of the Medieval Church*, Vol. I (Oxford: at the Clarendon Press, 1933).

The conclusion seems inescapable that the "dramatic instinct" of European man did not "die out" during the earlier Middle Ages, as historians of drama have asserted. Instead, it found expression in the central ceremony of Christian worship, the Mass. This being the case, an understanding of the medieval interpretation of the Mass should illuminate many hitherto obscure aspects of the history of European drama. . . . (p. 41) Just as the Mass is a sacred drama encompassing all history and embodying in its structure the central pattern of Christian life on which all Christian drama must draw, the celebration of the Mass contains all elements necessary to secular performance. (p. 79)

> O. B. HARDISON, JR., *Christian Rite and Christian Drama in the Middle Ages* (Baltimore: The Johns Hopkins Press, 1965).

5 Theatre and Drama in the Late Middle Ages

Not until the late Middle Ages (c. 1300–1500) were performances of religious plays commonly given outside of churches. But once the transition was made, productions became extremely elaborate, often extending over many days and drawing on the resources of the entire community. As in Greece and Rome, the theatre became once more a cooperative effort of church, state, and citizens.

The flowering of drama in the late Middle Ages can be traced in part to economic and political changes that had occurred during the high Middle Ages (c. 1050–1300), especially the formation of guilds and the growth of towns. Guilds originated during the eleventh and twelfth centuries as protective organizations against local feudal lords and for merchants when traveling. By the thirteenth century, many craftsmen—bakers, brewers, goldsmiths, tailors, and so on—had formed similar organizations to regulate working conditions, wages, the quality of products, and other matters affecting their well-being. These guilds were organized hierarchically. Each was governed by a council of masters (those who owned their own shops and supervised the work of others); under each master were a number of journeymen (those skilled in the trade but who worked for wages); and below the journeymen were apprentices (young men and boys who received room and board while learning a trade, usually over a period of seven years).

The rise of guilds was paralleled by the growth of towns. Originally towns were under the jurisdiction of local feudal lords, but as trade and manufacture grew the towns became sufficiently strong to win concessions, and eventually most of them became self-governing. Thereafter power resided primarily in the guilds, since they usually elected the mayor and the council from among their members.

The growth of guilds and towns brought a corresponding decline in feudalism. Kings and princes began to gain more control over subject lords, and as they did so the nations of modern Europe began to take shape. Princes were aided in this process by townsmen who contributed taxes in return for the ruler's protection and his maintenance of conditions favorable to manufacture and commerce.

The universities also played a significant part in shaping the late Middle Ages. Universities came into being during the twelfth century and soon replaced monasteries as the major seats of learning. Although not opposed to the church, universities stimulated interest in secular learning.

By 1300 the church's dominant role in society was being challenged, and throughout the late Middle Ages it had increasingly to share its position of authority with other institutions. The trend toward secularization was gradual but continuous. It was a time of transition and change during which medieval ideas and practices coexisted with others that would give rise to the Renaissance.

As groups other than the church gained in prominence, it was probably inevitable that they should come to participate in and eventually to dominate theatrical production. Nevertheless, throughout the late Middle Ages drama continued to be primarily religious, and the major theatrical conventions were those that had evolved within the church.

PERFORMANCES OUTSIDE THE CHURCH

Performances of religious plays outside the church seem to have begun during the twelfth century. Before the end of the fourteenth century lengthy vernacular religious cycles had come into being. It is usual, therefore, to consider the years between 1200 and 1350 as a time of transition during which liturgical drama was gradually transformed into vernacular plays. We know little about this transition since so little evidence has survived. The traditional view has been that vernacular drama came into existence through a gradual process in which individual short liturgical plays, having first been moved out of doors, were brought together to form long plays which were then translated into the vernacular tongues and performed by laymen.

The principal evidence for this view, apart from assumptions grounded in cultural Darwinism, is *The Mystery of Adam,* a play usually dated around 1150. Its detailed stage directions make it clear that it was staged outdoors but adjacent to the church. The text has three main parts: the first section concerns Adam and Eve; the second Cain and Abel; and the third is a traditional Prophets' play, in which a number of figures from the Old Testament foretell the coming of Christ. In the first two sections, the dialogue is in French, but the stage directions and choral songs are in Latin; in the final section, the scriptural passages spoken by the Prophets are given first in Latin and then paraphrased in the vernacular. It is unclear whether the actors were clergy or laymen, or where and when the play was produced. This work seems to look both backward to liturgical drama and forward to the vernacular cycles and to support the theory of gradual evolution. Unfortunately, there is little additional evidence on which to base an account of changes during the next 200 years. This lack of information is perhaps explained by the situation in which productions were no longer integral parts of church services but had not yet been taken over by secular organizations.

The traditional view of evolutionary development is not universally accepted. In recent years it has been challenged by V. A. Kolve and others who argue that the cycles developed quite independently of the liturgical drama and that the similarity between the two forms is attributable not to direct descent but to common sources—the Bible and other religious and devotional literature.

Whatever the truth, a number of significant changes occurred in religious drama in the years between 1200 and 1400. First, plays came to be staged outdoors primarily during the spring and summer months, in part because of the favorable weather but also because of the newly created feast of Corpus Christi. This festival was conceived by Pope Urban IV in 1264, given official sanction in 1311, and was being celebrated almost everywhere by 1350. Observed on the Thursday following Trinity Sunday, it varies in date from May 23 to June 24. Corpus Christi was instituted out of a desire to give special emphasis to the redemptive power of the consecrated bread and wine. Since it honored that mystery which to the medieval mind gave meaning to existence (the union of the human and divine in the person of Christ and the promise of redemption through his sacrifice) all Biblical events could be related to it without anachronism. Furthermore, if the meaning of Christ was to be made clear through drama, it seemed essential to include many events preceding Christ's birth, as well as those relating to his life, death, and resurrection. Often the Last Judgment (in which the ultimate human outcome is demonstrated) was also included. Thus, there grew up around Corpus Christi a cosmic drama which encompassed events ranging from the creation to the destruction of the world.

Obviously plays of such scope made demands in excess of those found in liturgical drama. Freed from the restrictions of church architecture and church liturgy, the producers of the outdoor plays were able to experiment. The result was great diversity in staging during the two hundred years between 1350 and 1550.

The feast of Corpus Christi was also motivated in part by the desire to make the church more relevant to the ordinary man and his life. Therefore, secular groups had to be assigned a role in the celebrations. Representatives of all ranks and professions (nobles, merchants, craftsmen, and churchmen) were included among those who participated in the central feature of the Corpus Christi festival: a procession through the town with the consecrated Host. Many scholars have seen in this cooperative venture the beginning of the layman's involvement that would eventually lead to his predominance in the staging of outdoor plays.

But if Corpus Christi supplied the impetus for presenting cyclical dramas, once established the plays did not always continue to be associated with that festival. Soon they were being given at other times, perhaps most often at Easter or Whitsuntide (seven weeks after Easter). In addition, some cities staged plays on the feast of their patron saints, and occasionally cities gave elaborate productions out of gratitude for deliverance from a plague, drought, or other disaster.

One of the most important changes made in drama at this time was the abandonment of Latin in favor of the vernacular tongues. This change, in turn, led to the substitution of spoken for chanted dialogue and facilitated the transition from clerical to nonclerical actors. The adoption of vernacular languages also indicated a major step toward national and away from international drama (which Latin had encouraged).

THE VERNACULAR RELIGIOUS DRAMA

It is impossible to determine when each change in dramatic practice first occurred, but it is clear that by the middle of the fourteenth century lengthy cycles of vernacular religious plays were coming into being. Between 1350 and 1550 the medieval theatre reached its peak. Our knowledge of it is most extensive in the late fifteenth century and especially the sixteenth century, for most of the surviving evidence dates from those years. Vernacular religious plays were performed throughout western Europe. In the British Isles, plays were produced by about 125 different towns at some time during the Middle Ages. Nevertheless, only a few texts survive. Most of the extant English works are parts of the cycles staged in four towns: York (48 plays), Chester (24), Wakefield (sometimes called the Towneley Plays, 32) and the *Ludus Coventriae* or N——town Plays (whose home is unknown although assigned by some scholars to Lincoln, 42). It is often assumed that these four cycles typify English practice, but such cosmic dramas can be clearly established in only twelve towns. It is certain that many cities never developed cycles.

The existing English cycles, all dating from about 1375, were performed until the mid-sixteenth century. During these 175 years, individual plays were rewritten,

new ones added and others dropped; consequently, they vary widely in dates of composition, as well as in quality. The surviving texts show the cycles as they existed near the end of their active production life. In addition to these cycle plays, ten other dramas in English and three in Cornish have survived from the British Isles.

A much larger number of plays from France are extant. They range from short works to those requiring twenty-five or more days to perform. Rather than covering material from the Creation to the Last Judgment like most of the English cycles, the French plays are usually more restricted in time. Most end with the death and resurrection of Christ. The Germanic territories and Spain were also very rich in vernacular religious plays. In Italy, Florence was the city most sympathetic to religious drama, which did not flourish in most parts of that country. Elsewhere in Europe religious drama was less extensively performed, although there is scarcely any country in which it was unknown.

While the length and scope of the dramas varied widely, they all dealt with the same basic subject matter: God's ordering of existence as revealed in the Bible, the Apocrypha, legends about Biblical figures and saints, writings of the church fathers, and collections of sermons. Consequently, regardless of where they were written, the medieval plays have many common characteristics.

The dramas seldom observe a clear-cut, cause-to-effect relationship among incidents. They are episodic, and there is no attempt to bridge the gaps between the short plays that make up long cycles. This loose structure probably did not offend the medieval audience, who believed that events occur because God wills them. The dramas display little sense of precise chronology, for Biblical characters often refer to things that happen long after their own times. Again, however, to medieval audiences temporal existence was merely a short preface to eternity, and the telescoping of past events only served to make the dramatic characters contemporary and to reinforce the message of the plays.

The religious dramas combine stylization with realism. They are written in verse, action is schematized, characterization is minimal, and the settings only sufficient to establish the place of action. On the other hand, some incidents, especially those dealing with miraculous occurrences, are presented with considerable realistic detail. Such incidents serve two purposes: they establish the relevance of the events to the medieval world, and they reinforce faith.

In spite of their essentially religious purpose,

many plays contain extended comic scenes, usually involving devils, villains, or buffoons. Most of the comic episodes depend upon the juxtaposition of reality with the ideal, of human failings with divine commandments, of the fashionable with the eternal, and thus remain relevant to the plays' didactic purposes. But, though always in part didactic, the plays were also highly effective theatrical entertainments.

PRODUCTION ARRANGEMENTS

Before the end of the fourteenth century, the production of plays had in most places passed out of the control of the church, although the scripts were still approved by church officials and were performed at religious festivals. Thus, though the church gave up its direct participation, it kept a watchful eye on the contents of the plays and their presentation.

There were many kinds of producing organizations in the late Middle Ages. On the continent, religious guilds, or confraternities, were the usual producers. The members of these groups, which began to appear about 1300, were mostly laymen, although some were clergymen. These guilds undertook charitable deeds and many of them presented plays as acts of devotion.

Although in England confraternities also frequently produced plays, the trade or craft guilds assumed much of this responsibility in the towns of northern England. While the trade guilds were primarily designed to protect the interests of craftsmen, they retained many religious connections: each helped to support a chapel, each had a chaplain and a patron saint, and, like the confraternities, the guilds undertook charitable deeds and sometimes presented plays as their contribution to religious festivals.

Other arrangements for theatrical productions include those in which responsibility was assumed by a town, the clergy, an individual, jointly by town and clergy, or by a temporary society formed for the express purpose of presenting a play. Thus, arrangements differed widely, but usually involved many persons working together. For the most part, the church was content with a passive role. In every case, however, its right to approve the scripts was probably understood.

The complex motives and arrangements are best summed up at Lucerne, where a passion play was presented at regular intervals for more than a century. Here the play was said to serve the purposes of honoring God, edifying man, and glorifying the city. The division of authority is revealed in these procedures: the proposal that the play be given came from the Brotherhood of the Crown of Thorns; after ratification by the city council, a public proclamation was made from the pulpit; the production was then placed under the supervision of a committee appointed jointly by the brotherhood and the city council, while the church reserved the right to approve the script.

The delegation of responsibilities and the methods of financing productions depended upon the type of organization. In northern England, the town council and trade guilds shared the responsibilities. The council decided whether performances would be given in a particular year; it assigned the plays to individual guilds, held the approved copy of the script, and demanded faithful adherence to it; it specified fines for guilds that did not produce their plays or did not perform them well; and it chose the playing places. The majority of the work and expense fell to the guilds. The plays were supposedly assigned on the basis of appropriateness: dramas about Noah were given variously to the shipwrights, watermen, and fishers, while the plays about the Three Kings were assigned to the goldsmiths, those showing the Last supper to the bakers, and so on. Each guild was then responsible for providing a pageant wagon, scenery, costumes, properties, special effects, actors, and supervisors. Two small or poor guilds might be given a joint assignment. Since each play was a self-contained unit (being mounted on its own wagon) and since the individual plays were performed in sequence, the entire cycle could be coordinated without great difficulty.

On fixed stages, where all episodes were performed on the same platform, an entire cycle often came under the direction of one man or a small committee. Double casting, crowd scenes, and elaborate scenery and special effects also were facilitated by the fixed stage. Such centralization, however, often led to complex financial arrangements. Sometimes a city corporation might make a grant; often those cast in the play were required to pay a fee and to furnish their own costumes and properties; sometimes the local chapter of clergy might provide part of the money. In some instances, admission was charged and salvaged materials were sold after the performances as a means of recovering expenses. At Valenciennes in 1547, where a cooperative society was formed to produce a play, the members raised the money and shared the considerable profits.

THE DIRECTOR

Such complex productions required careful organization, for the handling of casts that sometimes included as many as 300 actors, of complex special effects, and of large sums of money could not be left to chance. Consequently, the director (or stage manager, or pageant master) was of considerable importance.

Still, the director's duties varied considerably from one locale to another. In the guilds of northern England, the wardens of the companies were responsible to the town council for the proper staging of the plays, and they controlled finances and paid all bills. The wardens seldom did the actual work of play production, however, for normally they hired or appointed someone else to do this job. Often this position was given to a member of the guild, but in some instances a "pageant master" was put under comtract for a number of years at an annual salary. For example, at Coventry in 1454 the Smiths contracted for a period of twelve years with Thomas Colclow, who was to supply everything needed except the wagon and costumes. The pageant master secured actors, arranged rehearsals, and took charge of every phase of production. In addition, he supplied the men to move the pageant wagon from one location to another and to control the crowds during performances.

The director of plays on fixed stages needed even more skills, since an entire cycle was often under his direction. Technically, a committee of supervisors (often with as many as twelve members) was usually in charge, but they normally delegated their authority to one person or to a small group. At Lucerne in 1583 the committee turned over all details to the city clerk, Renward Cysat. At Vienna in 1505 much the same arrangement seems to have been used, since there Wilhelm Rollingen took complete charge. At Mons in 1501, four actor-managers, each with one assistant, were employed to stage the play. Some directors became sufficiently famous to be sought by many towns. After staging a cycle at Poitiers in 1508, Jean Bouchet was still in demand as late as 1532. In Spain, Lope de Rueda, a professional actor-manager, was put under contract by the city of Valladolid in 1552 to serve as pageant master for the Corpus Christi festivities. In the Tyrol region of Austria and Switzerland, Vigil Raber staged plays in a number of towns during the early sixteenth century.

The director's duties were outlined by Jean Bouchet: he must oversee the erection of a stage and the

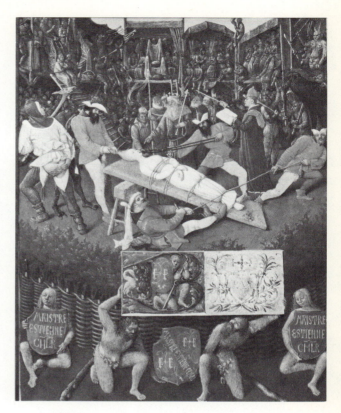

FIGURE 5.1 The Martyrdom of St. Apollonia. A miniature by Jean Fouquet, c. 1460. The figure at right center is often said to represent the director. Note the audience and raised mansions. Courtesy Musée Condé, Chantilly.

placement of scenery and machines; he must find persons to build and paint scenery and to construct seating for the audience; he must insure that all goods delivered are of the proper amount and quality; he must cast and rehearse the actors; he must discipline the actors and establish a scale of fines for those who infringe rules; he may act some roles himself; he must assign persons to take money at the entrances; he must address the audience at the beginning of the play and, after each intermission, give a résumé of previous happenings and promise greater marvels in the portions yet to come. Although not all directors had to cope with so many problems, many did. Consequently, the men given such positions had to be versed in every aspect of theatrical production.

Some historians have argued that the director was always on stage during performances, following the actors about, whispering their lines to them, and giving them directions. This theory, which seems most unlikely, is based almost entirely upon one anecdote of doubtful authenticity and a painting showing a scene from a play about St. Apollonia in which a figure with a book and staff stands in the middle of the stage. Some scholars identify this figure as the stage manager, although there seems no good reason to assume that he is not a character in the play. Considering the emphasis placed on learning lines and the fines levied against those who neglected to do so, it seems improbable that actors would have depended on the stage manager to supply each speech. On the other hand, the director or an assistant was probably in a position to give cues to actors and machinists and to prompt in an emergency.

A few records kept by directors in the Middle Ages have survived. From a play staged at Frankfurt-am-Main in 1350 we have the director's scroll (some 14½ feet long) giving all the actors' cues and complete stage directions. In addition, we have some detailed prompt-books. Those most readily available are from Mons (1501) and Lucerne (1583). Nothing in these books is left to chance; every detail has been prepared and recorded. They are the work of men who were stage directors in the modern sense.

ACTORS AND ACTING

The number of actors required for productions varied considerably. In the guild cycles of northern England, many of the individual plays include no more than five to ten characters. Thus, each guild needed only a few actors, but the total number of performers in the entire cycle was considerable. For the plays mounted on fixed stages, casting was more complicated. For *The Acts of the Apostles,* presented at Bourges in 1536, the 494 roles were distributed among 300 actors. But most plays of this scope date from the sixteenth century and seem to mark a considerable increase in numbers of roles over earlier works.

The majority of actors were drawn from the local population. Only in a few cases can we tell how they were selected. At York in 1476, the city council decreed that four of "the most cunning, discreet, and able players within this city" were to audition all persons who wished to act. No one was to appear in more than two plays. These provisions seem to indicate that guilds did not confine casting to their own members, and that actors might perform for two different guilds. At Seurre in

1496, the mayor, assisted by three other persons, cast the play. In 1540, heralds rode through the streets of Paris appealing for volunteers. At Lucerne in 1583, requests were made from the pulpit that all those interested in acting register with the city clerk, who then chose the cast with the aid of a committee. In those instances in which plays were repeated, an actor might play the same role many times over a period of years.

The majority of actors were chosen from the merchant or working classes, although members of the clergy and the nobility sometimes participated. Most were men or boys, but in France women and girls appeared occasionally. Doubling was a common practice. At Valenciennes in 1547 the more than 100 roles were assigned to 72 actors, and at Mons in 1501 about 350 roles were cast with approximately 150 players. On the other hand, sometimes a single role required more than one actor, as when a character grew from childhood to adulthood. For scenes of violence, such as beheadings and burnings at the stake, realistic effigies were substituted for live actors.

The good faith and discipline of the actors were insured by a number of devices. At Lucerne in 1583, each person was allowed fourteen days in which to decide if he wished to accept a role; once committed, he was bound by oath to continue. At Valenciennes in 1547, each actor was required to take an oath before a notary, in which he agreed to appear on the days of performance. Other provisions of the Valenciennes agreement are also revealing: each actor was required to accept the roles assigned to him and to attend rehearsals at the specified times; each agreed not to meddle in the affairs of the supervisory committee or to grumble against their decisions. There was also a schedule of fines for missing rehearsals or for other infringements of rules. Agreements from other towns indicate that jealousies, bickerings, and resignations were common, and that producers had learned by the sixteenth century to guard against them.

The time devoted to rehearsals was not great by modern standards. For example, although the play given at Mons in 1501 required four full days to perform, there were only forty-eight rehearsals. Two to five rehearsals were considered sufficient for the individual plays in the English cycles.

Something of the overall process can be inferred from the detailed records preserved from Lucerne in 1583 for a play that required twenty-four hours to perform in its entirety. Prior to the first rehearsals, a general meeting of the entire cast was held; the script was divided into twelve units for rehearsal; in addition to the regularly scheduled sessions, actors were urged to arrange other opportunities for working together privately; when the action presented unusual problems, extra rehearsals were called; changes in dialogue, action, and properties were frequently made during the preparatory period. Although the performances were given out of doors, rehearsals were held in a large hall. About eighty days elapsed between the first rehearsal and the performance of the play, but the total number of rehearsals is unclear.

The sponsoring organization usually supplied the actors with food and drink at rehearsals. If a participant had to miss work, someone was paid to replace him. This expense usually fell to the actor, but if he was too poor the producing group absorbed the cost.

It is uncertain whether dress rehearsals were customary. Each episode was probably prepared separately; but some plays were so long (as for example one at Bourges in 1536 which required forty days to perform) that a dress rehearsal in the modern sense would have been impossible. On the other hand, at Romans in 1509, after the dress rehearsal revealed that the playing time was much too long, extensive cuts were made. At Valenciennes in 1547, in a production taking up the afternoons of twenty-five days, the actors were required to report at 7 A.M. each morning for what was obviously a rehearsal of that day's episodes.

For the long plays given on fixed stages, actors assembled as a group and then went in procession to the site of the performance. Upon arrival, they marched around the playing area before taking their places inside or near the appropriate mansions. In many instances, the actors remained visible throughout, coming forward when needed and retiring to their places when no longer required. At Lucerne, elaborate plans were made so that the actors might slip away to change costumes and to eat during the two twelve-hour performances. At Valenciennes, the players agreed not to leave the stage during the performances without permission and to accept whatever food and drink might be passed to them there. At the end of the day's performance, the actors returned in procession to the place of assembly, where they were often served a banquet.

In some cycles, the individual plays supposedly were mounted on wagons and repeated at designated places throughout the town. In these presentations, procession alternated with performance.

Undoubtedly the quality of acting varied considerably. Many contemporary accounts praise certain actors lavishly, but others condemn the performers. In acting, voice seems to have been valued above all else. The chanting that had been typical in liturgical drama was abandoned in the vernacular plays in favor of a delivery resembling everyday speech. Since characters in the extant plays are lacking in subtlety, they did not require highly versatile performers. Most characters are typed and given a few clear-cut actions and emotions (such as adoration, joy, anger, or grief). Serious characters are usually restrained, but the comic roles allow much scope for improvisation and pantomime.

Attempts to be realistic occasionally exposed performers to considerable danger. At Metz in 1437, the actor playing Judas almost died while being hanged; at Seurre in 1496, Satan's costume caught fire, and actors in Hell scenes elsewhere were often injured by the cannons and other devices used to create noise, fire, and smoke.

By the sixteenth century, a number of actors were sufficiently skilled to be employed as coaches. The extent to which professionalism had arrived is a matter of controversy. Although the majority of players were clearly amateurs, a few were paid well for performing, although even they usually had other regular trades. Nevertheless, by the end of the Middle Ages, the professional actor was clearly in evidence.

COSTUMES

Most characters were dressed in garments like those worn by their counterparts in medieval life. For example, Roman soldiers were attired in medieval armor, and Jewish high priests wore the robes of Catholic prelates. Many of the Biblical characters closely associated with orthodox Christianity, though historically Jews, were dressed in clerical garb, but most other Jews normally wore clothing typical of the medieval Jew. God was costumed as an emperor or pope, and angels wore church robes to which wings were attached. Any important character, human or divine, might carry an identifying emblem (the Archangel Michael, for instance, always wielded a flaming sword). The devils were conceived most imaginatively, for they were made to resemble great birds of prey, monsters with animal heads, or creatures with scales, tails, horns, or claws.

In most instances, actors had to supply their own costumes, unless these differed markedly from those

FIGURE 5.2 Reconstruction of a performance of a cycle play on a pageant wagon. From Sharp, *A Dissertation on the Pageants or Dramatic Mysteries . . . at Coventry . . . .* **(1825).**

available in daily life. Consequently, the records of producing organizations show payments only for such exceptional garments as those of devils and effigies or for accessories and emblems. Actors often incurred heavy expenses, especially when playing wealthy personages. Double casting increased the outlay, particularly in the sixteenth century when stage costumes, even for lower-class characters, were often made of rich fabrics. Occasionally, as at Chalons-sur-Marne in 1507, nonparticipating wealthy citizens were required to buy costumes for actors unable to furnish their own. Other sources of supply include the clergy (who loaned or rented garments), other groups that regularly produced plays, and individuals (who occasionally contracted to outfit an entire production).

Because each actor usually supplied his own costume, supervision and coordination were needed. At Lucerne, the director gave each performer a detailed description of the appropriate dress for his character. It seems likely that similar procedures were followed elsewhere. Many of these practices extended to hand properties as well. Unless an item was not readily available, it was supplied by the actor who used it. Unusual articles were made at the expense of the producers.

THE STAGES

The stages upon which the vernacular plays were performed might be fixed or movable. Fixed stages were most common throughout Europe, but in England, Spain, and a few other places movable stages were sometimes used. Nevertheless, because most of the extant English plays were related to Corpus Christi processions which made use of pageant wagons, the movable stage is often treated as typical throughout England. The traditional view has been that each play in a cycle was mounted on a wagon and on the days of performance all were presented in succession at a number of different places in the town.

This view has recently been challenged by scholars who suggest that the plays themselves were not presented at various places but that the wagons in the Corpus Christi procession served much the same function as modern "floats" and that costumed characters on the wagons tried to convey the essence of each play as the wagons were drawn through the streets past the various stations set up for viewers. These scholars go on to argue that the plays themselves were presented at a single location, where the wagons served as mansions for the plays. If they are correct, the performances of plays in northern England would have resembled those given on the continent. This view, however, is still not widely accepted and for the most part the traditional view is followed here.

No one questions that in some English towns pageant wagons played a part in the Corpus Christi celebrations. Nevertheless, no clear description of an English pageant wagon has survived. Most modern discussions are based upon the account given by David Rogers in *A Breviarye, or Some Few Recollections of the City of Chester* (a manuscript of the late sixteenth or early seventeenth century). Rogers states that the pageant wagons "were a big scaffold with two rooms, a higher and a lower, upon four wheels. In the lower they appareled themselves, and in the higher room they played." (Another surviving version of this account states that the wagons had six wheels.) This description would seem to indicate a two-storied structure, with the lower part serving as a dressing room and the upper as the stage.

Roger's account, long accepted as accurate, is now questioned for two principal reasons. First, it is not certain that Rogers ever saw the plays performed. Second, the wagons he described would be extremely cumber-

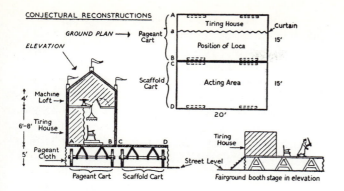

FIGURE 5.3 A reconstruction of an English pageant wagon and a ground plan of the overall playing arrangement. From Wickham, *Early English Stages,* Vol. I. Courtesy Columbia University Press and Routledge & Kegan Paul Ltd.

wagon was used by more than one guild, the scenic needs of the plays mounted on that wagon are very similar.

"Processional" staging was not confined to England; it seems to have been used in Belgium, the Netherlands, and especially in Spain. It is not known when wagons were first used in Spain, but they were clearly present by 1555 and were typical by the seventeenth century. In Spain, the wagons were used much as Wickham suggests. At each playing site in the town, a platform was available, and the wagons, or *carros,* were placed alongside this platform, which served as an acting area. The scenic investiture of these plays was relatively complex, and consequently from two to four wagons were required for each of the plays. (These Spanish practices are treated more fully in chapter 8.)

In Europe as a whole, however, fixed stages were

some. They would have been at least 15 feet tall (allowing for the wagon wheels, the dressing room space, and the scenery on the top level), but relatively narrow, since they had to be moved through alley-like streets. With the top level divided between the mansions and the playing space, the actors would have had to perform on a narrow ledge about nine feet above the street. Considering that a play such as the Chester cycle's "Last Judgment" depicts Heaven, Earth, and Hell, and includes more than twenty characters, this arrangement seems impractical. For these and other reasons, Glynne Wickham has argued in *Early English Stages* that the pageant wagon was a one-leveled structure taken up entirely by the mansions and "off-stage" space. The wagon served, he suggests, merely to provide a scenic background and dressing rooms, while the acting took place on a scaffold cart alongside which the wagon was drawn up. From stage directions, we also know that characters sometimes played on the street level. While Wickham's theory cannot be proven, it is a more persuasive solution to the problems of staging than those offered in earlier accounts. If the plays were given only once at a fixed location, as some contemporary scholars suggest, the actors could have used a single large platform and the scenery transported on the wagons could have been supplemented by additional structures.

The pageant wagons were not necessarily uniform in size or design. Since a guild always performed the same play, its wagon could be built to meet its special requirements. In those rare instances when the same

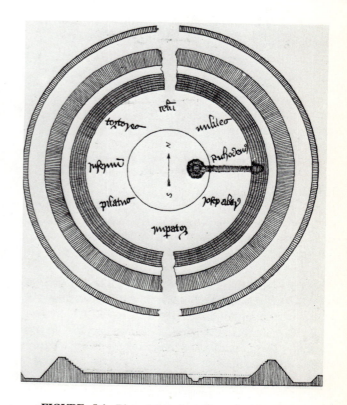

FIGURE 5.4 Plan (above) and section (below) of a "round" at Perranzabuloe in Cornwall (England). This structure, probably built in the fifteenth century, may have been used for dramatic performances. The drawing was made in the eighteenth century. From Albright, *The Shakesperian Stage* (1909).

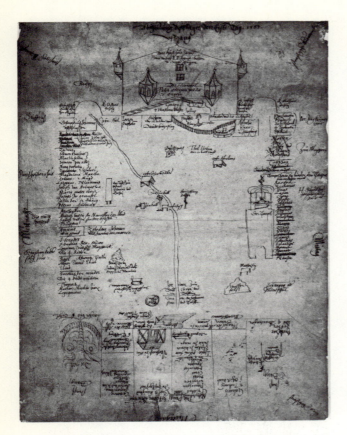

FIGURE 5.5 Renward Cysat's plan for the first day's performance of the Lucerne Passion Play, 1583. At the top is the building which served as Paradise with, at its base, the Garden of Eden. Down either side are mansions, each with a list of the characters assigned to it; at lower left is the Hell Mouth. Courtesy Burgerbibliothek, Lucerne.

The actor-audience spatial relationships varied considerably. In the amphitheatres and Cornish rounds, the audience may have viewed the action from all sides. At Lucerne, spectators were grouped around three sides of the playing area, while at Mons they viewed the stage from the front only.

Perhaps the most typical stage was a long rectangular platform set against a building or row of houses, although sometimes it extended down the middle of a square. Occasionally there was no platform, and the mansions were placed directly on the ground. The size of the stages also varied. At Autun in 1516 the platform was about 200 feet long, while at Romans in 1509 it was 120 feet long and 60 feet deep. At Lucerne, the playing space was irregularly shaped, being about 125 feet long but varying in depth from 80 to 60 feet.

In addition to outdoor stages, indoor platforms were used occasionally. For example, the Confrérie de la Passion in Paris played for more than 100 years in the Hôpital de la Trinité, where the stage was only about 40 feet wide.

FIGURE 5.6 Model showing Albert Köster's reconstruction of Renward Cysat's plan for the Lucerne Passion Play, 1583. Courtesy Theatermuseum, Munich.

certainly more common than wagons. The sites of fixed stages varied considerably. At Bourges and Rome, the ancient Roman amphitheatres were used. In Cornwall, the "Cornish rounds" offered similar playing arrangements. (These circular earthen embankments enclosing areas up to 120 feet in diameter may have been built as forts. They certainly were not constructed especially for the performance of plays.) Sometimes stages were erected in cemeteries adjoining churches. Courtyards of private residences (as at Valenciennes in 1547) or of monasteries (as at Romans in 1509) also were used. Most typical, however, were stages set up in large public squares, as at Frankfurt-am-Main in 1350, at Mons in 1501, and at Lucerne in 1583.

FIGURE 5.7 The stage used for the Valenciennes Passion Play, 1547. Note the Heaven mansion at the left and the Hell mansion (complete with Hell Mouth) on the right. The mansions between these two were changed each day as needed. Twenty-five days were required to perform the entire work. Courtesy Bibliothèque Nationale, Paris.

SCENERY

As in the church, the playing space was composed of two basic elements, the mansions and the *platea,* and as in liturgical drama, the locale of a scene was established by relating it to a mansion and then extending it to include as much of the adjoining stage space as was needed by the action. This convention was observed regardless of the type of stage.

Most pageant wagons carried only one mansion, although occasionally there might be as many as three. But, though the scenic investiture of individual wagons was limited, an entire cycle demanded considerable variety, for it often included more than 100 mansions.

To spectators, the fixed stages undoubtedly seemed more impressive than the movable ones, because on the former all of the scenery was visible simultaneously. This convention was somewhat modified, however, by other practices. Because of their scope, many of the plays were divided into parts (or *journées*), separated by intermissions varying in length from one to twenty-four hours. During these intervals, mansions were changed as needed; furthermore, the identity of a mansion might

be changed so that during the course of a production it represented more than one location. Consequently, it is difficult to know how many mansions were actually used to depict the places named in a script. In the play presented at Lucerne in 1583, about seventy different locales are indicated, but there seem to have been only thirty-two mansions.

The scenic complexity of a production might vary daily. For a passion play at Arras in the early fifteenth century, the number of mansions required by each of the four *journées* ranged from eight to fifteen. Other plays might require twenty or more mansions for a single *journée*. It was not taken for granted that the identity of mansions would be clearly evident. Therefore, the director usually appeared at the beginning of each *journée* and indicated (among other relevant information) what each structure represented. At times, labels were placed above mansions.

The two places most often represented on the fixed stages were Heaven and Hell. Characteristically, Heaven was placed at one end of the platform and Hell at the other. The earthly scenes were set between these poles, which symbolized man's dual nature and the

FIGURE 5.8 Hell Mouth and the interior of Hell as conceived by a medieval artist. A redrawing of a fresco in the Chapel of the Holy Cross, Stratford-on-Avon. From Sharp, *A Dissertation on the Pageants or Dramatic Mysteries . . . .* **(1825).**

and the whole was often gilded and brightly lighted with concealed torches to give the effect that golden light was emanating from it. In some instances, Heaven could open and close, and often machinery permitted angels to "fly" between Heaven and Earth, although stairs, either visible or concealed, were used in less elaborate productions. Above all, Heaven was made as inviting or awe-inspiring as possible.

Conversely, Hell was made as terrifying as possible. Just as Heaven was raised above the level of the stage, some portions of Hell were lower. At times Hell was treated as a fortified town, an especially effective device in those productions in which Christ forced open the gates of Hell to free the captive souls within. Hell was frequently divided into four parts: the Limbo of Biblical prophets and others who, according to medieval doctrine, were forced to languish there until Christ's redemptive power freed them; the Limbo of infants; Purgatory; and the pit of Hell, usually placed below stage level. The entrance to Hell was at times represented by the head of a monster (the "Hell mouth") that seemed to swallow those who entered there. Fire, smoke, noise, and the cries of the damned issued from Hell, and devils sallied forth from it to seize sinners and thrust them into eternal damnation.

The mansions representing earthly places were less elaborately depicted, although their complexity varied with dramatic need. Many were equipped with curtains that could be drawn to conceal or reveal interior scenes. The structures were of many sizes and shapes. Some were hexagonal, others were square or rectangular. Some were elevated a few steps above the stage floor. Often they were furnished with beds, tables, benches, altars, or thrones. Sometimes, as at Mons in 1501, they were lavishly outfitted with tapestries borrowed from wealthy families and churches.

A curtain representing the sky (sometimes complete with sun, moon, and stars) was often hung at the rear of the stage. Painted cloths representing clouds frequently concealed the overhead flying equipment and other devices for special effects. The stage was unframed, and one place flowed into another. Encompassing Heaven, Earth, and Hell, the medieval stage symbolized the entire universe.

Although a number of persons were required to build and paint the settings, few records pertaining to them have survived. Sometimes master artists were imported for the occasion, as at Mons in 1501. At Romans in 1509, the carpenters began work about four and one-

choices that faced him. Since these were both the most important and most permanent structures, not being replaced each day, they were also the most complex.

Of all the mansions, Heaven is the most difficult to reconstruct from the available evidence, for it seems to have impressed audiences with its splendor and magnificence, qualities not always evident in surviving illustrations. In the fifteenth and sixteenth centuries, Heaven was usually raised above the level of the other mansions. As a rule, it was supported structurally by an "earthly paradise" (the Garden of Eden), or a room beneath it at stage level. The size of Heaven was probably large, for it often accommodated many characters. At Rouen in 1474, God was accompanied by Peace, Mercy, Justice, Truth, and nine orders of angels. Sometimes Heaven included a series of intricately contrived turning spheres, half months prior to the performance. At Lucerne, the director of the play supervised the labor of city-employed workmen, who built the mansions, and of skilled artists, who painted the mansions, curtains, and effigies. Many other persons were required to operate the scenic effects during performances.

SPECIAL EFFECTS

Most of the realistic touches in medieval productions involved special effects. These grew in number and complexity during the fifteenth and sixteenth centuries as the machinists' abilities to contrive seemingly miraculous events increased.

Many special effects involved "flying." The fixed stages often were set against buildings so that pulleys and windlasses could be installed on the roofs and concealed with painted clouds or sky cloths. Additional flying machinery was concealed within the Heaven mansion. Using such devices, angels passed between Heaven and Earth; Lucifer lifted Christ to the top of the temple (a distance of up to forty feet); the souls released from Limbo floated up to Heaven; and devils and fire-spitting monsters flew about the stage. In some instances, characters rose or descended on platforms disguised as clouds.

Other effects depended upon devices operated from beneath the stage. Trap doors permitted sudden appearances, disappearances, and the skillful substitution of effigies for live actors in scenes of violence. In such episodes as the feeding of the multitudes through the miracle of the loaves and fishes, the baskets could be replenished from beneath the stage. Concealed mechanisms allowed the fig tree cursed by Christ to wither and permitted fountains to spring up at a magical touch.

Water was important in many plays. One of the most notable examples is the staging of Noah's flood. For this scene at Mons in 1501 sufficient water was stored in wine barrels on the roofs of adjoining houses to produce a continuous rain of five minutes. Other scenes included Christ walking on the sea and the apostles pulling in their nets filled with fishes.

In the frequent scenes of torture and executions, effigies were usually substituted for live actors. In a production showing Barnabas burned at the stake, an effigy was filled with bones and animal entrails to give a properly realistic smell. In another, showing the decapitation of St. Paul, the severed head bounced three times, and at each spot a well flowed; one with milk, one with blood, and the third with water.

Many animals were required. While some could be live, others had to be impersonated by actors or by effigies. Lions kneeled to St. Denis and tigers to St. Andrew. In one play, tigers sprang up out of the earth, pursued the apostles, and eventually were turned into sheep. The Serpent appeared in the Garden of Eden to tempt Eve. In other plays there were dragons, wolves, and wild or fanciful creatures.

Transformation scenes were popular. Moses' staff changed into a snake, Lot's wife into a pillar of salt, water into wine. Light also was treated as a special effect. As a nimbus or halo, it sometimes surrounded God, Christ, and saints. Normally this was achieved by reflecting the rays of concealed torches off gilded or highly polished surfaces. Sometimes a change from light to darkness was indicated by substituting a painted cloth depicting the sun for another showing the moon and stars. In a few plays, buildings were burned. For these, wicker structures covered with cloth were actually set on fire.

Many of the special effects required enormous skill and ingenuity. Thus, it is not surprising that by the sixteenth century accomplished machinists were in great demand. At Mons in 1501, two directors of "secrets" (as special effects were called) were imported from Chauny; eight master machinists were employed for a Passion Play at Vienna in the early sixteenth century. These men were aided by numerous assistants who operated the effects during the performance; at Mons, seventeen were required for the Hell scenes alone.

During the sixteenth century, the machinist was second only to the director in importance. He made detailed cue sheets and planned the operation of the effects as carefully as the director planned other parts of the production. The ultimate success of the plays depended much upon his skills.

MUSIC

Music was prominent in most medieval productions. Frequently it was played until the actors were ready to begin. During the plays, a chorus of angels (composed of choir boys and usually visible in the Heaven mansion) sang hymns. Angels played fanfares on trumpets to introduce God's proclamations, and the transitions between scenes might be bridged with instrumental or vocal music. Most plays included a number of songs ranging from popular secular tunes sung by individual actors to religious hymns sung by groups. The names and contents of songs, however, are seldom indicated in the scripts. While singing was usually done by choir boys or actors, instrumental music was played by professional musicians. At least 40 minstrels were hired at Chelmsford in 1562, and 156 musicians were employed at Lucerne in 1571. The musicians also kept the populace amused during the intermissions and in the evenings after the performances had ended.

AUDIENCES AND AUDITORIUMS

In most places, plays were not given every year. Even where the cycles were established, the interval between productions ranged from two to ten years. Some of the most elaborate performances were never repeated. In those years when plays were to be given, preparations extended over a period of months, and the days of playing were declared holidays.

Prior to performances, various devices acquainted the public with upcoming events. Invitations were usually sent to all the surrounding towns, posters were set up at the city gates, and a few days before the performance a procession, often with actors in costume, went about the town. On the days of performance, a herald rode through the city sounding a trumpet and summoning people to the play. The audiences were drawn from all classes and from both local and neighboring areas. In some places work was forbidden during the hours of performance, and special guards were set to protect homes and businesses against robbery.

The provisions made for spectators varied widely. In those parts of England where pageant wagons were used, a number of different viewing places were established. At York there were twelve to fifteen, at Beverley six. In most towns, performances lasted for several days. At Chester three days were required, and while York allotted only one, the festival there began at 4:30 A.M. It should be pointed out, however, that recently some scholars have argued that multiple viewing stations were used only for the processional portion of Corpus Christi and that the plays were all presented at a single location. If that is true, the arrangements would have been like those for fixed stages described below.

Spectators were probably admitted free to the English plays, for the only certain instance of fees being collected is found at Leicester in 1477. It has been suggested, however, that at York charges may have been made by the persons who controlled the playing places which were assigned according to bids received. It is possible, therefore, that successful bidders erected some kind of barrier and charged admissions. Distinguished citizens probably watched from the windows of surrounding houses and scaffold seating may have been erected for lesser personages, but the lower orders stood. These details are entirely conjectural, however, for there is no concrete evidence about how audiences were handled for English processional staging.

When a fixed stage was used, all spectators had to be accommodated in one place. Structures such as Roman amphitheatres or Cornish rounds provided ready-made seating; but in courtyards or city squares temporary auditoriums had to be improvised. In some instances, arrangements not unlike those that became typical in later professional theatres were used. For example, at Romans in 1509 standing room was available near the stage, and behind this there was scaffold seating which in turn was surmounted by a series of eighty-four boxes. At Vienna in 1560, private boxes could be rented for the entire performance. At Lucerne, scaffold seating surrounded three sides of the playing area, and the owners of adjacent houses probably rented space in their rooms and on the rooftops.

Entrance fees were not charged for many of the municipally sponsored productions. On the other hand, some productions were designed (in part) to make money. At Valenciennes in 1547, the members of the organization that produced the play divided the profits. Municipalities also sometimes charged fees in order to recover their outlay. Except when fees were charged, it is difficult to estimate attendance. If the available figures are typical, attendance was large. At Reims in 1490, 5,616 persons paid admissions; at Romans in 1509, 4,780 attended the first day, 4,420 the second, and 4,947 the third.

The hours of performance varied. In some cases, plays began about 7 A.M. and ran until 11; after an hour's intermission, they continued until about 6 P.M. In others, plays were presented in a series of afternoon performances; in still others, a production might proceed uninterrupted for as long as twelve hours. Often spectators began to take their places as early as 4 A.M., for usually seats were not reserved, except for officials, clergy, and important visitors. Sometimes children, elderly persons, and pregnant women were forbidden entry. A barrier of some kind (a ditch, a fence, water or guards) was used to prevent the audience from getting too near the stage. Guards were posted at night to protect the stage and its furnishings.

It is clear that by the sixteenth century the producers of plays had learned to cope with many problems. They had achieved a high level of technical excellence, as well as considerable sophistication in organizing and producing plays of great scope.

SECULAR DRAMATIC FORMS

Alongside the religious stage, a less elaborate secular theatre also existed and grew steadily. It evolved from many sources: mimes and entertainers of all sorts, stories and songs of *jongleurs,* and pagan rituals. Such antecedents seem to have existed throughout Europe, but they did not generate a secular drama until the thirteenth century, at about the time that religious plays were first being performed outdoors.

The oldest extant medieval secular drama, *The Play of the Greenwood,* was written by Adam de la Halle of Arras (France) in 1276/77. It mingles satirical scenes about the residents of Arras with such folk material as fairies and supernatural occurrences. Folk materials are even more evident in Adam's other work, *The Play of Robin and Marion* (c. 1283), a pastoral tale of the wooing of a shepherdess by a knight, the objections of her shepherd lover, and the eventual resolution of the conflict, followed by dances and games.

From the thirteenth century onward secular drama grew steadily. But, as with religious plays, the majority of the works that have survived were written after 1400. The secular entertainments of the late Middle Ages were of many types: farces, moralities, plays of the Chambers of Rhetoric, interludes, mummings and disguisings, tournaments, and royal entries.

FARCE

If the religious plays treat the triumph of virtue within an eternal order, the farces show imperfect man within the social order. Marital infidelity, quarreling, cheating, hypocrisy, and other human failings are the typical sub-

FIGURE 5.9   Pierre Pathelin and his wife. Woodcut from the edition of the play published in 1490.

jects. The clever man, even if a sinner, is usually the hero; the dupes deserve their fates because they are stupid or gullible. Sentiment is almost totally absent.

Farce began to appear during the thirteenth century. The oldest, *The Boy and the Blind Man,* written in a Flemish dialect, shows how a rogue deceives a blind man through ventriloquism, then robs and beats him. The cynical tone typical of medieval farce is already fully developed in this work.

The majority of extant farces are from France and Germany. Most of them are similar in tone and form. Typically they are short (no longer than a few hundred lines), are written in verse, and place considerable emphasis upon sex and bodily excretions. There are few characters; there is no complicated exposition, and the action develops rapidly and simply.

Most of the extant French farces are mere dramatized anecdotes, but one—*Pierre Pathelin* (c. 1470)—

FIGURE 5.10 Schembart revelers as depicted in a Schembart book of the sixteenth century. From Vogt and Koch, *Geschichte der Deutschen Literatur,* **Vol. I (1887).**

is now considered a minor masterpiece. It tells how a lawyer tricks a merchant out of a piece of cloth and is in turn cheated out of his fee by a supposedly stupid peasant, whom he has defended on a charge of stealing sheep. The play was so popular that it had gone through thirty editions by 1600.

Two variations on farce—*sotties* and *sermons joyeux*—also became popular in France. Both may have appeared because of the church's attempts to suppress the Feast of Fools, many features of which were expropriated in the fifteenth century by secular guilds or "companies of fools" called *sociétés joyeuses.* In some places the celebrations were taken over by the *basoches,* or society of lawyers, as one of their social activities. At other times, student groups staged a "festival of fools." The season for these celebrations was moved from Christmas to Mardi Gras, May Day, or the summer months. Although the activities took many forms, the most characteristic dramatic productions were the *sottie* and the *sermon joyeuse.* The latter was a burlesque sermon, while the former was a farce in which all the characters were fools. Often *sotties* were only thinly disguised political, social, or religious satires. The characters wore variations on the fool's traditional parti-colored garments, including a hood with ass's ears or a cock's comb. In Paris the *sotties* were made famous by two groups: the Basoche du Palais and les Enfants sans Souci. Pierre

Gringoire (1475–*c.* 1539) wrote the most celebrated *sotties,* among them *The Prince of Fools* (1512), a satire on the quarrel between Louis XII and Pope Julius II.

In Germany, farce seems to have grown out of folk festivals, especially the revels preceding Lent (thus early German farces are often called "Shrovetide" plays). Such plays can be found in southern Germany, Austria, Switzerland, and Holland. But most of the surviving farces are from Nuremberg. There plays came to be associated with the apprentices' revels (or *Schembartlaufen*) during the pre-Lenten carnival season. By around 1450 these revels, which centered around an elaborate and often riotous procession, had become an accepted part of Nuremberg life. As a part of the procession the apprentices performed short plays that required so little background they could be presented anywhere and repeated at various places along the way. Early writers of Shrovetide plays include Hans Rosenplüt and Hanz Folz. But by far the best known of such authors is Hans Sachs (1494–1576).

Sachs was a shoemaker but also a mastersinger, a form of artistry cultivated by the German trade guilds. As a singer, Sachs traveled widely and learned much about the poetry and drama of other areas. He was the author of 198 dramatic works, of which he classified only sixty-four as Shrovetide plays. Nevertheless, his other dramas are of slight worth and his reputation now rests almost entirely upon his farces. Of these, one of the best is *The Wandering Scholar and Exorcist,* in which a student convinces a man that he can call up the Devil, whom he forces a priest to impersonate as a price for concealing his illicit relationship with the man's wife; all bestow money on the student—the man to reward him for skill in exorcism, the priest and the wife to bribe him to remain silent about their adultery.

Sachs was also able to improve the quality of performances by removing the plays from the *Schembartlaufen.* With a company of amateur actors, he presented plays twice a week between Twelfth Night and Lent each year. His work marked the culmination of the medieval secular drama in Germany and established a foundation upon which a strong national tradition might have been built, had not political and religious wars interfered.

In England, farce first developed within the religious plays. For example, *The Second Shepherds Play* of the Wakefield cycle includes a fully developed farce within the framework of a nativity play. As an independent form, however, farce did not emerge in England until the sixteenth century with the work of John Heywood (*c.* 1497–*c.* 1580), whose most famous play, *Johan Johan* (1533), tells the story of a henpecked husband who, when ridiculed by his wife and her lover, a priest, drives them both from his house, only to worry about what they may be doing elsewhere.

In all countries, the conventions used in the staging of farces deviated in no important respect from those used for religious plays. Perhaps the most notable difference lay in the economy of means demanded by the farces, for rarely do they require more than two mansions or employ any complex special effects.

THE MORALITY PLAY

The morality play is the secular form closest in tone to the cycle plays. These didactic dramas first appeared in the fourteenth century as religious plays, but were gradually secularized and became one of the principal links between the religious and the professional stages.

The origin of the morality play can be traced to a number of influences. First, "Pater Noster" prayers, which were divided into seven petitions, each relating to the seven cardinal virtues and seven deadly sins, had established a framework of continual struggle between good and evil to possess man's soul. Second, popular outdoor preachers, in applying Biblical teachings to the problems of daily living, also adopted the concepts of the seven virtues and vices as a scheme for depicting the choices required of men. Third, literature, both religious and secular, had popularized allegory. One of the most influential of medieval works was the thirteenth century *Romance of the Rose,* a love story that included such allegorical characters as Slander, Danger, and Fair Welcome. Fourth, Christianity had become increasingly concerned with death and afterlife and was constantly admonishing men to "think upon their last ending." In the visual arts, Death's heads, skeletons, and similar devices were prominent; in drama this theme was epitomized in "The Dance of Death," in which Death summons representatives of all ranks and professions, from the pope to the lowest of peasants, in a demonstration that death is the lot of all mankind, whose only hope lies in salvation.

The immediate dramatic ancestors of the moralities are probably the Pater Noster plays performed in England at York, Lincoln, Beverley, and elsewhere, although these continued to be staged long after morality

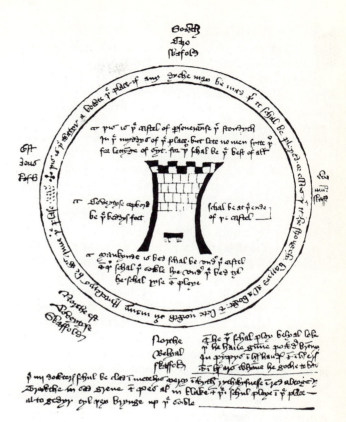

FIGURE 5.11 Plan of the mansions and playing area for *The Castle of Perseverance*. In the middle is the tower of Mankind. The legend enclosed within the circles reads: "This is the water about the place, if any ditch be made where it shall be played, or else let it be strongly barred all about." The location of five mansions is indicated outside the circles.

plays were well developed. Many of the Pater Noster plays were presented by municipalities and trade guilds under the same general arrangements as those used for the religious cycles. At Beverley in 1469 there were eight pageant wagons, seven of which transported plays about the seven deadly sins. Unfortunately, no Pater Noster plays have survived and consequently their precise relationship to the moralities cannot be determined.

As a distinct form, the morality play flourished between about 1400 and 1550. Although some examples have been found elsewhere the morality was for the most part an English and French phenomenon. The oldest extant morality is a fragment of *The Pride of Life (c.*

1400), in which the King of Life displays an overweening pride, from which he cannot be dissuaded. No doubt the lost portions showed his humiliation and repentance.

In terms of staging, one of the most interesting moralities is *The Castle of Perseverance* (c. 1425), which depicts Mankind's progress from birth to death and shows the final judgment on his soul. The play is long (more than 3,600 lines) and includes thirty-six characters. The manuscript provides some information about its performance. In a prologue, two heralds outline the action and declare that the play will be presented "on the green" beginning at 9 A.M. one week following the announcement. A diagram of the suggested playing arrangement is also included. It shows a circular area around the perimeter of which are placed five mansions; Mankind's castle is set in the center of the circle. Concerning the circle, a note declares: "This is the water about the place, if any ditch be made where it shall be played, or else let it be strongly barred about." It has usually been assumed that the water or fence referred to here was meant to enclose all of the mansions and audience areas and was intended to control paying spectators at a performance given by professional actors. Recently, however, it has been argued that the water or fence is meant only to enclose Mankind's castle and that it is a scenic element rather than a device for controlling crowds. This conclusion seems to be borne out both by the diagram and by the dramatic action of the play.

Originally, *Mankind* (c. 1470), of which only part survives, may have been a completely serious work, but if so it was later altered to include comic interludes and a number of songs and dances. In its final form, the play's action is interrupted to permit the actors to collect money from the audience. There are only seven roles and no scenery or complex properties. Thus *Mankind* demonstrates how the morality play was adapted to the needs of professional players and how the original didactic intention was altered out of a desire to attract a paying audience.

In France, on the other hand, moralities seem to have remained closer to the vernacular religious cycles both in terms of length and in approach to production. For example, *Well-Advised, Ill-Advised,* presented at Rennes in 1439, is some 8,000 lines long (about three times as long as Shakespeare's plays) with sixty characters and elaborate spectacle. As its title suggests, it contrasts the behavior of the well-advised and the ill-advised man. In its spectacular ending, Well-Advised is

FIGURE 5.12 *Everyman.* **Frontispiece to the edition published by John Sklot, c. 1530.**

carried off to Heaven by Angels, while Ill-Advised is consigned to Hell.

A similar contrast becomes the basis for *The Just Man and the Worldly Man,* written by Simon Bougoin (a member of Louis XII's household) and staged at Tarascon in 1476. It uses an extremely large number of episodes and myriad allegorical figures to demonstrate how the Just Man resists and the Worldly Man gives in to all manner of temptations. The play was so long that its performance extended over several days.

Unlike most French moralities, *Man the Sinner,* a play performed at Tours in 1494, develops the story of a single central figure in a relatively simple plot. It demonstrates the temptations that lie in wait for man and his inclination to submit to them. Nevertheless, the sinner eventually learns that true happiness lies in obedience to God, and his soul ascends to Heaven, leaving his body to decay on earth.

Perhaps the best known of all moralities is *Everyman* (*c.* 1500), an English play which is more restricted in its subject than most dramatic allegories of the time. In the play Everyman receives Death's summons, struggles to escape, and finally resigns himself to necessity. Seeking companions to accompany him on his journey, Everyman is quickly deserted by such former associates as Kindred, Goods, and Fellowship. Eventually only Good Deeds goes with him into the grave.

In the sixteenth century the morality underwent still other changes. In some instances, it was used to treat almost wholly secular subjects, as in John Skelton's *Magnificence* (*c.* 1516), which describes the lifestyle appropriate to a ruler, or in Nicolas de la Chesnaye's *Condemnation of the Banquet* (1507), which treats both mental and physical health and warns especially against the dangers of overeating. In other instances, the morality was adapted as a weapon in the religious controversies that swept Europe during the sixteenth century. Perhaps the best of these plays is John Bale's (1495–1563) *King John* (1538), in which the English ruler holds out against the evil forces of the pope. Here historical personages and events are integrated with the allegorical figures and struggles typical of the original moralities. Bale's drama is often said to mark a major step toward a serious secular drama and toward the English chronicle play.

As religious controversy grew, doctrinal plays also began to be written in northern Europe. The first great stimulus to this movement came in 1501 with the publication of the previously unknown plays of Hrosvitha, the tenth-century nun who had sought to write dramas in the manner of Terence but told stories about the "chastity of Christian virgins." Her works exerted considerable influence throughout the sixteenth century on a movement best summed up in the collective title used for Cornelius Schonaeus' plays, *Christian Terence, or Sacred Comedies* (1592).

During the sixteenth century these north European dramatists came to be divided between those who supported Protestantism and those committed to Catholicism. Among the Protestant dramatists, perhaps the most influential was Gnapheus, whose play on the prodigal son, *Acolastus* (1528), stimulated many other works on the same theme: the reclamation of those who have strayed from the paths of virtue. Many of the Protestant plays denounced Catholicism. Perhaps the most forceful of these was Thomas Naogeorgus' *Pammachius* (1538), which treats the struggle against Antichrist over a period of almost 1,000 years, ending with the glorification of Luther as a major target of Antichristian forces, epitomized in Bishop Pammachius.

Other changes in the morality play can be attributed to the introduction of classical subjects as interest in Greece and Rome and in learning for its own sake revived. This resulted in plays that were primarily philosophical, informative, and educational, best exemplified in Henry Medwall's *Nature* (*c.* 1500) and John Rastell's *The Four Elements* (*c.* 1518).

By the early sixteenth century, then, the morality play had become extremely diversified, and all of the various strains were to be found throughout the remainder of the century. The earliest type is still seen in such late works as George Wapull's *Tide Tarrieth for No Man* (1576) and T. Lupton's *All for Money* (1578), long after newer variations had become common. Elements of the morality play persisted into Shakespeare's time. But as the morality was increasingly secularized during the sixteenth century, the distinctions vanished between it and the type of play commonly labeled "interlude."

At first, morality plays were probably performed by amateurs, but gradually they were taken over by professionals, especially in England. The basic conventions of the religious drama were followed in staging, although as professionalism increased the number of actors and scenic elements declined. The emphasis on allegory was reflected in the costuming of such characters as Mercy, Kindred, and Good Deeds, abstractions that had seldom been seen in the cycle plays. The dress of allegorical figures was often very imaginative. The costume for Fame had eyes, ears, and tongues painted on it, while that for Vanity was covered with feathers of many hues, and that for Wealth was decorated with gold and silver coins. In the plays of religious controversy, each side drew on the allegorical tradition and dressed its adherents as the Virtues and its opponents as the Deadly Sins; such figures as Flattery and Ignorance were often costumed as priests of the opposing sect.

As dramas, the moralities mark the gradual evolution away from Biblical characters and events to ordinary men in their everyday surroundings. Consequently, they

FIGURE 5.13 Rhetoric stage at Antwerp, 1561. This stage is often considered to be one possible influence on the Elizabethan public theatre. From Wilhelm Creizenach, *The English Drama in the Age of Shakespeare* **(1916).**

1493 to 1570. Typically a question was posed, to which the various Chambers composed an answer in the form of an allegorical drama. These plays constituted the major dramatic expression of the Low Countries, since religious drama did not flourish there.

Although some of the plays were produced indoors, they were usually given outdoors on a stage which anticipated many features of the Elizabethan public theatre. At the back of a large platform, a fixed facade was erected. At the stage level there were normally three openings which could be closed with curtains or opened to reveal interior scenes. A second level included similar openings, while on the third level there was a throne for the figure (such as Wisdom, Lady Rhetoric, or the Virgin) in whose honor the festival was held. At the end of the contest, this figure was often flown to stage level to distribute the prizes.

The productions became increasingly lavish. The peak was probably reached in 1561 at a contest in Antwerp which lasted for one month. The nine competing societies made elaborate processional entries into the city using a total of 23 triumphal chariots and 197 pageant wagons. Plays were given over a period of fifteen days. To finance this festival, the city spent the enormous sum of 100,000 guilders, in addition to the funds provided by the competing societies.

Until the sixteenth century, the Chambers plays often sought to convey theological messages. But in 1516 Spain gained control of the Low Countries just as the Protestant movement was gaining force there. In an attempt to control the content of the plays presented by the Chambers of Rhetoric, an edict was issued in 1539 requiring all plays to be approved by Catholic church officials. As a result, dramatists turned increasingly to secular subjects. After 1625 the Chambers declined rapidly, as the professional theatre gained in popularity.

paved the way for the great secular plays of the succeeding period.

CHAMBERS OF RHETORIC

Closely related to the moralities are the plays performed by the Chambers of Rhetoric in the Low Countries. Orginating in the fourteenth century, these societies were concerned with poetry, music, and drama. By the sixteenth century practically every town in the Netherlands had at least one Chamber; Ghent had five.

Competitions among societies were being held by 1413 and were especially popular in the period from

INTERLUDES

Interlude is an imprecise term, since it was at various times applied to almost every type of play presented in the Middle Ages. Today it is normally used to designate the plays first presented indoors as a part of the entertainments of rulers, nobles, or rich merchants. The name probably derives from the practice of presenting plays between the parts of some other event, such as the courses of a banquet. The interlude might be of any type: religious, moral, farcical, historical. Often there was singing and dancing as well. Since it was often given in crowded banquet halls, the interlude used little scenery and few characters.

Like the morality play, the interlude was associated with the rise of the professional actor. From the eleventh century onward, most professional entertainers were grouped under the general heading of "minstrels," and various accounts speak of their popularity among the nobility and clergy throughout Europe. During the fourteenth century, as wealthy merchants began to emulate the nobility, demand for their services increased and minstrels took up permanent residence in larger towns. By 1350 many nobles were retaining their own companies of performers. As early as the thirteenth century, there had been attempts to classify minstrels according to their specialties, but not till the end of the fifteenth century did acting begin to be recognized as a distinct activity separate from minstrelsy, which thereafter came to be associated almost entirely with musical performances.

Since actors were more assured of a livelihood if they were attached to a noble household, many troupes became servants to kings or great lords. In England Richard III (reigned 1483–1485) and Henry VII (reigned 1485–1509) each maintained a company. There were probably many similar troupes by 1500. Most were permitted to tour under the names of their patrons when their services were not required at home. When they toured, the troupes presented their credentials to the mayor of a town, gave a performance before him and the aldermen, and, if approved, then gave other performances for a paying public in the town hall, an inn, or "on the green." In spite of their rising importance, however, professional players remained secondary to amateur performers until religious drama declined during the last half of the sixteenth century.

That professional actors were only beginning to appear in the late fifteenth century may explain why there are so few interludes prior to 1500. The oldest extant English play of this type, *Fulgens and Lucrece* by Henry Medwall, dates from 1497. Examples from the sixteenth century, however, are numerous.

The typical place for performing interludes was the "great hall" of a noble residence. These large rooms were constructed after a standard pattern: at one end was a raised platform for the table at which sat the nobleman, his family, and favored friends; at the opposite end was the "screen," a wall that separated the banqueting hall from the kitchen; this screen usually had two or three doors in it and above it a gallery for musicians; down the two sides of the room, and sometimes in the middle, were tables for less favored retainers and guests. Such an arrangement would have been typical when performances were given at banquets. On other occasions, the tables might be replaced by scaffold seating for spectators.

The basic scenic background was the screen, for each of its doors could represent a separate mansion or serve as an entrance. If there was a musicians' gallery, it might also be incorporated into the action. Elaborate mansions were often built at the king's court, but in other households the screen seems to have sufficed. There is little evidence of a raised stage until after 1550; instead, the actors performed on the floor of the hall. The acting space was often small and, as the lines of some plays attest, the audience frequently encroached upon it.

Most interludes were written for small troupes. In England, the title page of Phillip's *Patient Grissell* states that it may be played by eight persons. The printed versions of Lewis Wager's *Mary Magdalene* and *Wealth and Health* are said to be suitable for a company of four, and the title page of Preston's *Cambises* shows how the thirty-eight roles may be distributed among eight actors.

TOURNAMENTS, MUMMINGS, AND DISGUISINGS

Alongside the interludes, other courtly entertainments grew up around tournaments, mummings, and disguisings. Tournaments began in the tenth century as a means of training knights in warfare. Because a number of contestants had been killed, reforms in the conduct of tournaments were introduced during the thirteenth century, and by 1300 dramatic elements had begun to creep in. Soon, instead of merely seeking to unseat each other, knights were fighting to capture mansions representing such allegorical conceits as the Castle of Love inhabited by suitably costumed ladies and attendants.

At tournaments, spectators were carefully segregated according to sex and rank in galleries that surrounded the field of combat. At various points around this field were placed the elaborate mansions which established the allegorical context of the tournament. Among the favorite emblematic devices were mountains, castles, woods, fountains, ships, and chapels. For the most part, tournaments used the same visual symbolism found in the religious plays but often added a secular turn.

FIGURES 5.14 and 5.15 Two scenes from a tournament. Miniatures from a wedding chest, probably painted by Domenico Morone (fifteenth century). Courtesy National Gallery, London.

Tournaments were essentially noble or royal entertainments. Some were international events for which heralds were sent to foreign courts to issue challenges. In addition to the combats, there were elaborate processions, and in the evenings various forms of entertainment, including interludes. Many of these indoor celebrations were closely related to mumming and disguising.

Although by 1500 mummings and disguisings were principally court entertainments, they had their origins in such pagan ceremonies as sword and Morris dances. The sword dance may have been military in origin, but by the fourteenth century minstrels were performing it at weddings and other festivities. Sometimes it was called "the dance of the buffoons" for it usually included one or more comic dancers. In the similar Morris dance, the participants wore bells, and some blackened their faces (Morris may be a corruption of Moorish). A Morris troupe often included a clown, a fool, a hobby horse, and a man dressed as Maid Marion. At times a dragon appeared, and St. George was eventually introduced as the slayer of the dragon.

Out of these beginnings came the *mummers' play,* a term derived from a French word meaning to play in dumb show, mask, or disguise. In these plays, given at the Christmas season with Father Christmas as master of ceremonies or "presenter," at least one character is always killed in combat, after which a doctor arrives and brings the dead back to life through some grotesque device. Dances and songs were included in most performances. The actors often went from one house to another presenting their short pieces.

In addition to sword and Morris dances and mummers' plays, there were many other types of disguisings. Throughout the Christmas and carnival season preceding Lent, costumed and masked revellers of various sorts took to the streets. Some went from house to house presenting plays and pantomimes. Most took up collections, but some, wishing to show gratitude or respect to the king or other official, used this opportunity to offer gifts. Because such disguisings came to be used as a cover for criminal behavior, they were suppressed in England (except at court) in the fourteenth and fifteenth centuries. Elsewhere disguisings of various sorts continued among the common people; in many places they have persisted to the present day, especially in pre-Lenten carnival celebrations. In theatre, however, the most important offshoots of mummings and disguisings were to be such courtly entertainments as English masques, Italian *intermezzi,* and French *ballets de cour.*

FIGURE 5.16 Mummers play in the banqueting hall of Haddon Hall, Derbyshire, England. A nineteenth-century reconstruction. Note the hall screen in the background with the balcony above. This type of hall screen is often considered a major influence on the Elizabethan public theatre. From Joseph Nash, *The Mansions of England in Olden Times,* Vol. I (1869).

The disguisings given at court might be arranged for any special occasion. They were performed at banquets following tournaments, for visits of royalty, weddings, and on a variety of other occasions. Eventually they developed into complex spectacles. The first record of a courtly entertainment with elaborate scenic structures dates from 1377, when Charles V of France entertained the Emperor Charles IV. In England, disguisings were very popular under Henry VII (reigned 1485–1509) and Henry VIII (reigned 1509–1547). The scenic units were usually mounted on wheels so they could be brought into a hall between the courses of a banquet and removed for the dancing that followed. Thus, they were somewhat similar to the pageant wagons of religious cycles. The playlets were largely pantomimic, and were intended above all as ingenious allegorical compliments to the persons being honored.

Characteristically, the entertainment concluded in a dance. In England, performers did not at first mingle with the audience, but beginning in 1513 the dancers chose partners from among the spectators. Since this

FIGURE 5.17 Festival at Binche (Belgium) in 1549, given by the Queen Dowager Mary of Hungary for Prince Philip of Spain. Seen here are wild men interrupting a ball to take away ladies of the court to a nearby fortress which was stormed during the next day's festivities. Courtesy Bibliothèque Royale Albert Ier, Brussels.

practice was borrowed from the Italian courts, productions after this time were called "masques after the manner of Italy." In the English masques, courtiers served as actors and dancers, and professional musicians provided music and song. Since they required elaborate scenery and costumes, masques were far more costly to produce than were interludes, and the outlay increased steadily as time passed. In 1495, Henry VII spent only 13 pounds for a disguising, but by the time of Elizabeth I (reigned 1558–1603), the cost often mounted to 400 pounds. Henry VIII was especially fond of court entertainments and in 1527 had a House of Revels built in which to stage them. In 1545, in order to centralize control over court entertainments, he also created an Office of Revels. Under Elizabeth, the authority of this office was to be extended to cover all professional acting troupes in England.

Such court entertainments reached their peak in Italy during the sixteenth and seventeenth centuries and in England between 1603 and 1640. As integral parts of the Renaissance theatre, these descendants of medieval forms are treated at greater length in subsequent chapters.

ROYAL ENTRIES AND STREET PAGEANTS

Theatrical productions also came to be incorporated into the street pageants given by municipalities in honor of coronations, royal weddings, military victories, or visiting rulers. These celebrations followed a basic pattern: civic officials and representatives of the clergy and trade guilds met the person to be honored at a prearranged place outside the city; then they escorted the visitor along a carefully planned route through the town to the cathedral for a religious service, after which he was taken to his place of residence. It was an occasion upon which the city could demonstrate its loyalty, respect, or gratitude.

At first there was merely a procession, but gradually plays were added. These may have appeared as early as 1236, but were definitely being used by 1298, when the city of London honored Edward I's victory over the Scots. In Paris the first clear record of plays is found in 1313, when Edward II visited France. Gradually such celebrations spread throughout Europe. Although they still persist in a modified form, they ceased to be occasions for dramatic performances after the seventeenth century.

Plays were added to the entries at about the same time that religious dramas were first performed outdoors, and in the early years the subjects were almost identical with those at religious festivals. Beginning in the fifteenth century, the plays became increasingly allegorical or historical. These later works might take the form of elaborate compliments to the visitor, but they were often veiled lectures to a ruler on his duty to his subjects. Since they exploited the Bible, history, mythology, and allegory, the plays might resemble any of the major types of medieval drama: religious plays, morality plays, tournament plays, disguisings, or serious interludes. Despite these similarities, there was one major difference: most of these plays were pantomimic. Consequently, they are often called *tableaux vivants* (or living pictures).

In the beginning only a single tableau was mounted for an entry, but by the mid-fifteenth century there were often as many as six or more and there might be some dialogue or narration. Each play was complete in itself but all were connected by a common theme. In England during the sixteenth and seventeenth centuries, major dramatists (among then Nicholas Udall, John Lyly, Ben Jonson, Thomas Dekker, and John Webster) were commissioned to write them.

Each part was mounted on its own separate stage;

the procession halted at each stage to view the performance and then moved on to the next. The primary audience for the plays was the visitor and his party. On the other hand, for the city's populace, who lined the route, stood on housetops, or watched from windows, the attraction was the procession and the visitor. The stages erected for the tableaux varied in size and complexity; many were multi-storied. In equipment and conventions, they were similar in all important respects to those used for other dramatic types of the period.

Throughout Europe the planning and financing of these pageants were undertaken jointly by the city council and trade guilds. For example, at the entry of Katherine of Aragon into London in 1501, each tableau

FIGURE 5.18 Arch erected in Gracechurch Street for the entry of James I into London in 1604. Frontispiece to Vol. I of John Nichols, *The Progresses, Processions and Magnificent Festivities of James the First . . . .* (1828).

was assigned to a city alderman. He engaged workmen, obtained actors, and supervised all arrangements. The money was raised through taxes levied on the citizens. This method, or some variation on it, seems to have been typical.

THE DECLINE AND TRANSFORMATION OF MEDIEVAL DRAMA

In the 600 years during which it existed, the medieval drama became increasingly complex and diverse. From the simple liturgical plays and popular entertainments of the tenth century, it flowered into the great cycles, civic and court pageants, and secular plays of the sixteenth century. Yet during the sixteenth century the types of theatre that had been typical of the Middle Ages almost completely disappeared despite their obvious popularity and broad-based support. The reasons for this change were numerous, but a few were of special importance.

Perhaps most significantly, the church had been weakened by internal conflicts. It had reached the peak of its power around 1200, when the pope's supremacy in both religious and secular matters was almost universally accepted. But as nations began to take shape, princes sought ways of gaining control over religious affairs within their own territories. It soon became evident that the most effective means of control lay in the election of the pope, and rulers began intriguing to influence the choice, just as those elected often proved not to be immune from corruption. Between 1305 and 1377 the seat of the church was moved from Rome to Avignon, and the pope became a virtual captive of the French. Between 1378 and 1417 there were rival popes: at one time three competed for the papacy. By the fifteenth century, therefore, the church had been greatly weakened and many of its practices, perhaps most notoriously the selling of indulgences (or spiritual pardons) had led to demands for reform. Furthermore, as learning had revived with the rise of universities, a spirit of doubt and questioning had been fostered throughout Europe.

The elements in this ferment eventually came together in the sixteenth century in the Reformation, as dissident groups challenged the church's authority and set out to reform religious practice. Princes were drawn into the conflict, since they were called on by the church to enforce its decrees. Some did so, but others refused or were in the vanguard of dissidence. The civil wars and the

FIGURE 5.19 Scene staged for the royal entry of Charles V into Bruges, 1514. King Solomon's court is shown. From Bapst, *Essai sur l'Histoire du Théâtre* (1893).

political and religious realignments that resulted did much to shape modern Europe.

Obviously the theatre could not remain aloof from these events. In England, Henry VIII's break with the church of Rome in 1534 led to bitter controversies in which drama was used as a weapon to attack or defend particular dogmas. In an attempt to still the conflict, Elizabeth I, upon coming to the throne in 1558, forbade all religious plays. Although not immediately successful, Elizabeth's edict, except in rare instances, silenced the cycles after the 1570s.

Parallel events were underway in other counties. In the Netherlands the production of religious plays without prior sanction of church officials was forbidden in 1539, with the result that religious subject matter was generally abandoned. More important, the many Protestant secessions led the Catholic church to convene the Council of Trent (1545–1563) to cope with the issues. One of the results was the almost universal withdrawal of church sanction from religious plays. Production of the plays had virtually ceased in Italy by 1547, and in 1548 they were forbidden in Paris. In some Germanic areas they continued into the seventeenth century, but in most of Europe the religious drama had been abandoned by 1600. Only in Spain, where the Inquisition had established its unquestioned control over theology, did they continue.

The prohibition of religious subject matter led to other changes. First, dramatists had to turn to secular subjects. In doing so, they took advantage of the revived interest in Greek and Roman works, and in the process gained a new appreciation of dramatic form. The resulting blend of classical and medieval heritages did much to create the great secular drama of the Renaissance. Second, the abandonment of religious subject matter destroyed the last remaining basis for an international drama. Henceforth, each country developed its own national interests and characteristic style. Third, when the religious cycles were forbidden, the active support of the clergy, town councils, and merchant class, who had previously sanctioned and financed the most elaborate theatrical performances, was withdrawn. These groups made a clear distinction between productions motivated by religious and civic pride and the work of professional actors seeking to entertain for pay. The church had never rescinded the condemnation of professional actors pronounced in Roman times, and the censure was now reiterated.

Perhaps most important of all, the relationship of theatre to society underwent a drastic change at this time. In Greece, Rome, and medieval Europe, the theatre, in its most characteristic form, had enjoyed the active support of governmental and religious bodies. Theatre had been ceremonial and occasional, for it was essentially a community offering used to celebrate special events considered significant to all. Beginning in the sixteenth century, however, it was deprived of its religious and civic functions and henceforth it had to wage a fight for recognition on purely commercial and artistic grounds. In the beginning, it was sustained by noblemen and rulers, who continued the system of private patronage that had grown up in medieval times. With this help, the professional theatre gradually established itself throughout Europe, although in some countries the process was not to be completed for some 200 years.

LOOKING AT THEATRE HISTORY

Stage directions are often one of the historian's most useful sources. For example, the stage directions in *The Mystery of Adam* (c. 1150) provide the basis for arguments that plays were by that time being staged out of doors. Here is one of the crucial passages:

Then let God go to the church, and let Adam and Eve walk about, innocently delighting in the Garden of Eden. Meanwhile, let demons run back and forth through the square, making suitable gestures. . . .

Other major sources for the historian of medieval theatre are the municipal records kept by towns that were directly involved in the production of plays. One of the most complete accounts can be deduced from the records of the city of Mons (Belgium), which sponsored a passion play in 1501. Here are a few excerpts from those records. From the first we learn how many rehearsals were held, where they were held, and how the actors were notified:

To Jehan Billet, for the 48 days of summoning he has carried out in having assembled the players at all the rehearsals held since the beginning of the said play at the City Hall, as agreed upon, 6 1.

A second entry seems to refer to the four actor-directors who both performed and assisted in staging the play:

To Gille de Bievenne, Jaquemin Bozet, Jehan de Rocquegnies and Godeffroy de Bertaymont, in recompense for their work in the said Passion Play, has been paid out, on the order of the city magistrates, 12 February 1501, to the aforesaid de Bievenne, 9 1., to the aforesaid Bozet, 9 1., to the aforesaid Rocquegnies, 10 1., and to the aforesaid Godeffroy de Bertaymont, 40 s. Total, 30 1.

Another entry seems to suggest that the role of God was so demanding that the priest cast in it neglected his duties so fully that his payment went to the monastery:

To Master Jehan de Neele, bachelor of theology and priest in the Convent of St. Francis in this city of Mons, the 22nd of the said month of April, in recompense for what he has been required to do and what was undertaken by him, the role of the character of God in the said Mystery Play, in doing which he had devoted his time to learning the aforesaid role and neglected his position as preacher and other duties in carrying out the aforesaid role in consequence of which he has been dispossessed and therefore payment is put in the hands of Jehan de Francque [another priest at the Convent], to whom has been paid the agreed-upon amount of 12 1.

Translations by Lenyth Brockett. All of the accounts of this production can be found (in French) in Gustave Cohen, *Le Livre de Conduite du Regisseur . . . pour le Mystère . . . à Mons en 1501* (Paris, 1925).

There appear to have been a variety of professional entertainers during the Middle Ages and an equally varied moral response to them. Here is one account written by the Bishop of Salisbury (England) in the first half of the fourteenth century:

There are three kinds of histriones. Some metamorphose and transform their bodies through unseemly leaps and foul gestures, either exposing themselves shamefully or donning fearful masks, but surely all are damned unless they abandon their employment. Likewise there are others who work at nothing, . . . but follow after assemblies of great men and tell of disgraces and scandals so as to please others. They are also surely damned, for the Apostle forbids us to take food with such men. There is also a third kind of histriones who have musical instruments for delighting men, and of these there are two kinds. Some frequent public drinking bouts and licentious societies, and there they sing various songs so that men are moved to wantonness; these are to be damned as are the others. But there are also others, who are called jesters, who sing the deeds of rulers and the lives of the saints, and provide solace for men whether in their sicknesses or in low spirits, and they do not invent countless infamies as do the dancers and dancing girls and the others who play in shameful representations and cause apparitions to be seen through enchantments or by another method. But these . . . bring comfort to men. . . .

Thomas de Cabham, *Penetential*, trans. Barbara Spear.

One of the ever-present dangers in historical writing is that a single instance will lead one to generalize from it without due care for other evidence. This danger is well illustrated in the use to which the following passage has been put by some historians. On the basis of this statement and a painting of the Martyrdom of St. Apollonia (see page 105) some historians have concluded that the director was always onstage following the actors about and whispering each line to them. (For a discussion of this point, see pages 105–106.)

[For a miracle play in Cornwall] the players conne not their parts without booke, but are prompted by one called the Ordinary, who followeth at their back with the book in his hand, and telleth them softly what they must pronounce aloud. Which maner once gave occasion to a pleasant conceyted gentleman of practising a mery pranke. . . .

His turn came. Quoth the Ordinary, "Goe forth, man, and show thyself." The Gentleman steps out upon the stage, . . . cleaving more to the letter than the sense, pronounced these words aloud. "Oh" (sayes the fellowe softly in his eare), "you marre the play." And with this his passion, the Actor makes the Audience in like sort acquainted. Herein the prompter falles to flat rayling and cursing in the bitterest terms he could devise; which the Gentleman with a set gesture and countenance still soberly related, untill the Ordinary, driven at last into a madde rage, was faine to give over all. . . .

RICHARD CAREW, *Survey of Cornwall* (1811), p. 192.

6

The Italian Renaissance

Long before the medieval theatre came to an end in the late sixteenth century, the ideas and practices that came to be labeled the Renaissance had already emerged. In fact, the late Middle Ages and the early Renaissance co-existed, for historians usually date both from about 1300, although they recognize that medieval elements remained dominant until around 1500. In addition, the same forces that helped to destroy medieval culture were crucial in creating the Renaissance, for both the waning of the Middle Ages and the emergence of the Renaissance can be attributed to the decline of feudalism, the growth of cities, the increased power of princes, and challenges to church dominance over learning and life.

Perhaps most of all the Renaissance is associated with Humanism and the revival of interest in the classical world. Humanism, as the name implies, marked a return to concern for the worth of people and their earthly lives, not merely as preparation for eternity but as valuable in itself. The humanists were not irreligious, but they were not ascetics. They accepted the robust aspects of human nature and explored them sympathetically. They tended to view life both ideally and realistically and saw people both as deserving admiration and as prone to error. The Renaissance drew inspiration from the classical world, where humanism had first flourished, and it stimulated interest throughout Europe in Greece and Rome.

As these humanistic concerns grew, so did curiosity and the spirit of adventure. The Renaissance was an era of expansion, through geographical exploration, scientific experimentation, philosophical inquiry, and artistic creativity. In education the goal became the development of the universal man skilled in many fields: science, politics, sports, and art.

There are many reasons why the Renaissance first emerged in Italy. As the major terminus of trade routes to Asia and Africa, Italy was more strategically placed than the rest of Europe to absorb ideas from Byzantium, Islam, and other cultures. Trade also produced the wealth needed to support the arts and learning. As the seat of the Roman Catholic Church, Italy was strongly affected by the controversies that afflicted the papacy beginning in the late thirteenth century. The removal of the papal seat to Avignon in 1305 and the intrigues among rival popes from 1378 to 1417 raised skepticism about the church as a guide in daily life. The corruption of the papacy also subjected the church itself to numerous secular influences. In addition, since the fourth century the church had argued that the pope was the legitimate successor to the Roman emperors, and consequently it was not difficult in the early Renaissance to revive interest in the Roman Empire and its secular accomplishments. During the years of papal exile, many rulers of small Italian states sought to fill the gap created by the pope's absence, and they vied with each other for power and prestige. It soon became the mark of a ruler's enlightenment to support scholars, writers, and artists, and as patronage increased, the Renaissance flourished.

As appreciation for the individual and his potential

grew, the anonymous craftsmen and writers of the Middle Ages gave way to artists whose personal accomplishments were honored. Biblical and theological subjects were replaced by classical myths, history, and invented stories. In the arts the Renaissance may be said to have begun in Italy around 1300 with Dante (1265–1321) who—though he treated a theological subject—took Virgil for his guide in his *The Divine Comedy,* and with Giotto (1266–1337), who in painting broke with the stiff decorative style of medieval art. The Renaissance spirit was still more evident in the writings of Petrarch (1304–1374), who collected ancient manuscripts, urged scholars to study Greece, modeled his style after Cicero and Seneca, and championed human over theological subjects; and in the work of Boccaccio (1313–1375), who urged the study of the classics and celebrated man's lust for life in his collection of irreligious, bawdy tales, *The Decameron.*

In drama, the first sign of change was a new awareness of dramatic form that came from the study of Roman plays. Although the study of Latin plays had never been completely out of favor, Seneca's tragedies had been read principally as illustrations of moral lessons or rhetorical display and the comedies of Terence and Plautus as models of oral style. During the fourteenth century, however, a few men began to appreciate the plays for their dramatic values and to compose imitations of them. The earliest tragedy, Albertino Mussato's *Eccerinus* (*c.* 1315), used a modified Senecan form but drew its subject matter from Christian doctrine. But, beginning with *Achilles* (*c.* 1390) by Antonio Laschi, classical form and subject were united. Therefore, *Achilles* is frequently called the first true Renaissance tragedy. Comedy also began to appear during the fourteenth century. The oldest known example is Pier Paolo Vergerio's *Paulus* (1390), a satire on contemporary student life. A number of leading Humanists wrote comedies during the fifteenth century, although none produced plays of lasting interest.

All of the early comedies and tragedies were written in Latin and virtually none were performed. A vernacular drama did not appear until the early sixteenth century. By that time, other events had accelerated classical influence: in 1429, twelve of Plautus' lost plays were rediscovered; in 1453, the fall of Constantinople brought many scholars and many manuscripts of Greek plays to Italy; in 1465, the introduction of the printing press into Italy made the wide dissemination of classical texts possible, and between 1472 and 1518 all of the then-known Greek and Roman plays were published. During

this period, interest in classical drama, which until the late fifteenth century had been confined principally to scholars, spread to the courts of the many small states into which Italy was then divided. Around 1485, Italian rulers began to patronize dramatists and to finance productions of Roman plays or imitations of them. The desire to make the plays more accessible to courtly readers and spectators was probably the major motivation for translating the Roman plays into Italian and for writing new plays in the vernacular.

The vernacular drama was launched in 1508 with a production at the court of Ferrara of *La Cassaria (The Casket)* by Lodovico Ariosto (1474–1533). In this comedy, a favorite Roman plot (in which lovers are united following the discovery that the girl is the long-lost child of a rich father) is given a contemporary Italian setting. Ariosto went on to write other plays, including *The Counterfeits, The Charlatan, The Students,* and *The Bawd.* The development of vernacular comedy was also influenced by Bernardo Dovizi da Bibbiena's *La Calandria* (1513), a successful blending of Roman and con-

FIGURE 6.1 Map of Italy around 1500. Courtesy *World Book Encyclopedia.*

temporary elements. Based in part upon Plautus' *Menaechmi*, Bibbiena's play uses twins of different sexes and reunites them only after subjecting them to a complicated intrigue based on disguises and illicit love affairs. This combination of traditional and contemporary materials served as a model for those who came after. Another significant strain of comedy is exemplified by Niccolo Machiavelli's (1469–1527) *The Mandrake* (c. 1513–1520), in which the subject matter is original but the form borrowed from Roman comedy. Showing how a young wife and her lover cuckold the overcredulous husband, the play is similar in tone to medieval farce. By 1540 a native comedy was well established in Italy. Although few are now remembered, these dramatists were the first in Renaissance Europe to master the techniques of Latin comedy and to adapt them to contemporary taste. After 1575 their plays were read with increasing frequency in France and England and consequently they exerted considerable influence on the emerging drama of those countries.

The first important vernacular tragedy was *Sofonisba* (1515) by Giangiorgio Trissino (1478–1550). Following the example of the Greek tragedians, Trissino used a chorus of fifteen and avoided the division into acts. Trissino, with his deliberate attempt to counteract the all-pervasive influence of Seneca, launched a controversy that was to last for many years over the relative merits of Greek and Roman drama as suitable models for Italian authors. That this struggle was eventually won by the partisans of Rome was due in large part to the popularity of one author—Giambattista Giraldi Cinthio (1504–1573), whose *Orbecche* (1541), a tale of revenge in the Senecan manner, was the first tragedy written in Italian to be produced. After writing two other tragedies, *Dido* and *Cleopatra*, Cinthio turned to serious plays with happy endings because he found that audiences preferred this kind of plot. As a result, his late plays are essentially melodramas. Nevertheless, Cinthio influenced almost all of his successors, even those who avoided happy resolutions. No other serious dramatist rivalled Cinthio in popularity but several were admired both at home and abroad and did much to reestablish the tragic mode which had languished since Roman times.

In addition to comedy and tragedy, pastoral drama also thrived in Renaissance Italy. This form perhaps developed out of the interest in the satyr plays of antiquity, although in the Renaissance the boisterous and licentious world of Greek satyrs gave way to an idyllic society of shepherds, nymphs, and refined satyrs. The

FIGURE 6.2 Frontispiece to an edition of Ariosto's plays published in Rome in 1535.

principal subject was love, which usually triumphed over the many obstacles placed in its path. The first pastoral appeared in 1471, and the form reached the peak of its popularity in the late sixteenth century with Torquato Tasso's *Aminta* (1573) and Giambattista Guarini's *The Faithful Shepherd* (1590), both of which were admired and imitated throughout Europe.

During the 200-year period, then, between the late fourteenth and the late sixteenth centuries, Renaissance drama evolved in Italy. Today these Italian plays are of interest almost solely because they marked the first clear break with medieval practices and because they served as models for dramatists in other countries (especially England and France) where drama of more lasting value was to be written.

Around the middle of the sixteenth century the Italian Renaissance entered a new phase as its original vitality waned under the impact of the same forces that brought an end to medieval theatre. A new sense of purpose for the Catholic church had come out of the Council of Trent, which met between 1545 and 1563 to deal with the challenges posed by Prostestant secessions. The church adopted a number of means to discourage dissident opinion and to insure orthodoxy. Among these were the reinstitution of the Inquisition and the compilation of the *Index Expurgatorius* (a list of works the church sought to suppress by declaring it a sin to print, disseminate, or possess them). Thus, freedom of thought and conscience were curtailed. Italy also was forced to reassess its economic position. The fall of Constantinople had closed many trade routes to the East, and the geographical explorations undertaken by Spain, Portugal, and other nations from the late fifteenth century onward increasingly threatened Italy's primacy in trade and wealth.

For these and other reasons the second half of the sixteenth century was a time of anxiety for Italy. Art historians now use the term "mannerist" to describe the self-conscious and artificial visual style of that period. They also use the term "baroque" to describe the style that came into being around 1600. They consider the baroque to be in part an expression of the church's new self-confidence which took the form of monumental architecture and elaborate decoration. Historans also relate these changes in style to the growth of absolutism in government and the power of princes that found expression in grandiose palaces and other trappings of authority. The classical forms revived by the Renaissance lost their clean lines under baroque elaborations of S-curves and infinite decorative features. In music, melodic lines were embroidered with complex details and striking contrasts. In all the arts the movement was toward grandeur, richness, and monumentality. Most of these characteristics can be seen in the theatre, although their impact was not fully evident until around 1700.

THE NEOCLASSICAL IDEAL

In drama the new concern for authority was first felt through the formulation of the neoclassical ideal. This had been given full expression in Italy by 1570, and thereafter it spread to the rest of Europe, where it was to dominate criticism from the mid-seventeenth until the late eighteenth century.

Prior to 1550, interest in literary theory developed slowly and was concerned above all with two classical treatises: Horace's *Art of Poetry* and Aristotle's *Poetics*. While Horace's work had never been lost sight of since it was written in the first century B.C., Aristotle's was little known prior to 1498, when it was published in Italy in a Latin translation. During the sixteenth century, Aristotle came to be considered the supreme authority on literary matters. In 1548 the first commentary (by Robertello) on the *Poetics* was published, and in 1549 an Italian translation of Aristotle's treatise appeared.

Aristotle's authority was greatly increased when the Council of Trent adopted the teachings of St. Thomas Aquinas (who had drawn heavily on Aristotle's works) as the official position of the church. Thereafter, most commentators tended to accept Aristotle as the primary authority on all literary questions. Of the many treatises written after 1550, the most influential were those by three men: Antonio Minturno (? –1574), Julius Caesar Scaliger (1494–1558) and Lodovico Castelvetro (1501–1571). Although these and other writers differed on details, they were in general agreement on the basic precepts that constituted the neoclassical ideal.

In neoclassical doctrine, the fundamental demand was for verisimilitude, or the appearance of truth. A complex concept, verisimilitude may be divided into three subsidiary goals: reality, morality, and generality. In relation to reality, critics urged dramatists to confine their subjects to events that could happen in real life. Consequently, in practice, fantasy and supernatural events were usually avoided unless they were integral parts of some received story from myth, history, or the Bible, and even in these instances they were minimized as much as possible. Furthermore, such devices as the soliloquy and the chorus were discouraged on the grounds that it is unnatural for characters to speak aloud while alone or to discuss private matters in the presence of a group so large as the chorus. These devices were replaced by others, of which the most typical was the inclusion of a *confidant* (or trusted companion) for each of the main characters, so that he might believably reveal his inmost secrets. The demand for reality also led dramatists to keep battles, crowd scenes, violence, and deaths offstage on the grounds that it was too difficult to make such occurrences seem convincing.

The demand for faithfulness to reality was considerably modified by another—that drama teach moral lessons. Consequently, the dramatist was asked not merely to copy life but to reveal its ideal moral patterns. Since

God was said to be both omnipotent and just, it seemed only logical that the world over which God reigns should be represented in drama in such a way as to reveal his power and justice. This, in turn, meant showing wickedness punished and good rewarded. Those instances in life in which justice seemingly does not prevail were explained away as some part of God's long-range plans not fully comprehended by man but in which justice is certain eventually to prevail. Therefore, apparent aberrations in the workings of justice were thought unsuitable subjects for drama, which should depict that ultimate truth which is inseparable from morality and justice.

Both reality and morality were further modified by still another demand for abstraction or generality as the key to truth. Rather than seeking truth in a welter of surface details, the neoclassicist located it in attributes that are common to all phenomena in a particular category. Those characteristics which vary from one example to another were considered accidental and therefore not essential parts of truth. Thus, truth was defined as those typical and normative traits which are discoverable through the rational and systematic examination of phenomena, whether natural or man-made. Since these norms were considered to embody truth in its most essential form—one that remains unchanged regardless of historical period or geographical location—they were considered the foundation upon which all literary creation and criticism should rest.

The concept of verisimilitude, then, represents an attempt to define the reality that playwrights presumably should seek to mirror in their works. Out of this basic view developed a number of lesser principles, for the idea that truth is to be found in norms was extended to almost every aspect of dramatic composition. All drama was reduced to two basic forms, comedy and tragedy, and other types were considered inferior because they were "mixed." Consequently, purity of dramatic form—that is, no intermingling of comic and serious elements—was urged.

Comedy and tragedy were thought to have their own normative patterns. Comedy was said to draw its characters from the middle or lower classes, to base its stories on domestic and private affairs, to have happy endings, and to imitate the style of everyday speech. Tragedy was said to draw its characters from the ruling classes, to base its stories on history or mythology, to have unhappy endings, and to employ a lofty and poetic style. These norms mark several departures from Greek practice, but perhaps the most significant is the substitution of social rank for moral qualities in the description of characters.

The concept of norms was also extended to characterization, since the dramatist was expected to write about the permanent aspects of human nature rather than those peculiar to one time and place. In establishing norms (or the proper *decorum* for characters), all humanity was categorized according to age, rank, sex, and profession, and the attributes of each were described. As a result, neoclassical drama tended to depict types, who prosper if they observe the appropriate decorum and who are punished when they deviate from it.

All plays were said to have as their main functions "to teach and to please." Although the didactic ideal had often been stated in classical times, it was not given primary emphasis until the Humanists of the Renaissance found it necessary to justify the study and writing of literature at a time when learning was moving away from purely theological concerns. Because they wished to depict drama as a useful tool, they tended to emphasize the instructional over the pleasurable potentials of literature. Comedy was said to teach by ridiculing behavior that should be avoided and tragedy to show the horrifying results of mistakes and misdeeds. These ideas about the functions of drama were to dominate critical thought until the end of the eighteenth century.

The "three unities" of action, time, and place were also formulated during the sixteenth century. Unified action had been an ideal since Greek times, but unity of time was first advocated around 1543 and unity of place in 1570. It was Castelvetro who first stated all three as essential rules in 1570. He argued that since an audience knows that it has been in the theatre for only a few hours, it cannot be convinced that long periods of time have elapsed. Likewise, since the audience knows that it has been in only one place, it cannot accept any change of locale. After the 1570s, most critics demanded that a play have a single plot, take place in twenty-four hours or less, and be confined to one place, although the latter rule was often extended to include additional places if they could be easily reached without violating the twenty-four-hour rule. The division into five acts was also considered essential to regular drama. Horace had first stated this rule in Roman times, and it was adopted in the Renaissance as a norm of regular drama.

Although many of the neoclassical principles now seem arbitrary and restrictive, they were accepted as reasonable and desirable in the years from about 1570

FIGURE 6.3 Costume designs by Bernardo Buontalenti for an *intermezzo* at the Uffizi palace, Florence, 1589. Courtesy Theatre Museum, Victoria and Albert Museum.

until after 1750. As the neoclassical ideal took shape in Italy, drama became increasingly regular. Although some plays deviated from the rules, they were usually denounced as inferior and as unworthy of serious consideration.

During the sixteenth century the neoclassical rules were little known outside of educated circles and the plays written in accordance with them did not reach large audiences. Tragedy met a mixed reception even with educated groups, and comedy, which was produced primarily at court, was popular in part because of the *intermezzi* inserted between the acts.

INTERMEZZI AND OPERA

Intermezzi were descended from *mascherata* and the entertainments given at court on special occasions. (For a discussion of their early history, see chapter 4.) They were first coupled with comedies in the late fifteenth century. The principal appeal of *intermezzi* lay in the scenery, costumes, lights, special effects, music, and dance, for dialogue was used only when the allegorical plots had to be explained. Since entertainments were given at court primarily on such special occasions as betrothals, weddings, births, and visits of royalty, *intermezzi* were used to pay elaborate compliments to those

being honored. Thus, not only were they stunning as spectacle, they were instruments of power politics and diplomacy.

Four *intermezzi* became typical, since they filled the intervals between the five acts of regular drama. At first this interruption of a dramatic action with allegorical spectacle met considerable opposition, but by the 1570s the *intermezzi* had become more popular than the plays they accompanied. Originally, the various *intermezzi* seen on a single occasion had no connection with each other or with the play being performed. Gradually, however, they were related both to each other and to the theme of the main drama. By the late sixteenth century, they sometimes resembled loosely organized four-act works performed during the breaks of a five-act play, to which it was related through some common theme. Critics were fond of likening *intermezzi* to the choral interludes of Greek drama.

Since the *intermezzi* depended upon spectacle, they motivated many experiments with scenery. Furthermore, the need to change settings rapidly for the alternating segments of plays and *intermezzi* encouraged the development of new devices for shifting scenery. In the seventeenth century, the *intermezzi* were gradually absorbed into opera, although for a time they were performed between the acts of this new form as they had been with comedy. By 1650, they had virtually disappeared.

It was opera that was destined to become the most popular dramatic form in Italy. During the Renaissance, Italy had many "academies," or associations of men with common intellectual or artistic interests, and it was out of one of these, the Camerata of Florence, that opera came. Members of the Camerata, who were concerned with Greek music and its relation to drama, sought to create plays similar to ancient Greek tragedies. Their first full-length work, and the first "opera," was *Dafne* (1594), with text by Ottavio Rinuccini and Giulio Caccini and music by Jacopo Peri. The dialogue and choral passages were recited or chanted to a musical accompaniment which served merely to enhance the dramatic effectiveness of the dialogue. From this simple beginning, opera evolved into one of the major art forms of the baroque era.

The first great operatic composer was Claudio Monteverde (1567–1643), whose *Orfeo* (1607) enlarged the role of instrumental music and began the shift in interest from dramatic to musical values. Other composers continued these trends. Until 1637, however, opera remained principally an entertainment of the courts and academies. In that year, the opening of an opera house in Venice made the form available to the general public for the first time. So successful was this venture that between 1640 and 1700 four opera houses operated regularly in Venice, a city of about 140,000 population. From Venice, opera spread throughout Italy and then to the rest of Europe. As a popular entertainment, it underwent several significant changes. The melodious songs, or arias, increased in number as the passages of recitative and choral songs declined. Happy endings became typical and all of the scenic wonders of the court *intermezzi* were incorporated and elaborated. Consequently, when opera was imported into other countries, so also were Italian scenic practices.

THE DEVELOPMENT OF NEW SCENIC PRACTICES

Although interest in classical drama revived in the fourteenth century, none of the ancient works were performed until 1486, when the Roman Academy began its experiments. At about the same time the court at Ferrara also began presenting plays, and soon other courts and academies were competing for preeminence in staging. By the early sixteenth century, plays were considered suitable entertainment for almost all court celebrations and were being presented frequently by academies for their members and guests.

The production of plays was motivated in part by interest in Vitruvius' treatise on Roman architecture. Rediscovered in 1414 and printed in 1486, by 1500 *De Architectura* had assumed the position of authority on all matters relating to architecture and staging that Aristotle's *Poetics* was to gain in literature. Since the early producers wished to duplicate authentic Roman practices, they turned to Vitruvius for information about the auditorium and stage, about the appropriate scenery for tragedy, comedy, and satyr drama, and for justification of productions financed by rulers and wealthy citizens. But Vitruvius' somewhat cryptic remarks were easily misinterpreted, especially since his verbal descriptions were not accompanied by illustrations or plans. Because it was so ambiguous, *De Architectura* prompted many commentaries and critical editions, the most influential of which were those by Jocundus (1511) and Philander (1544).

FIGURE 6.4 Scene from Terence's *Adelphi*. Note the many doors, with the names of characters above them, an arrangement characteristic of the "Terence stage." From the edition of Terence's plays published at Lyon in 1493.

When members of the Roman Academy began staging plays around 1486, they turned to Vitruvius for guidance. Under the leadership of Pomponius Laetus (1424–1498), they sought to reconstruct the features of the Roman theatre for their productions. Young men from all over Europe came to study with Laetus and took many of his ideas back to their native lands.

From his study of Vitruvius, Laetus may have arrived at a stage similar to that shown in late fifteenth-century illustrated editions of Terence's plays. In these illustrations, a platform is backed by a continuous facade, either straight or angled and divided into a series of curtained openings, each representing the house of a different character. The first edition of Terence's plays to show this stage was printed at Lyon in 1493 and was edited by Godocus Badius, a Fleming who had studied with Laetus. The illustrations were imitated in a Venetian edition of 1511 and thereafter became current throughout Europe. Some scholars have argued that during the sixteenth century this "Terence stage" was in use almost everywhere, especially in schools. Contrarily, others have denied that its use was ever widespread.

If Laetus and others did employ a stage of this type, their practice was soon modified by the addition

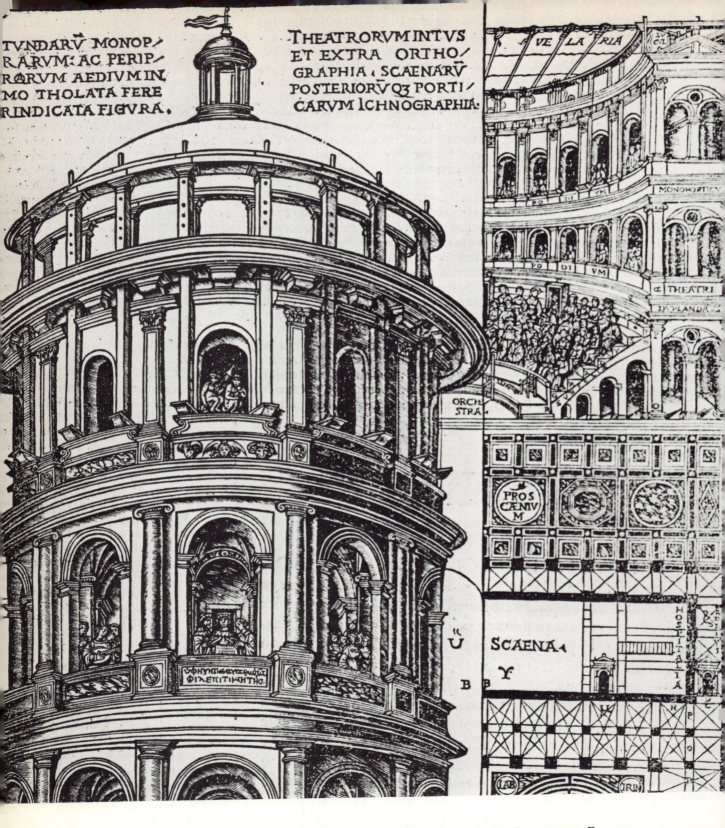

FIGURE 6.5 A Renaissance conception of the Roman theatre as a fully circular structure. From an edition of Vitruvius' *Architectura* published in 1521. Courtesy Lilly Library, Indiana University.

of perspective painting, whose influence was soon to outdistance that of Vitruvius. Although perspective developed over a long period, its principles were systematized by the architect Filippo Brunelleschi (1377–1446) and by the painter Masaccio (1401–1428) around 1425. But it was Leon Battista Alberti's *Della Pittura* (1435), the first treatise on the subject, that disseminated practical directions for making perspective drawings. Alberti's understanding of perspective was limited, however, for with his method all objects had to be drawn as if parallel to the picture plane. It was not until the time of Leonardo da Vinci (1452–1519) that space was seen to be spherical, curving away from the viewer in all directions. Even then, techniques had not yet been devised for transferring objects so perceived to the various flat surfaces of a stage setting and many of the later developments in scene design became practical only after much experimentation.

It is difficult now to appreciate the fascination that perspective drawing exerted on the Renaissance mind, for it seemed almost magical in its ability to manipulate illusion. Consequently, it is not surprising that perspective should soon find its way into the theatre, especially since scenery was usually designed by the leading painters and architects of the day. Although perspective settings may have been used as early as the 1480s, the first certain example is that by Pellegrino da San Daniele for Ariosto's *The Casket* at Ferrara in 1508, in which individual houses were placed in front of a painted backdrop. This arrangement, typical for many years, owed much to Vitruvius' description of theatrical settings: "Tragic scenes are delineated with columns, pediments, statues, and other objects suited to kings; comic scenes exhibit private dwellings with balconies and views representing rows of windows after the manner of ordinary dwellings; satyric scenes are decorated with trees, caverns, mountains, and other rustic objects delineated in landscape style." It also embodied another Renaissance interest derived from Vitruvius: the "ideal city." The overall purpose of *De Architectura* was to provide a guide for laying out towns. Renaissance artists, fascinated by the concept of the ideal city, sought in their stage settings to embody various aspects of it by depicting in the tragic scene the royal and ceremonial sections and in the comic scene those occupied by ordinary citizens.

The practices of the early sixteenth century are best summed up in Sebastiano Serlio's (1475–1554) *Architettura* (1545), the first Renaissance work to de-

FIGURE 6.6 The ancient theatre according to fifteenth-century humanists. Frontispiece to an edition of Plautus' plays published in Venice, 1511.

vote a section to the theatre. It also includes illustrations of the tragic, comic, and satyric scenes, based on Vitruvius' descriptions. Serlio was heavily indebted to other artists, especially Baldassare Peruzzi (1481–1537), with whom he had studied and who was the foremost early promoter of perspective settings. In his book Serlio seems to be describing practices typical of his time, and, since this treatise was circulated throughout Europe, it was a prime disseminator of Italian ideas abroad. Furthermore, after 1547 Serlio's perspective sketches of the tragic, comic, and satyric scenes were often reprinted in editions of Vitruvius' *De Architectura*, a practice that encouraged readers to transpose Vitruvius' descriptions into perspective settings.

FIGURE 6.7 Serlio's tragic scene. From Serlio's *Architettura,* Book 2, 1569 edition. Courtesy Fine Arts Library, Indiana University.

In *Architettura,* Serlio takes it for granted that theatres will be set up in already existing rooms, for in his day halls of state in palaces had become the usual places for staging plays. Thus, he fits Vitruvius' semicircular auditorium into a rectangular space by constructing stadium-like seating around an orchestra (used almost exclusively to seat the ruler and his attendants). The stage is raised to the eye level of the ruler and the perspective scenery is designed so that the ideal view of it is seen from his chair. The front portion of the stage floor is level, since it is intended for use by the actors, but back of this the floor slopes upward at a sharp angle so as to increase the illusion of distance. All scenery is placed on this raked portion.

Serlio considered his renderings of Vitruvius' three scenes adequate to meet the needs of all plays.

Each of his three sets has the same basic floor plan, for all require four sets of wings (the first three angled and the fourth flat) and a backdrop. The wings closest to the audience are given many three-dimensional details and some even have open arcades and galleries. Although Serlio mentions no framing device for his stage pictures, the downstage wings probably extended to walls of the hall, and a valance probably limited the overhead view to preserve the illusion.

Serlio's settings are conceived in architectural terms and were not meant to be changed. When *intermezzi* were performed, pageant wagons were drawn into the space just forward of the stage or portable set pieces were carried onto the platform. Shortly after Serlio's treatise was published, however, interest in spectacle had increased sufficiently that there arose a demand for settings that could be changed during performances.

The solution first adopted involved *periaktoi* (as described by Vitruvius and Pollux). The earliest known use of *periaktoi* in the Renaissance is by Aristotile de San Gallo (1481–1551) at Castro in 1543. They were in use at Florence by 1569, and in 1583 Vignola, in his *The Two Rules of Perspective Practice*, recommended as a means of changing scenes structures with from two to six sides.

Nicola Sabbattini's (1574–1654) *Manual for Constructing Theatrical Scenes and Machines* (1638), a major source of information about seventeenth-century practices, lists three principal methods of changing scenery. One requires *periaktoi*, but the other two are devices for changing the angled wings. In the first of these two methods, new wings are maneuvered around those already in place, and in the second, painted canvas is pulled quickly around the wings to conceal the pre-

viously visible surfaces. In addition, Sabbattini explains how to change the flat wings used near the back of the stage by sliding them in grooves or by mounting several in such a way that they can be turned like pages in a book. All of these devices demonstrate that wings had been considerably simplified during the century that separates Sabbattini's from Serlio's treatise, for by 1638 the three-dimensional details used by Serlio had been replaced almost completely by painted details.

The ultimate solution to scene shifting required that all angled wings be replaced with flat wings. This change had to await new developments in perspective drawing. Throughout the sixteenth century, the angled wings had been painted in position: the vanishing point was established on the back wall of the stage and a cord was anchored there; this cord was then stretched downstage and used to determine the relative height and size of all the details to be painted on the angled wings. Drawing, therefore, was relatively simple, for the two

FIGURES 6.8 and 6.9 Serlio's comic and pastoral scenes. Both from Serlio's *Architettura*, Book 2, 1569 edition. Courtesy Fine Arts Library, Indiana University.

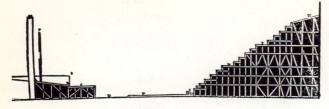

FIGURE 6.10   A cross section of Serlio's hall stage. From *The Second Book of Architecture* (1545).

faces of each wing were treated as different sides of a single structure, one parallel and the other at right angles to the picture plane. On flat wings, however, all details had to be depicted on a series of surfaces set parallel to the picture plane. The problems of transferring a perspective picture to a series of flat wings were not adequately solved until 1600, when Guido Ubaldus' *Six Books of Perspective* was published. The first application of Ubaldus' principles to stage settings composed entirely of flat wings was probably made by Giovan Battista Aleotti (1546–1636) at Ferrara in 1606. This new technique rapidly became popular and by 1650 had almost completely outmoded the angled wings.

Using flat wings, any number of settings could be easily shifted. At each wing position as many flats were set up, one immediately behind the other, as there were settings. Changes were accomplished simply by withdrawing the set of visible wings to reveal another set behind them. To support the flats and to permit their easy movement on and off stage, grooves were installed on the stage floor and overhead. The back scene was normally painted on two flats (or shutters) which met at the center of the stage, although cloths that could be rolled up were sometimes used.

Until about 1650 most scenes, following classical practice, showed exteriors. Consequently, overhead masking was usually painted to represent the sky or clouds. Sometimes an unbroken canvas was mounted to curve over the entire setting, but as flying machinery of various sorts became common, a bow-shaped border was hung above each set of wings. When interior settings were introduced, the borders were painted to represent ceilings, beams, domes, or other appropriate details.

By the early seventeenth century, then, the three basic elements of every setting were the side wings, back shutters, and overhead borders, and all could be changed simultaneously. At first, many stagehands were utilized

to make quick changes, but the results were not entirely satisfactory, since it was difficult to synchronize the movements of so many persons precisely.

The next significant step was taken by Giacomo Torelli (1608–1678), who perfected the chariot-and-pole system of scene shifting at the Teatro Novissimo in Venice between 1641 and 1645 (see Figure 6.13). Torelli cut slots through the stage floor so that upright supports (or poles) could pass through. These poles, on which flats were mounted above the floor level, were attached beneath the stage to "chariots" that ran in tracks parallel to the front of the stage. As the chariots rolled toward the center of the stage they carried flats into view, while the opposite movement took them out of sight. By means of an elaborate system of ropes, pulleys, and winches, every part of a setting could be changed simultaneously by turning a single winch. This

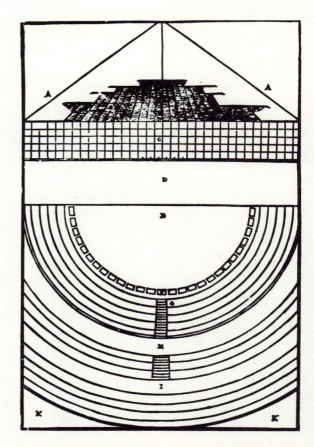

FIGURE 6.11   Ground plan of Serlio's hall stage. From *The Second Book of Architecture* (1545).

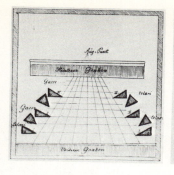
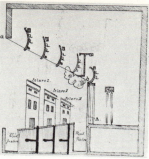

FIGURE 6.12 Joseph Furttenbach's plan and section of a stage showing the use of *periaktoi*, bow-shaped borders, and a rear pit for special effects. From *Die Theater Weins* (1899).

innovation, which at first seemed almost magical in its ability to produce transformations, was soon adopted almost universally in Europe, where it was to be the standard method of shifting scenery until the late nineteenth century. The older and simpler groove system persisted only in England, Holland, and America.

The advent of the flat wing coincided with and probably facilitated the development of the baroque visual style that began to take shape around 1600. As long as angled wings had predominated, each wing usually represented a separate building, a tradition that persisted for a time with flat wings. But this convention did not lend itself to effects of grandeur, and as the taste for monumentality grew during the seventeenth century, the former series of buildings gave way to a sequence of columns, porticos, or other architectural features which were treated as parts of a single structure. This change increased both the unity and the apparent size of stage settings. These trends toward monumentality were not completed until the eighteenth century, when the baroque style in scene design reached its fullest expression.

Since scenic design was long an adjunct of architecture or painting, many of Italy's finest artists designed scenery in the years between 1475 and 1650. Because they and their students moved about frequently, essentially the same scenic conventions were current throughout Italy. The prestige to be gained through lavish productions encouraged many rulers, notably those of Ferrara, Mantua, Urbino, Milan, and Rome, to patronize the theatre. Scenic grandeur was especially highly developed under the De Medicis at Florence, and prob-

ably reached its peak in the work of Bernardo Buontalenti (1536–1608), who served as architect and supervisor of entertainments at the Medici court for nearly sixty years. Buontalenti's work foreshadowed and probably helped create the visual style that was to become so elaborate during the baroque era. His finest work was done in 1589 in connection with the festivities honoring the marriage of the Grand Duke Ferdinand I, when an entire month was devoted to masquerades, animal hunts, a naumachia on the Arno River, comedies with *intermezzi*, and numerous other events. Buontalenti's fertile genius enriched the court spectacles with highly imaginative costumes, scenery, machinery, and special effects. He was succeeded by his pupil Giulio Parigi (*c.* 1570–1635), who designed major festivals in 1606, 1608, and 1616, of which many engravings have survived. It was from Parigi that Inigo Jones learned much that he was to apply in staging English masques between 1605 and 1640, and from Parigi Joseph Furttenbach (1591–1667) absorbed many of the ideas that he was to take back to Germany and disseminate through his books, *Civil Architecture* (1628), *Recreational Architecture* (1640), and *The Noble Mirror of Art* (1663).

FIGURE 6.13 Diagram illustrating the chariot-and-pole mechanism for shifting scenery. A—the tracks in which the chariots ride; B and C—chariots; D—the stage walls; E—the stage floor; F, G, H, and I—the lines, pulleys, and levers that operate the system. From Rees, *Cyclopedia*, XX (1803).

FIGURE 6.14 Torelli's setting for Act III of Strozzi's opera, *La Finta Pazza*, the work that launched Torelli's career in Venice in the early 1640s. Courtesy Theatersammlung, Osterreichische Nationalbibliothek, Vienna.

With the opening of the Venetian public opera houses, beginning in 1637, scenic splendor was made available to the general public for the first time since the decline of medieval religious plays. From opera it spread to the other dramatic forms and to the public playhouses. By the end of the seventeenth century, Italian scenic practices had been adopted almost everywhere in Europe.

DEVELOPMENT OF THEATRE ARCHITECTURE

In spite of the great interest in theatical production after the mid–1580s, plays were presented by courts and academies only on special occasions. Therefore, the need for permanent theatres was slow in arising. Many early productions were given out of doors in courtyards or gardens, but during the sixteenth century banqueting halls or other large rooms became the typical sites. These temporary theatres were usually arranged in the manner described by Serlio.

Although a few permanent structures may have been built earlier (allegedly a theatre at Ferrara burned in 1532), the oldest surviving Renaissance theatre is the Teatro Olimpico, built between 1580 and 1584 by the

Olympic Academy of Vicenza. Founded in 1555 to study Greek drama, this academy at first used temporary stages for its occasional productions. When the members decided to build a permanent theatre, Andrea Palladio (1518–1580), eminent architect, student of Vitruvius and of Roman ruins, and a member of the academy, undertook to reproduce a classical theatre inside a pre-existing building. In the Teatro Olimpico, semi-elliptical seating curves around a small orchestra. The rectangular stage is enclosed at the back and ends by a facade decorated with pillars, niches, statues, and bas-reliefs. Five openings pierce the facade, one at either end and three at the back. The overall effect is that of a miniature

FIGURE 6.15 First *intermezzo* of an evening's entertainment entitled *The Liberation of Tyrrhenus*, performed in Florence before the Medici court at carnival time, 1616. The setting on stage is by Guilio Parigi. Etching by Jacques Callot.

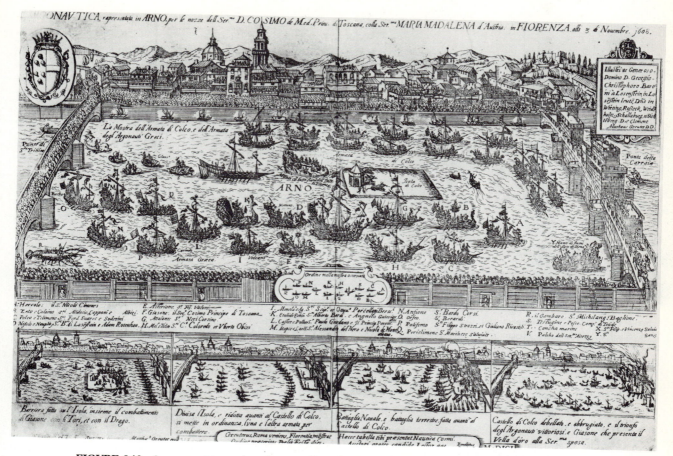

FIGURE 6.16 A *naumachia* on the Arno River in Florence given in honor of the marriage of Cosimo de' Medici to Maria Madalena of Austria in 1608. This *naumachia* was based on the story of the Argonauts. Engraving by Mathias Greuter. Courtesy Theatermuseum, Munich.

Roman theatre brought indoors. Palladio died before the theatre was completed, and for the opening production in 1585, Sophocles' *Oedipus Rex*, Vincenzo Scamozzi (1552–1616) placed street scenes built in perspective behind each of the stage openings to create the impression that the stage is a city square into which a number of streets lead. Each spectator has a view down at least one of the streets. These vistas still remain as permanent parts of the stage.

The Teatro Olimpico was not, however, in the main line of development, which is better represented by the small theatre built by Scamozzi at Sabbionetta in 1588. Here a complete theatre building was designed as a unit, although the interior still essentially followed Serlio's plan. Semi-circular seating faces a stage without

a proscenium arch, upon which angled wings are used for settings. As one of the few surviving Renaissance theatres, it is of considerable importance in showing the evolution of theatre architecture.

But the prototype of the modern stage is that of the Teatro Farnese at Parma, (designed by Giovan Battista Aleotti, completed in 1618 and first used in 1628), since it is the first surviving structure with a permanent proscenium arch. The orgins of the proscenium arch are obscure. Some scholars have suggested that the doorways of the Roman or "Terence" stages were gradually enlarged to permit playing scenes inside the openings, and that eventually all were merged into a single arch. Others have argued for a similar evolution out of the triumphal arches used in street pageants. Still

FIGURE 6.17 Interior of the Teatro Olimpico as it appears today.

others believe that the proscenium frame was borrowed from perspective painting, in which a central view was often framed by architectural side units (much as in Serlio's stage settings).

Any or all of these practices may have contributed to the proscenium arch, which was adopted to fill a need first clearly felt in the Renaissance. In the medieval theatre, Heaven, Hell, and Earth were shown simultaneously, since space was treated as unbounded and infinite. Contrarily, in the Renaissance, artists sought to depict only objects that could be seen from one fixed point; therefore, space was treated as finite, and consequently a framing device was needed to restrict the view of the audience. The proscenium arch, then, helped both to create the illusion of reality and to mask the mechanisms upon which it depended.

The proscenium came into use only gradually. In early sixteenth century settings the first pair of wings and an overhead valance provided sufficient masking. But as the desire to change settings increased, so did the need for downstage masking to conceal the changes. For a time, the first set of angle wings was neutralized to blend with the various settings; in some temporary theatres, an appropriate proscenium arch was erected for each new production. But in permanent theatres the desirability of a permanent framing device became

clear, especially after the flat wing was adopted. Consequently, during the seventeenth century the architectural proscenium arch became standard.

The usefulness of the arch was not restricted to the front of the stage, however, and the Teatro Farnese (as well as many later theatres) had two additional frames further back on the stage. This feature encouraged the use of settings of varying depths, since the openings made it easy to increase or restrict the visible stage space. The concept of internal arches increased in importance as the desire for grandeur and monumentality grew during the baroque era. The opening between the last set of wings came to serve as a second frame behind which a deep perspective vista was placed. Sometimes barriers were erected to prevent actors from moving too near the perspective backdrops and thereby destroying the illusion of distance, but with increasing frequency stages of great depth were also built to accomodate scenes of true immensity.

Although the stage of the Teatro Farnese was the prototype of virtually all those that were to follow during the next 300 years, its auditorium was still that of a conventional court theatre. In it, U-shaped, stadium-like seating surrounded a large open space that could be used for dancing or be flooded for water spectacles. The prototype of the later auditorium, therefore, is not to be found in the court but in the public theatres.

The professional public theatre began to emerge in Italy during the second half of the sixteenth century. The first record of a public theatre building there is found

FIGURE 6.18 Floor plan of the Teatro Olimpico. From Streit, *Das Theater* (1903).

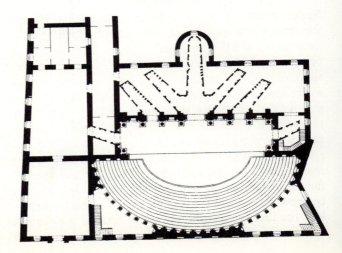

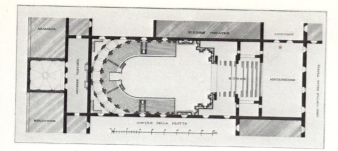

FIGURE 6.19 Floor plan of the Teatro Farnese, Parma. From Streit, *Das Theater* (1903).

in 1565 at Venice. By the early seventeenth century there were a number of public theatre buildings, although none was elaborate. Major architectural innovations did not come until opera began to be performed professionally in 1637. Venice was the logical place for the public theatre to develop, for it was the only Italian state not ruled by a monarch. Since its wealth depended upon commerce, it had a strong middle class capable of supporting a public theatre.

The auditorium of the Venetian public opera house was arranged to encourage attendance by all classes while permitting relative privacy for those who wished it. The San Cassiano, the first to be built, had five balconies each with thirty-one boxes. The first two levels, the most expensive, were patronized by the wealthier classes; the upper three were used by persons of lesser rank and wealth; the open area on the ground floor (the pit or *parterre*) attracted the lower classes or those to whom propriety was unimportant. The arrangement of tiers, one above the other, permitted large numbers of persons to be accommodated in a restricted space. The success of the San Cassiano was so great that by 1641 three other theatres had been opened, and the public performance of opera (and its attendant auditorium design) spread from Venice to other cities in Italy and elsewhere throughout Europe.

While the Venetian theatres popularized the "box, pit, and gallery" auditorium, they were not the first examples of it, for many of the theatres erected for the religious plays of the Middle Ages had employed this arrangement, and less elaborate versions of it were used for the public theatres of Paris, London, and Madrid before opera houses were opened in Venice. Nevertheless, the prestige of opera gave approval to the pattern that was to dominate auditorium design until the end

of the nineteenth century. Furthermore, since the Venetian opera houses also incorporated the proscenium arch, elaborate machines, and perspective scenery, they were the first public theatres to include all of the features that were to be most characteristic of the picture-frame stage.

MACHINERY AND SPECIAL EFFECTS

Much of the wonder inspired by the productions at courts and academies resulted from special effects. Building upon medieval practice, the Renaissance machinists arranged seemingly magical transformations, and made gods, monsters, and mythological creatures appear on the sea, in the air, in Heaven or in Hades. Just as playwrights turned to classical subjects, the machinists found justification for their work in Pollux' list of machines and Aristotle's inclusion of spectacle as one of the six basic parts of drama. Even in plays that observed unity of place, spectacle was often introduced to reduce the austerity imposed by a single setting. Typically, however, elaborate special effects were reserved for *intermezzi* or operas.

FIGURE 6.20 Proscenium wall of the Teatro Farnese, Parma, built in 1618. This is the first theatre known to have had a permanent architectural proscenium arch. From Streit, *Das Theater* (1903).

FIGURE 6.21 Auditorium of the Teatro Farnese, Parma. Note that the orchestra is left free so it may be used for dancing, water ballets, and other activities. The ducal box is located above the entrance at center left. From Streit, *Das Theater* (1903).

Much of the spectacle depended upon machinery for "flying." Gods appeared frequently to resolve the dramatic action, and these and other mythological characters were suspended above the stage in chariots, on clouds, or on the backs of animals or birds. From one to fifty figures might be shown in "the glory" of a brightly lighted paradise formed of clouds. To achieve these effects, appropriately shaped figures, such as chariots, horses, or clouds, were made of wood and canvas and then painted. Since the overhead space was limited in theatres of this period, beams and fulcrums at the sides of the stage were used for much of the flying. Some structures were hinged so that they might be collapsed within the overhead space. Ingenious riggings were invented for moving objects up and down stage while they were suspended in the air. In many productions transformations were masked by clouds that engulfed the stage (by lowering painted units from above or moving them on from the sides).

Other effects depended on trapdoors in the stage floor. Since the temporary theatres used platforms only about four to six feet high, the working space beneath the stage was restricted. Nevertheless, the effects were elaborate: mountains, rocks, trees, and other objects rose and sank; characters suddenly appeared or disappeared; objects and persons were transformed by means of substitutions from beneath the stage. To create the effect of ghosts rising through the floor, figures were painted on cloth, attached to poles, and slowly elevated through a slot. Fire and smoke were common. Sabbattini describes a device for making flames seem to rise out of the earth, and an arrangement of fire in front and in back of actors to make it appear that they are dancing in flames.

The popularity of sea scenes motivated the invention of several devices for simulating waves. In one, a large sheet of painted cloth was moved up and down rhythmically by means of cords attached to its under side; in another, a series of two-dimensional pieces shaped like waves as seen from the front were moved in such a way that as one group rose another fell to simulate the movement of the sea; in a third, a series of long, spiral cylinders was rotated one behind the other to create the sense of waves swelling and falling. Sometimes a sufficient number of units was utilized so that changes from calm to storm, from darkness to light, and various other conditions at sea could be simulated.

Ships, whales, and dolphins moved through the waves. To create the proper illusion, miniatures were usually mounted on poles and operated from beneath the stage. When ships had to accommodate a number of people, they were pulled across the stage by means

FIGURE 6.22 A public theatre of the early seventeenth century, thought to be in Cento (Italy). Drawing by G. F. B. Guercino. Courtesy British Museum.

FIGURE 6.23   Design by Bernardo Buontalenti for *The Harmony of the Spheres,* an *intermezzo* given at the Uffizi palace in Florence, 1589. This design also illustrates the use of "glories" in this period. Courtesy Theatre Museum, Victoria and Albert Museum.

of concealed ropes. One of the *intermezzi* designed by Buontalenti at Florence in 1589 showed Amphitrite moving through the waves on a shell accompanied by dolphins and Tritons; then a ship bearing twenty men sailed into view as a watchman in the crow's nest sang a song and a dolphin danced in the waves below.

Sometimes spectacles demanded that walls, fortified castles, or other buildings collapse. In these instances, the scenery was constructed in sections (like building blocks) and held together by concealed bars; when the bars were removed, the structures fell.

Sound was also important. Thunder was created by rolling cannon balls or stones down a rough channel; wind was simulated by whirling thin pieces of wood through the air rapidly. Music was played during scene

shifts and to disguise unwanted noises. It also accompanied the numerous songs and dances and much of the essentially pantomimic action of the *intermezzi.*

The front curtain might also be considered a special effect, since it was used to conceal the scenic wonders and to increase amazement when they were suddenly revealed. It was used only to begin performances and never to divide them into acts. At first, the curtain was dropped but, since this created too many hazards, the roll curtain was eventually adopted.

Although plays were the most usual entertainments, they were by no means the only ones, for the Italian courts revived many of the spectacles of the Roman Empire and continued others from the Middle Ages. Roman triumphal entries were transformed into

FIGURE 6.24 A carnival pageant, *The War of Love*, at the Medici court, 1615. The procession includes pageant wagons representing Africa and Asia. Etching by Jacques Callot.

trionfi, elaborate processions with pageant wagons, costumed classical or allegorical figures, and choreographed patterns used, like *intermezzi,* to celebrate some special occasion, such as a wedding, a betrothal, the birth of a prince, or an important state visit. Like other spectacles, they were also a symbol of power, wealth, and enlightenment. These *trionfi* were usually viewed from balconies and galleries of palaces, courtyards, or town squares. One of the most elaborate of these processions was *A Masque of the Genealogy of the Gods* (with 21 pageant wagons and 392 costumed mythological figures), given in Florence in 1566. *Naumachiae* were also revived. Usually they were presented on rivers, but at times flooded courtyards and other structures were used. Perhaps the most elaborate *naumachia* was *The Battle of the Argonauts,* given on the Arno River in Florence in 1608. In addition, there were various other kinds of processions, street revels, masquerades, carnivals, tournaments, and animal baitings. Most of these productions were unified by some dramatic or thematic framework that required costumes, properties, and scenic units. The love of spectacle seems to have been deep-seated and universal.

STAGE LIGHTING

When performances moved indoors, stage lighting became an important element of theatrical production for the first time. Although some of the medieval courtly entertainments had been performed indoors, it was not until the sixteenth century that indoor productions were common. At that time, techniques for lighting the auditorium and the stage had to be devised.

The illuminants available were candles and oil lamps. Candles were preferred for the auditorium because they smoked less and had a more pleasant odor than oil. Usually the auditorium was lighted by chandeliers hung just in front of the stage, illuminating both the auditorium and a portion of the platform.

FIGURE 6.25 Device for dimming candles. The hollow pipes could be lowered to obscure the light or raised to brighten it. From Sabbattini, *Manual for Constructing Theatrical Scenes and Machines* (1638).

The downstage acting area was also lighted by footlights, often mounted behind a parapet placed a short distance in front of the stage. Sabbattini states that the smoke from footlights and chandeliers often created a haze, and other writers comment upon the heat and fumes. The lights mounted on stage were usually concealed behind overhead or side masking pieces. Several oil lamps were placed in evenly spaced rings attached to vertical poles set up behind the proscenium and each of the wing positions. Other lamps were mounted on horizontal battens back of the front valance and each of the borders. To increase efficiency, reflectors made from tinsel, mica, or polished basins were placed behind the lamps.

At least three methods of darkening the stage were used: lamps were extinguished (although this was awkward if the lights had to brighten again); open cylinders were suspended above the lamps and lowered over them to darken the stage or raised to brighten it; or all lamps might be mounted on rotating poles that could be turned either toward or away from the visible portions of the stage. When exceptionally bright light was required, some scenic device such as a cloud, shell, or grotto was equipped with a downstage rim inside which lamps could be concealed and directed toward persons or objects inside the structure.

Sometimes the sun, moon, or lightning was shown. At Florence in 1539, San Gallo filled a crystal sphere with water and lighted it from behind with candles to form a sun that rose at the beginning of the play, moved across the sky, and set as the action closed. The moon was often represented in similar fashion. Bolts of lightning were made from jagged pieces of wood covered with tinsel and shot across the stage on wires. Occasionally attempts were made to color the light by placing containers filled with tinted liquids between the lamps and the stage. Since this reduced intensity markedly, it was normally reserved for such decorative devices as jewelled windows or festive lights mounted on top of buildings.

Since the intensity of lamps and candles was so limited, providing an adequate level of illumination took precedence over the other functions of stage lighting. Nevertheless, Renaissance theorists formulated several artistic principles similar to those advocated in modern times. Leone di Somi (1527–1592) argued that tragedy benefits from a lower level of illumination than that needed for comedy, and both he and Angelo In-

FIGURE 6.26 Scene from an Italian comedy of the early seventeenth century. From Rasi, *I Comici Italiana* (1895–1905).

gegneri (*c.* 1550–*c.* 1613) stated that the stage will appear brighter if it can be contrasted with a darkened auditorium. Sabbattini suggested that lighting the stage primarily from one side gives a more pleasing effect than even lighting from the front. For the most part, however, the Renaissance artist had to depend upon general illumination, for he had only limited control over color, distribution, and intensity. Nevertheless, he mastered most of the techniques that were to be typical until the late eighteenth century.

COMMEDIA DELL'ARTE

Productions at courts and academies were given for aristocratic audiences on special occasions. The plays were usually written by court poets and the scenery and cos-

FIGURE 6.27 Two *commedia* figures. From Jacques Callot's *Balli di Sfessania,* a series of twenty-four etchings made *c.* 1621–1622. The figures appear to be considerably exaggerated.

tumes were designed by court architects and painters. Acting was done by courtiers and music was supplied by court musicians. Thus, in spite of the high visual quality of the productions and their influence on later theatrical practice, they were essentially performances by amateurs given for very restricted audiences. The development of a public, professional theatre in Italy, therefore, was to come from other sources—primarily *commedia dell'arte.*

Commedia dell'arte (comedy of professional players), *commedia all'improviso* (improvised comedy), and *commedia a soggetto* (comedy developed from a plot, theme, or subject) are terms used to distinguish the plays performed by professional troupes from those presented by the amateur actors at courts and academies (the *commedia erudita* or learned comedy). Historians do not know when the *commedia dell'arte* came into being. The first clear records of it are found soon after 1550, but it may have existed long before that time. Several theories

have been advanced to explain its origin. One school seeks to trace it from the Atellan farce of Rome as preserved by wandering mimes during the Middle Ages. The principal evidence for this view is the similarity of stock characters in the two forms. A variation on this theory traces the *commedia* from troupes of Byzantine mimes who supposedly fled to the West when Constantinople fell in 1453. Other scholars have argued that it evolved out of improvisations on the comedies of Plautus and Terence. Still others have traced it to the Italian farce of the early sixteenth century.

Farce had appeared in Italy, as elsewhere, during the late Middle Ages, but its most extensive development came between 1500 and 1550, when it was especially popular with the general public; after this time, farce declined as *commedia dell'arte* rose in esteem. It reached its height in the work of Angelo Beolco (1502–1542), who began writing and acting around 1520. Disliking the *commedia erudita,* he turned for inspiration to the simple life and natural speech of northern Italy. Many of his plays center around the peasant Ruzzante, a role played by Beolco. The continuance of Ruzzante through several plays has been cited as a forerunner of the *commedia's* use of stock characters.

None of the theories about the origin of *commedia dell'arte* can be established or refuted. Many influences probably contributed to its development. Regardless of its source, before 1600 it had spread throughout Europe, where it was a typical and popular form of entertainment until about 1750.

The two fundamental characteristics of *commedia dell'arte* were improvisation and stock characters: the actors worked from a plot outline, on the basis of which they improvised dialogue and action, and each performer always played the same character with its fixed attributes and costume.

The earliest clear reference to improvisational playing is found in 1568, but if it was new at that time, it soon became standard. Historians have disagreed over the extent to which improvisation was used in performances. Certainly, several factors worked to reduce it. Each actor usually played the same character throughout his career, and this practice must have encouraged the repetition of lines and business which had been well received by audiences. Many bits of comic business (or *lazzi*) were sufficiently standardized to be indicated in plot outlines as *lazzi* of fear, hat *lazzi*, and so on. The rhymed couplets used to close scenes were probably memorized, and the actors playing the fashionable young lovers were encouraged to keep notebooks in which to record appropriate sentiments from poetry and popular literature. Consequently, most of the actors probably stored up lines and action which they repeated frequently. On the other hand, no actor could be sure what the others would say or do and thus he had to concentrate upon the unfolding action. As a result, performances must have created the impression of spontaneity.

The scenarios were refined over a period of time and passed down from one troupe to another. More than 700 have been preserved; the oldest 50 were published by Flaminio Scala (*fl.* 1600–1621) in 1611. By far the greatest number of scripts were comic, although a few were serious and many were melodramatic. The popularity of the troupes, however, rested primarily upon comedies revolving around love and intrigue, disguises, and cross-purposes. The *commedia* actors also performed occasionally in written plays.

Every troupe had its own set of fixed characters, each with a name and traits that set him off from similar characters in other companies. Nevertheless, the same character types tended to be repeated from one troupe to another. Consequently, although variations were numerous, the basic outlines remained relatively constant.

The character types in *commedia* can be divided into two general categories: the straight and the exaggerated. The straight roles were those of the young lovers, who served as a norm against which the peculiarities of other characters were seen. They were depicted as witty, handsome, well-educated young men and women; they dressed in the fashionable garments of the day and, unlike the other characters, were not masked. Each company had one or two pairs of lovers. The young man, the *innamorato* or *amoroso*, was often opposed in his love affairs by an older man, sometimes even his father. The young woman, or *innamorata*, was usually a sophisticated young lady courted by both young and old.

FIGURE 6.28 The Capitano of the *commedia dell'arte*. From Sand, *Masques et Bouffons* (1859).

The "character" roles can be divided into masters and servants. Of the masters, three types recurred most frequently: the Capitano, Pantalone, and Dottore. Originally the Capitano was one of the lovers and unexaggerated in manners and dress. Eventually, however, he was transformed into a braggart and coward who boasted of his great prowess in love and battle, only to be completely discredited in both. The sword, cape, and feathered headdress were standard features of his costume, though the degree of stylization varied considerably. He was often given such fanciful names as Spavento da Vall'Inferno, Coccodrillo, Rinocorente, or Matamoros. He frequently figured in the action as an unwelcome suitor to one of the young women, and his discomfiture was often a high point of the comedy.

Pantalone was always a middle-aged or elderly merchant. He spoke in a Venetian dialect, was fond of proverbs, and, in spite of his age, often posed as a young man and courted one of the young women. Typically, his costume included a tight-fitting red vest, red breeches and stockings, soft slippers, a black, ankle-length coat, a soft brimless cap with trailing wisps of hair, a brown mask with a large hooked nose, and a straggling gray beard.

Dottore was usually Pantalone's friend or rival and, like Pantalone, held an established place in society. He was a pedant, usually a Doctor of Law or Medicine, who spoke in a Bolognese dialect interlarded with Latin words and phrases. He loved to show off his spurious learning, but was often tricked by others because of his extreme credulousness. His dress was the academic cap and gown. He was a jealous husband, but was often cuckolded.

The most varied of all the *commedia* types were the servants, or *zanni*. Most scripts required at least two of these characters, one clever and the other stupid, but the number might vary from one to four. They usually figured prominently in the intrigues, and their machinations kept the plots moving as they sought to help or thwart their masters. Most of the servants were male, but there might be one or more maids, or *fantesca*, who served the *innamorata*. Typically young, coarsely witty, and always ready for an intrigue, they carried on their own love affairs with the male servants. Occasionally, they were older and might be the hostess of an inn, wife to a servant, or the object of an old man's affection.

Of the *zanni*, Harlequin (or Arlecchino) was by far the most popular after the mid-seventeenth century, although he did not figure prominently in the early

FIGURE 6.29 The lover of *commedia dell'arte.* Etching by Jacques Callot, 1618–1619.

scripts. He was a mixture of cunning and stupidity and was an accomplished acrobat and dancer. He was usually at the center of any intrigue. His costume underwent many changes. Originally, it was a suit with many irregularly placed patches, but these were gradually formalized into the diamond-shaped red, blue, and green pattern now associated with Harlequin. On his shaven head Harlequin wore a rakish hat above a black mask, and at his side he carried a wooden sword, or "slapstick," that figured prominently in the many fights and beatings of the *commedia*. Other related characters are Truffaldino and Trivellino.

Harlequin's most frequent companion was a cruel, libidinous, cynically witty servant who went by a variety of names. He was often called Brighella in the eighteenth century, when his mask had a hooked nose and mous-

FIGURE 6.30 Zanni, or Scapin. Etching by Jacques Callot, 1618–1619. Note the audience and performers in the background.

tache, and his trousers and jacket were ornamented with green braid. Other variations on this character included Buffetto, Flautino, Scapino, and Mezzetino.

Scaramuccia, another popular character, varied considerably in his attributes, sometimes resembling Harlequin, at others Brighella or the Capitano.

Pulcinello was always a Neapolitan, but his function in the plays varied. Sometimes he was a servant, or he could be the host of an inn or a merchant. He was a mixture of foolishness and shrewdness, villainy and love, wit and dullness. He had an enormous hooked nose, a humpback, and wore a long pointed cap. He was the ancestor of the English puppet character, Punch.

In addition to these common types, many other servants and incidental characters are listed in the scripts,

for each troupe tended to develop its own variations on the traditional approach.

In size, the troupes averaged ten to twelve members: seven or eight men and three or four women. A typical troupe included two sets of lovers, a servant girl, a Capitano, two *zanni*, and two old men (Pantalone and Dottore), but this pattern might be augmented or reduced according to the financial state of the group.

Productions were supervised by the leader or most respected member of a troupe. It was his responsibility to explain the characters, clarify the action, enumerate the *lazzi*, and acquire the properties needed. Although it is not clear whether the plays were actually rehearsed, pains were taken to see that each actor understood what was expected of him.

Most companies were organized on a sharing plan (under which the members assumed the financial risk and divided the profits), although some of the younger actors may have been salaried until they were granted full membership. The troupes traveled constantly, and at each new town they had to petition for the right to perform, a favor not always granted. Usually they hired large rooms in which to play, but they were equally at home on improvised outdoor stages and on indoor court stages. When perspective settings and elaborate effects were available, they were used, but the actors could perform just as easily with no scenery at all. Adaptability was one key to their success.

The *commedia* was most vigorous between 1550 and 1650, the period of the most famous troupes. The history of the various companies is often difficult to trace because of scanty records, frequent mergers and separations, and the similarity of names adopted by the troupes.

The first company of note was Alberto Ganassa's troupe which played in such diverse places as Mantua, Ferrara, Paris, and Madrid between 1568 and 1583. Eventually it was eclipsed in fame by the Gelosi ("zealous") troupe, which performed between 1569 and 1604. The outstanding members of the Gelosi were Francesco Andreini (1548–1624), originally an *innamorato* and later a Capitano, and his wife, Isabella (1562–1604), the most renowned *innamorata* of her day and a poet as well. After joining the Gelosi in 1583 they soon became its leaders and made it fashionable throughout Italy and France. They performed at the elaborate wedding celebrations in Florence for Ferdinando I in 1589 and were invited to France by Henri IV. The troupe disbanded upon the death of Isabella in 1604.

The Confidenti troupe performed between 1574

FIGURE 6.31 In the foreground characters of *commedia dell'arte* and in the background members of the French royal family. Seen at right are Pantalone and Harlequin. Painting attributed to Paul and Frans Porbus, 1572. Courtesy Bayeux Museum.

Italy, France was a second home, and troupes often traveled in Spain, Germany, Austria, and England. Wherever they went, they influenced native actors and writers.

By 1650 Italy had evolved the dramatic types, critical principles, and theatrical practices that were to dominate the European theatre for the next 150 years. The neoclassical ideal, classically inspired comedy and

FIGURE 6.32 Scene from the *commedia* play, *The Fairies, or the Tales of Mother Goose,* first performed at the Hotel de Bourgogne, Paris, 1697. Harlequin is depicted at center. From Gherardi, *Le Theatre Italien,* vol. VI (1741).

and 1621. Like others, it traveled widely, appearing throughout Italy, Spain, and France. Its many fine actors included Flaminio Scala, who published the oldest collection of *commedia* scripts. Because of internal bickering, the troupe declined considerably in quality after 1610. The Desiosi ("desirous") company played between 1580 and 1595. In spite of references to its high quality, we know little of its work. The Accesi ("flashing" or "inspired") troupe performed between 1590 and the 1630s, although its best work was done between 1600 and 1609 under the leadership of Pier Maria Cecchini (1575–1645), who played Fritellino. For a time, Cecchini shared leadership with Tristano Martinelli (*c.* 1557–1630), the first famous Arlecchino. The Accesi played in Italy, France, Austria, and Germany. The Fideli ("faithful") company was active from about 1598 until the 1640s. Its principal actors were Giambattista Andreini (*c.* 1578–1654), son of Francesco and Isabella Andreini, and his wife Virginia (1583–*c.* 1627/30). They made at least four trips to France and played as far north as Prague. In addition to these important troupes, others were patronized by the Dukes of Mantua throughout the seventeenth century. The most important troupes between 1650 and 1700 were attached to the courts of Parma and Modena.

The *commedia dell'arte* continued until about 1775, but never regained the prestige it commanded prior to 1650. Although it was always most popular in tragedy, opera, *commedia dell'arte*, theatre architecture, perspective scenery, indoor lighting techniques, complex special effects and stage machinery—all of these were to find their way to other countries, where they would be assimilated and adapted to local needs.

Despite these achievements, by 1650 Italy had lost its privileged position in Europe. As the seat of the Catholic Church, it had exerted profound influence on other western countries during the preceding 1000 years. Furthermore, its location had made it the bridgehead for trade with the East, and in turn this trade had brought it wealth and sophistication. In addition, under feudalism the small states into which it was divided could compete effectively with those elsewhere in Europe.

But during the Renaissance all this began to change. The schisms in the church weakened the position of Italy, especially during the time when the seat of the church was Avignon and after the many Prostestant secessions began. Although the papacy regained much of its prestige after 1550, its authority never equaled its influence of earlier centuries. In addition, as Mediterranean trade routes to the east were closed after 1453 and as new ocean routes were subsequently opened, Italy declined as a center of trade. With this decline went the basis of the wealth that had permitted Italy's ruling classes to patronize the arts and learning. This decline was not immediately evident, since Italy long remained a major banking center of Europe because of the capital it had accumulated through trade. Nevertheless, by 1700 Italy was economically a secondary power.

Italy also declined in political importance. In the tenth century the Holy Roman Empire had been revived as a confederation of German and Italian states. At times the emperor had attained effective control over subject princes, but during the fourteenth and fifteenth centuries the Italian states were almost totally independent of outside interference. Then, during the sixteenth century, Italy became a bone of contention among the strong nations that had developed in Spain, France, and Austria. For a time Spain gained dominance, and its troupes even sacked Rome in 1527. After 1559 Austria became the major force; most Italian states became dependencies of Austria until after 1850.

In the century following the Council of Trent the spirit of the Counterreformation motivated a final burst of creativity in church architecture and painting that produced the great baroque churches of Italy, including St. Peter's in Rome. In the theatre, the greatest of baroque creations was opera, which permitted Italy to remain a strong force in Europe's artistic life even after its drama had ceased to be significant. For the most part, however, Italy had become a backwater of Europe by the late seventeenth century. No longer important either politically or economically, Italy was forced to defer culturally to France.

LOOKING AT THEATRE HISTORY

In studying the theatre, the context in which we place events is crucial to our vision of their significance. This is well illustrated in Roy Strong's study of Renaissance courtly theatrical activities and festivals as reflections of royal power.

Through [festivals] the prince was able to manifest himself at his most magnificent in the sight of his subjects. By means of myth and allegory, sign and symbol, gesture and movement, festival found a means to exalt the glory of the wearer of the Crown. In such a way the truths of sacred monarchy could be propagated to the court and a tamed nobility take its place in the round of ritual. (p. 21)

For the modern reader the central thought tenet that motivated Renaissance court fetes is the least interesting *one. We can see them in retrospect for what they were: extravagant assertions of a mirage of power. They retain their fascination 350 years later only because through this alliance of art and power arose our modern opera and ballet and the theatre of illusion. In this century festivals have been studied seriously mostly as a curious ancestor of theatre, but they are in reality much more a branch of political history and thought. (pp. 247–248)*

ROY STRONG, *Splendor at Court: Renaissance Spectacle and Illusion* (Boston: Houghton Mifflin, 1973).

Accounts of ceremonies were often written to record the magnificence of court festivals. Much of our information comes from these books. Here are a few excerpts from Pavoni's account of the festivities accompanying the wedding of Christine of Lorraine to the Grand Duke of Tuscany in 1589. This section describes a mock sea battle staged in the courtyard of the Pitti Palace in Florence:

The courtyard was filled with water to a height of some five feet by means of underground water conduits . . . and . . . there entered . . . eighteen vessels. [Pavoni describes a sea battle between Christians and Turks, with the Turks defeated; then the Christians, still on their ships, attacked a Turkish castle at one end of the courtyard.] At last . . . rope ladders were attached to the walls by means of hooks . . . and other devices; and indeed many fell into the water. . . . [Finally] the Christians . . . won possession of the walls and the castle. And there, with many indications of happiness, songs, and dancing . . . they finished the festivities.

> GIUSEPPE PAVONI, *Diario descritto da Giuseppe Pavoni delle Feste Celebrate nella solenissime Nozze dell Serenissimi Sposi, il Sig. Gran Duchi di Toscanna* (Bologna, 1589). Longer excerpts (in a different translation) can be found in the Appendix to Glynne Wickham's *Early English Stages 1300–1660*, vol. I (New York, 1959).

By the late sixteenth century, Italian critics had set forth the basic tenets of neoclassicism. Minturno stated the fundamental concept that truth is unchanging, that it remains constant in all times and in all places:

[Some contemporary critics] are seeking to set forth a new art of poetry. . . . But if [Aristotle and Horace] have taught a true art, I do not see how another different from it can be established, for truth is single and what is once true must necessarily be true in every age . . . in everything Art abides by a law with which it is regulated and by which it directs everything.

> ANTONIO MINTURNO, *L'Arte Poetica* (1564), Book I, sections 32–33. Longer excerpts (in a different translation) may be found in Allan H. Gilbert, ed., *Literary Criticism: Plato to Dryden* (New York, 1940).

In 1571 Castelvetro reduced many of the tenets that were to dominate critical thought for the next 200 years to

strict rules. Here are a few key excerpts from his lengthy treatise:

Dramas do not show on the stage murders and other things that are difficult to represent with dignity, . . . such deeds should be done off stage and then narrated by a messenger. . . . A drama spends as many hours in performing things as was taken by the actions themselves . . . therefore tragedy and comedy . . . cannot last longer than the time permitted by the convenience of the audience, nor include more things than can occur in the space of time that the comedies and tragedies require in performance. . . . It is not possible to make the audience believe that several days and nights have passed when they have the evidence of their senses that only a few hours have gone by.

> LODOVICO CASTELVETRO, *The Poetics of Aristotle Translated and Annotated* (1571), sections 57 and 109. Longer excerpts (in a different translation) may be found in Gilbert, *Literary Criticism*.

One of the major sources of information about the *commedia dell'arte* is Perrucci's description of all aspects of the form. Here are some excerpts from his account of rehearsal practices:

The scenario is no more than the fabric of scenes woven from a plot, with brief hints of the action, divided into acts and scenes, which are to be acted extemporaneously by the performers. In the margins are indications as to where each character is to enter and . . . exit.

The manager or most experienced actor rehearses the scenario before it is acted, so the actors know the contents of the play, where the dialogue should end, and where new lazzi can be inserted . . . . he will plant the lazzi, . . . giving attention to the things needed in the play, such as letters, purses, daggers, and other properties. . . .

After the actors have been told what they must do . . . , they will be able to go through the scenes and rehearse new lazzi or material of their own invention. It is wise, however, not to depart from the plot so far that . . . the audience will lose the thread of the plot. . . . [Then] the actors ought to think about bringing in something . . . they have memorized for use in any play.

> ANDREA PERRUCCI, *Dell' arte rappresentativa, premeditata ed all' improvviso* (1699). Perrucci's treatise is most readily available in Enzo Petraccone, ed., *La Commedia dell'Arte, storie, tecnica, scenari* (Naples, 1927).

7

English Theatre from the Middle Ages to 1642

Because of wars and internal strife, England was scarcely affected by the Renaissance until the late fifteenth century. Since 1066, when England had been conquered by the Normans, its kings had also controlled extensive territories in France and had intermarried with the French ruling family. In 1337 England laid claim to the French throne, thereby precipitating a lengthy conflict (often called the Hundred Years' War) that was to continue until 1453. For a time England seemed to be winning the struggle, especially after 1415 when Henry V was named regent and heir to the French throne. But after his death in 1422 and the emergence of Joan of Arc in 1429 the English rapidly lost control. By 1453 England held only Calais in France. At about the same time a struggle for the throne of England began between the rival houses of York and Lancaster (the Wars of the Roses). The conflict continued until 1485 when Richard III was defeated by the Earl of Richmond, who united the dissident factions and as Henry VII founded the Tudor line that ruled England until the death of Elizabeth I in 1603. The Tudors brought political stability and a strong central government to England.

Under the Tudors the spirit of the Renaissance also began to be felt in England. Henry VII invited Italian Humanists to England, and they encouraged English scholars to study ancient literature and philosophy. The new interests soon affected dramatic writing. The oldest surviving English interlude, *Fulgens and Lucrece* (1497), by Henry Medwall, was written under the influence of humanism and produced at court. The new learning also began to alter the morality play, as can be seen in Medwall's *Nature* (c. 1500), John Skelton's *Magnificence* (c. 1516), and John Rastell's *The Four Elements* (c. 1518). All of these plays treat humanist subjects allegorically.

Humanism exerted even greater influence on drama through schools and universities. The key figure is John Colet (c. 1466–1519), who founded St. Paul's school around 1512. At schools that came under Colet's influence it soon became the custom not only to study but to produce plays, either Roman works or new ones written in imitation of them. Performances seem to have begun at Cambridge University around 1520 and soon thereafter became common elsewhere: at Eton about 1525, at St. Paul's about 1527, and at Oxford about 1535. Other important schools that presented plays include Westminster, Winchester, and the Merchant Taylors. Many of the plays were performed in Latin but others were given in English. The audiences were composed of students and invited guests.

Two of the school dramas are especially well known: *Ralph Roister Doister* and *Gammer Gurton's Needle*. Both are written in English but follow closely the techniques of Roman comedy. *Ralph Roister Doister* (c. 1534–1541) is the work of Nicholas Udall (1505–1556), Headmaster of Eton from 1534 to 1541 and at Westminster in 1555–1556. Heavily indebted to Plautus' *Braggart Warrior*, Udall's play shows the foolish posturings of a boastful coward and his discomfiture in his courtship of a widow. It demonstrates a command of dramatic construction far in advance of its time. *Gammer Gurton's Needle* by "Mr. S.," acted at Cambridge sometime between 1552 and 1563, fuses subject matter and characters similar to those typical of medieval farce with techniques borrowed from Roman comedy. It develops a series of misunderstandings (most of them initiated by Diccon, the bedlam or fool) between two neighboring households over the loss of a needle.

Despite classical influence, medieval practices and conventions continued to dominate English drama through most of the sixteenth century. Even the court interludes and many school dramas are more nearly medieval than classical in spirit and tone. Furthermore, the performers of interludes were for the most part professional players who acted both at court and for the general public, the latter of which was not much attuned to new trends. Aiming to attract a wide audience, the actors mingled elements of popular entertainment with subject matter drawn from many sources. Biblical stories were chosen for their romantic qualities, as in *Godly Queen Hester* (c. 1561) and *King Darius* (c. 1565). Foreign novels and chivalric tales were adapted in such plays as *Calisto and Melibea*, based upon a Spanish work. Classical myths were mingled with English historical and low-comedy figures in *Thersites* (1537) and *Horestes* (1567). The entire popular tradition is probably best summed up in Thomas Preston's (1537–1598) *A Lamentable Tragedy Mixed Full of Pleasant Mirth, Containing the Life of Cambises, King of Persia, from the beginning of his Kingdom, Unto his Death, His One Good Deed of Execution, after that Many Wicked Deeds and Tyrannous Murders, Committed by and Through Him, and Last of All, His Odious Death by God's Justice Appointed* (c. 1561). Although the play is set in Persia, many of the characters are mythological (Cupid and Venus), allegorical (Shame, Diligence, Trial, and Proof), or English (Hob, Lob, and Marian-May-Be-Good). It freely mingles the comic and the serious, ranges over a considerable period of time, and changes place with bewildering rapidity. The numerous bloody deeds, such as beheadings, flayings, and murders, are all shown on stage. As one of the most popular plays of the day, *Cambises* reveals much about the tastes of the audience that made a public theatre feasible. Its variety also illustrates the need for dramatists capable of unifying the diverse elements of which the interlude was compounded.

Many forces eventually shaped the great English drama of the late sixteenth century. One of the most important influences was the religious and political controversy that had raged in England from the time Henry VIII had broken with the Catholic Church in 1534. Following Henry's death, controversy became even more intense, especially after Mary sought to return England to Catholicism. During her reign (1553–1558) more than 300 persons were burned at the stake for heresy or sedition. In addition, Mary had married Philip II (1527–1598) of Spain, who after her death considered it a duty to remove the Protestant Elizabeth from the throne. In 1588 Philip sent what he considered an invincible fleet against England, not only because of religious differences but because the English were challenging Spain in the New World and were aiding the Netherlands in its attempts to throw off Spanish rule. The defeat of the Spanish Armada established England as a major maritime power. It is not entirely accidental that the period of great dramatic output in England coincided with the upsurge in national confidence in the late sixteenth century.

The 1580s also brought to a head the religious and political intrigues that surrounded Mary, Queen of Scots. Mary (1542–1587), who was descended from Henry VII, had been queen of Scotland (from the time she was one week old) and of France (in 1559–1560 as wife of Francis II), but had been forced by Protestant forces to abdicate the Scottish throne. In 1568 she fled to England, where she became the focus for Elizabeth's opponents and English Catholics. The intrigues surrounding Mary eventually led Elizabeth to agree to Mary's execution in 1587. Mary's death and the defeat of the Spanish Armada made English Protestantism relatively secure.

But these events did not end religious controversy, for English Protestants were divided into many factions. The best known of the dissident groups are the Puritans, who thought the official Church of England adhered too closely to Catholicism in its ceremonies and governance. They took an even dimmer view of the professional theatre that was beginning to take shape, and launched an attack on it. The first major assault came in John Northbrooke's *A Treatise Against Dicing, Dancing, Plays, and Interludes* (1577). This was soon followed by Stephen Gosson's *The School of Abuse* (1579). Both works railed in the harshest terms against the theatre as an instrument used by the Devil to encourage vice and to take people away from honest work and other useful pursuits. The attack was answered by Thomas Lodge in *A Defence of Poetry, Music, and Stage Plays* (1579), and especially by Sir Philip Sidney in *The Defence of Poesy* (1583), which argued that literature is the most effective of all human works in teaching morality and moving men to virtuous action. Sidney's treatise is also noteworthy as the first major statement in English of the neoclassical ideal. It was to exert a strong influence on writers of the next generation, especially on Ben Jonson (who sought to make English drama conform to classical and Italian Renaissance precepts). Although they were not able to suppress the theatre, the Puritans voiced the ideas that long dominated the governing councils of English towns, and for many decades theatre companies were to meet strong opposition from municipal authorities.

These religious and political controversies affected drama in several ways. Because drama had been used during the preceding reigns as a weapon, in 1559 Elizabeth forbade playwrights to treat religious or political subjects. In addition, she demanded that production of the medieval cycles cease. Although compliance with this edict came only gradually, it had been generally accepted by 1575. Consequently, drama in general was secularized. The Puritan attacks were important in focusing attention on the moral aspects of drama, and, though theological subjects were abandoned, plays continued to convey a strong sense of a moral force at work in the universe and in human affairs.

Among the influences on this developing drama was humanism as represented by schools, universities, and (perhaps most crucially) the Inns at Court: Gray's Inn, Lincoln's Inn, the Inner Temple, and the Middle Temple. Principally places of residence and training for lawyers, the Inns admitted young men, primarily recent graduates of Oxford and Cambridge, for further education. These wealthy and aristocratic students were taught music, dancing, and other graces, which were practiced in part through the presentation of plays. Most performances came during the Christmas "revels," which extended over a period of four weeks, but the Inns also gave many elaborate entertainments to honor their members, or on such special occasions as royal visits, or births and marriages in noble families. The audiences were aristocratic, well-educated, and abreast of the latest fashions in drama, both at home and abroad.

The first English tragedy, *Gorboduc* or *Ferrex and Porrex*, written by two students, Thomas Sackville

and Thomas Norton, was presented by the Inner Temple in 1561, with Queen Elizabeth in attendance. The subject, chosen from the legendary history of England, was treated in a pseudo-Senecan manner. The action is divided into five acts and treats the jealousy aroused between Ferrex and Porrex when their father, Gorboduc, decides to divide his kingdom between them. All of the principal characters eventually are killed and their fate is used to point a lesson for England about the dangers of leaving uncertain the order of succession to the throne. Although the play now seems weak, it made such a deep impression on educated men of the time that it had been printed five times by 1590. In comparison with earlier serious plays, it marked an enormous advance. The Inns also did much to popularize contemporary Italian drama. In 1566, Gray's Inn presented George Gascoigne and Francis Kinwelmarsh's *Jocasta*, a translation of Lodovico Dolce's *Giocasta* (1559), and Gascoigne's *The Supposes*, a translation of Ariosto's *I Suppositi*. Other plays given at the Inns show the contemporary interest in Italian novels and English history.

During Elizabeth's reign interest at universities and schools also shifted from classical drama to plays based on English history or recent Italian works. By 1600 the influence of schools and Inns had waned considerably, but by that time they had performed a crucial role by familiarizing students with plays of other times and places and with effective dramatic techniques. It was only when school-educated writers began to work for the professional troupes that English drama entered an era of true greatness.

THE UNIVERSITY WITS

During the 1580s all the strands of drama began to coalesce, primarily because a group of educated men, commonly called "the University Wits," turned to writing for the public stage. The most important of these writers were Thomas Kyd, Christopher Marlowe, John Lyly, and Robert Greene.

Thomas Kyd (1558–1594) is remembered primarily for *The Spanish Tragedy* (c. 1587), the most popular play of the sixteenth century. Its reception established the vogue for tragedy, previously given almost entirely for aristocratic audiences. In telling his sensational story of murder and revenge, Kyd places all of the important events on stage. But while the play ranges freely through time and place, it uses such Senecan devices as ghosts, the chorus, soliloquies, *confidants,* and the division into five acts. Most important perhaps, Kyd demonstrates how to construct a well-articulated plot to create a rapid, clear, and absorbing action. Although lacking in depth of characterization or thought, *The Spanish Tragedy* is a remarkable advance over preceding plays.

Christopher Marlowe (1564–1593), after obtaining a classical education at Cambridge, wrote a number of plays for the public theatre, including *Tamburlaine,* Parts 1 and 2 (1587–1588), *Doctor Faustus* (c. 1588), and *Edward II* (c. 1592). The focus in Marlowe's plays is on the protagonist, around whom an episodic story is organized to illuminate his complex motivations. *Edward II* was especially important in the development of the chronicle play, for with it Marlowe demonstrated how to construct a coherent story out of diverse historical events by rearranging, telescoping, and altering them to create a sense of causal relationships. Above all, Marlowe was a great poet and did more than any of Shakespeare's predecessors to perfect blank verse as a medium of drama.

John Lyly (c. 1554–1606) wrote primarily for boys' companies catering to aristocratic audiences. His most characteristic works are pastoral comedies that mingle classical mythology with English subjects. His is a fairy-tale world in which troubles vanish at the wave of a magic wand. All but one of Lyly's plays were written in the carefully balanced, refined, and somewhat artificial prose for which he is famous. Among his characteristic works are *Campaspe* (1584), *Endimion* (c. 1588), and *Love's Metamorphosis* (c. 1590). These delicate pastoral works established the tradition upon which Shakespeare built in *As You Like It* and *A Midsummer Night's Dream.*

Robert Greene (1558–1592) also wrote pastoral and romantic comedies, but his works are more varied than Lyly's, since he crowded many diverse elements into a single play. In his *Friar Bacon and Friar Bungay* (c. 1589) and *James IV* (c. 1591), stories of love and pastoral adventures are mingled with historical materials. Greene is especially noted for his charming and resourceful heroines, who, after wandering in disguise through a series of temptations, are rewarded in the fulfillment of their fondest desires.

Thus, by 1590, several dramatists who bridged the gap between the learned and popular audiences had appeared. Their successful blending of classical and medieval devices with compelling stories drawn from many

FIGURE 7.1 Illustration from an edition of Marlowe's *Doctor Faustus* published about 1620.

sources established the foundations upon which Shakespeare and his contemporaries built.

SHAKESPEARE AND HIS CONTEMPORARIES

William Shakespeare (1564–1616) is probably the greatest dramatist of all time. As a playwright, actor, and shareholder in acting troupes and theatre buildings, he was directly involved in more aspects of the theatre than any other writer of his day.

Shakespeare is credited with thirty-eight plays, some of which were written in part by others. Although difficult to date precisely, the plays have been given the following chronology by E. K. Chambers: *Henry VI,* Parts 2 and 3 (1590–1591), *Henry VI,* Part 1 (1591–1592), *Richard III* (1592–1593), *Comedy of Errors* (1592–1593), *Titus Andronicus* (1593–1594), *Taming of the Shrew* (1593–1594), *Two Gentlemen of Verona* (1594–1595), *Love's Labour's Lost* (1594–1595), *Romeo and Juliet* (1594–1595), *Richard II* (1595–1596), *A Midsummer Night's Dream* (1595–1596), *King John* (1596–1597), *The Merchant of Venice* (1596–1597), *Henry IV,* Parts 1 and 2 (1597–1598), *Much Ado About Nothing* (1598–1599), *Henry V* (1598–1599), *Julius Caesar* (1599–1600), *As You Like It* (1599–1600), *Twelfth Night* (1599–1600), *Hamlet* (1600–1601), *The Merry Wives of Windsor* (1600–1601), *Troilus and Cressida* (1601–1602), *All's Well that*

Ends Well (1602–1603), *Measure for Measure* (1604–1605), *Othello* (1604–1605), *King Lear* (1605–1606), *Macbeth* (1605–1606), *Antony and Cleopatra* (1606–1607), *Coriolanus* (1607–1608), *Timon of Athens* (1607–1608), *Pericles* (1608–1609), *Cymbeline* (1609–1610), *A Winter's Tale* (1610–1611), *The Tempest* (1611–1612), *Henry VIII* (1612–1613), and *Two Noble Kinsmen* (1612–1613).

It is impossible to do justice to Shakespeare in a short space, for no playwright's work has been more fully studied and praised. Thus, only a few characteristics of his dramaturgy can be reviewed here. Shakespeare borrowed stories from many sources (history, mythology, legend, fiction, plays) but reworked them until they became distinctively his own. Typically, situations and characters are clearly established in the opening scenes, and the action develops logically out of this exposition. A number of plots are usually interwoven, at first proceeding somewhat independently of each other but eventually coming together as the denouement approaches, so that the resolution of one leads to that of the others; in this way apparent diversity is given unity. The action ranges freely in time and space, normally encompassing months or years and occurring in widely separated places. This broad canvas creates a sense of ongoing life behind the scenes.

Shakespeare's large casts are composed of well-rounded characters who run the gamut from the inept and ridiculous to the commanding and heroic, from the young and innocent to the old and corrupt. Despite the enormous range of his characters, Shakespeare entered into most of them sympathetically and made them appear to be living individuals rather than mere stage figures. His penetrating insights into human behavior have remained valid for all succeeding generations.

No playwright uses language so effectively as Shakespeare. His poetic and figurative dialogue not only arouses specific emotions, moods, and ideas, it creates a network of complex associations and connotations that links the immediate dramatic situation with all creation.

Shakespeare was by far the most comprehensive, sensitive, and dramatically effective playwright of his day. He attempted almost all of the popular dramatic types and subjects of his time and in each instance gave them their most perfect expression. In his own day, nevertheless, Shakespeare's critical reputation was lower than that of Jonson or Beaumont and Fletcher. His fame began to grow in the late seventeenth century but it did

not reach its peak until the nineteenth century. Like most of his contemporaries, Shakespeare gave little thought to preserving his plays, which in his time were looked upon as momentary diversions (much as television dramas are today). Their survival may be credited in large part to the desire of Shakespeare's fellow actors, especially Henry Condell and John Heminges, to preserve his memory by publishing thirty-six of the plays. (This original edition, which appeared in 1623, is usually referred to as the First Folio.)

After Shakespeare, Ben Jonson (1572–1637) is usually considered the finest Elizabethan playwright. An actor for a time, Jonson began writing plays in the mid-1590s and by 1600 was the acknowledged leader of those authors who favored conscious artistry (that is, writing according to a set of principles or rules). More than any other English dramatist, Jonson turned attention to the classical precepts and sought to temper the excesses of native playwrights by recalling the practices of the ancients. Nevertheless, he was no slavish imitator of the past, for he frequently deviated from or altered classical principles.

Jonson gained the favor of the king and court, for whom he wrote more masques than did any other dramatist. His acceptance of a royal pension in 1616 made him the first "poet laureate" of England. Jonson also did much to change the English attitude about drama, previously looked upon primarily as mere diversionary entertainment, when in 1616 he prepared for publication a carefully edited collection of his plays (a practice which had been reserved by his contemporaries for poetry). In many ways, then, Jonson was the most influential writer of his time.

Of Jonson's plays, the comedies, especially *Every Man in His Humour* (1598) *Volpone* (1606), *The Alchemist* (1610), and *Bartholomew Fair* (1614), are now best known. The scope of these works is limited, for Jonson, concerned primarily with reforming human behavior, concentrated upon the foibles of contemporary types. Jonson's comedy is often described as realistic and "corrective" since the characters are supposedly based upon direct observation and are castigated for their shortcomings. Because Jonson does not arouse sympathy for his characters, the plays appear more harshly moralistic than do Shakespeare's. Jonson is also credited with popularizing the "comedy of humours." Since classical times it had been assumed that there were four bodily "humours" (blood, phlegm, and yellow and black bile) and that health depended upon a proper balance among them. In Elizabethan times, this medical concept was extended to human psychology. Jonson in particular attributed eccentricities of behavior to an imbalance of humours and created a wide range of character types based upon this scheme. Although the self-conscious use of humours waned after 1603, it continued as one basis for characterization until about 1700. Jonson also wrote two tragedies, *Sejanus* (1603) and *Catiline* (1611), both of which were among the most respected plays of the century (although they failed in the theatre).

Shakespeare and Jonson were surrounded by a host of less celebrated figures. Among the more important of these were George Chapman, John Marston, Thomas Dekker, Thomas Heywood, Thomas Middleton, and Cyril Tourneur. George Chapman (*c.* 1560–1634) wrote plays between 1595 and 1613, concentrating at first on comedy in the vein of Jonson and then on tragedy in the manner of Marlowe. In such plays as *May Day* (*c.* 1600) and *Sir Giles Goosecap* (1603), he mingled satirical and romantic elements with "humours" psychology to produce a moral comedy less biting than Jonson's. His most famous tragedies, *Bussy D'Ambois* (*c.* 1604) and *The Revenge of Bussy D'Ambois* (*c.* 1610), center around strong men of action who seem doomed to defeat. Perhaps Chapman's greatest fault lies in his diction, for it is lacking in variety and its figures of speech are often more distracting than enlightening.

John Marston (1576–1634) wrote his plays between 1599 and 1609. His preoccupation with man's imperfections is reflected in such comedies as *Histriomastix* and *What You Will*, and such serious plays as *Antonio and Mellida* and *The Malcontent*. In all of his works he lashes out at a world in which men have substituted their own desires for the Christian virtues, but he is most successful dramatically in *The Malcontent*, in which the discontent of the central character provides more effective motivation for the attack than is found in the other plays. Marston is also noted for his violent and original imagery, which influenced many of his successors.

Thomas Dekker (*c.* 1572–*c.* 1632) was generally content to please the popular audience. He wrote a vast number of plays, on many of which he collaborated with other leading dramatists of the day. Dekker tended to see humanity as essentially good and drew moral issues in broad strokes. His most famous work, *The Shoemaker's Holiday* (1599), depicts the unsophisticated world of apprentices and tradesmen, emphasizing only its pleasant aspects, in the story of an industrious tradesman who

becomes Lord Mayor of London. Like many of Dekker's plays, it appears to much better advantage on the stage than on the printed page.

Thomas Heywood (*c.* 1574–1641), like Dekker essentially a popular dramatist, claimed to have had a hand in more than 220 plays. He was especially good at arousing the pathetic emotions, but he seldom rose to those of tragedy. Today he is remembered primarily for *A Woman Killed with Kindness* (1603), which capitalized on the current vogue for plays about actual murders or other deeds of violence. Rather than basing his play on a specific case, however, Heywood captured the essence of the type in this story of a woman who, on the point of murdering her husband, repents and later dies of contrition because he treats her with great kindness after her confession.

Thomas Middleton (1580–1627) covered a range of moods and subjects second in diversity only to Shakespeare's. Like Shakespeare, he could enter into all characters and situations, but unlike Shakespeare, Middleton was often lacking in strong feeling or original insight. His early works are comedies, such as *The Family of Love*, *Michaelmas Term*, and *A Chaste Maid in Cheapside*. The last is especially noteworthy for its inventiveness, verbal wit, and vivid presentation of London life. Middleton came late to tragedy. With William Rowley (*c.* 1558–1625) he wrote *The Changeling* (1622) and *The Spanish Gypsy* (1623); his other tragic works include *The Game of Chess* (1624) and *Women Beware Women* (1625). In his serious plays, Middleton tends to show the destruction of a potentially great person through gradual corruption, but the tragic effect is blunted because the characters do not progress significantly in self-knowledge.

Cyril Tourneur (1579/80–1625/26) is unique among the dramatists of his time in seemingly accepting the world as inherently evil. In his three major plays, *The Revenger's Tragedy* (*c.* 1606), *The Atheist's Tragedy* (1611), and *The Nobleman* (1611–1612), he achieves a complete unity of mood through his handling of imagery, character, and events, but the overall effect is one of loathing and horror of life itself.

The plays of Shakespeare and his contemporaries display many technical similarities. Almost all use an early point of attack and follow a chronological organization, making little use of retrospection or of "messenger" scenes, since all important episodes are shown onstage. In most plays the short scene is the basic structural unit. Because they were written for a non-illusionistic stage, the plays are essentially placeless, although the locale is always specified in the dialogue when it is important to the action. The major concern is for developing action, in which time and place often shift rapidly. Tone also may vary frequently from serious to comic. Most of the plays are shaped in part by the belief in a moral order under which man is free to make his own choices but for which he is ultimately responsible to forces greater than himself. Although less obviously than in medieval drama, the characters are still caught in a struggle between good and evil. Much of this moral tone is established through poetic imagery, soliloquies, and *sententiae*, although the lesser writers resort to the straightforward statement of moral lessons.

JACOBEAN AND CAROLINE DRAMATISTS

Most critics agree that a significant change in English drama became evident around 1610. In part, the shift was one of subject matter, for the preoccupation with penetrating questions about man's nature and achievements abated in favor of interesting stories told for their own sakes. Thrills and excitement began to take precedence over significant insights or complex characterization. As tragicomedy increased in popularity, happy endings were contrived for otherwise serious plays, while the pathetic or sensational tended to replace the more genuinely tragic emotions.

At the same time, technical skill increased. The playwrights handled exposition more adroitly, compressed the action into fewer episodes, built complications to startling climaxes, and alternated quiet with tumultuous scenes. As a result, the plays of this later period are more skillfully contrived than those written before 1610, but they are often lacking in profundity. Of the many dramatists who worked between 1610 and 1642 the most important are Francis Beaumont, John Fletcher, Philip Massinger, John Webster, John Ford, and James Shirley.

By far the most successful of the new dramatists was John Fletcher (1579–1625), whose name is inextricably joined with that of Francis Beaumont (c. 1584–1616) because of the collection of about 50 plays published in 1647 and 1679 and attributed to their joint authorship. Although in actuality they collaborated on few of these works, between 1608 and 1613 they did produce a number of theatrically effective pieces—among them *The Maid's Tragedy*, *Philaster*, and *A King and No King*—that did

much to establish the tone and techniques of later drama. In many ways, *A King and No King* is typical of the trend toward sensationalism, for it depicts a brother and sister caught up in an apparently incestuous love, but the moral problem is resolved satisfactorily by the discovery that the lovers are not related.

After Beaumont's retirement, Fletcher continued to work alone and with others (among them Shakespeare, Rowley, and Massinger) and probably replaced Shakespeare as principal dramatist for the King's Men, the leading theatrical company of the time. He was one of the most successful playwrights of his day, for he knew how to shape every element in terms of dramatic effectiveness. His dialogue was especially admired by aristocratic theatregoers, who saw in it the epitome of the way they would like to speak. During the Restoration, Fletcher's plays were more frequently performed than those of either Shakespeare or Jonson. In later periods his *The Scornful Lady* (1616), *The Chances* (1617), *The Spanish Curate* (1622), *A Wife for a Month* (1624), and *Rule a Wife and Have a Wife* (1624) were especially popular. They were performed regularly into the nineteenth century.

Philip Massinger (1583–1639/40) often collaborated with Fletcher and he revised many of Fletcher's plays after his death. Consequently, it is difficult to distinguish their individual contributions. After 1625, Massinger became chief dramatist to the King's Men, for whom he wrote about two plays each year. Of all his works, *A New Way to Pay Old Debts* (1621/22) is by far the best known, since the role of Sir Giles Overreach, who goes from darkest villainy to madness and death, was a favorite with later actors.

John Webster (c. 1580–c. 1630) wrote many plays in collaboration with Dekker, Heywood, Middleton, Rowley, and others, but is remembered chiefly for *The White Devil* (1609–1612) and *The Duchess of Malfi* (1613/14), the Jacobean tragedies that rank closest to Shakespeare's in modern estimation. Webster's plays are flawed, however, by the obscurity of the action, which is always secondary to characterization. Because his protagonists are surrounded by corruption and do not themselves achieve any deep new insights, Webster's plays lack that sense of affirmation found in Shakespeare's tragedies. Thus, in spite of well-drawn characters and powerful dramatic poetry, they manage only to raise important issues without suggesting answers.

The plays of John Ford (1586–c. 1639) are usually cited as exemplifying the decadence that characterized Caroline drama, since *'Tis Pity She's a Whore* (1629–

1633) treats with apparent sympathy a love affair between brother and sister. Other significant plays among the seventeen attributed to Ford are *The Lover's Melancholy* (*c.* 1628) and *The Broken Heart* (*c.* 1627–1631). Scarcely noted in his own day, Ford is now admired for his treatment of essentially good characters caught in abnormal situations. His practice of illuminating evil by associating it with ordinary human beings has made Ford of special interest to modern critics.

James Shirley's (1596–1666) work is often said to be a precursor of Restoration drama, for his comedies, *Hyde Park* (1632) and *The Lady of Pleasure* (1635), depict the manners and fashions of aristocratic London society. Shirley considered his best work to be *The Cardinal* (1641), a tragedy similar to *The Duchess of Malfi.*

Many other writers might be cited, but these are the best known. Their work shows the trends toward greater polish and sophistication and decline in profundity. With the closing of the theatres in 1642, further developments in dramatic writing were postponed. Unfortunately, England has never again attained the heights reached between 1585 and 1642.

GOVERNMENT REGULATION OF THE THEATRE

The development of playwriting as a profession was made possible by the emergence of a public theatre that constantly required new plays. In turn, the stability of the theatre was heavily dependent on governmental regulations. When she succeeded to the throne, Elizabeth was faced with the challenge of gaining effective control over the numerous forces that made for divisiveness throughout English life. During her reign she slowly consolidated her power to the extent that the Stuarts (beginning with James I, son of Mary of Scotland) were able for a time to rule almost as absolute monarchs. The theatre was among those activities which the crown gradually gained control of, and since the attitude of the court was always more favorable to professional actors than that of local governments, the growth of the theatre paralleled the central government's assumption of authority over performances.

When Elizabeth came to the throne in 1558, any gentleman could maintain a troupe of actors. Any actor not employed by a nobleman was classed as a vagabond or rogue and was subject to severe penalties. Since even those troupes patronized by nobles were permitted to tour when not needed at home, actors were not always closely supervised and many illegal companies falsely claimed noble patronage or performed partisan plays that aggravated religious controversy. These conditions led Elizabeth to take a number of measures designed to bring order out of the chaos. In 1559 she banned the presentation of unlicensed works, forbade plays on religious or political subjects, and made local officials responsible for all public performances in their areas.

Since these regulations were not entirely effective, new measures were taken in the 1570s. The religious cycles, which had persisted in a few places, were now systematically suppressed. At the same time, actors were brought under closer supervision. In 1572, it was declared illegal for any nobleman below the rank of baron to maintain a troupe. Other companies could perform by obtaining a license from two Justices of the Peace, but since this license was good only in the locality where the Justices resided, a new license had to be secured in each town when troupes toured. On the other hand, the law specifically absolved licensed actors from charges of vagabondage, the indictment which had previously been used against them. The overall effect of the law was to reduce the number of troupes but to extend firm legal sanctions to licensed companies.

The authority of the crown was extended much further in 1574 when the Master of Revels, an official of the royal household, was made the licenser of all plays and acting companies. Technically, this move gave the crown complete control over the theatre, and any troupe licensed by it had a clear legal right to perform anywhere in the kingdom. Many local officials, however, believed that the crown was usurping authority which should reside with them, since they were responsible for health, conduct, and morals in their communities. Consequently, during the next thirty years local governments found many ways of evading the licenses held by actors. The most common reasons used in refusing permission to perform were the danger of plague, the rowdiness of crowds, and the drawing of persons from work or religious services. Even towns that had supported religious cycles resisted professional performers, and consequently without crown support, actors would have had little chance of survival. Around 1597, under pressure from city authorities, the crown seems to have agreed to a limit on the number of troupes but at the same time to have become firmer in its support of those that remained.

The Stuart monarchs, who succeeded the Tudor line in 1603, were strong believers in the divine right of kings and insisted on exerting authority more blatantly than Elizabeth had thought wise. In 1604 James I (reigned 1603–1625) took away the right of all noblemen to maintain troupes of actors. Therefore, between 1604 and 1642, all companies were licensed to members of the royal family. The new patents also specified the theatres in which troupes were to play, a provision which London officials seem to have accepted. Until 1608 all of the permanent theatres of London were outside the city limits, but after the crown assumed the right to specify playing places, companies began to move into the city, where at least five theatre buildings had been erected by 1642. The act of 1604 also deprived all provincial troupes of legal status. Although some companies continued for a time, the overall effect was to concentrate the theatre in London, except during times of plague, when London troupes made provincial tours.

Authority to supervise the theatre was delegated to the Master of Revels, who collected such handsome fees for his services that the office became a coveted one. Before the theatres were closed in 1642, he was receiving 2 pounds for each play licensed, besides 3 pounds a month and two annual benefit performances from each theatre. Sir Henry Herbert estimated that his income from this office just prior to 1642 was 4,000 pounds per year, an enormous sum for the time.

ACTING TROUPES

Although there were many acting troupes in England before the 1570s, little is known of them. For example, at least twenty different companies played at court between 1558 and 1574, but little information about them, beyond the bare mention of the performances, is recorded. In these early years, noblemen probably paid their actors a fixed yearly sum and allowed them to give public performances to earn additional money. Since the number of days upon which troupes could play varied with the place and season of the year, the actors led an uncertain existence.

During the 1570s, after new governmental decrees were issued, conditions for actors became more favorable, for it was probably the crown's sanction of daily performances that stimulated the building of permanent theatres in London and the assembling of larger companies. The first important troupe was the Earl of Leicester's Men, licensed in 1574. It was headed by James Burbage (1530–1597), also the builder of the first permanent theatre in London.

The next major troupe dates from 1583, when the Master of Revels chose the twelve best actors from several companies and named them the Queen's Men. This troupe was considered the best in England until 1593. The great plague of 1592–1593 forced many companies to dissolve or to amalgamate with others. Out of this crisis emerged two companies who thereafter were to vie for preeminence: the Lord Admiral's Men, under the leadership of Edward Alleyn and with the financial backing of Philip Henslowe; and the Lord Chamberlain's Men, a cooperative venture of the Burbage family and the leading actors of the company. When James I came to the throne in 1603, the latter company was renamed the King's Men, a title which it retained until 1642. Between 1603 and 1611 there were three adult troupes, and after that time four. Occasionally these were reconstituted or amalgamated, but all remained under the patronage of some member of the royal family. The more important troupes were Queen Anne's Men (1603–1619), Prince Henry's Men (1603–1612), Palsgrave's Men (1612–1631), Prince Charles' Men (1631–1641), Lady Elizabeth's Men (1611–1632), and Queen Henrietta's Men (1625–1642).

Royal patronage increased in still other ways after 1603. Elizabeth had seen an average of about five professional productions each year, for each of which she paid the companies a standard fee of 10 pounds. Although the Stuart kings paid the same basic fee, James I saw an average of seventeen and Charles I (reigned 1625–1649) an average of twenty-five productions each year. Thus, the income derived from performances at court greatly increased during the seventeenth century. Each actor in the royal companies was also paid by his patron a yearly fee of 5 pounds and he was given allowances for food, light, and fuel. Occasionally the troupes were given additional sums to buy new costumes or to tide them over during times when playing for the general public was impossible. In return, actors were called upon to help out with the court masques and to perform on special state occasions. Most court performances by professional troupes were given in the evening to avoid interfering with the public performances, which took place in the afternoons. Thus, the troupes benefited considerably from their attachments to the royal household. Since the plays given at court were usually those played for the general public, there was not that sharp division between the court and public theatres which characterized the Italian stage. On the other hand, some critics have suggested that increased concern for the taste of the court was partially responsible for the decline in vigor of the English drama after 1610.

Despite court patronage, companies relied primarily upon the public for support. But to produce the plays professionally required considerable financial resources. Most of the acting companies in the years between 1558 and 1642 were organized on the sharing plan, under which financial risk and profits were divided among the members. The number of sharers varied, for not all actors were shareholders. Originally the sharing system was probably used as a means of raising capital, but it later became a way of rewarding valued members of the company and insuring their continued service by including them in the management. Additional incentives were offered in some companies by making actors "householders," or part owners of the theatre building. Generous payments were also made to shareholders when they retired after a specified period of service.

The shareholders formed a self-governing, democratic body that selected and produced plays. Each shareholder also probably had some specific responsibility within the company, such as supervision of properties or costumes, business management, acting, or writing plays.

It is difficult to estimate the income of a sharing actor, for financial practices were complex. After each performance, the shareholders divided the money left after meeting all expenses (which included payments to authors, "hired men," and the fund out of which the "common stock" of costumes, properties, and other materials was purchased). In a court suit of 1635, one witness stated that shareholders in the King's Men earned about 180 pounds annually, although the actors themselves estimated their earnings at 50 pounds. Even the latter figure, however, is about twice the amount earned by skilled workers at that time. Undoubtedly the King's Men was the most affluent company, but so long as performances were not interrupted by forced closures, the major actors in all companies were probably well off.

More than half the members of each troupe were "hired men" employed under a two-year contract at a salary equivalent to that earned by a skilled laborer. In addition to acting, some hired men served as stage managers, wardrobe keepers, prompters, and musicians. The size of companies ranged from about ten to twenty-five persons; consequently, double casting was essential to fill all the roles.

The company was further augmented by boys apprenticed to well-established adult actors. It is normally assumed that boys played all of the women's roles, although this is by no means certain. Older women, especially the comic ones, may have been played by men. Little is known about the apprentices. The age of beginning has been estimated variously as from six to fourteen years, and that of termination from eighteen to twenty-one. The apprentices lived with their masters, who trained, fed, and clothed them. The masters were paid by the company for the boys' services. Some of the apprentices went on to become adult actors, but many followed other professions upon reaching maturity.

Most troupes sought to acquire a permanent home, and after 1603 most succeeded in doing so. Before that time and during forced closures, many had to tour. Companies often went bankrupt during closures, or, if they survived, they did so only by selling their stock of plays or by mortgaging their costumes.

Touring entailed many problems, for there were no permanent theatres outside of London. Thus, though it might have a license to perform, a troupe could be denied the right to play on the grounds that there was no suitable place, that the danger of plague was too great, or for other reasons. Upon arriving in a town, a company presented its credentials to the mayor, who usually requested that a performance be given before the council and other important persons. If the local group was pleased, it rewarded the actors with a payment from the council's funds and authorized additional performances for the public. Often the city hall was used for playing, but if refused its use, the troupe might perform in an inn or some other public place. In some cities, actors were welcomed, but in others they were paid not to perform. A number of troupes toured on the continent during closures, and it was from these itinerant English companies that the professional theatre in Germany descended.

Since companies both in and out of London changed their bills daily, they needed a sizable repertory. Plays were retained as long as they drew audiences and might be revised when they declined in popularity. The demand for new works made companies seek liaisons with dependable dramatists, many of whom worked under contract. Until about 1603 the average payment for a play was 6 pounds, but by 1613 the price had risen to 10 or 12 pounds. After about 1610, in addition to his fee, a playwright was given all of the receipts beyond a certain amount at the second performance. By the 1630s, a few writers were being paid a weekly salary and given one benefit performance for each play supplied to the company.

Once the playwright's fees had been paid, the play belonged to the troupe. Since there were no copyright laws, however, companies had no means of maintaining exclusive performance rights except by keeping plays out of the hands of others. The more popular works were often pirated by printers, and troupes sometimes sold publication rights during times of financial stress.

Every play had to be submitted to the Master of Revels for licensing before performance. The principal result was the elimination of passages thought to be morally, religiously, or politically objectionable. The company seems to have had only one complete copy of each play. In it (the promptbook) were made all necessary notes relating to performance: cues for sound, music, special effects, exits and entrances, and notations about properties. Actors were merely given "sides," which included only their own lines and cues.

Probably one of the shareholders rehearsed each play with the aid of the author, whose attendance was required, although his responsibilities are unclear. As a rule, a playwright knew in advance for which troupe he was writing and could tailor his work to the size of the company and to the skills of individual actors.

The prompter (sometimes called the bookholder or bookkeeper) was responsible for running performances, as well as for copying out the actors' sides and making lists of the necessary properties, costumes, and music. During performances a "plot," or skeletal outline of the action (indicating entrances, exits, properties, music, the names of players to be called, and similar information), was hung up backstage for quick reference. Seven of these plots have survived.

Each company had elaborate rules of conduct and fines for their infringement. For example, in 1614 Lady Elizabeth's Men agreed upon this schedule of fines: 1 shilling for lateness to rehearsals; 3 shillings for lateness to performance; 10 shillings for being intoxicated during a performance; 20 shillings for missing a performance; and 40 pounds for taking company property.

The names of many actors between 1558 and 1642 are known, but few performers achieved lasting renown. Richard Tarleton (? –1588), a member of the Queen's Men and an accomplished comic and musical performer, was the first English actor to win a wide following. The first great actor was Edward Alleyn (1566–1626), who created Marlowe's Faustus, Tamburlaine, and Barabbas, and Kyd's Heironimo. He gave up acting about 1604,

but continued in management with his father-in-law, Philip Henslowe. Other members of Alleyn's company were John Singer, Richard Jones, Thomas Towne, Martin Slater, Edward Juby, Thomas Downton, and Samuel Rowley.

The members of the Lord Chamberlain's Men gained more lasting fame because Shakespeare was one of their fellow players. The leading performer was Richard Burbage (*c.* 1567–1619), who created such roles as Richard III, Hamlet, Lear, and Othello, and was generally acknowledged to be the greatest actor of his age. Other members of the company included William Kempe (? –*c.* 1603), noted for his low comedy acting and jigs; Augustine Philips (? –1605); Henry Condell (? –1627); John Heminges (1556–1630), the business manager; William Sly (? –1608); Thomas Pope (? –1604); Robert Armin (*c.* 1568–1615), a celebrated clown; John Lowin (*c.* 1567–*c.* 1659), noted for his Falstaff and Henry VIII; Joseph Taylor (*c.* 1585–1652), who replaced Burbage when he died in 1619; and Nathan Field (1587–1620), considered by many as second only to Burbage.

In addition to the adult companies, there were a number of children's troupes. In the sixteenth century these were made up almost entirely of choir boys at court chapels or cathedrals. The boys were given a good education, and under the guise of training in elocution and deportment masters exploited their students' talents by staging plays, to which they charged admission. Following a scandal in the early seventeenth century, the use of choir boys in plays declined, but other school boys continued to make up the companies. Troupes of children were especially popular from about 1576 to 1584, and again from 1600 to about 1610. By far the best of these troupes was the Chapel Boys (after 1604, the Queen's Revels) between 1600 and 1608. The finest dramatists of the day, with the exception of Shakespeare, wrote for this company, which catered to a more educated and sophisticated audience than the adult troupes. The decline of child companies may be explained in part by the adult troupes' acquisition of both theatres and plays which had formerly been associated with the boys.

The acting style of the Elizabethan performer can only be guessed at. Some scholars have labeled it "formal" and others "realistic." Some of the conditions which suggest a "formal" style are the performance of female roles by male actors; the nonrealistic style of the scripts; the conventionalized stage background; and the large repertory, which would have made detailed characterizations difficult. Arguments for a relatively realistic style

FIGURE 7.2 The yard of the Tabard Inn, London. This sketch was made just before the inn was destroyed in the nineteenth century. Supposedly the yard had remained unchanged since the time of Elizabeth I. Although the Tabard was probably not used for plays, it illustrates the arrangement of the innyard in Elizabethan times. From Thornbury, *Old and New London*.

include Shakespeare's "advice to the players" in *Hamlet;* contemporary references to the convincing characterizations given by such actors as Burbage; the emphasis upon contemporary life and manners in many comedies; the truthfulness of human psychology portrayed in the serous plays; and the closeness of audience to actors during performances. Judging by contemporary accounts, many actors moved audiences with the power and "truth" of their playing, but this tells little about their style, for what is considered "truth in acting" varies markedly from one period to another. The most that one can say is that the better actors adapted well to contemporary conceptions of artistic truth.

THE PUBLIC THEATRES

In 1576 the first permanent theatres in England were opened. One, The Theatre, was an open-air structure designed for a general public; the other, the Blackfriars,

was remodeled from rooms in a former monastery for an aristocratic audience. It is customary to call structures of the first type "public," and those of the second "private" theatres. Both types were in use until 1642, and after 1610 the same companies might use both according to the time of the year.

By the 1570s there were two well-established traditions in staging: the outdoor and the indoor. The religious cycles, street pageants, tournaments, and morality plays had been given out of doors, and the companies attached to noble houses often played outside when on tour. On the other hand, mummings, disguisings, interludes, and special entertainments were normally given indoors; touring players often performed in town halls, manor houses, or inns. Consequently, there were many precedents upon which the Elizabethan troupes could draw when building permanent theatres.

The unroofed public theatres are usually traced from two sources, innyards and gaming arenas. It is certain that many troupes played in inns both before and after permanent theatres were built, and that at least six inns in London were used as theatres. The usual reconstructions of innyard theatres show a booth-like stage set up at one side of a courtyard, while the inn's permanent galleries provide seating on a raised level and the yard serves as a place where spectators can stand. The permanent theatre structures are then said to be a formalization of this arrangement. Recently some scholars have questioned the widespread use of innyards for playing, arguing that troupes normally played indoors. The principal arguments for indoor playing are that the use of the yards would have seriously disrupted the inn's normal activities, and that actors chose to play inside whenever they could. Certainly, all of the London inns known to have been used by actors were "carrier" inns (that is, they catered to drivers of wagons carrying goods to and from London). If wagons arrived at irregular intervals, closing off the yard would probably have interfered with this business. On the other hand, admission fees and the increase in tavern sales during performances may have been sufficiently profitable that the innkeeper abandoned the carrier trade or forbade drivers to arrive during playing hours. Although many of the performances at inns may have been indoors, especially during the winter months, some were certainly outdoors. Thus, the innyards could well have supplied a precedent for the permanent theatres.

The arenas used for bull or bear baiting and wrestling or fencing have also been cited as possible prototypes

FIGURE 7.3 A Renaissance conception of the Roman theatre. Note the several sides, galleries, and the label "Theatrum." This illustration from an edition of Terence's plays, printed in Lyons in 1493, was a possible influence on Burbage's The Theatre (1576). From Bapst, *Essai sur l'Histoire du Thèâtre* **(1893).**

influenced by gaming arenas or whether it influenced them.

Another possible source, less frequently cited, is illustrations published in editions of Terence's works. Some of these show open-air, galleried, circular structures labeled *"Theatrum."* Since the troupes were in the service of aristocrats and acquainted with many educated men, they may have had these illustrations brought to their attention and recommended to them as models for a playing space. Perhaps this explains why Burbage called his building The Theatre, a term not in common use at that time and certainly not normally applied to an amphitheatrical or round structure such as The Theatre supposedly was.

The stage itself is thought to have been derived from such diverse sources as the pageant wagons and fixed platforms of the religious plays and the booth stages of traveling players. The facade erected at the rear of the main acting area of public theatres seems to have much in common with the "screen" found in manor halls. It also bears a close resemblance to the Rhetoric stages then in use in the Low Countries. Thus, the possible influences on the public theatres are numerous, but no direct connection with any can be established.

The first permanent theatre was built by James Burbage in 1576 in Shoreditch, just outside the northern limits of London. It is usually assumed that the site was chosen to escape the London authorities, who frequently forbade performances within the city. But the choice may also have been influenced by the lack of available land in the city and the fact that Shoreditch was a popular recreational area. Regardless of his reasons, Burbage's decision to build a permanent theatre was revolutionary. It indicates a faith in the future of the theatre that was amply justified.

Burbage's success prompted others to follow his example. Not counting remodelings and reconstructions, at least nine public playhouses were built before 1642: The Theatre (1576–1597), The Curtain (1577–*c.* 1627), Newington Butts (*c.* 1579–*c.* 1599), The Rose (1587–*c.* 1606), The Swan (*c.* 1595–*c.* 1632), The Globe (1599–1613, 1614–1644), The Fortune (1600–1621, 1621–1661), The Red Bull (1605–1663), and The Hope (1613–1617). All were built outside the city limits, either in the northern suburbs or on the south bank of the Thames River. All but one was constructed between 1576 and 1605, and thus they predate the adult companies' practice of acquiring "private" theatres. After 1610 they came to be used principally as summer houses, secondary in im-

for the unroofed structures. Some scholars have argued that the theatres were formed merely by setting up a removable booth stage in an arena (which could be used for other purposes when not needed for plays). Such an argument depends upon the belief that baiting rings with multi-leveled galleries for spectators existed before 1576. That such was the case, however, is open to doubt. For example, the map views of London show baiting rings that appear to be more nearly corrals than galleried structures. Thus, it is uncertain whether The Theatre was

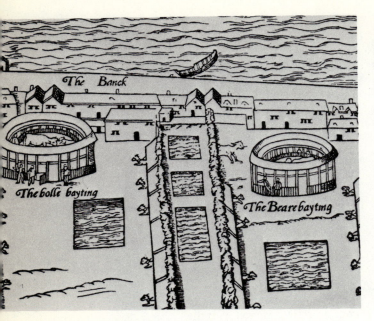

FIGURE 7.4 A portion of the Agas map of London (the sketches were made between 1569 and 1590, but not printed until 1631). Note that the bull- and bear-baiting rings appear to be more nearly corrals than three-tiered galleried structures.

portance to the private theatres used during the winter months. The most important of the public theatres were The Theatre and The Globe (because of their use by Shakespeare's company), and The Rose and The Fortune (operated by Edward Alleyn and Philip Henslowe).

Undoubtedly The Globe and The Fortune marked a considerable advance in design over The Theatre and The Rose. Some scholars have argued that all theatres prior to The Globe were multi-purpose structures with removable stages, because the theatre was too precarious a venture to justify buildings not easily adaptable to other uses. They suggest that The Globe, with its permanent stage, established the pattern adopted by subsequent theatres. Although it is impossible to verify that such a change occurred, it does seem likely that the public theatres were not uniform in design. Nevertheless, it is helpful to describe, insofar as possible, the typical features of the public playhouses.

Although the theatres varied in shape (circular, octagonal, square), their purpose was unvaried: to surround a playing area in such a way as to accommodate a large number of paying spectators. Most theatres had three roofed galleries, one above the other, surrounding the yard. At least some parts of one gallery were divided into private boxes or "lords' rooms." The other galleries, equipped with benches for seats, were undivided. The galleries encircled a large open area, or "yard," which was probably paved and may have sloped toward the stage to aid viewing.

The overall size of buildings varied. We know the dimensions of only one theatre, The Fortune. It was 80 feet square on the outside, and the yard was 55 feet square. Since the stage extended well into the yard in all theatres, no spectator was far removed from the performers. At The Fortune the stage was 27½ feet deep by 43 feet wide. This would have left an additional 27½ feet in front of the platform but only 6 feet on either side for spectators standing in the yard. The size and shape of the stage may have differed in other theatres, especially in those that were round or octagonal, but it is usually assumed that the platform jutted well into the yard and was viewed from three sides. A few scholars have argued that the galleries extended completely around the structure and that the action, therefore, was seen from four sides. The stage was raised 4 to 6 feet to improve the view for standing spectators and to provide understage space for trapdoors and special effects.

The stage in most, perhaps all, theatres was sheltered by a roof, commonly called "the shadow" or "the heavens," which served two purposes: to protect the stage from the weather and to house machinery and special effects. Thrones and other properties may have been lowered from it and such sound effects as thunder, alarum bells, and cannonades were operated within its attic space. In some instances, the sky, sun, moon, and signs of the zodiac were painted on the underside of the "heavens." In most theatres the stage roof was supported by two posts that rose from the front of the platform, but at The Hope the "heavens" were cantilevered so that the stage could be removed.

The rear of the stage was bounded by a multileveled facade. On the stage level, two large doors served as entrances and as passageways through which heavy properties and set pieces could be moved. These doors were the most essential part of the background because of their frequent and varied use. Changes of place were often indicated by the exit of characters through one door, followed by the entrance of others through the second. Usually the doors remained unlocalized, but at times they were used to represent houses, gates, castles, or other structures.

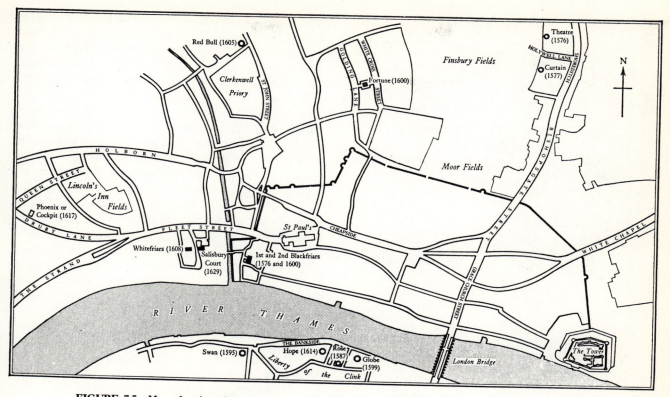

FIGURE 7.5 Map showing the location of London's playhouses. From Andrew Gurr, *The Shakespearean Stage, 1574–1642* **(1970). Courtesy Cambridge University Press.**

There was also a space for discoveries on the stage level. Most scholars have argued that the "discovery space" was located between the two doors at the rear of the stage. J. C. Adams calls the area the "inner below" or "study" and treats it as something like a miniature proscenium stage with a front curtain. He argues that it was used for staging interior scenes and that heavy properties were placed there and then revealed by drawing the curtain. Adams' view has been challenged by C. Walter Hodges and others. Hodges believes that the rear stage was a "pavilion" and that it jutted forward rather than receding into the facade. He argues that Adams' inner stage would be impractical because of its restricted sight-lines whereas a pavilion would be open to view from three sides. George Reynolds has suggested that the discovery space may have been raised slightly above the main stage and connected to it by one or more steps. He proposes this arrangement because of those scripts in which characters must go from one level to another

in full view of the audience, even though the theatre seems to have had no permanent visible stairway that connected the second level with the main stage.

Scholars also disagree about the permanency of the discovery space. Adams makes it an architectural feature of the building, while Hodges depicts it as removable. The latter theory has been adopted in part because the only surviving picture of a public theatre, a sketch made of The Swan in 1596, shows a blank space between the two doors of the facade. Furthermore, Reynolds insists that some plays require additional discovery spaces, and he suggests that in these instances structures similar to medieval mansions were erected on the stage itself. Richard Hosley has sought to reconcile all of the conflicting theories by arguing that the Swan drawing is correct in showing no separate discovery space because the area immediately behind each door could serve this function. Thus, he synthesizes many older views by suggesting that discoveries were made

FIGURE 7.6 Interior of The Swan Theatre, 1596. The original drawing, made by a Dutch visitor, Johannes de Witt, has not survived; this is a copy made of it by Arend van Buchell. The drawing was accompanied by a descriptive passage, which reads in part: "Of all the theatres, . . . the largest and most magnificent is . . . the Swan; for it accommodates . . . three thousand persons. . . . [It is] supported by wooden columns painted in such excellent imitation of marble that it is able to deceive even the most observant. . . . its form resembles that of a Roman work. . . ." Note the absence of a central "discovery space" and the human figures in the gallery above the stage. From Bapst, *Essai sur l'Histoire du Thèàtre* (1893).

have to be large enough to conceal such articles as a bed or table and chairs. Reynolds and Bernard Beckerman have shown that most properties were carried onto the stage or were "thrust forth" in full view of the audience. They also argue that the discovery space was seldom used.

Thus, historians agree that there was a discovery space in the public theatres but they disagree about its location, size, and use. The available evidence is insufficient to settle the controversy, although current opinion leans more toward Reynolds, Beckerman, and Hosley than toward Adams.

Similar arguments revolve around the second level of the stage facade. Almost all scholars agree that some type of acting space was located immediately above the stage doors. This space supposedly could be used to represent windows, balconies, battlements, or other high places. There is considerably less agreement, however, about the other features of this second level. Adams

FIGURE 7.7 J. C. Adams' reconstruction of The Globe theatre. Note the inner stages on both the first and second levels and the "musicians' gallery" on the third level. Courtesy Folger Library and Mr. Adams.

within permanent architectural units, that two simultaneous discovery spaces were always available, and that when no discovery space was needed it was "removable" (in the sense that the doors then reverted to conventionalized exits and entrances).

Another controversy centers around the use of the discovery space. Adams argues that numerous scenes were performed within the space and that most large properties were set up there while the curtains were drawn to conceal its interior. Other scholars believe that the discovery space was used only to establish locale and that virtually all action took place on the main stage. According to this view, the discovery space would only places a large bay window above each of the stage doors and between them a narrow railed area (the terrace or "tarras") backed by a curtained alcove (the "inner above") which corresponds to the inner below immediately beneath it. On the other hand, Hodges argues that the top of the removable pavilion (used when a discovery space was needed on the main level) served as a playing area. The drawing of The Swan merely shows what appears to be an open gallery on the second level.

Most historians agree that the second level was sometimes used as a playing area (as, for example, in the balcony scene of *Romeo and Juliet*). But they disagree about the number and kinds of scenes played there. One major theory about Elizabethan staging proposes a repetitive pattern in which the main stage, rear stage, and upper stage were used in orderly succession. Contrary theories hold that practically all scenes were played on the main stage and that other areas were rarely used. Leslie Hotson argues that the second level normally was employed to seat spectators. In each instance, the scholar's view about how the space was used dictates his attempts to reconstruct it, since he must make it sufficiently large in size and endow it with the facilities needed to accommodate the uses he proposes for it.

The stage facade in some theatres may have had a third level, although evidence to verify this theory is sketchy. Those who accept it usually call it the "musicians' gallery" because of its supposed primary use. If it existed, it may have been used occasionally by actors in scenes representing very high places.

Historians have paid little attention to the backstage space (or "tiring house") of the public theatre. Some reconstructions show this area as little more than a corridor, and virtually none make adequate allowances for storing the wardrobe, furniture, properties, and other equipment. Some companies owned adjoining structures that may have been used for storage and as dressing rooms. In general, however, we know little about the space used for preparing and maintaining productions.

Typically, modern scholars have depicted the public theatres as somewhat crude, half-timbered structures, although contemporary accounts speak of them as costly and sumptuous. DeWitt, describing The Swan in 1596, reports that the columns supporting the stage roof were painted to simulate marble. It seems likely that the theatres became more elaborate as the troupes became more prosperous. We would also do well to remember that the later descriptions of Elizabethan theatres as crude were written by admirers of the Italianate

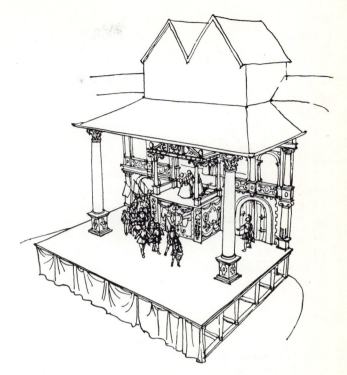

FIGURE 7.8　C. W. Hodges' reconstruction of the Elizabethan stage showing a pavilion at the rear. From Hodges, *The Globe Restored*. Courtesy of Mr. Hodges.

stage, to whom the disregard of illusionism seemed clear evidence of naiveté and simplicity.

Since few of the acting companies had sufficient capital to build their own theatres, most borrowed money to do so or rented theatres from those who had built them as a form of speculation. When Burbage built The Theatre, he borrowed money from John Brayne, a grocer who had earlier invested in a playhouse at the Red Lion Inn. Other speculators included Francis Langley, builder of The Swan, and Aaron Holland, chief investor in The Red Bull. Most important and successful of all, however, was Philip Henslowe, builder of The Rose, The Fortune, and The Hope. Henslowe not only built theatres, but often loaned money to the companies who played in them, and his surviving records of financial transactions contain our principal evidence about the operation of Elizabethan theatres. The pattern of ownership began to change in 1598, however, when the Burbages made Shakespeare and four other actors part owners of The Globe. The success of this arrangement led to its adoption at The Curtain, The Fortune, The Red Bull, and at some private theatres.

The owners, or "householders," were responsible for the upkeep of the building, payment of the rent on the land occupied by the building, and the salaries of the men who collected entrance fees. Although arrangements may have varied from one theatre to another, The Globe's division of receipts is usually taken as typical: the actors received all money collected for admission to the yard, while fees for entering the galleries were divided equally between the actors and the householders. Additional income was derived from renting the theatre to amateur actors, fencers, tumblers, and miscellaneous entertainers, and from the sale of various articles in the auditorium during performances. A major source of revenue for most theatres was a taphouse which dispensed beer, ale, and wine. The householders, and sometimes the actors, shared this additional income.

THE PRIVATE THEATRES

Although historians have usually treated the public theatres as those most typical of pre-Commonwealth England, it is likely that more performances were given indoors than outdoors in the years between 1558 and 1642. Many of these indoor productions were staged in manor houses, town halls, inns, or at court, but it is those at "private" theatres that are of major interest.

Many explanations have been offered for applying the term *private* to theatres open to the public. None is entirely satisfactory, but deviations from conditions at the public theatres help to clarify the usage: the theatres were roofed; they accommodated less than one-half as many spectators and charged considerably higher admission than did public theatres; they provided seats for all spectators; and they were lighted by candles. Other distinctions, based on location and troupes, may be of even greater importance. All of the early private theatres were located in the "liberties" of London. These areas —the principal ones were Blackfriars and Whitefriars— had originally belonged to monastic orders, but had been confiscated by the crown when the orders were dissolved in 1539. Although much of the property was later ceded to private individuals, the crown retained jurisdiction over the areas until 1608. Thus, though surrounded by the city of London, the liberties were not under municipal control. Furthermore, within the liberties the first theatres were set up in private dwellings, which were exempted from injunctions against playing. Perhaps most important of all, until 1608 the private theatres were used by children, who were technically amateurs and free from the stigma attached to professional actors. The most sophisticated playwrights, such as Lyly, Jonson, Chapman, and Marston, preferred to write for the boys' companies. Generally, then, the private theatres were more refined, exclusive, and expensive than their outdoor counterparts.

The first private theatre, the first Blackfriars, was opened in 1576, the same year in which The Theatre was built. At that time the boys' companies were still preferred by courtly and aristocratic audiences, perhaps because the adult companies had not yet attracted outstanding dramatists. Before 1576 the boys had usually given only one or two performances of each play; it was probably the desire to extend the runs to tap the relatively large audience of sophisticated Londoners that the Blackfriars theatre was built.

Since Blackfriars was one of the most fashionable residential areas, it was a logical choice for Richard Farrant, choirmaster of the Chapel Royal at Windsor, when he planned a theatre. In leasing the property, he stated that it would be used in teaching the children prior to their appearances before the queen; no mention was made of public performances. Farrant's concealment of his real intentions led to a series of lawsuits that put an end to the theatre in 1584. By that time, a number of different combinations of boys from various choir schools had performed there under a series of managements, Farrant having died in 1580. Although boys' companies continued to play elsewhere, no other "private" theatre existed until 1596.

By far the most important private theatre was the second Blackfriars, built in 1596 by James Burbage, whose lease on the site of The Theatre was due to expire in 1597. Though Burbage converted his newly acquired buildings in Blackfriars into a playhouse, the residents of that area secured an injunction against its use by an adult company. When Burbage died in 1597, he willed the Blackfriars to his son Richard, who was later to build The Globe. In 1600, Burbage leased the Blackfriars for 21 years to Henry Evans, who, in alliance with the master of the Chapel Royal, opened the theatre with a boys' company in that year. In 1604, after the accession of James I, this troupe was given the title "Children of the Revels of the Queen." Between 1600 and 1608,

FIGURE 7.9 A reconstruction of the second Black-friars Theatre, 1597. Note the curtained inner stages on both levels and the audience seated at the sides of the main platform. Drawing by J. H. Farrar. Courtesy the Architect to the Greater London Council.

the Blackfriars troupe was one of the most popular and successful in London, seriously challenging the adult companies. The willingness of the residents of Black-friars to accept a boys' company after rejecting an adult group says much about the disparity in contemporary attitudes about the two types of troupes.

Though popular, the Children of the Revels were frequently in trouble with the crown, usually for performing plays considered politically offensive. In 1608, James I became so enraged that he ordered the company disbanded. As a result, Burbage regained possession of Blackfriars. When the king's anger with the boys cooled, they were permitted to resume performances. They moved into a theatre that had been erected in Whitefriars about 1606 for another boys' company. They played there until 1614, and then moved into a new theatre in Blackfriars, Porter's Hall, even though they had been forbidden to do so. Probably because of this defiance, the troupe was disbanded in 1617. No more boys' companies were seen in London until 1637–1642, when Christopher and William Beeston ran a training company for youngsters (usually referred to as Beeston's Boys).

The private theatres were used exclusively by boys until 1610. After this time, the popularity of the children faded and the private theatres passed into the hands of adult troupes. The first important change came with Burbage's reassumption of the Blackfriars lease in 1608. James I now authorized the King's Men to play there, although because of a plague they did not begin until 1610. Their success led Christopher Beeston to convert a cockpit into a private theatre in 1616. Burned shortly afterward, it was rebuilt as The Phoenix. Occupied successively by Queen Anne's Men, the Prince's Men, Lady Elizabeth's Men, Queen Henrietta's Men, and Beeston's Boys, it continued in use until the Restoration. The Salisbury Court Theatre, built in 1629, was used by the King's Revels, Prince Charles' Men, and the Queen's Men. In addition, in 1629 Charles I had Inigo Jones convert the Royal Cockpit into a permanent theatre for the use of the King's Men when they played at court. (The plans for this theatre still exist.) Altogether, then, at least seven private theatres were built between 1576 and 1642.

The private theatres eventually became the primary homes of the adult troupes. The King's Men played from mid-October to mid-May at the Blackfriars and for the remaining five months at The Globe. Since the Blackfriars brought the company about two and one-half times more income at each performance than did The Globe, it is not surprising that the company preferred playing at the indoor theatre. As other private theatres were built, the public playhouses declined in importance although they were still regularly used during the summer months.

In terms of prestige and length of service, the second Blackfriars is by far the most important of the private theatres and has been the subject of most extensive inquiry. Irwin Smith's *Shakespeare's Blackfriars Playhouse*, the most detailed study of a private theatre, locates the second Blackfriars in a room measuring 101 feet by 46 feet, of which he assigns 35 feet to the tiring house, leaving for the auditorium and stage a space measuring 66 by 46 feet. Other scholars have thought the last dimensions, mentioned in a contemporary lawsuit, to be those of the entire theatre.

It is certain that the theatre had galleries (the number estimated varies from one to three), that there were some private boxes which could be locked, and that there were seats in the pit. Using as his standard the eye level of a person seated in the pit, Smith has estimated that the stage platform was raised 3 feet above the pit floor. (Hosley estimates the height as 4½ feet.) Smith's reconstruction of the stage facade is derived from J. C. Adams' study of The Globe and is open to the same objections. Nevertheless, most scholars, though they differ on details, agree that the stage background in the private theatres was similar in all important respects to that found in the public playhouses.

Estimates of the dimensions of the main stage at the Blackfriars range from 18½ feet deep by 29 feet wide to 25 feet deep by 46 feet wide. Thus, the measurements were probably somewhat smaller than those at The Fortune (27½ by 43 feet). The stage was open, having neither a proscenium arch nor a front curtain.

Although scholarly interest in private theatres has long centered on the second Blackfriars, because of its association with Shakespeare's company, it has begun to shift to The Cockpit at Court. Only recently has it been established that a set of plans (long known but little heeded) are those made by Inigo Jones when he converted the Cockpit at Court into a theatre in 1629–30.

The Cockpit was approximately 60 feet square; inside, the gaming area was octagon-shaped, and three sides of this octagon were converted into the stage. The king's box was located directly opposite the center door of the facade; other seats were placed in the pit and in two galleries shaped to follow the octagon. The stage was a semicircle, approximately 36 feet wide by 16 feet deep. It was backed by a two-storied facade stylistically reminiscent of the Teatro Olimpico, which had been designed by Palladio, an architect much admired by Jones. At stage level, there were five entrances; the largest, located upstage center, was arched and about four feet wide. None could be characterized as an "inner stage," although all could have served as "discovery spaces" from which properties or relatively small set pieces could be thrust out. The second level had only one opening (directly above the central doorway) that could be used as an acting space.

Since the productions given at the Cockpit at Court were imported from public and private theatres of the time, the features of this playhouse must have corresponded in all important respects with those found in other theatres. Consequently, some scholars now argue that Jones' drawings are the most reliable evidence we have for reconstructing all theatre buildings and stage practices of the period between 1576 and 1642. If this is true, the Cockpit at Court constitutes a serious argument against the notion that the Elizabethan theatre

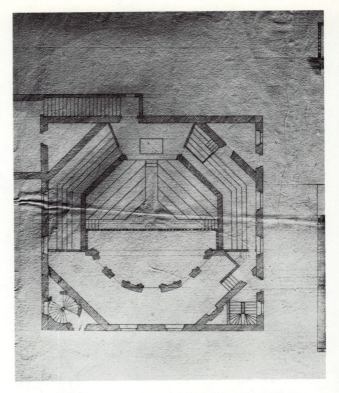

FIGURE 7.10   Floor plan of the Cockpit at Court. The King's chair faces the stage. Drawing by Inigo Jones. Courtesy Worcester College, Oxford.

had an inner stage and a complex acting area on the upper level.

SCENERY, PROPERTIES, AND SPECIAL EFFECTS

Although historians usually assume that the stage facade provided the background for all plays in this period, scenic practices are by no means clear. The principal sources of information about scenery are the play scripts, the accounts of the Master of Revels, and Henslowe's papers.

A number of scholars have analyzed the plays for scenic requirements, but their results conflict because they begin with different premises. One group assumes that the players relied primarily upon "spoken decor" (that is, they believe that places are mentioned only when dramatically relevant and because they were not scenically represented). Another group assumes that the audience would expect the things mentioned in the dialogue to be physically represented by some scenic piece. Probably neither of these views is correct. Reynolds' study of staging at The Red Bull concludes that the troupes were very inconsistent in their practices and varied them in accordance with available means rather than consistent theory. Nevertheless, all scholars agree that if scenic devices were used, they more nearly resembled medieval mansions than Italian perspective settings.

A recent study made by T. J. King of all plays staged between 1599 and 1642 shows that the following items were used on stage: banquets, tables, chairs, and stools; beds; carpets and cushions; hangings, curtains, and traverses; chairs of state and thrones; tents and canopies; altars and pulpits; stocks, scaffolds, and gibbets; biers, coffins, dead bodies, and litters; barriers and lists; chariots and vaulting horses; banks and caves; arbors, trees, bushes, boughs, and flowers. An inventory of 1598 preserved in Henslowe's papers lists similar articles: three trees, three rocks (two of which are "mossy banks"), two tombs, two steeples with bells, a Hell-mouth, a pair of stairs, Phaeton's chariot, a cage, a painted cloth showing the city of Rome, a stable, a wooden canopy, a bedstead, and other miscellaneous items. This list could be extended considerably by referring to other entries in Henslowe's diaries.

The Master of Revels' accounts of the late sixteenth century record items used for performances at court. When professional troupes played before the queen, the Revels office prepared a hall and supplied the necessary scenery. The items listed in the accounts include rocks, mountains, battlements, trees, and houses, all of which suggest that medieval-like mansions were in use. Numerous hangings, cloths, and curtains are also mentioned, but the majority of these were used to decorate the hall. Although staging at court was probably more elaborate than in the public theatres, the differences between them are unclear.

From the avilable evidence, however, it seems probable that Elizabethan scenic practices were adapted from medieval conventions. The large platform was essentially a *platea*, the identity of which could be altered by several devices. Most often treated as a neutral place, it could be localized either by the dialogue or by the use of set pieces such as trees, arbors, tents, altars, tombs,

FIGURE 7.11 Facade and plan of the stage of the Cockpit at Court, 1629–1630. The existing building was remodeled into a theatre for use by the public troupes when they played at court. Courtesy Worcester College, Oxford.

prison bars, beds, and thrones. Some scenic devices were so cumbersome that they were set on the main stage, where they remained throughout the performance, ignored except when relevant to the action. Other heavy pieces were revealed in or thrust forth from a discovery space. Smaller articles were brought on and off stage by servants as needed. Reynolds suggests that the number of set pieces employed in each play depended both upon the company's stock and the sequence of scenes, for the troupes suited their practice more to convenience than to principle. Neither audiences nor actors seem to have been bothered by inconsistencies.

The theatres retained and stored all scenic pieces, most of which could be used in a number of plays. There seems to have been no systematic attempt to increase the stock, articles being added at random. Thus, Henslowe's accounts show no regular payments to painters or carpenters. The scene stock was looked after by a "stage keeper," who was also responsible for the scenery, properties, and sound of each production.

Emphasis on spectacle increased after 1603 as the influence of the court grew. The actors could hardly have escaped knowledge of the Italianate conventions of the court masques, for professional troupes appeared at court on an average of from seventeen to twenty-five times yearly between 1603 and 1642, and individual actors were often called upon to perform speaking roles and to aid in the staging of the court masques. The boys' companies began to emphasize masque-like elements around 1605, and the adult troupes continued this trend when they took over the private theatres. The results were evident primarily in more elaborate set pieces, in the increased use of special effects, music, and dance, and in the more gorgeous costumes. But there was no attempt to copy the perspective settings used for the masques. Additional court influences are evident in the increased frequency with which characters were flown during performances and in the increased use of figures drawn from classical sources. The direction of change may be seen by comparing an early work by Shakespeare (such as *A Midsummer Night's Dream*) with one of his late works (such as *The Tempest*).

Music played a large part in English theatrical production from the beginning and was especially prominent during the years between 1558 and 1642. Incidental songs were inserted into many plays, and most performances concluded with a "jig" or some other entertainment involving music and dance. Trumpets sounded flourishes before entrances or to introduce proclamations, drums aided the battle scenes, and background music accompanied many episodes. The children's troupes offered concerts, up to one hour in length, before performances, a practice taken over by the adult troupes when they moved to the private theatres. Dance had a similar history. In the early days, it was designed to appeal primarily to the popular audiences and then became more sophisticated as the influence of aristocratic audiences increased.

COSTUMES

Because scenery and properties were used sparingly and because the actor was always of primary concern, costume

FIGURE 7.12 **A sketch allegedly made in 1595 of a scene from Shakespeare's *Titus Andronicus*. Some scholars argue that this is a nineteenth-century forgery. Courtesy Marquess of Bath.**

was probably the most important visual element in the Elizabethan theatre. Not only was it an integral part of each individual performer's appearance, it was crucial in such mass scenes as processions, battles, ceremonies, pantomimes, and masques.

The conventions that governed costuming between 1558 and 1642 differed little from those in effect during the Middle Ages. Most characters, regardless of the historical era in which they supposedly lived, were clothed in Elizabethan garments. Thus, by far the majority of costumes were contemporary dress such as was worn by persons in real life.

Other kinds of costume were used sparingly. The deviations from contemporary dress may be divided into five categories: (1) "ancient," or out-of-style clothing, used to indicate unfashionableness, or occasionally, to suggest another period; (2) "antique," consisting of drapery or greaves added to contemporary garments, used for certain classical figures; (3) fanciful garments used for ghosts, witches, fairies, gods, and allegorical characters; (4) traditional costumes, associated with a few specific characters such as Robin Hood, Henry V, Tamburlaine, Falstaff, and Richard III; and (5) national or racial costumes, used to set off Turks, Indians, Jews, and Spaniards. Although some of these costumes were conventionalized versions of garments from past periods, they were not historically accurate. With rare exceptions, even the "history plays" were costumed in Elizabethan dress.

Since costumes were seen at close range, the companies used authentic materials and fashions insofar as their finances permitted. Contemporary accounts mention the costliness and elegance of the players' costumes, and Henslowe's papers record numerous loans for the purchase of costumes, such as 7 pounds for "a doublet of white satin laid thick with gold lace" and 19 pounds for a cloak.

The troupes bought most of their costumes. Sometimes noblemen gave them garments, and frequently servants who had been willed their masters' clothing sold it to the actors. Occasionally the royal family made grants to the troupes to replenish their wardrobes. Since the actors relied heavily upon costumes, the acquisition and maintenance of a sizable wardrobe was important. Each company probably employed a tailor to keep the garments in good repair and to make new ones.

AUDIENCES

In the early part of Elizabeth's reign, the days upon which actors were permitted to perform varied considerably from one year to another. Then, in 1574, a royal decree proclaimed the right of companies to perform daily. This ruling remained in force until 1642 except for one modification—James I forbade playing on Sundays. But, even though it was legally possible for companies to play at almost any time, the actual number of performances given annually was considerably curtailed by forced closures attributable to plague, officially decreed mourning, certain religious observances, and unseasonable weather. It has been estimated that during the early seventeenth century performances were given on approximately 214 days each year (a total equivalent to about seven months).

Numerous devices were used to advertise plays. Posters were being set up within London as early as 1563, and handbills were in use by the seventeenth century. Occasionally a procession with drums and trumpets advertised performances, but this practice was largely restricted to companies touring outside London. Flags were flown from the roofs of London's theatres on the days when performances were to be given, and announcements of coming attractions were made from the stage during performances.

The capacity of the public theatres was large. Contemporary estimates suggest that about 3,000 persons was the average capacity, but modern scholars argue that it was more probably somewhere between 1,500 and

2,500. The private theatres probably seated about 500. Usually two or more theatres were open simultaneously in London, the population of which was about 160,000 persons. One historian estimates that the theatres normally played to half-filled houses.

To hold the interest of the relatively small theatregoing public, the companies changed bills daily and added new plays regularly. Henslowe's accounts for 1592–1603 show that the Admiral's Men produced a new play about every two and one-half weeks. In the 1590s a new play was performed once and then placed in the repertory, where it rotated with others until its popularity waned; the average number of performances given each play was ten. Between 1600 and 1642, however, many new plays were given several consecutive performances initially before being placed in the rotating repertory. The longest consecutive run, nine performances, was achieved by Middleton's *The Game of Chess* in 1624–1625. The number of plays in the active repertory at any one time also increased, rising from about 30 in 1600 to about 45 in 1640.

The usual starting time for performances was 2 P.M. so that spectators might return home before nightfall. At the public theatres, the plays were performed without intermissions, but at the private playhouses musical interludes often separated the acts. Wine, beer, ale, nuts, apples, cards, tobacco, and playbooks were all on sale, and the vendors of these items circulated freely during performances.

The theatres had no box office, tickets, or reserved seats. "Gatherers" collected money at the entrance to each of the three principal divisions of the auditorium: pit, public galleries, and private boxes (or lords' rooms). The public theatres catered to all classes, but the pit (or yard), which provided standing room only, was used primarily by the lower classes, while the public galleries, with their bench seats, were patronized especially by the middle classes, and the boxes were considered most appropriate for the aristocracy. By the end of the sixteenth century, a few spectators were being allowed to sit on the stage itself. As stage stools gained in prestige, the lords' rooms fell increasingly to prostitutes and others.

Some scholars have argued that after 1610 the private theatres catered to a sophisticated audience and that the public playhouses sought to attract a less refined group. The decline of vitality in dramatic writing is sometimes attributed to the companies' increased concern for the taste of those who attended the private theatres. But if the troupes expended their primary efforts

FIGURE 7.13 Entertainment given for Queen Elizabeth by the Earl of Hertford in 1591 at Elvetham in Hampshire. This is the second day's entertainment on a four-day visit. A crescent-shaped lake was dug especially for this water pageant. Queen Elizabeth's chair is at upper left. From John Nichols, *The Progresses and Public Processions of Queen Elizabeth,* Vol. II (1788).

on the indoor theatres, they did not abandon their concern for the public at large. The popularity of the theatre continued unabated until the playhouses were forceably closed in 1642.

In the late sixteenth century, admission to the yard was 1 penny, to the galleries 2 pennies, and to the private boxes 3 pennies. During the seventeenth century these prices rose to 2 pennies for general admissions, while private boxes sometimes cost as much as 20 pennies. Thus, at the public theatres the basic admission remained low, but the price of more desirable places increased considerably. At the private theatres, the lowest admission fee was 6 pennies, while a private box might run as high as 46 pennies. Consequently, in spite of their much smaller capacities, the private theatres regularly earned more money than did the public playhouses. Prices were raised on special occasions and were often doubled for premieres of new plays, perhaps because attendance at openings was much in vogue.

THE STUART COURT MASQUES

In addition to the public performances given for the paying patrons, many others open only to invited audiences were given at court. Most of the plays seen at court were presented by professional troupes who, though they might make use of scenery and costumes from the Master of Revels' stock, probably deviated little from the conventions they followed in the public playhouses. The court masques, on the other hand, introduced Italian ideals of staging into England and began that trend toward the proscenium-arch theatre that was to end in the abandonment of the facade stage after 1660.

Although masques had been popular at the court of Henry VIII, they were rarely given during the reign of Elizabeth, who contented herself with elaborate entertainments given in her honor by others. When James I came to the throne, masques were revived with ever-increasing splendor. Under James I an average of one masque was performed each year, and under Charles I this number increased to two, one at Twelfth Night and the other at Mardi Gras. The Carolinian masques were usually planned in pairs, one given by the king and the gentlemen and the other by the queen and the ladies of the court. In addition, the Inns of Court produced masques, usually in honor of the royal family or an important visitor or on some special occasion.

In *Splendor at Court,* Roy Strong uses such terms as "the theatre of power" and "the politics of spectacle" to describe the masque and other comparable forms produced at courts throughout Europe during the sixteenth and seventeenth centuries. In many ways, these productions symbolized the concentration of power in the hands of monarchs who saw themselves as ruling through divine right. Performances were more than entertainment: they were expressions of an entire political system in which the court considered its position pre-eminent and secure.

In England, as elsewhere, great sums of money were lavished on these productions. In 1618, James I spent 4,000 pounds on a single production, considerably more than on all the performances of plays given by professional companies at court during his entire reign. The most expensive of all masques, however, was given jointly by the four Inns of Court in 1634 to demonstrate their loyalty following an attack upon the theatre, and indirectly upon the crown, in *Histriomastix* by William Prynne, a member of Lincoln's Inn. This masque, *The Triumph of Love,* written by James Shirley and with scenery by Inigo Jones, cost 21,000 pounds. One of the participants, Bulstrode Whitlocke, preserved an account of this production so complete that it can still be reconstructed in all important details.

Considering the rewards both in prestige and money, it is not surprising that many leading dramatists (among them Marston, Chapman, Beaumont, Middleton, Daniel, Milton, and Davenant) wrote masques. The majority of the masques presented at the Stuart Court, however, were written by Ben Jonson and designed by Inigo Jones. Eventually, Jonson objected to the dominant role given to spectacle and after an open break with Jones in 1631 he was replaced by other writers.

The masque was similar in all important respects to the Italian *intermezzo,* since it was an allegorical story designed to honor a particular person or occasion through a fanciful comparison with mythological characters or situations. The text established a context for lavish spectacle. The serious speaking and singing roles were assumed by professional musicians, while the comic roles were played by professional actors. The major emphasis, however, was upon dance, which was performed by courtiers. This division in casting tells much about then-current attitudes towards actors: the courtiers refused to speak lines because they wished to maintain their amateur—and unsullied—status. Since courtiers were the principal performers, nonetheless, a minimum of dialogue was used in the masques so as not to detract from them.

Embedded in the masque's allegorical plot were usually three "grand masquing dances": an entry dance; a main dance, during which the performers usually went down into the hall to dance with selected spectators; and a "going out" dance. Many social dances of the period were incorporated into these productions, but the court dancing masters also invented elaborate symbolic formations. The dancers in a masque were all of one sex, except in those occasional double masques, in which equally balanced groups, one of men and the other of women, were used. Each dancer was usually accompanied by a "torchbearer" (that is, the carrier of a candelabrum) when the dancing took place in the auditorium. The torchbearers, usually young noblemen or children, often performed a special dance of their own. In addition, many productions included "anti-masques," first introduced in 1608 by Jonson to provide a contrast with the main story. Anti-masques introduced humorous or grotesque characters and dances, always performed by professionals. They also provided ample opportunity for the scenic designer to contrive striking transformations from ugliness to beauty.

The characters of the masques were usually either allegorical or mythological figures. The women might be goddesses, nymphs, queens, "The Beauties," or "The Graces." The men might be gods, ancient heroes, Signs of the Zodiac, "Sons of Peace, Love, and Justice," or

FIGURE 7.14 Inigo Jones' costume for a Fiery Spirit in *The Temple of Love*, 1635. Devonshire Collection, Chatsworth. Reproduced by permission of the Trustees of the Chatsworth Settlement.

form, raised about 6 feet above the hall floor, sloped upward toward the rear. A flat area was provided at the front for the performers, although they might occasionally go further back on the stage to that area reserved principally for scenic wonders.

The scenery, costumes, and special effects for most of the masques were by Inigo Jones (1573–1652), the first important English scene designer. Born in London, Jones went to Italy about 1600 to study, after which he worked for a time at the court of Denmark before returning to England around 1604. He designed his first masque for James I in 1605. He may have visited Italy again in 1607–1608, and certainly did in 1613–1615. In 1615, he was appointed Surveyor of His Majesty's Works, a post which he held until dismissed in 1643 by the Puritans.

Jones was thoroughly familiar with Italian artistic movements. At the court of Florence, he studied the work of Guilio Parigi, and his surviving copy of Palladio's treatise on architecture contains notes comparing Palladio's ideas with those of Serlio, Scamozzi, Vignola, and others. As the court architect and designer, Jones was the most influential English artist of his day. At his death, he willed his papers to his pupil and assistant, John Webb, who was to be a leading architect and scene

FIGURE 7.15 Inigo Jones' setting for Act V of Davenant's *Salmacida Spolia*, 1640. Note the "glory." Devonshire Collection, Chatsworth. Reproduced by permission of the Trustees of the Chatsworth Settlement.

representatives of various countries. The torchbearers might represent fiery spirits, Indians, Oceanae, or "antique" Britons. The anti-masques included satyrs, drunkards, gypsies, sailors, beggars, fools, and baboons or other animals.

The majority of Stuart masques were staged in the Banqueting Hall at Whitehall Palace until 1637, when Charles I had a "great new masquing room" built. All of the temporary theatres utilized a similar arrangement. Tiers of seats were set up along the sides and across the back of the hall. The royal dais was well back in the auditorium to provide the best view of the stage and to leave room forward of it for the dancers. Steps connected the hall with the stage.

The stages varied in size, but the average dimensions were about 40 feet wide by 28 feet deep. The plat-

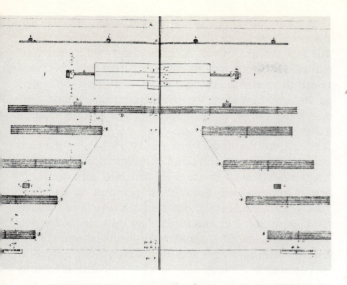

Between 1605 and 1610, Jones made other innovations. In 1606, for the *The Masque of Hymen*, the principle of the *periaktoi* was used to create a globe with no visible axle, which revolved to reveal eight dancers seated inside a "mine of several metals." In the same production, Jones suspended eight dancers in a cloud machine that moved from upstage to downstage. In 1608, for *The Hue and Cry After Cupid*, Jones made his first-known use of the proscenium arch and of scenery that parted in the middle to reveal another scene behind it. In the *Masque of Oberon* (1610), two sets of shutters were worked in grooves to reveal three successive scenes. After 1610 Jones tended to repeat the devices he had already perfected.

FIGURE 7.16 Inigo Jones' floor plan of the stage for *Salmacida Spolia*. Note the use of nested wings and back shutters, all of which could be changed by sliding them in grooves. This is probably the first instance of a completely changeable setting in England. Courtesy Trustees of the British Museum.

FIGURE 7.17 Jones' sectional plan for *Salmacida Spolia*. Courtesy Trustees of the British Museum.

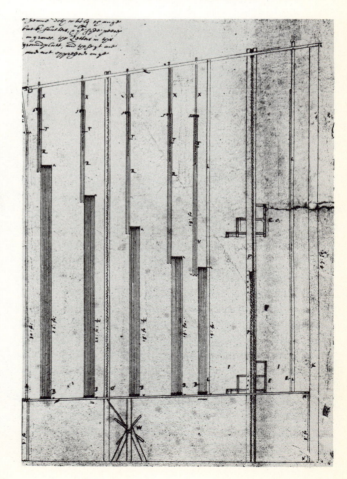

designer of the Restoration. Since William Davenant, one of the principal theatre managers of the Restoration, had written several of the last masques designed by Jones, and since Webb worked closely with Davenant after 1656, Jones also exerted considerable influence on Restoration scene design. To Jones, more than to any other artist, can be attributed the naturalization of the Italian ideal in England.

Jones' innovations were not all evident in his early designs, for some of the most important did not appear until 1640. Thus, it is helpful to examine the evolution of Jones' techniques. The nature of his contributions can be seen by comparing his designs with those used for the masques before he began his work at the Stuart court. The earlier masques had been staged with "dispersed decor" (that is, with mansion-like structures scattered around the hall). Thus, a new era began in 1605, when for Jonson's *The Masque of Blackness* Jones erected a stage at one end of the hall and placed all of the scenery on it. Furthermore, instead of mansions, he employed a perspective setting composed of angled wings and a backscene, all concealed until the beginning of the masque and then revealed suddenly by dropping a front curtain.

In the 1630s, however, he began to experiment once more. Perhaps his most important change was the abandonment of angled for flat wings. This innovation may have been made as early as 1634 but clearly was used in 1635 when Jones designed settings for Davenant's *The Temple of Love*. Jones' experiments reached their culmination in 1640 with Davenant's *Salmacida Spolia*, the last of the pre-Commonwealth masques. He set four sets of flat wings and several back shutters in grooves so that the settings could be changed rapidly. Thus, except for the chariot-and-pole system of scene shifting, Jones had by 1642 introduced into England all of the features that were to characterize the Italianate stage. When the English theatres reopened in 1660, Jones' practices were to triumph over those that had characterized the pre-Commonwealth public stage.

The extravagance of the court masques was one factor in the downfall of Charles I. Like his father, Charles I quarreled often with Parliament because he wanted to rule as an absolute monarch. From 1629 until 1640 he ruled without a Parliament. When financial difficulties forced him to call a session, Parliament declined to authorize any new funds until the king agreed to limits on his power. Charles refused, and in 1642 civil war broke out. Eventually Charles was defeated and in 1649 he was tried and beheaded.

Since the majority of the king's opponents were Puritans, the war also rekindled religious opposition to the theatre. The antipathy was intensified because all the acting troupes were licensed to members of the royal family. In 1642, Parliament used the disturbed state of the country as an excuse for closing the theatres for five years. When that time expired, the Puritans were in control of the government and they declared the closure to be permanent. Thus ended one of the most brilliant and productive periods the theatre has known.

LOOKING AT THEATRE HISTORY

One of the most revealing approaches to theatre history in any period can be made through reconstructions of its theatre buildings, either in drawings or scale models. Such an approach requires detailed information about the size, shape, and principal features of the structures. It also quickly reveals what we do not know, for in seeking to convert the available evidence into concrete visual terms we quickly learn that much information about the overall appearance, decorative detail, dimensions, and even the precise location of machinery and work space is often mere conjecture. Still, unless we can visualize the space in which plays were performed it is impossible to understand the theatrical practices of an age. In many ways, then, the attempt to reconstruct theatre buildings epitomizes the problem of the historian: how to make a meaningful whole out of the fragmentary remains of the past.

Because of the great interest in Shakespeare's plays and how they were originally staged, historians have been especially interested in reconstructing Elizabethan theatre buildings. Three examples of these efforts can be seen on pages 176, 177, and 179.

The principal visual evidence relating to English theatres prior to 1642 is reproduced on pages 176 and 180–181. In addition, two contracts for theatre buildings have survived, for The Fortune (1600) and The Hope (1613). Here are some excerpts from the latter, which describes a multi-purposed structure:

> [*The builder shall*] *set up one other Game place or Playhouse fit and convenient in all things, both for players to play in, and for the game of Bears and Bulls to be baited in the same, and also a fit and convenient tyre house and a stage to be carried or taken away, and to stand upon trestles good substantial and sufficient for the carrying and bearing of such a stage. . . . [He] shall also build the Heavens all over the said stage to be borne or carried without any posts or supporters to be fixed or set upon the said stage.*

Because it was so controversial, the theatre motivated numerous decrees, proclamations, petitions, and other documents during the reign of Elizabeth I. These public documents are among our most important sources of information about the theatre of that age. Most of the important documents are reprinted in two readily available sources: E. K. Chambers, *The Elizabethan Stage*, 4 vols. (London, 1923), and Glynne Wickham, *Early English Stages, 1300–1600*, 2 vols. (New York, 1959, 1972).

On May 16, 1559, Elizabeth issued a proclamation that effectively outlawed religious and political subject matter. In part it read:

> her majestie doth likewise charge every [official] . . . that they permit [no interludes] to be played wherein either matters of religion or of the governance of the estate of the common weale shall be handled or treated. . . .

On July 28, 1597, the Lord Mayor and Aldermen of London petitioned the Privy Council to suppress all performances in and around London, and they appended a list of arguments against plays:

> 1. They are a special cause of corrupting their Youth, containing nothing but unchaste matters, lascivious devices, . . . and other lewd and ungodly practices. . . .
> 2. They are the ordinary places for vagrant persons, masterless men, thieves, horse stealers, whoremongers, . . . contrivers of treason, and other idle and dangerous persons . . . which cannot be prevented nor discovered by the Governors of the City for that they are out of the City's jurisdiction.
> 3. They maintain idleness in such persons as have no vocation and draw apprentices and other servants from their ordinary works and all sorts of people from the resort unto sermons and other Christian exercises, to the great hindrance of trades and profanation of religion. . . .
> 4. In the time of sickness it is found by experience, that many having sores and yet not heart sick take occasion hereby to walk abroad and to recreate themselves by hearing a play. Whereby others are infected . . . .

Styles in acting are among the most difficult aspects of theatre to describe or define, in part because the same adjectives tend to be used in all ages but with divergent meanings. In most periods, the aim has been "to hold the mirror up to nature," but what is natural to one period is unnatural to others. The style of Elizabethan actors has been a source of considerable controversy. The evidence includes Hamlet's advice to the players (Act III, Scene 2), Thomas Heywood's *An Apology for Actors* (1608), and various comments by Ben Jonson and others. Here are some portions of a description of the excellent actor (attributed to John Webster, *c.* 1615). It suggests a realistic approach, but unfortunately we cannot be sure what that age found convincingly real and how its perceptions accord with ours.

> Whatsoever is commendable in the grave Orator is most exquisitely perfect in him. . . . He doth not strive to make Nature monstrous, she is often seen in the same Scene with him, but neither on Stilts nor Crutches; and for his voice tis not lower than the prompter, nor louder than the Foile and Target. By his action he fortifies morall precepts with example; for what we see him personate, we think truly done before us: a man of deep thought might apprehend the Ghosts of our ancient Heroes walked again, and take him (at several times) for many of them.

Salmacida Spolia (performed at Whitehall in January 1640), the last of the great Stuart masques, illustrates well the characteristic form. The subject was allegorical, as this summary by the author, William Davenant, indicates:

> Discord, a malicious fury, appears in a storm, and by the invocation of malignant spirits, . . . endeavors to disturb these parts [England], envying the blessings and tranquility we have long enjoyed. These incantations are expressed by those spirits in an Antimasque [composed of twenty ballet entries]: who on a sudden are surprised, and stopt in their motion by a secret power [Wisdom] . . . . This secret Wisdom, in the person of the King and attended by his nobles, and under the name of Philogenes or Lover of his people, hath his appearance prepared by a Chorus. . . . Then the Queen personating the chief heroine, with her martial ladies, is sent down from Heaven by Pallas as a reward of his prudence, for reducing the threatening storm into the following calm.

The scenery and costumes by Inigo Jones were typically lavish. Those for the third section are described as follows:

> . . . there came softly from the upper part of the heavens, a huge cloud of various colors . . . . which descending in the midst of the scene opened, and within it was a transparent brightness of thin exhalations, such as the gods are feigned to descend in: in the most eminent place of which her Majesty sat, . . . environed with her martial ladies. . . . The Queen's Majesty and her ladies were in Amazonian habits of Carnation, embroidered with silver, with plumed helms, baldricks with antique swords hanging by their sides, all as rich as might be, but the strangeness of the habits was most admired.

The final scene is depicted in the illustration on page 186. Davenant describes it thus:

> . . . the scene was changed into magnificent buildings composed of several selected pieces of architecture: in the furthest

part was a bridge over a river, where many people, coaches, horses, and such like were seen to pass to and fro: beyond this, on the shore were buildings in prospective, which . . . showed as the suburbs of a great city. From the highest parts of the heavens came forth a cloud far in the scene, in which were eight persons richly attired representing the spheres; this, joining with two other clouds which appeared at that instant full of music, covered all the upper part of the scene, and, at that instant beyond all these, a heaven opened full of deities, which celestial prospect with the Chorus below filled all the whole scene with apparitions and harmony.

The Dramatic Works of Sir William D'Avenant, vol. II (London, 1872).

8

The Spanish Theatre to 1700

As in England, the theatre in Spain flourished during the sixteenth and seventeenth centuries. In fact, the years between 1580 and 1680 were so productive that they are often called the Golden Age *(Siglo de Oro)* of Spanish drama. But the influences on Spanish drama differed markedly from those on English. Many of them are related to the Moorish occupation, which began in 711 and lasted until the fifteenth century. For almost 500 years the Moslems occupied all of the Spanish peninsula except the northern portion. The arts flourished in Spain during this period, since the Moors were far more advanced culturally than was feudal Europe. Their philosophers and scholars exerted strong influence on medieval universities elsewhere and their craftsmen were the envy of Europe.

Around 1200 the Christian kingdoms of northern Spain united to attack the Moors, and by 1276 had driven them from all but the southeastern portion. Spain was not to become a major power, however, until after 1479, when Aragon and Castile united under Ferdinand and Isabella. By 1492, these rulers had expelled the Moors entirely from Spain and had united most of the peninsula in a single nation.

Ferdinand and Isabella were also determined to Christianize Spain. In 1480 they instituted the Inquisition to hunt down and punish heretics. In addition to the Moors, all Jews were expelled from the country. Thus, while the Catholic Church was in general disarray else-where, in Spain it was able to establish and maintain a strict orthodoxy.

The influence of both the Moorish occupation and Catholicism are readily apparent in Spanish drama. The Moorish heritage can be seen in the attitude toward women and honor, while Catholicism is reflected in the emphasis on religious faith and doctrine.

Another important influence on drama was Spain's sense of its own position as a world power. Following Columbus' voyage of discovery in 1492, Spain became the dominant force in the New World; during the sixteenth century it acquired territory in northern Africa, the Netherlands, Portugal, Sicily, Italy, and elsewhere. By 1550 it was without question the most powerful nation in the world. By 1600 the decline of its empire had begun, although this was not fully evident until late in the seventeenth century. Nevertheless, in drama it was not decline that dominated so much as a sense of confidence, energy, expansiveness, and faith in God, church, and state.

THE RELIGIOUS DRAMA

Because of the Moorish occupation, religous drama in medieval Spain was extensive only in the northeastern areas. But as territory was recovered, plays were introduced in many places as a form of religious teaching.

FIGURE 8.1 Reconstruction by Richard Southern of an *auto sacramentale* in the Plaza Mayor, Madrid. It is based on a ground plan drawn in 1644. Note the two *carros* alongside a platform and the boxlike seating provided for the City Council and the Council of Castile. From *Le Lieu Thèâtrale à la Renaissance*. Courtesy Centre National de la Recherche Scientifique, Paris.

Until the mid-sixteenth century the Spanish religious plays were similar to those performed throughout medieval Europe, but after 1550 they assumed distinctive traits which they retained until performances were prohibited in 1765.

Perhaps because of the church's firm control over its content, Spanish religious drama grew in importance at the very time when it was being suppressed in other countries. Thus, during the last half of the sixteenth century plays came to be closely associated with Corpus Christi, a festival which emphasizes the power of the church's sacraments. Probably for this reason, the plays were labeled *autos sacramentales.*

The *auto sacramentale* combined characteristics of the morality and cycle plays. Human and supernatural characters mingled with such allegorical figures as Sin, Grace, Pleasure, Grief, and Beauty. Stories could be drawn from any source, even completely secular ones, as long as they illustrated the efficacy of the sacraments and the validity of church dogma.

Although production arrangements varied some-

what from one area to another, those in Madrid were typical enough to stand for all. Until 1550 trade guilds there were responsible for staging the plays, but at some time between 1551 and 1558 the City Council assumed control. Professional troupes were now employed to produce the plays, which were written by Spain's finest dramatists. Thus, after the mid-sixteenth century the connection between the public and religious stages was to be close.

By the end of the sixteenth century, production procedures had assumed the pattern that was to be followed thereafter, except for minor changes. Three *autos* were given each year until 1592, after which four were presented annually until 1647, when the number was reduced by two. The plays were sometimes new and sometimes old, except between 1647 and 1681, when all those given in Madrid were new and written by one author, Calderón. The plays were performed by a single company until 1592, after which two companies were employed. The troupes were chosen during Lent. In addition to being paid a sizable fee, these companies were awarded exclusive rights to give public performances in Madrid between Easter and Corpus Christi. After Corpus Christi, the actors also toured the *autos* to neighboring towns and performed them in the public theatres of Madrid as well. Thus, there were many incentives for the actors to participate in the festivals.

The plays were mounted on *carros,* or wagons, supplied by the city, which also furnished everything needed for the productions except the costumes and hand properties. Two *carros* were used for each play until 1647, when the number was increased to four. The two-storied *carros* were made of wooden frames covered with painted canvas and equipped according to instructions supplied by the dramatists. There is little information about the size of the wagons until the 1690s, when they were about 16 feet long by 36 feet tall. The facade of the upper story was often hinged so that it might open to reveal something within. Scenic devices might also rise out of the lower story, and many of the wagons included machinery for flying actors or objects. The *carros* served as entrances to the stage and as dressing rooms for the actors.

Until 1647 a portable stage (in the form of another wagon) accompanied the *carros* as an acting area. After 1647, when four wagons began to be used for each play, fixed platforms were erected at each playing place, since the portable stages were no longer large enough. Two *carros* were now drawn up at the back and one at either end of the stage, which was bare but equipped with trap-doors for special effects. The awkwardness of taking away the four *carros* used for one *auto* and bringing in four others for the next play led in 1692 to arranging all eight wagons around the platform throughout the performance. In the 1690s, the acting area was about 45 to 50 feet long by 36 feet deep.

Between eight and twenty days before Corpus Christi the actors were required to give a preview performance before the City Council. In some towns the first official performance was given inside the cathedral. By the early seventeenth century the latter practice had largely been discontinued, although in many places the first performance was still given just outside the church. There is no evidence that the plays were ever performed inside the churches of Madrid, and by the early seventeenth century even the performance in front of the church had been discontinued. Nevertheless, the *carros* were still included in the procession of the Host through the streets, and the plays remained an accepted part of the festival.

The City Council specified the playing places, often establishing so many that the performances extended over several days. After 1600, the first performance was usually given before the king in a palace courtyard. The plays were then presented in the square before the city hall, on one day for the Council of Castile (the most powerful of governmental groups), and on the next for the City Council. Several other state councils were also entitled to special showings and at least two performances were given for the general public. The *carros* were pulled from place to place by bullocks with gilded horns.

In addition to the *autos,* the actors also performed short farcical interludes and dances. Other performers were employed by the city to carry large carnival figures of giants and dragons about the streets and to perform the traditional dances. When the *autos* were finally forbidden in 1765, the reasons given were the predominance of the carnival spirit, the objectionable content of the farces and dances, and the undesirability of having religious plays performed by actors of questionable morality. All of these complaints had been voiced since the sixteenth century, however, and other reasons must have been equally important. Certainly interest had been declining since the death of Calderón in 1681, after which the *autos* became merely imitative of older works. The general loss of interest is probably also indicated by the abandonment of processional staging in 1705, after which

the *autos* were performed only in the public theatres. Regardless of the reason for their decline and prohibition, *autos* were an important adjunct to the professional stage for more than 200 years.

THE BEGINNINGS OF A SECULAR DRAMA

From about 1470 until 1550 the connections between Spain and Italy were close, and in these years the awakening interest in classical learning found its way into Spanish intellectual circles. In 1508 a university was founded at Alcala de Henares to encourage the study of Latin, Greek, and Hebrew, and this study soon led to an interest in classical drama. During the sixteenth century many Latin and Greek works were translated into Spanish and were widely disseminated through printing, which had been introduced into Spain in 1473.

By 1500 a secular drama had begun to emerge. Perhaps the most important early work is *The Comedy of Calisto and Melibea,* first published in 1499. A novel in dialogue rather than a true play, the edition of 1499 consisted of sixteen acts, but these were increased to twenty-one in the edition of 1502. Usually attributed to Fernando de Rojas (*c.* 1465–*c.* 1541), it may contain

FIGURE 8.2 Frontispiece to an edition of *Calisto and Melibea* published in Toledo in 1538.

sections written by others. Although *Calisto and Melibea* was not performed, it was so widely read that it influenced later writers through its examples of lifelike characters and situations. Especially famous were the low-life scenes portraying La Celestina, the go-between in the love affair of Calisto and Melibea.

Juan del Encina (1469–1529) is often called the founder of Spanish drama, since his early works predate *Calisto and Melibea*. After studying with the great Spanish humanist, Nebrija, Encina turned to writing "eclogues" in the manner of the Italian pastoral drama. But his early plays, dating from the 1490s, were still essentially religious, and it was not until he went to live in Italy that he turned to more purely secular works, such as *The Eclogue of Placida and Victoriano* (1513). His relatively simple plays were the first Spanish secular dramas to be performed. Bartolemé de Torres Naharro (c. 1480–c. 1530) at first imitated Encina's work but went on to write much more sophisticated farces and comedies. Like Encina, he lived for a time in Italy, where his plays were performed before being published in Spain in 1517 under the title *Propalladia*. The structure of Naharro's plays is primitive, for without the prologues the action of many would be unintelligible. His fluent verse and topical satire, however, won him a wide reading public. Gil Vicente (c. 1465–c. 1539) wrote primarily for the Portuguese court, but many of his plays were in Spanish. He is generally considered superior to his contemporaries because of his considerable lyrical gift, great range, comic sense, and spontaneity.

In addition to these native works, Italian plays were being performed with Italianate scenery at the Spanish court by 1548. All of the early secular drama in Spain was aimed at an aristocratic audience, and its influence on the professional theatre was negligible. Nevertheless, these plays established a foundation which later Spanish dramatists recognized as the source of their own practices.

THE EARLY PROFESSIONAL THEATRE IN SPAIN

As in other countries, in Spain the early history of professional playing is obscure. It is clear, nevertheless, that by 1454 actors were being paid to perform at Corpus Christi. In 1539, six men were employed to perform farces at the Cathedral in Toledo, and in 1529, 1535, and 1538 Italian companies appeared in Spain. Not until the 1540s, however, are notices concerning professional actors common. Although most of these relate to Corpus Christi festivities, it is clear that by 1550 a number of troupes were in existence.

The first important figure of the Spanish professional theatre is Lope de Rueda (c. 1510–c. 1565), of whom the first notice is found in 1542, when he appeared in religious plays at Seville. By 1551 he was sufficiently well known to be summoned by the governors of Vallodolid, then the capital of Spain, to perform before Philip II. From 1552 until 1558, Rueda was employed there at a considerable annual salary to supervise the Corpus Christi festivities. In addition, he performed frequently at court and toured widely. Rueda was also the first important writer of plays for popular audiences. A number of his works, including *The Frauds, Medora, Armelina,* and *Eufemia,* have survived. In their earthy humor and picturesque dialogue, they resemble medieval farces. Fools and simpletons (roles played by Rueda) are the most fully developed characters.

Cervantes states that Rueda's stage consisted of four or five boards set on benches backed with a blanket and that his costumes were "four white sheepskins trimmed with gilded leather." This statement has often been accepted as an accurate description of the professional theatre during Rueda's time. Even a cursory examination of contemporary records, however, will show that Cervantes oversimplified the situation, not surprisingly since he was recalling after fifty years a performance which he had seen as a boy. Rueda's contracts required him to supply costumes of silk and velvet for Corpus Christi productions, and it seems unlikely that he did not use them at other times, especially for his numerous court appearances. Probably Cervantes saw one of Rueda's clownish comedies, for which sheepskins and a crude background would have been appropriate.

No permanent theatres existed during Rueda's lifetime. Sometimes he acted in courtyards, sometimes indoors, sometimes in city squares, sometimes at court, for like his English and Italian counterparts, he could adapt to many conditions. Although Rueda is now almost universally considered the founder of the Spanish professional theatre, in actuality he was merely the most successful performer of his day. Nevertheless, it is his work which epitomizes the early years.

The popularity of the theatre mushroomed in the 1570s. Actors were welcomed throughout the country and permanent theatres began to appear. The major theatrical centers were Madrid (the capital of Spain after 1560) and Seville, but Barcelona, Valencia, Granada, Cordova, and other cities also boasted troupes.

Although the demand for new plays increased rapidly after Rueda's death, no writer of importance appeared until about 1590, when Lope de Vega began to write regularly for the stage. Between 1565 and 1590 plays were contrived primarily by the directors of theatrical companies, a fact which led to the continuing designation throughout the seventeenth century of managers as *autores de comedias* (or authors of plays). In these years, two dramatists—Cueva and Cervantes—achieved a measure of fame. Juan de la Cueva (1550–1610), working in Seville, was one of the first dramatists to draw on Spanish history in plays such as *The Seven Children of Lara*. He also wrote on classical subjects and on themes from everyday life. Miguel de Cervantes (1547–1616), remembered principally for his picaresque novel *Don Quixote,* also wrote about thirty plays, sixteen of which survive. The best of these are *The Siege of Numancia,* about a Roman attack on a Spanish town; *The Traffic of Argel,* concerning men captured by Algerian pirates; and *The Fortunate Ruffian,* a play of contemporary Spanish life. But Cervantes' plays, most of which were written between 1580 and 1600, came to seem stilted after Lope de Vega's works appeared.

By the end of the sixteenth century, several dramatic types had become popular. Since Spanish terminology is unique, a brief summary will facilitate later discussions. *Comedia* was used to describe any full-length play, whether serious or comic; most were divided into three acts, for the five-act form was never widely adopted in Spain. There were two major kinds of *comedias: capa y espada,* or "cape and sword," a name derived from the popular dress of gentlemen of minor ranks about whom the plays revolve; and *teatro, ruido* ("noise"), or *cuerpo* ("corpse"), terms applied to plays in which rulers, nobles, mythological characters, or saints are involved in actions set in remote places or periods. Until about 1615, every performance began with a *loa* ("compliment"), or prologue, which took the form either of a monologue or of a short dramatic sketch. It was designed to gain the good will of the audience, and it usually included singing and dancing. Although it declined in popularity after 1615, the *loa* was not abandoned for many years. *Entreméses* ("interludes"), or short topical sketches, were performed in the intervals between the acts of plays. Some *entreméses* were sung, others were spoken, and still others mingled speech and song. Around 1650, the term *sainete* came

into use for many short farces which earlier would have been called *entreméses*. Most Spanish dramatists wrote all of these forms.

LOPE DE VEGA AND HIS CONTEMPORARIES

By far the most prolific Spanish playwright was Lope Félix de Vega Carpio (1562–1635), whose personal life was as flamboyant as the plays he wrote. He was a member of the Spanish Armada, secretary to a nobleman, participant in many business and love affairs, and, after 1614, a priest. In spite of his many activities, he declared in 1609 that he had written 483 *comedias*. Estimates of his total output run as high as 1,800 plays, of which more than 450 have survived. Some were written in a couple of days, and near the end of his life Lope was regularly turning out two plays a week.

It is difficult to assess the quality of Lope's work because of its quantity. Nevertheless, some broad generalizations are possible. Above all, his plays are notable for clearly defined actions which arouse and maintain suspense. Many revolve around the conflicting claims of love and honor, a theme which Lope popularized and bequeathed to virtually all succeeding Spanish drama. Since he disliked unhappy endings, Lope usually found means for resolving conflicts happily. His characters include representatives of practically every rank and condition of mankind, into all of which Lope entered sympathetically. The female roles are among his best. He also extended the scope of the *gracioso,* or simpleton, a standard character in the plays of the day. Lope's dialogue is natural, lively, and appropriate; it ranges through many verse forms, for Spanish dramatists never developed an equivalent to English blank verse. In spite of Lope's achievements, however, he cannot be ranked with Shakespeare, to whom he is often compared. He never penetrates deeply into human nature, and the darker side of life is always glossed over in happy endings. Although the plays produce many surprises, they offer few new insights; they celebrate the variety of life without exploring its significance.

Lope was by far the most popular writer of his age. To modern audiences, his most appealing work is perhaps *Fuente Ovejuna (The Sheep Well, c.* 1614), in which a tyrannous feudal lord is killed by villagers, who refuse to confess even under torture and are saved by the intervention of the king. Many critics have seen revolutionary sentiments in the play, although it is more likely that Lope was praising the king for abolishing the feudal system. Among the best of Lope's lighter "cape and sword" plays are *The Gardener's Dog* (c. 1615), *Madrid Steel* (1603), and *A Certainty for a Doubt* (c. 1625).

Although Lope is now acknowledged to have been the foremost Spanish playwright of his time, he was surrounded by a host of lesser figures. The most important of these were Guillén de Castro, Tirso de Molina, and Juan Ruiz de Alarcón. Guillén de Castro (1569–1631), a friend and follower of Lope, wrote a number of plays but is now remembered almost entirely for his *Las Mocedades del Cid (The Youthful Adventures of the Cid)*, which was to serve as the basis for Corneille's *Le Cid*. Tirso de Molina (c. 1584–1648), a friar who gave up writing for the stage in 1625 following a rebuke from the Council of Castile, is said to have written about 400 plays, of which 80 survive. By far the most famous of these is *El Burlador de Sevilla (The Trickster of Seville)*, the first dramatic treatment of the Don Juan story. Juan Ruiz de Alarcón (c. 1581–1639), born in Mexico and educated in Spain, where he worked for the government, wrote 30 plays, in which he sought perfect finish at a time when other dramatists were noted for their facility. His best plays center around court life in Madrid. The finest is *La Verdad Sospechosa (The Suspicious Truth,* 1628), which explores the complications arising from the inability of a young man to tell the truth. In his plays, Alarcón makes characterization and subtle moral sentiments the bases of dramatic action.

CALDERON AND HIS CONTEMPORARIES

Before Lope de Vega died, his preeminence had been challenged by another writer, Calderón, who was to be ranked above Lope by many critics. Unlike Lope and his contemporaries, who were associated principally with the public theatres, Calderón and the best dramatists of his time wrote primarily for the court theatre. In this shift, many historians have seen a major cause of the decline of Spanish drama after 1650.

Pedro Calderón de la Barca (1600–1681), the son of a court official, received a university education and then entered the service of a nobleman. In 1651, after a series of personal disasters, Calderón became a priest, although he continued to write *autos sacramentales* for the city of Madrid and occasional plays for the court. Of his approximately 200 plays, about 100 have survived. Eighty of these are *autos*.

Calderón wrote practically all of his best secular plays between 1622 and 1640. These fall into two major categories: the "cape and sword" comedies, such as *The Phantom Lady* (1629), which depend on happily resolved love intrigues and misunderstandings; and the serious plays, many of which explore jealousy and honor. Of the latter type, the most famous is *The Physician to His Own Honor* (1635), a sympathetic treatment of a man who, in order to preserve his honor, manages to kill his wife in a manner that avoids scandal.

Calderón's most famous secular play, *Life Is a Dream* (c. 1636), is a philosophical allegory about the human situation and the mystery of life. The main character, Segismundo, a prince by birth, is reared in anonymity, taken to court while unconscious, and returned to his former state after being found unworthy; afterward, he believes that the interlude at court was a dream. In the chaotic years following 1640, when Catalonia and Portugal revolted against Spain, Calderón wrote only one outstanding *comedia*, *The Mayor of Zalamea* (c. 1642), the story of a peasant who seeks revenge for the violation of his daughter by an army officer. After 1652, all of Calderón's secular plays were written on demand for the court. They are short and light, often based on classical myths, with choral passages and much of the dialogue set to music. Because so many of them were performed at the royal hunting lodge, La Zarzuela, this type of musical comedy, which later was one of the most popular of Spanish dramatic forms, came to be called the *zarzuela*.

Above all Calderón is noted for his *autos sacramentales*, for he perfected the form. In his *autos*, Calderón effectively embodied Catholic dogma in symbolic stories told in lyrical dialogue of great beauty. Although he had written *autos* from the beginning of his career, he turned to them especially after 1647, writing two each year until his death. He was the author of all those presented in Madrid between 1647 and 1681. Nevertheless, his finest *autos*, *Devotion to the Cross* (1633) and *The Great World Theatre* (c. 1645), were written before he became a priest.

Of Calderón's contemporaries, two—Rojas Zorilla and Moreto—stand out. Francisco de Rojas Zorilla (1607–c. 1648) lived chiefly in Madrid, where he held a position at court and wrote primarily for the royal

FIGURE 8.3 A nineteenth-century reconstruction of the Corral del Príncipe. This sketch was made in 1888 to illustrate Ricardo Supelveda's *El Corral de la Pacheca* and is inaccurate in many details, although it manages to give a flavor of the interior. Unfortunately no visual evidence relating to the corrales can be found until the eighteenth century.

theatre. His best-known work, *Del Rey abajo Ninguno (All Equal Below the King)*, tells the story of a nobleman who is forgiven by the king for killing a man who sought to seduce his wife. In light comedy, Rojas Zorilla broke new ground with such works as *The Boobies' Sport* and *What Women Are*, in which a variety of pompous characters replace the traditional *gracioso* as the principal source of humor. Unfortunately, since Rojas Zorilla had no real followers, his breaks with tradition had little effect in Spain. His plays were greatly admired in France, however, and were adapted by Scarron, Thomas Corneille, and LeSage.

Augustín Moreto (1618–1669) was born in Madrid and spent most of his life at court, for which he

principally wrote. His best-known play is *Scorn for Scorn*, which served as the basis for Molière's *La Princesse d'Elide*. It tells the story of a woman who scorns all her lovers, only to be captured by one who pretends to scorn her. Moreto's delicate poetry, elegant and subtle wit, and interesting character portraits won him a wide following among aristocratic audiences. Most of his plays are adaptations of *comedias* by Lope de Vega and others.

The output of the Golden Age was phenomenal, for by 1700 an estimated 30,000 plays had been written. In quantity and vigor, the drama of Spain is comparable to that of England between 1585 and 1642. On the other hand, its failure to probe deeply into man's destiny, and its preoccupation with a narrow code of honor are limitations which make it inferior to the best English work. Nevertheless, many of the plays were widely known and imitated outside of Spain, and at home they established a lasting standard.

THE CORRALES

Although after 1625 the court attracted many of the finest dramatists, the majority of plays continued, as before, to be presented in the public theatres, or *corrales* (so called because they were originally adapted from existing courtyards). The *corrales* were at first under the direct control of confraternities like those which had presented religious plays throughout Europe during the Middle Ages. In Madrid, the public theatres were controlled by three charitable organizations. The Cofradía de la Pasión y Sangre de Jesucristo, founded in 1565 to feed and clothe the poor and to support a hospital, was the first to be granted the privilege of operating a theatre as a means of raising money. By 1568 it had opened a theatre in the Calle del Sol and soon added two others. In 1574, the Cofradía de la Soledad de Nuestra Señora, founded in 1567, petitioned to have one of the existing theatres placed under its control, a move which led to a sharing of revenues and expenses by the two *cofradías*. In 1583, the General Hospital of Madrid was also given a share in the revenues. These three organizations were to control the public theatres of Madrid until 1615. Similar arrangements were used in Barcelona, Zaragosa, Burgos, Vallodolid, Valencia, and Seville. Thus, the theatre was viewed as a means of raising money for charity, an attitude which saved it from closure on many occasions.

A new phase in the career of the theatres began in 1615, when the City of Madrid was ordered to pay the hospitals an annual subsidy, from which it could subtract a sum equal to the revenue which the *cofradías* received from the theatres. After this time, the *cofradías* gave up direct control over theatrical management and leased the theatres to entrepreneurs, normally for four-year periods. In 1638, ownership of the *corrales* passed to the City and two commissioners were appointed to oversee their operation, although the theatres continued to be leased as before. Despite some alterations in the system during the eighteenth century, the theatres were used to finance charities until the mid-nineteenth century. At no time during the Golden Age did the actors con-

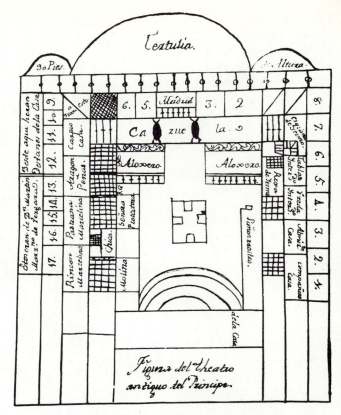

FIGURE 8.4 A rough plan of the Corral del Príncipe made about 1730. The stage is shown at the bottom, and the alehouse, *cazuela,* and Tertulia at the top; the side walls (showing the *aposentos* and *desvanes*) are drawn as though the various levels were side by side. From a plan published in 1881.

trol the *corrales*, which were occupied by them merely for short-term engagements under contracts with the theatres' lessees.

At first the *corrales* were temporary, at least five different ones being used in Madrid during the 1570s. The desirability of permanent theatres soon became evident, however, and in 1579 the Corral de la Cruz, the first permanent theatre in Spain, was opened in Madrid. It was followed by the Corral del Príncipe in 1583. After 1585 these were to be the only public theatres for drama in Madrid until the nineteenth century. Permanent theatres were also built in other cities.

Although the *corrales* were by no means uniform in design, they had many common features. Almost all were built around a square or rectangular courtyard. The only exception seems to have been the oval-shaped

Corral de la Montería, built in Seville in 1626. In most *corrales,* the courtyards were unroofed until the eighteenth century, but a few were covered during the seventeenth. When roofs were added, a row of windows just under the eaves provided light.

The large central courtyard, or *patio,* was occupied primarily by standing spectators, although by the end of the seventeenth century a few *lunetas,* or semi-circular rows of benches, had been set up near the stage. A raised and roofed platform equipped with benches (the *gradas*) extended along the side walls of the *patio.* At the rear of the *patio,* the *alojería,* or tavern, occupied the ground floor, while above it was the gallery for women (the *cazuela* or *corredor de las mugeres*). Above the *cazuela* were two other galleries, the first divided into boxes and assigned to the City of Madrid and the Council of Castile, while the upper, the *Tertulia,* was undivided and used primarily by clergymen and intellectuals. The side walls of the courtyard were taken up by boxes, or *aposentos,* which were in reality rooms in the surrounding houses from which the occupants could watch the plays from windows, typically covered with latticework or iron grilles. The third floor boxes were often called *desvánes* (attics) because of their location at the top of the buildings. On the first level, the *aposentos* were fronted by the *gradas,* while an open and railed gallery fronted the *aposentos* on the second level. Since the theatres in Madrid were converted from already existing courtyards, some of the *aposentos* were located in houses which were either rented or privately owned by persons having no connection with the theatre. In these cases, the occupants were required to pay a yearly fee for the use of the *aposentos* or to permit access to the *aposentos* through their houses.

Many of the theatres outside of Madrid deviated from this typical pattern. In some, the *aposentos* were replaced by open galleries divided into compartments like those later used in the Italian public opera houses; others had one row of *aposentos,* above which were open galleries. Nevertheless, the basic arrangement—an enclosed courtyard—was the same everywhere.

The two theatres had several entrances; at each there were two money takers, since two entrances fees were paid, one to the theatre lessee and one to the charities. About three-fifths of the combined total income went to the lessee and actors. The entrance fee entitled women to sit in the *cazuela* and men to stand in the *patio.* Additional fees were collected from the men if they wished to sit in the *aposentos, gradas,* or galleries. Some

of the *aposentos* were entered from the *patio,* but others were reached by passing through private houses. Many were rented permanently. The strict segregation of men and women was enforced by policemen. Women were forbidden in the *patio,* and men and women could occupy the same *aposento* only if they were known to be closely related.

Until the 1580s performances were confined to Sundays and feast days. But in 1579, Alberto Ganassa's visiting *commedia dell'arte* troupe was permitted to play on a weekday and this privilege was soon extended to Spanish companies. By the seventeenth century performances were allowed daily except on Saturdays. Sunday was always considered the best day for playing because of the larger potential audience. The theatrical season began in September and continued until Lent. All theatres were closed from Ash Wednesday until after Easter, when a new season began and extended until July, at which time the theatres were closed for the summer months. The theatres might also be closed during periods of official mourning, plagues, or war. It has been estimated that about 198 days each year were devoted to performances.

During the fall and winter seasons, performances began at 2 P.M., and during the spring season at 4 P.M. They were required to end at least one hour before nightfall. The daily bill began with music, singing, and dancing; next came the *loa,* or prologue, which was followed by another dance; then came the *comedia,* the acts of which were separated by *entreméses;* a dance concluded the performance.

Spectators, especially those in the *patio* and *cazuela,* were often noisy. The *mosqueteros* in the courtyard were usually the most unruly, but the women sometimes threw fruit at the actors, and both men and women carried such noisemakers as whistles, rattles, and bunches of keys. They were equally voluble in approval, which they demonstrated by applauding and shouting "Victor!" Refreshments such as fruit, wafers, and ale were sold throughout performances.

ACTING COMPANIES

It is difficult to estimate the number of acting companies that existed in Spain between 1550 and 1580, for many lasted only a single season and mergers or separations were frequent. The number increased so rapidly after permanent theatres were built that the government sought to regulate them. In 1603, the crown restricted the right to perform to eight companies, but in 1615, the number was raised to twelve. Such regulations seem to have been ignored, however, for records show that many additional companies played during those years.

There were two kinds of companies: sharing troupes *(compañías de parte)* and salaried actors working for a manager. Contracts usually ran for one or two years. The size of companies varied considerably. Augustín de Rojas Villandrando's *Entertaining Journey* (1604) describes troupes ranging in size from the single performer, who recited monologues or scenes from plays, to those with sixteen members and a repertory of sixty plays. Between 1610 and 1640, the period of the theatre's greatest popularity, the average company consisted of from sixteen to twenty actors. The troupes included both men and women. In addition, a few minors were usually serving apprenticeships.

Since most troupes preferred to play in Madrid or Seville, other cities sometimes had to employ agents to secure companies for their theatres. Even in Madrid, however, no troupe remained in the same theatre very long and almost all toured. Traveling was time-consuming and costly. In 1586, it took one company thirteen days to travel the 270 miles between Madrid and Seville. The mode of transportation, depending upon the company's finances, ranged from walking to using carts, pack animals, and coaches. Contracts often specified allowances for travel, as well as the type of lodging and food to be provided on the road.

Before performances could be given, a company had to obtain a license, which was usually granted only after civic officials had viewed a free performance. In addition, each play had to be licensed separately. After 1600 all plays were subject to censorship, and a dramatist could be excommunicated if he did not comply with recommendations. Since there were no copyright laws, a play could be performed by any company that could obtain a copy and a license.

Before 1590, many playwrights were attached to troupes as actors. After 1590, such close connections were unusual, and plays were bought outright for fees which varied according to the author's reputation. At the height of his career, Lope de Vega received about 500 reals for each play, at a time when an actor's average annual salary was about 6,000 reals. This disparity in income may explain why dramatists were so prolific.

By the 1650s, the payment had increased somewhat—to about 800 reals—for works by the best writers.

Payments to companies varied widely. Usually a troupe was given a fixed sum for each performance, and a percentage of the receipts was sometimes added for long engagements. Occasionally companies were paid entirely through a fixed percentage of receipts. If a company had to travel a long distance to keep an engagement, it might receive additional payments to defray expenses.

For *autos*, the companies received relatively high fees, since they were required to furnish expensive costumes. In addition, the troupes selected to perform *autos* were given exclusive performance rights in the town between Easter and Corpus Christi. After the festival, the *autos* were often presented in the public theatres. The city governments also hired actors to give free performances on special occasions.

Little is known of individual companies, although the names of many managers have survived. Among the most famous were Alonso Riquelme (*fl.* 1602–1621), Christobal Ortiz (*fl.* 1613–1626), Roque di Figueroa (*fl.* 1623–1650), and Antonio de Rueda (*fl.* 1628–1662). In addition to the Spanish troupes, Italian *commedia dell'arte* companies frequently visited Spain during the last quarter of the sixteenth century. Among the most famous of these were the troupes of Alberto Ganassa (1574–1584), Maximiliano Milanino (1581), and Tristano Martinelli (1587–1588).

ACTORS AND ACTING

The position of the professional performer in Spain was ambiguous. Since Roman times actors had been forbidden the sacraments of the church, and Alfonso X (1221–1284) declared that all actors were to be branded infamous. These strictures were not officially removed in Spain until the twentieth century. During the Golden Age the usual attitude was one of tolerance, however, so long as actors did not perform plays which contradicted church teachings; certainly many actors were married and buried in the church. Furthermore, they were employed by city officials to produce the *autos* given at Corpus Christi celebrations.

Nevertheless, many churchmen were opposed to the theatre, especiallly to the use of professional actors in religious plays. On many occasions, they petitioned the king to ban the public theatre and, in a few instances, were successful for short periods of time. Fortunately, the actors had strong allies in city officials, whose local charities depended upon the theatre for their funds. Consequently, closures were brief. The objections, however, did lead to closer supervision of the theatre.

A major source of dissatisfaction was the actress. Professional female performers in Spain can be traced back as far as the fifteenth century, and by the mid-sixteenth century, they were included in several acting troupes. Nevertheless, most women's roles were played by boys or men until 1587, when women were first licensed to appear on the stage. Churchmen secured a royal decree banning actresses in 1596, but it seems never to have been enforced. After a bitter controversy in 1598 and 1599, the royal council declared that no actresses were to perform unless their husbands or fathers were in the company, and that neither sex might appear in the dress of the other. Further attempts to still criticism probably lie behind the decree of 1608, which stated that only actors were to go backstage, forbade friars to attend the theatre, and banned the presentation of secular plays in churches or religious houses. At this time strict censorship was established over plays, and in 1615 it was extended to include dancing, which had given rise to many complaints.

Dance played an important role in both the *comedias* and the *autos*. Most actresses danced as well as acted, and the contracts of many actors specified that they must dance and sing. Many complaints against the theatre cited the *zarabanda*, introduced about 1588, as licentious and voluptuous. In addition, *bayles* (dances accompanied by couplets) were considered morally questionable by many persons. After the decree of 1615, dances became more sedate.

In 1631 the actors were allowed to form a guild similar to those of other recognized trades. Called the Cofradía de la Novena, it still exists and is open to all theatrical personnel. It did much to raise the social status of the actor.

We know the names of more than 2,000 actors of the Golden Age. Most performers were recruited from the common people, although occasionally members of the minor aristocracy went on the stage. Unfortunately, little is known about individual performers. Damien Arias de Penafiel (*fl.* 1617–1643), with his "pure, clear voice, vivacious manner, and excellent memory," was universally regarded as the finest actor of his time. Other outstanding performers included Nicolas de los Rios

(*fl.* 1570–1610), Antonio de Villega (*fl.* 1592–1613), Juan de Morales de Medrano (*fl.* 1595–1634), Alonso de Olmedo (*fl.* 1600–1651), and Cosme Perez (*c.* 1585–1673, the most famous comic actor of the age. Jusepa Vaca (*fl.* 1602–1634) was the most celebrated actress. Others included Juana de Villalba (*fl.* 1595–1619), Maria de Cordoba (*fl.* 1617–1643), María Calderón (*fl.* 1623–1635), and Maria de Riquelme (*fl.* 1620–1644).

In his *Entertaining Journey*, Rojas Villandrando describes the actor's life around 1600: the performer must rise early and study his roles from 5 until 9 A.M., after which he attends rehearsals until noon; after eating, he goes to the theatre to perform, completing his work about 7 P.M.; even then his time may still not be his own, for he may be summoned by officials or nobles to perform at night. Under Philip IV (reigned 1621–1665), the actors were much in demand at court, and Philip's practice of sending for companies on such short notice that they had to cancel public performances is sometimes cited as a reason for the public's loss of interest in the theatre.

The actors were usually paid after each performance. In sharing companies the receipts were divided after all expenses were subtracted. Salaried actors were paid by the day, and since the number of performances might vary widely from one year and troupe to another, it is difficult to calculate the average income. One historian has estimated it at about 6,000 reals per year, a rather liberal sum for the time. Most salaries were supplemented by a daily maintenance allowance, and additional payments might be made for traveling expenses and costumes. Thus, though the actor did not rank high in the social scale, he was in many ways better off than his French contemporaries, who were denied religious rights, or the English actors, who were always at odds with the civic authorities.

COSTUMES

The costume practices of the Spanish stage were similar to those of England during the same period. Contemporary clothing served in most cases, although historical and legendary figures were sometimes differentiated by outmoded or fanciful dress. Moors, toward whom the Spaniards felt a special antipathy, were always clearly distinguished from other characters.

Many actors owned their own costumes. Although

a sharing company usually maintained a wardrobe available to all its members, many actors supplied their own stage dress. Actors' contracts often specified allowances for costumes. The manager was responsible for the wardrobes of apprentices.

In most cases, actors seem to have dressed as lavishly as finances permitted. As early as 1534, Charles V issued a decree against extravagant dress on the stage, and government regulations recurred throughout the Golden Age. In 1653 actresses were forbidden to wear strange headdresses, decolleté necklines, wide hooped skirts, or dresses not reaching to the floor. In addition, they were restricted to one costume for each play unless the scripts clearly demanded a change.

Records of extravagance are numerous. In 1589, an actor paid 1,100 reals and in 1619 another paid 2,400 reals for a single costume, sums equivalent to about one-third of a typical actor's annual income. No doubt the minor performers were less richly dressed. The actor's wardrobe was considered his greatest financial asset, for it helped him secure employment and could be pawned in bad times.

The costumes for *autos* were probably more lavish than those used in the public theatres, for contracts usually specified costumes of silk and velvet. Often the actors petitioned civic officials for additional funds to pay for unexpectedly expensive garments, and their requests were frequently granted. In addition, towns voted special prizes to companies or actors who had distinguished themselves either through acting or costuming.

THE STAGE AND SCENERY

Like the costuming, the stage and scenery of the Spanish public theatre were in many ways similar to those of England. The stage was a raised platform without a proscenium arch or front curtain and was bounded at the back by a permanent facade. Since the *gradas* and second-level galleries extended up to the facade, the action was normally viewed from three sides, although most of the spectators sat or stood in front of the stage. Railings separated the *gradas* from the acting area.

The stage at the Corral del Príncipe was about 28 feet wide by 23 feet deep, not including the semi-circular projection at the front, which was about 5 feet deep at the center. Although the dimensions of the Corral de la Cruz are uncertain, its stage was probably about 26 feet wide by 29 feet deep, with a semicircular extension at the front. This open platform was backed by a facade of two levels. Two pillars divided the lower level into three openings, those at the sides serving as entrances and the larger central space primarily as a place for "discoveries." This discovery space was about 9 feet deep. The second level, essentially a gallery, could be used in a variety of ways, but normally represented towers, city walls, or hills. At times, discoveries were also made there by drawing the curtains. It was possible to go from the lower to the upper level in full view of the audience, but it is not clear how this was managed.

For the most part, staging conventions were simple and resembled those of the Elizabethan theatre. An exit and reentry was sufficient to mark a change of place. In addition, three different kinds of scenic background might be used. First, the facade sometimes served as the sole background for the action. Second, the curtains, which concealed the facade, were used when the locale was unimportant. They were drawn aside to reveal portions of the facade or scenic pieces set up in the discovery space when localization of the action was required. Third, medieval-like mansions were sometimes set up on the main stage. Surviving scripts clearly show that scenic pieces were used at times to represent gardens, fountains, rocks, trees, forts, and castles. Sometimes they are specified when not strictly required by the action, while in other instances the spectators are requested to imagine some place not shown. It seems likely that practice was inconsistent and was guided more by the availability of scenic pieces than by any conscious theory of stage decoration. On the other hand, as spectacle increased after 1650, painted flats and practicable windows and doors began to be set into the facade in lieu of curtains. Except in rare instances, however, there was no attempt to use perspective painting. The stage was equipped with several trapdoors, while the roof over the stage housed machinery for flying, which was increasingly popular after 1650. Essentially, however, scenic practices changed little during the course of the Golden Age.

COURT ENTERTAINMENTS

Although court entertainments like those found elsewhere in Europe had been seen in Spain since the thirteenth century, it was not until the reign of Philip III (1598–1621) that theatrical performances were given

FIGURE 8.5 **Stage setting for *Los Celos hacen estrellas* by Juan Velez de Guevara at the court in 1672. Courtesy Bildarchiv, Osterreichische Nationalbibliothek, Vienna.**

regularly at court. Philip's queen was especially fond of the theatre, and both professional productions and masques performed by courtiers were frequent until her death in 1611.

The court theatre reached its height during the reign of Philip IV (1621–1665), who between 1623 and 1653 saw about 300 different plays at court. Although Italianate scenery had been used occasionally since the sixteenth century, it was not until Cosme Lotti (? –1643) was imported from Florence in 1626 that it became usual. Until the 1630s most of the court entertainments were staged in a large hall at the Alcázar or in the gardens at Aranjuez; after 1633 the new palace, the Buen Retiro, became the center of court entertainments. After the opening of Buen Retiro, performances by courtiers declined rapidly, and most productions thereafter were acted by professional troupes.

Many lavish outdoor productions were staged on the palace grounds. One of the most famous of these was Calderón's *Love the Best Enchantment* (1635), for which Lotti built a floating stage on a lake. The special effects included a shipwreck, a triumphal chariot drawn across the water by dolphins, and the destruction of Circe's palace. The whole was lit by 3,000 lanterns and the king and his retinue watched from gondolas. In 1636, the three acts of Calderón's *The Three Great Prodigies* were given on three separate stages, each act being performed by a different professional troupe. In addition, there were many lavish masquerades, tournaments, and machine plays. For a carnival in 1637 Lotti designed huge wheeled structures measuring 22 feet in width, 32 feet in length, and 46 feet in height.

In 1640 a permanent theatre, the Coliseo, was constructed by Lotti in the Buen Retiro. This theatre

FIGURE 8.6   A play at the Spanish court of Carlos II, *c.* 1680. The king and queen are seated on the dais at right. Note the proscenium arch and the scenery, presumably composed of wings and shutters. From "Histoire de France" published at Antwerp by Philibert Buttats the Younger. Courtesy Bibliothèque Nationale, Paris.

seems to have resembled the public *corrales,* for it had a *patio,* three levels of *aposentos,* and a *cazuela.* The royal box was situated above the *cazuela.* On the other hand, the Coliseo was roofed and probably had a proscenium arch (often said to be the first in Spain), although this is by no means certain. The Coliseo was also frequently open to the public, who paid the same entrance fees as at the public *corrales.* Furthermore, the same percentage of the receipts were given to the charities. The plays were performed by troupes that normally appeared in the *corrales,* and the scenic demands for most of the plays were similar to those written for the public theatres. Other plays, however, were spectacular pieces that required Italianate scenery and special effects. Sometimes private court performances preceded those open to the public. The more intimate entertainments, however, were usually given in another room in the palace.

The 1640s saw a marked decline in theatrical activities, both at court and in the public theatres. The Catalan and Portuguese rebellions of 1640 ushered in a period of uncertainty, and, following the deaths of Lotti in 1643 and of the queen in 1644, court theatricals virtually came to an end. Between 1646 and 1651 the public theatres were closed as well.

By 1650, Philip had remarried and had settled many of his political problems; consequently, the Coliseo was reopened to the public in 1651, the same year in which the public theatres were permitted to resume performances. Another Italian designer, Baccio del Bianco, was imported in 1652, and the use of spectacular scenery increased markedly thereafter. Court performances were frequent until Philip's death in 1665. They were resumed about 1670 and the old practices were continued. In these years, a Spaniard, José Caudi, who replaced the Italians, became the first native scene designer of note. After the death of Carlos II in 1700, the court theatre declined rapidly.

Although productions were given at regular intervals from the 1620s until the end of the century, the court never employed a company of its own. Rather, actors were summoned from the public theatres of Madrid to rehearse and perform plays. Although the actors were well paid, the public theatres were often forced to cancel performances on short notice and to remain closed for some time.

By the late seventeenth century, the financial resources of Spain were virtually exhausted and Spain's political power was rapidly declining. The great dramatic impulse was also over, for after the death of Calderón in 1681 new writers sought merely to recapture a past glory instead of exploring new paths. As a consequence, the most vital and productive periods the Spanish theatre has known was clearly over by 1700.

FIGURE 8.7   An opera performed at the court, *c.* 1680. The suspended figures on stage indicate that the theatre was equipped with the Italianate machinery of the day. From "Histoire de France" published at Antwerp by Philibert Buttats the Younger. Courtesy Bibliothèque Nationale, Paris.

LOOKING AT THEATRE HISTORY

Public archives often contain some of the most valuable information concerning the theatre. This is especially true for a study of *autos sacramentales:* the Municipal Archives of Madrid contain numerous documents relating to the preparation and performance of Corpus Christi celebrations there. Many of the pertinent documents have been published by N.D. Shergold and J. E. Varey in a series of volumes (among them *Los Autos Sacramentales en Madrid en la Epoca de Calderón, 1637–1681,* Madrid, 1961). These are only some of the important theatrical documents scholars have found in their searches through the public records of countries throughout the world.

Other major sources of information are accounts written by visitors from other countries. Often they provide more graphic details of theatrical conditions than native writers who are so familiar with local situations that they consider it unnecessary to record them. One of the best descriptions of the Corpus Christi festivals in Madrid is found in an account written by the Dutchman Francis van Aerssen, who visited Spain in 1654–1665. His book was published in French in 1666 and in English in 1670.

. . . they begin by a procession, whose first ranks include several [musicians]; a great many habited in parti-colored clothes, skip and frolic as extravagantly as in a Morris dance. The King . . . after Mass, returns with a torch in his hand, following a silver Tabernacle, in which is the Holy wafer, attended by the Grandees of Spain and his several Councils . . . . before these . . . move Machines, representing Giants; these are Statues of Pasteboard carried by men concealed under them. . . . the Tarasca is a Serpent of enormous greatness in form of a Woman, moving on wheels, the body covered with scales, a vast belly, long tail, short feet, sharp talons, fiery eyes, gaping mouth, out of which extend three tongues, and long tusks. This Bulbeggar stalks up and down . . . and sometimes lays hold on Country fellows, whose fright moves laughter amongst the people. . . . The Procession having filed to the Piazza, returns by the . . . Calle Mayor, adorned by many tapestries waving on the balconies filled with men and women of all conditions. . . . In the afternoon about five o'clock, Autos are represented. . . . The two companies of Players that belong to Madrid at this time, shut their theatres, and for a month represent these Holy Poems: this they do every evening in publick on scaffolds erected to that purpose in the streets before the houses of the Presidents of several Councils. They begin at Court the day of the Solemnity. . . . the stage is

at the foot of these Scaffolds, and little painted booths are rolled to it, . . . and serve as tiring houses.

A Journey Into Spain (London, 1670), pp. 118–124.

In his account of a visit to Spain in 1659, François Bertaut describes the theatres:

. . . there are troupes of players in nearly all the towns, and they are better, in comparison, than our own [the French], but there are none in the pay of the King. They perform in a courtyard, where a number of private houses join together, so that the windows of the rooms . . . do not belong to the players but to the owners of the houses. They perform by day and without torches, and their theatres . . . have not such fine decorations as ours. . . . There are two places . . . in Madrid, which they call Corrales, and which are always filled with merchants and artisans, who leave their shops and repair thither. . . . Some of the spectators have seats close to the stage. . . . The women all sit together in a gallery at one end, which the men are not allowed to enter.

Relation de l'Estat and Gouvernement d' Espagne (Cologne, 1666), pp. 59–60.

In 1679 the Comtesse D'Aulnoy wrote a number of letters recording her impressions of her travels in Spain. In one she describes her visit to an opera *(Alcina)* at the court theatre located in the Buen Retiro palace:

I never saw such wretched machinery. The gods descended on horseback upon a beam which extended from one end of the stage to the other; the sun was lighted up by means of a dozen lanterns of oiled paper in each of which was a lamp. When Alcina practiced her enchantments and evoked the demons, the latter arose leisurely out of hell upon ladders. . . . The building is certainly very beautiful and handsomely painted and gilded; the boxes are furnished with blinds . . . [which] reach from top to bottom, so that they seem to form a kind of room.

Relation du Voyage d'Espagne (LaHaye, 1693), 10th letter.

Considerable information about the sharing companies of the seventeenth century can be gleaned from the contractual agreements made when the companies were formed. One contract dated June 1614 sets forth the agreement between Andrés de Claramonte and eleven other actors. Some of the provisions are these:

Andrés de Claramonte binds himself to furnish . . . as many as forty comedias and such others as the said company may require, besides the necessary entreméses, letras, *and* bailes.

Item: *That the various roles in the comedias shall be assigned amongst the members of the said company in such manner as shall seem most suitable to each in the opinion of the said company.*

Item: *During the said time the said members . . . are bound to attend with care and punctuality the rehearsals of all the comedias to be represented each day, at nine o'clock,* at the house of the said Andrés de Claramonte, where rehearsals are ordinarily to take place, and shall not fail to be present at any of the said rehearsals, under penalty of two reals. . . .

Item: *That if, during the said time, any member of the said company shall absent himself from it, he shall lose all that would have fallen to his share. . . .*

HUGO A. RENNERT, *The Spanish Stage in the Time of Lope de Vega* (New York, 1909), pp. 147–149.

LE NOVVEAV THEATRE DE LA TROVPPE ... ITALIENNE DE L'HOSTEL DE BOVRGOGNE

CASTIGAT RIDENDO MORES

9

The Theatre in France, 1500 to 1700

Like England, France began to feel the effects of the Renaissance in the late fifteenth century. From 1494 on it maintained close relationships with Italy and through a series of wars and marriages sought to extend its influence there. Francis I (reigned 1515–1547) was especially interested in the new artistic and literary movements and invited several Italian artists and scholars to his court, where they developed the style called the School of Fontainebleau. In 1546 Francis commissioned Pierre Lescot to rebuild the Louvre in Renaissance style, and it was during his reign that the great chateaux of the Loire region began to take shape.

THEATRE AT COURT AND IN SCHOOLS PRIOR TO 1600

Before the end of Francis I's reign neoclassical drama had made an impact both on schools and at court. As in other countries, the trend began with the study of Roman plays, continued with Latin imitations of classical works, and progressed to plays in French. It was in Lyons, France, in 1493 that the first illustrated edition of Terence's plays was published. The "Terence Stage" depicted in that edition probably provided the model for the staging of plays in French schools and at court until after the mid-sixteenth century.

Frenchmen also began to write plays in the classical manner. Between 1501 and 1524 Ravisius Textor composed a number of Latin *Dialogi* which were performed by students at the University of Paris, and in 1536 Roilletus published three Latin tragedies that had been acted by his students in Paris. At the College of Guienne in Bordeaux, Latin plays by George Buchanan and Muretus were produced between 1539 and 1545. Furthermore, around 1540, classical plays and critical treatises began to be translated into French. Plays by Sophocles, Euripides, Aristophanes, Seneca, Plautus, and Terence, and critical works by Aristotle and Horace had appeared before 1550. Recent Italian plays also were translated, as were Italian commentaries on Aristotle's *Poetics*.

Neoclassical influence accelerated after Henri II (reigned 1547–1559), who had married Catherine de' Medici (1519–1589), succeeded to the throne. By 1550 a group of seven French writers, headed by Pierre de Ronsard and known as the Pléiade, had assumed leadership. Seeking to develop French as the medium for a literature modeled on classical works, they formulated rules of grammar and prosody, enriched the language by inventing new words, and illustrated their ideals in their own literary works. Of necessity, the Pléiade addressed itself primarily to the educated classes. The first neoclassical plays in French came out of the Pléiade when in 1552 Etienne Jodelle (1523–1573) presented both the first tragedy, *Cléopatre captive,* and the first comedy, *Eugène,*

FIGURE 9.1 Catherine de'Medici's water fete given during the Festival at Bayonne, 1565. Drawing by Antoine Caron, who also probably designed the fete. Courtesy Pierpont Morgan Library, New York.

in the new vein before Henri II with Jodelle in the role of Cleopatra. Jodelle's tragedy is essentially narrative, since most of the action has occurred before the play begins. *Eugène* utilizes the conventions of Roman comedy in telling a story similar to those of medieval farce.

Jodelle's plays were performed in a hall of state in which an "antique" setting had been erected, but it is not clear whether this was a "Terence Stage" or a perspective setting. At this time either could have been used. Vitruvius' treatise on architecture had been known in France since around 1500; in 1542 Charles Estienne's preface to Terence's *Andria* had discussed the use of *periaktoi;* and in 1545 Serlio, then resident at the court of Francis I, had published his *Architettura* in France. In addition, perspective scenery had certainly been used in Lyons in 1548 for a production of Bibbiena's *La Calandria* given in honor of Henri II and Catherine. But, though the French obviously knew about Italian scenic practices, most of the spectacles at court used "dispersed decors," medieval-like scenic elements scattered around a hall rather than concentrated in a single, unified setting.

Jodelle's example was soon being followed by other dramatists who wrote for courtly or school audi-

ences, although the majority of these works probably was not performed.

By 1572, when Jean de la Taille published a preface advocating the three unities, the neoclassical ideal had been fully set forth in France, and most of the scholastic dramatists were following these precepts in their writing. By far the best of these playwrights was Robert Garnier (*c.* 1535–*c.* 1600), who wrote eight tragedies between 1568 and 1583. Although most of Garnier's plays are composed of scenes adapted from Euripides or Seneca, they are almost devoid of dramatic action, for Garnier restricted himself primarily to relating the suffering of his protagonists. Nevertheless, his plays were widely read and admired.

Garnier's most popular, though least characteristic, work is *Bradamante* (1582), a tragicomedy about a girl who can marry only the man who has overcome her in battle. It is indicative of changes that came over French scholastic drama after 1580 under the influence of novels and the popular theatre. For example, Beaubreuil's *Regulus* (1582) ignores the unity of time, and it places several battles on stage. Furthermore, in his preface Beaubreuil launched a vigorous attack on the unities. But though a few writers departed from the neoclassical mode, no marked trend toward irregularity developed, probably because no dramatist capable of commanding a wide following appeared.

Perhaps the most characteristic entertainments of this period were the court festivals. Both Francis I and Henri II were fond of tournaments, and Henri II met his death in 1559 while participating in one. His death left Catherine de' Medici in a position of power which was to last throughout the lives of her three sons: Francis II, husband of Mary of Scotland (reigned 1559–1560), Charles IX (reigned 1560–1574), and Henri III (reigned 1574–1589). Catherine was especially fond of royal entries and festivals of various sorts which she used as instruments to demonstrate France's power and to encourage alliances or reconciliations. The festivals arranged by Catherine began at Chenonceaux in 1563 and Fontainebleau in 1564; they were followed by a two-year ceremonial progress of the court through the various provinces of France, where every major town mounted a royal entry. An especially elaborate festival was held at Bayonne in 1565, when the main attraction was a water pageant offered by Catherine. These festivals were designed in part by Antoine Caron, several of whose drawings have survived. Other important celebrations were mounted for the entry of Charles IX into Paris in 1571; for the marriage of Catherine's daughter to Henry of Navarre in 1572; and for the visit of the Polish Ambassadors in 1573.

Through such spectacles, the *ballet de cour* (the French variation on Italian *intermezzi* and English masques) evolved. Their creators sought to unite dramatic plot, song, dance, and spectacle in the "antique manner." These experiments culminated in 1581 in the *Ballet Comique de la Reyne* with text by LaChesnaye, music by the Sieur de Beaulieu, scenery by Jacques Patin, and the whole planned and directed by Baltasar de Beaujoyeulx. It was based on the myth of Circe, who lures men into a life of vice and transforms them into beasts. The action was treated as a moral struggle between virtue and vice, with the King depicted as the deliverer. This story was developed through a series of *entrées* by various allegorical and mythological figures and ended with the triumph of reason and virtue and with praise for the wisdom of the kings of France. It was staged in the Salle du Petit Bourbon (located in a palace adjacent to the Louvre) which was to be one of the important court theatres of the seventeenth century. It measured about 49 feet wide by 177 feet long, with an apse extending another 44 feet. The king and courtiers sat at one end, while other spectators occupied two balconies extending around the side walls. The *Ballet Comique de la Reyne* is often said to be the first full expression of the *ballet de cour,* which was to be revived and extended in the seventeenth century. In the meantime, however, further developments were to be delayed by civil war.

THE PUBLIC THEATRE IN PARIS BEFORE 1595

While court spectacles and neoclassical plays were gaining in strength, the French public stage was at a low ebb. Its status was owing in part to the Confrérie de la Passion, a confraternity that had a monopoly on theatrical production in Paris. Organized in 1402 to produce religious drama, the Confrérie presented its occasional productions in a large hall at the Hôpital de la Trinité for many years. Forced to move in 1539, it had settled in the Hôtel de Flandres until that building was torn down in 1543. In 1548, after a series of relocations, the Confrérie began construction of a new building, probably the first perma-

FIGURE 9.2 *Ballet Comique de la Reine* as given at the Petit Bourbon in 1581. Note the dispersed decor and the placement of spectators. The king and his retinue are in the foreground. Courtesy Bibliothèque Nationale, Paris.

nent public theatre to be built in Europe since Roman times. Because it was located on land formerly owned by the Dukes of Burgundy, the theatre was called the Hôtel de Bourgogne. Before the theatre was completed, however, religious plays were banned. Nevertheless the Confrérie was given a monopoly on all theatrical production in Paris. Thus, while the traditional justification for the group's productions—the presentation of devotional dramas—had been removed, the Confrérie was given control over the secular theatre.

Few records of performances between 1548 and 1575 have survived. The Confrérie probably played at irregular intervals, but its popularity waned with its new repertory, principally farces. Consequently, it began to rent its theatre to other troupes. By the 1570s a number of professional companies had developed outside of Paris, possibly as offshoots of the confraternities formed to produce religious plays. Professional groups were performing at Rouen by 1556, at Amiens by 1559, at Dijon by 1577, and at Agen by 1585. Few played in Paris because of the Confrérie's monopoly. Outside of Paris, however, where no monopolies existed, conditions were more favorable.

In the 1570s visiting companies began to lease the Hôtel de Bourgogne for short periods and thereafter the theatre was operated increasingly by temporary occupants. Not all visiting companies played at the Hôtel de Bourgogne, but all had to pay fees to the Confrérie no matter where they performed within the city.

By this time both the public theatre and the court entertainments were being affected by the civil disturbances growing out of the struggle between Catholics and Protestants (or Huguenots). Persecution of Protestants had begun about 1540 but did not assume major proportions until 1572, when thousands of Protestants were murdered in the Massacre of St. Bartholomew's Day. Subsequently, as the Catholics gained strength under the leadership of the Duke of Guise, Henri III began to fear them and eventually had the Duke assassinated. In turn, he was killed in 1589, and since he left no heir, Henry of Navarre, a Protestant, succeeded to the throne as Henri IV (reigned 1589–1610). Open civil war followed and did not cease until Henri became a Catholic. Unable to enter Paris until 1594, Henri was not able to restore peace fully until after 1598 when he issued the Edict of Nantes granting almost complete autonomy to Protestants. During the disturbances, court entertainments were suspended, the neoclassical ideal forgotten, and public performances in Paris almost totally abandoned. As a result, French theatre almost had to begin anew in the late 1590s.

THE PUBLIC THEATRE, 1595–1625

When public theatrical performances resumed around 1595, French drama was still of little consequence. The neoclassical dramatists had catered to aristocratic audiences but had failed to produce any plays of lasting interest. Although a few of the learned dramas had been presented in the public theatres, the usual popular fare was farce, much of which was improvised under the influence of the *commedia dell'arte* troupes, which had played in Paris between 1572 and 1588 and were to return frequently after 1599.

These conditions began to change only with the appearance, in about 1597, of France's first professional playwright, Alexandre Hardy (*c.* 1572–1632). During the next thirty-five years, Hardy wrote about 500 plays, although only 34 have survived. Working for a popular audience, Hardy adapted his plays to its tastes. Thus, although he used such neoclassical devices as the five-act form, poetic dialogue, ghosts, messengers, and the chorus, he did not permit reverence for antiquity to interfere with his primary aim of telling an interesting story. He seldom observed the unities of time and place, and he put all important episodes, no matter how violent, on stage. At first he wrote tragedies, but since these did not please, he turned to tragicomedy and pastoral.

Although Hardy never achieved greatness, his accomplishment was considerable. Coming to the theatre when farce reigned, he paved the way for tragedy with his tragicomedies and for comedy with his pastorals. His success encouraged others to write for the stage. Not until after 1625, however, did any plays equal Hardy's in merit or popularity.

Hardy's early work was done primarily for Valleran LeComte (*fl.* 1592–1613), the first important French theatrical manager. Although a number of itinerant companies played in Paris after 1595, the arrival of Valleran in 1598 marks the first attempt to provide production of high quality. By this time, Valleran was already well established, having performed since 1592 in major provincial cities. In 1598 his troupe was already being called *Les Comédiens du Roi* ("The King's Players"), probably because it had at some time performed before Henri IV. The title, however, carried with it no special privileges or subsidy. Between 1598 and 1612, Valleran's was the most important company in Paris, although, like its competitors, it also toured elsewhere, for as yet no company was able to maintain itself permanently in the capital.

In the early seventeenth century, acting companies were bound together by two- or three-year contracts. All were organized on the sharing plan, under which profits were divided after each performance. The manager normally received two shares, while lesser actors might be allotted less than a full share. Companies ranged in size from eight to twelve members, sometimes supplemented by "hired men" and apprentices. By 1607, women were included in the companies. But if acting gained steadily in popularity between 1595 and 1625, the social and religious stigma attached to it led most performers to assume stage names when they went into the theatre.

In spite of the efforts of Valleran and Hardy, farce continued to be the most popular dramatic form, and between 1610 and 1625 the most famous actors in Paris were the players of the farcical types, Turlupin, Gaultier-Garguille, and Gros-Guillaume. Turlupin, acted by Henri LeGrand (*c.* 1587–*c.* 1637), who used the name Belleville in serious roles, was a rascally servant similar to Brighella of the *commedia dell'arte.* Gaultier-Garguille, acted by Hugues Guéru (*c.* 1573–1633), who played as Fleschelles in serious drama, was a tall, thin, bow-legged creature who could contort his body like a marionette. Gros-Guillaume, acted by Robert Guérin (*c.* 1554–*c.* 1634), who used the name LaFleur in serious roles, had a flour-whitened face and an obese body, emphasized by a belt above and below his enormous stomach. The practice of playing fixed characters with stock costumes and makeup suggests how close French farce of this period was to *commedia dell'arte,* a similarity which may have extended to improvisational playing. Associated for a time with Valleran's troupe, the players of Turlupin, Gaultier-Garguille, and Gros-Guillaume were the principal performers of the Hôtel de Bourgogne after Valleran left Paris in 1612, and they were probably most responsible for building up a theatregoing public.

The usual place for performances between 1595 and 1625 was the Hôtel de Bourgogne, since it was the only permanent theatre in Paris. Even though this building was used from 1548 until 1783, its dimensions are uncertain. The land acquired by the Confrérie in 1548 measured 101 by 108 feet, but part of this was sold before the theatre was built. One group of historians believes that the theatre was erected on a lot measuring about 42 by 108 feet, while another argues that it was 60 by 108 feet. Consequently, estimates of the theatre's width vary by almost 20 feet. Although it is difficult to choose between the claims, the interior dimensions of the Hôtel de Bourgogne were probably about 40 feet in width by 105 feet in length.

Around the walls of the auditorium ran two or three galleries, at least one of which was divided into boxes or loges. Above the loges facing the stage there was an undivided gallery (the amphitheatre or *paradis*). The first floor was taken up entirely by the pit, or *parterre,* in which there were no permanent seats (with the possible exception of a bench running along each of the side walls). The total capacity of the auditorium was about 1,600.

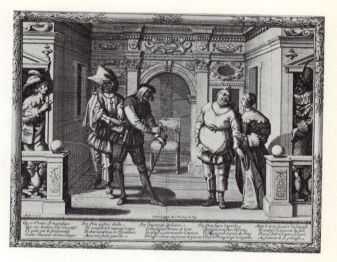

FIGURE 9.3 Farce actors at the Hotel de Bourgogne, *c.* 1630. On stage are Turlupin, Gaultier-Garguille and Gros-Guillaume. Engraving by Abraham Bosse. Courtesy Bibliothèque Nationale, Paris.

The stage was raised 5 or 6 feet above the pit. Although there was no proscenium arch, the side galleries, which extended to the stage, created a frame. The stage occupied the full width of the building, but the visible space was probably no wider than 25 feet. The depth of the stage is unknown, but estimates of it range from 17 to 35 feet.

Although the Confrérie probably used medieval mansions on this stage, the little that is known of scenic practices before 1625 can be summarized briefly: the Confrérie may have owned scenery which it rented with the theatre; Valleran's records show that he sometimes paid painters for scenic pieces; Hardy's extant plays require from three to seven locations, each probably represented by a separate mansion and all arranged around the periphery of the stage as they were in the 1630s; the few extant illustrations of farces show a stage with a compartment on either side, and either a cloth or doors at the back. Since all of the troupes were itinerant, none probably attempted elaborate settings.

Not all troupes performed at the Hôtel de Bourgogne, although the Confrérie collected a fee each day from all troupes appearing in Paris. For those who did not play at the Bourgogne, the usual choice was a tennis court. Since the Middle Ages, tennis (or *jeu de paume*) had been a favorite European game, and by the sixteenth century many courts were enclosed and roofed. Estimates of the number of courts in Paris in the seventeenth cen-

FIGURE 9.4 The second scene, "Garden of Delights," from *The Deliverance of Renaud,* produced at the French court in 1617. This seems to have been the first production in France to use angled side wings and back shutters. Courtesy Bibliothèque Nationale, Paris.

tury range from 250 to 1,800. By 1600, the measurements of tennis courts were standarized at about 90 by 30 feet. Thus, they did not differ markedly in size from the Hôtel de Bourgogne. A number of features recommended their use as theatres: the presence of a gallery for spectators along one side or end; the large open floor space; and the row of windows just below the roof which provided ample light. To convert a tennis court into a theatre, therefore, required merely the addition of a platform, an operation so simple that it was often done for a single performance. For more permanent conversions, the galleries were extended around the other walls and divided into boxes. Throughout Europe, the tennis court became the first choice of actors seeking buildings to convert into theatres.

In Paris, performances were given two or three times a week during the early seventeenth century. By

1600, posters were being used to advertise productions, and announcements of coming attractions were made from the stage. The starting times varied, but official regulations required that performances end sufficiently early that spectators might reach home before dark. Because the starting time was indefinite and spectators came early to secure good places, each company employed a "prologuist" to entertain the audience until the performance began. Bruscambrille (*fl.* 1610–1634) was famous in this role. The daily bill usually consisted of a long play followed by a farce, although an entire program might be made up of short plays. Music was a part of all performances.

The audience was drawn from all classes, but prior to 1625 it was largely undiscriminating in its search for entertainment. Many spectators wore swords or daggers, and fights in the pit were common. Probably there was much jostling and moving about by the approximately 1,000 persons who might be standing in the pit throughout a performance. The confusion was increased by the sale of food, drink, and other articles.

By 1625, the professional theatre had established a rather precarious foothold in Paris. Although still crude in comparison with those of England, Spain, or Italy, the French theatre was soon to undergo changes that would raise it above all others in the critical estimation of contemporaries.

THE TRIUMPH OF THE NEOCLASSICAL IDEAL

The stabilization and growth of the theatre paralleled political changes. Under Henri IV order had been restored but, like his predecessor, Henri was assassinated in 1610, bringing to the throne Louis XIII (reigned 1610–1643), then only nine years old. His mother and her ministers followed policies that stirred up trouble and the Huguenot question resurfaced because Protestant towns had become so independent that they constituted a nation within the nation. Beginning in the 1620s, the real power behind the throne was Cardinal Richelieu (1586–1642), who more than anyone else was responsible for concentrating almost unlimited power in the crown by taking it away from nobles and from the Protestant cities (though religious freedom was preserved).

With the return of stability in the 1620s came a resurgence of interest in neoclassicism. This renewed interest had already been felt, although weakly, in the early years of Louis XIII's reign. When the *ballet de cour* was revived in 1610 with *Alcine,* a unified setting in the Italian manner was definitely used for the first time. During the next ten years, largely due to the importation of such designers as Tomaso Francini, most of the Italian scenic innovations were seen at the French court. At first, sets were composed of painted cloths which could be dropped to reveal others. But in 1617 angled side wings and back shutters were introduced for *The Deliverance of Renaud.* By 1620, perspective scenery, unified settings, the raked stage, and scene shifting were in use. Around 1620, however, political unrest put an end to court productions and further developments had to wait until about 1640.

Soon, however, the neoclassical ideal was to find its way into the public theatres. There were several reasons for this development: a group of well-educated and technically proficient playwrights appeared; the audience came to prefer the new drama to the earlier farces; professional troupes gained a firm foothold in Paris; and political stability returned.

Of the dramatists who appeared around 1625, four were of special importance: Mairet, du Ryer, Rotrou, and Corneille. Jean de Mairet (1604–1686) came to Paris in 1625, the year in which his first play, *Chryséide and Arimand,* a tragicomedy, was performed. In 1626 he turned to writing pastorals, which he helped to popularize through such works as *Sylvie* (1628) and *La Sylvanire* (1631). Soon recognized as the leading dramatist of his day, he confirmed his reputation with *Sophonisba* (1634), the first tragedy of the new age to observe the neoclassical rules. It did much to revive interest in tragedy, which had been dormant since the first years of the century. Although Mairet's reputation has suffered because of his intemperate attack upon Corneille's *Le Cid,* he was as successful and often more highly regarded than Corneille in the 1630s. By the time he retired in 1640, he had probably done more than any other writer of his day to set drama on its new path.

Pierre du Ryer (*c.* 1600–1658), a well-educated government official, wrote prolifically in an attempt to overcome his perennial poverty. His early works were either irregular tragicomedies, such as *Clitophon* (*c.* 1629) and *Argenis and Poliarque* (1631), or farce vehicles for Gros-Guillaume. After coming under Mairet's influence about 1634, however, he turned to tragedy in the neoclassical mode. Of these later works, the best is *Scévole* (1644), which remained in the repertory for more than a century. Along with Mairet and Corneille, du Ryer established tragedy as a popular form.

Jean de Rotrou (1609–1650) began writing plays in 1628, and eventually succeeded Hardy as principal dramatist to the Hôtel de Bourgogne. Through Rotrou's adaptations of Spanish drama, the theme of love versus honor became a staple of the French stage. Interested primarily in rapid and absorbing actions, Rotrou failed to create characters of depth. Consequently, his plays now seem shallow, although in their day they did much to extend public interest in drama and offered Corneille his severest competition.

Despite the accomplishments of his contemporaries, Pierre Corneille (1606–1684) is now usually credited with establishing the neoclassical mode in France. Born in Rouen and educated for the law, he began to write plays after seeing the Montdory-LeNoir troupe perform in his home town. The result was *Mélite* (1629), a comedy unlike either farce or pastoral, the major comic forms of the time. Consequently, *Mélite* is often said to have set French comedy on a new path, one in which the intrigues and misunderstandings of lovers replaced the earlier emphasis on comic servants or sentimental love affairs. Until 1636, most of Corneille's plays were comedies and, though much admired, they served only to establish his reputation as a promising writer.

Le Cid (1636–1637) marked the turning point in Corneille's career and in French drama, for it precipitated a battle destined to clarify the conflict between the old and new ideals. Based upon Guillén de Castro's *Las Mocedades del Cid,* a play in six acts treating events occurring over many years and in many places, Corneille's play compresses the events into five acts, twenty-four hours, and four locations in a single town. Revolving around the theme of love versus honor, the action forces both the hero, Roderigue, and the heroine, Chimène, to choose between their love for each other and their duty to family and state. Although an enormous popular success, it was attacked by several critics, including Mairet and Georges de Scudéry (1601–1667), another leading playwright.

Several issues were raised. While the unity of time had been observed, verisimilitude had been strained by crowding numerous and complex incidents (including a war) into one day. Furthermore, Chimène's apparent agreement to marry Roderigue, who has killed her father less than twenty-four hours earlier, violated the neoclassical notion of decorum. The play did not fit any

FIGURE 9.5 Pierre Corneille's *Polyeucte.* In this scene pagan statues are being thrown down and destroyed. From the first edition of the play, 1643. Courtesy Lilly Library, Indiana University.

recognized dramatic type: it resembled tragicomedy in the number and variety of incidents, in the perils overcome by the hero, and in the happy ending; it resembled pastoral in the love story; and it resembled tragedy in its narrative and lyrical passages. The bitterness of the controversy prompted Cardinal Richelieu to request a verdict on the play from the newly formed French Academy. The results were destined to focus public attention on the neoclassical ideal.

After his rise to power, Richelieu had used his position to encourage the development of French literature and the arts so that France might become the cultural leader of Europe. To Richelieu, greatness seemed most likely to be achieved through following the Italian ideals of writing and staging. Consequently, through financial support and other incentives, he encouraged those authors who accepted the neoclassical ideal. Furthermore, in his own palace he built the first Italianate theatre in France. Perhaps most important, he promoted the formation of the French Academy as an arbiter of literary taste.

The French Academy originated in 1629 when a small group of men began meeting to discuss literature. Hearing of their work, Richelieu urged them to form an organization modeled after the Italian academies. In 1636 they reluctantly did as he wished, and in 1637 the French Academy received the state charter under which it still operates. Membership in the Academy was (and continues to be) restricted to forty, presumably the most eminent literary figures of the age. Upon its formation, the Academy took as its primary task the study and codification of French language and style.

It was to this newly formed group that Richelieu referred the controversy over *Le Cid.* The verdict, written principally by the group's leader, Jean Chapelain, was contained in *The Judgment of the Academy on The Cid* (1638). In it, Chapelain praised *Le Cid* insofar as it adhered to neoclassical doctrine and censured it for all deviations. He also restated the neoclassical ideal and urged its universal adoption.

Although Corneille later embraced neoclassical doctrine, he was stung by the reactions to *Le Cid* and wrote no more plays until 1640. Between 1640 and 1644, however, he produced the works now considered most characteristic of his style: *Horace* (1640), *Cinna* (1640), *Polyeucte* (1642–1643), and *The Death of Pompey* (1643). Each centers around a hero of indomitable will who chooses death rather than dishonor. Since Corneille's protagonists are never in doubt about their goals, they often appear one-sided; never divided within themselves, they are revealed in a series of episodes showing their reactions to external obstacles. Consequently, Corneille's characters are simple, but his plots complex. Beginning with *Rodogune* (1644), Corneille's stories often became so involved that they were difficult to follow. This trend toward complexity was not unique to Corneille's plays, for most dramatists of the time followed the same path until the 1660s when Racine's simplicity began a reaction against it.

While Corneille is the most celebrated tragedian of the 1640s, many others—including du Ryer and Rotrou—were also active in these years. In addition to tragedy, Corneille set the standard in comedy as well. His *The Liar* (1643), adapted from Alarcón's *The Suspicious Truth,* is considered the finest French comedy before Molière. Only one other comic writer, Paul Scarron (1610–1660), challenged Corneille's supremacy. Scarron paved the way for Molière by combining the comedy of intrigue, in which Corneille excelled, with farce, most notably in *Jodelet*, or *The Servant The Master* (1643) and *Jodelet Insulted* (1645), both written for the farceur Jodelet. In *The Scholar of Salamanca* (1654), Scarron introduced the character Crispin, who became so popular that other dramatists incorporated him into their plays. Scarron's novel, *A Comical Tale* (1651), which depicts the life of touring actors, is also noteworthy.

The vigor of the 1640s was followed by a decline in the 1650s. Tragedy lost its appeal and, after the failure of his *Pertharite* in 1652, Corneille gave up writing for many years. The decline can also be attributed in part to another civil war. Richelieu died in 1642 and Louis XIII in 1643. When Louis XIV (reigned 1643–1715) succeeded to the throne he was only five years old and his mother was named regent, although the major force was Cardinal Mazarin (1602–1661), her chief minister. Mazarin was unpopular not only because he used his position to enrich himself but because he was Italian. The nobility, sensing a chance to regain its old rights, joined together in a movement called La Fronde ("the sling") which developed into open rebellion in 1648. By 1652 the resistance of the nobility had been completely broken and thereafter those of the highest rank were forced to live at court where they could be watched. As a result, all authority was concentrated in the crown, where it was to remain until the Revolution of 1789. The civil war of 1648–1652 was followed almost immediately by French involvement in a Spanish conflict, which lasted until 1660. By that time the neoclassical ideal had completely triumphed.

ACTING COMPANIES, 1625–1660

The new vigor in playwriting after 1625 was paralleled by increased stability in acting companies. In contrast with the preceding period, when no troupe could maintain itself permanently in Paris, a company now settled in the Hôtel de Bourgogne, where it was to remain until 1680. Furthermore, by 1629 a second company had settled in Paris, and thereafter at least two theatres were always competing with each other.

The Bourgogne's troupe was descended from Valleran's. At first it included a number of actors who had worked for him and it assumed the title his troupe had held, The King's Players. Until their deaths in the 1630s, Turlupin, Gaultier-Garguille, and Gros-Guillaume were in the company. The leader and most important actor of the troupe, however, was Bellerose (Pierre le Messier, c. 1592–1670), who had begun as an apprentice in Valleran's company in 1609. After Valleran's death about 1613, Bellerose had toured with the remnants of the troupe until they returned to Paris in the early 1620s and amalgamated with the farce players then performing at the Hôtel de Bourgogne. Bellerose was a fine actor in both comedy and tragedy. He brought dignity to the theatre just as the new drama was achieving greater subtlety and as the taste for farce was declining. Noted for his natural style, he was nevertheless accused of affectation by some critics. His supremacy in the troupe remained unchallenged until his retirement in 1647.

The Comédiens du Roi soon had a rival in the troupe headed by Montdory (Guillaume des Gilleberts, 1594–1654) and Charles LeNoir (fl. 1610–1637). Montdory began his career about 1612 in Valleran's company, and, upon Valleran's death, joined the Prince of Orange's Players, with whom he remained for many years. In the late 1620s, he formed a company with Charles LeNoir, another actor-manager who had performed in Paris intermittently since 1610. After touring the provinces, they returned to Paris in 1629, bringing with them Corneille's first play, *Mélite*. They performed in a number of temporary theatres before settling in 1634 in a converted tennis court, the Théâtre du Marais, the first serious rival to the Hôtel de Bourgogne.

Because of his preference for the new drama, Montdory soon won the favor of Cardinal Richelieu, who awarded him a pension in 1634. In addition to *Le Cid*, many of the other outstanding plays of the 1630s were first played by Montdory. Sometimes called the first great French actor, Montdory was at his best in the roles of tragic heroes. Although a declamatory actor, he was capable of great emotion and is said to have brought conviction to all his parts. Under Montdory's leadership, the Marais became the leading theatre of Paris, a position which it was to hold until 1647. Unfortunately, Montdory suffered a partial paralysis in 1637 and was forced to retire.

Montdory was replaced at the Marais by Floridor (Josias de Soulas, 1608–1672), an aristocrat who had played in a touring company for many years. Upon Montdory's retirement, Floridor joined the Marais troupe as its leading actor until 1647, when he went to the Bourgogne to replace Bellerose. After Floridor's departure, the Marais declined, for Corneille and other leading dramatists now gave their plays to the Bourgogne. Floridor continued as the leading serious actor of Paris until his retirement in 1671. Floridor shared tragic roles with Montfleury (Zacharie Jacob, 1600–1667), who joined the Borgogne company in 1639 and rose rapidly to a position second only to that of Bellerose. Although he was enormously fat and employed a pompous delivery, he had a large following.

The farce tradition was continued by Jodelet and Guillot-Gorju. Jodelet (Julien Bedeau, *c.* 1600–1660) was a member of Montdory's troupe until ordered by Louis XIII to transfer to the Bourgogne in 1634. In the early 1640s he returned to the Marais, where he was so popular that a number of dramatists wrote plays especially for him. In 1659 he joined Molière, who created some roles for him, although Jodelet's death in 1660 made their association brief. Playing with a flour-whitened face in the manner of Gros-Guillaume, Jodelet was especially noted as the comic valet, a role which he raised to great popularity. Guillot-Gorju (Bertrand Hardouin de St. Jacques, 1600–1648) joined the Bourgogne troupe in 1633 upon the death of Gaultier-Garguille. In the role of the ridiculous doctor, he was famous for his witty repartee. He retired in 1641 to practice medicine, which he had studied prior to going on the stage.

After 1647, the Bourgogne troupe gained the ascendancy that it was to maintain until 1680. Meanwhile, the Marais, in an attempt to retain its popularity, turned increasingly to spectacle. Under the management of Laroque (Pierre Regnault Petit-Jean, *c.* 1595–1676), it fought a losing battle from 1647 to 1673, when the theatre was closed.

Both the financial and social position of the actor improved between 1625 and 1660. When Richelieu and others began to patronize the Marais troupe in the 1630s, Louis XIII granted the Comédiens du Roi a subsidy. All major troupes after this time received governmental assistance. Concern for the actor's dignity also began to grow around 1630. Gougenot's *La Comédie des Comédiens* (*c.* 1631), a play depicting a rehearsal, defends actors from the charge of immorality, and Georges de Scudéry's play of the same title, performed in 1632, takes the same position. Scudéry argues that actors, like the members of other professions, vary and that each should be judged on his merits. Scudéry also lists as qualifications of the good actor appropriate facial expression, impressive bearing, unconstrained movement, absence of

FIGURE 9.6 **Setting for Act V of** *Le Martyre de Sainte Catherine* **by Jean Puget de la Serre, produced at the Hotel de Bourgogne, 1643. In this production the basic structure remained fixed, while the view behind the central doorway and on the upper level changed with each act. The scene on the upper level apparently made use of the** *théâtre supérieure.* **From the original edition of the play. Courtesy Bibliothèque Nationale, Paris.**

extravagant posturing and provincial accent, a good memory, and sound judgment.

In 1641, Louis XIII sought to remove the stigma attached to acting by issuing a decree stating his desire that "the actors' profession . . . not be considered worthy of blame nor prejudicial to their reputation in society." But though it abolished certain legal restrictions, this decree did not alter the church's denial of its sacraments to actors.

THE PUBLIC THEATRES, 1625–1660

The major public theatres of Paris between 1625 and 1660 were the Hôtel de Bourgogne and the Théâtre du Marais. Presumably the physical attributes of the Bourgogne (already described) remained relatively unchanged from 1548 until 1647, when, by order of the King's Council, it was remodeled, probably in order to compete more effectively with the Marais.

Almost nothing is known of the first Théâtre du Marais, which was converted from a tennis court in 1634. When it burned in 1644, it was replaced immediately with a more elaborate structure which remained in use until 1673. The new Marais measured about 115 feet in length, 38 feet in width, and 52 feet in height. The pit, for standing spectators, was 61 feet by 38 feet; the side walls had three galleries, the first two divided into boxes, the third given over to the *paradis;* at the rear of the auditorium, the first gallery was divided into boxes, and above it rose the amphitheatre with its stadium-like seating. The capacity of the auditorium was about 1,500 persons.

The stage, raised about 6 feet above the *parterre,* sloped upward toward the back. It occupied the full width of the building and had a proscenium opening 25 feet wide. There was also a *théâtre supérieure,* or second stage, raised 13 feet above the main platform on 10 pillars. Semicircular, it curved upstage 6 feet at its center. But though documents clearly show that the Marais had a *théâtre supérieure,* scholars disagree about its size and placement. The reconstruction of the stage made by Deierkauf-Holsboer has the second stage begin only 6 feet back of the front edge of the main platform and consequently she shows the lower stage as being only 12 feet deep at its center. Bjurstrom, on the other hand, suggests that the lower stage was 29 feet deep at its center. Bjurstrom's reconstruction seems more logical, especially in light of the Marais' emphasis upon spectacle. On the other hand, much of the spectacle may have depended upon the upper stage. Since it might represent the "heavens," flying objects could rest on the upper stage in back of clouds used to conceal the platform. It is clear from many scripts, however, that not all flying was handled in this manner, and some scholars have questioned whether it was ever the usual method. Scholars also disagree about the use made of the second stage. Some argue that it was essential to almost every play, while others state that it was rarely employed. Although its precise use cannot be established, the *théâtre supérieure* was unquestionably available at both the Marais and the Bourgogne, although in the latter theatre it may have been removable.

It was probably the need to compete more effectively with the new Marais that led to the remodeling

FIGURE 9.7 Theatre built by Cardinal Richelieu in his palace in 1641. Seen in the foreground (from right to left) are Richelieu, Louis XIII, and the Queen. After Richelieu's death, this theatre was called the Palais-Royal.

of the Bourgogne in 1647. The imprecise contract for the changes still exist. It specifies that the stage is to be about 45 feet deep and "as wide as the building" (about 40 feet). The floor was raked upward toward the back and beams were installed at the front, probably to accommodate a curtain and to form a proscenium arch, neither of which apparently was used earlier. The stage opening was about 25 feet wide. In the auditorium, the galleries were curved into a U-shape to eliminate the former sharp angles at the rear corners. In spite of the remodeling, the Hôtel de Bourgogne remained the Parisian theatre least concerned with spectacle.

SCENIC PRACTICES AT THE PUBLIC THEATRES, 1625–1660

The scenic practices of the early 1630s are well documented in *Le Mémoire de Mahelot, Laurent, et des Autres Décorateurs . . . ,* one of the most valuable theatrical records of the seventeenth century. It is divided into three parts, each relating to widely separated years. The first part ends in 1635. Some scholars assume that it summarizes only the season of 1634–1635, while others argue that it records usage from about 1622 to 1635. It consists of seventy-one notices (that is, summaries of the scenic requirements) and forty-seven designs for plays in the repertory of the Hôtel de Bourgogne. Most scholars

FIGURE 9.8 **Setting for du Ryer's** *Lisandre and Caliste* **(c. 1635). Note the various locales represented simultaneously. From** *Le Mémoire de Mahelot.* **. . . Courtesy Bibliothèque Nationale, Paris.**

believe that the designs are by the compiler, Laurent Mahelot, although others have suggested that Mahelot was merely the theatre's machinist and that the designs are by George Buffequin, the major scenic designer of the period.

Mahelot's compilation demonstrates clearly that in 1635 scenic practices were still essentially medieval. Since the unity of place was not yet common, most plays required a number of locales, each of which was represented by a mansion. All mansions were present simultaneously, arranged along the sides and across the back of the stage to leave the center free for the actors. The back scene usually represented a single place, but typically there were two mansions on each side. Many of the mansions were of such a general nature—a house, a wood, a palace, a grotto, a cave, a tomb, a prison, a tent, a seacoast—that they reappeared in a number of different settings. When a play required more mansions than could be accommodated on stage at once, units were converted by removing painted canvas coverings or by opening curtains to reveal an interior. A few visual characteristics relate the settings to Italian practices: some of the painted backcloths are done in perspective; the balanced pairs of mansions resemble Serlio's arrangement of angled wings; and in some settings, decorative details are repeated to give greater unity to the whole. In spite of these superficial similarities, however, the effect is clearly more medieval than Italianate.

A few machines are mentioned by Mahelot. Boats with passengers move from one side of the stage to the other; gods and other supernatural characters appear above the stage; clouds, fire, smoke, and sound effects are specified. Such properties as human heads and sponges filled with blood are noted. Furniture is restricted to an occasional throne or stool.

Le Mémoire also gives some information about costumes, since it lists all items supplied by the company. It reveals that actors supplied their own garments except for monks, devils, ghosts, coachmen, and valets, or when a number of identical costumes were required. By the 1630s, considerable splendor in dress was evident. The inventory made of Charles LeNoir's wardrobe in 1637 appraised it at the modern equivalent of about $10,000.

The second part of the *Mémoire* lists seventy-one titles of works in the repertory of the Hôtel de Bourgogne in 1646–1647, but unfortunately it includes neither "notices" nor designs. It may be assumed that by this time scenic practices had gradually moved away from simultaneous settings to unified settings as the unity of place was increasingly adopted following the controversy over *Le Cid.* Certainly by 1680 settings were appreciably simpler than in 1635, a point which will be pursued later.

THE TRIUMPH OF THE ITALIAN IDEAL IN SCENERY, 1640–1660

Although Italianate scenery had been introduced at court before 1625, it was not exploited there until after 1640. Perhaps to provide a model, Cardinal Richelieu had the architect LeMercier construct the first theatre in France with a permanent proscenium arch and a stage designed to use flat wings. This theatre, commonly called the Palais-Cardinal, had a stage 59 feet wide by 46 feet deep, and an auditorium 59 feet wide by 65 feet deep. Two undivided galleries surrounded the hall, while most of the ground floor was taken up by an amphitheatre that rose in broad steps from a small pit. Since the theatre was intended only for invited guests, the auditorium did not follow the arrangement used in the public theatres.

The Palais-Cardinal was opened in January 1641 with *Mirame,* with scenery and special effects designed by Georges Buffequin. Since *Mirame* required only one setting, the potentialities of the theatre were not fully displayed until later in 1641 when the *Ballet de la*

Prospérité des Armes de la France, with nine settings, was produced. When Richelieu died in 1642, the theatre came under the control of the crown and thereafter was called the Palais-Royal.

Richelieu's successor as Chief Minister, Cardinal Mazarin, had a taste for opera, a form that he sought to promote in France. His first production in 1645 set in motion a series of events which were to bring Giacomo Torelli to Paris. A visiting *commedia dell'arte* troupe, knowing the power of opera, became so anxious over Mazarin's plans that it begged the queen to import a designer and choreographer from Italy to insure the appeal of their own productions. Consequently, the queen wrote to the Duke of Parma, who sent Torelli in response to her request.

By 1645, Torelli was probably the most famous scene designer in Italy because of his productions at the Teatro Novissimo in Venice. Torelli accepted the royal summons without realizing that he was to work with *commedia dell'arte* players. Upon learning the truth, he at first refused to cooperate, but eventually he agreed upon the condition that he be allowed to design operatic productions as well. For his first opera in Paris, he chose *La Finta Pazza,* the work that had made him famous in Venice. Staged at the Petit Bourbon in December, 1645, before the court, it was a complete success. Most historians date the triumph of the Italian ideal in France from this production.

To house this opera, Torelli had also converted the Petit Bourbon into an Italianate theatre. He erected a platform 6 feet high to make a stage about 49 feet wide by 48 feet deep, somewhat larger than the one he had used in Venice. He also installed his chariot-and-pole system of scene shifting, probably his only major improvement over Richelieu's theatre.

In 1646, Torelli remodeled the Palais-Royal to accommodate the chariot-and-pole method of shifting, and in 1647 *Orphée* was staged there at a tremendous cost, which Mazarin paid out of state funds. The presence of so many Italians, the hostility which the French nobles felt against Mazarin, and the use of state money to finance operas aroused considerable resentment. Mazarin, seeking works more compatible with French taste, then commissioned Corneille to write *Andromède,* which when finished was labeled a "machine play" since it differed considerably from Italian opera. *Andromède* was like regular drama in that its story progressed through spoken episodes, but resembled opera in that each act provided an excuse to introduce elaborate machinery and special

FIGURE 9.9 *La Prospérité des Armes de la France* **as given at Cardinal Richelieu's new theatre in 1641. Note the figures atop the walls and the chariot in the sky. Courtesy Theatre Museum, Drottningholm.**

effects during a pantomimic episode accompanied by music. Most of the scenery and machinery used for Corneille's play had already appeared in *Orphée*. Staged at the Petit Bourbon in 1650, *Andromède* was successful enough to begin a vogue for machine plays, one that the Marais sought to meet with such productions as *The Golden Fleece, The Loves of Jupiter and Semele, The Loves of Venus and Adonis,* and *The Marriage of Bacchus and Ariadne.* Eventually the Marais was virtually bankrupt by the sums required to mount these spectacles.

In the late 1640s, ballet began to recapture the popularity it had enjoyed at court before 1620. It was especially prominent between 1651 and 1669, when Louis XIV appeared in many of the productions. Called *ballets d'entrées,* these entertainments did not require the technical proficiency of modern ballet. They were allegorical stories, explained by a spoken libretto and pantomimed by performers in movements based upon ballroom dances of the time, although these dances were often given elaborate choreographic patterns. One of the most characteristic works, *The Ballet of the Night* (1653), was divided into forty-three "entries," featuring such groups as hunters, bandits, shepherds, gypsies, astrologers, the Four Elements, Venus, and Aurora, each related crown's power was so firmly established that Louis could convincingly declare, "I am the State." During the years that followed, French artists developed their own distinctive version of the baroque visual style, appropriately called Louis Quatorze.

The innovations in scenic practice that had been introduced by Torelli were strengthened by the prepara-

FIGURE 9.10 Giacomo Torelli's setting for Act II of Pierre Corneille's *Andromède* at the Petit Bourbon, 1650. Engraving by François Chauveau. Courtesy Bibliothèque Nationale, Paris.

to a different phase of the night. Finally, the Sun, danced by Louis XIV, appeared to disperse the darkness. This piece of transparent flattery was one of many works that helped to create the image of Louis XIV as the "Sun King" (around which everything revolves), a symbol promoted assiduously throughout his reign.

In 1654, Mazarin, seeking once more to adapt opera to French taste, commissioned Isaac Bensérade (1613–1691), who had composed the librettos for the majority of the court ballets, to write an opera with ballets interspersed between the acts. For this production, *The Marriage of Peleus and Thetis*, Torelli designed seven sets and a number of spectacular special effects. Louis XIV appeared in six roles.

By 1660, the Italian ideal had clearly triumphed in France.

THE NATURALIZATION OF THE ITALIAN IDEAL, 1660–1700

In 1660 Louis XIV married Marie Thérèse of Spain, and in 1661 Mazarin died. These two events mark the coming of age of Louis, who thereafter assumed complete control over governmental affairs. By this time, the

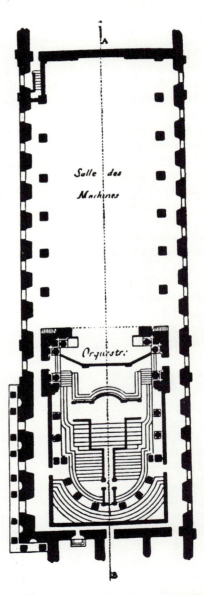

FIGURE 9.11 Plan of the Salle des Machines designed by Gaspare Vigarani and opened in 1662. From L. P. de la Guepière, *Théâtre et Machine* (1888).

tions made for the marriage of Louis XIV. In 1659, Mazarin sent to Italy for Gaspare Vigarani (1586–1663), famous at this time as a scenic designer and builder of theatres. The Petit Bourbon was torn down, and a new wing was added to the Tuileries Palace. Within this wing Vigarani set up the largest theatre in Europe, the Salle des Machines. Although only 52 feet wide, the new theatre was 232 feet long; of this length, only 92 feet were occupied by the auditorium, leaving 140 feet of depth for a stage which had a proscenium arch only 32 feet wide. This enormous depth is symptomatic of the trend then underway toward settings of ever-increasing size. Completed in 1660, the Salle des Machines was inaugurated in 1662 with the opera *Hercules in Love,* a transparent compliment to the king. Interlarded with ballets, the opera featured Vigarani's scenery and machines, on one of which, 60 feet deep by 45 feet wide, the entire royal family and their attendants were flown. This ma-

chine was used again in *Psyché* (1671) to display 300 deities surrounded by clouds. Despite this auspicious beginning, the Salle des Machines was seldom used after the 1660s because of its size and poor acoustics.

When Mazarin imported Vigarani, he had not intended to exclude Torelli, but the latter's enemies rallied around Vigarani, and after Mazarin died in 1661 Torelli was ordered to leave France. He returned to his native Fano, where he later built a theatre. There he staged his last production in 1677, the year before he died. Although Torelli left Paris under a cloud, the primary credit for establishing the Italian ideal in France must go to him.

When Vigarani died in 1663, his post as court designer was given to his son, Carlo (1623–1713), who retained it until 1680. Carlo Vigarani's principal work was done at the opera in Paris and at the court at Versailles.

After 1660 Louis XIV's attention turned increasingly to the palace he was building at Versailles twelve

FIGURE 9.12 Design by Vigarani, *c.* 1660. Courtesy National Museum, Stockholm.

FIGURE 9.13 One of the entertainments from the first day of *Pleasures of the Enchanted Island,* given by Louis XIV at Versailles in 1664. Here a stage has been erected in the middle of a lake to represent the palace of Alcine; after an elaborate ballet was performed there, the palace was destroyed by fire, thus breaking the enchantment which had held the hero, Roger, captive. A contemporary engraving by Israel Silvestre. In the possession of the author.

miles outside of Paris. Eventually this palace would be more than a half mile long with several wings and hundreds of rooms. While it was being built, Louis staged several festivals there, using temporary theatres set up at various spots in the palace grounds. One of the most spectacular of the celebrations was that of 1664, called "The Pleasures of the Enchanted Island," which extended over three days, and included processions, tournaments, ballets, and plays.

Throughout the 1660s, "comedy ballets," in which scenes in dialogue alternate with ballet entries, were a favorite with Louis. Many of these were written by Molière and Jean-Baptiste Lully (1632–1687), destined to become the founder of French opera. Lully was born in Italy, but came to France when only twelve years old. Appointed a court musician in 1653, by 1661 he was superintendent of all court music. In this capacity, he worked closely with Molière and others on court entertainment, and his experience with ballets, machine plays, and other forms familiarized him with French musical taste. In 1672 he obtained a monopoly on musical performances in Paris from Louis XIV, and in 1673 after Molière's death, he wrested control of the Palais-Royal from Molière's widow to use as the home of his Royal Academy of Music and Dance (commonly called the Opéra). Although the terms of Lully's monopoly were vague, he interpreted them to cover any performance that required more than six instruments, two trained singers or elaborate spectacle. The latter provision is indicative of the period's association of spectacle with opera, for, as the neoclassical ideal triumphed, the staging of drama had become increasingly simple. Lully's monopoly put an end to the "machine plays" at the Marais and thus further weakened that company, which had steadily declined since 1647.

Between 1672 and 1687, Lully created a series of works considered to mark the beginnings of French opera. His principal collaborator was Phillippe Quinault (1635–1688), author of fourteen librettos, of which the most famous are *Atys* (1676) and *Armide* (1686). Until 1680, when he returned to Italy, Vigarani designed the scenery for these operas.

Vigarani was succeeded by Jean Berain père (1637–1711). Educated entirely in France, Berain is credited with the first complete realization of the visual style associated with the reign of Louis XIV. Employed at court in 1671 to design embroidery, tapestry, woodcarving, and furniture, he succeeded Henri Gissey as "Designer of the Cabinet of the King" in 1674. Since Gissey

FIGURE 9.14 Jean Berain's design for *Armide,* 1680. Courtesy National Museum, Stockholm.

had customarily designed costumes for the opera, Berain also assumed this job. After 1680, Berain was principal designer for the court and the opera until his death, when he was succeeded by his son, Jean Berain *fils* (1678–1726), who held the posts until 1721. To the Berains goes the credit for establishing a distinctively French style of design emphasizing heavy lines, reverse curves, and encrusted ornamentation. In his stage designs, Berain usually restricted himself to one set for each act, but he employed many machines and special effects. This combination of static scenery and dynamic machinery was to remain typical of French operatic design through the eighteenth century.

In 1682 Louis moved the seat of government to Versailles, and forced all of France's leading noblemen to live there so he might keep an eye on them. By this time the nobility had become relatively powerless, though it had been deprived of none of its major privileges. Forced to live at court, the nobles lost touch with lesser ranks, especially those in the provinces. Versailles not only became the symbol of the king's absolute power, but it also epitomized many of the conditions that underlay the French Revolution a century later.

By the time the court moved to Versailles, the Italian ideals of staging had been completely naturalized, and France had replaced Italy as the cultural center of Europe. Court taste had been decisive in this process. After 1682, however, the influence of the court on the Parisian stage declined, no doubt because courtiers no longer made up a significant part of the audience.

FRENCH DRAMA, 1660–1700

Court taste also played a crucial role in the development of French drama. Following its decline during the Fronde rebellion, drama began to recover in the late 1650s. Tragedy returned to favor with *Timocrate* (1656) by Thomas Corneille (1625–1709), younger brother of Pierre Corneille. Author of more than forty plays, the best of which are *Ariane* (1672), *The Statue's Banquet* (1673), and *The Count of Essex* (1678), Thomas Corneille was one of the most successful dramatists of his time, although his reputation has suffered by comparison with that of his brother. Pierre Corneille also returned to writing in 1659 with *Oedipe* and continued until 1674.

Although many of Pierre Corneille's late works are of unquestioned merit, they are overshadowed by

FIGURE 9.15 Berain's costume design for an Indian in *The Triumph of Love,* 1681. From Adolphe Jullien, *Histoire du Costume au Théâtre* (1880).

Jean Racine's (1639–1699) plays, with which French tragedy reached its peak. Racine received an excellent education which instilled in him a lasting admiration of the Greek dramatists, whose example he sought to follow. His first tragedy, *La Thébaïde*, was produced in 1664 by Molière, who, in spite of the financial failure of the play, also produced Racine's second work, *Alexander the Great* (1665). Dissatisfied with the production, Racine permitted the Hôtel de Bourgogne to present the same play two weeks later, an unprecedented breach of contract. Furthermore, Racine allegedly induced Mlle. DuParc, Molière's principal tragic actress, to join the Hôtel de Bourgogne troupe. This double treachery led to a permanent rupture between the two men.

Racine's reputation, established by *Andromaque* in 1667, grew steadily during the next ten years with *Britannicus* (1669), *Bérénice* (1670), *Bajazet* (1672), *Mithridate* (1673), *Iphigénie* (1674), and *Phèdre* (1677). After *Phèdre*, Racine gave up playwriting, perhaps because his enemies had contrived to make a success of

FIGURE 9.16 Scene from Racine's *Bérénice*, first performed in 1670 at the Hôtel de Bourgogne with Mlle. Champmeslé in the title role. Engraving from the edition of Racine's plays published in 1676.

actions out of the internal conflicts of his protagonists. In contrast with Corneille's use of simple characters and complex plots, Racine constructed simple plots and complex characters. Because Racine's protagonists vacillate between two courses of action, torn between their sense of duty and their uncontrollable desires, dramatic interest is centered on the inner struggle rather than on the external events, which are important only as they contribute to the inner crisis. The plays usually begin some time after the protagonist has become aware of his dilemma. In a state of high emotion, he usually lays his soul bare to a *confidant* during the opening scene. Although no information is withheld, neither the audience nor the characters can foresee the outcome. The protagonist's psychological struggle makes up the dramatic action. Therefore, Racine was able to express his tragic vision adequately within the confines of the neoclassical ideal.

Upon Racine's retirement, tragedy began a long decline, which was not immediately apparent, since at the time other writers seemed worthy successors. The most important of these were Campistron, Longpierre, and LaFosse. Jean Galbert de Campistron (1656–1723) wrote seven tragedies between 1683 and 1691 which led critics to consider him the leading tragedian of his time. His most popular plays were *Andronic* (1685), which reverses the situation in *Phèdre* by having a man fall in love with his stepmother, and *Tiridate* (1691), a play about incestuous love. Campistron concentrated upon the victims of tragedy, and consequently his effects are essentially pathetic. After 1691, he retired to enter the king's service.

Hilaire Bernard de Roqueleyne Longpierre (1659–1731) also concentrated upon pathetic situations, although, like Racine, he placed major emphasis upon internal psychological conflicts. His major work is *Medée* (1694), notable in part because the fourth act is entirely a monologue. Antoine de LaFosse (1653–1708) did not begin writing until 1696 and composed only four tragedies. Nevertheless, many critics believed that, had he begun earlier, he would have surpassed Racine. Today he is remembered primarily for *Manlius Capitolanus* (1698), which remained in the repertory of the Comédie Française until 1849. In spite of these new writers, the tragic impulse was nearly over by 1700.

Like tragedy, comedy reached its peak in the 1660s and 1670s. As Racine represents the summit in tragic writing, so does Moliére in comic drama. Building upon the comedy of intrigue popularized by Corneille and Scarron, Moliére added interest above all through

Jacques Pradon's (1632–1698) *Phèdre*, produced simultaneously with Racine's play, and his own a relative failure. At about this time, Racine was appointed historiographer to Louis XIV and abandoned his literary life. Some years later, he wrote *Esther* (1689) and *Athalie* (1691) for Mme. de Maintenon's (Louis XIV's second wife) school for girls at St. Cyr. Neither play was performed profesionally during his lifetime. In addition to his tragedies, Racine wrote one comedy, *The Litigants* (1668), based in part on Aristophanes' *The Wasps*.

Racine's reputation is based upon the tragedies written between 1667 and 1677, of which *Phèdre* is the acknowledged masterpiece. Racine's greatness stems in part from his ability to develop compelling dramatic

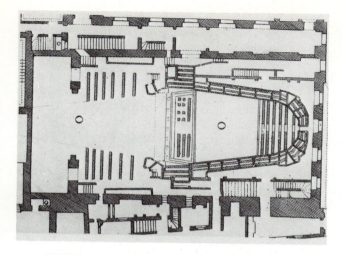

FIGURE 9.17 Plan of the Palais-Royal. This theatre was built by Richelieu and remodeled by Torelli. It served as the home of Molière's company from 1660 until 1673, and was used by the Opéra from 1673 until 1763, when it was destroyed by fire. Note the stage at left with its inner stage; also note the seatless pit (marked O at right). From Blondel, *Architecture Française* (1754).

characterization. With his work, comedy was raised to a level equaling tragedy.

Molière (Jean-Baptiste Poquelin, 1622–1673), the son of a prosperous upholsterer and furniture maker, was given an excellent education and was destined for a court position until he joined with nine other young people to form the Théâtre Illustre in 1643. Having failed in Paris, the troupe set off in 1646 on a tour of the provinces which lasted until 1658. At this time, about twelve or fifteen other companies were touring in France, and Molière's company soon joined with that of Charles Dufresne (*c.* 1611–*c.* 1684). By 1651, Molière was head of the troupe. He now turned to writing plays; his first important work was *The Blunderer,* performed at Lyons in 1655. The turning point in the troupe's fortunes came in 1658, when it was invited to court by the king's brother, who had seen it perform in the provinces. The company was sufficiently well received to be granted the title Troupe de Monsieur and the use of the Petit Bourbon for public performances.

The company was not very successful with the public, however, until it presented Molière's *Les Precieuses Ridicules* (*The Affected Ladies,* 1659), a satire on contemporary affectations. After this production, its

fortunes were assured. When the Petit Bourbon was torn down, Molière was allowed to use the Palais-Royal, built by Richelieu and remodeled by Torelli. Here the company played from 1660 until 1673, enjoying a position of preeminence in comedy similar to that attained by the Bourgogne in tragedy. The Marais was soon relegated to the third rank.

The reputation of the Palais-Royal troupe derived primarily from Molière's plays, the core of its repertory. Now remembered principally for his comedies of character, Molière wrote other kinds of plays as well. Many of his works are farces in the manner of the *commedia*

FIGURE 9.18 Scene from Molière's *Learned Ladies,* first performed at the Palais-Royal in 1672 with Molière in the role of Chrysale (seen here at left). From the edition of Molière's plays published in 1682.

dell'arte, by which he was much influenced. Some of the most popular of these were *Sganarelle, or The Imaginary Cuckold* (1660), *The Doctor in Spite of Himself* (1666), and *The Tricks of Scapin* (1671). Other works were written especially for court festivities, although most were later performed for the general public. A large number of these were "comedy ballets," such as *The Bores* (1661), *The Forced Marriage* (1664), *The Princess of Elide* (1664), and *Monsieur de Pourceaugnac* (1669). Others, such as *Amphitryon* (1668) and *Psyché* (1671) were "machine plays" with much spectacle. For most of the court plays, Molière collaborated with Lully, who provided the music. Occasionally Molière attempted serious drama, as in *Don Garcie de Navarre* (1661), but with little success.

Molière's great achievements are his comedies of character and manners, such as *The School for Husbands* (1661), *The School for Wives* (1662), *Tartuffe* (1664, 1667, 1669), *The Misanthrope* (1666), *The Miser* (1668), *The Learned Ladies* (1672), and *The Imaginary Invalid* (1673). His observations on contemporary manners and character types in these works embroiled him in much controversy. The first important battle was precipitated by *The School for Wives* (1662), which treated the upbringing appropriate to young girls who are to be faithful wives. Although enormously popular, the play was attacked on both artistic and moral grounds. Molière answered in two plays: *The Critique of The School for Wives* (1663) and *The Rehearsal at Versailles* (1663). Louis XIV's grant of an annual pension to Molière did much to silence the criticism. By far the bitterest controversy, however, centered around *Tartuffe,* an attack upon hypocrisy interpreted by many as a condemnation of all religion. After the play was forbidden, Molière rewrote it twice, in 1667 and in 1669, before it was deemed acceptable. When the final version was produced in 1669 it had an initial run of thirty-three performances, a record for the time. Louis XIV's attitude toward the quarrel is probably indicated by his grant to Molière's company in 1665 of an annual subsidy and the title, The King's Troupe.

These quarrels clearly indicate that Molière had made comedy a vital reflection of contemporary life and manners. Still, there is little bitterness in his plays, for though he ridiculed customs and character types, he did not believe that men could be changed; thus, he shows human nature being deformed by various kinds of deviant behavior but he does not imply that it can be perfected. Consequently, his characters remain much the same at the end of the plays as at the beginning. This probably explains why his resolutions, usually brought about by some external force, are open to criticism. When, as in *The Misanthrope,* no external power intervenes, the action remains unresolved.

In his long plays, Molière usually conforms to the neoclassical ideal of five acts and the unities. Some of the plays are written in verse, others in prose. While his language is varied, it is rarely witty for its own sake; aptness to character and situation is the secret of his dialogue. Many of the plays are set in drawing rooms, a clear departure from previous comedy, which had usually been placed out of doors in the manner of Roman comedy. With Molière, the settings are a reflection of the manners and characters depicted, and his example did much to popularize the interior setting for comedy. Molière wrote for his own company and knew who would play each character. Furthermore, he directed his own plays and often played the leading role himself. Hence, details were probably added during rehearsals that are not explicitly stated in the scripts.

ACTING COMPANIES, 1660–1700

When Molière died in 1673, Paris had five professional troupes: Molière's, Lully's opera company, a *commedia dell'arte* troupe, and the companies at the Hôtel de Bourgogne and at the Marais. All received some financial assistance from the government. By 1700, only two were left.

At Molière's death, many doubted his company's ability to continue. To allay anxieties, the troupe resumed performances after one week. Soon, however, a number of actors seceded, and Lully was able to evict the troupe from the Palais-Royal. Another theatre was found in the rue Guénégaud, but the Marais troupe also wished to buy it. Louis XIV now intervened by ordering the closing of the Marais and the amalgamation of the two companies. The combined groups opened at the rue Guénégaud in July 1673.

This situation continued until 1679, when Mlle. Champmeslé, the Bourgogne's principal tragic actress, left that company to join the troupe at the Guénégaud. This crisis was also resolved by a crown order joining the two companies. Thus came into existence the Comédie Française, the world's first national theatre. The new company gave its first performance on August 25, 1680, at the theatre in the rue Guénégaud.

FIGURE 9.19 Angelo Constantini receiving Arlequin's mask and baton from Columbine. In the background are seen the figure and tomb of Domenico Biancolelli, the Arlequin who has died. This is the *commedia dell'arte* company that played at the Hotel de Bourgogne from 1680 to 1697. Watercolor by Lichery, 1688. Courtesy Bibliothèque Nationale, Paris.

Upon its formation, the Comédie Française was given a monopoly on the performance of all spoken drama in French. (The rights of the Confrérie de la Passion had finally been abrogated in the 1670s.) Almost immediately, however, an exception to this monopoly was granted the *commedia dell'arte* troupe headed by Tiberio Fiorillo (1608–1694) that had made Paris its permanent home since 1660 and had for some time been performing plays in French. Other famous actors in this company were Domenico Biancolelli (*c.* 1637–1688),

a favorite of Louis XIV and the popularizer of Arlequin in France; Marc'Antonio Romagnesi (*c.* 1633–1706), who at first played the lover and later Dottore; and Angelo Costantini, who made many innovations in the character Mezzetin. When the Comédie Française was installed at the rue Guénégaud in 1680, the *commedia* troupe was assigned the Hôtel de Bourgogne as its home.

Periodically, the *commedia* troupe was in trouble because of the audacity of its plays, but it overcame all difficulties until 1697, when it was expelled from Paris following an alleged attack upon Mme. de Maintenon, Louis XIV's second wife, in *The False Prude*. There were to be no more Italian troupes in Paris until 1716. Thus, in 1697, the Parisian theatre was reduced to the Comédie Française and the Opéra.

THE ORGANIZATION OF FRENCH ACTING COMPANIES

All of the French acting companies of the seventeenth century were organized on the sharing plan, under which all regular members participated in the management and divided the profits. The number of members varied with the company's prosperity. Before 1650, there were usually eight to twelve; when Molière returned to Paris in 1658, his troupe included ten members, but was increased to twelve (eight men and four women) in 1659. When the Comédie Française was formed in 1680, 21¼ shares were divided among twenty-seven members (17 full shares, 7 one-half shares, and 3 one-quarter shares). Thus, an actor's share varied according to his importance in the company.

Since the number of shares in the Comédie Française was fixed by the First Gentlemen of the Chamber (the court officials who superintended the troupe), not all the actors were sharing members (or *sociétaires*) No new member could be admitted as a sharer until an actor resigned, retired, or died. When a vacancy occurred, the *sociétaires* elected a new member, usually from among the *pensionnaires* (the actors who worked for the troupe on salary). If a performer desired a position with the Comédie Française, he was required to play a series of roles in regular public performances; if the troupe wished to retain him, they placed him on salary until a vacancy in membership occurred, although many *pensionnaires* never became *sociétaires*. When he became a *sociétaire*, an actor bound himself to the company for twenty years

FIGURE 9.20 The expulsion of the Italian actors from Paris in 1697. An engraving based on a painting by Watteau. Courtesy British Museum.

and made himself liable to a heavy fine if he quit. The *sociétaires* had a voice in all matters of policy, including the acceptance of new plays. The actor with the longest service acted as head (or *doyen*) of the troupe. The Comédie Française also continued the pension system that had evolved among the earlier troupes. Under it, an actor could retire after twenty years of service with an annual pension of 1,000 francs. The government also continued to provide the troupe with an annual subsidy.

A member of the Comédie Française had considerable security. His assured position as a *sociétaire*, however, encouraged complacency and arrogance. The opportunities for employment had also been considerably restricted, since after 1680 Paris had only one troupe for drama.

Of the actors who achieved fame in the years between 1660 and 1700, several were associated with Molière. Madeleine Béjart (1618–1672) was already an established provincial actress when Molière met her. She is credited with inducing him to become an actor and was intimately involved in his work until her death. In the early years, she played tragic heroines, but later turned to the saucy maids of Molière's comedies. Geneviève (c. 1622–1675), Joseph (c. 1620–1659), who played young lovers, and Louis Béjart (1625–1678), who played comic valets, were also members of the troupe. Armande Béjart (1642–1700), who became Molière's wife in 1662, made her debut in 1663 and thereafter played the heroines in his plays. A versatile actress, she did much to hold the company together after her husband's death. In 1677, she married Isaac François Guérin d'Étriché (c.

1636–1728), who acted until he was past eighty and had become *doyen* of the Comédie Française.

Perhaps even more than Molière's wife, LaGrange (Charles Varlet, c. 1639–1692) was responsible for the continuation of Molière's company. Employed in 1659 to replace Joseph Béjart as the young lover, he also kept the company's records until 1685. His *Registre*, which records receipts, performances, and all deliberations, is the principal source of information about Molière's troupe and the early years of the Comédie Française. LaGrange also wrote the only contemporary biography of Molière, published in 1682 in the first edition of Molière's works.

Of tragic performers, the most important were Mlle. DuParc, Mlle. Desoeillets, Mlle. Champmeslé, and Michel Baron. Mlle. DuParc (1633–1668) joined Molière's troupe in the provinces and remained with him until 1666, when Racine is said to have lured her to the Borgogne, where she was the leading tragic actress until her death. Mlle. Desoeillets (1621–1670) served a long apprenticeship in the provinces before coming to Paris around 1660. Playing first at the Marais, she moved to the Bourgogne in 1662; there she was the leading performer until Mlle. DuParc joined the company in 1666, and again after Mlle. DuParc died. Short and not very pretty, she nevertheless gave moving performances which won her a devoted following. Mlle. Champmeslé (1642–1698) came to the Marais in 1669, also after a career in the provinces. Within six months she was considered the finest tragic actress in Paris and had moved to the Bourgogne. She retained her position of supremacy until her death, creating such great tragic roles as Phèdre. Supposedly her desertion of the Bourgogne motivated the formation of the Comédie Française. She passed on her declamatory style to two of her pupils, Mlle. Desmares and Mlle. Duclos, the leading tragic actresses of the early eighteenth century.

The void left at the Bourgogne by the death of Montfleury in 1667 and the retirement of Floridor in 1671 was not filled until Michel Baron (1653–1729) deserted Molière's troupe in 1673. Baron had been a child actor even before Molière took him into his home in 1666 and trained him further. His adult career began in 1670 as Domitien in Corneille's *Titus and Bérénice*. By the time of Molière's death, Baron was noted as a fine serious actor of the natural school; soon after he joined the Bourgogne in 1673, he was recognized as the leading tragic actor of the day and continued to be so regarded until he retired in 1691. His return to the stage in 1720 will be considered later. To many, Baron was the epitome of great acting and the finest serious actor of the seventeenth century.

Although an actor tended always to play the same type of role, he was not as yet employed to play a specified range of characters, as he was to be in the eighteenth century. The casting of a new play was done by the author, and actors were forbidden to refuse a role. Old plays were cast by the company in consultation. Rehearsals, perfunctory by modern standards, were held in the late morning. Although authors allegedly staged their own plays, they probably relied heavily upon the advice of a leading actor. Once a play had been performed, the actors were considered ready to present it at any time thereafter. A company in this period usually had about seventy plays in its active repertory, and these plays were rotated in a daily change of bill.

Until the 1650s, an author was paid a fixed sum for each play. Later, he was assigned shares for the initial run, after which he received no further payments. As long as the play remained unpublished, it was considered the exclusive property of the company that had bought it; after publication, any company could produce it without paying a fee.

The expenses of a company were subtracted before the sharing actors were paid. The troupe, however, did not supply costumes. Although most characters were dressed in contemporary garments, others, expecially classical, Near-Eastern, and Indian figures, were usually played in elaborate and costly costumes quite unlike those worn in daily life. The typical dress of classical heroes, the *habit à la romaine,* an adaptation of Roman armor, tunic, and boots, accompanied by a full-bottomed wig and plumed headdress, cost about 2,000 livres, a sum roughly equivalent to one-third of the actor's annual income. This financial burden was somewhat relieved by the royal practice of paying actors 400 livres for each costume they provided in plays mounted especially for court. In spite of his expenses, the actor of the late seventeenth century was well paid by the standards of the time.

Until 1680, the troupes played only three or four days each week, the preferred days being Tuesday, Friday, and Sunday. After 1680, the troupes began to play daily; in the 1682–1683 season, the Comédie Française gave 352 performances. After 1680 the usual starting time was 4 or 5 P.M. Attendance was not high, the average at the Comédie Française between 1680 and 1700

FIGURE 9.21   Theatre in the rue Guénégaud, used by the amalgamated Molière-Marias troupe from 1673 until 1680 and by the Comédie Française from 1680 until 1689. It was built in 1670 and originally was used for opera. Note the chandeliers over the stage and the spectators on stage and in the boxes. Courtesy Bibliothèque Nationale, Paris.

being about 450 persons in theatres designed to hold 1,500 to 2,000 persons. Spectators still stood in the pit and moved about freely. Others sat on the stage, a practice which some scholars date from the first production of *Le Cid* in 1636. By the late seventeenth century, benches installed on either side of the stage reduced the

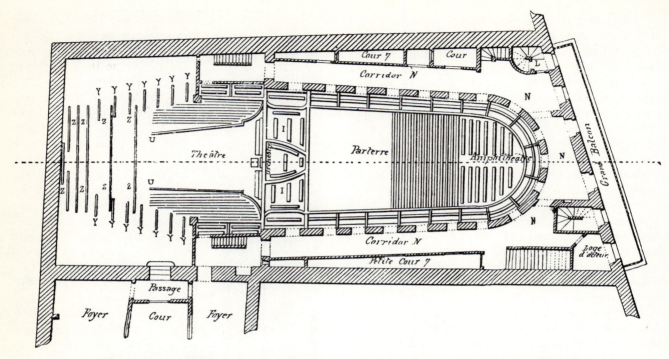

FIGURE 9.22 Plan of the theatre used by the Comédie Française from 1689 until 1770. It opened 18 April 1689 with *Phaedra* and *The Doctor in Spite of Himself.* Note the benches on stage for spectators. From Adolphe Jullien, *Les Spectateurs sur le Théâtre* (1875).

playing area to about fifteen feet in width. All entrances and exits had to be made from upstage. This confined acting area and the presence of spectators on three sides undoubtedly affected the acting style and the sense of illusion.

THEATRE ARCHITECTURE AND SCENIC PRACTICES, 1660–1700

The public theatres of Paris remained relatively unchanged from the 1640s until after Molière's death. In 1673, the Marais was abandoned, and the Palais-Royal was refurbished for the Opéra. Little is known of the theatre in the rue Guénégaud, occupied by the Marais-Molière troup from 1673 to 1680 and by the Comédie Française from 1680 until 1689. Built in 1670 by the Marquis de Sourdéac, it housed Lully's operatic productions until he gained control of the Palais-Royal.

The Comédie Française was ordered to leave the rue Guénégaud in 1687, when the Sorbonne decided to built a new college nearby. Not until 1689 was it able to acquire a new home, the Etoile tennis court in the rue Neuve-des-Fossés in the St. Germain-des-Prés quarter of Paris. Remodeled by the architect Francois d'Orbay at a cost of 200,000 livres, it put the company in debt for many years. It was to be the home of the Comédie Française until 1770.

D'Orbay ignored the exterior walls of the tennis court and constructed inside them a horseshoe-shaped auditorium. On the ground floor, a standing pit was backed by an amphitheatre raised about 6 feet above it. Along the walls, two levels of nineteen boxes were surmounted by an undivided gallery. The total capacity of the auditorium was about 2,000.

The stage was about 41 feet deep by 54 feet wide, but the available acting area was considerably restricted by five rows of benches on either side of the stage. A few benches were also placed in the orchestra pit, which was not used by the musicians because of objections raised by the Opéra. When musicians were needed, they were placed in a box at the rear of the auditorium. The stage was equipped for flat wings and shutters, but since changes of scene were seldom required, the machinery was minimal.

This stage reflects the changes which had occurred in scenic practices since the 1630s. *Le Mémoire de Mahelot, Laurent, et d'Autres Décorateurs,* the last part of which was compiled between 1678 and 1686, contains notices of fifty-four plays performed at the Hôtel de Bourgogne between 1678 and 1680, and sixty-nine notices of plays staged at the rue Guénégaud between 1680 and 1686. Most of these notices were written by Michel Laurent.

The principal change indicated by Laurent's notices of 1678 to 1686, in comparison with those by Mahelot in 1634 and 1635, is the trend toward simplicity. By Laurent's time, most settings represented a single place and were composed of flat wings. Shutters may have been pierced by doors, since entrances from the sides were almost impossible because of onstage spectators.

The typical background for tragedies was the *palais à volonté,* a neutral setting suited to the action but without particularizing details. Consequently, it could serve as a background for all scenes in the same town without any changes, for it was usually so anonymous that it might represent a street, a square, a vestibule, or a palace. A variation showed tents near a battlefield, often with a sea or city in the background. For comedy, the *chambre à quatre portes* (or room with four doors) was typical. It differed in no important way from the *palais à volonté,* except that it depicted domestic architecture, usually an interior, whereas the *palais à volonté* was more formal. The unity of place was never completely adopted, however, for in some plays the settings changed with each act. In others, a shutter or curtain was opened to reveal another place behind the one previously shown. By the end of the seventeenth century, the typical setting at the Comédie Française supplied a suitable, though neutral, background which placed little emphasis upon illusion and concentrated attention upon the actor.

THE CLOSE OF THE SEVENTEENTH CENTURY

By 1700, then, two Parisian troupes with monopolistic privileges divided the whole range of drama between them. The Opéra depended much upon Italianate scenery and machines for the effectiveness of its musical dramas and ballets. The Comédie Française relied little on spectacle, although it too had adopted the Italian mode in scenery and the neoclassical ideal in drama.

The vigor of earlier years had been replaced by a spirit of conservatism. Rather than searching for new horizons, dramatists looked to the past for standards. The prevailing mood can be seen in the "Battle of the Ancients and Moderns" which raged in the French Academy and elsewhere after 1688 over the relative merits of classical and seventeenth century French writers. The battle had many political overtones as well, since Louis XIV could not help being flattered if the cultural level of his reign was declared superior to that of Greece and Rome. Perhaps it is not surprising, then, that in general the battle, which continued into the eighteenth century, was decided in favor of French authors. In practice, this meant that Corneille and Racine replaced the Greek tragedians as standards for tragedy and that Molière replaced Plautus and Terence as models for comedy. But attempts to maintain the glory of the seventeenth century inevitably led to stagnation and decline. Although for another century French drama continued to set the standard for Europe, its period of greatest vitality was over by 1700.

These changes, in turn, were reflections of political and social developments. In 1685, Louis XIV revoked the Edict of Nantes that had guaranteed freedom of conscience, and subsequent persecutions led some 200,000 Huguenots to emigrate, a serious loss to the nation in wealth and talent. Louis also became increasingly puritanical. He gave up attending the theatre altogether, and this no doubt helped to provoke a number of attacks on the theatre as immoral. The enormous sums expended on building Versailles and conducting a series of wars depleted the country's resources. In addition, Louis' attempts to extend his power throughout Europe had been checked by alliances among other countries. In 1700 France was still the most powerful country in Europe, both politically and culturally, but thereafter its energies were to be devoted more to maintaining the *status quo* than to seeking new paths.

LOOKING AT THEATRE HISTORY

One effective way of studying theatre history is to read novels and plays that have theatrical backgrounds, since they often give details and provide local color that make more factual, less lively treatments come alive. A number of such fictional works were written in France during the seventeenth century. Le Sieur Gougenot's *The Comedy of the Comedians* (*c.* 1631) depicts Gros Guillaume, Turlupin, Bellerose, and other actors as they are preparing a play for presentation at the Hôtel de Bourgogne. Similarly, Georges de Scudéry's play of the same title (1632) depicts the performers at the Marais (thinly disguised under other names) and provides considerable information about contemporary theatrical conditions. Later in the century, Molière treated the critical attitudes of his day in *The Critique of 'The School for Wives'* (1663), written in answer to the storm of protest raised by his play, and in *Rehearsal at Versailles* (1663) he reveals much about his approach to rehearsals and about his ideas on acting. Paul Scarron's novel, *A Comical Romance* (1651, 1657), follows the fortunes of a band of strolling actors as they travel through France. In the opening chapters, the company sets up a stage in a tennis court and gives a performance. Its subsequent adventures are detailed in the course of the two-volume work.

From France in the seventeenth century we also have one of the earliest attempts to describe in factual detail precisely how a company functioned. Written by a playwright, Samuel Chappuzeau, it treats almost all aspects of theatrical production in the 1670s. Here is his summary of rehearsal practices:

The roles being duly distributed, each actor goes off to memorize his part, and if time is pressing and a special effort is made, a full length play can be memorized in a week. There are some fortunate persons with good memories for whom a role, however difficult, does not take more than three mornings. . . . when they feel themselves secure in their parts, they gather for the first rehearsal, which serves only to give a rough sketch of the whole, and it is not until the second or third rehearsal that it is possible to judge what success the play may have. They do not risk producing a play until it has been perfectly memorized and well staged, and the final rehearsal ought to be exactly like a regular performance. Ordinarily the author attends these rehearsals and instructs the actor if he falls into some error, if he fails to

grasp the sense, if he fails to be natural in voice and gesture, if he expresses more or less emotion than the action demands. Intelligent actors are allowed to give their opinions in these rehearsals, without offending their comrades, since it is a question of the common good.

> Le Théâtre François (Paris, 1674),
> book II, ch. 17.

During the seventeenth century French scenic conventions underwent a complete transformation. The scenic practices of the Hôtel de Bourgogne are well documented in *Le Mémoire de Mahelot, Laurent, et des autres Décorateurs. . .* , the first part of which ends in 1635. Here is Mahelot's summary of the requirements for DuRyer's *Lisandre and Caliste.* (The sketch of this simultaneous setting is reproduced on page 222.)

It requires at the center of the stage the little castle of Saint Jacques and a street where the butchers are located, and in one of the butcher's houses a window which is directly across from the grilled window of the prison, from which Lisandre can speak to Caliste. This must be hidden during the first act, and it should be made to appear during the second act and to close again during the same act; in closed position it serves as the palace. At one side of the stage a hermitage on a mountain and a cavern below from which a hermit enters. On the other side of the stage, there should be a room into which one enters from behind, raised by two or three steps. Some helmets, bucklers, shields, trumpets, and an unsheathed sword. It is also necessary in one scene for it to be night.

By the mid-century the Italian ideal had triumphed, largely because of Torelli's work after 1645. Torelli's settings for Corneille's *Andromède* (presented at the Petit Bourbon in 1650) are described in the playwright's script and are depicted in a series of contemporary engravings. Here are the descriptive passages for Act II. The engraving of this setting is shown on page 224.

The public square vanishes in an instant to give way to a delightful garden; and the great palaces are changed into so many white marble vases, which alternately bear statues from which jets of water spring, others blossoming with jasmine, and other plants of that nature. On each side stands a line of orange trees in similar vases, which form an admirable bower in the middle of the stage, and separates it into three paths, which the ingenious art of perspective makes appear more than a thousand feet deep. . . .

Here thunder commences to sound with so great a noise with lightning redoubled so quickly that it arouses astonishment with its naturalness. Meantime one sees Eolus

descend with eight winds, of which four are at either side. . . . two [winds] . . . descend, seize Andromède by the arms and lift her into the clouds.

Oeuvres de Pierre Corneille,
vol. VI (Paris, 1821).

10

The Theatre of the Orient

While the Middle Ages and Renaissance were underway in Europe, the theatres of China, Japan, and Southeast Asia were developing the forms and conventions that have been characteristic of those nations ever since. The years between 1300 and 1700 were marked by innovation and creativity so different from that of the West that the two traditions have remained almost wholly distinct, for they were not to interact until the twentieth century, and then only sporadically.

CHINA

Ironically, it was not until the Mongols conquered China in the thirteenth century that drama began to flourish there. The Mongols, whose empire stretched across Asia into Europe, established the Yüan Dynasty, which was to rule China from 1279 until 1368. (It was during this time that Marco Polo visited China and alerted Europeans to the marvels of this rich and highly civilized country.)

Historians often say that advances in literature under the Yüan rulers are explained by the exclusion of Chinese intellectuals from government posts, the traditional outlet for their talents. Supposedly, they then began to practice and perfect native folk arts, including drama. Especially attracted to earlier forms of music-drama, these intellectuals wrote plays usually considered

the foundation of the classical Chinese theatre. In the course of less than a century, Chinese drama reached its peak. Thus, despite political and social repression, China enjoyed something of a golden age in drama, perhaps because the wealth and taste of the foreign rulers created conditions favorable to it.

Yüan dramatists drew their stories from history, legend, novels, epics, and contemporary events. The characters ranged through the entire spectrum of humanity, although the most important roles usually were those of emperors, scholars or students, government officials, generals, rebels, wives, daughters, or concubines. The plays advocated the virtues of loyalty to family and friends, honesty, and devotion to work and duty. They often showed a world out of joint, but one in which poetic justice usually prevailed, and even plays that ended unhappily for the protagonists often showed the villains being discovered and punished. In the final scenes, lovers or long-separated relatives were reunited or reconciled, deserving officials were rewarded, and wealth or honor was restored. Overall, the plays provided a wide and rich panorama of Chinese life, much of it based on the past but always made relevant to the contemporary scene.

Through most of the Yüan period the best dramatists lived in northern China, especially Peking, where they developed a style usually labeled "northern." Each play in this style consisted of four acts with from ten to twenty songs or arias, all sung by the protagonist. The rest of the characters spoke or recited their lines. Yüan

The simple, unadorned accompaniment used a seven-tone scale and was usually played by an orchestra consisting of gong, drum, clapper, and *p'i p'a* (a plucked instrument similar to a lute). The action typically extended over months or years, only rarely was it confined to one place, and it occasionally ended unhappily, although poetic justice usually prevailed.

The many stage directions included in the texts, contemporary references, and a still-extant wall painting

FIGURE 10.1 Silk scroll painting made during the twelfth century A.D. showing a theatre in use during a Chinese festival. From a copy made in the eighteenth century.

FIGURE 10.2 A wall painting from northwestern China, *c.* 1324, showing that many features of the traditional Chinese theatre had already been established by that time. Note the hangings at the rear of the stage, the character entering at rear left, and the costumes and accessories of the figures in the foreground. Courtesy Professor Wu-chi Liu.

dramatists drew their melodies from an existing repertory of about 500 tunes that can be grouped into nine modes according to musical quality and evocative powers. The writers were governed by strict rules which demanded that all songs in a single act use melodies from the same mode and that all lyrics make use of the same rhyme; the mode and rhyme used for one act could not be used for any other act of the same play.

If the dramatic action could not be represented in four acts, a wedge *(chieh tze)* could be added as a prologue or interlude. The wedge was short, with no more than two arias, which might be sung by some character other than the protagonist. At the end of the play a rhymed couplet or quatrain summed up the story. One of these final lines also served as the title for the piece.

(dated about 1324) indicate that many of the now-traditional staging practices of the Chinese theatre were already in use by the fourteenth century. The stage was essentially bare, with one door on either side at the rear for entrances and exits. Between the two doors hung an embroidered, purely decorative wall piece (the extant picture shows this in two pieces which meet at the center). In the painting the performers wear colorful costumes, some with long and extremely wide sleeves, makeup, and beards. Properties—such as fans, swords, and belts—are also in evidence. Both male and female performers were included in the companies, many of which were named for the leading actresses of the time.

It is unclear how many plays were written during the Yüan period, but more than 700 titles are recorded; about 170 of these have survived. Some 550 dramatists are known to have written at this time, but little information about them (often not even life dates) has come down to us. One of the best of these authors is Kuan Han-ch'ing, often called the father of Chinese drama. He wrote sixty-seven plays, of which eighteen survive. Perhaps the best known of these plays is the domestic tragedy, *The Injustice Done to Maid Tou,* based on a real-life murder and trial. It shows the suffering, courage, and virtue of a chaste widow wrongfully accused of murder by a wicked rejected suitor. After she has been executed, her spirit appears to a judge, who reopens the case and punishes the villain. Maid Tou epitomizes the virtuous Chinese woman, and her moral courage is intended to provide a lesson for all.

The most popular of Yüan dramas is *Romance of the West Chamber* by Wang Shih-fu. Unique among northern dramas, it is composed of twenty acts, although the traditional form is preserved by casting it into five parts, each with four acts. Based on a novel, it traces the trials and joys of a pair of ideal lovers, the beautiful Ying Ying and the talented Student Yang, and shows their reunion after long separation. It is noted especially for its characterizations and its poetic excellence, variety, and beauty.

Another well-known play of this period is *The Orphan of the House of Chao,* probably by Chi Chün-hsiang, which concerns a child who is saved at great sacrifice to his rescuer so he can grow up to avenge his family, who have been exterminated by a corrupt general. This was the first Chinese play widely known in the West, although only through Voltaire's adaptation of it as *The Orphan of China* (1755). An even more influential play in the West has been *The Story of the Chalk Circle*

FIGURE 10.3 A scene from *Romance of the Western Chamber* showing a rendezvous between Ying Ying and Student Chang as the maid Hung Niang keeps watch. From an edition published during the Ming dynasty. Courtesy Professor Wu-chi Liu.

by Li Ch'ien'fu. It tells of two women who both claim to be the mother of a young child and family heir; the judge places the child inside a chalk circle and orders the women to pull him out; he awards the child to the one who shows her love by refusing to hurt him. This drama was to serve as a basis for A. H. Klabund's *The Circle of Chalk* (1923) and Bertolt Brecht's *The Caucasian Chalk Circle* (1944). Other plays of this period deal with the religious and supernatural (as in Ma Chih-yüan's *Dream of the Yellow Millet*), bandit heroes (as in Kao Wen-hsiu's *The Black Whirlwind*), and many other topics.

Before the middle of the fourteenth century, another school of drama, the "southern," began to emerge in the area around Hangchow, where the northern style was little understood or appreciated. Of the Yüan dramas from this area, the best known is *Lute Song* (c. 1350) by Kao Ming. Its forty-two acts tell the story of Chao Wu-niang, a virtuous wife who stays at home when her scholar husband, Ts'ai Po-chieh, sets off for the emperor's court. There he succumbs to the allure of fame and wealth and marries the daughter of a prime minister. After Ts'ai Po-chieh's parents die, Chao Wu-niang makes her way to the court, where she recalls her husband to his duty. They are reconciled and he places her on an equal footing with his second wife. *Lute Song* is noted especially for its pathos, poetry, and songs of great beauty.

The founder of the Ming dynasty (1368–1644), who ousted the Mongol rulers, admired *Lute Song* so much that he demanded to see it often. His patronage increased the prestige of the southern drama and helped to make it the dominant style.

Important innovations in southern drama were made in the early sixteenth century by Wei Liang-fu, who after studying earlier operas and their music for some ten years introduced changes based on the music of K'un-shan (the region near Soochow). These changes were so popular that by 1600 they dominated the stage. By that time the southern style had also assumed all of its characteristic features, markedly different from those of the northern style.

A southern play may have as many as fifty or more acts, each with its own title. In the opening act, usually called the argument or prologue, a secondary character sets forth the author's purpose and explains the story. Succeeding acts introduce many plot strands; all are happily resolved by the final scene. Any of the characters may sing, and there are solos, duets, and even choruses. The music is composed from a five-tone scale (except for tunes borrowed from northern drama). The melodies are usually soft and slow (four to five times as slow as in northern drama). The basic accompaniment is played on a horizontal bamboo flute *(ti tzu)*, noted for its lingering and emotionally evocative effects. The orchestra also includes other (especially percussion) instruments.

For the most part this later southern drama followed the traditions established by Kao Ming in *Lute Song*. The main changes lay in greater harmony between words and melody, more elaborate and standardized musical scores, and the exclusive use of the Soochow dialect (noted for its sweet, liquid sounds) in the dramatic songs. Although northern dramas continued to be written after 1600, they were mainly poetic exercises.

The best of the Ming dramatists was probably T'ang Hsien-tsu (1550–1616) whose four plays, collectively called the "Four Dreams," all develop the theme that life is but an illusion. *The Peony Pavilion* is the most admired of the four. In fifty-five acts it tells a complex story of a girl who pines her life away for a lover she has seen only in a dream; later, when he actually appears at her grave she is resurrected. Her father, believing that a deception is being practiced on him, has the lover arrested and beaten before harmony is restored. The play has great variety—a trial in Hades, combats, farcical episodes, suspense, and rescues—but it is most renowned for its love scenes and poetry. T'ang Hsien-tsu's greatest rival was Shen Ching (1553–1610), an expert in prosody whose most lasting contribution was a treatise on the musical patterns of southern drama, long the standard work on the subject.

Although in the beginning southern drama was a vital theatrical form, it gradually became mere closet drama. The scripts were often too long to be produced in their totality; the language was too formal and filled with allusions to be understood by anyone other than scholars; and the writers followed prescribed rules of prosody so slavishly that spontaneity suffered. Nevertheless, the southern style continued to dominate literary output until well after the Manchu invaders from the north established the Ch'ing Dynasty (1644–1912). The most important dramatists of the Ch'ing period are Kung Shang-jen (1648–1718), whose *The Palace of Long Life* shows a series of tragic episodes during the closing years of the Ming dynasty, and Hung Sheng (c. 1646–1704), whose *Peach Blossom Fan* deals with the love of a T'ang emperor for his concubine.

Alongside these literary works there were others intended primarily for theatrical performance. The best of the popular writers was Li Yü (1611–c. 1680), noted especially for his intricate comedies of situation, such as *Ordained in Heaven* and *Be Circumspect in Conjugal Relations*. He was a master craftsman who invented his own plots based on the ludicrous situations of everyday life. Although extremely effective, these works were largely ignored by the literary men of the time. It is ironic, therefore, that Li Yü, through his *A Temporary Lodge for My Leisure Thoughts* (1671), came to be known as China's first and only notable dramatic critic.

Unfortunately neither Li Yü nor his more liter-

FIGURE 10.4 The orchestra of Peking Opera. Note the variety of stringed and percussion instruments. From *Peking Opera* by Rewi Alley (Peking, 1957).

arily inclined contemporaries could stem the decline of southern drama, although it continued to be the principal type until 1853, when Soochow, its primary home, was destroyed during a rebellion. Still, southern drama must be admired for the resiliency that permitted it to survive for some 500 years. Even after 1853, its theatrical traditions and texts were to influence its successor, the Peking Opera.

Peking Opera, the dominant theatrical form of China since the mid-nineteenth century, came to the fore only gradually. As the southern style lost its vitality and its appeal during the late eighteenth century, a number of local styles emerged which mingled traditional stories with melodies based on folk tunes. The most highly developed regional forms were found in the provinces of Chiang-si (in the north), Hupeh (in central China), and Shensi (in the northwest). In 1790, to celebrate the eightieth birthday of Emperor Ch'ien-lung, the best performers from various regions were brought to Peking. Many of these performers remained in the capital where features from various regional styles gradually amalgamated to become Peking Opera. By the mid-nineteenth century this new style had become the dominant popular entertainment throughout much of China.

Unlike its predecessors, Peking Opera was primarily a theatrical rather than a literary form; its emphasis was upon rigidly controlled conventions of acting, dancing, and singing rather than upon the text. Instead

of a single work, an evening's program in Peking Opera is usually made up of a series of short pieces, many of them acts or portions of longer works (including traditional southern or northern plays), intermingled with acrobatic displays. There are no intermissions and usually the scenes are arranged to insure that the best actors are saved for the final episodes.

The plays of Peking Opera are usually classified under two headings: civil plays (dealing with social and domestic themes) and military plays (involving the adventures of warriors or brigands), although the two are often mingled. The dramas are derived from earlier literary plays, novels, history, legend, mythology, folklore, and romance. All end happily. The text of a work is seldom strictly followed, for all great actors make changes at certain points, and each troupe has its own version of standard works. The dramatic action in a Peking Opera is often obscure because beginnings and endings are neglected, for the primary interest lies in the high points of the story. A play, however, is merely an outline for a performance, and the audience goes to see a production rather than to hear a literary text. The names of the dramatists are not even listed on the programs.

Above all, Peking Opera is characterized by the conventions it inherited from earlier periods and developed into a strict system. Since they differ so markedly from Western practices, these conventions need to be described in some detail. Many are related to the architectural features of the playhouse. The earliest stages were probably the porches of temples—simple platforms with an ornate roof—and the influence of the temple stage continues to the present time. The stage of the traditional Chinese theatre is an open platform, often almost square, covered by a roof supported by lacquered columns. Raised a few feet above the ground and surrounded by a wooden railing about 2 feet high, the stage is equipped only with a carpet, two doors in the rear wall (the one on stage right is used for all entrances and that on stage left for all exits), between which hangs a large embroidered curtain. The only permanent properties are a wooden table and a few chairs.

This simplicity allows for rapid changes of place, which are indicated through speech, action, or properties. In addition to statements about place, actors may pantomime knocking at gates, entering rooms, or climbing stairs. To circle the stage indicates a lengthy journey. The table and chairs may be used to symbolize a law court, banqueting hall, or other interior scene, for each of which furniture is arranged according to a prescribed formula. The significance of the table and chairs is further extended through their combination with other simple properties: an incense tripod on the table indicates a palace; paper and an official seal indicate an office; an embroidered divided curtain hung from a bamboo pole signifies a general's tent, an emperor's chamber, a drawing room, or a bride's bedroom, depending upon the other properties with which it is combined. The table and chairs may also be used less representationally. Two chairs back to back may stand for a wall; chairs placed with backs to the end of a table may form a bridge; a chair may represent a tree or the door of a prison; a table may stand for a hill, cloud, or other high place.

Other properties serve to clarify setting and action. A wall painted upon a blue cloth may represent a fort, city gate, or mountain pass; a whip indicates that an actor is riding a horse; two yellow flags with wheels painted on them signify a chariot or wagon; four pieces of cloth carried by an actor running across the stage represent the wind; a banner with a fish design indicates water; a stylized paddle is used to mime rowing. A rolled water banner on a tray becomes a fish, while a corpse is represented by a paddle wrapped in a garment. Weapons, although modeled after real ones, are made of bamboo, wood, or rattan and are decorated. Thus, the audience's imagination is stimulated, but much is left to be filled in. The overall conventionalization is well illustrated by the presence on stage throughout the performance of assistants who help the actors with their costumes and bring on, remove, or rearrange properties as needed. No attempt is made to disguise their presence; in contrast with the gaudily attired actors, they wear ordinary street clothes, often of an extremely informal type.

Traditionally, the musicians also remain in full view throughout the performance and are dressed in the same style as the stage assistants. They come and go freely and are never considered part of the stage picture. (In contemporary China, the musicians are often seated in an orchestra pit and kept offstage.) Music is an integral part of every performance. It provides an atmospheric background, accompanies the many sung passages, controls the timing of movements, and welds the performance into a rhythmical whole. Since Chinese musical notation is very imprecise, theatre musicians learn their parts by rote. Most music used in the Peking Opera has been worked out collaboratively between actors and musicians; most is borrowed from already existing sources and recombined according to the requirements

FIGURE 10.5 The contemporary Chinese actress Hung-yen Hu in a *tan* role from Peking Opera. Courtesy Performing Arts Program of the Asia Society.

of a particular play. Although they may be classified as string, wind, and percussion, the instruments of the Chinese orchestra have no counterparts in the West. The leader of the orchestra plays a drum which establishes the time and accentuates the rhythm. Gongs, cymbals, brass cups, flutes, stringed instruments, and more exotic items complete the orchestra. Songs are accompanied only by flute and strings, but entrances and exits are signaled by deafening percussion passages. Much of the onstage action is performed to a musical background.

It is the actor, however, who is at the heart of the Peking Opera. On a bare stage furnished only with a few properties and served by drably clothed stage attendants and musicians, the lavishly and colorfully dressed actors speak, sing, and move according to rigid conventions. Acting roles are divided into four main types: male, female, painted face, and comic. The male roles (*sheng*) include scholars, statesmen, patriots, and similar types. They range from young to old and from the dandy to the warrior. They are subdivided according to whether they involve fighting and acrobatics or are restricted to singing and dancing. Actors playing these roles wear simple makeup and, except for young heroes, beards. The female roles *(tan)* are subdivided into six types: the good and virtuous wife or lover; coquettish types; warrior maidens; young unmarried girls; women of evil character; and old women. Originally all *tan* roles were played by women, but from the late eighteenth century until the twentieth century actresses were forbidden. Perhaps as a result, the *tan* roles were always considered secondary until Mei Lan-fang (1894–1961), the most famous of Chinese actors, raised them to prominence. After 1911, actresses returned to the stage and now have largely supplanted the male *tan* actors. The painted face *(ching)* roles are so called because of the brilliant and elaborate patterns painted on the actors' faces. The *ching* roles include warriors, bandits, courtiers, officials, gods, and supernatural beings, but the basic attribute of all is their swagger and exaggerated strength. They are also subdivided according to whether they are good or evil, whether fighting and gymnastics are required, and so on. The comic actor or clown *(ch'ou)* speaks in an everyday dialect, is free to improvise, tells many jokes, and is the most realistic of the characters. He may be a servant, businessman, jailer, watchman, soldier, shrewish mother-in-law, or matchmaker. He combines the skills of the mime and the acrobat.

Upon his first entrance, each important character describes his basic nature and appearance in a half-spoken, half-chanted passage. This is often followed by other lines in which he explains the story, tells his name and family background, and gives other essential information. Such speeches clarify situation and character quickly and leave the dramatist time to develop fully the moments of high interest.

The actor's delivery of lines is rigidly controlled by conventions. Each role has its prescribed vocal timbre and pitch, and syllables are often drawn out without regard for conversational usage in order to maintain the appropriate rhythm. Even spoken passages are governed by strict rhythms and tempos. Chanted and sung passages are freely inserted into spoken monologues or dialogues. Thus, the lines are rendered in an extremely stylized manner.

All stage movement is related to dance, since it is rhythmical, mimetic, and symbolic. Furthermore, each word is accompanied by movement intended to enhance or explain its meaning. Such stage gesture has been fully codified. There are seven basic hand movements, many special arm movements, more than twenty different

pointing gestures, more than twelve special leg movements, and a whole repertory of sleeve and beard movements. Methods of walking or running vary with each role. The prescribed gestures and movements are combined according to character, mood, situation, or other conditions.

Costumes, most of which are heavily patterned and gaudy in color, are also extremely important in the Chinese theatre. Each of the more than 300 standard items is designed to describe its wearer's character type, age, and social status through color, design, ornament, and accessories. Color is always used symbolically: red for loyalty and high position, yellow for royalty, dark crimson for barbarians or military advisors, and so on. The designs also have symbolic significance: the dragon is the emblem of the emperor; the tiger stands for power and masculine strength; the plum blossom indicates long life and feminine charm. Headgear is almost as varied as the garments, but the approximately 100 variations are

FIGURE 10.6 A *wu sheng* (military role) character, noted for acrobatics and excellent physical coordination. From Alley, *Peking Opera* (Peking, 1957).

mance requires long and rigorous training. The would-be actor enters a school between the ages of seven and twelve, where he undergoes a period of strict discipline for six years. At first his training is generalized, but as the student shows a suitability for a particular type of role his training is specialized. If an actor is to achieve fame, he must remain within the prescribed conventions of his role but somehow endow it with his own personality.

The peculiar flavor of the Chinese theatre also owes much to the audience. Most of the early public theatres were temporary, but in the seventeenth century actors began to perform in teahouses where customers were seated at tables. When permanent theatres were built, this arrangement was retained and the ground floor was fitted out with tables and stools at which spectators were served tea while watching the play. The permanent theatres also included a raised platform around the sides and back of the auditorium where poorer spectators sat on benches. A balcony, divided into sections much like the boxes of a Western theatre, was also added. In some periods the balcony was occupied by the wealthy class, but in others it was reserved entirely for women.

FIGURE 10.8 Scene from a Peking Opera, *The Wild Boar Forest,* showing the hero (center) and his companion (right) buying a sword. From Alley, *Peking Opera* (Peking, 1957).

all used symbolically. Most costumes are made of rich materials regardless of the wearer's rank, but occasionally linen or cotton is used for very poor characters or clowns.

The visual appearance is completed by makeup. Bearded *sheng* actors and old women wear very little makeup. For other female roles, the face is painted white and the eyes surrounded by a deep red, shading into pink. A similar makeup, although with less marked contrasts, is used for the unbearded *sheng* roles. The clown's distinguishing feature is the white patch around the eyes; the various types of clowns are differentiated by distinctive black markings. By far the most complex makeup is that of the *ching* roles, the entire face being painted in bold patterns symbolic of the particular character.

Such a complex and formalized system of perfor-

FIGURE 10.9 Examples of face painting in Peking Opera. From top left, clockwise: an heroic face, an unstable character, a dragon character, a fierce but stupid general. From *Peking Opera* by Alley (Peking, 1957).

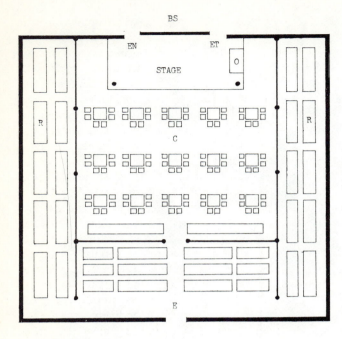

FIGURE 10.10 Ground plan of a traditional Chinese theatre. BS—Backstage, EN—Entrance to stage, ET—Exit from stage, O—Orchestra, E—Main entrance to auditorium, R—Raised side seats, C—Tables and stools for audience. Drawing by Douglas Hubbell.

After the Chinese Republic was formed in 1912, the traditional arrangement of the auditorium began to change and now most urban theatres are furnished with Western style chair seating. Audience behavior has changed little, however, for the spectators carry on conversations, eat and drink, and come and go freely. Audiences are usually familiar with the plays; each member has his favorite passages to which he attends carefully, only to ignore others. Like the playwright, the spectator is more concerned with significant moments than with overall effect.

Peking Opera is by no means the only form of traditional theatre in China, for there are many regional variants. Such variations were probably encouraged by the upheavals in Chinese life that have been almost continuous since about 1840 when China was forcibly opened to Western trade and influence. Thereafter wars and rebellions gradually weakened the power of the Manchus, and in 1912 the empire was replaced by a republic. This change did not result in peace, however,

for not only were there internal struggles for power, but in 1931 Japan set out to take over China. The subsequent fourteen-year war with Japan was merely a prelude to another civil conflict which ended only when the Communists won control of the mainland and the Nationalists retreated to Taiwan in 1949.

Under these unsettled conditions, it is not surprising that many local styles of drama developed. Two of the most interesting varieties are found in Canton and Shanghai. In Canton, there was no theatre until about 1850, when during the wars with westerners it was imported by generals from the north. The companies soon translated their plays into the Cantonese dialect, and at the same time they adopted musical forms and instruments more familiar to the Canton public. Under Western influence, the Cantonese theatre later also adopted painted scenery and illusionistic backdrops. In Shanghai, the Shao-sing operas developed under the influence of the West. Their makeup was relatively natural and their costumes more delicate than in Peking Opera, and both lighting and scenery were realistic. The Shanghai plays were confined to lyrical scenes and love stories, and the music was played primarily on wind and string instruments.

Western style drama also made considerable gains in China after the overthrow of the empire. At first this form was called "new drama" or "modern drama," but since the late 1920s it has most often been labeled "spoken drama" to distinguish it from the essentially operatic mode of traditional forms. Originally many spoken dramas were translations or adaptations of foreign works, especially those by Shakespeare, Chekhov, Shaw, Galsworthy, and Ibsen. A number of native authors also attempted the new style, but the first to win both critical and commercial success was Ts'ao Yu (1910-), usually considered the finest Chinese dramatist of the twentieth century. His works, such as *Thunderstorm* (1933), *Sunrise* (1935), and *The Bridge* (1945), deal with contemporary social problems, especially the conflict between old and new standards.

Since the Communists assumed control over the Chinese mainland in 1949, a number of changes have been made in Peking Opera. The reforms are designed primarily to make subjects and ideas conform to Communist goals, but they also extend to some of the theatrical conventions. To clarify its standards, the government has encouraged the production of "model" and "revolutionary" works to serve as guides to authors and theatrical troupes. In its traditional form, Peking Opera is now most fully preserved on Taiwan and (to a somewhat lesser degree) in Hong Kong and Singapore.

Similarly, since 1949 the majority of Chinese spoken drama, whether written on the mainland or on Taiwan, has dealt with ideological positions. In these melodramas, characters are usually heroes or villains, depending upon their political convictions, and invariably the enemy is exposed and routed. But if spoken drama has grown steadily in volume, it is still Peking Opera which most fascinates Westerners, who remain little familiar with the great dramas of the Yüan and Ming periods.

JAPAN

The early history of Japan and its theatrical forms are shrouded in mystery since the first written account, *Records of Ancient Things,* was not compiled until 712 A.D. Before that time, however, there were numerous rituals, many of them related to Shintoism, which began in nature and ancestor worship. All these rituals are now usually grouped together under the general label *kagura;* some have persisted to the present day. During this early period a form of rhythmic movement set to music—*sangaku,* "miscellaneous" or "scattered" music—was also being performed at court. Jesters were also common.

During the sixth century A.D. Japan began to undergo profound change after Prince Shotoku (573–621) imported Buddhism. A period of some 200 years followed when continental culture, especially from Korea, China, and India, was enthusiastically embraced. Writing and numerous forms of music were among the imports, as were masked dances that soon became regular features of Japanese festivals. By the eighth century three forms—*gigaku, bugaku,* and *sarugaku*—had won special favor with the Japanese. All were patronized by the court and given official recognition within the Imperial Department of Music, which trained performers in these forms. Since it no longer exists, *gigaku* is little understood. Most of our information comes from a work on music written in 1233. A form of masked dance set to music and presented at religious festivals, *gigaku* probably came to Japan with Buddhism. About 200 *gigaku* masks have survived. After about 800, it virtually disappeared, and along with *sarugaku,* was abandoned by the Imperial Department of Music.

Bugaku was more fortunate, for it has continued to be performed to the present day on important state occasions at the imperial court. (A version is also performed in some Shinto shrines.) *Bugaku* now means any dance performed to classical court music by dancers whose art has been passed down through generations of families with hereditary rights. It includes some purely Japanese dances but most are derived from continental Asia, especially from Korea, China, and India. The dances are usually divided into two categories: "Dances of the Right," derived from Korea; and "Dances of the Left," derived from China or Southeast Asia. Despite these labels, the dances are now almost wholly Japanese in character. *Bugaku* performers are also divided into two groups: "Dancers of the Music on the Right," dressed in predominantly green costumes and performing to accompaniment played primarily on percussion instruments; and "Dancers of the Music on the Left," dressed predominantly in red costumes and performing to accompaniment played primarily on woodwinds. The rhythms vary from the stately to the lively. *Bugaku* is a symbolic representation of one part, the most interesting, of a whole story and is structured in terms of introduction, development, and climax. It probably exerted considerable influence on the early development of Noh drama.

But Noh owes most to *sarugaku-no* and *dengaku-no. Sarugaku-no* probably originated when ritualistic elements, music, and dance from the continent were mingled with tumbling, dancing, and mimicry. The result was a kind of noisy merrymaking (*sarugaku* means "monkey music"). It was extremely varied, even circus-like. An early treatise, *New Notes on Sarugaku* (c. 1060), considers *sarugaku* to be an inclusive term for all kinds of comic entertainment. *Dengaku-no* may have been imported from Korea but it came to be associated primarily with harvest rituals. It was both acrobatic and rural in character. The first reference to it as a dramatic performance is found c. 1023 when it is said to be made up of rustic dances and songs.

Around the beginning of the twelfth century, *sarugaku-no* was adapted by Buddhists as a way of demonstrating their teachings. Thus, it was given a role similar to that of the medieval mystery and morality plays of Europe. At first the plays were acted by priests, but as performances came to attract large numbers of people to the temples professional players began to imitate the temple performances at times other than festivals. As the skill of the professionals grew, some temples began to employ them to replace the actor-priests. *Den-*

FIGURE 10.11 A *Bugaku* Dance of the Left, Tagyuraku, based on an ancient polo-game. The dancer is Mr. Tsuji Toshio, Assistant Chief Court Musician. From Robert Garfias, *Music of a Thousand Autumns* (Berkeley: University of California Press, 1976). Courtesy Mr. Garfias and the University of California Press.

gaku-no was developed in much the same way, primarily in connection with Shinto shrines.

After a time performers had proliferated so much that controls were needed. As a result guilds *(za)* were formed. *Dengaku* guilds can be traced back as far as 1150 and *sarugaku* guilds to about 1270. Most of these guilds were attached to some powerful shrine or temple which granted them a monopoly on performances in its area. In return the players gave at least some free performances during ceremonies and festivals. By the beginning of the fourteenth century, then, there were numerous groups of well-organized players who gave performances that mingled mimicry, song, and dance, although their performances were probably not yet fully dramatic.

During the fourteenth century Japanese theatre underwent what was probably its most crucial change, a development that can best be understood within the sociopolitical context of the time. In 1192 the emperor ceded his secular powers to a *shogun* (military dictator), a post that became hereditary, although new families won possession of the title from time to time in civil wars.

Under the shogunate, Japan developed a strict feudal system that lasted until the late nineteenth century. Within this rigidly organized society, the highest rank was held by the *samurai* (warriors), with the *shogun* at their head. Beneath the *shogun* were *daimyo* (feudal chiefs), directly responsible to him; below the *daimyo* were the *hatamoto* (or lesser warriors), many with their own fiefs but all receiving an annual allowance of rice according to their ranks. The distinctive badge of the *samurai* was the right to wear two swords. (Many Japanese plays involve a search for a stolen sword, symbol of the family's honor.) A *samurai* followed a strict code of behavior which demanded that he always be ready to face death, fulfill his filial duty, and be absolutely loyal to his lord and his class. If a *samurai* lost his position because of disgrace or poverty, he and his followers became *ronin* (men adrift), common figures in Japanese drama. Below the *samurai* were the other ranks: *shonin* (merchants), *shokunin* (artists and craftsmen), and *hyakusho* (farmers and peasants)—all with numerous subdivisions. These lesser ranks were usually denied access to the pleasures of the *samurai*, a fact that was to have considerable effect on Japanese theatre.

In 1338 the Ashikaga family assumed the shogunate and held it until the late sixteenth century. It was during the Ashikaga period that Japan, after centuries of domination by imported culture, rediscovered its own heritage. The result was a period of great creative energy during which foreign and native elements were mingled in new and distinctive ways. During this time the shoguns patronized the arts and the *daimyo*, perhaps in emulation, sought to demonstrate their cultural sophistication.

It was out of this context that the first great Japanese theatrical form, Noh, came in the late fourteenth century. At this time Kannami Kiyotsugu (1333–1384) was a major performer of *sarugaku-no*. In 1374 he appeared before the *shogun* Yoshimitsu Ashikaga (1358–1408), who was so impressed that he took Kannami and his son Zeami Motokiyo (1363–1444) under his patronage and granted them favors that placed them among the highest officials of his court. Within this rather refined atmosphere, Noh assumed its characteristic form.

Kannami was probably the great innovator, for he seems to have amalgamated elements of *sarugaku*, *kusemai* (a popular form of song and dance), and Zen Buddhist ideals to create a form suited to the tastes of the *shogun* and his followers. It remained for Zeami to perfect the form, whose triumph was rapid. Consequently, *dengaku-no* quickly declined in popularity and eventually disappeared. As a result, *sarugaku-no* after a time came to be called merely *no* (Noh). Zeami is usually considered the greatest of all Noh dramatists. He wrote more than 100 of the approximately 240 plays that make up the active Noh repertory today. Furthermore, it was Zeami who summed up Noh's aesthetic goals and described its practices in three theoretical treatises. Consequently, Noh is above all a product of the fourteenth and fifteenth centuries.

The major influence on Noh was Zen Buddhism. From this spiritual source Zeami adopted the conviction that beauty lies in suggestion, simplicity, subtlety, and restraint. Virtually all of his premises are summed up in the complex term *yūgen*, which, essentially, means gentle gracefulness, the mysterious beauty of impermanence in which elegance is always accompanied with awareness of its fragility. In later years, Zeami extended his conception of *yūgen* to include the feeling of tranquil loneliness and the peaceful acceptance of old age.

It is the qualities summed up in *yūgen* that Noh seeks to capture. Because it relies on indirectness, suggestion, simplicity, and restraint, Noh makes enormous demands on its audience, for it is not easy to comprehend fully or to enter the realm it embodies. It is not essentially storytelling; rather, it seeks through retrospection about some past event to evoke an emotional state or mood. A musical dance-drama, the written script of a Noh play (typically shorter than the average one-act drama of the West) serves merely as a framework for choreographically ordered movement. All Noh plays culminate in a dance, and the dialogue and song that precede it serve primarily to outline the circumstances that motivate it. A chorus sings the actor's lines while he is dancing and also narrates many of the events during the rest of the play. Most of the lines (which are partly in verse and partly in prose) are either sung melodically or intoned. The few spoken passages—usually less than one-third of the total—are recited in a highly stylized manner. Ordi-

FIGURE 10.12 A *Bugaku* Dance of the Left, the Music of Great Peace, in which the dancers represent warriors who return to the capital in time to prevent a revolt and maintain peace. Courtesy Mr. Garfias and the University of California Press.

nary speech is used only when a player comes on stage between the parts of a two-act piece to summarize what has happened during the first act.

Noh dramas are classified into five types: *kamimono*, or plays praising the gods; *shuramono*, plays about warriors; *kazuramono*, plays about women; *kuruimono*, miscellaneous plays, most often about mad persons or spirits but sometimes about unmasked "living persons"; and *kirinomono*, plays about demons, devils, or other supernatural beings. Traditionally, a program was made up of one play of each type performed in the order listed above. In recent years, however, it has become common to have programs composed of only two or three plays.

The number of roles in a Noh play is small. Every play includes at least the *shite* (or principal character) and the *waki* (or supporting character), but sometimes there are as many as six roles. The *shite* may be a supernatural being, an aristocrat, lady, or ghost, but he always dominates the performance. He may have one or more companions (attendants, maids, or courtiers). The *waki* is most often a priest, and he too may have companions or attendants. There are also occasionally noble child roles *(kokata)* and commoners. All of the performers are male.

FIGURE 10.13 Scene from a Noh play. Note the audience seated at the front and side of the main platform. At upper center left is the *hashigakari* (or bridge). The orchestra may be seen at the rear of the main stage; an actor stands by the upstage pillar. From Haar, *Japanese Theatre in Highlight*. Courtesy Charles E. Tuttle Co., Tokyo.

Normally the *shite* and his companions wear masks of painted wood, many of which have been handed down for generations. Masks fall into five basic types—aged, male, female, deities, and monsters—although each may have many variations. In addition, special masks are sometimes used.

Costumes, rich in color and design, are based upon the official dress of several centuries past but have been adapted to give an air of grandeur and to increase the performer's stature. Most are made of silk decorated with elaborate embroidery, but they are never as gaudy as those used in the Chinese theatre. The garments may be divided into four categories: the outer garments; garments worn indoors or without an overdress; lower garments, such as divided skirts; and headdresses. Each category has many variations, but the same garments may be combined with others for use in different roles. Thus, costumes are less rigidly conventionalized in color

and design than in the Chinese theatre. Costumes are often changed or adjusted on stage.

Hand properties are few and conventionalized. The fan is by far the most important, for it can be used to suggest the blowing of the wind, the ripple of water, a rising moon, falling rain, and many subtle emotional responses. The meaning of the fan is determined by the actor's movement and the music. Occasionally the actor may use a sword or spear. Stage properties are also simple. A miniature wooden or bamboo structure may represent a palace, mountain, bedchamber, or other place; a bamboo frame represents a boat. Usually no more than one or two stage properties are present at once. There is no machinery or scenery.

The Noh stage has been standardized since about 1615. Its two principal areas, the stage proper *(butai)* and the bridge *(hashigakari)* are both roofed like the shrines from which they are descended. The stage roof is supported by four columns, each with its own name and significance. At the upstage right pillar, *shitebashira* (principal character's pillar), the *shite* pauses when he enters to announce his name and where he comes from. While reciting this speech, he faces the pillar at the downstage right corner, the *metsukebashira*. The pillar at the downstage left corner is called *wakibashira* because of its association with the secondary character. The upstage left pillar, *fuebashira* (flute pillar), indicates the flute player's position on stage.

The stage is divided into three principal areas, although none is marked off architecturally except by the pillars. The largest area, the mainstage, is enclosed within the four pillars and is about 18 feet square. The floor of this area is specially constructed of polished cypress, and sounding jars are placed beneath it to make the rhythmic and emphatic stamping of feet, a distinctive feature of Noh, more effective. Back of the upstage pillars is the rear stage *(atoza)*, occupied by an orchestra composed of two or three drummers and a flute player. To stage left of the main stage is the *waki-za*, occupied by the chorus of six to ten members.

There are two entrances to the stage. The principal one, the bridge *(hashigakari)*, is a railed gangway about 6 feet wide and from 33 to 52 feet long leading from the dressing room. In front of this bridge are three small pine trees symbolizing heaven, earth, and man. The bridge is used for all important entries. The other entrance, the "hurry door," upstage left and only about 3 feet high, is used by subordinate characters, the chorus, musicians, and stage assistants, and for the exit of dead

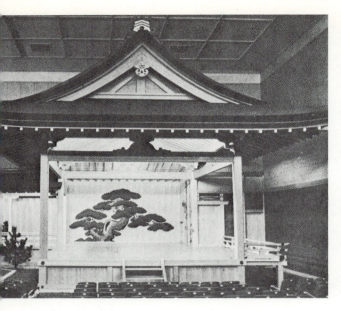

FIGURE 10.14 The Noh stage and auditorium as they appear today. Note the Western-style seating. The bridge is at left.

when Toraaki Okura (? –1662) recorded 203 of them. These have remained important in the *kyōgen* repertory. In 1660, Okura also published the first treatise devoted wholly to *kyōgen*.

Kyōgen covers a wide range of comic subjects that place more emphasis on situation than character. It shows the unexpected dilemmas in which the drunkard, cowardly samurai, ignorant lord, sly servant, greedy monk, shrewish woman, and others find themselves. Sometimes the plays parody Noh; occasionally subjects are taken from folklore with animals, gods, or devils as characters. *Kyōgen* plays seldom include more than three characters and rarely use musical accompaniment, since all the dialogue, except for a few short chanted passages, is spoken. But though *kyōgen* depends on humorous dialogue and pantomime, it is performed according to strict conventions. Its performers also appear in Noh plays as villagers, peasants or commoners, thereby adding an earthy and occasionally humorous touch to otherwise stately plays.

Although during the middle ages Noh and *kyōgen* were from time to time given publicly for "subscription" audiences, they were essentially aristocratic entertainments. The *shoguns* took Noh under their protection, accorded the performers *samurai* status, and granted them a stipend raised through a system of national requisitions.

characters. The rear walls of the stage and bridge are made of wood. On the wall back of the orchestra is painted a pine tree and on the stage-left side wall bamboo, perhaps as reminders of the natural scenery which formed the background of the earliest performances. The audience views the stage from two sides: from in front of the main stage and from the side in front of the bridge.

The Noh performance is one of the most carefully controlled in the world. Every movement of hands and feet and every intonation follows a set rule. The orchestra supplies a musical setting and controls the timing. Every episode is drawn out to great length to extract the full flavor of the ritualistic action.

Noh is intimately bound up with *kyōgen* (mad words), short farcial pieces used as interludes between the acts of Noh plays. *Kyōgen*, like Noh, is descended from *sarugaku*, but unlike Noh it maintains the comic tone that characterized the earlier form. Again, like Noh, *kyōgen's* conventions were probably set by Zeami, who declared that *kyōgen* should be restrained, subtle, and never vulgar.

By the sixteenth century there were three main school of *kyōgen* performers: Okura, Sagi, and Izumi. None of their plays was written down until 1638 to 1642,

FIGURE 10.15 Ground plan of a Noh stage. A— Audience, B—Bridge, DR—Dressing room, H—Hurry door, RS—Rear stage, S—Main stage, W—Waki-za. Drawing by Douglas Hubbell.

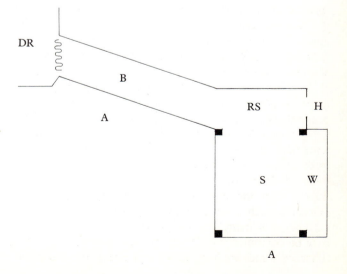

Five schools, or branches, of Noh were recognized and the headship of each made hereditary. These schools still exist. When the shogunate fell in 1868 Noh lost its privileged position and survived through the difficult period immediately following primarily because of the patronage of societies organized for that purpose. Since World War II it has been recognized as a national treasure and placed on a more secure footing. It has gained increased support among the general populace as well and its survival now seems assured.

While Noh was assuming its role as a major aristocratic art form, other entertainments were being addressed to more plebeian audiences. But major popular forms did not emerge until the era of the Tokugawa-family shogunate (1603–1867). As with Noh, the new forms can best be understood within the sociopolitical context of the time. Through most of the Tokugawa era, Japan was at peace. As a result, the *samurai* declined in importance while the lesser ranks improved their economic position. Beginning in the early seventeenth century, the shoguns also expelled all foreigners and deliberately isolated Japan from outside influences. The resulting emphasis on native social and artistic forms encouraged the elaboration of ceremonials and entertainments of all kinds just when the increased wealth of the lesser classes permitted them to patronize the arts. This conjunction of events helps to explain why during the course of the seventeenth century there evolved two of Japan's most distinctive theatrical types—the doll theatre and Kabuki.

The doll theatre *(ningyo shibai)* first came to prominence during the seventeenth century as an amalgamation of numerous earlier influences, although some types of puppet performances can be traced back to the Heian era (781–1185). In 1100, Oe Tadafusa published his *Book of Puppeteers;* thereafter some type of puppet theatre was always practiced by wandering entertainers.

Even before this doll theatre came to the fore there was another entertainment in which stories or legends were recited or chanted to the accompaniment of a stringed instrument, the *biwa.* After 1560 this form underwent a major change when another stringed instrument with quite different qualities, the *samisen,* was introduced from the Ryukyu Islands. By far the most popular work in this altered genre treated the love story of Joruri, the daughter of a wealthy family. It became so dominant that the form itself came to be called *joruri.*

The first major step toward a mature doll theatre was taken sometime between 1596 and 1614 when doll

FIGURE 10.16 Japanese puppets and their handlers. From Haar, *Japanese Theatre in Highlight.* Courtesy Charles E. Tuttle Co., Tokyo.

performances were combined with *joruri* narration. This combination became increasingly popular, especially after 1648 when Toraya Gendayu established a company in Tokyo. The perfection of the form, however, had to await Takemoto Gidayu (1650–1714), who founded a company in Osaka in 1685. His style was to dominate the doll theatre thereafter. Takemoto's popularity owed much to the plays of Chikamatsu Monzaemon (1653–1724), Japan's greatest playwright, who began writing specifically for Takemoto in 1686. Chikamatsu wrote many kinds of works but was noted especially for his five-act history plays and his three-act plays on contemporary life. He came to be admired above all for his dramas about the double suicides of lovers, his sensitive characterizations, and his beautiful language. Among his best known plays are *The Double Suicide at Sonezaki* (1703), *Drumming of the Waves at Horikawa* (1707), and *Battle of Kokusenya* (1715).

The dolls used in these performances underwent many changes, becoming ever more complex. Originally the puppeteers used a head only, but later hands and feet were added, and by 1678 rather complete figures were in use. In 1730, a mechanism was introduced that allowed the dolls to move their eyes; in 1733 jointed and movable fingers were added; later, the puppets were fitted with movable eyebrows. As the figures grew in complexity, the number of operators increased. Originally one handler, hidden from view, was sufficient, but after 1734 each doll was operated by three men, all entirely visible to the audience. One person manipulated the head and right arm, a second the left arm, and a third the feet. In 1736, the figures were doubled in size to their present height of 3 or 4 feet.

The stage also grew in complexity. The use of movable stage settings after 1715 soon led to the invention of stage machinery which has since been adopted throughout the world. In 1727, elevator traps were introduced to raise scenery through the floor, and after 1757 they were used to create different stage floor levels.

The doll theatre reached the height of its popularity in the eighteenth century. Its most popular playwrights at that time were Takedo Izumo (1691–1756) and Chikamatsu Hanji (1725–1783). Most of the conventions were also fixed at this time. Around 1780 the doll theatre began to decline as it was overshadowed by Kabuki. Some of its vitality was restored after Uemura Bunrakuken (1737–1810) came to Osaka sometime between 1789 and 1800. The name Bunraku, used by present-day doll theatres, was derived from him. Despite Bunrakuken's work, the doll theatre was to lead a precarious existence throughout the nineteenth and twentieth centuries. Its future now seems secure, however, for in 1963 the Bunraku Association was formed to manage all phases of the art. Since then the doll theatre has been under the sponsorship of the National Commission for the Protection of Cultural Properties, the Osaka prefectural and municipal governments, and the Japan Broadcasting Corporation. In addition to performing in Osaka, this troupe also plays four months each year in a small theatre created especially for it within the National Theatre in Tokyo, opened in 1966.

Like Noh, Bunraku has its own fixed conventions. The long and narrow stage of the theatre is divided into three levels from front to rear, each indicated by low partitions between which the handlers sit. All locales are represented scenically and changed as required by the story. Numerous properties are used. At the right side of the auditorium just forward of the stage is a platform for the narrator and *samisen* player. This platform is equipped with a turntable which is revolved to bring the narrator and *samisen* player into position. At the end of each act a new team replaces the earlier one.

A puppet performance begins with the appearance of an announcer clad in black and wearing a hood (this costume is worn by all the stage assistants except the principal handlers, the musicians, and the narrator), who proclaims the title of the play and the names of the *samisen* player and the narrator. The *samisen*, a three-stringed instrument related to the lute, has a skin-covered base and is simultaneously plucked and struck. Extremely varied in sound, it can follow the rise and fall of the voice, give special emphasis, and provide punctuations to the narration and action. Its accompaniment is considered essential in the puppet theatre. The narrator tells the story (the handlers do not speak) and expresses the feelings of each puppet. He smiles, weeps, starts with fear and astonishment.

The handlers and the puppets occupy center stage. The puppets vary somewhat in size and complexity according to their importance in the play. The female figures ordinarily do not have feet, although these are suggested by the way the kimono is handled. Minor puppets do not have movable mouths, eyes, and eyebrows. The handlers seek to become one with their puppets and to absorb themselves in the drama. They undergo long and arduous training before appearing on stage, first learning to operate the feet (usually about ten years is spent mastering this operation), then progressing to the left hand (requiring another ten years), and then to the head and right arm. Their artistry has exerted considerable influence upon Kabuki.

Even as the doll theatre was developing in the seventeenth century, Kabuki was taking shape. Of the three major Japanese theatrical forms, Kabuki is the least "pure," for it has always borrowed freely from Noh, the doll theatre, and other sources. Thus, it is the least fixed of the forms and has long been the most popular.

Kabuki is usually traced back to 1603 when Okuni, a female dancer from the Izumo Grand Shrine, began to give public performances on an improvised stage set up in the riverbed at Kyoto. Her programs seem to have been composed of playlets interspersed with dances. Most of the performers were women, although they sometimes dressed as men, and they were obviously erotic. The programs caught on rapidly, and by 1616 there were seven licensed theatres in Tokyo. They came to be associated with prostitution, however, and in 1629 the *shogun* forbade women to appear on the stage. Women's Kabuki was succeeded by Young Men's Kabuki, which was suppressed in 1652, for the boys proved to be as seductive as the women. Next, came Men's Kabuki, destined to be the permanent form, al-

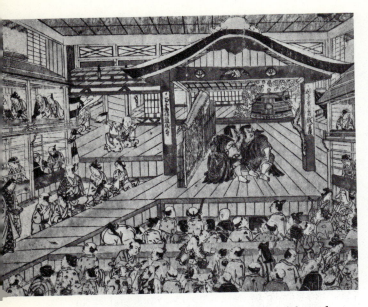

FIGURE 10.17 A Kabuki theatre in the eighteenth century. Note that the stage still retains some features of the Noh, although they have been modified, and that the *hanamichi* has been added. An eighteenth-century print. Courtesy British Museum.

though the men were required to shave their foreheads and to eschew any emphasis upon physical charms.

Kabuki developed rapidly, and between 1675 and 1750 evolved most of its characteristic techniques. New methods of acting were introduced, fully developed plays replaced the former improvised entertainments, and artistry replaced personal appeal. Many practices and much of the repertory were borrowed from the puppet theatre, which Kabuki had surpassed in popularity by the end of the eighteenth century. Many purists consider that true Kabuki ended in 1868, when the emperor resumed his authority from the shogunate and Western influence began to be extensive.

Under the impact of Western ideas Kabuki underwent several changes. Since the Second World War ticket prices have made Kabuki something of a luxury, while the patronage of tourists has brought alleged debasements of the traditional practices. Nevertheless, Kabuki remains the most popular of Japanese theatrical forms, and its future now seems assured since the Japanese National Theatre was opened in 1966.

Kabuki drama has undergone many changes. Originally, improvised sketches were inserted into dance performances, and it was not until the second half of the seventeenth century that works of a more ambitious nature began to appear. The first two-act play was given in 1664 but no important writer emerged until the 1670s, when Chikamatsu Monzaemon began to write for the Kabuki troupes. In twenty-seven years he provided between 25 and 50 plays, although none now exists in its original form, and none ranks with the works he wrote for the doll theatre. Many of his approximately 100 doll plays were later taken into the Kabuki repertory.

Next to Chikamatsu, the most important Kabuki dramatist is Takedo Izumo (1691–1756), who worked with Chikamatsu and succeeded him as principal writer for the Osaka doll theatre. His masterpiece is *Chushingura* (1748), originally a doll play but now the most popular of all Kabuki dramas. Eleven acts long, it requires a full day in performance. Based upon an actual event, it tells of forty-seven faithful *ronin* who avenge the wrongs done to their master.

As drama increased in importance, the staff of each troupe came to include a playwright and a number of assistants apprenticed to him. When a new work was needed, the dramatist outlined a plot and his assistants then worked together on it, a practice which continued until 1868. Only one dramatist after Izumo is of special importance. Kawatake Mokuami (1816–1893) bridged the old and the new system (under which writers worked alone) to become famous for his domestic plays, especially those about thieves and other low-life characters, such as *Benten Kozo and His Gang of Thieves* (1862) and *Gorozo the Dandy* (1864). Kawatake's dramas have remained so popular that it is rare to see a Kabuki program today that does not contain a selection from his approximately fifty plays.

Kabuki drama is not considered to be literature, however, for, like most Eastern dramatic forms, it serves merely as a basis for performance. Kabuki writers never thought in terms of precisely defined forms and no clear line was drawn between comic and serious works as in Noh and *kyōgen*. Nevertheless, Kabuki has few purely comic plays, and most of these are dance pieces in one act. Other works are sometimes called comedies because they end happily. Most Kabuki plays are essentially melodramas, although they vary considerably in mood. Most are made up of loosely connected episodes joined together to create works of many acts and of considerable length. More interested in a series of climaxes than in a complete story, the playwrights often wrote strong scenes without being much concerned about the connection

FIGURE 10.18 Scene from a Japanese doll theatre performance. The principal puppeteer is seen at left and three others can be glimpsed at right. Courtesy Performing Arts Program of the Asia Society.

between episodes in the same play. This practice of composing relatively discrete episodes probably explains the modern convention of presenting programs made up of parts of plays (often even parts of acts) rather than of complete works.

Kabuki programs have traditionally been lengthy. From around 1650 until after 1850 they usually lasted about twelve hours. In this period it was customary to arrange programs according to a four-part division: First came a historical play *(jidaimono)* that glorified the traditions and values of the *samurai;* a dance (either with or without a story but with a strong emotional flavor) either

came next or was included within the *jidaimono;* then a domestic drama *(sewamono)* set in the milieu of merchants, traders, or artisans was presented; and the performance concluded with a striking one-act dance drama, often humorous. All of the parts of the performance were related thematically whenever possible. In 1868, the maximum length of performances was reduced to eight hours a day. (Night performances were not given until 1878, when gas lighting was introduced.) Since the Second World War, it has been customary to give two programs a day, one lasting from about 11 A.M. until 4 P.M., and the second from about 4:30 P.M. until 9:30 P.M. But, though the length of performances has been reduced and complete full-length plays are now seldom performed, the four-part arrangement is still usually followed.

Many critics consider dance to be the basis of Kabuki, although dance must be understood to include rhythmical movement, studied posture, and conventionalized gesture. Originally only the female roles were danced, but by the late eighteenth century dance was such an essential part of all performances that a professional choreographer was added to each company. Since then dance has grown more complex and new forms have been specially created for Kabuki. The choreographers founded schools and granted licenses to students when they reached a certain level of proficiency. Many of the present schools date back to the eighteenth century.

Dance in Kabuki is always expected to reflect the verbal text. It seeks to distill the essence of real emotions and deeds into stylized gesture, movement, and posture. Thus, weeping becomes a rhythmical movement of the head accompanied by precise hand gestures. Kabuki dance is accompanied by narrative and descriptive music that helps to establish its character but always remains subordinate. The music for each play is traditional. Because Kabuki has borrowed from several sources, the placement of the musicians on stage varies: sometimes they sit upstage, sometimes they are at stage left, sometimes at stage right. Onstage musicians wear ceremonial dress of the *samurai* (divided skirt, kimono, and stiff horizontal shoulder pieces). When not performing, they sit upright and motionless. In addition to the onstage musicians, others provide special musical effects from behind a screen on stage right. Although the orchestra includes flutes, drums, bells, gongs, cymbals, and strings, the most essential instrument is the *samisen*. Singing and narration to its accompaniment is one of the most characteristic features of Kabuki.

Song and narration are important in Kabuki, especially in dance plays or those taken from the puppet theatre. Since actors never sing, in these works a narrator sets the scene, comments on the action, and speaks part or all of the dialogue as in the puppet theatre. In plays in which most of the lines are spoken by actors, the narrator or chorus still sings or recites some passages. Even the actor's spoken lines follow conventionalized intonational patterns.

Kabuki acting is a combination of speaking and dancing. Because it follows established rules, it requires long and diligent study. The actor begins his training at the age of six or seven, first studying dance and then

FIGURE 10.19 Ichikawa Danjuro V in the role of Kagemasa Gongoro in the Kabuki play, *Shibaraku* (1697). Depicted is one of the characteristic features of Kabuki acting, the pose struck and held (*mie*). In this play the character exits along the *hanamichi* through a series of these poses. The popularity of the play and this exit were such as to motivate woodcuts of the type shown here. Woodcut by Katsu Shunsho, 1770. Courtesy Rietberg Museum, Zurich.

proceeding to diction, intonation, and the wearing of costumes. Since there are many children's roles, the student is usually on stage from the beginning of his career and learns his profession at first hand. Most of the leading performers come from a few families for whom acting is a hereditary profession. Each family has an elaborate system of stage names, some of which are so honored that they are awarded only to those considered undisputed masters of their art. An actor is almost never judged mature until after he has reached middle age.

The roles in Kabuki are divided into a few basic types: *tachiyaku*, loyal, good, and courageous men; *katakiyaku*, villainous men; *wakashukata*, young men, who if mild in disposition are called *nimaime; dokekata*, comic roles, including comic villains; *koyaku*, children's roles; and *onnagata*, women's roles of various kinds, all played by men.

Kabuki actors do not wear masks, but some roles require boldly patterned makeup to exaggerate the muscular conformation of the face. Red and black patterns are normally painted upon a white base, although demons and evil characters may use blue or brown. The *onnagata* draws in false eyebrows and adds rouging at the corner of the eye and to the mouth but otherwise leaves the face completely white. Married women blacken their teeth and obliterate their eyebrows. For some of the more athletic male roles, the arms and legs are made up in a conventional pattern. The makeup of each role is symbolic of the character.

Every role also has its traditional costume. Most are based upon historical garments which have been altered for dramatic purposes. Dress from different periods is often seen in a single play, for historical accuracy is of no importance in Kabuki. Pattern and color are usually subdued. Some costumes weigh as much as fifty pounds and stage attendants must assist the actors in keeping them properly arranged on stage.

In visual style Kabuki lies somewhere between the conventionalism of the Noh stage and the illusionism of the Western theatre. This combination can be seen most clearly in the properties, stage, and scenery. Properties range from the symbolic to the relatively realistic. The fan is used much as in Noh and can indicate riding a horse, shooting a bow and arrow, the rising of the moon, or opening a door. A scarf serves a multitude of similar purposes. On the other hand, many properties are representational, although none is intended to be convincingly real. The Kabuki horse probably best exemplifies the degree of illusionism; a wooden framework shaped like

FIGURE 10.20 Scene from a Kabuki play at the present-day Kabuki-za in Tokyo. Note the mingling of representational and conventionalized elements. From *Décor de Théâtre dans le Monde depuis 1935.*

a horse, covered with velvet and ridden by an actor, is supported by two actors, whose legs clearly show. Many other properties—armor, swords, human heads, tigers, elephants, monkeys, household goods—are treated in much the same fashion.

The stage also marks a compromise between convention and illusionism. Originally the Kabuki performers used the Noh stage, but by the 1660s they had already widened the bridge and added a curtain to conceal the stage. But not until 1724 were the Kabuki players allowed to have buildings complete with roofs. After that time machinery began to be used for special effects. A small elevator trap was installed in 1736, but soon more elaborate devices were exploited. In 1753 Namiki Shozo invented the large elevator stage and in 1758 he introduced the revolving stage (first used at the Kado-za in Osaka). After 1827 the revolving stage was sometimes constructed in two sections, one revolving inside the other, and worked independently. A forestage had become a permanent feature of the Kabuki theatre by 1736 and was the principal acting area after 1745. Some scenic pieces began to appear in the late seventeenth century and grew ever more complex thereafter.

Some time between 1724 and 1736 one of the Kabuki's most distinctive features, the *hanamichi*, was introduced. A raised gangway which connects the stage with a small room at the rear of the auditorium, the

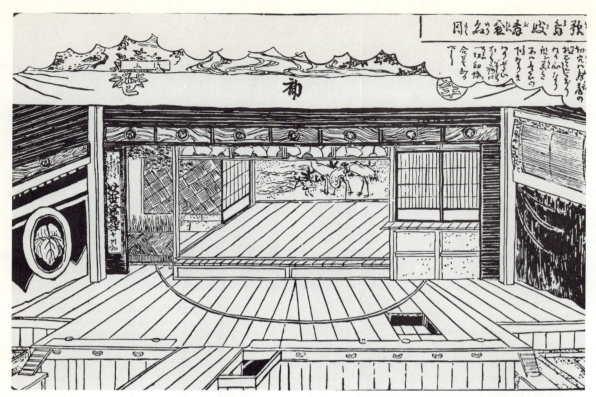

FIGURE 10.21   A Kabuki stage of the nineteenth century showing the revolving stage (first used in 1758) and a small elevator trap (first used in 1736). At center left is the *hanamichi*. Note also the screens at either side of the stage, the one at right raised like a venetian blind. A woodcut published in *Scribner's Magazine,* vol. 7 (1890).

FIGURE 10.22   The Nakamura-za in 1859 during a Kabuki performance. Note the two *hanamichi* and the arrangement of the auditorium. A contemporary engraving.

hanamichi is used for all major entrances and exits, as well as for many important scenes. The *hanamichi* was so popular that a second had been introduced by the 1770s. By 1830, the Kabuki stage had achieved its characteristic form. The Noh roof had been abandoned, and the stage now occupied the full width of the auditorium and was equipped with revolving stage and elevator traps. The area between the two *hanamichi* was divided into numerous square enclosures, or floor boxes, in which spectators sat on mats. Another row of these boxes ran along each side of the auditorium.

After 1868, several changes were made as a result of Western influence. The proscenium arch was introduced in 1908 and became standard after 1923, as did Western-style seating. The second *hanamichi* was eliminated, although it is still sometimes installed temporarily when required for a particular play. Except for the introduction of flying machinery, electric lighting, and the proscenium arch, however, the stage has remained relatively unchanged. The proscenium arch of the present Kabuki-za in Tokyo is 90 feet wide but only about 20 feet high, and the auditorium is only 60 feet deep. Thus the spatial relationship between stage and audience differs considerably from that of the typical Western theatre.

Unlike Noh, Kabuki uses a great deal of scenery, although it decorates the stage rather than conceals it. Every locale in a Kabuki play is suggested scenically. The scenery is changed in full view of the audience by means of the revolving stage, elevator traps, grooves, or by visible stage attendants. Perhaps because Kabuki emphasizes lateral composition, no more than two sets are erected on the revolving stage at once; sets are never pie-shaped and almost all scenery is placed parallel to the front of the stage. Painting is usually flat and is not intended to appear three-dimensional. Typically the stage is enclosed at the rear by flats painted with a distant view, but illusionism is avoided by letting the cracks between individual flats show and by using a black curtain to cut off the top of the scene.

Sometimes relatively realistic Japanese buildings are erected on stage, but the entry gates to houses are often removed by stage assistants when they are no longer needed, and other theatrical conventions constantly remind the audience of the contrivance. Many scenic pieces are used symbolically. White mats represent snow, blue mats water, gray mats the ground; different kinds of trees indicate changes of locales. This mingling of the familiar with the conventional makes Kabuki, among all the traditional Oriental forms, most accessible to Westerners.

After the end of Japan's isolation and the fall of the shogunate in the late nineteenth century, many of the earlier restrictions on the theatre were removed. Women were now allowed to appear on the stage and entrepreneurs to open new theatres. The major novelty, however, was the introduction of Western-style drama and theatrical conventions. The earliest productions in this mode came in the 1880s, but *shimpa* (as this movement was called) reached its peak between 1904 and 1909, and then rapidly declined. Since World War II there have been attempts to revive the early *shimpa* style, but the results have generally been unsatisfactory and are now treated with considerable condescension because the plays have typically been sentimental, romantic, or melodramatic.

Another attempt to promote familiarity with Western drama was initiated in 1909 with the formation of the Free Theatre Society, which staged plays by Shakespeare, Ibsen, Shaw, Chekhov, Strindberg, and others. The leader of this movement, Tsubouchi Shoyo, also established a theatre museum at Waseda University in Tokyo which has become a major center for theatre research.

Still another offspring of the Western movement is *shingeki* (or new theatre). Long committed to realism and to Konstantin Stanislavksy's methods, *shingeki* has in recent years become eclectic in outlook and experimental in approach. Consequently, it is now attuned to the major international artistic currents. But despite all trends toward Westernization, the traditional forms—Noh, the doll theatre, and Kabuki—continue to command the greatest respect both in Japan and abroad.

OTHER ORIENTAL COUNTRIES

Every Oriental country has its own dramatic traditions, often quite diverse and highly developed. Korea's theatrical forms are related to Chinese and Japanese modes, although they had their own distinct characteristics, which exerted considerable influence on Japanese forms. Ritualistic performances in Korea can be traced back to the third century A.D. but they may be even older. Eventually Korea produced various types of dance-drama, puppet shows, farces, pantomimes, and, after 1908, a Western-style drama.

One of the most interesting of Korea's theatrical

FIGURE 10.23 The masked dance-drama of Pongsan, Korea. In the background are seen the musicians. Courtesy Performing Arts Program of the Asia Society.

wayang kulit. It is unclear when or where it originated. Some scholars argue that it is purely indigenous, others that it came from India, and still others that it came from China. Regardless of its origin, it had by the eleventh century A.D. developed into a highly complex art quite unlike the forms seen in India or China. Between the thirteenth and seventeenth centuries, the Indonesian and Malaysian shadow puppets evolved to their present size and shapes and by the nineteenth century their visual features and the conventions of performance had become fixed.

The *wayang kulit* uses flat puppets made of leather that are cut and decorated to create intricate patterns of light and shadow when images of the figures are cast on a screen. The puppets, which range in size from 6 inches to more than 3 feet, are mounted on sticks of buffalo horn. The major characters in the dramas, most of which

FIGURE 10.24 Shadow puppet from Malaysia representing Hanuman (the monkey king). From the private collection of Ruth and Walter Meserve.

forms is the mask dance-drama of Pongsan, now some 200 years old and the inheritor of numerous earlier traditions. Originally the purpose of this dance-drama was to exorcise evil spirits and to insure a good harvest and the safety of the village, but it is now performed primarily as entertainment. Through vigorous dance, gesture, jesting, and singing, it comments on hypocritical monks, aristocratic privilege, male-female relationships, and the lot of the common man. The accompaniment is played on woodwind, string, and percussion instruments.

The theatre of Southeast Asia is allied to that of India, perhaps because the peoples of that area share the heritage of Hinduism, the Hindu epics, and Buddhism. Dance-drama, especially, is highly developed in Indonesia, Thailand, Cambodia, Laos, and Burma. But there are as well many other theatrical forms in Southeast Asia—folk drama, operetta, spoken drama, pantomime, improvised plays, shadow puppet plays, doll puppet plays, and Western-style drama.

Perhaps the most distinctive form of Asian drama is the shadow play, which is widely performed in Indonesia, Malaysia, and Thailand in numerous local variations. This form seems to have been cultivated most fully on the island of Java in Indonesia, where it is called are based on *Mahabharata* or *Ramayana*, are differentiated through size, shape, color, and costume, but minor figures are differentiated only according to type (ogre, clown, god, and so on). A complete set of *wayang kulit* puppets includes 300 to 400 figures. All the puppets used during a performance are manipulated by one person, who also speaks the dialogue (much of it improvised) and narrative passages (many of them fixed and traditional), sings songs, provides many sound effects, and gives cues to the musical ensemble (composed of various kinds of xylophones, percussion and stringed instruments, a flute, and a number of singers). By tradition, performances begin at 8:30 P.M. and last until dawn (nine to ten hours). Only on special occasions are performances given during daylight hours.

A *wayang kulit* nighttime performance is divided into phases related to the passing hours: first, a problem or situation is established; then an intrigue begins, usually in the stronghold of the hero's enemies; next, the hero appears, accompanied by clown-servants (this happens at midnight); the action reaches its climax in a battle fought between the hero and several powerful giants (this phase of the story usually begins about 3 A.M.); and the action is resolved at dawn with the triumph of the hero over the forces of evil. The drama is accompanied throughout by music, which also varies according to the phase of the story and the hour of the night. The performances are usually given in an open pavilion. The audience sits on both sides of the screen—those on one side see the puppets themselves, those on the other side the shadows cast by an oil lamp.

A number of dramatic types have been derived from the *wayang kulit*. One variation *(wayang golek)* uses three-dimensional doll puppets. Another *(wayang orang)* uses human performers, as does *wayang topeng,* a masked dance drama that makes use of many different kinds of stories. The variations are numerous indeed.

In India, theatrical forms are extremely varied. Historians have long believed that the production of Sanskrit plays ceased in the thirteenth century, but they have learned in the twentieth century that Sanskrit performances continued to be given in the southwestern Indian state of Kerala by actors and musicians who were part of a hereditary temple-service caste. Until the 1960s, these performances were given only at yearly temple festivals. Then a series of public performances was arranged, and eventually a systematic study of these dramas began.

The traditions in Kerala can be traced back to at least the tenth century A.D. For each play in the repertory

FIGURE 10.25 Shadow puppet from Malaysia representing Seri Rama (the hero). From the private collection of Ruth and Walter Meserve.

there is a manual that describes the staging, acting, and costuming. These have yet to be translated, but eventually they will add much to our knowledge about Sanskrit drama and its staging.

The temples in which the plays are performed also provide architectural evidence about performance spaces and traditions. The temple-theatres vary in size, with proportion being more important than dimensions, since each part of the whole is symbolic. There is a good deal of sculptural decoration, the most elaborate reserved for the stage.

FIGURE 10.26 *Wayang topeng* mask of wood for the role of Pandji, Prince of Djenggala. From Java, eighteenth century. Courtesy Rietberg Museum, Zurich.

others, they are light farces, dance dramas, or devotional plays. Regardless of type, almost all have common characteristics. A narrator usually sets the scene, calls out each character as needed, and describes events not shown on stage. All are performed on an open stage surrounded on three sides by the audience. No scenery is used. The acting is stylized, but uses conventions fully understood by the audiences of the area. Music accompanies the entire performance. Most plays continue all night in the light of flickering torches.

The puppet and folk plays kept Indian traditions alive during the centuries of Muslim and English domination. Similarly, dance traditions were preserved by temple dancers, especially in the state of Madras from the

FIGURE 10.27 Performer in the *wayang topeng* masked dance theatre of Bali. Courtesy Performing Arts Program of the Asia Society.

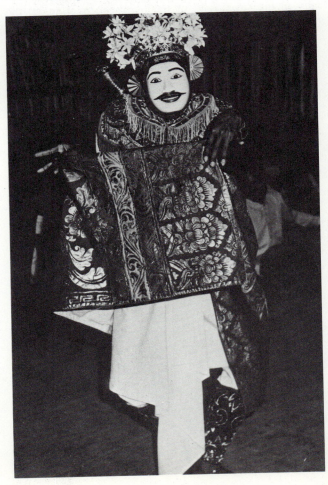

The square stage is equipped only with stools, a single bronze lamp, a removable curtain, and drums set between the two doors that lead to the dressing room back of the stage. (Clifford Jones provides considerable detail about the architectural features in an article published in the *Journal of the American Oriental Society* in 1973.) What has been published so far about the Kerala performances is helpful (although it tells little about the actual productions), but it will probably be many years before the new evidence is fully evaluated.

In modern India the folk play tradition has been far more popular than the Sanskrit. It probably had its roots in the plays performed for the common people during the early Christian era, but its definite history can be traced no further back than the fifteenth or sixteenth centuries. Each area of India has its own characteristic folk plays; the variations are extremely numerous. In some locales, they assume operatic form and feature legendary heroes or themes of love and chivalry; in

FIGURE 10.28 **Chhau dancer of northeastern India. Courtesy Performing Arts Program of the Asia Society.**

fifteenth century onward. When Indian nationalism began to reassert itself in the 1890s, this traditional dance form, now called the *Bharatanatyam*, came into prominence once more and has since been highly prized in the Madras area. Although originally probably performed by more than one dancer, it is now a woman's solo dance noted for its grace. Classical dance also survived in the Kathak, characterized by intricate footwork and precise rhythms; the Manipuri, noted for its swaying and gliding movements, and in innumerable local variants throughout India. Two of the most interesting variants are the Chhau and Kathakali.

The Chhau masked dances are found in northeastern India, where for centuries they have been a part of the spring festival given in honor of the god Shiva. Encompassing solos, duets, and dance-dramas which interpret mythology, sacred history, legend, and nature subjects, they are performed throughout four nights, usually in a courtyard lighted by torches and lanterns. Chhau makes use of the conventions described in *Natyasastra* but adds many of its own. The dancers wear gold and silver brocaded costumes in rich colors, elaborate headdresses, and intricate molded and painted masks

made of *papier-mâché* and wood. The dances are performed entirely by men to the precise rhythms of drums.

Kathakali, now about 300 years old, is restricted to southwestern India. Its subject matter is taken primarily from the Hindu epics. Perhaps because it is pantomimic, Kathakali has exaggerated many of the features found in Sanskrit drama and has brought violence and death onto the stage. Its stories center around the passions and furies of gods and demons, or the loves and hates of superhuman characters; the forces of good and evil clash in desperate struggles, but good always wins. The actors rely entirely upon dance, mime, costume, and makeup, although musicians also help to tell the story through song and instrumental accompaniment. The gestural language includes more than 500 separate signs. Characters fall into about seven basic types, each with its own costume and symbolic makeup, which takes hours to apply. Because it is so energetic, Kathakali uses boys to perform female roles. The Kathakali dancer must begin his training as a child and is not considered mature until he has performed a role for about twenty years. Kathakali is presented in a temple courtyard or other open space, upon a stage about 16 feet square covered

FIGURE 10.29 Kathakali performers. Note the heavily stylized makeup and costume, especially on the figure at the left. From Gargi, *The Theatre in India*. Courtesy Theatre Arts Books.

century. In the nineteenth century Indian plays written in the Western style began to appear. Of the modern playwrights, Rabindrinath Tagore (1861–1941) has been most successful in blending Indian and Western traditions in such plays as *Chitra* (1894), *King of the Dark Chamber* (1914), and *The Cycle of Spring* (1917).

Although the revival of the Indian national consciousness redirected attention to Sanskrit drama and other classical forms, the great diversity of local languages and customs has not yet permitted the development of a characteristic modern style. The Indian theatre is now extremely diverse, ranging through productions of the Sanskrit plays and folk drama to modern realistic works. The influence of India on other countries, nevertheless, continues to derive primarily from its classical forms.

The Western world for the most part remained ignorant of the Eastern theatre until the nineteenth century. The Sanskrit plays were the first to be translated and read, but Oriental theatrical conventions were unappreciated until Eastern companies began to appear in the West. A Chinese troupe played in Paris in 1895; a Japanese group appeared in London in 1900; and individual performers toured with some frequency thereafter. Nevertheless, it was not until such Western producers as Meyerhold, Vakhtangov, Brecht, and Artaud began to advocate them as alternatives to the Western emphasis on illusionism that Eastern conventions began to affect Western practices. At first viewed as perverse or exotic, the innovations have been increasingly accepted since the Second World War, largely because of the influence of Brecht and Artaud. Although it is still doubtful that most Westerners truly understand the Oriental theatre, they have been stimulated by it to seek new theatrical means.

with a flower-decked canopy and lighted by torches. Performances last all night.

Western-style drama is also common in present-day India. Western plays were first introduced by the British when they arrived in India in the eighteenth

LOOKING AT THEATRE HISTORY

In studying the theatre of other cultures, it is important to become familiar with the context out of which it has emerged, for otherwise it will seem merely quaint rather than a vital expression. Obviously, it is difficult to enter fully into another culture, which is a compound of elements often quite unlike those we know. It is possible to

gain insight into other ways of life, however, by reading social and cultural histories and by examining the arts these cultures have produced. This kind of approach is especially important if Westerners are to develop an appreciation for Eastern theatrical forms.

The following brief passage points out the relationship between Chinese drama and the three great Chinese philosophies, Confucianism, Buddhism, and Taoism:

Whatever native ingredients and alien elements entered into the melting pot of Chinese civilization, its main component has been essentially Confucianism. . . . A practicable moral philosophy that teaches the rules of personal cultivation and virtues of human relationship, Confucianism has molded the Chinese national character and pervaded every aspect of Chinese society, the family, literature and the arts. . . . but when the country was in disorder, Taoism and Buddhism took over [since] disappointments bred . . . a desire to wander astray in . . . otherworldliness. The majority of Chinese writers, however, have been conformists to the grand Confucian tradition. To them, literature has been a vehicle for the communication of the aim of Confucian doctrine: to teach and influence people to be good. . . . The three great Chinese doctrines merged in the common belief in retribution . . . [which] deterred the growth of anything like the Western concept of tragedy. . . . From the Chinese point of view it would be a blemish in the literary work not to give its readers a sense of satisfaction in the ultimate vindication and triumph of the good and virtuous.

WU-CHI LIU, *An Introduction to Chinese Literature* (Bloomington: Indiana University Press, 1966), pp. 4–5

Similarly, in his study of Kabuki, A. C. Scott points out the influence of Buddhism, Shintoism, and Confucianism on Japanese life and theatre. He also discusses domestic architecture, dress, food, social relationships, etiquette, and other aspects of daily life that have contributed to theatrical subjects and conventions:

Formerly, everything and everybody in Japan was bound by a strict code of etiquette. There were correct ways of eating, drinking, wearing clothes and moving about according to time and place. . . . This fact, coupled with their characteristic manner of living, such as for instance sitting, dining and sleeping on the tatami *[reed mats] created gestures and movements which were individual in style, and these translated into terms of stage technique have developed a very special visual effect, both in the case of the single actor or group composition. . . . the legends, customs, habits, religion, loves and hates of the Japanese people are drawn upon freely and woven into the pattern of construction of this colorful drama.*

The Kabuki Theatre of Japan (London: George Allen and Unwin, Ltd., 1955), pp. 32–33.

Even with a knowledge of the intellectual and cultural context, a Western observer often has difficulty, at least in the beginning, with many conventions of the Oriental theatre. Among these are the color symbolism and face painting of Peking Opera. (For some examples, see the illustrations on page 247.)

The more admirable characters are usually painted in relatively simple colors. Enemy leaders or very special people have more complicated designs on their faces—toughs, bandits, hardened soldiers, rebels. A lot of red indicates courage, loyalty, straightforwardness; more black denotes impulsiveness, while a blue face is a cruel one. A crook who is completely untrustworthy is given a white, often twisted face.

Musical modes are also apt to seem strange, and to the Westerner the orchestra has "a superabundance of gongs, cymbals, and drums."

The accompaniment for the voice is played on the "ching hu"—the two-stringed fiddle. . . . Flutes are also used, the bamboo kind, held parallel to the face when played. The "sheng" or reed flute is really a small organ and has chords. Then there are the moon guitars and three-stringed guitars, a kind of Chinese clarinet . . . ; big and small drums, a bell, cymbals and the "pan" or wooden time-beater which does for the orchestra what the conductor does for his musicians in a Western performance. . . . Entrances and exits have a musical accompaniment. An actor, before breaking into song, will speak his last words in a certain way so that the orchestra knows the song is about to begin.

REWI ALLEY, *Peking Opera* (Peking, 1957).

In the advice he gave to Noh actors in his *Works*, Zeami emphasizes restraint, which is to be accomplished in part through the reconciliation of opposites:

In representing anger the actor should yet retain some gentleness in his mood, else he will portray not anger but violence.

When the body is in violent action, the hands and feet must move as though by stealth. When the feet are in lively motion, the body must be held in quietness.

Translated by Arthur Waley in his *The No Plays of Japan* (New York: Alfred A. Knopf, 1922), p. 26.

A number of works that give advice to actors or preserve anecdotes about acting in Kabuki have survived from the late seventeenth and early eighteenth centuries. In "The Words of Ayame" there is this passage about the *onnagata* (female) role, at that time always played by men:

> The *onnagata* role has its basis in charm, and even one who has innate beauty, if he seeks to make a fine show in a fighting scene, will lose the femininity of his performance. . . . if he does not live his normal life as if he was a woman, it will not be possible for him to be called a skillful *onnagata*.

From "A Sequel to 'Dust in the Ears'" comes this account of playwriting prior to the late seventeenth century:

> The normal way of working was that after the discussion of a new play and a decision upon it, the construction of each scene was worked out. Then the actors in a scene were called together, placed in a circle, and taught the speeches orally. They stood there until they made their exit, and then either rehearsed it again . . . or the authors worked out the speeches for the next section, and got them fixed by repetition.

> *The Actors' Analects*, ed., trans., and with an introduction and notes by Charles J. Dunn and Bunzo Torigoe (New York: Columbia University Press, 1969), pp. 53, 118.

11 The English Theatre, 1642–1800

Because of the civil war between the Royalists and Puritans, life in England was very unsettled during the 1640s. England did not return to peace until 1649, when Charles I had been captured, tried, and beheaded by the Puritans. For a time England was governed by a committee appointed by Parliament, but after 1653 Oliver Cromwell was a virtual dictator. When he died in 1658, his son was chosen as his successor but he could not maintain control. In 1660 the Stuarts were restored to the throne.

THEATRICAL ACTIVITY, 1642–1660

During the eighteen years between 1642 and 1660, the Puritans sought to stamp out theatrical activity. As a result, few records relating to performance have survived, although playing certainly continued intermittently. At first the actors complied with the law passed in 1642 suspending performances for a period of five years. The King's Men sold its wardrobe, and its Globe Theatre was torn down. Actors soon began to perform surreptitiously, however, and by 1647 performances were being given at the Fortune, Cockpit, and Salisbury Court theatres. Although Parliament ordered officials to halt the violations, suppression was sporadic and ineffectual. When the law prohibiting performances expired in 1647, open playing was immediately resumed. But in 1649,

Parliament passed a new law ordering that all actors be apprehended as rogues; the interiors of the Fortune, Cockpit, and Salisbury Court were dismantled. The actors continued to perform, nevertheless, using The Red Bull, which had escaped demolition, or, when that appeared too dangerous, private houses, tennis courts, or inns. Often officials were bribed to ignore violations. In these years, the usual form of entertainment seems to have been the "droll," a short farcical play condensed from a longer work.

Apparently, the actors believed that the theatre would eventually be legalized. Around 1650, William Beeston, (c. 1606–1682) acquired The Salisbury Court, rebuilt it, and began to train a company of boys. The Cockpit passed into the hands of John Rhodes, a bookseller, who also organized a young company. Perhaps most significantly, William Davenant, who in the 1630s had succeeded Jonson as the principal writer of court masques, began openly to stage what have been called England's first operatic productions. His initial offering, *The First Day's Entertainment at Rutland House*, was presented in May 1656.

The production of *The Siege of Rhodes*, also in 1656, is a far more important event, however, for it marks the first clear use in England of Italianate scenery for a public performance. Designed by John Webb (1611–1672), pupil and son-in-law of Inigo Jones, the settings were mounted on a stage measuring only 22 feet in width, 18 feet in depth and 11 feet in height. Behind the prosce-

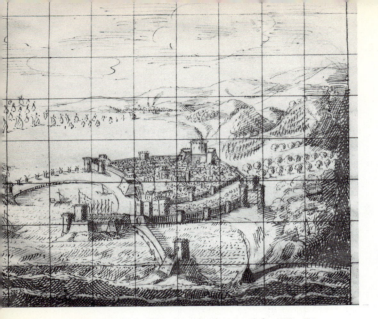

FIGURE 11.1 The first background for *The Siege of Rhodes,* a distant view of Rhodes and the harbor. The drawing is divided into squares to facilitate the transfer of the design to the shutters. Devonshire Collection, Chatsworth. Reproduced by permission of the Trustees of the Chatsworth Settlement.

nium, a series of fixed wings, painted to represent rocky cliffs, terminated in movable shutters which, in combination with set pieces, depicted the various places required by the action.

These first entertainments were given in Rutland House, Davenant's residence, but in 1658 and 1659 Davenant presented at least three others at The Cockpit, in which a proscenium arch was erected. Although some opposition was expressed, by this time the restoration of the monarchy was imminent and no action was taken. On the other hand, Davenant was not violating any law, for his pieces were "musical entertainments," which had not been forbidden.

THE REESTABLISHMENT OF THE THEATRE

In 1660 Charles II (reigned 1660–1685) was restored to the throne. (Thus, the period from 1660 to 1700 is usually called the Restoration, even though it extended considerably beyond Charles' reign.) Under Charles, England rejected the strict puritanism of the Commonwealth, so much so that the Restoration became noted for its permissiveness, even libertinism. Charles maintained an easy political truce with Parliament, since neither wished to give up any rights or to engage in another open conflict. Charles' belief in his rights as a monarch are

nowhere more evident than in his relation to the theatre, which he treated as a royal property to dispose of as he saw fit.

And it was soon disposed of. As soon as it became evident that the monarchy would be restored, preparations began for reopening theatres. In March 1660, Davenant leased Lisle's Tennis Court and went to France to urge his claims to a license with Charles II. Sir Henry Herbert resumed the position of Master of Revels, which he had held under Charles I, and licensed three companies: one under John Rhodes at The Cockpit, another under Michael Mohun at The Rud Bull, and a third under William Beeston at The Salisbury Court. Meanwhile, Charles II, unaware of Herbert's actions, had awarded a monopoly on theatrical production in London to Davenant and Thomas Killigrew (1612–1683), who had grown up in the English court, had written a number of plays before 1642, and had been with the royal family throughout its exile. Not until late 1660 were Davenant and Killigrew able to suppress the troupes licensed by Herbert. At first they ran a company jointly, but they soon formed two troupes. Killigrew, as head of the King's Company, took the older, more experienced actors, while

FIGURE 11.2 The proscenium and side wings for *The Siege of Rhodes* as designed by John Webb and presented by William Davenant at Rutland House in 1656. The wings, representing cliffs, remained fixed throughout and scenic units were changed behind them. This perspective setting with movable units is the first known use of Italianate scenery on the public stage in England. Devonshire Collection, Chatsworth. Reproduced by permission of the Trustees of the Chatsworth Settlement.

Davenant's Duke's Company was left with the younger performers.

The monopoly granted Davenant and Killigrew was challenged almost immediately by George Jolly (*fl.* 1648–1673), who during the Commonwealth years had headed a touring company in Germany. It was there in 1655 that he had performed for the future Charles II and had received some kind of commitment from him about the future. As a result, in late 1660, the king granted Jolly a license to perform in London. In 1662, Davenant and Killigrew rented Jolly's license, and he went on a tour of England. During his absence, the two managers convinced the king that they had bought Jolly's license and in 1664 they secured new grants giving them exclusive rights to perform in London. Following this treachery, Jolly returned to London and resumed performances until 1667, when the king finally silenced him. Perhaps to avoid further trouble, Jolly was employed by Davenant and Killigrew to head a training school for actors. After 1673, no more is heard of him.

Davenant and Killigrew also had difficulties with Sir Henry Herbert, who sued them for usurping many privileges formerly held by the Master of Revels. Eventually Herbert was deprived of the right to license theatres and companies in London, although he continued to authorize companies outside of London and to license all new plays. Thus, Davenant and Killigrew established almost complete control over theatrical performances in London. The patents issued to them by Charles II were to remain in effect until 1843, seriously hampering the growth of the English theatre.

FIGURE 11.3 A drawing, probably showing a composite of the stages used during the Commonwealth for "drolls." Note that characters from several plays are shown. Note also the use of chandeliers and footlights. From Kirkman, *The Wits,* a collection of drolls, published in 1672.

ACTING COMPANIES, 1660–1700

Although Killigrew began with the advantage of experienced actors, his company did not prosper as did Davenant's. Killigrew devoted little attention to the theatre, delegating authority to three of his actors. Perhaps as a result, the company was wracked by constant dissension. Davenant, on the other hand, supervised his theatre closely until his death in 1668, after which the actors Betterton and Harris assumed artistic direction under the control of the Davenant family. By 1682 Killigrew's company was in such serious financial difficulties that the two troupes were merged.

The United Companies continued until 1695, when several actors seceded to form another troupe after a series of events had placed them in an untenable position. In 1688, Charles Davenant had sold the controlling interest in the theatre to his brother Alexander; in 1693, when Alexander fled England to escape his creditors, it was revealed that his financial support had come from Christopher Rich and Sir Thomas Skipworth. Rich, a lawyer without any theatrical experience, seized control of the company and proved himself so unpleasant, by withholding salaries and favoring those actors who catered to his whims, that the major performers, under Betterton's leadership, secured a license from William III to form a second troupe. This separation was to last from 1695 until 1707.

In addition to the London companies, a number of troupes were licensed to perform in the provinces. The most important provincial center was Dublin, perhaps because it had its own Master of Revels. In 1637, John Ogilby (1600–1676) had been given a license to open a theatre in Dublin and was named Master of Revels for Ireland. Ogilby's patent, dormant after 1641, was renewed in 1661, and in 1662 he opened the Smock Alley, the first theatre built in Great Britain after the Restoration. Upon Ogilby's death, the patent passed to Joseph Ashbury, who maintained the finest company outside of London for the next forty-five years.

ENGLISH DRAMA, 1660–1700

One of the problems facing managers in 1660 was a suitable repertory. At first they depended on pre-Commonwealth plays, which the Master of Revels divided between the companies. Of these, the works of Beaumont and Fletcher were the most popular; Jonson's, though much admired, were seldom produced. Several of Shakespeare's plays were revised to bring them into line with contemporary tastes. Many of the older works soon proved too outmoded, and they were dropped from the repertory as soon as new ones were available. Others, however, remained favorites.

Several types of serious plays were written between 1660 and 1700. Until 1680 the dominant mode was "heroic" tragedy, which, heavily indebted to Spanish and French authors, emphasized stories centering around the rival claims of love and honor. This type first reached popularity through the works of Roger Boyle, Earl of Orrery (1621–1679), especially *The Tragedy of Mustapha* (1665), *The Black Prince* (1667), and *Tryphon* (1668). Other popular writers of this genre were Elkanah Settle (1648–1724), author of *Cambyses, King of Persia* (1671), and *The Empress of Morocco* (1673); Nathaniel Lee (1653–1692) with *The Rival Queens* (1677); and John Dryden (1631–1700) with *The Indian Queen* (1664), *The Indian Emperor* (1665), *The Conquest of Granada*, parts 1 and 2 (1669–1670), and *Aureng-Zebe* (1675). In these works, typically an idealistic hero and a beautiful heroine are faced with a situation in which the fulfillment of their mutual love will precipitate other events apt to bring ruin or dishonor to themselves, their families, or country. Often the background is martial, and frequently a happy ending is contrived. Filled with ranting

FIGURE 11.4 Dryden's *All for Love*. From Dryden's *Dramatick Works*, Vol. IV (1735).

speeches in rhymed couplets, the plays now seem hopelessly stilted. The genre was dealt a heavy blow in 1671 by *The Rehearsal*, written by George Villiers, second Duke of Buckingham (1628–1687), which burlesqued the typical themes, plot devices, and staging conventions of heroic tragedy. Buckingham's play outlived its target, remaining in the repertory until the late eighteenth century.

As the heroic mode declined, it was replaced by tragedy written in blank verse and according to the neoclassical rules. Using relatively simple plots and observing the three unities, the form first gained popularity through Dryden's *All for Love* (1677), a "regularization" of Shakespeare's *Antony and Cleopatra*. It was to remain the dominant mode through the remainder of the century. English neoclassicism was always more liberal than the version that prevailed on the continent. Unity of action was interpreted to permit a number of related subplots, and the unity of place was thought to have been adequately observed if the characters could move easily between the various locales without violating the 24-hour time limit.

The combined influence of neoclassicism and of Shakespeare are evident in the work of the best serious playwright of the age, Thomas Otway (1652–1685), whose *The Orphan* (1680) and *Venice Preserv'd* (1682) remained in the repertory until the late nineteenth century. The first of these plays focuses on a girl who is loved by two brothers, one of whom she marries secretly, upon which the other brother, suspecting an illicit relationship, brings ruin to them all. *Venice Preserv'd* deals with a conspiracy to overthrow the government of Venice and ends in death for the three principal characters, Pierre, Jaffier, and Belvidera. But though in Otway's plays pathos has not yet replaced true tragic pity, a trend toward the tearful was already evident and would thereafter accelerate.

Building upon Davenant's Commonwealth "entertainments," opera also flourished during the Restoration. It differed from heroic tragedy primarily in the addition of music, song, and spectacle, and it departed from the conventions of Italian opera by substituting spoken passages for recitative. Not only were Shakespeare's *Macbeth, The Tempest,* and *A Midsummer Night's Dream* adapted to the operatic mode, but such original works as Dryden's *Albion and Albianus* (1685) and *King Arthur* (1692) also achieved considerable popularity. This English strain of opera was to decline rapidly after the vogue for Italian opera began around 1705.

But the Restoration is noted above all for its diverse comic drama: comedies of humours, comedies of intrigue, farces, and comedies of manners. Because of Jonson's reputation, "humours" were much exploited during the Restoration. Of the major authors, Thomas Shadwell (1642–1692) was the most successful writer of humorous comedy with *The Sullen Lovers* (1668), *The Humourists* (1670), *The Squire of Alsatia* (1688), and *Bury Fair* (1689). Each of these plays introduces a series of eccentric characters in a story of contemporary life, told with frank and outspoken dialogue.

Perhaps because of the influence of Corneille and the Spanish dramatists, the comedy of intrigue was also popular in these years. The best examplar of this genre was Mrs. Aphra Behn (1640–1689) with such plays as *The Rover*, parts 1 and 2 (1677–1680). Farce reached its height in the works of Edward Ravenscroft (*fl.* 1671–1697), whose *London Cuckolds* (1681) and *The Anatomist* (1697) were played throughout the eighteenth century.

Above all, however, the Restoration is noted for its sprightly comedy of manners. Dryden, the most versatile dramatist of the age, contributed to its formation with such works as *Sir Martin Mar-All* (1667), *The Mock Astrologer* (1668) and *Marriage à la Mode* (1672),

FIGURE 11.5 Congreve's *The Way of the World.* At center is seen Lady Wishfort and her nephew from the country. From an edition of Congreve's plays published in 1753.

each of which includes a pair of carefree, witty lovers. The fully developed comedy of manners, however, is usually traced to the plays of Sir George Etherege (c. 1634–1691), who, after a somewhat erratic beginning in *Love in a Tub* (1664), set the pattern for later writers with *She Would if She Could* (1668) and *The Man of Mode* (1676). Here for the first time we find the elements that were to be typical of the type: characters drawn from the upper classes, a preoccupation with seduction, arranged marriages, and the latest fashions and witty repartee.

Of the later writers in this vein, Wycherley and Congreve were of special importance. William Wycherley (1640–1715) began writing for the stage in 1671 with *Love in a Wood*, and continued with *The Gentleman Dancing Master* (1672), *The Country Wife* (1675), and *The Plain Dealer* (1676). Although these plays are well constructed and present subtly depicted characters, their moral tone has offended many critics. *The Country Wife*, in which the hero circulates the rumor that he is sexually impotent in order to facilitate his seductions, is often cited as evidence of the moral laxity of Restoration comedy. The comedy of manners reached its peak in the plays of William Congreve (1670–1729), whose *Love for Love* (1695) and *The Way of the World* (1700) are still considered masterpieces, because of their brilliant scenes, sparkling dialogue, and clear-cut characterizations. *The Way of the World*, in which the witty lovers Millamant and Mirabell reach their own unique marital agreement based on their knowledge of the ways of their world, inhabited primarily by intriguers, fops, and fools, is usually thought to be one of the finest of all English comedies.

The subject matter and tone of the Restoration comedies of manners has led to much debate over their moral viewpoint. In them the wise are rewarded and the foolish are duped; virtue consists of unsentimental self-knowledge. The self-deceived are ridiculed and gulled, often by protagonists who use their own superior (if somewhat cynical) insights to justify their treatment of the fools. Discussions about the acceptability of these standards of behavior have often obscured the remarkable accomplishments of the Restoration dramatists.

By 1700 changes in English life and drama were becoming evident. When Charles II died, he was succeeded by his brother James II (reigned 1685–1688), who sought to reassert the power of the monarchy and to reestablish Catholicism. Despite his unpopularity, he was tolerated until a son was born to him, raising the

FIGURE 11.6   Scene from Farquhar's *The Beaux' Stratagem.* From an edition of the play published in 1733.

threat that his policies would be perpetuated. A group of leading politicians then invited James's Protestant daughter Mary and her husband William of Orange, ruler of the Netherlands, to assume the throne of England. William invaded England; James fled; and Parliament declared Mary II (reigned 1689–1694) and William III (reigned 1689–1702) co-rulers of England. At the same time, Parliament passed and the new rulers accepted a bill requiring Parliament's consent on all important matters and giving it the right to determine the succession to the throne. In effect, this legislation converted England into a constitutional monarchy and put an end to absolute monarchy, thereby resolving the major cause of the dissension that had plagued England for half a century. It was also an important step in guaranteeing the rights of the people, although primarily the upper and middle classes. Perhaps most of all it is indicative of the strength of the mercantile class, which was rapidly becoming the major source of England's wealth and power.

It is not surprising, then, that the middle class should begin to make its tastes felt in the theatre or, since it was morally conservative, that when it did Puritan sentiment would surface again. This reawakened conservatism was expressed through several attacks on the theatre during the 1690s, but none was truly effective until Jeremy Collier's *A Short View of the Immorality and Profaneness of the English Stage* (1698) appeared. Collier succeeded where others had failed because he began with the accepted neoclassical doctrine that the purpose of drama is to teach and to please and went on to show the disparity between theory and practice. Most dramatists found it impossible to answer Collier effectively, since they too had accepted moral teaching as the basic aim of drama. A few playwrights, among them Dryden, made public recantations; Congreve, though not solely because of Collier's attack, gave up playwriting altogether. Even as the controversy raged, English drama began to move in new directions.

FIGURE 11.7 The "screen scene" from Sheridan's *The School for Scandal* at Drury Lane in 1777. A contemporary print.

ENGLISH DRAMA, 1700–1750

The transition toward a new approach is best seen in the plays of Cibber and Farquhar, in which the characteristics of the established comic types are modified considerably by a more conservative moral outlook and by greater sentimentality. In Colley Cibber's (1671–1757) *Love's Last Shift* (1696), *The Careless Husband* (1704), *The Double Gallant* (1707), and *The Lady's Stake* (1707), profligate characters pursue their fashionable follies until the fifth act, when they undergo rapid and sentimentalized conversions. George Farquhar (1678–1707) preserved much of Congreve's wit, but set his plays in the country and resolved them in a manner which removed all moral objections. His best plays are *The Constant Couple* (1699), which introduced Sir Harry Wildair, one of the most popular characters of the eighteenth century, *The Recruiting Officer* (1706), and *The Beaux' Stratagem* (1707), the latter two still perennial favorites.

The trend in comedy toward sentimentality and toward protagonists drawn from the middle class first reached full expression in *The Conscious Lovers* (1722) by Sir Richard Steele (1672–1729). Based on Terence's *Andria*, Steele's play transfers the action to eighteenth century London. The play's penniless heroine, Indiana, after withstanding many trials, is discovered to be the daughter of a rich merchant, thus making a happy resolution possible. The few humorous scenes fall to the servants. In Steele's play, the purpose of comedy has been seriously altered: rather than seeking to arouse laughter or ridicule, it sought to arouse noble sentiments through the depiction of trials bravely borne by sympathetic characters who are rescued from their sufferings and handsomely rewarded. As Steele put it, he wished to arouse "a pleasure too exquisite for laughter."

Today the drama of the eighteenth century is usually called "sentimental," for the characters appear unnaturally good and their problems seem too easily overcome. These plays were accepted in the eighteenth century, nevertheless, as truthful representations of human nature. The disparity in attitude is explained by our changed view of psychology. Eighteenth-century philosophers conceived of man as good by nature, a state which he could retain by following his instincts, but from which bad examples might divert him. Consequently, it was thought possible to reclaim men from vice by appealing to those virtuous human feelings that had been glossed over by thoughtless or callous behavior. For this reason, characters could be reformed quickly if their "hearts"

FIGURE 11.8 Scene from Gay's *The Beggar's Opera.* Polly and Lucy are pleading for Macheath's life. Note the spectators on stage. An engraving by William Blake after William Hogarth's painting of 1729. Courtesy Harvard Theatre Collection.

could be touched. Pathetic situations were also considered to be useful devices because they demonstrated the goodness of the characters who withstood all trials and because they provided the spectator with an occasion for displaying his own goodness, since to be moved by the sight of virtue in distress was a sign of a properly sensitive and moral nature.

Although Steele was to have no important successors in comedy until after 1750, this new vein in drama was exploited effectively in tragedy much earlier. In the early eighteenth century, Nicholas Rowe (1674–1718) had written a number of pathetic tragedies, such as *The Ambitious Step-Mother* (1701), *Tamerlane* (1701), *The Fair Penitent* (1703), and *The Tragedy of Jane Shore* (1714), which were to hold the stage until the nineteenth century. Other important serious playwrights included Ambrose Philips (1675–1749), whose *The Distrest Mother* (1712), based upon Racine's *Andromaque*, remained a popular vehicle for actresses for over a century; Joseph Addison (1672–1719), whose *Cato* (1713) was considered a masterpiece; and James Thomson (1700–1748), whose *Sophonisba* (1729) was one of the most admired plays of its time. These tragedies, however, were all based upon historical or mythological subjects and drew their characters from the ruling classes. A significant new direction was taken in 1731 when George Lillo (1693–1739) wrote *The London Merchant,* in which the hero-apprentice, George Barnwell, is led astray by a prostitute, kills his kind uncle, and ends on the gallows in spite

of his abject repentance. Lillo chose his subject from everyday life because he believed that the lessons of traditional tragedy, with its characters drawn from the nobility, were not sufficiently applicable to the ordinary man. It is clear that he was considered successful, for until well into the nineteenth century the apprentices of London were sent each year during the Christmas season to see this play as a warning against going astray. Although Lillo had many imitators, none achieved his success.

During the eighteenth century, a number of minor dramatic types (pantomime, ballad opera, comic opera, and burlesque) contributed to the decline of neoclassicism. Pantomime combined elements from *commedia dell'arte* and farce with topical satire and stories drawn from classical mythology. *Commedia dell'arte* troupes had appeared occasionally in England since the sixteenth century, and *commedia* types had been incorporated into the dances and entr'acte entertainments of English performers since the late seventeenth century. Then in 1702 John Weaver arranged the dances into a connected story. It remained for John Rich (1692–1761), son of Christopher Rich and manager of Lincoln's Inn Fields and Covent Garden theatres, to establish the accepted pattern of English pantomime with such works as *Harlequin Executed* (produced during the season of 1716–1717) and *Amadis, or the Loves of Harlequin and Columbine* (1718). In Rich's pantomimes, serious scenes based on classical mythology alternated with comic episodes featuring *commedia* characters. The comic scenes were mute, but the serious plot used dialogue and song. Music accompanied much of the action. But the dominant feature was spectacle, motivated by Harlequin's acquisition of a magic wand that could transform places or characters. Unlike most pantomimes, Rich's were long-lived. In forty-five years he created only about twenty, thirteen of which were first performed between 1717 and 1732. Nine pantomimes became mainstays in his repertory; they were refurbished at regular intervals and were alternated from season to season. Under the name Lun, Rich was also the most famous and the most accomplished English pantomimist of the eighteenth century.

By 1723, pantomime was the most popular form of theatrical entertainment. Although they served only as afterpieces, many pantomimes were more popular than the plays they accompanied. Prices were always raised when new pantomimes were offered, and several had initial runs of forty to fifty performances. Rich trained a number of other pantomime players. The most

FIGURE 11.9   A pantomime at the Haymarket Theatre in the late eighteenth century. Note also the theatre's architecture: proscenium doors, wide apron, stage box, and backless benches in the pit. From Wilkinson, *Londina Illustrata* (1825).

famous was Harry Woodward (1717–1777), who deserted Rich in 1738 and for the next twenty years mounted pantomimes at Drury Lane in competition with his former master.

Rich is also associated with the rise of ballad opera, since he produced the first one, *The Beggar's Opera* (1728) by John Gay (1685–1732), after it had been refused by Drury Lane. Ballad opera emerged in part out of the vogue for Italian opera, which began around 1705 and accelerated in 1710 with the arrival of George Frederick Handel (1685–1759) in England. In 1719, the Royal Academy of Music was founded as the home of opera. Although always in financial difficulties after 1730, the opera continued to enjoy great prestige with the aristocracy through the remainder of the century. Gay's ballad opera drew upon many operatic conventions (even as it satirized them) but it departed from them by alternating spoken dialogue with lyrics sung to popular tunes. Gay's work was more than popularized opera, however,

for its story of London low-life commented satirically on the political situation of his time and set the tone for much of the minor drama of the next ten years. No subsequent ballad opera, however, achieved the popularity of the first one.

The satirical burlesque, which differed from ballad opera principally in the absence of sung portions, appeared in the 1730s. The finest writer of this form was Henry Fielding (1707–1754), who began his dramatic career with adaptations from Molière and then turned to topical satire in his burlesque of contemporary tragedy, *Tom Thumb, or the Tragedy of Tragedies* (1730). His later plays, such as *Pasquin* (1736), *Tumble-Down Dick* (1736), and *The Historical Register of 1736* (1737), burlesqued the major figures and events of the day. Other famous burlesques include Henry Carey's *The Tragedy of Chrononhotonthologos* (1734) and *The Dragon of Wantley* (1737). Like ballad opera, burlesque waned after the passage of the Licensing Act in 1737.

GOVERNMENTAL REGULATION OF THE THEATRE

The Licensing Act of 1737 was an outgrowth of both political and theatrical conditions. During the reign of Queen Anne, sister of Mary II, political parties developed as the role of Parliament increased. Her successor, George I (reigned 1714–1727), was a German prince who spoke no English and permitted his chief minister, Sir Robert Walpole (usually said to be Britain's first prime minister), to run the government. George I's practice was continued by his son, George II (reigned 1727–1760). Thus, after 1714 political factions and government officials and policies provided fertile ground for satire. Dramatists did not fail to capitalize on this opportunity, especially during the 1720s and 1730s.

By this time, the legal status of the patents issued by Charles II was also being debated. William III had raised the question in 1695 when he granted Betterton's troupe a license despite the monopoly held by Christopher Rich. The two companies in existence after 1695 continued in opposition until 1707, when they were reunited by crown action. Rich immediately returned to his oppressive policies and, after ignoring orders to meet his actors' demands, was silenced in 1709. Rich still held both of the original patents, however, and, biding his time, he moved his headquarters to the Lincoln's Inn Fields Theatre, upon which he had taken a lease.

The Drury Lane was reopened in 1710 under a license, and with the exception of the years between 1715 and 1719, when a patent was granted to Sir Richard Steele, it was to operate under a renewable license thereafter. Upon the death of Queen Anne in 1714, the ban against Rich was raised, and his son John opened the Lincoln's Inn Fields Theatre under the original patents.

By 1720, the validity of patents was being questioned because Charles II's grants had never been confirmed by Parliament, and because the crown itself had made so many exceptions to them. This doubt led several men to defy the patents. The first serious challenge came from John Potter, who opened the Haymarket Theatre in 1720. By the 1730s four unlicensed theatres were operating in London. The confusion was compounded in 1733 when the courts dismissed the legal actions brought by the two licensed theatres against actors who had seceded from the Drury Lane to act elsewhere. Since this decision seemed to deny the validity of the patents, clarification was needed.

The immediate motivation for the Licensing Act, however, was Prime Minister Walpole's sensitivity to the political satires being offered at unlicensed theatres. Following a particularly scurrilous attack on Walpole, a bill was rushed through Parliament. Since it was not thoughtfully devised, it created as many problems as it solved. The main provisions of this bill, the Licensing Act of 1737, were simple: (1) it prohibited the acting for "gain, hire, or reward" of any play not previously licensed by the Lord Chamberlain, and (2) it restricted authorized theatres to the City of Westminster (the official seat of government). The Drury Lane and Covent Garden thus were confirmed as the only legitimate theatres in England, for no provisions were made for troupes in any other city. This law had an immediate and lasting effect both on drama and theatrical activity.

At first the law was obeyed, but in 1740, Henry Giffard, who had managed the best of the unlicensed troupes between 1731 and 1737, reopened the Goodman's Fields Theatre. Ostensibly charging admission only for concerts, to which plays were added free, Giffard sought to evade the Licensing Act by interpreting literally the prohibition against unauthorized acting for "gain, hire, or reward." The attention drawn to this theatre by David Garrick's debut in 1741 soon brought its closure. Others were to use similar ruses; Samuel Foote offered his "free" entertainments to those who paid for a "Dish of Chocolate" or to attend an "Auction of Pictures." Such ventures were tolerated for a time but most were eventually for-

FIGURE 11.10 **Strolling actors dressing in a barn. Note the many stage props, bits of scenery, costumes, and the preparations for performance. An engraving by William Hogarth. Courtesy Indiana University Libraries.**

bidden. It was the closure of the New Wells Theatre that prompted William Hallam to send a troupe to America in 1752, an event usually said to mark the true beginning of the American theatre.

Other public entertainments did not require licensing until 1752, when abuses led to the passage of a new bill. Under this legislation all places of entertainment within a twenty-mile radius of London were required to secure licenses from local magistrates. Although regular drama was expressly forbidden, the permissible kinds of entertainment were left undefined.

No law as yet provided for theatrical entertainments outside of the area adjacent to London. Nevertheless, the provincial theatre had continued to operate (either by ignoring the law or by using various ruses to circumvent it), and a number of regular circuits had grown up. By the 1760s, the larger towns were objecting to being denied lawful theatres. As a result, Parliament began to authorize theatres in specific towns: in Bath and Norwich in 1768, in York and Hull in 1769, in Liverpool in 1771, and in Chester in 1777. By the end of the century, almost every major town had a "theatre royal," or crown-authorized theatre.

In London, no exception to the monopoly held by Drury Lane and Covent Garden was made until 1766, when, in recompense for having been crippled by a prank instigated by the Duke of York, Samuel Foote was granted a license to present plays at the Haymarket Theatre between May 15 and September 15, a period during which the patent houses presumably would be closed. Although Foote's license was granted only for his lifetime, he sold it to George Colman in 1777 and it was renewed thereafter until 1843. Thus, the Haymarket became a third legitimate theatre, though it was restricted to playing during the summer months.

Still another bill was passed in 1788 that permitted magistrates outside the twenty-mile radius of London to license theatres for legitimate drama. As a result, the theatre was once again legitimized throughout the British Isles. After the act of 1788, the possibilities of confusion were almost as great as before 1737, for there were now four distinct licensing authorities: (1) the Lord Chamberlain, who licensed all plays and theatres in the city of Westminster; (2) local magistrates within twenty miles of London, who licensed places of minor entertainment; (3) local magistrates outside the twenty-mile radius, who licensed legitimate theatres in their districts; and (4) Parliament, who authorized "theatres royal" in specific towns. The confusion was not to be

FIGURE 11.11 Opening scene of Isaac Bickerstaffe's *The Maid of the Mill*. The setting is by Inigo Richards, one of the major scene designers of the late eighteenth century. From *The Magazine of Art* (1895).

exploited until the nineteenth century, when changing conditions led managers to search for ways to evade the legal restrictions.

ENGLISH DRAMA, 1750–1800

Drama was seriously affected by the Licensing Act of 1737, since thereafter it had to pass the scrutiny of a censor. The minor forms suffered most, for topical and political satire were strongly discouraged. Consequently, both ballad opera and burlesque declined rapidly. Ballad opera was replaced by a new musical type, comic opera, that had sentimental plots and original music. The most famous writer of the new type was Isaac Bickerstaffe (1735–1812), with such works as *The Maid of the Mill* (1765) and *Lionel and Clarissa* (1768). Other works in this vein include Richard Brinsley Sheridan's (1751–1816) *The Duenna* (1775), John O'Keeffe's (1747–1833) *The Poor Soldier* (1783), and George Colman the Younger's (1762–1836) *Inkle and Yarico* (1787).

Few burlesques were written in the last half of the eighteenth century and for the most part their authors chose literary and dramatic works rather than politics as their targets. By far the best of the burlesques was Sheridan's *The Critic* (1781), a satire on tragedy, critics, authors, and the vogue of spectacle. It replaced Buckingham's *The Rehearsal*, and it was regularly performed until the end of the nineteenth century.

Pantomime was little affected by the Licensing

FIGURE 11.12 Scene from *She Stoops to Conquer* as produced at Covent Garden in 1773. Shown here are Edward Shuter and Mrs. Green as Mr. and Mrs. Hardcastle and John Quick as Tony Lumpkin. Painting by Parkinson. Courtesy Theatre Museum, Victoria and Albert Museum.

was to develop in the nineteenth century into melodrama.

Robust comedy did not altogether die out. Between 1720 and 1760, however, "laughing" comedy was restricted primarily to farce, usually short plays performed as afterpieces. Samuel Foote (1720–1777) did much to keep the comic spirit alive through such works as *The Knights* (1749), *The Orators* (1762), *The Minor* (1760), and *The Maid of Bath* (1771), for all combine farcical wit and situations with satire on such contemporary targets as the rising Methodist religion.

After 1760 a few writers began to oppose sentimentalism. George Colman the Elder (1732–1794) approached the spirit of Restoration comedy in *The Jealous Wife* (1761) and other plays. The most important of the later comic writers, however, were Goldsmith and Sheridan. Oliver Goldsmith's (1730?–1774) *The Good Natur'd Man* (1768), an attack upon the style of Kelly, Cumberland, and others, is somewhat stilted and structurally weak, but *She Stoops to Conquer* (1773) is a comic masterpiece. Subtitled *The Mistakes of a Night*, it shows how two young men are duped into mistaking the home of a country gentleman for an inn, their consequent ill-mannered treatment of their host, and the misunderstandings, intrigues, and discoveries that eventually lead to the satisfactory conclusion of the love affairs of the principal characters. Its skillful manipulation of an amusing and rapid action was an effective argument in favor of a return to "laughing" comedy.

Richard Brinsley Sheridan (1751–1816) is noted primarily for *The Rivals* (1775) and *The School for Scandal* (1777), which recall Congreve's comedies of manners with their sparkling and witty dialogue and their vivid pictures of the fashionable society of the day. But Sheridan is more morally conventional than was Congreve, for he always made true virtue triumphant. In *The School for Scandal*, for example, though he permitted his scandalmongers to murder reputations through witty gossip and comic intrigue and to promote the sentiment-spouting but hypocritical Joseph Surface at the expense of his rakish but openhearted brother Charles, eventually Joseph is exposed, Charles is united with the virtuous Maria, and the strong-willed but naive Lady Teazle is recalled to her duty to her elderly and comically crotchety husband, Sir Peter.

Goldsmith and Sheridan did much to recapture the brilliance of English drama, and, with the exception of Shakespeare's, their plays have held the stage more consistently than have those by any other English dramatists. Unfortunately, Goldsmith and Sheridan had no

Act, but no deviser of this form stands out in the last half of the century. The major change is seen after 1760 in the waning popularity of Harlequin and the rise of the more sentimentalized Clown. But pantomime continued to be the most popular of all theatrical entertainments.

After 1750 domestic tragedy declined in favor. The only work of this type to win continuing fame was Edward Moore's (1712–1757) *The Gamester* (1753), which depicted the downward career of a gambler.

As domestic tragedy declined in popularity sentimental comedy flourished, perhaps because audiences preferred to see characters rescued from misfortune rather than punished for mistakes. The most important later writers were Hugh Kelly (1739–1777), whose *False Delicacy* (1768) treats the disentanglement of three pairs of unsuited lovers; Richard Cumberland (1732–1811), whose *The West Indian* (1771) tells the story of a young rake who, after being reformed by marriage, is rewarded by the discovery that his wife is an heiress; and Thomas Holcroft (1745–1809), whose *The Road to Ruin* (1792) shows a gambler so touched by his father's shame that he is restored to virtue. Such sentimental drama, with its emphasis upon moral teaching through poetic justice, successful emulators, and after 1780 English drama moved steadily toward melodrama.

The eighteenth-century theatre was by no means restricted to production of contemporary plays. The pattern followed throughout the eighteenth century had been set during the Restoration, when a company's repertory of thirty-five to forty plays was divided about equally between pre-Commonwealth plays and new plays or successes from recent seasons. By the early eighteenth century, the repertory had increased to forty to seventy-five plays, and by the last quarter of the century to about ninety works. After 1750, about one-third of the repertory was drawn from Shakespearean and other pre-Commonwealth plays, another third was made up of Restoration or early eighteenth-century works, and the remaining third was composed of recent successes or new plays. Consequently, playgoers were offered more plays from the past than from recent years, and new plays constituted the smallest portion of the repertory.

THE PLAYWRIGHT

Although the repertory offered much variety, the demand for the contemporary dramatist's work was not great. Not only were the opportunities for production few, but the financial rewards to the playwright were uncertain. For a time after the Restoration, a few playwrights were attached to companies at a fixed salary or as a shareholder. Dryden, for example, held a share in the King's Company from 1668 until 1678, in return for providing three plays each year. As the supply of plays began to exceed the demand, however, other financial arrangements became more economical. After 1680, dramatists were paid by the "benefit" system, under which they received the proceeds (less house expenses) of the third night of the initial run. After 1690, they might also be given a benefit on the sixth night, if the play ran so long, and in the eighteenth century on every third night of the original run. Few plays ran beyond the third night, however, and some did not run that long.

Normally, a playwright was able to increase his income by selling the copyright to his play. After 1709 works could be copyrighted for a period of fourteen years. Usually the theatre bought the copyright to protect its investment, for once a play was printed any other theatre could produce it. Occasionally the playwright sold the copyright to a publisher. In either case, he was paid no royalty beyond the initial sum. After fourteen years (if he were still alive) the copyright reverted to the author and could be renewed for an additional fourteen years.

Although occasionally they were paid set sums by theatres for their plays, throughout the eighteenth century dramatists depended primarily upon benefit performances for their income, since copyright payments were relatively small. A few plays brought their authors considerable financial rewards, but these were exceptional.

The greatest demand for new plays came during the ten years preceding the passage of the Licensing Act in 1737, for during this time a number of minor theatres were open, some of them specializing in new plays. This act, which brought strict censorship and the closure of many theatres, was to reduce the playwright's opportunities to have his plays produced during the remainder of the century.

FINANCIAL POLICIES

By 1700 theatre managers had evolved most of the financial policies that were to remain in use for the next 150 years. In these policies, shares played a heavy role. There were two kinds of shares: in buildings and in companies.

From the Restoration on, theatres in England were normally erected on leased land with money obtained by the sale of shares in the buildings. In return for their investment, shareholders were paid a fixed sum for each day the theatre was used for performances. Often they also had the right to attend the theatre free of charge.

The second type of sharing involved an investment in a company and its productions. For a time after 1660, the old system under which actors shared in the company's risks and profits was revived, but as the theatre declined in prosperity actors came to prefer a fixed salary to the indefinite income derived from sharing. Consequently, by 1690 the sharing arrangement had been abandoned in London. It was revived by Betterton's troupe from 1695 to 1707, but after that time it disappeared almost altogether in London, although it continued to be used in most provincial theatres until well into the nineteenth century.

As the actors' control declined, the power of outside investors increased. Davenant and Killigrew established the pattern that eventually prevailed when they mortgaged their patents, scenery, and costumes in order to raise capital. When the mortgages were not redeemed, partial ownership of the companies passed to persons who had little or no interest in the theatre except as a commercial investment. The danger of this system first became evident in 1693 when Christopher Rich, ostensibly to protect the investors, assumed control of the United Companies, even though he had had no theatrical experience of any kind. He was merely the first of many similar persons who were to gain control over theatres in London and elsewhere.

Although there might be many investors in a company, the financial risk fell almost entirely on the man who leased the theatre and ran the company (that is, on the manager of the troupe). Few managements survived long, and consequently few in the eighteenth century are significant. Among the most important were those of the Rich family. Although Christopher Rich was evicted from Drury Lane in 1709, his son John managed Lincoln's Inn Fields from 1714 to 1732 and Covent Garden from 1732 to 1761. Thus, from 1693 until 1761, the Rich family played a crucial role in London's theatrical life. After 1767, when Rich's heirs sold their interest, Covent Garden was weakened by dissensions among the owners. Then, in 1771, control passed to Thomas Harris, who retained it into the nineteenth century.

Between 1710 and 1733 the Drury Lane was very successful because of the policies of the "triumvirate" of actor-managers, Colley Cibber, Robert Wilks, and Thomas Doggett (replaced after 1713 by Barton Booth). After 1733, however, Drury Lane was in grave financial difficulty until 1747, when stability was restored under David Garrick and John Lacy. With Garrick assuming responsibility for staging and Lacy for finances, this management was to be the most admired of the eighteenth century. After Garrick's retirement in 1776, control passed to a group under the leadership of Richard Brinsley Sheridan. Most of the production duties, however, fell to Thomas King, an actor. But he was given so little authority that the theatre had declined considerably by 1788, when John Philip Kemble replaced King.

The Haymarket Theatre was under many short-lived managements until 1766, when it became the third licensed house. From 1766 until 1777 it was managed by Samuel Foote, and after 1777 by George Colman. Both men supervised their companies closely.

The success of theatre management, then, was somewhat erratic. Most of the failures can be attributed to managers who either knew little of the theatre and were unwilling to delegate authority to experienced persons, or to businessmen who sought merely to exploit

FIGURE 11.13 Stage of the Dorset Garden Theatre. The proscenium doors can be glimpsed at the extreme sides. The scene is from Settle's *The Empress of Morocco,* produced in 1673. From Wilkinson, *Londina Illustrata* (1825).

the theatre. But despite some setbacks, the theatre on the whole became increasingly prosperous during the eighteenth century.

Despite occasional retrenchments, the trend between 1660 and 1800 was toward larger companies and more carefully mounted productions, both of which demanded greater financial resources. Whereas the typical acting company of the Restoration had included thirty-five to forty persons, the troupe of 1800 had about eighty. In addition to actors, each company employed a treasurer, ticket takers, "numberers" (people who counted spectators as a check on the ticket takers), prompters, dancers, musicians, bill distributors, scene painters, candle snuffers, stagehands, wardrobe keepers, dressers, laundresses, and maintenance personnel. In the late eighteenth century, the major troupes were employing more than 200 people.

Expenses were calculated in terms of a single playing day. This was necessary in part because by the eighteenth century benefits were an important feature of theatrical life and a manager had to state the amount to be deducted from the receipts as the theatre's expenses on these occasions. In the early eighteenth century, the average daily expenses were about 40 pounds; by 1735 they had risen to 50 pounds, and by 1790 to 105 pounds.

Since the manager depended primarily upon ticket sales for income, only two paths were open to him as his expenses increased: to raise the price of tickets, or to increase attendance. Although at times he did both, he was cautious about raising prices. Consequently, the scale of entrance fees did not change markedly. During the Restoration the basic charges were: boxes, 4 shillings; pit, 2 shillings 6 pence; middle gallery, 1 shilling 6 pence; upper gallery, 1 shilling. In the late eighteenth century, the comparable prices were 5 shillings, 3 shillings, 2 shillings, and 1 shilling. The normal prices were raised for premieres, or when expenditures for new costumes or scenery were thought to justify a temporary increase. On special occasions, such as a benefit for a particularly popular actor, portions of the pit were converted into boxes and additional seating was erected on the stage. Such alterations were also accompanied by a considerable increase in the prices charged for those sections, although little of the additional income went to the manager.

Beginning in the 1690s spectators were allowed to enter at the end of the third act at "half price," except when a new pantomime or other attraction was to be given as an afterpiece. On the other hand, if prices were raised because of the afterpiece, the spectator who left at the end of the main piece was refunded the additional charge. Besides tickets, the managers realized some income from the sale of concession to those who hawked food, drink, playbooks, and playbills in the theatre.

Steadily increasing expenses, however, forced most managers to enlarge their theatres to accommodate additional spectators. Most of the changes in theatre auditoriums were motivated by this need, whereas alterations of the stage resulted from changing fashions in spectacle.

THEATRE ARCHITECTURE

Although following the Restoration the Salisbury Court, Cockpit and Red Bull theatres were used for a short time, none was thought sufficiently suited to the Italianate scenery which was then coming into vogue. Consequently, Killigrew used Gibbons' Tennis Court only until his Theatre Royal in Bridges Street was ready for occupancy in 1663. Little is known of the latter building, which burned in 1672. Another structure, usually called the Drury Lane Theatre, was erected on the same site. Opened in 1674 and used until 1791, it measured 58 feet by 140 feet.

In 1661, Davenant converted Lisle's Tennis Court into the Lincoln's Inn Fields Theatre. Measuring only about 30 by 75 feet, it became increasingly inadequate for the operatic spectacles that Davenant favored. Consequently, in 1671 it was replaced by the Dorset Garden Theatre, a structure measuring 57 by 140 feet, designed by Christopher Wren. The Dorset Garden was seldom used after the union of the troupes in 1682 and was torn down in 1709. When Betterton's company was licensed in 1695, it reopened the Lincoln's Inn Fields Theatre.

Thus, in London between 1660 and 1700 there were three theatres of importance: Drury Lane, Lincoln's Inn Fields, and Dorset Garden. They varied in size and detail, but they shared common features that established

FIGURE 11.14 Sectional plan of a theatre, believed to be Drury Lane, as designed by Christopher Wren in 1674. The auditorium is at left. Note the backless benches in the raked pit; the deep apron with two proscenium doors; and the relatively shallow stage behind the proscenium. Copyright the Warden and Fellows of All Souls College, Oxford.

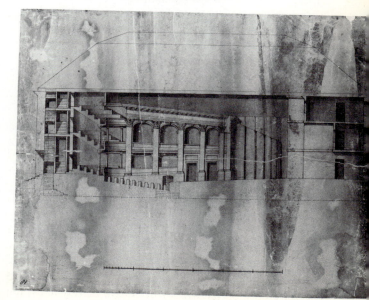

FIGURE 11.15 The auditorium of the Drury Lane Theatre after it was remodeled and redecorated in 1775. Engraving by R. and J. Adams. Courtesy Theatre Museum, Victoria and Albert Museum.

the pattern for English playhouses until the nineteenth century.

In these theatres the auditorium was divided into pit, boxes, and galleries. Unlike its French equivalent, the English pit was raked to improve sightlines and equipped with backless benches for all spectators. There were two or three galleries. The first was partitioned into boxes; the uppermost was undivided and equipped with benches; the middle gallery, when present, might be partially devoted to boxes and the remainder to benches. The early theatres were small. At the Drury Lane, for example, the distance from the front of the stage to the back of the auditorium was only about 36 feet. Seating capacity was limited. In the seventeenth century, the Drury Lane held only about 650 persons and Lincoln's Inn Fields even fewer. Thus, these were relatively intimate theatres.

If the auditorium resembled that of the continental theatres, the stage differed, for it included both a proscenium arch and an open platform forward of the proscenium. The Drury Lane of 1674 had a stage about 34 feet deep, divided into two roughly equal parts by the proscenium. Two (and in one instance three) doors, surmounted by balconies, opened onto the forestage at either side. These doors were the customary entrances for all characters, since most of the action took place on the forestage. As in Elizabethan times, an exit through one door and reentry through another was sufficient to indicate a change of place. Thus, the forestage thrust the action into the auditorium, rather than confining it behind the picture frame. In its combination of features of the pre-Commonwealth and Italianate stages, it fore-

shadowed in many respects the thrust stage of the twentieth century.

The floor of the stage sloped upward from the front of the forestage to the back wall of the stagehouse. Behind the proscenium, grooves were installed to accommodate wings and shutters, while trapdoors and flying machinery were provided for special effects. With minor changes, these basic characteristics were to continue through the eighteenth century.

Between 1700 and 1800 only a few theatres were important: Drury Lane, Lincoln's Inn Fields, the King's Theatre, the Haymarket, and Covent Garden. The Drury Lane was altered several times during the eighteenth century; in 1790 it seated about 2,300 as compared to 650 in 1700. When Lincoln's Inn Fields was abandoned in 1705, Christopher Rich razed it and erected a new theatre on the site. This building, which seated about 1,400, was used from 1714 until 1732, when it was replaced with Covent Garden. The King's Theatre (until 1714 called the Haymarket or Queen's Theatre), built in 1705, was devoted entirely to opera from 1707 until 1789, when it was gutted by fire. At the time of its destruction, it had a capacity of more than 3,000 persons. The Haymarket, built in 1720, was used by unlicensed companies until 1766, after which it took its place as a major theatre. In the late eighteenth century it held about 1,500. The Covent Garden, built in 1732 to replace Lincoln's Inn Fields, remained in use until 1808. Originally it seated about 1,300 to 1,400, but by the 1780s it had been enlarged to hold about 2,500 and in 1793 to hold about 3,000. (This final renovation was made in part because Drury Lane was being rebuilt at that time to hold 3,600.) Thus, the size of auditoriums increased throughout the eighteenth centry, although the trend toward largeness did not accelerate until after 1760. In spite of the increase in size, however, the basic arrangement remained constant. All the theatres continued to be divided into pit, boxes, and galleries, and until the 1790s none had more than three levels of galleries.

As the auditorium grew in size, so did the stage. Around 1700, the stage back of the proscenium at Drury Lane was increased to about 30 feet, and by 1790 some theatres had stages more than 50 feet deep. At the same time, the forestage dwindled. Around 1700, Rich removed one set of proscenium doors and shortened the forestage (to make room for more seats in the pit). Consequently, throughout the eighteenth century there was usually only one proscenium door on either side of the stage. The forestage, now reduced to about 12 feet in

FIGURE 11.16   Setting by James Thornhill for *Arsinoe*, Act 1, scene 1, in 1706. This setting is supposed to be seen by moonlight. Courtesy Theatre Museum, Victoria and Albert Museum.

depth, remained the favorite playing area, however, until at least 1765, after which it was used less extensively.

The work areas needed for production were also enlarged during the eighteenth century by remodeling the existing structure or by acquiring or constructing smaller buildings adjoining it. These spaces included dressing rooms, greenrooms, storage of various kinds, areas used in the construction of scenery and for costumes and properties. In spite of all additions and alterations, by 1790 most of the theatres were considered inadequate, and soon after they were to be replaced by larger, more elaborate buildings.

SCENIC PRACTICES

After 1661 the scenic practices of the English stage differed little from those then in use in Italy and France. Wings, borders, and shutters were the standard units,

although after 1690 roll drops were sometimes used in the place of shutters. Sets were shifted by means of grooves installed on the stage floor and overhead. Stagehands made the necessary changes upon a whistled signal from the prompter. (For reasons that are unclear, the chariot-and-pole system, the standard method of shifting scenery in continental theatres, was seldom used in England, except at the opera house.) Since the front curtain was raised after the prologue was spoken and not lowered until the end of the performance, all changes were made in full view of the audience. Even entr'acte entertainments were given in front of a full stage setting until about 1750, after which an "act drop" was used as a background. Heavy properties or furniture could be set up and removed behind the shutters. Occasionally they were brought on by servants in full view of the audience.

Between 1660 and 1800 each theatre accumulated a stock of scenery that was used over and over again. When a new theatre was built, settings were commissioned even before the repertory was fixed. This practice was made possible by the neoclassical attitude that specific time and place are irrelevant in drama, and that attempts to particularize only diminish universality. The aim was to capture the essence of a type of place rather than to recreate the features of a particular place. Thus, settings were so anonymous that they could be used in many different plays. One author, writing about 1750, lists the necessary scenes as: (1) temples, (2) tombs, (3) city walls and gates, (4) palace exteriors, (5) palace interiors, (6) streets, (7) chambers, (8) prisons, (9) gardens, and (10) rural prospects. He adds that other settings are needed only occasionally. During the Restoration, a few comedies depicted well-known places in London, but this type of particularity diminished markedly during the eighteenth century, except in those minor dramatic types, such as pantomine, in which spectacle played a major role. Even in these instances, however, the scenery created for them was reused extensively in other plays.

The development of spectacle was retarded by the presence of spectators on the stage. Although well established before 1642, this practice was not revived until about 1690, and was not usual until about 1700. It continued until 1762, when Garrick banished the audience from the stage. Between 1700 and 1762, rows of benches extended upstage from the proscenium, and at benefits additional amphitheatrical seating often was erected across the back of the stage. On the other hand, the audience was sometimes forbidden to sit on the stage if a production depended heavily on spectacle.

Because most plays were performed in stock scenery, ticket prices were raised when new sets were introduced. The additional revenue which this provided may be one reason why spectacle increased, for Rich's successful exploitation of spectacle in pantomimes led him to experiment with it in regular drama. In the 1730s he added a procession and coronation scene to *Henry VIII*, in 1750 a funeral procession to *Romeo and Juliet*, and in 1761 the coronation of George III to several of Shakespeare's history plays. Elaborate spectacle was ordinarily reserved for the minor genres, however, until about 1765, when Garrick returned from the continent with new ideas of staging. Through the remainder of the century, scenery was to become more particularized and new settings more common. Of the thirty-seven new plays presented at Drury Lane between 1765 and 1776, nineteen were given entirely new scenery.

The increasing interest in spectacle was accompanied by a change in the status of the scene painter. From 1660 until about 1735, no theatre had a scene painter on its regular staff; settings were usually commissioned as needed from easel painters. But by the late eighteenth century, two or more scene painters were attached to each major theatre. This probably explains why so little is known of scene designers before 1760. During the Restoration, John Webb worked with Davenant, and Samuel Towers, Robert Robinson, and Robert Streeter painted settings for Killigrew. It seems probable that the principles of transferring a complex design to flat wings were not yet well understood in England, since some painters took so long and were paid so well for creating perspective settings. For example, in 1669 Killigrew was sued by Isaac Fuller, who claimed that he had not been paid for one setting, which he testified had taken him six weeks to paint; the court awarded him 335 pounds for his work (at a time when a leading actor was paid about 2½ pounds per week). In 1674–1675, another painter was paid 800 pounds to do settings for one play. By the early eighteenth century, however, payments were considerably less, perhaps because the painters now had greater facility. Since before 1760 scenery was commissioned only sporadically, the average yearly expenditure for settings was small. Covent Garden spent only 253 pounds in the season of 1746–1747, and until after 1760 only about one-tenth of a company's budget was ever spent on settings. From occasional references we know the names of many scene painters of the first half of the eighteenth century. Some of the more important are James Thornhill, who flourished in the early years of the century; John DeVoto, who worked between 1719 and 1744; George Lambert, a landscape painter who did settings for Rich at Lincoln's Inn Fields and Covent Garden and some of whose settings remained in use until 1808; and Francis Hayman and Thomas Lediard, who painted settings for Drury Lane in the 1730s.

The situation began to change in 1749, when Rich began to import designers from the continent. The most significant of these was Jean-Nicolas Servandoni (1695–1766), famous for his work at the Paris Opéra and elsewhere in Europe. Rich seems to have had Servandoni paint some settings for which he had no immediate use, for one was introduced at Covent Garden as late as 1773 as never having been used before. Other important artists who worked at Covent Garden include Giovanni Battista Cipriani, a Florentine painter who came to London in 1755; Nicholas Thomas Dall, a Dane who settled in England around 1760, considered one of the finest painters of his age; and John Inigo Richards

FIGURE 11.17 A sketch by DeLoutherbourg for the battle scenes in Shakespeare's *Richard III*. Note the tent at left and others in the background. From *The Magazine of Art* (1895).

(?–1810), a distinguished English painter noted especially for his picturesque landscapes.

The most important designer of the late eighteenth century, however, was Philippe Jacques DeLoutherbourg (1740–1812), a French artist who had studied with Boucher and Boquet of the Paris Opéra. Engaged by Garrick in 1771 to oversee all elements of spectacle, he continued in this position until 1781, when he resigned because Sheridan proposed to cut his salary of 500 pounds. DeLoutherbourg continued to design settings occasionally until 1785. Between 1771 and 1785, he prepared more than thirty productions, of which a few are of special importance: *A Christmas Tale* (1773), with its subtle lighting effects; *The Wonders of Derbyshire* (1779), which depicted actual places in England and established the vogue for "local color"; and *Omai, or a Trip Around the World* (1785), a "travelogue" based on Captain Cook's voyage. In other productions, De-Loutherbourg recreated such recent events as the Portsmouth Naval Review (1773) and a fashionable outdoor festival (1774). From 1781 to 1786, he maintained a miniature theatre, the Eidophusikon, where, on a stage 6 by 8 feet, he created remarkable illusions of specific places and weather conditions through painting, lighting, sound effects, and music.

DeLoutherbourg's contributions were many. He popularized reproductions of real places on the stage. To increase illusion, he broke up the stage picture with ground rows and set pieces to gain a greater sense of depth and reality, and to avoid the symmetrical composition imposed by parallel wings and shutters. He used miniature figures at the rear of the stage to depict battles, marching armies, and sailing vessels; and sound effects, such as waves, rain, hail, and distant guns, to increase the illusion of reality. He revamped the lighting system, installing overhead battens, using silk screens and gauze curtains to gain subtle variations in color and to simulate various weather conditions and times of day. Perhaps most important of all, DeLoutherbourg achieved unity of design by overseeing all the visual elements of productions. Before DeLoutherbourg's time, the various settings for a single play were often done by different painters. Furthermore, a play might be given one new set and have others taken from stock. Thus, although a manager probably had a vague agreement with his painters about the kind of scenes to be provided, there seems to have been little attempt to co-ordinate efforts. DeLoutherbourg's practices established a standard that was not to be fully achieved by his successors until well into the nineteenth century.

The work of DeLoutherbourg and others reflects the growing interest in both local color and history. The rediscovery of Herculaneum in the early eighteenth century aroused public curiosity about past civilizations, and soon an interest in picturesque places and customs began to replace the neoclassical preoccupation with generalized, universalized times and places. Settings became more specific, and composition began to move away from the symmetrically balanced settings typical of the preceding period. These new interests were not fully exploited, however, until after 1800.

Little is known of lighting practices during the Restoration. Performances were given in the afternoon, and windows probably provided some illumination. Chandeliers hung above the apron and behind the proscenium. Pepys, in his *Diary*, often complains of headaches produced by looking into the candles. Footlights were certainly in use by 1673, for they are depicted in an illustration printed in that year. Since most of the action occurred on the apron, both auditorium and stage were illuminated throughout performances.

By 1744, lights were apparently being mounted on vertical "ladders" behind each wing and dimmed by "scene blinds" (that is, by shields that could be manipu-

FIGURE 11.18 The "Fitzgiggo riots" at Covent Garden in 1763. The actors are dressed for Arne's *Artaxerxes*. Note the men's Near Eastern clothing as compared with the women's fashionable English dress. Note also the chandeliers above the stage. Courtesy Theatre Museum, Victoria and Albert Museum.

lated to intervene between the light source and the stage), for an inventory made at Covent Garden in that year lists 12 pairs of "scene ladders," 24 "scene blinds" and 192 tin candlesticks. Footlights were mounted on pivots which allowed them to be lowered below the stage level for dimming. Lamps were used in some positions, since reflectors made candles wilt. It is difficult to say when these arrangements began. Possibly they date from the Restoration, for similar practices were clearly in use on the continent by that time.

Although Garrick is credited with reforming stage lighting in 1765, the nature of his reforms is unclear. He seems to have removed all visible light sources from the stage and to have increased brightness, perhaps with improved lamps and reflectors. During the 1770s, DeLoutherbourg made other changes. Using silk screens to reflect light, and perhaps transparent silk filters, he gained considerable control over color for the first time. This increased concern for lighting is reflected in the costs: in 1745, theatres were spending about 340 pounds a year on lighting, while during the 1770s expenses rose to 1,970 pounds.

Lighting improved after the introduction in 1785 of the Argand, or "patent," lamp. Using a cylindrical wick and glass chimney to control the relative pro-

portions of oxygen and oil, this lamp produced a much brighter and steadier light than had earlier instruments. After this time, oil largely superseded candles for stage lighting. Since the chimneys could be colored, experimentation with color effects also increased.

Improvements in lighting and increased emphasis upon illusion encouraged managers to place more of the action behind the proscenium arch. This trend was not fully completed during the eighteenth century, however, and the auditorium continued to be lighted as a part of the total picture.

COSTUME PRACTICES, 1660–1800

For the most part, the principles governing costume between 1660 and 1800 differed little from those of pre-

FIGURE 11.19 The play-within-the-play scene from *Hamlet* as shown in a painting by Francis Hayman, who also painted scenery for the Drury Lane Theatre during the 1730s. At center Claudius is rising from his seat; Hamlet is seated on the floor in the lower right corner. Note the costumes. Courtesy the Folger Shakespeare Library, Washington, D.C.

Commonwealth times or from those of seventeenth-century France. Since time and place were considered unimportant, most characters wore contemporary garments. Furthermore, since neoclassicism tended to idealize nature, most actors dressed their characters as sumptuously as possible. As in the earlier period, however, some deviations from contemporary dress were usual. Classical heroes wore the *habit à la romaine,* while Near-Eastern characters were identified by turbans, baggy trousers, and long fur-trimmed gowns. On the other hand, actresses playing classical or Near-Eastern roles merely added feathered headdresses or a few exotic touches to otherwise contemporary dress. Until about 1750, actresses often wore black velvet in tragedy, but after that time they appeared increasingly in the latest fashions.

Conventionalized costumes continued for a few characters, notably Falstaff (played in ruff and Cavalier boots), Richard III (dressed in Elizabethan pumpkin hose), and Henry VIII (clothed after the manner of Holbein's portrait). Other conventions included costuming Hamlet in black, adding ermine trim to Lear's otherwise contemporary dress, and playing Macbeth in the uniform of a British army officer.

Concern for greater realism and appropriateness began in the 1740s. In 1741, Charles Macklin clothed Shylock in a black gabardine gown, long trousers, and red hat (which he considered realistic Jewish dress). After 1750, Garrick occasionally attempted to costume pre-Commonwealth plays in Elizabethan garments, although he continued to perform all those written after 1660 in eighteenth-century dress. Garrick's costumes were neither historically accurate nor consistent, but his concern indicates the awakening interest in history and the desire to reflect it in costuming. At first, there were no guides to historical costume, but in 1757 there appeared in London *Recueil des Habillements,* a collection of designs taken from paintings by Holbein, Van Dyke, Hollar, and others, "to which are added the habits of the principal characters on the English stage." In 1775, Joseph Strutt was to provide more accurate information in *The Dress and Habits of the Peoples of England.* As with scenery, however, costuming was not significantly altered by these trends until the nineteenth century.

Between 1660 and 1800, the principal sources for costumes were the company's wardrobe and the actor's own garments. Each company maintained a "common stock" of costumes, which were preserved and added to

FIGURE 11.20 A scene from Whitehead's *The Roman Father* at Drury Lane in 1750. At center is Garrick. Note the *habit à la romaine* worn by the men, and the few exotic touches at the shoulder and waist on the women's dresses. Courtesy the Folger Shakespeare Library, Washington, D.C.

regularly. Throughout the eighteenth century, companies always spent more on costumes than on scenery and in time wardrobes became extremely large, since nothing was thrown away and costumes were frequently refurbished. In staging a coronation scene in 1761, Garrick is said to have used garments that had been in stock since 1727. In the late 1760s, the Covent Garden wardrobe had grown so large that it had to be moved to an adjoining separate house.

At a glance, these practices suggest that a company provided adequate costumes for its repertory, but this is not completely true. In the second half of the eighteenth century, a company added to its stock only an average of about twelve new women's and twelve new men's outfits each year. Since an acting company included seventy to eighty performers and a repertory of seventy-five to eighty plays, this rate of acquisition would probably have left most actors rather shabbily dressed if all had depended on the company's wardrobe.

It is probably for this reason that actors with sufficient means supplied most of their own costumes. Some demanded and received a special allowance from the manager for this purpose. The actors' desire to dress as sumptuously as possible led to intense rivalries. As a result, costumes often reflected the actor's purse rather than the character's position, and a queen played by a poor actress might appear shabby alongside an attendant played by a performer of greater means.

Nevertheless, the company's wardrobe was available to all actors. Wardrobe keepers checked out costumes to players, who were free to select whatever they wished to wear. In the late eighteenth century this freedom of choice was considerably curtailed as concern for appropriateness grew and as managers began to give wardrobe keepers more authority to decide what garments should be worn. Nevertheless, by modern standards the costume practices of the eighteenth century were at best haphazard.

In addition to looking after the costumes, wardrobe keepers made and altered garments, purchased supplies and took an inventory annually. Laundresses to keep the clothes clean and "dressers" to assist the actresses during performances were also employed.

ACTORS AND ACTING, 1660–1800

A major innovation of the Restoration was the introduction of women into acting companies. By 1661 both Davenant and Killigrew had a full complement of actresses, and after this time men appeared only in such female roles as witches and comic old women, a practice that persisted through the eighteenth century.

Between 1660 and 1800 actors usually entered a company on a probationary status and learned by observing established performers. In the 1660s and 1670s, Davenant and Killigrew maintained a training company, and in the 1740s Macklin ran an acting school, as did Thomas Sheridan somewhat later, but none of these operations was a marked success. At Drury Lane between 1710 and 1730, the young actors had to attend three sessions a week to learn singing and dancing, and the established actors in that company were sometimes paid to teach the beginners. After 1750 Garrick instructed his young actors, and Rich trained several pantomime players. Such attempts were sporadic, however, and most performers learned through trial and error.

The beginner, or "utility" actor, played an enormous number of small roles each season and eventually discovered the types for which he was best suited. After

a few years, he advanced into a "line of business" (a limited range of character types) in which he usually remained for the rest of his career. It is impossible to determine when lines of business were first recognized, for they may extend back to pre-Commonwealth times. By the late eighteenth century four clearly distinguishable ranks existed: (1) players of leading roles, (2) players of secondary roles, (3) players of third-line parts (often called "walking ladies" or "walking gentlemen"), and (4) general utility performers. The first rank was usually restricted to players of heroes and heroines of tragedy and light comedy, although an unusually popular performer in another line might command a salary of the highest rank. The lesser ranks included specialists in such lines as low comedy roles, "singing chambermaids," fathers and elderly men, eccentric types, witches, and hags.

The extent to which an actor specialized depended both upon his versatility and the size of the company in which he performed. A small, provincial company required its actors to play a wider range of parts than did the large London troupes. Most actors had a serious and a comic line, although they were seldom equally good in both. Lines of business were not related to an actor's age. Garrick played Hamlet until he was fifty-nine, and actresses often performed Juliet throughout their lives. Lines of business led to the "possession of parts," since once an actor was cast in a role he continued to play it as long as he remained in the company. Under the repertory system, each actor was assigned a large number of roles which he was supposedly able to perform on 24-hours' notice. Actors jealously guarded their parts and crises often developed when established actors were brought into a company and roles had to be redistributed as a consequence. This problem increased in the late eighteenth century, when troupes began to employ more than one performer in a single line of business. The number of parts that a leading actor had in his active repertory at any time varied. Mrs. Oldfield had an average of about twenty-six, Barton Booth about thirty-five, and Garrick, ninety-six.

The lesser actors in a company were employed by the season but leading actors were usually put under contract for a longer period, although almost never exceeding five years. On the other hand, after 1743 Macklin usually performed only under short-term engagements, a practice which foreshadowed the "starring" arrangements that were to dominate the nineteenth-century theatre. The concept of starring engagements also re-

FIGURE 11.21 The closet scene from *Hamlet* as it appeared in the early eighteenth century. Note the contemporary dress worn by Hamlet and the Queen. From Rowe's edition of Shakespeare's works, Vol. V (1709).

received about 70 pounds a year; by the 1740s a top-ranking actor earned about 180 pounds; in the 1760s the four ranks of actors were paid 287 pounds, 148 pounds, 70 pounds, and 42 pounds; by 1790 several leading performers were receiving well above 300 pounds.

This stated salary, however, was usually augmented by at least one benefit annually. Benefit performances for groups of actors were instituted in the 1660s and were first accorded to individuals in the late 1680s. After 1695 Betterton began offering benefits as an inducement to actors to remain with his company; after 1700 this custom was gradually extended until it included every employee of the playhouse. Major performers had separate benefits, but lesser actors and most of the nonperforming personnel usually shared benefits. Typically, the beneficiaries received all the receipts in excess of house expenses, although there were many variations on this arrangement. At first the benefits were scattered throughout the season, but after 1712 they were normally concentrated in the period between March and the summer closing.

A well-attended benefit might bring a performer more income in a single evening than he made throughout the rest of the year, especially since spectators often voluntarily paid higher admission fees and presented gifts of money or jewelry to popular performers. On the other hand, the receipts sometimes did not meet the house expenses and the actor lost money. The lure of a profitable benefit, however, probably permitted managers to pay actors considerably less than might otherwise have been demanded.

Usually an experienced actor (called the "acting manager") was appointed to stage the plays when the theatre manager was not qualified for this task. Betterton was acting manager of the companies in which he worked for most of the years between 1668 and 1709; at Drury Lane between 1710 and 1732, the triumvirate of actor-managers divided the rehearsal duties; John Rich staged pantomimes and spectacles, but employed such actors as James Quin, Lacy Ryan, and James Lacy to rehearse the regular drama; Charles Macklin was acting manager at Drury Lane from 1734 to 1743, and Garrick was in charge of the repertory and staging at that theatre from 1747 until 1776.

The first three rehearsals of a new play fell to the dramatist, who presumably helped the actors with interpretation. The acting manager had complete responsibility for all revivals. Rehearsals were few by modern

ceived considerable impetus from those eighteenth-century performers who made brief appearances with provincial troupes during the summer months when the major theatres in London were closed.

The income of actors varied considerably. Salaries, though quoted by the week, were paid only for those days upon which the theatres were open; any closure brought a proportionate deduction from the actors' pay. Except for leading performers, little is known about actors' salaries prior to 1750. In the 1690s, Mrs. Barry

FIGURE 11.22 David Garrick as Macbeth and Mrs. Pritchard as Lady Macbeth just prior to the murder of Duncan. Note that Macbeth is costumed as a British army officer, while Lady Macbeth wears eighteenth-century fashionable garments. Courtesy Theatre Museum, Victoria and Albert Museum.

standards; they were held from about 10 A.M. until 1 P.M. and seldom extended beyond two weeks. Garrick was sometimes more meticulous and occasionally prolonged rehearsals to eight weeks. Little time was spent on blocking or movement patterns. Actors learned by experience how to move about the stage and when to give the dominant positions to the major performers. Most scenes were played on the forestage or near the front of the main stage, and lines were addressed to the audience as much as to the other characters. Since furniture was seldom used, actors stood throughout and gave little thought to creating realistic stage pictures. During rehearsals, the players seldom attempted to give full portrayals. Consequently, innovations were usually not revealed until the first performance, when they surprised fellow actors as much as the audience. The typical brief rehearsals usually meant that on opening night actors were often still uncertain of their lines and depended much on improvisation. Furthermore, their relatively secure positions seem to have made many actors neglectful. As a result, managers sought to impose discipline through an elaborate system of fines for such faults as tardiness at rehearsals, failure to learn lines, refusal of roles, and a variety of other lapses.

The orderly operation of a company depended much upon the prompter, whose dutes included securing licenses for the plays, copying out the actors' "sides," holding rehearsals when requested to do so, and assessing fines. During performances he gave cues for scene shifts and music, dispatched call boys for actors, and prompted as necessary. Some of these men, notably John Downes, William Chetwood, and Richard Cross, have left invaluable records of the theatres in which they served.

Acting was a mixture of tradition and innovation. Roles were passed down from one generation to the next, and with them went the traditional interpretation. When one actor succeeded another, he was expected to learn the business used in that company, since the repertory could not be restaged to suit him. Because so much of playing became traditional, new conceptions of characters, or even new line readings, often produced sensations. Thus, Charles Macklin greatly altered the conception of Shylock in 1741 by departing from the traditional low-comedy interpretation. On the other hand, Garrick built his reputation through the unique qualities he was able to achieve without altering the basic tradition of his roles.

The style of acting varied from formal to realistic. Until about 1750, the dominant approach was oratorical, as epitomized in the playing of Betterton, Booth, and Quin. Then Macklin and Garrick urged the adoption of a style based upon direct observation of life, although they too probably idealized reality. The two styles came into direct conflict in the 1740s when Quin and Garrick were the leading performers of London. The triumph of Garrick served to establish the more realistic approach as a standard for the remainder of the century. Garrick's victory parallels the changes evident in the other theatre arts, since it marks a movement away from the idealized generality of neoclassicism, which Quin favored, to a more specific and individualized characterization. The neoclassical and oratorical style persisted, however, even among Garrick's troupe, and two rather distinct styles were often seen in the same play.

Despite changes, however, some conventions remained relatively constant, and they most clearly distinguish the "realism" of the eighteenth century from that of today. First, whenever possible actors played at the front of the stage. Furthermore, as one reporter stated: "They never turn their backs on the public, and seldom show their faces in profile." They seem also to have exchanged stage positions after each speech. As one observer put it, "An actor passes invariably to the right as his interlocutor passes to the left, and vice versa." Other customs included "affected prolongation of certain cries and exclamations, the sort of 'organ-point' by which all of the oh's and ah's are emphasized; the frequent transports in which the actors feel compelled to precipitate themselves full length to the floor, and the frightful noise of these oft-repeated plunges."

During the early part of the century, actors seem to have observed the meter of verse in a long intoned chant, but from Garrick's time onward they attempted to disguise the verse so as to make it sound as "natural" as possible. Throughout the century actors seem in speaking to have distinguished between less important passages and highpoints by delivering the former in a manner called "level speaking" and the latter with great vehemence. Actors sought and expected to receive applause as they made "points" throughout the play. (Since there were no curtain calls at the end of the play, this applause had to suffice.) Taken altogether, the performance style of the eighteenth-century actor probably more nearly resembled what we see now in opera than in drama.

The period between 1660 and 1800 is noted above all for its actors. In fact, so many outstanding performers appeared during this time that only a few can be noted here. Of the pre-Commonwealth actors who returned at the Restoration, the most important were Michael Mohun (c. 1620–1684) and Charles Hart (? - 1683), leading members of Killigrew's company. Of the younger group, the most famous were Edward Kynaston (c. 1640–1706), at first the player of women's roles and then of heroic parts; James Nokes (? -1696), actor of foolish old husbands, clumsy fops, and ridiculous old women; Cave Underhill (c. 1634–1710), noted for his low comedy playing; Henry Harris (?-c. 1682), friend and rival of Betterton; William Mountfort (1664–1692), portrayer of the heroes of Restoration comedy; and John Lacy (? -1681), outstanding in ridiculous characters. By far the most important actor of the Restoration, however, was Thomas Betterton (c. 1635–1710). On the stage from 1660 until 1709, he excelled in heroic and tragic parts and was universally considered the greatest actor of his day. Betterton performed a wide range of roles, both comic and serious, although he was probably best in such parts as Hamlet, Othello, Hotspur, and Brutus. He remained completely in character throughout a performance and commanded universal attention with his restrained but powerful action and speech. His somewhat formal and elocutionary style established the model for others. Three of the actresses were outstanding: Nell Gwynn, Mrs. Barry, and Mrs. Bracegirdle. Nell Gwynn's

(1650–1687) acting career was brief, 1665 to 1669, but sufficient to establish her fame as a comedian (especially in roles requiring male attire), dancer, and speaker of witty prologues and epilogues. Elizabeth Barry (1658–1713) played leading tragic roles opposite Betterton. Anne Bracegirdle (c. 1663–1748), trained by Betterton, excelled in comedies of manners from 1680 until 1707, when she retired at the height of her career.

Between 1710 and 1735 the outstanding actors were Colley Cibber, Robert Wilks, Thomas Doggett, Barton Booth, and Anne Oldfield. Cibber (1671–1757) entered the United Companies in 1690. Remaining with Rich when the more experienced actors seceded in 1695, he was soon playing leading roles and writing popular plays. From 1710 until 1733, he was one of the managers and leading performers of Drury Lane. In 1740, he published his autobiography, a principal source of information about the English theatre between 1690 and 1735. As an actor, Cibber was best in the roles of fops. Robert Wilks (c. 1665–1732), who began his acting career in Ireland in 1691, was well established at Drury Lane by 1698, where he played leading roles and served as acting manager. From 1710 until his death he was one of the managers of Drury Lane. Although successful in tragedy, he was especially admired as the dashing young hero of comedy. Thomas Doggett (c. 1670–1721) was considered the finest low comedian of his day. He began his career in Dublin and several provincial companies before coming to London in 1691. He went with Betterton to Lincoln's Inn Fields in 1695. Taken into the management of Drury Lane in 1710, he resigned in 1713 and seldom acted afterward. Barton Booth (1681–1733) began his career in Dublin about 1698 and came to London in 1700. He played secondary roles until 1713, when he made a great sensation in Addison's *Cato*. By royal order, he was admitted to the management of Drury Lane. From 1713 to 1727, when ill health forced him to retire, he was considered the finest tragic actor of London and Betterton's true successor. Anne Oldfield (1683–1730) went on the stage in 1700 and achieved her first success about 1704. After the retirement of Mrs. Barry and Mrs. Bracegirdle she was considered the finest actress of her time. She played both comic and serious roles, but was especially admired in high comedy. She was buried in Westminister Abbey, the first actress to be so honored.

By 1733 these actors were either dead or retired. During the next ten years there was a dearth of outstanding performers. The leading actor was James Quin (1693–1766), who began his career in Dublin in 1712,

FIGURE 11.23 Charles Macklin as Shylock and Mrs. Pope as Portia in the trial scene of *The Merchant of Venice.* Macklin's manner of playing and dressing the part created a sensation because it departed so markedly from earlier treatments. Note the contemporary garments worn by the other characters. Courtesy the Folger Shakespeare Library, Washington, D.C.

came to Drury Lane in 1714, and in 1718 joined John Rich, for whom he worked as acting manager. He returned to Drury Lane in 1734 and retired in 1751. Although his declamatory style in tragedy led to unfavorable comparisons with Garrick, he was universally admired in such comic roles as Falstaff. Despite Garrick's reputation, Quin was at the height of his popularity when he retired.

Although Garrick is often credited with inaugurating the more natural style of acting, he was anticipated by Charles Macklin (1699–1797). Born in Ireland, Macklin began acting about 1719 and continued until 1789. He first came to London about 1725, but his style was considered too prosaic and he returned to the provinces until 1730. He served as acting manager at Drury Lane from 1734 until 1743, when he and other actors, includ-

ing Garrick, seceded. Refused a license, they capitulated, but the manager would not employ Macklin again. For a time he ran an acting school, and thereafter for the most part played short engagements in London and elsewhere. Macklin's reputation was based primarily upon a few roles, especially Shylock and the protagonists of his own comedies, such as *Love à la Mode* (1759) and *The Man of the World* (1781). Although he was more devoted to naturalistic acting than Garrick, Macklin's limited range as an actor and his quarrelsome nature restricted his success. He specialized in bluff, hearty old men, and eccentric characters.

From the 1740s until 1776, David Garrick (1717–1779) dominated the English stage. After making his London debut at Goodman's Fields Theatre in 1741, he alternated between Drury Lane and Covent Garden until 1747, when he became joint manager of Drury Lane, a position which he held until his retirement in 1776. Garrick influenced the theatre through his managerial policies as much as through his acting, for in addition to being a careful and devoted director, he was responsible for several significant innovations. As an actor, he had an extremely wide range, playing almost every kind of character, although he was considered best as Lear, Macbeth, and Hamlet. He had a mobile face, piercing eyes, and expressive body, all of which he used to great effect in the pantomimic byplay for which he was famous. His agreeable and well-controlled voice was somewhat lacking in fullness. Through intense concentration upon the immediate situation, Garrick made whatever he did seem compellingly real. Above all, he seemed to grasp the complexities of each role, and he gave them fuller expression than did any of his contemporaries. Garrick is often said to have been the greatest English actor of all times.

Garrick's fame has overshadowed the many other fine performers of the late eighteenth century. Among the acresses who worked with him were Peg Woffington (c. 1714–1760), noted especially for her portrayal of spirited heroines of comedy and for "breeches" parts (roles played in male attire); Kitty Clive (1711–1785), who began her career in 1728 and remained a favorite with audiences in farce and spirited comedy; and Frances Abington (1737–1815), noted for high comedy roles. Equally important were Mrs. Cibber and Mrs. Pritchard. Susanna Cibber (1714–1766), daughter-in-law of Calley Cibber, began her career as a singer but turned to acting in 1736. Appearing almost entirely in tragedy, she modified her declamatory style somewhat after joining Garrick in 1753. Mrs. Hannah Pritchard (1711–1768) was universally considered the finest tragic actress of her time. So thoroughly did she make Lady Macbeth her own that Garrick never appeared in the play after she died.

Garrick's greatest rival was Spranger Barry (1719–1777), who began his career in Ireland in 1743 and came to London in 1746. From 1750 to 1758 he played at Covent Garden in competition with Garrick. Although Garrick outshone him in most roles, Barry was considered superior as the romantic lover. From 1766 until his death, he often appeared with Garrick at Drury Lane.

Other performers of note include: George Ann Bellamy (c. 1727–1788), remembered principally as Garrick's Juliet; Mary Ann Yates (1728–1787), who replaced Mrs. Cibber in tragedy; Edward Shuter (1728–1776), famous for his comic old men and for his entr'acte entertainments; Richard Yates (1706–1796), a low comedian and Harlequin; Thomas King (1730–1805), a player of comic old men and acting manager under Sheridan at Drury Lane; John Henderson (1747–1785), considered Garrick's successor, but whose early death prevented him from establishing a lasting reputation; and Elizabeth Farren (1759–1829), an outstanding actress of fine ladies, who left the stage to marry the Earl of Derby in 1797. By the 1790s the leadership in acting was passing to the Kemble family, who were to dominate the next generation.

AUDIENCES AND PERFORMANCES

During the Restoration, the theatrical season ran from October to June; in the eighteenth century, it opened in mid-September and continued until the end of May or early June. After about 1750, the theatres played two or three times a week in the fall until mid-October, when they began to perform daily except Sundays. All theatres were closed on certain specified occasions: Christmas Eve, Christmas night, January 30 (the anniversary of the death of Charles I), Ash Wednesday, Holy Week, and Whitsun Eve. Plays were also forbidden on Wednesdays and Fridays during Lent, but after 1740 oratorios were permitted on those days. Other closures were decreed on days of national thanksgiving or during periods of mourning. Thus, the number of annual performances during the regular season might vary considerably, but the average was between 170 and 200.

Playing in the summer only gradually came into vogue. During the Restoration, it was restricted almost altogether to occasional programs given by apprentice actors. In the 1740s several illegal companies gave summer performances but these were usually not allowed to continue for long. It was only after 1766, when the Haymarket was licensed to perform from May 15 to September 15, that London regularly had a summer season.

Performances were advertised in various ways: posters set up around the city; handbills distributed at coffee houses, private homes, and elsewhere; advertisements in newspapers, after these began to appear in the early eighteenth century; and announcements made from the stage each evening. The performance time was gradually moved from midafternoon to early evening. During the Restoration, the beginning time was 3 or 3:30 P.M.; by 1700, it had been moved to 4 or 5; between 1700 and 1710, the time varied from 5 to 5:30 to 6; after 1710, the usual hour was 6 P.M.; by the last quarter of the eighteenth century it had become 6:15 or 6:30. The unauthorized theatres, however, often played at other hours. The doors of the theatres were usually opened long before performances began and, since seats were not reserved, many persons came early or sent servants to hold seats. By the 1730s, tickets for boxes could be bought in advance, but specific seats were not reserved. Each part of the house—boxes, pit, and galleries—had its own entrance, ticket sellers, and ticket takers. Since seats were unnumbered, squabbles over places often occurred.

The evening's bill was complex. In the Restoration, it consisted of a full-length play, with singing and dancing between the acts. Around 1700, Christopher Rich added acrobats, trained animals, and other circus-like performers in an attempt to compete more effectively with Betterton's troupe; this kind of entertainment was never completely absent from the theatre thereafter. Around 1715, the afterpiece was introduced and soon became standard. Thus, after 1720, a typical evening's bill was arranged in this way: approximately one-half hour of music preceded the performance; then came the prologue, followed by a full-length play; the intervals between acts were filled with miscellaneous variety entertainment; following the main play, an afterpiece (a pantomime, farce, or comic opera, all usually in two acts) was performed; and the evening concluded with a song and dance. Performances lasted from three to five hours.

The relationship between audience and performers was close. Actors often took their grievances to the spectators, who sometimes refused to let performances proceed until explanations from alleged offenders were forthcoming. Riots, precipitated by changes in casting, in the evening's bill, or well-established customs, were not uncommon. Thus, spectators believed firmly in their rights and did not hesitate to exert their power to correct any grievance, actual or supposed.

Throughout the eighteenth century the theatre gained steadily in popularity as commercial prosperity enlarged the potential playgoing public. Consequently, by the 1790s the theatre buildings had grown too small to accommodate all those who wished to attend. Also by this time new values had undermined neoclassicism. England was on the threshold of new developments in both its theatre and drama.

THE PROVINCIAL THEATRE

During the eighteenth century, theatre in the British Isles was not confined to London. Dublin was especially important as a theatrical center; it not only supported thriving companies but supplied London with many of its most prominent playwrights and actors. The theatre in Dublin prospered in part because Ireland was exempted from the provisions of the Licensing Act of 1737, and consequently until the 1760s it maintained the only legitimate theatres in the British Isles outside of London.

Nevertheless, though they lacked legal sanction, companies continued to perform throughout England and Scotland after 1737. They evaded the law by advertising their programs as medleys of songs, dances, and dramatic scenes. Provincial officials ignored the infringements of the law, except on those rare occasions when citizens instituted legal proceedings against the actors. After the 1760s, when Parliament began to authorize provincial troupes, the theatre outside of London prospered. The best companies were those of Edinburgh, Bath, York, Norwich, Liverpool, Manchester, Bristol, Newcastle, and Brighton. They were the training ground for most of Britain's actors, and they offered a steady supply of new talent to London's companies. Together, the provincial troupes provided entertainment for virtually the whole of the British Isles.

THE THEATRE OF COLONIAL AMERICA

Until 1776, when they declared their independence, the American colonies were controlled by the British, and the American theatre was merely another—though remote —provincial circuit. In the colonies the theatre developed slowly but along lines then customary in the parent country.

At first, life in the American colonies was too harsh to permit theatrical activities. The earliest record of a performance is not found until 1665, when three men in Virginia were hauled into court for performing a playlet, *The Bear and the Cub*. No other instances are noted until the end of the century, when students presented plays at Harvard College and at William and Mary. In New York sometime between 1699 and 1702, Richard Hunter obtained permission to give theatrical entertainments, but it is not certain that he did so. In 1703 Anthony Aston, the first professional actor to arrive in America, gave a few performances in Charleston and New York to earn money for his return passage to England. In 1714, the first extant American play, *Androboros* (or "Maneater"), written by Robert Hunter, Governor of New York, was published. A rather crude satire, it ridiculed Hunter's political opponents.

Between 1715 and 1735, theatrical activities increased. In 1716, William Levingston of Williamsburg, Virginia, built the first theatre in America, and here until about 1732 Charles and Mary Stagg arranged entertainments, the precise nature of which is uncertain. In Philadelphia, strolling players performed in 1723 and 1724; in Lancaster, performances were given irregularly between 1730 and 1742; and in New York, amateur players staged plays and fitted out a theatre between 1730 and 1733. In Charleston, South Carolina, amateurs gave a season of three plays in 1735 and built a theatre for performances in 1736 and 1737. This flurry of activity came to an end in the late 1730s, however, probably because of the religious fervor that accompanied the appearances of George Whitefield and John Wesley in the colonies.

A significant new beginning was made in 1749, when a company under the leadership of Walter Murray and Thomas Kean made its initial appearance in Philadelphia. Almost nothing is known about the origin or qualifications of the actors in this company. Most of the players probably were amateurs. This troupe played in Philadelphia until 1750, and then moved on to New York and various towns in Virginia and Maryland. Little is heard of it after 1752. Regardless of its artistic stature, the Murray-Kean company was the first to present seasons of some length in several towns. It established a precedent which was to be followed by its more important successor, the Hallam troupe.

Before turning to the Hallams, however, it is necessary to glance briefly at Jamaica, where theatrical performances had been given sporadically since about 1680.

The arrival in 1745 of John Moody, an English strolling player, marked a significant change. After playing with an amateur group, he returned to England in 1749 to recruit professional actors, and in 1751 he sent a company, headed by David Douglass (? –1786), to Jamaica. It was probably Moody who alerted English actors to opportunities in the colonies at a time when the Licensing Act had seriously curtailed the theatre in England. His news came at an especially crucial moment in the career of the Hallams.

William Hallam, one of a large family of actors, had opened the New Wells Theatre in Goodman's Fields, London, in 1740. At first he presented only minor entertainments, but in 1744 turned to more ambitious works in spite of the Licensing Act. Although he prospered for several years, in 1751 his theatre was closed. It was at this time that Hallam conceived the idea of sending a troupe to America. The new company was headed by his brother, Lewis Hallam (1714–1756), an actor of secondary roles, with Mrs. Lewis Hallam as the leading actress. Consisting of twelve adults and Hallam's three children, the troupe was organized on the sharing plan, which was then still typical of English provincial troupes. Upon arriving in America, they fitted out a theatre at Williamsburg and opened in September, 1752. From this date can be traced the effective beginning of the professional theatre in America.

In addition to Williamsburg, the Hallams played in New York, Philadelphia, and Charleston before sailing to Jamaica in 1755. When they arrived, David Douglass was preparing to leave for England to recruit new actors, and the amalgamation of the troupes solved difficulties for both companies. Lewis Hallam died in 1756, and in 1758 Mrs. Hallam married Douglass, who remained head of the troupe until the Revolution. From 1758 to 1764, Douglass' company played in the mainland colonies. During these years, Mrs. Douglass continued as the leading actress, while Lewis Hallam, Jr. (c. 1740–1808) was now the leading man. Between 1759 and 1761, Douglass performed in New York, Philadelphia, Annapolis, Williamsburg, and elsewhere, and in 1761–1762, his presentations of "moral dialogues" in Rhode Island were the first professional performances in New England.

After another interval in Jamaica, Douglass returned to the mainland from 1766 to 1775. By now, he had developed considerable optimism about the future and began to build substantial permanent playhouses. The first, the Southwark Theatre in Philadelphia, was opened in 1766. In 1767, he built the John Street Theatre in New York, and thereafter erected theatres in major towns between New York and Charleston. During these years, Douglass also performed the first American play to be given a professional production, Thomas Godfrey's (1736–1763) *The Prince of Parthia*. A neoclassical tragedy with echoes of many Shakespearean works, it was given in Philadelphia in 1767. At the outbreak of the Revolution in 1774, the Continental Congress called for the cessation of theatrical entertainment. In 1775, Douglass sailed for Jamaica. Although many members of his company were to return after the war, Douglass' theatrical career soon ended.

The colonial theatre between 1752 and 1774 differed little from the English provincial theatre of the day. The Hallam-Douglass company had to tour, for as yet there was no center capable of supporting a permanent theatre. The expense and inconvenience of travel made it necessary to keep the troupe small and the scenic investiture simple. The performers were at best third-rate; they doubled in roles and appeared in entr'acte entertainments as well. Thus, while the artistic level was not high, the company established the foundations upon which later and more substantial companies would build.

During the Revolution, there were no professional performances, although British soldiers presented plays in Boston, New York, and Philadelphia, and American troops performed on a less ambitious scale. American playwrights were more active than performers. Mercy Otis Warren (1728–1814) satirized British sympathizers in *The Adulateur* (1773) and *The Group* (1775), Hugh Henry Brackenridge (1748–1816) wrote a blank-verse play, *The Battle of Bunker Hill* (1776), and to John (or Joseph) Leacock is attributed the five-act prose work, *The Fall of British Tyranny* (1776). The most effective play of the period is Robert Munford's (c. 1730–1784) *The Patriots* (c. 1776–1777), a satire on "super patriots" who label all opponents enemy agents. Although the literary output of the period is slight, it is still significant as the first flurry of dramatic writing in America.

When the peace treaty that made America fully independent was ratified in 1783, theatrical activity was just beginning to revive in the new nation. Thereafter, it would grow steadily and spread widely as new territories were opened up. But though political freedom had been won, it would be many years before the theatre would deviate significantly from the patterns it had inherited from its English ancestor.

LOOKING AT THEATRE HISTORY

In recent years, quantification and computers have become significant tools in historical research. In one sense, quantification has always played a large role in historical writing, since it is difficult to avoid such terms as "few," "numerous," "majority," and "percentage," all of which refer to quantity. But in most instances these terms have been used impressionistically, since they are not based on precise data. This is understandable, for it is difficult to assemble examples in sufficient quantities to permit wholly accurate generalizations. But, as William O. Aydelotte points out in *Quantification in History* (Reading, Mass.: Addison-Wesley Publishing Co., 1971), "The apparent disadvantages of quantitative research, the impediments to generalization that it presents, are actually advantages for they call attention to limits in knowledge or to flaws in reasoning that might not otherwise be perceived or fully appreciated" (page 60). In other words, it should make us wary of generalizations based on inadequate numbers of examples.

Nevertheless, many problems do lend themselves to quantification. For example, we can now answer many questions about the theatre in London between 1660 and 1800 with far greater precision than in the past because relatively complete information about all performances in London during those years has been recorded and computerized so that quantifiable information can be retrieved within the space of a few moments or hours. As one example, this computer can supply a list of all the roles (a total of 1,610) performed by David Garrick, with information about dates, places, and theatres, a feat that would require months of research using traditional methods. With such data, much more precise generalizations can be made.

Obviously a computer's reliability depends upon the accuracy of the data entered into it. Also, what questions it will answer depend on what it has been programmed to do. Computers cannot replace human beings, but they can aid them. We must also recognize that not all knowledge is quantifiable. But in almost all situations data banks and retrieval systems can speed the process of finding information and reduce errors in reporting it.

These tools have not yet been widely applied to theatrical materials and problems, but the example of "The London Stage, 1660–1800" (the data bank for which is housed at Lawrence University in Appleton, Wisconsin) suggests their great potential.

The student of theatre history needs to be aware that the versions of plays performed in the theatre are not necessarily those now commonly available for reading. This is especially true in dealing with Shakespeare's plays. Restoration and eighteenth-century audiences found many of Shakespeare's scripts unacceptable and preferred adaptations of them. Thus, when an eighteenth-century actor appeared in *King Lear* (to name only one conspicuous example), he did not perform the text we know. The student can gain considerable insight into eighteenth-century taste from reading the *King Lear* that held the stage through that century. Written by Nahum Tate and first performed in 1681, it makes Cordelia and Edgar lovers from the outset, and omits the Fool altogether. At the end, Lear is restored to the throne, Goneril and Regan die of poison, and Cordelia and Edgar are united in marriage. Thus, the neoclassical demand for poetic justice was upheld.

Neoclassicism also motivated the use of generalized scenery, as this passage makes clear:

> The stage should be furnished with a competent Number of painted scenes sufficient to answer the Purposes of all the Plays in the Stock, in which there is no great variety, being easily reduced to the following classes.
> 1st. Temples
> 2ndly. Tombs
> 3rdly. City Walls and Gates
> 4thly. Outsides of Palaces
> 5thly. Insides of Palaces
> 6thly. Streets
> 7thly. Chambers
> 8thly. Prisons
> 9thly. Gardens and
> 10thly. Rural prospects of Groves, Forests, Desarts, &c.
> All these should be done by a Master, if such can be found: otherwise they should be as simple and unaffected as possible to avoid offending a judicious eye. If for some particular purpose, any other Scene is necessary, it can be got up occasionally.
>
> *The Case of the Stage in Ireland*
> (Dublin, 1758).

During the course of the eighteenth century, pantomime did much to cultivate a taste for more spectacular scenery as can be seen from this stage direction in *Harlequin a Sorcerer* (one of John Rich's pantomimes, first presented in 1725 and revived often thereafter):

the Curtain rises, and discovers dark rocky Caverns, by the
Side of a Wood, illumin'd by the Moon: Birds of Omen
promiscuously flying, Flashes of Lightning faintly striking.

Under his stage name of Lun, Rich also perfected pantomimic acting. Here is a description of his portrayal of the scene in *Harlequin a Sorcerer* in which Harlequin is hatched from an egg:

This certainly was a masterpiece in dumb show. From the first chipping of the egg, his receiving motion, his feeling the ground, his standing upright, to his quick Harlequin trip around the empty Shell, through the whole progression every limb had its tongue, and every motion a voice, which "spoke with most miraculous organ" to the understandings and sensations of the observers.

JOHN JACKSON, *The History of the Scottish Stage* (Edinburgh, 1793), pp. 367–368.

By the mid-eighteenth century, tastes in acting and costuming began to change. Here is a description of a performance in which both Quin (the major exponent of the older school) and Garrick (the major exponent of the newer school) appeared:

Quin presented himself . . . in a green velvet coat embroidered down the seams, an enormous full bottomed periwig, rolled stockings and high-heeled square-toed shoes, with very little variation in cadence, and in a deep full tone, accompanied by a sawing kind of action, which had more

of the senate than of the stage in it, he rolled out his heroics with an air of dignified indifference. . . . Garrick, then young and light and alive in every muscle and in every feature, came bounding on the stage . . . it seemed as if a whole century had been stept over in the transition of a single scene; old things were done away, and a new order at once brought forward, bright and luminous, and clearly destined to dispel the barbarisms and bigotry of a tasteless age, . . . superstitiously devoted to the illusions of imposing declamation. . . . yet in general [the audience] seemed to love darkness better than light, and . . . bestowed far the greater show of hands upon the master of the old school than upon the founder of the new.

RICHARD CUMBERLAND, *Memoirs* (London, 1806), pp. 59–60.

Before the end of the century, dissatisfaction with anachronistic costuming was becoming more intense. Here is one complaint about the mixture of modes in *Richard III*:

King Richard's troops appear in the present uniform of the soldiers in St. James's park, with short jackets and cocked-up hats. King Richard wears indeed the habiliments of his time, but Richmond is dressed à la vraie moderne; . . . The Lord Mayor . . . . figures in his own character, but the other attendants in the play not so. . . . How is it possible to reconcile Macbeth or Hamlet dressed in our fashionable short coats, with the idea of habits of ages so far anterior?

Gentleman's Magazine (May, 1789).

12 Italy, France, and Spain in the Eighteenth Century

By 1700, Italy was of little consequence in European politics. Most of its several states were included within the Holy Roman Empire, which from 1559 until 1806 was almost always headed by a member of the Hapsburg family that ruled Austria. Consequently, Austria came to dominate Italy. It controlled some parts directly and the remainder through local princes loyal to it. In effect, then, Italy was a dependency of Austria.

THE EVOLUTION OF ITALIAN SCENIC DESIGN

By 1700 Italian scenic practices had been adopted throughout most of Western Europe. Proscenium arches, perspective settings (composed of flat wings, shutters, and borders), rapid shifts of scenery, and spectacular special effects had become common almost everywhere. In 1700 the visual conventions were still those popularized by Torelli and Vigarani. Thus, typically, settings were symmetrically arranged perspective alleys depicting a series of large buildings terminating in a view of a distant prospect.

Through most of the seventeenth century the important centers for theatrical design were Venice, Parma, Bologna, Florence, Milan, Turin, Rome, and Naples. But after 1650 the Imperial court at Vienna challenged the Italian cities for supremacy since it could provide significant rewards both in money and prestige for outstanding designers. Here between 1652 and 1707, Giovanni Burnacini (1600–1665) and Ludovico Ottavio Burnacini (1636–1707) staged some of the most lavish entertainments in Europe and gained international reputation. Of their more than 115 productions, the most elaborate was probably *The Golden Apple* (1668), which opened the lavish new opera house. It required twenty-three settings and thirty-five machines; in the final scene, three groups of dancers performed simultaneously—one in the sky, one on the sea, and one on land.

Throughout the seventeenth century there was a noticeable trend toward increased size and splendor in stage settings. These and other changes seem first to have reached full expression, however, in the work of the Bibiena family, perhaps the most influential designers of the eighteenth century. Of the many Bibienas, the most

FIGURE 12.1 Design by Burnacini for *The Golden Apple,* Act I, scene 2: The Palace of Paris. Above the stage are seen the goddesses who insist that Paris judge their beauty. Courtesy Theatersammlung, Osterreichische, Nationalbibliothek, Vienna.

auditorium, and the scenery had been proportioned accordingly. Thus, in Torelli's settings the tops of the buildings were always visible. Furthermore, the rectangular alignment of the auditorium was continued by the central perspective alley created by the scenery. Bibiena, on the other hand, divorced his settings from the auditorium both in terms of angle and of scale. Consequently, since a scene could now be depicted from any eye point, the former symmetrical arrangement was no longer necessary. Furthermore, the wings near the front of the stage were painted as though they were merely the lower portion of a building too large to be contained in the narrow confines of the proscenium. In addition, vanishing points were placed extremely low so as to increase apparent size of the settings. As a result, Bibiena's designs often seem so vast that they create a mood of fantasy and unreality.

In spite of its apparent size, a setting using angle perspective often required less space than one with a central alley, for the effect of vastness was created in part by side vistas not fully shown. Many of the settings divide the stage into a foreground, intended for the actors, and a background representing distant objects. A drop,

FIGURE 12.2 Design by Giuseppe Galli Bibiena for *Costanza e Fortezza* as presented at the royal palace in Prague, 1723. Courtesy Theatermuseum, Munich.

important were Ferdinando (1657–1743), Francesco (1659–1739), Giuseppe (1696–1757), Antonio (1700–1774), and Carlo (1728–1787). The family's reputation was first established widely through Ferdinando's work at Bologna and Parma. By 1708 he was sufficiently famous to be summoned to Barcelona, where he staged the festivities for the marriage of the future Emperor Charles VI, and in 1711, Charles VI appointed him court architect at Vienna to succeed Burnacini. Thereafter the Bibienas were in demand wherever an interest in opera developed. During the eighteenth century they were employed in such major cities as Paris, Lisbon, London, Stockholm, Berlin, Dresden, and St. Petersburg.

The contributions of the Bibiena family to scenic design were numerous. Around 1703, while working at Bologna, Ferdinando introduced angle perspective (*scena per angolo*), perhaps his most significant innovation. Rather than a single vanishing point located at the rear of a setting, Bibiena used two or more vanishing points at the sides. Whereas previous designers emphasized a central vista, Bibiena (while he did not give up the earlier practice altogether) characteristically placed buildings, walls, statues, or courtyards at the center of the picture and relegated vistas to the sides.

Bibiena also altered the scale of settings. Before his time, the stage had been treated as an extension of the

FIGURE 12.3 Setting by Ferdinando and Giuseppe Galli Bibiena for *Angelica, Vincitrice di Alcina* **as performed out of doors in the Favorite Park, Vienna, in 1716. Courtesy Theatermuseum, Munich.**

cut to form arches or a series of columns, often delimits the acting area at the rear and provides a frame through which distant prospects are seen. The chariot-and-pole system of scene shifting also aided composition, since an obelisk, tree, or other seemingly freestanding object could be moved at any point on the stage. (Unlike the groove system used in England, the chariot-and-pole did not require any overhead support for a scenic piece set at mid-stage nor did it require a stagehand to come into view to move it to the right position since it could be handled from offstage through mechanical means.) Despite the great number of extant pictures of stage settings, it is difficult to recreate the floor plans of eighteenth-century scenic designs, for engravings give few clues about how the visual elements were divided among wings, shutters and borders.

Virtually all of the practices for which the Bibienas are now noted were extensions of the baroque style, which had begun to appear in the late sixteenth century. The baroque marks a departure from the dominant mode of the Renaissance, which was characterized by restraint, order, symmetrical balance, and rectangular space. Baroque art, on the other hand, was extravagant, asymmetrical, and mingled rectangular and curvilinear space. While, as in the Renaissance, the principal architectural elements in the baroque era continued to be columns, arches, and pediments, these were now altered by twisting the columns, entwining them with garlands and by other additions; S-curved supports were added to beams and

pediments; and the whole structure was often encrusted with carving, statuary, and painting. By a careful juxtaposition of mass and space, by using such new materials as stucco and plaster out of which to create swirling details, and by such devices as foreshortening and forced perspective, the whole structure was given a sense of activity and movement. The overall effect was one of monumentality, grandeur, and richness. It is these qualities, by 1700 typical in architecture, which the Bibienas exploited in their scenic designs of the early eighteenth century.

Although the *scena per angolo* was popularized by Ferdinando Bibiena, it seems also to have been developed quite independently by Filippo Juvarra (1676–1736), who adopted angle perspective in Naples around 1706. After working in Rome, Juvarra moved to Turin, where he became the leading architect of northwestern Italy.

Juvarra's settings differ from Bibiena's because they are essentially curvilinear. Thus, the eye of the observer is led in a circle and always back to the foreground rather than off to the sides, as was often the case with Bibiena's side alleys. It may be for this reason that

FIGURE 12.4 Stage setting by Giuseppe Galli Bibiena for a production given at the betrothal of members of the ruling houses of Poland and Saxony in 1719. Courtesy Metropolitan Museum of Art, Harris Brisbane Dick Fund, 1951.

FIGURE 12.5 Design by Filippo Juvarra. At the bottom are two variants on the setting, probably indicating that this is a permanent setting with changeable back scenes. Courtesy Theatre Museum, Victoria and Albert Museum.

and elsewhere. The Quaglio family, beginning with Giulio (1601–1658) and ending with Eugen (1857–1942), continued as designers through six generations. Although of Italian origin, they worked principally in Austria and Germany. From 1778 until 1917 they maintained headquarters at Monaco, where the museum perserves many of their designs. The Galliari family, whose most famous members were Bernardino (1707–1794) and Fabrizio (1709–1790), were active from the early eighteenth century until 1823. Although they worked in many cities, they were associated primarily with Turin and Milan.

The visual style established between 1700 and 1750 underwent many changes in the late eighteenth century as new interests emerged. For example, as comic opera grew in popularity, domestic and rustic settings became common. Comic opera evolved in Italy out of the *intermezzi* which were often performed with serious operas. The first Italian comic opera to achieve widespread fame was Pergolesi's *The Servant the Mistress* (1733). Variations on comic opera appeared throughout Europe (in England the ballad opera, in Germany the *singspiele*, in France the *opéra comique*). The type was so popular by the late eighteenth century that many of the larger opera houses were maintaining what amounted to two separate troupes, one for comic and one for serious opera.

An increased interest in history also affected scenic design during the late eighteenth century. The rediscovery of Herculaneum in 1709 and of Pompeii

FIGURE 12.6 Design dating from about 1780 by Giuseppino Galliari. Note the classical forms in a state of picturesque ruin. Courtesy Museo Civico, Turin.

Juvarra's settings also seem less monumental and fantastic than do Bibiena's.

Juvarra did considerable experimentation in settings. For example, he sometimes used unit settings, in which the background elements were altered behind a fixed foreground. He also created some settings entirely of draperies, and in others he included what were then very exotic elements, such as tropical foliage and Near-Eastern architectural forms. In designing his settings, Juvarra appears to have worked from floor plans, for they are often included at the bottom of his drawings.

In addition to the Bibienas, several other families of scenic designers were active in the eighteenth century. Members of the Mauro family worked in the principal theatrical centers of Italy and Germany from the seventeenth century until 1820. Beginning with Gaspare Mauro (*fl.* 1657–1719), the family designed settings in Venice, Turin, Parma, Monaco, Milan, Dresden, Vienna, in 1748 captured the imagination of Europeans and called attention to the "pastness" of classical civilizations. Engravings of classical ruins were widely circulated, and many aristocrats had ruins constructed in their gardens as visual centerpieces. Similarly, scenic designers began to show classical structures in various stages of deterioration, with shrubs and vines growing from fissures.

This renewed interest in history also stimulated the writing of works based on the post-classical national past and on folk materials. Many of these works were set in the Middle Ages and thus they brought Gothic architecture into the theatre, where previously classical forms had been seen almost exclusively.

The late eighteenth century also brought a rebellion against baroque music and art with all its ornamentation and nonfunctional details. This reaction was perhaps best captured in the work of the composer Christoph Willibald Gluck (1714–1787), who through such works as *Orpheus and Eurydice* (1762) sought to recapture the simplicity of early Florentine opera and to synthesize action and music. The popularity of his works helped to initiate a new "classical" era in music during the last quarter of the eighteenth century. This trend was paralleled in architecture and scenic design by an attempt to return to pure classical forms devoid of extraneous ornament and detail.

But perhaps the most important innovation of the late eighteenth century was the introduction of "mood" into design. Before the late eighteenth century, settings were for the most part painted so that every detail was depicted clearly. Now designers began to emphasize the atmospheric values of light and shadow. The key figure in this trend probably was Gian Battista Piranesi (1720–1778). Although he designed many stage settings, Piranesi's influence was exerted primarily through the more than 1,000 engravings of Roman ruins and contemporary prisons he published between 1745 and 1778. His drawings of ruins contributed much to the interest in "ruined" antiquity, and his prisons, with their marked contrasts in light and shadow, accelerated interest in atmospheric qualities. Scene designers began to depict picturesque places as seen by moonlight or interiors illuminated by a few shafts of light. Color played only a minor role in this trend, for the palette was limited. Settings were painted in sepia or pastel shades of green, yellow, and lavender. Mood, therefore, was achieved primarily through the juxtaposition of masses of light and shadow.

In spite of the trend toward greater visual variety, the types of places represented in late eighteenth century

FIGURE 12.7 Piranesi's engraving of the Forum of Nerva. Note the emphasis on light and shadow. From Giovanni Battista Piranesi, *Le Antichita Romane Opera* (1765). Courtesy Lilly Library, Indiana University.

operas can be reduced to about ten. Because each locale was idealized, settings could be reused for a number of different works. The basic compositional techniques remained unchanged, however, for the *scena per angolo* continued to dominate. The many innovations after 1750, especially in new visual content and the increased concern for mood, are indicative of the dissatisfaction with the strictures that had been imposed by the neoclassical outlook. Perhaps more important, they are harbingers of romanticism, which soon was to become the dominant style.

ITALIAN DRAMA OF THE EIGHTEENTH CENTURY

If Italy's designers dominated the theatre of Europe, the same cannot be said for its dramatists, for few of them achieved fame. Because of the prestige of opera, most Italian playwrights were content to compose librettos, and the most prized honor was the post of poet to the Imperial Court of Vienna. Here the two most famous Italian writers of the early eighteenth century worked. Apostolo Zeno (1668–1750), author of more than sixty opera librettos, was considered the leading author of the years 1700 to 1725. But he was soon overshadowed by his successor, Metastasio (Pietro Trapassi, 1698–1782), honored as the greatest poet of his age. Metastasio prided

FIGURE 12.8 Scene from Alfieri's *Saul*. From the edition published in Florence in 1824.

himself on writing librettos that could be performed effectively without music. Thus, his plays resemble neoclassical tragedies, with the exception that they are in three acts and end happily. Since the characters are either good or evil and virtue is always triumphant, they are essentially melodramas. Although Metastasio wrote only about thirty librettos, the most famous of which are *Adriano* (1731), *Issipile* (1732), and *The Clemency of Titus* (1734), they were set to music more than 1,000 times before 1840. The shallowness of these works by modern standards makes it difficult to understand the eighteenth-century admiration, bordering on worship, of Metastasio.

Except for opera, serious drama was not popular in eighteenth-century Italy. Prior to 1750, the only tragedy of note was *Merope* (1713) by Francesco Scipione di Maffei (1675–1765). It is based on the classical story of Merope, who, on the verge of slaying her unknown son, discovers the truth and is able to effect revenge upon the real cause of her misery.

Italy's most famous tragedian, Vittorio Alfieri (1749–1803), came to the fore around 1775. Alfieri sought to present the most powerful emotions in the simplest possible dramatic form. In his plays everything not essential is pared away. As a result, his tragedies are closer to those of Racine than to typical eighteenth-century works. Of his dramas, which include *Oreste* (1776), *Antigone* (1783), and *Mirra* (1789), the acknowledged masterpiece is *Saul* (1782). In it, attention is concentrated upon Saul, the remnant of a great man, now vacillating between madness and sanity, petty tyranny and greatness. The action is simple, for it grows out of Saul's inner torment as he watches David grow in esteem as his own influence wanes. Only in the face of death does he rise once more to greatness. Most of Alfieri's works are flawed by his strong political convictions, which sometimes led him to place too great emphasis upon doctrinal messages, for he was a strong advocate of independence for Italy and a firm foe of all tyranny. Nevertheless, it was Alfieri's political ideas that influenced most of his successors in the nineteenth century, although none rose to his artistic level.

FIGURE 12.9 Goldoni's *The Servant of Two Masters*, Act I, scene 7. From Carlo Goldoni, *Commedie*, Vol. XIV (1824).

Comedy fared somewhat better than tragedy. Until 1750, the comic impulse was largely channeled into the *commedia dell'arte*. Unfortunately, after 1700 this formerly vital form grew repetitious. Minor characters, music, and spectacle were added to increase its variety, but, as sentimentalism grew, *commedia* came to seem crude and unfeeling. It was in this atmosphere that Carlo Goldoni (1707–1793), Italy's greatest comic dramatist, appeared. He began his career in 1734 by writing scenarios for *commedia* troupes in and around Venice, the last stronghold of the *commedia dell'arte*. From the first he objected to many of the form's conventions and in 1738 he began his program for reform by writing out the principal role in his *Man of the World*. This was sufficiently well received that by 1743 he was writing out all of the parts, and by 1749 was beginning to alter the traditional character types.

In 1750, Goldoni's *The Comic Theatre* attacked the antiquated methods of the *commedia*, called for abandoning masks (because they prevent subtle facial expression), adopting better stage speech, and substituting subjects based on life for the conventionalized situations of *commedia*. Since he had already abolished most improvisation, his program advocated altering virtually all of the form's essential characteristics. By 1761, when he left Venice, Goldoni had done much to banish fantasy, vulgarity, and nonrealistic devices from the *commedia* and to substitute for them humor, sentiment, and realism (both in incident and treatment). The stock characters had been humanized and softened. Pantalone, for example, was no longer the ridiculous, miserly, and lecherous old man of the traditional scenarios, but an honest merchant, good father, and solid citizen. Through such means, Goldoni did much to obliterate the distinctions between *commedia* and regular comedy. Among Goldoni's *commedia* plays, perhaps the best is *The Servant of Two Masters*. In 1762 Goldoni settled in Paris, where, until his retirement in 1773, he wrote for the Comédie Italienne.

Goldoni's interests were by no means restricted to *commedia* or even to comedy. One of the most prolific writers of the century, he turned out 10 tragedies, 83 musical dramas, and about 150 comedies. Many of these are mere trifles, but others are among the finest works of the age. Goldoni was enormously inventive, and found many ingenious ways of unifying plots. Sometimes he used a place, as in *The Coffee House*, at others an object, as in *The Fan*, or character type, as in *The Women's Gossip*, to weld together a number of actions. Although

FIGURE 12.10 A performance in the Roman amphitheatre at Verona. About this, Goldoni writes in his *Memoirs*: "Spectacles of all kinds are given: courses, jousts, bull-fights; and in summer, plays are even represented. . . . For this purpose . . . there is erected, on very strong supports, a theatre in boards, which is taken down every winter and refitted again in the fine season." Painting by Marco Marcola, 1772. Courtesy the Art Institute of Chicago.

Goldoni depicted almost every profession and class, he favored the middle and lower classes, and often characterized the nobility as decadent and useless. Above all he idealized his female characters, as his most famous play *The Mistress of the Inn* (1753) illustrates well. The sentimental strain is found throughout Goldoni's work, but there is always sufficient wit and humor to avoid the cloying sentimentality that afflicts many plays of the era. Nevertheless, Goldoni's work, despite its charm and vivacity, is lacking in true depth.

Carlo Gozzi (1720–1806) strongly objected to Goldoni's alterations of the *commedia*, his sentimentalism, and his denigration of the upper classes. Gozzi's counter-attack took the form of *fiabe,* or satiric fairy tales written for the *commedia* masks. Gozzi emphasized the elements that Goldoni sought most to suppress: fantasy, enchantment, and inprovisation. Thus, he chose his subjects from fairy tales or legends (which provided many opportunities for spectacular effects) and used them to satirize the sentimental trends of current literature. As a result of this topicality, a modern reader can only guess at their effectiveness, especially since all leave some portions to be improvised. Although his *The Love for Three Oranges* (1761), *King Stag* (1762), *Turandot* (1762), and *The Magic Bird* (1765) were extremely popular in the eighteenth century, Gozzi's fame was not lasting. He brought a new life to the *commedia* for a few years, but after 1770 its strength rapidly declined. Thereafter, Italian comedy was to reflect the major European trends and to confine itself to types of drama found elsewhere.

FRENCH DRAMA OF THE EIGHTEENTH CENTURY

Throughout the eighteenth century, France remained a major power, but its former position of dominance was considerably weakened by a series of wars and by disastrous economic policies. The War of Spanish Succession, which resulted when Louis XIV sought to unite France and Spain by placing his grandson on the Spanish throne, pitted France against most of the rest of Europe between 1701 and 1713. The proposed succession was eventually permitted after France agreed that Spain and France would never be united, but France had suffered a number of humiliating defeats by England and Austria, who thereafter kept France in check. After 1750 France lost its major territories in the New World to England. These wars put a heavy strain on France's economy, with the burden falling primarily on the middle and lower classes, since the nobility and clergy were exempted from taxation. Such conditions created increasing unhappiness, which eventually erupted in the revolution of 1789.

Despite its problems, France continued to be the major cultural center of Europe throughout the eighteenth century, and its drama was the standard against which all others were judged. Still, French drama tended to be backward-looking, taking its standards from the seventeenth century. Most eighteenth-century tragic writers sought to follow in Racine's footsteps, but per-haps because they substituted involved plots and complex character relationships for his emphasis upon internal conflicts, their work failed to achieve greatness. The major trends can be seen in the work of LaGrange-Chancel, Crébillon, and Voltaire.

Joseph de LaGrange-Chancel (1677–1758) wrote fourteen plays after 1694. The most popular, *Ino and Mélicerte* (1713), tells the story of Ino, now a slave in the household of her former husband, the king, who believes her to be dead. The present queen is plotting to kill Ino's son, Mélicerte, who is unaware of his own identity. A number of other complex relationships are clarified in a series of recognition scenes, which thwart the evil queen and restore Ino to happiness. The trend toward melodrama, evident in this plot, was accelerated by Prosper Jolyot Crébillon (1674–1762). Many of Crébillon's extremely complex dramas were designed to arouse horror in the spectator, as in *Atreus and Thyestes* (1707), in which Thyestes is served a drink concocted from the blood of his sons. Crébillon's preference for complex plots is well illustrated by *Electre* (1707), in which Aegisthus is provided with a son and daughter to motivate complications based on the love of Aegisthus' children for Electra and Orestes. Crébillon's best play is *Rhadamisthe and Zénobie* (1711), in which the unrecognized heroine is loved by Rhadamisthe (her cruel husband, who is present in disguise although he is presumed to be dead), her unscrupulous father-in-law, and her brother-in-law, Arsames. After numerous recognition scenes and the death of Rhadamisthe, Zenobie finds happiness in marriage to the virtuous Arsames. This play, considered one of the finest of the eighteenth century, held the stage until 1830.

Voltaire (François-Marie Arouet, 1694–1778) dominated tragedy in the eighteenth century, as he did virtually all French literature and thought. Beginning with *Oedipe* (1718), he wrote fifty-three plays, more than half of them tragedies. Although superior in many respects, Voltaire's tragedies continue the trend toward complex plots, involved character relationships, and sudden reversals based upon recognitions.

Voltaire's best work, *Zaïre* (1732), set in the Middle East at the time of the Crusades, tells the story of the slave, Zaïre, who is loved by her master, the Sultan Osman. Her discovery that she is the daughter of Lusignan, the Christian former king of the area and a fellow-slave, is kept from the sultan, who grows insanely jealous of her meetings with Nerestan, Zaïre's recently-discovered brother, and kills them both. Voltaire's philosophical

FIGURE 12.11 Scene from Regnard's *The Universal Heir* at the Comédie Française, 1708. From the original edition of the play.

interests are reflected in many of his plays. For example, *Alzire* (1736), a complex story about the Spaniards in Peru, argues that a religion should be valued only to the extent that it produces humanitarian results. The trend toward sentimentalism is reflected in Voltaire's frequent use of the *voix du sang* (an instinctive attraction to blood relatives) as a dramatic device to foreshadow recognition scenes.

After living in England from 1726 to 1729, Voltaire came to consider the French neoclassical ideal overly restrictive and he sought thereafter to liberalize it. His reforms, however, were confined to introducing ghosts and a limited amount of violence onto the stage, to widening the range of permissible subjects, and to increasing spectacle. But Voltaire's attempts to use spectacle more effectively were frustrated by the presence of spectators on the stage, and it was largely due to his influence that the practice was abolished in 1759. This innovation, coming at just the time when public interest in history and local color was growing, encouraged the exploitation of spectacle in the regular drama. Voltaire's *Tancrède* (1760) turned attention to the Middle Ages and began a vogue for plays about the French national past, which

was exploited in such later popular works as Pierre Laurent de Belloy's *The Siege of Calais* (1765) and *Gaston and Bayard* (1771).

In his desire to liberalize the French stage, Voltaire called attention to Shakespeare's works, previously neglected in France. But though thereafter they were sometimes read in their original form, Shakespeare's plays were considered much too "irregular" for the stage without severe alteration. Even the drastic adaptations of them made by Jean-François Ducis (1733–1816), several of which were produced after 1769, were too exotic for French taste. This response illustrates how solidly entrenched neoclassicism continued to be, in spite of the reforms introduced by Voltaire and others.

Comedy, perhaps because of its less privileged position, underwent more changes than did tragedy. The influence of Molière, dominant until about 1720, is seen in the comedies of Dancourt, Regnard, and LeSage, the major comic authors of the early eighteenth century. Florent-Carton Dancourt (1661–1725) made his debut as an actor at the Comédie Française in 1685 and eventually became the leader of the troupe. Of his more than fifty comedies, two are of special importance, *The Fashionable Gentleman* (1687) and *The Fashionable Middle-Class Women* (1692). The first introduces a type that was to be prominent in later plays, the *chevalier d'industrie* or gigolo, while the second satirizes the attempts of merchants' wives to become ladies of fashion. In such plays, Dancourt reflects the rise (much as in England at this time) of an ambitious mercantile class. His other plays, most of them comedies of manners, treat a wide range of character types and social customs of his day. From 1688 to 1694, Jean-François Regnard (1655–1709) wrote for the *commedia* troupe then resident in Paris. His later plays were intended for the Comédie Française. His finest works are *The Gambler* (1696), a comic portrait of a compulsive gambler, and *The Universal Heir* (1708), a farce about a valet who seeks to make his master and himself heirs to an irascible old uncle. Alain-René LeSage (1668–1747), after adapting plays by Lope de Vega, Rojas Zorilla, and Calderón, launched a remorseless attack upon contemporary tax collectors in *Turcaret* (1709). Often called the first great French comedy of manners, it depicts a world of clever rascals who prey upon each other. Under the surface lurked a thinly disguised criticism of Louis XIV's economic policies which permitted the privileged and unscrupulous to thrive at the expense of lesser and more honest citizens. The controversy aroused by the play left

LeSage estranged from the Comédie Française. As a result, he confined himself thereafter to novels and comic operas, produced by the illegitimate theatres at the Parisian fairs.

The trend toward sentimentalism, which, as in England, began around 1720, is most evident in the works of Destouches, Marivaux, and LaChaussée. The reputation of Philippe Néricault Destouches (1680–1754) is based primarily upon two plays, *The Married Philosopher* (1727) and *The Conceited Count* (1732), both of which have many traits in common with Steele's *The Conscious Lovers.* (The similarities may be explained in part by Destouches' residence in England during the 1720s.) The trend of Destouches' work is perhaps best seen in *The Conceited Count,* in which a penniless but arrogant nobleman reforms following an emotional appeal made to him by his father, who later comments, "My son is proud, but his heart is excellent; that makes up for all."

Pierre Carlet de Chamblain de Marivaux (1688–1763) came to prominence in 1720 with *Arlequin Refined by Love.* This play was presented by the Italian troupe that had been readmitted to France in 1716 following the death of Louis XIV. The majority of Marivaux's thirty-five plays were produced by this company, whose acting style was much better suited than that of the Comédie Française to Marivaux's subtle presentation of emotion. Most of Marivaux's plays are concerned with awakening love. Unlike earlier comedies, in which lovers are kept apart by some external force (usually parents or guardians), the obstacles in Marivaux's plays arise from the inner conflicts of the characters. For example, in *The Game of Love and Chance* (1730) two friends arrange a marriage between their children, but only on the condition that the boy and girl are willing to accept each other; the young couple, who have never met, are skeptical about the match and each hits upon the idea of changing places with a servant to observe the other; then, each irresistibly and against his will falls in love with a supposed servant. Here, as in most of Marivaux's plays, interest is focused on subtle changes in feelings within characters rather than upon external intrigue. Consequently, Marivaux is sometimes likened to Racine. He is also noted for his distinctive prose style, often labeled *marivaudage.* With his emphasis on feeling, Marivaux contributed significantly to the development of sentimentalism, but his charm and wit raise him far above his contemporaries. Because of his interest in inner psychological conflicts,

his critical stature has grown steadily since the late nineteenth century. In France today, among the classics his comedies are second in popularity only to those of Molière.

With *False Antipathy* (1733) and *The Fashionable Prejudice* (1735), Pierre Claude Nivelle de LaChaussée (1692–1754) established the *comédie larmoyante,* or tearful comedy, perhaps the most popular dramatic type in France from the 1730s until about 1750. In LaChaussée's works a virtuous protagonist is faced with a set of obstacles designed to arouse sympathy and compassion and from which he is rescued by the revelation of previously unknown facts and rewarded for his constancy. Thus, his plays resemble contemporary tragedy in the use of plots based on concealed information and in their use of verse dialogue, and comedy in their happy endings. The overall effect was one of considerable refinement and delicacy. Several other authors, among them Voltaire with such works as *The Prodigal Son* (1736) and *Nanine* (1749), also contributed significantly to the development of sentimental comedy.

After 1750, *comédie larmoyante* was absorbed into other types as a few writers, most notably Denis Diderot (1713–1784), demonstrated and sought to win acceptance for an enlarged range of dramatic genres. At this time virtually all traditional concepts, including those about drama, were being reevaluated by a group of advanced thinkers (the *philosophes*) through controversial essays in the *Encyclopédie,* edited by Diderot and published in twenty-eight volumes between 1748 and 1772. Diderot's own ideas about drama are expressed primarily in a few dialogues and in two plays, *The Illegitimate Son* (1757) and *The Father of a Family* (1758). Diderot argued that neoclassicism was too narrow in restricting the acceptable dramatic types to comedy and tragedy, and that additional "intermediate" genres— the *drame,* or domestic tragedy, and a comedy concerned with virtue—should be added. He also suggested many innovations in staging, for he believed that drama would move an audience profoundly only if it created a complete illusion of reality. Consequently, he advocated subject matter chosen from everyday life and presented in settings that duplicated real rooms. He urged the use of prose dialogue, detailed pantomime, and the "fourth wall" convention in acting (that is, behavior which takes no cognizance of the audience). Diderot's ideas, which foreshadow realism, were not to be fully exploited until the late nineteenth century.

Diderot did inspire a number of disciples, however, who sought additional inspiration in English sentimental drama. Bernard-Joseph Suarin (1706–1781) adapted Moore's *The Gamester* as *Beverlei* (1768), and Louis-Sebastien Mercier (1740–1814) adapted *The London Merchant* as *Jenneval* (1769), as well as writing such original works as *The Judge* and *The Indigent Man*. The best of the *drames* was *A Philosopher Without Knowing It* (1765) by Michel-Jean Sédaine (1719–1797). Its subject, the story of a young man who survives an unwanted duel to become the friend of his former enemy, is a typical one, but the play rises above other *drames* because of its superior characterization and less obvious didacticism. Since the Comédie Française did not encourage it, the *drame* had little chance to develop, except in the minor theatres, where it was to mingle with pantomime and music and emerge in the nineteenth century as melodrama.

The late eighteenth century produced only one major French dramatist, Beaumarchais (Pierre-Augustin Caron, 1732–1799). Now remembered chiefly for his comedies, Beaumarchais also wrote a number of *drames*, such as *Eugénie* (1767) and *The Two Friends* (1770). But his assured fame rests on *The Barber of Seville* (1775) and *The Marriage of Figaro* (1783). The former, a comedy of intrigue in which an elderly guardian's plans to marry his young ward are thwarted, introduces Figaro, the culmination of all the comic servants of French drama. Although *The Marriage of Figaro* includes many of the characters found in the earlier play, its tone is quite different, for intrigue is now subordinated to commentary upon society and class relationships. It is a far more complex play than *The Barber of Seville*. Although the setting ostensibly is Spain, *The Marriage of Figaro* clearly reflects contemporary France, for by this time the nobility had become superfluous and Louis XVI's (reigned 1774–1793) attempts to curb its privileges had proven wholly ineffectual, much to the chagrin of the middle and lower classes who bore the burden of taxation, even though they enjoyed few civil rights. Beaumarchais recaptured the spirit of "laughing" comedy, much as Goldsmith and Sheridan had done in England, but he added to it a sense of political and sociological concern.

In the late eighteenth century, however, the typical plays continued to be sentimental in tone. Many also capitalized on the growing interest in history and local color. All of these trends are epitomized in Charles Collé's (1709–1783) *The Hunting Party of Henri IV*

FIGURE 12.12 Final act of Beaumarchais' *The Marriage of Figaro.* **From the 1785 edition of the play. Courtesy Lilly Library, Indiana University.**

(1774), in which the disguised king mingles with the common people and helps resolve their problems.

By 1790, then, French drama had taken a few tentative steps away from neoclassicism. Nevertheless, though the typical subject matter and treatment often differed considerably from those of 1700, no startling innovations had been made before the Revolution inaugurated a new era in France.

PARISIAN ACTING TROUPES

In 1700 there were only two legitimate troupes in Paris, the Opéra and the Comédie Française, each with monopolistic privileges. These companies were to remain the major ones throughout the century, although they were to encounter considerable competition. The first challenge came from the illegitimate theatres at the fairs, especially those of St. Germain, which ran from February 3 until Easter, and St. Laurent, which ran from the end of June until near the end of October. Together they were open about six months each year. The fairs had featured entertainers, such as acrobats, dancers, and exhibitors of trained animals and freaks, since the sixteenth century. In the late seventeenth century, they introduced crude dramatic skits and *commedia dell'arte* plays, and when the Italian company was expelled from France in 1697, they seized the opportunity to enlarge their activities. After 1698, the Opéra and the Comédie Française strove continuously to suppress these troupes, which used various ruses to evade the monopolies.

FIGURE 12.13 Scene from a fair theatre play, *The Quarrel of the Theatres*, satirizing the Comédie Française (represented by the figure on the right) and the Comédie Italienne (represented by the figure on the left) for plundering the fair theatres of their stock in trade. From *Le Théâtre de la Foire, ou l'Opéra Comique* by Le Sage and D'Orneval, Vol. III (1723).

Because of their desire to offer entertainments not prohibited by the monopolies, the fair companies experimented continuously with dramatic forms, and the popularity of their "irregular" plays did much to undermine the neoclassical ideal in France.

The first significant minor form to emerge was the comic opera. Forbidden to use dialogue, the fair troupes condensed the necessary exposition and speech into couplets, which were printed on placards held by small boys dressed as cupids and suspended above the stage; the couplets, set to popular tunes, were than sung by confederates planted in the auditorium. By 1714, the Opéra was in such financial difficulties that, in return for a sizable fee, it authorized one of the fair troupes to use music, dance, and spectacle. After this time, the entertainments were called *opéras comiques*. Between 1713 and 1730, LaSage, who was no longer able to write for the Comédie Française after the controversy over *Turcaret*, exploited this form so successfully that he is often called the founder of French comic opera. In his works, spoken dialogue alternates with verses set to popular tunes much as in English ballad opera somewhat later. Featuring *commedia* characters, these short pieces parodied tragedies and operas and satirized current events and fashions. The fair companies' bills, which always included sideshow variety acts, contrasted sharply with the staid performances of the Comédie Française and the fashionable offerings of the Opéra.

The Parisian theatre was further diversified in 1716, when the Duc D'Orleans, Louis XIV's libertine brother and Regent for the young Louis XV (reigned 1715–1774), invited a *commedia dell'arte* troupe back to France. Installed in the Hôtel de Bourgogne, the Italians were led by Luigi Riccoboni (*c.* 1676–1753), who in 1713 had attempted unsuccessfully to establish a national theatre in Italy. By 1716 Riccoboni had already recognized that *commedia* was declining, and he sought to diversify his offerings. Thus, when the company's initial popularity in Paris slackened, he began to perform such works as Maffei's *Merope* and Italian translations of French tragedies and tragicomedies. In 1718 he added a few works in French, and in 1719 he began to present parodies in the manner of the fair troupes. By 1721, Riccoboni had added four French actors to his company and had induced such authors as Marivaux to write plays for him.

The turning point in the company's fortunes came in 1723, when it was made a state theatre with the official

FIGURE 12.14   The Italian company of actors, *c.* 1720. Painting by Antoine Watteau. Courtesy Kress Collection, National Gallery of Art, Washington, D.C.

title Comédiens Ordinaires du Roi (although it was almost always referred to as the Comédie Italienne). At the same time the company was granted an annual subsidy and placed under a set of governing rules similar to those of the Comédie Française. At this time its repertory was restricted to *commedia dell'arte* scripts, comedies, and parodies.

The fair companies, which had been suppressed in 1718, although they had continued to perform surreptitiously, resumed open playing in 1723, after Louis XV (who that year had been declared of age) attended a performance. This apparent sanction won them many years of unmolested prosperity. After 1723, then, Paris had three legitimate troupes, plus a number of semilegitimate fair companies.

In the 1740s *opéra comique* began to drop its farcical and satirical subject matter in favor of more sentimental stories. Charles-Simon Favart (1710–1792) was especially successful with the new type. His *Acajou* (1744) was so popular that the Opéra suspended the fair troupe's right to use music and spectacle, which it had granted the minor company in return for an annual fee, and sought to take control of *opéra comique*. This led to such a violent controversy that the crown issued an injunction against all performances of comic opera. Between 1745 and 1751, the years during which the injunction was in effect, English pantomime was introduced to fill the void. It was received so enthusiastically that it remained a staple of the Parisian minor theatres for the rest of the century.

Two significant innovations were made in *opéra comique* after its revival in 1751. First, ordinary characters began to replace the *commedia* figures. As a part of this shift, local color, in the form of picturesque characters, places, and customs, came into the minor theatres long before it was common at the major houses. Second, following the great success of Pergolesi's *The Servant the Mistress* in 1752, original music began to replace the popular tunes to which couplets had been sung prior to that time. Possibly because these innovations brought the form greatly increased popularity, *opéra comique* was lost to the fair troupes in 1762, when in that year the reorganized Comédie Italienne was awarded a monopoly on comic opera. At the same time, Goldoni was also imported from Italy to write plays for the troupe. *Opéra comique* and Goldoni's comedies proved so popular that between 1769 and 1780 French plays were dropped altogether from the Comédie Italienne's repertory.

When the fair troupes were deprived of *opéra comique*, they returned to the original form of comic opera, in which songs were set to popular tunes. Now called *comédies-en-vaudevilles*, plays of this type were to retain their appeal until well into the nineteenth century. Pantomime also increased in popularity as it became more melodramatic with mood music underscoring emotional scenes of innocence persecuted and rescued from villainy. By 1780, dialogue had been introduced into this previously silent form and such anachronistic labels as *pantomimes dialoguées et parlées* (with dialogue and speaking) had become common. After 1769, when the Comédie Italienne dropped its French repertory, the minor companies also began to perform *drames* and comedies, perhaps because French playwrights now had no other market if their works were refused by the Comédie Française.

After 1760 the fair troupes began to relocate on the Boulevard du Temple, a fashionable recreational spot, although they continued to play part of each year at the fairs. Thus, they became year-round companies. Of the troupes that moved to the Boulevard, four were especially important: Audinot's, Nicolet's, the Théâtre des Associés, and the Variétés Amusantes. (The location of these theatres was to supply the term which is still applied to Parisian companies catering to popular audiences—boulevard theatres.)

During the 1780s the minor theatres had to make a number of adjustments, primarily because of actions taken by the major companies. Some changes were ini-

FIGURE 12.15 Charles Simon Favart in the role of a shepherd in a sentimental opéra-comique. From *Die Theater Wiens,* Vol. II, pt. 1 (1899).

tiated by the Comédie Italienne, which after Goldoni's retirement in 1773 had declined in popularity. Consequently, in 1780 it was reorganized once more and both its Italian plays and performers were dropped, thus severing its last connections with Italy. At this time, French comedies and *drames* were returned to the repertory. Since the boulevard theatres were not allowed to compete directly with the state companies, they had to adjust their offerings; the result was an increased emphasis on pantomime. Other changes were initiated by the Opéra. Seeking to solve its perennial financial problems, in 1784 it petitioned for and was granted authority over the minor companies. Those agreeing to pay a substantial yearly fee were permitted to continue performances, but those who defied the grant were expropriated or suppressed.

This situation continued up to the time of the Revolution. Then, in 1791 the National Assembly abolished all monopolies, thus freeing the theatres from former restraints. Although other restrictions were soon to be imposed, the act of 1791 marks the end of an era.

Throughout all the controversies of the eighteenth century, the Comédie Française maintained its monopoly on "regular" comedy and tragedy. Consequently, most of the major playwrights wrote for it, since only the lesser and "irregular" forms were permitted at the Comédie Italienne and the fairs. These restrictions often meant that a play refused by one company had to be rewritten to meet the genre restrictions placed on another troupe. The limited demand for new works sometimes led to the acceptance of plays years before they were produced. It is probably for this reason that in the late eighteenth century the Comédie Française was required to produce one new play or revival each month.

Of all the troupes, the Opéra enjoyed the greatest prestige. For this reason, it was allowed to exploit other companies. After 1714 it collected considerable revenue by licensing other theatres to use music, dance, or elaborate spectacle. After 1762, the Comédie Italienne paid

FIGURE 12.17 Various kinds of acrobatic entertainments used as incidental diversions at Nicolet's theatre on the Boulevard du Temple in the late eighteenth century. From Pougin, *Dictionnaire du Théâtre* (1885).

FIGURE 12.16 The Fair of St. Ovid, one of the lesser Parisian fairs. In the foreground are seen two booth theatres. On the right is Nicolet's booth. Note the balconies on which *parades* (brief skits used to entice customers inside) were performed. From Pougin, *Dictionnaire du Théâtre* (1885).

the Opéra from 20,000 to 54,000 francs yearly for the right to present musical plays, and after 1784 the boulevard theatres were subsidiaries of the Opéra.

The Comédie Française and the Comédie Italienne were organized as sharing companies. When the Comédie Italienne became a state troupe in 1723 it was placed under the supervision of the Gentlemen of the Chamber, who also oversaw the Comédie Française, and under regulations similar to those governing the older company. Ostensibly, all decisions were made at weekly meetings of the actors. After 1759, even the *pensionnaires* were included in deliberations. On the other hand, the Gentlemen of the Chamber had to ratify all decisions, including the choice of plays and actors, changes in financial procedures, and alterations in the theatre buildings. They sometimes ordered the admission of actors as *sociétaires* (even if this forced others to retire), redistributed shares, and interfered in other ways.

The Opéra was organized along entirely different lines. Although the crown provided a subsidy and laid down the rules under which it functioned, the management was farmed out to an enterpreneur. Because of its

FIGURE 12.18   Pen drawing by Boquet of costumes for a *pas de deux* at the Opéra, danced by M. Gardel as Hippomene and Mlle. Asselin as Atalanta, 1769. From Adolphe Jullien, *Histoire du Costume au Théâtre* (1880).

large expenses, the Opéra was always in financial difficulties, and by 1749 had accumulated a debt of more than one million francs. In that year, it was ceded to the City of Paris. Having failed to achieve a sound fiscal policy, the city also farmed out the management after 1757. By 1780 the situation was so chaotic that the crown resumed its control and placed a court official in charge. This arrangement continued until the Revolution. In spite of its abysmal financial and managerial record, the Opéra was the favored troupe with aristocratic audiences throughout the century. It presented the most spectacular productions in Paris, and after 1775 was considered the finest opera company in Europe. The fair and boulevard theatres were run entirely as private ventures. Each was operated by a manager, who assumed both risks and profits.

The troupes increased in size during the century. In 1713, the Opéra had 121 performers (singers, dancers, and musicians), but by 1778 it had grown to 228. By the 1770s, the Comédie Française included about 50 actors and the Comédie Italienne about 70. Although growth brought increased expenses, it was probably less responsible for the troupes' constant financial difficulties than were their strange fiscal policies. Both the Comédie

Française and the Comédie Italienne received subsidies (ranging from 12,000 to 15,000 francs), required each new *sociétaire* to invest from 8,000 to 15,000 francs in the company, and collected large sums in annual rentals for private boxes. Most of this money, however, was divided among the *sociétaires* rather than going into a common fund, with the result that the troupes were never able to meet unexpected expenses. Consequently, the Comédie Françasie owed 487,000 francs in 1757 and the Comédie Italienne 400,000 in 1762, even though *sociétaires* were sometimes receiving as much as 30,000 francs a year, as compared to a *pensionnaire's* salary of less than 2,000 francs. Thus, while the troupes in theory were sharing companies, they appear to have shared income more than expenses. Occasionally the crown made special grants or ordered economies to reduce indebtedness, but no effort was made to reform fiscal policies.

The dramatic troupes played daily. At first the season extended from November 2 until Easter, but after 1766 it ran from November 15 until May 15. In 1700, the curtain time was 5 P.M.; it later changed to 5:15 or 5:30. Each theatre was required to list its bill two weeks in advance. Normally a different play was offered each day, except when a popular new piece was produced. At the Opéra, performances were given only three days a week. Its season was divided into two parts: October to Lent, and Easter to mid-May. In 1700, performances began at 4, but after 1714 at 5:15. The Opéra ran each production as long as it drew an audience and sometimes performed no more than four or five works in a season.

The evening's bill was simpler than in a London theatre. The Comédie Française normally presented a long play and an afterpiece. After 1757, ballets were given as entr'actes. The Comédie Italienne often gave programs made up of several short pieces, and its bills were organized to reserve certain days of the week for each of the genres it was permitted to perform. In the 1740s it added a dance troupe, and after 1750 pantomimes and displays of fireworks became typical offerings. The Opéra normally presented one major work along with incidental ballets. After the 1770s, when Jean-Georges Noverre (1727–1810) became the ballet master, ballet increased in importance at the Opéra. Noverre began his career in 1743 in *opéra comique* and later worked in several major European cities. In 1760 he published his revolutionary work, *Letters on the Dance and Ballet*, which was instrumental in transforming ornamental and spectacular dances into story-telling works that were the forerunners of modern ballets. At the fair theatres, variety was the key, for there the carnival atmosphere predominated. Thus, the Parisian theatre included as wide a range of entertainment as did the English, although the restrictions on the French companies led to more specialization by each troupe.

THE DRAMATISTS

In the eighteenth century, the payment of authors was also regulated by the government. After a dramatic troupe's daily expenses and a poor tax (ranging from $\frac{1}{6}$ to $\frac{5}{18}$) had been deducted from receipts, the author was paid $\frac{1}{9}$ (after 1781, $\frac{1}{7}$) of the revenue for a long play and $\frac{1}{18}$ (after 1760, $\frac{1}{12}$) for a short play. This arrangement continued until the receipts fell below a prescribed amount, after which the dramatist received no further payment. Since the Opéra sought long runs, its scheme of payments differed. For long works, the librettist and composer each were paid 100 francs for the first ten performances and 50 francs for the next twenty; for short pieces, 60 francs for the first ten and 30 francs for the next twenty.

Although this scheme guaranteed the playwright an income for his work, the actors found ways of decreasing it. The most significant was the exclusion from their calculations of income from annual box rentals. Beaumarchais' objections to this practice led him in 1777 to found the Bureau Dramatique (the origin of France's present-day Society of Authors) to represent dramatists. Largely because of this organization's efforts, the National Assembly in 1791 passed the world's first law relating to royalty payments. It secured to authors and their heirs complete control over dramatic works until five years after the author's death and made it possible for the playwright to collect fees for each performance of his works.

ACTORS AND ACTING

The eighteenth century also brought the first successful attempt to establish an orderly system for training actors. Until the 1780s, most French actors received their training while playing utility roles in a provincial troupe. A few beginners were accepted into the Parisian companies after being coached by leading actors (who were paid 500 francs for each pupil taken into the company). These methods were eventually judged insufficient, however, and in 1786 the Royal Dramatic School, forerunner of the present Conservatoire, was founded as an adjunct to the Comédie Française.

Admission to a major Parisian troupe was difficult. An applicant had first to be approved by a committee of actors; he then played at least three roles in public performances; if deemed successful, he was accepted as a *pensionnaire* until a vacancy occurred among the *sociétaires*. By the late eighteenth century, a *pensionnaire* either had to be admitted as a *sociétaire* or released by the end of his second year with the troupe. This rule often led to reassignments of shares or forced retirements in order to make room among the *sociétaires* for desirable performers.

A young actor often began as understudy, or *double*, to a major performer. As in England, most casting was governed by "lines of business." The major lines in tragedy were kings, tyrants, lovers, princesses, mothers,

FIGURE 12.19 The actors of the Comédie Française, *c.* 1720. Note the *habit à la romaine* worn by the actor in the foreground. At right rear an actor is dressed as one of Molière's characters, some of whom continued to be costumed in seventeenth-century dress. Oil painting by Antoine Watteau (1684–1721). Courtesy Metropolitan Museum of Art, Jules S. Bache Collection, 1949.

and female lovers, while the major lines in comedy were old men, lovers, valets, peasants, old women, coquettes, and soubrettes. In addition, there were a number of secondary lines, and the bottom rank was made up of general utility players. Certain tragic and comic lines were usually filled by the same actors. For example, the *jeune premier* (or leading male performer) played the lover in both comedy and tragedy, while the actress who played princesses in tragedy normally assumed the roles of coquettes in comedy. As a rule, an actor remained in the same line of business throughout his career.

The eighteenth century produced many distinguished performers, most of them members of the Comédie Française. Between 1700 and 1720, a period noted for its formal and oratorical style, the major actors were Mlle. Desmares, Mlle. Duclos, and Beaubour. Charlotte Desmares (1682–1753) succeeded Mlle. Champmeslé, her aunt, as leading actress of the Comédie Française in 1698 and retained that position until she retired in 1721. Her principal rival was Mlle. Duclos (Marie-Anne de Chateauneuf, 1668–1748), Mlle. Champmeslé's understudy and pupil. After the vogue in acting style changed around 1720, she lost most of her following; by the time she retired in 1736, she was judged very old-fashioned. Pierre-Trochon de Beaubour (1662–1725) replaced Baron at the Comédie Française in 1691. His good looks and excellent declamation assured him the position of leading actor until he retired in 1718.

FIGURE 12.20 **Crowning a bust of Voltaire during a performance of his *Irène* at the Comédie Française in 1778. At this time the Comédie was performing at the Théâtre des Tuileries. From Pougin,** *Dictionnaire du Théâtre* **(1885).**

Around 1720, the performance style became more realistic, partially because of Michel Baron's return to the stage from 1720 to 1729. The trend toward realism was also strengthened by Adrienne Lecouvreur (1692–1730), who made her debut in 1717 and became the leading actress of the company after the retirement of Mlle. Desmares in 1721. She died suddenly in 1730 and was refused Christian burial, being interred in some unknown spot in the same year that Mrs. Oldfield was buried in Westminster Abbey. Aside from Baron, the leading actor of this period was Quinault-Dufresne (1693–1767), admitted to the Comédie Française in 1712 as understudy to Beaubour, whose roles he inherited in 1718 and retained until his retirement in 1741.

In the succeeding period, the leading performers were Mlle. LaGaussin, Grandval, and Mlle. Dangeville. Mlle. LaGaussin (Jeanne-Catherine Gaussens, 1711–1767), daughter of Baron's valet, was accepted into the Comédie Française in 1731 and was its leading actress until overshadowed by Mlles. Dumesnil and Clairon. Her ability to express tenderness and grief made her especially effective in "tearful comedy." Charles-François de Grandval (1710–1784) began in 1729 as understudy to Quinault-Dufresne, whose roles he inherited in 1741. He remained the company's leading actor until 1768. Marie-Anne-Botot Dangeville (1714–1796) was admitted to the Comédie Française in 1730 and was its principal comedienne until her retirement in 1763. Garrick thought her the finest actress on the French stage.

Perhaps the most famous players of the eighteenth century were Mlle. Dumesnil, Mlle. Clairon, and Lekain. Mlle. Dumesnil (Marie-Françoise Marchand, 1713–1803) began her acting career in the provinces around 1733. Accepted as an understudy at the Comédie Française in 1737, she became a *sociétaire* in 1738 and was soon the leading performer of such strong tragic roles as Clytemnestra and Medea. In his *Paradox of Acting*, Diderot depicts her as an erratic performer dependent on inspiration and thus sometimes magnificent and at others mediocre. She retired in 1776. Mlle. Clairon (Claire-Josèphe-Hippolyte Léris de la Tude, 1723–1803) began her career in 1736 at the Comédie Italienne and, after performing in the provinces and at the Opéra, was admitted to the Comédie Française in 1743 as understudy to Dumesnil. Diderot idealizes her as an artist conscious of every detail in performance. Voltaire and Garrick also considered her superior to Dumesnil. At first declamatory in style, Clairon was persuaded by the critic Marmontel in 1753 to assume a more conversational tone. This change made her question the old traditions of costuming and in 1755 she began to adopt more realistic and historically accurate stage dress. She retired in 1766 at the height of her career. Mlle. Clairon's reforms were supported by Henri-Louis Lekain (1729–1778), who was admitted to the Comédie Française in 1750 largely because of Voltaire's influence. He worked hard to overcome his vocal and physical shortcomings, but was not awarded a full share in the company until 1758. His talents were not fully recognized until after Grandval's retirement in 1768. Thereafter, Lekain was considered the greatest tragic actor of his age. Together he and Mlle. Clairon did much to bring greater realism to the acting of the time.

Lekain's principal successors were Larive and Molé. Larive (Jean Mauduit, 1747–1827) was appointed understudy to Lekain in 1775 and succeeded to many of his roles in 1778. But in spite of his handsomeness and fine voice, he never achieved Lekain's reputation. He retired in 1788. François-Rene Molé (1734–1802), after several years in the provinces, was admitted to the Comédie Française in 1760. Thereafter he was the leading player of young comic heroes and inherited as well several of Lekain's serious roles. He left the troupe in 1791.

The principal tragic actresses of the late eighteenth century were Mme. Vestris and Mlle. Raucourt. Mme. Vestris (Françoise-Marie-Rosette Gourgaud, 1743–1804), after studying with Lekain, was admitted to the company after the retirement of Clairon and Dumesnil. Mlle. Raucourt (1756–1815) made her debut in 1772 as understudy to Mme. Vestris. Dismissed in 1776 following a scandal, she was readmitted in 1779. She was excellent in stern tragic roles but lacking in tenderness.

The finest comic actor of the late eighteenth century was Préville (Pierre-Louis Dubus, 1721–1799), who played in the provinces before joining the Comédie Française in 1753. Préville revolutionized the playing of low comedy roles, which had previously been treated as fat and alcoholic bunglers. Préville, who was handsome, slender, and graceful, used these qualities in his carefully differentiated characterizations. He retired in 1786.

Although most of the famous actors were associated with the Comédie Française, a few achieved fame at the Comédie Italienne. Luigi Riccoboni, leader of the original troupe, was excellent as the "first lover," and Giovanna Benozzi, the second *amoureuse*, was the inspiration for many of Marivaux's heroines. Perhaps the most famous performer of the Comédie Italienne was Marie-Justine Favart (1727–1772), wife of Charles-

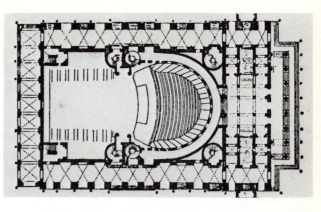

FIGURE 12.21 Plan of the theatre built for the Comédie Française in 1782. It later became the Odéon. Note the horseshoe-shaped auditorium; also the seated pit, an innovation in France. Note too that the stage is deeper than the auditorium. From Donnet and Kaufmann, *Architectonographie des Théâtres* (1836–1857).

Simon Favart. After playing at the fairs, she joined the Comédie Italienne in 1749 and continued there until 1771. A performer of great versatility, she was also a leader in costume reform. But the restriction of the Comédie Italienne to minor forms and the frequent reorganization of the company prevented the development of strong traditions and an outstanding ensemble.

With the coming of the Revolution, the French actor achieved full civil and religious rights. The National Assembly forbade discrimination against players, and though this act did not make performers socially acceptable universally, it removed the legal grounds which had encouraged prejudice in the past.

THEATRE ARCHITECTURE

The major theatre buildings of Paris remained virtually unchanged until after 1750, when interest in theatre architecture increased. Articles appeared in Diderot's *Encyclopédie,* and Dumont's *Comparison of the Most Beautiful Theatres of Italy and France* (1763) contrasted the outmoded French structures with their newer Italian counterparts. Perhaps as a result, the new buildings which replaced the old ones followed the Italian trends toward the ovoid auditorium and the enlarged stage.

FIGURE 12.22 The theatre designed by Victor Louis in the 1780s for the Opéra but never used by that company. When this engraving was made *c.* 1790 it was the home of the Variétés Amusantes. Note the emphasis on spectacle with the practicable suspended bridge. This theatre was the home of the Comédie Française throughout the nineteenth century. Courtesy Bibliothèque Nationale, Paris.

The first major change in the Parisian theatres came in 1763 when the Palais-Royal (home of the Opéra) burned. From 1763 until 1769, the opera company performed in the Théâtre des Tuileries, converted from the stage (an area 52 by 140 feet) of the disused Salle des Machines. With its three tiers of boxes, it recreated the principal features of the Palais-Royal. The Opéra's new theatre opened in 1769 and burned in 1781. The troupe then moved to the new Porte-Saint-Martin Theatre, where it remained until 1794.

The Comédie Française continued to use its converted tennis court until 1770. Alterations to it were minor. Several large boxes were divided into smaller ones that could be rented by the year; about 180 seats were installed at the front of the pit when spectators were banished from the stage in 1759, but at the same time, in order not to diminish the space allotted to standing spectators, the amphitheatre was reduced in size. In 1770 the troupe moved to the Théâtre des Tuileries recently vacated by the Opéra, until its new theatre, on the site of the present-day Odéon, was opened in 1782. The new building provided seats for all spectators and wholly abolished the standing pit for the first time in a Parisian theatre devoted to nonoperatic performances.

The auditorium was ovoid in shape and the stage much better equipped than that of its predecessor.

The Comédie Italienne played in the Hôtel de Bourgogne from 1716 until 1783, when this theatre, built in 1548, was abandoned. Changes in the Bourgogne during the eighteenth century paralleled those made at the Comédie Française. A number of large boxes were subdivided in 1760, and in 1765 benches were installed at the front of the pit to accommodate the spectators who were banished from the stage at that time. Perhaps out of a desire to compete with the Comédie Française, the Comédie Italienne moved into a new building in 1783. It, too, incorporated the latest Italian features, but it retained a "standing pit" sufficiently large to hold 650 spectators. In 1788, the attempt to furnish this area with benches was met with such opposition that the plan was abandoned. Not until the early nineteenth century was the seated pit fully accepted in Paris.

The boulevard theatres also began to acquire elaborate theatres in the late eighteenth century. The

FIGURE 12.23 A performance at the Hotel de Bourgogne in 1769, a time when the repertory of the Comédie Italienne was restricted to *opéra-comique* and Italian comedies. On stage is a scene from an *opéra-comique*. Note the footlights, prompter's box at front-center of stage, and the orchestra. Note also that most of the action is placed on the platform forward of the proscenium. There are a few benches at the front of the auditorium but the remainder of the spectators in the pit are standing. Drawing by P. A. Wille the Younger. Courtesy Bibliothèque Nationale, Paris.

Variétés Amusantes, designed by Victor Louis and originally intended for the Opéra, opened in 1785. At that time, it was probably the finest theatre in Paris and after 1799 was to be the home of the Comédie Française.

By the time the Revolution began, all the major theatres of Paris had been modernized. The changes appear to have been motivated by the desire to improve sightlines, to provide better facilities for spectacle, and to increase seating capacity.

SCENIC PRACTICES

Although as early as the 1730s Voltaire urged the use of more appropriate spectacle, little could be done to implement his suggestions in nonoperatic productions until 1759, when spectators were banished from the stage. Thus, until about 1760 the *palais à volonté* and the *chambre à quatre portes* continued to be the usual settings.

The removal of spectators from the stage was motivated primarily by the desire to use more elaborate settings. An important turning point in the attitude toward spectacle can be seen in the Comédie Française's productions of Voltaire's *The Orphan of China* (1755), which was billed as having new and accurate Oriental costumes and settings. During the 1750s the Comédie Italienne also began to introduce local color, and as soon as spectators were removed from the stage both companies markedly increased their use of spectacle. In 1760 Voltaire's *Tancrède* directed attention to the Middle Ages, and soon other plays were being set in such locales as Norway, Russia, Spain, America, and the Near East and in many different periods. Diderot's plea (made in the 1750s) for greater fidelity to everyday life was also met in a few plays, such as Voltaire's *The Scots Girl* (1760), set in the common room of an inn, and Beaumarchais' *Eugénie* (1767), which sought to reproduce a domestic background in all its details. In spite of these innovations, however, the majority of plays continued to be presented in stock scenery.

At the Opéra considerable emphasis was placed on spectacle throughout the century. After the retirement of Jean Bérain in 1721, the most important designer was Jean-Nicolas Servandoni (1695–1766), a Florentine who worked for the Opéra from about 1728 to 1746. His principal contributions to French design were the *scena*

FIGURE 12.24 The auditorium of the Comédie Française, 1726. Note the audience on stage peering through and around the curtain. Note also the standing pit. From Adolphe Jullien, *Les Spectateurs sur le Théâtre* **(1875).**

per angolo and monumentality in the manner of the Bibienas. Servandoni is also noted for his "mute spectacles," mounted in the Salle des Machines between 1738 and 1742 and again from 1754 to 1758. In these, he recreated faithfully a number of well-known places, and the naturalism of these actorless spectacles probably did much to motivate the other theatres of Paris to improve their settings.

Servandoni's successors at the Opéra changed so rapidly that none was able to establish a dominant style. Among the later designers the most important were François Boucher (1703–1770), who worked for a number of theatres after 1740 and who was noted for his idyllic landscapes; Louis-René Boquet (1717–1814), famous for ballet costumes as well as scenery in which Chinese decorative motifs were prominent; and Pietro Algieri, who designed settings from about 1748 to 1761 and turned attention away from the fantasies of Boucher and Boquet to more formal architectural settings. Many of the best-known French painters, such as Gillot, Saint-Aubin, Wailly, and Moreau the Younger, also designed settings. Nevertheless, scenic design in France seldom rose to the level achieved by the Italian designers of the

FIGURE 12.25 A stage setting by Jean-Nicolas Servandoni, who naturalized the *scena per angolo* in France. From Bapst, *Essai sur l'Histoire du Théâtre* (1893).

period. The frequent changes in management and the constant financial difficulties at the Opéra, the continued adherence to the neoclassical ideal, and the reticence of the actors to authorize large expenditures for scenery at the Comédie Française did much to keep scenic practices in old paths. Although new directions had been suggested before the Revolution, they had not yet been fully exploited.

COSTUME PRACTICES

Costume practices in France differed little from those of England. Most characters were dressed in contemporary garments and as sumptuously as the performers could afford. Ordinary fashionable garments were used in both comedy and tragedy until 1727, when Adrienne Lecouvreur adopted the much more elaborate court dress for tragedy. Her practice soon became standard for all tragic heroines. The actors also adopted court dress for tragedy except in classical roles, for which the *habit à la romaine* was retained, although it, too, grew more elaborate and conventionalized, as the plumed helmet was replaced by a three-cornered hat and the skirt of the tunic was hooped. The use of traditional costumes for a

few roles continued through the eighteenth century. Molière's ridiculous characters, such as Harpagon, Sganarelle, Scapin, and Gros-René, were most subject to this treatment, for all continued to be costumed in the style of the mid-seventeenth century when the plays were written.

As in England, costumes came from two sources: the company's wardrobe and the actor's privately owned garments. Each company owned an extensive wardrobe, but since it was reused constantly, the costumes were often threadbare. As a result, it was used primarily by the lesser performers. By 1730 the major actors were engaging in bitter competition to outdo each other in the lavishness of their stage dress. When Adrienne Lecouvreur died, her wardrobe was sold for 40,000 francs, and Mlle. Raucourt was given a wardrobe valued at 20,000 francs when she made her debut in 1772.

The ideal of lavishness began to be challenged in the 1750s. The first significant change came in 1753, when Mme. Favart wore an authentic peasant dress as the heroine of *The Loves of Bastien and Bastienne*. In 1761, she supposedly sent to Constantinople for an authentic dress to wear in *The Three Sultans*. The new trend came to the Comédie Française also in the 1750s, under the leadership of Mlle. Clairon and Lekain. For his *The Orphan of China* (1755), Voltaire asked the artist Joseph Vernet to design clothing which, though based on Chinese dress, would not provoke laughter. The results were more nearly Turkish than Chinese in appearance. The innovation was favorably received, nevertheless, and thereafter Clairon and Lekain sought to dress each role appropriately. In 1756, Lekain outraged audiences by appearing in *Sémiramis* with bare arms, disarrayed hair, and bloody hands. Voltaire disapproved of so much realism, calling it "too English." Voltaire's *Tancrède* (1760) introduced medieval costumes, and thereafter other periods and locales were occasionally represented in costumes. The increased concern for costume is seen at its peak perhaps with Beaumarchais, who described in detail the dress for each of his characters, even when the plays had contemporary settings.

None of these reforms had far-reaching effects. Many of the actors refused to accept the changes and others were inconsistent in their use of them. By 1790, the reforms had amounted to little more than the abandonment of hooped petticoats for classical figures and plumed headdresses for all characters, and the adoption of sixteenth-century garments for all historical periods other than classical or contemporary. Since, with rare exceptions, each actor chose his own costumes, inconsistencies abounded. The state of costuming is well illustrated in Levacher de Charnois' *Costumes et Annales des Grand Théâtres de Paris* (1786–1789), in which pictures of actors in their costumes are followed by historically accurate drawings of the same garments.

Nevertheless, the seeds of change had been planted. The conflict between the old outlook, in which art was expected to idealize, and the new, in which art was expected to copy life, had begun. As yet, neoclassicism still reigned, but its foundations had been undermined.

By 1790 France was involved in radical change of a more fundamental sort. In 1789 the country had been in such financial distress that Louis XVI had been forced to call a meeting of the States-General (the French national assembly) for the first time since 1614. When one group within the assembly demanded a constitution and basic social reforms, Louis attempted to disband the States-General, thereby precipitating the march on and fall of the Bastille, which initiated the French Revolution. Ultimately the conflict was over the divine right of kings versus equality among men. At stake was the class system that had existed since the Middle Ages. The new doctrine of equality and of government as a social contract had been forcefully stated by the American Declaration of Independence in 1776, but its impact was to be far more radical in France which was still governed by an absolute monarch. But the true revolution lay not so

FIGURE 12.27 Mme. Favart in the costume she supposedly imported from Constantinople to insure authenticity of dress in *The Three Sultans,* 1761. From *Costumes et Annales des Grand Théâtres de Paris* (1786–1789).

much in the violent events of the 1790s as in the ideas about social organization and human rights, for they give the common man a new vision of himself and his worth.

FIGURE 12.26 Lekain and Dusmesnil in Voltaire's *Sémiramis.* Although this play is set in ancient Assyria, Mlle. Dusmesnil wears an elaborate court dress of the eighteenth century and Lekain a formalized costume similar to that used for classical heroes. An English print of 1772.

SPANISH THEATRE, 1700–1800

Following the War of Spanish Succession (1701–1713), Spain rapidly became a backwater of European politics, living on its past glories. It was much the same in drama, for from the death of Calderón in 1681 until well into the eighteenth century, writers sought unsuccessfully to recapture the glory of the Golden Age, and theatres drew their repertories primarily from the past. During the eighteenth century, many attempts were made to turn attention to the neoclassical ideal. Under Philip V (reigned 1700–1746), Louis XIV's grandson, who had been the cause of the war, a Spanish Academy was formed, and Ignacio de Luzán (1702–1754) sought through his critical treatises to familiarize his countrymen with neoclassical principles. Despite these efforts, no playwright adopted the new mode until after 1750.

FIGURE 12.28 Mlle. Clairon's costume for *The Orphan of China* (1755). Although it marked a change to more accurate costuming, it fell considerably short of authenticity. From a contemporary print.

Under Carlos III (reigned 1759–1788), *autos sacramentales* were abandoned in 1765 and the public theatres were forbidden to perform religious plays. By the end of his reign, the popularity of seventeenth-century plays was at last being challenged by neoclassical dramas. Most of the new works were translations, but native tragedy was accepted after the appearance of Vincente García de la Huerta's *La Raquel* (1778) and Lopez de Ayala's *Destruction of Numancia* (1778), while neoclassical comedy was established by Tomás de Iriarte's *The Pampered Youth* (1788) and *The Ill-Bred Miss* (1791).

By far the most important dramatist of the eighteenth century was Leandro Fernández de Moratín (1760–1828). Son of a writer, he spent some time in Paris in the 1780s before writing his own plays between 1786 and 1805. Moratín's acknowledged masterpiece is *The Consent of Young Maidens* (1805), which tells of the rivalry between an uncle and nephew for the hand of

a young girl. Unlike most plays on this theme, Moratín's concentrates upon character rather than intrigue; all of the complications stem from the inability of the young people to be frank with their elders. Because of its truthful observation and sincerity, *The Consent of Young Maidens* is considered the best Spanish play between 1680 and modern times.

If Moratín was the finest playwright of his age, Ramón de la Cruz (1731–1794) was the most popular. Originally a writer of comedies, in 1764 he turned to the *zarzuela,* which he transformed by banishing the mythological figures and replacing them with contemporary character types. In this form, the *zarzuela* has continued to be one of the most popular Spanish dramatic genres. Cruz also achieved renown for his *sainetes,* or one-act farces performed between the acts of longer works.

Theatrical conditions changed little during the eighteenth century. In Madrid, the Corral de la Cruz and the Corral del Príncipe continued to be the only public

FIGURE 12.29 The final scene from Moratín's *The Consent of Young Maidens.* From the original edition of the play.

theatres performing Spanish drama. In the 1740s the original structures were replaced (the Teatro de la Cruz in 1743 and the Teatro del Príncipe in 1745), but the only important change was the addition of a proscenium arch. Moratín states that the scenic practices and other customs continued to resemble those of the Golden Age.

A third theatre, the Caños del Peral, was built by an Italian troupe in 1708. After 1715, it was used entirely for opera, then in great favor with the court and aristocracy. Farinelli (Carlo Broschi, 1705–1782), the greatest opera singer of his age, came to Spain in 1737 and staged lavish operas at the Buen Retiro palace between 1747 and 1759.

During the last part of the eighteenth century many attempts were made to reform the public theatres, but almost nothing was accomplished until Isodoro Maiquez (1768–1820) came to the fore. Son of an actor, Maiquez made his debut at the Teatro del Príncipe in 1791 after playing in the provinces. Before 1800 he was the leading performer of Madrid. He then went to Paris, where he is said to have studied Talma's techniques and to have brought them back to Spain. Thereafter he did much to discourage the old declamatory style and to promote more natural delivery. Unfortunately he had no strong successors and it was still to be many years before the Spanish stage underwent lasting reforms.

LOOKING AT THEATRE HISTORY

It is often helpful to think of the theatre not merely as an autonomous art but as one among several related arts. Familiarity with the painting, music, and literature of a period can clarify much about the theatre of the age, especially its stylistic qualities and conventions. Thus, the more fully one knows the other arts, the more insights one gains into the theatre. This is true in part because the arts of an age are usually based on shared theoretical foundations. For example, Arnold Hauser in *The Social History of Art* argues that all baroque art has common characteristics that grow out of an uneasy world view brought about by Copernicus's discovery that the earth (and therefore man) is not the center of the universe. "The whole of the art of the baroque is full of this shudder. . . . The impetuous diagonals, the sudden foreshortenings, the exaggerated light and shade effects, everything is the expression of an overwhelming unquenchable yearning for infinity."

A. Hyatt Mayor theorizes that stage design offered an ideal outlet for the baroque imagination, whose conceptions were so grandiose that few of its architectural fancies could be realized in stone. "The wise heads of the time must have seen that the new visions of space and grandeur . . . remained uninhabitable dream palaces. . . . the Bibienas, in designs as arbitrary as the mandate of the autocrats they served, summed up the great emotional architecture of the baroque." (*The Bibiena Family*, pp. 27–28.)

As a branch of theatre, opera is especially im-

portant in the study of scenic design and theatre architecture. In fact, the majority of extant pictorial evidence about scenery between the Renaissance and the nineteenth century is from opera, which means that studies of scenic design emphasize musical more than nonmusical production. This is especially true of the eighteenth century, during which the Bibiena family dominated operatic design. In 1785, Stefano Arteaga wrote of Ferdinando Bibiena's contributions:

The art of making tiny space seem vast, the ease and speed of changing sets in a twinkling of an eye, . . . and above all buildings seen at an angle brought the science of illusion to the highest possible pitch. . . . the change from perspectives that limit sight and imagination by running to a central vanishing point was like opening a new world to busy the imagination. . . . and could represent and ennoble the real things of this world. . . .

> From A. HYATT MAYOR, *The Bibiena Family* (New York: H. Bittner and Co., 1945), p. 24.

Just as Italy was the traditional home of opera, so too it was of *commedia dell'arte*. But before the middle of the eighteenth century the *commedia* was beginning to be repetitious and out of tune with the sentimental tastes of the age. In his *Memoirs*, Goldoni tells of his attempts to reform it:

The mask must always be very prejudicial to the action

of the performer . . . and however he may gesticulate and vary the tone, he can never convey by the countenance . . . the different passions. . . . [For this and other reasons, I attempted] the reform of the Italian Theatre, and to supply the place of farces with comedies. . . . I undertook to produce a few pieces merely sketched, without ceasing to give comedies of character. I employed the masks [in some] and I displayed a more noble and interesting comic humor in the others. . . . with time and patience I brought about a reconciliation [of the two]; and I had the satisfaction, at length, to see . . . my own taste [become] in a few years the most general and prevailing in Italy.

> CARLO GOLDONI, *Memoirs*, trans.
> John Black (London, 1814), II,
> pp. 56–57

In France, as elsewhere in Europe, sentimentalism became a dominant strain in drama during the eighteenth century. Its foundation in the belief in man's goodness is clearly demonstrated in this passage by Denis Diderot:

[Human nature] is very good. . . . everything in nature is good. . . . It is our misguided conventions that distort and cramp man. . . . [Our responses to the theatre] depend upon the degree to which our hearts are open to it.

Diderot did not find the two forms of drama sanctioned by neoclassicism sufficient and he proposed two "middle genres" to enlarge the range to four types:

laughing comedy, whose purpose is to ridicule vice; serious comedy, whose function is to depict virtue and duty; the kind of tragedy that is concerned with domestic troubles; and finally, the kind of tragedy that deals with public catastrophes and the misfortunes of the mighty.

In addition, Diderot wished to reform theatrical production to make it as illusionistic as possible and he became the first to propose the "fourth wall" conception of the stage:

Regardless of whether you are writing or acting, think no more about the audience than if it did not exist. Imagine a wall across the front of the stage, dividing you from the audience, and act precisely as if the curtain had not risen.

> DENIS DIDEROT, *On Dramatic Poetry*
> (1758).

During the early eighteenth century in France monopolies on stage production—the Comédie Française's on comedy and tragedy, and the Opéra's on musical drama and spectacle—drove other would-be producers to strange expedients in their attempts to circumvent the law. Here is a police report on a performance at a Parisian fair in 1711, when such entertainers were forbidden to use dialogue:

We . . . noted that there is a stage elevated about four or five feet, with chandeliers above and an orchestra below the said stage, in which there were seven or eight . . . instruments. . . . that upon the said stage came actors and actresses dressed either in French garments or as Harlequin or Pierrot or other disguises; that they performed silent scenes on different subjects with placards which were held by two small boys suspended in the air, who were raised and lowered by means of ropes and machines; that the said placards contained songs which were sung by several persons in the audience as soon as they were given the tune by the violin; which songs, written on both sides of each placard, served as a rule as responses one to another and thus gave an explanation of the silent scenes.

> Reprinted in EMILE COMPARDON,
> *Les Spectacles de la Foire* (Paris,
> 1877), I, p. 91.

In France in the 1750s reforms began to be made in acting and costume to achieve greater naturalness. Here is a brief comment by Marmontel on one of the first attempts:

I went to see [Mlle. Clairon] in her dressing room, and, for the first time, I found her dressed in the habit of a sultana; without hoop, her arms half-naked, and in the truth of Oriental costume. . . . The event surpassed her expectation and mine. It was no longer the actress, it was Roxane herself . . . . The astonishment, the illusion, the enchantment, was extreme. . . . [The audience] had heard nothing like it. I saw her after the play . . . . "Don't you see that it ruins me? In all my characters, the costume must now be observed; the truth of declamation requires that of dress; all my rich stage-wardrobe is from this moment rejected. . . ."

> JEAN FRANCOIS MARMONTEL, *Memoirs*
> (London, 1805), pp. 44–45.

13

Theatre in Northern and Eastern Europe During the Eighteenth Century

Although by 1700 the professional theatre was firmly established in England, France, Italy, and Spain, it had scarcely begun in Northern and Eastern Europe. The slowness of Northern Europe to develop a professional theatre can be attributed in large part to unsettled religious and political conditions dating back to the early sixteenth century. The conflict between Protestants and Catholics at that time had led to the Treaty of Augsburg in 1555, but the results were never wholly satisfactory and in 1618 open warfare broke out again. Usually called the Thirty Years War, this conflict was to continue until 1648. By 1635 it had become more political than religious, and France, under Cardinal Richelieu's guidance, actively aided the Protestant faction out of a desire to curb the power of Austria. By the time the Peace of Westphalia was concluded in 1648 the population and resources of Germanic territories had been so seriously depleted that it would take almost 150 years for full recovery. In addition, the area was divided into more than 300 independent units, some large but others only a few square miles in size. Under these political, economic, and religious conditions, an adequate professional theatre could come into existence only gradually. In this struggle for survival, professional troupes received little encouragement, since the policies of both court and church discouraged rather than assisted the spoken drama.

THE COURT THEATRES OF GERMANY

France's decisive role in negotiating an end to the Thirty Years War gave it considerable prestige throughout Germany, where soon every ruler was seeking to create his own version of the French court. As a result, opera, ballet, and theatrical spectacles of all sorts became a regular part of court life. The more affluent rulers imported Italian and French designers, musicians, and singers, but the less prosperous had to rely on native Germans to copy the foreign models.

Austria set the pattern when in 1652 the emperor imported Ludovico Burnacini from Venice to stage court entertainments. At Vienna an elaborate court theatre was opened in 1668 and to serve it the most famous composers and librettists of the age were brought from Italy. As a result, Vienna was to be the most important center for operatic production in Europe from about 1660 to 1740.

Other German rulers followed the Austrian example. At Munich, Francesco Santurini, one of Italy's most outstanding designers, opened a court theatre in 1654 and thereafter mounted numerous lavish spectacles. An opera house was built in Dresden sometime between 1664 and 1667 and another in Gotha about 1683. By the end of the seventeenth century, opera and

FIGURE 13.1 The opera house at Vienna designed
by Lodovico Burnacini. On stage is seen part of
The Golden Apple. On the dais are the Emperor
Leopold I and his retinue. Engraving by Franz
Geffels, 1668. Courtesy Bildarchiv, Osterreichische
Nationalbibliothek, Vienna.

portment. Many plays were presented in Latin, others in
the vernacular.

The school drama reached its peak in the Catholic
schools run by the Jesuits. The Society of Jesus, an outgrowth of the Counterreformation, was founded in 1534
(given papal sanction in 1540) to combat heresy and to
strengthen the authority of the church. It viewed education as a primary tool whereby to influence those most
likely to become the future leaders of church and state.
By 1600 it had established 200 schools, universities, and

FIGURE 13.2 Map of Germany. This map shows
the present-day divisions, but it is helpful for locating the numerous cities that have figured prominently in German theatre history since the eighteenth
century. Courtesy *World Book Encyclopedia.*

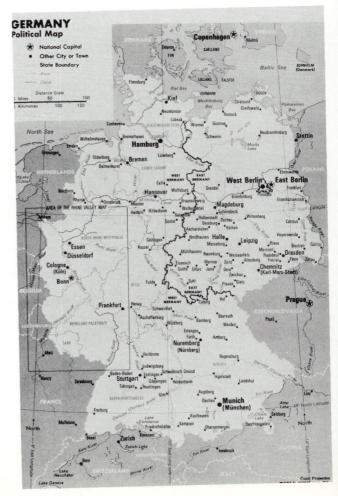

Italianate scenery were to be seen at practically every
court in Germany. Although rulers occasionally witnessed spoken drama, they confined their financial support for the most part to opera, ballet, and foreign
troupes.

Considering its favored position with the ruling
class, it is not surprising that opera also became the most
admired form with the prosperous middle class. Before
the end of the seventeenth century, some of the populous commercial centers had been able to establish
public opera houses. Hamburg had a company from
1678 until 1738 and Leipzig from 1693 until 1720,
although both performed only sporadically. Nevertheless, with both the aristocracy and the bourgeoisie opera
was the favorite form until well after 1750 and spoken
drama only gradually won their support.

THE JESUIT THEATRE

In the seventeenth century, numerous German schools,
both Protestant and Catholic, presented plays, since
drama was thought effective not only for teaching doctrine but also for providing training in speaking and de-

FIGURE 13.3   Costume designs by Burnacini. From Alexander von Weilen, *Die Theater Wiens*, Vol. II, pt. 1 (1899).

seminaries, and by 1706 the number had increased to 769. In some parts of Europe, it achieved a virtual monopoly over education. It was especially successful in France, Austria, and southern Germany.

With the Jesuits the educational theatre reached its highest peak prior to modern times. The first recorded Jesuit production occurred in 1551, but soon almost every Jesuit school was performing at least one play a year and often more. Students made up the casts; often the plays were written by professors of rhetoric; and the audiences were composed of members of the courts, municipal authorities, church dignitaries, parents, and others.

At first the plays were presented in Latin and kept by piety within narrow confines, but gradually the vernacular, low comedy, music, and ballet crept in. Furthermore, the Terence stage, used in the beginning, gave way in the seventeenth century to well-equipped proscenium theatres, complete with perspective scenery, machinery, and special effects. Out of the Jesuit schools came many of the most important works on theatrical practice published in the seventeenth and eighteenth centuries, among them Dubreuil's *Treatise on Perspective* (1649), Pozzo's *Pictorial and Architectural Perspective*

(1693–1700), and Lang's *Dissertation on Stage Acting* (1727). The height of the Jesuit theatre was reached during the seventeenth century. By the eighteenth century a decline in vigor was apparent and the order had begun to make powerful enemies because of its political intrigues and attempts to gain a monopoly on education. As a result, in 1773 it was suppressed. Although later revived, it never regained its former power.

In the seventeenth and eighteenth centuries, the Jesuit theatre could be found wherever the order established schools, but it was especially highly developed in Austria and southern Germany, where it gave the most elaborate productions to be seen in those areas outside the courts. There through such plays as Jakob Bidermann's *Cenodoxus* (1602), Jakob Balde's *Jephtias* (1637) and Jakob Masen's *Androphilus* (1647), it sought to teach piety and contempt for worldly pursuits.

The Jesuit theatre probably reached its peak in Vienna with Nikolaus of Avancini's *Pietas Victrix* (1659), presented before Leopold I, whom it glorified by associating him with the subject of the play, the victory of the Christian Emperor Constantine over the pagan Emperor Maxentius. This production included battles on land and sea, visions, angels and spirits of

FIGURE 13.4 Design by Francesco Santurini for *Antiopa Justificata* as presented in Munich, 1662. Courtesy Theatermuseum, Munich.

hell, and the eventual enthronement of Constantine as an angel hovered overhead on a cloud. On the frame of the proscenium the Hapsburg emblem was prominently displayed, thus making it clear that the Austrian Empire rested on Constantine's victory for the Christian faith. *Pietas Victrix* was staged with money provided by the court and was designed by Giovanni Burnacini, the court architect and one of the leading scenic designers of Europe.

Despite their theatrical sophistication, the Jesuits did not encourage the professional theatre, which, in their view, all too often led the faithful astray. Consequently, they contributed little to its development. In fact, by setting high standards in production and by raising expectations of a high moral tone, they probably did much to deter attendance at performances by German professional troupes, who until well into the eighteenth century fell far short of the standards set by the Jesuit theatres.

THE EARLY PUBLIC THEATRE IN GERMANY

If the Jesuit and court theatres prospered after 1650, the same cannot be said for the troupes of professional actors, who had to depend primarily upon unsophisticated playgoers for their support. This had not always been true, for prior to 1650 some companies had been patron-

ized by rulers. These early troupes were English in origin, and consequently the German professional theatre can be said to descend from those Elizabethan actors who began to tour widely on the continent around 1586. Among these early companies the most important were those of Robert Browne (from about 1590 to 1606), John Spencer (from 1605 to 1623), and John Green (from 1606 to 1628). These troupes often moved from one German court to another, taking with them letters of recommendation. Some enjoyed considerable reputation with the ruling classes. Since they traveled widely and played wherever they could, they also were popular with the common people. Until after 1650, the designation of a company as "English" was synonymous with high quality.

Still, the lot of these troupes was not always easy. To attract a German-speaking audience, the English-speaking actors had to adapt their plays (most of them drawn from the London public theatres) by simplifying plots and by adding low comedy elements, pantomime, music, song, and dance. Perhaps because he depended little on language, the clown became a special favorite with audiences, and English actors developed such stock comic fools as John Posset, Stockfish, and Pickelherring.

FIGURE 13.5 Scene from Nikolaus of Avancini's *Pietas Victrix,* a Jesuit play performed before the emperor of Austria in 1659. The setting is by Giovanni Burnacini. From *Die Theater Wiens* (1899).

FIGURE 13.6 Strolling players performing on the Anger in Munich in the eighteenth century. A painting by Joseph Stephan, *c.* 1770. Courtesy Theatermuseum, Munich.

In seeking to increase their appeal, the English actors also soon added German phrases, speeches, and entire scenes, and by 1626 had begun to include German actors in their troupes. By 1650 a few companies were composed entirely of Germans. The last important English group was that headed by George Jolly, who performed in Germany during the 1650s when the English theatre was closed. By 1680 virtually all English actors had disappeared from the continent.

The first outstanding German troupe was that managed by Carl Andreas Paulsen from 1650 to 1687. More significant was that of Johannes Velten (1640–1695), a well-educated man who sought to raise the level of the German theatre by adapting the plays of Corneille, Molière, and others for his company. He could accomplish little, however, under the existing theatrical conditions. Since there were no cities of any size, troupes were forced to travel constantly in search of new audiences. They competed vigorously for the right to perform at fairs held annually in the major towns, since it was here that the largest crowds assembled. But wherever they played, they were required to contribute up to one-fourth of their receipts to local charities. Since there were no permanent theatres, the actors set up their stages in town squares, riding schools, inns, fencing grounds, rooms above markets, and tennis courts. They had to change their bills daily and replenish their repertories often in order to attract the small potential audience. (Velten's troupe usually had eighty-five to ninety plays in its repertory.)

At the end of the seventeenth century, a program was made up of a long play and an afterpiece, both of which might include such incidental entertainment as songs, dances, and acrobatic feats. The main offering, called the *Hauptaktion* (chief play) or *Haupt-und-Staatsaktion* (chief and state play), might be either serious or comic. The afterpiece, or *Nachspiel*, was usually a farce. It is unclear who wrote these plays. Most of the long works were hodgepodges of serious and comic scenes, of bombast and violence, villainous machinations and fortunate escapes. No matter how serious the play, the clown was usually the central figure.

By 1707 all of the earlier clowns had coalesced in the character Hanswurst. Given his distinctive traits by Joseph Anton Stranitzky (1676–1726), Hanswurst was compounded of many elements: Harlequin, familiar to German audiences because of the tours of *commedia dell'arte* troupes; the medieval fool; and the various

FIGURE 13.7 Stranitzky (in the foreground) as Hanswurst. From *Die Theater Wiens* (1899).

clowns introduced by English actors. Stranitzky's Hanswurst was a jolly, beer-drinking peasant with a Bavarian accent. His costume consisted of a green pointed hat, red jacket, long yellow trousers, and white neck ruff. Although Hanswurst's attributes and dress varied from one part of Germany to another, the broad outlines of the characterization established by Stranitzky were retained.

Stranitzky worked primarily in Vienna, where he virtually created the public theatre. Until his death he was the mainstay of the Karntnertor, Vienna's first permanent public theatre, built by the town council in 1708. Here Stranitzky established such a vigorous tradition of improvisation that regular drama made little headway until after 1750.

In the early eighteenth century, then, several factors contributed to the theatre's low state: a repertory designed to attract an unsophisticated audience; the uneducated actors, who were little better than sideshow performers; and conditions which made it impossible

to rehearse and mount plays with care. Under the circumstances, it is not surprising that aristocrats and churchmen held the professional theatre in contempt.

THE REFORMS OF GOTTSCHED AND NEUBER

The first significant steps toward reform were taken in the 1720s by Johann Christoph Gottsched (1700–1766), who, after being educated at the University of Königsberg, rapidly became the intellectual leader of Germany. The development of German as a medium for literary expression ranked high among his many interests, for Latin was still the language of the universities (the first lecture in the vernacular had not been given until 1687), while French was favored by the aristocracy. Above all, Gottsched was interested in raising the intellectual level and refining the artistic taste of Germans, not only of the educated and aristocratic but also of the common man. The theatre attracted him because he saw in it a means of reaching the masses who could not read.

Gottsched was not the first well-educated German dramatist, for the schools had produced many. A few of their plays, among them some by Andreas Gryphius (1616–1664) and Daniel Caspar von Lohenstein (1635–1683), had been performed by professional troupes. But these earlier writers had no close connections with professional actors and many would have thought it immoral to do so. Gottsched, on the other hand, actively sought liaisons with those professional companies that came to play in Leipzig, where he lived. His overtures were unsuccessful until 1727, when he met the Neubers.

The daughter of a lawyer and government official, Carolina Neuber (1697–1760) had run away from home in 1717 with Johann Neuber, whom she married in 1718 after joining an acting troupe. For a time they were members of the troupe headed by Johann Caspar Haacke and Karl Ludwig Hoffman, but they formed their own company in 1727. They also acquired the title, "Royal Polish and Electoral Saxon Court Comedians," which brought with it the right to play during the annual fair at Leipzig, then the intellectual capital of Germany and Gottsched's home.

In 1727, the Neubers and Gottsched agreed to work together toward the reform of the theatre. This liaison, which was to last until 1739, is significant as the first alliance between a leading literary figure and

FIGURE 13.8 Gottsched's pastoral drama, *Atalanta, or The Disdainful One Defeated by Disdain.* Frontispiece to a printed edition of the play. From *Die Theater Wiens,* Vol. II, pt. 1 (1899).

careful rehearsals and the abandonment of improvisation; she assigned each actor additional duties, such as painting scenery, making handbills, or sewing costumes; she policed the performers' personal lives in an attempt to overcome moral prejudices against actors. She was doomed to disappointment, however, for it was impossible to attract a new kind of spectator rapidly enough to replace those alienated by the new drama. In order to survive, she was forced to compromise, much to the impatience of Gottsched. In 1735, more than half of her afterpieces still included Hanswurst and, although in 1737 she banished him from the stage in a short play of her own composition, by 1738 he had crept back into many of her productions under another name and in different garb. Furthermore, the company still had to tour, for Gottsched's followers were too few to support a year-round theatre in Leipzig, and elsewhere enthusiasm for the reforms was not yet strong. Her problems are illustrated by an eight-month season in Hamburg, second only to Leipzig as a cultural center, where in 1735, her 203 performances included 75 full-length and 93 one-act plays. Considering the problems of maintaining such a large repertory, it is not surprising that her performances did not always achieve the polish she so optimistically promised.

Although Frau Neuber attracted some powerful supporters, notably the ruler of Schleswig-Holstein, she did not succeed as she had hoped, and after 1735 began to rebuke audiences publicly for their lack of taste. She alienated many of her supporters in Hamburg and

FIGURE 13.9 A company believed to be that of Carolina Neuber in Nuremberg, *c.* 1730. Note the heroic figures at center flanked on either side by clownish figures. Courtesy Theatermuseum, Munich.

a professional acting company in Germany. Unfortunately, it was easier to formulate high ideals than to achieve them. First, a completely new repertory had to be obtained, for Gottsched wished to eliminate *Haupt-und-Staatsaktion* plays, improvisation, burlesque afterpieces, and Hanswurst. Gottsched and his circle set out to supply the new works, principally by translating or imitating French neoclassical plays, which to them represented the ideal form of drama. The most famous of the new works was Gottsched's *The Dying Cato* (1731), reprinted ten times before 1756; adaptations of plays by Destouches, LaChaussée, Voltaire, and others also came to be performed regularly.

As her contribution, Frau Neuber sought to raise the level of theatrical performances. She insisted upon

Leipzig, and in 1739 broke with Gottsched. Thereafter, her career declined. In 1740 she went to St. Petersburg, but the death of the Empress Anna six months after her arrival led to the closure of her theatre. Returning to Leipzig in 1741, she found Schönemann, one of her former actors, established in her theatre. There followed a pitched battle, in the course of which Neuber satirized Gottsched and his ideas. Although her attack signaled the end of Gottsched's leadership, it did not aid her. She remained in Leipzig for a few years, then moved on to Vienna and elsewhere until her death in 1760.

Although Gottsched and Neuber were not always successful, neither were they failures. By the 1740s regular drama was being performed by all companies, much of it taken directly from the six volumes of plays published by Gottsched between 1740 and 1745 under the title, *The German Stage*. Furthermore, Neuber's production techniques were being adopted by other troupes. Thus, though Gottsched and Neuber were often ridiculed by later dramatists and actors, they made the future gains possible.

ACTING TROUPES, 1740–1770

Between 1740 and 1770, Neuber's principles were perpetuated and extended by a number of troupes. The earliest of these was formed in 1740 by Johann Friederich Schönemann (1704–1782), who had entered the Neuber troupe in 1730. Originally a clown, Schönemann played comic valets in Neuber's company. When he formed his own group, he borrowed Frau Neuber's methods and repertory. The vitality and refinement of his young and relatively well-educated actors attracted much support in Leipzig and three of the performers—Sophie Schröder, Konrad Ackermann, and Konrad Ekhof—were to become famous. Sophie Schröder (1714–1792), a well-educated woman in need of employment after leaving her husband, was persuaded by Ekhof to take up acting. Although she had no theatrical experience, she immediately became the leading actress of the Schönemann company. Her career is thereafter inextricably tied to that of Konrad Ackermann (1710–1771), whom she was to marry in 1749. Although he did not begin acting until he was almost thirty years old, Ackermann achieved success quickly, perhaps because his family background and fine education encouraged in him that stately presence for which he was noted. If Frau Schröder and Ackermann

prospered immediately, the same cannot be said for Konrad Ekhof (1720–1778), who, short and homely, had to work hard to win acceptance. Frau Schröder and Ackermann left Schönemann after one season, but Ekhof remained with him for seventeen years. By 1752, he was the company's leading man. He was also the first important theorist of the German stage, and in 1753 sought to establish a school in Schwerin to train actors. Although he was able to institute his plan (which he described in twenty-four articles), classes were soon abandoned because of the indifference and mockery of fellow actors.

After Schönemann's troupe was given the title "Court Comedians to the Duke of Schwerin" in 1751, it divided its time between Schwerin and Hamburg. This comparative stability, however, encouraged Schönemann to pursue his mania for horsetrading, with the result that the company declined. In 1757, after Ekhof had resigned in protest, the company collapsed and Schönemann retired. Ekhof was induced to return, but having little interest in management, he requested Heinrich Koch to take charge. New friction caused Ekhof to join Ackermann's troupe in 1764.

Heinrich Koch (1703–1775) entered Neuber's company in 1728 and remained with her until she left Leipzig in 1749. Obtaining her former license, he toured in that area until he joined the Schönemann troupe in 1758. Between 1758 and 1763, Koch succeeded in playing most of each year in one city, Hamburg, a feat not yet accomplished by any troupe. In 1766, following the Seven Years War, he returned to Leipzig, where he built that city's first permanent theatre. (In spite of the city's importance as the cultural center of Germany, all previous theatres had been temporary.) Koch played at the court theatre in Weimar from 1768 to 1771 and in Berlin from 1771 until his death in 1775. He was probably the first German manager fully to achieve Neuber's ideals. Paying careful attention both to staging and to public taste, he was eventually able to abandon touring and establish a company in one location.

The third major company was that of Konrad Ackermann. With Sophie Schröder, he worked in a number of companies, touring as far afield as Russia, before establishing a more stable organization in 1753. In 1755, he built a permanent theatre in Königsberg (in East Prussia, now a part of Russia), perhaps the first in Germany intended for sole use by a dramatic company. Unfortunately, in 1756 the Seven Years War (in which Prussia and Austria fought for supremacy between 1756 and 1763, with Prussia emerging as leader of the German

FIGURE 13.10 Exterior view of the building, constructed by Konrad Ackermann in 1765, that served as the home of the Hamburg National Theatre from 1767 to 1769. A nineteenth-century print.

a businessman and friend of Sophie Hensel, the business manager. The actors, with a few exceptions, were drawn from Ackermann's company. G. E. Lessing, by this time considered Germany's finest playwright, was induced to become resident critic and advisor to the company and to edit a theatrical journal designed to create interest in the repertory and to educate the public.

The Hamburg National Theatre was opened with high hopes in April 1767. Lowen soon lost authority over the actors, however, and only Ekhof could maintain some discipline. Furthermore, in spite of the stated goal of presenting drama of higher quality than had previously been seen, the theatre was forced to add variety acts to keep up attendance. The venture came to an inglorious end in 1769. The only lasting achievement of the Hamburg National Theatre was Lessing's theatrical journal, *Hamburg Dramaturgy,* now considered one of the major critical works of the eighteenth century. Although it accomplished little, the Hamburg National Theatre remains a landmark as the first German attempt to establish a theatre on noncommercial lines. While it was not truly a "national" theatre, it popularized the notion that Germany needed such theatres and paved the way for those which were soon to appear.

states) forced Ackermann to flee to the West, where he played in Switzerland, Alsace, and elsewhere before coming to Hamburg in 1764. In this year, Ekhof joined the company. Because of the Ackermanns, Ekhof, Sophie Hensel (1738–1789), and young Friedrich Schröder, the troupe was probably the finest in Germany at this time. In 1765 Ackermann built Hamburg's first permanent theatre. Unfortunately, rivalries within the company led to friction. It was probably for this reason that Ackermann agreed to give up his company and rent his theatre to the newly created Hamburg National Theatre.

The Hamburg National Theatre grew out of ideas set forth by Johann Friedrich Löwen, Schönemann's son-in-law, in a pamphlet on the state of the German theatre. He blamed the low repute of the theatre on uncultivated managers and actors, the profit motive, the lack of state support, the necessity of touring, and the shortage of German dramatists. To remedy the situation, he proposed the establishment of a permanent, subsidized, nonprofit theatre, run by a salaried manager; he advocated establishing an academy to train actors, high salaries and a pension system to attract the best performers, and prizes to encourage dramatists. Löwen persuaded twelve businessmen to back his venture; he was to be the artistic director and Abel Seyler (1730–1801),

GERMAN DRAMA, 1740–1787

By the 1740s, Gottsched and his circle had laid the foundations for a new repertory but had provided no plays of lasting value. As their influence waned, a new group of dramatists appeared. Among the most important of these were Johann Elias Schlegel (1719–1749), who wrote a number of comedies and tragedies, of which the best is *Hermann* (1743), a tragedy based on early German history, and C. F. Gellert (1715–1769), who championed tearful comedy and domestic tragedy.

But the finest playwright of this period was Gotthold Ephraim Lessing (1729–1781), Germany's first truly significant dramatist. Lessing began his career in 1748 with *The Young Scholar,* performed by the Neuber troupe, and won his first widespread fame in 1755 with *Miss Sara Sampson,* a domestic tragedy that swept Germany and won a resounding triumph for sentimental drama. The way for Lessing's tragedy had been paved not only by Gellert's works but by translations of such English plays as Lillo's *The London Merchant* and Moore's *The Gamester.* In writing *Miss Sara Sampson,*

FIGURE 13.11 Scenes from Lessing's *Minna von Barnhelm.* Engravings by Daniel Chodowiecki. Courtesy Theatermuseum, Munich.

Lessing drew upon the Medea myth but modernized it and set it in contemporary England. He also changed the focus of the story by making the victim of Medea's wrath the central figure. His play tells the story of a naive and loving young girl who is persuaded by a rakish young man to run away with him; when the young man's mistress learns that she has been deserted, she contrives to poison Sara and to escape across the English channel. First performed by Ackermann's troupe, *Miss Sara Sampson* was soon the most popular play in Germany and the most widely imitated. Such "middle-class drama," which was given still further impetus when Lessing translated Diderot's works, was able to attract a large audience of the bourgeoisie to the theatre for the first time in Germany. Because Lessing had only gradually come to believe that English drama was the most suitable model for German writers, it was not until about 1760 that he broke completely with Gottsched's emphasis upon French models. Thereafter, Lessing sought to discredit Gottsched and the French neoclassicists and to elevate English drama both through his plays and criticism, especially the *Hamburg Dramaturgy* (1767–1769).

Lessing's second influential play, *Minna von Barnhelm* (1767), is often called Germany's first national comedy. Treating events immediately following the Seven Years War, the play presents lovers drawn from opposing sides who symbolize current problems and divisions within Germany. The union of the lovers at the end of the play, therefore, has a significance beyond the literal meaning. In spite of its topical subject, it is one of the most durable of eighteenth-century comedies, for, though the play is sentimental, Minna's resourcefulness and humor give it freshness. Like *Miss Sara Sampson, Minna von Barnhelm* became exceptionally popular and stimulated numerous imitations.

Lessing's third influential drama, *Emilia Galotti* (1772), adapts the classical story of Appius and Virginia to an eighteenth-century background. By avoiding the sentimentality of *Miss Sara Sampson,* it approaches more nearly the spirit of tragedy. Lessing's depiction of the despotic ruler of a small state led many to interpret his work as a criticism of contemporary political and social conditions and as an attack on the morality of the aristocracy.

Lessing's last important work, *Nathan the Wise* (1779), a dramatic poem not intended for the stage, is considered by many the greatest philosophical drama of the eighteenth century. In it, he depicts characters representing Judaism, Islam, and Christianity to demonstrate that universal love is the only fruitful doctrine. Probably because it was not written for performance, its structure is much freer than that of Lessing's other plays. It is also the first major German work to be written in blank verse (previously plays had been cast either in the alexandrine or in prose). After Goethe adopted Lessing's innovation, blank verse became standard in German tragedy. *Nathan the Wise* was soon performed and has continued to be one of the most frequently produced German works.

Thus, Lessing, through his plays and criticism, established a new standard by leading drama away from Gottsched's narrow path and by demonstrating that a native playwright could attract a wide following. It would be a mistake, however, to assume that the repertory had been transformed by the time Lessing died in 1781. The majority of plays continued to be adaptations or close imitations of foreign works. Nevertheless, the hold of French drama had been broken, and the English drama had replaced it as a model.

In spite of Lessing's reforms, he had remained within the mainstream of eighteenth-century rationalism, which viewed the universe as ruled by a benevolent god, man as essentially good, and the human mind as capable of solving all important problems through the exercise of reason. His own plays, while freer in structure than the French dramas of the period, merely represent a "revised classicism" rather than a markedly new approach. His criticism, however, had served to undermine the hold of neoclassicism. Consequently, before he died a new and more radical group of dramatists had appeared.

The revolt of dramatists against the past was centered in the *Sturm und Drang* (Storm and Stress) school of writers. Traditionally dated from 1767 to 1787, the Storm and Stress movement reached its peak in the 1770s. Among its major writers and works are Goethe's *Goetz von Berlichingen* (1773), Jacob M. R. Lenz's (1751–1792) *The Tutor* (1774) and *The Soldiers* (1776), Heinrich Leopold Wagner's (1747–1779) *The Child Murderess* (1776), Johann Anton Leisewitz's (1752–1806) *Julius von Tarent* (1776), Friedrich Maximilian Klinger's (1752–1831) *Storm and Stress* (1776), and Friedrich Schiller's *The Robbers* (1782), *Fiesko* (1782), and *Intrigue and Love* (1783).

The Storm and Stress plays have often been described as completely formless rebellions against neo-

FIGURE 13.12 Scene from Klinger's *The Twins*, a "storm and stress" play. Engraving by Albrecht. Courtesy Osterreichische Nationalbibliothek.

classicism, primarily because *Goetz von Berlichingen*, with its fifty-four scenes and tangle of plots, and *Storm and Stress*, with its rhapsodic emotionalism, have been taken as typical of the school. In actuality, most of the plays are written in five acts; as many observe the unities of time and place as violate them. Storm and Stress was a frankly experimental movement of young men in revolt against eighteenth-century rationalism. Since they agreed upon no alternative philosophy, the plays show wide variations both in thought and expression. *The Robbers* displays a liberal, Rousseauistic outlook, while *The Soldiers* upholds the need for class distinctions; *Julius von Tarent* is written in a strict neoclassical form, while *Goetz von Berlichingen* uses a loose, episodic struc-

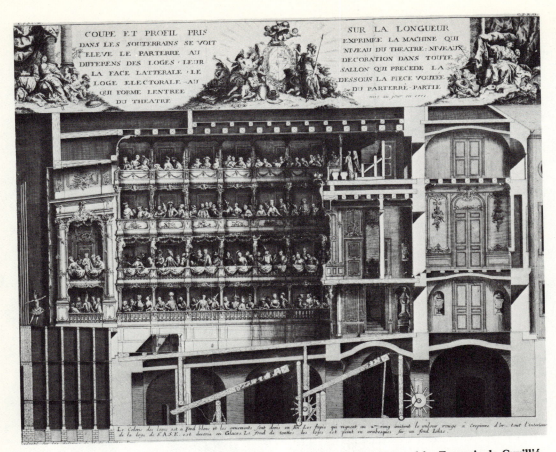

FIGURE 13.13 Cross section of the Residenztheater, Munich, 1771, designed by François de Cuvillié *père*. The forward part of the stage and space beneath it can be seen at left. The pit floor could be raised so that it was level with the stage to use for balls and on similar occasions. The machinery used to lower and raise the floor is seen at bottom center. The ruler's box is shown center right. Engraving by Valerian Funck. Courtesy Theatermuseum, Munich.

ture; the naturalistic subject matter of *The Child Murderess* contrasts sharply with the lyrical subjectivism of *Storm and Stress;* and the diction ranges from the formal verse of *Julius von Tarent*, through the staccato, expressionistic outbursts of *Storm and Stress,* to the conversational prose of *The Tutor*. The very diversity of the plays was bewildering to audiences, for the young authors seemed to be challenging all artistic and social values. The subject matter was often shocking. *The Soldiers* proposes a state-sponsored system of prostitution, while in *The Child Murderess* a rape occurs just off stage and a child is killed on stage. The plays made many new demands on staging. For example, *Goetz von Berlichingen* moves from one place to another as rapidly as does any movie scenario, and other plays call for detailed settings, clearly described in lengthy stage directions.

Few Storm and Stress plays were produced, and even fewer were well received. The major exceptions were *Goetz von Berlichingen* and Schiller's early works. Nevertheless, Storm and Stress plays were widely read and discussed. Consequently, they helped to break down old barriers and to pave the way for other writers who adapted many of the new ideas and techniques to popular tastes. They also probably aided in gaining acceptance for Shakespeare's plays, then being introduced on the German stage, for to many critics they seemed similar in structure and outlook. Out of these beginnings, a more mature drama was to come between 1785 and 1805.

THE ESTABLISHMENT OF
NATIONAL THEATRES, 1770–1800

While the drama was breaking new ground in the 1770s, the theatre was consolidating its former gains. Several periodicals kept the scattered troupes in touch with each other and helped to create common ideals of theatrical production. The number of troupes also increased. From about six in Neuber's time, they had grown to about fourteen in 1776. Most important, state-supported theatres were founded.

The first state theatre was established at Gotha in 1775 from the remnants of the Hamburg National Theatre troupe. When the Hamburg theatre closed in 1769, Abel Seyler had formed a new company, including Sophie Hensel and Ekhof, which, after touring for a time, had settled in Weimar between 1772 and 1774. When the Weimar theatre burned, Seyler moved to Gotha. There in 1775 a scheme for the formation of a state theatre was proposed and carried out. Although Seyler left, Ekhof and the better actors remained.

The Gotha Court Theatre was a nonprofit organization, in which each member was a state employee with pension rights. Ekhof, who was responsible for staging the plays, was at this time the most respected actor in Germany. He brought to Gotha a number of talented young men who received fine training and later became the leading actors of Germany after Ekhof's death. Ekhof was very conservative in his tastes, however, and did nothing to forward the new drama. In 1779, upon Ekhof's death, the theatre was closed.

Before the Gotha venture ended, a far more important state theatre had begun in Vienna. Although it had always been the most powerful Germanic city, Vienna had lagged behind others in the development of a public theatre. While the court had spent lavishly on opera, it had almost completely ignored German drama, considered so inferior that the Empress Maria Theresa (1717–1780) never saw a German play until 1771. Dramas at court were usually given by French actors, who performed in the Burgtheater, converted from a tennis court in 1741.

The general public had been served by the Karntnertor theatre since 1708, but because of the traditions established by Stranitzky and his successors, Gottfried Prehauser and Joseph von Kurz, improvised drama had been the usual fare until about 1750. Written drama began to gain a foothold after Koch appeared in Vienna in 1748, but it was not until the 1760s, when Professor

Joseph von Sonnenfels waged a campaign in its favor, that regular drama was widely accepted. A new era in the Austrian theatre was inaugurated in 1776, when the Emperor Joseph II founded the Imperial and National Theater (more commonly called the Burgtheater after the building in which it performed). Its organization and procedures were modeled after those of the Comédie Française. Although the Burgtheater encountered many difficulties in its early years, it gradually moved to the forefront of the German theatres because generous state support permitted it to assemble a fine company. By 1825, it was considered the best of all the German troupes.

A third state theatre was founded at Mannheim in 1779, when the ruler, Karl Theodor, succeeded to the Electorate of Bavaria and moved his court to Munich. As a gift to compensate his subjects in Mannheim, he created the Hof-und-Nationaltheater. Under the supervision of Baron H. von Dalberg, the company was an amalgamation of Seyler's troupe and the recently disbanded Gotha company. At first, Seyler had primary re-

FIGURE 13.14 John Goodwin, one of the English actors who performed in Germany during the seventeenth century. He is seen here as Harlequin. Courtesy British Museum.

FIGURE 13.15 Konrad Ekhof and Hensel in *School for Fathers* **by Romanus as presented at the Gotha Court Theatre in 1776. Engraving by Liebe after a painting by G. M. Kraus. Courtesy Theatersammlung, Universität Hamburg.**

voted to French culture, had engaged a French troupe for his private theatre and had supported lavish operatic productions. Neither Schönemann nor Koch received any recognition from the court when they played in Berlin. A new era did not begin until 1786 when Frederick William II (reigned 1786–1797) established a subsidized state troupe. Prussia's position of leadership in Germany made its theatre especially influential after 1800.

Thus, in the years between 1775 and 1800 far-reaching changes occurred in the German theatre. In contrast with the period between 1725 and 1740, when troupes were virtually ignored by the aristocracy, rulers now vied with each other in establishing theatres, much as they had formerly competed in supporting opera. The theatre was now viewed as a cultural institution to be made available to all the people and as an instrument for unifying Germans. Perhaps fortunately, the continued division of Germany into many states perpetuated a decentralized theatre with excellent resident companies scattered throughout Germanic territories.

The establishment of state theatres was paralleled in the same period by the building of permanent theatres in towns other than the seats of state governments. Before 1800 there were permanent theatres in Linz, Innsbruck, Brunn, Frankfort-on-Main, Augsburg, Nürnberg, Altona, Breslau, Riga, and elsewhere. By the 1790s there were more than seventy Germanic companies, over half of them permanently located. Touring was now restricted to minor troupes.

sponsibility for production, but after 1781 Dalberg took charge and made the theatre one of the finest in Germany, especially between 1784 and 1795.

After 1780 state theatres were established throughout German-speaking areas. Among the most important were those at Cologne, Mainz, Salzburg, Weimar, and Passau. The theatre formed in Berlin in 1786 was destined to become the most important one. As in other states, drama had been given little encouragement in Prussia during the early eighteenth century, although Frederick the Great (reigned 1740–1786), who was de-

F. L. SCHRÖDER

The most influential troupe in the years between 1770 and 1800 was that of Friedrich Ludwig Schröder (1744–1816). The son of Sophie Schröder, he was on the stage from the time he was three years old. Separated from the Ackermanns at the time of the Seven Years War, he learned to fend for himself by joining with itinerant performers, who taught him acrobatics and dancing. Later, he rejoined his parents and came into contact with Ekhof, who first made him realize what great acting might be. When the Hamburg National Theatre was formed in 1767, Schröder left the company and performed for a time with Kurz, from whom he learned improvisational playing. Schröder returned to Ackermann's Hamburg troupe in 1769 and became artistic director of the company when his stepfather died in 1771.

FIGURE 13.16   The Margrave's Opera House, Bayreuth, designed by Giuseppe and Carlo Galli Bibiena, 1748. This theatre captures Baroque splendor at its highest. Gouache by Gustav Bauernfeind, 1879. Courtesy Theatermuseum, Munich.

The challenge of management seems to have transformed Schröder. Previously a careless performer who could scarcely be induced to rehearse, he now became a firm disciplinarian who insisted upon perfection in every detail. Consequently, his was the first company in Germany to become a truly integrated ensemble. Furthermore, he produced a distinguished repertory. Not only did he perform Lessing's works, but he was the first manager to champion Shakespeare and the Storm and Stress writers. In 1774 he gave the premiere of *Goetz von Berlichingen,* a play which most managers considered unproducible. Beginning in 1776 with *Hamlet,* Schröder had by 1779 performed eleven of Shakespeare's plays, although in severely adapted versions.

In addition to his managerial duties, Schröder performed about thirty-nine new roles each year, and between 1771 and 1780 he translated, adapted, or wrote twenty-eight plays. Although he remained a versatile actor, he gradually moved away from light comedy to tragic roles. By 1780, he was universally recognized as Germany's greatest actor.

Despite his success, Schröder remained merely the employee of his mother, who retained complete financial control over the company. In 1780 she was still

FIGURE 13.17 Schröder in the role of Falstaff. From *Literatur und Theaterzeitung* (1780).

paying him the same salary as in 1771. For this and other reasons, Schröder resigned his post in 1780 and for the next six years played at leading theatres elsewhere, especially in Vienna.

Meantime, the Hamburg company rapidly declined. Thus, when in 1786 Schröder returned, he assumed complete control of the company. For the next twelve years he made it the most respected troupe in Germany. In spite of continuing acclaim, however, his major contributions had already been made, for now Schröder seemed content merely to repeat his earlier successes. He retired in 1798 while at the height of his career.

Schröder is still considered by many the greatest actor Germany has known. In his lifetime he played more than 700 roles. Historically, he is perhaps most important for creating what came to be called the "Hamburg school" of acting and production in which character and setting were carefully delineated and differentiated. It was the Hamburg style that Goethe sought to counteract at Weimar through his own distinctive approach. During the early nineteenth century, theatres throughout Germany struggled to resolve the conflicts that had been created by the Hamburg and the Weimar schools.

EVOLUTION OF STAGING IN THE EIGHTEENTH CENTURY

The trend during the eighteenth century toward greater security is reflected in every aspect of the theatre. As audiences increased in size, the companies could reduce the number of plays in the repertory. This change, in turn, permitted more careful preparation. Nevertheless,

FIGURE 13.18 The closet scene from *Hamlet*, performed in Berlin in 1778. The adaptation was by F. L. Schröder. Seen here are J. F. H. Brockmann as Hamlet and Mme. Hencke as Gertrude. Engraving by Daniel Chodowiecki. Courtesy Theatermuseum, Munich.

FIGURE 13.19   A middle-class theatre of the second half of the eighteenth century. Note the pit, boxes, footlights, prompter's box, and wings of the interior setting. Note also that upstage a door has been set between the wing and backshutter, a practice that would later lead to the fully developed box set. Courtesy Theatermuseum, Munich.

not until the last part of the century was ensemble playing achieved, largely because of Schröder's influence. He began the practice of reading each play to the assembled cast and guiding them in their characterization. He demanded strict order and punctuality at all rehearsals and performances. The superior quality of his productions led other companies to adopt his procedures.

The acting style moved increasingly toward realism. In Neuber's time, good acting was considered to be quite unlike everyday behavior. Ekhof and Schröder, however, turned to life as the standard, and Schröder especially sought to make his characters convincingly natural on the human level. As a result, even the great tragic figures came to be portrayed as ordinary creatures.

So long as there were no permanent theatres, spectacle was not extensively developed. Furthermore, during the early years the necessity of touring forced companies to rely upon a few settings which might be adapted for almost any play. Before 1725, three sets were considered sufficient: a wood for all exterior scenes; a hall for palaces; and a cottage room for domestic interiors. After 1750, the typical stock settings were somewhat more numerous: a Prachtsaal (or *palais à volonté*), a street, a village, several middleclass rooms, a prison, and several hills and shrubs. Changes of place were difficult

to handle before permanent theatres were built. Consequently, up to the 1770s many companies hung a curtain about half way back on the stage so that shallow and full stage scenes could be alternated while changes were made behind the curtain.

The 1770s brought significant innovations in spectacle. Permanent theatres introduced the chariot-and-pole system of scene shifting just when changing standards created a demand for more appropriate, varied, and detailed settings. The success of *Minna von Barnhelm* (1767) and the subsequent vogue for plays with war backgrounds brought the first attempts to create authentic settings and costumes. For these productions, managers often sought the cooperation of local army garrisons. Schröder, for example, is said to have borrowed eighty soldiers to use as supernumeraries in one of his productions in 1771.

Concern for historical accuracy was stimulated by *Goetz von Berlichingen* and the series of chivalric plays (or *Ritterstücke*) which it stimulated. Schröder's production of *Goetz* in 1774 was the first to use scenery and costumes intended to evoke a historical milieu. Although inaccurate in detail, they were sufficiently effective to make historical spectacle standard for plays in the Ritterstücke tradition. Dalberg extended the principle in the

FIGURE 13.20   A German theatre of the late eighteenth century. Note the arrangement of the auditorium and the wings of the stage setting. Courtesy Theatermuseum, Munich.

ager supplied him a coat and waistcoat. This basic costume, used in practically all roles, was adapted by the addition of simple accessories: a king carried a scepter and wore a feathered headdress; a classical hero draped a scarf diagonally across his chest and wore a helmet. Actresses wore the most fashionable garments they could afford. Lace was often made from cut paper.

As the influence of French drama increased, the costuming conventions of the Parisian troupes were adopted. Most tragic heroes and heroines were played in French court dress, while classical heroes wore the *habit à la romaine,* and Near-Eastern characters adopted baggy trousers and turbans. Performers sought to accumulate their own wardrobes, and managers to increase the common stock.

Beginning with Gottsched, intermittent attempts were made to introduce a measure of historical accuracy. Gottsched recommended the use of Roman togas in classical plays and, after their break, Frau Neuber revenged herself on him by following his prescriptions for costuming *The Dying Cato,* much to the great amusement of audiences who were reduced to uncontrollable laughter. In 1766, Koch created a considerable stir when he opened his new theatre in Leipzig with Schlegel's *Hermann* done in period dress. It was not until the 1770s, however, that historical costumes became common. For

FIGURE 13.21   The first production of *Hamlet* in Germany, performed in Berlin in 1778. J. F. H. Brockmann is seen as Hamlet seated on the floor at right. In the background is the play within the play. After an engraving by Daniel Chodowiecki. From *Die Theater Wiens,* Vol. II, pt. 1 (1899).

1780s, when he staged Shakespeare's *Julius Caesar* at Mannheim with unprecedented attention to antiquarian detail and picturesque splendor.

By the 1790s dramatists were writing plays that demanded the use of practical bridges, walls, and other complex set pieces. Doors and windows began to be set up between wings, thus marking the first steps toward the box set. As elsewhere, however, the trends toward greater realism and accuracy of detail were not to be fully exploited until the nineteenth century.

Costumes followed the same general trends. Before 1725, extreme simplicity was the rule. Each actor was expected to own a pair of black breeches, while the mana-

his production of *Goetz* in 1774, Schröder dressed the knights in armor, the monks and bishops in appropriate ecclesiastical garments, and the courtiers, citizens, and gypsies in allegedly accurate clothing. This is the feature of the production, considered a major innovation, that seems most to have impressed critics of the day. Thereafter the Ritterstücke plays accepted historical costuming as necessary. All of these plays, however, used garments of a single period—the sixteenth century—no matter the supposed time of the action. In 1776, Roman dress was adapted for some classical plays at Gotha, and in the 1780s Dalberg introduced it at Mannheim.

In the 1770s, authors of domestic plays began to prescribe the costumes to be worn by their characters, often enumerating the colors and details at length. Thus, before 1800 managers were becoming aware of the need for individualized costumes, although earlier practices probably continued to dominate.

Other theatrical customs also changed. Through much of the eighteenth century, performances were not permitted on Saturdays, Sundays, holidays, or during Lent and Advent. Gradually the strictures were relaxed, but it was not until about 1800 that daily playing throughout the year was permitted. As in other countries, the starting time was moved to later hours. The Neubers' performances began at 4 or 4:30 P.M.; by the 1770s the usual hour was 5, and by 1800, 5:30.

IFFLAND AND KOTZEBUE

Just as the theatre of Germany achieved full acceptance between 1775 and 1800, so too its drama attained maturity. In these years the theatre attracted audiences from every class in large part because of the plays of Iffland and Kotzebue, although true distinction was reserved for Goethe and Schiller.

August Wilhelm Iffland (1759–1814) began his acting career in the Gotha company under Ekhof and joined the newly created Mannheim state theatre in 1779. During Iffland's tenure, the Mannheim theatre was one of the most vital in Germany. Schröder played there in 1780 and introduced Shakespeare into the repertory; Schiller's first three plays were first produced there and for a time Schiller was the resident dramatist; and Dalberg made numerous innovations in theatrical practice.

Iffland rapidly came to the fore, both as actor and dramatist. From 1784, when his *Crime from Ambition*

FIGURE 13.22 Iffland and Madame Bethmann in a scene from *The Family Friend*. A contemporary engraving.

established his fame as a writer, until 1796, when he left the troupe, Iffland was the most influential member of the Mannheim company. Thirty-seven of his plays were first performed by this theatre, and Iffland's enormous reputation, which extended throughout Germany, served to elevate this theatre in public esteem. As Iffland's plays became widely known, he began to be in great demand for starring engagements, and thereafter he traveled extensively. From 1796 until 1814 he was head of the Berlin state theatre, which he welded into one of the finest ensembles of his time.

After Schröder's retirement in 1798, Iffland was usually considered to be Germany's leading actor. As a performer, he depended especially upon his expressive body and face, for his voice was weak. Because his major strength lay in the portrayal of sentiment, he is often said to form a bridge between the neoclassic and romantic styles.

Iffland's own plays provided him with his best acting vehicles. Offering idealized portraits of ordinary men and women, their touching situations tended to romanticize the simple life, as in *The Hunters* (1785), which contrasts unsophisticated country people with scheming city dwellers. Although Iffland now seems a precursor of romanticism, he opposed the new movement and sought to keep the romantic drama out of the reper-

FIGURE 13.23 Kotzebue's *Menschenhass und Reue (The Stranger).* **The final scene of reunion as shown in the edition of the play published in 1790. Courtesy of the Osterreichische Nationalbibliothek, Vienna.**

tory at Berlin. Nevertheless, his own sentimental portraits of humanity paved the way for the romantic school.

August Friedrich von Kotzebue (1761–1819) was even more popular than Iffland as a playwright. From 1787, when he won his first success with *Misanthropy and Repentance,* until his death, he was the most popular playwright in the world. Between 1787 and 1867, one-fourth of all the Burgtheater's performances were of Kotzebue's plays; at other theatres the proportion was often higher. Thirty-six of the plays were translated into English, and several remained starring vehicles throughout the nineteenth century. Kotzebue's more than 200 plays range through domestic drama, historical spectacle, verse plays, and farces.

Kotzebue's success can probably be explained by his ability to adapt new trends to public tastes. Thus, while he used many of the themes and devices introduced by Storm and Stress dramatists, he was successful where they had failed. He knew how to titillate audiences without shocking them and how far he could depart from accepted conventions without confusing unsophisticated spectators. He combined sensational subjects, striking spectacle, and humanitarian sentiments so successfully that he helped to create the vogue for melodrama that was to dominate the nineteenth century stage. Largely because of Kotzebue's plays, German drama was by 1800 considered the most vital and popular in the world.

GOETHE, SCHILLER, AND WEIMAR CLASSICISM

If Iffland and Kotzebue raised German drama to the peak of its popularity with the theatregoing public, Goethe and Schiller were to be remembered as Germany's greatest playwrights. In their joint work at Weimar, they also created a distinctive style of production which spread the fame of that small town throughout Germany.

Johann Wolfgang von Goethe (1749–1832) is usually considered the greatest literary figure Germany has known. A "universal genius," Goethe's interests ranged through almost every field and to most he made significant contributions. He began his literary career at a very early age, but it was his play *Goetz von Berlichingen* (1773) and his novel *Werther* (1774) that made him the most famous young writer of his time and the center of the Storm and Stress school. Throughout Europe,

FIGURE 13.24 The Court Theatre at Weimar as it appeared when Goethe was manager. A contemporary engraving.

Goethe's *Werther* came to epitomize the longings of the new generation.

In 1775, at the request of the young ruler, Duke Karl August, Goethe settled in Weimar, which he made one of the cultural centers of Germany. Arriving shortly after Seyler and Ekhof had departed, Goethe became the leader of the amateur group that provided the town's only theatrical entertainment. After the enthusiasm of the amateurs waned, the ducal theatre, which had been built in 1780, was leased in 1784 to a professional troupe under the direction of Joseph Bellomo. Given a small subsidy and a limited supply of scenery and costumes, Bellomo's troupe remained in Weimar until 1791.

Goethe's visit to Italy from 1786 to 1788 marks a turning point in his outlook. His new appreciation of the classical past made him reject his former Storm and Stress period and write for a time in the classical mode. His *Iphigenia in Tauris* (1787) is often considered one of his greatest achievements. Within the framework of the ancient myth, it depicts man's ethical evolution from a narrow concern for self to an awareness of the broader claims of humanity.

In 1791, Karl August dismissed Bellomo's troupe and established a state theatre like those which had been appearing elsewhere. Since the population of the city of Weimar was only 6,000, the duke could not afford a first-rate company. Failing to attract a suitable director, he appointed Goethe to the post. The Weimar Court Theatre opened in 1791 with a mediocre company under the artistic direction of Franz Fischer, an actor. Goethe took little interest in the theatre until 1796, when a visit from Iffland gave him a vision of what the troupe might become if given sufficient guidance. This interest was deepened by Schiller, who stimulated Goethe to take over the active direction of the company.

Friedrich Schiller's (1759–1805) career had developed along quite different lines than Goethe's. The son of an army officer, Schiller had been forced by the Duke of Württemberg to enter military school. When, following the success of his first play, *The Robbers* (1782), Schiller was forbidden to write, he fled to Mannheim; there he was appointed resident dramatist to the state theatre and wrote for it *Fiesko* (1783) and *Intrigue and Love* (1784). Like Goethe, Schiller underwent a significant change during the 1780s. While working on *Don Carlos* (1787), he began to reassess his values in the light of his study of history. He wrote no plays between 1787 and 1798, devoting himself instead to historical studies. His *The Revolt of the Netherlands* and *A History of the Thirty Years War* won him fame as a historian and an appointment as professor of history at the University of Jena, only five miles from Weimar. Goethe and Schiller gradually became close friends and began to exert a strong influence on each other. In 1799, Schiller left Jena and settled in Weimar, where he assisted Goethe. Between 1798 and 1805 Schiller wrote his mature works and Goethe made the Weimar theatre one of the most famous in Germany.

Although in many ways Goethe and Schiller were almost opposite in temperament, they were united by a common artistic view. Now often grouped with the romantic school, they considered themselves quite distinct from it. To them, the romantics seemed content either to reproduce the life they saw around them or to escape into emotionalism or fantasy, while Schröder, Kotzebue, and Iffland seemed bent on reducing all experience to the level of domestic drama. Goethe, under the impact of his visit to Italy, and Schiller, after his study of history and philosophy, sought to counter the major artistic trends of their day. Although both wrote some plays in the classical style, it was not the formal characteristics of ancient drama which attracted them so much as its spirit. For them, the formal conventions of Greek tragedy served merely as devices to "distance" the spectator from the play's events so that they might perceive the ideal patterns behind everyday reality. Thus, Goethe and Schiller argued that drama should transform ordinary experience rather than create an illusion of real life. Consequently, they adopted verse, conventionalized structural patterns, and stylized production techniques in order to lead spectators beyond their normal perceptions into the realm of ideal truth. Out of these views came "Weimar Classicism."

Schiller's late plays are extremely complex works in which philosophical, historical, and personal problems are interwoven to produce many layers of meaning. For most, Schiller chose subjects which represent turning points in history. *Wallenstein's Camp* (1798), *The Piccolomini* (1799), and *Wallenstein's Death* (1799) form a trilogy on the Thirty Years War conceived on a vaster scale than any work since the time of Shakespeare. *Mary Stuart* (1800), *The Maid of Orleans* (1801), and *William Tell* (1804) treat decisive events in English, French, and Swiss history.

Goethe turned his attention to transforming the second-rate Weimar troupe into a true ensemble. The actors' geographical origins and lack of education were evident in every performance because of the wide range of accents and stage behavior. Since they had so many roles to learn, most of them had come to depend upon improvisation. To remedy this situation, Goethe laid down a set of rules which, without a knowledge of the actors' problems, might seem elementary. They cover proper enunciation, ways of overcoming regional dialects, control of tempo and tone, principles of movement and grouping, posture and stance, and social behavior. All aim at achieving grace, dignity, and ease.

Since he did not trust either the taste or previous training of his actors, Goethe became an absolute dictator. He began each new production with a series of reading rehearsals during which he corrected errors in line readings, pronunciation, and interpretation. He also gave considerable attention to the proper speaking of verse. To aid blocking, he divided the stage into squares and specified the actors' movements in relation to them. He often consulted painters about pictorial composition, and he was so concerned with rhythm and cadence that on occasion he allegedly beat time with a baton. Rather than seeking to create the illusion of reality, Goethe attempted to achieve a harmonious and graceful picture which, in combination with intelligent and euphonious line readings, would attune the spectator to an ideal beauty. By requiring absolute adherence to his directions, Goethe achieved the most perfect ensemble yet seen anywhere. Because of his working methods, he must be considered one of the world's first directors in the modern sense. At the time, however, critics varied widely in their opinions about the theatrical effectiveness of Goethe's productions. Goethe's numerous admirers praised the results extravagantly; others found the performers so uniform that they might exchange roles without any noticeable effect.

Goethe treated the audience as autocratically as he did the actors. He forbade them to express approval except by applause or disapproval except by silence. Sometimes he reprimanded the audience from his box in the theatre if they responded incorrectly and he ordered their arrest if they misbehaved. He assumed the role of schoolmaster to all Weimar.

The remodeled Weimar theatre was opened in 1798 with Schiller's *Wallenstein's Camp*. The combined fame of Goethe and Schiller attracted many visitors and

FIGURE 13.25 Schiller's *Fiesko* as performed at Weimar in 1805. Aquatint by J. C. E. Müller after a painting by G. E. Opitz. Courtesy Theatermuseum, Munich.

soon "Weimar Classicism" was famous throughout Germany. Despite Goethe's ideals, the repertory was not confined to plays of the type admired by him and Schiller. Since the state subsidy covered only about one-third of the company's expenses, Goethe had to arrange the repertory so as to insure popular support. Consequently, of the three weekly performances, one was usually devoted to musical plays or opera, one to popular drama (especially that of Kotzebue and Iffland), and the third to plays that Goethe admired. The actors complained, probably with good cause, that Goethe spent two-thirds of the rehearsal time on plays of the last type. Goethe often experimented with unusual production devices or plays. He used half masks in Terence's *The Brothers*, revived some *commedia dell'arte* scripts, and presented plays by Shakespeare, Calderón, and other authors not normally found in the repertories of the period.

After Schiller died in 1805, Goethe gradually lost interest in the theatre. In 1807 the troupe was invited to Leipzig, where it was much admired for its ensemble. The actors were now much in demand and, joining other troupes, they disseminated the Weimar style widely during the first half of the nineteenth century. As a result, German theatrical practice was caught between the de-

mands of idealism (epitomized by Weimer Classicism) and the demands of realism (epitomized in the Hamburg style). Goethe gradually lost control of the Weimar troupe to Caroline Jagemann (1777–1848), an actress and the duke's mistress. He resigned his post in 1817, and the Weimar theatre slowly sank back into obscurity.

Of Goethe's later dramatic works, the most famous is *Faust,* the first part of which was published in 1808 and the second in 1831. Not intended for the stage, this dramatic poem seeks to depict man's search for fulfillment and to suggest that man finds salvation through such striving. Its episodic structure and philosophical viewpoint are similar in all important respects to the work of the romantic playwrights. Thus, while Goethe stands as the culmination of German classicism, he also contributed much to the romanticism which came to the fore after 1798.

THEATRE AND DRAMA IN OTHER COUNTRIES OF NORTHERN EUROPE

By 1800 Germany had assumed a position of leadership in the European theatre, but other countries of Northern Europe continued to play a subordinate role. Nevertheless, the theatres of Belgium and Holland could boast a continuous history since the Middle Ages, when spectacular religious dramas had been staged in Belgium and Chambers of Rhetoric had flourished in Holland.

Beginning in the sixteenth century, Belgium was something of a political pawn passed among Spain, Austria, France, and the Netherlands. Not until 1830 did it become an independent nation. But, since its educated classes were for the most part French-speaking, its theatre was most influenced by French practices. The Academy of Music, the first opera house in Belgium, was established in Brussels in 1687. In 1700, the Théâtre de la Monnaie was opened, and, though altered many times, continues to be a principal theatre of Brussels. In 1705, the first permanent dramatic troupe was assembled. Since that time the Belgian theatre has, with a few interruptions, enjoyed a continuous history.

The Flemish and Dutch areas of the Low Countries were especially prosperous during the seventeenth century. They had declared their independence from Spain in 1581, although their new status was not recognized by treaty until 1648. During the last half of the seventeenth century, the Netherlands became the world's

FIGURE 13.26 Interior of the Schouwburg, Amsterdam, built in 1638. Engraving by S. Savry, 1658. Courtesy Toneelmuseum, Amsterdam.

greatest maritime power and Amsterdam the world's major commercial city, the center of an empire that reached into the New World and the Far East.

By the beginning of the seventeenth century, the Chambers of Rhetoric were in decline, and in 1617 the only two remaining societies in Amsterdam were united under the more fashionable name, The Academy. In 1618, the city of Amsterdam gave The Academy a building which was soon christened the Schouwburg (or the Playhouse). In 1638, the city itself assumed responsibility for the Schouwburg, thus making it the first municipal theatre of modern times.

Designed by Jacob von Campen, who had studied in Italy, the stage of the Schouwburg was a compromise between those used by the Rhetoric and Italian theatres. Raised about 7 feet above the auditorium floor, it had no proscenium arch or front curtain. Along the sides and across the back there were pilasters at intervals with space between them to set flats, each of which might represent a different locale or, less frequently, parts of a single place. At times the pilasters across the back were used to form an open colonnade. The stage picture, therefore, varied from multiple settings similar to those used at the Hôtel de Bourgogne in the early 1630s to modified perspective settings in the Italian manner. Some of the flats were doubled-sided to permit quick changes. When needed, the central portion of the rear facade could be used as an inner stage. The main stage was divided into two parts by a curtain hung about halfway back; this curtain could be closed to permit quick changes behind it or opened to indicate a shift in locale. At times mansion-like structures were set up on the stage. There was also a permanent upper stage in the form of a balcony extending across the back and part way down the sides. Like the *théâtre supérieure* of the Théâtre du Marais in Paris, the upper stage might be treated as part of a unified setting or used to represent one or more separate locales. The ovoid auditorium consisted of a standing pit, 46 feet wide by 23 feet deep, surrounded by a row of ten raised boxes, and above the boxes, an open gallery.

In this period the major Dutch dramatist was Joost van den Vondel (1587–1679), author of thirty-two plays, many of them imitations of Plautus and Terence but others on Biblical or historical subjects, such as *Lucifer*, *Jeftha*, and *Maria Stuart*. His best known play is *Gysbrecht van Aemstel*, a glorification of the city of Amsterdam, still played annually in Holland at New Year's or Twelfth Night.

In 1664, the old theatre was torn down and replaced by the Nieuwe Schouwburg, a wholly Italianate structure. During the eighteenth century, the Netherlands declined as a world power, but it remained relatively

FIGURE 13.27 Scene from *Gysbrecht van Aemstel* as presented in 1775. Setting by A. van der Groen. This illustration also shows the interior of the Nieuwe Schouwburg, built in 1664. Courtesy Toneelmuseum, Amsterdam.

prosperous and its theatre thrived, although for the most part thereafter it merely reflected major trends current elsewhere in Europe.

Farther north, the professional theatre was slower in appearing. Until the eighteenth century, Norway and Denmark (unified as a single country until 1814) were dependent upon French, English, and German troupes. Beginning in the late seventeenth century, the court maintained a French troupe, but the general populace had to content itself with traveling companies of the type then common in Germany.

The turning point came in 1720, when Frederick IV dismissed his French company. Its leader, René Magnon de Montaigu, had been in Denmark since 1686 and wished to remain. Consequently, he joined with Étienne Capion, another Frenchman and former actor, in a petition to the king asking permission to open a public theatre. Upon receiving a favorable response, they built a small theatre (seating about 400) and opened it in 1722. This venture ended in bankruptcy in 1727. Montaigu then received permission to use the court theatre and was given a small subsidy. But in 1730, under pressure from puritan forces, all theatrical activity was banned.

In spite of these difficulties, native drama dates from these years when Ludwig Holberg (1684–1754) became the first dramatist to write plays in the vernacular language. Not only was Holberg well educated, he had traveled throughout Europe and had seen the best companies of England, France, and Italy. In 1718 he was appointed a professor at the University of Copenhagen. Soon afterwards he began his literary career with *Peder Paars,* a literary satire usually considered to mark the beginnings of literature in the Danish language. To write in the vernacular was revolutionary, for Latin was still the accepted medium for scholars and French for the court.

Since Holberg was the only writer to have used the vernacular successfully, it is only natural that Montaigu and Capion should commission him to supply their newly created company with dramas suited to a Danish audience. Between 1722 and 1727, Holberg wrote twenty-six plays. Of these, *Jeppe of the Hill* (1722) and *Erasmus Montanus* (printed 1731) are probably the best known. Many of Holberg's plays resemble robust medieval farces, although he always appended moral lessons to them. For example, *Jeppe of the Hill* tells the story of a henpecked peasant who is kidnapped while in a drunken stupor and is then led to believe that he

FIGURE 13.28 Scene from Ludwig Holberg's *The Busy Man.* **From an eighteenth-century edition of the play. Courtesy Teaterhistorisk Museum, Christiansborg.**

is a great lord before being returned to his village during another bout of drunkenness. This comic story concludes with the argument that class barriers must be maintained, since, as Jeppe has shown, the lower classes would become tyrannical if given power. But not all of Holberg's comedies are medieval in tone, for he borrowed freely from Plautus, Molière, and *commedia dell'arte,* although he always recast his borrowings until they seemed native in their origins. Holberg's works were to be the backbone of the Danish repertory, but they also were extremely popular throughout northern Europe.

When Frederick V came to the throne in 1746 he lifted the ban against playing and in 1748 a new theatre was opened. At this time, Holberg wrote seven plays, but they lacked the vitality of his earlier work. The fortunes of the new theatre were as uncertain as those of the old until 1772, when the Royal Danish Theatre, still the national theatre of Denmark, was created.

The bulk of the late eighteenth-century repertory was foreign, for Holberg had few successors. Johan Herman Wessel (1742–1785), a prolific translator, also gained considerable fame by writing parodies of foreign works. Johannes Ewald (1743–1781), Denmark's first important serious playwright as well as one of its greatest lyric poets, provided *Rolf Krage* (1770), the first significant Danish tragedy, and *The Fishermen* (1780), the first serious Danish play to treat ordinary people sympathetically. Ewald also called attention to the rich heritage of North European folklore and legend and laid the foundations for the succeeding romantic movement.

The theatre of Sweden has a long if somewhat undistinguished history. Although school plays were being written in the vernacular by about 1550, they did not lead to significant developments, perhaps because Sweden was involved in a series of conflicts (including the Thirty Years War). Around 1690 public performances began to be seen in Stockholm, and in 1773 the court theatre, inaugurated in 1737, was transformed into a national theatre.

During the eighteenth century, the Swedish theatre received considerable impetus during the reign of Gustav III (1771–1792), who established a Swedish academy, wrote plays, encouraged native writers and performers, and in general sought to reshape native arts along French lines. Unfortunately, the results were for the most part mere lifeless imitations of foreign models.

Despite its considerable accomplishments, Gustav's reign is now remembered primarily because of the theatre at Drottningholm, a royal residence near Stockholm. Erected between 1764 and 1766, this theatre was used extensively during the late eighteenth century but was closed upon Gustav's death in 1792. Until 1921, when it was rediscovered, it remained untouched and virtually forgotten. As a result, thirty stage settings, the stage and its machinery, and the auditorium survived intact. As one of the few truly authentic eighteenth-century theatres now in existence, it has become one of the world's major theatrical museums. It is used occasionally for performances of eighteenth-century works. The theatre at the royal residence at Gripsholm has also survived but it is less typical of its age.

THEATRE IN RUSSIA TO 1800

The eighteenth century also saw the establishment of theatre and drama in Russia. As in other parts of Europe, folk and ritual drama in Russia can be found from the earliest times and wandering entertainers can be traced back as far as the tenth century. If an extensive liturgical drama ever existed there, however, few traces of it have survived. In the seventeenth century, drama was introduced into the Jesuit schools of the Ukraine, and until well into the eighteenth century students from these schools toured plays as far east as Siberia.

The first clear record of theatre in Moscow is found in 1672 during the reign of Alexis (1645–1676), who, after he failed to secure a theatrical troupe from the West, persuaded Johann Gottfried Gregory, a Lutheran minister and schoolteacher in the resident German colony, to produce plays for the theatre that Alexis had built in his palace. Although Gregory's productions were Haupt-und-Staatsaktion plays (complete with the clown Pickelherring), Alexis was so enthusiastic about them that he forced the aristocracy to attend. He also established a subsidized theatre school to train additional performers. But, upon Alexis' death in 1676 both the theatre and school were abandoned.

The theatre then lay fallow until Peter the Great (reigned 1682–1725) decided to use it in his campaign to westernize Russia. In 1702, he imported Johann Kunst's company from Danzig and installed it in a theatre on what is now Red Square. Since few of his people understood German, Peter selected several Russians to be trained by the foreign actors. This theatre, already disrupted by the movement of the capital to St. Petersburg (a city built by Peter beginning in 1703) was abandoned upon Peter's death.

Between 1725 and 1750 theatrical activities were largely confined to the court. For the coronation of the Empress Anna (reigned 1730–1740), the Polish king sent a *commedia dell'arte* troupe. Their success led to the demand for other Western forms, and consequently Francesco Araia, a Neapolitan operatic composer, was imported in 1735 and Jean-Baptiste Landet, a French dancing master and founder of Russian ballet, in 1738. In 1740, the Neuber troupe was invited to St. Petersburg, but their engagement was cut short by the death of the Empress Anna.

Under the Empress Elizabeth (reigned 1741–1762), the Italians and French struggled for supremacy

FIGURE 13.29 Interior view of the theatre at Drottningholm as it appears today. On stage is a *palais à volonté* setting designed by Carlo Bibiena in 1774. Note the wave machine in the background. Courtesy Drottningholms Theatermuseum, Stockholm.

in the court theatre. Eventually a French company was employed to perform plays twice a week, while the Italians continued their spectacular operatic productions. By 1750, the Russian court was conscious of the latest Western trends. There was as yet, however, neither a public theatre nor a native Russian repertory.

Around 1750 a number of developments began a new era in the Russian theatre. First, a talented Russian dramatist, Alexander Sumarokov (1717–1777), began to write plays on Russian subjects but cast in French neoclassical form. His tragedies and satirical comedies mark the beginning of the Russian classical school. In 1749, the success of the cadets at the Academy of the Nobility with Sumarokov's first play, *Khorev* (1747), induced them to present other works by Sumarokov.

Another major train of events was set in motion around 1750 when Fyodor Volkov (1729–1763), a merchant's son who had seen theatrical performances in St. Petersburg, decided to present plays in his native Yaroslavl. Assembling a troupe from among his family and friends, Volkov fitted up a barn as a theatre. Enthusiasm was so great that he had moved into more adequate quarters before being summoned to play for the empress in 1752. Impressed by their work, the empress sent some of the actors to the Academy of the Nobility for further education and permitted them to give performances for the general public. Thus, Volkov is usually considered the founder of the Russian professional theatre.

The next significant development came in 1756, when the empress established a state theatre for Russian plays. The troupe, made up primarily of Volkov's actors, was placed under the direction of Sumarokov, although ultimate authority resided in a court official. The relatively slight value placed on this Russian company, however, is indicated by its subsidy of 5,000 rubles as compared with the 20,000 given the French actors and the 30,000 granted the Italian opera troupe. The Russian plays, treated condescendingly by the court, were attended primarily by the middle class.

Under Catherine II (reigned 1762–1796) the theatre spread throughout Russia. Playwrights increased, although few won lasting fame. Leadership passed from

FIGURE 13.30 Interior of the Bolshoi Theatre, St. Petersburg, in the late eighteenth century. A contemporary engraving.

operated under regulations established by the crown. Although opera continued to be the favored form with the aristocracy, the dramatic troupes achieved increased security. In 1776 a pension system was inaugurated, and after 1789 the companies were allowed four annual benefit performances, the proceeds of which were divided among all the actors. In 1779 an acting school was established, and in the 1790s a second state theatre was opened in St. Petersburg. In general, acting companies followed "lines of business" similar to those current in France. A state document of 1766 lists the lines as follows: first, second, and third comic and tragic lovers, noble fathers, comic fathers, first and second domestics, moralizers, clerks, confidants, first and second tragic and comic female lovers, first and second chambermaids, old women, and confidantes.

After the death of Volkov in 1763, the most famous actor was Ivan Dmitrevsky (1734–1821), who began his career in Volkov's Yaroslavl troupe. In 1765 and 1767 he went abroad, where he is said to have studied the acting of Clairon, Lekain, and Garrick. He acted only rarely after 1787, but became an influential teacher. In 1791 he was appointed supervisor of all performances in the state dramatic troupes. A carefully controlled performer who planned every effect, Dmitrevsky was best in the classical repertory. Yakov Shusherin (1753–1813), on the other hand, was famous for his portrayal of sentimental roles. Between 1787 and 1810 he was the most popular actor on the St. Petersburg stage.

By the end of the eighteenth century, itinerant companies were touring to all of the principal cities of Russia. Many privately owned theatres also had appeared; some gave public performances, while others were maintained by nobles for private entertainments. Few of those giving public performances were successful. In Moscow, for example, the public theatre was open only sporadically. When one venture failed, after lasting only from 1759 to 1761, there was no professional troupe there until 1786, when M. E. Medox's company opened and struggled along until 1796. Moscow was not to be given a state-supported theatre until the nineteenth century.

By far the majority of the privately owned theatres were maintained by the great landowners. With the encouragement of Catherine II, the aristocracy began to patronize the arts as a sign of their enlightenment, and many nobles established small courts of their own. Several maintained theatrical troupes composed of their serfs.

Unlike the rest of Europe, where it had largely

Sumarokov to his son-in-law, Yakov Kniazhnin (1742–1791), who after 1769 wrote seven tragedies and a number of comedies in the neoclassical style. But the best of the eighteenth-century Russian dramatists was Denis Fonvizin (1745–1792), who began writing in 1761 and achieved his first significant success in 1766 with *The Brigadier General,* a satire on the newly rich and on the Russian tendency to praise everything from Western Europe and to disparage everything Russian. His lasting reputation rests principally on *The Minor* (1781), a satirical picture of the brutish, uneducated rural gentry.

The majority of the plays in the repertory, however, were translations, and, after the 1760s, as the works of Diderot, Destouches, Mercier, Lillo, Lessing, and Beaumarchais were imported, domestic tragedy and sentimental comedy were the most popular types. Musical plays in the manner of ballad opera or *opéra comique* also gained an enormous following. The most popular of these works was A. Ablesimov's (1742–1783) *The Miller, the Witchdoctor, the Cheater and the Matchmaker* (1779), which held the stage through the nineteenth century.

Under Catherine, the state continued its firm control over the theatre. All plays were subject to strict censorship, and the court- and state-subsidized theatres disappeared during the Renaissance, in Russia serfdom was not established until the late sixteenth century, when a series of decrees bound the peasants to the land. Thereafter, serfdom became the principal basis of the Russian economy, and a landowner's wealth was measured primarily by the number of serfs bound to his estate. During the late eighteenth century many nobles began to select serfs and train them as performers. Thus, they owned their own troupes. In 1797 in Moscow alone there were fifteen serf theatres, many of which rivaled in quality the court and state theatres of St. Petersburg. Prince Yusopov, owner of 21,000 serfs, established separate ballet, opera, and dramatic companies and a training school. Count Peter Sheremetyev built three separate theatres, one of which had three tiers of boxes. His principal troupe had 230 members. He retained an agent

in Paris to keep him abreast of all the latest developments in Western Europe, and his productions, famous for their lavishness, were attended by the royal family, important nobles, and foreign dignitaries. Sometimes landowners sold entire companies or rented them out for public performances. The most important serf companies operated between 1790 and 1810, but some continued to operate until serfdom was finally abolished in 1861.

By 1800, then, Russian theatre and drama had gained a relatively firm foothold. Few important dramatists had appeared and the theatre was still largely imitative of French and Italian practices, but the basis for future developments was clearly evident. The Russian situation also shows that by 1800 the professional theatre had spread throughout Europe. It remained for the nineteenth century to bring it to full flower.

LOOKING AT THEATRE HISTORY

The study of theatre history can be enhanced by a knowledge of geography, which is concerned, among other things, with configurations of the land (such as rivers, plains, and mountains) and with conditions that affect economic life (such as the soil, climate, and natural resources). These factors are important in theatre history, for the division of territory into political units, the distribution of population and wealth, and physical hazards of travel seriously affect theatrical conditions. Perhaps in no period have geographical considerations been so crucial to the theatre as in eighteenth-century Germany. About Germany in this age, Bruford writes:

Germany was not at this time . . . a single national state, but . . . a loose confederation of states, the boundaries and authority of which were so ill-defined that it is for many purposes misleading to speak of the "Germany" of that age. . . . Many general causes have been suggested for the [overall divisiveness]. . . . The one least in dispute is the geography of the country. The abundance of barriers in the interior and the absence of clearly marked natural boundaries on its borders made the centralisation of authority much more difficult in Germany than it was in either England or France. . . . (pp. 1–2)

Bruford goes on to describe the diversity in size, govern-

ment, and power among the numerous states that made up the Germanic territory:

[There were] kings of European importance like those of Austria and Prussia, the electoral princes, 94 spiritual and lay princes, 103 counts, 40 prelates, 51 Free Towns, in all some 300 separate "Territories," each jealous of its time-honoured privileges and little affected by any memories of a common inheritance. (p. 7)

W. H. BRUFORD, *Germany in the Eighteenth Century* (Cambridge: at the University Press, 1965).

In the early eighteenth century, when Germanic rulers disdained the native drama, the theatre was at a low ebb, as this account by Konrad Ekhof testifies:

Travelling troupes of mountebanks, going from one fair to another all over Germany, amused the mob with low farces. . . . the performance of the plays was just as ridiculous as their plots. One very frequently presented everywhere was entitled Adam and Eve, or the Fall of the First Men. *. . . I remember seeing it acted at Strasbourg. You saw a fat Eve, in tights made of coarse flesh-colored linen, to which a narrow girdle of fig-leaves was attached. The costume of Adam was equally ridiculous, while God the Father ap-*

peared in an old dressing gown . . . . The comic element
was provided by the devils. . . . the old German plays . . .
were not written out in full. The actors usually had just a
scenario and played everything extempore. Hanswurst
above all found abundant scope for his sallies. . . . A
miserable wooden hut served as playhouse; the scenery was
lamentable. . . . In a word, the theatre was an amusement
for the mob.*

Quoted in F. J. VON REDEN-ESBECK,
Caroline Neuber und ihre Zeitgenossen
(Leipzig, 1881), p. 37.

Meantime, Germanic rulers were presenting some
of the most lavish operatic spectacles to be seen in all
Europe. In 1716, the Emperor Charles VI, on the occasion of his son's birth, presented *Angelica, Vincitrice
di Alcina* out of doors at night in the Favorite Park,
Vienna. The settings were by Ferdinando and Giuseppe
Bibiena (see the illustration on page 305). Here is an
eyewitness account from a letter written by Lady Mary
Wortley Montagu:

*Nothing of that kind ever was more magnificent; and I can
easily believe what I am told, that the decorations and
habits cost the emperor thirty thousand pounds sterling.
The stage was built over a large canal, and, at the beginning of the second act, divided into two parts, discovering
the water, on which there immediately came, from different
parts, two fleets of little gilded vessels, that gave the representation of a naval fight. . . . The story of the opera
is the Enchantments of Alcina, which gives opportunity
for a great variety of machines, and changes of scene, which
are performed with a surprising swiftness. The theatre is
so large, that it is hard to carry the eye to the end of it;
and the habits in the utmost magnificence, to the number
of one hundred and eight. No house could hold such large
decorations.*

*The Letters of Lady Mary Wortley
Montagu* (London, 1861), vol. I,
letter to Alexander Pope, dated
14 September 1716.

Lessing, Germany's first major critic and playwright, more than any one else was responsible for turning German taste away from the French neoclassical
ideal championed by Gottsched and his circle. In the
final numbers of his *Hamburg Dramaturgy* (1767-1769),
he sums up his fundamental views:

*I set myself the task of judging . . . some of the most cele-
brated models of the French stage. For this stage is said to*

be formed quite in accordance with the rules of Aristotle,
and it has been particularly attempted to persuade us Germans that only by these rules have the French attained to
the degree of perfection from which they can look down on
all the stages of modern peoples. We have long so firmly
believed this, that with our poets, to imitate the French
was regarded as much as to work according to the rules of
the ancients.*

*Nevertheless this prejudice could not eternally stand
against our feelings. These were fortunately roused from
their slumbers by some English plays, and we at last experienced that tragedy was capable of another quite different
effect from that accorded by Corneille and Racine. . . . No
nation has more misapprehended the rules of ancient drama
than the French.*

GOTTHOLD EPHRAIM LESSING,
Hamburg Dramaturgy, trans. Helen
Zimmern (New York: Bohn's
Standard Library, 1890).

F. L. Schröder, Germany's greatest actor of the
eighteenth century, was instrumental in establishing
the Hamburg school of "realistic" acting. Here is a statement by him about his standards:

*It appears to me that only he has reached the standard of
true art who conceives each character in such a way that
nothing alien enters into it, that it not merely suggests a
type, but distinguishes itself from kindred characters by
individual features, which the performer finds in his own
experiences. . . . I hope that by consulting no other mirror
than that of the truth, I shall be able to satisfy the reasonable
demands of a judge of human character.*

F.L.W. MEYER, *Friedrich Ludwig
Schröder*, vol. I, page 337, quoted in
Karl Mantzius, *A History of Theatrical
Art*, vol. V (London, 1909), p. 163.

By the end of the eighteenth century, Weimar's
theatre was one of the best known in Germany because
of Goethe and Schiller. In one of his many conversations
with J. P. Eckermann, Goethe describes some of his
methods that lay behind what came to be called Weimar
Classicism:

*I did not look to magnificent scenery and a brilliant ward-
robe, but . . . to good pieces. . . . By means of good pieces
I educated the actors. . . . I was, also, constantly in personal contact with the actors. I attended the readings of the
plays, and explained to every one his part; I was present at
the chief rehearsals, and talked with the actors as to any
improvements that might be made; I was never absent from*

a performance, and pointed out the next day anything which did not appear to me to be right.

*Conversations of Goethe with
Eckermann and Soret,* trans. John
Oxenford (London, 1874), conversa-
tion of 22 March 1825.

Two actors who were coached by Goethe, Pius Alexander Wolff and Karl Franz Grüner, set down precepts they learned from their teacher. These were later arranged by Eckermann and published as Goethe's "rules for actors." Here are a few of the ninety-one rules:

35. . . . the actor must understand that he not only should imitate nature but present it ideally . . . uniting the true with the beautiful.

36. . . . the actor must gain complete control over every part of his body so that he may use each part freely, harmoniously and gracefully as expression demands.

39. The actors should not out of a mistaken idea of naturalness play to each other as if no third person were present. They should never play in profile or turn their backs to the audience. . . .

91. These rules are to be observed primarily when noble and worthy characters are to be represented. . . .

Johann Wolfgang von Goethe,
Werke, vol. 40 (Weimar, 1901).
A different and full translation of the
rules can be found in the *Quarterly
Journal of Speech,* XIII (1927),
247–256, 259–264.

14 Theatre in Europe and America During the Early Nineteenth Century

The nineteenth century was to bring the most radical social and political changes since the Renaissance. Most of the period from 1790 to 1850 was taken up with a struggle between those seeking to maintain the sociopolitical *status quo* and those working for a more democratic society. France played the key role in this struggle since the French Revolution had been its principal motivating force.

What had begun in France in 1789 as a relatively modest demand for a constitutional monarchy soon became more radical, especially after other countries, worried that the Revolution might spread, declared war on France and its royal family was accused of aiding the enemy. By 1792 France had been declared a republic, and in 1793 Louis XVI was guillotined. There followed the "reign of terror" during which thousands of persons were executed, many on mere suspicion of treason or lack of sympathy with the Revolution. This bloodbath finally ended in 1795, but by then most of the Revolution's major leaders had themselves been executed. Thereafter revolutionary fervor abated, but France's affairs, both internal and external, continued in disarray until Napoleon (1769–1821) seized power in 1799 and brought order out of chaos. In 1804 Napoleon was named emperor, and between 1805 and 1812 he gradually became master of practically all Europe, where he placed members of his family or army on the thrones of such countries as Spain and Holland, and many German and Italian states. Gradually he assembled the most extensive empire since

Roman times. Within this empire he made many reforms. He abolished the Holy Roman Empire, reduced the number of German states to less than forty, and put an end to serfdom in parts of eastern Europe.

But by 1810 the vision of a democratic order had degenerated into dreams of empire. Many who had considered Napoleon a deliverer developed nationalist sentiments that were to dominate Europe throughout the nineteenth century.

In 1812 the tide began to turn against Napoleon. In 1814 he was defeated at Waterloo; in 1815 he made a brief comeback, and was then permanently exiled. The aftermath was another blow to liberal sentiments, for the Congress of Vienna (1814–1815) sought above all to restore the sociopolitical conditions that had existed before 1789, although it did not hesitate to alter national boundaries or to award territory to its major participants. The result was that after 1815 repressive regimes returned to power throughout Europe, and most of them sought to insure that the French experience would not be repeated.

Unfortunately, the period after 1815 was one of great economic hardship, since the Napoleonic wars had severely depleted Europe's resources. Industrialization was also beginning to make itself felt as such inventions as the power loom, the steamship, and the locomotive promoted the factory system over the individual craftsman. Factories forced people to move into towns in order to be near their work; thus large population centers developed. With urbanization came wretched living conditions that cried out for social legislation at a time when conservative governments viewed any request for reform as a prelude to revolution. Therefore, it is not surprising that around 1830 frustrations boiled over into a series of uprisings throughout Europe. Most were unsuccessful, and in most instances even more intense repression resulted. Not until after another series of revolutions in 1848 and 1849 would significant change begin.

It is within this context that the theatre operated during the first half of the nineteenth century. Until about 1830 the movement called romanticism, with its idealistic views and yearnings for natural man and equality, dominated both artistic and social thought. But the failure of the 1830 uprisings turned this idealism, already weakened by earlier events, into disillusionment. Thereafter pessimism grew. Around 1850 a new movement—realism—began to replace the romantic vision. Still, between 1800 and 1850 romanticism was the dominant mode, even though it varied considerably from one country to another and from one decade to another.

THEORETICAL FOUNDATIONS OF ROMANTICISM

The eighteenth century had witnessed the gradual decline of the neoclassical ideal as the former emphasis upon man as a rational creature had been undermined by a growing faith in feeling and instinct as guides to moral behavior. Writers had begun to idealize the distant past when man allegedly had lived in a natural state, free from the shackles of despotic rulers. These changes contributed to shaping a new view of human nature, political theory, and literary forms. Most of these trends came together around 1800 and were eventually labeled romanticism.

As a conscious movement, romanticism began in Germany, but ultimately it affected all the Western world in varying degrees. Romanticism was first used as a descriptive term by a group of writers in Berlin in their literary journal, *Das Athenaeum* (1798–1800). These German romantics were not in revolt against a stagnating drama, as their French counterparts were to be, for they appeared at the very time when Goethe and Schiller were at the peak of their creativity. Rather, they saw themselves as clarifying and developing concepts derived from the Storm and Stress school of writers

and from Goethe and Schiller. They also borrowed liberally from the writings of Immanuel Kant (1724–1804) and other idealist philosophers in formulating the theoretical bases of a "romantic" art.

The philosophical foundations of romanticism are complex, but the fundamental tenets can be summarized briefly. First, the romantics (especially in Germany) argued that behind all earthly phenomena lies a higher truth than that of everyday social forms and natural phenomena, for all that exists has been created by an absolute being (variously called God, Spirit, Idea, Ego). Consequently, all creation participates in eternal truth and all things are parts of the whole and of each other. Truth, then, is defined in terms of the infinity of existence, rather than in observable norms, as the neoclassicist had held.

Second, since all creation has a common origin, a thorough and careful observation of any part may give insights into the whole (essentially a democratic idea). The less spoiled a thing is—that is, the less it deviates from its natural state—the more likely it is to embody some fundamental truth. Hence, the romantic writer preferred as subjects nature and unspoiled natural man or man in rebellion against the unnatural restraints of a highly structured and bureaucratic society.

Third, human existence is compounded of dualities: the body and the soul, the physical and the spiritual, the temporal and the eternal, the finite and the infinite. Because of his dual nature, man is divided against himself, for he must live in the physical world although his spirit strives to transcend this limitation. Thus, he longs for some ideal existence or society but is kept from achieving it by selfishness or other human limitations. In this scheme, art is of enormous significance, for it allows man to be "whole again," since during the aesthetic experience he is freed momentarily from the divisive forces of everyday existence. Art makes the "supersensuous sensuous" by giving a higher, eternal truth concrete, material form so that it can be apprehended by the limited human sensory apparatus; through these glimpses of ultimate truth, man becomes more fully aware of his potential—artistically, socially, and politically.

Fourth, to perceive the final unity behind the apparently endless diversity of existence requires an exceptional imagination, one found fully active only in the artist-genius and the philosopher. Thus, art like philosophy is a superior form of knowledge and the artist a truly superior being capable of providing guidance for others willing to listen.

FIGURE 14.1 Scene from Werner's *The Twenty-Fourth of February*, Act V. From *Le Monde Dramatique*.

Romantic theory implies that complete happiness and truth are to be found only in the spiritual realm and thus that they are impossible to attain fully during earthly existence. Furthermore, since spirit, as a part of the absolute, is eternal and infinite, the human mind with its physical limitations can never encompass truth in its totality. Therefore, the romantic playwright was faced with an impossible task, for not only was the highest truth always just beyond his grasp, but the profound intuitions granted him as a genius could never be embodied adequately because the means he had to use were necessarily too limited. (Similarly, the ideal society and state remained more nearly visions than attainable goals because of human weaknesses.) The demands of the physical stage were often viewed as too restrictive, and many dramatists refused to write with them in mind, preferring instead the freedom for imaginative flights permitted by "closet" drama.

Given these conceptions, it is not surprising that the romantics rejected the unities of time and place, the strict separation of drama into genres, the rationalistic outlook, and narrow didacticism. To them, Shakespeare's plays seemed most nearly to approach the desired goal; consequently, they adopted them as models to be followed in writing. For many writers, however, Shakespeare merely meant freedom from restraint, and they justified their own disorganized and episodic works

by his example. This subjectivity and lack of discipline alienated Goethe and Schiller, who in other respects had much in common with the romantic authors, for even though Goethe called romanticism "sickly," his *Faust,* with its enormous scope, its picture of eternal human striving, and its attempt to encompass the infinite variety of existence, epitomizes much of romantic thought and sums up much of his own and German literary experience between 1770 and 1830.

The ideas of the German romantics were eventually disseminated throughout Europe and America, although seldom were they articulated so completely or consciously. But everywhere playwriting and production were gradually altered by these views, which for the most part undergird dramatic and theatrical practice in the years between 1800 and 1850.

ROMANTIC DRAMA IN GERMANY

In Germany, among those who called themselves romantics, only two, Schlegel and Tieck, were deeply concerned with drama. August Wilhelm Schlegel (1767–1845) formulated and disseminated romantic theory in Germany and elsewhere through his lectures and essays. Samuel Taylor Coleridge adapted Schlegel's ideas in England, and Mme. de Staël popularized his views in France and Italy through *Of Germany.* Schlegel was perhaps the first critic to use classicism and romanticism as polar terms and it was largely through his influence that they passed into currency almost everywhere. Schlegel considered Shakespeare to be the greatest of all dramatists and he translated seventeen of the plays. His translations, and those of Shakespeare's other plays made later by members of the Tieck-Schlegel circle, have been mainstays of the German repertory since the early nineteenth century. In his criticism, Schlegel paid little attention to dramatic form, preferring instead to discuss tragic and comic "moods" as states of perception out of which differing approaches come. Thus, mood, emotion, and character were for him the main ingredients of drama, and plot a mere contrivance used by lesser playwrights to keep a story moving. This conception of dramatic elements has dominated critical thought since Schlegel's time and has served to divert attention from structure to vision.

Ludwig Tieck (1773–1853) had already developed a profound interest in Elizabethan drama before he met the other early romantics. This interest continued throughout his life, and he was perhaps more instrumental than anyone else in familiarizing Germans with the works of Shakespeare and his contemporaries. Among his own dramatic works were a number of "fantastic comedies" in the manner of Gozzi's *fiabe*, based on such fairy tales as "Little Red Riding Hood" and "Puss in Boots" but serving as springboards for his satirical comments on eighteenth-century rationalism and theatrical practices. These comedies are surprisingly modern in tone, for they break dramatic illusion frequently and call attention to the theatrical medium and to contemporary artistic taste. Tieck also wrote tragedies. Of these, *Kaiser Octavianus* (1802) is perhaps the best known. Set in the Middle Ages, its basic subject is the development of Christianity and the union of all men in a universal church. Its extremely episodic plot is held together primarily by the allegorical figure, Romance. The prologue to this play became famous for its evocation of twilight as that time when the logic of daylight fades into the mystery and magic of night. Tieck's contemporaries considered this passage so characteristic of the romantics that they dubbed them the "twilight men."

The early romantics were held together by close personal ties, but as their ideas spread and as they separated, the movement became increasingly diverse. Consequently, literary historians now divide the German romantics into groups, such as the Heidelberg Romantics, the Berlin Romantics, and so on. Few of their plays were produced, and even fewer found favor with the German public. The movement made an impact on the ordinary theatregoer primarily through the work of such popularizers as Kotzebue or through the writers of "fate tragedy," which was in great vogue between 1810 and 1820. It was initiated by Zacharias Werner's (1768–1823) *The 24th of February* (1809), which tells of a series of widely separated tragic events, all stemming from a curse and all occurring on the 24th of February. This play also spread the influence of Schiller, who previously had been derided by the romantics because of his attempt to unite literature and the theatre, a task which they thought impossible because of the limitations that production placed upon the playwright's genius. The phenomenal success of Werner, who had taken his inspiration from Schiller's *The Bride of Messina*, wrought a change of attitude and led to many imitations of Schiller's plays. Other popular writers of fate tragedy include Gottfried Müllner (1774–1829) with *The Debt* (1813) and Ernst von Houwald (1778–1845) with *The Portrait* (1820).

The best German dramatist of the early nineteenth century, Heinrich von Kleist (1777–1811), had no direct connection with the romantics, and critics disagree as to whether he should be considered one of them. Receiving little encouragement as a writer, Kleist committed suicide without having seen any of his plays produced. He remained virtually unknown until Tieck published his collected works in 1826. But by 1900 his reputation far exceeded that of any of the romantics, and his plays still figure prominently in the German repertory.

Kleist's best known dramas are *The Broken Jug* (1806), *Penthesilea* (1808), and *The Prince of Homburg* (1810). *The Broken Jug,* a long one-act play about a Falstaffian judge who seeks to hide his involvement in a case being tried before him, is one of the few comedies from the romantic era that remain playable. *Penthesilea*, essentially a psychological study of lust and the irrational element in love, is set during the Trojan War and shows the destruction of self-centered characters by uncontrollable desires. *The Prince of Homburg,* Kleist's masterpiece, tells of a young army officer who is sentenced to die even though his disobedience of an order has led to a military victory. Following a scene in which he begs for his life and admits that his action was motivated by ambition, he is pardoned. Kleist here seems to be concerned with the conflict between selfishness and selflessness. Kleist probably failed to achieve recognition in his own time because, unlike the self-conscious romantics, he often emphasized man's sensual (rather than his spiritual) nature.

POST-ROMANTIC GERMAN DRAMA

A change in the German consciousness seems to have occurred around 1805–1806 as Germany and Austria came under Napoleonic dominance. Thereafter, a sense of nationalism increased and interest in the Teutonic past burgeoned. Nevertheless, little nationalistic drama of importance was written, perhaps because censorship was so strict both during and following the Napoleonic years. Because innovation was frowned upon, the repertory came to be made up of classics (including works by Lessing, Goethe, Schiller, and Shakespeare) and innocuous new dramas by such writers as Kotzebue, who lived until 1819. Among the new dramatists, Ernst Raupach (1784–1852) most nearly equaled Iffland and Kotzebue in popularity. He wrote 117 plays after 1821; during the

1830s his works, including 14 spectacular history plays, dominated the repertory in Berlin and elsewhere. Other popular dramatists included Charlotte Birch-Pfeiffer (1800–1868), an actress who gave up the stage in 1828 to adapt popular novels, such as *The Hunchback of Notre Dame* (1837); Friedrich Halm (1806–1871), who wrote sentimental poetic dramas such as *Griseldis* (1834); and Eduard von Bauernfeld (1802–1890), who presented witty scenes of Viennese life in such plays as *The Confession* (1834) and *Middle Class and Romantic* (1835).

In the rather fallow years between 1815 and 1830, two dramatists—Grabbe and Grillparzer—stand out. Christian Dietrich Grabbe (1801–1836) was virtually ignored during his lifetime but is now recognized as a precursor of expressionism, epic theatre, and absurdism. In revolt against the optimism of the preceding years, Grabbe used a chaotic structure in *Comedy, Satire, Irony and Deeper Meaning* (1822) to depict his own views of society as a tangle of selfish interests, outworn clichés, and static conventions; in the final scene he appears as a character. In *Don Juan and Faust* (1829), Grabbe uses the principal figures to symbolize such contemporary polarizations as the masses and the intellectuals, the sensual and the spiritual. Most of Grabbe's plays are difficult to stage; for example, *Napoleon, or the One Hundred Days* (1831) demands the European continent as a stage and an army as actors. Only one of Grabbe's plays was produced during his lifetime, and his fame did not begin to grow until after 1875.

Franz Grillparzer (1791–1872) was Austria's first important serious playwright. He began his career in 1817 with *The Ancestress* (a work likened by critics to the fate tragedy then in vogue) and thereafter wrote regularly for the stage (despite almost continuous difficulty with the censor) until 1838, when the banning of one of his works led to his decision to withhold his plays from production. Consequently, many were not staged until after his death. His plays range through classical subjects, as in *Sappho* (1818) and *The Golden Fleece* (1821); history, as in *The Fate and Fall of King Ottokars* (1824) and *The Jewess of Toledo* (1837); and philosophical fantasy, as in *Der Traum ein Leben* (1834) based on Calderon's *Life is a Dream*. Grillparzer was the first significant playwright to express the sense of disillusionment that followed the Congress of Vienna. In his plays, the protagonists usually are rootless or alienated from their society. Motivated by some high ideal, they strive for reconciliation with others or self but usually end in disaster. More than any other writer of his time, Grillparzer captured in his poetic

FIGURE 14.2 Scene from Grillparzer's *Life is a Dream,* Act IV. Engraving by Andreas Geiger. Courtesy Bildarchiv, Osterreichische National-bibliothek, Vienna.

works the prevailing sense that idealism is ineffectual against the forces of society and destiny.

The Austrian temperament found more characteristic expression, however, in the folk and peasant play, which had been the dominant dramatic type since Stranitzky had introduced Hanswurst. This long tradition culminated in the nineteenth century in the plays of Raimund and Nestroy. Beginning in 1823, Ferdinand Raimund (1790–1836) wrote a series of plays for the Leopoldstadter Theater (founded in 1781), where he acted from 1817 until 1830. In these works realistic scenes of peasant life are interwoven with supernatural and fairy-tale elements. Regional dialects, folklore, allegory, and farce are the major ingredients of such plays as *The Barometer-Maker and the Magical Island* (1823) and *The Alpenking and the Misanthrope* (1828). Johann Nepomuk Nestroy (1801–1862), a comic actor, began writing plays about 1832, most of them (with leading roles for himself) for Carl Karl's (1782–1854) company at the Theater am der Wien, where he worked for some twenty years. His early work, such as *The Evil Spirit Lumpazivagabundus* (1833), resembled traditional folk drama in its use of the supernatural, but his subsequent plays abandoned the fairy element. Typical of the later

FIGURE 14.3 Nestroy's *The Ground Floor and the First Floor,* showing the use of two settings simultaneously, one above the other. Engraving from *Theaterzeitung.* Courtesy Bildarchiv, Osterreichische Nationalbibliothek, Vienna.

works is *The House of Temperaments* (1837), which used four apartments simultaneously to show four families headed by fathers of different temperaments. Nestroy also wrote dialect farces and parodies. One of his plays was to serve as the basis for Thornton Wilder's *The Matchmaker.* After about 1835 Nestroy was the most popular Viennese playwright of his day.

Following the abortive revolutions of 1830 a new movement—Young Germany—came to the fore and provided some of the most controversial plays of the 1830s and 1840s. In many ways quite diverse, its members were united by their scorn for abstraction and the idealism of the romantics. They championed social awareness and the relevance of ideas to contemporary affairs. In drama the leaders were Gutzkow and Laube. Karl Gutzkow (1811–1878) began writing plays in 1835 but had no work produced until 1839 when *Richard Savage,* in which a poet struggles with class prejudice, was given in Frankfurt. His most enduring play was to be *Uriel Acosta* (1847), which treats religious prejudice through a story about a young Jew. Heinrich Laube (1806–1884) began writing plays in 1841 with *Mondaleschi.* His best work probably is *The Karls Schoolboy* (1846), concerning Schiller's conflict with the Duke of Wurttemberg (who forbade him to

write). In these and other Young Germany works the concern for contemporary problems was only feebly masked under stories from other times and places. Consequently, the writers were often in trouble with the censor, and only after the revolution of 1848 were their works widely produced. By that time Gutzkow was literary advisor to the theatre at Dresden and Laube director of the Burgtheater in Vienna. But Young Germany plays were so firmly tied to the contemporary situation that they were soon dropped from the repertory.

Far more enduring fame was won by Georg Büchner (1813–1837), a writer somewhat tenuously related to Young Germany. Büchner wrote only three plays, *Danton's Death* (1835), *Leonce and Lena* (1836), an ironic comedy, and the uncompleted *Woyzeck* (1836). *Danton's Death,* an episodic drama set during the "reign of terror" following the French Revolution, has as its central character an idealist who, seeing his highest aims wrecked by pettiness, comes to suspect that his ideals were merely a disguise for sensual appetites. His superior sensitivity, which causes him to question the meaning of existence, will permit no resolution of his doubts, and he ends in despair and death. *Woyzeck,* one of the first plays to treat a lower-class protagonist sympathetically, shows the gradual degradation of a man trapped by heredity and environment. The play foreshadows naturalism in its subject matter and expressionism in its structural devices and dialogue. Because his outlook and techniques were considerably in advance of his time, Büchner seemed very modern when his plays were rediscovered by Max Reinhardt around 1900. Since then Büchner has been considered one of the major dramatists of the nineteenth century.

After 1840 the German playwright most praised by contemporary critics was Friedrich Hebbel (1813–1863). Largely self-educated, Hebbel began his playwriting career in 1839 with *Judith.* Among his most important works are *Genoveva* (1841), *Maria Magdalena* (1844), *Herod and Miriamne* (1849), and the trilogy *The Niebelungen* (1855–1862). Like many of his contemporaries, Hebbel underwent a serious crisis in belief after first accepting the romantic outlook. Unlike Büchner, who never passed beyond pessimism, Hebbel found consolation in his own version of G.W.F. Hegel's philosophical position. Thus, he came to view society as a reflection of Absolute Spirit, which lies behind human existence and works out its own perfection through humanity. In Hebbel's view, the most significant human problems arise because values tend to harden into con-

FIGURE 14.4 Friedrich Hebbel's *Agnes Bernauer* at the Burgtheater, Vienna, in 1868. The performers are Friedrich Krastel as Albrecht and Friederike Bognar as Agnes. Courtesy Osterreichische Nationalbibliothek, Vienna.

triumph of the position that has seemingly been defeated. Through such a view, Hebbel reconciled his sense of the world's current imperfections with the possibility of improvement. His most famous play, *Maria Magdalena*, is now usually studied as a forerunner of realism because its characters are drawn from ordinary life, its dialogue is in prose, and its story ends in the suicide of the heroine, a victim of society's narrow-mindedness. Thus, the play can be viewed as a realistic depiction of nineteenth-century German life. Nevertheless, like Hebbel's other plays, it too embodies the conflict between old and new values, and the heroine's death serves to make way for the new by raising serious doubts about the old. After Hebbel's death in 1863, German drama entered a period of decline from which it did not recover until the 1890s.

THEATRICAL CONDITIONS IN GERMANY

The vitality of the German theatre between 1805 and 1815 was curtailed by the French occupation, during which many state troupes lost their subsidies. While the downfall of Napoleon brought the reinstatement of financial aid, it also brought greater political control. Government officials, many with no theatrical experience, were appointed as superintendents of state theatres on the grounds that they could mediate between the public good and the sometimes self-serving practices of theatre workers. As a result, the stage manager's authority was undermined and a bureaucratic organization was imposed on each company. Initiative soon declined and routine efficiency tended to replace innovation. Censorship, which in many states was quite severe, also contributed to mediocrity by discouraging anything considered potentially offensive or dangerous. As a result, the German theatre of the nineteenth century tended to be competent but rarely inspired.

   If few companies were truly outstanding, the theatre in general prospered. In subsidized troupes actors were relatively secure because they were now civil servants with pension rights; company deficits were made up by governments, which also supplied buildings with good facilities. By 1842, Germany had sixty-five permanent theatres employing about 5,000 actors, singers, and musicians. By 1850 both state and municipal governments took it for granted that they should support the theatre, and because of this attitude each sizable city had a troupe of reasonably good quality. On the other hand,

ventional patterns rather than remaining flexible to meet changing situations. Consequently, advances in morality are accomplished only after a violent conflict has destroyed worthwhile human beings seeking a better way of life; death serves to raise doubts about the old patterns, however, and to make way for new ones. Since the new values will rigidify in their turn, the process must be repeated. Thus, Hebbel viewed history as a series of conflicts and his plays reflect this preoccupation with moral evolution.

   In Hebbel's works, the main characters are representative of the old and the new orders. Since the old has the power of established authority behind it, the new, which can rely only upon faith or love, is usually destroyed. This destruction, however, foreshadows the

FIGURE 14.5   Scene from Nestroy's *Lumpazivaga-bundus* (roughly *Rascal Vagabond*) in 1833. Nestroy is at left, and the actor-manager Karl Carl at center. The exaggerated comic costumes are typical of the period. From *Schriften der Gesellschaft fur Theatergeschichte* (1908).

decentralization made it difficult for any theatre to become dominant.

Nevertheless, two cities—Berlin and Vienna—stood out above the others during these years. In the beginning, Berlin was dominant, perhaps because of Iffland, who ruled over the National Theatre there until his death in 1814. Here Iffland mounted the most sumptuous productions (primarily of Schiller's works, sentimental plays and operas) to be seen in Germany. With them, Iffland (working with his designer, Bartolomeo Verona) extended the trend begun by Schröder and others toward historical accuracy. For example, his production of Schiller's *The Maid of Orleans* in 1801 was especially admired for its coronation procession of more than 800 persons in period dress set before a Gothic cathedral. Iffland was succeeded from 1814 to 1828 by Count Karl Bruhl (1782–1837), a court official who was even more insistent upon accuracy in costumes and settings, although he was not insistent upon ensemble acting. After 1816 his principal designer was Karl Friedrich Schinkel (1781–1841), a leader in the classical revival then underway. It was also Schinkel who designed the company's new theatre, opened in 1820 and used till 1944, which, with its half-circle auditorium and extensive work space, influenced almost all subsequent theatre architecture in Germany.

After 1815 primacy passed to the Burgtheater in Vienna, largely because of Josef Schreyvogel's (1768–1832) leadership between 1814 and 1831. The Burgtheater's eminence was stimulated in part by being the first German state theatre to restrict its repertory (beginning in 1810) to spoken drama. (Others continued to mingle drama and opera for some time thereafter.) Despite strict censorship, Schreyvogel was able to build the finest repertory and the best ensemble of any German theatre. His outstanding company included Sophie Schröder (1781–1868), the greatest tragic actress of her day; Heinrich Anschütz (1785–1865), noted for performances in middle-class comedy, drama, and tragedy; and Ludwig Costenoble (1769–1837), one of the best comic actors of the time. In production, Schreyvogel sought a middle ground between Weimar's spare, declamatory style and Berlin's sumptuous, spectacular style. Consequently, he emphasized beauty and grace in acting and pictorial composition but he did not stint on decor and costumes. Between 1810 and 1848 the Burgtheater's

FIGURE 14.6   The coronation procession from Schiller's *The Maid of Orleans* as staged by Iffland at the Berlin National Theatre in 1801. This production was one of the first anywhere to emphasize historical accuracy in costumes and scenery, although even here many elements were more nearly sixteenth than fifteenth century, the time of the action. From Weddigen, *Geschichte der Theater Deutschlands* (1904).

decor was under the supervision of Philipp von Stuben-rauch, an expert on all historical periods who did much to insure accuracy in both costumes and settings.

A similar trend toward historical accuracy was evident in virtually all the theatres of Germany at this time. Nevertheless, in costuming, five periods were considered sufficient for all plays set in past eras: classical, medieval, sixteenth century, seventeenth century, and mid-eighteenth century. More precise treatment was not to come until after 1850, when additional information became available in Jakob Weiss' authoritative histories of costume (published between 1856 and 1872).

While most settings continued to be composed of wings and drops, the box set was used occasionally for interiors. Apparently the box set began to evolve in the late eighteenth century when a door or window was set up between two wings. Gradually other units were added, until the acting area was completely enclosed. The first fully developed box set in Berlin was used in 1826. By the 1830s Nestroy, in his *The House of Temperaments*, could demand a setting which showed two rooms on the stage level and two above. Nevertheless, the box set did not become usual for interior scenes until about 1875.

The kind of ensemble attained by Schröder and Goethe seems to have declined after 1830 as emphasis shifted to starring performers, perhaps because of the romantic glorification of individual genius. Starring engagements, popularized in the eighteenth century by Schröder and Iffland, grew in number during the nineteenth century, especially after the opening of the first railroad in 1835. Managers thought it necessary to engage a series of stars, for, while the theatre was the favorite form of entertainment, the German public was not attracted by the standard repertory unless performed by noted actors. Since the visitors seldom rehearsed extensively with the local companies and often insisted that other roles be curtailed so as not to detract from their own, ensemble effect was difficult to attain.

During the first half of the nineteenth century, Germany produced many outstanding actors. Its greatest romantic actor was Ludwig Devrient (1784–1832), who made his debut in 1804 but achieved success only after turning to character roles. He was especially noted for his Richard III, Shylock, Falstaff, Lear, and Franz Moor (in Schiller's *The Robbers*). Devrient came to Berlin at the time of Iffland's death, but because of conflict between him and the company's leading tragic actor, Pius A. Wolff (1782–1828), who had been trained by Goethe, Bruhl appointed Devrient stage manager for comedy.

FIGURE 14.7 **Ludwig Devrient as King Lear in the storm scene. From Weddigen,** *Geschichte der Theater Deutschlands* **(1904).**

Thus, after his initial season in Berlin Devrient was confined to acting comic roles at the very time when he was at the height of his powers. In 1828 he went to the Burg-theater and for the next four years electrified Viennese playgoers with his passionate and versatile acting. Unfortunately his powers were soon exhausted and he died at the age of forty-eight.

Throughout this period the conflict between acting styles, often within the same company, was evident. Two of Devrient's nephews, Eduard (1801–1877) and Emil (1803–1872), epitomize the conflict. Eduard performed in a natural, realistic style, while Emil was a disciple of Weimar Classicism. Another outstanding performer in the classical style was Ferdinand Esslair (1772–1840), after 1820 leading actor at Munich, although he spent

FIGURE 14.8 Ludwig Tieck's production of *A Midsummer Night's Dream* in Berlin, 1843. Note the tapestries downstage on either side; note also the steps that curve up to form an inner stage between them. A contemporary lithograph.

much of his time touring with his interpretations of Schiller's protagonists. The realistic style was championed by Karl Seydelmann (1793–1843), who made his reputation at Kassel between 1822 and 1828 and toured extensively in such roles as Iago, Shylock, and Mephisto before joining the Berlin company in 1838; and by Bogumil Dawison (1818–1872), a Polish actor who created tormented portraits of such characters as Richard III, Iago, and Shylock, both as a touring star and as a member of companies in Vienna and Dresden. Not until after mid-century was the conflict in styles resolved in favor of the realistic school.

Not everyone was content with the prevailing conditions. Among those who sought reform, the most important were Tieck and Immermann. Ludwig Tieck's interests extended far beyond the playwriting which had first introduced him to the theatre. By the 1820s he was considered Germany's leading authority on the theatre because of his critical essays and his performances as a

platform reader. Nevertheless, his ideas about production were considered impractical, and, though he served as literary advisor to the Dresden troupe from 1824 until 1842, his influence was restricted to improvements in the repertory. It was not until 1841, when he was sixty-four years old, that Tieck was given a chance to implement his ideas about staging.

The difficulties which Tieck encountered are explained by the dominance of Weimar Classicism and realistic spectacle in German theatres of the period. Since Tieck advocated psychologically realistic acting on a simple platform stage, he called for an approach at variance with the two dominant styles of the time. Many of Tieck's ideas stemmed from his intensive study of Shakespeare. In 1836, with the architect Gottfried Semper, he reconstructed the Fortune Theatre, the first attempt of this kind. In his novel, *The Young Master Cabinetmaker* (1837), Tieck described a performance of *Twelfth Night* on an Elizabethan public stage. He was the first modern critic to advocate a return to the open stage, for he believed that true illusion results from convincing acting and is destroyed by pictorial realism. He also believed that every element of a production should be supervised by a single and autocratic director.

Tieck's chance to try out his ideas came in 1841, when William IV of Prussia decided to devote his court theatre at Potsdam to experimental productions. He summoned Tieck to stage Sophocles' *Antigone,* an innovation in itself, since professional productions of Greek tragedies were practically unknown at this time. Tieck was given complete authority over the production. He extended the apron over the orchestra pit in a semicircle and constructed a Greek *skene,* which served as the only background for the action. After its success at Potsdam, the production was moved to the state theatre in Berlin and was soon adapted by companies at Dresden, Leipzig, Mannheim, Munich, and Karlsruhe.

Tieck's most famous production was of Shakespeare's *A Midsummer Night's Dream,* presented in 1843 with incidental music by Felix Mendelssohn. For it, Tieck adapted Elizabethan conventions to the proscenium theatre. Letting the forward part of the stage form a large open space, he constructed a unit at the rear, with curving stairs leading to an acting area 8 feet above the main stage. The two stairs framed an inner stage on the lower level. The sides of the stage were masked by tapestries hung at right angles to the proscenium. This production was repeated forty times during the first season at the Berlin theatre, and was imitated by numerous troupes throughout Germany. Because of illness, Tieck was never able to complete another production. *Henry V,* which he planned to do without any set changes, had to be abandoned.

Tieck's work was made possible only because William IV ordered all theatrical personnel to follow Tieck's orders. Bypassing the permanent managers created considerable friction, and after Tieck's retirement the old methods were resumed. Nevertheless, Tieck's ideas were to be revived and pursued more consistently at the end of the century.

Karl Immermann (1796–1840) combined the ideas of Goethe and Tieck, for while he advocated a declamatory acting style, he accepted many of Tieck's theories about spectacle. Immermann believed that the salvation of the theatre lay in drama of high quality and productions controlled by a single artistic consciousness. Immermann, originally a law-court official, began his theatrical work around 1829 with amateurs. In 1834 he took over the management of the Dusseldorf Municipal Theatre, where he presented plays by Calderón, Goethe, Schiller, Lessing, Kleist, and others, although the majority of the works were light, ephemeral pieces, perhaps understandably so since in four years Immermann presented 355 plays. By the standards of the time, his productions were prepared with great care, though he usually had no more than ten rehearsals. In some instances he employed painters to design settings, and he made extensive use of carefully-posed tableaus, many based on well-known paintings. Despite Immermann's high ideals, he was forced by economic pressures to give up management in 1837, but his theatre was long considered to be a model by others.

Ironically, Immermann is now remembered primarily for a single private production of Shakespeare's *Twelfth Night* given in 1840. The architect Wiegman designed a special stage for this production with a fixed facade around three sides of an open space. At each end were entrances and across the back an inner stage and other smaller openings. Historically it is significant as the first important attempt to return to a stage like that for which Shakespeare wrote, even if the results more nearly resemble the Teatro Olimpico than the Globe.

Throughout the first half of the nineteenth century the German theatre enjoyed considerable popularity and prosperity. In general it was prosperous, and the number of companies steadily increased. Not only were theatres opened in cities previously without them, but in such major centers as Vienna and Berlin several theatres

FIGURE 14.9 Immermann's stage for Shakespeare's *Twelfth Night,* 1840. The forestage remained fixed but some scenic elements were changed within the openings at the rear. Courtesy Theatermuseum, Munich.

were in operation simultaneously before 1850. They would continue to grow in number during the second half of the century.

THE FRENCH THEATRE, 1789–1815

During the period of political uncertainty in France which followed the fall of the Bastille in 1789, the minor theatres grew ever bolder in their encroachments on the privileges of the major troupes, who protested in vain. After the monopolies were abolished in 1791, numerous new companies were formed in Paris. It is difficult to chronicle their development, for many soon expired, and others adopted new names with bewildering frequency in the desire to reflect changing political currents and to remain in favor with the ruling factions. Estimates of the number of troupes between 1791 and 1800 range from 50 to 100.

Most of the theatres catered to mob tastes by offering a wide range of popular entertainments combined with appeals to patriotic sentiment. The first burst of freedom, during which censorship was lifted, gave way during the "reign of terror" to repressive measures and severe punishments for any alleged opposition to the Revolution. Consequently, little drama of merit appeared. By far the most popular playwright of the Revolution was

Marie-Joseph Chénier (1764–1811), whose *Charles IX* (1789) and *Henri VIII* (1791) set the political tone for others. In spite of their revolutionary sentiments, however, Chénier's plays remained clearly within the neoclassical tradition.

During the 1790s the former crown theatres lost much of their prestige. In 1791, the Comédie Française, already weakened by internal strife, split into two troupes. The actors sympathetic to the Revolution, including Talma and Mlle. Desgarcins, joined those of the Variétés Amusantes to form the Théâtre de la République in 1792. After 1793, when the actors at the Comédie Française were imprisoned, this company was considered the finest in Paris. The Comédie Italienne, renamed the Théâtre Favart, was dangerously weakened by its fierce competition with the Théâtre Feydeau. The Opéra survived only because it was taken over by the city of Paris.

By 1799 when Napoleon came to power France was weary of intrigues and fanaticism. Napoleon immediately made clear his opposition to partisan drama by suppressing several plays favorable to his own cause. As a result, the theatre began to turn away from political subjects.

The changed atmosphere also brought renewed stability to the major troupes. In 1799, the fragments of the Comédie Française were reunited; in 1800 its theatre was declared state property and its use ceded to the troupe; in 1801, its pensions and subsidies, interrupted in 1791, were reinstated. In 1801, the Théâtre Feydeau and the Théâtre Favart were united in the state-subsidized Théâtre National de l'Opéra-Comique. In 1802, the Opéra was brought under state control once more and in 1803 was granted a subsidy.

The favors shown the major troupes were paralleled by repressions of minor theatres, for which Napoleon had little respect. In 1806, he decreed that works in the repertories of the state troupes could not be performed by any other theatres, that all plays must be passed by a censor, and that no new theatres might be established without special permission. In 1807, he took more drastic measures. First, he authorized four state-supported theatres: the Comédie Française (for regular comedy and tragedy); the Théâtre de l'Impératrice, later the Odéon (for lesser drama); the Opéra (for grand opera and serious ballet); and the Opéra-Comique (for light opera and comic ballet). These troupes (in varying guises) were to continue into the twentieth century. Second, he ordered the closure of all minor theatres except four: the Théâtre de la Gaîté and the Ambigu-Comique (both to perform melodramas and pantomimes); and the Théâtre des Variétés and the Vaudeville (both to perform short plays, parodies, and *comédies-en-vaudevilles*). Other theatres, such as the Porte-Saint-Martin and the Cirque Olympique, were eventually allowed to reopen, but they too were restricted to minor genres. Napoleon's strictures were continued under the restored monarchy from 1815 until 1831, when a new uprising forced a change. Between 1807 and 1831 the number of theatres in Paris was strictly controlled and each was restricted to entertainments of specific types. Thus, theatrical conditions differed little from those of the 1780s. As before the Revolution, the principal innovations were to come from the boulevard theatres.

FRENCH DRAMA, 1800–1850

Just as Napoleon sought to pattern his empire after Rome, so too he favored a classical drama. It is often said that in return for supporting the theatre he expected a new masterpiece each year. Beginning in 1804 he offered annually prizes of 10,000 and 5,000 francs for the best tragedy and the best comedy performed at the Comédie Française. Unfortunately, few of the prize works found lasting favor. Probably the best playwright of the time was Népomucène Lemercier (1771–1840), author of *Pinto* (1800) and *Christophe Colomb* (1809), but the latter work was performed at the Odéon billed as a "Shakespearean comedy" because of its defiance of the unities and its mixture of genres.

Ironically, it was the boulevard theatres that produced the only truly popular plays, and these were melodramas rather than the tragedies for which Napoleon longed. Although melodramatic works, most often in the form of tragicomedy or pastoral, can be traced back to classical Greece, the term "melodrama" did not come into widespread use until after 1800. While all of the characteristic elements of melodrama had long been present in many boulevard theatres, it was René Charles Guilbert de Pixérécourt (1773–1844), in *Victor, or The Child of the Forest* (1798), *Coelina* (1800), and other works, who gave them their typical form. The popularity of Pixérécourt's works (in combination with Kotzebue's) established melodrama as the dominant dramatic type of the nineteenth century.

The basic characteristics of melodrama can be summarized briefly: a virtuous hero (or heroine) is relentlessly hounded by a villain and is rescued from seemingly insurmountable difficulties only after he has undergone a series of threats to his life, reputation, or happiness; an episodic story unfolds rapidly after a short expository scene; each act ends with a strong climax; all important events occur on stage and often involve elaborate spectacle (such as battles, floods, earthquakes) and local color (such as festivals, dances, or picturesque working conditions); the typical plot devices include disguise, abduction, concealed identity, and strange coincidence; strict poetic justice is meted out, for, although he may succeed until the final scene, the villain is always defeated; comic relief is provided by a servant or companion to one of the principal characters; song, dance, and music provide additional entertainment or underscore the emotional values of scenes. Melodrama, with its simple, powerful stories, unequivocal moral tone, and elements drawn from popular entertainment, could be understood and enjoyed by the least sophisticated of theatregoers. Probably for this reason, melodrama was largely responsible for bringing into the nineteenth-century theatre a large popular audience comparable to that enjoyed by motion pictures and television in the twentieth century.

Although Pixérécourt, with his more than 120 works, was the most successful of the melodramatic playwrights, he had many competitors. Of these, the most influential were Victor Ducange, author of such plays as *Thirty Years, or the Life of a Gambler* (1827), and Louis Caigniez, author of such plays as *The Hermit of Mont-Pausilyse.*

Melodrama paved the way for French romantic drama by popularizing departures from neoclassical precepts and by creating a large potential audience for it. Furthermore, melodrama's plot devices were taken over by the French romantics to such an extent that many of their plays can be distinguished from melodrama only because of a few differences: romantic drama employs the five-act form (as opposed to melodrama's three acts); it avoids the happy ending; and it is more dependent upon diction. In broad outline, nevertheless, the characteristic French romantic drama was often merely elevated melodrama.

The romantic movement was slow in getting underway in France because of political conditions. Its first important impetus came with the publication of Mme. de Staël's *Of Germany.* Born Germaine Necker, Mme. de Staël (1766–1817) was the daughter of Louis XVI's minister of finance and wife to the Swedish ambassador

FIGURE 14.10 Setting by Gué for the third act of Pixérécourt's *The Marseilles Plague,* produced at the Théâtre de la Gaiëté, Paris, 1928. Courtesy Bibliothèque de l'Arsenal, Paris.

to France. A bitter enemy of Napoleon, she spent the years of his reign in Germany, where she became familiar with romanticism, especially through her acquaintance with A. W. Schlegel, who for a time was tutor to her children. *Of Germany,* which described the new literary movement, was published in France in 1810 but was immediately suppressed. Following Napoleon's downfall in 1814, it was quickly reissued. The notoriety of Mme. de Staël's feud with Napoleon brought the book much publicity and gave its ideas wide currency. Thereafter debate over the relative merits of neoclassicism and romanticism raged in earnest.

Stendhal (Marie-Henri Beyle, 1783–1842) contributed to the controversy with *Racine and Shakespeare* (1823–1825), in which he declared Shakespeare's plays to be more suitable as models for dramatists than those of Racine. But the major French statement of romantic doctrine came in Hugo's preface to his play *Cromwell* (1827). Victor Hugo (1802–1885) set forth few ideas not already current in Germany, England, and elsewhere. He called for the abandonment of the unities of time and place, denounced the strict separation of genres, and advocated emphasizing the specific historical milieu of an action. Perhaps most important, he insisted that art should go beyond the neoclassicist's "idealized nature" to one that included both the sublime and the grotesque. Since for Hugo the sublime was related to man's spiritual qualities and the grotesque to his animal nature, he argued that a truthful depiction of humanity requires that both be represented in every literary work.

The culmination of the debate came in 1830 with the production of Hugo's *Hernani* at the Comédie Française. A pitched battle between the romantics and traditionalists, during which the actors were scarcely heard, raged for several nights. The bitterness of the contest is probably explained by the feeling on both sides that principles involving the future course of literature were at stake. Several events had accelerated the trend toward romanticism in France after 1827: Charles Kemble's troupe of English actors had performed Shakespeare's plays to admiring Parisian audiences in 1827; W. C. Macready had appeared in Paris in English romantic plays in 1828; Sir Walter Scott's novels were attracting an ever-wider reading public throughout France; and Shakespeare's plays were being read and produced in France with increasing frequency. Furthermore, by 1829 French romantic plays had made their way into the repertory of the Comédie Française: Alexandre Dumas *père's Henri III and His Court*, Casimir Delavigne's *Marino Faliero*, and Alfred de Vigny's adaptation of *Othello* as *The Moor of Venice* were all produced in 1829. By opposing *Hernani*, the conservative audience hoped to halt this trend.

In *Hernani*, Hugo deliberately violated many of the rules which the advocates of neoclassicism sought to retain. First, he made innovations in the alexandrine, which had been the accepted verse form for tragedy since the seventeenth century. Second, he used many words which had long been considered beneath the dignity of tragedy. Third, he broke the unities of time and place. Fourth, he showed deaths and violence on stage. Fifth, he shifted the mood of his scenes frequently and mixed humor with seriousness.

Hernani is essentially a melodrama with an unhappy ending. It tells the story of the noble outlaw Hernani and his attempt to wed Dona Sol over the opposition of the king and her guardian, both of whom also love her. Eventually he succeeds and a happy future seems to lie ahead when he is reminded of a pledge made to the guardian earlier in a moment of crisis—that Hernani would give his life if the guardian ever demanded it. When the vindictive guardian asks that the pledge be redeemed, the couple choose suicide above a dishonored oath.

It is usual to date French romanticism from the triumph of *Hernani*. The upsurge in the production of

FIGURE 14.11 The battle over *Hernani* (1830). Onstage is the final scene. From Grand Carteret, *XIXe Siècle* (1892).

romantic plays is probably also explained by the lifting of censorship and genre restrictions following the Revolution of 1830. In addition to Hugo, whose popularity continued to increase with such plays as *Marion Delorme* (1831), *The King Amuses Himself* (1832), and *Ruy Blas* (1838), other important dramatists of the school include Dumas *père*, Vigny, and Musset.

The plays of Alexandre Dumas *père* (1802–1870) are of two types: historical spectacles, such as *Henri III and His Court, Christine* (1829), and his dramatization of *The Three Musketeers;* and domestic dramas, such as *Antony* (1831). Although Dumas had a surer sense of dramatic situation than did Hugo, he lacked Hugo's poetic gift, and, when he attempted to express profound emotion or significant thought, often lapsed into puerility.

Alfred de Vigny (1797–1863) began his dramatic career by adapting the works of Shakespeare and went on to write historical spectacles, such as *The Marshal of Ancre*. He is now remembered primarily for his *Chatterton* (1835)—the story of a poet-martyr outcast from society because of his special insight—which epitomizes the romantic idealization of the misunderstood genius.

Of French romantic dramas, those by Alfred de

Musset (1810–1857) have fared best, although originally they were virtually ignored. After the failure of his first play, *A Venetian Night* (1830), Musset ceased writing for production. Consequently, his later works shift time and place freely and depend little upon spectacle. Like Racine and Marivaux, Musset is primarily concerned with the inner feelings of his characters, especially their inability to resist love's compelling force. Musset's characters are essentially selfish, however, and seek desperately to protect their egos by forcing others to reveal their feelings first. But since the others also are loathe to lay themselves open to hurt or rejection, the participants indulge in a series of ploys and counterploys. Sometimes the results are happy, as in *A Door Should Either Be Shut or Open,* and sometimes tragic, as in *No Trifling with Love.* Musset seldom strayed from his preoccupation with love, but his *Lorenzaccio,* the story of a Hamlet-like character who seeks to right the Florentine state, is one of the finest historical dramas of the nineteenth century. Musset's plays, most of which were written between 1830 and 1840, did not begin to be produced until 1847. Since that time, they have never been absent from the repertory.

Following the removal of genre restrictions, romantic drama found a ready home in the boulevard theatres. There it mingled with melodrama and absorbed still more melodramatic traits even as it helped to elevate melodrama. But by the 1840s the enthusiasm for romantic drama had waned. The failure of Hugo's *Les Burgraves* in 1843 is usually considered to mark the end of the romantic era in France.

Romanticism was succeeded by the "Theatre of Common Sense," which sought a middle ground between neoclassicism and romanticism. The leader of the new group was François Ponsard (1814–1867), who came to prominence in 1843 with *Lucrèce.* But, as with most compromises, the Theatre of Common Sense soon lost its appeal. By the 1850s it was giving way to still another movement—realism.

THEATRICAL CONDITIONS IN FRANCE, 1800–1850

The number of theatres in Paris grew steadily during the first half of the nineteenth century. Although the government retained firm control over licensing, the eight companies authorized by Napoleon in 1807 had grown to twenty-eight by 1855. Of these, the four state-supported

FIGURE 14.12   A sketch by Hugo for his play, *The King Amuses Himself.* **Hugo often supplied designs for his plays. Here he shows a scene at night outside a tavern. From Loliée,** *La Comédie Française* **(1907).**

troupes commanded the greatest prestige. After genre restrictions were removed in 1831, the Odéon and Opéra-Comique often rivaled the Comédie Française and Opéra in the quality of works presented and in the mounting of their productions. Throughout the century, the boulevard theatres were the most experimental, often championing new playwrights or methods of production long before they were accepted by the state troupes. Of the secondary theatres, the most influential were the Vaudeville, Gymnase, Porte-Saint-Martin, Gâité, and Ambigu-Comique.

Apart from the Comédie Française, all of the Parisian troupes (with a few minor exceptions) were run by managers who hired actors on contract. The Comédie Française, on the other hand, continued to be a sharing company, operating under rules much like those in effect before the Revolution. The new regulations, established by Napoleon in 1812 by the "Decree of Moscow," sought through 101 articles to correct some of the earlier problems. A reserve fund was established to insure pensions and to take care of deficits. Each *sociétaire* was now guaranteed a minimum annual wage and, in addition, was paid a small fee for each day he performed. As in earlier years, the government provided a generous subsidy. Ostensibly the actors were responsible for all policy decisions, but the supervisor, who replaced the Gentlemen of the Chamber, often assumed considerable authority. Furthermore, in the 1830s problems became so pressing that the actors ceded much of their authority to a manager.

The other state theatres were let (under renewable contracts) to managers who had full control over the performers and the repertory, although their work was subject to close governmental scrutiny. The Opéra continued to be the favored troupe. Not only was its subsidy often four times as great as that of the Comédie Française, but between 1811 and 1831 it was allotted up to 1/20 of the receipts of all private theatres.

All the Parisian theatres retained the repertory system until after 1850, although the long run began to alter the old patterns. In the early years of the century, only unusually popular plays were performed for a number of consecutive evenings; typically the bill was changed every day. But as early as 1835 a run of 100 nights had been achieved, although this was not to be common until the 1870s.

Spectators at Parisian theatres had to present their tickets to three persons: the theatre's official ticket taker, the government employee who made a record of the poor tax, and the representative of the Society of Dramatic Authors who calculated royalties. The Society of Dramatic Authors, which succeeded the Bureau Dramatique in 1829, was a "closed shop" that boycotted any theatre refusing to accept its authority over contracts. The standard contract specified the maximum permissible delay between the acceptance and production of a play, required that each play be performed at least three times, and allowed a cessation of rehearsals for ten days so that the author might revise his work. Dramatists received from 10 to 15 percent of each performance's receipts. The society also established a pension fund for playwrights who had been members for more than twenty years, and who had had more than a minimum number of plays produced. French playwrights were the first in the world to collect a royalty for each performance of their works and to achieve the financial security of a pension fund.

Every theatre had a paid claque to insure correct and adequate response. Some actors even specified in their contracts the amount of applause they were to receive at their first entrance in each play. As a result of this paid approval, other spectators tended to restrict overt response to disapproval.

DIRECTING AND ACTING IN FRANCE, 1800–1850

In France, melodrama initiated a concern for "directing," for much of its effect depended upon the precise manipulation of coincidence and spectacle. Plots often revolved around overheard conversations, fortunate entrances, and spectacular feats of physical courage, and the resolutions often saw the villain foiled by an earthquake, a volcanic eruption, or some other fortuitous cataclysm. The effectiveness of many melodramas, therefore, depended upon the precise coordination of many elements. It was for this reason that Pixérécourt insisted upon absolute control over the staging of his works. He later declared that his preeminence as a dramatist was due to his care in production.

Pixérécourt's example was followed by several of the romantics, and above all by Hugo and Dumas. But, whereas Pixérécourt had been concerned primarily with the coordination of special effects, Hugo was additionally concerned with the actor's stage positions and the overall composition. Prior to 1830, French actors had tended to form a straight line or semicircle at the front of the stage near the prompter's box, for though furniture had begun to proliferate by the 1820s, it was seldom used by the actors and was treated primarily as decoration. Contrary to earlier practices, Hugo in *Hernani* utilized the entire stage space, replaced the usual long diagonal movements with short curved movements, and even had an occasional actor play a scene with his back to the audience. But the *sociétaires* at the Comédie Française did not approve of these innovations and when Hugo began to take his plays to other theatres they returned to their old practices. But by 1835 critics were noting that in the boulevard theatres actors had begun to sit on the arms of chairs, to lean on tables, and even to remain seated while speaking. Still, most directors were more concerned with picturesque local color, historical accuracy, or precision of stage business than with creating an illusion of real life. Those who did move toward greater lifelikeness met considerable opposition from critics, who argued that art should idealize rather than copy life. Even those who approved of the trend usually denounced any attempt to represent sordidness on the stage.

Throughout the first half of the nineteenth century French actors continued to be employed according to lines of business. But, as elsewhere, there was a trend toward stars. Even at the Comédie Française leading

FIGURE 14.13   Talma as Titus in Voltaire's *Brutus* in 1791. From Adolphe Jullien, *Histoire du Costume au Théâtre* (1880).

stant source of friction because of his dissatisfaction with the troupe's acting style, costuming practices, and politics. He attained his first success in 1789 in Chénier's *Charles IX*, a work which contributed to the separation of the company in 1791. After the troupe was reunited in 1799, Talma remained its acknowledged leader until his death. He was a favorite of Napoleon, who often summoned him to play before the rulers of Europe. Talma was devoted to authenticity in costume (at least for classical roles) and to detailed study of every role. To this care, he joined intense feeling and vigor. It is sometimes said that he was by temperament a romantic but by circumstance doomed to perform in neo-classical plays.

Mlle. Duchenois (Catherine Rafuin, *c.* 1777–1835) was Talma's usual companion in tragedy. In 1802 her debut as Phèdre was so successful that the play was repeated for eight nights. Although she was notoriously ugly, her "profound tenderness and melodious sorrow" won her a devoted following. She seldom played after Talma's death and retired altogether in 1830.

While Talma and Mlle. Duchenois dominated tragic acting, Mlle. Mars and Fleury were the most famous performers of comedy. Mlle. Mars (Anne Boutet, 1779–1847), on the stage from childhood, joined the Comédie Française in 1799 and after 1805 was the idol of Paris. All critics spoke of her in glowing terms. Although noted for her shrewishness offstage, as an actress she seemed the ideal woman. (She created Dona Sol in *Hernani.*) When the Comédie Française began to go into debt in the 1830s, she resigned as a *sociétaire* so that she might demand an exorbitant salary as a *pensionnaire*, thus setting a precedent that was to plague the troupe through much of the century. She continued to play young heroines until her retirement at the age of 62.

Abraham-Joseph Fleury (1750–1822) joined the Comédie Française in 1778 and taught at the Conservatoire from its founding in 1786. His elegant manner in comedy made him a fit companion for Mlle. Mars. He retired in 1818.

Mlle. George (Marguerite Weymer, 1787–1835), daughter of a provincial manager, made her debut at the Comédie Française in 1802 at the age of fifteen. Her rivalry with Mlle. Duchenois was intensified when Napoleon took her as his mistress, and the Empress Josephine retaliated by taking Mlle. Duchenois under her protection. In 1808, Mlle. George left Paris to play in St. Petersburg, Stockholm, and elsewhere before returning in 1813. After Napoleon's downfall, she fled

actors were listed on the bills after 1805 as a means of stimulating audience interest.

Between 1790 and 1850 France produced a number of outstanding actors. Prior to 1825 the leading performers were Talma, Mlle. Duchenois, Mlle. Mars, Fleury, and Mlle. George. François-Joseph Talma (1763–1826), often called the greatest of all French actors, spent much of his youth in England, but returned to France in 1785 and was one of the first students at the Ecole Royale Dramatique when it opened in 1786. Entering the Comédie Française in 1787, he was a con-

France once more until 1822. After this time her career was bound up with that of Jean-Charles Harel, manager of the Porte-Saint-Martin and Odéon theatres. Harel was very sympathetic to the romantics and in the 1830s produced many of their plays. In these, Mlle. George played the heroines and did much to popularize the new drama.

Melodrama and romantic plays brought many boulevard actors to the fore. Of these, the most popular were Mme. Dorval, Bocage, and Deburau. Mme. Dorval (Marie Delaunay, 1798–1849), after studying at the Conservatoire, played for a time in the provinces before joining the Porte-Saint-Martin troupe in 1818. Here she played in melodrama until the theatre was permitted to perform other genres. An intuitive actress, she was best at portraying vehement emotion and seductive charm. From 1835 to 1837 she played at the Comédie Française, but she encountered so much opposition (primarily from the partisans of Mlle. Mars) that she returned to the more compatible boulevard theatres.

Bocage (Pierre-François Touze, 1797–1863), a weaver in his youth, was admitted to a provincial company largely because of his handsomeness. After being refused an engagement at the Comédie Française in 1821, he turned to the boulevards, where he was soon regarded the greatest stage lover of his day. He appeared at the Comédie Française briefly in the 1830s but found the atmosphere so hostile that he soon left. After 1845 he served as manager of the Odéon.

Jean-Gaspard Deburau (1796–1846) was born into a family of touring acrobats. In 1811, he settled in Paris, where he was associated principally with the Théâtre des Funambules. His fame came after 1825 as he developed the character Pierrot, a pale, lovesick, ever-hopeful seeker after happiness. In this role, he became one of the most popular performers in Paris.

The most renowned romantic actor of France, Frédérick Lemaître (1800–1876), entered the Conservatoire at the age of fifteen, and performed at the circus in pantomime and melodrama while still undergoing this rigorous classical training. In 1823, he achieved renown by turning the villain of a melodrama into a comic caricature. Thereafter he took considerable liberties with his roles until he was employed by Harel at the Odéon and Porte-Saint-Martin, where he became a dedicated performer. Lemaître was the most versatile actor of his day, for he refused to be bound by the usual lines of business. He delighted in astonishing audiences by novel interpretations and passionate outbursts. The

FIGURE 14.14 Rachel's farewell appearance during a highly successful engagement at Her Majesty's Theatre in London, 1841. Courtesy Theatre Museum, Victoria and Albert Museum, London.

peak of his popularity was reached between 1830 and 1850, but he went on acting until his death, long after his popularity had waned.

Of similar temperament but performing an entirely different kind of repertory, Rachel (Elisabeth Félix, 1821–1858) epitomized the tempestuous actress. The daughter of a peddler, she was befriended while a child street singer and sent to a dramatic school. Withdrawn by her father who wished to exploit her talent, she made her professional debut in 1837 at the Gymnase. In 1838, she was engaged at the Comédie Française, where she soon became its major attraction. She insisted on an enormous salary (sometimes equaling that of France's Prime Minister). Her performances revived the popularity of the classical repertory, which had declined markedly after romanticism came to the fore, and contributed in its turn to the decline of romanticism. While she filled the Comédie Française on the nights when she played, she impoverished the company by taking most of the receipts and by going on extended tours. Largely because of this experience, the Comédie has since that time refused to give any performer star billing and has listed all actors according to seniority.

Rachel's repertory was not large, and only one of her major roles, Scribe's *Adrienne Lecouvreur*, was from a contemporary play. She was unsuited to comedy and could not portray convincingly tenderness, womanly softness, gaiety, or heartiness; her strength lay in scorn, triumph, rage, malignity, and lust. Within her range, however, she had no peers. Her death throes as Adrienne Lecouvreur aroused both admiration and horror because of their lifelikeness. By 1841 she was in demand for foreign tours and began to play throughout Europe; in 1855 she appeared in America. Tuberculosis brought a decline in her powers, and in her last years she conserved her strength for the great moments and rushed through other scenes. Nevertheless, her intensity and power established a standard remembered through the rest of the century.

SCENERY, COSTUME AND LIGHTING IN FRANCE, 1800–1850

Although local color and historically accurate motifs had been introduced before the Revolution, they were not exploited fully until the nineteenth century. During the 1790s many managers sought to recreate actual places and real events, but a consistent emphasis upon spectacle first became evident in the boulevard theatres between 1800 and 1830. Here it served at least two major functions: as a plot device in dramatic action and as a novelty designed to attract audiences. Both promoted the increased use of detailed settings and special effects.

Early nineteenth-century melodramas often depended upon natural disasters to forward the plot. For example Pixérécourt's *The Exile's Daughter* shows a flood uprooting trees, inundating the stage, and carrying the heroine away on a plank. Similarly, his *Death's Head* uses a volcanic eruption to engulf the stage and foil the villain. The Cirque Olympique, under the direction of Laurent Franconi, recreated famous battles, using more than 100 persons and 30 horses, in which a troupe of cavalry not uncommonly arrived at the crucial moment. Thus, many of the boulevard plays depended heavily upon spectacle to keep plots moving or to resolve them.

Emphasis was also placed on the novelty of the spectacle. Playwrights sought to include new places or examples of local color never before represented on the stage. Consequently, a variety of historical periods, exotic locales, and fantastic settings was introduced.

Spectacle was so highly developed by 1828 that the new Ambigu-Comique opened with a play in which the "Muse of the Mise-en-Scène" demanded admission to Mount Parnassus. As evidence of her worth, she displayed all the scenic marvels of the theatre and so impressed the other Muses that she was granted admission to their ranks. Nevertheless, spectacle did little to enrich characterization, for usually it merely gave variety to an otherwise routine story.

During this period two designers, Daguerre and Ciceri, laid the foundations for many later developments. Daguerre is especially important for his work with the panorama and diorama, which brought illusion ever closer to reality. The panorama, invented and patented by Robert Barker in 1787, was first seen in Edinburgh in 1788 and in London in 1792. Robert Fulton (1765–1815), an associate of Barker and later the inventor of the steamboat, secured a French patent on the panorama in 1799. He then sold it to an American, James Thayer, who opened two panoramas in Paris in 1800. Panoramas were displayed in circular buildings in which the audience, occupying a central platform, was completely surrounded by a continuous painting. To the spectator, the total effect was that of being set down at a spot from which he had a commanding view in every direction.

Louis-Jacques Daguerre (1787–1851) began his career as an assistant to Pierre Prévost (1764–1823), one of the first painters of panoramas, but his interest

FIGURE 14.15 **Setting by Daguerre for the third act of** *Elodie* **as produced at the Théâtre de l'Ambigu Comique, Paris. Courtesy Bibliothèque Nationale, Paris.**

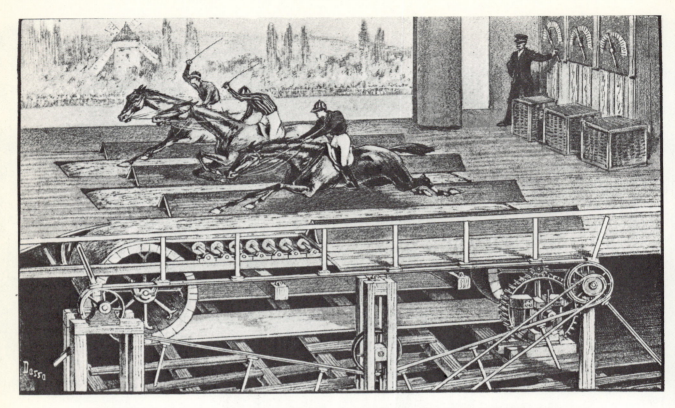

FIGURE 14.16   A horserace on stage at the Union Square Theatre, New York, 1889–1890, with a moving panorama and treadmills run by electric motors, the speed of which was controlled by the man at upper right. From Georges Moynet, *La Machinerie Théâtrale* (1893).

in optics, which was to culminate in his invention of the first effective form of photography (the Daguerro-type) in 1839, led him to experiment with variations on the panorama. Thus, in 1822 he began to display his diorama. Here the spectator was not surrounded by the painting, but rather sat on a platform which revolved every 15 minutes to show him one of two different paintings, each about 71 feet wide by 45 feet high, on proscenium-like stages. Daguerre's improvement lay in his ability to create the illusion of constant change. While Daguerre's partially transparent scenery remained stationary, he varied its appearance by manipulating (with a system of screens and shutters) the direction, intensity, and color of the natural light which entered through overhead openings. By controlling light, he was able to depict the gradual change from fair weather to storm, from day to night, and other conditions. Daguerre was not long content with his accomplishment, and soon perfected the *diorama à double*

effet. Here some details were painted on the front and some on the rear of a transparent cloth. Through changes of light, Daguerre could make details visible or invisible. One of his most famous dioramas, "Midnight Mass at St. Etienne-du-Mont," showed the church empty by day, then gradually filling with people for the midnight mass, and finally returning to emptiness.

Panoramas were displayed throughout the world during the nineteenth century and were soon adapted to theatrical uses. The panorama was always more useful in the theatre than the diorama because it did not depend upon the manipulation of stage lighting. On the other hand, the panorama had to be altered considerably for stage purposes, since it could no longer surround the audience; thus, it assumed the shape which Daguerre adopted for his dioramas. Perhaps for this reason, after the 1820s the terms panorama and diorama were often used interchangeably.

Moving panoramas were introduced into the

theatre in the early nineteenth century. A continuous scene was painted on a cloth of enormous length, suspended from an overhead track, and attached at either end to an upright roller, or "spool." When the spool was turned, the cloth moved across the stage. In this way, characters, ships, horses, and carriages, while remaining in full view, apparently moved from one place to another without any abrupt change in the setting, as would have been necessary had wings and drops been used. Before the end of the nineteenth century, the moving panorama was coupled with "treadmills" for such scenes as the chariot race in *Ben Hur,* for which the stadium was painted on a panorama and moved past the galloping horses, which were kept on stage by the treadmills.

The panorama and diorama also permitted designers to dispense with sky borders, which by the early nineteenth century were considered unsatisfactory, since they destroyed illusion by making breaks in the sky. Panoramas permitted a new arrangement. Flats representing architectural units or natural objects were erected near the front of the stage to form an arch, through which was seen a distant view painted on a panorama curving across the back and down the sides of the stage. Not only did this eliminate sky borders, but an entire scene, with the exception of the downstage masking pieces, could be painted on a continuous surface. This practice eventually led to the development of the neutral cyclorama to surround the acting area.

The panorama and diorama, then, contributed in many ways to illusionism. In Paris, their theatrical uses were first fully exploited at the Panorama-Dramatique where, between 1821 and 1823, panoramic spectacles with only two characters made up the entire repertory.

While Daguerre contributed to scenic practices primarily through his experiments with optical illusion, Pierre-Luc-Charles Ciceri (1782–1868) was the most influential designer of the period, probably because of his ability to depict the favorite visual themes of the time: quaint local color, nostalgic ruins, and picturesque historical milieus. From about 1810, Ciceri was the Opéra's principal designer, but he also worked for the Opéra-Comique, Comédie Française, Porte-Saint-Martin, Panorama-Dramatique, and other theatres. After 1822, he was in such demand that he opened the first scenic studio in Paris. Here he eventually employed specialists (one for architectural details, another for landscapes, and so on), a practice which was to prolong the use of different designers for a single production. From Ciceri's time, the independent scenic studio began to

FIGURE 14.17 Design by Pierre-Luc-Charles Ciceri for Donizetti's *Robert le Diable* at the Paris Opera in 1831. Seen here is a cloister in which was danced the ballet of dead nuns. Courtesy Bibliothèque de l'Opéra.

replace those maintained by individual theatres. Ciceri's students were to dominate stage design in France for the rest of the century.

Interest in spectacle accelerated after 1820. The new Opéra, opened in 1822, incorporated all of the latest developments, including gas lighting and a water system for creating realistic fountains and waterfalls. After 1825, when Baron Taylor was appointed its supervisor, even the Comédie Française began to follow the new trends. Taylor, previously director of the Panorama-Dramatique, employed Ciceri in 1826 to provide historically accurate settings for a number of plays, among them *Hernani.*

After 1828, the increased interest in spectacle led to the publication of *livrets scéniques,* or promptbooks, describing in detail the scenery and special effects used in the Parisian theatres, with suggestions for simplifying spectacle in less well-equipped theatres. After 1830 concern for historical accuracy also increased, for the romantic playwrights were scornful of the inconsistencies often seen in productions of melodramas. Hugo consulted the Commission on Historical Monuments and other sources before making the sketches which he provided for productions of his plays. Dumas *père* often publicly castigated those producers who failed to provide sufficiently accurate spectacle for his works. From 1847 to

FIGURE 14.18 The opening performance in Alexandre Dumas *père's* Théâtre Historique in Paris, 1847. From *The Illustrated London News* (1847). Courtesy Hoblitzelle Theatre Arts Collection, University of Texas, Austin.

1850 he headed his own Théâtre Historique where he staged productions so lavish they almost bankrupted him.

By 1840, dramatic critics were writing detailed accounts of scenery, costumes, and lighting and often even criticized fairy-tale pantomimes for alleged inaccuracies. The classical repertory, for which the *palais à volonté* had continued in use, largely escaped the trend toward historical accuracy until 1842, when the revival of *Le Cid* with six settings established a new pattern.

Although local color and historical accuracy were the most popular forms of scenic illusionism, realism of daily life also made headway. Under its impact, the box set, complete with ceiling, gradually came into use for interior scenes. It is impossible to say when the box set was first used, but by the 1820s it was no longer unusual. Only gradually, however, was it furnished with complete realism, for until 1850 most of the properties and furniture were mere painted cut-outs. In 1846, *Pierre Fevrier* created a sensation with its real furnishings and its decorated floor cloth, simulating black and white marble squares, the first seen in Paris.

As with scenery, costumes between 1790 and 1850 became increasingly realistic. In the early years, Talma did much to popularize historical accuracy in tragic costuming. As early as 1787 he startled audiences by appearing in a toga and with bare arms and legs, the first attempt in France to achieve true authenticity in classical dress. Although a consistent approach was long in developing, progress was steady, especially in serious plays. Comedy continued to be performed in contemporary dress until 1815. Then, seventeenth-century garments were gradually adopted for Molière's plays, although Mlle. Mars refused to accept the changes and continued to wear the latest fashions. Baron Taylor, who became superintendent of the Comédie Française in 1825, placed considerable emphasis on accuracy of spectacle, a view which the romantic dramatists strongly favored. Consequently, by 1840 critics were almost universally scornful of anachronisms in dress.

In lighting, eighteenth-century practices were continued until 1822, when the Opéra introduced gas. The flexibility and greater intensity of gaslight soon led other theatres to adopt it, although the Comédie Française did not install it until 1843. Even then, the Comédie retained its oil footlights because the actresses considered gas light too harsh. Allowing greater control over intensity and direction, gas encouraged more realistic lighting effects. Since spotlights had not yet been invented, however, stage lighting still consisted primarily of general illumination.

The movement toward more specific illumination dates from the 1840s, when experiments with the carbon arc and limelight began in France. In 1846 a carbon arc was used at the Opéra to create the effect of a rising sun, and in 1860 a carbon arc was equipped with a hood and lens to create the first effective spotlight. Originally used as "follow" spots or for special effects, these spotlights were only gradually exploited in the modern manner; their full potentialities were not to be realized until the twentieth century.

ITALY AND SPAIN IN THE EARLY NINETEENTH CENTURY

Between 1800 and 1861, Italy was preoccupied with political developments. During the Napoleonic Wars, it was overrun by France, which merged many of the smaller states and reduced the power of the church over temporal affairs. During this period, the national consciousness was also awakened for the first time. The fall of Napoleon in 1815 brought the return of conditions much like those that had existed before 1800, but the reestablishment of Austrian dominance over

FIGURE 14.19 Costumes for Dumas' *Don Juan de Marana* **(1836). From** *Revue du Théâtre* **(1836).**

many states served to keep alive the desire for independence. Following a series of rebellions in 1848, the demand for unification increased and in 1861 Italy became a nation.

Until 1815, for the most part, tragedy followed the model established by Alfieri and comedy that popularized by Goldoni. Immediately after the fall of Napoleon, however, Mme. de Staël's *Of Germany* was published in Italy and hastened the trend toward romanticism. Since it was associated in the popular mind with liberalism and nationalism, romanticism tended to unite literary and political interests.

Nevertheless, only a few important dramatists appeared. Ugo Foscolo (1778–1827), with *The Tombs* (1807) and *Ajax* (1809), is usually considered a precursor of romanticism. Partially because he was forced to flee Italy for political reasons in 1815, Foscolo was popular with liberal elements throughout the early nineteenth century. The first important Italian romantic dramatist, Alessandro Manzoni (1785–1873), combined religious themes and liberal political sentiments in such plays as *The Count of Carmagnola* (1820) and *Adelchi* (1822). By far the most famous writer of the period, however, was Giambattista Niccolini (1782–1861), a Florentine professor who wrote in the style of Alfieri before turning to romanticism. His plays, by pointing clear parallels between present and past events, consistently urged liberation from foreign rule and church influence. Although they now seem dull, his *Giovanni da Procida* (1830) and *Arnaldo da Brescia* (1843) inspired Italians with their sense of national destiny.

Scene design in Italy followed the same general trends as in France. Among the more important designers were Lorenzo Sacchetti (1759–1829), who worked in

Venice, Vienna, and Prague; Alessandro Sanquirico (1777–1849) of the Teatro alla Scala in Milan; and Antonio de Pian (1784–1851), who worked in Venice and Vienna. Although Italy continued to be a leader in opera, its influence lessened. The outstanding Italian composers spent much of their lives in France and elsewhere, but worldwide demand for Italian performers and scenic artists declined. In Germany, where Italian opera troupes had been common since the seventeenth century, the last foreign company was dismissed in 1832. Elsewhere, native performers gradually replaced Italians. Stars continued to be welcomed everywhere, but other Italian personnel were less popular. Opera continued to dominate the theatrical life of Italy, nevertheless, and the few dramatic companies only managed to survive by touring.

In Spain, as elsewhere, the theatre was heavily influenced by political events. In 1815, Napoleon's brother, who had been crowned king of Spain in 1808, was replaced by one of the most repressive regimes in Europe. Consequently, many of Spain's writers lived abroad until conditions eased after the death of Ferdinand VII in 1833. Most spent the years of exile in Paris, where they witnessed the romantic revolution.

The Spanish counterpart of the battle over *Hernani* came in 1835 with the production of Angel de Saavedra's (1791–1865) *Don Alvaro, or The Force of*

FIGURE 14.20 Act V of Alessandro Manzoni's *The Count of Carmagnola*, **first performed in 1828. From A. Manzoni,** *Opera varie* **(1845).**

FIGURE 14.21 **Setting by Sanquirico for Meyer-beer's** *The Crusader in Egypt* **at the Teatro alla Scala in Milan, 1826. From Sanquirico,** *Raccolta di Varie Decorazioni Sceniche* **(1828).**

Destiny. Although its success established romanticism in Spain, the vogue was short-lived and declined rapidly after 1840. Among the more important romantic dramatists were Martínez de la Rosa (1787–1862) with *Venice Conspiracy* (1834), Antonio García Gutiérrez (1812–1884) with *The Troubador* (1836), José Zorilla (1817–1892) with *Don Juan Tenorio* (1844), Antonio Gil y Zárate (1796–1861) with *Carlos II* (1837), and Mariano José de Larra (1809–1837) with *Macías* (1834).

As the popularity of drama grew in the 1830s, so did the number of theatres. But they were still used to support charities, as in the Golden Age. Not until this practice was abandoned in 1849 were significant reforms introduced.

RUSSIAN DRAMA AND THEATRE, 1800–1850

From 1805 onward Russia was one of France's major foes during the Napoleonic era, and it was during his Russian campaign that Napoleon suffered his first major defeat. As elsewhere, nationalist sentiment steadily grew in Russia during these years. The most popular play-wright of the time was Vladislav Ozerov (1770–1816), probably because his works appealed to patriotic sentiment at a time when Russia was endangered by France. Written in the neoclassical style, his plays, most notably *Dmitri Donskoi* (1807), were extravagantly praised but soon forgotten.

As in other countries of Europe, in Russia the end of the Napoleonic era brought new repressions. Alexander I (ruled 1801–1825) talked of freeing the serfs and making other reforms, but when it became evident that nothing would be done revolutionary groups began to organize. After Nicholas I (ruled 1825–1855) came to the throne this dissatisfaction boiled over into open rebellion in 1825. The revolt was quickly put down, and to prevent reoccurrences the Czar established a secret police force and the most stringent censorship in Europe. Although his reign was one of great creativity, the best plays were almost always severely mutilated before they were licensed for production.

Alexander Griboyedov (1795–1829) is remembered primarily for *Woe from Wit* (1822–1825), one of the masterpieces of Russian drama and sometimes said to be the only significant Russian play in the neoclassical style. As in Molière's *The Misanthrope*, the disillusioned hero of *Woe from Wit* seeks to make others aware of the shortcomings of a materialistic and hypocritical society. To demonstrate his point, Griboyedov brings together a gallery of character types representative of Moscow life. This emphasis upon characterization probably explains the comedy's lasting appeal. Unfortunately it was completed just as censorship was tightened following the revolt of 1825. As a result, it was long kept from the stage. The complete version was not seen until 1869; since then, it has never been absent from the Russian repertory.

By the time Griboyedov's play was written, romanticism was emerging. Alexander Pushkin (1799–1837) is usually given major credit for establishing the new style. His *Boris Gudonov* (1825), with its variety, magnitude, poetic strength, and historical subject, marks the first victory of romanticism over neoclassicism. Sometimes called the first Russian play on a political theme, it deals with the relationship of a ruler to his subjects. Censorship kept the play out of print until 1831 and from production until 1870. Mussorgsky's operatic version, presented in 1873, has largely supplanted the original text in the theatre. Mikhail Lermontov (1814–1841), one of Russia's finest romantic poets, also wrote a few plays after 1830, when his *The*

FIGURE 14.22   Scene from Griboyedov's *Woe from Wit*. At center Mikhail Shchepkin is seen as Famusov. From Komissarzhevsky, *Moscow Theatres* (1959).

writers cultivated the taste. The *comédie-en-vaudevilles*, a one-act comedy with couplets sung to familiar tunes, was especially popular. It reached its high point in the work of Alexander Pisarev (1803–1828), but many other writers followed his example through the remainder of the century.

A more realistic drama began to appear in the 1830s with the work of Nikolai Gogol (1809–1852). As a playwright Gogol is now remembered primarily for *The Inspector General* (1836), the story of a young man mistaken for an official from St. Petersburg. Satirizing the corruption and boorishness of provincial officials, the play was original for its time, since it included neither a love story nor sympathetic characters. Its claim to realism lies almost entirely in its grotesque characterization and its preoccupation with pettiness, hypocrisy, and corruption. Its production, allegedly after the personal approval of the czar, encouraged other authors to turn to more realistic portraiture, but this new trend was not fully evident until after 1850.

During the nineteenth century the Russian theatre expanded constantly, but always under close government supervision. Prince Alexander Shakhovskoy (1777–1846), Director of Repertory in the Imperial Theatres from 1801 to 1826, initiated several important changes. In 1805 a state theatre was opened at last in Moscow, for which the crown purchased a company of seventy-four serf actors from A. E. Stolypin and others from

FIGURE 14.23   Interior of the Bolshoi Theatre, *c.* 1850. From Barkhin, *Architektura Teatra* (Moscow, 1947).

Spaniards appeared. He is now remembered primarily for *Masquerade* (1835), in which corrupt society is blamed for a man's murder of his wife. Censorship kept this play from the stage until the 1860s.

Given the severity of censorship, it is not surprising that most Russian plays were either innocuous or flattering to the ruler. Consequently, romanticism flourished primarily in the patriotic spectacles encouraged by Nicholas I. One of the most successful writers of such plays was Nestor Kukolnik (1809–1868), whose *The Almighty's Hand the Fatherland Has Saved* (1834) depicts the election of Michael Romanov, Nicholas I's ancestor, to the throne. Nikolai Polevoy (1796–1846) exploited the same vein, although he achieved his greatest success with melodrama, which had become popular in Russia following the production in 1829 of Victor Ducange's *Thirty Years*. Polevoy's greatest contribution, however, was the introduction of Shakespeare to the Russian stage through his translation of *Hamlet* in 1837. Thereafter, the works of Shakespeare became increasingly prominent.

As elsewhere, the repertory in Russia was dominated by melodrama and musical plays. A large number were translations, especially of French works, but native

Prince Volkonsky. In 1809 a training school was added; gradually, the Moscow troupes grew in theatrical importance, although the companies in the Russian capital, St. Petersburg, continued to receive favored treatment and higher subsidies. Shakhovskoy, after visiting Paris and other Western theatrical centers, also attempted to raise the level of production, and worked out regulations for governing the troupes which were to remain in effect from 1825 until 1917.

Throughout this period the imperial theatres had a total monopoly on theatrical production in St. Petersburg and Moscow. St. Petersburg had three theatres: the Bolshoi, used mainly for ballet and opera; the Maly (replaced by the Alexandrinsky in 1832), used primarily for drama; and the Mikhailovsky, devoted primarily to foreign works. Moscow had two theatres, one for opera and ballet and the other for drama. Both Moscow companies were originally housed in temporary buildings, but in 1824 a permanent home for spoken drama, the Maly, was opened; it remains in use. In 1825 the Bolshoi was inaugurated for opera and ballet; after it burned in 1853, it was replaced in 1856 with the present building. Because of their prestige, the state troupes set the standard for all Russia, which for the most part depended upon touring companies of poor quality.

Between 1800 and 1850, actors in the state troupes were still hired according to lines of business adopted from French usage. State-approved rules governed rehearsals, the behavior of actors, and every aspect of their lives. In 1839, they were placed under civil service and divided into three ranks according to length of service.

The actors in the St. Petersburg troupes were long considered superior to those in Moscow. Semyonova and Yakovlev were especially admired. Yekaterina Semyonova (1786–1849), trained by Dmitrevsky, played leading roles in both comedy and tragedy, although she excelled in the latter; she was unsuited to domestic drama. Because of her popularity, she was paid considerably more than other performers and given a special allowance for costumes. When Mlle. George arrived from Paris in 1808, a bitter battle for supremacy raged until the French actress left in 1811. Aleksey Yakovlev (1773–1817), also trained by Dmitrevsky, made his debut in 1799. An impulsive actor who depended primarily upon inspiration, Yakovlev was especially popular in Ozerov's tragedies, then at the height of their vogue. During the second quarter of the nineteenth century, the St. Petersburg stage was dominated by Vassily Karatygin (1802–1853). Tall, handsome, and vocally gifted, he played roles of almost every type. He was a master technician who paid careful attention to costume, makeup, and every detail of his performances.

After 1825, however, the lead gradually passed to Moscow. Among the early performers there the most important were Mochalov and Shchepkin. Paul Mochalov (1800–1848) was on the stage from the age of seventeen. An uneven, emotional actor, he swept audiences away when he was at his best. He was especially admired in melodrama and in such roles as Richard III and Hamlet. According to Stanislavsky, Mikhail Shchepkin (1788–1863) was the first great Russian actor. Born a serf, Shchepkin spent his early career in a serf troupe. He began to travel with a professional company in 1808 and obtained his freedom in 1821. By 1823 he was a member of the Maly troupe in Moscow with which he remained the rest of his life. After 1832 he taught at the dramatic school and toured frequently throughout Russia. Shchepkin was a painstaking technician who strove for naturalness in acting. Because of his influence, ensemble effects were achieved at the Maly long before they were usual elsewhere in Russia. He initiated the practice of reading the play to the company before the roles were cast and guided other actors in their characterizations. He excelled in Gogol's comedy, and his natural style is said to have encouraged playwrights to draw more realistic characters.

In general, the Russian theatre was very conservative in its scenic practices, and for the most part it continued to depend on a limited range of stock settings made up of wings and drops. The box set was introduced in the 1830s but it found little favor until much later in the century.

Opera, which had been primarily an aristocratic entertainment, began to win a wider following in the 1830s, when Mikhail Glinka (1804–1857) initiated the Russian school of composers. Nevertheless, foreign influence remained dominant throughout the century. Ballet was also under foreign influence. Between 1801 and 1829, Charles Didelot, a Frenchman, introduced Noverre's reforms into Russia. He emphasized vertical movement, replaced the soft shoe with one permitting difficult turns, introduced leotards, and shortened skirts. Foreign stars, such as Marie Taglioni (1804–1884), the most celebrated ballerina of her day, were imported beginning in the 1830s and gave further emphasis to technical excellence. Not until the late nineteenth century, however, was Russian ballet to be given its distinctive form.

FIGURE 14.24   One of the many new theatres built in London between 1810 and 1840, the Royal Coburg, as it looked when it opened in May 1818. It later came to be called the Old Vic and as such is still in use. From Wilkinson, *Londina Illustrata* (1825).

TRENDS IN ENGLISH THEATRE, 1800–1843

In the years between 1790 and 1815, England, more than any other country, opposed France. Its policies were aimed at isolating the French. (Its attempt to interrupt all shipping to France precipitated the War of 1812 with the United States.) The Industrial Revolution, which began in the late eighteenth century, had made England the leading manufacturing and trading nation of the world by the early nineteenth century. Nevertheless, the Napoleonic Wars severely strained English resources and thereby emphasized the long-standing need for social and political reforms. But as elsewhere, the post-Napoleonic era was one of governmental conservatism. As a result, England underwent financial stress and social upheaval during the 1820s and 1830s. Fortunately, Britian was more flexible than other European countries, and made a number of significant Parliamentary and

labor reforms. Nevertheless, from the 1790s until about 1840 England was almost always in a state of unrest because of war, economic conditions, urbanization, and social conditions.

By 1800 London was the world's largest city, and by 1843 its population had doubled—to two million. During these years the working classes began to attend the theatre in large numbers for the first time and to exert important influences on it. The results were several.

First, the patent theatres were enlarged. The seating capacity of Covent Garden was increased in 1792–1793 to about 3,000, and in 1794 Drury Lane was rebuilt to accommodate more than 3,600. Second, minor theatres were opened. The first were licensed in the 1780s by magistrates outside the City of Westminster (the official seat of government) under the provisions of the law of 1752. After 1804, when the Earl of Dartmouth became Lord Chamberlain, an important change occurred. He interpreted the Licensing Act as authorizing minor theatres within the City of Westminster, so long as they did not infringe upon the rights of the patent houses. Consequently, beginning in 1807 he issued a number of permits for new theatres. By 1843, there were twenty-one companies in the London area as compared to six in 1800. Furthermore, the Lord Chamberlain authorized longer seasons for the Haymarket, originally restricted to five months during the summer. By 1812, it was open seven months, and by 1840 ten months. Third, the repertory was affected. While only the patent houses (Covent Garden, Drury Lane, and the Haymarket) were authorized to perform regular drama, other theatres were permitted to give the lesser forms and incidental entertainment. In an attempt to retain audiences in the face of the new competition, the patent theatres increased their offerings of minor drama. Furthermore, in seeking to cater to all tastes, the evening's bill was extended until it lasted five or six hours. Sometimes as many as three plays were performed on the same evening; a bill composed of two full-length plays, an afterpiece, and numerous variety acts was not unusual between 1820 and 1843. Many persons felt that the patent theatres had abdicated their responsibility for producing regular drama by adopting a repertory not unlike that seen in the minor houses. Consequently, around 1810 and again in the 1830s, attempts were made to establish a "third theatre" which would be devoted entirely to the standard repertory. Although nothing came of these efforts, they focused attention upon the need for reform. As the repertory of the major theatres changed, especially after 1810, a number of the former spectators deserted the drama for opera at the King's Theatre, where even the frequenters of the pit were required to wear formal evening dress. The audience that remained faithful to drama seemed to care little for poetic plays, and by 1843 it was widely believed that Shakespeare's plays brought ruin at the box office.

Although the patent houses were free to perform the minor genres, other theatres could not play regular drama. Consequently, they sought loopholes in the Licensing Act which would allow them to compete more effectively with the major theatres. Two dramatic types, the burletta and the melodrama, came to their rescue. By 1800 burletta, imported into England in the mid-eighteenth century as a type of comic opera, had become such an ambiguous label that the Lord Chamberlain accepted as a burletta any work that had no more than three acts, each of which included at least five songs. This ambiguity was first exploited by Robert Elliston,

manager of the Surrey Theatre. One of the finest actors of his day, Elliston was not content to perform in the usual fare of the minor theatres. Consequently, in 1809 he transformed Farquhar's *The Beaux' Stratagem* into a burletta and followed it with *Macbeth* presented as a "ballet of action." Thereafter, almost any work might be altered to meet the licensing requirements.

Melodrama, which most minor theatres were allowed to perform, offered a similar loophole. Characteristically it was written in three acts and was accompanied by a musical score. Thus, regular plays could be made into melodramas by dividing them into three parts and adding musical accompaniment. This ruse became so perfunctory that *Othello* is said to have been performed as a melodrama with the mere addition of a chord struck on the piano every five minutes.

Although minor theatres were occasionally penalized for such evasions, the distinctions between patent and minor theatres became increasingly blurred. The demand for reform became so insistent that action was at last taken by Parliament. In 1843, the Theatre Regulation Act abolished the privileges of the patent houses that had been in effect since the 1660s. Thereafter any licensed theatre could perform works of any type. The new law did not affect the demand that plays be licensed in advance by the Lord Chamberlain. This form of censorship was to remain in effect until 1968.

ENGLISH DRAMA, 1800–1850

While most of the major English poets of the early nineteenth century wrote plays, few of their works were intended for production, and few had any success when presented. Most of the poetic plays written between 1800 and 1850 were neo-Elizabethan in subject matter and approach, for they treated historical themes and sought to recapture Shakespeare's glory.

One of the most admired playwrights of the early nineteenth century was Joanna Baillie (1762–1851), who between 1798 and 1812 published three volumes entitled *Plays of the Passions*, each drama treating one dominant emotion. While the verse is of high quality, the plays are unsatisfactory because character and story are subordinated to a single motivation. Only *DeMontfort* (acted 1800) achieved any success in the theatre, although Miss Baillie's works were extravagantly praised by other writers.

FIGURE 14.25 Astley's Amphitheatre as it appeared in the early nineteenth century. Both the ring and the stage could be used for dramatic performances. This theatre was noted for its equestrian melodramas. From Wilkinson, *Londina Illustrata* (1825).

Most of the romantic poets attempted drama. Samuel Taylor Coleridge (1772–1834), the major theorist of romanticism in England, wrote *Remorse* (1813), William Wordsworth (1770–1850) *The Borderers* (1795–1796), and John Keats (1795–1821) *Otho the Great* (1819). Percy Bysshe Shelley (1792–1822) was probably the best poetic dramatist of the time, but his plays *The Cenci* and *Prometheus Unbound* were not acted until the twentieth century. *The Cenci* (1819), which tells of Beatrice Cenci's revenge upon her father for his inhuman behavior, comes closer to Jacobean drama than does any play of its period. George Gordon, Lord Byron (1788–1824), was the most successful of the romantic poets in the theatre. Not only did he write more plays, but more were suited to the stage. As a member of the governing committee of Drury Lane, Byron probably had more knowledge and interest in production than did his contemporaries. Nevertheless, only *Marino Faliero* (1821) was acted during his lifetime (and that over his objections), but all of his plays were eventually performed. *Sardanapalus* (1821) offered such producers as Charles Kean irresistible opportunities for historical spectacle, while *Werner* (acted 1830), the

story of a man destroyed by his obsession with revenge, became one of Macready's vehicles.

Although Sir Walter Scott (1771–1832) had an abiding interest in the theatre and wrote several plays, his influence came primarily through his novels, most of which were adapted by others for performance. With their emphasis on local color and history, they helped to establish the vogue for the historical romance. Robert Browning (1812–1889), author of many "dramatic" poems, seemed ideally fitted for writing dramas and, at Macready's urging, he accepted the challenge. But *Strafford* (1837), *A Blot on the 'Scutcheon* (1843), and *Colombe's Birthday* (1853) gained no marked success, perhaps because they concentrate on the eccentric and thus fail to achieve universality. For many years Thomas Noon Talfourd's (1795–1854) *Ion* (1836), based upon classical myth, was hailed as the long-awaited masterpiece. Macready performed it regularly until about 1850, but its reputation faded rapidly thereafter.

At the time, the writer who seemed most clearly destined for greatness was the actor-dramatist James Sheridan Knowles (1784–1862), who first gained renown with *Virginius* (1820), soon a standard play in theatres throughout England and America. Knowles consolidated his fame with *William Tell* (1825), *The Wife* (1833), and *The Hunchback* (1832). His success stemmed from a skillful blending of melodramatic stories with a pseudo-Shakespearean form. For many years he enjoyed a considerable critical and popular following.

If serious playwriting did not fare well, melodrama did. Although many melodramatic elements can be found in the sentimental comedy and domestic tragedy of the eighteenth century, they were not fully developed until the end of the cnetury, when the impact of Kotzebue's work turned attention to the form. Thirty-six of Kotzebue's plays were translated into English, and *The Stranger* and *Pizarro* remained in the repertory throughout the nineteenth century. Melodrama also received considerable impetus from native playwrights, expecially Matthew Gregory Lewis (1775–1818), usually called "Monk" Lewis because of his famous novel, *Ambrosio, or the Monk* (1795). Dramatized many times, this novel and *The Castle Spectre* (1797) began a vogue for "Gothic" melodramas. Set in the Middle Ages, these plays often transpired in mysterious ruined castles or abbeys and featured outcasts, ghosts, long-lost relatives, and long-concealed crimes. In 1802, Thomas Holcroft (1745–1809) gave the trend toward melodrama new strength with *A Tale of Mystery* (an adaptation of Pixérécourt's

Coelina), the first play in English to be labeled a melodrama. Soon this new form was attracting large audiences and thereafter they were a mainstay of the minor theatres.

Until the 1820s the majority of melodramas were rather exotic, either because they were set in some remote time or place, or because they featured the supernatural or highly unusual. Pierce Egan's *Life in London* (1821), dramatized by Egan and others as *Tom and Jerry, or Life in London,* began a trend toward melodramas of contemporary life and local color. Egan's work featured a number of well-known places in London and told a story based on everyday events.

The trend begun by Egan was developed by Jerrold, Fitzball, and Buckstone. Douglas William Jerrold (1803–1857) began his playwriting career in 1821 and gained his greatest success with a series of "nautical" melodramas; *Black-Eyed Susan* (1829) was to become one of most popular plays of the century. Although remembered primarily for his melodramas, Jerrold wrote many kinds of plays, including blank verse tragedy but, after 1841, he largely gave up dramatic writing to work on the magazine *Punch.* Edward Fitzball (1792–1873) had dramatized a number of Scott's novels before turning to original compositions; soon his nautical melodramas rivalled those of Jerrold. He is now especially remembered, however, because he initiated the vogue for melodramas based on actual crimes. His *Jonathan Bradford or the Murder at the Roadside Inn* (1833) had an initial run of 160 nights, a record not broken until 1860. One of the most prolific playwrights of the century, Fitzball continued to turn out plays until his death. John Baldwin Buckstone (1802–1879), a popular actor and manager, wrote or adapted more than 200 plays between the 1820s and the 1870s. His early work, especially *Luke the Labourer* (1826), helped to popularize the "domestic" melodrama. Many of Buckstone's later plays were farces, pantomimes, or dramatizations of recent novels.

Although the older exotic melodrama continued, domestic themes began to dominate after 1830. A number of other types also appeared. Astley's and the Royal Circus featured melodramas which incorporated daring feats of horsemanship, and Sadler's Wells had a water tank installed in 1804 so that it might perform "aquatic" plays featuring sea battles and rescues from drowning.

Until around 1840, melodrama made its greatest appeal to the unsophisticated theatergoer. With the work of such men as Bulwer-Lytton and Marston, however, there appeared a "gentlemanly" melodrama which was to

FIGURE 14.26   A water spectacle at Sadler's Wells Theatre in the early nineteenth century when the stage was equipped with a water tank. From *Microcosm of London,* Vol. 3 (1902)

attract a more discriminating audience with works both theatrically effective and critically acceptable. Although many of Knowles' plays fall into this category, it was Edward George Bulwer-Lytton (1803–1873) who established the type. Already noted for his novels, Bulwer-Lytton was persuaded by Macready to turn to playwriting. Three of his works, *The Lady of Lyons* (1838), *Richelieu* (1839), and *Money* (1840), which owe much to Macready's suggestions, held the stage throughout the nineteenth century. John Westland Marston (1819–1890) also helped to establish the type with *The Patrician's Daughter* (1842) and *Anne Blake* (1852), both of which treat contemporary subjects in poetic dialogue but in a melodramatic form. With "gentlemanly" melodrama, the theatre began to regain its former prestige with the upper classes.

ENGLISH THEATRICAL CONDITIONS, 1800–1843

Between 1800 and 1817, the English theatre maintained its stability largely because of the work of John Philip

Kemble (1757–1823). When Kemble became acting manager of Drury Lane in 1788, it had fallen considerably from the height to which Garrick had lifted it. Richard Brinsley Sheridan, the manager, had devoted himself increasingly to politics but had failed to delegate sufficient authority to Thomas King, who ran the theatre in his absence. Although Kemble did much to reestablish the reputation of the Drury Lane, he tired of coping with crises induced by Sheridan's frequent financial difficulties, and in 1802 he moved to Covent Garden, where he remained until his retirement in 1817. During his tenure Covent Garden became the leading theatre of the English-speaking world.

By the time Kemble retired, England, as a result of the Napoleonic wars, was in a financial crisis that was to last until 1840. Scarcely a theatrical management escaped bankruptcy between 1817 and 1843. The rapid decrease in income can be seen at Drury Lane, where receipts diminished from 80,000 pounds in 1812–1813 to 43,000 pounds in 1817–1818. Nevertheless, the owners of theatres were slow to lower their rental charges. At Drury Lane between 1819 and 1827, Robert Elliston paid 10,000 pounds annually for his lease, and it was only in 1832, after Elliston and several of his successors had failed, that the rent was lowered to 6,000 pounds. Pressure on the managers was reduced somewhat by a decline in other expenses. At Covent Garden, nightly expenses fell from 300 pounds in 1809 to 154 pounds in 1836. Still between 1833 and 1835 the major theatres were in such straits that Alfred Bunn (1798–1860) was able to lease both Drury Lane and Covent Garden and run them with a single company. Of the patent houses, only the Haymarket, a small theatre free from major competition during the summer months, remained relatively prosperous.

Some of the difficulties during these years are explained by the greater financial outlay required by the increasingly elaborate spectacle. It is sometimes suggested that the enormous auditoriums made subtlety in acting impossible and shifted emphasis to visual effects. Covent Garden was destroyed by fire in 1808 and Drury Lane in 1809. In the new Covent Garden (1809) the distance from the stage to the back of the upper gallery was 104 feet, and at the new Drury Lane (1812) only slightly less. Such size, coupled with the growing interest in melodrama, local color, and history, undoubtedly encouraged greater emphasis upon the visual elements.

Increased concern for spectacle was evident as early as the 1790s, when Kemble began to mount Shakespearean revivals with the same care previously lavished

FIGURE 14.27 Interior of Drury Lane as it appeared before it was destroyed by fire in 1809. From *Microcosm of London,* **Vol. 1 (1902).**

upon minor drama by Garrick and DeLoutherbourg. The major designer of the Kemble era was William Capon (1757–1827), who came to the fore when the Drury Lane was reconstructed in 1794. This theatre had a stage 85 feet wide and 92 feet deep, with a proscenium opening 43 feet wide by 38 feet high. One of

FIGURE 14.28 Interior of the Covent Garden Theatre after it was rebuilt in 1809. From *Microcosm of London,* **Vol. 3 (1902).**

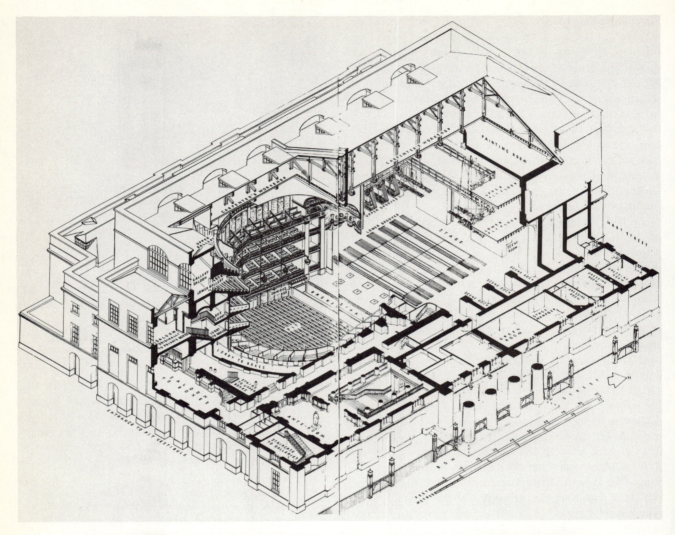

FIGURE 14.29 **The Covent Garden Theatre in 1824. Scale reconstruction by Richard Leacroft. From Leacroft,** *The Development of the English Playhouse* **(1973). Courtesy Eyre Methuen and Cornell University Press.**

Capon's sets in 1799 showed the nave, choir, and side aisles of a fourteenth-century cathedral; it measured 56 feet in width, 52 feet in depth, and 37 feet in height. Capon continued as principal designer at Drury Lane until it burned in 1809, after which he worked at Covent Garden. Some of his scenery was in use as late as 1840. Unlike DeLoutherbourg, Capon designed primarily for regular drama and was one of the first important advocates in England of historical accuracy in scenery. Nevertheless, consistency had not yet been attained, for often several different designers, each working independently, provided settings for a single play, and frequently

one act was newly mounted while the others were performed in stock scenery.

Kemble's attitude toward scenery and costumes marks a transition from the generality favored by the neoclassicists to the individuality advocated by the romantics. Thus, although he often clothed the major characters in pseudo-historical garments, the minor personages usually wore traditional costumes taken from the company's wardrobe. Similarly, while Mrs. Siddons discarded fashionable dress in tragedy, she substituted for it conventionalized "draperies" of no particular era. Furthermore, Kemble always put theatrical effectiveness above archeological accuracy. For example, he set *Coriolanus* in late rather than in early Rome because he thought audiences were unprepared to accept the architecture of the earlier period, and for *King Lear* the costumes were given merely a "Saxon tendency." Consequently, while he acknowledged the desirability of historical and individualizing detail, Kemble applied it sporadically and inconsistently.

During Kemble's lifetime, complex practical scenic pieces also increased markedly in number. For example, Sheridan's *Pizarro* (1799) required a gorge spanned by a bridge which could be cut loose so that the hero might escape. Such devices became common as melodrama grew in popularity. In 1811, under the influence of equestrian drama, Kemble even employed a troupe of mounted cavalry. He also made increased use of processions, coronations, and other mass effects. By the time he retired in 1817, it was accepted that all drama should be "illustrated" as completely as possible.

Robert Elliston (1774–1831), manager of Drury Lane from 1819 to 1826, continued the emphasis upon spectacle. His *King Lear* (1820) featured trees that actually bent in the wind and storm noises so realistic that Lear could not be heard. Elliston installed a water system to achieve greater illusion of fountains and waterfalls, and one of his principal designers, Clarkson Stanfield (1793–1867), introduced moving dioramas (panoramas had been used in London theatres since about 1800).

A major step toward antiquarianism came in 1823, when James Robinson Planché (1796–1880) persuaded Charles Kemble (1775–1854), manager of Covent Garden from 1817 to 1832, to use historically accurate costumes for every role in Shakespeare's *King John*. Although the actors feared that they would be laughed at, the audience allegedly welcomed the innovation. In 1824, both historically accurate costumes and scenery were used for Kemble's production of *Henry IV, Part I*. In spite of the success of these productions, Kemble did not repeat the experiment until 1827, and it was not until Macready accepted it in 1837 that authenticity was consistently exploited. Thus, while Planché's work in 1823 must be considered a landmark, it did not bring an immediate revolution in theatrical practice.

Planché continued to be a leader in the movement toward antiquarianism. Finding it difficult to obtain information for his costume designs, he undertook extensive research which resulted in his *History of British Costume* (1834), long the standard English work in this

FIGURE 14.30 Gothic stage setting designed by William Capon for J. P. Kemble's Shakespearean revivals at Covent Garden after 1809. From *The Magazine of Art* (1895).

field. He continued his study of heraldry and was frequently consulted by producers. Thus, Planché not only provided impetus to authentic staging, but also supplied the information that made it possible.

By the 1830s it was assumed that each theatre would prepare a number of handsomely mounted productions each season. The increased financial outlay

FIGURE 14.31 A costume design by J. R. Planché for Henry IV in Charles Kemble's production of 1824. From J. R. Planché, *Costume of Shakespeare's King Henry IV, Parts 1 and 2* (1824). Courtesy Lilly Library, Indiana University.

FIGURE 14.32 An engraving based on the painting by G. H. Harlow (1819) showing various members of the Kemble family in *Henry VIII* by Shakespeare, although they probably never all appeared together in this play. At front Mrs. Siddons as Queen Katherine; at left John Philip Kemble as Cardinal Wolsey; seated at table center Charles Kemble as Cromwell; upstage center Stephen Kemble as Henry VIII. Courtesy Theatre Museum, Victoria and Albert Museum.

meant, however, that longer runs were required to justify the investment. Consequently, from this time the trend toward long runs accelerated, although it was not to be widely exploited until after 1850.

Between 1800 and 1843 a number of important actors appeared on the English stage. Until 1815, it was dominated by the Kemble family. Almost all of the twelve children of Roger Kemble (1721–1802), a provincial actor-manager, became actors, but lasting fame was achieved only by John Philip and Sarah Kemble Siddons (1755–1831). As an adult, John Philip Kemble was on the stage from 1776. After coming to London in 1783, he only gradually gained favor, but from 1790 until his retirement he was considered to be the leading actor of the English-speaking world. Mrs. Siddons was on the stage from childhood; attaining no success at Drury Lane in 1775, she returned to the provinces until 1782. From her reappearance in London until her retirement in 1812, she was recognized as the greatest tragic actress of her day.

Kemble and Mrs. Siddons established a style usually called "classical" because of its emphasis upon stateliness, dignity, and grace. In Kemble, this style often gave the impression of coldness and he was truly excellent only in such roles as Cato, Coriolanus, Cardinal Wolsey, Brutus, Rolla, and the Stranger. His characterizations were always worked out studiously and sustained with

care. As a result, he was often accused of self-consciousness. Mrs. Siddons, while attaining a comparable dignity, rose far above her brother because of her greater emotional intensity. She was especially noted for her playing of Lady Macbeth, Queen Katharine, Volumnia, and Mrs. Haller.

Other members of the Kemble family included Stephen (1758–1822), who acted primarily in the provinces but became famous in London for his Falstaff; Eliza Kemble Whitlock (1761–1836), who, after performing in the provinces, migrated to America in 1794 to become one of the most noted actresses in the new country; Charles, who excelled as the young heroes of John Philip Kemble's productions and later managed the Covent Garden theatre. Much of Charles Kemble's later fame was associated with his daughter, Frances Anne Kemble (1809–1893), a popular leading lady from her debut in 1829 until her retirement in 1834. Charles

FIGURE 14.33 John Philip Kemble as Hamlet in a provincial theatre. Note the grave trap and the low-comedy antics of the Gravedigger. Engraving by George Cruikshank from *Memoirs of Joseph Grimaldi*, ed. by Boz (Charles Dickens), Vol. 1 (1838).

Kemble retired in 1836 and later served as Examiner of Plays for the Lord Chamberlain.

The Kemble school of acting was continued by Charles Mayne Young (1777–1856), who succeeded to many of John Philip Kemble's roles until his retirement in 1832; J. M. Vandenhoff (1790–1861); J. W. Wallack (1791–1864), who became a leading figure in the American theatre; and Eliza O'Neill (1791–1827), considered by many to be Mrs. Siddons' true successor.

The classical approach was challenged after 1814 by the romantic school. Although Edmund Kean was the greatest exponent of the new style, he was preceded in it by George Frederick Cooke (1756–1812). On the stage from 1776, Cooke did not appear in London until 1800 when his powers were already declining. Addicted to drink, Cooke was unreliable and sometimes disappeared for long periods. When in full possession of his powers, no one could so captivate an audience. At his best in villainous roles such as Richard III and Iago, he cared little for grace or nobility but was unequaled at portraying hypocrisy and evil. He favored realistic acting and even wrote out poetic dialogue as prose so as to avoid emphasizing rhythm or rhyme. His last years, 1810 to 1812, were spent in America; as the first major English actor to undertake a starring tour of the United States, he established a precedent that was to have important consequences.

If Cooke prepared the way for romantic acting, Edmund Kean (1787–1833) perfected the style. On the stage as the child prodigy Master Carey, Kean began his adult career at fourteen in a provincial company. He did not appear in London until he was twenty-seven, but from his debut there in 1814 he was considered a major star and, after Kemble's retirement, the foremost actor of his day. Like Cooke he excelled in somewhat villainous roles, such as Richard III, Shylock, Sir Giles Overreach, and Barabas; he seldom appeared in comedy. Although it is sometimes said that Kean depended upon inspiration, this is a misconception. He worked out every movement and intonation with care. Once set, a role was much the same at every performance, although Kean sometimes revised a characterization, and his intentions were often subverted by his alcoholism. In later years, he was inclined to save his strength for great moments and to slight the remainder of a role. Unlike Kemble, Kean did not value grace and dignity; he was willing to cringe or crawl on the floor if he thought it necessary to convey the proper effect. Thus, he tended to emphasize realism of emotion, whereas Kemble had sought to

FIGURE 14.34 Edmund Kean in the role of Richard III. A contemporary engraving.

convey an ideal nobility. Kean's style pleased the new audiences, but his erratic behavior had lowered his popularity considerably before his death in 1833.

Largely because of Kean's example, starring engagements became the norm for major performers after 1815. In London, Kean was never a regular member of an acting company after the early 1820s. Instead, he frequently demanded 50 pounds or more for each time he performed. (Kemble had never received more than 36 pounds a week, and Mrs. Siddons never rose above 30 pounds a week.) His demonstration that a star could command a high salary with a limited repertory established a precedent followed by many of his successors.

Although no comic actors achieved the lasting fame enjoyed by Kemble and Kean, many won popular acclaim. In addition to his importance as a manager, Robert Elliston was universally admired as the young hero of comedy and later in such character roles as Falstaff. Charles Mathews the Elder (1776–1835) was noted especially for his "At Homes," in which he por-

FIGURE 14.35 Most English actors in the early nineteenth century began their careers in the provinces. Both in the provinces and London, the actor still depended on benefits for much of his income. Shown here is a poorly attended benefit in a provincial theatre. Also depicted are many architectural and staging features of the time. From Pierce Egan, *The Life of an Actor* (1825).

trayed a succession of character types based upon observation. Beginning around 1808, this superior kind of mimicry made him a leading attraction throughout England and took him to America for tours in 1822 and 1834. Above all, however, it was the era of the low comedian. For the first time, such performers as Joseph Munden (1758–1832), John Liston (1776–1846), and Robert Keeley (1793–1869) commanded salaries equaling or exceeding those of major serious actors. Other outstanding stars included Tyrone Power (1795–1841), noted for his comic Irish portrayals, and T. P. Cooke (1786–1864), famous as the hero of nautical melodramas.

Audiences were also attracted by the eccentric and unusual, and the early nineteenth century brought a craze for child actors, of which the most famous was William Henry West Betty (1791–1874), often called the Young Roscius. When Master Betty came to London in 1804 after winning fame in the provinces, his following became so great that Kemble and Mrs. Siddons gave up playing for a time. On one occasion, Parliament was adjourned so that its members might see him perform. Betty's fame soon passed, and after 1811 he sank into obscurity.

Except during starring engagements, actors were still employed by the season at a weekly salary and a yearly benefit. Although "lines of business" continued to be the norm, specialization increased. After 1809,

Kemble employed the equivalent of three troupes, one for serious drama, one for comedy, and one for music and dance. Thereafter, the trend in large companies was to hire actors who were outstanding in a limited range, whereas diversity was achieved because each troupe included so many specialized performers.

Rehearsals were still perfunctory. Although Kemble aimed at ensemble effects, he did little beyond holding line rehearsals, probably because by this time conventional groupings and movement served in most instances. It was customary for actors to space themselves an arm's length apart so as not to inhibit gestures. Because the footlights had a large cluster ("the rose"), an actor moved to this bright spot each time he had an important speech. After delivering his lines, he then moved three steps to the left or right to make way for the next speaker. This continuous shifting of places was typical of acting through most of the early nineteenth century.

MACREADY AND VESTRIS

In the 1830s two English managers, Macready and Mme. Vestris, began to bring order out of the near-chaos which had reigned since about 1815 and to lay the foundations for the recovery of the theatre.

William Charles Macready (1793–1873) had no intention of going on the stage until a financial crisis in his father's theatre at Birmingham forced him to leave school in 1810. By 1816 he was playing in London, where he was soon considered a serious rival to Kean, although it was not until Kean's death that he was acclaimed England's foremost actor. As a performer, Macready combined much of Kemble's dignity and studiousness with Kean's fire. Unlike Kemble, however, he sought to give an illusion of everyday life, and included many domestic and familiar details in his stage business. He was famous for his lengthy pauses, during which he seemed to reflect and compose his responses.

Macready's profound dissatisfaction with theatrical conditions eventually led him into management as the only effective means of reforming them. From 1837 to 1839 he managed Covent Garden and from 1841 to 1843 Drury Lane, each with more artistic than financial success. In spite of difficulties, however, Macready introduced many innovations which were to form the basis of later practices.

Macready was one of the early directors in the modern sense. He did not allow actors to choose their own stage positions, but sought instead to impose blocking upon them. He was often derided and defied, but he did not give up. Furthermore, Macready insisted upon acting during rehearsals rather than "saving himself" for performances, the usual practice of the day. While he did not convert all of his company, his superior success as a performer and director won many converts.

Macready paid attention to every detail of his productions. Although he presented stock plays which were repeated many times each season, he introduced and lavished attention upon a few new productions each year. He was the first director who consistently sought historical accuracy in both costumes and scenery. His usual designer was Charles Marshall (1806–1880), one of the finest landscape artists of the day, but he also employed many other noted designers. For *Henry V*, Clarkson Stanfield designed a moving diorama to illustrate the sea voyage from Southampton to Harfleur, and Col. Hamilton Smith (1776–1859), a noted antiquarian, was often consulted on costumes.

Macready sought to improve the repertory. He placed considerable emphasis upon Shakespeare's plays and claimed much credit for restoring the original texts, although he was not always scrupulous in this matter.

FIGURE 14.36 W. C. Macready's production of *King Lear*, 1838. Macready at center as Lear; to his left Priscilla Horton as the Fool (a role often played by women in the 19th century). From George Scharf, *Recollections of the Scenic Effects of Covent Garden Theatre, 1838–1839* (1839).

He persuaded some of the foremost literary figures of his time to write for the stage and from these efforts came "gentlemanly" melodrama. Macready also considered it a point of integrity to perform no work more than four times a week, regardless of its popularity. (From this policy stemmed many of his financial difficulties.)

Macready maintained a company of high quality. Helen Faucit (1817–1898), an actress of the Kemble school who made her London debut in 1836, was generally considered the finest actress of the day. Mrs. Mary Warner (1804–1854) was recognized as the leading performer of such mature roles as Lady Macbeth. Samuel Phelps, soon to attain fame as a manager, was second only to Macready in the company.

Continually disappointed in his efforts to achieve a stable theatre of high quality, Macready gave up management in 1843 and thereafter was a touring star. His last appearance in America in 1849 was marred by the Astor Place riot, stemming from his rivalry with Edwin Forrest, during which twenty-two people were killed. Macready retired in 1851.

Whereas Macready's influence came through his productions of regular drama, Mme. Vestris' most significant work was done with minor forms. Born Lucia Elizabetta Bartolozzi (1797–1856), in 1813 she married Armand Vestris (1788–1825), a famous dancer of the time. In 1815 she went on the stage, playing in both London and Paris. She achieved her first outstanding

FIGURE 14.37   The Olympic Theatre as it appeared in the 1820s. From Wilkinson, *Londina Illustrata* **(1825).**

success in a "breeches role" in *Giovanni in London* (1821), a burlesque of Mozart's *Don Giovanni*. She remained one of the most popular performers of light comedy and burlesque until her retirement in 1854.

Mme. Vestris' importance, however, stems from her work as a manager, notably at the Olympic Theatre from 1831 to 1839. Here she had the assistance of J. R. Planché, who wrote many of the plays in her repertory, which was restricted to burlesques, extravaganzas, and similar minor types. At this time, the burlesque was a broad caricature of popular drama, myth, or current events. In its original form, the extravaganza was a whimsical treatment of a myth or fairy tale placing special emphasis upon dance and spectacle. Both burlesque and extravaganza usually made considerable use of music. Because of their common characteristics, they were eventually intermingled and the type designations lost their specificity. Burlesque seems to have appealed to the nineteenth-century taste for broad humor, while extravaganza was a precursor of musical comedy. Both were extremely popular, especially between 1830 and 1870. Planché, one of the most prolific writers of these forms, turned out about 175. With their whimsy and wordplay, Planché's works were to be a major influence on the comic operas of Gilbert and Sullivan.

As a manager, Mme. Vestris is important for several reasons. First, she paid close attention to every element of production and coordinated them into an integrated whole. Second, she gave special consideration to spectacle and is usually credited with introducing the box set into England. The origin of the box set is obscure, but it probably came into being gradually. In 1808, Monk Lewis' *Venoni* required two rooms simultaneously, a demand repeated in George Colman's *The Actor of All Work* in 1817. Fitzball's *Jonathan Bradford* (1833) utilized four rooms simultaneously, two above and two below. While it is unclear how these scenic requirements were met, they suggest some version of the box set. Nevertheless, Mme. Vestris was probably the first producer to use this type of setting with some consistency; she may also have been the first to enclose the acting area completely. There is much dispute over the date when the box set was introduced at the Olympic, but 1832 seems most likely. By 1834 it had been seen at Drury Lane and by 1837 was in use at Covent Garden. Nevertheless, the box set remained something of a novelty and was not widely adopted until after 1870.

Not only did Mme. Vestris use box sets, she equipped them like rooms in real life. Rugs were laid on the floor, knobs were attached to doors, and bookcases, books, and bric-a-brac were included to give the appearance of reality. This care extended to costumes. With Planché's encouragement, Mme. Vestris substituted garments like those worn in real life for the ridiculously exaggerated costumes that had become typical for burlesque. Thus, she was the first producer to treat minor drama with the respect formerly reserved for the classics.

Mme. Vestris was also instrumental in simplifying the evening's bill. She curtailed her offerings so that the program ended no later than 11 P.M., a drastic measure since programs at this time usually lasted until 1 or 2 A.M. The popularity of the innovation began the trend which eventually led to the one-play bill.

In 1838 Mme. Vestris gave up the Olympic Theatre and married Charles Mathews the Younger (1803–1878), a performer of light comedy roles in her company. Together they managed Covent Garden from 1839 to 1842 and the Lyceum from 1847 to 1856. At both they continued the policies begun at the Olympic. At the Lyceum, they were assisted by William Roxby Beverley (c. 1814–1889), one of the finest designers of the day. Their insistence upon the highest quality in every detail led them into financial difficulties, and both managerial ventures ended in bankruptcy. Nevertheless, their reforms were to inspire others and to produce important results in the 1860s.

Thus, by 1850 the English theatre was in a state of transition. The Theatre Regulation Act of 1843 had removed many obstacles to initiative and innovation. Soon a marked change would become evident.

THE AMERICAN THEATRE, 1782–1815

In America, theatrical performances resumed soon after the Revolutionary War ended. In 1782, Thomas Wall, a former member of Douglass' troupe, appeared in Baltimore, and in the next year he joined forces with Dennis Ryan to form the "American Company," which played between New York and Charleston during the next few years. In 1784 Lewis Hallam brought a company to the new nation, and in 1785 John Henry (1738–1794), another of Douglass' players, came with his. In 1785 Hallam and Henry joined forces to create the "Old American Company," the new country's major troupe until 1794 and the basis of a permanent theatre in New York.

Between 1794 and 1815, however, Philadelphia was to be the dominant theatrical center. It began with little promise, for the prohibition against acting, instituted in 1774, was not rescinded until 1789. In 1791 Thomas Wignell (1753–1803), Hallam and Henry's principal low comedian, and Alexander Reinagle, a musician, set out to establish a company there. Desiring to create a theatre of high quality, they erected the Chestnut Street Theatre, the finest in America. Designed by Inigo Richards, one of England's leading scene designers and Wignell's brother-in-law, it seated about 1,200 and had a stage 71 feet deep with a proscenium opening about 36 feet wide. While it was being built, Wignell sailed for England, where he engaged the best company yet seen in America. Among his recruits were Eliza Kemble Whitlock (1761–1863), sister of John Philip Kemble and Mrs. Siddons; Mrs. Oldmixon (? 1835/36), a favorite singer at Covent Garden; and James Fennell (1766–1816), an actor of enviable reputation both in Edinburgh and London.

The troupe was further strengthened in 1796 with the addition of Mrs. Merry, Warren, and Cooper.

FIGURE 14.38 Mme. Vestris and Charles Mathews the Younger (both at left) in W. B. Bernard's *The Conquering Game* at the Olympic Theatre, 1832. This setting is usually considered to be one of the earliest box sets on the English stage. Drawing from the title page of the acting edition, *Duncombe's British Theatre,* Vol. 35 (c. 1865).

Anne Brunton Merry (1768–1808) had been the leading actress at Covent Garden before retiring upon her marriage in 1792. Financial reverses soon made it necessary for her to return to the stage; the lack of a suitable engagement in England brought her to America, where she remained at the head of her profession until her death at the age of forty. After her first husband died, she married successively Wignell and then William Warren (1767–1832), an actor of old men's roles, who was connected with the Chestnut Street Theatre from 1796 until 1829 and who from 1806 until 1827 shared in its management. Thomas Abthorpe Cooper (1776–1849), one of England's most promising young actors, came to America in 1796 because he was unable to find a suitable engagement at home. Within a few years he was considered America's leading actor. Essentially a tragic performer, he popularized the Kemble style in America. In 1797, Wignell added John Bernard (1756–1828) to his troupe. A performer of heroes in high comedy, Bernard had played at Covent Garden and elsewhere before coming to America. In Philadelphia, Boston, New York, and Albany, Bernard did much to raise the level of performance before returning to England in 1819. With this superior company and under sound management, the Chestnut Street Theatre forged to the front. Its high standards were maintained by Wignell and Reinagle's successors, Warren and William Wood (1779–1861), joint managers of the company from 1810 to 1826.

The secondary position of the New York theatre between 1794 and 1815 is explained in part by dissensions within its company. In 1792, John Hodgkinson (*c.* 1765–1805), a versatile and ambitious provincial actor, joined the troupe, and by 1794 had replaced Henry in the management. By this time, Hallam's popularity was declining, and his jealousy of Hodgkinson seems to have interfered with the orderly operation of the theatre. Perhaps for this reason, William Dunlap (1766–1839), the leading playwright of the period, was induced to join the management. Shortly afterward, Hallam gave up his share, as did Hodgkinson in 1798, although both continued to act with the company and to create dissension. Thus, by the time Dunlap became sole manager in 1798, the troupe was in serious difficulty despite attempts to strengthen it with new talent. In 1793, Mrs. Charlotte Melmoth (1749–1823), an actress who had won considerable fame at Covent Garden and Drury Lane, had arrived to play principal tragic roles, and in 1795, Joseph Jefferson I (1774–1832), a popular comic actor who was to found an important theatrical family, joined the company. In spite of these and other additions, factions within the troupe made it difficult to maintain discipline and to achieve high artistic standards.

The New York theatre had also been weakened financially by Hodgkinson's insistence upon taking the company to play in New England and by competition from the Chestnut Street troupe, which still made occasional visits to New York. Furthermore, by 1798 the John Street Theatre was inadequate and a new home had to be built. In 1798 the Park Theatre, destined to be New York's leading theatre until the 1840s, was opened. As sole manager, Dunlap struggled along until 1805, when bankruptcy overtook him. In 1807, Thomas A. Cooper became manager, and the Park entered a period of prosperity, especially after 1808–1809 when Cooper sold a share in the company to Stephen Price (1783–1840), a lawyer and businessman who proved to be a

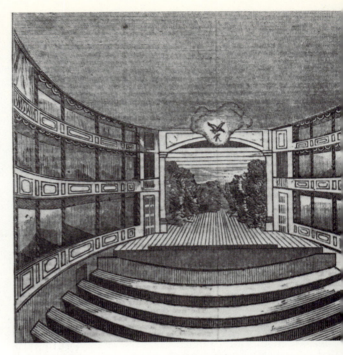

FIGURE 14.39 **Interior of the Chestnut Street Theatre, Philadelphia, 1794. From a plate published in the** *New York Magazine,* **1794. Courtesy Hoblitzelle Theatre Arts Collection, University of Texas, Austin.**

skillful manager. After Price demonstrated his abilities, Cooper spent an increasing amount of time on starring tours, and by 1815 had given up management altogether.

It was Cooper and Price who did the most to popularize tours by starring actors, a practice that would eventually undermine resident troupes. Although leading actors had played short engagements with companies other than their own since about 1800, it was their importation of George Frederick Cooke in 1810 which created a demand for stars of the first magnitude. Cooper and Price served as Cooke's agents in America and engaged Dunlap to travel with him to Boston, Philadelphia, and Baltimore. This tour was so profitable that others were inevitable, although the War of 1812 (the American portion of the Napoleonic conflicts then underway in Europe) prevented immediate successors.

The 1790s also introduced the professional theatre in Boston where the puritan outlook until that time had been able to outlaw it. Performances seem to have begun in 1792, although the prohibition against acting was not actually lifted until 1793. The Federal Street Theatre was erected in the latter year and Charles Stuart Powell assembled an inferior company for it in England. Managements changed often and conditions remained unsettled until 1802, when Snelling Powell (1774–1843) assumed control. The company was especially strong between 1806 and 1811, when John Bernard shared in the management and attracted a number of outstanding players.

Charleston emerged as the fourth important theatrical center of the 1790s. While the Ryan-Wall troupe had played in Charleston as early as 1785, no continuing company settled there until 1795, when John Joseph Sollee assumed control of the City Theatre. Much of the vitality of the Charleston theatre came from the influx of French refugees, both at the time of the French Revolution and following the slave uprising in Santo Domingo in 1793. In the 1790s many plays were performed in French, and many outstanding actors were of French origin. Perhaps the most important French artist was Alexandre Placide (c. 1750–1812), a dancer, acrobat, and pantomimist from the Parisian fair and boulevard theatres, who appeared with all of the major troupes in America before becoming manager of the Charleston theatre from 1798 until 1812.

By the 1790s, then, the theatre was firmly established along the Atlantic seaboard where most of the nation's four million inhabitants were concentrated. Four main circuits were established: the Charleston troupe controlled all of the towns northward to Richmond; the Philadelphia troupe controlled Baltimore, Annapolis, and later Washington; the New York company toured for a time in the adjacent area, but after 1800 tended to remain fixed; and the Boston troupe dominated New England. While there were other lesser ones, these were the principal companies until 1815. After 1790, the major troupes abandoned the sharing arrangement in favor of salaries and a yearly benefit, although lesser groups continued the older tradition through much of the nineteenth century. Performances were still given only three times a week, and the length of seasons in each town was variable, since most troupes toured and yellow fever and the discomfort of winter cold and summer heat often required the suspension of playing.

For the most part the repertory was English. Nevertheless, American playwrights, notably Tyler, Dunlap, and Payne, laid the foundations for a native drama. Royall Tyler (1757–1826) is remembered now

FIGURE 14.40 Interior of the Park Theatre, New York, *c.* 1805. Courtesy Hoblitzelle Theatre Arts Collection, University of Texas, Austin.

FIGURE 14.41 Final scene from Tyler's *The Contrast* (1787). The Yankee character Jonathan is seen at center. From the first edition of the play (1790). Courtesy Humanities Research Center Library, University of Texas, Austin.

cident involving a British spy during the Revolutionary War. The majority of Dunlap's plays were written before 1812, after which he devoted his time primarily to painting. Dunlap is also important for his *History of the American Theatre* (1832) and the first history of American art (1834).

John Howard Payne (1791–1852) came to public attention when only fourteen years old as the publisher of *The Thespian Mirror*, a critical journal. In the following year, his first play, *Julia* (1806), was acted at the Park Theatre, and in 1809 he made his acting debut, billed as a child prodigy. With Stephen Price as his manager, he enjoyed a considerable vogue for a short time, but by 1811 his popularity had waned. In 1813, he went to England, where he spent the next twenty years as dramatist and critic. Payne wrote or adapted between fifty and sixty plays. His best known plays were *Brutus* (played by Edmund Kean in 1818), *Charles II* (performed by Charles Kemble in 1824), and *Clari* (1823), famous for the song, "Home, Sweet Home." Payne was America's first internationally successful dramatist. After 1832, he ceased writing for the stage.

THE EXPANDING AMERICAN THEATRE, 1815–1850

Following the War of 1812 the westward movement of American settlement accelerated. In 1803 the territorial limits of the United States had been greatly extended when Napoleon, in need of money, sold France's lands west of the Mississippi to the United States (the Louisiana Purchase). Thereafter the nation continued to expand with the acquisition of Florida in 1819, and Texas, the southwest, and California in the 1840s. By 1850, it occupied, with the exception of small portions of Arizona and New Mexico, all of the contiguous territory it now does. Thus, during a period of about fifty years, the nation had added lands extending from the Mississippi River to the Pacific Ocean, thereby more than tripling in size.

When settlers began to move into this new territory, the theatre followed. Although there had been a few theatrical performances west of the Alleghenies before 1815, these had been given primarily by amateurs. Only in New Orleans, where a French theatre was opened in 1791, had there been extensive dramatic activity.

primarily for *The Contrast* (1787), the first American comedy to be professionally produced. Owing much to Sheridan's plays, it is saved from mere imitativeness by the Yankee servant, Jonathan, whose frank and naive responses to New York social life illuminate the manners of the period.

Tyler's success may have inspired William Dunlap to turn to playwriting. Dunlap had spent the years between 1784 and 1787 in England and had seen most of the important performers and plays of the time. After the success of *The Father* (1789), he went on to write some sixty plays, at least thirteen of which were adapted from works by Kotzebue. His most famous original drama, *André* (1798), is based on an actual in-

FLOATING PALACE

FLOATING PALACE

SPALDING & RODGERS CIRCUS CO
ON BOARD FLOATING PALACE,
WILL Exhibit in Terre Haute on Saturday, April 23d, at 2 and 7 o'clock, P. M.
PRICE OF ADMISSION.

Dress Circle, all armed Chairs..........................50 cer
Family Boxes, Cushioned Seats....................... ....25 "
Gallery..25 "
Gallery for Colored persons.............................50 "
The Company will perform at the following places:
Monday 18, Mt. Carmel at 2 & 7 p. m.
Tuesday 19, Vincennes at 2 & 7 p. m.
Wednesday 20, Russelville at 2 & 7 p. m.
Thursday 21, Hudsonville at 2 & 7 p. m.
Friday 22d at Darwin at 2 & 7 p. m.
April 9, '53 33 3t.

FIGURE 14.42   Advertisement for a showboat circus in 1853. From Hulbert, *The Ohio River* (1906).

The first major step toward a professional theatre in the "West" came in 1815 when Samuel Drake (1769–1854) took a company overland from Albany to Pittsburgh and down the Ohio River to Kentucky. Here Drake established a circuit, including Lexington, Louisville, and Frankfort, although he ventured at times into Ohio, Indiana, Tennessee, and Missouri. His scenery was designed to meet all situations. An adjustable cut-drop served as a proscenium that could be erected in any large room; a roll drop served as a front curtain; three sets of wings (one for exteriors, one for fancy interiors, and a third for plain interiors) and six roll drops (garden, street, wood, palace, parlor, and kitchen) served all scenic demands. Plays were altered so that they could be performed by his company of ten actors, who also doubled in backstage capacities. Drake's work is typical of all the pioneers who came after him, for like the Hallams he improvised to meet whatever situation he encountered and remained in each town as long as attendance permitted. Typically, troupes began by touring over a large area and, as the population increased, gradually confined themselves to an ever smaller territory until touring could be given up altogether.

Drake soon had a number of competitors. The most important between 1820 and 1840 was James H. Caldwell (1793–1863), an English light comedian who came to America in 1816. Appearing first in Charleston and Richmond, he moved to New Orleans in 1820. Between 1825 and 1835, Caldwell dominated the theatre in the Mississippi Valley, for he controlled theatres in Natchez, St. Louis, Nashville, and elsewhere. Thus, Caldwell could offer attractive contracts to touring stars as they came to include the West in their tours around 1830. After suffering serious financial losses during the depression of 1837, he gave up his theatrical interests in 1843.

Caldwell was succeeded by Ludlow and Smith. Noah Ludlow (1795–1886) came west with Drake, and in 1817 set off to tour through Tennessee, Alabama, and elsewhere, giving the first theatrical performances ever seen in many areas. He alternated between management and acting engagements until 1835, when he formed a partnership with Solomon Smith (1801–1869), who had begun his acting career in 1823 and had played for a number of managers in the West before joining Ludlow. Between 1835 and 1853 they dominated the St. Louis theatre, controlled the Mobile theatre until 1840, and from 1843 to 1853 succeeded to Caldwell's

FIGURE 14.43   The auditorium of the showboat "Dixiana" *c.* 1920, at the very end of the showboat era. From the Robert Downing Collection, Hoblitzelle Theatre Arts Collection, University of Texas, Austin.

position of preeminence in New Orleans. Thus, during the 1840s they were the most powerful managers in the West. Ludlow and Smith are also important for having written accounts of their experiences, major sources of information about the "frontier" theatre.

This westward expansion was facilitated by improvements in transportation. During the early nineteenth century canals and toll roads were constructed; in 1830 the first railroad began operation and others soon followed. But during this period the most common mode of travel was by water. The steamboat was invented in 1807, and by 1846 some 1,200 steamboats were in operation on the Mississippi and its tributaries alone.

Most theatres in the West were situated on rivers easily reached by boat. Few were located north of the Ohio River. Chicago did not see a professional production until 1833 and had no permanent theatre until 1847. Small itinerant companies were to be found almost anywhere, however, for just as the new territory provided a buffer against financial crisis and overpopulation in the East, so too it offered a chance to actors who had been unsuccessful in the major theatrical centers. Most itinerant companies set up temporary theatres in each town they visited. In the 1830s, however, a new answer, the showboat, was conceived. While actors had long traveled by water, no one seems to have thought of fitting out a boat as a theatre until 1831, when William Chapman (1764–1839), an English actor who had come to America in 1827, converted a flatboat, and gave performances on it while floating downstream from Pittsburg to New Orleans. Unfortunately, flatboats had to be abandoned when they reached the end of the trip, and it was not until 1836 that a steamboat, which could return up-river, was converted into a theatre. Showboats were eminently practical, for they allowed traveling companies to take well-equipped theatres wherever there was a navigable river. Interrupted by the Civil War, showboating resumed immediately afterward. The most lavish "floating palaces" were in service between 1875 and 1900, when A. B. French, E. A. Price, and E. E. Eisenbarth dominated the river. Showboats continued in regular use until about 1925, after which they became quaint relics.

While the frontier was being settled, the eastern cities continued to grow. The population of New York increased from 60,000 in 1800 to 312,710 in 1840, and Philadelphia grew from 41,000 in 1800 to 93,665 in 1840. Much of this growth can be attributed to the rapid industrialization of the East after 1820.

FIGURE 14.44 A performance at the Park Theatre, New York, in 1822. On stage are Charles Mathews the Elder and Ellen Johnson in a scene from *Monsieur Tonson*. Courtesy New York Historical Society.

The demand for theatrical entertainment resulting from this growth was met in several ways. Existing theatres were enlarged. The Chestnut Street Theatre, which originally seated 1,200, was remodeled in 1805 to hold 2,000, and the Park Theatre in New York was enlarged in 1807 to accommodate 2,372. After both theatres burned in 1820, they were rebuilt for audiences of between 2,000 and 2,500. In New York, the Bowery Theatre, built in 1826, seated 3,000. The number of weekly performances was also increased. In 1820, the Park Theatre began to play six times a week, a move which was adopted in 1823 by the Chestnut Street Theatre. Others soon accepted the new trend.

New companies were also established. By 1825 there were about twenty resident troupes in America, and by 1850 about thirty-five. In addition, there were countless temporary or itinerant groups. In the major cities of the East, expansion followed a typical pattern. Usually a second theatre began as an amphitheatre or circus, which at first gave occasional theatrical entertainments and then progressed to a full season of plays. New York gained its second theatre in 1812, when a circus was converted into the Olympic Theatre (later called the Anthony Street and then Pavilion Theatre). By the 1830s, New York had four theatres playing regularly and the number increased steadily thereafter. In spite of competition, the Park Theatre retained its preeminence. By 1815, the management had passed to Stephen Price and Edmund Simpson (1784–1848), an English actor who came to New York in 1809. After 1840 Simpson was sole manager until 1848, the year in which the Park Theatre burned, thus ending its dominance of New York theatrical life. One of the most ambitious of the Park's competitors was the Bowery Theatre, the largest in the country when it opened in 1826. It soon turned to melodramas so gory that it came to be called the "slaughter house." When it was rebuilt in 1845 it could seat 4,000 persons.

A similar pattern can be seen in Philadelphia. In 1812, a former circus began to offer occasional dramatic entertainments and later became the Walnut Street Theatre. When the Arch Street Theatre opened in 1828, a three-way struggle for supremacy left all of the companies weakened. William Wood, who had left the Chestnut Street Theatre in 1826, headed the Arch Street Theatre, but both he and Warren, who had continued to manage the Chestnut Street, were bankrupt before the season of 1828–1829 ended. Both then retired. Nevertheless, after 1828, Philadelphia usually had at least three theatres in operation. The Chestnut Street's preeminence passed to the Arch Street during the 1830s, and after 1850 the Walnut Street came to the fore. The Chestnut Street was closed in 1855.

In Boston, the Federal Street Theatre encountered its first competition in 1827 when the Tremont Street Theatre was opened. The two companies were amalgamated in 1829, but new competition appeared in 1832 with the opening of the National Theatre. Thereafter, Boston always had more than one troupe. The most important company was to be that of the Boston Museum. Opened in 1841 as a collection of sideshow exhibits, the Museum included a music salon in which short entertainments were given. By 1843, regular plays were being offered, and in 1846, following the enormous popularity of *The Drunkard* (1844), a melodrama written by the company's stage manager, William H. Smith

(1806–1872), a regular theatre was erected. This was to house one of America's leading companies until 1893.

The rapid expansion of the theatre during a period of financial crisis brought many bankruptcies and frequent changes of management. The battle for audiences was reflected in many ways, but perhaps most importantly in the increased use of visiting stars after Edmund Kean's visit to America in 1820–1821. Then considered the finest actor of the English-speaking world, Kean set an example that made it easy to persuade other major actors to cross the Atlantic. After 1820, Price spent much of his time in London recruiting performers for American tours. Stars came with ever-increasing frequency: Charles Mathews the Elder in 1822 and 1833–1835; Macready in 1826–1827, 1843–1845, and 1849; Charles Kean in 1830, 1839, and 1845–1847; Charles and Fanny Kemble in 1832–1834; Mme. Vestris and Charles Mathews the Younger in 1838. At first, tours were restricted to the Atlantic Coast, but as transportation improved, stars ventured to New Orleans and up the Mississippi River.

In the beginning, visits from major actors served to elevate the quality of local companies, but after 1830, as starring engagements came to be a mark of distinction, lesser actors began to tour. Consequently, few good actors were content to remain within the confines of a local troupe. The quality of performances also began to suffer, for stars usually arrived too late for adequate rehearsals, performed only in vehicles adapted to their talents, and relegated local leading actors to secondary roles. Often stars demanded enormous salaries and one or more benefits, leaving the managers with little profit from their visits. Nevertheless, managers were soon trapped by the system, for audiences were loathe to attend unless some novelty were offered. While these evils were not immediately evident, the resident stock company was eventually undermined by them.

The struggle for survival was also reflected in the repertory. Entr'acte entertainments increased in number and variety, novelties (such as child actors, animals, and specialty performers) abounded, and melodrama and minor forms composed an ever-larger part of the repertory. While this pattern did not differ markedly from that current in England, it was complicated by the American ambivalence toward foreign plays and performers. As Americans developed their national consciousness, especially after the War of 1812, the mass audience tended to be suspicious of anything foreign, while the better educated and more sophisticated groups

FIGURE 14.45 Edwin Forrest in the role of Virginius. Courtesy Hoblitzelle Theatre Arts Collection, University of Texas, Austin.

trained. The dominant performer up to 1825 was Cooper, but his "classical" style was less admired as Kean's approach triumphed. Of the new school, perhaps the most important was Junius Brutus Booth (1796–1852). On the stage from 1813, Booth came to America in 1821 and remained for the rest of his life. Although he managed theatres for brief intervals, he was essentially a touring star, one of the first to appear in the Mississippi Valley and the first major actor to play in California. It is sometimes said that Booth did more than any other performer to create a taste for tragic acting. His erratic behavior made him undependable, however, and lessened his potential influence in the major theatrical centers. Other English actors who contributed significantly to the American stage in this period were Mary Ann Duff and the Wallacks. When Mary Ann Duff (1794–1857) came to America in 1810, she had had little experience or training, and did not emerge as a leading player until 1818. Edmund Kean, Forrest, and Cooper all acclaimed her the greatest tragic actress of her day, and Kean declared her superior to any actress on the English stage. Henry J. Wallack (1790–1870) and James Wallack (1791–1864), actors in the Kemble tradition, divided their time between England and America after 1818, serving with distinction both as actors and managers.

Although there had been many native-born actors before his time, Edwin Forrest (1806–1872) was the first American performer to win lasting fame. On the stage from the age of fourteen, Forrest gained much of his early experience in frontier theatres. He made his New York debut in 1826 and by 1828 was the major attraction at the Bowery Theatre. Thereafter, he was considered America's leading actor. Following the Astor Place Riot of 1849 and his sensational divorce, his popularity diminished somewhat and after 1852 he appeared infrequently. He retired in 1872.

Forrest established an "American" style of acting (sometimes called the "physical" or "heroic" style). A man of powerful physique and great vocal strength, he disliked the repressed acting of the Kemble and Macready schools. His athletic and uninhibited performances made him the idol of unsophisticated theatregoers, but he won only grudging admiration from others. Forrest was always more vigorous than most of his contemporaries, many of whom sought to emulate him.

The first native-born actress to win international fame was Charlotte Cushman (1816–1876). Originally an opera singer, she turned to drama when her voice failed. After serving as a utility actress at the Park The-

looked to Europe for their standards and gave only condescending attention to native talent. Consequently, after 1815 American dramatists and performers gained recognition only gradually and were usually accepted by the mass audience before winning critical approval. Acceptance was won more easily after 1830 as "Jacksonian democracy" encouraged faith in the tastes of the common man and native institutions.

Until around 1830 the majority of actors, both major and minor, were English-born and English-

FIGURE 14.46 Charlotte Cushman in the role of Meg Merrilies in Act II, scene 4 of an adaptation of Sir Walter Scott's *Guy Mannering*. This was one of Miss Cushman's most popular roles. Courtesy Hoblitzelle Theatre Arts Collection, University of Texas, Austin.

atre from 1837 to 1840, she played leading roles in Philadelphia and New York. Appearing with Macready in 1843, she was much affected by his methods, which she adopted so successfully that she was often called the "female Macready." In 1845, she went to London, where she won immediate and lasting fame, soon being considered the finest tragic actress of the English-speaking world. After 1852 she appeared only sporadically and confined herself to a restricted repertory, notably Lady Macbeth, Queen Katherine in *Henry VIII,* and Meg Merrilees in *Guy Mannering.* In some ways, Cushman's

acting style was not unlike Forrest's, for it depended upon energy and constant motion, but her intelligent line readings and emotional control won her a much wider following among sophisticated audiences. James E. Murdoch (1811–1893) also gained wide recognition both in America and England. On the stage from 1829 until the late 1850s, Murdoch exerted considerable influence on others through his textbooks on elocution as well as through his performances.

Between 1815 and 1850, a number of American dramatists achieved limited fame. James Nelson Barker (1784–1858) wrote ten plays, of which five survive. The first to be acted was *Tears and Smiles* (1807), a comedy of manners, not unlike *The Contrast,* on Philadelphia society. His *The Indian Princess* (1808), a romantic drama about Pocahontas, was the first play about Indians to reach the stage. His best play, *Superstition* (1824), treats witchcraft in New England. Mordecai Manuel Noah (1785–1852) contributed a number of patriotic plays, such as *She Would Be a Soldier* (1819), *The Siege of Tripoli* (1820), and *Marion, or the Hero of Lake George* (1821). Simply written, Noah's plays depend much upon spectacle and action. Richard Penn Smith (1799–1854) wrote twenty plays, fifteen of which were performed, ranging from farce to romantic tragedy. While most of his comic works were adapted from French sources, several of his serious plays, notably *William Penn* (1829) and *The Eighth of January* (1829), treated American themes. Samuel Woodworth (1785–1842) wrote a number of domestic dramas, such as *The Deed of Gift* (1822) and *The Widow's Son* (1825), but is remembered now primarily for *The Forest Rose* (1825), which introduced the popular Yankee character Jonathan Ploughboy.

Several native dramatists were encouraged by Edwin Forrest, who after 1828 offered prizes for plays by American authors. The most important of the dramatists who wrote for Forrest were Bird and Stone. Robert Montgomery Bird (1806–1854) began his playwriting career in 1827 with *The City Looking Glass,* one of the first American plays of local color and low-life. He subsequently supplied Forrest with some of his most lasting vehicles, *The Gladiator* (1831), *Oralloosa* (1832), and *The Broker of Bogota* (1834). John Augustus Stone (1801–1834) is remembered primarily for *Metamora* (1829), a play about a noble Indian chief in which Forrest performed throughout his career. Other dramatists who provided Forrest with plays include Robert T. Conrad (1824–1871) with *Jack Cade* (1835), and George H. Miles (1824–1871) with *DeSoto* (1852).

FIGURE 14.47   Charles Mathews the Elder as the various characters in one of his "at homes," *Invitations.* **From Anne J. Mathews,** *Memoirs of Charles James Mathews,* **vol. 3 (1842).**

Between 1800 and 1850 the percentage of American plays in the repertory increased from about 2 percent to about 15 percent. As elsewhere, melodrama was the most important dramatic type. Its emphasis upon suspenseful plots, theatrical effects, and moral preaching made it especially appealing to the unsophisticated audiences that flocked to the theatre increasingly. It was also a medium into which commentary about current concerns (such as slavery, the rights of workers and slum life) could be inserted, so that despite its oversimplifications it served to reflect contemporary conditions, while its happy endings reassured audiences that their faith in justice and democracy was justified.

American plays of the early nineteenth century popularized two important native types: the Indian and the Yankee. The Indian was presented sympathetically, following the romantic tradition of the "noble savage," and provided strong roles for serious performers. The Indian had been introduced in American drama as early as 1766 in Robert Rogers' *Ponteach*, but Barker's *The Indian Princess* sketched the outline which was to be followed by others. The vogue for Indian dramas was given its major impetus by George Washington Parke

Custis' (1781–1857) *The Indian Prophecy* (1827) and *Pocahontas* (1830). Between 1825 and 1860, more than fifty Indian plays were performed in America, many by Forrest. The type was dealt a serious blow by John Brougham's burlesque, *Po-ca-hon-tas* (1855), but not until after 1870 was the "noble savage" tradition abandoned.

The Yankee character was the province of the comic actor or "specialty" performer. Although the Yankee had appeared in many plays after his introduction in *The Contrast* (1787), the idea of making him the central character seems to have stemmed from Charles Mathews' *A Trip to America* (1824), a work satirizing various American types. (With his "At Homes," Mathews also did much to popularize the "specialty" performer in America.) After 1825, the Yankee became a favorite character and a number of "specialists" appeared. The Yankee was the symbol of the American common man, simple and naive on the surface, but upholding democratic principles and despising pretense and sham. The first important actor of Yankee roles was James H. Hackett (1800–1871), who conceived the character Solomon Swap in *Jonathan in England* (1828), the first im-

FIGURE 14.48 George Handel Hill, one of the leading Yankee specialists in the 1830s and 1840s. Here he is seen in *The Yankee Pedlar*. An aquatint published in 1838.

portant Yankee play. Hackett gave up Yankee roles in 1836, but continued his distinguished career as manager and actor, being especially noted for his portrayal of Falstaff. Hackett was succeeded by George Handel Hill (1809–1849), by 1832 considered the best of the Yankee specialists. In addition to monologues and skits, Hill performed full-length plays, such as J. S. Jones' *The Green Mountain Boy* (1833) and *The People's Lawyer* (1839). With Hill, the Yankee became more sympathetic and sentimental. Dan Marble (1810–1849) achieved fame after 1836 in the role of Sam Patch, a more generalized American type, while Joshua Silsbee (1813–1855) was the acknowledged master of Yankee roles after the deaths of Hill and Marble. Silsbee turned the type once more toward broad and eccentric humor. Of the later specialists, John E. Owens (1823–1886) was the most famous. Ultimately, the vogue for the Yankee, which reached its height between 1830 and 1850, is perhaps most important for its role in establishing a native American comedy.

The black, another important native type, also fell to specialists. The black may be found in American drama from the beginning as a faithful servant or comic caricature, but the popularity of the type dates from about 1828 when Thomas D. Rice (1808–1860) introduced his "Jim Crow" song and dance. Soon a major star, Rice spawned a host of imitators, most notably Barney Williams, Jack Diamond, Barney Burns, and Bob Farrell. Rice's success also helped to create the Minstrel Show. In an effort to enlarge his repertory, Rice began to offer "Ethiopian Operas" around 1833. Building upon these, Dan Emmett (1815–1904) put together a full-length entertainment, "Virginia Minstrels," in 1843, and in 1846 the Minstrel Show was given its distinctive form by E. P. Christy (1815–1862).

The Minstrel Show was divided into two parts. In the first, the performers were arranged in a semicircle, the tambourine player at one end and the "pair of bones"

FIGURE 14.49 Thomas D. Rice as Jim Crow. Courtesy the Albert Davis Collection, Hoblitzelle Theatre Arts Collection, University of Texas, Austin.

player at the other. These "end" men came to be called Tambo and Bones. The "middle" man, or Interlocutor, served as Master of Ceremonies and exchanged jokes with the end men between musical numbers. The second part, or "olio," consisted of specialty acts and songs. The Minstrel Show reached the peak of its popularity between 1850 and 1870. After 1870, companies began to increase in size, some including more than 100 performers. The popularity of the form declined, nevertheless, and by 1896 only ten companies remained. By 1919 there were only three, and soon the Minstrel Show was a mere curiosity.

Despite such caricatures, the black was able to make his own mark during the early nineteenth century. In 1821 the first known company of black actors in America was assembled in New York by James Brown, who presented occasional theatrical performances at the African Grove, an outdoor tea garden, and later at an indoor theatre. The repertory included *Richard III, Othello* and other plays, and starred James Hewlett, a native of the West Indies. It also included the first known American play written by a black author, Brown's own *King Shotaway,* which dealt with an insurrection on the island of St. Vincent. Unfortunately, the company was plagued by white rowdies and perhaps because of these difficulties it fades from surviving records after 1823.

The African Company left one important legacy, however, for it seems to have provided Ira Aldridge (1807–1867) with his first acting experience. Unable to pursue a theatrical career in America, Aldridge went to London, where he made his debut in 1825; within a few years he was known throughout England as "the celebrated African Roscius." In 1852 he undertook his first European tour and aroused such enthusiastic response that he spent much of his time thereafter on the continent. Noted for his performances of Othello, Shylock, Macbeth, and Lear, he was decorated by the rulers of Prussia, Russia, and Saxe-Meiningen. He died while performing in Poland. By all indications, Aldridge was one of the great actors of his age, but racial barriers prevented him from ever showing his great powers in the land of his birth.

Another native type, the city boy, came into prominence in the 1840s, perhaps to give the increasing urban population its own folk hero. City low-life had appeared on the stage occasionally since Pierce Egan's *Tom and Jerry, or Life in London* was adapted in the 1820s as *Life in Philadelphia, Life in New York,* and so on. The city boy was not popular, however, until Ben-

FIGURE 14.50 Frank Chanfrau as Mose the Bowery Boy and volunteer fireman. This character was a popular stage figure from the 1840s to the 1860s. Courtesy Hoblitzelle Theatre Arts Collection, University of Texas, Austin.

jamin Baker's *A Glance at New York* (1848) introduced the volunteer fireman and good-natured roughneck, Mose the Bowery Boy. The phenomenal success of this play led to many sequels in which Mose visits various countries and becomes embroiled in new situations. Frank S. Chanfrau (1824–1884) spent much of his career acting this role. The Bowery Boy faded in popularity after the 1860s, but was assimilated into other plays about city life.

By the 1840s, American writers and actors were no longer novelties. Perhaps for this reason, Anna Cora Mowatt (1819–1870) won immediate and widespread acceptance with *Fashion* (1845), a comedy of manners about New York social life. Of a well-to-do family, Mrs. Mowatt turned to writing around 1840 when her husband lost both his fortune and his health. Since playwriting paid little, Mrs. Mowatt went on the stage in 1845. With no previous experience, she was a star from the first. In such roles as Juliet and Rosalind, she won fame both in America and England before retiring in 1854.

Between 1815 and 1850 spectacle began to be given greater emphasis. For the most part, plays continued to be staged in stock settings, but occasionally an effort was made to provide more specific and elaborate backgrounds. Interest in historical accuracy is first found in John J. Holland's Gothic settings for Joanna Baillie's *De Montfort,* presented at the Park Theatre in 1809. Archeological detail did not make a deep impression, however, until 1845–1846, when Charles Kean staged *Richard III* and *King John* at the Park Theatre. Thereafter, accuracy was gradually accepted as an ideal.

Panoramas and dioramas were introduced in an attempt to gain greater realism. Nontheatrical panoramas had been seen in New York since the 1790s, and in the 1820s Daguerre's dioramas were regularly shown there. Perhaps as a result, Dunlap was commissioned by the Bowery Theatre in 1827 to write *A Trip to Niagara,* in which a journey by steamboat up the Hudson River was depicted. During her tour in 1838, Mme. Vestris allegedly attracted attention to more detailed settings and properties, and it is possible that she introduced the box set into America at that time.

In 1816 the Chestnut Street Theatre became the first in the world to light its stage with gas. This new medium had been demonstrated in England by William Murdoch in the late eighteenth century but it had not then been sufficiently perfected as an illuminant. It was adopted for exterior lighting at Covent Garden in 1815 and may have been installed in the auditorium of the Lyceum in the same year. It was first used for lighting the stages of Covent Garden and Drury Lane in 1817. By the early 1820s, gas was being used experimentally in most countries of the Western World.

Gas did not win immediate acceptance, however, for it presented many problems. Since there were as yet no gas mains, each theatre had to install and maintain its own plant, an expensive undertaking. Furthermore, gas gave off unpleasant fumes and oppressive heat; the danger of fire was always great. It was not until the 1840s, when a dependable supply became available, that gas was widely adopted.

Gas eventually triumphed because of its advantages over candles and oil. For the first time, the stage could be lighted as brightly as desired. Since the burners did not have to be trimmed, as did the wicks of candles and lamps, they could be distributed more advantageously. As a result, border lights were used more extensively. Furthermore, complete control over intensity was now possible. At first each gas pipe was controlled separately, but in the 1840s the "gas table," comparable to the modern control board, made it possible for an operator to control all lights from one position. After 1850 many of the objections to gas were eliminated by the "fishtail" burner, which increased efficiency and reduced fumes by controlling the relationship of the fuel to oxygen. In the 1880s, an incandescent mantle made gas even safer, but by this time electricity had begun to replace it.

Two lighting instruments, the limelight and carbon arc, were of special importance during the nineteenth century. The limelight ("calcium" or Drummond light) was invented by the Englishman Thomas Drummond in 1816. It consisted of two cylinders of compressed gas, one of hydrogen and one of oxygen, which were directed against a column of lime so as to heat it to incandescence. Placed inside a hood and fitted with a lens, the limelight was the prototype of the spotlight. Macready was the first to recognize its potentialities for the stage, but after using it for a time in 1837 he gave it up as too expensive. Nevertheless, by the 1850s it had been adopted widely and played a prominent role in productions thereafter. Its mellow and brilliant rays were first used for creating such atmospheric effects as sunlight or moonlight; only gradually was its potentiality for lighting the acting area developed. Eventually it came to be used primarily as a "follow" spot to emphasize starring performers. The major disadvantage of the limelight was its need for constant supervision: since the lime had to be kept in proper alignment with the gases and flame, it required a separate operator for each instrument.

The carbon arc was first demonstrated in 1808 by Sir Humphrey Davy, but the lack of a satisfactory source of power left its theatrical uses unexplored until the 1840s. By 1860, it had been placed in a housing and equipped with a lens to create a spotlight. It was not widely used, however, until after 1880, when electricity began to replace gas. To create a carbon arc, each electrical pole was attached to a stick of carbon; when the carbons were brought into close juxtaposition, the current leaped between them, creating an incandescence. Giving off a rather harsh light, the carbon arc also tended to be noisy and to flicker. Many of the drawbacks were eliminated with the invention in 1876 of the Jablochkoff Candle, which kept the carbon in proper alignment without the aid of an operator. The carbon arc served the same purpose as the limelight.

These innovations—gas, gas table, limelight, carbon arc, and the various refinements on each—revolutionized stage lighting in Europe and America between 1815 and 1880, although the artistic principles needed to guide usage were yet to be formulated.

Between 1800 and 1850, then, the theatre underwent many changes. During this time the last vestiges of neoclassicism almost wholly disappeared under the onslaught of romanticism. In some countries the romantic ideal was self-consciously followed and in others it was little known, but everywhere the melodramatic and pseudo-Shakespearean mode in playwriting, local color and historical accuracy in settings and costumes, and emotional and psychological realism in acting had made themselves felt and had combined to create a theatre in 1850 quite unlike that of the late eighteenth century. But by 1850 the romantic outlook itself had come to pall, and new forces, destined to lead to realism, were already coming to the fore.

LOOKING AT THEATRE HISTORY

In theatre history there is a tendency to judge an era by the excellence of its drama. In most instances the best plays come to be treated as typical, while all lesser works and entertainments are swept aside as unimportant. This approach results in considerable distortion, for it suggests that "popular culture" is insignificant. Yet the entertainments of the masses are more apt to represent the norm of the age than is the elitist art of "high culture." The popular arts almost always offer important insights into their time. As Leo Lowenthal says in *Literature, Popular Culture and Society* (1961), "By studying the organization, content, and linguistic symbols of the mass media, we learn about typical forms of behavior, attitudes, commonly held beliefs, prejudices, and aspirations of large numbers of people."

Concern for "popular culture" is especially pertinent in studying nineteenth-century theatre history, since the repertory was dominated by melodrama and minor forms usually scorned by literary critics. Thus, nineteenth-century drama and theatre are often treated condescendingly or passed over lightly as unworthy of serious attention. David Grimsted is one of those who has sought to counter the typical approach; he demonstrates how melodrama can be a key to understanding the nineteenth century:

The aesthetically poor quality of its plays has encouraged stage historians to view the period's theatrical history as a strange interlude either preparatory to twentieth-century improvements or simply full of quaint plays, practices, and anecdotes. Seen as a product of particular intellectual and social preconceptions . . . . the melodrama becomes less an inexplicable monstrosity and more an emotionally valid attempt to dramatize an era's faith. (p. x)

At the end of his study, Grimsted concludes:

[Melodrama's] conventions were false, its language stilted and commonplace, its characters stereotypes, and its morality and theology gross simplifications. Yet its appeal was great and understandable. It took the lives of common people seriously and paid much respect to their superior purity and wisdom. . . . And its moral parable struggled to reconcile social fears and life's awesomeness with the period's confidence in absolute moral standards, man's upward progress, and a benevolent providence that insured the triumph of the pure. (p. 248)

> DAVID GRIMSTED, *Melodrama Unveiled: American Theatre and Culture, 1800–1850* (Chicago: University of Chicago Press, 1968).

Melodrama, like pantomime before it, helped to bring to drama the kind of spectacular effects that since the Renaissance had been associated primarily with opera. Pixérécourt, the "father of melodrama," was a master of spectacle. The second act of his *Daughter of the Exile*, for example, includes a flood in which the heroine escapes by floating away on a plank. Here is a contemporary review of the production:

The scenery of the second act must be considered a marvel of perspective and mechanics. The progressive heightening of the waves, the falling of snow and of rocks, the uprooting of trees, the balancing of the plank on the surface of the waters, all is a striking and realistic imitation.

Journal des Debats, March 16, 1819.

Spectacle became even more realistic with the introduction of moving panoramas and dioramas. Daguerre's dioramas *à double effet*, especially, created a great sensation, since on a single canvas, through the manipulation of painting and lighting, more than one picture could be made to appear and to alter its appearance before one's eyes. These dioramas were one step in the development of the motion picture. Daguerre has left a detailed description of the process he used in creating these dioramas, of which only a few excerpts are given here. Other passages tell precisely how the painting is to be done and the lighting controlled:

> . . . one indispensible essential is to employ [cloth] which is exceedingly transparent. . . . it is necessary to prime it, on both sides, with at least two coats of parchment size. The first effect, which ought to be the clearer of the two, is executed on the right side of the canvas. . . . The second effect is painted on the wrong side of the canvas. . . . The first effect . . . is lighted . . . only by a light which comes from the front, while the second effect . . . receives its light . . . from behind only. . . . we may employ both lights at once, in order to modify certain portions of the picture.

> L. J. M. DAGUERRE, *An Historical and Descriptive Account of the Various Processes of the Daguerrotype and the Diorama* (London, 1839), pp. 81–86.

During this period the introduction of gas, with its brilliance and ease of control, gave stage lighting previously unknown potential. Here is an account of the inauguration of gas lighting at Drury Lane in London in 1817:

> . . . gas lights . . . are introduced not only in front of the stage, but at the various compartments on each side: Their effect, as they appear suddenly from the gloom, is like the striking of daylight; and indeed it is in its resemblance to day that this splendid light surpasses all others. It is as mild as it is splendid—white, regular, and pervading. . . . if it is managed as well as we saw it on Friday [it] will enable the spectator to see every part of the stage with equal clearness. If the front light could be thrown, as daylight is, from above instead of below (and we should like to hear the reasons why it cannot) the effect would be perfect.

> Review by LEIGH HUNT in *The Examiner,* September 7, 1817.

This was also an era of great actors, many of whom developed international followings much like those of movie stars today. One of the most famous was the French actress, Rachel. Here is a review of her performance in Racine's *Phaedra:*

> Her entrance as she appeared, wasting away with the fire that consumed her, standing on the verge of the grave, her face pallid, her eyes hot, her arms and hands emaciated, filled us with a ghastly horror. . . . In the second act, where she declares her passion, Rachel was transcendent. There was a subtle indication of the diseased passion, of its fiery but unhealthy—irresistible and yet odious—character, in the febrile energy with which she portrayed it. It was terrible in its vehemence and abandonment. . . . when she left the scene our nerves were quivering with excitement almost unsupportable.

> J. FOSTER and G. H. LEWES, *Dramatic Essays* (London, 1896), pp. 84–85.

The fame of such actors created a desire to see them in person, and extensive tours were arranged for them. Soon lesser actors were emulating them, much to the detriment of resident companies, which began to disintegrate. Here are the American manager William Wood's comments on this situation:

> When the performance of great leading parts were claimed by Cooke or Kean as stars, the regulars [in the resident company] never, in my experience, showed dissatisfaction. . . . But when we had cast upon us, as stars . . . actors of all grades, the case became widely different. The companies here found, night after night, some new person they had never before heard of, announced in big letters—all their own plans deranged, themselves forced into extraordinary and severe study, and their whole time absorbed . . . merely that they might act as subsidiaries . . . to some foreign adventurer, who possessed no merit half so great as their own; while he took away in one night twice as much as they could earn as their whole weekly wages. . . . accordingly men who, up to this time, had been perfectly contented with their wages, and with their home reputation of clever stock actors . . . now abandoned that safe position for the attractive honors of the star.

> WILLIAM B. WOOD, *Personal Recollections of the Stage* (Philadelphia, 1855), pp. 446-447.

15 Theatre and Drama in Europe and America During the Late Nineteenth Century

The last half of the nineteenth century brought many changes to western Europe. The revolutions of 1848 had demonstrated the overwhelming desire for political, social, and economic reform. Initially, governments were frightened into promising change, but after the violence abated most of them declined to implement their pledges. The republic established in France in 1848 gave way to another empire under Napoleon III from 1852 until 1871, and throughout Europe it was not until late in the century that the demands made in 1848 began to be met. England was probably the most compliant: in 1867 it greatly extended the franchise; in 1872 it introduced the secret ballot; and in 1884 it finally extended the vote to all adult males; in 1870 Parliament also made government appointments dependent on examination rather than patronage. But all such reforms were bitterly opposed by those who championed a benevolent despotism of the privileged over the working classes.

The late nineteenth century was also the heyday of nationalism and imperialism. On the European continent the number of independent states declined markedly as they were brought into the German empire, the kingdom of Italy, the Austro-Hungarian empire, or the Russian empire. This trend toward centralization at home was paralleled by overseas expansion, motivated in part by the need for raw materials and markets to support rapid industrialization. Much of Africa and Asia came under the direct control of European nations. Bri-

tain acquired the largest empire, but it was followed closely by France and Germany.

Industry and trade encouraged technological advances, and each new invention increased the peoples' faith in science and engineering to solve human problems. Nevertheless, benefits were not evenly distributed, and the working classes had to fight for every increase in their rights. Unionization and strikes became their principal weapons, especially after the 1860s, but even then success came only through costly work stoppages and violence. It was a time when the common man began to assert himself through programs of action other than revolution and to demand that his worth and dignity be recognized and respected.

Reformers no longer expected to achieve changes overnight. In search of pragmatic solutions, they rejected the idealistic and utopian visions of the romantics. It was out of this pragmatism that a new artistic movement—realism—gradually emerged.

THE BEGINNINGS OF REALISM

Realism owed much to the "positivism" of Auguste Comte (1798–1857), author of *Positive Philosophy* (1830–1842) and *Positive Polity* (1851–1854). Comte classified the sciences according to their relative simplicity, placing the demands for authenticity of spectacle and psychological motivations. All of the approaches before 1850, however, had emphasized "beautiful" nature, norms, picturesque local color, or pleasing contrasts. Even Hugo, who had demanded the inclusion of the grotesque in art, avoided the sordid in his own practice. Around 1850, however, critics began to advocate a close and objective observation of life, no matter how squalid or elevated.

As a conscious movement, realism is first discernible around 1853 in France. By 1863 the theoretical foundations had been fully expressed there in such periodicals as *La Révue de Paris, L'Artiste, Le Figaro, Réalisme* (first published in 1856), and *Le Présent*. The main tenets of the new movement were: art must depict truthfully the real, physical world; truth can be attained only through direct observation; only contemporary life and manners can be observed directly; and the observer must strive to be as impersonal as a scientist.

FRENCH DRAMA, 1850–1900

It was also in France that dramatists first consciously sought to implement the realists' aims. Among these pioneering playwrights, the most important were Dumas *fils* and Augier. But they owed much to their predecessors and perhaps most to Eugène Scribe (1791–1861), for he had popularized the structural pattern which they were to appropriate. Between 1811 and 1861, Scribe contributed over 300 pieces to Parisian theatres, 23 of them to the Comédie Française. He ranged through *comédies-en-vaudevilles*, opera libretti, comedies, and serious drama. Perhaps the best of his works were *Marriage for Money, A Glass of Water*, and *Adrienne Lecouvreur*. Today, Scribe is remembered primarily as the popularizer of the "well-made play" formula. Often used as a term of derision and sometimes said to apply only to Scribe's own works, "well-made play" can perhaps best be understood as a combination and perfection of dramatic devices common since the time of Aeschylus: careful exposition and preparation, cause-to-effect arrangement of incidents, building scenes to a climax, and use of withheld information, startling reversals, and suspense. Because they sacrifice depth of characterization and thought to intrigue, Scribe's plays now seem shallow. To theatregoers of the nineteenth century, however, they appeared more substantial, probably because they manipulate so skillfully the attitudes and prejudices of that

FIGURE 15.1 Scribe's *The Glass of Water,* Act V, scene 7, first performed at the Comédie Française, 1840. From *Oeuvres Completes de M. Eugène Scribe,* vol. 5 (1847).

sociology at the apex as the most complex and important of the sciences. Since to him the ultimate aim of all knowledge was the betterment of human life, Comte argued that all the sciences must contribute to sociology, which, after the rigorous application of the scientific method, would supply the necessary knowledge for predicting human behavior and controlling society. Comte's arguments fell on willing ears, not only among scientists and philosophers, but also among many artists, who sought to make art "scientific." Out of these attempts, realism emerged.

The realistic mode in art had been attempted sporadically since the time of the Greeks. Beginning in the Renaissance, pictorial illusion had dominated the theatre. Melodrama and romanticism had accelerated

FIGURE 15.2   Final scene of *La Dame aux Camelias* by Alexandre Dumas *fils,* first performed at the *Théâtre Contemporain Illustré* (1867).

time. Although Scribe was not associated with the realistic movement, his well-made play formula, emphasizing as it did the seemingly logical development from cause to effect, supplied Dumas *fils* and Augier a suitable form for their ideas.

Alexandre Dumas *fils* (1824–1895) came to public attention with a dramatization of his own novel, *The Lady of the Camellias* (now usually referred to as *Camille*). Although today *Camille* (performed 1852) seems merely an idealized treatment of the "prostitute with a heart of gold," it was forbidden production for three years because of its realism. Set in Paris in the 1840s, the play used prose dialogue and depicted a protagonist based upon a well-known courtesan of the time. Hugo's *Marion Delorme* had also treated a courtesan but its story was historical and its dialogue poetic. Consequently, it had not aroused the objections which greeted Dumas' work.

By 1855, Dumas had undergone a change of attitude and in *The Demi-Monde* he treated unsympathetically the same kind of characters that are presented sentimentally in *Camille*. He now set out to show that "women with a past" must be prevented from marrying into good families. After this time, Dumas wrote "thesis plays" about current social problems, utilizing Scribe's well-made play formula to create suspenseful and entertaining stories. His works are marred by didacticism,

for in most a message is clearly stated by an articulate *raisonneur,* or author's mouthpiece. In spite of this lack of objectivity, Dumas considered himself a realist and his duty the betterment of society. In an open letter to the critic Sarcey, he wrote: ". . . if I can exercise some influence over society . . . if I can find some means to force people to discuss the problem, and the law-maker to revise the law, I shall have done more than my duty as a writer, I shall have done my duty as a man."

Emile Augier (1820–1889) was a more versatile writer than Dumas *fils.* He began his career in 1844 as an adherent of the "theatre of common sense" but, after seven verse plays, adopted the realistic style. One of his first prose works, *Olympe's Marriage* (1855), was intended as a direct reply to Dumas' *Camille,* for it shows the disastrous results of a courtesan marrying into an aristocratic family. It is Augier's most didactic play. His more characteristic works are comedies of manners, such as *M. Poirier's Son-in-Law* (1854) in which Augier depicts the struggle for supremacy between the impoverished but proud nobility and the well-to-do and ambitious middle class. Others of his plays treat the power of money, the influence of the church on politics, and numerous additional problems.

Although they occasionally shocked audiences, Dumas and Augier were viewed not as extremists but as

FIGURE 15.3   Augier's *Giboyer's Son,* Act IV, scene 6, at the Comédie Française, 1862. Courtesy Bibliothèque de l'Arsenal, Paris.

FIGURE 15.4 Scene from Sardou's historical spectacle, *Fatherland!*, directed by Sardou at the Théâtre de la Porte Saint-Martin in 1868. Setting by Cambon. Courtesy Bibliothèque de l'Arsenal, Paris.

sane citizens seeking to raise the moral tone of their times. Their plays treated subjects of concern to the middle-class citizenry of Napoleon III's materialistic and conservative Third Empire. Thus, Dumas and Augier were rapidly assimilated into the mainstream of drama not only in France but throughout Europe. It would be left to their more uncompromising successors, the naturalists (to be discussed in a later chapter) to bring hitherto unacceptable topics and techniques onto the stage. Furthermore, perhaps because they used Scribean techniques, Dumas and Augier did not seem at the time to differ markedly, except in tone, from their less serious contemporaries, such as Sardou and Labiche.

Victorien Sardou (1831–1908), Scribe's true heir, was one of the world's most popular playwrights between 1860 and 1900. Like Scribe, he used the well-made play formula and adapted it to almost every dramatic type. His early successes included comedies, such as *A Scrap of Paper* (1860) and *Our Intimates* (1861), and satires on contemporary life, such as *The Family Benoiton* (1865). He later wrote a number of plays for Sarah Bernhardt, including *Fedora* (1882) and *Tosca* (1887), and some of the most lavish historical spectacles of the nineteenth century, such as *Fatherland!* (1869) and *Theodora* (1884). The latter works elicited praise even from the naturalists for their faithful recreation of particular

milieus. To George Bernard Shaw, however, Sardou's shallow dramas seemed to epitomize the decadence and mindlessness into which the late nineteenth-century theatre had descended, a state he labeled "Sardoodledom."

Eugène Labiche (1815–1888) was one of the finest writers of farce in the nineteenth century. Uninterested in theories, Labiche wrote for the popular audience and only reluctantly agreed to the publication of his plays. Most of his works, of which *The Italian Straw Hat* (1851) is representative, appear delightfully irresponsible, but others, such as *M. Perrichon's Journey* (1860) and *Dust in the Eyes* (1861), make penetrating observations on human nature. Many of his plays have worn better than those of his more self-consciously serious contemporaries.

Of the minor forms, the most popular in France during the late nineteenth century was operetta, which as a distinct form emerged around 1848. A mixture of song and speech, fantasy, buffoonery, and irreverent subject matter, operetta made its mark above all through the work of Jacques Offenbach (1819–1880), especially *Orpheus in the Underworld* (1858) and *La Belle Hélène* (1865).

THEATRICAL CONDITIONS IN FRANCE, 1850–1900

The playwrights discussed here are only a few of those who sought to fill Parisian theatres, which sometimes numbered as many as fifty and seldom fewer than thirty during the last half of the century. Until the 1880s most of the stable minor houses tended to specialize in one of five genres—melodrama, comedy, vaudeville, spectacle drama, or operetta—perhaps because most of them assembled companies best at performing a particular kind of play and sought authors who wrote that type. Beginning in the 1880s, however, this pattern broke down for many reasons. Among the most important was the increase in the length of runs. By 1880 no play was considered successful unless it was given at least 100 performances; many were given 300 or more times. In turn, length of run as a standard of success led managers to search for works likely to attract large audiences; it also led them to replace the resident company with performers hired only for the run of a play to which their talents were especially fitted. The long run meant as well that each theatre needed to produce only a few works each

FIGURE 15.5 Setting by Chaperon for *Oedipus Rex.* From *Revue des Arts Decoratifs* (1881–1882).

year to fill out its season. Furthermore, the provincial theatre was so undermined by touring companies that by 1900 Paris had become virtually the only theatrical center in France. Near the end of the century, one writer complained that about twenty-five authors had come to monopolize the market, since the demand for new plays had been so much reduced and since managers favored works by proven authors. Censorship also encouraged conservatism in the choice of plays.

Overall, the theatre during the last half of the century was prosperous. After 1875 matinee performances were added, and by 1900 ticket agencies had appeared and were being accused of buying up seats to popular plays so they might resell them at inflated prices.

During this period, then, the French theatre was characterized by conservatism motivated in part by material prosperity but also by taste. It was this conservatism which eventually stimulated the concern for reform which gave rise to the "modern" era in French theatre.

Throughout the last half of the nineteenth century, two demands—for increased realism (and a consequent need for greater control over production) and for virtuosity (which tended to encourage defiance of control)—were evident and often in conflict. Of the two, the trend toward realism is perhaps most apparent, for it can be seen clearly in every aspect of production. It was certainly one of the decisive elements in the development of directing.

Both Sardou and Dumas *fils* credit Adolphe Montigny (1805–1880), director of the Gymnase, with first treating directing as an art in France. According to Du-

mas, Montigny, beginning around 1853, placed a table downstage center in order to prevent the actors from taking up the semicircular formation then typical. Next, he put chairs around the table, seated the actors, and made them speak to each other rather than to the audience, as had been typical in the past. Finally, he furnished his settings like real rooms and placed properties, such as cigar boxes, handkerchiefs, or letters, about the stage to motivate movement from one place to another. In this way, he gradually arrived at an illusion of real life. According to Sardou, Montigny's success encouraged others to adopt his innovations.

Most of Montigny's work was done with contemporary plays written in the realistic mode. Thus, it was left to Sardou, who supervised the production of his own plays, to perfect historical spectacle, which he insisted be absolutely faithful to fact. Such care for detail extended as well to some revivals at the Comédie Française (for example, *The Marriage of Figaro* in the early 1880s had seventy rehearsals, an unusually large number for that time). By the end of the century practically all companies employed a director and gave him two or three assistants to oversee the various aspects of staging and performance.

The movement toward realism is also evident in scenery and costuming. In terms of archeological accuracy, it reached its peak in Sardou's spectacles, which were so detailed in their *milieux* that even the naturalists praised them. For *Hatred* (1874), set in medieval Siena, unprecedented sums were spent on armor, costumes, and scenery. *Theodora* (1884), laid in Byzantium, was given an even more elaborate mounting; in their reviews of this piece, some critics spoke of virtually nothing except the scenic marvels.

Realistic details from daily life also proliferated. For example, *My Friend Fritz,* produced at the Comédie Française in 1876, featured a farmyard in which real water flowed from a pump and real cherries were picked from trees; in another scene, real food and drink were served and consumed on stage.

The visual style and favored motifs differed little from those of earlier years because the major designers were those who had begun their careers before 1850 or their students: A. A. Rubé, Philippe Chaperon, C. A. Cambon, J. B. Lavastre, Edouard Despléchin, Jean Daran, and Eugene Lacoste.

By the end of the nineteenth century, methods of obtaining scenery had become relatively standardized. The director, after consultation with the playwright,

FIGURE 15.6 Backstage at a theatre in the late nineteenth century. Note the division of the floor; note also the poles supporting the flats. From Pougin, *Dictionnaire du Théâtre* (1884).

gave a summary of requirements to the scenic designers, who then made cardboard models of the sets. When these were approved, scale drawings were made to guide the theatre's carpenters, who built the settings. After completion, the scenery was sent to one of Paris' five or six scenic studios for painting. Each theatre hired a relatively small number of stagehands, for since French plays almost never changed place within acts, shifting was usually confined to intermissions when haste was not of major concern.

For costumes, theatres began after 1850 to employ special designers for historical plays and to increase their staffs of tailors and seamstresses to construct and maintain garments. Special supply houses were founded to meet the growing demand for armor and other articles

too difficult to be made by the theatres. Professional wig makers supplied wigs and several hairdressers were hired to assist the actors. By the late nineteenth century, Racinet's *Le Costume Historique* (completed 1888) had become the standard guide for the design of costumes.

In acting, realistic touches also increased. Actresses began to knit, actors to smoke or perform other familiar business. One performer at the Comédie Française in the 1870s consulted toxicologists in order to make a death scene more convincing (it was judged one of the most realistic ever seen on the French stage); in 1890 a realistic blood transfusion was performed on stage. Such instances could be extended almost indefinitely.

There was also at least one important attempt to revolutionize training so that acting might become a more precise mode of communication. At this time most French actors still received their training while in service, although the Conservatoire became increasingly important as the repertory system began to decline. But even at the Conservatoire students learned primarily by imitating their teachers, and thus they perpetuated earlier acting techniques and styles. Given the temper of the nineteenth century, it was probably inevitable that someone would try to approach acting analytically and scientifically. And so it was that François Delsarte (1811–1871) set out to demonstrate that the laws of stage expression are discoverable and these laws can be formulated as precisely as mathematical principles.

Delsarte sought to analyze emotions and ideas and to determine how they are outwardly expressed. He divided human experience and behavior into the physical, mental, and emotional-spiritual, and he related these to each action, thought, and emotion. He also divided and subdivided the body into parts and related each to the physical, mental, and emotional-spiritual. Eventually he arrived at an elaborate scheme whereby he sought to describe how the feet, legs, arms, torso, head, and every other part of the body are used in communicating particular emotions, attitudes, or ideas.

Although Delsarte's system eventually became overly mechanistic, it remains important as the first significant attempt to reduce every aspect of the actor's training to method. By the end of the nineteenth century it was being taught virtually all over the world and, though it is now usually treated derisively, it has contributed to most subsequent attempts to formulate training programs for actors.

If many forces encouraged realism in the late

FIGURE 15.7   Constant-Benoît Coquelin as Cyrano de Bergerac, a role created for him by Edmond Rostand. The original production in 1898. From *Le Théâtre* **(1898).**

nineteenth-century French theatrical production, perhaps an equal number worked against it. In scenery, for example, in 1900 the same settings were still being used for several different plays. Thus, while a company might have many more settings than in the eighteenth century, it did not consider it necessary to have specially designed scenery for each play. Furthermore, since the various settings for a single production were often designed by different artists, unity was lacking. Similarly, in costume many actors continued to supply their own wardrobes, and actresses were often outfitted by *couturiers*. Even when a manager employed a costume designer, the leading actors felt free to supply their own dress and were often praised by critics for their novel touches. Although consistency was most nearly achieved in historical spec-

tacles, even here it was seldom complete. As with scenery, the same costumes were used for many different plays.

But earlier practices were probably most evident in acting. Until near the end of the nineteenth century, actors were employed according to lines of business and thus they tended to build up a repertory of tricks and business which they drew on in every role. Contrarily, supernumeraries were almost always recruited off the streets, and they rarely rehearsed with the company before performing. Most theatres employed someone to secure and rehearse the supernumeraries and to provide leadership on stage during performances. Often the group differed each night.

But, most significant, the late nineteenth century glorified starring performers. Consequently, most productions were built around them. If the star had a strong artistic conscience, this practice could lead to excellent results, but all too often it brought the subordination of everything to his whims. Even the Comédie Française did not escape this trend, and bickerings and jealousies there did much to undermine that company's ensemble.

Stars were legion during the late nineteenth century, but among the most important were Got, Coquelin, Mounet-Sully, and Réjane. Edmond Got (1822-1901), who performed at the Comédie Française after 1844, was noted for his excellent characterizations in classical and, especially, contemporary comedy. Constant-Benoît Coquelin (1841–1909) performed at the Comédie Française from 1860 to 1886, after which he toured throughout the world before returning to Paris. In the early 1890s Coquelin created a major scandal when he defied the rule which forbade any actor who left the Comédie Française to perform elsewhere in Paris. (Bernhardt had also defied this rule, but she had been such a troublemaker at the Comédie that no one wished her to remain in the company.) Coquelin's example tended to undermine the Comédie's discipline by making it easy for any disgruntled actor to leave its ranks. In 1897 Coquelin became manager of the Porte-Saint-Martin, where he created the role of Cyrano de Bergerac, written especially for him. At his best in Molière's comic roles or in flamboyant romantic parts, Coquelin was noted for his technical proficiency, about which he wrote extensively in such works as *The Art of the Actor* (1889).

Mounet-Sully (Jean-Sully Mounet, 1841–1916) had been trained at the Conservatoire and had played at the Odéon before he entered the Comédie Française

FIGURE 15.8   Sarah Bernhardt at center in Sardou's *Theodora* in a 1902 revival in Paris. From *Le Théâtre* (1902).

in 1872. He was soon acknowledged the finest tragic actor of his time. With his striking physique, beautiful voice, and fiery temperament, he brought considerable originality to all the great tragic roles in both the classical and romantic repertory.

Gabrielle Réjane (1857–1920) made her first appearance in 1875 and soon was considered the finest player of comedy of her age. She seldom ventured outside light contemporary drama, but in that she was unsurpassed. She appeared with considerable success in London, New York, and elsewhere before she retired in 1915.

But the most famous French star of the late nineteenth century was Sarah Bernhardt (1844–1923). She made her debut in 1862 and after performing in several minor theatres and at the Odéon was engaged at the Comédie Française in 1872, where she soon became a great attraction and a source of controversy. After considerable unpleasantness, she left the company in 1880. The rest of her career was devoted to starring tours throughout the world and to the management of a series of Parisian theatres. Noted for her slim figure, dark eyes, "golden" voice, and her portrayals of seductiveness, pain,

tearful rage, and death, she achieved her greatest success as Camille, Tosca, Adrienne Lecouvreur, Phaedra, Dona Sol in *Hernani*, and the title role in Rostand's *The Eaglet*. Her mastery of the techniques of acting and her magnetic personality combined to create an image that epitomizes the "grand actress." Many still consider her the greatest actress of her age.

The tension between tradition and change, so evident in every area of production, was also reflected in theatre architecture. During the 1860s, many new theatres were built as Napoleon III's scheme for an elaborate network of "grand boulevards" took shape. As one result, the Boulevard du Temple, the original home of the boulevard theatres, disappeared. The new theatres that replaced the old ones retained many traditional features but included some innovations. In the auditorium, the area immediately forward of the stage was fitted out with comfortable armchairs (a practice begun at the Opéra-Comique in the 1840s) but behind this area there continued to be, as in the past, a section (the pit or *parterre*) equipped only with benches. This ground level was surrounded by a row of boxes (or *baignoires*), above which rose two or three additional galleries. The first contained two or three rows of chairs and behind these a row of boxes; the second gallery was usually devoted entirely to boxes, and the third entirely to benches. The more fashionable theatres had a number of lavish *loges à salon,* fitted up like sitting rooms complete with bell cords so that the occupants could ring for service during the performances. The seating capacity of the theatres averaged from 1,200 to 2,000. Not until near the end of the century was there much concern for safety. The aisles were narrow and often filled with folding chairs; fire exits were inadequate and ventilation poor. After 400 persons perished in the fire which destroyed the Opéra-Comique in 1887, attention was at last turned to achieving greater safety.

The proscenium arch was usually very high in order to provide adequate sightlines for spectators in the galleries, which not only rose to the ceiling but extended along the sides of the auditorium to the proscenium. The proscenium arch was also usually very thick, for in most theatres a box was set into it on the level of each gallery. This thickness created a wide apron which was much used by the actors, especially before realism was fully established. The prompter was housed in a box at the front of the apron. The floor of the stage raked up toward the rear. The chariot-and-pole system remained the usual method of scene shifting, although it was supplemented by flying and the movement of set pieces by hand. During the nineteenth century, space above and below the stage was greatly enlarged to permit more effective handling of the increasingly detailed settings, and in several theatres elevator traps were installed.

Perhaps no theatre summed up earlier tradition so thoroughly as did the Paris Opéra, completed in 1874. Designed by Charles Garnier and begun in 1862, the Opéra cost about 40 million francs. Enormous foyers and stairways led to the auditorium with its four levels of galleries and seating capacity of 2,100 persons. A proscenium arch 55 feet wide framed a stage 175 feet wide by 85 feet deep. The depth could be increased to about 150 feet by including the dance salon immediately behind the stage. The floor from the front of the stage to the back of the dance studio was raked upward two inches in every 40 inches. Above the stage there was 119 feet of space, and below it 50 feet. The stage floor was divided from front to back into ten sections, or *plans,* each of which was subdivided into (1) several slots about 1½ inches wide, (2) narrow traps about 18 inches wide, and (3) larger traps about 40 inches wide. Any

FIGURE 15.9 Sectional plan of the Paris Opéra, opened in 1874. The stage house is at right. Note the many levels below the stage. Note also the enormous amount of space given over to lobbies and other audience uses. From *Monde Illustré* (6 February, 1875).

part of a subdivision or entire plan could be opened the width of the proscenium arch. This flexibility permitted the operation of almost any effect from beneath the stage. Scenery was shifted by chariots, each about 10 feet long and equipped with four upright poles upon which flats could be mounted. In addition, scenery could be flown or moved through the stage traps. When it was built, this was the most elaborate theatre in the world. Ironically, this enshrinement of the past practices was completed just as Wagner's Festspielhaus in Bayreuth, which initiated a new ideal, was being built.

In France, then, the late nineteenth century brought increased attention to every aspect of theatrical endeavor. At the same time, an uneasy tension between innovation and tradition was evident. Still lacking was a theory of theatrical production capable of welding the diverse elements into a unified whole. During the last years of the century this need began to be met. The results will be the subject of later chapters.

ENGLISH DRAMA, 1850–1890

In England, drama was at a low ebb during the second half of the nineteenth century, although a number of writers achieved contemporary fame with melodramas, light comedies, burlesques, and musical dramas. Among

FIGURE 15.10 Scene from Tom Taylor's *The Ticket-of-Leave Man* as produced at the Olympic Theatre, London, 1863. At center Horace Wigan is seen as Hawkshaw, perhaps the first stage detective. Courtesy Theatre Museum, Victoria and Albert Museum.

the popular dramatists of this period were Taylor, Byron, and Boucicault.

Between 1844 and 1878, Tom Taylor (1817–1880) wrote more than seventy plays ranging through almost every type, but he was at his best in comedy and domestic drama. Among his most famous works were *Masks and Faces* (1852), based on the life of Peg Woffington; *Still Waters Run Deep* (1855), which created a stir because of its discussion of sex; *Our American Cousin* (1858), made famous by E. A. Sothern's playing of Lord Dundreary; and *The Ticket-of-Leave Man* (1863), a story of low-life featuring the detective Hawkshaw.

Between 1857 and 1882 Henry James Byron (1834–1884) wrote nearly 150 plays ranging from sentimental comedy to burlesque-extravaganza. *Our Boys* (1875) achieved a run of 1,362 performances, a record which stood for many years. Byron's plays epitomize the general level of dramatic entertainment in the late nineteenth century, for they seldom penetrated beneath the surface of conventional ideas or stock characters.

Perhaps the most successful dramatist of the period was Dion Boucicault (1822–1890), who began his career in 1841 with *London Assurance,* a sprightly comedy of manners, and continued to write prolifically thereafter for the remainder of his life. From 1844 to

1848 he lived in France, where he mastered the techniques of French romantic drama and melodrama. He spent the years between 1853 and 1860 in America and thereafter divided his time between the United States and England. During the 1850s Boucicault perfected the basic ingredients of his plays—sentimentality, wit, sensationalism, and local color—and seldom varied them thereafter except in details. His major works, such as *The Corsican Brothers* (1852), *The Sidewalks of New York* (1857), *The Octoroon* (1859), *The Colleen Bawn* (1860), *Arrah-na-Pogue* (1864), and *The Shaughraun* (1874), all tell suspenseful and melodramatic stories set in picturesque locales and most are resolved through scenes of sensational spectacle, such as fires, explosions, snowstorms, or avalanches. Not only was Boucicault one of the most skillful playwrights of his age, his penchant for making the latest scientific inventions important elements in his plots exerted considerable influence on theatrical production.

Not until the 1860s did a dramatist interested in the realistic mode appear. Thomas William Robertson (1829–1871), son of a provincial actor, was originally a performer and for a time Mme. Vestris' stage manager. He began writing in 1851 but had little success until 1864 when *David Garrick* was produced. The plays upon which his reputation rests—*Society* (1865), *Ours* (1866), *Caste* (1867), *Play* (1868), and *School* (1869)— all tell stories of contemporary life and take place in highly particularized locales, every detail of which is meticulously described in the scripts. Furthermore, many

FIGURE 15.11 Slave market scene in Boucicault's *The Octoroon,* first produced in 1859. A contemporary engraving.

important points are made primarily through pantomime and stage business which recreate everyday domestic events, such as making, serving, and drinking tea. As produced by the Bancrofts, these plays also popularized several innovations in performance. Robertson cannot be labeled a great dramatist but among his contemporaries he was unique. Unfortunately, he had no immediate successors, and consequently the realistic vein was not exploited by English writers until the 1890s.

In terms of popular appeal, the most favored forms between 1850 and 1900 were pantomime, burlesque-extravaganza, and musical entertainments. During these years pantomime underwent significant change as the traditional short form was enlarged into full-length entertainments. This transformation owed most perhaps to the playwright E. L. Blanchard (1820–1889) and to the Vokes family of performers at Drury Lane between 1869 and 1879. During the 1880s, Augustus Harris (1851–1896) made still other changes when he began to import music hall performers to Drury Lane to play the "principal boy" (a breeches role) and the "dame" (played by a man) and to present numerous specialty acts as a part of the pantomime. After this time comedy gained the ascendancy and the fairy tale element became merely a skimpy framework holding together the comic routines, dances, and spectacle. It is in this form that the English Christmas pantomime has survived to this day.

At mid-century the most popular of all dramatic types was burlesque-extravaganza. Almost all theatres performed it, and a few built their repertory around it. By this time Planché's light touch and delicate irreverence had given way to broad travesties of popular plays, operas, myths, and fairy tales, all filled with topical allusions, low comedy business, and anachronisms. Puns appeared in almost every line of the doggerel verse in which they were written. Numerous songs set to already existing music and elaborate spectacle, including a magical transformation scene, completed the appeals. In addition to H. J. Byron, other masters of the genre were William Brough (1826–1870) and F. C. Burnand (1836–1917).

By the 1870s burlesque-extravaganza had begun to decline in popularity, although it continued to be performed until the end of the century. As it declined, its place was taken by comic opera, especially that of Gilbert and Sullivan. William Schwenck Gilbert (1836–1911), encouraged by Robertson to take up dramatic writing, was the author of some forty plays, mostly comedies, quite independent of Sullivan's music. Several of these—

FIGURE 15.12 A pantomime based on "Puss in Boots" as seen at the Drury Lane Theatre in 1887. The script was by E. L. Blanchard. The setting is by Wilhelm. From *The Graphic* (7 January 1888).

most notably *Pygmalion and Galatea* (1871), *Sweethearts* (1874), *Broken Hearts* (1875), and *Engaged* (1877)—enjoyed considerable success. But Gilbert is now remembered primarily for the comic operas he wrote with Arthur Sullivan (1842–1900). Their first important work, *Trial by Jury* (1875), also brought an alliance with Richard D'Oyly Carte (1844–1901), who in 1881 built the Savoy Theatre to house their plays. Among their many collaborations, some of the best are *H.M.S. Pinafore* (1878), *The Pirates of Penzance* (1879), *The Mikado* (1885), *The Gondoliers* (1889), and *Utopia Limited* (1893). Eventually a quarrel between Gilbert and Sullivan disrupted their partnership, but their comic operas have continued to hold the stage. With their lighthearted melodies and whimsical humor, they turned extravaganza into a form of satire sometimes said to be the nineteenth-century equivalent of Aristophanic comedy.

The success of Gilbert and Sullivan prompted still other developments in musical drama, most notably in the work of George Edwardes (1852–1915). Business manager of the Savoy Theatre for a time, in 1885 Edwardes became manager of the Gaiety Theatre. Here, beginning with *In Town* (1892) and *The Shop Girl* (1894), Edwardes established a type of musical comedy in which a sketchy plot provided an excuse for songs, elaborate production numbers performed by beautiful chorus girls, and specialty acts. In this form, musical

FIGURE 15.13 The new Haymarket Theatre, opened in 1821 to replace the older structure torn down in 1820. It is still in use. The floor plan is seen at the bottom of the picture. From Wilkinson, *Londina Illustrata* (1825).

up throughout England. A number of circuits were created—the most famous being that of Edward Moss and Oswald Stoll—and from time to time there was an attempt to substitute the term "variety" for "music hall." This form of entertainment remained a favorite with the British public until after World War I, when the motion picture began to replace it.

ENGLISH THEATRICAL CONDITIONS, 1843–1860

When the Theatre Regulation Act was passed in 1843, the London stage seemed at a low ebb. Many persons

FIGURE 15.14 Young Joe Grimaldi as a monkey performing with his father, an eccentric buffoon, at Sadler's Wells. Seen here is an accident in which a broken chain precipitated Young Joe into the audience. Engraving by George Cruikshank. From *Memoirs of Joseph Grimaldi*, ed. by Boz (Charles Dickens), vol. 1 (1838).

comedy was to flourish without significant change until the First World War.

The music hall also prospered in the late nineteenth century, as regular drama was separated from the incidental entertainment which had accompanied it since around 1700. Music halls developed out of the "music rooms" attached to taverns, but it was not until about 1850 that Charles Morton (1819–1904) took the significant step of erecting a separate building to house entertainment. Other tavern owners followed his example, but it was many years before the link with taverns was broken. Gradually, however, the separation came and the entertainment was made acceptable to middle-class audiences. Sketches and short plays were added to the bills, and famous actors and concert artists were induced to appear in the music hall theatres that sprang assumed that the new law would bring rapid change and that many new theatres would be built. In actuality, the period between 1843 and 1860 was to be one of reassessment and gradual recovery. Unlike the years between 1810 and 1843, when many new buildings were erected, no new theatre was built in London until after 1860. Yet in retrospect, out of the years 1843–1860 grew an unprecedented prosperity and new prestige.

After 1843, Drury Lane and Covent Garden rapidly lost their positions of dominance. Covent Garden soon became the home of opera, while Drury Lane turned increasingly to spectacle and musical drama; both have continued these specialties to the present day. Of the patent theatres, only the Haymarket retained its stability; between 1843 and 1850 it was London's foremost home for regular drama. From 1837 to 1853, the Haymarket was managed by Benjamin Webster (1797–1882), a former member of Mme. Vestris' troupe, who in 1844 also acquired the Adelphi, which specialized in melodramas, most notably those of J. B. Buckstone. In 1853, Webster ceded the management of the Haymarket to Buckstone, who retained it until 1876. Under Buckstone, the Haymarket maintained its reputation for comedy, but it lost its privileged position in serious drama except when visiting stars performed there. Webster rebuilt the Adelphi in 1858 and remained at its head until 1874.

But, Webster and Buckstone were continuers of tradition rather than innovators. Major new developments were to come at Sadler's Wells and the Princess' Theatre. In 1844, Sadler's Wells was a remote house noted for its bloodthirsty melodramas. Since about 1730 it had been offering theatrical entertainments and it had been the principal target of the bill of 1752, which required the licensing of all places of entertainment. In the early nineteenth century it had gained renown for its aquatic dramas and later as the summer home of Joseph Grimaldi (1778–1837), the most famous clown of pantomime.

It is unclear why Samuel Phelps (1804–1878), an actor since 1826 and Macready's principal support since 1837, chose this out-of-the-way, rundown theatre for his experiment in management, but it is probably explained by the low rent. Contrary to expectations, not only was Phelps financially successful but he made Sadler's Wells the principal home of poetic drama in London between 1844 and 1862. Phelps' significance lies in his demonstration—at a time when it was almost universally believed that only popular entertainment could attract a large audience—that fine drama could be suc-

FIGURE 15.15 Samuel Phelps as Macbeth, Act II, scene 1, just before the murder of Duncan. Courtesy Hoblitzelle Theatre Arts Collection, University of Texas, Austin.

cessful. The source of Phelps' popularity was unmistakable, for his repertory was composed almost entirely of poetic drama. Except for six of the minor works, Phelps produced all of Shakespeare's plays in versions more complete than any since Shakespeare's time. Unlike his successors, who rearranged the plays to avoid scene shifts and made drastic cuts to allow scope for spectacle, Phelps made only minor cuts and transpositions.

Although he mounted his productions with care, Phelps' lack of funds precluded sumptuous costumes and settings, and, while he sought historical accuracy, he never sacrificed dramatic values. Perhaps his most famous production, *A Midsummer Night's Dream* with settings by Frederick Fenton, used a moving diorama to shift the scene from one part of the forest to another;

FIGURE 15.16 Scene from Lord Byron's *Manfred* at Drury Lane, 1863. The Steinbach Waterfall, haunt of the Witch of the Alps. Samuel Phelps appeared in this production after he left Sadler's Wells. From *The Illustrated London News* (1863). Courtesy Hoblitzelle Theatre Arts Collection, University of Texas, Austin.

much of the action took place behind a scrim which created a misty atmosphere.

Phelps suffered most from the lack of first-rate actors. For the first two seasons, Mrs. Warner played leading roles; she was followed by Isabella Glyn and several lesser actresses. Perhaps because of their inexperience, the actors were coached extensively by Phelps, who also played many leading roles ranging from Lear to Bottom. As a performer, Phelps was universally praised for his judgment, taste, absence of tricks, and faultless elocution (which Macready and Charles Kean were slighting in their attempts to achieve greater realism). His faults were monotonous pace and slow delivery. Despite its mediocre company, Sadler's Wells had the most devoted audience of any theatre in London.

It is sometimes charged that as a manager Phelps merely continued Macready's work. While this is partially true, Phelps succeeded where Macready failed, and it was he who reestablished that faith in poetic drama which Macready's financial troubles had undermined. After he gave up Sadler's Wells in 1862, Phelps toured widely, and for a time in the 1860s restored Drury Lane to its former glory with a series of Shakespearean productions. He continued on the stage until 1877, by which time his style was considered old-fashioned.

If Phelps revived poetic drama, Charles Kean (1811–1868) perfected pictorial realism and brought

the fashionable audience back to the theatre. Son of Edmund Kean, he went on the stage in 1827 but, lacking his father's powers, he gained little recognition until 1838. In 1842, he married Ellen Tree (1806–1880), his leading lady thereafter. His first experience as a director came in 1841, when he staged *Romeo and Juliet* for Webster. During his third tour of America between 1845 and 1847, he produced *King John* and *Richard III* in New York, following Macready's promptbooks closely. The most detailed productions yet seen in America, their success probably encouraged Kean to go into management, and in 1850 he leased the Princess' Theatre in London.

The Princess' was the last theatre opened in London before the passage of the Theatre Regulation Act. During the 1840s it was noteworthy primarily because it presented the American actors Edwin Forrest, Charlotte Cushman, Anna Cora Mowatt, and E. L. Davenport. Its period of glory, however, was to come with Kean's management between 1850 and 1859.

Kean's work is significant for several reasons. First, it brought fashionable audiences back to the theatre. Probably much of the credit should go to Queen Victoria, who in 1848 revived the office of Master of Revels and appointed Kean to it. Queen Victoria requested many theatrical performances for Windsor Castle and also began to attend the Princess' Theatre. The combination of her prestige and the respectable tone of Kean's management soon made his theatre a fashionable resort.

FIGURE 15.17 One of the witches scenes from Charles Kean's production of *Macbeth* in 1853 at the Princess' Theater, London. Courtesy Hoblitzelle Theatre Arts Collection, University of Texas, Austin.

FIGURE 15.18 Setting for the banquet scene in Charles Kean's production of *Macbeth*, 1853. This was the first production for which Kean supplied the audience a list of the sources he had consulted in order to insure the historical accuracy of all the visual elements. Courtesy Folger Shakespeare Library, Washington.

Second, Kean influenced changes in the evening's bill. Because fashionable playgoers tended to dine late, Kean opened some productions with a short piece to offset the effect of late arrivals. Gradually this practice caught on and the curtain-raiser replaced the afterpiece in many theatres. Furthermore, he dispensed with all incidental entertainment. Thereafter, variety acts were increasingly relegated to the music halls, and each theatre began to specialize in a limited range of theatrical entertainment.

Third, Kean hastened the trend toward "gentlemanly" melodrama begun by Macready. Although now remembered primarily for his Shakespearean productions, Kean presented fewer than half of Shakespeare's plays, and his greatest success as an actor came in such melodramas as Boucicault's *The Corsican Brothers* and *Louis XI*, both adapted from French works which blend romantic drama and melodrama. Such plays were to enjoy enormous popularity through the remainder of the century.

Fourth, and probably most important, Kean developed antiquarianism further than did any English producer. His first significant attempt to insure accuracy in every detail came in 1852 with *King John*. Beginning with *Macbeth* in 1853, he provided the audience with a printed list of the authorities he had consulted in his search for authenticity. Kean considered his election in 1857 to the Society of Antiquaries one of his greatest honors. Despite his care for details, however, Kean could never induce Ellen Tree to abandon the hooped petticoats she wore under garments of every period.

Often called the "illustrator" of Shakespeare's texts, Kean cut many of the finest descriptive passages and replaced them with spectacle and pantomime, and he often rearranged texts so as to avoid scene changes. For settings, Kean had the services of such gifted designers as Thomas Grieve, William Telbin, and Frederick Lloyds. About 400 watercolor sketches of Kean's productions have survived to provide one of the most complete records of any nineteenth-century producer's work.

Finally, Kean helped to establish the director as the primary artist in the theatre. Other than himself and his wife, he employed no stars. He gained his effects

FIGURE 15.19 Charles Fechter as Hamlet in the graveyard scene, Act V, scene 1. Courtesy Hoblitzelle Theatre Arts Collection, University of Texas, Austin.

primarily through care for details and the coordination of the whole. Despite his fame, Kean was not financially successful, for he always spent more than he made. Any deficit, however, can be attributed to his high standards rather than to lack of patronage, for his theatre was always well attended. After his retirement from management, Kean toured throughout the world in starring engagements.

ENGLISH THEATRICAL CONDITIONS, 1860–1880

By 1860 the major work of both Phelps and Kean was over, and the theatre was well on its way to recovery. For the first time since 1843, new theatres began to be built, and by 1870 the twenty-one theatres of 1860 had increased to thirty. The population of London also grew from 3,316,932 in 1864 to 4,766,661 in 1881. This growth brought a number of changes in theatrical production, especially through the work of Fechter, Boucicault, and the Bancrofts.

Charles Fechter (1824–1879), born in London to a German father and French mother, made his debut at the Comédie Française in 1844. Soon dissatisfied, he left to play for a time in Berlin and London before returning to Paris in 1848. He was soon regarded the foremost stage lover of his day (he was the original Armand Duval in Dumas' *Camille*), and for a time was joint manager of the Odéon. Resigning after a disagreement, he decided to go to London.

Fechter opened at the Princess' Theatre in 1860 and there in 1861 created a sensation with his production of *Hamlet*. Unfamiliar with the English tradition, Fechter's interpretation of Hamlet was markedly different from any previously seen. Playing in the familiar style of gentlemanly melodrama and in settings furnished like ordinary rooms, he made the play seem contemporary. From 1863 to 1867, Fechter managed the Lyceum Theatre, where he featured translations of French plays and won a reputation as one of the finest actors of his time. In 1870 he went to America, but failed to gain a wide following because by then his powers were fading. In 1876 he retired.

Fechter's influence was considerable. First, he extended the vogue for gentlemanly melodrama begun by Macready and Kean. Second, he popularized a more realistic acting style, for he played the classics in precisely the same manner as he did contemporary drama. Thereafter, poetic drama grew in favor largely because it was merged with the nineteenth-century taste for spectacular melodrama. Third, Fechter revived interest in the box set, which he used for most interiors. He gave up the practice of entering between the wings, which English actors traditionally had done even when the wings represented solid walls. While Fechter did not bring about a revolution in theatrical practice, he encouraged more rigorous concern for illusionism.

After Dion Boucicault returned to England in 1860, he helped to gain acceptance for several innovations. He contributed to the vogue of the "out-of-town tryout" when *Arrah-na-Pogue* was played in the provinces before opening in London in 1865. He was also one of the first to employ actors for the run of the play rather than on a season's contract, for he seems early to

FIGURE 15.20 Duel scene from Boucicault's *The Corsican Brothers* as performed at the Princess' Theatre, London, 1852. Charles Kean is seen at left as the dying Louis dei Franchi. Kean also played Louis' twin brother, Fabien, who avenges his brother's death. Courtesy Theatre Museum, Victoria and Albert Museum, London.

have grasped the implications of a long-run policy. Additionally, Boucicault was the first English playwright to achieve financial security from his writing. During the early nineteenth century the traditional practice of paying authors through benefit performances had gradually been replaced by the payment of set sums (normally 100 pounds for a five-act play and proportionately less for shorter works) on the third, sixth, and twentieth nights of the original unbroken run. Few playwrights between 1810 and 1860, however, had received even 300 pounds for a single play. Jerrold testified that for *Black-Eyed Susan,* one of the most popular works of the nineteenth century, he had received a total of 70 pounds. By 1830 dissatisfaction with this situation had prompted the formation of the Dramatic Authors' Society, and largely because of its efforts Parliament in 1833 passed England's first copyright law relating to plays. But, while the act protected dramas written after 1823, it did not cover dramatizations of novels, and the force of the bill was further reduced by a court decision which declared that the acting rights to printed plays belonged to their publishers. Thereafter, many dramatists sought to keep their works out of print. Thus, the

new bill gave authors some protection but did not greatly improve their lot.

Boucicault's innovation did not stem from any new legal sanction. Rather, because of the popularity of his plays, he demanded and received a percentage of the receipts from every performance. Consequently, *The Shaughraun* is said to have earned him $500,000. In 1865, the Bancrofts began to pay Robertson a set fee for each performance of his works; thereafter, the royalty system gradually gained in favor. The playwright's legal position did not become secure, however, until near the end of the nineteenth century, for copyright did not extend beyond national boundaries. In 1886 an International Copyright Agreement, under which each subscribing nation pledged to uphold the copyright provisions of all others, was prepared, and by 1900 most of the world's major countries had accepted it. Loopholes in earlier national laws were also gradually eliminated. Largely for these reasons, playwriting at last became a profitable profession. Boucicault was one of the first to benefit from the changes.

Probably the most significant management between 1860 and 1880 was that of the Bancrofts at the Prince of Wales' Theatre, for here many earlier trends came together. Although it is difficult to discover a practice which they initiated, the Bancrofts combined a number of innovations to create a theatre quite unlike any other of the period.

Mrs. Bancroft, born Marie Wilton (1839–1921), was on the stage as a child, appearing with both Macready and Charles Kean. Her success as an adult actress began in burlesque-extravaganza in 1856. Then, at the age of twenty-six, she decided to manage her own company. The only theatre she could afford to rent was the out-of-the-way Queen's Theatre, so run-down that it was known as the "dust hole." Nevertheless, after indemnifying him against loss, she induced the popular dramatist H. J. Byron to join her as co-manager and to supply the theatre with plays. Now called the Prince of Wales', the theatre opened in 1865. In securing Byron's services, Miss Wilton obviously intended to present a repertory composed primarily of burlesques and light comedy. It was at Byron's urging that she produced Robertson's *Society,* a play previously refused by several other managers. Its run of 150 nights began an association which soon made Byron superfluous, and in 1867 he withdrew from the management. In the same year, Miss Wilton married Squire Bancroft (1841–1926), her leading

FIGURE 15.21 Robertson's *Caste* as produced by the Bancrofts at the Prince of Wales' Theatre, 1879. Courtesy Enthoven Collection, Victoria and Albert Museum.

man. Bancroft had made his debut in 1861 and had played in the provinces until he joined Miss Wilton's company in 1865. From 1867 until 1879 the Bancrofts were joint managers of the Prince of Wales' Theatre, and from 1880 until they retired in 1885, of the Haymarket.

It is difficult to distinguish the Bancrofts' contributions from those of Robertson, for not only was he their major playwright, he also directed the plays during the formative years. On the other hand, Robertson had little success with any other troupe. Consequently, it would appear that their joint success stemmed from compatibility.

The distinctive Robertson-Bancroft style—a form of domestic realism—first appeared with *Caste* (1867). While several earlier producers had emphasized realistic visual detail, they had used spectacle primarily as embellishment. In Robertson's plays, on the other hand, character and stage business are inseparable, for the attitudes and emotions of his personages are revealed primarily through the minutiae of everyday life. Without spectacle Robertson's plays scarcely exist, and the printed versions require lengthy and detailed stage directions to be comprehensible. They marked the advent of a new kind of realism in England.

Robertson worked with the actors of the Bancroft troupe on every detail; he substituted understatement for bravura acting and emphasized ensemble effects. Lines of business, still dominant in other companies, were ignored, the company had no stars, and even the Bancrofts often played small roles. Perhaps fortunately, most of the actors were young and welcomed these breaks with tradition.

The Bancrofts' contributions came primarily in contemporary drama. Only two of their productions were of classics and these were unsuccessful, for the company's acting style was not suited to period plays. Nevertheless, the prestige of the Bancroft company was comparable to that enjoyed earlier by Charles Kean, and contemporary drama was raised considerably in critical esteem.

The Bancrofts embraced the long run. In their twenty years of management they produced some thirty long plays, and almost half of all performances were of Robertson's works. After they began to present a series of plays for extended runs, they employed many of their actors on a "run of the play" contract. They abandoned benefits for actors, then still prevalent in most theatres, and raised salaries markedly. When other managers were paying actors five to ten pounds weekly, the Bancrofts were offering 60 to 100 pounds.

The Bancrofts also helped to establish several other important innovations. Their production of *Caste* in 1867 was among the first in England to tour with a full company and with all scenery and properties. Thereafter touring increased rapidly and by 1880 provincial resident companies were beginning to disappear. The Bancrofts also helped to establish the single-play bill by dropping the curtain-raiser and after-piece. Although some theatres retained the longer bill, audiences no longer demanded it. Additionally, the Bancrofts aided in establishing matinee performances. Used occasionally after the 1850s, matinees became usual with the Bancrofts during their production of Sardou's *Diplomacy* in 1878. Matinees were adopted for Gilbert and Sullivan's comic operas in the 1880s and were standard in most theatres by 1900.

Many of the Bancrofts' contributions involved spectacle and theatre architecture. More than any other management of the nineteenth century, they won acceptance for the box set. Because of their example, most theatres after 1875 devoted as much care to accuracy in modern as in period plays. The Bancrofts also firmly anchored acting behind the proscenium arch. The retreat from the forestage had begun with Garrick, but, despite several attempts to abandon the proscenium doors, they were not removed at Drury Lane until 1822 and at Covent Garden until 1823. In 1831 the Olympic became the first minor house to dispense with them. The apron persisted, however, and actors continued to use it. But, after 1867, the "fourth wall" was always respected at the Prince of Wales' Theatre. When the Bancrofts moved to the Haymarket in 1880, they extended the gilded proscenium arch across the bottom of the stage to emphasize the picture frame. By 1900 the use of the apron had been seriously curtailed in virtually all of London's theatres.

The Bancrofts were also instrumental in establishing the orchestra as the favored seating area. In 1800, the pit still consisted only of backless benches. The King's Theatre, which was used for opera, converted some of its benches into seats with backs in the 1820s, and in 1822 The Drury Lane added a few of these "stalls." Gradually other theatres accepted the change, although the stalls were restricted to a few rows at the front, and the pit continued to occupy the remainder of the ground floor. In 1863, The Haymarket replaced its stalls with upholstered chairs, and the last pit benches were removed when the Bancrofts took over the Hay-

market in 1880. Other theatres gradually followed this example. With the introduction of chair-style seating came the numbering and reservation of places. In turn, the practice of reserving seats reenforced the long run, since popular plays encouraged the booking of seats in advance and advance sales encouraged the extension of runs.

These changes are representative of many others in auditorium design. Since the Restoration, the pit had been surrounded by boxes only slightly raised above it. Around 1820, however, the Adelphi Theatre established a new trend when the boxes were raised sufficiently to permit the extension of the pit to the outside walls. Other changes came after 1860. Probably most important was the movement away from large houses. The Criterion, opened in 1874, held only 660, and the Prince of Wales' seated only 600. Few theatres built after 1875 held more than 1,500. This reduction in size meant fewer galleries, while the growing prestige of stall seating motivated the replacement of boxes with open balconies, usually called the Dress Circle, Upper Circle, and Gallery. Furthermore, the balconies were foreshortened on the sides so that they no longer extended to the proscenium wall. As a result, the proscenium arch could be lowered. The cantilevering of balconies, which began in the late nineteenth century, permitted the removal of supporting posts. All of these changes did much to improve sightlines and comfort. Many of these innovations stem from the work of C. J. Phipps (1835–1897), designer of about forty theatres in England.

ENGLISH THEATRICAL PRACTICE, 1880-1900

Between 1880 and 1900 the English theatre was dominated by the actor-manager, Henry Irving (1838-1905). Born John Henry Brodribb, Irving played in the provinces from 1856 to 1866 and then in London with several leading actors before going to the Lyceum Theatre in 1871 as leading man and stage manager. At that time, the Lyceum was under the management of H. L. Bateman (1812-1875), an American who had taken the theatre to star his daughters, Kate (1843-1917), Virginia (1853-1940), and Isabel (1854-1934). Kate and her sister Ellen (1844-1936) had achieved acclaim in America as child prodigies in such roles as Richard III, Macbeth, and Shylock. Ellen had retired at the age of sixteen, but Kate had won considerable fame as an adult performer before

FIGURE 15.22 Henry Irving (foreground) as Mathias in *The Bells* seeing a vision of the Polish Jew he has murdered. Irving played this role, one of his most admired, for more than thirty years. A contemporary engraving.

the family came to London. After Bateman died in 1875, his wife continued as manager until 1878, when the Lyceum passed to Irving. Under Irving's management from 1878 to 1898, the Lyceum became the foremost theatre of London. Irving also played throughout England and made eight tours of America. He retired in 1902.

As an actor, Irving gained his first outstanding success in 1871 as Mathias in *The Bells,* a thrilling melodrama about a man who confesses under hypnosis to the murder of a Jewish pedlar. This role remained one of Irving's most popular throughout his career. He continued to build his reputation in such melodramas as W. G. Wills' (1828–1891) *Charles I* (1872) and *Eugene Aram* (1873). In 1874, his *Hamlet* ran for 200 nights, a new record for a Shakespearean play. By the time he became a manager, he was considered the finest serious actor in London. By 1878 he had already been on stage for more than twenty years and his success had been won only through long and diligent work. Irving had few natural attributes upon which to build; throughout his career critics voiced grave reservations about his playing. He mispronounced many words, walked, as one critic put it, like a man trying to get over a plowed field hastily,

and at times interpreted roles in a bizarre fashion. On the other hand, he was a master of byplay which clarified every reaction and thought. His roles were boldly conceived and carefully portrayed. Like Charles Kean, Irving was at his best in melodrama, for though he is now remembered chiefly as a Shakespearean actor, the only Shakespearean role in which he consistently appeared with success was Shylock. Irving promoted no new playwrights and never appeared in the new realistic drama.

Irving's fame is bound up with that of his leading lady, Ellen Terry (1847–1928), who came from a large family of actors, two others of whom were well known. Kate (1844–1924), on stage with Ellen as a child in Charles Kean's company, went on to perform Ophelia to Fechter's Hamlet before retiring in 1867. She was to be the grandmother of John Gielgud. Fred Terry (1863–1933), outstanding in romantic roles in the Lyceum company, managed his own troupe from 1900 to 1930. As an adult, Ellen Terry had played in the provinces, for the Bancrofts, and at the Court Theatre before joining Irving in 1878. She remained Irving's leading lady until he retired in 1902. She then managed the Imperial Theatre for a time, where she allowed her son, Gordon Craig, to try out many of his ideas. After 1907 she performed only occasionally, although she did not retire fully until 1925. At her best in such roles as Beatrice in *Much Ado About Nothing,* Olivia in *Twelfth Night,* and Portia in *The Merchant of Venice,* Miss Terry had an excellent sense of timing and great command of stage movement and speech. To all of her roles she brought freshness and vitality.

Despite the personal fame of Irving and Ellen Terry, the reputation of the Lyceum rested upon the total effect of its productions. Building upon the tradition of Macready and Charles Kean and stimulated by the London appearance of the Meiningen Players in 1881, Irving's work climaxed the trend in England toward pictorial realism. Although never the stickler for accuracy that Kean had been, Irving often employed archeologists to aid him, as in *Cymbeline* (1896) and *Coriolanus* (1901), for both of which the costumes and scenery were by Sir Lawrence Alma-Tadema (1836–1912). At other times he commissioned designs from such famous painters as Edward Burne-Jones (1833–1898). In addition, he had on his staff the finest scenic artists of the day, Hawes Craven and Joseph Harker. Craven (1837–1910) had worked in London since 1857 for such producers as Fechter and the Bancrofts, and to him probably should go much of the credit usually given Irving. Craven was later to open a scenic studio which supplied many theatres with settings. Joseph Harker (1855–1927) began his career as an assistant to Craven and later took major responsibility for many of Irving's productions. After leaving Irving he became Herbert Beerbohm Tree's principal designer. Continuing to work into the 1920s, Harker was one of the major links between Victorian and modern scenic practices. But if Irving employed the finest artists available, he had no consistent policy. Sometimes a single artist designed the scenery and costumes for a production, but more frequently the tasks were divided among a number of designers.

Many of the innovations at the Lyceum resulted from changes in the method used to shift scenery. In 1881, Irving took a revolutionary step—he abandoned the grooves that had been the standard method of shifting scenery for more than 200 years. By adopting "free plantation," Irving could place scenery wherever he desired and achieve complete flexibility. Irving's solution was the culmination of many earlier trends. Since the beginning of the century, heavy set pieces had proliferated and many of them had been shifted by means of large elevator traps located upstage, so that while a "short scene" occupied the forward part of the stage, a "set scene" could be arranged behind a drop and revealed when needed. In this way, heavy pieces could be shifted without the necessity of closing the front curtain. Other complex changes were often made while the "act drop" was serving as a background for the entr'acte entertainment. Irving was the first English producer who consistently used the front curtain to mask major changes of scenery, although he too continued the alternation of short and long scenes to avoid breaks in the action.

During the nineteenth century, as the requirements of spectacle increased, the layout of the stage floor grew ever more complex. Thus, after 1850 the stage was usually constructed in the following manner. The supporting joists, which ran parallel to the footlights, were arranged in groups of three or four set about 1½ to 2 inches apart. The spaces between the joists could be covered with narrow strips of wood or left open to form "cuts," through which pieces of scenery, such as ground rows, might be raised or lowered. Occasionally, a vertical moving panorama ran from overhead through a cut to aid the illusion, for example, of climbing a cliff or falling from a height. The groups of joists were spaced about four feet apart. Between them were laid floorboards, some of which could be removed for the insertion of traps or all to form "bridges" the width of the proscenium through

FIGURE 15.23 Henry Irving's production of *King Lear*, Act I, scene 1, at the Lyceum Theatre, 1892. Design by Hawes Craven. From the souvenir program. Courtesy Hoblitzelle Theatre Arts Collection, University of Texas, Austin.

which large set pieces could be raised or special effects manipulated.

Many traps were required by nineteenth-century plays. The "vampire" trap, named for Planché's *The Vampire* (1820), consisted of two spring-leaves that parted under pressure and immediately reclosed. It could be set into the floor to permit an actor seemingly to sink into the earth or set into a flat to permit the illusion of walking through a solid wall. The "Corsican" trap (so-called because of its use in *The Corsican Brothers*) or "ghost glide" was more complex. For it, a "bridge" was removed the full width of the stage. The flooring removed to create the bridge was replaced by a covering like that of a roll-top desk. Beneath the bridge an inclined track was installed. As a wheeled platform moved up this track, the actor standing on it was forced up through a "bristle" trap (an opening covered with bristles colored to match the floor). The roll-top covering over the bridge was geared to move with the platform so that no opening in the floor was ever seen by the audience. Thus, figures appeared to rise from or sink into the earth while gliding through space.

As the desire for complete illusion grew, so did the use of three-dimensional scenic elements. Charles Kean had still depended primarily upon two-dimensional painted pieces, and it was not until the 1870s that steps, platforms, and similar three-dimensional units were common. Edward Godwin (1883–1886), father of and he rehearsed them as throughly as he did his actors. Irving's innovation was soon to outmode the raked floor, on which it was difficult to handle scenery not mounted parallel to the footlights.

Irving also paid careful attention to costumes, but his chief improvement over his predecessors lay in the care given to minor characters. Even Kean had dressed the supernumeraries in armor made of zinc and tinsel and had substituted glazed cotton for satin. Irving allegedly applied the same standard to all costumes and consequently achieved a more unified effect.

FIGURE 15.24 Section drawing showing the operation of a star trap. Note how the flexible parts of the trap covering fit around the actor's body as he passes through; these parts conceal the opening when it is not in use. From Georges Moynet, *La Machinerie Théâtrale* (1893).

FIGURE 15.25 An English stage of the late nineteenth century. Note how the stage floor is divided; note also the sinking trap, the overhead grooves, and the strong beam of light (either a limelight or a carbon arc). Footlights are visible in the extreme lower right corner, as is a row of vertical lights just back of the proscenium arch. From *The Magazine of Art* (1889).

Gordon Craig, seems to have contributed to the trend when he served as artistic advisor for the Bancrofts' *The Merchant of Venice* in 1875. Godwin later built a Greek stage inside a circus, anticipating Max Reinhardt's experiments by many years. It was probably Irving's desire to make more effective use of three-dimensional pieces that motivated his removal of the grooves, which were suited only to flat wings. Since he then had to depend primarily upon manual shifting, Irving employed about 135 persons to "arrange and conduct the scenes,"

Irving was probably the first English producer to make an art of stage lighting, for while the many technical advances (such as the introduction of gas, the gas table, limelight, and the carbon arc) had created new potential for stage lighting, few directors had explored its artistic applications.

Irving's improvements were gained through care for details. He broke up the footlights and borders into short sections, each of which was equipped with different colors and controls. He experimented with transparent lacquered glass to achieve varied hues and with several means of distributing light more effectively. Critics almost always commented on his lighting, although many termed it arbitrary and distracting because each moment had obviously been contrived for beauty and effectiveness. Irving also introduced black masking pieces at the front of the stage to prevent "light spill" and was the first English producer consistently to darken the auditorium during performances. It required thirty "gas men" to mount and operate the lights at the Lyceum.

Until the end of his career, Irving used gas, even though by that time he was in the minority. In 1879 Edison's invention of the incandescent lamp had made it possible to light the entire stage electrically and almost immediately the changeover began, in part because several disastrous theatre fires made managers anxious to adopt the first illuminant yet developed that did not require an open flame. In 1881 the Savoy Theatre became the first in London to be lighted throughout with electricity, and by 1900 almost all English theatres had followed its example. Because early incandescent lamps could be made only in very low wattages, the carbon arc and limelight at first continued to be important supplements. Beginning in 1905, significant improvements in the filaments of lamps made higher wattages possible and, as the potential intensity of lamps increased thereafter, the carbon arc and limelight were used less frequently, though they remained important until after World War I.

Irving's care with each element of production was crowned by even greater care for coordinating them into an integrated whole. It was for this reason that Irving's work was superior to that of his English contemporaries. His practices as a director pointed the way toward the future, even if his emphasis on pictorial realism was merely the culmination of the nineteenth-century tradition.

Irving's greatest success came between 1878 and 1888. The relative failure of *Macbeth* in the latter year marked the beginning of his decline, though his most

FIGURE 15.26 The final scene of Irving's production of *Romeo and Juliet* in 1881. The tomb setting is by William Telbin. Note the extensive use of three-dimensional scenery and the effective use of lighting. This was Irving's first production after abandoning wings and grooves in his theatre. From *The Illustrated London News* (1882).

lavish production, *Henry VIII,* did not come until 1892. In 1896 his health began to fail, and in 1898 he gave up management but continued to perform until 1902.

In 1895 Irving became the first performer in English history to be knighted, an indication that actors had at last achieved social acceptance and that Irving was considered preeminent in his profession. In 1897 Squire Bancroft was knighted, and by 1914 such performers as John Hare, Johnston Forbes-Robertson, and Herbert Beerbohm Tree had been similarly honored. Comparable awards were not given to women until 1925, when Ellen Terry was named Dame Commander of the British Empire.

THE THEATRE IN ITALY AND SPAIN, 1850–1900

After the unification of Italy in 1861, political sentiments no longer provided dramatists with themes capable of

FIGURE 15.27 Despite Irving's advances, he still clung to many past conventions. For example, in his production of *Macbeth* in 1888 (seen here) he used the chorus of witches that had been interpolated into the play in the late seventeenth century. From the souvenir program. Courtesy Hoblitzelle Theatre Arts Collection, University of Texas, Austin.

transcending regional interests. Because each area clung to its own customs and dialect, most playwrights wrote with a particular region in mind. Since 1861 Italian writers have only rarely captured the national consciousness, and even fewer have achieved international fame.

During the late nineteenth century, Italy made its greatest impact internationally through touring stars, especially Ristori, Salvini, and Rossi.

Adelaide Ristori (1822–1906) was on the stage from the age of twelve and at fourteen was already playing leading roles in the company of Giuseppe Moncalvo (1781–1859). In 1838 she joined the Royal Theatre at Turin, where she received formal training in classical poetic drama. By 1850 she was famous throughout Italy for her studious and regal performances and in 1853 took her company to Paris. From that time until 1885, when she retired, she toured throughout Europe; she also made four visits to America and in 1874 went around the world. Although she made no striking innovations, she raised the received tradition to new heights.

Tommaso Salvini (1829–1915) began his career at the age of fourteen in the troupe of Gustavo Modena (1803–1861) at Padua. By 1848 he was in Ristori's

company in Rome, where he won his first fame as Alfieri's Orestes. Around 1860 he began a series of international tours. Salvini excelled as Macbeth, Lear, Alfieri's heroes and, above all, as Othello. An actor of great passion and energy, he is said to have terrified his leading ladies because of his complete absorption in his roles. Throughout the world, Salvini's name became synonymous with fiery tragic acting. He retired in 1890.

Ernesto Rossi (1829–1896) entered the theatre in 1846, replacing Salvini in Modena's company. He later performed with Ristori, and in 1857 took his own troupe to Vienna. After that time, he toured all over the world in plays by Alfieri and Shakespeare. A polished performer, he was considered by many too studied, an opinion which probably explains his failure to rival the fame of Ristori and Salvini.

Italy's contribution to theatre and drama in the late nineteenth century, then, was minor. For the most part, it merely followed traditions already established elsewhere.

In Spain, the period from 1840 to 1875 saw the transition from romanticism to a tentative realism in drama. Among the important writers of this period were Ventura de la Vega (1807–1865), whose *Man of the World* (1845) followed Moratín's style; Manuel Tamayo y Baus (1829–1898), whose *Love's Madness* (1855) develops the story of Queen Juana's jealousy and whose *The Positive One* (1862) treats domestic and social problems; Adelardo López de Ayala (1828–1870), whose *A Copy for a Hundred* (1861) and *Consuelo* (1878) are reminiscent of Augier's plays. By 1875, the foundations had been laid for

FIGURE 15.28 Interior of a Spanish theatre about 1845. From a contemporary print.

the more complete realism which would be developed by "modern" Spanish playwrights.

In the Spanish theatre, conditions were by 1849 so chaotic that a state council was created to establish guidelines for its regulation. This council was to accomplish the first significant reforms since the seventeenth century. At this time, the Teatro del Príncipe was renamed the Teatro Espagñol and made the Spanish national theatre, a position which it still holds. Its building was remodeled, gas lighting was installed, and its production methods modernized. (The Teatro de la Cruz was abandoned in 1856.) The use of theatres to support charities was now discontinued so that the revenue might be used to raise the level of performance. All theatres were classified into three ranks, and each was restricted to particular dramatic genres.

Although the latter provision was never fully enforced, it encouraged the growth of minor dramatic types. In 1870, only eight of Madrid's thirty-two theatres were devoted to regular drama. Furthermore, the major theatres found it difficult to compete with the minor houses, which soon established the custom of offering an evening's bill composed of four distinct entertainments. This flexibility in the length of programs and the hours of attendance greatly increased the popularity of the minor houses. This custom has continued to plague theatres wishing to present full-length plays and has seriously affected playwriting.

During the nineteenth century, then, the theatre of Spain burgeoned, growing from a few companies in 1800 to more than fifty by 1875. From an antiquated institution, it had been brought more nearly into line with current practices in other European countries. Nevertheless, it retained much of its insularity, participating in major international movements only at a distance.

RUSSIAN THEATRE AND DRAMA, 1850–1900

During the late nineteenth century Russia wavered between reform and harshness. Alexander II (ruled 1855–1881) initiated a series of changes, including loosening censorship, freeing the serfs (in 1861), and extending the educational system. But after an attempt on his life in 1866, he lost his zeal for reform, and his assassination in 1881 led Alexander III (ruled 1881–1894) to reinstitute strict censorship and to strengthen the power of the

FIGURE 15.29 Setting by A. Roller for a ballet. From Syrkina, *Russkoe Teatralne Dekoratsione Iskusstvo.*

aristocracy. Thus, Russia remained somewhat isolated from the rest of Europe.

It is surprising, therefore, to find that realism appeared in Russian drama even earlier than in French, and that it was more uncompromising. It was first fully realized by Ivan Turgenev (1818–1883), considered Russia's major author after 1852, when his collection of short stories, *A Sportsman's Sketches*, appeared. After 1863, Turgenev lived abroad, where he became the best known of all Russian authors. Most of his plays were written between 1843 and 1852, but their influence on other dramas came much later since his finest work, *A Month in the Country* (1850), was not produced until 1872. Turgenev's major concern in this play is the inner life of the characters. He renders the daily routine of a country estate faithfully, but he does so only as a means of showing the permanent psychological changes wrought in several characters by the presence of a young tutor. Turgenev's contribution to realism comes from his use of domestic detail to reveal inner turmoil. Upon his work, Chekhov was to build.

Before Turgenev's plays appeared on the stage, realism had already been popularized through the work of Alexander Ostrovsky (1823–1886), Russia's first professional playwright and the first Russian writer to confine himself exclusively to drama. Ostrovsky wrote his first play in 1847, and from 1853 until his death completed at least one new drama each year. Working primarily from observation, Ostrovsky is often credited with creating a peculiarly Russian drama free from Western influence. Although he wrote in a variety of forms and used a wide range of subjects, his major works draw on the life he knew best, that of the middle class. He sought to eliminate Gogol's penchant for caricature and to avoid stage tricks and irrelevant spectacle by concentrating upon characters and their relationships to each other and to a particular milieu. Ostrovsky is perhaps best known for *Enough Stupidity in Every Wise Man* (sometimes called *The Diary of a Scoundrel)* and *The Thunderstorm.* The former is the comic chronicle of a man's rise through his manipulation of other people's vanities, while *The Thunderstorm,* which shows the tragic outcome of parental tyranny, is noteworthy for its use of the storm as a symbol of turmoil in human affairs. In his use of symbolism, Ostrovsky anticipates Chekhov.

Ostrovsky was instrumental in founding the Russian Society of Dramatic Authors and Composers in 1866. Until this time, the dramatist usually received no pay for his work beyond a set fee from the state troupes; provincial companies did not pay at all. After 1866, playwrights gradually won full copyright protection.

Of Ostrovsky's contemporaries, the most important were Pisemsky, Sukhovo-Kobylin, and Saltikov-Shchedrin. A. F. Pisemsky (1820–1881) wrote many kinds of plays but is now remembered primarily for one of the most naturalistic works of the nineteenth century, *A Bitter Fate* (1859), which antedates by many years the Naturalist movement in France. The story is simple: a peasant learns that his wife has been seduced by a wealthy landowner; he kills the child born to her and turns himself over to the authorities. A masterfully written work, it more nearly realizes the aims of the French naturalists than does any of their own dramas. Alexander Sukhovo-Kobylin (1817–1903) is noted primarily for a trilogy of plays treating the Russian legal and bureaucratic systems, with which he was personally entangled. *Krechinsky's Wedding* (1854) is relatively lighthearted, but *The Case* (1861) and *Tarelkin's Death* (not produced until 1917) seem intended to arouse shudders rather than laughter. The work of Mikhail Saltikov-Shchedrin (1826–1889) is related to that of Sukhovo-Kobylin, for he too gives a satirical picture of corruption in his *The Death of Pazukhin* (1857, banned until 1900).

Near the end of the nineteenth century, Leo Tolstoy (1828–1910), already famous as a novelist, turned to playwriting. Of his dramas, the most important is *The*

FIGURE 15.30 Setting by M. A. Shishkov for Griboyedov's *Woe from Wit.* **From Syrkina,** *Russkoe Teatralne Dekoratsione Iskusstvo.*

Power of Darkness (1886, first performed in Russia in 1895), a story of greed and murder among Russian peasants. Like *A Bitter Fate,* it is one of the most effective of naturalistic plays. *The Fruits of Enlightenment* (1889, produced 1892) satirizes the preoccupation of the nobility with trifles and superstitions, while *The Living Corpse* (1900), or *Redemption* is a problem play about the conflict between marriage laws and the Christian demand for self-sacrifice.

Although the major Russian plays of the late nineteenth century fall into the realistic school, they were by no means the standard fare of the public theatres, which continued to favor melodrama, farce, musical drama, and romantic spectacles. Of the writers outside the realistic trend, probably the most important was Alexey K. Tolstoy (1817–1875), whose plays idealized the Russian past and emphasized the clash of strong personalities against picturesque historical backgrounds. His trilogy, *The Death of Ivan the Terrible, Tsar Fyodor Ivanovich,* and *Tsar Boris* (written between 1865 and 1870) are among the finest of their genre.

Thus, during the late nineteenth century Russia produced a number of outstanding playwrights, many of them still little known in the West. It is difficult to avoid speculating about the heights which might have been reached had censorship been less strenuous and theatrical conditions more favorable.

Perhaps because it did not arouse official displeasure, Russian ballet reached a peak of perfection during the last half of the century under the influence of Marius Petipa (1822-1910). Born in France, Petipa came to Russia in 1847 and was appointed ballet master of the Imperial Schools in 1862. After 1870 he was the virtual dictator of ballet in Russia. He choreographed seventy-four long works and thirty "entertainments," in which considerable emphasis was placed on sets and costumes as well as upon storytelling dance. By the time he retired in 1903, Russian ballet had assumed the characteristics for which it is still noted.

Russian theatrical conditions changed little until after 1882, when monopolies were abolished. In actuality, the monopolies had been violated for many years by performances disguised as private entertainments. The Nobility Assembly, the Painters Club, the Merchants Club, and others had regularly scheduled "dramatic evenings," and "family reunions" often featured theatrical entertainment. By 1875 about twenty-five such groups were performing regularly in Moscow and St. Petersburg.

After the monopolies were rescinded, the public theatre expanded rapidly, although the state troupes continued to command the greatest prestige. The quality of the provincial theatres also improved. Prior to the 1880s, even the best companies had to tour and, even then, felt it necessary to import stars to increase their appeal. As soon as a provincial actor established a reputation, he was hired by the Imperial troupes. Costumes and scenery were meager, and amateurs were often employed as stagehands. By the 1870s permanent buildings had been built in eight provincial cities, but not until about 1890 were companies able to settle down permanently. The first provincial troupe to establish a repuation for excellence was that of N. N. Solovtsov (1857-1902), which performed in Kiev and Odessa between 1892 and 1902. Aside from a few large towns, however, Russia continued to be served by touring groups. In 1897 the provincial theatres held the first All-Russian Convention of Theatrical Workers to discuss common problems.

The trend toward accuracy in settings and costumes, which in Western Europe had preceded the development of realism in character and situation, was slow to develop in Russia. In 1853, one of Ostrovsky's plays is said to have startled audiences with its simple and accurate spectacle when the heroine appeared in a cotton dress and with natural hair rather than the usual fashionable garments and coiffure. Thereafter, realism of detail grew steadily, especially at the Maly, upon which Os-

trovsky exerted considerably influence. In 1885, the final year of his life, Ostrovsky was made head of the theatre, the first time that a professional had been appointed to such a post, but he died before he could implement the reforms he envisioned.

It was not until the 1880s that theatres began to be much concerned about accurate settings. Until then, most theatres used conventionalized settings, devoid of national or period flavor. Such decor had been popularized by Andreas Roller (1805-1891), a German designer who dominated Russian scenic practices, since he, his pupils or disciples held the major posts in the state theatres. Nevertheless, archeologically correct settings began to appear sporadically after the 1860s. In 1865, the Alexandrinsky Theatre employed an archeologist to assist with historically accurate settings and costumes for Tolstoy's *The Death of Ivan the Terrible,* and after 1870 such major Russian painters as Bocharov and Shishkov began to turn attention to accuracy of detail. In 1880, Shishkov organized a special class in theatrical design at the Art Academy, and by the 1890s a number of prominent painters were working for the private theatres. Nevertheless, Ostrovsky's response to the Meiningen Players when they played in Moscow in 1885 tells much about Russian attitudes of the time: he labeled them a talented group of amateurs who placed far too much emphasis upon spectacle except in the admirable crowd scenes. On the other hand, Stanislavsky was deeply impressed by the Meiningen troupe's attention to pictorial values, which contrasted so sharply with the typical Russian approach. Stainslavsky states that in Russia around 1890 three sets of period costumes were considered sufficient for all plays, and that, since these were used repeatedly, they were usually old and dirty. He adds that actresses still insisted upon wearing stylish and inappropriate clothing and that the secondary characters could always be identified by their drabness.

In acting, the troupe at Moscow's Maly continued to be superior to those in St. Petersburg. Shchepkin's major successor was Prov Sadovsky (1818-1872), who was so effective in Ostrovsky's plays that the Maly came to be called "the House of Ostrovsky." Discovered in the provinces by Shchepkin, in 1839 Sadovsky came to the Maly, where he played minor roles until Ostrovsky's plays offered him parts suited to his style of performance. While Shchepkin had excelled at external detail, Sadovsky's ability to project both internal and external realism created more fully rounded characterizations than any previously seen.

Other important actors of the Maly included Shumsky, Fedotova, Yermelova, Lensky, and Yuzhin. Sergei Shumsky (1821–1878) was a follower of Shchepkin and continued his tradition of careful attention to detail and technical excellence. Glikeria Fedotova (1846–1925), on the stage from the age of sixteen, was at her best in Ostrovsky's character roles. Maria Yermelova (1853–1928), after beginning her career in ballet, changed to drama in 1870 and achieved her first important success in 1876 in Lope de Vega's *The Sheep Well*. She continued on the stage into the Soviet period and was the first actress to be named a "People's Artist." Alexander Lensky (1847–1908) went on the stage in 1865 and in 1876 settled in Moscow, where he became a noted stage lover and excellent teacher. After 1898 he served as a director and teacher at the Novy Theater. Alexander Yuzhin (1857–1927) was an outstanding interpreter of heroic roles and a staunch defender of realistic detail. In 1909 he became director of the Maly.

The St. Petersburg troupes were more inclined than was the Maly to cultivate popular taste and to ignore ensemble effects. Perhaps for this reason, they produced fewer outstanding actors than did the Maly. Among the most important performers were Martynov, Davidov, and Savina. Alexander Martynov (1816–1860), a pupil of Karatygin, was noted principally for comic acting, in which he developed a realism similar to that practiced by Shchepkin. Vladimir Davidov (1849–1925) played in the provinces from 1867 until 1880, when he came to St. Petersburg. He remained on the stage until 1922. Noted primarily for comic playing, he combined realistic detail with broad theatricality. Maria Savina (1854–1915), on the stage as a child, played at the Alexandrinsky Theatre after 1874. She was noted for her truthful playing and avoidance of clichés. At her best as society women, she appeared in works by Gogol, Turgenev, Ostrovsky, and Tolstoy.

Until the 1860s, actors were trained either in service or at the state dramatic schools, which combined the course of study for actors, dancers and singers. After the private Russian Musical Society opened a conservatory in St. Petersburg in 1862 and another in Moscow in 1866, the state schools reevaluated their approach. Training for opera and ballet were separated from acting, and graduates were no longer automatically eligible for employment in the imperial theatres. In 1882, lines of business were abandoned as the basis of employment in the state troupes. Although type casting continued, greater flexibility became possible.

But true ensemble effects of the type exemplified by Saxe-Meiningen's company in Germany were not to be achieved in Russia until after 1898, when the Moscow Art Theatre was founded. Prior to this time, however, a few Russian companies had pointed the way. Especially important was the troupe founded in 1882 by O. A. Korsh (1852–1921) in Moscow. Korsh maintained a high standard of production, introduced many significant plays from Western Europe, established matinee performances in Russia, and trained a number of actors later to be famous. The company continued until 1932, many years after Korsh's death. In Korsh's theatre, the early productions achieved a consistent style and all roles were cast and prepared with care. By the 1890s, however, this meticulousness had begun to fade. Nevertheless, by 1898 the conditions and possibilities of a new theatre had been established. It remained for Stainslavsky and Nemirovich-Danchenko to consolidate the gains and to inaugurate a new era in the Russian theatre.

GERMAN AND AUSTRIAN THEATRE, 1850–1900

Germany produced few dramatists of note in the second half of the nineteenth century. The major playwrights of the 1850s were Otto Ludwig (1813–1865) and Gustav Freytag (1816–1895). Ludwig sought a middle ground between idealism and naturalism. He opposed the political and social stance of Young Germany and sought to substitute a realism lacking in tendentiousness. His best plays are *The Hereditary Forester* (1850), a middle-class tragedy which reflects *Othello* in its treatment of a misunderstanding between friends, and *The Maccabees* (1854), which treats the revolt of Judas Maccabeus against Antioch. Freytag is remembered primarily for *The Journalists* (1853), a good-humored view of politics in a small town. In addition, his *The Technique of Drama* (1863) was long considered to be a major treatise on dramatic structure.

Following the death of Hebbel in 1863, German-language drama entered a state of decline from which it did not recover until the 1890s. Perhaps the general level of serious drama in this period is indicated by the works of Ernst von Wildenbruch (1845–1909), an ardent admirer of the Hohenzollern rulers and of the Teutonic heritage. His plays gained wide popularity following the unification of Germany in 1871. Wildenbruch had a

FIGURE 15.31 Interior of the Burgtheater in the late nineteenth century. From *Die Theater Wiens* (1893).

considerable gift for writing crowd scenes and for depicting picturesque working-class life, but much of his drama, such as his trilogy *Heinrich and Heinrich's Family* (1896), now seems poor indeed.

In Austria, the peasant play was kept alive by Ludwig Anzengruber (1839–1889), who gave it a more serious turn by using it to present a faithful picture of rural life. *The Priest of Kirchfield* (1870) reflects the controversy over the recently promulgated doctrine of papal infallibility, while his *The Double Suicide* (1875) is reminiscent of *Romeo and Juliet*. But Anzengruber was not always serious; his *The Cross Signers* (1872), for example, is a variation on *Lysistrata*. Because of his realism, Anzengruber was little appreciated until the end of his life, when the rise of naturalism called attention to his depiction of characters rooted in particular environments. His fame aroused new interest in peasant drama, as a result of which a theatre was founded in Bavaria in 1891 especially to produce and tour folk plays.

During the late nineteenth century variety theatres, cabarets, summer theatres, and pleasure gardens flourished. Operetta also became increasingly popular,

especially in Vienna. The vogue began around 1858 with the importation of Offenbach's works. The first important native composer was Franz von Suppé (1820–1895) with such pieces as *Fatinitza* (1872) and *The Devil on Earth* (1878), but he was soon surpassed by Johann Strauss (1825–1899) with *Die Fledermaus* (1874), *A Night in Venice* (1883), *The Gypsy Baron* (1885), and many others. Operetta was long to be one of Vienna's major attractions.

The lack of significant new dramatists was not keenly felt, since the plays of Shakespeare, Lessing, Goethe, and Schiller were prominent in the repertory and those of Kleist began to assume the status of classics. Following Grillparzer's death in 1872, directors vied in giving his works lavish productions.

After 1850, foreign plays, especially those of Scribe, Sardou, Augier, and Dumas *fils,* also made up an increasingly large part of the German and Austrian repertory and helped to compensate for the lack of good native plays. The period of stagnation was ultimately broken around 1890 with the emergence of the "modern" school.

In contrast to changes then underway elsewhere, in Germany resident companies did not decline markedly in number or prestige during the last half of the nineteenth century, perhaps because the major troupes were supported by state or municipal governments. Such theatres were little affected by the unification of Germany in 1871, since individual states retained their identities and many of their functions. Nevertheless, after 1871 Berlin increasingly became the political and cultural center of Germany, although not until the 1880s, when the Deutsches Theater, Berliner Theater and Lessing Theater were opened, did true distinction return to the theatre there.

During the late nineteenth century the major German-language theatre was Vienna's Burgtheater, in large part because of Laube and Dingelstedt. Heinrich Laube (1806–1884) was a well-known playwright of the Young Germany school before he was appointed director of Vienna's Burgtheater, a post he held from 1849 until 1867. Laube placed primary emphasis on the text and especially on diction and characterization. Under his direction, the Burgtheater regained the preeminence it had enjoyed under Schreyvogel. Its ensemble was the finest of any German-language company, including among its members Bogumil Dawison, Adolf Sonnenthal (1834–1909), especially admired for his work in drawing-room drama, and Charlotte Wolter (1833–1897), one of

FIGURE 15.32 The final scene of the second play in Hebbel's trilogy, *The Niebelungen,* as produced at Weimar by Franz Dingelstedt in 1861. From *Leipziger Illustrirte Zeitung* (1861).

the great international stars of the age. Laube was opposed to elaborate historical settings because he thought them distracting and "operatic." On the other hand, he was the first German producer consistently to use the box set, which he adopted because it increased the sense of immediacy and intimacy. Nevertheless, he never permitted more furniture on stage than was demanded by the action. His was a rather austere realism aimed at riveting attention on the actor rather than on the spectacle. In the history of German directing, Laube holds a position comparable to Montigny's in France.

Laube was followed at the Burgtheater between 1870 and 1881 by Franz Dingelstedt (1814–1881), who, unlike his predecessor, emphasized lavish and historically accurate decor. Dingelstedt had become well known throughout Germany because of his work in Munich between 1851 and 1857 and in Weimar between 1857 and 1867. In Munich in 1851, he staged Sophocles' *Antigone* with the assistance of some of the most respected scholars, artists, and musicians of his day. The high point of his work in Munich probably came in 1854 with a festival (held in conjunction with the Munich Industrial Exposition) during which outstanding German actors presented plays by Goethe, Schiller, Lessing, and others. This venture aroused such enthusiasm that thereafter festivals began to appear throughout Europe. At Weimar Dingelstedt restored the reputation of the company which had been in continuous decline since Goethe's time. He was especially noted for his staging there of Schiller's *Wallenstein* trilogy in 1859, Hebbel's *Niebelungen* trilogy in 1862, and almost all of Shakespeare's plays during a single week in 1864 (which motivated the for-

mation of the German Shakespeare Society). In 1870 he became director of the Burgtheater, where with his costumer Franz Gaul (1837–1906) and scene designer Herman Burghart (1834–1901) he presented some of the most lavish productions of the age. Perhaps his major achievement came in 1875 with the presentation of Shakespeare's history plays as a connected cycle.

Another major director of the period was Friedrich Haase (1827–1911), especially at Coburg-Gotha's theatre from 1866 to 1868 and at the Leipzig Municipal Theatre from 1870 to 1876. Through his work at these theatres and elsewhere he came to be especially noted for his staging of such Shakespearean plays as *Hamlet* and *The Merchant of Venice* in the manner of Charles Kean, whose influence he freely acknowledged. As a major star, Haase extended his own influence through engagements with other companies.

By 1875 historical accuracy was accepted as an ideal by almost all German troupes. Nevertheless, the same settings were still reused for different plays of the same historical period, and inconsistencies abounded. Perhaps the greatest needs were for ensemble playing and for a controlling artistic consciousness. It was to these problems, above all, that the two major innovators of the

FIGURE 15.33 Friedrich Haase as Hamlet in his own production at Leipzig. Shown here is the play-within-the-play scene. Woodcut by Knut Ekwall, 1871. Courtesy Theatermuseum, Munich.

period—Wagner and Saxe-Meiningen—addressed themselves so effectively that they laid the foundations for the modern movement.

WAGNER AND SAXE-MEININGEN

Richard Wagner (1813–1883) was brought up in a theatrical family (his stepfather and four of his brothers and sisters were employed in the theatre). His first opera, *Die Feen,* was written in 1831, but he did not achieve critical success until 1842 with *Rienzi,* which also brought him an appointment as conductor at the Dresden opera house. Banished for his part in the revolution of 1848, he spent twelve years in exile, during which he formulated those theories which were to influence the course of the modern theatre.

Wagner rejected the contemporary trend toward realism, arguing that the dramatist should be a mythmaker rather than a recorder of domestic affairs. To him, true drama was concerned with the ideal world, which is left behind as soon as spoken dialogue is admitted. He suggested that drama should be "dipped in the magic fountain of music" to combine the greatness of Shakespeare with that of Beethoven. He also argued that music, through melody and tempo, permits greater control over performance than is possible in spoken drama, in which interpretaion is subject to the performers' personal whims. Thus, for Wagner the effectiveness of music-drama depended upon performance as well as upon composition, and he argued that the author-composer should supervise every aspect of production in order to synthesize all the parts into a *Gesamtkunstwerk,* or "master art work." From these ideas were to stem much of modern theory about the need for a strong director and unified production.

In addition to his theories, Wagner's practice also exerted considerable influence, especially on theatre architecture. To house his idealized music-drama, Wagner created a new kind of theatre. The structure which he eventually built is said to have been suggested as early as 1841 by Schinkel. The first concrete plans were made in 1864 by Gottfried Semper, who had worked with Tieck on his reconstruction of the Fortune theatre, and were later reworked by several persons, including the architects Wilhelm Neumann and Otto Brückwald and the machinist Karl Brandt. Originally planned for Munich, the opera house was built in Bayreuth.

Begun in 1872 and opened in 1876, the new

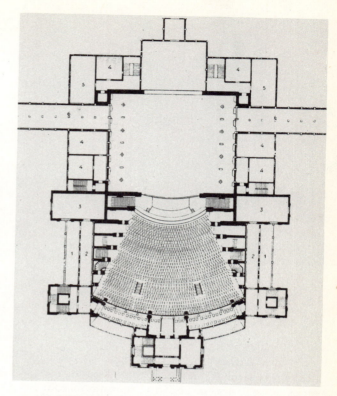

FIGURE 15.34 Plan of Wagner's theatre at Bayreuth. From Sachs, *Modern Opera Houses and Theatres* **(1896–1898).**

opera house was soon famous throughout the world and was to inspire many reforms in architectural design. Since Wagner wished to create a "classless" theatre, he abandoned the box, pit, and gallery arrangement. The main part of the auditorium had thirty stepped rows of seats; there were no side boxes or center aisle, and each row led directly to a side exit. At the rear of the auditorium was a single large box surmounted by a small gallery. The total seating capacity was 1,745. To insure good sightlines, the auditorium was shaped like a fan, measuring about 50 feet across at the proscenium and 115 feet at the rear of the auditorium. Since all seats were said to be equally good, a uniform price was charged. The orchestra pit was hidden from view, much of it extending underneath the apron of the stage. This feature helped to create a "mystic chasm" between the real world of the auditorium and the "ideal" world of the stage, an effect reenforced by darkening the auditorium during performances and by framing the stage with a double proscenium arch.

FIGURE 15.35 The auditorium and stage of the Bayreuth Festival Theatre. On stage can be seen a setting for *Parsifal* designed by Max Brückner. From *Le Théâtre* (1899).

The arrangement of the auditorium was the theatre's greatest innovation, since the stage was essentially conservative in design. The stage floor was raked upward toward the back, and the chariot-and-pole system of scene shifting was retained. The principal innovation was a system of steam vents to create realistic effects of fog and mist and a "steam curtain" to mask scene changes. The proscenium opening, about 40 feet wide, gave onto a stage 80 feet deep by 93 feet wide. About 100 feet of overhead space and 32 feet of below-stage space were provided. The building also included ample workshops, storage, dressing rooms, and rehearsal space.

Although Wagner's theories later inspired several nonillusionistic approaches, his own productions aimed at complete illusion. He forbade the musicians to tune their instruments in the orchestra pit and allowed no applause during performances or curtain calls at the end. He sought precise historical accuracy in scenery and costumes and employed such devices as moving panoramas. His taste for minute detail may be seen in *Siegfried*, for example, in which he used a dragon with realistic scales and movable eyes and mouth. To Wagner, the ideal was to be reached through total illusion. Thus, Wagner's theatrical practice was grounded solidly in the nineteenth-century tradition. Nevertheless, his conceptions of the master artwork, the director, the unified production, and theatre architecture were to inspire many pioneers of the "modern" theatre.

While Wagner's opera house was being constructed, another potent force, the Meiningen Players, came to the fore. Although plays had been performed in the Duchy of Meiningen since the late eighteenth century, a permanent court theatre was not opened until 1831, and the productions there remained commonplace until Georg II (1826–1914) succeeded to the throne in 1866. Georg II, Duke of Saxe-Meiningen, had received extensive art training, had been at the Prussian court in Berlin at the time when Tieck worked there, and had seen Charles Kean's Shakespearean productions in London, Friedrick Haase's in Coburg-Gotha, and the superior ensemble of the Burgtheater. Thus, his intense interest in the theatre was well developed before a Prussian invasion of Meiningen forced his father to abdicate in his favor.

Upon succeeding to the throne in 1866, Georg II immediately began to change the repertory of the court theatre and to take a personal interest in its affairs. In managing the troupe, the duke at first depended heavily on Friedrich von Bodenstedt (1819–1892), and after 1871 on Ludwig Chronegk (1837–1891). Trained as a singing comedian, Chronegk had been employed at Meiningen in 1866 as a comic actor. His appointment as director came as a surprise to the company, for there seemed little in his background to justify it. Nevertheless, the fame of the troupe probably owes as much to Chronegk as to Saxe-Meiningen, since not only was he an indefatigable worker, he conceived and arranged the tours which made the company famous. A third major influence was Ellen Franz (1839–1923), an actress who in 1873 became the duke's third wife. After this time she assumed responsibility for proposing the repertory, adapting the texts, and supervising stage speech. Thus, it is difficult to assign credit for the company's accomplishments, although it is now typical to allot sole responsibility to the duke.

From 1866 until 1874 the company played entirely in Meiningen, and when it appeared in Berlin in 1874 it took the astonished spectators completely by surprise. After its initial success, the company began a long series of tours. Between 1874 and 1890, it played in thirty-eight cities in nine countries, including Russia, Sweden, Austria, Denmark, Belgium, Holland, and England, giving about 2,600 performances of forty-one plays. By 1890, when it gave up touring, the Meiningen

FIGURE 15.36 Anthony's oration over the body of Caesar in Saxe-Meiningen's production of *Julius Caesar* as performed at Drury Lane, London, 1881. From *The Illustrated London News* (1881). Courtesy Theatre Museum, Victoria and Albert Museum, London.

for a few performances, the other contemporary plays in the repertory were mostly poetic, romantic works.

The Meiningen Players also resembled other groups of the time in emphasizing pictorial illusion, in which it excelled all previous standards because of its greater accuracy. The duke divided each century into thirds and further distinguished among national differences within each time period. As a result, his productions attained unprecedented authenticity. Accuracy was further insured by the duke's refusal to permit actors to tamper with their costumes. In most theatres of the time, the stars either supplied their own garments or altered as they saw fit those provided by the theatre. Actresses often wore crinoline petticoats under dresses of all periods. Furthermore, the duke insisted upon authentic materials in place of the usual cheap substitutes. He used heavy upholstery fabrics, many imported from France and Italy and some made to his specifications; he introduced genuine chain mail, armor, swords, axes, halberds, and other instruments. In Roman plays, the actors wore togas of enormous length. Authentic period furniture was always used. The success of the Meiningen Players led to the establishment of theatrical supply houses which manufactured furniture, properties, costume materials, and armor to meet the new demand from other troupes.

Saxe-Meiningen designed all of the costumes, scenery, and properties used by his troupe. The settings were usually painted by the Brückner brothers of Coburg, who also designed Wagner's and Haase's settings. Strong colors were used in scenery for the first time, reversing the former practice of having actors play against pastel scenery. This innovation probably accounts for the adverse comments by critics on the "garishness" of the Meiningen settings. The duke was opposed to sky borders and used foliage, beams, banners, or other devices as overhead masking. He avoided symmetrical balance, for he thought this unnatural, and was careful to keep each detail in correct proportion and to blend painted and three-dimensional elements convincingly. He was also one of the first artists consistently to treat the stage floor as part of the design, breaking it up with fallen trees, rocks, hillocks, steps, and platforms.

While its use of scenery and costumes was probably superior to that of other troupes, the company's principal sources of power were totality of effect and, especially, ensemble acting. The duke maintained as complete authority over his actors as over the scenic

commanded the greatest respect of any company in the world.

The accomplishments of the Meiningen Players were due to its methods rather than to its aims. The duke, like most producers of his day, sought to create the illusion of reality with accurate spectacle and lifelike acting. His repertory, composed primarily of works by Shakespeare, Schiller, Grillparzer, and nineteenth-century romantic playwrights, was not unlike that of other producers except in its inclusion of more plays of high merit. Although Ibsen's *Ghosts* was presented

FIGURE 15.37 Saxe-Meiningen's sketch for Act 2 of Julius Winding's *Pope Sixtus V*. Courtesy Theater-museum, Munich.

investiture. Because he could not afford major performers, his company was composed either of beginners or of older actors who had not attained outstanding success. Although guest actors sometimes performed with the troupe, they had to conform to the company's rules against stars. Perhaps to discourage any tendency toward the "star complex," Saxe-Meiningen required all actors not cast in leading roles to appear as supernumeraries. This, in turn, made possible the effective crowd scenes for which the company was noted. Saxe-Meiningen used no supernumeraries who were not permanent members of the troupe. While this limited the number of persons available for crowd scenes, the effect of large masses was achieved by settings kept sufficiently small to force many of the actors into the wings (thus suggesting that great numbers were out of sight offstage) and by diagonal and contrasting movements to create effects of confusion and agitation. In rehearsing

crowd scenes, the duke divided his actors into small groups, each under the charge of an experienced performer who aided in training those under him. Furthermore, each member of a mob was given individualizing characteristics and specific lines; then all were carefully coordinated. The results obtained in this manner, contrasting sharply with the usual mob scenes, were considered revolutionary.

Fortunately, the duke could depend upon long rehearsal periods. Since Meiningen had a population of only 8,000, the theatre was open only twice a week for six months of the year. This schedule and the duke's authority made it possible to rehearse in a way quite different from that in use elsewhere. Each work was rehearsed from the first with full settings, furniture, and properties. Costumes were not always available from the beginning, but were always used for some time prior to the premiere. Actors were required to "act" from the first day rather than merely "walking through" the part as was typical in many theatres. Rehearsals, held in the evening after the duke's state duties were completed, often lasted five or six hours and continued until the play was judged ready for performance, even if this required several months. Because he did not work against a deadline, the duke conceived many details as he went along, and rehearsals were frequently delayed while furniture was rearranged or new plans made.

The impact of the Meiningen Players came from the complete illusion attained in every aspect of the production. Thus, the company stands as the culmination of trends that had begun in the Renaissance. More important, it stands at the beginning of the new movement toward unified production, in which each element is carefully selected because of its contribution to the total effect; the actor had given way to the director as the dominant artist in the theatre. Saxe-Meiningen's example influenced such men as Antoine and Stanislavsky, who were to figure significantly in the formation of the modern theatre. By the time the Meiningen Players discontinued touring in 1890, the theatre was already entering the new era which they had helped to inaugurate.

THE AMERICAN THEATRE, 1850–1870

During the late nineteenth century America was involved in the same movements then underway in Europe. It too was extending its territories and consolidating its power, although most of its energies were expended on preserving the nation and filling up the continent over which it had won control. The most important event of the half-century was the Civil War, which brought an end to slavery and the influence of the rural South; it insured the preservation of the union, but at great human and financial sacrifice. The empty reaches of western land, however, always held out the lure of wealth and security; consequently, adventurers and settlers streamed westward in search of mining strikes and free homesteads, displacing the Indians as they went.

This westward movement and the needs of commerce and industry motivated the development of networks of railroads, which by the end of the century extended throughout the land. The first transcontinental railroad was completed in 1869 and by the 1880s there were others. This expansion of the transportation system

was paralleled by a race to gain control over the country's resources and to exploit them. During this era America was looked upon by many Europeans as a brawling giant lacking in refinement and culture, but to the common man everywhere it was the "land of opportunity" and immigrants streamed in, contributing to the labor force and slum population, but also bringing diversity and talent. As in Europe, the American government was not prepared to deal with such complex developments and consequently the rapacious made enormous fortunes at the expense of others. But the cry for reform grew—in labor conditions, women's rights, education, civil rights, and protection against exploitation by "robber barons" —although it was not to be effectively answered until the twentieth century.

During this period the theatre continued to expand. In the cities, companies often resembled their European counterparts, but elsewhere they retained their pioneering quality as actors who could not find steady employment in urban centers tried their luck in mining camps and small towns. Thus, like the country itself, the theatre was diverse.

FIGURE 15.38 Sketch by Saxe-Meiningen for the funeral oration scene in *Julius Caesar*. This drawing shows how carefully Saxe-Meiningen considered composition and groupings. Compare this with the drawing of the actual performance (Fig. 15.36). Courtesy Theatermuseum, Munich.

FIGURE 15.39 An unpopular actor being pelted with fruit and vegetables at Baldwin's Theatre, San Francisco, *c.* 1870. From the Albert Davis Collection, Hoblitzelle Theatre Arts Collection, University of Texas, Austin.

As the westward movement accelerated, especially after the discovery of gold in California in 1848, the theatre kept pace. In California, the first professional performances in English were given in 1849, when Sacramento's Eagle Theatre began to offer three programs each week to the miners. In San Francisco, the first theatre was opened in 1850 and throughout the following decade there were usually four in operation. After this time, San Francisco was to be the major theatrical center of the Far West. From 1853 to 1856, Catherine Sinclair (1817–1891), Edwin Forrest's divorced wife, ran the Metropolitan Theatre with the first outstanding company seen in that area. All these early efforts, however, were eclipsed by the California Theatre, one of the best in the entire country when it was opened in 1869 by John McCullough and Lawrence Barrett.

Despite tedious journeys overland or by sea, stars began to visit the new territory almost immediately. Among the first were Junius Brutus Booth, Frank Chanfrau, and J. W. Wallack, Jr. Most stars came from the East, but one native performer, Lotta Crabtree (1847–

1924), was to gain national fame. On the stage from the age of eight, she was a major star and had embarked on her first eastern tour by the age of seventeen. In vehicles written especially for her, she usually played several characters to demonstrate her versatility. In many of the plays she portrayed a ragged waif who regenerates drunken miners. All allowed her to display her talents for singing, dancing, and playing the banjo.

New mining strikes led to still further expansion of the western theatre. The Comstock Lode, discovered in 1859, had by the mid-1860s spawned five legitimate theatres and six variety houses in Nevada City, Nevada. Similarly, mining towns attracted actors to Idaho, Montana, and Colorado. In the late 1850s touring groups began to appear in Oregon, where a theatre was established at Willamette in 1861. Washington saw its first professional troupe in 1862, but no permanent theatre was established there until 1879.

In Utah, the Mormons began to produce plays as early as 1850, and in 1862 they erected the Salt Lake Theatre, the first major structure built in Salt Lake City. Performances were at first given by amateurs, but in 1863 professional actors began to be added and a permanent company was maintained after 1865. The theatre in all these western areas was considerably strengthened with the opening of transcontinental railroads beginning in 1869.

Between 1850 and 1870 the number of resident companies increased throughout America. The thirty-five of 1850 had grown to about fifty in 1860, and remained constant until after 1870. Countless itinerant groups played in less populous areas. The dependence upon visiting stars continued, although a number of managers sought to counteract its adverse effects. Among these the most important were Mitchell, Burton, and Wallack. At the Olympic Theatre in New York between 1839 and 1850, William Mitchell (1798–1856) maintained an outstanding theatre without using starring performers. He specialized in light entertainment, however, and it remained for William E. Burton (1804–1860) to extend Mitchell's policy to standard drama. Born in London, Burton had been a low comedian in the English theatre from 1821 to 1834, when he came to America. A popular actor and successful manager in Philadelphia until 1848, he then opened Burton's Chambers Street Theatre in New York, where between 1848 and 1856 he maintained the most respected company in America. Because the Chambers Street Theatre seated only 800, in 1856 Burton moved to the Metro-

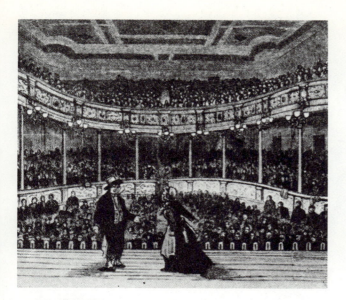

FIGURE 15.40 Auditorium of Burton's Chambers Street Theatre, New York, in the 1850s. Burton is seen on stage. Note the numerous posts used to support the balcony, since cantilevering had not yet been perfected. Courtesy Hoblitzelle Theatre Arts Collection, University of Texas, Austin.

politan Theatre, one of the largest in the world. Success did not follow him, and he soon had to import stars. He gave up management in 1858 and retired in 1859. With his excellent company and broad-ranging repertory Burton demonstrated at the Chambers Street Theatre that success did not require stars. He also gained much prestige with his productions of Shakespeare's plays in historically accurate settings and costumes.

Before Burton retired, his preeminence had already been seriously challenged by James W. Wallack, who in 1853 had taken over the Lyceum Theatre and renamed it Wallack's Lyceum. From 1855 until the 1880s, Wallack's was the leading theatre of America. He was succeeded as manager by his son, Lester Wallack (1820–1888), a fine romantic leading actor, who continued his father's policies until 1887. Also prominent in the troupe was James W. Wallack, Jr. (1818–1873), a performer of tragic roles. Maintaining a high standard of production, Wallack's presented a repertory made up primarily of standard works.

Another outstanding company was assembled by Laura Keene (c. 1820–1873), an English actress who had worked for Mme. Vestris. Following her American debut in 1852, she played for Wallack before going on tour.

Between 1855 and 1863, she ran her own theatre in New York, serving as manager and leading actress in a series of lavishly mounted productions in the style of Mme. Vestris. After 1863 she toured and was playing at Ford's Theatre in Washington on the night of President Lincoln's assassination.

Not all of the major troupes were located in New York. The Boston Museum, one of the finest in the country, owed much of its prestige to William Warren, Jr. (1812–1888), who performed there from 1847 until 1883. Because of his wide range, Warren is considered by many critics the finest comic actor of his age. Philadelphia's Arch Street Theatre, under the direction of Mrs. John Drew (1820–1897), became famous throughout America for its fine company and the training it gave young actors. Born Louisa Lane, Mrs. Drew was on stage as a child, came to America in 1827, and married John Drew (1827–1862), an actor of Irish roles, in 1850. Although she retained the management of the Arch Street from 1860 until 1892, the theatre's reputation was made during the 1860s. After 1870, Mrs. Drew toured widely, especially in the role of Mrs. Malaprop. In Chicago, John H. McVicker (1822–1896), after working for Ludlow and Smith and inheriting Dan Marble's Yankee roles, formed his own company in 1857. Until his death, his Chicago theatres were among the finest outside of New York. In St. Louis, Ludlow and Smith were succeeded by Ben DeBar, who dominated the theatre there from 1853 until the 1880s.

While the resident stock company continued to be the standard theatrical organization between 1850 and 1870, it was gradually undermined by several innovations. One of the most damaging was the introduction of the long run. Before 1850, successful new plays had usually been given no more than 15 times and then placed in the repertory to alternate with other plays. In 1852–1853, *Uncle Tom's Cabin* was played for 300 consecutive performances. Although atypical, this run is symptomatic of the new trend toward extended engagements even in well-established stock companies. At the Boston Museum, for example, the average run in the 1860s was 14 to 40 performances, in the 1870s, 20 to 50, and in the 1880s, 50 to 100.

The increase in the length of runs brought a decrease in the size of the repertory. In 1851–1852, the Boston Museum gave 140 plays (68 full-length and 72 afterpieces), but by 1875 the number had declined to 75 and by 1893 to 15. At Wallack's Theatre in 1855–1856, 60 plays were performed, but by the mid-1870s only 15

FIGURE 15.41 *Uncle Tom's Cabin* as produced by William Brady in 1901. This scene shows Eliza ready to cross the frozen river. The use of horses and dogs had become usual in productions of this play by the late nineteenth century. Note the cut wings used to represent trees. Courtesy Harvard Theatre Collection.

to 25, and in the mid-1880s only 5 to 10. While some of the decrease can be attributed to the gradual abandonment of the afterpiece around 1870, it is indicative as well of a new approach to repertory playing under which a series of plays was given for long runs, while the older scheme of alternating plays was retained merely in the intervals between successful productions.

With the extended run came greater emphasis upon new plays. Although between 1850 and 1870 Shakespearean and other standard works continued to make up a sizable portion of the repertory, the majority of long-running plays were new works. Adaptations of recent novels, melodramas, extravaganzas, and burlesques were prominent. Probably the most popular play of the period was *Uncle Tom's Cabin,* based on Harriet Beecher Stowe's novel. Although it was adapted many times, the most popular version was George L. Aiken's, first played in Troy, New York, in 1852 as two separate plays and then combined into a single six-act work. It was written for the Howard family (George C. Howard as St. Clare, Mrs. Howard as Topsy, and their daughter, Cordelia, as Little Eva), who played it until 1887. Although the

craze for *Uncle Tom's Cabin* died down before 1860, it revived in the 1870s, when about fifty traveling companies were performing it. In 1927 there were still twelve touring companies who performed only this play.

It is ironical that Mrs. Stowe's tale should have been so phenomenally popular while *The Escape* (1858), the oldest extant American play by a black author, William Wells Brown (c. 1816–1884), a historian and former slave, should never have reached the stage. Brown had to content himself with reading his work about the dilemma of the slaves Glen and his wife Melinda to literary societies and abolitionist meetings.

Even more ironical, black performers were permitted on the American stage during the last half of the nineteenth century only as caricatures of a caricature—that is, as members of all-black troupes of minstrels. The first of these companies was formed in 1852, but many others followed. Circumstances forced them to imitate their white counterparts, even to blacking their faces, reddening their lips and wearing kinky wigs, but they managed nevertheless to introduce many new specialty numbers. Furthermore, beginning in the 1890s black musical plays were to evolve out of this form.

As in England between 1850 and 1870, burlesque-extravaganza was one of the most popular dramatic types. Parodying well-known types of plays, performers, or topical events, and featuring songs and dances, it appealed to the taste for broad comedy and spectacle. Probably the most successful writer of burlesques was John Brougham (1810–1880), an Irishman who had worked for Mme. Vestris before coming to America in 1842. A popular comic actor, Brougham tried his hand unsuccessfully at management several times, adapted many popular novels for the stage, and wrote numerous original works. Of all his plays, perhaps the most famous was *Po-ca-hon-tas,* or *The Gentle Savage* (1855), a burlesque of the "noble savage" tradition, popular especially since the 1820s. Many others also wrote and performed in burlesques. George L. Fox (1825–1877), one of the most talented comic actors of the nineteenth century, was famous for his travesties of *Macbeth, Richard III,* and *Hamlet.* He also revitalized pantomime with his *Humpty Dumpty* (1868), in which he played Clown more than 1,200 times. Mrs. John Wood (1831–1915) was probably the best burlesque actress of the day, winning special acclaim in *The Sleeping Beauty* and *The Fair One with the Golden Locks.*

Of the serious dramatists of this period, the best was George Henry Boker (1823–1890). Son of wealthy parents, he began to write plays about 1848. His first work, *Calaynos,* was produced in London by Phelps in 1849. His *Francesca da Rimini* (1855) is considered by many the finest poetic tragedy of the nineteenth century. Boker worked hard to secure more adequate legal protection for dramatists. Although probably not due to his efforts, a copyright act was passed in 1856. Unfortunately, it failed to give effective protection because it merely provided for the registration of works in local courts. The transfer of registration to the Library of Congress in 1870 did much to correct the weaknesses, but full protection of the American playwright was not to come until the acceptance by the United States of the International Copyright Agreement in 1891 and the passage of a revised American Copyright Act in 1909.

THE AMERICAN THEATRE, 1870–1895

The years between 1870 and 1895 brought enormous changes to the American theatre as the resident company

FIGURE 15.42 Niblo's Theatre, New York, 1872. On stage is a ballet-extravaganza. Courtesy Hoblitzelle Theatre Arts Collection, University of Texas, Austin.

was undermined by touring groups, as New York became the only major center of production, and as the long run superseded the repertory system. By 1870, the resident stock company was at the peak of its development in America. The fifty permanent companies of 1870, however, had dwindled to twenty by 1878, to eight by 1880, to four by 1887, and had virtually disappeared by 1900.

While the causes of this change are numerous, probably the most important was the rise of the "combination" company (that is, one that travels with star and full company). Sending out a complete production was merely a logical extension of touring by stars. By the 1840s, many major actors were already taking along a small group of lesser players, for they could not be sure that local companies could supply adequate support in secondary roles.

There is much disagreement about the origin of the combination company. Boucicault claims to have initiated it around 1860 when he sent out a troupe with *Colleen Bawn,* but this was in England. A book published in America in 1859 speaks of combination companies as already established. Joseph Jefferson III also declared that he was a pioneer in the movement. The practice probably began with the Howard-Aiken com-

FIGURE 15.43 Boucicault's *Colleen Bawn.* Drawing from an acting edition of the play, *c.* 1865.

pany's production of *Uncle Tom's Cabin* in 1852. Its development was interrupted by the Civil War, but it mushroomed in the 1870s, as the rapid expansion of the railway system made it increasingly feasible to transport full productions. In 1872, Lawrence Barrett took his company, but no scenery, on tour; in 1876, *Rose Michel* was sent out with full company, scenery, and properties. By the season of 1876–1877 there were nearly 100 combination companies on the road, and by 1886 there were 282.

During the early years of the combination system, local managers maintained companies to perform during the intervals between traveling productions. Often the local company toured small towns in the vicinity while the visitors occupied its theatre. As local support was withdrawn from the resident troupes and given to touring productions, managers dismissed their actors and became mere landlords. The new system did not end the emphasis upon stars, but now they traveled with full productions. Henry Irving toured America eight times between 1883 and 1902; Salvini five times between 1872 and 1889; Coquelin three times between 1889 and 1900; and Sarah Bernhardt nine times between 1880 and 1918. While foreign stars usually played a small repertory,

American troupes most frequently performed a single play.

These changes did not occur overnight, and several of the major companies held out against the new system for many years. Nevertheless, Wallack's closed in 1888, the Arch Street Theatre in 1892, and the Boston Museum in 1893. Most of the significant contributions of the years between 1870 and 1895, nevertheless, came from those managers who maintained permanent troupes. Of these, the most important were Edwin Booth, Augustin Daly, and Steele MacKaye.

As a young man, Edwin Booth (1833–1893) accompanied his father, Junius Brutus Booth, on his tours and made his own acting debut in 1849 in Boston. From 1852 to 1856 he played with various companies and toured in California, Australia, and the southern United

FIGURE 15.44   Backstage at Booth's Theatre, 1870. Note the use of traps (hydraulic lifts) to raise and lower heavy props and pieces of scenery. This was one of the first stages anywhere to have a level floor and to dispense with grooves. Note the stage braces used to support the scenery now that grooves are no longer available for that purpose. From *Appleton's Journal,* vol. 3 (May 28, 1870).

FIGURE 15.45 The "ghost scene" from the first act of *Hamlet* in Edwin Booth's production at Booth's Theatre. From a sketch by Thomas B. Glessing, *c.* 1870. Courtesy the Walter Hampden-Edwin Booth Theatre Collection and Library, New York.

States before appearing at Burton's Theatre in New York. From 1856 until his death, he was one of the country's major stars. In 1863, he leased the Winter Garden Theatre in New York and gave a number of Shakespearean productions which surpassed in quality any yet seen in America. His *Hamlet* ran for 100 nights, a record not broken in America until the twentieth century. When his brother killed Lincoln, Booth retired from the stage for a time. In 1869, his Booth's Theatre, built to his specifications, introduced several innovations. The stage floor was flat and had no grooves. Several elevators were used to raise set pieces from the 50 feet of working space below the stage, and flying machinery raised other pieces into the 76 feet of overhead space. Thus, Booth introduced "free plantation" of scenery many years before it was adopted by Irving in England. Booth's Theatre also had no apron, and box settings were used extensively to increase the illusion of reality. Booth produced on such a lavish scale that by 1874 he was bankrupt. From then until his retirement in 1891, he played starring engagements in America and abroad.

Booth believed that the theatre should confine itself to the best drama and that the actor's function is to reveal the beauty and wisdom contained in great plays. He studied his roles tirelessly and executed them with infinite care. He was noted for his elegant and graceful movements, the use of vocal tone to reveal mood and meaning, the combination of emotional intensity with clarity of interpretation, the consistency of his characteri-

zations, and his freedom from mannerisms. Not having great physical strength, he depended much upon his flexible and expressive voice. At his best in serious roles, notably Hamlet, Iago, Othello, and Richelieu (in Bulwer-Lytton's play), Booth is considered by many historians the greatest actor America has produced.

Augustin Daly (1836–1899) was a critic before winning fame with *Leah the Forsaken* (1862), adapted from a German play, Mosenthal's *Deborah*. His first original work, *Under the Gaslight* (1867), also saw his debut as a producer. In 1869 he leased the Fifth Avenue Theatre and formed his own company. From that time until his death he was one of the most influential figures in the American theatre. His most important work was done after 1879, when he opened Daly's Theatre, his company's third home. After playing in London several times successfully, he opened his own theatre there in 1893.

Daly's significance derives from several sources. He contributed much to the development of realism. Many of his works were adaptations of plays by Dumas and Sardou. Some of his original plays emphasized real-

FIGURE 15.46 Interior of Daly's Fifth Avenue Theatre, New York. Note that all but a few boxes have been replaced by open balconies. Note also the chair seating in the orchestra and the center aisle. The apron has virtually disappeared. From the Albert Davis Collection, Hoblitzelle Theatre Arts Collection, University of Texas, Austin.

FIGURE 15.47 Act I of Daly's production of Shakespeare's *The Merchant of Venice*. Note the attempt to reproduce actual places in Venice. At left is seen the Grand Canal, complete with boats. Courtesy Harvard Theatre Collection.

istic special effects (the hero tied to the tracks in the path of an approaching train; the heroine locked in the stateroom of a burning steamboat) and new subject matter. His *Horizon* (1871) was the first work to present the Indian as villain and to emphasize the difference between standards of conduct in America's East and West. More important, Daly helped to establish the director as the major force in the theatre. He retained absolute control over every element of his productions. In many ways, he was comparable to Saxe-Meiningen in Germany, and Irving and the Bancrofts in England. Daly assumed the right to coach his actors in interpretation, stage business, and blocking, and he abandoned the traditional practice of casting according to lines of business. Because of his working methods, Daly usually attracted young performers, many of whom he raised to stardom. Consequently, he was one of the earliest "star makers." Daly's first star was Agnes Ethel (1852–1903), who with almost no previous experience played the leading role in *Frou-Frou* (1870), Daly's first important production. She retired from the stage in 1874. Next came Fanny Davenport (1850–1898), daughter of E. L. Davenport (1815–1877), one of the most versatile actors of the nineteenth century. After an apprenticeship in Mrs. Drew's company, she came to Daly in 1869, emerged as a leading actress in 1875, and then left Daly to star in her own productions.

Daly's most famous discovery was Clara Morris (1846–1925), who came to the fore when Agnes Ethel left the company. Catapulted to fame in 1872 by her performance in *Article 47,* she too soon left the company. At her best in roles of pathetic suffering, she was so realistic in her emotional outbursts that she was called the "Queen of Spasms." Her style palled after 1890, and ill health forced her to give up the stage soon afterward.

Daly's mainstays after 1879 were "the big four": Ada Rehan (1860–1916) and John Drew II (1853–1927), players of leading roles; James Lewis (1840–1896) and Mrs. G. H. Gilbert (1822–1904), chief comic actors. Between 1879 and 1892 they helped Daly create the finest ensemble in America. Both Drew and Miss Rehan had been trained by Mrs. Drew and continued to perform together until 1892, when Drew left Daly's company. For Daly, Miss Rehan played more than 200 roles, of which her best was Katherine in *Taming of the Shrew*. Her personal magnetism and beautiful voice made her one of the most popular actresses of her day. Unable to adapt to other working conditions after Daly's death, she retired in 1905.

Steele MacKaye (1842–1894), actor, playwright, director, inventor, designer, and teacher, was more versatile than Daly but probably less influential because few of his enterprises were sustained long enough to demonstrate their worth. As an actor and teacher, he is remembered primarily for introducing the Delsarte method into America. After studying with Delsarte in France, MacKaye came to believe that Delsarte's system could reform the stage and he promoted it in America

FIGURE 15.48 Augustin Daly's production of *The Taming of the Shrew* in 1886. A room in Baptista's house. Courtesy Hoblitzelle Theatre Arts Collection, University of Texas, Austin.

FIGURE 15.49 Sectional drawing of the Madison Square Theatre, opened in 1879. Note the two stages, one above the other, mounted in elevators and operated by counterweights. From *The Scientific American* (April 5, 1884).

cant in the development of realism, for although essentially melodramatic, it contained no villain and all the characters were drawn with sympathy and fidelity. *Paul Kauvar* was noted for its crowd scenes staged in the manner of the Meiningen company.

MacKaye was one of the most fertile inventors of the late nineteenth century. His Madison Square Theatre, opened in 1879, had two elevator stages, each 22 feet wide by 31 feet deep, which permitted complete scene changes in forty seconds. His Lyceum Theatre in 1885 was one of the first to use electric lighting and to emphasize safety devices. At Madison Square Garden, in a play on the westward movement written and staged for "Buffalo Bill" Cody, MacKaye created a realistic cyclone and stampede. But many of MacKaye's grandest schemes were never realized. For the Chicago Exposition of 1893, he designed a "Spectatorium" with twenty-five stages on which to portray Columbus' voyage to the New World and the subsequent story of America's development. A financial panic prevented its completion, but the surviving plans show that his conception was feasible. Few American producers have been so inventive, and few have been dogged by so many misfortunes.

Other important managers of this period include Daniel Frohman and A. M. Palmer. Daniel Frohman (1851–1941), who succeeded MacKaye at the Lyceum Theatre, maintained one of the finest companies in New York until 1902. Many of his brother Charles Frohman's stars established their reputations in the Lyceum company. Daniel Frohman succeeded to the management of the extensive Frohman enterprises upon his brother's death in 1915. A. M. Palmer (1838–1905) also maintained outstanding companies at the Union Square Theatre from 1872 to 1896, at the Madison Square Theatre from 1884 to 1891, and at Wallack's from 1891 to 1896. Palmer's success stemmed primarily from his executive ability, for he left the production work to others. Although his selection of plays was not daring and he hired actors only after they had proven their abilities elsewhere, he recognized and rewarded proven merit and maintained high standards.

As the emphasis shifted to new works, playwriting emerged as a full-time profession in America. Bronson Howard (1842–1908), America's first professional dramatist, began his playwriting career in 1864, but did not attract wide attention until his *Saratoga* (1870) ran for 101 nights. Of his eighteen plays, *The Banker's Daughter* (1878), *Young Mrs. Winthrop* (1882), and *Shenandoah* (1888) are the best known. *Shenandoah*,

through a series of acting schools. In 1872–1873 he created a short-lived training program, probably the first in America, at his St. James' Theatre in New York. His greatest contribution, however, came in 1884, when at his Lyceum Theatre he began another training program which was to become the American Academy of Dramatic Art. Two of MacKaye's students founded other schools: Samuel S. Curry created the Curry School of Expression, and Charles W. Emerson the Emerson School of Oratory. As the most important of the early American acting schools, these three spread MacKaye's and Delsarte's system.

MacKaye also wrote or adapted nineteen plays, three of which were especially successful: *Hazel Kirke* (1878–1880), *Won at Last* (1877), and *Paul Kauvar* (1887). After achieving an initial run of 486 performances in New York, *Hazel Kirke* was taken on the road by fourteen different companies in 1884. It is also signifia play set against the background of the Civil War, launched Charles Frohman on his producing career. Howard was one of the first dramatists to receive regular royalty payments, and in 1891 he founded the Society of American Dramatists and Composers, the forerunner of the present-day Dramatists' Guild.

Much of the drama of this period illustrates the trend toward realism. While fidelity of spectacle had been increasing throughout the century, realism of character and situation were slower in arriving. One step toward more daring subject matter was taken in 1857 with the production of *Camille*. Considered by many too bold, the play had first been presented by Laura Keene as a terrible dream from which the heroine awakens. Matilda Heron (1830–1877), on the other hand, translated the play faithfully and played it without idealizing the characters. It ran for 100 nights, and Miss Heron was hailed for her naturalistic acting.

But realism was usually confined to local color. Building upon the popularity of Bret Harte and Mark Twain, such works as Bartley Campbell's (1843–1888) *My Partner* (1879) exploited frontier life. Local color was also emphasized in Augustus Thomas' (1857–1934) plays, *Alabama* (1891), *In Mizzoura* (1893), and *Arizona* (1897). Thomas' best works, however, turned in other directions. *The Witching Hour* (1907) deals with hypnosis and telepathy, while *The Copperhead* (1918) tells the story of a northern patriot who pretends to be a southern sympathizer in order to aid his country during the Civil War.

Local color of a quite different sort appears in the plays of Edward Harrigan (1845–1911), a comic writer who extended the "Bowery Boy" tradition and whose early fame was gained in variety houses in partnership with Tony Hart (Anthony Cannon, 1857–1891). Harrigan began by writing sketches and went on to full-length plays about life among various immigrant groups in New York. Combining knockabout farce and realism, most of the plays end with some outrageous denouement, such as the explosion of a fireworks factory followed by bodies falling through the ceiling. Harrigan performed in his own works and mounted them with absolute fidelity of background and dress. After 1895, Harrigan performed only rarely. Little appreciated by contemporary critics, he is now recognized as a faithful observer of his milieu.

In this period realism was developed most extensively in the plays of Gillette and Herne. William

FIGURE 15.50 Miss Whitlock, who played the leading role in the original production of *The Black Crook* at Niblo's Garden, 1866. From the Albert Davis Collection, Hoblitzelle Theatre Arts Collection, University of Texas, Austin.

Gillette (1855–1937), on the stage after 1875, wrote his first play, *The Professor*, in 1881. Of his twenty works, the most important are *Held by the Enemy* (1886), the first major play on a Civil War theme, *Secret Service* (1895), and *Sherlock Holmes* (1899). Gillette's most realistic drama, *Secret Service*, also has a Civil War background. Built around minutiae, the play's stage directions take up more space in printing than does the dialogue. One act requires an authentic telegraph office, complete with a working telegraph key. Although Gillette's plays are essentially melodramas, they create the illusion of real life through the accumulation of external details. Gillette was also one of the finest actors of his day. By concentrating upon the moment-by-moment development of the action, he sought to create the "illusion of the first time" regardless of how often he had performed a role.

James A. Herne (1839–1901) began his career in 1859 as an actor. During the 1870s while serving as a stage manager in San Francisco, he adapted several plays, some in collaboration with David Belasco. He first attracted favorable critical attention with *Drifting Apart* (1888), a work about the evil effects of drink on a Massachusetts fishing village. Encouraged by William Dean Howells and other realists, Herne thereafter consciously sought fidelity to life in writing, staging, and acting. His most important play, *Margaret Fleming* (1890), is usually considered the most realistic American drama of the nineteenth century. It tells the story of a woman who, upon learning of her husband's infidelity, takes his illegitimate child to rear with her own. While it includes much realistic visual detail, its major emphasis is upon psychological conflicts. Its subject matter made it unacceptable to commercial managers, and Herne had to present it in halls and out-of-the-way theatres. After suffering heavy financial losses, he recovered his fortunes with *Shore Acres* (1892), a play about a quiet, lovable, New England character. Although in the realistic mode, it did not offend moral sensibilities and was soon a popular favorite. Not a great playwright, Herne nevertheless did more than any other American dramatist of his day to establish the realistic mode.

Despite the trend toward realism, the majority of theatres continued to emphasize more popular fare. After 1870, minor dramatic forms were combined with variety acts to create new conceptions of burlesque and vaudeville. Burlesque began to change in 1866 when a troupe of ballet dancers, stranded in New York, were incorporated into *The Black Crook*. The resulting combination of spectacular scenery, lightly clad girls, music, dance, and song was so popular that it ran for sixteen months and spawned many imitations. This vogue was given further impetus in 1869 by the appearance of Lydia Thompson and her "British Blondes" in burlesques which emphasized feminine charms more than parody, the previous domain of burlesque. Soon burlesque had assumed its modern form: a collection of variety acts mingled with musical numbers featuring beautiful women. With its sexual overtones it came to appeal primarily to male audiences. Burlesque reached the height of its popularity just prior to the First World War, but it was not until around 1929 that the "striptease" be-

FIGURE 15.51 The Macgilton's Eccentric Dancers in *The Black Crook* at Niblo's Garden, New York. Various groups were worked into this production from time to time. From the Albert Davis Collection, Hoblitzelle Theatre Arts Collection, University of Texas, Austin.

came a feature which placed burlesque on the fringes of legality.

Modern vaudeville grew out of the same movement. In the 1880s, Tony Pastor (1837–1908) reshaped the burlesque to make it suitable for the family audience. From about 1890 until 1930, vaudeville was one of the most popular of theatrical entertainments. Essentially a collection of variety acts, it also featured sketches and short plays in which leading actors often performed.

Most of the major actors of the period have already been mentioned, but a few others deserve attention. Joseph Jefferson III (1829–1905), one of the most

FIGURE 15.52 Joseph Jefferson III as Rip Van Winkle, a role he played for some forty years. From the Albert Davis Collection, Hoblitzelle Theatre Arts Collection, University of Texas, Austin.

the age of fifteen. From 1861 to 1866 he played secondary roles to Forrest, whose approach he adopted. After playing in San Francisco from 1866 until 1875, McCullough came under Mackaye's influence and altered his acting style. By the time he died, he was considered second only to Booth as a tragic actor. Lawrence Barrett (1838–1891) had few attributes to recommend him for the stage. Accepted into Burton's company in 1857, he worked his way up slowly. Virtually illiterate when he began, Barrett perfected his knowledge until he came to be known as the "scholar" of the American theatre. In the 1880s, he became Booth's partner and co-star. Noted for his clarity of conception, he was somewhat faulty in execution because of his self-consciousness and artificial elocution. Richard Mansfield (1854–1907) went on the stage in 1880 and achieved his first success in 1883 as Baron Chevrial, a doddering lecher in *A Parisian Romance.* After 1886, he maintained his own company and each year added a new role to his repertory, alternating long runs of new works with his repertory of past hits. Best in melodramatic and eccentric parts, his lack of subtlety limited his success in major tragic roles. With his lavishly mounted productions, Mansfield was often compared to Irving as actor and manager.

By 1895 the actor's position in the theatre had changed radically. Benefits had been abandoned in the 1870s in favor of straight salary payments. With the triumph of the traveling company, actors now had to go to New York to seek employment. Furthermore, they were hired for the run of a play rather than by the season, and since there was as yet no union to protect their rights, they received no salary during rehearsal periods and were often stranded when productions closed on the road. From the position of dominance which he had held for some 200 years, the actor was now subordinate to both the director and the producer.

By the late nineteenth century numerous theatre artists in Europe had become so dissatisfied with existing conditions that they were promoting far-reaching innovations. Out of their work would come attitudes and practices that continue to influence the theatre.

beloved actors of the nineteenth century, was on the stage from the age of four. He early established a reputation for comic playing, but *Rip van Winkle* was to be the mainstay of his repertory after 1865. Noted for ease, expressive action, and inventive byplay, he mingled pathos and humor in a unique combination. John McCullough (1832–1885) came to America from Ireland at

LOOKING AT THEATRE HISTORY

One way of studying theatre history is through an examination of the technology available for creating the effects demanded by playwrights, directors, and designers. All ages, from the Greek to the present, have made use of technological devices, and an understanding of the available means and how they were used can do much to clarify the stylistic and visual qualities of theatrical art in any period. Few periods have been as self-conscious as the late nineteenth century about the application of scientific knowledge to stage production. Perhaps the most obvious results were in stage machinery, but in all areas of production a major goal was to create illusion so true to nature that it could withstand the scrutiny of the most demanding observer. Stage technology became a frequent subject in periodicals, perhaps most notably in *The Scientific American*. Albert A. Hopkins, for many years editor of that magazine, drew heavily on articles first published there for his *Magic: Stage Illusions and Scientific Diversions* (1897), a section of which is devoted to "Science in the Theatre." It is a valuable source of information about the theatre technology of that time.

Among the devices described in *Magic* is the elevator stage installed in MacKaye's Madison Square Theatre (see the illustration on p. 459):

> The shaft through which the huge elevator moves up and down measures one hundred and fourteen feet from the roof to the bottom. . . . The whole construction is fifty-five feet high and twenty-two feet wide and thirty-one feet deep, and weighs about forty-eight tons. . . . Only about forty seconds are required to raise or lower the stage in position, and the entire structure is moved by four men at the winch. The movement is effected without sound, jar or vibration, owing to the balancing of the stage and its weight with counterweights. . . . The borders and border lights are supplied to each of the movable stages, and each stage has its own trap floor. . . . (p. 271)

Hopkins also describes MacKaye's Spectatorium, Lautenschlager's revolving stage (shown in the illustration on p. 501), the horse race illustrated on page 382, and various other devices, including many required by Wagner's operas (such as floating the Rhine Maidens in *The Rhinegold* and making and operating the dragon in *Siegfried*).

One technological milestone of the period was the development of electricity as a motive force for stage machinery and lighting. Here is a report concerning the Savoy Theatre, built to house Gilbert and Sullivan's comic operas:

> . . . an attempt will be made here for the first time in London to light a theatre entirely by electricity. The system used is that of the "incandescent lamp". . . . About 1,200 lights are used, and the power to generate a sufficient current for these is obtained from large steam engines, giving about 120 horse power, placed on some open land near the theatre. The new light is used not only in the audience part of the theatre, but on the stage for footlights, side and top lights, etc. . . . What is being done is an experiment, and may succeed or fail.

> *The Times*, 3 October 1881.

The nineteenth century also sought to apply scientific (that is, precise) knowledge to the design of scenery and costumes so as to insure their accordance with fact. Charles Kean sometimes even supplied his audiences with an account of the sources he had consulted and the reasoning that had led to his decisions. Such an account (some parts of which follow) was first used by him with his production of *Macbeth* in 1853:

> The very uncertain information . . . which we possess respecting the dress worn by the inhabitants of Scotland in the eleventh century, renders any attempt to present this tragedy attired in the costume of the period a task of very great difficulty. . . . In the absence of any positive information I have borrowed materials from those nations to whom Scotland was contantly opposed in war. . . . I have introduced the tunic, mantle, cross gartering, and ringed byrne of the Danes and Anglo-Saxons. . . . The coats of mail appear to have been composed of iron rings or bosses, sewn upon cloth or leather, like that of the Anglo-Saxons. . . . The . . . architecture previous to the Norman conquest has been adopted throughout the play. . . . On this subject I have availed myself of the valuable knowledge of George Godwin, Esq., F. R. S. of the Royal Institute of Architects, to whose suggestions I take this opportunity of acknowledging my obligation.

> *Shakespeare's Tragedy of Macbeth, . . . Arranged for Representation at the Princess's Theatre, with Historical and Explanatory Notes by Charles Kean* (London, 1853), pp. v–ix.

Acting did not escape the scientific trends of the time, for in France Delsarte sought to reduce it to laws that would permit it to be taught with precision:

I had learned how vain is advice dictated by the caprice of a master without a system. . . . I knew that certain laws existed. . . . I had the nucleus of the science . . . and I did not despair of formulating it.

One of his disciples sums up the basic assumptions on which the system rested:

There is no science without principles which give a reason for its facts. Hence to teach and to learn [this subject] it is necessary: 1. to understand the general law which controls the movement of the organs; 2. to apply this general law to the movements of each particular organ; 3. to understand the meaning of the form of each of these movements; 4. to adapt this meaning to the various states of the soul.

> *The Delsarte System . . . with the Literary Remains of Francois Delsarte (New York, 1887).*

Delsarte and his followers subdivided the body and developed rules for using each to express all the basic human emotions and spiritual states. This system was to dominate actor training in Europe and America in the late nineteenth and early twentieth centuries.

It was the demand for precision in every aspect of production that coalesced in the work of the Meiningen company, which toured widely in Europe from 1874 until 1890. In 1881 the company appeared in London. Reviewers were not impressed by all aspects of the productions, since they thought that in some areas the English did as well or better, but they found much to recommend as models for emulation. Here are portions of a review of *Julius Caesar* (see the illustration on page 449):

It may . . . be maintained that no spectacular play of Shakespeare, such as "Julius Caesar" may claim to be considered, has ever been put upon our stage in a fashion equally effective. . . . the principal gain is in the manner in which those who are little or nothing more than supernumeraries wear the costumes of a bygone age, and take intelligent part in actions and movements of which they can have had no experience in real life. . . . the openly manifested desire to obtain an ascendancy over his fellows, which has been the disgrace of the English actor, is kept out of sight. . . .

In the case of "Julius Caesar" the most noteworthy features consisted of the arrangement of the tableaux and the disposition of the supernumeraries when as in the case of the oration of Antony over the body of Caesar, strong and growing emotion has to be expressed. From the picturesque standpoint these things were perfect.

> *The Athenaeum, June 11, 1881, p. 796.*

16 The Beginnings of the Modern Theatre, 1875–1915

For the most part, the theatre during the late nineteenth century was merely a logical outgrowth of what had gone before. But after 1875 several writers and directors made a marked break with the past and initiated the "modern" theatre—an era still underway. Nevertheless, in the beginning the changes were essentially intensifications of the realistic vision, for in many ways Ibsen—the "founder of modern drama"—was merely the first playwright to achieve fully the goals that had been set forth by the realists. But it was Ibsen who made the public aware that a new era in the theatre had begun.

IBSEN

Henrik Ibsen (1828–1906), after publishing his first play in 1850, was appointed resident dramatist and stage manager at the newly created Norwegian National Theatre in Bergen in 1851. By 1857 he had assisted in staging 145 plays, and had written seven of his own. From 1857 until 1862, he worked at the Norwegian Theatre in Christiania (now Oslo). After 1864, he lived abroad except for brief intervals.

Between 1850 and 1899, Ibsen wrote twenty-five plays. Most of the early works are romantic verse-dramas about the Scandinavian past. These include *Lady Inger of Ostraat* (1855), *The Vikings* at *Helgeland* (1858), and *The Pretenders* (1864). The most important early works, however, are *Brand (1866) and Peer Gynt* (1867). *Brand*, a dramatic poem, depicts an uncompromising idealist who sacrifices everything, including his family, to his vision. It established Ibsen's reputation, and the financial security which it brought made it possible for him to work as he pleased. *Peer Gynt* contrasts sharply with *Brand*, for its protagonist is a man who avoids issues by skirting them. A skillful blending of fantasy and reality, *Peer Gynt* was interpreted by many as a satire on the Norwegian character.

In the 1870s Ibsen made a sharp break with his past. He now declared his intention of abandoning verse because it was unsuited to creating an illusion of reality. The future direction of his work first became apparent with *Pillars of Society* (1877), but it was with *A Doll's House* (1879), *Ghosts* (1881), and *An Enemy of the People* (1882) that Ibsen established his reputation as a radical thinker and controversial dramatist. Above all, it was *A Doll's House* and *Ghosts* that shocked conservative readers and served as a rallying point for supporters of a drama of ideas. In *A Doll's House*, Nora, upon realizing that she has always been treated as a doll, chooses to leave her husband in order to become a person in her own right. In *Ghosts*, Mrs. Alving, conforming to traditional morality, has remained with a depraved husband only to have her only son go mad, presumably from inherited syphilis. Thus, both plays questioned the inviolability of marriage, while the allusion to venereal disease in *Ghosts* made it such a storm center

FIGURE 16.1 Eleanora Duse (at left) in Ibsen's *Rosmersholm* at the Norwegian National Theatre, Oslo, 1906. From *Bühne und Welt* (1906).

throughout the world that it was forbidden production in most countries.

Ibsen soon turned in new directions. In *The Wild Duck* (1884), *Rosmersholm* (1886), *The Master Builder* (1892), *John Gabriel Borkman* (1896), and *When We Dead Awaken* (1899) he made increasing use of symbolism and of subjects more concerned with personal relationships than with social problems. In actuality, the basic theme of Ibsen's plays remained relatively constant: the struggle for integrity, the conflict between duty to oneself and duty to others. Mrs. Alving of *Ghosts* discovers too late that she had destroyed her life by overvaluing duty to others, whereas in many of the late plays the protagonists, while pursuing some private vision, destroy the happiness of others and finally their own.

Much of Ibsen's work contributed to the development of realism. In the prose dramas, he refined Scribe's "well-made play" formula and made it more fitting to the realistic style. Ibsen discarded asides, soliloquies, and other nonrealistic devices, and was careful to motivate all exposition. Most often a character who has just arrived elicits information in a manner which appears completely natural by asking questions about happenings during his absence. All scenes are causally related and lead logically to the denouement. Dialogue, settings, costumes, and business are selected for their ability to reveal character and milieu, and are clearly described in stage directions. Each role is conceived as a personality whose behavior is attributable to hereditary or environmental causes. Internal psychological

motivations are given even greater emphasis than external visual detail. In these ways, Ibsen provided a model for writers of the realistic school.

Ibsen's late plays were to influence nonrealistic drama as extensively as the earlier prose plays did realistic works. In them, ordinary objects (such as the duck in *The Wild Duck*) are imbued with significance beyond their literal meaning and enlarge the implications of the dramatic action. Furthermore, many of the works border on fantasy. In *Rosmersholm,* a phantom white horse is significant, and in *When We Dead Awaken* the mountain heights exert an irresistible pull. This sense of mysterious forces at work in human destiny was to be a major theme of idealist drama.

Whether realistic or idealistic, almost all dramatists after Ibsen were influenced by his conviction that drama should be a source of insights, a creator of discussion, a conveyor of ideas, something more than mere entertainment. He gave playwrights a new vision of their role. Almost everywhere Ibsen's plays came to epitomize the break with the past and to be a rallying point for producers seeking new paths.

ZOLA AND THE FRENCH NATURALISTS

Even as Ibsen was writing his prose plays, the French naturalists, working quite independently, were also demanding a new drama. The naturalists considered heredity and environment to be the major determinants of man's fate. This doctrine was grounded (at least in part) in Charles Darwin's *The Origin of Species* (1859), which had set forth two main theses: (1) all forms of life have developed gradually from a common ancestry; and (2) the evolution of species is explained by the "survival of the fittest." These theories have several important implications. First, they make heredity and environment the causes of everything man is or does. Second, since behavior is determined by factors largely beyond his control, no individual can truly be held responsible for what he does. If blame is to be assigned, it must go to a society that has allowed undesirable hereditary and environmental factors to exist. Third, Darwin's theories strengthened the idea of progress, since if man has evolved from an atom of being to the complex creature he now is, improvement appears to be inevitable. Nevertheless, it was argued, progress can be hastened by the

FIGURE 16.2 Mrs. Fiske as Hedda Gabler with George Arliss as Judge Brack in the final scene of Ibsen's *Hedda Gabler*. Courtesy Hoblitzelle Theatre Collection, University of Texas, Austin.

consistent application of scientific method. Fourth, man is reduced to the status of a natural object. Before the nineteenth century man had been set apart from the rest of creation as superior to it. Now he lost his privileged status and became merely another object for study and control.

Naturalism also attracted many adherents because of contemporary political and economic conditions. The Franco-Prussian War of 1870–1871 was a severe blow to French pride, for not only was France defeated, but it lost Alsace and Lorraine to Germany. The war also brought an end to Napoleon III's empire. In Paris, a commune was established, but this was soon overthrown and France once more became a republic. The war and its aftermath served to emphasize that the working man enjoyed few privileges, and during the last quarter of the nineteenth century socialism began to gain support throughout Europe as many came to believe that only this form of social organization could insure equality to all. Such pressures motivated several European governments to adopt constitutions at last; by 1900 every major country in Europe except Russia had some degree of constitutional government. This interest in the lot of the working classes and the rights of the common man was to provide the main focus of

the naturalist movement. As means of dealing with contemporary problems, science and technology were considered the major tools, and the naturalists argued that all problems could be solved if only the scientific method were applied systematically.

Naturalism as a conscious movement first appeared in France in the 1870s. Its primary spokesman was Emile Zola (1849–1902), an admirer of Comte and an advocate of the scientific method as the key to all truth and progress. Believing that literature must either become scientific or perish, Zola argued that drama should illustrate the "inevitable laws of heredity and environment" or record "case studies." He wished the dramatist, in his search for truth, to observe, record, and "experiment" with the same detachment as the scientist. Zola compared the writer with the doctor, who seeks the causes of a disease so that it may be cured; he does not gloss over infection, but brings it out into the open where it can be examined. Similarly, the dramatist should seek out social ills and reveal them so they may be corrected.

Zola's first major statement of the naturalist doctrine came in 1873 in the preface to his dramatization of his novel *Thérèse Raquin;* he expanded his views in *Naturalism in the Theatre* (1881) and *The Experimental Novel* (1881). Some of Zola's followers were even more radical than he in their demands for theatrical reform,

FIGURE 16.3 Ménessier's adaptation of Zola's novel, *The Earth,* as directed by Antoine at the Théâtre Antoine, 1902. Note the many naturalistic details, including the chickens in the foreground. From *Le Théâtre* (1902).

arguing that a play should merely be a "slice of life" transferred to the stage. Thus, in their zeal to approximate scientific truth, they often obliterated virtually all distinction between art and life.

Naturalism, like many movements before it, was handicapped by a lack of good plays embodying its principles. Although a few plays, such as *Henriette Maréchal* (1863) by Edmond and Jules Goncourt and *L'Arlesienne* (1872) by Alphonse Daudet, were produced, they made little impact. Even Zola's *Thérèse Raquin* failed to live up to his critical precepts except in the setting, for rather than a slice of life it was more nearly a melodrama about murder and retribution.

Ironically, it was Henri Becque (1837–1899) who most nearly captured the naturalist ideal, even though he and Zola were equally contemptuous of each other. Becque's *The Vultures* (1882) shows the fleecing of a family of women by their supposed friends following the death of the father; there are no sympathetic characters, the ending is pessimistic and ironical, and there are no obvious climaxes, merely a slow progression toward the cynical outcome. *La Parisienne* (1885) depicts a wife who considers her infidelity an asset to her husband's advancement in business. In these plays, Becque raised French naturalism to its highest point.

That *The Vultures* was presented by the Comédie Française, a bastion of conservatism, would on the surface suggest that by the 1880s naturalism had been fully accepted in Paris. But Becque's play was ineffectually produced because he refused to comply with the company's request for revisions that would have brought the work more nearly into conformity with contemporary tastes. Because virtually all naturalist dramas that received a hearing failed to raise any serious questions about traditional values, the complacency of neither the public nor theatrical workers was seriously challenged. Something more was needed if significant change was to come. This new element was to be added by Antoine at the Théâtre Libre, where after 1887 naturalistic staging and writing were used for the first time.

ANTOINE AND THE THÉÂTRE LIBRE

André Antoine (1858–1943) seemed a most unpromising source of revolution in 1887, for he was merely a clerk in a gas company, and his theatrical experience was limited to supernumerary acting with Parisian pro-

FIGURE 16.4 Antoine's setting for Ibsen's *The Wild Duck* at the Théâtre Libre, 1891. Courtesy Bibliothèque de l'Arsenal, Paris.

fessional companies and occasional appearances with an amateur group. When Antoine sought to produce a program of new plays, including a dramatization of Zola's *Jacques Damour,* his amateur circle refused its sanction and Antoine set off on his own. In search of a name for his company, he adopted Théâtre Libre (or "Free Theatre"). The success of his first program won him the endorsement of Zola and other influential figures. His second program was attended by major theatrical critics, who wrote lengthy reviews. Before the end of 1887, Antoine was famous. He gave up his clerk's job and thereafter until 1914 devoted himself to theatrical production.

Organized on a subscription basis, the Théâtre Libre was open only to members and therefore was exempt from censorship. As a result, many of the plays available to Antoine were those that had been refused licenses, and most were naturalistic. Much of the notoriety of the Théâtre Libre stemmed from its *comédies rosses* (plays in which the usual principles of morality are reversed), many so extreme that they repelled even Antoine's tolerant audience. It was largely because of these works that naturalism gained a reputation for depravity, but the publicity they attracted also gradually paved the way for greater freedom in established and conservative theatres.

In 1888 Antoine also began to produce one foreign work each year. After Tolstoy's *The Power of Darkness,* he went on to Ibsen's *Ghosts* and *The Wild Duck.* In this way, controversial foreign as well as domestic plays were given their first Parisian performances.

In addition to serving as a showcase for new dramas, the Théâtre Libre also became the proving ground for production techniques. Although Antoine had used a realistic approach from the beginning, he intensified his search for authenticity after witnessing the Meiningen Players and Irving's company in 1888. He now sought to reproduce environment in every detail. In *The Butchers* (1888), for example, he hung real carcasses of beef on the stage. The "fourth wall" was observed consistently; in designing settings, he arranged rooms as in real life and only later decided which wall should be removed. Often furniture was placed along the curtain line, and actors were directed to behave as though there were no audience. Through his belief in the importance of environment, Antoine helped to establish the principle that each play requires its own setting quite distinct from that of any other work. After witnessing the Meiningen company, Antoine also gave special attention to ensemble acting. Although most of his performers were amateurs, he coached them carefully and autocratically. He discouraged conventionalized movement and declamatory speech, seeking natural behavior instead.

Antoine's success worked against him, for as soon as a playwright or actor established his worth, he was employed by a major company. Furthermore, Antoine's high standards of production kept him constantly in debt. Even at the height of its popularity, the Théâtre Libre gave no production for more than three performances. By 1893, the company began to weaken and in 1894 Antoine left it. By then he had presented sixty-two programs composed of 184 plays. In addition to playing in Paris, he had toured in Belgium, Holland, Germany, Italy, and England. His fame was worldwide, and the example he had set was to be followed in several other countries.

Antoine did not stay away from the Parisian theatre long. In 1897 he opened his Théâtre Antoine, run as a fully professional theatre, and in 1906 he was appointed director of the state-subsidized Odéon, which he completely modernized. Although he practiced it less assiduously, realism still dominated his work. Probably his most famous productions of this era were of French classical dramas, in which he attempted to recreate the theatrical conventions of the seventeenth century. Costumed actors served as onstage audience, chandeliers were hung over the stage, and candle footlights were conspicuous. Through this approach, he helped to establish a realism based upon past theatrical conventions rather

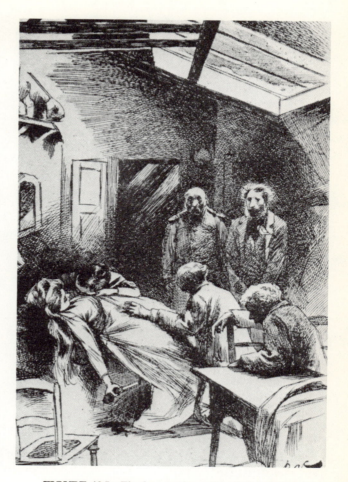

FIGURE 16.5 Final scene from Antoine's production of Ibsen's *The Wild Duck* at the Théâtre Libre. From a contemporary lithograph.

than upon architecture and dress, as had been usual with other producers. Antoine also directed several outstanding productions of Shakespeare's plays. Near the end of his tenure at the Odéon, he staged a few works in which stylization (based on visual sources) was clearly evident, but he resigned his post before this new trend was fully explored. By 1914 he had presented a total of 364 works. No one else had influenced the French theatre of the period so profoundly as had Antoine.

After 1890, most of the major new French dramatists were realists and many of these were given their first hearing by Antoine. Among these the most important were Porto-Riche, Curel, and Brieux. Georges Porto-Riche (1849–1930) was noted for subtle characterizations which emphasized internal conflicts. Probably his best play is *Infatuated* (1891) in which a husband tries to rid himself of his wife by arousing her interest in another man, only to discover that he cannot give her up. François de Curel (1854–1928) had his first play produced by Antoine in 1892. He made few concessions to popular taste, and his disregard for ordinary principles of dramatic construction often obscured his intentions. His concern for internal psychological conflicts, however, did much to forward realistic subject matter. Among his best works are *The Fossils* (1892), depicting a decaying aristocracy, and *The Lion's Feast* (1898), in which the protagonist attempts to improve the lives of workingmen. Eugène Brieux (1858–1932) was said by Shaw to be the most important dramatist in Europe after the death of Ibsen. Given his first production by Antoine in 1892, Brieux went on to write *The Red Robe* (1900), showing the difficulty of obtaining justice from judges concerned primarily with promotion, *Damaged Goods* (1902), concerning syphilis and its transmission to a child, and *Maternity* (1903), in which a blistering attack is launched on a society which does not permit legal birth control. As Brieux's plays reveal, subjects which had been unacceptable to the general public when Ibsen began his work were to be seen in commercial theatres by 1900.

THE FREIE BÜHNE AND GERMAN REALISM

The pattern that emerged in France was repeated in Germany. The first step toward theatrical reform came in 1883, when the Deutsches Theater was opened in Berlin by Adolf L'Arronge (1838–1908) and Ludwig Barnay (1842–1924), with a company headed by Josef Kainz (1858–1910), who had worked in the Meiningen troupe, and Agnes Sorma (1865–1927), later to be Germany's leading actress. Here a repertory of old and new plays was produced in the manner of the Meiningen Players. In 1888, Barnay left the Deutsches Theatre to found the Berliner Theater, and in the same year Oskar Blumenthal (1852–1917) founded the Lessing Theater. Thus, by 1890 Berlin had several companies of excellent quality. Nevertheless, their choice of plays was severely restricted by censorship.

Meanwhile, a group calling itself "Youngest Germany" had begun to advocate a new art based upon an objective observation of reality, while another calling itself *Durch* (or "Through") went even further than Zola in its demands for a naturalistic drama. Both groups found inspiration in Ibsen's plays, sixteen of which had been translated into German by 1890.

As in France, however, the new movement lacked focus until an "independent" theatre was formed. Taking its inspiration from the Théâtre Libre, the Freie Bühne (or "Free Stage") was organized in Berlin in 1889. Unlike Antoine's company, however, the German group was a democratic organization with officers and a governing council. Otto Brahm (1856–1912), a dramatic critic, was elected president and became its guiding spirit. In order to secure the services of professional actors, the Freie Bühne gave its performances on Sunday afternoons since its actors and most of its personnel were regularly employed by established theatres, especially the Deutsches Berliner, and Lessing. Each production usually involved different actors, over whom Brahm had little control. Thus, the Freie Bühne exerted little influence on theatrical production. Its major contribution was made by giving a hearing to plays forbidden by the censor. The opening production of *Ghosts* was followed with plays by Hauptmann, the Goncourts, Zola, Becque, Tolstoy, Anzengruber, and Strindberg. After the season of 1890–1891, regular performances were discontinued, although occasionally programs were arranged when a worthy play was forbidden a license. The Freie Bühne came to an end altogether in 1894, when Brahm was named director of the Deutsches Theater.

The only truly important German dramatist introduced by the Freie Bühne was Gerhart Hauptmann (1862–1946). The furor which greeted his *Before Sunrise* (1889), the story of a Silesian family which sinks into viciousness after the discovery of coal on their land, established Hauptmann as a major new playwright. During the next fifty years he wrote about thirty plays. Of the early works, the best is *The Weavers* (1892), remarkable for its group-protagonist of workers engaged in an abortive revolt. Like Ibsen, Hauptmann went on to write plays in a more symbolic vein, notably *The Assumption of Hannele* (1893) and *The Sunken Bell* (1896). After 1912, his plays became increasingly nonrealistic. Before his death, Hauptmann lost much of his prestige because of his passive acceptance of Hitler's regime. All of Hauptmann's work shows great compassion for human suffering, but his protagonists, who are victims of circumstances beyond their control, are more pitiable than heroic.

The Freie Bühne stimulated the formation of several other stage societies in Germany. Although none achieved the fame of the original group, they helped to pave the way for a new drama. Perhaps of equal importance, a "people's" theatre was organized by socialist groups (the ban on which was lifted in 1890) interested in raising the cultural standards of the working classes. Using the Freie Bühne as a model, the Freie Volksbühne was organized in Berlin in 1890 to produce plays at Sunday matinees, for which season tickets were distributed by lot at a nominal price. Beginning with 1,150 members, the organization included 12,000 by 1908. In 1892, the Neue Freie Volksbühne, founded by the former director of the original group, began a similar program. By 1905, it was offering its subscribers a choice among productions at several major theatres. Before the First World War the two groups had amalgamated, and their membership of 70,000 was soon to open one of the most modern theatres in Germany with its own permanent company. The workers' theatre movement flourished throughout Germany and Austria. To it must go considerable credit for creating the broad-based theatregoing public which continues in Germany even today.

Before 1900, the new realistic drama was being accepted almost everywhere. At the Burgtheater in Vienna a wide selection of recent works was presented between 1890 and 1898, when Max Burckhardt (1854–1912) was director of the theatre. His successor, Paul Schlenther (1854–1916), a friend and admirer of Hauptmann, continued his policies. A somewhat similar pattern was followed elsewhere, for as public interest in the new plays grew the repertory expanded to include them.

In addition to Hauptmann, other important new dramatists including Sudermann, Halbe, Hirschfeld, and Fulda. Hermann Sudermann (1857–1928) was even more instrumental than Hauptmann in making realism acceptable to the public, for he tended to retain the well-made play techniques and to conform more nearly to accepted morality while writing about "advanced" subjects. His most popular play, *Magda* (1893), concerning a singer whose bohemian life brings her into conflict with her father, became a favorite vehicle of actresses. Sudermann continued to write until well into the twentieth century, although his reputation declined markedly after 1905. Max Halbe's (1865–1944) work is typified by *Youth* (1893), the story of a young girl killed by her half-witted brother while he is seeking to destroy her lover. George Hirschfeld (1873–1943),

a strong exponent of naturalism, is most famous for *The Mothers* (1896), the story of a working-class girl who leaves a composer when she realizes that she cannot fit into his life. Ludwig Fulda (1862–1939) won fame for *Comrades* (1894), a satire on the "new" woman, and *The Lost Paradise* (1890), a naturalistic play about class conflicts.

In Austria, Schönherr, Bahr, and Schnitzler were probably the best dramatists. Karl Schönherr (1867–1943), writing in the vein of Anzengruber, painted realistic pictures of Tyrolean peasant life in such works as *Earth* (1908) and *The She-Devil* (1914). Hermann Bahr (1863–1934) demonstrated his firm grasp of all the new movements in his more than 80 works. His most popular play is *The Concert* (1909), a comedy about a wife's attempt to cope with her pianist-husband's amorous adventures. But by far the most important Austrian dramatist of this period was Arthur Schnitzler (1862–1931), a recorder of the melancholic world-weariness that characterized the turn of the century, and of the shallow sexual attitudes that accompanied it. The most famous of his works is *Anatol* (1893), a series of short plays, each of which records a different love intrigue. Even in the midst of happiness, Anatol knows that his momentary pleasure will dissolve into jealousy and boredom. A similar, though more shocking work to audiences, is *Reigen* (1900, variously translated as *Hands Around, La Ronde,* and *Round Dance*), with its ten characters who engage in a series of love affairs. Schnitzler, a friend of Freud, was much concerned with the centrality of sexual behavior, but was also convinced that love cannot be built upon pure ego satisfaction. While he seldom strayed from this theme, Schnitzler occasionally wrote on other subjects, as in *Professor Bernhardi* (1912), a play about anti-Semitism.

THE INDEPENDENT THEATRE AND REALISM IN ENGLAND

After the death of Robertson in 1871, the English theatre was given over largely to works in the tradition of Boucicault and Sardou or to lavish productions of the classics. A new direction was not evident until the 1890s, when Jones and Pinero appeared. These writers hold a place in English drama comparable to that of Dumas *fils* and Augier in French, for both were sufficiently new to be slightly scandalizing, yet both were

FIGURE 16.6 Scene from Act I of the original production of Pinero's *The Second Mrs. Tanqueray,* with Mrs. Patrick Campbell and George Alexander. From *The Graphic* (1893).

sufficiently conventional to be acceptable to the censor and the theatregoing public.

Henry Arthur Jones (1851–1929) began his playwriting career with a successful melodrama, *The Silver King* (1882), and did not turn to more serious drama until after 1890 with *The Dancing Girl* (1891), *The Liars* (1897), and *Mrs. Dane's Defence* (1900). His most unusual play, *Michael and His Lost Angel* (1896), treats a love affair between a minister and one of his parishioners. Although Jones had high ideals for drama, he was not an original thinker. He aroused suspense and titillation without giving any significant new insights.

Arthur Wing Pinero (1855–1934) began his career in 1874 as an actor and turned to writing in 1877. His first major success came with a farce, *The Magistrate* (1885), a form in which he excelled. Although Pinero never professed interest in a "drama of ideas," it was his *The Second Mrs. Tanqueray* (1893), the story of a "woman with a past," which brought the first change in public attitudes, for when it proved a popular hit, producers began to look more favorably upon "Ibsenesque" drama. Pinero continued to write for another thirty years,

turning out such successful plays as *The Notorious Mrs. Ebbsmith* (1895), *Iris* (1901), and *Mid-Channel* (1909), but his popularity declined steadily after 1910.

While Jones and Pinero paved the way for public acceptance, the development of a more significant drama owes most to Ibsen. By 1880, William Archer and others had begun to translate Ibsen's plays and by 1890 all those then written were available in English. In 1889, Janet Achurch (1864–1916) presented *A Doll's House,* the first unadapted version of a play by Ibsen seen in England. Miss Achurch was to be one of the new drama's most ardent champions, appearing in many plays by Ibsen, Shaw, and others. Her production of *A Doll's House* reminded critics of how far behind the continent English drama had fallen and supplied one of the motivations for founding the Independent Theatre.

Modeled on the Théâtre Libre and the Freie Bühne, the Independent Theatre was headed by J. T. Grein (1862–1935), a Dutch-born critic who had lived in London for many years. Like its predecessors on the continent, the Independent Theatre was organized on a subscription basis to avoid censorship, and like the Freie Bühne it gave its productions on Sundays in order to gain the cooperation of theatre managers and actors. The opening play in 1891, *Ghosts,* prompted more than 500 articles, most of them vituperative. The second program, Zola's *Thérèse Raquin,* created almost as great a storm. This publicity began to make the general public aware of the new drama for the first time.

Between 1891 and 1897, the Independent Theatre presented twenty-six plays, mostly translations. It did little in the way of mounting the plays. Thus, like the Freie Bühne, it served primarily as a rejuvenator of drama rather than as an influence upon production. Grein had hoped to produce new English plays, for he was convinced that the low state of English drama was attributable to the conservatism of producers. He soon found, however, that no significant plays were available. His disappointment prompted Shaw to complete *Widower's Houses,* the production of which in 1892 launched Shaw's career as a dramatist.

George Bernard Shaw (1856–1950), previously a novelist and critic, wrote regularly for the theatre from 1892 until his death. Unlike most of the new writers, who tended to be gloomy and intensely serious as a reaction against the shallowness of their predecessors, Shaw wrote primarily in the comic form. This choice may be explained in part by Shaw's interest in persuasion, which was best served by having characters

FIGURE 16.7 Shaw's *Caesar and Cleopatra* at the Savoy Theatre, London, 1907, under the management of Vedrenne and Barker. Forbes Robertson as Caesar, Gertrude Elliott as Cleopatra. From *Play Pictorial*, vol. 10 (1907).

Although Shaw is related to the realistic movement through his concern for ideas and social problems, he differed markedly from most of the writers of this school. While acknowledging the importance of heredity and environment, Shaw always implies that man had freedom of choice. Furthermore, although his characters often speak in dialect, they are always articulate and seldom follow closely the patterns of everyday speech. Shaw was not objective, for he chose his characters and invented his stories to illustrate a point of view. His comic method eventually won a wide audience for the drama of ideas.

Shaw was not immediately successful, however, for at first his unconventional ideas and paradoxical situations only puzzled or irritated audiences. His reputation was built slowly through the efforts of organizations which succeeded the Independent Theatre. The first of these was the Incorporated Stage Society, founded

FIGURE 16.8 Shaw's *Mrs. Warren's Profession* in its original English production, a private performance by the Incorporated Stage Society in 1902. Granville Barker is seen at the left. Courtesy Enthoven Collection, Victoria and Albert Museum.

arrive at perceptions that remove the barriers to a happy resolution. Shaw also delighted in using paradoxes to make both characters and audiences reassess their values. Thus, *Arms and the Man* (1894) punctures romantic notions about love and war, while *Major Barbara* (1905) upholds a munitions manufacturer as a greater humanitarian than an officer in the Salvation Army, because the Salvation Army prolongs an inequitable system by caring for victims whereas the manufacturer provides his workers with the means whereby to better themselves. Many of Shaw's plays, notably *The Doctor's Dilemma* (1906) and *Getting Married* (1908), are essentially extended discussions of specific problems. Other works, such as *Man and Superman* (1901) and *Back to Methuselah* (1919–1921), show Shaw's interest in "creative evolution" and the "life force," which he believed were striving to create a "superman" by working through superior individuals. In still other plays, as in *Caesar and Cleopatra* (1899) and *Saint Joan* (1923), Shaw sought to correct popular misconceptions of historical figures and events. Perhaps his least characteristic work is *Heartbreak House* (1914–1919), a parable about the failures of Europe at the time of the First World War. Shaw labeled it a play in the Chekhovian manner, perhaps to indicate its difference from his other works.

in 1899 to present modern plays. At first its programs were given on Sunday afternoons but, as its membership grew from the original 300 to 1,500 by 1914, it added Monday matinees as well. By the time the group disbanded in 1939 it had presented about 200 works, many of which would otherwise not have been seen. It served as an experimental theatre which kept the English theatrical world abreast of the latest movements both at home and abroad.

The most significant company in this period was that at the Court Theatre, where between 1904 and 1907 Harley Granville Barker (1877–1946) and John Vedrenne (1863–1930) gave the new drama its first full hearing in a public theatre. Barker had begun his career as an actor in 1891, had worked with several organizations, including the Incorporated Stage Society, and had established himself as a dramatist before being invited to assist Vedrenne with a production of *Two Gentlemen of Verona.* This beginning soon developed into a permanent arrangement, under which one play was offered each evening for several weeks while another little-known or seldom-performed work was given at matinees. If the matinees engendered enough enthusiasm, the play was moved to evening performances. Even successes, however, were not played consecutively for more than a few weeks. Between 1904 and 1907, the Court presented thirty-two plays by seventeen different authors, including Euripides, Hauptmann, Ibsen, Galsworthy, and Yeats. The mainstay of the theatre, however, was Shaw, eleven of whose plays were presented in productions directed by Shaw himself. These productions established Shaw's popularity with the British public.

The Court made other important contributions. It was noted for ensemble acting by a company which included some of the best actors of the period: Lillah McCarthy, Edith Wynne Matthison, Louis Calvert, Lewis Casson, and Godfrey Tearle. There were no stars. Since Barker believed that it is the director's primary task to give a thoughtful interpretation of the playwright's script, he sought to find in each work the style suited to it. Nevertheless, the dominant style of the Court productions was a subtle realism which avoided bravura. Simplicity and suggestion were the keynotes of both the acting and scenery. In 1907, Barker and Vedrenne moved to the Savoy Theatre, but closed after one season because of lack of attendance and trouble with the censor. When Charles Frohman established a repertory company at the Duke of York's Theatre in 1910, he employed Barker to head it. After presenting seventeen plays in seventeen weeks and incurring a sizable deficit, Barker resigned.

In spite of these failures, the Barker-Vedrenne experiments engendered several imitators, especially in the provinces, where repertory companies began to be opened once more. The first important company was established by Miss A. E. F. Horniman (1860–1937) in 1907 in Manchester. Until it was discontinued in 1921 this was to be one of the best theatres in England, offering a wide variety of English and continental plays. Its encouragement of local writers gave rise to the "Lancashire School," of which Stanley Houghton (1881–1913), author of *Hindle Wakes* (1912), and Harold Brighouse (1883–1958), author of *Hobson's Choice* (1916), were the most important. Other vigorous repertory companies were founded at Liverpool in 1911 and at Birmingham in 1913. The Birmingham Repertory Company, under the direction of Barry Jackson (1879–1961), was to be especially influential after the First World War.

In addition to Shaw, a number of other dramatists in the realistic vein appeared after 1900. John Galsworthy (1867–1933), already one of England's most successful novelists, turned to playwriting in 1906 with *The Silver Box,* in which the justice meted out to a poor and a rich man for the same crime is contrasted. His later plays, *Strife* (1909), *Justice* (1910), and *Loyalties* (1922), were in the same vein. All are objective treatments of social problems and demonstrate Galsworthy's considerable gift for creating dramatic dialogue and clear-cut conflicts. Harley Granville Barker won fame as a dramatist with such plays as *The Marrying of Ann Leete* (1902), *The Voysey Inyeritance* (1905), *Waste* (1907), and *Madras House* (1910). Similar to Shaw in his interests, Barker lacked Shaw's sense of the comic, and his discussions now seem cold and deficient in intensity. St. John Hankin (1869–1909) was the most gloomy dramatist of the period. In such works as *The Return of the Prodigal* (1905) and *The Last of the DeMullins* (1908), he attacked abuses but offered no alternatives to the conditions depicted.

THE CONTINUING TRADITION IN ENGLAND, 1900–1914

Despite these "modern" trends, pictorial realism continued to be the principal goal in England until the First World War. Furthermore, most of the major figures of the London stage between 1900 and 1914 had been trained in the Bancroft-Irving tradition, and they made few innovations. Of the actor-managers, the most important were John Hare, the Kendals, Forbes-Robertson, Martin-Harvey, Wyndham, and Tree.

John Hare (1844–1921) had won a considerable following before he left the Bancrofts in 1875 to manage the Court Theatre. In partnership with the Kendals, he managed St. James' Theatre from 1879 to 1888, when he moved to the Garrick. He retired in 1911. Hare was considered one of London's most versatile actors and most careful managers.

Madge Kendal (1848–1935), Robertson's sister, and her husband William Hunter Kendal (1843–1917) played for the Bancrofts and Hare before entering management in 1879. They retired in 1908. Mrs. Kendal was noted for her technical skill and subtle playing in the Bancroft tradition. Both were considered models of personal and professional behavior.

Johnston Forbes-Robertson (1853–1937) differed from most of the major actors of his day in being an excellent speaker of verse, an art which he had learned from Samuel Phelps. On the stage from 1874 until 1913, Forbes-Robertson acted with Phelps, the Bancrofts, and Irving. He also served as leading man to Helena Modjeska (1844–1909), the Polish actress who appeared with great success in England and America between 1877 and 1905, and to Mary Anderson (1859–1940), an American actress who won fame in England between 1883 and 1889 for her Shakespearean performances. Occasionally Forbes-Robertson undertook management, but his reputation rested primarily upon his acting. Some critics (including Shaw, who wrote *Caesar and Cleopatra* for him) consider him the finest Hamlet of all time.

John Martin-Harvey (1863–1944) made his debut in 1881 and after 1882 played for Irving, whom he succeeded as manager of the Lyceum Theatre. In his first independent production, an adaptation of Dickens' *A Tale of Two Cities,* he won such popularity that he was condemned to play the role of Sidney Carton through most of his remaining career. He gained new fame in 1912 for his performance in Reinhardt's London production of *Oedipus Rex.* Until about 1910, Martin-Harvey continued Irving's practices, but gradually accepted modern trends and after the First World War abandoned pictorial realism altogether. More than any other producer, he successfully bridged the Victorian and the modern stage.

FIGURE 16.9 Beerbohm Tree's production of Shakespeare's *A Midsummer Night's Dream* at Her Majesty's Theatre, London, 1900. Oberon stands in front of the tree center; Titania is at left surrounded by fairies. Courtesy Enthoven Collection, Victoria and Albert Museum.

Charles Wyndham (1837–1919) became an actor in 1862 but did not achieve success until he opened the Criterion Theatre in 1874. He made this theatre and those which he later acquired—Wyndham's (1889) and the New Theatre (1903)—famous for light drama. His productions were considered impeccable. Wyndham is also credited with replacing the short handbill with the modern theatre program.

The most famous actor-manager between 1900 and 1914 was Herbert Beerbohm Tree (1853–1917). On the stage from 1878, he assumed the management of the Haymarket in 1887. From the profits made there on melodramas and light contemporary plays he built Her Majesty's Theatre in 1897. Although he had had little previous experience with Shakespearean drama, Tree's new theatre was to be the principal home of Shakespeare in London between 1900 and 1914. Tree continued, and even extended, the trend toward actualistic detail. His *A Midsummer Night's Dream* in

1900 featured live rabbits and a carpet of grass with flowers that could be plucked; although the scene changes added forty-five minutes to the playing time, the production's literal realism attracted more than 220,000 spectators, perhaps the largest number ever to witness any Shakespearean play in London. Beginning in 1905, Tree annually held a festival of Shakespeare's plays in which many other companies took part.

Although not a very good actor, Tree often starred in his own productions. On the other hand, he employed the best performers available, and he worked on every production with unbounded enthusiasm. As the repertory system declined, Tree became concerned about the lack of effective training for young actors, and in 1904 he established the acting school which was to become the Royal Academy of Dramatic Art, still the most prestigious in England.

Following the outbreak of the war in 1914, Tree gave up his theatre. Before the hostilities ended, he was dead. With him died much of English tradition, for after the war the actor-manager system, the dominant type of organization since 1700, was largely abandoned, and pictorial realism, long the standard of perfection, had come to seem old-fashioned.

THE MOSCOW ART THEATRE AND REALISM IN RUSSIA

Russia also had to await the "independent theatre" movement before needed reforms were to come. Although such Russian dramatists as Turgenev, Ostrovsky, and Pisemsky had already inaugurated a realistic school of writing, theatrical production still preserved conventions inherited from the eighteenth century, and the visit of the Meiningen Players in 1885 and 1890 had revealed to many Russian producers how far behind they were. Little significant progress was made, however, until the formation of the Moscow Art Theatre by Konstantin Stanislavsky (1863–1938) and Vladimir Nemirovich-Danchenko (1858–1943) in 1898.

The Moscow Art Theatre differed from the other independent theatres in being a fully professional organization from the beginning and in emphasizing theatrical production reather than neglected plays. Its first program, Alexei Tolstoy's *Tsar Feodor Ivanovich*, created a sensation because of its painstaking recreation of the

FIGURE 16.10 Act I of Chekhov's *The Sea Gull* at the Moscow Art Theatre, 1898. Setting by V. A. Simov. From *Moscow Art Theatre, 1898–1917* (Moscow, 1955).

Russia of 1600, its ensemble acting, and its absence of stars. Public interest waned, however, until the production of Chekhov's *The Sea Gull* established the originality of both the author and the company.

Anton Chekhov (1860–1904) began his dramatic career with vaudeville sketches and short plays in the comic-pathetic vein and then went on to long plays. When *The Sea Gull* (1896) was performed at the Alexandrinsky Theatre in St. Petersburg, it was a failure because the actors did not understand their roles and had not learned their lines. As a result, Chekhov was determined to give up playwriting. After reluctantly permitting the Moscow Art Theatre to perform *The Sea Gull*, he went on to provide it with three other plays: *Uncle Vanya* (1899), *The Three Sisters* (1901), and *The Cherry Orchard* (1904). Chekhov's reputation rests primarily upon these four plays.

Each of Chekhov's four major plays is set in rural Russia and depicts the monotonous and frustrating life of the landowning class. All of the characters aspire to a better life, but none knows how, or has the initiative, to achieve his goals. The plays are built upon infinite detail, the connection among which is not always obvious. Yet gradually a unifying mood, clearly delineated characters, and a complete and simple action emerge. The absence of startling climaxes, strong suspense, and clear purpose has caused many readers to misunderstand the plays, which require detailed study and attention to nuance if the pattern behind the surface is to become clear.

The methods of the Moscow Art Theatre were well adapted to the demands of Chekhov's plays. Stanislavsky always undertook a long study of each play before rehearsals began. He insisted upon careful attention to detail from each actor, and he sought to recreate the milieu only after visiting the site of the play's action, or after extensive research.

Despite its success with *The Sea Gull*, the Moscow Art Theatre ended its first season in debt and was saved only by the generosity of patrons. With the new support, it was able in 1902 to build its own theatre, with workshops and such up-to-date equipment as a revolving stage. It increased its acting company from 39 to 100 members. Thereafter, it staged from three to five new plays each year, while keeping successful works in the repertory. The influence of the Moscow Art Theatre was soon felt throughout Russia, and by 1906 it was sufficiently well known abroad that it undertook a foreign tour.

Stanislavsky is now remembered above all for his attempts to perfect a method of acting. He became fully aware of the need in 1906 and made the first outline of his ideas in 1909, but he did not set down his system in writing until he published *My Life in Art* (1924) and *An Actor Prepares* (1936). The entire plan was not available outside of Russia until the appearance of *Building a Character* (1949) and *Creating a Role* (1961). Because of this piecemeal publication, the ambiguities in the theory, and the many changes made by Stanislavsky as he refined upon the method, many conflicting interpretations of "the Stanislavsky system" have arisen.

Although no summary is entirely acceptable to all of Stanislavsky's admirers and critics, the system includes the following principles. (1) The actor's body and voice should be thoroughly trained so they may respond efficiently to all demands. (2) The actor should be schooled in stage techniques, since he must be able to project his characterization to an audience without any sense of contrivance. (3) The actor should be a skilled observer of reality, out of which he builds his role. (4) The actor should seek an inner justification for everything he does on stage. In doing so, he depends in part upon "the magic 'if'" (that is, the actor says, "If I were this person faced with this situation, I would . . ") and "emotion mem-

ory" (a process by which the actor relates the unfamiliar dramatic situation to some analogous emotional situation in his own life). (5) If the actor is not merely to play himself, he must undertake a thorough analysis of the script and work within the "given circumstances" found there. He must define his character's motivations in each scene, in the play as a whole, and his relationship to each of the other roles. The character's primary "objective" becomes the "through line" of the role, around which everything else revolves. (6) On stage, the actor must focus his attention upon the action as it unfolds moment by moment. Such concentration will lead to the "illusion of the first time" and will guide the actor in subordinating his ego to the artistic demands of the production. (7) An actor must continue to work to perfect himself as an instrument.

Various aspects of this method have been emphasized by different interpreters. Taken as a whole, it is an attempt to analyze each phase of the actor's work and to make it as efficient as possible. Stanislavsky was never fully satisfied with his system and he continued to refine it up to the time of his death. He also cautioned others against adopting it without making changes required by different artistic needs and cultural backgrounds.

Although the Moscow Art Theatre had no stars, a number of outstanding actors came to the fore. In addition to Stanislavsky, these included Moskvin, Kachalov, and Knipper. Ivan Moskvin (1874–1946), a small man, was best suited to self-effacing characters such as Epikhodov in *The Cherry Orchard*. His was the art of understatement in which a few subtle touches brought out the emotional values of a scene. Vassily Kachalov (1875–1948), a tall, handsome man with a beautiful voice, was at his best in the roles of romantic heroes, rebels, or intellectuals. Olga Knipper (1870–1959), Chekhov's wife, played a wide variety of roles, but was best known as Madame Ranevskaya of *The Cherry Orchard*.

In addition to Chekhov, the Moscow Art Theatre also encouraged Maxim Gorky (1868–1936), already famous as a writer of realistic stories. *The Lower Depths* (1902), set in a flophouse and featuring a collection of characters defeated by life, became one of the troupe's greatest successes. Other plays include *Summer Folk* (1904) and *Enemies* (1907). Gorky was much involved in the political struggles of the day, including the Revolution of 1905, which though largely unsuccessful won a small measure of representational government. Gorky's activities caused him to be exiled, but his reputation

as a champion of the proletariat would later give him
enormous influence among the Soviets.

THE REVIVAL OF IDEALISM IN FRANCE

The realistic and naturalistic outlook did not go unchallenged. Although the intellectual climate between 1850
and 1900 was largely anti-idealistic, the sweeping claims
made for science at this time brought several protests.
The most significant of these came from the symbolists,
who launched their counterattack in 1885 in a "manifesto." Taking its inspiration from the works of Edgar
Allan Poe, Baudelaire's poems and criticism, Dostoev-
sky's novels, and Wagner's music and theory, symbolism
attracted representatives from all the arts. To the symbolists, subjectivity, spirituality, and mysterious internal
and external forces represented a higher form of truth
than that to be derived from the mere observance of
outward appearance. This deeper significance, they
argued, cannot be represented directly but can only be
evoked through symbols, legends, myths, and moods.
The principal spokesman for the movement was Stephane
Mallarmé (1842–1898), whose views of drama—as an
evocation of the mystery of existence through poetic
and allusive language, performed with only the most
essential and atmospherically appropriate theatrical aids,
for the purpose of creating a quasi-religious experience—
set the tone for the antirealistic works of the 1890s.

     As with naturalism, symbolism made no marked
impression in the theatre until an "independent" group,
modeled on the Théâtre Libre appeared. In 1890, Paul
Fort (1872–1962), a seventeen-year-old poet, founded
the Théâtre d'Art, where by 1892 he had presented works
by forty-six authors, ranging from readings of poems and
adaptations of portions of the *Iliad* and the Bible to
modern plays. Most of the programs were given only
one performance, and the actors, primarily amateurs,
were often inadequate. Unlike Antoine, Fort received
predominantly hostile critical notices, perhaps because
his productions seemed incomprehensible to those ac-
customed to illusionism.

     When Fort left the theatre in 1892, his work was
carried on by the Théâtre de l'Oeuvre, headed by Auré-
lien-Marie Lugné-Poë (1869–1940). An actor and stage
manager at the Théâtre Libre for a time, Lugné-Poë was
converted to the idealist outlook after seeing and ap-

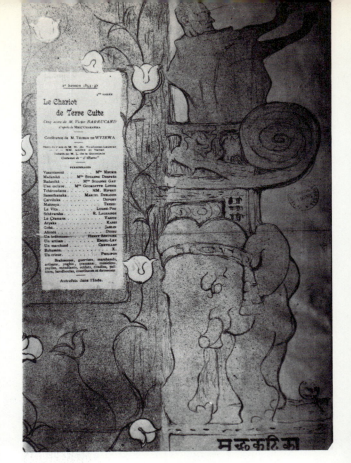

**FIGURE 16.11 Program for *The Little Clay Cart*,
an adaptation of the Sanskrit drama by Victor Bar-
racund for Lugné-Poë's Théâtre de l'Oeuvre in the
season of 1894–1895. The program and some of
settings were designed by Toulouse-Lautrec. Courtesy Bibliothèque de l'Arsenal, Paris.**

pearing in some of the productions at the Théâtre d'Art
and while sharing an apartment with the painters Edouard
Vuillard, Maurice Denis, and Pierre Bonnard. The
Théâtre de l'Oeuvre gave its first performance in 1893.
From that time until 1897 Lugné-Poë used a similar style
for virtually all of his productions. Guided by the motto
"the word creates the decor," he reduced scenery to simple compositions of lines and color painted on backdrops.
Using settings by Toulouse-Lautrec, Denis, Vuillard,
Bonnard, Odilon Redon and others, Lugné-Poë sought
to create a unity of style and mood rather than of milieu.

     The opening production, *Pelléas and Mélisande*,
was typical. No properties or furniture were used; the
stage was lighted from overhead and most of the action
passed in semidarkness; a gauze curtain, hung between
the actors and the audience, gave the impression that

mist enveloped the stage; backdrops, painted in grayed tones, emphasized the air of mystery; costumes were vaguely medieval, although the intention was to create draperies of no particular period. The actors spoke in a staccato chant like priests and, according to some critics, behaved like sleepwalkers; their gestures were strongly stylized. Given this radically new approach, it is not surprising that many spectators were mystified.

Lugné-Poë's repertory was made up primarily of French plays but with these he mingled some works by Ibsen, Hauptmann, Sanskirt dramatists, and others. Of the French dramas, those by Maeterlinck were the best. Maurice Maeterlinck (1862–1949), after coming to Paris from Belgium, turned to playwriting in 1889 and by 1896 had written *The Intruder* (1890), *The Blind* (1890), and *The Death of Tintagiles* (1894). Of his early work, the best known is *Pelléas and Mélisande* (1892), in which a young woman, after marrying a prince who has found her in a forest, falls in love with his brother and dies of grief. The interest does not reside in the triangular relationship, however, but in the mood of mystery which envelops it and which is evoked through a multitude of symbols, such as a wedding ring dropped into a fountain, doves that fly away from a tower, subterranean pools and grottoes, enveloping shadows, and blood stains that cannot be washed away. In the early 1890s, Maeterlinck argued that the most dramatic moments are those silent ones during which the mystery of existence, ordinarily obscured by bustling activity, makes itself felt. After 1896, Maeterlinck revised his view and modified his style to include more straightforward action. The most famous of his later plays is *The Blue Bird* (1908), an allegory about the search for happiness.

In 1896 Lugné-Poë presented Alfred Jarry's (1873–1907) *Ubu Roi*, sometimes called the first absurdist drama. Jarry's play is related to symbolist works in being antirealistic but its moral topsyturvydom more nearly resembles that of the naturalists' *comédies rosses*, although it completely avoids their scientific bias and realistic techniques. *Ubu Roi* shows in all its grotesqueness a world without human decency. Its central figure, Ubu, is violent, stupid, totally devoid of moral scruple; he is the epitome of all that Jarry found inane and ugly in bourgeois society, of all that is monstrous and irrational in man. The action of the play shows how Ubu makes himself king of Poland and keeps his power by killing and torturing all those who oppose him; eventually he is driven from the country but he promises to continue his

FIGURE 16.12   Jarry's *Ubu Roi* at the Théâtre Antoine, 1908. Gémier directed the play and appeared as Père Ubu. From *Figaro* (16 February 1908).

exploits elsewhere. Jarry wrote two other plays about Ubu, *Ubu Bound* (1900) and *Ubu the Cuckold* (published 1944), but these were not produced during his lifetime. At first Jarry's influence was negligible, but in the 1920s he attracted a following among the surrealists and since World War II his grotesque vision of man has won him a place of honor as a major prophet of the absurdist movement.

The first major phase of the antirealistic movement came to an end in 1897 when Lugné-Poë broke with the symbolists after concluding that most of their plays were immature and that his commitment to a single style of production was too limiting. His decision was influenced by his admiration for Ibsen, whose plays he found unadaptable to the extreme stylization favored by the symbolists.

The Théâtre de l'Oeuvre closed in 1899, but Lugné-Poë was to revive it in 1912 and again after the First World War and to continue his work there until 1929. Nevertheless, it is his symbolist productions of the 1890s that constitute his most significant contribution to the theatre. Through tours with his company and articles written about his work, Lugné-Poë influenced almost every departure from realism between 1893 and 1915.

FIGURE 16.13 Design by Adolphe Appia for the sacred forest in Wagner's *Parsifal*, 1896.

APPIA AND CRAIG

At about the time that Lugné-Poë was closing down the Théâtre de l'Oeùvre in 1899, two other men, Appia and Craig, working independently of each other, were beginning to lay the theoretical foundations of modern non-illusionistic theatrical practice. Adolphe Appia (1862–1928), born in Switzerland, first came into contact with the theatre through his musical studies. Deeply impressed by Wagner's music-dramas and theoretical writings, Appia recognized that the usual mounting of the operas did not properly embody Wagner's theories. After years of thought, he published *The Staging of Wagner's Musical Dramas* (1895), *Music and Stage Setting* (1899), and *The Work of Living Art* (1921). In these, he set forth ideas about theatrical production that were eventually accepted almost universally.

Beginning with the assumption that artistic unity is the fundamental goal of theatrical production, Appia sought to analyze failures to achieve it. He concluded that stage presentation involves three conflicting visual elements: the moving three-dimensional actor; the perpendicular scenery; and the horizontal floor. In painted two-dimensional settings he found one of the major causes of disunity and recommended that they be re-placed with three-dimensional units (steps, ramps, platforms) that enhance the actor's movement and blend the horizontal floor with the upright scenery. Above all, however, Appia emphasized the role of light in fusing all of the visual elements into a unified whole. Since to him light was the visual counterpart of music, which changes from moment to moment in response to shifting moods, emotions, and action, Appia wished to orchestrate and manipulate light as carefully as a musical score. Attempts to implement this theory, which require control over the distribution, brightness, and color of light, have led to much of modern stage-lighting practice. Appia also argued that artistic unity requires that one person control all of the elements of production. Thus, his ideas strengthened the role of the director.

In 1906 Appia met Emile Jacques Dalcroze (1865–1960), who, next to Wagner, was to be the greatest influence on Appia's work. Dalcroze was the inventor of "eurythmics," a system under which students were led to experience music kinesthetically by responding physically to the rhythms of musical compositions. Under Dalcroze's influence Appia came to believe that the rhythm embedded in a text provides the key to every gesture and movement to be used on the stage and that the proper mastery of rhythm will unify all the spatial and temporal elements of a production into a satisfying and harmonious whole. Appia worked with Dalcroze on a few productions at Dalcroze's school at Hellerau, and for this school Appia designed the first theatre of modern times to be built without a proscenium arch and with a completely open stage.

In the 1920s Appia began to win his long-delayed recognition. In 1923 he staged *Tristan and Isolde* in Milan and in 1924–1925 two parts of the *Ring* cycle in Basel. Nevertheless, it was not through practice but through theory that Appia was to exert lasting influence on the modern theatre.

Gordon Craig (1872–1966), son of Ellen Terry and Edward Godwin, began his career as an actor in Irving's company. His first important experience as a designer was gained in his mother's company at the Imperial Theatre in London in 1903. An exhibit of his work in 1902 and the publication of his book, *The Art of the Theatre* (1905), created such controversy that within a few years he was well known throughout Europe. In 1904, he designed a play for Brahm in Berlin, in 1906 one for Eleanora Duse in Florence, and in 1912 one for the Moscow Art Theatre. Everywhere controversy followed him. He continued to set forth his provocative

FIGURE 16.14 Craig's setting for *Hamlet* at the Moscow Art Theatre, 1912. The screens were supposed to be sufficiently mobile that the appearance of the setting could be changed quickly and without closing the front curtain. Unfortunately they never functioned as envisioned. From *Moscow Art Theatre, 1898–1917,* Moscow (1955).

and original ideas in *On the Art of the Theatre* (1911), *Towards a New Theatre* (1913), *The Theatre Advancing* (1919), and *The Mask,* a periodical issued sporadically between 1908 and 1929. In 1908 he settled in Florence, where he ran a school for a time. Although Appia had set forth many of the same ideas, it was Craig who publicized them. To many conservative producers, Craig seemed as dangerous "a crank" as Ibsen had in the 1880s.

Craig thought of the theatre as an independent art and argued that the true theatre artist welds action, words, line, color, and rhythm into a product as pure as that of the painter, sculptor, or composer. He acknowledged the kind of theatre in which a craftsman-director, beginning with a literary text, coordinates the work of several other craftsmen, but he sought a higher form in which the master-artist, without the medium of a literary text, would create every part of a wholly autonomous art.

Craig's influence was felt most heavily in design, perhaps because he conceived of the theatre primarily in visual terms. He argued that the public goes to see rather than to hear a play. His own drawings show a marked predilection for right angles and almost an obsession with parallelism. Their most notable feature, however, is height and the resulting sense of grandeur.

Perhaps Craig's favorite project was the mobile setting. Throughout most of his life he experimented with screens, out of which he hoped to create a setting which, by invisible means, could move in ways analogous to the actor and to light.

Craig always refused to assign a hierarchy to the theatrical elements and blamed many faults of the past on the dominance of one or another part. Thus, he often denounced the dramatist, upon whom he blamed the overemphasis upon the spoken word. Similarly, he often blamed starring actors for the low state of the theatre, since they sought to aggrandize themselves and to interject their own conceptions between those of the director and the public. Consequently, he once suggested that ideally the master artist should use an *Ubermarionette,* a superpuppet without any ego but capable of carrying out all demands. No idea voiced by Craig aroused a greater storm.

Although Appia and Craig arrived at many of the same ideas, there were also important differences. Appia's

FIGURE 16.15 Design by Gordon Craig for *Electra,* 1905. From City of Manchester Art Gallery, *Exhibition of Drawings and Models by Edward Gordon Craig* (1912).

artist was to be primarily an interpreter of the composer-dramatist's work; Craig's was a full-fledged artist in his own right. Appia assigned a hierarchy to the theatrical elements; Craig refused to do so. Appia thought in terms of successive settings (a different setting for each locale); Craig sought a single setting capable of expressing the spirit of the entire work or of reflecting changes through mobility.

Appia and Craig were often denounced as impractical men who knew little of the workaday theatre and whose ideas were useless in practice. But they championed ideals and goals that practical men of the period could not provide. Together they forced their contemporaries to reconsider the nature of the theatre as an art, its function in society, and its elements (both separately and in combination). They influenced the trend toward simplified decor, three-dimensional settings, plasticity, and directional lighting—toward evocation rather than literal representation. At first highly controversial, their theories were to prevail after World War I.

STRINDBERG AND FREUD

The first decade of the twentieth century also brought works of another type that were to be a major influence on modern drama: the nonrealistic plays of the Swedish dramatist, August Strindberg (1849–1912). Strindberg had already established his reputation as a realistic dramatist with *The Father* (1887) and *Miss Julie* (1888), both of which demonstrate his preoccupation with what he considered to be the elemental and inevitable conflict between men and women. *Miss Julie* especially won high praise for its emphasis upon heredity and environment, its unusual setting (a triangular view of one corner of a kitchen), and its use of pantomimes to replace intermissions. Many critics considered it an excellent exemplar of naturalistic principles.

Powerful as these plays are, they were not to be as influential as those Strindberg wrote after undergoing a bout with insanity during the 1890s. Partially because of his recent experiences and partially under Maeterlinck's influence, Strindberg now began to write "dream plays," of which he said: "The author has tried to imitate the disconnected but seemingly logical form of the dream. Anything may happen; everything is possible and probable. Time and space do not exist. On an insignificant background of reality, imagination designs and embroiders novel patterns, free fancies, absurdities and improvisations. The characters split, double, multiply, vanish, solidify, blur, clarify. But one consciousness reigns above them all—that of the dreamer; and before it there are no secrets, no incongruities, no scruples, no laws." In such plays as *To Damascus* (a trilogy, 1898–1901) and *The Dream Play* (1902), Strindberg reshaped reality according to his own subjective vision. Time and place shift frequently and without regard for logical sequence, the real and the imaginary blend, and the seemingly commonplace is invested with a sense of significance. In these late works, Strindberg treats with great compassion alienated man, lost and rootless, seeking meaning in an incomprehensible universe, trying to reconcile the most disparate elements: lust and love, body and spirit, filth and beauty.

From 1907 to 1910, Strindberg was associated with August Falck (1882–1938), an actor and producer, at the Intimate Theatre in Stockholm. Seating only 161, this theatre was intended as a home for Strindberg's plays, and for it he wrote five "chamber plays," of which the best known is *The Ghost Sonata* (1907), a work which echoes many of the ideas found in *The Dream Play*.

By the time Strindberg died in 1912 he was one of the most famous writers in the world. Although his plays have never been widely popular in the theatre, they have never ceased to be a source of controversy and inspiration. His vision of man as tortured and alienated was to attract many later writers, and his technical devices were to show others how psychological states and spiritual intuitions might be externalized. As the first dramatist to make extensive use of the unconscious, he was to be a major influence on subsequent playwrights.

Strindberg's acceptance was probably aided by widespread interest in the psychoanalytic theories of Sigmund Freud (1856–1939), who in such books as *The Interpretation of Dreams* (1900) and *Three Contributions to the Theory of Sex* (1905) sought to analyze the structure of the mind, to describe its functionings, and to suggest means for dealing with abnormal behavior. Freud's explanation of human behavior, with its emphasis upon the unconscious mind, dreams as a key to understanding suppressed desires, and the human propensity for telescoping experience, gave strong authority for Strindberg's dramaturgy. Furthermore, just as Comte, Zola, and others had placed primary emphasis upon social environment as a determinant of human behavior, Freud turned attention toward equally powerful psychological causes. His interest in aggression and sexual drives as keys to human behavior also did much to break down taboos about suitable subjects for drama.

Freud's pervasive influence on modern drama is also explained in part by his quasi-scientific explanation of behavior that in idealist drama had been attributed to "the mystery of fate," "intuition," or other equally vague and subjective concepts. By locating the source within the human mind, Freud made it possible for realistic dramatists to portray behavior previously considered irrational because it had no verifiable basis. Freud's conception of reality which intermingles the rational and irrational, the conscious and unconscious, the objective and subjective, the real and the fantastic, was to break down many of the barriers between realistic and nonrealistic drama.

IDEALIST THEATRE AND DRAMA IN GERMANY

In Germany, a number of dramatists, most notably Hauptmann and Sudermann, eventually were to write alternately in realistic and nonrealistic styles. But others, among them Hofmannsthal and Wedekind, fall more clearly into the antirealist camp. Hugo von Hofmannsthal (1874–1929) is usually considered an exponent of neo-romanticism, a movement which in Germany roughly parallels symbolism in France. His early plays are mostly short, as in *The Fool and Death* (1893) and *The Adventurer and the Singing Girl* (1899), and written in a verse that led many critics to praise him as the finest poet since Goethe. Around 1900 he underwent a crisis during which he came to believe that words are meaningless. Although he moved beyond this belief, he thereafter reworked existing materials, as in *Elektra* (1903), *Everyman* (1912), and *The Great World Theatre* (1922), or wrote opera librettos, such as *Die Rosenkavalier* (1911) and *Ariadne auf Naxos* (1912), in collaboration with Richard Strauss. Some of his plays continue to be mainstays of the Salzburg Festival.

Franz Wedekind (1864–1918) is more nearly related to Strindberg than to the French symbolists. After working as a journalist, publicist, and actor, Wedekind toured Germany in a repertory of his own plays, which were never widely appreciated during his lifetime. Wedekind's first important play, *Spring's Awakening* (1891), is the story of two adolescents' struggle with sexual awareness. One commits suicide, and the other is saved from a similar fate only by the mysterious "Man

FIGURE 16.16 Design by Julius Diez for Shakespeare's *Twelfth Night* at the Munich Art Theatre, 1908. Director Albert Heine. Courtesy Theatermuseum, Munich.

with the Mask." The play is interesting in part because of its intermingling of naturalism and symbolism, of brutal frankness and lyrical expression. Wedekind's interest in sexual themes continued in *Earth Spirit* (1895) and *Pandora's Box* (1904), both treating the same protagonist, Lulu, who cannot distinguish between lust and love; in the first play Lulu prospers, but in the second she gradually descends until she is murdered by Jack the Ripper. Many of Wedekind's other plays also show his preoccupation with sex, but in such late works as *Samson* (1914) and *Herakles* (1917) the treatment sometimes borders on lunacy. Wedekind's plays are of such uneven quality that it is difficult to judge them fairly. But after 1900 his reputation grew steadily and he exerted considerable influence on the expressionists, who were attracted both by his rebellion against conventional values and by his experiments with stylistic elements.

After 1900 German producers also came to be increasingly interested in nonrealistic staging. Some of the most important innovations were made at the Munich Art Theatre, founded in 1907 and headed by George Fuchs (1868–1949), a critic and theorist, with Fritz Erler (1868–1940), as designer. In two books, *The Theatre of the Future* (1905) and *Revolution in the Theatre* (1909), Fuchs expressed the need for a theatre to meet the needs

FIGURE 16.17 Design by K. Walser for Max Reinhardt's production of Wedekind's *Spring's Awakening* at the Kammerspiele, Berlin, 1906. This design is for Act III, scene 6. Courtesy the Max Reinhardt Archive, State University of New York, Binghamton.

of modern man and declared pictorial illusionism outmoded. Under the slogan "retheatricalize the theatre," he sought to unite all the arts in a new kind of expression.

For the project, Max Littmann (1862–1931) designed a theatre with an auditorium and sunken orchestra pit similar to those at Bayreuth. The stage, however, differed markedly from that at Bayreuth. The acting area could be extended into the auditorium by covering over the orchestra pit, while an adjustable inner proscenium, containing a door at stage level and a balcony above, made it possible to adjust the size of the stage opening. The stage floor was broken into sections, each of which was mounted on an elevator, permitting the floor to be arranged into levels. The stage was backed by four cycloramas, each of a different color, which could be changed electrically.

The most controversial aspect of the productions was the acting, which typically was confined to the plane outlined by the inner proscenium, while the area back of this plane was reserved for scenery or for crowd scenes.

The aim was to keep the performer close to the audience so as to establish a sense of community and to emphasize his plasticity by framing him against a simplified background.

Erler sometimes used the adjustable proscenium as the principal scenic element; sometimes he used it in combination with other pieces, but often he employed it merely as a frame for the area behind it. His effects were achieved primarily with simple forms, painted drops, and the play of colored light.

Like Appia and Craig, Fuchs believed that rhythm fuses all the elements of production. Unlike them, however, he placed the actor in front of the setting rather than within it and so tended to mute the three-dimensionality they so avidly sought. Still, as the work of the Munich Art Theatre became widely known, Fuchs' theories reenforced those of Appia and Craig and helped to establish the trend toward stylization in all theatrical elements.

Ultimately virtually all of the ideas and innovations—whether realistic or idealistic—introduced between 1875 and 1900 came together in the work of Max Reinhardt (1873–1943). On stage as an actor from the age of nineteen, Reinhardt was brought to the Deutsches Theater by Otto Brahm in 1894. While acting with Brahm's troupe, Reinhardt experimented with staging at a cabaret and developed a strong appreciation for its intimate atmosphere. His first experience as a producer was gained between 1902 and 1905 at the Kleines Theater, where he presented nearly 50 plays drawn from many countries and styles. His major work began in 1905, when he succeeded Brahm as director of the Deutsches Theater. In 1906, he opened the Kammerspiele, a small theatre, in conjunction with the larger house. The flexibility in programming and style of production which this arrangement permitted was to influence almost all state theatres in Germany and eventually the educational theatre in America.

Reinhardt's influence came in large part through his diversity. Unlike major producers who preceded him, almost all of whom had used the same style for every play they presented, Reinhardt believed that each play requires a different style. His eclecticism, therefore, reconciled many conflicting movements, for with him each style had its uses. With Reinhardt, each new production became a problem to be solved, not through the employment of proven formulas but through clues found within the work itself. Furthermore, his conception of theatrical style included the physical arrangement of the theatre and the spatial relationship of the audience to the performers. In his view, some plays required intimate surroundings, others large spaces; some needed a proscenium, others an open platform. For example, he staged *Oedipus Rex* in a circus, because this arrangement seemed most appropriate to the spirit of Greek tragedy. He was to extend such experiments with styles of production and theatre architecture after the First World War.

Reinhardt believed that the director must control every element of production. For each play he prepared a *Reigiebuch* (or promptbook) in which he recorded each detail of movement, setting, properties, sound, lighting, and costume. Some critics charge that Reinhardt's actors were mere puppets that he manipulated, while others maintain that Reinhardt was so sensitive that he knew exactly how to help each performer. In any case, Reinhardt worked closely with his actors to achieve performances world-famous for their stylistic excellence. Among his actors, the best known were Alexander Moissi

(1880–1935), noted especially for his Shakespearean and Greek roles; Max Pallenberg (1859–1934), a versatile comic actor; Albert Bassermann (1867–1952), famous for his performances in Ibsen's plays and later as an actor in American films; Werner Krauss (1884–1959); and Emil Jannings (1887–1950).

Reinhardt also worked closely with his scene designers, notably Ernst Stern (1876–1954), Alfred Roller (1864–1935), Oscar Strnad (1879–1935), and Emil Orlik (1879–1932). Often his productions centered around a motif, a ruling idea, or the staging conventions of a past period; they ranged through every style from naturalism to extreme stylization. Reinhardt has been accused of debasing the ideas of others, but he did more than anyone

FIGURE 16.18 Design by Ernst Stern for Reinhardt's production of Friedrich Freska's pantomime *Sumurun*, at the Kammerspiele, Berlin, 1910. Courtesy Harvard Theatre Collection.

FIGURE 16.19 John Martin-Harvey in the title role of Sophocles' *Oedipus Rex* as staged by Max Reinhardt at Covent Garden, London, 1912. Courtesy the Max Reinhardt Archive, State University of New York, Binghamton.

to make new movements and techniques acceptable to the general public.

THE NONREALISTIC THEATRE IN ENGLAND

In England, few playwrights departed markedly from the realistic mode. Oscar Wilde (1856–1900), a member of the "Art-for-Art's Sake" or "Aesthetic" movement which paralleled French symbolism, rejected the idea that drama should be utilitarian or that the popular audience is a suitable judge of merit. He suggested that life should seek to become a work of art rather than art imitating life. Nevertheless, of Wilde's plays only *Salomé* (1893), resembles French symbolist drama, although his phenom-

enally popular comedy, *The Importance of Being Earnest* (1895), illustrates his general outlook through its parody of the stock devices of comedy and its epigrams which puncture the conventional sentiments of his time. On the surface, *Lady Windermere's Fan* (1892), *A Woman of No Importance* (1893), and *An Ideal Husband* (1895) appear to be much like Pinero's social dramas, but a closer examination will show that Wilde deliberately lets the machinery of his plots show until the plays become near-parodies.

J. M. Barrie (1860–1937), after beginning as a journalist and novelist, turned to drama in 1892 and wrote regularly for the stage until 1936. Through all of his work shines an optimistic, whimsical view of life in which humor is infused with sentiment. His most successful play is *Peter Pan* (1904), a sentimental fantasy which romanticizes childhood and the child's view of reality. Other popular works by him include *The Admirable Crichton* (1902), *What Every Woman Knows* (1908) and *Dear Brutus* (1917).

While few English plays departed from the realistic mode, several innovations in staging were to lead away from illusionism. Many of these stemmed from interest in staging Shakespeare's works. An early step toward more simplified staging was taken by Frank Benson (1858–1939), who after acting with Irving, founded his own troupe in 1883 and continued to tour the prov-

FIGURE 16.20 J. M. Barrie's *Peter Pan*, the original production at the Duke of York's Theatre, 1904. Seen here is the pirate's ship. Courtesy Theatre Museum, Victoria and Albert Museum, London.

inces in a Shakespearean repertory until 1933. Benson produced almost all of the plays seen at the annual festival at Stratford-on-Avon (instituted in 1879) between 1886 and 1913, and after 1900 gave a few performances in London each year. Benson began by producing plays in the style of Irving, but by 1900 he had reduced the scenic background to a few stock settings and was placing primary emphasis upon the actors. Although his solution was at best a compromise, Benson helped to make simplified staging acceptable to the public.

A more drastic reform was sought by William Poel (1852–1934). After his debut as an actor in 1876, Poel worked for Benson and others before undertaking those experiments with staging Shakespeare's plays for which he is now remembered. In this work, Poel had, between 1894 and 1905, the support of the Elizabethan Stage Society, of which he was the guiding spirit.

In staging Elizabethan drama, Poel did not always use the same solution but he is now considered noteworthy almost entirely because of his attempts to reconstruct the Elizabethan public stage. He also popularized several conventions: dressing the actors in Elizabethan garments to reflect Shakespeare's own day rather than the historical epoch of the dramatic action; using costumed pages to draw the curtains of the inner stage and to arrange properties and furniture; and employing an on-stage audience to emphasize the audience-actor relationships of the Elizabethan era. But, above all, Poel desired continuity of action and lively pace. Although his productions did not generate much enthusiasm, they demonstrated the advantages of unbroken playing and of concentrating attention upon text and performers. Poel's approach represents another form of antiquarianism, one which sought to substitute the theatrical conditions of a past era for historical accuracy in the older sense. It is typical of similar approaches then being tried in several countries. At the Royal Court Theatre in Munich in 1889, Karl von Perfall and Jocza Savits had attempted to approximate the Elizabethan plan on a picture-frame stage by using a deep apron behind which a playing space was enclosed by an architectural facade with several doors and at center back a curtained inner stage where furniture and realistic scenic pieces could be set and revealed as needed. This and a similar attempt made in Munich in 1909–1910 by Julius Klein and Eugene Kilian differed little from the solution used in 1840 by Immermann. In a somewhat similar vein, Antoine staged a number of seventeenth-century French plays at the Odéon between 1907 and 1910 for which

FIGURE 16.21 Poel's production of *Measure for Measure* in 1893. Shown here is Act II, scene 2. Note the costumed spectators on either side of the stage. Courtesy Theatre Museum, Victoria and Albert Museum.

he sought to reproduce the playing conditions and conventions of the original productions.

Many of the earlier experiments in staging Shakespeare's plays were synthesized by Granville Barker in productions at the Savoy Theatre in London between 1912 and 1914 of *A Winter's Tale, Twelfth Night,* and *A Midsummer Night's Dream.* Barker, who had worked for Poel before going to the Court Theatre, amalgamated Poel's continuous staging with the visual simplicity advocated by Craig and others. He remodeled the Savoy Theatre by adding an apron and doors forward of the proscenium. Back of the proscenium the stage was divided into a main acting area and a modified inner stage, raised a few steps and equipped with curtains. This division of the stage into three parts allowed a continuous flow of action and eliminated the extensive cutting and rearrangement of the scripts usual in illusionistic staging. Barker employed such artists as Norman Wilkinson (1882–1934) and Albert Rutherston (1884–1953) to design scenery and costumes. Settings were composed primarily of painted, draped curtains, while the costumes were of no certain period. Such bright colors as magenta, scarlet, and lemon replaced the somber tones usual in Shakespearean productions. The forest of *A Midsummer Night's Dream* (presented in 1914) contained no three-dimensional trees; rather, it was suggested by painted drapery. Similarly, Titania's bower

FIGURE 16.22 Harley Granville Barker's production of *A Midsummer Night's Dream* at the Savoy Theatre, London, 1914. Note that the forest is represented by trees painted on draperies and that Titania's bower is formed of gauze hanging from a wreath. Courtesy Theatre Museum, Victoria and Albert Museum, London.

was made of gauze suspended from a crown of flowers. The fairies were gilded and directed to move like marionettes in order to set them off from the mortals. Although many conservative critics were deeply offended by Barker's productions, his approach set the tone for work that would be done after the war.

THE IRISH RENAISSANCE

Around 1900 Ireland began to assert its artistic independence from England. From the time of Henry VIII onward, England had ruled Ireland, although it had never been able to suppress Roman Catholicism or to command the full loyalty of the people. As elsewhere in Europe, in Ireland nationalistic sentiment became especially strong during the nineteenth century, and as a result its Gaelic and Celtic heritage assumed increasing importance. This interest eventually made its way into the theatre.

Although Dublin had been one of the major English theatrical centers since the seventeenth century,

no attempts were made to create an indigenous Irish drama until the 1890s. The first significant step was taken in 1898, when the Irish Literary Society was established in Dublin. Between 1899 and 1902, this group produced seven short plays and demonstrated the possibility of creating an Irish theatre. The leaders of the Society were William Butler Yeats (1865–1939), Lady Augusta Gregory (1863–1935), George Moore (1853–1933), and Edward Martyn (1859–1923).

Meantime, another organization, the Ormond Dramatic Society, headed by W. G. Fay (1872–1947) and Frank Fay (1870–1931), was also presenting plays with an Irish flavor and eventually the two amalgamated to form the Irish National Theatre Society. An appearance by the new group in London in 1903 won the support of Miss A. E. F. Horniman, who acquired a building for the company and remodelled it into the Abbey Theatre, opened in late 1904. Until 1910 Miss Horniman also provided the troupe with a subsidy.

Originally the group gave only three performances a month, but after it obtained a permanent home it began to present a different play each week. Not until 1908, however, was it able to pay royalties or actors' salaries. Nevertheless, its finest achievements came before 1910, after which many of its best authors and actors began to defect.

Of the Abbey's playwrights, three—Yeats, Lady Gregory and Synge—were most important. Yeats wrote about thirty plays between 1892 and 1938. Much of his early work resembled that of the French symbolists, many of whom he had known in Paris. Of the early plays, the best known is probably *Cathleen ni Houlihan* (1902), in which the spirit of Ireland, incredibly old but forever lovely, is embodied in the figure of an old woman who is transformed into a young girl. Around 1910 Yeats ceased to write specifically for the Abbey and soon afterwards came under the influence of Japanese Noh drama. Thereafter he made increasing use of masks, dance, music, and chant. Among the late works, one of the best is *At the Hawk's Well* (1917), in which a chorus describes the action as two characters await the appearance of waters that will confer immortality. Yeats disliked realistic drama and sought to arouse a community of feeling and ideals among spectators through poetic plays based on Celtic myth or legend.

From the first there were two conflicting styles at the Abbey: the poetic-mythic (best represented by Yeats) and the realistic-domestic (best represented by Lady Gregory). Most of Lady Gregory's dramatic writing

FIGURE 16.23   William Butler Yeats' *The Hour Glass.* **Design by Gordon Craig. From Yeats,** *Plays for an Irish Theatre* **(1911).**

was done between 1902 and 1912, although she did not cease altogether until 1926. She was most at home in one-act peasant comedies, such as *The Spreading of the News* (1904). But she also virtually invented the Irish folk-history play based primarily on oral tradition, as in *Kincora* (1905). Only rarely did she venture into the fully serious realm, as in *The Gaol Gate* (1906). Though she does not rank in critical stature with Yeats, she was far more successful than he was with audiences, perhaps because she wrote about familiar subjects and in a style familiar to them.

It remained for John Millington Synge (1871–1909) to fuse the two styles represented by Yeats and Lady Gregory, for he made the mythic seem familiar, raised the familiar to the level of myth, and wrote in a lilting, poetic prose fashioned from speech familiar to the Irish people. But Synge was also the most controversial of the Abbey's writers. *In the Shadow of the Glen* (1903) was denounced as a slander on Irish womanhood because it showed a wife happily leaving home to go away with a tramp after her husband has ordered her from the house. Here as in others of his plays Synge is concerned with the conflict between a repressive life and the urge toward joy and freedom. *The Playboy of the Western*

World (1907) aroused even greater wrath, for its story, in which a young man becomes a village hero after boasting of killing his father, was considered an insult to the national character. Wherever it played riots occurred. Not all of Synge's plays were controversial. Many critics consider *Riders to the Sea* (1904) to be the finest short play in the English language. In it Maurya loses the last of her six sons to the sea, but she achieves a new peace, for now fate can do no more to her. Although Synge is now considered the finest Irish dramatist of his day, at the time his plays did much to create dissension in the company and motivated many actors and playwrights to desert the Abbey.

Lesser dramatists encouraged by the Abbey include Lord Dunsany (1878–1957), whose *The Glittering Gate* (1909) and *If* (1921) helped to win acceptance for nonrealistic drama; St. John Ervine (1883–1971), whose *Jane Clegg* (1913) and *John Fergusson* (1915) present powerful character studies in the realistic vein; and Lennox Robinson (1886–1958), whose *The Whiteheaded Boy* (1916) and *The Far-off Hills* (1928) developed native Irish themes. Robinson was long one of the leaders of the Abbey Theatre, especially in the years following the First World War.

The Abbey Theatre gained international fame for its ensemble acting. In addition to the Fays, associated with the troupe until 1908, the company included Dudley Digges (1879–1947), destined to become one of the mainstays of the Theatre Guild in New York after 1919; Arthur Sinclair (1883–1951), who performed with the troupe until 1916; Sinclair's wife, Maire O'Neill (1887–1952), and her sister, Sara Allgood (1883–1950), later a well-known film actress in America. Although in the 1920s the Abbey was to recapture some of its former glory with the plays of Sean O'Casey, its major contribution had been made by 1915.

RUSSIAN IDEALISM

In Russia, the revolts against realism were centered at first around *The World of Art*, a periodical begun in 1898 by Sergei Diaghilev (1872–1929). In addition to keeping Russians abreast of events in the artistic centers of Europe, the magazine sought to encourage Russian artists and composers. Diaghilev's major contribution, however, was to stem from ballet. After Petipa retired, Prince Sergei Volkonsky, Director of the Imperial Theatres, and Mikhail Fokine (1880–1942), choreographer at the Mariinsky Theatre, introduced several innovations. Fokine disliked the long narrative works which Petipa had favored, and sought more limited subjects which offered greater opportunity for novel choreographic design. Using music by such composers as Igor Stravinsky, he emphasized complex rhythms and an overall harmony of mood.

Meanwhile Diaghilev had been arranging exchanges of art with other countries, and in 1909 he took opera and ballet companies, including Fokine's, to Paris for a six-week season. The ecstatic response led Diaghilev to form his Ballets Russes, which then toured throughout Europe. Everywhere they were praised both for their dancing and for their scenic design. When the Revolution came, many members of the company remained in the West.

The scenic style of the Ballets Russes did not depend upon any new technical devices, for it relied upon painted wings and drops. Nevertheless, it departed markedly from illusionism, since line, color, and decorative motifs were considerably stylized to reflect moods and themes rather than specific periods or places. Costumes also emphasized exaggerated line, color, and

FIGURE 16.24 Leon Bakst's design for the Ballet Russes' *Tamar,* **1912. From the souvenir program.**

mass. Thus, although the artists drew on familiar forms and decorative motifs, they created a sense of exoticism and fantasy through stylization. The influence upon European scenic art of the Ballets Russes' designers— among them Leon Bakst, Alexandre Benois, Alexander Golovin, Mstislav Dobuzhinsky, and Natalie Gontcharova—is incalculable. Bakst and Benois later settled in Paris and continued to work there.

During the 1890s the symbolist ideal began to be expounded in Russia but not until about 1905 did it make a deep impression. From that time until 1917 it was to be the major literary mode. Shortly after 1900 Stanislavsky became interested in Maeterlinck and in 1904–1905 presented a bill of his short plays. This experience helped to convince Stanislavsky that his company needed to enlarge its approach, and in 1905 he established a studio to experiment with nonrealistic styles. To supervise the work, Stanislavsky employed Vsevelod Meyerhold (1874–1940), a former member of the Moscow Art Theatre who had left in 1902 to form his own troupe. A number of productions were planned for the new studio, but Meyerhold's subordination of the actors to his directorial concepts displeased Stanislavsky so much that he discountinued the experiment.

Nevertheless, the Moscow Art Theatre went on to produce other nonrealistic works, including Maeterlinck's *The Blue Bird* in 1908 and *Hamlet* in 1912, the latter with scenery by Gordon Craig. It also encouraged Leonid Andreyev (1871–1919), Russia's foremost nonrealistic dramatist. After beginning in the realistic mode, Andreyev was converted to symbolism in 1907, the year in which he wrote his most famous play, *The Life of Man,* an allegory which seeks to summarize the human experience. Stanislavsky staged it against black curtains, using rope to outline windows, doors, and walls, and with considerable stylization in acting. Andreyev later turned to writing in a more concrete style, although *He Who Gets Slapped* (1915), a drama with a circus background, demonstrates his continuing penchant for allegory.

In 1911, the Moscow Art Theatre established the First Studio, under the direction of Leopold Sullerzhitsky (1872–1916), primarily to give training in the Stanislavsky system, but also to encourage nonrealistic approaches. Here a number of future leaders, notably Richard Boleslavsky, Mikhail Chekhov, and Eugene Vakhtangov, received their training. But, if Stanislavsky experimented with nonrealistic approaches, any marked departure from realism was ultimately unacceptable to him since all tended to "dematerialize" the actor.

The most important early experiments with nonrealistic staging in Russia were undertaken in the company maintained by Vera Kommissarzhevskaya (1864–1910). On the stage from 1891, she attracted an enormous following and opened her own theatre in St. Petersburg in 1904. Interested in new approaches, she employed Meyerhold when he left Stanislavsky. For his production of Ibsen's *Hedda Gabler,* Meyerhold assigned each character a costume of distinctive color and devoid of realistic detail. Furthermore, each character was restricted to a limited number of sculpturesque gestures and a pose to which he always returned. The setting and furniture were greenish-blue and white. Ibsen's stage directions were completely ignored. For Wedekind's *Spring's Awakening,* Meyerhold placed everything to be used in the production on stage at once and spotlighted each area as needed. When audiences did not respond favorably to these and other experiments, perhaps because Meyerhold did not exploit the considerable talents of Kommissarzhevskaya, Meyerhold was asked to leave. Immediately afterward he was employed by the Director of Imperial Theatres. With the state troupes he continued his experiments. When he staged Molière's *Dom Juan* at the Alexandrinsky Theatre in 1910, he removed the front curtain and footlights, extended the forestage into the auditorium, kept the house lights on throughout the performance, used stagehands to change properties and scenery, and set the actors' dancing movements to Lully's music. After the enormous success of this production, he went on to stage several operas, among them Wagner's *Tristan and Isolde.*

Between 1910 and 1914, Meyerhold also established studios where he experimented with circus and *commedia dell'arte* techniques. In one studio the performers mingled with the audience and converted the entire auditorium into an acting area. Actors worked out their own scripts and experimented with geometrically patterned movement, improvisation, and rhythm. Meyerhold also became interested in Oriental theatre and began to turn the scenic background into a mere apparatus for acting—a collection of steps and levels. He was to continue and extend his work after the Revolution. In these early years, Meyerhold clearly believed that the director is the major creative force in the theatre and that a script is merely material to be moulded and reworked as the director wishes. His was probably the most persistent exploration of the possibilities and limitations of the theatre as a medium of expression to be found anywhere at that time.

At Kommissarzhevskaya's theatre, Meyerhold was succeeded by Nikolai Evreinov (1879–1953). Although equally opposed to realism, Evreinov sought to enlarge the actor's place in the theatre by emphasizing flamboyance, theatricality, and the grotesque. Evreinov is probably most famous for his "monodramas," the basic principle of which was first set forth in his "Apology for Theatricality" in 1908. He suggested that man's inborn theatrical instinct leads him into "role playing" and makes him seek to transform reality into something better. Consequently, he argued, the theatre should not imitate life, but life should seek to become like theatre at its best. In his "monodramas," he aimed to help the audience achieve its desires by making it the alter-ego of the protagonist. Through identification, the audience supposedly participated directly in the experience and was led to perceptions of the higher reality. In staging, Evreinov sought to treat everything as seen through the mind of the protagonist. Lighting, sound, and scenery reflected the character's changing moods and emotions. The most famous of the monodramas was *The Theatre of the Soul* (1912). Although never very popular, Evreinov's monodramas contributed to expressionism and to motion picture techniques. Evreinov considered illusionism mistaken and in several ways sought to provide examples of more profitable alternatives: he staged two seasons of works from the Middle Ages and the Spanish Golden Age; he conducted experiments with *commedia dell'arte;* and he promoted cabaret theatre.

Theodore Kommissarzhevsky (1874–1954) worked with his sister, Evreinov, and others before open-

FIGURE 16.25 Tairov's production of Wilde's *Salomé* at the Kamerny Theatre, 1917. Costumes and setting by Alexandra Ekster. Each costume combined materials of varying color and texture to create the effect of figures taken from stained glass windows.

ing his own theatre in 1910. Probably the most balanced Russian producer, he sought to remain faithful to each playwright's intention, an attempt which led to a thoroughgoing eclecticism. His eclecticism extended further than that of Reinhardt, however, for he adopted a working method that might be called "internal eclecticism." Rather than choosing a historical period or single style for a play and then staying consistently within it, Kommissarzhevsky believed that each character and action has its own qualities for which the director must find some meaningful visual metaphor that will set up the right associations for contemporary audiences. Thus, his productions often combined elements from many periods and styles. Kommissarzhevsky was associated with numerous theatres between 1910 and 1919 (when he emigrated to the West); at one time he was head of four theatres and a training school. He later was to continue his work in France, England, and America.

Alexander Tairov (1885–1950) worked for a number of producers before opening his own theatre, the Kamerny (or Chamber) Theatre in Moscow in 1914. Tairov argued that there is no relationship between art and life and that the theatre must be viewed as analogous to the sacred dances of an ancient temple. Like Meyerhold, he viewed the text as an excuse for creativity, although he objected to Meyerhold's suppression of the actor, who, according to Tairov, is the basic creative force in the theatre. Because he was concerned with rhythmical movement, Tairov's settings were essentially architectural, being composed primarily of sculptural elements, steps and levels. Productions were approached as if they were musical compositions; speech was a compromise between declamation and song, and movement always tended toward dance. The effect was nearer to ritual than to the usual dramatic performance. By the time of the Revolution, Tairov had staged fourteen plays drawn from a wide variety of countries and dramatic types. Most productions featured his wife, Alice Koonen, his ideal intrepreter. Tairov was to continue his work after the Revolution.

By 1917, Russian experimenters had introduced techniques far removed from those employed by Stanislavsky in 1898. Some methods were as determinedly nonrealistic as have ever been devised. One of the least advanced countries of Europe at the end of the nineteenth century, Russia had witnessed some of the most daring theatrical experiments, although, with the exceptions of the Ballets Russes and the Moscow Art Theatre, the work had made little impact outside its borders.

THE REVIVAL OF IDEALISM IN FRANCE

After the closing of the Théâtre de l'Oeuvre in 1899, Paris settled once more into its somewhat complacent conviction that it was the artistic capital of Europe. Antoine's productions became the standard, and nonrealistic experiments were few and sporadic. Thus, the appearance of the Ballets Russes in 1909 came almost as a revelation. A new wave of experimentation was given further impetus by the publication in 1910 of *Modern Theatre Art* by Jacques Rouché (1862–1957). After describing the work of Fuchs, Erler, and Reinhardt in Germany, of Meyerhold, Stanislavsky, and Kommissarzhevskaya in Russia, and the theories of Appia and Craig, Rouché went on to call for similar experiments in France. Not only was his book widely read and discussed, Rouché himself set out to implement his ideas at the Théâtre des Arts between 1910 and 1913. Rouché did not aim at extreme stylization, but sought a simplicity in which color and line characterize a milieu and mood without calling attention to themselves. He found his ideal designer in Maxime Dethomas (1867–1929). Rouché was the first French producer to be truly eclectic. He went on to become director of the Opéra, where between 1914 and 1936 he renovated the repertory and brought to it a new generation of scene designers.

Rouché's work had important consequences. Lugné-Poë revived the Théâtre de l'Oeuvre, where he

FIGURE 16.26 *Hamlet* at the Théâtre de l'Oeuvre, 1913. Directed by Lugné-Poë and Gémier. Setting by Jean Variot. The structure in the foreground remained throughout, and set pieces were changed behind the central opening. From *Le Théâtre* (1913).

inner proscenium, but no machinery except for a set of curtains and asbestos hangings which could be moved on rods to effect rapid changes of locale. To these curtains were added only the most essential furniture and set pieces. In 1913–1914, before the war forced him to stop, Copeau presented fifteen plays, including works by Shakespeare, Molière, Heywood, Claudel, and others. In 1917 Copeau was asked to revive the troupe and take it to New York. There between 1917 and 1919 he presented plays for American audiences before returning to Paris to reopen his theatre. It is impossible to overrate the importance of the Théâtre du Vieux Colombier, for with its formation the leadership of the French theatre passed from Antoine to Copeau, who was to dominate the postwar theatre in France.

presented a series of plays with designs by Jean Variot, who reenforced Rouché's influence. More important, Rouché inspired Jacques Copeau (1879–1949) to open his own theatre. A dramatic critic, Copeau gained his first practical experience at the Théâtre des Arts when his adaptation of *The Brothers Karamazov* was produced there in 1911. Copeau was convinced that Rouché's suggested reforms put too much emphasis upon visual elements and that no significant progress could come except through the drama itself.

In 1913, Copeau published a manifesto for a new theatre. In it, he adopted a position almost opposite to that of Meyerhold and Tairov, for he argued that the director's primary task is the faithful translation of the dramatist's script into a "poetry of the theatre." Furthermore, he stated that the actor, as the "living presence" of the author, is the only essential element of theatrical production, and that a rejuvenation of the drama depends upon a return to the bare platform stage.

Copeau assembled a company of ten actors, including Louis Jouvet, Charles Dullin, Suzanne Bing, Romain Bouquet, and Valentine Tessier, all of whom were to be significant in the postwar theatre, and retired to the country to perfect his first productions. Meanwhile, with the assistance of Francis Jourdain, Copeau converted a small hall into the Théâtre du Vieux Colombier, seating only 400. It had a forestage forward of an

THE THEATRE IN ITALY AND SPAIN, 1875–1915

Between 1875 and 1915, both Italy and Spain were more emulative than innovative. Italy's major creative energies continued to be poured into opera. In drama, realism arrived first in the works of Paolo Ferrari (1822–1889), a writer in the vein of Dumas *fils,* and then through the "Verist" (or naturalistic) school. Since Italy was still divided by differences in dialect and customs, the Verists are usually separated into groups centered in Milan,

FIGURE 16.27 Scene from Copeau's adaptation of Dostoyevsky's *The Brothers Karamazov* at Rouché's Théâtre des Arts, 1911. At center Charles Dullin is seen as Smerdiakov. Setting by Maxime Dethomas. From *Le Théâtre* (1911).

FIGURE 16.28 Eleanora Duse in the title role of D'Annunzio's *Francesca da Rimini* at the Teatro Constanzi, Rome, 1902. From *Le Théâtre* (1902).

Turin, and Naples. Of the Milanese school, Marco Praga (1862–1929), with such dark, hopeless plays as *The Virgins* (1889), was the most famous. At Turin, Giuseppe Giacosa (1847–1906) was the dominant figure with his Ibsenesque plays *The Rights of the Soul* (1894) and *Like Falling Leaves* (1900). Of the Neapolitan school, Roberto Bracco (1862–1943), with his dramas about victimized women, as in *Maternity* (1903) and *Nellina* (1908), was the best. In Sicily, Giovanni Verga (1840–1922) won fame with his Zolaesque plays of brutal violence, *Cavalleria Rusticana* (1884) and *The She-Wolf* (1896). Neoromanticism found its major exponent in Gabriele D'Annunzio (1863–1938), who, under the influence of Maeterlinck, wrote such plays as *The Dead City* (1898), *La Giaconda* (1898), and *Francesca da Rimini* (1902).

The strong Italian acting tradition was continued by such outstanding players as Ermete Zacconi (1857–1948), Giovanni Grasso (1875–1930), and Ruggero Ruggeri (1871–1954). By far the most renowned, however, was Eleanora Duse (1859–1924). On the stage from the age of four, she became Rossi's leading lady in 1879. After touring South America in 1885, she formed

her own company and played throughout the world. She retired in 1909, but returned to the stage in 1921 and died in Pittsburgh while on tour. Duse played an extremely wide range of roles, many of them favorites of Bernhardt, with whose flamboyance her quiet style contrasted sharply. Noted for subtlety, she used simple means to convey complex conceptions. She scorned makeup and prided herself on her ability to make unaided the physical adjustments required by each role. To many discerning critics, she was the greatest of modern actresses.

In Spain, the realistic drama found its first important exponent in José Echegaray (1848–1927), notably in *The Son of Don Juan* (1892), patterned on Ibsen's *Ghosts,* and *The Great Galeoto* (1881), a play about the power of gossip to ruin lives. After the war of 1898 had stripped Spain of her last shreds of glory, a new movement, "the Generation of '98," sought to revitalize literature. The most famous of the new writers was Jacinto Benavente (1866–1954), a versatile dramatist who composed nearly 300 works ranging through every style and form. Of his realistic plays, the best is probably *The Passion Flower* (1913), the story of a man's love for his stepdaughter, while of the nonrealistic works *The Bonds of Interest* (1907), a philosophical work using *commedia dell'arte* conventions, is the best known.

For the most part, however, Spanish drama tended to remain sentimental and melodramatic underneath a facade of realistic detail. Serafín Álvarez Quintero (1871–1944) and Joaquín Álvarez Quintero (1873–1938) wrote more than 150 plays of this type, such as *The Merry Heart* (1906) and *Malvoloca* (1912). In much the same vein, Gregorio Martínez Sierra (1881–1947) wrote *Cradle Song* (1911) and *The Kingdom of God* (1916).

The modern movement in Spain was helped considerably by the Teatro Intim, founded in imitation of the "independent theatres" of Europe by Adria Gual (1872–1932) in 1898 at Barcelona. Here a cross section of drama from Aeschylus to the present was offered for more than thirty years. With his experiments in production styles, Gual brought many of the new trends to Spain.

The major Spanish actors of this period were María Guerrero (1868–1928) and her husband, Fernando Diaz de Mendoza (1862–1930). From 1896 until 1909 they managed the Teatro Espagñol, and from 1909 until 1924 the Teatro de la Princesa (later renamed the Teatro María Guerrero). The Mendoza-Guerrero company toured South America twenty-two times and elsewhere with less frequency.

THE AMERICAN THEATRE, 1895–1915

The new trends made little impact on the American theatre prior to 1915. By 1895, the traveling road show had become the usual source of theatrical entertainment in America. While a few resident troupes remained, the long-run hit had become the goal, and New York was virtually the only theatrical center. These conditions brought many new problems. Perhaps the most obvious difficulties were those connected with booking. The manager of a local theatre now had to go to New York to arrange a season of attractions. If he wished to schedule a forty-week season, he often had to deal with forty different producers, each of whom was negotiating with many other local managers. Thus, booking was difficult and haphazard and, because producers often defaulted on their agreements, local theatres were frequently faced with sudden cancellations. To remedy these ills, new approaches evolved. Theatres in a restricted area joined together to arrange bookings, and agents began to serve as middlemen between managers and producers.

In this confusion, a small group of men saw the possibility of gaining control of the American theatre. In 1896 Sam Nixon and Fred Zimmerman of Philadelphia, Charles Frohman, Al Hayman, Marc Klaw, and Abraham Erlanger of New York formed the "Theatrical Syndicate." Of these men, only Frohman was directly involved in theatrical production, the others being booking agents or theatre owners. The new organization began by offering a full season of stellar attractions, on the condition that local managers book exclusively through the Syndicate. This offer was welcomed by many managers, for it permitted them to deal with a single agent and to obtain outstanding productions. Managers who refused to deal with the Syndicate were systematically eliminated through simple, if ruthless, maneuvers. The Syndicate did not seek to gain direct control over all theatres in the country; rather, it concentrated on key routes between large cities, for unless productions could play along the way, touring was financially impossible. Where it could not gain control over key theatres, the Syndicate built rival houses and booked into them the finest productions at reduced prices until the competing theatres were bankrupt. New York producers who refused to cooperate were denied bookings and many actors were "blackballed," since the Syndicate would not send on tour any production in which they appeared. By 1900, the Syndicate was in effective control of the American theatre. Now in a position to influence the choice of plays, it refused to accept works not likely to appeal to a mass audience and favored productions which featured stars with large personal followings. As a result, between 1900 and 1915, the American theatre became largely a commercial venture.

Of the Syndicate members, Charles Frohman (1854–1915) was by far the most important, since he was the only one directly involved in theatrical production. Working his way up from program seller to business manager and agent, Frohman had entered management in 1889. In 1893, he opened the Empire Theatre in New York, where he maintained a fine stock company for many years. In 1896, he extended his interests to London and later controlled five theatres there. At the height of his power he employed some 10,000 persons. As an entrepreneur, Frohman was guided by two convictions: public taste is infallible, and stars are necessary to attract audiences. Thus, he sought to provide the mass public with works which would please, and he launched many new stars.

Several of Frohman's stars were already well-established performers when he engaged them. These included John Drew II, William Faversham (1868–1940), a popular matinee idol, Viola Allen (1869–1948), noted primarily for her Shakespearean performances, and Otis Skinner (1858–1942), outstanding in romantic dramas and sentimental comedies. Other Frohman stars were Henry Miller, Margaret Anglin, Maude Adams, Ethel Barrymore, E. H. Sothern, and Julia Marlowe. Henry Miller (1860–1925) had played in several companies before becoming the leading actor in Frohman's Empire stock company. In 1897 Miller went on the road, but in 1906 he formed his own company and in 1918 he opened his own theatre in New York. Closely associated with Miller through much of his career was Margaret Anglin (1876–1958), leading acctress of the Empire troupe. After 1910, her interests turned increasingly to standard drama, and she made an enviable reputation with her Greek and Shakespearean productions. Maude Adams (1872–1953) was on stage from childhood, but her fame rests upon her work in Frohman's productions. Now remembered primarily for her appearances in J. M. Barrie's plays, she was Frohman's greatest money maker for many years, perhaps because she accepted only roles showing optimism and wholesomeness. Retiring from the stage in 1918, she returned for occasional engagements after 1931. Ethel Barrymore (1879–1959) had served a brief apprenticeship with her

FIGURE 16.29 Mrs. Fiske and Holbrook Blinn in Edward Sheldon's *Salvation Nell,* 1908. Courtesy Hoblitzelle Theatre Arts Collection, University of Texas, Austin.

uncle, John Drew II, and with Henry Irving before becoming a star overnight in *Captain Jinks of the Horse Marines* in 1901. By the 1920s she was considered America's leading actress, even though she had appeared in no significant plays and depended primarily upon her own forceful personality. From the 1920s, she worked almost exclusively in films. After 1904 the careers of E. A. Sothern (1859–1933) and Julia Marlowe (1870–1950) were bound up together. Previously Sothern had toured with McCullough and had been a leading actor in the Lyceum company, while Miss Marlowe, on the stage from childhood, had gained considerable fame for roles in standard works. From 1904 to 1924, they were the principal purveyors of Shakespeare to American audiences. Although inferior to many of their predecessors, they kept the classical tradition alive at a time when most of their contemporaries were appearing in new plays.

Despite the Syndicate's strength, it did not go unopposed. James A. Herne, Mr. and Mrs. Harrison G. Fiske, James O'Neill, David Belasco, and others held out, although with the exception of the Fiskes all eventually came to terms with the Syndicate. Minnie Maddern (1865–1932) was on the stage from the age of three and had achieved considerable fame by 1889, when she mar-

ried Harrison Grey Fiske (1861–1942), a dramatist and editor of the most influential theatrical newspaper of the day, *The New York Dramatic Mirror.* After she returned to the stage in 1893, Mrs. Fiske championed the new realistic drama and was the first American to give Ibsen an extensive hearing through her productions of *A Doll's House, Hedda Gabler, Rosmersholm, Pillars of Society,* and *Ghosts.* When the Syndicate closed its theatres to her, she and her husband leased the Manhattan Theatre, where from 1901 to 1907 they produced many outstanding plays in which they sought to subordinate stars to ensemble effect. As a performer, Mrs. Fiske relied upon direct observation of life and a close study of psychology. She moved away from lines of business and encouraged actors to play as wide a range of roles as possible. She probably did more than any other American performer of her day to pave the way for the modern theatre.

James O'Neill (1847–1920), now remembered as the father of Eugene O'Neill, was one of America's most popular actors from the 1880s until the First World War. Despite great promise, he became identified with the leading role in *The Count of Monte Cristo,* which he first played in 1883, and rarely appeared in other works.

But the most significant opposition to the Syndicate came from David Belasco (c. 1854–1931), a producer and dramatist who shared many of Frohman's ideals. Born in San Francisco, he was on the stage as a child and wrote his first play at the age of twelve. By the time he left California in 1882, he had written or adapted over 100 works and had staged some 300. In New York he served as manager of the Madison Square Theatre after MacKaye left it, and later was MacKaye's stage manager at the Lyceum. Between 1887 and 1890 he collaborated with Henry C. DeMille (1850–1893) on four very successful plays for the Lyceum, and during the 1890s continued to build his reputation as a dramatist with such hits as *The Girl I Left Behind Me* (1893), *The Heart of Maryland* (1895), and *Zaza* (1899). Although he had produced plays occasionally during the 1890s, it was not until 1902 that he acquired his own theatre. In 1907 he opened the Stuyvesant Theatre (renamed the Belasco in 1910), where every modern improvement was installed. Here he continued his work until 1928. Belasco never maintained a stock company and always worked on the single-play principle.

As a producer, Belasco is now remembered for three reasons: his power as a star maker, his realism in staging, and his opposition to the Syndicate. Like Frohman, Belasco depended much on stars, many of whom he

FIGURE 16.30 David Belasco's production of Edward Locke's *The Case of Becky,* 1912. Note the meticulous attention to detail. Courtesy Hoblitzelle Theatre Arts Collection, University of Texas, Austin.

crowd scenes were famous for their authenticity and power. In collaboration with Louis Hartman, he experimented extensively with stage lighting. In *Madame Butterfly,* the passage of night was shown realistically through a twelve-minute sequence that moved through sunset to night to dawn. Around 1915, Belasco replaced footlights with spotlights mounted in the auditorium and developed new color media. In his search for perfection, however, Belasco remained firmly within the nineteenth-century tradition, for he sought merely to bring the maximum of illusion to a repertory in the Boucicault tradition.

Belasco first came into conflict with the Syndicate when he sought to take *The Auctioneer* on the road in 1902. Further difficulties led to a court battle in 1906. By 1909 Belasco's productions were in such demand that the Syndicate was forced to accept Belasco's terms, even though he refused to book exclusively through it. Its concessions to Belasco marked the first important break in the Syndicate's power.

The willingness of the Syndicate to make concessions had been hastened by the rise of the Shuberts. Three brothers, Sam (1876–1905), Lee (1875–1954), and Jacob J. (1880–1963), after beginning in Syracuse, New York, leased a theatre in New York City in 1900. When the Syndicate closed its theatres to their productions in 1905, the Shuberts began to establish a rival chain. By this time, the high-handed methods of the Syndicate had created much dissatisfaction, and the Shuberts were welcomed by many local managers as allies. By 1908 several theatres had defected to the Shuberts, and the revolt accelerated after 1910 when the

coached carefully and for whose capabilities he tailored plays. Among his stars were Mrs. Leslie Carter (1862–1937), featured in many of Belasco's works from 1895 to 1905; Blanche Bates (1873–1941), noted especially for her appearances in Belasco's *Madame Butterfly* (1900) and *The Girl of the Golden West* (1905), and later in many of Frohman's productions; Frances Starr (1886–1973), a versatile actress who starred in such works as Belasco's *The Rose of the Rancho* (1906) and Eugene Walter's *The Easiest Way* (1909); and David Warfield (1866–1951), a burlesque performer until Belasco transformed him into a leading dramatic actor in such plays as *The Auctioneer* (1902), *The Return of Peter Grimm* (1911), and *The Merchant of Venice* (presented in 1922).

Above all, Belasco is now remembered for his staging. Like Daly and MacKaye, Belasco insisted upon controlling every aspect of his productions. With him, naturalistic detail reached the peak of its development in America. For *The Governor's Lady* (1912), a Childs Restaurant was reproduced on stage and the Childs chain stocked it daily with food which was consumed during the performance. For *The Easiest Way,* Belasco bought the contents of a boardinghouse room, including the wallpaper, and had it transferred to his stage. His

FIGURE 16.31 Belasco's production of *The Governor's Lady* showing the replica of Childs Restaurant which he erected on stage. From *The Theatre* (1912.)

FIGURE 16.32 The first act of William Vaughan Moody's *The Great Divide,* with Henry Miller and Margaret Anglin, Princess Theatre, New York, 1906. Courtesy Hoblitzelle Theatre Arts Collection, University of Texas, Austin.

National Theatre Owners Association was formed. The struggle between the Shuberts and the Syndicate reached its peak in 1913, after which the Syndicate's grip was broken. Further weakened by the death of Charles Frohman in 1915, the Syndicate ceased to be an effective force after 1916. Unfortunately, the Shuberts became as dictatorial and monopolistic as the Syndicate had been. As producers, they were noted for lavish musicals with little substance. Although they largely gave up producing plays after 1945, they continued to control "the road" until 1956, when the government ordered them to sell many of their theatres.

Although the American theatre was dominated by commercial interests, a few groups sought to bring a new vision to the theatre. Among these were the Criterion Independent Theatre (1897–1900) in New York, Arnold Daly's (1875–1927) two-month season of Shaw's works in New York in 1905, and the New Theatre (1906–1907) in Chicago. Nevertheless, these ventures made little impact.

Under the conditions which governed the American theatre between 1895 and 1915, it is not surprising that significant playwriting did not flourish. Probably the most successful dramatist was Clyde Fitch (1865–1909), who, after being commissioned by Richard Mansfield to create *Beau Brummel* (1890), wrote about sixty plays, of which the most important were *Barbara Frietchie* (1899), *Captain Jinks of the Horse Marines* (1901), *The Girl with the Green Eyes* (1902), *The Truth* (1907), and *The City* (1909). During the season of 1900–1901, ten of Fitch's works were being played

in New York or on the road. A careful observer, Fitch reflected the life of his times. Noted for his quiet, intense scenes, he probably failed to achieve true depth because of the haste with which he wrote. As the first American playwright to publish his works regularly, he established a pattern continued until the present.

During the first decade of the century Willam Vaughan Moody (1869–1910) seemed the dramatist with greatest promise. Moody was a professor at the University of Chicago and a poet of stature when he began writing closet dramas about 1900. His first produced work, *The Great Divide* (1906), performed by Henry Miller and Margaret Anglin, was considered a landmark because it combined considerable literary merit with an exciting action which dramatized the "great divide" between the effete and self-conscious East and the rough and open-hearted West. Moody's only other play to reach the stage, *The Faith Healer* (1909), was not well received, perhaps because of its rather unconvincing protagonist. Moody's early death blighted the hopes of those who saw in his work the source of a truly significant American drama.

By 1915, the theatre was beginning to decline in popularity. While increased ticket prices were partially responsible, effective competition, most notably from spectator sports and motion pictures, was also appearing. Soon after Thomas A. Edison demonstrated the "kinetoscope" in 1894, "penny arcades" began to show short motion pictures. Only one person at a time could be served, however, until George Eastman's flexible film and Thomas Armat's projector made it possible to show movies to an assembled audience.

In 1905, the first of the "nickelodeons" was opened in McKeesport, Pennsylvania, and by 1909 there were 8,000. The early theatres seated only about 100 and offered only short films. In 1914, the Strand Theatre in New York, with its 3,300 seats, began the trend toward larger houses. But it was not until D. W. Griffith's *The Birth of a Nation* (1915) surpassed Belasco's realism and melodramatic power that films became a serious competitor to the theatre. With their superior ability to capture spectacle and their markedly lower admission costs, motion pictures began to draw away that audience which had sought illusionism and thrills in the theatre. Unfortunately, the commercialization of the theatre had alienated a large part of the more discriminating spectators, leaving no effective buffer against disaster.

The competition from films did not bring an over-

FIGURE 16.33 The first revolving stage used in the West. It was designed by Karl Lautenschläger for the Residenz Theater, Munich in 1896. Courtesy Theatermuseum, Munich.

night revolution. In 1915, there were still about 1,500 legitimate theatres outside of New York and the number of theatrical productions on Broadway continued to increase until the season of 1927–1928. The invention of sound motion pictures in 1927 and the depression of 1929 dealt serious blows, however, and by 1930 only 500 theatres remained outside of New York. Thereafter, the number steadily declined.

Although these new directions were not readily apparent in 1915, it was already clear to many that the old production methods were outmoded and that commercialization had gradually reduced the repertory to works calculated to appeal to the mass audience. Reassessment, new methods, and changing ideals were in the offing.

MAJOR TECHNICAL INNOVATIONS, 1875–1915

Between 1875 and 1915 several important technical innovations were introduced, the majority in Germany.

Many were motivated by the need to shift the heavy three-dimensional settings which were replacing the wings and drops designed for movement by the chariot-and-pole system. One of the most important of the new devices was the revolving stage. The first one was installed at the Residenz Theater in Munich in 1896 by Karl Lautenschläger (1843–1906). Its ability to accommodate several settings and to change them merely by revolving the turntable, led to its wide adoption after 1900. Another solution, the rolling platform stage, was introduced by Fritz Brandt (1846–1927) at the Royal Opera House in Berlin around 1900. With it, settings could be mounted on a large platform offstage and then moved on stage by means of rollers set in tracks. The elevator stage also was widely adopted. At the Munich Art Theatre, the Burgtheater, and elsewhere, the stage was divided into segments, each of which could be adjusted to create a variety of levels for the action or to raise heavy objects from beneath the stage. A still more complex arrangement was installed in the Dresden state theatre by Adolf Linnebach (1876–1963) in 1914 by combining sliding platforms with elevators. These complex mechanical devices were supplemented with flying, manual shifting, and with small wagons mounted on casters. The new stage machinery was adopted more widely in Germany than elsewhere probably because of two factors: the expense, absorbed in Germany by the state; and the decline of realism before the devices were widely adopted elsewhere, for the growing emphasis upon simplified settings made complex machinery less essential.

Many German theatres of this period also installed a plaster dome (or *kuppelhorizont*) which curved around and over the stage to give the effect of infinite space and eliminated the need for overhead and side masking pieces. To fulfill the same function, other theatres used a cloth cyclorama hung from a batten which curved around the stage.

Many experiments with stage lighting also were conducted. Light bridges and other new mounting positions were tried. After 1907, improvements in the filaments of incandescent lamps made it possible to increase wattage. By 1913, 1,000-watt lamps were available in Europe, and color media and spotlights were beginning to be common. Consequently, footlights were gradually replaced by spotlights mounted in the auditorium. One of the most ambitious lighting systems of the period was devised by Mariano Fortuny (1871–1949), who directed strong lights against colored silk

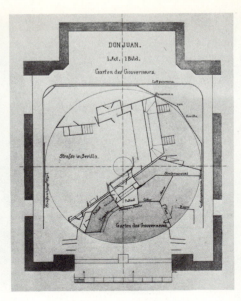

FIGURE 16.34 **The first revolving stage as used for Mozart's** *Don Giovanni* **at the Residenz Theater, Munich, in 1896. At left is a plan showing two settings in place: the Commandant's Garden, and a street in Seville. At right is a drawing of the setting for the first of these. Courtesy Theatermuseum, Munich.**

panels, which reflected the light onto a *kuppelhorizont* and then onto the stage. With elaborate machinery for changing the panels and controlling the light, the system gave the most subtle variations of any then known, but its complexity and cost prevented its widespread adoption. Nevertheless, it is indicative of the growing interest in lighting as an important element of design.

Auditoriums also underwent considerable change, largely under the influence of Wagner's theatre at Bayreuth. Boxes tended to disappear and the number of balconies to decrease (sometimes there was none); center aisles were eliminated, and sightlines were improved. As the interest in breaking down the barriers between performers and audience grew, the apron stage returned to favor and in a few instances the proscenium arch was eliminated. Thus, the Italianate theatre, dominant since the seventeenth century, was challenged for the first time.

By 1915, the standards of production that had been accepted almost universally in 1875 had begun to seem outmoded. Although pictorial realism still dominated the popular theatre, it had been undermined by a host of experiments. A common theme ran through all of the experiments: the need for unified production, a strong director, and artistic integrity, so that the theatre might once more assume the role it had played in ancient Greece as a source of insight and a place of communion. Although the war interrupted developments, it provoked reassessments, out of which new convictions and renewed vigor came in the postwar years.

LOOKING AT THEATRE HISTORY

One way of studying theatre history is through reconstructing specific productions. Obviously, one cannot recapture a performance completely, but one can regain much more than might be expected. Such an approach requires that one collect information about the entire context: the prevailing theatrical conditions and conventions, the dramatist, the script, the director, the actors, the theatre building, the settings, the costumes, the lighting, the music, the rehearsals, the performances, the audiences, and the critical response. One needs also to read any accounts left by participants or eyewitnesses and to gather all the visual evidence that has survived. With such materials in hand, one can gain a reasonably complete understanding of the elements that went into the production and can trace the performance, scene by scene. Such study will illuminate not only the specific production but the theatre of that age.

Among the best sources of information about productions are prompt scripts, especially those made after 1850, for before that time few details about blocking and stage business were recorded in the prompt-copy, as such matters were considered to lie within the actor's domain. But since the mid-nineteenth century prompt scripts usually have recorded highly specific information about almost all production elements.

Charles Shattuck has published a list of the Shakespearean promptbooks that are available in libraries and collections in *The Shakespeare Promptbooks: A Descriptive Catalogue* (Urbana, Ill., 1965). In addition, Shattuck's studies of specific Shakespearean productions are models of how performances can be reconstructed. These include *William Charles Macready's "King John"* (Urbana, Ill., 1962) and *The Hamlet of Edwin Booth* (Urbana, 1969). Although his are full-length books, other reconstructions need not be so thorough to be enlightening.

A study of the critical responses to new plays and production styles between 1875 and 1915 can be very revealing, since it helps us understand the great uproar caused by scripts or productions that now seem uncontroversial. As a playwright, Ibsen was a special focus for contention. Here are some of Clement Scott's responses to *Ghosts:*

If people like the discussion of such nasty subjects on the stage . . . if it is desirable to drive decent-minded women out of the playhouse, and to use the auditorium as a hospital-ward or dissecting-room, let it be so. . . . But in our hurry to dramatize the Contagious Diseases Act let us first set about writing a good play. Who in their senses can say that Ghosts is a good play? . . . If, by the examples we have seen, Ibsen is a dramatist, then the art of the dramatist is dead indeed. . . .

> *The Illustrated London News,*
> 21 March 1891.

Similarly, when Granville Barker attempted to do away with illusionistic scenery in his Shakespearean productions, he met considerable derision. Here are portions of a review of *A Midsummer Night's Dream* written in 1915 (for an illustration of one setting, see page 490):

Let it be said that it represented the last cry in the new stage decoration. . . . The . . . changes of scene were indicated by curtains that waved, to the loss of all illusion. . . . No human being . . . can be expected to be anything but worried and annoyed by pink silk curtains that are supposed to be the roofs of houses, or green silk curtains that are supposed to be forest trees. . . . I hope this is not indicative of what will happen when stage setting ceases to be scenery and becomes only decoration.

> Review by G. C. D. ODELL,
> reprinted in his *Shakespeare from Betterton to Irving* (New York, 1920), II, 467–468.

Probably the most extreme departure from the realistic mode was seen at Paris' Théâtre de l'Oeuvre, where more startling than the abandonment of illusionistic scenery was the highly stylized acting:

The most simple and sensible things take on a different appearance in passing through the mouths and gestures of the l'Oeuvre's actors under the direction of Lugné-Poë. They have a continual ecstatic air of perpetually being visionaries. As if hallucinatory, they stare before them, far, very far, vaguely, very vaguely. Their voices are cavernous, their diction choppy. They seem to be attempting to give the air that they are fools.

> *Moniteur Universel,* 5 March 1894.

Perhaps the most notable feature of the period between 1875 and 1915 was the attempt to redefine the the "art of the theatre." In this effort, the leaders were Appia and Craig. Here are some excerpts from one of Appia's essays. After pointing out the weaknesses of the nineteenth-century theatre (which he blames on the disparity between the static, two-dimensional painted scenery, the flat stage floor, and the three-dimensional, moving actor), he goes on to ask:

What would happen if we began with . . . the plastic, moving human body? . . . An object is three-dimensional to our eyes only because of the light that strikes it. . . . [Furthermore] human movement . . . requires obstacles if it is to be fully expressive. Therefore, the actor's mobility cannot be used to artistic advantage except when it is integrally related to objects and the floor. Thus the two basic conditions required for the artistic use of the human body on the stage are: light that reveals its plasticity, and its harmonization with the setting so as to enhance its attitudes and movements. . . .

The effects of lighting are limitless. . . . [When it is used properly] the actor no longer walks about in front of painted light and shade; he is enfolded in an atmosphere destined for him. . . .

Scenic illusion may be defined as the living presence of the actor.

. . . [If we are to create the appropriate scenic illusion] we must greatly simplify [the setting] . . . completely re-arrange the stage floor, and above all make adequate provisions for lighting. . . .

> "Comment Reformer Notre Mise en
> Scène," *La Revue,* 50 (June 1, 1904),
> 342–349.

Craig wished to establish that theatre can be an autonomous art created by a master artist, rather than an assemblage of other arts put together by craftsmen:

The Art of the Theatre is neither acting nor the play, it is not scene nor dance, but it consists of all the elements of which these things are composed: action, which is the very spirit of acting; words, which are the body of the play; line and colour, which are the very heart of the scene; rhythm, which is the very essence of dance. . . .

When [the director] interprets the plays of the dramatist by means of his actors, his scene-painters, and his other crafts-men, then he is a craftsman—a master craftsman; when he will have mastered the uses of actions, words, line, colour, and rhythm, then he may become an artist. Then we shall no longer need the assistance of the playwright—for our art will then be self-reliant.

> *On the Art of the Theatre* (Chicago:
> Browne's Bookstore, 1911),
> pp. 138, 148.

During this period, Stanislavsky began to evolve his system of acting, probably the most influential of all times. In *My Life in Art,* he tells how his system took shape over many years, beginning in 1906 when he became concerned over his inability to remain fresh in his roles:

How was I to save my roles from bad rebirths, from spiritual petrifaction, from the autocracy of evil habit and lack of truth? There was the necessity not only of a physical make-up but of a spiritual make-up before every performance. (pp. 460–461)

As he experimented with a system capable of meeting the actor's problems, his ideas began to attract others:

For the young people who came to seek my help I founded a Studio [in 1911]. . . . here we gathered all who wanted to study the so-called Stanislavsky System. . . . I began to give a full course of study in the shape in which I had at that time formed it. Its aim was to give practical and conscious methods for the awakening of superconscious creativeness. (p. 531)

About his system, Stanislavsky warned:

My system cannot be explained in an hour or in a day even. It must be systematically and practically studied for years. It does good only when it becomes the second nature of the actor, when he stops thinking of it consciously, when it begins to appear naturally, as of itself. (p. 529)

> CONSTANTIN STANISLAVSKY,
> *My Life in Art,* trans. J. J. Robbins
> (New York: Theatre Arts Books,
> 1948).

The Theatre in Europe and America Between the Wars

The period between 1915 and 1940 was bounded by the two most destructive and costly wars of modern times. World War I grew out of problems inherited from the nineteenth century: the desire of each ethnic and language group to have its own nation; the competition among the great powers for territory, markets, and spheres of influence; military alliances that had been formed to insure a balance of power; and secret diplomacy that created suspicion among nations. The war utilized not only the largest armies ever assembled up to that time, but new and improved instruments of destruction—tanks and other mechanized vehicles, airplanes and bombs, submarines and torpedoes. Some 8,300,000 men died and more than $337 billion were spent. To many thoughtful people the war seemed an exercise in madness.

The war ended in a wave of optimism as republics replaced monarchies, as small ethnic groups were allowed to form their own nations, and as a League of Nations and a World Court were established to arbitrate national disputes. But optimism soon declined because of the great economic problems created by human and material destruction and because of the vindictive treatment of the losing nations. Rampant inflation in the 1920s was followed by severe depression in the 1930s. In several countries conditions became so chaotic that dictators were able to gain complete control: Mussolini of Italy in 1922, Stalin of Russia around 1928, Hitler of Germany in 1933, and Franco of Spain in 1939. During the 1930s, conflicts—over ideologies, territorial claims, and imperi-

alistic designs—increased steadily. The League of Nations proved ineffective, and the great powers set about rearming. In 1939 the tensions erupted into a second World War that was to be even more destructive than the first.

World War I seems to have had a liberating effect, however, in many realms, perhaps most notably in moral standards, codes of dress and behavior, women's and workers' rights, and artistic experimentation. Through the last of these especially, the theatre was deeply affected.

GERMAN THEATRE AND DRAMA, 1915–1940

During World War I the German theatre continued without interruption and, unlike its English, French and American counterparts, did not turn primarily to popular entertainment. When Germany became a republic at the end of the war, the former "royal" theatres were rechristened "state" theatres, but there were few changes in organization or policy, for they continued to offer seasons composed of varied plays performed by permanent companies. After 1920, as economic conditions worsened and inflation skyrocketed, nonsubsidized groups found it increasingly difficult to survive except by abandoning the repertory system in favor of new works tailored to popular tastes.

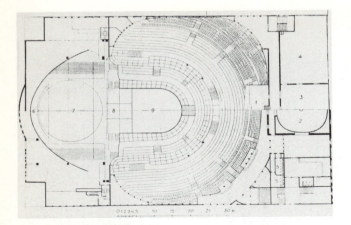

FIGURE 17.1 Plan of Reinhardt's Grosses Schauspielhaus, remodeled from a circus building. At left note the full proscenium stage, complete with revolving stage. Forward of the proscenium are a platform and arena. The theatre seated about 3,500. From Barkhin, *Architectura Teatra,* Moscow (1947).

Of the prewar producers, Max Reinhardt remained the most important. While continuing his management of the Deutsches Theater and the Kammerspiele, he also remodeled the Circus Schumann into the Grosses Schauspielhaus (seating more than 3,500), where between 1919 and 1922 he presented a series of monumental productions, most notably the *Oresteia, Julius Caesar,* and *Danton's Death.* The venture ultimately failed, perhaps because the theatre's great size discouraged subtlety and because the compromises demanded by the combined open and picture-frame stages were never entirely satisfactory.

From 1922 to 1924, Reinhardt maintained his headquarters in Austria, where he had annually produced von Hofmannsthal's *Everyman* and *The Great Theatre of the World* at the Salzburg Festival since its founding in 1920. In 1922 he became director of Vienna's Theatre in dem Redoutensaal, converted from an imperial ballroom of the 1740s, where against a background of screens he presented plays and operas of the eighteenth century. The intimacy of this theatre contrasted markedly with the immensity of the Grosses Schauspielhaus. Although he retained and extended his Austrian enterprises, in 1924 Reinhardt returned to Berlin where he continued his manifold activities until Hitler's rise to power forced him to flee in 1933. Between 1905 and 1933 Reinhardt had personally directed 136 plays and through his experi-

ments with production styles and theatre architecture had exerted a pervasive influence on the German stage. In the United States after 1933, Reinhardt directed a few plays and films, but he never fully adjusted to his new situation.

Reinhardt's postwar activities were essentially continuations of practices he had begun before 1914. But other directors championed a new mode—expressionism—which for a few years dominated the German stage. The term expressionism first gained currency in France around 1901 as a label used to distinguish the kind of painting done by Van Gogh and Gauguin from that of the impressionists, who sought to capture the appearance of objects as seen under a certain light at a particular moment. In contrast, expressionism was thought to emphasize strong inner feelings about objects and to portray life as modified and distorted by the painter's own vision of reality.

Around 1910 expressionism as a term was introduced into Germany, where shortly afterward it was picked up by critics and popularized as a label for tendencies already underway in literature and the arts. Since almost any departure from realism soon came to be labeled "expressionism," the movement is difficult to define. Nevertheless, its basic premises may be outlined. An

FIGURE 17.2 Reinhardt's Redoutensaal theatre, Vienna, 1922, created within the ballroom of an eighteenth-century palace. Note that the stage has been erected without disturbing the walls of the ballroom. There is no proscenium arch or curtain. From *Le Théâtre* (1922).

anthropomorphic view of existence led expressionists to project human emotions and attitudes into all objects, and to seek truth in man's spiritual qualities rather than in external appearances. Expressionists opposed realism and naturalism on the grounds that they focused attention upon surface details and implied that the observable phenomena of contemporary materialistic and mechanistic society represent fixed truths. The expressionists argued that external reality is alterable and should be changed until it harmonizes with man's spiritual nature, the only significant source of value. Many expressionists sought merely to focus attention upon these inner qualities, but others took a more militant view and worked to transform social and political conditions so that they would no longer mechanize and distort man's spirit and prevent his attainment of happiness.

Since the expressionists' "truth" existed primarily within the subjective realm, they had to seek new artistic means to express it. Distorted line, exaggerated shape, abnormal coloring, mechanical movement, and telegraphic speech were devices commonly used to lead audiences beyond surface appearances. Often everything was shown through the eyes of the protagonist, whose view might alter emphases and impose drastic interpretations upon the events. Most expressionist plays were structurally episodic, their unity deriving from a central idea or argument, often one suggesting the possibility of a future Utopia.

The first true expressionist play—*The Beggar* by Reinhard Johannes Sorge (1892–1916)—was published in 1912. It shows the struggle between established conventions and new values, between the older and younger generations, and the attempt of a visionary poet to achieve fulfillment in a materialistic and insensitive society. Much the same idea is found in Walter Hasenclever's (1890–1940) *The Son* (1914), in which the protagonist threatens to kill his father because his freedom to experience life in all its glory is restricted by his puritanical and hypocritical parents; it was probably intended as a symbolic treatment of the need to rid the world of those old values and social forms standing in the way of the "new man."

With the coming of World War I, expressionism began to change and the emphasis to move away from personal concerns to warnings of impending universal catastrophe or pleas for the reformation of man and society. For example, Hasenclever's antiwar play *Antigone* (1916) suggests that love is the only path to happiness but that it cannot be followed until unjust and autocratic rulers are overthrown. Similarly, Fritz von

FIGURE 17.3 Settings by Otto Riegbert for Hasenclever's *The Son* at Keil in 1919. Courtesy Theatermuseum, Munich.

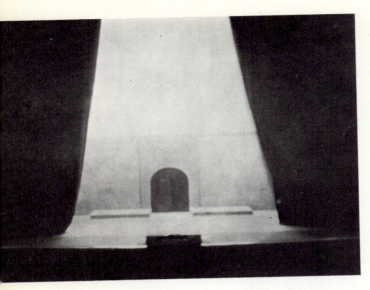

FIGURE 17.4 Jessner's production of Shakespeare's *Richard III* at the Berlin State Theatre in 1919. Setting by Emil Pirchan. Courtesy Theatermuseum, Munich.

Unruh's (1885–1970) *One Race* (1918) shows how mistaken values and deeds (especially war) have dehumanized man, and it ends with a plea to storm "the barracks of violence" as a prelude to a better world.

In 1918 widespread revolution overthrew the German government and brought an end to the war and the monarchy. Until that time few expressionist plays had been produced in Germany because of the strict censorship. Beginning in 1913 a few private readings and dramatic performances had been presented by Herwarth Walden (1878–1941) as an extension of his periodical *The Storm*. But no public performance of an expressionist play was given until 1916, and when the war ended only a few plays had been seen and these only by limited audiences. When peace came, however, expressionism flourished. For example, the ten German-language expressionist periodicals of 1917 had grown to 44 in 1919. Similarly, beginning in 1919 theatres began to take expressionist plays into their repertories and until 1924 the new mode was to remain dominant. But the optimism that accompanied the end of the war (and which seemed to promise the possibility of achieving the expressionists' ideals) soon gave way to disappointment and disillusionment. By 1924 expressionism was virtually dead. This shift from optimism to pessimism is especially evident in the work of the two major expressionist playwrights—Kaiser and Toller.

Georg Kaiser (1878–1945) began his playwriting career in 1911 but his first important work in the expressionist vein was *From Morn to Midnight* (1916), in which a machine-age Everyman searches for the meaning of life only to become a martyr to callousness and greed. But, though the world is not yet ready for the hero's message, Kaiser seems to believe that he has pointed the way. He next wrote a trilogy of plays—*Coral* (1917), *Gas I* (1918) and *Gas II* (1920). In the first, the protagonist gradually comes to recognize the primacy of the soul, and in the second his son sets out to regenerate society. Though in neither play is the protagonist fully successful, both works are essentially optimistic about the future. But in *Gas II* Kaiser seems to have despaired of man and when the play ends the world is undergoing a cataclysmic destruction. After this time Kaiser abandoned the expressionist mode.

Ernst Toller (1893–1939) wrote his first play, *Transfiguration* (1918), while serving a prison term for antiwar activities. It shows the gradual evolution of its hero from a naive patriotic soldier to ardent antiwar revolutionary seeking to help man fight his oppressors. Toller's most influential work was to be *Man and the Masses* (1921), the story of a woman's struggle to aid workers, and her defeat by those who place ideological position above humanitarian principles. By the time Toller wrote *Hurrah, We Live!* (1927) his disillusionment was complete. It shows former idealists, now settled into comfortable lives, repeating the mistakes they once

FIGURE 17.5 Jessner's production of Blut's *Lucius' Insurrection* at the Berlin State Theater. Setting by Emil Pirchan. Note the steps and levels for which Jessner was famous. From *Theatre Arts* (1924).

rebelled against. In protest against such madness, the protagonist commits suicide.

Between 1919 and 1924, expressionism also became a major style of production, especially as applied by Jessner and Fehling. Leopold Jessner (1878–1945) had worked in Hamburg and Königsberg before becoming director of the Berlin State Theatre in 1919. Here he won international fame for his imaginative use of flights of steps *(Jessnertreppen)* and platforms as the major compositional elements in his productions. His principal designers, Emil Pirchan and Cesar Klein, discarded representational scenery for stylized pieces which, along with costumes and lighting, were selected primarily for their emotional and symbolic qualities. Jessner's production of *Richard III* is typical of his approach; the blood-red costumes and light used at the peak of Richard's power dissolved into white costumes and light as Richmond's forces came to the fore. Despite his fame as an "expressionist" director, Jessner worked primarily with the classics. In 1933, he emigrated to the United States.

Unlike Jessner, Jürgen Fehling (1890–1968) made his reputation with expressionist drama, beginning with Toller's *Man and the Masses* at Berlin's Volksbühne in 1921. Fehling sought to arouse intense emotional response in spectators. In his production, bankers fox-trotted to the sound of jingling coins; the workers did a wild dance, which, set to the tune of a concertina and accompanied by constantly shifting colored lights, gave the impression of a witches' sabbath; throughout, the masses were used to create striking effects with movement and sound. Fehling was more eclectic than Jessner, both in the kinds of plays he directed and in the devices he used. He remained in Germany under the Nazis and served as director of the Berlin State Theatre.

As expressionism declined, a more militant approach, eventually to be called "Epic Theatre," arose. Its first major practitioner, Erwin Piscator (1893–1966), after working with the Proletarian Theatre in 1920 and the Central Theatre from 1921 to 1924, was appointed a director at the Volksbühne, where between 1924 and 1927 he sought to create a "proletarian drama," as opposed to merely producing standard plays for a working-class audience. His reshaping of texts into propaganda, however, aroused such controversy that he resigned in 1927 to found the Piscator Theatre. There in 1927–1928 he perfected many of the techniques later associated with Epic Theatre. For Toller's *Hurrah, We Live!*, a reworking of Alexei Tolstoy's *Rasputin*, and an adaptation of Jaroslav Hacek's novel, *The Good Soldier Schweik,*

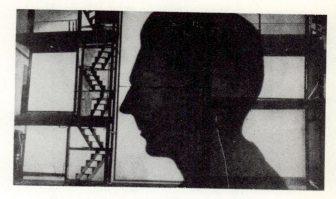

FIGURE 17.6   Piscator's setting for Toller's *Hurrah, We Live.* From *Theatre Arts* (1932).

Piscator used filmed sequences, cartoons, treadmills, segmented settings, and other devices to draw strong parallels between the dramatic events and real-life situations, thus arguing the need for social and political reforms. Piscator left Germany in 1933 and in 1939 went to America, where until 1951 he taught at the New School for Social Research and staged a number of plays in New York and elsewhere.

Despite Piscator's pioneering work, Epic Theatre is now associated primarily with Bertolt Brecht (1898–1956), the movement's major theoretician and dramatist. Brecht entered the theatre as a director in Munich and

FIGURE 17.7   Brecht's *Drums in the Night* as presented at the Kammerspiele in Munich, 1922. Directed by Otto Falckenberg, setting by Otto Riegbert. Courtesy Theatermuseum, Munich.

FIGURE 17.8 Brecht's *Im Dickicht der Städte* as presented at the Residenztheater, Munich, 1923. Directed by Erich Engel, design by Caspar Neher. Courtesy Theatermuseum, Munich.

later worked for Reinhardt in Berlin. As a playwright, he experimented with dadaism and expressionism in such early plays as *Baal* (1918) and *Drums in the Night* (1922) before arriving at his more characteristic style with *Man is Man* (1926). His first major success came with *The Three-Penny Opera* (1928), which, with music by Kurt Weill and settings by Caspar Neher (1897–1962), ran for 400 performances. In 1933, Brecht went into exile, during which he wrote most of his major works: *The Private Life of the Master Race* (1935–1938), twenty-eight scenes demonstrating Nazi inhumanity; *Mother Courage* (1937), emphasizing both the endurance and the brutalization of a woman during the Thirty Years' War; *Galileo* (1938–1939); *The Good Woman of Setzuan* (1938–1940), *Herr Puntila* (1940–1941), *The Resistible Rise of Arturo Ui* (1941), and *The Caucasian Chalk Circle* (1944–1945), Brecht's last major play. Because of his exile, Brecht's works were little produced until he returned to Germany in 1947, but since then they have been increasingly important throughout the world.

Although Brecht's plays have gained a devoted audience, his theory probably is even more widely known. Brecht called his approach "epic" in order to indicate its broad sweep and its mixture of narrative and dramatic techniques. He wished to assign the spectator an active role in the theatre by making him watch critically rather than passively. Consequently, he arrived at the concept of "alienation" *(verfremdungseffekt)*, or making stage events sufficiently strange that the spectator will ask questions about them. To create this thoughtful contemplation and to prevent the spectator from confusing stage events with real-life events, Brecht wanted the

theatrical means (such as lighting instruments, musicians, scene changing) to be visible. He also deliberately separated episodes by inserting songs and narrative passages between them. Through these and other devices he called attention to the theatrical nature of the experience and sought to create the alienation that he thought would induce critical evaluation of the dramatic situations. Brecht hoped in this way to lead the audience to relate what they saw on the stage to social and economic conditions outside the theatre; ultimately, he wished the audience to apply its new perceptions by working for changes in the social and economic system.

Unlike Appia and Craig, Brecht did not believe that all the theatrical elements should be synthesized into a master work with a complete unified effect. This, he suggested, was a redundant use of the various elements, each of which should make a different comment on the action. He also rejected Stanislavsky's approach to acting and advised performers to think of their roles "in the third person" so they might comment upon the characters' motivations and actions. Brecht's theories have been subjected to many conflicting interpretations, but they have stimulated directors throughout the world.

Still another experiment of the 1920s—the Bauhaus—was to have considerable international impact. In 1919, Walter Gropius (1883–1969) established at the Staatliches Bauhaus in Weimar a School of Fine Arts and of Arts and Crafts in which he attempted to break down the traditional barriers between the artist and the craftsman and to unite architecture, painting, sculpture, and other arts into a communal expression. Ultimately the Bauhaus wished to shape daily surroundings into a "master art work" in which everything from the landscaping to the house, its furnishings, decorations, and even its kitchen utensils are conceived as parts of a total design for living. It sought to make the functional artistic, and the artistic functional. It wished to end the elitist status of art, under which it had been confined primarily to museums or the homes of wealthy, and to make it a part of daily life.

From 1923 until 1929 the Bauhaus' stage workshop was under the direction of Oskar Schlemmer (1888–1943), who was concerned primarily with three-dimensional figures in space. Rather than trying to adjust stage space to the natural form of man, he sought to unify the human body with the abstract stage space, and consequently he attempted to alter the human shape through three-dimensional costumes that transformed actors into "ambulant architecture" and to control their movement

FIGURE 17.9 Brecht's *Threepenny Opera*, the original production at the Theater am Schiffbauerdamm, Berlin, 1928. Directed by Erich Engel, setting by Caspar Neher. Courtesy Theatermuseum, Munich.

be used as an acting area, and scenery could be shifted on it by means of wagons. A wide stage house also permitted rolling platforms to move horizontally. Spaced around the perimeter of the auditorium were twelve columns, between which could be mounted screens. A translucent cyclorama at the rear of the proscenium stage also provided a surface for projections, and other screens were mounted in the auditorium above the heads of the spectators. Gropius declared that he wished to place the

through mathematical precision. Schlemmer ignored the verbal element, but he systematically analyzed each visual element (empty space, the human figure, movement, light, and color) both in isolation and in various combinations. Like much of the Bauhaus' work, Schlemmer's can probably best be viewed as a form of basic research, the results of which can be applied in various ways to practical problems. Since the 1950s, his experiments have been especially influential on dance.

In theatre architecture, the Bauhaus' most important work was done by Gropius, who in 1927 designed a "total theatre" for Piscator. Although never built, its design has continued to be influential on theatre architecture. According to Gropius, there are only three basic stage forms—the arena, thrust, and proscenium—and in his total theatre he sought to accommodate all. He mounted a segment of seats and an acting area on a large revolvable circle forward of the proscenium. When this acting area was moved to a position contiguous with the proscenium, it formed a thrust stage, and when rotated 180 degrees it became an arena. From the wings of the proscenium stage ran an open platform which continued completely around the edge of the auditorium. It could

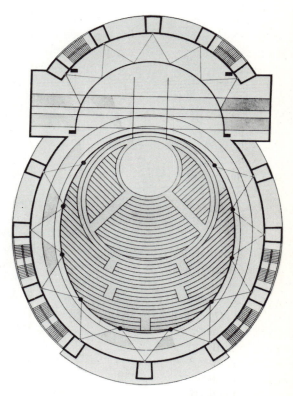

FIGURE 17.10 Gropius' "total theatre." Note that the white circle (a playing area) joins the proscenium to form a thrust stage. This circle (along with the seating shown on the larger circle) can be revolved to place the acting area in the middle of the auditorium to create an arena stage. Note the ramp, which also may be used for acting, that completely surrounds the auditorium. Note also the projectors (the beams of which are represented by triangular lines) placed around the auditorium and back of the cyclorama, thus making it possible to enclose the audience within a projected setting. From Barkhin, *Architectura Teatra*, Moscow (1947).

audience in the midst of the action and "to force them to participate in experiencing the play."

The Bauhaus was always controversial and when the Nazis came to power it was forced to close. Its members dispersed throughout the world, but their influence upon design and architecture has been so pervasive that its source is seldom recognized.

Although Epic Theatre and the Bauhaus now seem the major German contributions of the 1920s, at the time another movement—usually called *Neue Sachlichkeit* or neorealism—dominated the theatre. It came into being around 1923 in reaction to the excesses of expressionism and consequently concentrated on such mundane problems as the difficulties of adjusting to peacetime, the overly rigid legal system, and the traumas of adolescence and school life. Unfortunately, though neorealistic plays were numerous, few now bear reading. Among the best writers were Friedrich Wolf (1888–1953), with *Cyanide* (1929), an attack on abortion laws, and *The Sailors of Cattaro* (1930), a documentary drama about an uprising in the Austro-Hungarian navy during World War I; and Ferdinand Bruckner (1891–1958), with *The Malady of Youth* (1926), about the disillusionment of young people, and *The Criminals* (1928), a study of the legal system. (Bruckner later won international fame with his plays about historical figures, such as *Elizabeth of England*.) The best of the neorealist writers was Carl Zuckmayer (1896–   ). His *The Merry Vineyard* (1925), an earthy comedy set against the background of a wine festival, was a resounding success. His most enduring work has been *The Captain of Kopenick* (1931), a satirical treatment of Prussian bureaucracy, showing how a petty criminal takes over a town merely by putting on a uniform and thereby commanding unquestioning obedience.

With the advent of Hitler in 1933, many important theatre artists left Germany. Many of those who remained underwent what has been called an "inner emigration" by writing or staging historical works or by deliberately distancing their work from the contemporary scene. The Nazis encouraged plays about the Teutonic past and a production style calculated to evoke a grandiose, larger-than-life picture of an all-powerful, all-Nordic world. But theatrical personnel were seldom overtly required to comply with Nazi ideology, and several were able to retain relative independence. Among these, the most important were Heinz Hilpert (1890–1967), who succeeded Reinhardt as head of the Deutsches Theater from 1933 to 1945, Karlheinz Martin

(1886–1948), Berthold Viertel (1885–1953), and Jürgen Fehling. Perhaps the best of the designers were Traugott Müller, Rochus Gliese, Cesar Klein, Caspar Neher, Wilhelm Reinking, and Karl Gröning. For the most part, however, the German theatre between 1933 and 1945 was subordinated to political demands.

THEATRE AND DRAMA IN FRANCE, 1915–1940

The First World War severely curtailed theatrical activities in France. Practically all able-bodied actors were inducted and others spent much of their time performing for the armed forces. The Parisian companies were so depleted that even the Comédie Française had to fill out casts with students from the Conservatoire. The wartime mood turned the theatre toward popular entertainment, a direction which continued to dominate the "boulevard theatres" after the war. Of the boulevard producers, the most successful was probably Sacha Guitry (1885–1957), author of about 150 plays, most of which he produced, directed, and starred in.

At the opposite extreme, a series of revolts against tradition—fauvism, cubism, futurism, constructivism, dadaism, and surrealism—helped to break the hold of realism and to turn attention to new forms. During the war many artists and political dissenters sought refuge in Switzerland, where dadaism, the most extreme of the revolts, was launched in 1916. The principal spokesman for dada was Tristan Tzara (1896–1963), who published seven manifestoes between 1916 and 1920. Dada was grounded in a thorough-going skepticism about a world that could produce a global war. Since insanity seemed to them the world's true state, the dadaists sought in their actions to replace logic and reason with calculated madness and in their art to substitute discord and chaos for unity, balance, and harmony. They presented a number of programs composed of lectures, readings, "sound poems," dances, visual art, and short plays. Often several things were going on simultaneously. As the war drew to a close, the dadaists dispersed. For a time, the movement thrived in Germany, but it received its greatest support in Paris. But everywhere it had begun to decline by 1920 and shortly afterwards disappeared. Much of what it stood for was to resurface in the 1960s and to be developed under other names.

In France, dadaism was succeeded by surrealism, which drew much of its inspiration from the works of

Jarry and Apollinaire. Guillaume Apollinaire (1880–1918), friend to almost all *avant-garde* writers and painters after 1900 and the principal spokesman for cubism, influenced surrealism largely through his play, *The Breasts of Tiresias* (1903, revised and produced in 1917), subtitled a "drame surréaliste." Purporting to be a plea for the repopulation of France, the play concerns Thérèse, who after releasing her breasts (balloons, which float away) is transformed into Tiresias. Her husband, now forced to take over her functions, eventually discovers the means of creating children (sheer willpower) and becomes the parent of more than forty thousand offspring. This work exemplifies many of Apollinaire's theories; he rejected everyday logic and suggested that comedy, tragedy, burlesque, fantasy, acrobatics, and declamation should be mingled with music, dance, color, and light to create a new form of expression.

André Breton (1896–1966) soon assumed leadership of the surrealists and issued the movement's first "manifesto" in 1924. Freud's considerable influence upon Breton is evident in his definition of surrealism as "pure psychic automatism, by which is intended to express, verbally, in writing, or by other means, the real process of thought. Thought's dictation, in the absence of all control exercised by the reason and outside all esthetic or moral preoccupation." Thus, the subconscious mind in a dreamlike state represented for Breton the basis of artistic truth. After his conversion to communism in 1926, Breton sought to make surrealism more militant, and his second manifesto (1929) denounced many of the movement's former members. Thereafter, surrealism declined, although its crowning achievement did not come until 1938, when an international exhibition of painting demonstrated the movement's considerable accomplishments.

Surrealism's impact on the theatre was essentially indirect. The most effective uses of its techniques were made by Jean Cocteau (1892–1963), who began his theatrical work with *Parade* (1917), a ballet staged by the Ballets Russes, and *The Ox on the Roof* (1920), a pantomime performed by the Fratellini family of circus clowns. His finest plays, *Antigone* (1922), *Orpheus* (1926), and *The Infernal Machine* (1934), based on the Oedipus legend, are reworkings of myths. Cocteau's power came in part from the manner in which he juxtaposed the familiar with the legendary. For example, in *Orpheus* the protagonists are a modern young married couple, but the introduction of a mysterious glazier and a horse who delivers messages evokes a sense of mystery and significance, by means of which the ancient myth is given contemporary relevance. Although Cocteau never escaped the charge of charlatanism, he was a source of inspiration to other artists throughout his life.

Many of the new movements in the visual arts came into the theatre through the Ballets Russes, which commissioned settings from Picasso, Matisse, Juan Gris, Marie Laurencin, and Braque. The Ballets Suédois, which played in Paris between 1920 and 1925 under the direction of Rolf de Maré (1888–1964), also commissioned settings from Léger, de Chirico, and Picabia. This company extended the traditional conceptions of ballet as well through such works as Cocteau's *The Married Couple of the Eiffel Tower* (1921), in which dialogue was spoken by actors costumed as phonographs.

Of all the *avant-garde* figures between the wars, Antonin Artaud (1896–1948) was to be the most important. Associated with the theatre from 1921, Artaud had worked with Lugné-Poë, Dullin, and Pitoëff before founding the Théâtre Alfred Jarry in 1926 in association with Roger Vitrac, a surrealist playwright. Devoted entirely to nonrealistic drama, this theatre lasted only two seasons. Artaud's significant contributions were to be made after 1931, when the stimulation of a Balinese dance troupe motivated him to formulate his theory of the theatre, published in 1938 as *The Theatre and Its Double*.

According to Artaud, the theatre in the Western world has been devoted to a very narrow range of human experience, primarily the psychological problems of individuals or the social problems of groups. To Artaud, the more important aspects of existence are those submerged in the unconscious, those things that cause divisions within people and between people and lead to hatred, violence, and disaster. He believed that if given the proper theatrical experiences, man can be freed from ferocity and can then express the joy that civilization has forced him to repress, for the theatre can evacuate those feelings which are usually expressed in more destructive ways. Or, as Artaud put it, "the theatre has been created to drain abcesses collectively."

Artaud was certain that his goals could not be reached through appeals to the rational mind. Rather, it would be necessary to operate directly upon the senses (for the conscious mind has been conditioned to sublimate many human impulses) and break down the audience's defenses. Artaud sometimes referred to his as a "theatre of cruelty," since in order to achieve its ends it would have to force the audience to confront itself. But the cruelty he advocated is not primarily physical but moral or psychological.

Artaud's intention to operate directly on the nervous system led him to suggest many innovations in theatrical practice. Among these was the replacement of the traditional theatre building with remodeled barns, factories, or airplane hangars. He wished to locate acting areas in corners, on overhead catwalks, and along the walls. He was much impressed by Eastern practices and argued that the West needed to develop symbolic and ritualistic devices similar to those used in the Orient. In lighting, he called for a "vibrating, shredded" effect, and in sound he favored shrillness, abrupt changes in volume, and the use of the human voice to create harmonies and dissonances. Thus, Artaud wanted to assault the audience, to break down its resistance, to purge it morally and spiritually, and he sought to do this through devices "addressed first of all to the senses rather than to the mind," for "the public thinks first of all with its senses."

Like Appia and Craig, Artaud was a visionary rather than a wholly practical man, and like them he was at first little appreciated. Many of their ideas are similar, but Artaud differed drastically in his conception of the theatre's ultimate purpose. Appia and Craig tended to value art for its own sake, whereas Artaud saw in it the salvation of mankind. Theirs is a world of idealized beauty, his a region of cruel torment. Consequently, as the post-World War II view of man darkened, the influence of Appia and Craig declined as that of Artaud increased.

Somewhere between the commercial and *avant-garde* figures were Gémier, Hébertot, and Copeau. Firmin Gémier (1869–1933) began his acting career with Antoine in 1892 and later worked with groups ranging from the Théâtre de l'Oeuvre to melodrama troupes. Perhaps for this reason, Gémier was to follow an eclectic approach not unlike that of Reinhardt. From 1906 until 1922 he served as director of the Théâtre Antoine, and from 1922 until 1930 as director of the Odéon. Under Gémier, the Odéon became almost an *avant-garde* theatre, in part because his designer, René Fuerst, drew upon practically all of the recent movements. Despite Gémier's fine work as a director, his significance probably lies in his continuing attempts to bring the theatre to all the people.

The desire to make cultural activities available to the common man had led in the 1890s to the Volksbühnen of Germany and the less ambitious "people's

FIGURE 17.11 Jean Cocteau's surrealistic play, *Antigone*, as produced by Charles Dullin at the Atelier, Paris, in 1922. From *Le Théâtre* (1923).

theatres" of France. In 1903, Romain Rolland's *The Theatre of the People* outlined a program under which local groups would perform plays for their fellow citizens as in Greek times. Attracted by this movement, Gémier sought to make the best professional productions available to provincial audiences through his Théâtre Ambulant, which between 1911 and 1913 toured through France with a tent theatre. In 1920, Gémier persuaded the government to create the Théâtre National Populaire. Given only a token subsidy, Gémier had to rely on other companies to contribute occasional productions to the TNP. Although it never became a significant force during Gémier's lifetime, the TNP was to become one of France's finest theatres after the Second World War. Gémier's interests in a popular theatre also led him into other experiments. In 1919 he took over the Cirque d'Hiver, where he staged *Oedipus, King of Thebes* by Bouhélier and *The Great Pastoral,* a Provençal nativity play. In this and other ways, Gémier's work in France paralleled that of Reinhardt in Germany.

Jacques Hérbertot (1886–1971) exerted his primary influence as an entrepreneur. In his three contiguous theatres, the Théâtre des Champs-Elysées, the Comédie des Champs-Elysées, and the Studio des Champs-Elysées, between 1920 and 1925, he employed the most imaginative directors of his age. Furthermore, he imported such companies as the Moscow Art Theatre, the Kamerny, and others. Thus, Hébertot made the best of both domestic and foreign theatre available to the Parisian public.

The most pervasive influence on the theatre between the wars was exerted by Jacques Copeau, who reopened the Vieux Colombier in 1919 and rededicated himself to the ideals he had set forth before the war. Unlike Gémier, Copeau thought it impossible to maintain high standards while appealing to the masses. Consequently, he was often accused of snobbery and of treating the theatre as a religion. Eventually, Copeau found it difficult to reconcile his high standards with a full schedule of public performances; in 1924 he left Paris to open a school in Burgundy, where he hoped to perfect his ideas.

Although Copeau performed for only five years after the war, his ideals were to be continued by four other producers—Jouvet, Dullin, Pitoëff, and Baty—who dominated the Parisian theatre until the Second World War. In 1927, they formed an alliance, commonly called the Cartel des Quatre, under which they agreed to counsel each other, to share publicity, and to negotiate jointly with theatrical unions.

Louis Jouvet (1887–1951) began his career in Rouché's Théâtre des Arts, where he met Copeau, for whom he acted minor roles in 1913–1914. Accompanying Copeau to New York in 1917, he remained with him until 1922 when Hébertot employed him as a director. After achieving a major success with Romains' *Dr. Knock* in 1923, Jouvet formed his own company in 1924, taking into it many members of Copeau's recently disbanded troupe. Jouvet did not prosper, however, until 1928, when he began his collaboration with Giraudoux. In 1934, he moved his company to the Théâtre de l'Athenée, a boulevard house, where he remained until 1941, after which he went into voluntary exile until 1945. Jouvet, like Copeau, put primary emphasis upon the text. Above all, he respected language and its nuances. He demanded lucid analysis and careful attention to detail from his actors. In the early years, he designed his own scenery, which was always tasteful without being innovative. At the Athenée, he usually worked with Christian Bérard (1902–1949), one of the finest designers of the period.

Charles Dullin (1885–1949) had played at many minor theatres before joining Rouché and then Copeau. After returning to Paris in 1919, he worked for Gémier before establishing his own theatre, l'Atelier, in 1922.

FIGURE 17.12 **Stage of the Vieux Colombier in use. Here it has been adapted for Shakespeare's** *Twelfth Night.* **Note how the basic form has been partially disguised. From** *Theater Arts Magazine* **(1924).**

He remained in this small, out-of-the-way theatre until 1939. Dullin was extremely eclectic, presenting works ranging from the Greeks to the present and from tragedy to farce. Through painstaking analysis of the text, he sought to let each play dictate the proper approach to it. His aim was to capture the "inner poetry" through honesty and unity. He refused to do any play which he thought depended upon machinery or upon a director's

FIGURE 17.13 **Bérard's setting for Jouvet's production in 1937 of Molière's** *School for Wives.* **From** *Décor de Théâtre dans le Monde depuis 1935.*

FIGURE 17.14 Pitoëff's production of *Romeo and Juliet*. Note the strong emphasis on triangular shapes and converging lines, giving an expressionistic effect. From *Theatre Arts* (1935).

tricks. Nevertheless, he put considerable emphasis upon visual design and employed some of the best artists of his time: Louis Touchagues, Lucien Coutaud, Georges Valmier, Jean-Victor Hugo, Michel Duran, and André Barsacq. Music, dance, and mimed spectacle also figured prominently in practically all of his productions. Dullin's perennial hope of attracting a wider audience led him in 1941 to become director of the Théâtre Sarah Bernhardt, where he struggled along until 1947. His last years were spent in Geneva as director of the theatre section of the Maison des Arts. Ultimately, Dullin's impact on the theatre was to come in large part through his school, in which such significant later figures as Barrault and Vilar received their early training.

Georges Pitoëff (1884–1939) had performed widely in his native Russia before emigrating to Switzerland in 1914. He and his wife, Ludmilla (1896–1951), who had studied at the Conservatoire, came to Paris in 1922 and worked for Hébertot until 1925, after which they formed their own company and played in a number of Parisian theatres and toured abroad. Pitoëff was noted for his knowledge of foreign drama, of which he was the principal producer in France. As a director, Pitoëff placed primary emphasis upon the text. For him, the most powerful element was perhaps rhythm, which he sought to find and project for each character and scene. He designed his own scenery, which ranged stylistically from the abstract to the realistically pictorial. Characteristically, however, he used a few indispensable set pieces which he invested with symbolic significance. Of all the members of the Cartel, Pitoëff was probably the most versatile and experimental.

Gaston Baty (1882–1951) was the only member of the Cartel who was not an actor and who did not place primary emphasis upon the text. He began his career under Gémier in 1919, managed the Studio des Champs-Elysées from 1924 to 1928, and then settled in the Théâtre Montparnasse in 1930. After 1935, Baty became extremely interested in marionettes, as a result of which his productions became increasingly stylized. Through much of his career, Baty was assisted by Marguerite Jamois (1903–1964), who starred in many of his productions and directed others. To Baty, the director was the major theatrical artist. In his productions a mysterious

FIGURE 17.15 Baty's production of his own adaptaion of *Madame Bovary* (1936). The actors are Lucien Nat and Marguerite Jamois. From *Theatre Arts* (1936).

and poetic world, created by the skillful manipulation of mood, seemed to lurk behind a realistic surface. His emphasis upon costumes, scenery, properties, music, and lighting was sometimes criticized, but he was also known as the "magician of the *mise-en-scène.*"

The influence of Copeau was reenforced in the 1930s by several new groups. In 1930, students from Copeau's school formed the Compagnie des Quinze under the direction of Michel Saint-Denis (1897–1971), Copeau's nephew, and from 1931 to 1933, they played at the Vieux Colombier. After the company disbanded, Saint-Denis opened the Theatre Studio in London, which, in combination with his directing work at the Old Vic and elsewhere, served to carry Copeau's influence into the British theatre. Léon Chancerel (1886–1965), another of Copeau's students, worked primarily with student groups in schools and universities and with children's theatre. His Compagnie des Comédiens-Routiers (1929–1939) played primarily for Boy Scout groups, while his Théâtre de l'Oncle Sébastien (1935–1939) presented plays for children.

Three other directors, Barsacq, Dasté, and Jacquemont, were also to be of considerable importance. André Barsacq (1909–1973) had studied at the School of Decorative Arts and with Dullin before becoming one of Paris' leading scene designers. In 1937, he joined with Dasté and Jacquemont to form the Compagnie des Quatre Saisons, but left in 1940 to assume control of the Atelier when Dullin relinquished it. Barsacq continued to direct that theatre until his death, maintaining Dullin's high standards. Jean Dasté (1904–   ), Copeau's son-in-law and pupil, was a member of the Compagnie des Quinze before joining the Compagnie des Quatre Saisons. In 1940 he went with Barsacq to the Atelier, where he was one of the theatre's principal directors. Maurice Jacquemont (1910–   ) was trained by Chancerel and had worked with several companies before the formation of the Compagnie des Quatre Saisons, with which he continued until 1942. In 1944 he became head of the Studio des Champs-Elysées, a position he was to hold until 1960.

Copeau returned to a more active role in the theatre during the 1930s. In addition to directing both in Paris and abroad, he was associated with the Comédie Française after 1936 and served as its director in 1939–1940 until dismissed by the Vichy government. Under Emile Fabré's direction between 1915 and 1936, the Comédie Française had steadily declined, in large part because of low subsidy and political interference. After

FIGURE 17.16   André Barsacq's setting for Dullin's production of *Volpone,* 1929. From *Décor de Théâtre dans le Monde depuis 1935.*

1936, the new director, Edouard Bourdet, was able to make many improvements. Not only was the subsidy doubled, but Bourdet imported Copeau, Dullin, Jouvet, and Baty to direct several revivals. For the first time in its history, the Comédie Française came to list each play's director on its programs. By the time the war began, the prestige of the company was fully revived. In spite of the company's conservative nature before 1936, it included some of the best actors in France: Béatrix Dussane (1888–1969), Berthe Bovy (1888–   ), André Brunot (1879–1973), Charles Grandval (1882–1943), Pierre Fresnay (1897–1975), Marie Bell (1900–   ), and Madeleine Renaud (1903–   ).

Although France produced few truly outstanding playwrights between the wars, a number achieved considerable renown. Henri-René Lenormand (1882–1951) was one of the first French writers to emphasize the subconscious mind and the relativity of time and space through such works as *Time is a Dream* (1919) and *The Eater of Dreams* (1922). Henri Ghéon (1875–1944) sought to revive religious drama and for many years toured with his Compagnons de Notre-Dame. Of his approximately 100 plays, the best known are *The Poor Under the Stairs* (1921) and *Christmas in the Market*

Place (1935). André Obey (1892–   ) was associated with the Compagnie des Quinze, which produced his first plays, *Noah* and *The Rape of Lucrece,* in 1931. Perhaps his best work is found in *Man of Ashes* (1949), a retelling of the Don Juan story. Armand Salacrou (1899–   ) was one of the most versatile dramatists of the period, ranging through surrealist fantasies, light comedy, drama, and historical plays. He came to public attention with *Patchouli* (1927), and did his best work with *The World Is Round* (1935), a history in miniature of the recurrent struggle between the flesh and the spirit.

Of the satirical writers, the best were Jules Romains (1885–1972), whose *Doctor Knock, or the Triumph of Medicine* (1923) shows the exploitation of man's anxieties about his health, and Marcel Pagnol (1895–1974), whose *The Merchants of Glory* (1925) satirizes the business schemes built around the war dead, and *Topaze* (1928), the story of a schoolmaster who prospers only after he abandons his principles. Pagnol is now better known for his romantic trilogy about Marseilles waterfront life, *Marius* (1929), *Fanny* (1931), and *César* (1937). Surrealistic farce was exploited by Fernand Crommelynck (1888–1970), whose *The Magnificent Cuckold* (1921) tells of a man who, upon becoming suspicious of his wife's fidelity, insists on testing it endlessly but never to his satisfaction; and Roger Vitrac (1899–1952) who derided all traditional values in *Victor, or Children in Power* (1928) and *The Secret Hawker* (1936). Vitrac's reputation has grown considerably since 1963 when *Victor* was revived in Paris to critical acclaim. Marcel Achard (1899–1974) excelled in stylized romantic comedy, notably *Voulez-Vous Jouer avec Moi?* (1923), *Jean de la Lune* (1929), and *The Pirate* (1938), in which, typically, a devoted lover subdues the frivolity of a coquette. The most bitter plays of the period were written by Steve Passeur (1899–1966), who delighted in reversing the normal pattern of relationships. In his most famous play, *The Woman Buys* (1930), a woman buys a husband and subjects him to a daily round of torment until they hate each other.

The plays of the Belgian dramatist Michel de Ghelderode (1898–1962) resemble those of Jarry, the surrealists and expressionists, and his theories recall those of Artaud. Throughout his more than thirty plays runs his vision of man as a creature whose flesh overpowers his spirit. Corruption, death, and cruelty are always near the surface, although behind them lurks an implied criticism of degradation and materialism and a call to repentance. But in his works faith is apt to be approached through blasphemy and suffering through ludicrous farce. Like Artaud, Ghelderode downgrades language in favor of spectacle. Place is apt to shift rapidly and unexpectedly; characters are usually exaggerated and many are descended from the clowns of music hall, circus, and fair. His scorn for traditional dramaturgy is shown by the labels he applied to his works: "tragic farce," "burlesque mystery," "tragedy for the music hall," and so on. Of his many dramas, the best known are *Escurial* (1927), *Chronicles of Hell* (1929), *Pantagleize* (1929), and *Hop, Signor* (1935). Since 1949, when he came to the attention of the absurdists, Ghelderode's reputation has steadily risen.

Probably the most important French dramatist between the wars was Jean Giraudoux (1882–1944), a novelist and member of the Foreign Service, who in 1928 began his theatrical career with a dramatization of his novel *Siegfried.* In Jouvet, Giraudoux found his ideal interpreter and he wrote most of his important works for him: *Amphitryon 38* (1929), *Judith* (1931), *The Trojan War Shall Not Take Place* (1935), and *Ondine* (1939). Giraudoux often took his subjects from familiar sources but gave them novel interpretations, for he delighted in pointing out the simple in the complex and the surprising in the familiar. His works turn on antitheses—peace and war, fidelity and infidelity, life and death, liberty and destiny—and their reconciliations. His dramas take place at the moment when men are faced with a choice between two contradictory positions; he explores the contradictions and usually suggests means whereby they can be reconciled, often through some novel perception. Language, which he considered the highest expression of human reason, is Giraudoux's primary means. Writing at a time when the playwright had been subordinated to the director, Giraudoux sought to reaffirm the literary worth of drama. He wrote in a euphonious and highly expressive prose, with a marked disposition for fantasy, irony, and humor. Throughout all his work runs a deep faith in man.

Giraudoux's position of preeminence was to be challenged after the war by Jean Anouilh (1910–   ), who began as Jouvet's secretary and turned to writing in 1932 under Giraudoux's inspiration. His first success came in 1937 with *Traveller Without Baggage,* presented by Pitoëff. Most of Anouilh's later works, such as *Carnival of Thieves* (1938), *Rendezvous in Senlis* (1941), and *Antigone* (1943), were produced by Barsacq. Anouilh has divided his plays into the serious, or "black" pieces, and the comic, or "red" pieces. In the former, typically a

FIGURE 17.17 Jouvet's production of Giraudoux's *The Trojan War Shall Not Take Place.* Jouvet is seen at the right. From *Theatre Arts* (1936).

young, idealistic, and uncompromising protagonist is able to maintain his integrity only by choosing death. *Antigone* is perhaps the best-known example. In the "red" plays, although the characters are in many ways similar, a fairy-tale atmosphere permits a happier resolution. Anouilh was to be one of France's most prolific postwar writers.

With the coming of war in 1939 and the surrender of Paris to the Nazis, theatrical activities were at first seriously curtailed. Some major figures went into exile and those who remained were subject to close surveillance. For the most part, the theatre was reduced to politically inoffensive plays or popular entertainments, but a few productions were to attain true eminence despite all strictures.

ITALIAN THEATRE AND DRAMA, 1915–1940

Many major Italian artists during this period were adherents of futurism, a movement launched in Italy in 1909 by Filippo Tommaso Marinetti (1876–1944). Like the expressionists, the futurists rejected the past and

wished to transform man. But, whereas the expressionists associated the past with soul-destroying materialism and industrialism, the futurists deplored the veneration of the past as a barrier to progress. Consequently, they glorified the energy and speed of the machine age and sought to embody them in artistic forms. From 1910 onward they gave performances during which they proclaimed their manifestoes, gave concerts, read poems, performed plays, and exhibited works of visual art—at times several of these simultaneously. Sometimes they moved about among the spectators, using various parts of a room sequentially or concurrently. They especially outraged audiences with their demands that libraries and museums be destroyed as the first step toward creating a more dynamic future.

Among the art forms championed by the futurists were "picture poems" (or concrete poetry), kinetic sculptures, colleges, and *bruitisme* (or "dynamic music," based on the sounds of everyday life). As for theatre, they denounced past practices and declared music halls, nightclubs, and circuses to be better models on which to base future forms. They found earlier drama too lengthy, analytic, and static and proposed instead a "synthetic drama" which would compress into a moment or two the essence of a dramatic situation. In 1915–1916 they published seventy-six of these short plays.

During World War I, futurism lost many followers because it glorified war as the supreme example of energy. After the war it received new vitality, perhaps because many of its tenets were compatible with Mussolini's program of aggressive action. The principal exponent of futurism in the 1920s was Enrico Prampolini (1894–1960), who demanded that the painted scene be replaced by "stage architecture that will move." He also wished to substitute luminous forms for human actors. He conceived of the stage as a multidimensional space in which spiritual forces (represented by light and abstract forms) would play out a drama of semireligious significance.

After 1930 interest in futurism declined. Though it never became a major theatrical movement, it pioneered innovations that would be revived and extended in the 1950s: (1) the attempt to rescue theatrical art from a museum-like atmosphere; (2) direct confrontation and intermingling of performers and audiences; (3) the exploitation of modern technology to create multimedia performances; (4) the use of simultaneity and multiple focus; (5) an antiliterary and alogical bias; and (6) the breaking down of barriers between arts.

FIGURE 17.18   A Futurist pantomime, *The Merchant of Hearts,* **staged by Enrico Prampolini at the Théâtre de la Pantomime Futuriste in Paris, 1927. Note the mingling of performers with various non-human shapes and forms.**

During the First World War, a new school of writing, usually called "the theatre of the grotesque," appeared in Italy. Its name was derived from *The Mask and the Face* (1916), "a grotesque in three acts," by Luigi Chiarelli (1884–1947). Turning upon the contrast between public and private role-playing, this comedy tells the story of a man who, after confessing the murder of his wife because he thought her unfaithful, is tried and acquitted, although in actuality she is merely locked up at home. Of the many other writers who exploited this ironical vein, the best was probably Pier Maria Rosso di San Secondo (1887–1956), with *Marionettes, What Passion!* (1918) and *The Sleeping Beauty* (1919).

Luigi Pirandello (1867–1936) was by far the greatest Italian playwright of the period. After winning fame with his novels and short stories, Pirandello turned to playwriting in 1910 and after 1915 devoted himself increasingly to the theatre. From 1924 to 1928 he headed the Art Theatre of Rome, with which he presented many significant Italian and foreign plays. Here he was assisted by Marta Abba (1906-   ), who played leading roles, and a company which included Ruggero Ruggeri, one of Italy's most respected actors.

Pirandello's plays, of which the best are *Right You Are—If You Think You Are* (1916), *Six Characters in Search of an Author* (1921), *Henry IV* (1922), *Naked* (1922), *Each in His Own Way* (1924), *Tonight We Improvise* (1930), and *As You Desire Me* (1930), usually turn upon a question of fact which cannot be resolved because each character has his own version of the truth. Thus, Pirandello raises doubts about the validity of the

scientific approach to truth—the direct observation of reality. He seems to suggest that "truth" is necessarily personal and subjective.

Pirandello was also concerned about the relationship between art and nature. Since truth means continual change and since a work of art is fixed forever, he found the theatre the most satisfying form of art, for it necessarily differs at each performance. Thus, he likened the theatre to a living statue. Since for him even the most realistic play could only give a travesty of truth, he thought the only remedy lay in writing philosophical plays that show reality as everchanging. Pirandello made a profound impression on his age. Probably no other writer did so much to popularize the philosophical view that was to be espoused by dramatists of the post-World War II period.

Italy's most eclectic director between the wars was Anton Guilio Bragaglia (1890–1960), who from 1922 to 1936 ran the Teatro degli Independenti in Rome, where on a tiny stage he presented a wide-ranging program of works by Strindberg, Wedekind, Jarry, Maeterlinck, Pirandello, and others, including the futurists. For the most part, however, the Italian theatre was made up of touring companies playing the latest hits. A step toward improvement was taken in 1936 with the formation of the Academy of Dramatic Art in Rome under the direction of Silvio D'Amico. Here the principles of Stanislavsky, Copeau, and Reinhardt were taught. The coming of the war interrupted the Academy's work, however, and its impact was not to be felt until after 1945.

THEATRE AND DRAMA IN SPAIN, 1915–1940

In the years between 1915 and 1940, Spain's popular playwrights continued to be Benavente, the Quinteros, and Martínez Sierra. But the most significant native drama of the immediate postwar years was written by Unamuno and Valle-Inclán. Miguel de Unamuno (1864–1936), one of Spain's most respected philosophers, first expressed his theory of drama in *The Tragic Sense of Life* (1913). His declaration that tragedy stems from a conflict between man's desire for immortality and skepticism about its possibility was to contribute much to existentialist drama following the Second World War. Because of censorship, Unamuno's plays, such as *Fedra* (1917) and *Dream Shadows* (1931), were not widely produced until after 1950. Similarly, the plays of Ramón del Valle-Inclán (1869–1936), perhaps because of their similarity to absurdist drama, have only recently come to the fore. Valle-Inclán, noted primarily as a novelist, wrote several verse plays, satirical dramas, and farces, of which the best are probably *Divine Words* (1913), *The Farce of the True Spanish Queen* (1920), and *The Horns of Don Friolera* (1925). Valle-Inclán labeled his method *esperpento,* or a systematic deformation designed to show the grotesque reality beneath the surface of Spanish life.

A new spirit began to enter Spanish literature with the "Generation of '27," a group which blossomed especially after censorship was eased under the second Republic, proclaimed in 1931. Of the new dramatists, the most significant were Lorca and Casona. Federico García Lorca (1899–1936) wrote his first play, *The Butterfly's Crime,* in 1920. After its failure, he returned to Granada, where he cultivated his interests in symbolism, surrealism, music, painting, and Spanish folklore, and wrote a number of puppet plays. After his *Mariana Pineda* was performed in Barcelona in 1927 by Margarita Xirgu, one of Spain's outstanding actresses, Lorca resumed an active interest in the theatre.

But Lorca's major plays were written only after he had worked closely with a theatre group, La Barraca, a troupe composed of university students and subsidized by the government under its program to bring cultural events to the people. Formed in 1932, La Barraca played Golden Age dramas to rural audiences, and it was the enthusiastic response of these unsophisticated spectators that influenced Lorca to turn to similar themes of love and honor. The results may be seen in *Blood Wedding* (1933), *Yerma* (1934), and *The House of Bernarda Alba* (1935). Blending poetic imagery with primitive passions, these plays are usually considered the finest Spanish works since the Golden Age.

In many ways, the career of Alejandro Casona (1903–1966) paralleled that of Lorca. Between 1931 and 1936, he too directed a government-sponsored troupe, The People's Theatre, which toured Spanish villages. Casona's troupe played primarily short, humorous plays, but like Lorca, Casona was inspired by his experiences to write for this audience. *The Siren Washed Ashore* (1934) and *The Devil Again* (1935) show that blend of realism and fantasy for which Casona was to be noted. In all his works an air of optimism suggests that human problems can be solved.

The Civil War of 1936 brought profound changes. Lorca was killed and Casona emigrated to Argentina.

Until 1939 the theatre served primarily as an instrument of propaganda for both sides of the conflict, and following the victory of Franco's forces it suffered from severe censorship. The plays of Lorca, Casona, and Unamuno were forbidden, and the Spanish theatre entered another period of isolation.

THEATRE AND DRAMA IN RUSSIA, 1917–1940

The most drastic changes brought by World War I were felt in Russia, where the czar's policies had been unpopular for many years. The economic hardships created by the conflict fed the unrest, which in early 1917 broke into open rebellion, thereby ending more than 300 years of rule by the Romanovs. Moderate socialists controlled the government at first, but in late 1917 the Communists seized power. Civil war continued, however, until the early 1920s, by which time more than 20 million people had died and Russia's economic resources were severely depleted. For several years thereafter the government was so preoccupied with rebuilding the nation that the theatre was left free to experiment with new forms.

The Communists viewed the theatre as a national treasure, formerly reserved for the middle and upper classes, to be made available to the proletariat. It was also considered a major tool of instruction and, as such, was placed under the authority of the Commissar of Education, Anatole Lunacharsky (1875–1932). Not only was attendance at professional productions encouraged, but amateur groups were organized among peasants, workers, and soldiers. By 1926, there were about 20,000 dramatic clubs among the peasants alone. Between 1918 and 1922, amateurs also figured prominently in the many mass spectacles that recreated major events in the Revolution. The most famous of these was *The Taking of the Winter Palace,* staged in 1919 by Evreinov on the site of the actual event with a cast of about 8,000 soldiers, sailors, and workers.

The new regime proceeded slowly in its nationalization of the theatre. By 1922–1923, only 33 percent of the theatre plants belonged to the state. By 1925–1926, the percentage had increased to 63, but the process was not to be completed until 1936. Similarly, it was long before theatrical personnel were subjected to political domination.

FIGURE 17.19 Setting by Lyubov Popova for Meyerhold's production of Crommelynck's *The Magnificent Cuckold*, 1922. The action of this play occurs in and around a mill, suggested here by various wheels all of which turned at speeds that varied according to the rhythmical and emotional demands of the scene. This is a good example of Meyerhold's constructivistic productions.

Many of the most enthusiastic supporters of the Revolution were members of the *avant-garde,* who saw in the new regime the opportunity to break with the past and to create new theatrical forms. Meyerhold soon emerged as the leader of this faction. In 1920 he was appointed head of the theatre section in the Commissariat of Education, a position that made him nominal head of the theatre in Russia. At the same time, he continued his own work as a director, staging *The Dawns* (written in 1898 by the Belgian symbolist, Emile Verhaeren) as a Soviet propaganda piece, in which real news bulletins were read from the stage and a public meeting was held with the audience taking part. When this production was denounced by the Central Committee of the Communist Party as foreign to the needs of the proletariat, Meyerhold resigned his government post, but later that year he was appointed head of the state's workshop for directors and in 1922 he acquired a theatre of his own. This series of events is indicative of the power of the *avant-garde* even in the face of official disapproval.

Between 1921 and 1930, Meyerhold perfected techniques with which he had experimented before the Revolution. He now developed more conscious and systematic methods, to which he applied such terms as *biomechanics* and *constructivism.* Biomechanics referred primarily to Meyerhold's approach to acting, intended to create a style appropriate to the machine age. His performers were trained in gymnastics, circus movement, and ballet in order to make them as efficient as machines in carrying out "an assignment received from the outside." Basically what Meyerhold had in mind is a variation on the James-Lange theory: particular patterns of muscular activity elicit particular emotions. Consequently, the actor, to arouse within himself or the audience a desired emotional response, needs only to enact an appropriate kinetic pattern. Thus, Meyerhold sought to replace Stanislavsky's emphasis on internal motivation with one on physical and emotional reflexes. To create a feeling of exuberant joy in both performer and audience, Meyerhold thought it more efficient for the actor to plummet down a slide, swing on a trapeze, or turn a somersault than to restrict himself to behavior considered appropriate by realistic social standards.

Constructivism was a term taken over from the visual arts, where it had first been applied about 1912 to sculpture composed of intersecting planes and masses without representational content. Similarly, Meyerhold frequently arranged nonrepresentational platforms, ramps, turning wheels, trapezes, and other objects to create a "machine for acting," more practicable than decorative.

Meyerhold applied his theories about biomechanics and constructivism most thoroughly in the years between 1922 and 1925, but he steadily softened them. His most famous production of the 1920s was Gogol's *The Inspector General,* presented in 1926. Meyerhold transferred the scene to a large city, reshaped all of the characters and invented several new ones. Costumes, scenery, and properties were based on stylized nineteenth century motifs, and the action was accompanied by period music. The most striking scene was one in which Meyerhold arranged fifteen doors around the stage, and an official emerged simultaneously from each door to offer the inspector a bribe.

Next to Meyerhold, the most influential Russian director of the 1920s was Tairov, who continued the methods he had introduced before the war. Following the Revolution, Lunacharsky had divided theatres into two groups: the well-established or "academic" theatres, which the government subsidized and allowed relative autonomy; and the unproven theatres, which were permitted to exist but given little encouragement. Thus, the government favored pre-Revolutionary groups, a practice bitterly opposed by Meyerhold. Under this scheme, the Kamerny Theatre was classified as an "academic" theatre. Until 1924, Tairov took little notice of the Revolution, producing such works as Wilde's *Salomé,* Scribe's *Adrienne Lecouvreur,* and Racine's *Phèdre* in the style he had always followed. Unlike most producers of the period, who clothed actors in uniform-like garments similar to those worn by the spectators, Tairov sought to lift audiences above the drabness of everyday life. After 1924, Tairov occasionally produced Russian classical and contemporary plays, but his theatre remained the principal link with the West. In addition to its predominantly Western repertory, the troupe also toured in Western Europe in 1923, 1928, and 1929. When Tairov turned to contemporary Russian works, he often ran into difficulties. In 1929 his production of Mikhail Levidov's

FIGURE 17.20 Meyerhold's adaptation of Gogol's *The Inspector General,* 1926. Shown here is the "bribery" scene. The set could open at the back to allow wagons to move in and out.

Plot of the Equals, a play about the degeneration of the French Revolution into the Reign of Terror, was removed after one performance. Thereafter, Tairov's influence declined.

Another important innovator in these early years was Yevgeny Vakhtangov (1883–1922), who had become the artistic leader of the First Studio of the Moscow Art Theatre after Sullerzhitsky died in 1916. Vakhtangov's reputation rests primarily upon four productions: Maeterlinck's *The Miracle of Saint Anthony* (performed by the Third Studio of the Moscow Art Theatre in 1921); Strindberg's *Erik XIV* (given at the First Studio in 1921); Ansky's *The Dybbuk* (performed by the Habimah Theatre in 1922); and Gozzi's *Turandot* (produced at the Third Studio in 1922).

Vakhtangov began as a faithful follower of Stanislavsky, but his strength came from his effective blending of the Moscow Art Theatre's realistic approach with Meyerhold's theatricalism. From Stanislavsky he preserved the emphasis upon concentration and the exploration of each character's biography and of hidden meanings; to this he added a heightened and stylized use of movement and design not unlike that of the German expressionists. In *Erik XIV,* for example, which was conceived as a death knell for monarchy, all of the courtiers and bureaucrats were played as automatons while the proletariat was treated realistically. Vakhtangov's greatest achievement came with *Turandot,* throughout which the actors seemed to be improvising effortlessly. This production was retained in the repertory as a memorial to Vakhtangov, who died shortly after it opened. Because he worked with several student groups and trained so many actors, Vakhtangov's influence was considerable. His approach was continued by such associates and students as Yuri Zavadsky (1894–   ), Boris Shchukin (1894–1939), Reuben Simonov (1899–1968), Boris Zakhava (1896–   ), Nikolai Akimov (1901–   ), and Alexander Popov (1892–1961). Most of these men were to be important leaders into the 1960s. In the post-Stalinist era, Vakhtangov's methods were to offer the most acceptable alternative to Soviet realism.

In 1924, the First Studio became an independent organization, the Second Moscow Art Theatre, headed by Mikhail Chekhov (1891–1955), a nephew of Anton Chekhov. After entering the Moscow Art Theatre in 1910, Chekhov soon found the Stanislavsky method inadequate and later worked closely with Vakhtangov, winning considerable fame for his portrayal of Erik XIV. Chekhov thought that Stanislavsky's system restricted the actor to copying nature instead of emphasizing what might be. Thus, he came to stress inspiration above analysis as the actor's primary tool. His conceptions were always somewhat mystical, however, and in 1927 seventeen of his associates resigned from the troupe and published a denunciation. Chekhov then left Russia and settled in the United States, where he ran an acting school for many years and published *To the Actor*. The Second Moscow Art Theatre was dissolved in 1936.

Although the innovators of the 1920s attracted most attention, the conservative groups, notably the Maly Theatre in Moscow and the Alexandrinsky Theatre in Leningrad, were favored by political leaders and most of the public. Meyerhold disliked the Maly Theatre's realistic productions so much that in 1921 he recommended that the troupe be liquidated. In response, Alexander Yuzhin, the Maly's director, launched an attack on "formalism" that began a struggle not to be resolved until the 1930s.

Between 1917 and 1925, the Moscow Art Theatre played only a minor role in Russian theatrical life. It mounted only two new productions and its troupe was decimated in 1919 by the defection of several actors to the West. In 1922, it was granted permission to tour abroad, and in 1923–1924 the troupe performed in America to universal praise. When the company returned to Russia in 1924, it was at its lowest ebb. Its studios were alienated, and the company was so depleted that Stanislavsky had to add eighty-seven new members. Then the process of rebuilding began. In 1926, it achieved its

FIGURE 17.21   Design by I. Nivinsky for Vakhtangov's production of Gozzi's *Turandot*, 1922.

first postwar success with Ostrovsky's *The Burning Heart*, and in 1927 presented Vsevelod Ivanov's *Armored Train 14–69*, its first important Soviet play. From this time, the company's fortunes steadily improved.

Around 1927, the Soviet attitude toward the theatre also began to change. After Lenin died in 1924, Stalin had gradually gathered power into his hands and in 1928 began his campaign to industrialize Russia and to collectivize farming. Concessions formerly granted dissident elements were withdrawn and the central government extended its power over all aspects of Soviet life. In 1927, a training program to equip party members to manage theatres was initiated and "artistic councils" within each theatre were given considerable power over repertory, style, and policy. Nevertheless, attacks on nonconformists in the theatre came primarily from the Russian Association of Proletarian Writers (RAPP), a radical group that sought to abolish everything not deriving directly from the proletariat. Its violence sufficiently alienated party leaders that it was disbanded in 1932 and replaced by the Union of Soviet Writers, headed by Gorky. At first, greater freedom seemed to be in store, but in 1934 "Socialist Realism" was declared the proper style for all art, and pressure began to be exerted to discourage "formalism." In 1936, all theatres were placed under the Central Direction of Theatres, and after 1938 the "stabilization" of companies made it almost impossible for workers to change jobs without specific government approval.

The new policies meant the gradual suppression of the *avant-garde* troupes and greater prestige for the Maly, Alexandrinsky (now renamed the State Academic Pushkin Theatre), and the Moscow Art Theatre, which after 1932 was called "the House of Gorky." The non-realistic groups attempted to adapt to the new demands. Tairov began to alternate Soviet plays with productions in his older style. In 1933, he won considerable praise for his staging of Vishnevsky's *The Optimistic Tragedy,* but by 1937 he was so out of favor that his company was merged for a time with that of the Realistic Theatre. Reopening in 1939, the Kamerny gained approval for some productions but was sent to Siberia during the war years. Meyerhold adopted a style usually called "impressionistic," exemplified in his productions of Dumas' *Camille* in 1934 and Tchaikovsky's *Queen of Spades* in 1935. In neither did he alter the text or use biomechanics; both were given lavish, if somewhat stylized, decor and both were popular successes. Nevertheless, Meyerhold's completely nonpolitical interpretations displeased officials even more than his formalism, and in 1938 his theatre was closed. In 1939, he made his last official appearance; in a speech to the First All Union Congress of Directors he is reported to have admitted errors, but to have added: "The pitiful and wretched thing called socialist realism has nothing in common with art. . . . Where once there were the best theatres in the world . . . in hunting formalism, you have eliminated art." Shortly afterward he was arrested and disappeared.

Despite these repressions, stylization received official approval when it was used to convey clear political messages. The most significant experiments of the 1930s were those of Nikolai Okhlopkov (1900–1966) at the Realistic Theatre. Originating as the Fourth Studio of the Moscow Art Theatre in 1921, the Realistic Theatre attained independent status in 1927. Okhlopkov, who had worked with both Meyerhold and Tairov, was appointed its director in 1932. He eliminated the platform stage and placed all action in the auditorium. Although he often used a central playing area, Okhlopkov also staged scenes around the periphery of the auditorium or on a bridge overhead. Realistic set peices might be placed almost anywhere, and sound effects from many directions made the audience feel at the center of events. Okhlopkov preferred to work with dramatizations of novels, and all of his productions were "cinematic" in their rapid cutting from one scene to another. But while

FIGURE 17.22   A production of *The Beginning* at Okhlopkov's Realistic Theatre in Moscow, 1932. Note the two levels and the placement of the audience.

his selection of plays was acceptable, his production approach was considered too anarchic. For a time his theatre was merged with Tairov's. In 1943 he was named head of the Theatre of the Revolution, where he was to be one of the most important directors of the postwar period. Yuri Zavadsky's career followed a similar path. After Vakhtangov's death he operated a studio for a

FIGURE 17.23   Mayakovsky's *Bedbug* as produced by Meyerhold in 1929.

FIGURE 17.24 Final scene from Trenyov's *Lyubov Yarovaya* at the Maly Theatre, Moscow, 1926. This was the first Soviet play to win widespread popularity.

time, and in 1932 was appointed director of the Red Army Central Theatre. Here he did several fine productions, but in 1935, after refusing to merge his studio with the larger troupe, he was exiled to the provinces until 1939. Zavadsky was succeeded at the Red Army Central Theatre by Alexei Popov, who was more responsive to official demands.

Considering the uncertainties of the early years and the political pressures of the 1930s, it is not surprising that few significant playwrights emerged. Gorky was the only pre-Revolutionary author who played an important role under the Communists and even he was alienated from the regime for many years. Consequently, his plays were little performed until 1927, after which they came to be considered models of appropriate style. After Gorky was named head of the Union of Soviet Writers in 1932, his works came to be almost obligatory parts of each theatre's repertory. After the Revolution, Gorky wrote only two plays and these not till the 1930s— *Yegor Bulichev and Others* (1932) and *Dostigayev and Others* (1933)—and even these concern life before the Soviet regime began.

In the years immediately following the Revolution, leadership passed to the futurists, militant enemies of old forms and strong advocates of a utilitarian art suited to the needs of a machine age. The major playwright of the movement was Vladimir Mayakovsky (1894–1930), a close friend of Meyerhold, who staged all of his plays. Mayakovsky's *Mystery-Bouffe* (1918) parodied the Bible and ended with the proletariat entering the promised land, while *The Bedbug* (1929) and *The Bathhouse* (1930) satirized Soviet bureaucracy. His last two plays were received so adversely that Mayakovsky committed suicide in 1930.

Most Soviet plays were either farces or melodramas upholding the Revolution and denouncing its opposers. Among the best of the early dramatists were Vsevelod Ivanov (1895–1963), with *Armored Train 14-69* (1927); Mikhail Bulgakov (1891–1940), with *The Days of the Turbins* (1925); and Constantin Trenyov (1884–1945), with *Lyubov Yarovaya* (1926). Trenyov's play was the most popular of the early Soviet works, probably because it combined humor, melodrama, and sentiment. Of the later writers, the best were Nikolai Pogodin (1900–   ), with *Aristocrats* (1934), *The Man with the Gun* (1937), and *Kremlin Chimes* (1942); Alexander Afinogenov (1904–1941), with *Far Taiga* (1935) and *On the Eve* (1941); Alexander Korneichuk (1905–1972), with *Truth* (1937) and *The Front* (1942); and Vsevelod Vishnevsky (1900–1951), with *The Optimistic Tragedy* (1932) and *At the Walls of Leningrad* (1941).

By the beginning of the Second World War, the Russian theatre had been subjugated to political pressures. Nevertheless, no country in the world took its theatre more seriously as a medium of ideas and as an integral part of society.

ENGLISH THEATRE AND DRAMA, 1915–1940

The First World War brought major changes to the English theatre. With it, the actor-manager system virtually disappeared, to be replaced by the commercial producer and the long run. During the war, popular entertainment dominated the stage. Tree's theatre, for example, the home of Shakespeare since 1900, was in 1916 given over to *Chu Chin Chow*, a musical version of *Ali Baba and the Forty Thieves*, which ran for 2,238 performances.

Probably the most significant occurrence of the war years was the emergence of the "Old Vic" as the principal producer of English classics. Built in 1818 as the Royal Coburg and later renamed the Royal Victoria, the Old Vic was taken over in 1880 by Emma Cons, a social reformer, who converted it into a "temperance Music Hall." In 1898, Miss Cons' niece, Lilian Baylis (1874–1937), became manager of the theatre and began to present operas. It was not until 1914, however, that Shakespearean plays were added. During the war years, the repertory was under the direction of Ben Greet

FIGURE 17.25 The Old Vic's production of *The Tempest* in 1934. At the back as Prospero is Charles Laughton, in front of him Elsa Lanchester is seen as Ariel. Courtesy Debenham Collection, British Theatre Museum, London.

1971) was appointed administrator and operated it with distinction until 1945. Guthrie had made his debut as an actor in 1924, but had soon turned to directing. His first London production came in 1931, but his finest prewar work was done with the Old Vic. As a director, Guthrie was noted for his novel interpretations of standard works (sometimes considered merely bizarre by critics), and the restless and vital quality of movement. By 1939, the Old Vic was the most respected troupe in England. With its own theatre, a permanent company, and a policy of producing the finest plays at reasonable prices, it set a standard for the entire country.

Several other producers in London helped to raise the level of performance between the wars. Among these, the most important were the Lyric Theatre, the Gate Theatre, and the Mercury Theatre. The Lyric Theatre, Hammersmith, one of the many houses built in the suburbs during the heyday of music halls, had fallen upon hard times when Nigel Playfair (1874–1934) leased it in 1918. Although Playfair presented many kinds of plays,

FIGURE 17.26 Tyrone Guthrie's production of *Twelfth Night* at the Old Vic in 1933. From *Theatre Arts* (1933).

(1857–1936), who, in the tradition of Frank Benson, had long been performing Shakespearean works for both English and American audiences.

After the war, Greet was succeeded by Robert Atkins (1886–1972) from 1920 to 1925, Andrew Leigh (1887–1957) until 1929, and Harcourt Williams (1880–1957) until 1934. In 1931, the Old Vic acquired the Sadler's Wells Theatre, and a ballet company was formed under the direction of Ninette de Valois (Edris Stannis, 1898–), who had been trained in the Diaghilev company and had later established her own school. Between 1931 and 1935, the opera and ballet company and the dramatic company alternated between the Old Vic and Sadler's Wells every week. When this arrangement became too cumbersome, drama was confined to the Old Vic, and opera and ballet to Sadler's Wells. The Sadler's Wells Ballet Company was to become the finest in England, and was rechristened the Royal Ballet after the Second World War, and its opera troupe developed into the present-day English National Opera Company.

When Miss Baylis died in 1937, it was feared that the Old Vic would close, but Tyrone Guthrie (1900–

FIGURE 17.27 *The Beggar's Opera* at the Lyric Theatre, Hammersmith, 1920. Setting by Claud Lovat Fraser. The unit at front remained throughout, while pieces were changed behind the arches. Courtesy Theatre Museum, Victoria and Albert Museum, London.

did much to reestablish the intimate revue, which had declined since the 1920s.

The Mercury Theatre was established in 1931 as the Ballet Club and was licensed as a public theatre in 1933 to Ashley Dukes (1885–1959), who emphasized poetic drama at a time when commercial managers were uninterested in it. Closely associated with Dukes was E. Martin Browne (1900–   ), who continued the theatre into the 1940s.

Of the several important groups outside of London, perhaps the best was the Birmingham Repertory Company, which, under Barry Jackson's direction between 1913 and 1935, produced about 400 plays ranging through the entire history of drama. Between 1922 and 1934, Jackson also presented 42 plays in London, many remarkably successful despite their departure from commercial formulas. Through his productions of *Hamlet*

FIGURE 17.28 Peter Godfrey's production of Kaiser's *From Morn to Midnight* at the Gate Theatre, London, in 1928. Courtesy Enthoven Collection, Victoria and Albert Museum.

his reputation rests upon his productions of Restoration and eighteenth-century works, most notably *The Beggar's Opera* (which opened in 1920 for a run of 1,463 performances), *The Way of the World* (1924), *The Rivals* (1925), *The Beaux' Stratagem* (1927), and *Love in a Village* (1928). Most of his productions were decorative, gay, stylized caricatures. For a time, the Lyric was the most fashionable theatre in London, but as Playfair's approach hardened into a formula, popularity declined, and in 1932 the company was dissolved. The Lyric was noted above all for its sense of style, first established by Claud Lovat Fraser (1890–1921), whose sensitive use of color and period motifs profoundly influenced others.

The Gate Theatre was opened in 1925 by Peter Godfrey (1899–1971), a former circus clown and Shakespearean actor. Unable to secure a license for the only hall he could afford, Godfrey ran his theatre as a private club. In nine years, he produced over 350 plays. His most characteristic productions were of expressionist plays or those with a psychoanalytic bias. Using set pieces against black drapes, unusual lighting effects, and stylized acting techniques, Godfrey was the principal exponent of expressionism in London. In 1934, the Gate Theatre passed to Norman Marshall (1901–   ), who presented many works forbidden by the censor. He also

(1925), *Macbeth* (1928), and *Taming of the Shrew* (1928), Jackson began the vogue for playing Shakespeare in modern dress. When Jackson transferred ownership of his theatre to the City of Birmingham in 1935, it became England's first civic theatre.

Jackson also founded the Malvern Festival in 1929, thereby giving considerable impetus to the summer festival movement. Operated primarily by the Birmingham Repertory Company until 1939, the Malvern Festival had no clear policy, some seasons being devoted to plays of a particular era, others to plays by specific authors, especially Shaw. All, however, were of high quality. The festival was discontinued between 1939 and 1949.

Two other provincial troupes—the Cambridge Festival Theatre and the Oxford Repertory Company—were outstanding. The Cambridge Festival Theatre was established by Terence Gray (1895–) in 1926 with the avowed purpose of undermining realistic acting and production, a policy that was followed consistently. The theatre had no curtain, proscenium arch, or orchestra pit. Scenery normally consisted of ramps or other constructions set against a cyclorama, upon which patterns of light were projected. The actors' movement was often described as "choreographic" and was always highly stylized. Gray thought the text an excuse for a director's improvisations. He performed *Romeo and Juliet* in flamenco costumes; put some characters in *Twelfth Night* on roller skates; and had the Judge in *The Merchant of Venice* play with a yo-yo. Gray's productions generated much controversy but had little immediate result. The theatre closed in 1933.

The Oxford Repertory Company, headed by J. B. Fagan (1873–1933) from 1923 to 1929, presented twenty-one plays a year drawn from many countries and periods. The schedule meant that productions were often rough, but all had vitality and clear interpretations. Little scenery was used, for the theatre had only a small stage fronted by a large apron, upon which most of the action transpired. The importance of this company rests in part upon the many young actors, most notably Tyrone Guthrie, John Gielgud, Raymond Massey, Flora Robson, and Glen Byam Shaw, who received their first major experience under Fagan.

The Stratford-on-Avon seasons of Shakespeare's plays also gained in prestige after they resumed in 1919. Until 1934, most of the plays were directed by W. Bridges-Adams (1889–1965), who worked under adverse

FIGURE 17.29 *Gammer Gurton's Needle* **at the Malvern Festival. Setting by Paul Shelving. From** *Theatre Arts* **(1933).**

conditions. There were no shop or storage facilities, the Festival Committee controlled policy, and six plays were opened on six successive evenings. After the old theatre burned in 1926, the company played in a motion picture house until the present building was completed in 1932. Although the new auditorium was largely satisfactory, the stage was a conventional picture-frame structure; its sliding platform stages could not move entirely out of sight and the elevator stages only sank 8 feet. Such blunders have required several remodelings, the most recent in 1972. Bridges-Adams resigned in 1934 and was succeeded until 1942 by B. Iden Payne (1881–1976), whose most characteristic productions were in the style of Poel—using an Elizabethan structure and Elizabethan costumes. Other directors, most notably Theodore Kommissarzhevsky, brought novel conceptions to the plays. Kommissarzhevsky's production of *The Merchant of Venice* utilized *commedia dell'arte* conventions and his *The Merry Wives of Windsor* was given a Viennese background. London critics largely ignored the Stratford company, which did not achieve its current critical stature until after the Second World War.

The little theatre movement burgeoned in England after the First World War. The British Drama League, founded in 1919 and headed by Geoffrey Whitworth (1883–1951) until 1948, organized conferences, sent out costumes and properties, aided in play selection, and held annual festivals of plays. Although many of these groups did excellent work, none equaled the quality achieved by Nugent Monck (1877–1958) at the Madder-

FIGURE 17.30 Terence Gray's production of *Henry VIII* at the Festival Theatre, Cambridge, 1931. Note the abstract setting and the playing-card costumes.

market Theatre in Norwich, noted throughout England for its high level of performance.

During this period many performers of high merit appeared. Of the actresses, the best were probably Sybil Thorndike (1882–1976) and Edith Evans (1888–1976). Miss Thorndike began her career in Ben Greet's company and after 1914 acted often with the Old Vic troupe. She was especially noted in the 1920s for her portrayal of Shaw's Saint Joan, although her performances ranged from Greek tragedy to modern comedy. Miss Evans began her career with Poel and gained fame as Millamant in the Lyric Theatre's production of *The Way of the World*. She also appeared frequently with the Old Vic, at the Malvern Festival, and in many London commercial theatres. Other outstanding actresses included Lilian Braithwaite (1873–1948), Marie Tempest (1864–1942), Flora Robson (1902–   ), Gertrude Lawrence (1898–1952), and Peggy Ashcroft (1907–   ).

Of the actors, the most important was John Gielgud (1904–   ), who made his debut in 1921 and won major acclaim with Hamlet in 1934. He soon became one of England's major directors as well. In 1937–1938, he leased the Queen's Theatre, assembled a company that included Peggy Ashcroft, Michael Redgrave, and Alec Guinness, and produced a repertory of classics. By the time the war began, Gielgud was accepted as England's finest actor. Other outstanding performers included Cedric Hardwicke (1893–1964), who worked closely with Barry Jackson after 1922, Donald Wolfit (1902–1968), who played at the Old Vic, Stratford, and with his

own company, and Maurice Evans (1901–   ), who played for Terence Gray and the Old Vic before emigrating to America in 1935. A number of young men, who would be of greater importance after the war, also established their promise: Laurence Olivier (1907–   ), who had played with the Birmingham Repertory Company, Gielgud, and the Old Vic; Michael Redgrave (1908–   ), on the stage after 1934; Ralph Richardson (1902–   ), Alec Guiness (1914–   ), who made his debut in 1934; Anthony Quayle (1913–   ), on the stage after 1931; and Glen Byam Shaw (1904–   ), who played with the Oxford Repertory Company and Gielgud.

Few major dramatists emerged between the wars, although a number of older ones, such as Shaw, Barrie, Galsworthy, Pinero, and Ervine, continued to write. During the 1920s, three authors—Maugham, Lonsdale, and Coward—excelled in sophisticated comedy. Sommerset Maugham (1874–1965) wrote his first play in 1904 and until 1933 was one of England's most prolific playwrights. His major achievement came with his comedies of manners, *Our Betters* (1917), *The Circle* (1921),

FIGURE 17.31 Laurence Olivier as Romeo, Edith Evans as the Nurse, and John Gielgud as Mercutio in Gielgud's production of *Romeo and Juliet*, 1935. From *Theatre Arts* (1936).

The Constant Wife (1927), and *The Breadwinner* (1930), in which sardonic humor and unusual personal outlooks never descend into trite happy endings. Often compared with Maugham, Frederick Lonsdale (1881–1954) drew a wide following with his amusing situations and effective dialogue in *The Last of Mrs. Cheyney* (1925), *On Approval* (1927), and *The High Road* (1929). Noel Coward (1899–1973) captured the spirit of the postwar era with such works as *Fallen Angels* (1925), *Hay Fever* (1925), *Bittersweet* (1929), *Private Lives* (1930), and *Design for Living* (1932), in which unconventional behavior was combined with sophisticated wit.

Of the serious writers, J. B. Priestley (1894–   ) gained the greatest prestige. He began his dramatic career in 1932 with *Dangerous Corner* and went on to *Time and the Conways* (1937) and *An Inspector Calls* (1946). Although he wrote many kinds of plays, Priestley is most noted for his compression or distortion of time to illuminate characters and ideas. Of the sentimental and melodramatic school, Emlyn Williams (1905–   ) was perhaps the most successful. After writing two sensational plays, *A Murder Has Been Arranged* (1930) and *Night Must Fall* (1935), he presented *The Corn Is Green* (1938), a sentimental story about a Welsh teacher and her star pupil.

This period also brought several attempts to revive poetic drama. Gordon Bottomley (1874–1948) wrote *King Lear's Wife* (1915), *Britain's Daughters* (1922), and *Laodice and Danae* (1930), and W. H. Auden (1907–1973) and Christopher Isherwood (1904–   ) collaborated on *The Dog Beneath the Skin* (1935) and *The Ascent of F6* (1936). The most lasting achievement was that of T. S. Eliot (1888–1965) with *Murder in the Cathedral* (1935), the story of Thomas à Becket's martyrdom. Eliot went on to write *The Family Reunion* (1939) and, after the war, several other verse plays. In general, however, the attempt to revive poetic drama was ineffective, primarily because of shortcomings in the plays rather than because of any opposition to poetry.

The revue was one of the most popular theatrical forms between the wars. C. B. Cochran (1873–1951), its most famous producer, began his work with "intimate revues" in 1914 and then turned to large-scale, lavish productions between 1918 and 1931. André Charlot (1882–1956) also presented many revues between 1916 and 1923, bringing Beatrice Lillie (1898–   ) to fame. The intimate revue was revived at the Gate Theatre in the 1930s, especially through the writing of

FIGURE 17.32 T. S. Eliot's *Murder in the Cathedral* at the Mercury Theatre, London, in 1935. Directed by E. Martin Browne. Robert Speaight is seen at right as Becket. Courtesy Debenham Collection, British Theatre Museum.

Herbert Farjeon (1887–1945) and the performances of Hermione Gingold (1897–   ).

To Ireland, England's deep involvement in World War I offered the chance to throw off British rule. Consequently, in 1916 it began a rebellion, which was put down after much bloodshed. But the demand for independence grew and in 1919 Ireland declared itself a republic. Three years of armed conflict ensued before a treaty was signed in 1923 which granted independence to all but six northern counties.

This struggle provides the context for the early plays of Sean O'Casey (1884–1964), Ireland's most important post-war playwright. O'Casey turned attention away from folk and legendary subject matter to the urban life of his time. The plays that established his fame—*The Shadow of a Gunman* (1923), *Juno and the Paycock* (1924), and *The Plough and the Stars* (1926)—were realistic in tone and dealt with the effects of the rebellion on the lives of ordinary people. After this time O'Casey adopted expressionistic techniques in such works as *The Silver Tassie* (1928), *Within the Gates* (1934), *Red Roses for Me* (1943), and *Purple Dust* (1945). His change of style precipitated a break with the Abbey Theatre in 1928, after which O'Casey lived in England. O'Casey's works have been more widely read than produced, largely because, in spite of many powerful scenes, the dramatic action is sometimes obscure. Nevertheless, his characterizations, vivid use of language, and human compassion make him one of the finest writers of modern times.

AMERICAN THEATRE AND DRAMA, 1915–1940

The United States was able to remain aloof from World War I until 1917, when it was drawn into the conflict. Not only was it decisive in the outcome of the war, it was a leader in founding the League of Nations and in establishing independent states for the ethnic and language groups of Europe. Following the war, however, America entered another period of isolationism, during which it sought to divorce itself from foreign affairs and imposed tariffs to reduce imports. The economic results were disastrous for farmers and workers and ultimately were instrumental in bringing on the Great Depression of the 1930s. It was during the post-war period that women won the right to vote and that mass production and new developments in transportation and communication revolutionized American life.

During the 1930s the energies of the nation were devoted to overcoming economic problems. For the first time, the government assumed a key role in social planning and began such programs as social security and public works. By 1940, American life was vastly different from what it had been in 1915. The United States had become one of the world's great powers and an industrial giant. It had also won a measure of respect in artistic and cultural affairs for the first time.

Not until around 1915 did America begin to be aware of innovations that had long been underway in the European theatre. This awareness came about in large part through nonprofessional groups. Around 1912, several "little theatres" were established in emulation of the independent theatres of Europe. Among the most important of these were the Toy Theatre, opened by Mrs. Lyman Gale in Boston in 1912; the Chicago Little Theatre, formed by Maurice Brown in 1912; the Neighborhood Playhouse, established in New York by Irene and Alice Lewisohn in 1915; the Washington Square Players, formed in New York in 1915; the Provincetown Players, organized in Provincetown, Massachusetts, in 1915; and the Detroit Arts and Crafts Theatre, opened in 1916. By 1917 there were at least fifty of these groups. For the most part they depended upon unpaid volunteers for personnel and upon subscribers for fi-

FIGURE 17.33 Robert Edmond Jones' design for Granville Barker's production of *The Man Who Married a Dumb Wife,* 1915. This setting is usually said to be the first important native expression of the "new stagecraft" in America. From *The Theatre* (1915).

nancial support; most produced a series of plays each year, using techniques already widely accepted in Europe. The little theatre movement made its greatest contributions between 1912 and 1920 by preparing audiences to accept the new drama and production methods.

After 1920, the little theatres began to be indistinguishable from community theatres. Originating like its European counterpart in attempts to revive the spirit of ancient Greece, the community drama movement had begun in America around 1905. Its most ardent supporter was Percy MacKaye (1875–1956), whose *The Civic Theatre* (1912) and *Community Drama* (1917) outlined a program and whose outdoor pageants provided texts designed to involve several thousand participants. Interest in mass spectacles soon declined, however, and after 1920 most local groups turned to the performance of recent Broadway hits. By 1925, nearly 2,000 community or little theatre companies were registered with the Drama League of America, an organization which encouraged local interest in drama. The number has continued to grow.

Drama programs also began to be introduced into colleges and universities. Although plays had been produced by students since the seventeenth century, no courses in theatre were offered until about 1900. The first important change came in 1903, when George Pierce Baker (1866–1935) began to teach playwriting at Radcliffe College. Later opened to Harvard University students, the course was enlarged in 1913 to include a workshop for the production of plays. Baker attracted many of America's most talented young men, including Eugene O'Neill, S. N. Behrman, and Robert Edmond Jones, instilled in them high standards, and helped them to acquire skills. In 1925, Baker moved to Yale University where he established a drama department which was to provide professional training for many later theatre workers. In 1914 at the Carnegie Institute of Technology, Thomas Wood Stevens (1880–1942) instituted the country's first degree-granting program in theatre, and in 1918 Frederick Koch (1877–1944) founded the influential Carolina Playmakers. Many other programs

soon followed. By 1940, theatre education was an accepted part of most American universities.

In the years following 1910, the "new stagecraft," as the European trends were called in America, began to find its way into the commercial theatre. Winthrop Ames (1871–1937), who had gone to Europe in 1907 to study new developments there, was employed in 1909 to manage the New Theatre in New York, an ambitious nonprofit repertory company. The large theatre soon proved both financially and artistically unsatisfactory, however, and Ames then built the Little Theatre, seating only 300, where in the years preceding the First World War he presented a number of plays in the new style. In 1912, he imported Reinhardt's production of *Sumurun*, which also aroused much interest in European ideas.

In 1912, the Boston Opera Company hired Joseph Urban (1872–1933), a well-established Viennese designer of the new school, to mount its productions. Urban later

FIGURE 17.34   Robert Edmond Jones' setting for the banquet scene in *Macbeth*. Arthur Hopkins' expressionistic production, 1921. Note the masks above the stage. From *Theatre Arts Magazine* (1924).

worked in New York, where he was famous for the fresh coloring and simplicity of his settings. In 1915, the New York Stage Society invited Harley Granville Barker to direct a series of plays for its members. For Barker's production of *The Man Who Married a Dumb Wife,* Robert Edmond Jones (1887–1954) provided settings usually considered the first native expression of the "new stagecraft." Jones was one of several young men, including Lee Simonson and Sam Hume, who had studied in Europe between 1912 and 1915 and had been impressed by the changing theatrical trends. In 1914, Hume arranged an exhibit of continental scene design which was shown in New York, Detroit, Chicago, and Cleveland. Hume later was associated with the Detroit Arts and Crafts Theatre; here his associate, Sheldon Cheney (1886–   ) in 1916 launched *Theatre Arts Magazine,* which until 1948 was to be the principal disseminator of new ideas in America. Visits of the Abbey Theatre in 1911, the Ballets Russes in 1916, and Copeau's troupe from 1917 to 1919 also helped to stimulate interest in foreign movements. Nevertheless, when the war ended in 1918 the American theatre was only beginning to be aware of European practices.

The triumph of the new ideal owes most to the Provincetown Players, the Theatre Guild, and to Arthur Hopkins. After presenting a few programs on Cape Cod, the Provincetown Players moved to New York in 1916. In its early years, the company concentrated upon plays by American playwrights and by 1925 had presented ninety-three plays by forty-seven authors. After 1923, the group split into two branches. One continued the older practices, while the other, under Eugene O'Neill, Robert Edmond Jones, and Kenneth Macgowan, performed foreign and period plays along with the noncommercial works of O'Neill and others. Although it succumbed to financial pressures in 1929, the Provincetown Players had served an important role as an experimental theatre both for new plays and for new production techniques.

In 1918, the Washington Square Players was disbanded, but some of its members then formed the Theatre Guild, a fully professional company, with the avowed purpose of presenting plays of merit not likely to interest commercial managers. After an uncertain beginning in 1919, it soon became America's most respected theatre, presenting a number of plays each year to an audience of subscribers. In 1928 it also began a subscription series in six other cities. The Guild was governed by a board of directors, and for a time maintained a nucleus company

FIGURE 17.35 Norman Bel Geddes' project for staging Dante's *The Divine Comedy.* Courtesy Hoblitzelle Theatre Arts Collection, University of Texas, Austin.

of actors. It adopted an eclectic approach to staging; its principal director, Philip Moeller (1880–1958), and its principal designer, Lee Simonson (1888–1967), drew upon several European movements, although their most typical style was a modified realism. During the 1930s the company gradually curtailed its activities because of financial problems and by World War II was merely another commercial producer investing in long-run hits.

In 1918 Arthur Hopkins (1878–1950) began a series of productions which were to mark him as the most adventurous of New York's commercial producers. Working with Robert Edmond Jones, Hopkins presented plays by Tolstoy, Ibsen, Gorky, Shakespeare, O'Neill, and others. In 1921, his production of *Macbeth* created a sensation with its expressionistic use of tilted arches, and in 1922, *Hamlet,* staring John Barrymore (1882–1942), was declared one of the best productions of the century. After Hopkins and the Guild demonstrated the commercial viability of the "new stagecraft," it was gradually adopted by others and by 1930 had become the standard approach.

The "new stagecraft" was primarily a visual movement, and the total effect of most productions might best be described as "simplified realism." In addition to

Jones and Simonson, the major influence on scene design was Norman Bel Geddes (1893–1958), a visionary not unlike Appia. Geddes' plan for staging Dante's *The Divine Comedy* on a series of terraces (published in 1921) is still considered one of the most brilliant conceptions by an American designer. His penchant for steps, platforms, and imaginative lighting is also seen in his productions of *Hamlet* (1931) and Werfel's *The Eternal Road* (1936), in which the platforms soared to a height of 50 feet. Other important designers included Cleon Throckmorton (1897–1965), Mordecai Gorelik (1899–   ), Boris Aronson (1900–   ), Aline Bernstein (1882–1955), Howard Bay (1912–   ), Donald Oenslager (1902–1975), and especially Jo Mielziner (1901–1976), who was to be America's most prolific and respected designer after 1945. While all did not follow the same style, they shared a respect for simplicity and a desire to capture the spirit of a text.

Continental influence continued to be felt in the 1920s through a series of visitors: the Moscow Art Theatre toured America in 1923–1924; Reinhardt presented *The Miracle* (with designs by Geddes) in 1924 and staged a season of plays in 1927–1928; and Copeau directed *The Brothers Karamazov* for the Theatre Guild in 1927. Two of Stanislavsky's actors, Richard Boleslavsky (1889–1937) and Maria Ouspenskaya (1881–1949), were induced to head the American Laboratory Theatre between 1923 and 1930. Here the Stanislavsky system was taught in a version later popularized by Boleslavsky's book *Acting, the First Six Lessons* (1933). Among the more than 500 students who studied at the American Laboratory Theatre were Stella Adler, Lee Strasberg, and Harold Clurman.

Between 1925 and 1940 several groups tried to escape the commercial pattern. From 1925 to 1930, Walter Hampden (1879–1955) revived the actor-manager system with his repertory company. Although the depression forced him to give up his theatre in New York, Hampden continued to tour with his troupe for many years. Between 1926 and 1933, Eva Le Gallienne (1899–   ) managed the Civic Repertory Theatre, produced thirty-four plays and built up a subscription list of 50,000. Despite its excellent repertory and wide following, the company was always in debt and could not survive the depression.

The most distinguished troupe of the 1930s was the Group Theatre, launched in 1931 by Lee Strasberg (1901–   ), Harold Clurman (1901–   ), and Cheryl Crawford (1902–   ) on the model of the Moscow Art

FIGURE 17.36 Drawing showing the arrangement of the stage of the Manhattan Opera House, New York, for Max Reinhardt's production of Franz Werfel's *The Eternal Road* in 1937. The design is by Norman Bel Geddes, who worked with Harry Horner on this production. Courtesy Max Reinhardt Archive, State University of New York, Binghamton.

Theatre, whose methods and ensemble approach it emulated. With a company including Stella Adler (1904–   ), Morris Carnovsky (1898–   ), and Elia Kazan (1909–   ), it presented plays by Paul Green, Maxwell Anderson, Sidney Kingsley, Irwin Shaw, William Saroyan, and others, although its reputation rests especially upon its productions of Clifford Odets' dramas. Ultimately the troupe foundered because of disagreements over policy. In 1941 it was disbanded. Its influence has continued, however, through the work of many former members, several of whom were instrumental in popularizing the Stanislavsky system in America.

The depression motivated the creation of a unique experiment, the Federal Theatre Project, which was established in 1935 to combat unemployment. Headed by Hallie Flanagan Davis (1890–1969), at its peak it employed 10,000 persons in forty states. About 1,000 pro-

FIGURE 17.37 Norman Bel Geddes' setting for *The Miracle* at the Century Theatre, New York, 1924. For this production, directed by Max Reinhardt, Bel Geddes converted the theatre into a cathedral. The accompanying sectional plan shows how the scenery and machinery were arranged. From *The Scientific American* (1924).

ductions of all types were mounted, 65 percent of them free. In spite of its diversity, it is now remembered primarily for developing the "Living Newspaper," a cinematic form which integrated factual data with dramatic vignettes. Each script centered around a problem: *Triple-A Plowed Under* (1936) dealt with agriculture, *Power* (1937) with rural electrification, and *One-Third of a Nation* (1938) with slum housing. Most of the plays had as a central character the "little man" who, upon raising questions about a current problem, was led through its background, human consequences, and possible solutions. Much of the dialogue was taken from speeches, newspaper stories, or other documents. Many of the techniques were borrowed from Epic Theatre. The political tone of many works eventually alienated Congress, which in 1939 refused to appropriate funds for its continuance.

The Federal Theatre motivated the formation of the Mercury Theatre in 1937, when Orson Welles (1915–) and John Houseman (1902–) decided to present Marc Blitzstein's *The Cradle Will Rock* after it was withdrawn from production by the Federal Theatre. Welles had already established a reputation as an actor with his portrayal of Doctor Faustus and as an imaginative producer with *Macbeth*, which he set in Haiti and performed with an all-black cast. Between 1937 and 1939, the Mercury Theatre presented works by Büchner, Dekker, Shaw, and Shakespeare. Its greatest success came with *Julius Caesar*, played as a comment upon fascism.

The Federal Theatre also promoted black theatre, which, though not extensive between the wars, was laying the foundations for later developments. In the years between 1890 and 1915 a few musicals had been written for black casts, a few stock companies had performed sporadically in New York and elsewhere, and (after 1910) one black performer—Bert Williams (1876–1922)—had won stardom on Broadway in musical pieces.

An important step was taken in 1915 when Anita Bush organized the All-Colored Dramatic Stock Company in New York, which, after one season, passed to the control of Robert Levy at the Lafayette Theatre. Most of the company's repertory was taken from Broadway, but it gave black actors their longest continuous employment in regular drama to that time. Around this time, a few dramatists also began to write sympathetically about blacks. The first serious plays for black actors to be seen on Broadway were Ridgely Torrence's *Three Plays for a Negro Theatre* (1917), which not only marked a turning away from the stereotyped treatment of blacks but also the first time that blacks were welcomed into Broadway audiences. There followed such works as O'Neill's *The Emperor Jones* (in which a black actor played the leading role in a serious American play on Broadway for the first time), DuBose and Dorothy Heyward's *Porgy*, Marc Connelly's *The Green Pastures*, and Paul Green's *In Abraham's Bosom*, all by white authors.

There were as well several black authors, although they were given relatively little encouragement. Among the best of the plays were Willis Richardson's *The Chipwoman's Fortune*, Frank Wilson's *Sugar Cane*, Hall Johnson's *Run Little Chillun*, and Langston Hughes' *Mulatto*. There were also a number of musical plays, among the most successful of which were Noble Sissle and Eubie Blake's *Shuffle Along, Chocolate Dandies,* and *Runnin' Wild*. All of these plays helped such black

FIGURE 17.38 Howard Bay's setting, a tenement house, for *One Third of a Nation,* "a living newspaper" about inadequate housing, staged by the Federal Theatre Project in 1938. From *Theatre Arts* (1938).

performers as Richard Harrison, Frank Wilson, Rose McClendon, and Abbie Mitchell to demonstrate that they could compete with the best actors of the period.

Black theatre received a major boost from the Federal Theatre, which in several cities established black units that presented seventy-five plays in four years. Unfortunately, most of the hopes were dashed when the project ended in 1939.

By World War II, many plays about black life had found their way onto the stage. Perhaps the most disturbing of these was *Native Son,* Paul Green and Richard Wright's adaptation of Wright's novel, which showed the terrible effects of social evils on the life of the protagonist. But, if there was still a long way to go, there had been much improvement since 1915. The black theatre artist had made his presence felt, even if he had not yet been permitted to demonstrate his full potential.

The depression also gave impetus to the "workers' theatre" movement, which had begun in 1926 with the Worker's Drama League. In 1932 a national organization was formed, later called the New Theatre League. Most of the member groups were amateur, but in 1933, a fully professional organization, the Theatre Union, was formed in New York and provided leadership for the

entire movement. After the failure of the Theatre Union in 1937, the League declined and by 1942 had virtually ceased to exist. For the most part, the workers' theatres presented socialistic propaganda plays designed to arouse protest.

As the depression deepened, it became increasingly difficult for playwrights to get unusual works produced. Largely for this reason, the Playwrights' Company was created in 1938 by Maxwell Anderson, Elmer Rice, Sidney Howard, Robert E. Sherwood, and S. N. Berhman. In addition to their own plays, they also presented works by other authors. The Playwrights' Company was to be a major producing organization until 1960.

These dissident groups had little effect upon the basic pattern of the commercial theatre. The length of runs steadily increased, reaching a peak with *Tobacco Road* (1933), which played for seven years. The number of new productions also grew each season until 1927–1928, when about 300 plays were mounted, but rapidly declined after 1930, having fallen to 80 by 1939–1940. Theatrical production was complicated in these years by the emergence of powerful labor unions. The stage hands' union, the National Alliance of Theatrical Stage Employees, had achieved full recognition during the season of 1910–1911, and in 1918 the United Scenic Artists was formed. Actors Equity Association, founded in 1912, was recognized in 1919; it became a "closed

FIGURE 17.39 Orson Welles' version of *Macbeth,* set in Haiti. It was produced by the Federal Theatre Project. Setting by Nat Karson. From *Theatre Arts* (1936).

shop" in 1924 and was able to establish a minimum-wage scale in 1933. The Dramatists' Guild, formed in 1912, became the bargaining agent for all playwrights in 1926. As each group bettered working conditions, it also demanded considerably higher pay for its members and thereby contributed to the economic problems of the theatre. Despite all difficulties, a number of producers and directors were able to maintain high standards. Among the producers, the best were Gilbert Miller, Jed Harris, John Golden, William A. Brady, and Sam Harris. Among the directors, the most outstanding were Guthrie McClintic, Worthington Minor, Herman Shumlin, Brock Pemberton, and George Abbott.

Between 1915 and 1940, American dramatists began to command international respect for the first time. Few were members of any particular movement, but most shared a dislike for romantic melodrama with realistic trappings. Only one American dramatist—O'Neill—achieved genuine stature. Eugene O'Neill (1888–1953), son of James O'Neill, turned to playwriting around 1912, attended Professor Baker's playwriting classes for a time, and in 1915 had his first works presented by the Provincetown Players. The group continued to encourage him through the 1920s by performing those works rejected by commercial producers. His first full-length play, *Beyond the Horizon*, brought him to Broadway in 1920. After 1934, although he continued to write, no new works were performed until 1946.

O'Neill wrote about twenty-five full-length plays of uneven quality. Many were artistic failures, and even the best often suggest that more was intended than achieved. Nevertheless, his protagonists' search for some significance in life gives the plays a tone of high seriousness. O'Neill also experimented with many novel theatrical devices and dramatic techniques. In *The Great God Brown* (1926), *Lazarus Laughed* (1926), and *Days Without End* (1934) he made use of masks; in *Strange Interlude* (1928) he employed lengthy "interior monologues" to express the characters' inner thoughts; in *Mourning Becomes Electra* (1931) he gained scope by adopting the trilogy form. O'Neill also ranged through many styles. The devices of expressionism were adopted for *The Hairy Ape* (1922) and *The Great God Brown*, those of symbolism for *The Fountain* (1922) and to a lesser extent for almost all the plays; those of realism for *Beyond the Horizon, Anna Christie* (1921), and *Desire Under the Elms* (1924). O'Neill's strength lay in complex characterization, strong dramatic situations, and seriousness of purpose.

Probably O'Neill's greatest rival was Maxwell Anderson (1888–1959), who after achieving renown for his antiromantic war play, *What Price Glory?* (1924), turned to blank verse drama in *Elizabeth the Queen* (1930), *Mary of Scotland* (1933), *Winterset* (1935), and other plays. Although dramatically effective, Anderson's plays offered few new insights, being merely skillful retellings of familiar stories. Other serious playwrights included Elmer Rice (1892–1967) with *The Adding Machine* (1923), an expressionistic drama about the dehumanization of man, and *Street Scene* (1929), a naturalistic play set in the New York slums; Sidney Howard (1891–1939), with *They Knew What They Wanted* (1924), an antiromantic comedy about three people who get their wishes by accepting compromises, *The Silver Cord* (1926), about a mother's attempt to retain her control over her newly married son, and *Yellow Jack* (1934), a semidocumentary play about the fight to control yellow fever; Paul Green (1894–   ), with his tragedies, *In Abraham's Bosom* (1926) and *The House of Connolly* (1931), and the expressionistic antiwar play, *Johnny Johnson* (1936); Sidney Kingsley (1906–   ), with *Men in White* (1933), dealing with the medical profession, and *Dead End* (1935), a naturalistic play of slum life; and Lillian Hellman (1905–   ), with such moral fables as *The Little Foxes* (1938), a story of rapacious greed among the rising industrialists of the new South around 1900.

The comedy of manners was well represented by Phillip Barry (1896–1949) with *Paris Bound* (1927) and *The Philadelphia Story* (1939), both treating divorce among the upper classes; S. N. Behrman (1893–1973), with *Biography* (1932), *Rain from Heaven* (1934), and *End of Summer* (1936), all of which contrast tolerance with inhumanity; and John van Druten (1902–1957), with *There's Always Juliet* (1931) and *The Voice of the Turtle* (1943), sophisticated stories of sex and love. Among the writers of farce, the best was George S. Kaufman (1889–1961), who worked with a number of collaborators, most successfully with Moss Hart (1904–1961) on *You Can't Take it With You* (1936) and *The Man Who Came to Dinner* (1940). William Saroyan (1900–   ) glorified the simple life in such plays as *My Heart's in the Highlands* (1939), *The Time of Your Life* (1939), and *The Beautiful People* (1941), all of which depict eccentric characters living on the fringes of society who find beauty and redemption.

The drama of social consciousness was most persistently practiced by John Howard Lawson (1895–   ), whose *Roger Bloomer* (1923), *Processional* (1925),

Internationale (1928), and *Marching Song* (1937) were experimental in form and militantly propagandistic in theme. Clifford Odets (1906-1963) followed something of the opposite development, for his early plays, *Waiting for Lefty* (1935) and *Awake and Sing* (1935) call for group action, while his later works, *Paradise Lost* (1935) and *Golden Boy* (1937), take a more complex view of social conditions. Odets was essentially a chronicler of family relationships; his strength lay in his ability to create believable characters struggling to achieve more than life will give them.

Two of the finest dramatists of the 1930s were Sherwood and Wilder. Robert E. Sherwood (1896-1955) in *The Petrified Forest* (1935) created an allegorical cross section of American life, in *Idiot's Delight* (1936) depicted through melodramatic farce the horrors of war and the spiritual bankruptcy which gives rise to it, and in *Abe Lincoln in Illinois* (1938) sought to remind Americans of the high ideals upon which their country had been founded. Thornton Wilder's (1897-1975) reputation was created primarily by two plays, *Our Town* (1938), which seeks to point out the eternal patterns of human experience behind seeming progress, and *The Skin of Our Teeth* (1943), a testimonial to man's ability to survive all disasters. Wilder's frank theatricality and simplicity have won him a wide following both at home and abroad.

Much popular entertainment between the wars took the form of musical comedy and revues. Every year between 1907 and 1931, Florenz Ziegfeld (1869-1932) mounted a new edition of the *Ziegfeld Follies,* each more lavish than the last. Musical comedy, long merely the excuse for presenting beautiful chorus girls, began to move in a new direction after 1928, when Jerome Kern and Oscar Hammerstein II placed the major emphasis in *Showboat* upon a coherent story. This new direction reached its culmination in Richard Rodgers' and Oscar Hammerstein's *Oklahoma* (1943), in which music, story, dance, and setting were fully integrated to tell a semi-serious story. With the triumph of the new approach, the old type of musical largely disappeared.

Of America's many outstanding performers, only a few can be mentioned: Jane Cowl (1884-1950), on the stage from 1903 but most famous for her portrayals of Juliet, Cleopatra, and the heroines of van Druten and Sherwood; Pauline Lord (1890-1950), especially remembered for her performances in *Anna Christie* and *They Knew What They Wanted;* Laurette Taylor (1884-1946), one of the most versatile actresses of her day, whose last major appearance was made as Amanda in Williams' *The Glass Menagerie;* Ina Claire (1895-   ), who appeared in many *Ziegfeld Follies* before playing the heroines of Behrman's comedies; Helen Hayes (1900-   ), noted especially for her appearances in Barrie's plays, Anderson's *Mary of Scotland,* and Housman's *Victoria Regina;* Katherine Cornell (1898-1974), who gave outstanding portrayals in *Candida, The Three Sisters, The Barretts of Wimpole Street,* and many other plays; Lynn Fontanne (1887?-   ), an English actress, who came to America in 1910 and whose later career was tied up with that of her husband, Alfred Lunt (1893-   ), with whom she appeared in *The Guardsman, Reunion in Vienna, Amphitryon 38,* and many other works.

The Second World War, like the first, interrupted the theatre's normal patterns. The war also raised serious doubts about a world which had created such horrors as the Nazi extermination camps and such destructive weapons as the atomic bomb. Out of the questioning would come new experiments in theatre and drama.

LOOKING AT THEATRE HISTORY

One of the ways of studying theatre history is through the theories of art that lie behind practice. Perhaps for no period is this more helpful than the twentieth century, which has seen artistic movements come and go with bewildering rapidity. The proliferation of movements was especially evident between 1910 and 1925. Many movements of that time introduced ideas and techniques that were to reappear in the theatre of the 1960s. Because they are often based on unfamiliar premises, modern artistic movements have seemed merely perverse, bizarre, or incomprehensible to those unaware of their goals. If we are to understand artistic movements, therefore, we must explore the perceptions about truth that underlie them. Only then will we see why they depict human experience as they do and why the techniques they employ are consistent with their intent. Understanding may not cause us to admire the artistic products of movements, but it will prevent us from reaching uninformed judgments. It will also help us to understand the forces that have helped to create the extremely varied theatre of the twentieth century.

Immediately following World War I, the movement with the greatest impact on the theatre was expressionism. An excellent overview of the movement can be gained from John Willett's *Expressionism* (New York, 1970), but little of the theory has been translated into English. Here are some excerpts from a statement written by Yvan Goll in 1918 about his vision of a new "superdrama":

> [*It will depict*] *man's battle against everything that is thing-like and animallike around and within him. . . . The writer must recognize that there are realms quite different from that of the five senses. . . . His first task will be to destroy all external form. . . . Man and objects will be stripped as clean as possible and looked at through a magnifying glass for greater effect. . . . The theatre must not restrict itself to "real" life; it will become "superreal" when it learns what lies behind things. Pure realism was the worst mistake ever made in literature. . . . Art, if it wishes to educate, improve, or be effective in any way, must destroy everyday man . . . . to make him become once more the child he once was. The easiest way to do this is through the grotesque. . . . Consequently, the new theatre must use technological means that are equivalent to the ancient mask. . . . the phonograph to distort the voice, masks . . . which typify through . . . physical distortions [equivalent to] the inner distortions of the plot. . . . We are searching for the Superdrama.*

> YVAN GOLL, Preface to *The Immortal Ones* (Cologne, 1920).

The futurists made less immediate impact than the expressionists, but in their manifestos they set forth ideas that were harbingers of future developments. Here are some excerpts from a manifesto that glorifies the variety theatre.

> *Futurism exalts the Variety Theatre because: . . . .*
> *4. The Variety Theatre is unique today in its use of cinema which enriches it with an incalculable number of visions and otherwise unrealizable spectacles. . . .*

> *5. The Variety Theatre . . . naturally generates what I call "the Futurist marvelous," produced by modern mechanics [which includes] all the new significations of light, sound, noise, and language, with their mysterious and inexplicable extensions into the least-explored part of our sensibility. . . .*
> *8. The Variety Theatre is alone seeking the audience's collaboration. It doesn't remain static like a stupid voyeur. . . . the action develops simultaneously on the stage, in the boxes, and in the orchestra. . . .*
> *16. The Variety Theatre destroys all our conceptions of perspective, proportion, time, and space. . . .*

> "The Variety Theatre,"
> September 29, 1913. From *Marinetti, Selected Writings*, edited and with an introduction by R. W. Flint (New York: Farrar, Straus and Giroux, 1971), pp. 116–122.

The most influential theoreticians of the theatre between the two world wars were Brecht and Artaud. They were united in their dislike for conventional, realistic theatre, but divided in their conceptions of the ideal theatre. Brecht's theories took shape over many years. (His writings have been collected in John Willett's *Brecht on Theatre*.) Perhaps the most systematic statement of his theoretical views is "A Short Organum for the Theatre." In it Brecht states his dislike for the traditional theatre which lulls the spectator into a belief that social conditions are fixed, and he proposes to replace it with one which distances him (the Alienation effect) from the stage events in a way that will make him judge them critically:

> *42. . . . A representation that alienates is one which allows us to recognize its subject, but at the same time makes it seem unfamiliar. . . .*
> *43. . . . The new alienations are only designed to free socially-conditioned phenomena from that stamp of familiarity which protects them from our grasp today.*
> *47. In order to produce A-effects the actor has to discard whatever means he has learnt of getting the audience to identify itself with the characters which he plays. . . .*
> *48. At no moment must he go so far as to be wholly transformed into the character played. . . . He has just to show the character. . . .*
> *74. So let us invite all the sister arts of the drama, not in order to create an "integrated work of art" in which they all offer themselves up and are lost, but so together with the drama they may further the common task in their differ-*

ent ways; and their relations with one another consist in this: that they lead to mutual alienation.

> "A Short Organum for the Theatre," *Brecht on Theatre,* trans. by John Willett (New York: Hill and Wang, 1964), pp. 179–205.

Brecht later sought to clarify his position on alienation in acting with this note:

> The contradiction between acting (demonstration) and experience (empathy) often leads the uninstructed to suppose that only one or the other can be manifest in the work of the actor (as if the Short Organum concentrated entirely on acting and the old tradition entirely on experience). In reality it is a matter of two mutually hostile processes which fuse in the actor's work. . . . His particular effectiveness comes from the tussle and tension of the two opposites, and also from their depth. . . .

> "Appendices to the Short Organum," *Brecht on Theatre,* pp. 276–281.

Artaud's major essays on theatre were collected in *The Theatre and Its Double* (1938). Here are some excerpts from his "Theatre of Cruelty, First Manifesto":

> The theatre will never find itself again . . . except by furnishing the spectator with the truthful precipitates of dreams, in which his taste for crime, his erotic obsessions, his savagery, his chimeras, his utopian sense of life and matter, even his cannibalism, pour out, on a level not counterfeit and illusory, but interior. . . .

> Every spectacle will contain . . . cries, groans, apparitions, surprises, theatricalities of all kinds, . . . costumes taken from certain ritual models; resplendent lighting, incantational beauty of voices, . . . physical rhythm of movements whose crescendo and decrescendo will accord exactly with the pulsation of movements familiar to everyone. . . .

> We abolish the stage and the auditorium and replace them by a single site, without partition or barrier of any kind. . . . A direct communication will be reestablished between the spectator and the spectacle, . . . from the fact that the spectator placed in the middle of the action, is engulfed and physically affected by it. . . .

> There will not be any set. . . .

> We shall not act a written play, but we shall make attempts at direct staging, around themes, facts, or known works. . . .

> Without an element of cruelty at the root of every spectacle, the theatre is not possible. In our present state of degeneration it is through the skin that metaphysics must be made to re-enter our minds. . . .

> ANTONIN ARTAUD, *The Theatre and Its Double* trans. M. C. Richards (New York: Grove Press, 1958).

18

Theatre and Drama, 1940–1960

World War II was the most extensive war ever fought in terms of people killed, property destroyed, and the number of countries involved. It made use of the most deadly weapons yet devised, including bombers, ballistic milsiles, and the atomic bomb.

The causes of the war were numerous, including problems left unsolved by World War I, the rise of totalitarian governments with their denial of civil liberties and, in some instances, programs of genocide, and the territorial ambitions of such countries as Germany, Italy, and Japan. The German extermination camps are one of the great blots on human history. At the end of the war Europe was divided into sectors, with the east dominated by Russia and the west dominated by the United States. There followed a "cold war" as the two nations sought to maintain or extend their influence. As a result, during the 1950s the world lived under the threat of an atomic war capable of ending life on earth. It was an age of anxiety and stress. The major stabilizing force was the United Nations, which replaced the League of Nations. It provided a forum for debate and international cooperation, but, like its predecessor, the U.N. was often ineffective, since several major powers had the right to veto its actions.

The theatre was heavily influenced by the horrors of the war and the threats of impending disaster. Serious questions were raised about man's capacity to act responsibly or even to survive. Anxiety and guilt became major themes, although as in most periods much entertainment sought merely to distract audiences from cares.

FRENCH THEATRE AND DRAMA, 1940–1960

During the war years, the theatre in Paris was relatively prosperous. Productions were numerous and well attended, although with the exceptions of those by Dullin, Baty, Barsacq, and the Comédie Française, few were outstanding. The end of the war brought many stresses, as production costs rose and films and television drained away audiences. The new government, attempting to play a more decisive role than its predecessors, took steps to aid the theatre. In 1946, the Ministry of Arts and Letters began to subsidize productions of selected new plays and a few new companies; an annual competition was also inaugurated among the new troupes for the best production and direction. Furthermore, the state theatres were reorganized. The Opéra and Opéra-Comique were placed under a single management, and the Comédie Française and Odéon were merged, the Odéon being called the Salle Luxembourg and the main house the Salle Richelieu. At first, the Salle Luxembourg was restricted to new or recent plays, but this scheme proved impractical and both branches came to present similar repertories. When Pierre Dux (1908–   ), Administrator of the Comédie Française from 1944 to 1947, instituted new regulations designed to reduce his actors' film appearances and other outside commitments, many of the leading *sociétaires*, including Jean-Louis Barrault, Madeleine Renaud, Marie Bell, Renée Faure, and Aimé Clairond, resigned. As a result, the troupe lost much of its strength, and, although it slowly rebuilt under the administrations of Pierre-Aimé Touchard (between 1947 and 1953) and Pierre Descaves (between 1953 and 1959), its prestige suffered seriously.

The government also encouraged decentralization of the theatre, which by 1945 was restricted almost entirely to Paris. Consequently, subsidized regional dramatic centers began to be established in 1947. The first, the Dramatic Center of the East, based at Strasbourg, was placed under the direction of Andre Clavé (succeeded in 1953 by Michel Saint-Denis and in 1958 by Hubert Gignoux), and a second was opened almost immediately at St. Étienne under Jean Dasté. In 1949, Le Grenier, a troupe which had been performing since 1945 under the direction of Maurice Sarrazin, was designated the Dramatic Center for Toulouse, and in the same year a fourth center was established at Rennes, under Hubert Gignoux (succeeded in 1958 by Guy Parigot). Other centers were inaugurated at Aix-en-Provence (1952), Tourcoing (1960), and Bourges (1963). In addition to performing in its home theatre, each troupe made several annual tours to towns in its region. Both national and local authorities aided the many dramatic festivals founded after 1945, most notably at Avignon (beginning in 1947) and Aix-en-Provence (beginning in 1948). By the 1960s more than fifty festivals were being held annually.

Despite these steps toward decentralization, Paris continued to be the principal theatrical center and the boulevard theatres, with their long-run policy, the typical organizations. The most influential theatres, however, departed from this pattern. For a few years after the war, three members of the Cartel continued their work: Dullin remained in Paris until 1947, Baty until 1951, and Jouvet from 1945 until his death in 1951. But by 1952, all of the members of the Cartel were dead. Of the younger prewar leaders, André Barsacq (at the Atelier after 1940) and Maurice Jacquemont (at the Studio des Champs-Elysées until 1960) were probably the most important. To this group should be added Marcel Herrand and Jean Marchat, who, after acting with Pitoëff's company, had formed the Rideau de Paris in the 1930s. Upon Pitoëff's death in 1939, they took over his Thé-

FIGURE 18.1 Jean-Louise Barrault's production of Claudel's *Christophe Colomb* at the Théâtre Marigny (1953). Photograph by Agence de Presse Bernand.

âtre aux Mathurins. Until 1952, they presented there excellent productions of foreign works, as well as many new French plays.

The major leaders in the postwar years were to be Barrault and Vilar. Jean-Louis Barrault (1910–   ), after studying with Dullin and working with Artaud and the pantomimist Étienne Decroux, had attained an enviable reputation as an actor in both the theatre and films before the war began. In 1940, he became a *sociétaire* at the Comédie Française, where in 1943 his production of Claudel's *The Satin Slipper* was the first important example of what came to be called "total theatre." Claudel's play, written between 1919 and 1924, had previously been considered unplayable because of its length and complexity, for the events span a century and occur in Spain, Italy, Africa, America, and at sea. At one point, the hemispheres converse, and at another the earth is represented as one bead on a rosary. A drama of love and salvation, *The Satin Slipper* was shaped by Barrault into a theatrical experience of such a high order that it was to influence other directors for a long time. Although Barrault was later to refine his ideas, in 1943 he had already formulated his basic outlook. He has declared that the text of a play is like an iceberg, since only about one eighth is visible. It is the director's task to complete the playwright's text by revealing the hidden portions through his imaginative use of all the theatre's resources. Thus, Barrault arrived at something like a synthesis of Copeau's and Artaud's approaches.

In 1946, after resigning from the Comédie Française, Barrault (with Madeleine Renaud, whom he had married in 1936) formed the Compagnie Madeleine Renaud–Jean-Louis Barrault. With such major actors as Jean Desailly, André Brunot, Jacques Dacqmine, Edwige Feuillère, and Pierre Brasseur, Barrault produced about forty plays ranging from the *Oresteia* to contemporary *avant-garde* works before he gave up his Théâtre Marigny in 1956.

Jean Vilar (1912–1971), a fellow student of Barrault at Dullin's school, was much slower in achieving recognition, and had worked in a number of companies before being employed to organize the festival at Avignon in 1947. His work there and his fine performances in Paris (most notably as Pirandello's Henry IV in Barsacq's production) led in 1951 to his appointment as director of the Théâtre National Populaire, then on the verge of collapse. He assembled a company that included Maria Casarès, Georges Wilson, and Daniel Sorano, and was most fortunate in attracting Gérard Philipe (1922–1959), who, after a brief career in the theatre, had been one of France's major film stars. Although not immediately successful, by 1954 the TNP was one of the most popular troupes in France. Vilar's productions always placed major emphasis upon the actor, reenforced by costume and lighting. Scenery was usually restricted to platforms or a few set pieces. Vilar was the first producer to achieve wide popularity with the approach advocated by the Cartel (whose following had always been limited). Although the TNP's principal home was at the Palais de Chaillot in Paris, it also played at the Avignon Festival and toured throughout France. It soon commanded greater popular support there than any of the other state troupes, all of which played exclusively in Paris.

Many changes in the postwar theatre were intimately connected with experiments in dramaturgy, most notably those of the absurdists. This movement did not come to the fore until the 1950s, however, and much of the major writing of the postwar period was to come from dramatists well known before 1940. Among these, the most prolific was Jean Anouilh, with such works as *Invitation to the Chateau* (1947), *Waltz of the Toreadors* (1952), *The Lark* (1953) and *Becket* (1960). In these plays Anouilh continued to explore the problem of maintaining integrity in a world based upon compromises.

Other prewar dramatists who made important contributions after 1945 include Marcel Achard, with *Patate* (1957) and *Eugene the Mysterious* (1964), and Armand Salacrou, with *Nights of Wrath* (1946) and *Boulevard Durand* (1960).

The most respected of the new dramatists was Henry de Montherlant (1896–1972), whose novels had won a wide following before the war. Although he had written a few minor plays, Montherlant's first produced work was *The Dead Queen* (1942), directed by Barrault at the Comédie Française. Its success led him to write *The Master of Santiago* (1948), *Port-Royal* (1954), *The Cardinal of Spain* (1960), and *The Civil War* (1965). *The Master of Santiago* is often considered Montherlant's most characteristic work because of its simple external action, complex psychology, and elevated style. The motif of sacrifice and the harsh rejection of all mediocrity runs through it. In all of Montherlant's work, the interest resides as much in the intellectual positions taken up by the characters as in their psychological traits and actions. His plays illustrate well the large role played by philosophical concerns in postwar French drama.

The enormous influence of postwar French drama, however, came from existentialist and absurdist

FIGURE 18.2 Vilar's production of Marivaux's *Triumph of Love* at the Théâtre Nationale Populaire (1956). Setting by Leon Gischia. Courtesy Agence de Presse Bernand.

FIGURE 18.3 First production of Beckett's *Waiting for Godot*, Théâtre de Babylone, Paris, 1953. Directed by Roger Blin. Photograph by Pic.

plays. Following the war, existentialism as a philosophical outlook attracted considerable attention, especially through the essays and plays of Jean-Paul Sartre (1905–). A philosopher and novelist, Sartre turned to drama in 1943 with *The Flies,* and went on to write *No Exit* (1944), *Dirty Hands* (1948), *The Devil and the Good Lord* (1951), and *The Condemned of Altona* (1959). All illustrate Sartre's existentialist views. Denying the existence of God, fixed standards of conduct, and verifiable moral codes, Sartre argues that each man must choose his own values and live by them regardless of prevailing ideas, for to conform unquestioningly to the conventions established by others is the immoral response of a robot rather than the responsible act of a true being. Sartre's plays show characters faced with choices which require them to reassess their outlooks and to forge new personal standards. In the uncertainty that followed the war, Sartre attracted a wide following, for he cast doubt upon

the conformism that had made possible the Nazi atrocities. But Sartre also believed that it is necessary for man to be politically "engaged," even though the choices open to him are seldom ideal. In *Dirty Hands,* he argues that to participate in political action invariably means that one's hands will get dirty, but that to refuse to become engaged merely means that others will make the choices that determine the direction of events.

The work of Albert Camus (1913–1960) was to be of equal importance. Before turning to drama, Camus had been a theatre worker in his native Algeria, a journalist, and the editor of a clandestine newspaper during the German occupation of France. His dramatic output was small: *Cross-Purposes* (1944), *Caligula* (performed 1945), *State of Siege* (1948), *The Just Assassins* (1949), and a few adaptations. His influence on the theatre came in part from his essay, "The Myth of Sisyphus" (1943), in which his discussion of the "absurd" was to supply the name for the absurdist movement. In this essay Camus argues that the human condition is absurd because of the gap between man's hopes and the irrational universe into which he has been born. For Camus, the only remedy lies in each man's search for a set of standards (admittedly without any objective basis) that will allow him to bring order out of this chaos. Although Camus denied being an existentialist, his conclusions were similar to those of Sartre.

Camus and Sartre differed most in their ideas about "engagement," for Camus rejected the conclusion advocated by Sartre in *Dirty Hands* and denied the validity of choosing between two immoral positions. Their difference on this point led to a prolonged and bitter debate. Between them, nevertheless, they supplied the philosophical basis for the absurdist movement which began to emerge in the early 1950s.

Although Sartre and Camus reject rationalistic views of the universe, their plays retain the traditional dramatic forms. Since they begin with the assumption that the world is irrational and then go on to create order out of chaos, their works have clear dramatic actions. On the other hand, the absurdists, while for the most part accepting Sartre's philosophical outlook, tend to concentrate upon the irrationality of human experience without suggesting any path beyond. By employing a succession of episodes unified merely by theme or mood instead of a cause-to-effect arrangement, they arrive at a structure paralleling the chaos which is their usual dramatic subject. The sense of absurdity is heightened by the juxtaposition of incongruous events producing seriocomic and

FIGURE 18.4   Madeleine Renaud in Genet's *The Screens*, Théâtre de France (1966). Photograph by Pic.

ironical effects. Because they view language as the major rationalistic tool, the absurdists often demonstrate its inadequacy and subordinate it to nonverbal devices. Of the absurdists, four—Beckett, Ionesco, Genet, and Adamov—were to be most important.

Samuel Beckett (1906-   ), although not the earliest of the absurdists, was the first to win international fame, and it was his *Waiting for Godot* which in 1953 brought absurdism its first popular attention both in France and elsewhere. Irish by birth, Beckett first went to Paris in the 1920s and settled there permanently in 1938. Beckett began writing around 1930 but he did not turn to the dramatic form until he wrote *Waiting For Godot*. Since then he has written *Endgame* (1957), *Krapp's Last Tape* (1958), *Happy Days* (1961), *Play* (1963), *Come and Go* (1966), *Not I* (1973), and *That Time* (1976). In many ways, Beckett seems the characteristic dramatist of the 1950s, a decade made anxious by the threat of the cold war and of total destruction by an atomic holocaust. In fact, Beckett's characters often seem to be set down in a world that has already undergone the ravages of disaster and in which man's very existence is in question. Beckett is not so much concerned with

man as a social and political creature as with the human condition in a metaphysical sense. His spiritual derelicts are usually isolated in time and space; they torture and console each other and themselves, raise questions which cannot be answered, and struggle on in a world which seems to be disintegrating around them. Probably more than any other writer, Beckett expressed the postwar doubts about man's capacity to understand and control his world.

Eugène Ionesco (1912-   ), a Roumanian by birth, labeled his first work, *The Bald Soprano* (1949, performed 1950), an "anti-play" to indicate a rebellion against conventional drama. The early works, which include *The Lesson* (1950) and *The Chairs* (1952), attracted little attention at first, but steadily grew in reputation after 1953, when Anouilh published an article praising *Victims of Duty*. These early plays, as well as *Amedée* (1954) and *The New Tenant* (1957), are mainly negative, for they concentrate upon the clichés of language and thought, the dominance of materialism, and the irrationality of values. Later works, such as *The Killer* (1959), *Rhinoceros* (1960), *A Stroll in the Air* (1963), *Hunger and Thirst* (1966), *Macbett* (1972), and *The Man with the Suitcases* (1975), have taken a somewhat more positive view by showing protagonists who hold out against conformity, although they cannot offer any rational basis for their actions.

Unlike Beckett, Ionesco is concerned primarily with man's social relationships, most typically those of middle-class characters in family situations. Two themes run through most of his work: the deadening nature of materialistic, bourgeois society, and the loneliness and isolation of the individual. Perhaps ultimately his vision of man's condition differs little from Beckett's, but it is conceived in more domestic terms. All of his plays seek to discredit clichés, ideologies, and materialism. His characters tend to be unthinking automatons oblivious of their own mechanical behavior, just as material objects tend to proliferate and take over the space that should be occupied by people. Ionesco is especially antipathetic to the notion that drama should be didactic. To him truth means the absence of commitment, either ideologically or esthetically, for commitment involves a fatal step toward conformity.

Jean Genet (1910–   ) spent much of his life in prison, a background that figures prominently in much of his writing. His first plays, *The Maids* (presented by Jouvet in 1947) and *Deathwatch* (produced by Herrand in 1949) were at first unsuccessful, and his reputation was to be made with *The Balcony* (1956), *The Blacks* (1959), and *The Screens* (1961, not produced in France until 1966). Genet's characters rebel against organized society and suggest that deviation is essential if man is to achieve integrity. They also imply that nothing has meaning without its opposite—law and crime, religion and sin, love and hate— and that deviant behavior is as valuable as the accepted virtues. Genet, viewing all systems of value as entirely arbitrary, transforms life into a series of ceremonies and rituals which give an air of stability and importance to otherwise nonsensical behavior.

Arthur Adamov (1908–1971), born in Russia and educated in Switzerland, was attracted early to surrealism, a movement that has influenced all absurdist drama. After he turned to playwriting in 1947, Adamov's first work was produced in 1950. The early plays, for example *The Invasion* (1950), *Parody* (1952), and *All Against All* (1953), show a seriocomically cruel world of moral destructiveness and personal anxieties in which the characters are condemned to be eternal failures by their inability to communicate with each other. Time and place are usually indefinite, as in dreams. Adamov's later plays became progressively more socially oriented,

especially after 1956, when he denounced his earlier work and adopted a Brechtian form. His new outlook is reflected in *Paolo Paoli* (1957), a commentary upon the materialism and hypocrisy which preceded the First World War, and *Spring '71* (1960), which idealizes the men who created the Paris Commune in 1871. But with this change in mode went a decline in popularity for Adamov's work and by the time of his death his reputation was considerably lower than that of the other three major exponents of absurdism.

Absurdism was never a conscious, clearly defined movement. The label was popularized by Martin Esslin's book *The Theatre of the Absurd* (1961). Since it was not a conscious movement, it is difficult to specify those authors who should be included within its ranks. As a label, absurdism is clearly not broad enough to encompass all of the experimental dramatists of the time, of which there were many in France. Among those who probably should not be labeled absurdists, some of the best were Jacques Audiberti (1899–1965), whose *Quoat-Quoat* (1946), *The Black Feast* (1948), *The Landlady* (1960), and *The Sentry-Box* (1965) stress the power of evil and of sex over human affairs; Georges Schéhadé (1910–   ), whose *Evening of Proverbs* (1954), *Tale of Vasco* (1956), and *The Journey* (1961) are often reminiscent of Giraudoux's work in their combination of fantasy, precise language, and love for humanity; and Jean Tardieu (1903–   ), who has concentrated upon one-act "chamber" plays, such as *The Information Window* (1955) and *The ABC of Our Life* (1959), treating man's enslavement to social conventions.

Most of the *avant-garde* drama was first produced in small, out-of-the-way theatres by adventurous young men, many of them heavily influenced by Artaud and later to be among France's most respected directors. Of these, perhaps the most important was Roger Blin (1907–   ), a disciple of Artaud, who, after working with Dullin and Barrault, was closely associated with the absurdist movement after 1949. He is especially noted for his staging of Beckett's plays. Other important directors include André Reybaz (1922–   ), who introduced Audiberti, Ghelderode, and Ionesco to Parisian audiences and worked with a number of *avant-garde* theatres before becoming director of the Dramatic Center at Tourcoing in 1960; Georges Vitaly (1917–   ), who worked with Reybaz before founding the Théâtre LaBruyère in 1953; Jean-Marie Serreau (1915–   ), a pupil of Dullin who directed the first productions of Adamov's plays before opening the Théâtre de Babylone with Blin in 1952 and going on to direct at many other theatres; and Jacques Fabbri (1925–   ), who worked with Vitaly and Reybaz before forming his own company, with which he has won special renown for his staging of farces. To this group should be added Nicolas Bataille (1926–   ), Marcel Cuvelier (1924–   ), Michel de Ré (1925–   ), Jacques Polieri (1928–   ), and Jacques Mauclair (1919–   ). Beginning as members of the *avant-garde,* most of these directors were later to work regularly with such established troupes as the Comédie Française and the Théâtre de France.

By the time General DeGaulle came to power in 1959, French theatre and drama had almost fully recovered from the effects of the war years. By then, they enjoyed perhaps the greatest critical esteem of any in the world. In 1959, the DeGaulle government instituted a series of policies that would affect the French theatre deeply after 1960.

FIGURE 18.5 Wieland Wagner's production of *Tannhäuser* at Bayreuth, 1954. Note the absence of three-dimensional scenery and the dependence on light and projections. This approach outraged those who favored the three-dimensionality that had prevailed at Bayreuth prior to World War II. From *Décor de Théâtre dans le Monde depuis 1935.*

GERMAN THEATRE AND DRAMA, 1940–1960

When Germany surrendered to the Allies in 1945, all theatres were closed for a time but soon they began to reopen under the surveillance of occupation forces. After 1945, the German theatre grew steadily and by the 1960s was one of the most stable in the world. Although Germany was divided after 1945, the theatre in the two areas shared many common characteristics. In both, the system of state-supported resident companies was continued. By the early 1960s, there were 175 professional theatres in West Germany, of which 120 were publicly owned, and in East Germany there were about 135 theatres, all state-owned. Almost every city had a dramatic company and an opera and ballet troupe of good quality. All of the subsidized troupes in a single town were under one manager (or Intendant), appointed by the city or state, and all shared a staff of directors and designers. A "dramaturg" advised the companies on the choice of plays and other artistic matters.

Among the outstanding directors of the postwar period were Boleslaw Barlog, Fritz Kortner, Willi Schmidt, Wolfgang Langhoff, Wolfgang Heinz, and Benno Bessen in Berlin; Harry Buchwitz in Frankfort-on-Main; Gustav Gründgens and Oscar Fritz Schuh in Hamburg; Karlheinz Stroux in Düsseldorf; Heinz Hilpert in Göttingen; Rudolf Sellner in Darmstadt and Berlin; Günther Rennert in Munich; Hans Schalla in Bochum; and Karl Kayser in Leipzig. In 1951, Erwin Piscator returned to Germany, where he directed for numerous troupes, as well as being manager of the Freie Volksbühne in West Berlin until his death in 1966. The most influential designers were Caspar Neher (1897–1962) and Teo Otto (1904–1968), both attuned to Brecht's approach. They moved design in the direction of theatricalism—the frank manipulation of stage means. Although they often used realistic elements, they normally suggested place through decorative screens, projections, a few architectural details, and lighting which created mood and atmosphere. Among the other fine designers were Max Fritzsche, Karl Gröning, Helmut Jürgens, Wilhelm Reinking, Rudolf Heinrich, and Karl von Appen.

Although more than 100 theatre buildings were destroyed during the war, a phenomenal rebuilding program after 1950 replaced most of them. In the new buildings, sightlines were considerably improved, boxes were eliminated, and the number of balconies reduced. The prewar emphasis upon complex stage machinery continued. For example, the Schiller Theater, opened in West Berlin in 1951, has a revolving stage, elevators, and rolling platform stages. Most of the theatres are of the conventional proscenium-arch type. A few small theatres intended as second houses are more flexible, but there has been little experimentation with spatial relationships.

In addition to permanent resident troupes, festivals were of considerable importance in postwar Germany. The most famous was still the Bayreuth Festival (revived in 1951 under the direction of Wieland Wagner until his death in 1966, and then under Wolfgang Wagner). After the war, Wagner's operas were performed for the first time at Bayreuth with simple scenic investiture much like that advocated by Appia, instead of the historical realism which had been used since Wagner's time. Bitterly opposed by traditionalists, the new methods won wholehearted approval from others. In 1973 the Wagner family relinquished much of its control over the festival and archival materials when the Richard Wagner Foundation was formed. This foundation will maintain, but not run, the festival, and a member of the Wagner family is to direct future festivals "if no better qualified applicants come forward." In 1976 the one-hundreth anniversary of the festival was celebrated with great fanfare. The centenary also motivated numerous assessments of Bayreuth's achievements and speculations about its future.

Of all the German companies, two in East Berlin—the Berliner Ensemble and the Komische Oper—achieved the greatest renown. The work of the Berliner Ensemble is bound up with Brecht's late career. After he returned to Europe in 1947, Brecht's plays rapidly found their way into the repertories of most German troupes and his theory was soon known throughout the world. His fame was confirmed through the work of the Berliner Ensemble. Opened in 1949 with *Mother Courage*, the Berliner Ensemble for a time shared the Deutsches Theater with another troupe. In 1954, it was given the Theater-am-Schiffbauerdamm, the house in which Brecht's *Threepenny Opera* was first produced in 1928. With its appearances in Paris in 1954 and 1955, the Berliner Ensemble became internationally famous and has since been considered one of the world's finest troupes. After Brecht's death in 1956, the company continued under the direction of Helene Weigel (1900–1971), Brecht's wife, who had been its director from the

FIGURE 18.6 The Berliner Ensemble's production of Brecht's *The Caucasian Chalk Circle*. Setting by Karl von Appen. From *Décor de Théâtre dans le Monde depuis 1935*.

beginning. Brecht's methods were also retained by the company's principal directors.

Much of the Berliner Ensemble's achievement stemmed from its long and careful rehearsals, sometimes extending over five months. When each production was ready, a *Modellbuch* containing 600–800 action photographs was made. The published *Modellbücher* have influenced many producers who have never seen the company perform. The Berliner Ensemble did much to establish the validity of Brecht's theories, while the humanitarian and social emphases of his plays suggested an alternative to the absurdists (who tended to dramatize personal anxieties). On the other hand, since Brecht used nonrealistic devices and, like absurdists, emphasized irony and humor, the two influences have since 1960 sometimes merged.

Upon Miss Weigel's death in 1971, Ruth Berghaus became director of the company. But by the time the troupe celebrated its twenty-fifth anniversary in 1974, it had begun to lose much of its vitality. To prevent it from becoming merely a Brecht museum, Miss Berghaus attempted to revitalize it through highly experimental productions of such plays as Wedekind's *Spring's Awakening* and Strindberg's *Miss Julie*. Her efforts met with considerable opposition, being damned by some critics as "self-indulgent formalism." It remains to be seen if the Berliner Ensemble will be able to maintain the strengths on which its world-wide fame rests.

The Komische Oper was founded in 1947 by Walter Felsenstein (1901–   ), who established the company's style, a highly selective realism. Through lengthy and rigorous rehearsals and complete control over every artistic element, Felsenstein's productions contrasted sharply with those usually seen in opera houses. The Komische Oper rapidly became one of East Germany's most popular theatres. Its appearances elsewhere have also won it a reputation only slightly below that of the Berliner Ensemble. Felsenstein's reputation as a director has brought him many opportunities to direct nonmusical works, perhaps most notably at Vienna's Burgtheater.

In Austria, the pattern of postwar reconstruction paralleled that in Germany. By the 1960s there were thirty-six theatres in Austria, twenty of which were located in Vienna. Four of these were state theatres, the Staatsoper and the Volksoper for opera, the Burgtheater and the Akademietheater for drama, while the Theater-in-der-Josefstadt and the Volkstheater were subsidized by the city of Vienna. The festival at Salzburg, reopened in 1946, also resumed its position as one of the finest in the world.

If Germany and Austria rebuilt one of the best systems of subsidized theatres in the world, they were less successful in developing significant new dramatists,

FIGURE 18.7 Walter Felsenstein's production of Mozart's *The Magic Flute* at the Komische Oper (1954). Setting by Rudolf Heinrich. Courtesy *World Theatre*.

for until the late 1950s the major German dramatist was Brecht, all of whose major works were written before 1946. Zuckmayer returned to Germany, but his *The Devil's General* (produced in 1948), depicting the inhumanity of the Nazi hierarchy, *The Cold Light* (1956), about the dilemma of an atomic physicist, and *The Pied Piper* (1975), a reworking of the fairy tale with added topical political overtones, never equaled the popularity of his prewar satire, *The Captain from Koepenick*. Wolfgang Borchert (1921–1947) won fame with one play, *The Man Outside* (1947), about a returning soldier trying to adjust to civilian life, but died before he could fulfill the promise shown by that work. Fritz Hochwalder (1911–   ) found a wide audience at home with *The Holy Experiment* (1943), *The Fugitive* (1945), and *The Public Prosecutor* (1949), all of which pose questions of individual responsibility and public guilt, but he never won a following outside of German-speaking territories.

The major drama in German during the 1950s was written by two Swiss playwrights, Frisch and Duerrenmatt, both of whom were encouraged by Kurt Hirschfeld and Oskar Walterlin of the Zurich theatre, one of the best in Europe during the Nazi regime because so many refugees settled in Switzerland. Max Frisch (1911–   ) was trained as an architect but turned to writing in 1944. His reputation rests primarily upon *The Chinese Wall* (1946), *Biedermann and the Firebugs* (1958), and *Andorra* (1961), all of which treat questions of guilt. In each play the past is reviewed and the characters construct elaborate rationalizations for their actions; none is really willing to accept responsibility. Although it is clear that Frisch longs for a world of integrity, he seems to suggest that it is unattainable because men do not learn from their mistakes. Through techniques borrowed from Wilder, Strindberg, Brecht, and others, he embodies his search and disillusionment in symbolic and nightmarish fantasy.

Friedrich Duerrenmatt (1921–   ) began writing plays in 1947. Of his many works, the most successful have been *The Visit* (1956) *The Physicists* (1962), *Play Strindberg* (1969), and *The Collaborator* (1973). Like Frisch, Duerrenmatt is concerned with moral questions, which he suggests will not be solved satisfactorily because man is so readily corrupted by promises of power or wealth. Duerrenmatt is much more detached than Frisch. He emphasizes the grotesqueness of the human condition, which he expresses through a rather dark comedy. Although he is concerned with moral dilemmas,

FIGURE 18.8 Duerrenmatt's *The Physicists* at the Kammerspiele, Munich (1962). Directed by Hans Schweikart. Courtesy *World Theatre.*

he shows the human instinct for good corrupted either by power and greed or by chance. He avoids bitterness by standing at a distance and viewing events sardonically.

Because the majority of significant postwar German drama dealt with questions of guilt related to larger political and social issues, it differed considerably in tone from the French absurdist drama, which attracted few German exponents. Of those who wrote in the absurdist vein, probably the best was Günter Grass (1927–   ), with such plays as *The Wicked Cooks* (1957), in which rival factions seek to discover the recipe of a soup, apparently symbolizing significant human experience, so that it can be reproduced according to a formula. In the 1960s Grass abandoned the absurdist for the Brechtian mode. In *The Plebeians Rehearse the Revolution* (1966) Grass sets the uprising of East Berlin workers in 1953 within the framework of a rehearsal of Brecht's *Coriolanus,* a device which allowed him to comment upon the present by drawing parallels with the past.

Thus, while Germany established a strong postwar theatre, it was less successful in producing a significant new drama. Nevertheless, through the work of Brecht and other socially conscious writers, the German theatre exerted strong influence on postwar developments.

AMERICAN THEATRE AND DRAMA, 1940–1960

After World War II the most influential figures in the American theatre were probably the director Elia Kazan and the designer Jo Mielziner, for through their joint work on such plays as Williams' *A Streetcar Named Desire* (1947) and Miller's *Death of a Salesman* (1949) they established the productional approach that was to dominate until about 1960. Under Mielziner's influence, stage settings turned away from realism, although they retained clearly representational features. This "theatricalized realism" was essentially an extension of the new stagecraft of the 1920s. On the other hand, acting moved increasingly toward psychological truth as found in the characters' inner motivations. It was an extension of the Group Theatre's approach as taught at the Actors Studio.

Founded in 1947 by Robert Lewis, Elia Kazan, and Cheryl Crawford (although Lee Strasberg was to be the dominant figure), the Actors Studio was designed to permit selected actors to work and develop according to the Stanislavsky system. Marlon Brando (1924–   ), with his characterization of the inarticulate, uneducated, and supremely self-confident Stanley Kowalski of *A Streetcar Named Desire,* came to epitomize in the popular mind the Actors Studio style. The novelty of serious acting based upon substandard speech, untidy dress, and boorish behavior captured the public imagination and began a vogue for this approach. It also, probably quite mistakenly, created an image of the Actors Studio as merely encouraging actors to explore their own psyches while ignoring the skills needed for projecting a characterization. Although much of the criticism is clearly exaggerated, Strasberg did place primary emphasis upon "inner truth" as the basis of good acting, and much of the Studio's training was determined by this goal. In 1956, the Studio began a program to assist playwrights and in 1960 it added a workshop for directors. By the 1960s, however, the influence of the Actors Studio had begun to decline as interest turned toward nonrealistic and period drama, for which the Studio's approach seemed too limited. Nevertheless, it remained a powerful force.

FIGURE 18.9 Scene from Tennessee Williams' *A Streetcar Named Desire,* with Marlon Brando, Kim Hunter, Karl Malden, and Jessica Tandy. Directed by Elia Kazan, setting by Jo Mielziner. Photo by Graphic House, Inc.

After the war, the theatre was seriously threatened by the rapid development of television. In 1948 there were only 48 stations, but by 1958 there were 512 and over 50 million television sets. The free entertainment provided by the new medium came at just the time when production costs in the theatre were rapidly increasing. Between 1944 and 1960 the price of tickets doubled, and the costs of mounting a show increased at a still faster rate. Under these circumstances, producers tended to seek vehicles with broad appeal, and to avoid both plays and production styles that might offend or confuse spectators.

The Broadway theatre continued the decline which had begun before the war. It reached the lowest point in the season of 1949–1950, when only fifty-nine new productions were mounted, but then slowly climbed to about seventy, a number which could not be greatly increased because of the relatively small number of theatres available (about thirty in the 1950s).

In the late 1940s, the reduction of the American theatre to a small number of Broadway productions served to motivate several attempts to diversify the theatre. One of the most important efforts was to be the off-Broadway movement. By playing in out-of-the-way theatres or improvised auditoriums, production costs could be cut considerably, and works which would not appeal to a mass audience could be played for more restricted groups. Although its main force was to be felt during the 1950s, the off-Broadway movement can properly be traced back to the little theatres of the World War I era. It had declined markedly during the 1930s but began to revive during World War II. In 1943, the city of New York acquired the Mecca Temple on 55th Street and converted it into the City Center, where opera, musical comedy, ballet, and drama were played for limited engagements at moderate prices. Under the general direction of Jean Dalrymple (1910–   ), the City Center was to build enviable ballet and opera troupes before moving to Lincoln Center in 1966. Then in 1946–1947, Eva Le Gallienne, Margaret Webster, and Cheryl Crawford established the American Repertory Company (modeled on Miss Le Gallienne's earlier Civic Repertory Company), which performed a season of six plays before being forced to close.

The more typical off-Broadway groups, however, were begun by relatively unknown directors. The first

FIGURE 18.10 Jo Mielziner's settings for Arthur Miller's *Death of a Salesman* (1949). The design above shows the set as it appeared in the opening scene and for subsequent scenes that take place in the present. Below is the setting as it appeared during flashback scenes, which were identified by the projected leaf pattern. Photographs by Peter A. Juley & Son. Courtesy Mr. Mielziner.

to attract attention was New Stages, a group founded in 1947 by David Heilweil, who in 1950 also opened an arena theatre in the ballroom of the midtown Edison Hotel. But, the major upturn in prestige came in 1952, when the Circle in the Square presented Williams' *Summer and Smoke*, a failure on Broadway, to high critical praise. Soon off-Broadway was viewed as a workable alternative to Broadway's commercialism. By 1955–1956, there were more than ninety off-Broadway groups, and they, rather than Broadway companies, gave the first performances in New York of works by such authors as Brecht, Ionesco, and Genet.

Of the off-Broadway groups, two—Circle in the Square and the Phoenix Theatre— were of special importance during the 1950s. The Circle in the Square was opened in 1951 by José Quintero (1924–   ) and Theodore Mann (1924–   ). In this former nightclub, the actor-audience relationship was entirely flexible, although spectators normally were seated around three sides of a rectangular acting area. Here such performers as Geraldine Page, Jason Robards, Jr., George C. Scott, and Colleen Dewhurst came to prominence. After his triumph with O'Neill's *The Iceman Cometh* in 1956, Quintero was asked to direct the Broadway production of *Long Day's Journey into Night*. Its cumulative record made the Circle in the Square one of the most respected theatres of the 1950s. It has continued to play an important role, but not so fully as during the first decade of its existence.

The Phoenix Theatre was inaugurated in 1953 by Norris Houghton (1909–   ) and T. Edward Hambleton (1911–   ) in an out-of-the-way but fully equipped conventional theatre. It presented a diverse program of plays by such authors as Aristophanes, Shakespeare, Turgenev, Ibsen, Shaw, Pirandello, Ionesco, and Montherlant. It also attempted to use a different director for each play and frequently attracted such outstanding actors as Siobhan McKenna and Robert Ryan. Beginning in the late 1950s, the Phoenix employed a permanent acting company, which under the direction of Stuart Vaughan presented a series of plays each season. This arrangement lasted until the early 1960s, when Houghton and Hambleton formed a liaison with the Association of Producing Artists and thereafter became primarily producers of that company's offerings.

For the most part, off-Broadway theatres in the 1950s were little concerned with experimentation in staging except in their use of arena and thrust stages. They were most interested in repertory, seeking to do a higher level of drama than that favored by Broadway. Their goals were essentially artistic.

After the war there were also a number of attempts to decentralize the theatre. One leader in this area was the American National Theatre and Academy (ANTA), which had been chartered by Congress in 1935 to stimulate the rejuvenation of the theatre outside of New York and to form an academy to train personnel. Because of lack of funds, little was accomplished, although ANTA became the principal American center for collecting and exchanging information about the theatre. After the war, the attempt to found regional theatres was given its first important impetus by Margo Jones (1913–1955), who successfully established an arena theatre in Dallas in 1947. Other pioneering groups include the Alley Theatre, founded in Houston in 1947 by Nina Vance; the Arena Stage, opened in Washington in 1949 by Edward Mangum and Zelda Fichandler; and the Actors' Workshop, begun in 1952 in San Francisco by Jules Irving and Herbert Blau. At first, most of the groups struggled along with semiprofessional personnel while gradually building audiences. Then, in 1959 the regional theatre movement was considerably strengthened by the Ford Foundation's decision to give financial support to resident companies that had demonstrated the greatest strength. Thus, although the accomplishments of the 1950s were not great, the foundations were laid for more ambitious projects in the 1960s.

Summer festivals also added diversity. At Stratford, Ontario, a Shakespearean Festival was inaugurated in 1953. Here Tyrone Guthrie used an open stage; the success of this festival and its spatial arrangements were to be influential throughout North America. An American Shakespeare Festival was instituted at Stratford, Connecticut, in 1955; since then it has annually offered a fifteen-week season of plays. The New York Shakespeare Festival was established in 1954 by Joseph Papp, and since 1957 has played free of charge in Central Park, where the municipally owned Delacorte Theatre (seating 2,263) was inaugurated in 1962. Other Shakespearean festivals were held annually at Ashland (Oregon), San Diego, and elsewhere. Summer theatres, most of them in resort areas, also steadily increased in numbers. Additionally, by the early 1960s approximately 1,500 colleges and universities were offering courses in theatre. Thus, various groups sought to compensate for the concentration of the professional theatre in New York.

For a time after the war, America seemed to be rich in playwriting. Its stature increased considerably

FIGURE 18.11   O'Neill's *Iceman Cometh* at the Circle in the Square (1956). Directed by Jose Quintero. Photograph by Jerry Dantzic.

with the return of O'Neill's plays to the repertory following the success of *The Iceman Cometh* in 1956. *A Long Day's Journey into Night* (produced 1957) was one of the most impressive plays of the 1950s, and other works by O'Neill were performed to critical acclaim. Although he declined in power, Maxwell Anderson also continued to write such plays as *Joan of Lorraine* (1946), *Anne of the Thousand Days* (1948), and *The Golden Six* (1958). Clifford Odets regained some of his former strength with *The Country Girl* (1950) and *The Flowering Peach* (1954), William Saroyan returned with *The Cave Dwellers* (1957), Lillian Hellman with *The Autumn Garden* (1951) and *Toys in the Attic* (1960), S. N. Behrman with *The Cold Wind and the Warm* (1959) and *But for Whom, Charlie* (1962), and Thornton Wilder with *The Matchmaker* (1954).

The most outstanding new writers were Williams and Miller. Tennessee Williams (1911–   ) achieved his first success in 1945 with *The Glass Menagerie* and rapidly consolidated it with *A Streetcar Named Desire* (1947), *The Rose Tattoo* (1951) *Cat on a Hot Tin Roof* (1954), *Orpheus Descending* (1957), and *Sweet Bird of Youth* (1959). But by the late 1950s Williams was being accused of repeating himself and thereafter both his

critical stature and his output declined, although he continued to write such works as *Night of the Iguana* (1961), *The Milk Train Doesn't Stop Here Anymore* (1962), *Slapstick Tragedy* (1966), and *This Is [an Entertainment]* (1976).

Williams' strength lies in his ability to create interesting characters caught in critical or violent situations as they seek to recover a past or create a future more satisfying than the vulgar and materialistic present. As the dramatic action progresses, the protagonist is usually forced to abandon his illusions, often after physical or moral degradation at the hands of callous or vicious characters. Williams' sensational situations have often obscured his moral concern for the survival of love and beauty in a materialistic world. To achieve his effects, Williams has used theatrical means imaginatively, manipulating them, sometimes quite obviously, to focus attention on the inner truth of character and situation. No American playwright commanded so wide an audience as did Williams between 1945 and 1960.

Arthur Miller (1916–   ) achieved his first success with *All My Sons* (1947), an Ibsenesque play about a manufacturer of airplane engines who has put profit above the safety of wartime pilots. Miller's reputation now rests primarily upon *Death of a Salesman* (1949), *The Crucible* (1953), and *A View from the Bridge* (1955). Of his later works, which include *After the Fall* (1964), *Incident at Vichy* (1964), and *The Creation of the World and Other Business* (1973), only *The Price* (1968) achieved any real success. Through most of Miller's plays run the same ideas. His characters stray because of overly narrow (often materialistic) values and find peace in some more meaningful understanding of themselves and of their roles in society. Miller is often called a "social" dramatist, but his interests have always been moral. Though society may encourage false values, it remains the individual's responsibility to sort out the true from the false. Miller clearly implies that it is possible to maintain one's integrity within the framework of society. Of Miller's work, *Death of a Salesman* is usually considered most significant, perhaps because it dramatizes so successfully the conflict in the American consciousness between the desire for material success and for adventure and happiness.

Few other new playwrights lived up to their initial promise. William Inge (1913–1973) gained a considerable following with such works as *Come Back, Little Sheba* (1950), *Picnic* (1953), *Bus Stop* (1955), and *The Dark at the Top of the Stairs* (1957), but his work now seems essentially a more naive version of Williams'. Other popular dramatists of the time include Robert Anderson (1917–   ) with *Tea and Sympathy* (1953) and *You Know I Can't Hear You When the Water's Running* (1966); Arthur Laurents (1918–   ), with *Home of the Brave* (1948) and *A Clearing in the Woods* (1957); and Paddy Chayefsky (1923–   ) with *The Tenth Man* (1959) and *Gideon* (1961).

Musical drama continued to be one of the most popular of forms. For the most part, successful works were adapted from well-known novels, plays, or stories. Rodgers and Hammerstein, with *Carousel* (1945), *South Pacific* (1949), and *The King and I* (1951), established the pattern which was followed by others, such as Alan Jay Lerner and Frederick Loewe with *Brigadoon* (1947) and *My Fair Lady* (1956), and Frank Loesser with *Guys and Dolls* (1950) and *Most Happy Fella* (1956). For a time it appeared that a musical drama of greater depth might develop. Gian Carlo Menotti won a considerable following on Broadway with his operas, *The Medium* (1947) and *The Consul* (1950), but his later works proved less successful. Marc Blitzstein turned Hellman's *The Little Foxes* into an opera, *Regina,* and Leonard Bernstein collaborated with Miss Hellman on *Candide* (1956),

a musical play based upon Voltaire's novel, and with Arthur Laurents on *West Side Story* (1957), an adaptation of *Romeo and Juliet* to the world of New York's juvenile gangs. Despite the prestige gained by these pieces, the musical continued to be aimed for the most part at the mass audience.

By the late 1950s, American drama seemed to be at a standstill, for the earlier promise had been dissipated and no new dramatists of significance had yet made their power felt. But new developments, both in theatre and drama, were in the making, and the 1960s were destined to bring renewed vigor to the American scene.

ENGLISH THEATRE AND DRAMA, 1940–1960

With the coming of the war in 1939, the English theatre was soon at a virtual standstill. At the height of the Ger-

FIGURE 18.12 *Measure for Measure* at the American Shakespeare Festival, Stratford, Connecticut in 1973. The actors in the foreground are Lee Richardson and Christina Pickles. Directed by Michael Kahn. Courtesy American Shakespeare Festival.

FIGURE 18.13 T. S. Eliot's *The Cocktail Party* in its original production. Rex Harrison is seen at center as Harcourt-Reilly. Photo by Anthony Buckley.

man blitz, only one theatre remained open in London. The Old Vic retreated to the provinces, Donald Wolfit organized lunch-time programs, and a few others attempted to keep the theatre alive, but for the most part English theatrical life was almost completely disrupted.

Following the war, the English commercial theatre developed along lines reminiscent of America's Theatrical Syndicate. In 1942 Prince Littler, owner of several provincial theatres, acquired the Stoll Theatre Corporation and began to form alliances with several other theatre owners and producers. By 1947 his "The Group" controlled 75 percent of the theatres in England and owned the majority of shares of H. M. Tennant, Ltd., London's largest producing organization. "The Group" then demanded 30 to 40 percent of the gross weekly earnings of a play as a condition for leasing its theatres and reserved the right to close any play which fell below a specified weekly income.

Under these circumstances, it is not surprising that postwar English drama was innocuous. The leading dramatist was Terence Rattigan (1911–   ), who began to write plays in 1933, achieved his first popular success with *French Without Tears* (1936), and after the war turned to more serious subjects in *The Winslow Boy* (1946), *The Browning Version* (1948), *Separate Tables* (1955), and *Ross* (1960). Although Rattigan created compelling situations and interesting characters, the "drawing room" atmosphere of his plays perpetuated conservative traditions.

The commercial theatre also took poetic drama under its wing for a time during the 1950s, after E. Mar-

tin Browne had generated considerable response through his work at the Mercury Theatre. Browne's production of *A Phoenix Too Frequent* (1946) called attention to Christopher Fry and led to John Gielgud's production of *The Lady's Not for Burning* (1949), which established Fry's reputation and revived interest in poetic drama. Fry (1907–   ) went on to write *Venus Observed* (1949), *The Dark is Light Enough* (1954), *Curtmantle* (1961), *A Yard of Sun* (1970), and several adaptations. T. S. Eliot also returned to playwriting with *The Cocktail Party* (1949), which enjoyed a considerable popular success following its production at the Edinburgh Festival, and went on to write *The Confidential Clerk* (1953) and *The Elder Statesman* (1958). By 1955 interest in poetic drama was on the wane, for it too had come to seem merely an old formula dressed in poetic dialogue.

After the war, the Old Vic and the Shakespeare Festival Company were the most respected groups in England. The Old Vic returned to London in 1944, having spent the war years in the provinces. At first it had to play in the New Theatre, for its own building had been partially destroyed by bombing. At this time, the management passed from Tyrone Guthrie to Laurence Olivier, Ralph Richardson, and John Burrell, who presented a series of brilliant productions that made the Old Vic one of the most admired companies in the world. In 1946, the Old Vic also established a theatre school under the direction of Michel Saint-Denis, assisted by George Devine and Glen Byam Shaw, who utilized principles drawn primarily from Copeau. Closely allied with this school was a company—the Young Vic, under the direction of George Devine—which performed for children. After 1946 the Old Vic also had a second branch in Bristol.

Unfortunately, after 1948 the Old Vic began to decline, as Olivier and Richardson began to devote increasing amounts of time to outside commitments. In 1949 the management passed to Hugh Hunt (1911–   ), who had served as director of the Bristol Old Vic since its formation. The return of the company to the repaired Old Vic Theatre in 1950 created considerable conflicts with the school and the Young Vic troupe, and in 1952 both of the latter were dissolved. From 1953 to 1958 the Old Vic was headed by Michael Benthall (1919–   ). The company was still good though relatively young (the leading players were John Neville, Barbara Jefford, and Paul Rogers). But the days of greatness were over, although they were recaptured briefly in 1960 with Franco Zeffirelli's brawling, lusty production of *Romeo*

FIGURE 18.14 Franco Zeffirelli's production of *Romeo and Juliet* at the Old Vic in 1960. From *Scene Design Throughout the World Since 1950*.

tions also came to be accepted as the norm rather than as aberrations. It was out of this atmosphere that still other innovations would come in the 1960s.

After the war, repertory seasons in London were also sponsored occasionally by commercial managers. With the backing of H. M. Tennant, John Gielgud presented a notable series of plays at the Haymarket in 1944–1945, and from 1945 to 1956 the Lyric Theatre, Hammersmith, housed some outstanding revivals which were later sent on tour. Despite much fine acting, however, by 1956 the English theatre seemed merely to be looking toward the past. Many critics considered it doomed. Then, in 1956, a revolution began which soon transformed the English theatre.

The change can be attributed to two producing organizations, the English Stage Company and the Theatre Workshop, and to the dramatists with whom they worked. The English Stage Company was founded in 1956 under the direction of George Devine (1910–1966), who began his career as an actor in 1932, taught at Michel Saint-Denis' London Theatre Studio from 1936 to 1939, and directed the Young Vic Company after the war. When Devine took over the Royal Court Theatre, once the home of Granville Barker's troupe, he intended to

FIGURE 18.15 Osborne's *Look Back in Anger* at the Royal Court Theatre (1956). Directed by Tony Richardson. The actors are Kenneth Haigh, Alan Bates, and Mary Ure. Photograph by Houston Rogers.

and Juliet. In 1963, the Old Vic was dissolved and its headquarters became the home of the National Theatre.

As the Old Vic declined, the Stratford Festival Company gained in prestige, largely because of several reforms made by Barry Jackson, head of the theatre between 1946 and 1948. Under his management, the company became a self-contained producing organization with its own technical staff providing costumes and scenery; storage space was added and the stage was remodeled. Jackson also gained control over the entire festival so that its activities could be coordinated, and he enlivened the troupe by the addition of such vital young directors and actors as Peter Brook (1925–   ) and Paul Scofield (1922–   ). Between 1948 and 1956 the management was assumed by Anthony Quayle (1913–   ), who was joined in 1953 by Glen Byam Shaw. Such outstanding actors as Gielgud, Olivier, Redgrave, and Peggy Ashcroft appeared often, and in 1951 the number of productions given annually was reduced to permit more careful preparation. For the first time, London's critics attended the performances regularly and soon Stratford was being elevated in their reviews above the Old Vic. During this decade, novel interpreta-

FIGURE 18.16 John Arden's *Sergeant Musgrave's Dance* in its production at the Royal Court Theatre, London, in 1965. Photo by Zoë Dominic.

emphasize new English plays and foreign works not yet seen in England. Failing to uncover a backlog of unproduced English dramas, Devine placed a notice in *The Stage* which induced John Osborne (1929–   ) to submit *Look Back in Anger*. The production of Osborne's play in 1956 is usually considered the turning point in postwar British theatre.

Osborne's break with the past is not to be found in his dramaturgy, for *Look Back in Anger* is straightforwardly realistic, but in his attack upon class distinctions and upon the complacency and inertia of all classes. Its protagonist, Jimmy Porter, seems to have no positive solution to suggest but merely denounces a long list of moral, social, and political betrayals by those who go on mouthing Edwardian platitudes. Although the play is essentially negative in tone, it caught the contemporary rebellious mood so well that Jimmy soon became a symbol of all the "angry young men." Osborne's next play, *The Entertainer* (1957), has as its protagonist a disintegrating music hall performer (originally played by Laurence Olivier). Here England's progressive decline in vigor and values is symbolized in three generations of the Rice family of entertainers. Osborne seems to have been influenced by Brecht, for he alternates realistic scenes with vaudeville routines.

Osborne's work since 1960 has been very uneven in quality. Among his successful plays have been *Luther* (1961), a psychological study of the religious reformer, and *Inadmissible Evidence* (1965), a moving evocation of the wasted life of an outwardly successful, middle-aged lawyer. But Osborne has also written a number of unsuccessful works, among them *A Patriot for Me* (1965), *Hotel Amsterdam* (1968), *West of Suez* (1971); and *Watch It Come Down* (1976). Despite the critics' fondness for declaring that he has failed to live up to his early promise, Osborne must be considered one of the most important of postwar dramatists.

Next to Osborne, the Royal Court's most important dramatist of the early years was probably John Arden (1930–   ), author of *Live Like Pigs* (1958), *Sergeant Musgrave's Dance* (1959), *The Happy Haven* (1960), *Armstrong's Last Goodnight* (1964), and several other plays. Arden's work has been both praised highly and judged to be confused. Because he treats contemporary problems but does not seem to take sides, audiences have found it difficult to decide what he intends. But practically all of the plays pursue the same themes—the conflict between order and anarchy, between conformity and freedom, between those who wish to impose some pattern or principle and those who resist such efforts.

Among the Royal Court's other dramatists were N. F. Simpson (1919–   ) with such absurdist works as *A Resounding Tinkle* (1956), *One Way Pendulum* (1959), *The Cresta Run* (1965), and *Glorious Miles* (1975) and Ann Jellicoe (1928–   ) with *The Knack* (1961), an entertaining story of the struggle over a girl between two men, one too naive and the other too experienced.

Although the Royal Court made its principal contribution through its advocacy of new works, it also presented a wide range of older plays, such as *Lysistrata*, *The Country Wife*, *Major Barbara*, and *The Good Woman of Setzuan*.

The Theatre Workshop was founded in 1945 by a group of young people dissatisfied with the commercial theatre on both artistic and social grounds. Joan Littlewood (1914–   ) soon became its leader. Having no financial resources, the company toured England and the continent before settling in 1953 in a London suburb, Stratford, a working-class district. It did its important work between 1955, when it gained international recognition through an appearance at the world festival in Paris, and 1961, when Miss Littlewood resigned.

Two playwrights, Behan and Delaney, were especially associated with the Theatre Workshop. Brendan Behan's (1923–1965) first play, *The Quare Fellow*, written in 1945, was presented by the Theatre Workshop in 1956. A mixture of the comic and serious, it shows a

FIGURE 18.17 Joan Littlewood's production of *Oh, What a Lovely War!* at the Theatre Workshop in 1963. Design by John Bury. Photo courtesy *The Report.*

cross section of prison life on the eve of a prisoner's execution. Similarly, *The Hostage* (1958) is built around varying attitudes toward the impending death of an I.R.A. agent and the hostage who is to be killed in reprisal. Many diversions (songs, dances, and character vignettes) enliven the play. Shelagh Delaney's (1939–   ) *A Taste of Honey* (1958) is the story of a young girl and her slatternly mother set against a closely observed background. The charge that Miss Littlewood had a strong hand in reshaping the plays of both Behan and Delaney is supported in part by the failure of both to produce significant work except with the Workshop.

The Theatre Workshop is also noted for its production style, perhaps best exemplified in *Oh, What a Lovely War!* (1963), a biting satire on the First World War. As the director of more than 150 of its productions, Miss Littlewood was responsible for establishing the company's approach. She drew heavily on Brechtian and music hall conventions, but also on Stanislavsky, especially "through lines" of action and improvisation. Her ultimate aim was to create a theatre to which the working classes would go with the same regularity and enthusiasm as to fun palaces or penny arcades. She sought to imbed some lasting message or significant content within a framework of techniques borrowed from popular entertainments.

Several of the troupe's successful productions were moved to commercial theatres, and this practice so weakened the company that Miss Littlewood eventually resigned. Since then she has returned occasionally to direct productions for the Workshop, but it can no longer be considered the vital force that it unquestionably was during the years between 1955 and the early 1960s.

Not all important new playwrights were attached to the English Stage Company or the Theatre Workshop. Among those who were not, one of the most important was Arnold Wesker (1932–   ), perhaps England's most socially conscious playwright of the late 1950s. His best known works are the trilogy—*Chicken Soup with Barley* (1958), *Roots* (1959), and *I'm Talking About Jerusalem* (1960)—which trace the declining sense of purpose in the socialist movement and seek to show that workers have settled for too little and have chosen the wrong paths in seeking to remedy ills. In *The Kitchen* (1958), Wesker explores working-class conditions through the microcosm of a kitchen in a large restaurant, and in *Chips with Everything* (1962) he uses an air force camp to show that enlisted men are exploited and systematically deprived of all that is best in entertainment, art, and living conditions.

In 1962 Wesker became the leader of a working-class artistic movement, Center 42 (so named from the Trades Union Congress resolution number 42 which in 1961 called for the popularization of the arts among workers). With Center 42 Wesker intended to supply plays and music of high quality for festivals throughout the country, but after a brief burst of energy in 1962 the movement subsided, and from 1966 to 1970 it was almost wholly confined to the Roundhouse, a converted railroad shop located in north London. In 1971, Center 42 was disbanded. After 1962 Wesker wrote little, and such works as *The Four Seasons* (1966), *The Friends,* (1970), and *The Old Ones* (1972) had little success, perhaps because they were so unlike Wesker's early work, upon which his reputation still rests.

Another important dramatist, Peter Shaffer (1926–   ), also began his career during the 1950s. Shaffer has written quite diverse plays, ranging through the realistic *Five Finger Exercise* (1958) to such absurdist comedies as *The Private Ear and The Public Eye* (1962) and *Black Comedy* (1965). He is most admired, however, for *The Royal Hunt of the Sun* (1964), a story about the Spanish conquest of Peru but which Shaffer has described as "an attempt to define the concept of God,"

FIGURE 18.18 Peter Shaffer's *Royal Hunt of the Sun* in its original production at the National Theatre, London, in 1964. Courtesy National Theatre, London.

and *Equus* (1973), a psychological study of a boy who has blinded several horses and of the psychiatrist who treats him. In these plays Shaffer has demonstrated a masterful control of his medium, and he continues to be one of the most versatile dramatists of our time.

Of the many other dramatists, those who attracted most attention include John Whiting (1915–1963), with *A Penny for a Song* (1951) and *Marching Song* (1954), plays which puzzled audiences when first presented but which later found favor; Bernard Kops (1928–   ), with *Hamlet of Stepney Green* (1956), a retelling of Shakespeare's play in a modern setting, and *Enter Solly Gold* (1962), a comedy about a Jewish trickster; Graham Greene (1904–   ) with plays about moral and religious questions as in *The Living Room* (1953), *The Potting Shed* (1957), and *The Complaisant Lover* (1959); and Robert Bolt (1924–   ), with *The Flowering Cherry* (1957), a quasi-Chekhovian study of self-deception and failure, and *A Man for All Seasons,* based on the life and martyrdom of Sir Thomas More.

Much of the English theatre's accomplishment during the 1950s was made possible by a change in attitude toward subsidies. Until the Second World War, no direct governmental aid had ever been given the arts. Then, in 1940, the Council for the Encouragement of Music and the Arts (CEMA) was given 50,000 pounds to assist in wartime work. In 1945, CEMA became the Arts Council, an independent organization financed by government funds, which decides how the support will be distributed. It has never had much money (in the 1960s it had only about one million dollars annually for drama), but it has used it to encourage organizations which seem capable of providing leadership. In 1948, Parliament also authorized local governments to allot a percentage of their revenues to support the arts. As a result, several municipalities began to provide subsidies for local resident companies, of which by the 1960s there were more than fifty in Great Britain, most performing a mixed repertory of classics and recent works.

Festivals—such as those at Edinburgh, Chichester, Malvern, Glyndebourne, Canterbury, and Aldeburgh—also added considerably to the vitality of the English theatre during the 1950s. Overall, the British theatre had by 1960 become one of the finest in the world.

THEATRE AND DRAMA
IN ITALY AND SPAIN, 1940–1960

After World War II the position of the Italian playwright remained as difficult as it had been a century earlier, for there was still a conflict between the demand for realism (which required the use of some regional dialect) and for universality (which required a more literary speech). Consequently, playwrights normally wrote with one specific region in mind. Occasionally a dramatist was able to attract a national following, but only one, Betti, achieved international stature in the postwar years. Ugo Betti (1892–1953) began writing plays in 1927, but his reputation rests primarily upon his late works, *Corruption in the Palace of Justice* (1948), *The Queen and the Rebels* (1951), and *The Burnt Flower Bed* (1953). All of Betti's plays are concerned with crises of conscience, especially among those who have gained influence through bureaucratic means. His preoccupation with guilt and power struck a responsive chord in the postwar consciousness.

Two other dramatists, Fabbri and de Filippo, won lesser international recognition. Diego Fabbri (1911–   ) has upheld the teachings of the church through dramas of traditional form. Of his plays, *Christ on Trial* (1955), showing the difficulties created by Christ's presence in the world, is probably the best known. Eduardo de Filippo (1900–   ) began writing around 1930. Although set in Naples and written in the Neapolitan dialect, his plays achieve universality because they show characters struggling to survive in the face of poverty, disease, and strained family relationships. They mingle the serious, comic, and pathetic with closely observed local detail. Among his best works are *Naples' Millionaires* (1946), *Filumena* (1955), *Saturday, Sunday,*

FIGURE 18.19 Goldoni's *Servant of Two Masters* at the Piccolo Teatro, Milan. Directed by Giorgio Strehler; setting by Ezio Frigerio. From *Scene Design Throughout the World Since 1950.*

and Monday (1959), and *The Boss* (1960). De Filippo, also a fine actor, worked for many years with his brother, Peppino de Felippo (1903–   ), one of Italy's most popular performers.

In production, touring companies continued to dominate, but a few men were able to establish permanent resident companies. The most important of these permanent troupes was the Piccolo Teatro, established in Milan in 1947 by Giorgio Strehler (1921–   ) and Paolo Grassi (1919–   ). It was given a rent free theatre by the city of Milan and later became the first dramatic company in Italy to receive a governmental subsidy. The Piccolo Teatro was a self-contained organization with a permanent troupe of twenty to thirty actors and a training school. Strehler directed about three-fourths of the plays but invited well-known foreign directors to stage others. He leaned heavily toward Brechtian techniques, as did his designers, Gianni Ratto until 1954 and then Luciano Damiani. Partially because of its foreign tours, the Piccolo Teatro came to be considered not only Italy's finest troupe but one of the best in the world. Permanent theatres were also established elsewhere in Italy. Perhaps the best of these were the Teatro Stabile in Genoa, founded in 1952 and headed by Luigi Squarzina, and the Teatro Stabile, founded in Turin in 1955 and headed by Gianfranco de Bosio. By the 1960s there were ten of these resident companies in Italy.

Nevertheless, most cities had to depend on touring companies. Of these, three were especially important. Vittorio Gassman, who won an international reputation as a film star but is known in Italy as a major classical

actor, from time to time assembled companies with which he presented outstanding works from the past. The Compagnia deLullo-Falk—with Giorgio deLullo as leading man and director, Rosella Falk as leading lady, and Romolo Valli and Elsa Albani as character actors—was after 1955 the best of the touring groups. Its preeminence was later challenged by the Compagnia Proclemer-Albertazzi, run by the actor-directors, Anna Proclemer and Giorgio Albertazzi, perhaps Italy's most famous acting team. These companies toured throughout Italy.

Two Italian directors won international fame in the postwar years. Luchino Visconti (1906–1976) was one of the originators of the neorealism that gave Italian film much of its renown during the 1950s, and he brought the same stylistic quality to his stage productions. His best known work was done in opera, especially in a series of productions starring Maria Callas. Franco Zeffirelli (1923–   ) began his career as a designer for Visconti, perhaps the greatest influence on his work. He turned to directing in 1953, at first primarily in opera, and by 1958 was being invited to direct abroad. He built a reputation for bringing classics down to earth (his productions of *Romeo and Juliet* and *Hamlet* were especially well re-

FIGURE 18.20 Vittorio Gassman in his own production of Alfieri's *Oreste* (1957). Setting by Gianni Polidori. Courtesy *World Theatre.*

FIGURE 18.21 Valle-Inclán's *Divine Words* at the Teatro Bellas Artes, Madrid (1961). Directed by José Tamayo. Courtesy *World Theatre.*

ceived). In most of his productions (which he also designs), Zeffirelli has used neorealistic settings and business, an approach which has led on the one hand to accusations that he swamps the text with visual details and on the other to praise for bringing a sense of concreteness to works which all too often remain remote from audiences.

In Spain, the theatre was isolated from the rest of the world until the 1950s by severe censorship, which was administered largely by priests, who, working without any clear guidelines, were often capricious in their rulings. Despite this situation, however, a revival of Spanish drama began to be evident around 1950. The change is usually dated from the production of *The Story of a Stairway* by Antonio Buero Vallejo (1916–   ) in 1949, the first time after the Civil War that a new play was considered worthy of the Lope de Vega Prize. This work spans a period of twenty-eight years in the lives of four working-class families who live on the same floor of an apartment house. Since 1949 Buero Vallejo has written steadily and is now considered Spain's leading dramatist. Until 1958 most of his works were realistic, but since then he has branched into fantasy, symbolism, and history.

Joaquín Calvo Sotelo (1905–   ) continued the realistic tradition with such works as *Plaza de Oriente* (1947), *The Visitor Who Didn't Ring the Bell* (1950), and *The Power* (1965). *The Wall* (1954), dealing with a man's difficulties with his family when he decides to give up his wrongfully acquired wealth, created more debate in Spain than any play since Echegaray's Ibsenesque plays in the late nineteenth century. Miguel Mihura (1909–   ), with such plays as *Sublime Decision* (1955) and *Maribel and the Extraordinary Family* (1959), was the most popular writer of comedy, while Alfonso Paso (1926–   ) seemed the author destined to replace Benavente as a prolific purveyor of popular entertainment. Beginning his writing career in 1952, Paso was soon turning out as many as ten plays a year. Among his most popular works are *The Poor Little Thing* (1957), *The Girl's Wedding* (1960), and *Dear Professor* (1965).

Perhaps Spain's most controversial playwright was Alfonso Sastre (1926–   ), who advocated a "theatre of anguish" designed to make the audience face the problems of modern life. Such plays as *The Condemned Squad* (1953), *Gored* (1960), and *Anna Klieber* (1962), concerned as they are with social, moral, and political issues, have been more read than produced in Spain.

During the 1950s there was some decrease in censorship. As a result, the works of such foreign authors as Williams, Wilder, O'Neill, Claudel, Anouilh, and Montherlant were introduced into the repertory. The plays of Lorca and Casona were also produced for the first time since the Civil War and interest grew in the work of Valle-Inclán and Unamuno. Nevertheless, by 1960 Spain still remained extremely conservative in comparison with her neighbors.

RUSSIAN THEATRE AND DRAMA, 1940–1960

During the war years the Russian theatre was devoted primarily to building morale. Since governmental supervision was considerably relaxed, many thought that the end of the war would bring still greater freedom. Instead, restrictions even more severe than those of the 1930s were imposed in 1946, and in 1948 all subsidies, except those granted to a few favored theatres, were stopped.

FIGURE 18.22 Scene from Pogodin's *Sonnet of Petrarch* at the Mayakovsky Theatre, Moscow, 1957. From Komissarzhevsky, *Moscow Theatres* (1959).

The loss of governmental financial support was a severe blow, since 450 of Russia's 950 theatres had been destroyed during the war. By 1953 only about 250 were left.

Artistic restrictions were imposed by making Socialist Realism the only acceptable style and the Moscow Art Theatre's methods standard. Political control was strengthened in 1949 when party-appointed Administrative Directors were placed in complete charge of each theatre. Most Western plays were removed from the repertory, and new Russian works were expected to uphold governmental policy. A large number of plays, such as Anatoly Safronov's *The Muscovite Character* (1949), show the reeducation of persons who have stood in the way of party goals, while Constantin Simonov's *Alien Shadow* (1949) and Nikolai Pogodin's *The Missouri Waltz* (1950) are typical of the numerous anti-American plays. Other postwar drama, such as Vsevelod Vishnevsky's *1919—The Unforgettable Year* (1949) and A. Stein's *Prologue* (1952), glorifies Stalin's role in the development of Communism.

Following Stalin's death in 1953 many changes occurred. Although periods of freedom and restrictions alternated thereafter, in general there was a steady relaxation of the former rules, especially after Khrushchev's denunciation of Stalin in 1956. Censorship in the sense of prior judgment was no longer practiced, although many

pressures were still exerted on drama, most notably through the governing boards of theatres. Realism remained the dominant style and didacticism the the dominant aim, but neither was enforced and both steadily declined in popularity. In new plays, romantic or family situations were treated more frequently, as in Pogodin's *Sonnet of Petrarch* (1957), while the theme of vindication from unjust charges, typified by Alexander Volodin's *Factory Girl* (1957), became common. The conflict between generations, exemplified in Victor Rozov's *The Unequal Struggle* (1960), also became a popular subject. Anti-American plays largely disappeared from the repertory, while many previously banned Russian plays became popular. The penchant for reshaping classics to bring out propagandistic themes also lessened considerably.

The changes of the 1950s meant a loss of prestige for the Moscow Art Theatre, although it continued to be at the head of its profession in terms of subsidies, salaries, and other governmental standards. Despite its official position, the Moscow Art Theatre was by 1960 looked upon by the public as something of a museum. Much the same might be said of the Maly Theatre, which retained an official position only slightly lower than that of the Moscow Art Theatre.

As these theatres declined in prestige, others rose. Some of the changes can be attributed to the abandonment in 1956 of the fixed pay scales and ranks and the prohibitions against changing companies which had hampered actors since the 1930s. Other changes can be attributed to shifts in taste. Of the older theatres, the Vakhtangov, under the direction of Reuben Simonov, became the most popular, for Vakhtangov's methods provided the most acceptable alternative to Socialist Realism. The Theatre of Satire, under Valentin Pluchek, also grew in esteem after it created a sensation in 1954 with productions of Mayakovsky's *The Bedbug* and *The Bathhouse* in a style not unlike Meyerhold's.

At the Mayakovsky Theatre (formerly the Theatre of the Revolution), Nikolai Okhlopkov returned to his prewar experimentation with performer-audience relationships. In the late 1950s he restaged Pogodin's *Aristocrats,* with the audience surrounding the playing area as in his productions of the 1930s. The most famous of Okhlopkov's postwar productions was probably *Hamlet* (1954), in which the setting was divided into compartments and the whole action treated as Hamlet's attempt to escape from a prison-like world. Two other prewar directors, Yuri Zavadsky at the Mossoviet Theatre and

Alexei Popov at the Central Theatre of the Soviet Army, also continued to be important.

In Leningrad, the Pushkin Theatre occupied a prewar position comparable to that of the Moscow Art Theatre in Moscow and during the 1950s its prestige suffered similarly. Ths most admired theatre in Leningrad became the Gorky Theatre, after 1956 under the direction of Georgi Tovstogonov (1915–   ), noted for giving classics contemporary significance. Using realistic set pieces, Tovstogonov often dispensed with walls, ceilings, and similar details, and employed such cinematic techniques as moving the action forward on platforms for "close-up" effects. At the Leningrad Comedy Theatre, Nikolai Akimov (1901–   ), as both director and designer, also maintained high standards. Despite his fine work, Akimov's official position was probably reflected by the theatre in which he worked, a large room over a grocery.

By 1960, then, the Russian theatre was moving away from the restrictions and standards imposed during the Stalinist era. But the pressures to conform to party needs were still evident, and the government continued to make its presence felt when deviations became more than it wished to countenance. Nevertheless, a recovery had begun and would continue during the 1960s.

INTERNATIONAL DEVELOPMENTS

At the end of the Second World War, international cooperation was sought in every aspect of life. The formation of the United Nations was followed by many other organizations designed to promote international understanding. The International Theatre Institute (ITI), was founded in 1947 under the auspices of the United Nations Educational, Scientific, and Cultural Organization (UNESCO), which provided it with a yearly subsidy. From 1950 to 1968 the ITI published *World Theatre,* a periodical designed to disseminate information. The ITI also held frequent international meetings, and since 1954 has sponsored an annual festival, the Théâtre des Nations. Other organizations have also promoted the

FIGURE 18.23 Okhlopkov's production of *Hamlet* at the Mayakovsky Theatre, Moscow, 1954. Note the setting used to create the impression that Hamlet's world is a prison.

exchange of ideas. Among these are the International Association of Theatre Technicians, the International Association of Theatre Critics, and the International Federation for Theatre Research.

International cooperation also encouraged the development of the theatre throughout the world, for newly created nations sought to display their national culture to advantage. Consequently, theatres were established in parts of the world where there formerly were few or none. In geographical scope, therefore, the theatre became more extensive after 1945 than at any time in the past.

By the 1960, the theatre had rather fully recovered from the destruction of the war years. For the most part, however, it had continued along lines that had been established earlier, although there were a few notable exceptions, especially in France and England. But during the 1950s, new tensions and outlooks began to gather strength, and by 1960 the theatre was entering a period of both enormous vitality and enormous controversy.

LOOKING AT THEATRE HISTORY

In studying theatre history we need to be concerned about the "intellectual climate" of an age. Is it a period in which there is agreement on values and goals? Are there sharp divisions? If so, over what? What is being defended or attacked? What is so much taken for granted that it need not be questioned or discussed? What kinds of authority are cited to uphold beliefs or doubts: the supernatural order, scientific knowledge, cumulative human experience? In no one period is there total agreement on values and goals, but in many there is sufficient likeness to provide the cohesiveness needed for stability. In others, there is enough disagreement to produce disarray. In either case, the theatre cannot help but be affected.

In general, disarray has marked the years since 1940. The horrors of the Nazi concentration camps and the atomic bomb, the threat of world destruction that lurked behind the "cold war" of the 1950s, and other events raised doubts not only about man's ability to act rationally but about the possibility of finding any system of belief on which to build a sane and cohesive society.

It was out of the crisis in belief that the absurdist movement emerged. The crisis is perhaps most clearly defined by Albert Camus:

A world that can be explained even with bad reasons is a familiar world. But, on the other hand, in a universe suddenly divested of illusions and lights, man feels an alien, a stranger. His exile is without remedy since he is deprived of the memory of a lost home or the hope of a promised land. This divorce between man and his life . . . is properly the feeling of absurdity. . . . Of whom and of what indeed can I say: "I know that!" This heart within me I can feel, and I judge that it exists. This world I can touch, and I likewise judge that it exists. There ends all my knowledge, and the rest is construction. . . .

I said that the world is absurd, but I was too hasty. This world in itself is not reasonable, that is all that can be said. But what is absurd is the confrontation of this irrational and the wild longing for clarity whose call echoes in the human heart. . . .

The absurd is born of this confrontation between the human need and the unreasonable silence of the world.

ALBERT CAMUS, "The Myth of Sisyphus," *The Myth of Sisyphus and Other Essays,* trans. Justin O'Brien

(New York: Alfred A. Knopf, 1967), pp. 6, 19, 21, 28.

It was Martin Esslin who in 1961 first invented a label, Theatre of the Absurd, for the group of plays that seemed to stem from the position set forth by Camus:

The hallmark of [the Theatre of the Absurd] is its sense that certitudes and unshakable basic assumptions of former ages have been swept away, that they have been tested and found wanting, that they have been discredited as cheap and somewhat childish illusions . . .

This sense of metaphysical anguish at the absurdity of the human condition is, broadly speaking, the theme of the plays of Beckett, Adamov, Ionesco, Genet, and the other writers discussed in this book. But it is not merely the subject-matter that defines what is here called the Theatre of the Absurd. . . . [That Theatre also] strives to express its sense of the senselessness of the human condition and the inadequacy of the rational approach by the open abandonment of rational devices and discursive thought. . . . [It seeks] to achieve a unity between its basic assumptions and the form in which they are expressed.

MARTIN ESSLIN, *The Theatre of the Absurd,* revised and updated edition (Woodstock, N.Y.: The Overlook Press, 1973), pp. 4–6.

Eugène Ionesco has been not only one of the most successful but one of the most argumentative of absurdist playwrights, often taking issue with the directors of his plays and with critics. (Many of his comments are collected in *Notes and Counter Notes.*) Here are some reactions motivated by the American production of *Rhinoceros* in 1961:

I have read the American critics on the play and noticed that every one agreed that the play was funny. Well, it isn't. . . . The production reveals not only an absence of style . . . but above all intellectual dishonesty. . . . [The play] is a fairly objective description of the growth of fanaticism, of the rebirth of a totalitarianism that grows, propagates, conquers, transforms a whole-world. . . . I really tried to say this to the American director; I clearly indicated in the few interviews I was able to give that. . . . it cannot be anything else but painful and serious.

Some critics blame me for denouncing evil without saying what good is. . . . but it is so easy to rely on a system of thought that is more or less mechanical. . . . an unworkable solution one has found for oneself is infinitely more valuable than a ready-made ideology that stops men from thinking. . . .

One of the great critics of New York complains that, after destroying one conformism, I put nothing else in its place, leaving him and the audience in a vacuum. That is exactly what I wanted to do. A free man should pull himself out of vacuity on his own, by his own efforts and not by the efforts of other people.

> *Notes and Counter Notes, Writings on the Theatre,* trans. Donald Watson (New York: Grove Press, 1964), pp. 207–211.

During the 1950s dissatisfactions were not expressed wholly through absurdist drama. In England, the most powerful impact was made by the "angry young men," who expressed themselves in relatively traditional dramatic forms. Although it is now usual to suggest that Osborne's *Look Back in Anger* was recognized immediately as a turning point in English drama, most reviewers voiced serious reservations about it. Here are some excerpts from one of the most negative reviews*:

We should be very frank about this. If more plays like tonight's Look Back in Anger *are produced, the "Writer's Theatre" at the Royal Court must surely sink. I look back in anger upon a night misconceived and mis-spent. . . . The principal character is self-pitying, uncouth, cheaply vulgar. . . .*

> J. C. Trewin in *The Birmingham Post,* 8 May 1956.

Fortunately, others were more perceptive:

If I were Mr. George Devine I should regard Look Back in Anger *as something of a test case. This is just the sort of play which the English Stage Company was created to produce. . . . If there is . . . an audience [for what Devine is trying to do] let them show their interest by filling out the performances of the play. . . .*

Of course, Look Back in Anger *is not a perfect play. But it is a most exciting one, abounding with life and vitality and the life it deals with is life as it is lived at this very moment—not a common enough subject in the English theatre. . . . Not a pleasant play, then. . . . All the same, don't miss this play. If you are young, it will speak to you. If you are middle-aged, it will tell you what the young are feeling. . . .*

> T. C. Worsley in *The New Statesman.*

Between 1945 and 1960, the dominant production style in America was exemplified in the combined work of Elia Kazan (as director) and Jo Mielziner (as designer). Here, in his review of Tennessee Williams' *Cat on a Hot Tin Roof* (1955), Eric Bentley gives a good description of their work:

Jo Mielziner's setting consists of a square and sloping platform with one of its corners, not one of its sides, jutting towards the audience. A corner of a ceiling is above, pointing upstage. On the platform are minimum furnishings for a bed-sitting room. Around the room, steps and space suggest the out of doors. The whole stage is swathed in ever-changing light and shade. . . .

Such is the world of Elia Kazan, as we know it from his work on plays by more authors than one. The general scheme is that not only of Streetcar *but also of* Salesman: *an exterior that is also an interior—but, more important, a view of* man's *exterior that is also a view of his interior, the habitat of his body and the country of his memories and dreams. A theatre historian would probably call this world a combination of naturalism and expressionism. . . .*

It is one of the distinctive creations of American theatre. . . . with the means of the new American theatre (school of Lee Strasberg and Harold Clurman) it does reach the cherished end of the older theatre (true grandeur of performance) at a time when the older theatre itself . . . is failing to do so. . . .

I do not think the reason for this resides in the formality itself. The effectiveness of this grandeur results . . . from the interaction between formality in the setting, lighting, and grouping and an opposite quality . . . in the individual performances. The externals of the physical production belong . . . to the old theatre, but the acting is internal, "Stanislavskyite." Within the formal setting, from the fixed positions in which they are made to stand, the actors live their roles with that vigilant, concentrated, uninterrupted nervous intensity which Mr. Kazan always manages to give. . . .

> *The New Republic,* April 4, 1955.

---

*Both reviews reprinted in *John Osborne: Look Back in Anger, A Casebook,* edited by John Russell Taylor (London: Macmillan and Company, 1968). The first review appears on p. 45 of this book, the second on pp. 51–53.

19 Theatre and Drama Since 1960

The 1960s saw enormous stresses develop in almost every country in the world. In America, these stresses were at first concerned primarily with the drive for civil rights. Spearheaded by Martin Luther King and his doctrine of passive resistance, the struggle progressed through demonstrations, sit-ins, and other forms of nonviolent protest. These techniques were so effective that they were soon taken over by other groups, especially those disenchanted by America's involvement in Viet Nam. As protests gained in popularity, they moved away from nonviolence toward guerrilla tactics. Consequently, from 1968 onward violence became increasingly a part of daily life.

These patterns of protest and violence were symptomatic of deepseated doubts about the validity of long-standing conventions and traditional values and the ability of social institutions to respond efficiently to changing needs. Individuals and groups began to elevate their own ideals above existing laws, to assert their obligation to live by their own standards, and to demand the alteration or destruction of anything contrary to their views. The result was a fragmented society lacking in strong common purposes: a tendency toward anarchy. Such conditions were most evident in the United States, but they existed almost everywhere.

The theatre could not remain aloof from the stresses of the time. It was caught in a struggle between those who wished to maintain tradition and those who championed innovation and change. This conflict was especially strong in the late 1960s and provoked much controversy over the nature and function of theatre. The old conception of art as detached contemplation (or as the pursuit of some superior beauty and order) was challenged by those who wished to make it reflect immediate social and political pressures and to use it as an instrument for reform. This struggle was more evident in some countries than in others. In a relatively insulated nation such as Russia the stresses were seldom intense, but elsewhere—especially the United States—they often led to frenetic experimentation. Throughout the 1960s economic prosperity gave the theatre considerable stability, for it was easy to gain financial support both for traditional and innovative work. Thus, it was a decade in which the old and the new coexisted, sometimes in uneasy alliance, but often in radical opposition.

In the early 1970s, however, a mood of hesitation and doubt began to replace the climate of defiance and challenge, and the future began to appear highly uncertain. Thereafter, conservatism, both political and economic, reasserted itself. As the financial situation worsened, the exuberance of the 1960s faded. The effect on the theatre is still being assessed.

THEATRE AND DRAMA IN ITALY SINCE 1960

During the 1960s the Italian theatre achieved greater stability than it had previously enjoyed. In the mid-1960s there were ten resident troupes, with the best in Milan, Genoa, Turin, and Rome. But by the late 1960s, Italy, like other countries, was undergoing considerable stress, which inevitably affected the theatre. In Milan, Giorgio Strehler resigned his post at the Piccolo Teatro in 1968 when it failed to get the building he had been seeking and when it was not named a national theatre as had seemed likely. The company continued under the direction of Paolo Grassi (with Strehler as occasional guest director). In 1972 Grassi was named head of the LaScala opera company and Strehler resumed his former position at

FIGURE 19.1 Luca Ronconi's production of *Orlando Furioso*, first performed at the Festival of Two Worlds, Spoleto, in 1969. Note the wheeled wagons on which the performers stand surrounded by the audience. Photograph by Pic.

the Piccolo. At this time the two companies agreed to link their ticket offerings and to give special priority to attracting a working-class audience.

Strehler is now considered to be Italy's most distinguished director. He is also much in demand internationally. He has served as artistic advisor to the Salzburg Festival and has directed at the Paris Opéra, Vienna's Burgtheater and elsewhere. In addition, he has received numerous awards and honorary degrees. He is also one of the world's most extravagant directors. The Piccolo Teatro has accumulated a debt of more than 350,000,000 lire, and Strehler resigned his post at Salzburg in 1974 after he was censured for overspending.

The stresses that began in the late 1960s caused some resident companies to be disbanded, but there are still eight. Aside from Milan the best of these are in Genoa (headed by Luigi Squarzina and Ivo Chiesa) and in Turin (headed by Aldo Trionfo).

Most cities in Italy, however, still depend on commercial theatres dedicated to the long run and to touring. In the mid-1970s there were eighty such companies in Italy.

Of all European countries, Italy appears to glorify most the virtuoso performer, even though it provides few opportunities for actors to acquire sound technical training. These conditions make for poor ensemble work, and consequently, outside a few companies, the general level of acting remains poor. The best of the touring companies are those headed by Anna Proclemer and Giorgio Albertazzi and a cooperative venture of Giorgio DeLullo, Rosella Falk, Romolo Valli, Elsa Albani, Rina Morelli, and Paolo Stoppa.

Since the late 1960s, the most innovative directors in Italy have been Fo and Ronconi. Dario Fo began working in the theatre in the 1950s and soon turned to broadly farcical political satire, such as *He Had Two Pistols with Black and White Eyes*, intended to appeal to middle-class audiences. But in the late 1960s Fo came to champion a proletarian revolution and since than he has sought to attract a working-class audience with agit-prop plays satirizing capitalism, the Italian Communist party, the Italian state, the church, and other enemies of the Maoist communism he champions. Fo's productions are theatrically imaginative, often making use of oversized puppets and devices drawn from practically all forms of popular entertainment. His company performs in factories, gymnasiums, and out of doors; it takes up a collection rather than charging admission, and divides the receipts among its members.

Among Fo's most popular productions are *Mistero Buffo* (1969), which combines elements from medieval farce, mime, and contemporary life, and *We're All in the Same Boat—But That Man Over There, Isn't He Our Employer?* (1974), based on Italian political events between 1911 and 1923, when Mussolini came to power. Since it is so wide-ranging in its criticism, Fo's company, the Collettivo Teatrale della Commune, is now so disliked by both the political right and left in Italy that it has difficulty in finding a permanent home and has been evicted from several buildings. Fo's company has toured widely in Europe where it has won an enviable popular and critical following.

Luca Ronconi came to international prominence in 1969 with his production of *Orlando Furioso,* seen first in Spoleto and later in Belgrade, Milan, Paris, New York, and elsewhere. The text was adapted by Edoardo Sanguineti from Lodovico Ariosto's sixteenth-century epic poem, an enormously long work about chivalric adventures involving mythical creatures, enchanted castles, sorcerers, and other fanciful beings. Rather than performing the episodes in strict sequence, two or more progressed simultaneously in different parts of the theatrical space, since Ronconi believed that this achieved the same effect of disorder and fantasy induced by a reading of the poem. About fifty wheeled wagons were used in a large open space, which was also occupied by the audience, who moved about choosing what to watch.

Ronconi's subsequent productions are less well known but equally imaginative. In *XX* (1971), he divided the audience into groups and placed each in separate rooms, the walls between which were gradually removed. Each group saw a few disturbing events and heard voices and sounds elsewhere. When all the walls were gone, a *coup d'état* was announced and the audience was ordered to disperse. Ronconi declared that he had sought to show how dictatorial power can be assumed almost unnoticed until it is too late. His *Oresteia* (1972), a six-hour-long production, was highly praised for its impressive visual imagery but faulted for its acting. Ronconi has continued to build an international, though controversial, reputation through his innovative use of space and his metaphorical theatricality in such productions as *The Barber of Seville* (1974) and *Utopia* (1975), an adaptation of Aristophanes' *The Birds.*

Italy has been less fortunate in writers than in directors. Virtually no contemporary Italian playwright has been able to win international recognition, although

a number of competent dramatists have been at work since 1960. Among these are Diego Fabbri (perhaps the best known abroad), Carlo Terron, Federico Zardi, Franco Brusati, Giuseppe Patroni-Griffi, and Luigi Squarzina. At a conference held in the mid–1970s, several reasons were advanced for this lack of significant playwrights. Among these were the absence of literary advisors to companies and the lack of artistic trust which would encourage writers to take chances.

Like many other European countries, Italy in the 1970s began to be concerned about theatre for children and youth. This concern was strengthened in 1974 by the establishment of a national festival of youth theatres.

During the past few years the extreme inflation that has plagued Italy has posed a serious threat to its theatres, many of which are now hard pressed to survive. Thus, the gains made during the 1960s now seem to hang in the balance.

RUSSIAN THEATRE AND DRAMA SINCE 1960

The thaw in Russia that began after Khrushchev's denunciation of Stalin in 1956 continued after 1960, although the government from time to time applied pressures to keep the theatre within acceptable limits. One result of relaxed strictures was the presentation for the first time of many foreign plays in Russia. For example, in 1960 Brecht's works began to be introduced into the repertory, and soon plays by Miller, Osborne, Williams, and others were being produced with some frequency. On the other hand, few absurdist dramas were presented, probably because they were considered too "formalistic." Another result was revived interest in Meyerhold and Tairov. During the 1960s a complete edition of Meyerhold's writings was published, and exhibits were mounted of his and Tairov's productions. In 1974, the centenary of Meyerhold's birth was celebrated with special exhibits, performances, articles, conferences, and commemorative stamps. Thus, he was restored to official favor, although many of his methods were still considered unacceptable in a socialist state. Nevertheless, the renewed interest in Meyerhold is symptomatic of a general decline in prestige for Socialist Realism, although it continues to be the dominant mode. After 1956, Vakhtangov's methods also grew in popularity, perhaps because they were considered an

FIGURE 19.2 Yefremov's production of Aksenov's *Always on Sale* at the Contemporary Theatre, Moscow, 1966.

acceptable compromise between the approaches of Stanislavsky and Meyerhold.

Despite all changes, the Moscow Art Theatre has continued to enjoy the greatest official prestige and its actors are still the highest paid. Although by the 1960s it had come to be viewed by many Russians as more nearly a museum than as a vital institution, its standing with the government is indicated by the new and lavish theatre built for it in 1968–1969 in honor of its seventieth anniversary.

In terms of innovation, two companies—the Contemporary and the Taganka—took the lead after 1960. The Contemporary Theatre, founded in 1957, was the first new company to be authorized in Russia since the 1930s. Under the leadership of Oleg Yefremov until 1970 and then under Oleg Tabakov, the Contemporary has drawn most of its personnel and methods from the Moscow Art Theatre or its training school. The principal departures of the new company lie in its concentration on plays (such as those by Brecht, Osborne, Shatrov, and Rozov) thought to be relevant to present-day life and in its use of simplified settings rather than the elaborate mountings typical at the Moscow Art Theatre. The Contemporary also did much to revive the reputation of Yevgeny Schwarz (1897–1958), author of satirical fables based on fairy tales and legends, among them *The Naked King* (1933, based on "The Emperor's New Clothes"), *The Shadow* (1941), and *The Dragon* (1943), works alternately banned and permitted by Soviet

authorities because of their ambiguous political overtones. By 1970 the Contemporary Theatre had achieved sufficient stature that Yefremov was appointed to head the Moscow Art Theatre in an attempt to revive that troupe's waning prestige and vigor. In 1974 the Contemporary received a new theatre (a remodeled cinema with rehearsal rooms and workshops) but retained its old quarters in order to enlarge its activities. In recent years, this company has also produced some plays that seem part of a trend in Soviet drama—semi-documentary plays, such as Shatrov's *Tomorrow's Weather* and Zakharov's *Autotown 21*—about life in Russia's industrial towns.

The Moscow Theatre of Drama and Comedy (usually called the Taganka after the suburb in which it is located) was founded in 1964 by Yuri Lyubimov, formerly a teacher at the Vakhtangov Theatre's training school. It now enjoys the reputation of being Russia's most experimental troupe. Many of its techniques are reminiscent of Meyerhold's. It makes liberal use of dynamic movement, dance, mime, masks, puppets, and projections, and it frequently reshapes scripts. In 1970 at the congress of the All-Union Society of Theatre Workers, it was the only theatre to be singled out for censure. The Taganka is especially popular with young audiences.

One of the Taganka's most popular productions in recent years has been *Fasten Your Seat Belts* (1975), written by Lyubimov and G. Baklanov, treating World

FIGURE 19.3 A setting by Nisson Chifrine for a dramatization of a novel by Sholokhov at the Theatre of the Red Army, Moscow, 1957. From *Scene Design Throughout the World Since 1950*.

FIGURE 19.4 Josef Svoboda's setting for an adaptation of Maxim Gorky's novel, *The Last Ones,* at the National Theatre, Prague, in 1966. Directed by Alfred Radok. Photograph copyrighted by Jaromir Svoboda.

War II soldiers thirty years later and exploring the problem of the individual seeking to maintain his integrity in the face of authoritarian demands. It is such themes (on the edge of permissibility) and unusual production techniques that have kept the Taganka at the forefront of the contemporary Soviet theatre. It is indicative of Lyubimov's current standing that in 1975 he was permitted to stage a production in the West (in Italy), a rarity for a Soviet director.

Another of Russia's controversial directors is Anatoly Efros, largely because he gives novel interpretations to scripts that sometimes call official attitudes into question. Several of his productions, though popular, have been withdrawn from the repertory (although some have later been returned). Nevertheless, Soviet authorities seem more interested in controlling than in forbidding the work of such directors as Efros and Lyubimov.

Despite these innovators, the Russian theatre as a whole remains rooted in the Stalinist era. Perhaps the most notable overall change from the previous years can be seen in the current dominant mode in scenery. Rather than representing each place in detail, it is now more common to use one fixed background representative of a play's overall mood, and to change small realistic set pieces in front of it. Among the best of recent de-

signers have been Alexander Tychler, Nisson Chifrine, Evgeny Kovalenko, Alexander Vassiliev, Yuri Pimenov, B. R. Erdman, I. G. Sumbatashvili, and M. S. Saryan.

Seemingly the theatre is now as popular in Russia as anywhere in the world. Moscow's approximately thirty theatres are usually filled each night, and government statistics indicate that attendance is on the increase throughout the country. In 1975 there were 560 theatres in Russia, about 100 of which had companies that play exclusively for children and youth. During the summer months the major companies of Moscow and Leningrad tour the provinces, and provincial troupes come to play in these major cities. Trains are also being used to bring live theatre to areas without resident companies. Thus, the theatre seems to be firmly entrenched in Russian life.

THEATRE AND DRAMA IN CZECHOSLOVAKIA SINCE 1960

Following World War II, most of Eastern Europe came under the domination of Russia. As a result, theatre in these countries was subjected to restrictions similar to those imposed in the USSR. Following the break with Stalinism in 1956, however, strictures were considerably relaxed and experimentation flourished, especially in Czechoslovakia and Poland.

Czechoslovakia has made its greatest international impact in the field of technology and design and above all through the work of Josef Svoboda (1920–   ). Although he began his career around 1945, Svoboda was unable to demonstrate his great versatility until the late 1950s when Socialist Realism was no longer the standard mode. Much of his work is an extension of experimentation begun with multimedia in the 1930s by E. F. Burian (1904–1959) and Miroslav Kouril (1911–   ). It is also heavily indebted to the Prague Institute of Scenography, founded in 1957 and headed by Kouril, for its staff and facilities did much of the experimentation.

The turning point in Svoboda's career came in 1958 when he began collaborating with the director Alfred Radok on two projects—Polyekran and Laterna Magika, both using a number of screens on which still and moving pictures were projected. Laterna Magika also integrated live actors into the performance. Both of these forms were shown at the Brussels World's Fair in 1958 and elicited considerable praise and excitement. In 1959 Svoboda began to carry over many of the technical devices into his stage work. Since then he has experimented

FIGURE 19.5 Setting by Josef Svoboda for *Their Day* by Josef Topol at the National Theatre, Prague (1959). Note the use of projections on screens of varying sizes. This was Svoboda's first attempt to apply the techniques of the Laterna Magika in theatrical production. Photograph copyrighted by Jaromir Svoboda.

continuously with means to create a completely flexible stage which can change from scene to scene as the needs of the drama change. In addition to screens and projections, he has also developed platforms and steps that can move vertically, horizontally, and laterally to alter the spatial relationships and size of the acting area. He has also explored the potentials for stage use of such materials as mirrors, plastic, and various kinds of netting, and has used most of these as surfaces on which to project images (or in some instances to reflect the action as seen from above, behind, or at an angle). He has designed settings in every conceivable style and is now perhaps the best known and most influential designer in the world, although he continues to be associated especially with the development of multimedia techniques.

Svoboda's work has done much to call attention to the high quality of the Czech theatre as a whole. In the 1960s there were about fifty-six companies in Czechoslovakia, but those best known abroad (aside from the Prague National Theatre) were a group of small theatres in Prague, most of which came into existence after 1962 when the government created the State The-

atre Studio to assist experimental companies. Of these, three were especially outstanding. The Theatre Behind the Gate, founded in 1965 by Otomar Krejča, shared its 435-seat theatre with the Laterna Magika, for both of which Svoboda was principal designer. It was noted for its imaginative staging and thoughtful interpretation of Czech and foreign plays. The Cinoherni (Actors' Club), founded in 1965 and headed by Jaroslav Vostry, performed in a theatre seating 220. Its primary emphasis was on ensemble acting (probably the best in Czechoslovakia) and a wide-ranging repertory drawn from world drama. The Theatre on the Balustrade, founded in 1958 and headed from 1962 until 1969 by Jan Grossman, seated about 200. This company was the primary home of absurdist drama in Czechoslovakia and had as its resident playwright Václav Havel (1936–   ), often considered the leading contemporary Czech dramatist. His bitingly satirical treatments of bureaucracy, *The Garden Party* (1963), *The Memorandum* (1965), and *The Conspirators* (1974) have come to be known and admired throughout the world.

The Soviet invasion of Czechoslovakia in 1968 dealt a sharp blow to the theatre. Beginning in 1969 censorship was reimposed. In that year Grossman and Havel also resigned their posts at the Balustrade, and the Činoherni was forced to change many of its policies. In 1971 Krejča was removed as director at the Gate and in 1972, reportedly because the actors remained loyal to him, the Gate was disbanded. In 1976, Krejča was permitted by authorities to leave the country for a permanent post in West Germany. The Prague Institute of Scenography has also been closed. In these and other ways the theatre has been brought increasingly into line with the government's outlook. Svoboda, perhaps because of his international reputation, enjoys much the same freedom as before, but most organizations have been forced to abandon their liberal policies. Regardless of the future, however, the Czech theatre was during the 1960s one of the most vital in the world.

THEATRE AND DRAMA IN POLAND SINCE 1960

The Polish theatre followed a path not unlike that seen in Czechoslovakia. It too had developed a sophisticated and technically advanced theatre between the wars and it too came under Soviet domination after 1945. Poland was the first of the East European countries to ease restraints, and from 1956 until the late 1960s its government exerted little direct pressure on the theatre.

After 1956 the dominant dramatic mode was absurdism, although it took a more satirical and didactic turn than in France. The vogue was initiated with the plays of Stanislaw Ignacy Witkiewicz (1885-1939), a previously neglected surrealist writer of the interwar years, whose works such as *The Water Hen, The Mother,* and *The Madman and the Nun* have won increasing acceptance throughout the world as major *avant-garde* dramas. In addition to Witkiewicz's plays, Beckett's *Waiting for Godot* helped to establish the taste for absurdist drama. Soon a new school of dramatists appeared, of whom the most important were Rósewicz and Mrozek. Tadeusz Rósewicz (1921-   ), already famous as a poet, began writing plays in 1960. His *The Card Index* (1960) and *He Left Home* (1964) did much to establish the pattern that would be followed by subsequent writers, with whom the most common theme was the search for a lost order even as they rejected the concept of absolutes. He has continued to explore this theme in such plays as *The Laocoon Group* (1974) and *White Marriage* (1975).

Although within Poland Rósewicz is perhaps the most respected of contemporary dramatists, abroad he has been overshadowed by Slawomir Mrozek (1930-   ), whose plays depend rather heavily on caricature. For example, *The Police* (1958), one of Mrozek's numerous short plays, shows how the secret police, having been so successful that they are in danger of being abolished, order one of their own men to become an enemy agent so they may survive. Mrozek has also written a few full-length plays, of which the best known is *Tango* (1965), one of the most popular of all recent plays in Europe. *Tango* is a parable about the decay of values, which has become so complete that only brute force is truly effective; consequently those who are most willing to exercise power, ruthlessly and without regard for humanistic principles, become the rulers. Mrozek has continued this vein in *A Happy Event* (1971), in which he depicts left-wing anarchist youth in the form of a grown-up baby who tyrannizes his parents, blows up their house, and ends up helpless in the ruins; in *The Emigrés* (1974), a two-character play which suggests that the left-wing intellectual and the worker depend on each other to give their lives significance; and in *Slaughterhouse* (1975), which concerns an artist's loss of faith in art, his obsessive search for some new truth, and his eventual suicide.

But Poland is perhaps best known for its innovative production rather than its writing. Within Poland,

Erwin Axer and Konrad Swinarski (until his death in 1975) have been the most admired directors. Both have promoted foreign and recent Polish drama and gained considerable renown for their imaginative productions. Henryk Tomaszewski has also won an enviable reputation at home and abroad with his Pantomime Theatre.

But in international reputation all of these directors have been far outstripped by Jerzy Grotowski (1933-   ), director of the Polish Laboratory Theatre. Founded in Opole in 1959, Grotowski's company moved to Wroclaw (Breslau) in 1965 and was designated the Institute for Research in Acting. Until 1965 Grotowski was little known, but since then his reputation has mushroomed. His company has performed in various countries and Grotowski himself has worked with many foreign troupes and has lectured widely about his methods. His work has also been publicized through a collection of essays by and about him, *Towards a Poor Theatre* (1968).

Ironically, Grotowski began to alter his approach just as he won international acceptance. Thus, his work can be divided into two principal phases: that of the 1960s and that of the 1970s. During the first phase, Grotowski began with the premise that the theatre has borrowed too heavily from other media, especially film and television, and thus has violated its own essence, to which he sought to return by eliminating everything not truly

FIGURE 19.6 Axiometric view of Grotowski's plan for Slowacki's *Kordian,* 1962. Grotowski redesigns the actor-audience relationship for each production. Here the black figures represent actors, white figures spectators. Courtesy *World Theatre.*

required by it. He called his approach "poor theatre," since it avoided all machinery and minimized all spectacle not created by the actor. His performers were not allowed to use makeup or to change costume in order to indicate a change in role or within a character; all music had to be produced by the actors themselves; he used no scenery in the traditional sense, although a few functional properties might be rearranged or used in various ways as the action demanded; he abandoned the proscenium-arch theatre in favor of a large room which could be rearranged for each production. In this way, the actor (the essential theatrical element) was thrown back on his own resources.

During this period, it was the training of the actor that lay at the heart of Grotowski's concerns. In his work he drew heavily from many sources—Stanislavsky, Yoga, Meyerhold, Vakhtangov, Delsarte, Dullin, and others. His system required that the actor gain absolute control over himself physically and vocally and to an extent psychically, so that during performances he might completely transform himself as demanded by the production. His actors had to be willing to give of themselves fully and expose themselves psychically when necessary. According to Grotowski, actors should arouse a sense of wonder because they can go so far beyond what the spectators are able to do.

In this early phase, Grotowski looked upon the theatre as something like a ritual to which spectator-witnesses are admitted. He believed that the audience is the other essential ingredient of a performance and that it must be put in a position which permits it to play its role unselfconsciously. (He argued that attempts to involve the audience directly in the action make it self-conscious.) Therefore, for each production he decided how the audience should respond psychologically and then designed the spatial arrangement to create the appropriate psychic distance.

In preparing a production, Grotowski searched in a script to find those patterns that he considered to have universal meaning for audiences today. Much of the script might be abandoned and the remainder rearranged. The ultimate aim was to make the actors and the audience confront themselves in something resembling a religious experience. The results were appraised variously. Some critics found Grotowski's productions among the most significant of the age, whereas others thought them incomprehensible or pretentious. No one, however, denied the technical excellence of Grotowski's actors.

By 1970 Grotowski had come to believe that his group had reached the end of its search for technical mastery and he decided to create no new productions. He realized that while his actors had been able to eliminate the blocks that stood in their way as performers, they had not broken down the blocks between performer and audience. He then set out to eliminate "the idea of theatre," in the sense of an actor playing before an audience, and to find a way of incorporating spectators into the disarmament process. In 1973 he stated: "We came to the conclusion that we must abolish . . . payments, and that those who came to us would come to a special place where they could leave their daily lives behind. . . . We call this period of time 'Holiday,' or the day that is holy. . . . What is possible then together? A meeting, not a confrontation; a communion, where we can be totally ourselves. . . ."

Around 1970, Grotowski reorganized his company, took into it five young people with no previous professional theatrical experience, and thereafter worked to develop a "special project" with six subgroups, each headed by a member of the original company. Each subgroup has been concerned with a different problem, but all are related to the main purpose: to lead participants back into the elemental connections between man and his body, his imagination, the natural world, and other human beings.

The first major revelation of the new work came during the summer of 1975 when approximately 500 people from all over the world attended a "research university" organized by Grotowski at Wroclaw under the sponsorship of the Théâtre des Nations, which that year was staged in Warsaw. The group included students, teachers, and journalists, as well as several famous directors—among them Peter Brook, Jean-Louis Barrault, Luca Ronconi, Joseph Chaikin, and André Gregory. Everyone who attended had to participate. Some of the activities involved groups going into the woods for twenty-four hours during which they were led through ritualized relivings of basic myths, archetypes, and symbols including fire, air, earth, water, eating, dancing, playing, planting, and bathing. Through this process, participants were expected to rediscover the roots of the theatre in pure ritualized experience, as well as to discover their own true being. Since this was Grotowski's first attempt to involve large numbers of people in his current work, it is uncertain how he will proceed in the future. Still, it is clear that his current approach differs markedly from his productions of the 1960s, and it is the subject of lively debate both in Poland and elsewhere.

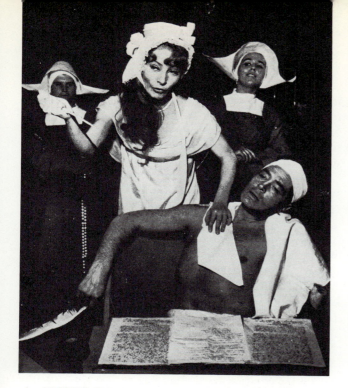

FIGURE 19.7 Weiss' *Marat/Sade* at the Schiller Theater, Berlin (1964). Directed by Konrad Swinarski, designed by Peter Weiss. Photograph by Heinz Köster.

In 1968 the theatre in Poland underwent a crisis when many theatrical workers objected to their nation's participation in putting down Czech liberalization. As a result, several leading critics went into exile, and Mrozek's plays were banned. By the mid-1970s, restrictions had lessened considerably. Mrozek's plays had been returned to the repertory and several new theatres were being built or remodeled for Poland's seventy-four dramatic, eighteen musical, and twenty-five puppet companies. Concern was being expressed, nevertheless, over the theatre's lack of appeal to young people and workers. Between 1970 and 1974 the number of tickets sold declined by 376,000. But the government's strong commitment to the theatre was evidenced in increased subsidies and prizes given for plays about contemporary life and for artistic innovation. And despite a decline in popularity, Poland's companies presented 400 different productions to an audience of 9 million people in 1975.

THEATRE AND DRAMA IN GERMANY SINCE 1960

After 1960 the popularity of Brecht in Germany grew steadily and by the 1970s his plays had surpassed even those of Shakespeare in numbers of annual performances. Many playwrights who had begun their careers earlier—among them Frisch, Duerrenmatt, Hochwalder, and Grass—continued to be productive. But the most characteristic German form in the 1960s was "documentary drama" or the "theatre of fact" in which actual events, often quite recent, were used to explore the by-then characteristic concern for guilt and responsibility in public affairs and morality. The best known writers of the form are Hochhuth, Weiss, and Kipphardt, although all have written other types of plays as well.

Rolf Hochhuth (1931–   ) came to prominence with *The Deputy* (1963), which seeks to place much of the blame for the extermination of German Jews on Pope Pius XII's refusal to take a decisive stand against Hitler's policies. This accusation made the play controversial wherever it was performed, and in many countries it was forbidden. *The Soldiers* (1967) also aroused considerable consternation because of its suggestion that Winston Churchill conspired in the death of General Sikorski, president of the Polish government in exile, because he endangered the Anglo-Russian alliance. In the late 1960s, Hochhuth seemed to tire of factual material. *The Guerrillas* (1970) is set sometime in the future and centers around a *coup d'état* in the United States, which Hochhuth suggests could come about only through someone so well placed as to be beyond suspicion. Hochhuth's first comedy, *The Midwife* (1972), has as its protagonist a woman who leads a double life (as pensioned widow and as member of the town council) in order to help the homeless, since bureaucracy has bogged down either in corruption or indifference. In *Lysistrata and NATO* (1974), Hochhuth adapts Aristophanes' basic situation to a story about an attempt to block the use of a Greek island as a NATO base. All of Hochhuth's plays are long and diffuse and must be cut severely in production. Perhaps for this reason, he has yet to win full critical acceptance. Nevertheless, he has been one of the most controversial writers, primarily because his use of recent historical figures (to whom he attributes questionable motives) has raised serious ethical questions about the limits to which a dramatist may go without becoming libelous.

Peter Weiss (1916–   ) worked as a graphic artist, filmmaker, and journalist before winning fame as a playwright. Although he began writing in the 1940s, his first play was not produced until 1962. His international reputation dates from 1964 with the production of *The Persecution and Assassination of Jean-Paul Marat as*

FIGURE 19.8 Peter Handke's *Kaspar* as presented by the Chelsea Theatre Center in 1973. Directed by Carl Weber; video by Video Free America. The actors are Guy Boyd, Christopher Lloyd, Randal Chicoine, Robert Einenkel, and Veronica Castang. Photograph by Amnon Nomis. Courtesy Chelsea Theatre Center.

Performed by the Inmates of the Asylum of Charenton Under the Direction of the Marquis de Sade (usually shortened to *Marat/Sade*). Set in 1808 in the asylum at Charenton where the Marquis de Sade is confined, it shows the presentation of a play written by de Sade for performance by the inmates before a fashionable audience from nearby Paris. The play that de Sade has written is Brechtian in form (making use of a presenter to introduce scenes and of songs to reflect upon the action), and the whole is intended by Weiss to provoke thought about political and social justice. The asylum serves as a metaphor for the world, and the play's ending (in which the inmates get out of hand) suggests what happens when the sensual and anarchistic outlook of a de Sade is given full rein. Peter Brook's production of *Marat/Sade* (seen first in London and then in New York) was to be one of the most

influential of the decade, since it drew forceful attention to devices of the "theatre of cruelty," while Weiss' play provided a model on which many other playwrights were to build by imbedding social and political arguments within a context of swirling visual and aural effects.

Marat/Sade is only partially factual, but in his next play, *The Investigation* (1965), Weiss passed over completely into documentary drama. Set in a courtroom, *The Investigation* utilizes dialogue taken from the official hearings into the extermination camp at Auschwitz. Weiss' subsequent documentary plays include *The Song of the Lusitanian Bogey* (1967), about the suppression of native Africans by the Portuguese in Angola, and *A Discourse on the Previous History and Development of the Long War of Liberation in Vietnam as an Example of the Necessity for the Armed Fight of the Suppressed Against Their Suppressors as Well as the Attempt of the United States of America to Destroy the Foundations of the Revolution* (1968).

Like Hochhuth, Weiss in the late 1960s began to retreat from documentary drama, although his work has continued to be based on historical sources. *Trotsky in Exile* (1970) uses material from Trotsky's life to stimulate thought about his ideas and to raise questions about our own political perspectives. *Hölderlin* (1971) is based on the life of the nineteenth-century German poet who spent much of his time locked away from the world. It shows the protagonist in flight from a world he considers deranged, and through his plight Weiss suggests that society has a tendency to destroy its visionaries. Its form resembles that of *Marat/Sade* and indicates that Weiss may be moving back toward his earlier, most successful approach.

Heinar Kipphardt (1922–   ) first won international renown with *In the Case of J. Robert Oppenheimer* (1964), all the dialogue for which is excerpted from the United States government's hearings into the loyalty of Oppenheimer after he resisted development of the hydrogen bomb. Kipphardt's primary concern, however, is with the conflict between a scientist's responsibility to his country and his duty to humanity at large—a familiar issue in postwar German drama. In *Joel Brand* (1965) Kipphardt treats the attempt of the Germans during World War II to exchange one million Hungarian Jews for 10,000 Allied trucks and the failure of the attempt because the Allies could not be convinced that the offer was made in good faith. In 1973 he treated the Uruguay Tupamaros in *Who's Looking After the Guerrilla?*

The success of documentary drama in Germany

seems to have stimulated playwrights in other countries to adopt the form. Consequently, many contemporary events were brought onto the stage, among them the *Pueblo* incident, the trial of the "Chicago Seven," and various aspects of the Vietnam war. But by the early 1970s, interest in the "theatre of fact" was on the wane, above all in Germany.

Not all German dramatists of the 1960s wrote documentary plays. Among those who did not, two of the best were Walser and Dorst. Martin Walser (1927–) in his early works, such as *Oak and Angora* (1962) and *The Black Swan* (1964), treats the familiar theme of guilt and evasion. For example, *The Black Swan* contrasts the younger generation, who seem overly sensitive about the Nazi period, with the older generation, who lead seemingly placid lives despite their own involvement in Naziism. Most of Walser's subsequent plays, such as *The Battle of the Bedroom* (1967) and *Children's Game* (1971) have treated more private subjects. But in *The Pig Play—Scenes from the Sixteenth Century* (1975), he makes historical events reflect the political fears and lack of certainty among today's workers and intellectuals.

Tankred Dorst (1925–) began writing plays in the 1950s but was not widely acclaimed until the 1960s. One of his most characteristic works is *Freedom for Clemens* (1961), which shows how an imprisoned man gradually realizes that freedom is an internal state rather than external circumstances. In *Toller* (1968), Dorst uses material about the expressionist playwright to explore the relationship of the artist to political action. In *Little Man, What Now?* (1972), a revue based on a novel by Hans Fallada, Dorst evokes a sense of the early 1930s with his middle-class characters who evade reality through a pursuit of popular culture idols of the time even as the political situation disintegrates. More recently, he has begun a series of plays about the German middle class from the 1920 to the present. The first, *On Chimborazo* (1975), is set on a hill near the border with East Germany where the characters reminisce and come to understand themselves as they wait to light a signal fire to friends on the other side of the border.

In the late 1960s a new group of playwrights came to the fore, most of them seemingly weary of the preceding generation's preoccupation with guilt. The most admired of the new writers has been Peter Handke (1942–), who has been concerned above all with language and its relationship to reality and behavior. He began his playwriting career in 1966 with *Offending the Audience*, in which four unnamed and undifferentiated

speakers make a series of statements to the audience about the clichés concerning theatregoing and the nature of theatrical illusion. Ultimately he argues that a theatrical performance is not a reflection of reality but is the reality of that moment. Probably Handke's best known work is *Kaspar* (1968), in which a young man who has been brought up in total isolation (and therefore without speech) is gradually reduced to conformity through language; at the end he is indistinguishable from a host of almost identical figures. In these and other plays, such as *My Foot My Tutor* (1969), *The Ride Across Lake Constance* (1971), and *The Unreasonable Are Dying Out* (1974), Handke has been preoccupied with how human beings are brutalized and dehumanized by conventions that reduce everything to conformity and are punished when they try to break out of mechanistic patterns.

In the late 1960s there was also a renewed interest in the folk play tradition. One of the writers who has exploited its conventions most effectively has been Martin Sperr (1944–), noted especially for a trilogy of plays that treat successively peasant life, small town life, and city life: *Hunting Scenes from Lower Bavaria* (1966), *Tales of Landshut* (1967), and *Munich Freedom* (1971). All depict man as selfish, corruptible, and cruel.

Among the younger writers, the most frequently produced and most popular is Franz Xaver Kroetz (1946–), who has written more than twenty plays and film scripts since 1970. Most of his early works are pessimistic, but his recent dramas, such as *Dear Fritz* and *The Nest*, point to positive solutions of contemporary problems.

By the 1970s Germany had almost fully recovered from the dearth of dramatic talent that had marked the immediate postwar period. Among current writers some of the best are Peter Hacks, Leopold Ahlsen, Jochen Zeim, Hartmut Lange, Hans Gunter Michelsen, Karl Wittlinger, Rainer Werner Fassbinder, Siegfried Lenz, Wolfgang Bauer, Helmut Baierl, Rolf Schneider, Thomas Bernhard, and Heiner Müller.

During the 1960s the basic organizational patterns of the German theatre remained unchanged. Virtually every town of any size had one or more subsidized theatres which performed a cross section of world drama. Not until the late 1960s was this arrangement seriously challenged. Perhaps the greatest source of unhappiness was the almost unlimited decision-making power of the state-appointed theatre managers *(Intendanten)*. The dissatisfaction came to a head in 1969 when in several cities actors disrupted performances with demands for

FIGURE 19.9 Planchon's production of *Dead Souls*, adapted by Adamov (1960). Théâtre de la Cité, Villeurbanne. Setting by René Allio. Photograph by Pic.

a greater voice in the theatre's affairs. This crisis was met in various ways. Cologne appointed a triumvirate of directors, each with his own group of performers, working under a single supervisor; Wuppertal turned to a six-man directorate under a supervisor; Frankfurt and Kiel attempted a participatory directorate, in which every member of the company was involved; and in West Berlin a commune was established (the most widely publicized solution). Nevertheless, most companies continued under the old system, although a large proportion are now headed by new or young directors who are more sensitive to the problems than were their predecessors. In 1972 more than twenty companies received new Intendants, among them Hans Lietzau in Berlin, Ulrich Brecht in Dusseldorf, Peter Zadek in Bochum, Gunther Rolf in Hanover, and Wolf Dieter Ludwig in Mainz. Of West Germany's many theatrical centers, the most active now are Hamburg, Berlin, and Munich. Berlin is especially noted for its diversity, in large part because of Peter Stein, Germany's most admired director. In East Germany, Rostock, with its five theatres under the direction of Anselm Perthen, is currently the most active theatrical center.

As elsewhere in the late 1960s in Germany there was much argument over the extent to which the repertory should be made relevant to the immediate social and political scene. It was often charged that the typical season seemed more concerned with preserving the past

than reflecting the present. But the attempt of some directors to politicize the repertory led to factionalism and dissension. To take care of the demand for relevance, most companies began to place increased stress on experimental theatres where innovation in techniques and subject matter could be more easily accommodated than in the large houses. The 1970s, however, brought renewed interest in the past, not in the old sense but as a confrontation with the roots of the present, especially those from which contemporary problems have sprung. Overall, the repertory grew more conservative, and light comedy began to be a major element, though it was often interpreted as a commentary on bourgeois values.

Dissension in the late 1960s also led to a decline in attendance, and some theatres began to experience financial difficulties. In the early 1970s doubts were voiced that West Germany really needed all of the approximately 200 subsidized stages then in existence. It was suggested that some should be abandoned. (Oberhausen decided to discontinue its permanent company at the end of 1973 but no others have done so.) It was also suggested that companies in close proximity to each other should be combined. More typical, however, was the exploration of schemes for cooperation among companies. In some areas plans have been made under which productions will be exchanged, costumes and settings be shared, and information and publicity will be handled cooperatively. There have also been proposals for a system of vouchers which purchasers could exchange for tickets at any participating theatre.

In the 1970s, the theatres of West Germany and Austria encountered still other problems as inflation increased and as the work week for employees in subsidized theatres was reduced from forty-two to forty hours. The latter action resulted in reduced rehearsal time and, in some theatres, closure for one evening each week. The problems of the subsidized theatres stimulated the growth of private companies, so that by the mid-1970s there were about eighty-five, many of them touring widely. Subsidized theatres began to book touring productions into their houses as a way of saving money, but this created considerable controversy over indirect subsidization of private companies—no small concern since only about 19 percent of the costs of state-subsidized theatres is covered by box-office receipts. East German theatres have had to face few of these problems, since the state maintains almost complete control over wages and other economic factors. In 1975 East Germany had fifty-three state companies (playing in seventy-nine theatre buildings and twenty-three auxiliary spaces), most of which performed both drama and opera.

The stresses of the late 1960s also led to the formation of free theatres, cooperatives (which linked a number of small companies), and lunch-time theatres. They seem also to have stimulated interest in children's theatre as a means of reaching and building future audiences. Formerly, most theatres had performed one children's play each year (usually at Christmas and most often based on a fairy tale). During the 1970s, some companies were formed to play exclusively for children and youth. Of these, the best known is the Grips Theatre in West Berlin. Like several other troupes, Grips has abandoned fairy tales for material related directly to the children's own lives. This approach is usually referred to as "emancipatory theatre," since it seeks to free its audience from false conceptions and traditional repressions. A number of theatres also cater exclusively to adolescents. Such theatres are not numerous but they are growing in popularity. In 1976 the Alliance for Children's and Young People's Theatre was formed to help the companies deal with common problems and concerns.

As elsewhere, in Germany the theatre in the 1970s was beset with problems, but it remained one of the most fully decentralized and best supported in the world.

THEATRE AND DRAMA IN FRANCE SINCE 1960

After General DeGaulle came to power in 1959 his minister of culture, André Malraux, retained many of the previous government's policies but also made a number of reforms. He continued to subsidize promising new dramatists and companies and sought to extend decentralization. In addition to founding several new "dramatic centers," the Gaullist regime also promoted municipal cultural centers *(maisons de la culture)* and supplied 50 percent of the funds necessary to finance them. The first of the cultural centers was opened in 1962 and others are still being completed. In addition to theatrical performances, these centers include facilities for films, music, dance, the visual arts, and public lectures. Some of these centers are located in the suburbs of Paris, for it became clear that the residents of those areas were too far removed from the center of the city to benefit adequately from its resources.

Malraux also reorganized the state theatres. He removed the Odéon from the control of the Comédie Française, renamed it the Théâtre de France, and installed Barrault's company in it. Similarly, the Théâtre National Populaire (TNP) was elevated to a rank equal with the other state theatres. Jean Vilar continued to head the TNP until 1963, when he was succeeded by George Wilson, a long-time member of the company.

Among the new directors who came to the fore in the early 1960s, the most important were Planchon, Bourseiller, and Béjart. Roger Planchon (1931–   ) after 1957 was head of the Théâtre de la Cité in Villeurbanne, an industrial suburb of Lyons, where he was very successful in attracting the working-class audience he sought. In his productions, Planchon borrowed many techniques from film (since he considered this medium most familiar to his unsophisticated theatregoers) and from Brecht. He made liberal use of projections (captions, commentaries, and pictures) and often utilized turntables to show the action from different angles, as in the cinema. He presented plays by Molière, Marivaux, Shakespeare, Kleist, Marlowe, Racine, Brecht and other major writers, but he usually gave them working-class interpretations. Consequently, his productions were often controversial. But their liveliness, richness, clarity, and novelty won Planchon one of the largest followings in France.

Antoine Bourseiller (1930–   ) came to prominence in 1960 when he won the prize offered annually for the best production by a young company. He then

FIGURE 19.10 Maurice Béjart's production of Berlioz' *The Damnation of Faust* **at the Paris Opéra (1964). Photograph by Pic.**

became head of the Studio des Champs-Elysées and staged a number of critically praised productions for other companies, including Barrault's. In 1966 he was appointed director of the dramatic center in Aix-en-Provence and has directed there and elsewhere in France since that time. Bourseiller declared his desire to shock audiences into reassessing their preconceptions and has become noted for novel interpretations of standard works. Probably his most controversial production has been of Molière's *Dom Juan,* presented by the Comédie Française in 1967.

Maurice Béjart (1937–   ) is noted primarily for his work with the Twentieth Century Ballet Company, which since 1959 has been based in Brussels. He is not so much concerned with traditional dance forms as with using dance to bridge the gulf between men of all nations. His work is often denounced by purists because it mingles so many diverse elements, but if his dance vocabulary is limited, his use of it has aroused intense emotional response. Béjart has not confined his work to dance, having directed opera and drama. He is perhaps most important for breaking down the barriers between the performing arts and for experimenting with means whereby to involve the entire sensory apparatus in a type of "total theatre."

In the late 1960s the wave of dissatisfaction which swept the world brought a number of changes in the French theatre. In May 1968 an uprising of workers and students virtually paralyzed the country and prompted DeGaulle to retire. At this time Barrault resigned as head of the Théâtre de France and, since the troupe was under contract to him, the Odéon was left without a company. The Odéon remained virtually unused, except for visiting companies, until 1970 when it was assigned to the Comédie Française. That company has used the Odéon primarily as a home for new and *avant-garde* works and has sought thereby to broaden its appeal. In 1975 the rules governing the Comédie Française were revised: the number of *sociétaires* was increased from thirty to forty; the length of contracts was reduced from twenty to ten years; the percentage of the profits going to the company was increased and for the first time the *pensionnaires* were included among the beneficiaries; and greater freedom to perform elsewhere was granted the actors.

Upon leaving the Théâtre de France, Barrault conceived and directed *Rabelais* (1968), a three-hour adaptation of material drawn from Rabelais' writings and intended as a timely commentary on repression and revolution. Drawing liberally on practically all recent trends in staging, the production was originally presented in a sports arena in Paris before being seen in London, New York, and elsewhere. In 1970, Barrault attempted to duplicate this success with a project based on Jarry's life and writings, *Jarry sur la Butte,* but the results were disappointing. In 1971 Barrault became director of the Théâtre des Nations, an international festival which until recently was always held in Paris. (It is now held in a different country each year.) In addition to productions from various countries, the festival also features workshops, lectures, and discussions designed to provoke thought and to encourage understanding and innovation. Barrault also continued his own company, which since 1974 has been housed in the new 900-seat Théâtre d'Orsay, constructed inside a former railway station. In addition to his own productions there, he hosts other companies, especially foreign, each season.

Under President DeGaulle's successors, the French government has continued the policy of decentralization. In the early 1970s it reorganized the national theatres and for the first time designated companies outside Paris as national theatres. These include the Théâtre National de Strasbourg (a former dramatic center); the Théâtre de l'Est Parisien (in a suburb of Paris); and Planchon's troupe in Villeurbanne, now called the Théâtre National Populaire, under the direction of Planchon and Patrice Chereau. (The Parisian troupe that had held the title Théâtre National Populaire was retained but renamed the Théâtre National du Palais de Chaillot.) Planchon has sought to justify his company's status as a national theatre by performing for a month at a time in several of France's larger towns, while giving a full season of plays in his home theatre.

Governmental attempts to assist the theatre did not meet universal approval. Dissatisfaction was often expressed about the way subsidies were distributed, and a major crisis developed in 1974 when the Minister for Cultural Affairs announced a reshuffling of directors among several state theatres and dramatic centers. As a result of the controversy, the government articulated a number of policies and goals: greater mobility among directors with contracts running from three to no more than ten years; increased aid for new plays and their production; help for young companies by associating them with dramatic centers; increased funds for cultural activities; and the creation of an office to encourage the diffusion of culture. While most of these goals were applauded, they did not silence complaints, especially

FIGURE 19.11 Arrabal's *The Automobile Grave-yard* as directed by Victor Garcia at the Théâtre des Arts, Paris, in 1967. Photo by Bernand.

about the arbitrary assignment of directors and subsidies.

The unrest of the late 1960s also provoked dissatisfactions with traditional organizational patterns. One result was the establishment of several theatres in the suburbs of Paris as the potential for audiences there began to be recognized. By the 1970s there were more than twenty of these "theatres on the periphery." Within cities, other groups began to give performances in cafés, artists' centers, and other nontheatrical environments.

One of the most interesting and innovative of these groups is the Grand Magic Circus, headed by Jerome Savary, who began his career in 1967 as a director but soon grew dissatisfied with conventional theatre. It was while working in New York with the La Mama company that he conceived the Grand Magic Circus. He began to attract wide favorable attention in 1970 with *Zartan*, "the story of Tarzan's deprived brother," described by Savary as the "marvelous story of colonialism from the Middle Ages to the present." Savary then conceived *The Last Days of Solitude of Robinson Crusoe* (1972) as the story of a modern Everyman freed from loneliness, passivity, and speechlessness, and went on to produce *Goodbye Mr. Freud, From Moses to Mao,* and *Adventures in Love.* Although Savary's productions are thinly veiled commentaries on the contemporary world, he does not consider these messages primary. Rather, for him the function of the theatre is to be a "life show"—a pretext for people to come together in a joyous celebration. He dislikes the theatre of Grotowski and the Living

Theatre (both of which he labels "cerebral") and seeks to appeal to all types of audiences in a very direct manner. His company plays on beaches, in hospitals, in parks—almost anywhere except in traditional theatres. He has won a considerable following with his productions that have the zest of children's theatre, circus, and carnivals created by extensive exchanges between audience and performers, improvisations, acrobatic feats, satirical thrusts, and stunning effects of all sorts.

Festivals also continued to grow in number. The most important, nevertheless, remained that at Avignon, which in 1976 celebrated its thirtieth anniversary. During the 1970s Avignon became a major showcase for provincial theatres, new plays, and experimental productions. During some seasons, there were as many as sixty performances a day.

Of the directors who have come to prominence since 1965 two of the most important have been Mnouchkine and Garcia. Ariane Mnouchkine (1940-   ) works with the Théâtre du Soleil, a commune composed of about forty members. Until it was torn down in 1968, the Cirque d'Hiver was the company's home and there it created a considerable stir with productions of Wesker's *The Kitchen* and Shakespeare's *A Midsummer Night's Dream.* The group is probably best known for *1789—The Revolution Must Stop Only with the Perfection of Happiness—Saint Just,* originally presented in Milan in 1970 and then moved to an abandoned cartridge factory just outside Paris. This production dealt with the early years of the French Revolution and argued that the Revolution was frustrated by those who became more concerned about property than justice. Staged on platforms surrounding a standing audience (which was treated as the mob), it was highly praised and extremely successful. It was followed by *1793* (1972), a much less effective treatment of later phases of the Revolution, and *The Age of Gold* (1975), which as the title suggests deals with various aspects of materialism.

Victor Garcia (1934-   ) came to Paris from his native Argentina in the early 1960s and has since worked with companies throughout the world. He made his first deep impression in 1966 with a production of Arrabal's *The Automobile Graveyard,* which ran for two years. Since then he has directed in Spain (where for Nuria Espert he has staged Genet's *The Maids* and Lorca's *Yerma*), England (where for the National Theatre he directed Arrabal's *The Architect and the Emperor of Assyria*), in Brazil (where he gutted a theatre in order to create a spirally arranged setting and seating for

Genet's *The Balcony*), and elsewhere. He has come to be considered one of the most imaginative directors anywhere.

Though the theatrical scene in France remained lively after 1960, few new playwrights of importance appeared. Older writers, such as Anouilh, Montherlant, Ionesco, Beckett, Adamov, and Sartre, continued to write, but few won international fame. Those who did include René de Obaldia (1918–   ), who in such works as *The Agricultural Cosmonaut* (1965), *In the End the Bang* (1968), and *The Baby Sitter* (1971), treats the inanities and concealed lies of life, which he brings to the surface and treats as wholly logical; Romain Weingarten (1926–   ), in whose best known play, *Summer* (1966), childhood experience is counterpointed with the quarrels of two lovers and the comments of two cats on humanity and life; Françoise Sagan (1935–   ), whose *Castle in Sweden* (1960), *The Vanishing Horse* (1966), and *Piano on the Lawn* (1971) are characterized by penetrating psychological insight, bittersweet lyricism, and elegant diction; and Marguerite Duras (1914–   ), who after a notable career in films and as a novelist turned to dramas of minute internal dissection, usually of female characters, in such plays as *Entire Days in the Trees* (1965) and *A Place Without Doors* (1969). But the best known of all French playwrights since 1960 has been Fernando Arrabal (1932–   ), who was born in Spain, moved to Paris in 1955, and has written all of his plays in French. His early plays emphasize a childish, thoughtless cruelty couched in a form similar to that used by the Absurdists. For example, in *Fando and Lis* (1958) the two childlike protagonists seek to reach the town of Tar but always arrive back at the same place. Fando both loves and resents the paralyzed Lis because she is wholly dependent upon him, but he also is very proud of her beauty, so much so that he leaves her exposed for strangers to view. As a result of exposure, Lis becomes ill and when she falls and breaks his drum, Fando beats her so cruelly that she dies. Fando then misses Lis but fails to comprehend his part in her death.

Around 1962 Arrabal became interested in what he called *théâtre panique*, "a ceremony—partly sacrilegious, partly sacred, erotic and mystic, a putting to death and exaltation of life, part Don Quixote and part Alice in Wonderland." Among his later works are *Solemn Communion* (1966), *The Architect and the Emperor of Assyria* (1967), *And They Handcuffed the Flowers* (1970), *A Tortoise Called Dostoyevsky* (1973), and *Young Barbarians Today* (1975). Of these, the second is perhaps the best known. It includes only two characters, who enact a series of ritualized human situations: master and slave, judge and criminal, mother and child, male and female, sadist and masochist, and so on. Eventually one decides that he must be punished and asks the other to kill and eat him. When this is done, they seem somehow to merge. But now a new figure appears, apparently beginning the whole cycle over again. Through such plays, Arrabal not only challenges all values, he ferrets out all the hidden corners of the human psyche.

In the 1970s Jean-Claude Grumbert (1940–   ) was probably the most admired of young writers. His *Dreyfus* (1974) is set in a Jewish ghetto in a Polish town around 1930 where amateurs, while rehearsing a play about the Dreyfus affair, explore the phenomenon of anti-semitism. It won the critics award as the best play of the 1974–1975 season. *On the Way Back from the Paris Exposition* (1975) treats the French working-class movement at the turn of the twentieth century. Grumberg's popularity seems to suggest that there is a renewed concern underway in France for socially conscious drama.

Despite this considerable number of competent writers, however, the overall impression is that France has declined in dramatic vigor since the 1950s, when its plays were perhaps the most admired in the world.

ENGLISH THEATRE AND DRAMA SINCE 1960

After 1960 three companies were especially important in English theatrical life: the Royal Shakespeare Company, the National Theatre, and the English Stage Company. In 1961 the Stratford Memorial Theatre was given a new charter and a new title, The Royal Shakespeare Company (RSC). Its new status owed most to Peter Hall (1930–   ), who after beginning his directing career in 1955, had worked at Stratford since 1957 and had been named head of its company in 1960. Upon assuming the new post, Hall at once set out to overcome one of the troupe's principal problems: the inability to hold a company together and build an ensemble because the season at Stratford lasted only about six months each year. To remedy this situation, Hall took a lease on the Aldwych Theatre in London and transformed the organization into a year-round operation. Since then the company has divided its time between Stratford and

London. Hall also broadened the repertory to include plays other than those by Shakespeare so that actors would have diversified experience.

By 1962 the RSC's activities had been so enlarged that Peter Brook and Michel Saint-Denis were added to the management. The RSC also began an experimental program, and in 1963–1964 Brook, in collaboration with Charles Marowitz, produced a series of programs under the overall title, "Theatre of Cruelty." It was out of this season that Brook's production of Weiss' *Marat/Sade* came. By the mid-1960s the RSC was London's major *avant-garde* troupe, noted both for its innovative techniques and for its wide-ranging repertory, with plays by Hochhuth, Pinter, and numerous continental and British dramatists of the past and present. The Aldwych also became the home of the World Theatre Season, an arrangement under which each spring major companies from throughout the world come to London for limited engagements.

In 1968, Hall, Brook, and Saint-Denis resigned their posts as directors of the RSC and were succeeded by Trevor Nunn, assisted by an advisory board. After that time most of the directing has been done by Nunn, Clifford Williams, Terry Hands, and John Barton (and occasionally by Hall and Brook), plus younger directors brought in from time to time.

In the 1970s the RSC was plagued by the rampant inflation then besetting England. In contrast with the subsidized theatres of Germany, in which less than 20 percent of costs were covered by box-office receipts, the RSC had to support approximately 80 percent of its expenditures through ticket sales. Nevertheless, it continued its extremely ambitious program, producing well over 100 plays in a five-year period. Not only has it renewed the past through outstanding productions of plays by Gorki, Gillette, Boucicault, and others (including Shakespeare), but it has continued its experimentation through work at The Other Place and Studio Theatre in Stratford and at the Roundhouse and elsewhere in London. Without doubt, the RSC has established itself as one of the world's major companies. Nevertheless, it is faced with the specter of retrenchment because of financial difficulties, even though it is heavily subsidized and plays to full houses almost constantly.

After leaving the RSC in 1968, Hall served for a time as co-director of the Royal Covent Garden Opera company, and in 1973 was named successor to Laurence Olivier as head of the National Theatre. Of the RSC'S directors, however, Peter Brook (1925–   ) has been

FIGURE 19.12 Peter Brook's production of *King Lear* at the Memorial Theatre, Stratford-on-Avon, 1962. Seen here are Paul Scofield as Lear, Alec McCowan as the Fool, and Irene Worth as Goneril. Reproduced by permission of the Governors of the Royal Shakespeare Theatre.

the most influential. He began directing while still in his teens and first worked at Stratford in 1946. During the 1950s he built an enviable reputation with productions starring such actors as Olivier, Paul Scofield, and the Lunts, and with plays by such authors as Shakespeare, Fry, Anouilh, Eliot, Duerrenmatt, and Genet. But he is now best known for a series of productions after 1960, including *King Lear* (1962), *Marat/Sade* (1964), *The Tempest* (1968) and *A Midsummer Night's Dream* (1970). As a director, Brook has not been so much an innovator as an eclectic who has transformed borrowings from many sources into his own vital expression. For example, for *A Midsummer Night's Dream*, he borrowed from Meyerhold, *commedia dell'arte*, circus, and radical theatre groups of the 1960s, but the results were uniquely his own. For this production, Brook sought to divest the play of its romantic aura of fairies and haunted woodlands and to make it more immediately relevant to our time. He interpreted the script as an exploration of love, and consequently he used the same pair of actors as Theseus and Hippolyta and Oberon and Titania, and treated the enchanted scenes as lessons on love for the betrothed royal couple. The stage was enclosed on three sides by white, unadorned walls broken only by two nearly invisible doors at the rear. The forest was suggested by loosely coiled metal springs attached to fishing

FIGURE 19.13 Peter Brook's production of Shakespeare's *A Midsummer Night's Dream* with the Royal Shakespeare Company in 1970. Alan Howard as Oberon and John Kane as Puck on trapezes; Sara Kestelman as Titania and David Waller as Bottom. Design by Sally Jacobs. Photograph by permission of the Royal Shakespeare Theatre.

rods. The flying was accomplished with trapezes lowered and raised to varying heights within the setting. Most of the performers wore a kind of coverall but there was a sprinkling of *commedia dell'arte* and circus costumes. Despite all these distinctive features, the text was given its full poetic value. It is such novel and imaginative approaches that have made Brook one of the most effective and respected directors of the age.

In 1971 Brook assumed direction of the International Center for Theatre Research, based in Paris and including participants from all over the world. In the summer of 1971 the group gave its first performance, *Orghast,* in Iran at the Persepolis Festival. It received a mixed reception, in part because the play used an invented language. The company then worked on Handke's *Kaspar* and a twelfth-century Persian poem. In 1972, it traveled and played in Africa; in 1973 it appeared in America where it worked with El Teatro Campesino and

the National Theatre of the Deaf. In 1974–1975 it prepared Shakespeare's *Timon of Athens* and *The Ik* (a play based on a book about an African tribe whose hunting grounds are turned into a national park) and performed them in Paris, London, and elsewhere. Through this work Brook has sought to discover acting and directing devices and techniques that can transcend the barriers created by differences in language and culture. These experiments will probably continue since the French government has provided the Center with a theatre until 1979.

Beginning in the 1960s the RSC had a powerful rival in the National Theatre. England was one of the last European countries to establish a national theatre, though it had long contemplated such a move. Parliamentary approval for the company was given in the late 1940s but it was not implemented until 1963, when the Old Vic company was dissolved and its building assigned to the new troupe. Laurence Olivier was named director and Kenneth Tynan literary advisor. The National Theatre rapidly built a reputation for excellence through its extremely eclectic choice of plays and production styles. It sought to assemble for each production the team best suited to that script. Consequently, it utilized numerous English and foreign directors (among them Brook, George Devine, Jonathan Miller, Franco Zeffirelli, Ingmar Bergman, and Victor Garcia) and designers (among them Motley, Sean Kenny, Josef Svoboda, and René Allio). It has also from time to time staged seasons of experimental plays, and in 1972 began to tour throughout England with productions able to play almost anywhere. Its constantly expanding program also necessitated enlarging its supervisory staff, which has included Paul Scofield, Frank Dunlop, Bill Bryden, John Dexter, Albert Finney, and Michael Blakemore.

In 1970 the National Theatre added the Young Vic troupe, designed to appeal primarily to children and youth. It soon became something of a focus for the growing interest in theatre for the young and served as host for a National Festival of Theatre for Young People. Its significance was recognized in 1975 when it was separated from the National Theatre to become an independent organization.

In 1973 Peter Hall replaced Laurence Olivier as director of the National Theatre. (Olivier's great service to the theatre was recognized in 1970 when he became the first actor in English history to be raised to the nobility.) In 1976 the company began its move from the Old Vic (the future of which remains uncertain) to its new building, designed by Denys Lasdun and built at a cost of some $32 million. One of the most advanced theatre plants anywhere, it includes three performance spaces: the 890-seat Lyttleton proscenium theatre; the 1,160-seat Olivier open-stage theatre with a revolving stage 40 feet in diameter divided into two parts that can be lowered to workshops 45 feet below; and the 400-seat Cottesloe laboratory theatre. There are more than 100 dressing rooms, several stage-sized rehearsal rooms, and numerous workshops. Hall expects to employ a company of eighty to ninety performers, all of whom will be kept busy. He also plans to bring the best work from the provinces and create a ferment of activity that will justify the great expenditures made on the new facility, a source of considerable controversy. Since the National Theatre now receives more than twice as much subsidy as any other company in Britain, much is expected of it.

The English Stage Company (more commonly called the Royal Court after the theatre in which it is housed), founded by George Devine in 1956, continued after 1960 to be the principal champion of new playwrights. Of the writers launched during the 1960s, perhaps the most important were Edward Bond, Joe Orton, and David Storey. Upon Devine's retirement in 1965, the management passed to William Gaskill (1930–   ), assisted by Lindsay Anderson, Anthony Page, and Peter Gill. In 1969, the company enlarged its program when it opened the Theatre Upstairs, devoted entirely to short runs of new plays. (The parent company continued to produce a mixed repertory of new and established works.) Although the management has changed rather often (in 1976 the directors were Nicholas Wright and Robert Kidd), the company's basic goals have remained rather constant. Thus, a large share of the credit for England's strength in playwriting must go to the Royal Court. Nevertheless, in the mid-1970s this role was being threatened by inflation, which forced the company to reduce its program.

Outside of London the number of resident companies increased after 1960 to more than fifty. Perhaps the best of these were at Bristol, Birmingham, Manchester, Nottingham, Coventry, and Glasgow, all subsidized by local governments. Nevertheless, the English theatre remained within relatively conservative limits until 1968, when the censorship that had been in effect since 1737 was abolished. A number of plays previously forbidden were produced immediately, among them *Hair* (banned because of nudity and obscenity), Osborne's *A Patriot for Me* (forbidden because of homosexual

scenes), Hochhuth's *The Soldiers* (banned because it was considered offensive to Churchill's memory), and Edward Bond's plays (forbidden because they were considered immoral).

More important perhaps, the change in law seems to have given impetus to small groups (comparable to American off-off-Broadway companies) which up to that time had made little impact. After 1968 these "fringe" groups increased rapidly, and by the early 1970s there were more than thirty in London performing in pubs, playgrounds, meeting halls, or almost anywhere an audience could be assembled, and at lunchtime or late at night, as well as at more traditional hours. Their great flexibility (in approach, place, and time of performing, subjects, and desired audiences) did much to bring variety to the English theatre. By the mid-1970s these companies were protesting the smallness of subsidies awarded them and were mounting strong campaigns to have their merit recognized through financial support. Of the fringe groups, the one with the most extensive program has been Interaction, a commune founded by Ed Berman in 1968. It operates a mobile theatre (the Fun Art Bus), a street theatre (Dogg's Troupe), two *avant-garde* companies (the Ambiance and The Other Company) which

FIGURE 19.14 The National Theatre's production of Strindberg's *The Dance of Death* (1967). The actor's are Geraldine McEwan, Robert Stephens, and Laurence Olivier. Photograph by Zoë Dominic.

FIGURE 19.15 Pinter's *The Homecoming* as directed by Peter Hall for the Royal Shakespeare Company in 1965. Seen here are Michael Craig as Teddy, Terence Rigby (seated) as Joey, and Ian Holm as Lenny. Courtesy Royal Shakespeare Company.

crease in their minimum weekly wage from an absurdly low $48 (which it was often charged had amounted to an indirect subsidy for producers) to $72. Other increases in production costs, combined with rapid inflation, served to drive ticket prices ever higher. Subsidized theatres made frequent appeals for supplementary grants to avoid serious deficits. Regional arts associations were also formed throughout Britain to deal with financial crises, encourage cooperative ventures, and promote the arts in their areas. In the mid-1970s, a number of theatres were cutting back on their seasons, the sizes of casts, and overall personnel, others were turning to plays calculated to have a wider appeal, and several were threatened with complete collapse.

Despite its current problems, the English theatre has long been and continues to be among the best in the world. Much of its strength can be attributed to its excellent playwrights. Among these, the one with the greatest critical reputation has been Harold Pinter (1930–), who, after beginning his career as an actor, turned to playwriting in 1957 with *The Room*. Since then he has written regularly for the theatre, television, and films. His stage works include *The Dumb Waiter* (1957), *The Birthday Party* (1958), *The Caretaker* (1960), *The Homecoming* (1965), *Old Times* (1970), and *No Man's Land* (1975). Although there is much variety among them,

FIGURE 19.16 David Storey's *The Contractor* as performed at the Royal Court Theatre, London, in 1970. Directed by Lindsay Anderson. Photo by Tom Murray.

play at the Almost Free Theatre, and a theatre for the elderly. Through such varied activities Berman hopes to make the arts a vital part of an urban community. Other important fringe groups include the People Show, the Pip Simmons Theatre, the Freehold, the Portable Theatre, and Triple Action. Such companies have contributed enormously to the vitality of the English theatre, especially through their appeal to audiences that had previously ignored the theatre. These "alternative" theatres were not restricted to London. A descriptive directory published in 1976 listed 133 companies of which approximately forty were based outside the capital city.

Part of the appeal of the English theatre during the 1960s lay in its relatively cheap admission prices, which permitted audiences to attend the theatre as easily as movies. During the 1970s, however, this advantage began to fade. A "value added" (or sales) tax imposed in 1972 increased ticket prices by some 10 percent, and in 1974 they were further affected when actors won an in-almost all of Pinter's plays have in common a few characteristics: everyday situations that gradually take on an air of mystery or menace; unexplained, unrevealed, or ambiguous motivations or background information; and authentic, seemingly natural though carefully wrought dialogue. With Pinter silence is an integral part of language, and he treats all speech as one type of stratagem whereby characters seek to cover their psychological nakedness. Thus, an "unspoken subtext" is often as important as the dialogue. In Pinter's plays everything may at first seem amusing or pleasantly ambiguous, but gradually the tone changes to anxiety, pathos, or fear as the characters confront some predicament and seek to defend themselves against some unknown, often undefined danger from outside or within the room in which the action occurs. As a dramatist Pinter falls somewhere between Beckett and Chekhov. Like Beckett, he isolates characters and lets them wrestle with their anxieties in an unverifiable universe; like Chekhov, he creates a realistic texture of background and dialogue in which surface act and speech are merely evasions or disguises of deeper conflicts and uncertainties.

Probably the most controversial contemporary English playwright is Edward Bond (1935–   ), who achieved overnight notoriety in 1965 with a private performance at the Royal Court of *Saved*, in which a baby is stoned to death in its carriage by its father and his roustabout friends. Even more shocking perhaps was *Early Morning* (1968), a surrealistic farce about Victorian life in which Florence Nightingale and Queen Victoria are involved in a lesbian relationship and virtually all the characters indulge in cannibalism. Bond's first play to receive a public performance, *Narrow Road to the Deep North* (1968), is set in Japan and avoids the more shocking features of the earlier works, although it too emphasizes the callousness of mankind. *Lear* (1971) uses many of the characters and situations from Shakespeare's play but alters them to make a despairing statement about human brutality and inhumanity. *The Sea* (1973), set in a seaside resort in 1907, depicts a society where apparent peace and harmony are mere disguises for the inhumanity of a rigidly structured society. *Bingo* (1973) has as its protagonist Shakespeare after he has retired to Stratford, and shows him caught between the idealistic impulses that inform his plays and the selfishness of common humanity. Using the nineteenth-century poet John Clare as his subject, Bond shows in *The Fool* (1975) a dogmatic and violent society treating genius as madness. Bond has been denounced by many critics

FIGURE 19.17 Tom Stoppard's *Rosencrantz and Guildenstern Are Dead* as performed at the National Theatre, London, in 1967. Photograph by Anthony Crickmay.

as sensational, decadent, and overly preoccupied with violence, but ultimately his plays are based on moral concerns about a world in which the lack of love and compassion has bred a callousness that accepts the horrible as normal.

Joe Orton (1933–1967) also won a reputation for sensationalism, but was less philosophically inclined than Bond. In *Entertaining Mr. Sloane* (1964), he shows a brother and sister encouraging a young murderer to rid them of their senile father and when he has done so, thinking he will then be able to blackmail them, they turn the tables and agree to divide him sexually between them six months at a time. This amoral tale is given its distinctive tone in part because it is set within the framework of conventional drawing-room drama with its decorous speech and manners. Similarly, *Loot* (1966) parodies the conventions of the detective thriller through a story of murder, robbery, and chicanery in which the criminals and police eventually agree to share the loot; and *What the Butler Saw* (produced 1969) treats a series of complex family and sexual relationships through the conventions of bedroom farce. More than any other English playwright, Orton has achieved commercial success with subjects almost wholly amoral.

Among the most successful of current dramatists is David Storey (1933–   ), who began his career as a

FIGURE 19.18 Tom Stoppard's *Travesties* as performed by the Royal Shakespeare Company, 1974. Photograph by Sophie Baker.

novelist and turned to playwriting in 1967 with *The Restoration of Arnold Middleton*. Since then he has written *In Celebration* (1969), *The Contractor* (1970), *Home* (1970), *The Changing Room* (1971), *The Farm* (1973), and *Life Class* (1974). Stylistically, Storey's plays bear a distant resemblance to those of Pinter and Chekhov in their surface realism and their absence of clear-cut meaning, but they lack the sense of menace found in Pinter's works. Storey is concerned above all with various kinds of alienation: class from class, person from person, man from himself, the reality from the ideal, and so on. These various forms of alienation are perhaps most fully developed in *Home*, set in an asylum where the four main characters, through seemingly random dialogue, point up the ironic implications about alienation contained in the play's title (which may mean country, dwelling, or sense of belonging). Storey also often gives focus to his concerns through detailed physical activity. In *The Contractor*, a group of working men put up a tent for a wedding in the first act and take it down during the last act; during this process a cross section of attitudes and relationships are demonstrated by the workmen and their employers. Similarly, in *The Changing Room*, members of a semiprofessional rugby team (all of whom

have other jobs during the week) change into their uniforms in the first act and back to their street clothes in the final act; class, social distinctions, and purposelessness are similarly divested and reassumed after a short period of community achieved by a harsh ritual. Probably no writer today has so precisely recreated the detail of real life situations or has used them to imply so much about modern man and social conventions as has Storey.

Other prominent English dramatists of today include Stoppard and Nichols. Tom Stoppard (1937–) came to prominence in 1967 with *Rosencrantz and Guildenstern Are Dead*, a play reminiscent of Beckett's works, for Stoppard makes protagonists of two attendant lords from *Hamlet*, and though they sense that important events are going on around them they are killed without understanding anything about the life of which they have been a part. Stoppard has continued this highly theatrical and brilliant exploration of the nature of reality in such plays as *The Real Inspector Hound* (1968), *Jumpers* (1972), and *Travesties* (1974).

Peter Nichols (1929–) achieved his first stage success with *A Day in the Death of Joe Egg* (1967), which deals with the attempts of a schoolteacher and his wife to cope with their spastic child, whom they view as a joke played on them by life but who ultimately serves as a catalyst to bring to the surface their suppressed anxieties and frustrations. This mixture of humor, compassion, and astringent observation is continued in *The National Health* (1969), a play about elderly patients who drag out their lives in a hospital ward against a background of television programs which romanticize medical practice, and *Forget-Me-Not Lane* (1971), in which the protagonist recalls growing up during World War II and eventually realizes that he is repeating all of the mistakes that he so clearly despised in his own parents.

England now has a large number of young writers who promise to keep its stage vital. Among the best of these are Christopher Hampton with *The Philanthropist* (1970) and *Savages* (1973), David Hare with *Knuckle* (1974) and *Teeth 'n' Smiles* (1975), Trevor Griffiths with *The Party* (1972) and *Comedians* (1974), and Stephen Poliakoff with *Heroes* (1975) and *City Sugar* (1976).

Other fine dramatists since 1960 include Peter Terson, Henry Livings, David Mercer, Charles Wood, David Campton, David Rudkin, Frank Marcus, Howard Brenton, Snoo Wilson, and Alan Ayckbourn. They illustrate the considerable depth now evident in English dramatic writing and help to show why in the mid-1970s the English theatre was among the best anywhere, although clearly not without its problems.

AMERICAN THEATRE AND DRAMA SINCE 1960

After 1960 production costs in New York continued to soar with the result that Broadway ticket prices became ever more expensive. The consequent need for mass appeal tended to increase the emphasis on musicals, light comedy, or plays already proven elsewhere, either at one of the regional theatres or (especially) in London.

The musical remained the most vital and innovative form on Broadway. Some attempts were made in the 1970s to achieve greater unity in musicals by reducing the emphasis on spectacle and by making the chorus and the principals the same, as in *Company* (1970) and *Chorus Line* (1975). There were also several experiments with presentational techniques, perhaps most successfully demonstrated in the revised version of *Candide* (1973) and in *Pacific Overtures* (1976).

Although since 1960 Broadway has declined considerably in importance as a producer of new plays, it has retained its status as the primary home of America's

FIGURE 19.20　Scene from *Chorus Line* (1975) as directed by Michael Bennett. Photograph by Martha Swope.

commercial theatre. In the early 1970s it underwent a considerable slump, but it made a rapid recovery in the seasons of 1974–1975 and 1975–1976, when it had the highest box-office sales in its history. The most successful writer for the Broadway stage has been Neil Simon (1927–　　), who after a somewhat tentative beginning with *Come Blow Your Horn* (1961) turned out a string of hits, among them *Barefoot in the Park* (1963), *The Odd Couple* (1965), *The Last of the Red Hot Lovers* (1970), *The Sunshine Boys* (1972), *God's Favorite* (1974), and *California Suite* (1976), all combining zany humor with eccentric characters.

The most prestigious American playwright of the 1960s was Edward Albee (1928–　　), whose first four plays, all short, were produced off-Broadway in 1960–1961. These early works, especially *The Sandbox* (1959) and *The American Dream* (1960), were thought to ally Albee with the Absurdists; but with *Who's Afraid of Virginia Woolf?* (1962), his first full-length play and first Broadway success, Albee, through his exploration of tortured psychological relationships, demonstrated an affinity to Williams and Strindberg. In *Who's Afraid of Virginia Wolf?*, the facades of the characters are gradually stripped away during the course of an all-night drinking bout to show people creating hells for each other through inability to accept weaknesses. Most of Albee's

FIGURE 19.19　Edward Albee's *A Delicate Balance* as presented by the Royal Shakespeare Company in 1967. Courtesy Royal Shakespeare Company.

subsequent work has been concerned with values. *Tiny Alice* (1964), a puzzling parable, seems to suggest that man reconciles himself to his lot by constructing unverifiable systems to explain why he has been martyred by life; *A Delicate Balance* (1966) shows several characters seeking to escape anxieties and how the protagonist comes to recognize that friendship is more important than self-protectiveness; *Box* and *Quotations from Chairman Mao Tse-tung* (1968) appear to point up the dangers of triviality, boredom, conflicts among ideologies and between rich and poor, which, if not corrected, may reduce the world to something like an empty box; *All Over* (1971) seems to argue that if we do not develop inner strengths (which must include self-knowledge, compassion, and the will to act on conviction), it will soon be all over with mankind, since external authoritarian guides are dying out; and *Seascape* (1974) suggests that human beings have lost their vitality and that the future belongs to other creatures (here shown as two amphibians who crawl out of the water onto the beach) as they discover love and consideration. In these complex plays, Albee has become increasingly abstract until in his latest works the relationship between story and meaning is often purely

FIGURE 19.21 **Scene from the film *Paradise Now: The Living Theatre In Amerika* by Marty Topp; produced by Universal Mutant, Ira Cohen, producer; distributed by Universal Movement Theatre Repertory.**

conjectural. Consequently, in recent years critics have tended to downgrade Albee's importance. Nevertheless, during the 1960s he was almost universally considered the American dramatist of greatest stature.

In the early 1960s, Arthur Kopit (1938–   ) was often ranked with Albee. He first came to prominence in 1960 with *Oh, Dad, Poor Dad, Mama's Hung You in the Closet and I'm Feeling So Sad*, a parodistic work reminiscent of Tennessee Williams' more bizarre creations but treated through absurdist techniques. In it, Mme. Rosepettle, whose household includes piranhas, venus fly traps, and the stuffed body of her dead husband, tries to protect her son from life's harsh realities only to have him break free from her domination. Kopit had little further success until 1968 with *Indians,* in which he used Buffalo Bill's Wild West Show as a framework for suggesting how the Indians' betrayal has been transformed into entertainment, thus permitting us to ignore the reality. It is a variation on the by-now familiar theme of the American dream gone awry.

An oft-expressed need has been for a permanent resident company in New York like those found in major European cities. In the 1960s an effort was made to remedy this lack with the Lincoln Center for the Performing Arts (with facilities for opera, ballet, concerts, and plays). In anticipation of the Center's completion, a repertory company was formed in 1963 under the direction of Elia Kazan and Robert Whitehead. Expectations were high, since at that time Kazan was considered America's finest director and since he was promised new plays by Arthur Miller *(After the Fall* and *Incident at Vichy)* and S. N. Berhrman *(But for Whom, Charlie).* The results were so disappointing that after one season Kazan and Whitehead resigned. They were replaced by Herbert Blau and Jules Irving, who had been outstandingly successful at the Actors' Workshop in San Francisco. In 1965 the company moved into its newly completed home (the Vivian Beaumont Theatre, designed by Eero Saarinen and Jo Mielziner) at Lincoln Center. But Blau and Irving soon ran into difficulties and in 1967 Blau resigned. Thereafter Irving continued slowly to build a company, though it seldom rose to true distinction. Eventually the artistic and financial problems became so great that in 1973 Irving resigned.

For a time New York also had a second repertory company, the Association of Producing Artists (APA). Founded in 1960 by Ellis Rabb, the APA formed a liaison in 1964 with the Phoenix Theatre, which thereafter served as its producer. The APA won high critical praise but because of financial difficulties had to be disbanded in 1970. Its repertory was impressive, ranging through works by Shaw, Chekhov, Pirandello, Shakespeare, Ionesco, and others. The company was sometimes accused of being too conservative because it only produced already proven works, but for a time it provided the most impressive cross section of drama to be seen in America.

During the 1960s the New York theatre continued to be enlivened by off-Broadway. Of the many off-Broadway groups, the most influential was to be the Living Theatre, founded in 1946 by Judith Malina (1926-   ) and Julian Beck (1925-   ). Originally they were interested in poetic drama and nonrealistic production techniques and during the 1950s also came under the influence of both Artaud and Brecht. The turning point in their work came in 1959 with their production of Jack Gelber's *The Connection,* a drama that pretends that the audience is being allowed to watch the making of a documentary film about real dope addicts. The overall effect was that of a naturalistic slice of life. The production won a number of awards in New York and in Paris at the Théâtre des Nations. Another important production was Kenneth Brown's *The Brig* (1963), which recreates the repetitive and senseless routine of a day in a Marine prison camp.

In 1963 the company lost its theatre because of failure to pay taxes and in 1964 it went abroad. Thereafter it toured throughout Europe and became increasingly committed to anarchy and revolution. Although it performed Genet's *The Maids* and a version of *Antigone,* its major productions after 1964 were works of its own creation: *Mysteries and Smaller Pieces, Frankenstein,* and *Paradise Now,* all advocating total freedom from restraints. Its best known production is probably *Paradise Now* (1968), in part because it coincided with and mirrored a period of great unrest in Europe and America. The action of the piece is divided into eight parts designed to increase the audience's political perceptions and to move ever nearer the present, when it is hoped the audience will move into the streets to continue the revolution begun in the theatre. All barriers between actors and spectators were eliminated and both roamed the stage and auditorium indiscriminately. The performers were intensely aggressive, confronting spectators, and seeking to overcome, through insults and obscenities, all opposition. The overall effect was that of an inflammatory political meeting.

When the Living Theatre returned to the United States in 1968 it received enormous publicity and aroused intense controversy. After returning to Europe it split into three groups in 1970. The Becks took their contingent to Brazil, where they were jailed for several months before returning to the United States in 1971. At that time they announced plans for a new work, *The Legacy of Cain,* to be performed in the streets over a period of several weeks. These plans have yet to be implemented.

Perhaps no group was better known or more influential in the late 1960s than the Living Theatre. For a time the disaffected almost everywhere echoed its attitudes and practices: denigration of any text that could not be transformed into an argument for anarchy and social change; downgrading language in favor of Artaudian techniques; athleticism in performance; insistence on confronting and overriding audiences; evangelical tone; and freewheeling lifestyle. As social conditions changed in the 1970s, however, the Living Theatre's influence waned rapidly. Hoping to regain its prestige, in 1976 the company once more was seeking to establish a permanent base in Europe.

By the time the Living Theatre left the United States in 1964 the off-Broadway theatre was beginning to undergo many of the same economic pressures felt on Broadway, and consequently it began to be less adventurous than in earlier years. By the mid-1970s it cost about $75,000 to produce even a simple play off-Broadway and it was increasingly difficult to recover the initial investment. In 1975, while selling out nightly, *Chorus Line* lost $18,000 each week before it was moved to Broadway. Thus, off-Broadway has lost most of its former appeal.

As it declined, it was replaced by off-off-Broadway. It is usual to date off-off-Broadway from 1958 when Joe Cino began to use his Café Cino as an art center. By 1961 plays were a regular part of his offerings and others had begun to take up the idea. Soon plays were being presented wherever space could be found. Most of the participants were unpaid and budgets were infinitesimal, but nevertheless by 1965 some 400 plays by more than 200 playwrights had been seen off-off Broadway.

The most influential of the off-off-Broadway producers was to be Ellen Stewart, who began to present plays in a basement room in 1961. After running into trouble with fire inspectors, she created the La-Mama Experimental Theatre Club (ostensibly a private organization and therefore exempt from many regulations governing public performances). By 1967 she had produced 175 plays by 130 writers. During the season of 1969–1970 LaMama alone produced more plays than were seen on Broadway that year. In 1969 the LaMama organization acquired its own building with two theatres and in 1974 quadrupled its space through the acquisition of an annex.

Beginning in 1964, Miss Stewart also took productions abroad, where her freewheeling experiments attracted such favorable attention that she was invited to found branches in several countries. Thus the LaMama organization has come to be known throughout the world. Miss Stewart considers LaMama to be a playwright's theatre intended to nourish talent. Her encouragement of innovation has meant that many LaMama plays have been amateurish, but it has also meant that many talented writers have been given a hearing that might otherwise have been denied. Nevertheless, LaMama illustrates well the perils of off-off-Broadway in the 1960s—the determined pursuit of novelty and the lack of standards by which to judge it.

LaMama's dedication to experimentation also required new directorial approaches, the results of which were manifested most clearly in the work of Tom O'Horgan, who worked for LaMama before winning renown around 1968 with productions of *Hair, Futz,* and *Tom Paine.* O'Horgan has tended to place primary emphasis on frantic physical activity, pulsating light effects, electronic sound, and gimmickry of various sorts. His productions have been colorful, unabashedly frenetic, and joyful. But his tendency to subordinate script to directional embellishments led to a break with LaMama. For a time O'Horgan suffered a decline in reputation but made a forceful comeback in 1971 with *Lenny* and *Jesus Christ Superstar.* Although controversial, many of O'Horgan's techniques were important because so many plays of the time were verbally inarticulate and required the "physicalization" he used so liberally.

In the 1970s LaMama has been concerned especially with ensemble companies, some of which have produced plays of particular interest to ethnic groups (Puerto Rican, Black, and Native American). The best known of all these ensembles is headed by Andrei Sherban, who has worked with Greek mythic material, invented language, and ritualized action to create productions of enormous emotional impact in *Medea, The Trojan Women,* and *Electra* (all first performed in 1974).

Many devices and attitudes in the off-off-Broadway theatre were closely related to developments in "happenings," which revived many of the techniques of the futurists, dadaists, and surrealists. The key figure in this movement is Allan Kaprow (1927–   ), a painter and art historian, who in the 1950s became interested in "environments" (that is, the extension of the concept of art to include the entire setting in which it is seen or in which it occurs) and, believing that all those who attend an exhibit become a part of the total context, he gradually began to give the spectators things to do. In 1959 he published an outline for an artistic event that he labeled a "happening" because he considered the term to be neutral. Later that year he gave the first public showing of such an event—*18 Happenings in 6 Parts.* The gallery was divided into three compartments and various things went on simultaneously in each while images were projected on a variety of surfaces, and music and sound effects provided a background. All those who attended became a part of the event as they carried out instructions passed out to them when they entered.

Many persons other than Kaprow were interested in happenings, and the term eventually came to be used as a designation for any event in which improvisation and chance plays a large role. Though happenings were not always theatrical, many of their characteristics were carried over into theatrical practice and goals during the 1960s. First, as "institutionalized art" came under attack, there were many attempts to transcend the confines of the theatre, museum, or concert hall and to put art into more readily accessible and familiar surroundings. There were also attempts to enlarge the audience by removing art from the atmosphere of fixed places and fixed attitudes which had made it the preserve of the privileged classes. Second, emphasis was shifted from observation to participation—from the product to the process—as event and spectator were brought into closer relationship. Sometimes the audience and the performers were the same. Third, emphasis shifted to awareness and away from the artist's intention. Fourth, simultaneity and multiple focus tended to replace orderly sequence and cause-to-effect arrangement. Usually there was no pretense that everyone could see and hear the same things at the same time. Fifth, since happenings were essentially nonverbal, they promoted the retreat from the conceptual into the perceptual. Thus, they tended to be multimedia events appealing to the total sensory apparatus.

Many of these ideas were synthesized in *environmental theatre,* a term popularized by Richard Schechner, then editor of *The Drama Review.* In 1968, Schechner published six "axioms" designed to clarify environmental theatre. First, he declares that events may be placed on a

FIGURE 19.22 *Commune* as presented by the Performance Group in 1970. Photograph by Elizabeth LeCompte.

continuum with "Pure/Art" at one end and "Impure/Life" at the other and extending from traditional theatre at one pole through environmental theatre to happenings and ending with public events and demonstrations at the other pole. Thus, he locates environmental theatre somewhere between traditional theatre and happenings. Second, in environmental theatre, "all the space is used for performance; all the space is used for the audience." Spectators are both "scene-makers" and "scene-watchers," for, as in a street scene from daily life, those who watch are part of the total picture, even when they consider themselves to be mere spectators. Third, "the event can take place either in a totally transformed space or in a 'found' space." In other words, space may be converted into an "environment" or a place may be accepted as it is and the production adapted to it. Fourth, "focus is flexible and variable." Fifth, "all production elements speak their own language" rather than being mere supports for words. Sixth, "a text need be neither the starting point nor the goal of a production. There may be no text at all." The key concept here is an extension of Kaprow's idea of environments, so that the site of a performance is

made an integral part of the whole, encompassing both actors and spectators so that they may interact as an entity. Such an attempt almost automatically means abandoning traditional theatre architecture in favor of places already suitable as environments or that may easily be converted. Furthermore, focus almost automatically becomes multiple or variable. Schechner considers the Polish Laboratory Theatre, the Living Theatre, the Open Theatre, and several other groups to be environmental.

In 1968 Schechner formed his own company, the Performance Group, to carry out some of his ideas. Their theatre is a converted garage with towers and platforms scattered about it (the arrangement changes somewhat from one production to another) all of which may be used by both actors and spectators. Their first production was *Dionysus in 69,* a reworking of Euripides' *The Bacchae* into a series of rituals, most of them relating to the flesh and sex or to freedom and repression. Overall, the production became a plea for greater freedom coupled with a warning against blindly throwing off restraints. Subsequently the group presented *Makbeth* (based on Shakespeare's play), *Commune* (1970), a company-created work about the American past and present, and Sam Shepard's *The Tooth of Crime* (1973), a play about rivalries in the pop music world treated in terms of gangsterism. Its greatest success was won with the production in 1975 of Brecht's *Mother Courage.*

One of the groups cited by Schechner as a major example of environmental theatre—the Open Theatre—attracted a large following during the 1960s. Founded in 1963 by Peter Feldman and Joseph Chaikin, the Open Theatre was more nearly a workshop than a producing organization, and showed its work publicly only at irregular intervals. It was concerned especially with exploiting those aspects of the theatre that distinguish it from films and television—the sense of direct human contact and its constantly changing components. It drew heavily on "role playing" and "games" theories of human behavior, especially as they relate to "transformation" (that is, the idea that reality constantly shifts as we take on and discard roles in relation to the changing context). The Open Theatre utilized many techniques reminiscent of Grotowski's "poor theatre": the actors wore rehearsal clothes which remained unchanged throughout a performance; they used no makeup and few properties; scenery was almost nonexistent and lighting minimal; actors performed in a large open space; and they moved freely out of one role into another in a series of transformations.

The relationship between the Open Theatre and its playwrights was close. Typically, the writer supplied an outline, scenes, situations or motifs; working from this base, the actors explored the possibilities through improvisations, metaphorical associations, and other techniques; the playwright then selected those results that seemed most effective. Some of these experiments came to nothing, but others yielded outstanding results, especially in collaboration with Terry and Van Itallie. Megan Terry (1932–   ) is probably best known for *Viet Rock* (1966), a play about the horrors of war in Vietnam. She also used transformational techniques in works not written for the Open Theatre, most notably in *Approaching Simone* (1970), which traces the life of the French philosopher and mystic Simone Weil. Perhaps Jean-Claude van Itallie's (1936–   ) best work is *The Serpent* (1969), which mingles material from the Bible with recent events, such as the assassinations of John F. Kennedy and Martin Luther King, and suggests that the serpent is that impulse within man that makes him break the limits set on him, whereas God is an idea invented by man to set limits on himself.

In 1970 the Open Theatre was reconstituted as a collective and thereafter performed primarily for university and prison audiences. It was dissolved in 1974. Chaikin has since worked on a production of *Electra*, and with Van Itallie he created *A Fable* (1975), concerning a journey in search of the "golden times." Megan Terry founded her own company, the Omaha Magic Theatre, which she seeks to root in the community. Other former members of Chaikin's group established the Medicine Show Theatre Ensemble. Thus, though the Open Theatre has been dissolved, its influence continues.

Other important off-off-Broadway groups of the 1960s included the Judson Poets' Theatre (founded in 1961 by Al Carmines and especially important for promoting small-scale musicals, most of them written by Carmines); the American Place Theatre (founded in 1964 by Wynn Handman to rejuvenate the American theatre by encouraging outstanding authors to write plays, and now housed in one of the mid-Manhattan skyscrapers which, owing to tax incentives, have included theatres); and Theatre Genesis (established in 1964 by Ralph Cook and housed in St. Mark's in the Bowery).

In the 1970s off-off-Broadway was subjected to many of the same stresses that earlier had afflicted off-Broadway. In 1975 Actors Equity, in an attempt to improve the economic position of its members, sought to end showcase productions, a major element in off-off-Broadway. Under the showcase arrangement, a company could present a play for a limited number of performances without paying any of those involved. This permitted many plays and actors to be seen that could not have been financed under union restrictions. The Equity proposal was roundly rejected by its members. Thus, the showcase arrangement has survived and off-off-Broadway continues, at least for the time being, to be the most lively part of New York's theatre.

There are about 150 off-off-Broadway groups of one sort or another, and among them they produce an average of fifty plays each week. Many companies are linked through the Off-Off-Broadway Alliance, formed in 1972 to assist members with common problems. The companies are so numerous that only a few can be named here. Some of the best are the Chelsea Theatre Center (headed by Robert Kalfin at the Brooklyn Academy of Music and noted especially for its outstanding program of foreign plays); the Ridiculous Theatrical Company (which specializes in outrageous parodies of popular cul-

FIGURE 19.23 David Rabe's *Streamers.* Directed by Mike Nichols. Photograph by Martha Swope.

FIGURE 19.24 Scene from *The Domestic Resurrection Circus* as performed by the Bread and Puppet Theatre in Vermont, 1974. Courtesy Craig Hamilton.

ture myths); the Manhattan Project (headed by André Gregory and noted especially for its improvisations on *Alice in Wonderland* and *Endgame*); Mabou Mines (headed by Lee Breuer), creator of "animations" in which narrations accompany experiments with music and words; the Manhattan Theatre Club, which since 1970 has sought to assist new playwrights through readings and productions in its three theatres; the CSC Repertory and Circle Repertory Theatre Company, both of which present plays in rotation; and Richard Foreman's Onto-logical-Hysteric Theatre, which in its visually oriented presentations seeks to subvert the familiar and open up new perceptions. Together these groups cover an enormous range.

The work of Robert Wilson stands somewhat apart from these off-off-Broadway groups. Wilson, primarily a visual artist, calls his productions—among them *Deafman Glance* (1970) and *Letter to Queen Victoria* (1974)— "operas." Typically they are very long (most around twelve hours, although one required 168 hours), one of the most prominent traits being slow motion (it often takes more than an hour for a character to complete a single sequence), through which Wilson seeks to alter perceptual awareness and place the audience and

the performers in touch with their own inner consciousness and reveal their obsessive fantasies.

Of all the off-off-Broadway groups, the New York Shakespeare Festival Public Theatre is now the most important. It is the creation of Joseph Papp (1921-   ), who began work in 1954 with the New York Shakespeare Festival, which since 1957 has given performances free of charge in Central Park, where the municipally owned Delacorte Theatre was inaugurated in 1962 to accommodate it. In 1964 Papp began to take some of his productions into New York's neighborhoods, since one of his goals was to reach unsophisticated audiences and prove to them that theatre could be both entertaining and relevant. In 1967 Papp acquired the Astor Library and converted it into the Public Theatre with five auditoriums. It opened with *Hair* (which after its initial run was restaged on Broadway by O'Horgan to become one of the greatest hits of the decade). Since then Papp has run an increasingly complex program and has become one of the principal suppliers of hits to Broadway, among them *Two Gentlemen of Verona* and *Much Ado About Nothing*, the Pulitzer Prize winning plays *No Place to Be Somebody* (by Charles Gordone) and *That Championship Season* (by Jason Miller), and the musical *Chorus Line*.

601

Furthermore, Papp's productions have garnered a large number of the awards given annually for excellence in the theatre. Nevertheless, Papp has been dogged by financial problems and on several occasions has been threatened with closure. These problems were eased after 1971 when the city of New York purchased the Public Theatre and leased it back to Papp for one dollar per year. In 1973 Papp was named to replace Jules Irving at Lincoln Center, but this has not curbed Papp's other work.

Together the off-Broadway and off-off-Broadway theatres have produced plays by a vast number of young dramatists. Unfortunately, few of these writers have lived up to their promise. Those who have been most successful include Sam Shepard, author of more than 100 plays, such as *Chicago* (1965), *Operation Side-winder* (1970), and *The Tooth of Crime* (1973); Rochelle Owens, with *Futz* (1961) and *Beclch* (1969); Paul Foster, with *Balls* (1964) and *Tom Paine* (1968); Terrence McNally, with *Sweet Eros* (1968), *Next* (1969), and *Whiskey* (1973); David Rabe, with *The Basic Training of Pavlo Hummel* (1971), *Sticks and Bones* (1971), and *Streamers* (1976), Lanford Wilson with *The Rimers of Eldritch* (1967), *Hot L Baltimore* (1973) and *The Mound Builders* (1975); Ronald Ribman with *Harry, Noon and Night* (1965), *The Ceremony of Innocence* (1968) and *The Poison Tree* (1976); Israel Horovitz with *The Indian Wants the Bronx* (1968), *Line* (1968), and *The Primary English Class* (1976); and Robert Patrick with *Kennedy's Children* (1973) and *Play by Play* (1975).

The off-Broadway and off-off-Broadway playwrights have been more important as a group than individually, for together they have done much to shift American drama toward experimentation with form and toward disaffection from the mores and values of the past in subject matter. Virtually all have abandoned the cause-to-effect arrangement of incidents leading from exposition to complication, crisis, and resolution, in favor of organizational patterns more nearly musical—that is, the introduction of a theme followed by variations on it. Characteristically, these works are episodic and loosely organized; most downgrade language in favor of nonverbal sound, song, music, and metaphorical spectacle, the whole usually intended to convey some perception about popular attitudes, political or social conditions or lifestyle. The plays have also done much to lessen earlier strictures on acceptable subject matter, behavior, and language in the theatre. Perhaps the most notable changes came with the introduction of nudity and obscenity, both of which made their first great impact in 1968 with the appearance of *Hair* on Broadway. In 1969 *Che!* brought explicit sexual acts on stage and later that year *Oh, Calcutta* included a large number of scenes performed entirely in the nude. By the early 1970s, although the limits of permissibility were still somewhat vague, almost any sexual theme or obscenity had become potential material for stage use.

The kind of theatrical activity associated with off-off-Broadway was not confined to New York. During the 1970s small nonprofit professional companies sprang up throughout the country as working on one's own terms came to seem more important than commercial success in the traditional theatre. "Alternative theatre" came to be the term used to describe these companies. In 1975 a periodical, *Alternative Theatre*, was launched as a voice for the approximately ninety affiliated groups. Some of the best groups outside of New York have been the Iowa Theatre Lab, the ProVisional Theatre and the Berkeley Stage Company (in California), the Otrabanda Company (in Louisiana), and the Cambridge Ensemble (in Massachusetts).

A number of alternative theatres grew out of the political and social unrest of the 1960s, when they were most usually referred to as "radical theatres." Of these, the most sophisticated artistically was the Bread and Puppet Theatre, founded in 1961 by Peter Schumann and based in New York until 1970 when it moved to Vermont. Using puppets of varying sizes, live actors, and stories based on myths, the Bible, and well-known tales, it seeks to promote love, charity, and humility and to denounce the evils of materialism and deception. Other important radical theatres were the San Francisco Mime Troupe (founded in 1959 by R. G. Davis to perform silent plays, radicalized in 1966, after which it rejected Davis and presented agit-prop spoken plays about current issues performed in a broad caricature style); El Teatro Campesino (founded in 1965 by Luis Valdez to dramatize the plight of grape pickers in California and later used to encourage pride in Mexican-Americans); and the Free Southern Theatre (founded in 1963–1964 by Gilbert Moses and John O'Neal as an extension of the civil rights movement). During the 1960s a number of people also became interested in "guerrilla" theatre—seizing on a gathering or occasion and presenting unscheduled, brief, pithy, attention-getting skits as means of arousing interest in some issue. As the mood of the country changed in the 1970s, guerrilla theatre declined rapidly and the radical theatres tended to lose their uniqueness as alternative groups grew in number.

One of the most encouraging developments after 1960 was the emergence of a strong black theatre movement. It differed from its forerunners in accepting the integrity of the black experience and in its unwillingness to compromise because of white sensibilities. It began in 1963 with the Free Southern Theatre and received additional impetus in 1964 when LeRoi Jones and others founded the Black Arts Repertoire Theatre School in New York, although this organization soon came to an end because the radical tone of some productions brought a cessation of government funding which had partially supported it. Other organizations soon sprang up throughout the country. By the late 1960s there were more than forty groups, three of them of special importance. The Negro Ensemble Company (NEC), founded in New York in 1968 and directed by Douglas Turner Ward, Robert Hooks, and Gerald S. Krone, produced a wide range of plays meaningful to blacks though not necessarily written by blacks. The quality of its work has generally been high, but it has often been accused of insufficient dedication to the black cause, a charge which it has in recent years tried to disprove. Nevertheless, it is the only one of the three groups that still survives as a significant force in the theatre. The New Lafayette Theatre, founded in 1967 by Robert Macbeth, served as something of a cultural center for Harlem. After 1969 it received several grants intended to encourage plays about black life. It also served as a clearing house for black groups throughout the country through an information service and through *Black Theatre Magazine.* Unfortunately, dissension within the company brought its dissolution in 1973. Neither of these groups was sufficiently separatist to suit LeRoi Jones (now called Imamu Amiri Baraka), who, totally alienated from whites, headed the Spirit House in Newark, dedicated to a wholly black culture. These three groups inspired a great many others, although some were not able to survive. But in the mid-1970s there were numerous black theatre companies in the United States, most of them linked through the Black Theatre Alliance.

The upsurge in black theatrical activity brought a corresponding increase in opportunities for black actors (among them James Earl Jones, Ruby Dee, Diana Sands, Claudia McNeill, Ossie Davis, Roscoe Lee Brown, Moses Gunn, Robert Hooks, Ron O'Neal, Clifton Davis, and Cicely Tyson) and directors (among them Michael Schultz, Robert Macbeth, Lloyd Richards, and Melvin van Peebles). Furthermore, the number of black dramatists increased yearly. Some representative writers are

FIGURE 19.25 Scene from Joseph A. Walker's *The River Niger,* as produced by the Negro Ensemble Company, 1972. Photograph by Bert Andrews.

Hansberry, Jones, Bullins, Ward, Elder, Walker, and Gordone.

Lorraine Hansberry (1930–1965) won recognition with *A Raisin in the Sun* (1959), a compassionate drama about a hardworking black family in Chicago whose dreams are shattered but whose values mature in the process. Before her untimely death, Miss Hansberry completed only one more play, *The Sign in Sidney Brustein's Window* (1964), concerning a naive idealist who is too busy to recognize the problems within his own family. Some of Miss Hansberry's uncompleted works have also been assembled by her husband, Robert Nemiroff.

LeRoi Jones (Imamu Amiri Baraka, 1934–   ) is one of the most important of black writers both for the quality of his work and because his career illustrates the movement of many black writers away from interest in integration to a desire for separatism. His early plays, such as *The Toilet* (1964) and *Dutchman* (1964), treat black-white relationships—often sympathetically, sometimes bitterly, but with considerable understanding and compassion. After the mid-1960s Jones became increasingly anti-white, an attitude reflected in such plays as

FIGURE 19.26 Interior of the Tyrone Guthrie Theatre, Minneapolis. Note the thrust stage and steeply banked seating. Sir Tyrone Guthrie's 1963 production of Chekhov's *The Three Sisters,* The Guthrie Theatre, Minneapolis/St. Paul.

Home on the Range and *The Death of Malcolm X.* One of the most powerful of his later plays is *Slave Ship* (1969), which traces the black experience from African days to the present and seeks to build solidarity among blacks and a total rejection of white society.

The most prolific of black writers has been Ed Bullins (1935-   ), formerly resident playwright at the New Lafayette Theatre and editor of *Black Theatre Magazine,* and from 1971 till 1973 associate director of the New Lafayette. After leaving the New Lafayette, he headed a workshop for playwrights at Papp's Public Theatre. His work is varied in subject and tone, but it is unified by a concern for and pride in blackness. He is now writing a lengthy cycle of plays about black life in the industrial North and West, of which *In the Wine Time* and *In New England Winter* have been shown with considerable success. One of Bullins' prime targets is the black pseudointellectual, as in *The Electronic Nigger*

(1968) and *Clara's Old Man* (1965), although the latter play is more deeply concerned with how life has forced a woman to assume responsibilities abdicated by others. Other plays by Bullins include *The Pig Pen* (1970) and *The Taking of Miss Janie* (1975). Of current black writers, Bullins is probably the most respected.

The Negro Ensemble Company has achieved considerable success with the plays of Ward, Elder, and Walker. Douglas Turner Ward, the NEC's artistic director, through such works as *Day of Absence* (1967) and *The Reckoning* (1969), has used broad caricature to show blacks outwitting whites and to suggest that they have been forced into deception in order to survive. Lonne Elder III, director of the NEC's playwriting program, is noted for one play, *Ceremonies in Dark Old Men* (1969), a compassionate play about life in Harlem and the ceremonies men enact in order to escape their unpleasant situation. One of the NEC's greatest successes was won with Joseph A. Walker's *The River Niger* (1972), which, using three generations of a black family in Harlem, seeks to trace the black man's odyssey. Ultimately it is a debate drama about racial obligations and roots and an argument for the importance of action. Its high point is a poem, "The River Niger," written by the sixty-year-old, near alcoholic father, which metaphorically depicts the African stream reaching all the way into Harlem.

Charles Gordone is noted for one play, *No Place to Be Somebody* (1969), a Pulitzer Prize winning drama about a black man's attempt to start his own version of the Mafia and the violence his plan engenders. The strength of the play, however, lies in its characters and their interrelationships.

Other black playwrights who might be mentioned include Richard Wesley, Ben Caldwell, Ron Milner, Ossie Davis, Adrienne Kennedy, Melvin van Peebles, Ted Shine, Philip Hayes Dean, Vinette Carroll, and Leslie Lee. By the mid-1970s the emphasis in black playwriting was shifting away from defining the black experience through negative comparisons with whites and toward viewing blacks in relation to other blacks. Perhaps most encouraging, it now appears that black theatre and drama may for the first time in American history be able to sustain themselves on a continuing basis.

In addition to blacks, other ethnic groups, especially Puerto Rican, Mexican-American, and Native American, have become increasingly concerned with theatre during the 1970s. Many of these theatres seek to promote social action and to establish a close relationship with the communities they serve. Still other theatres have been established to express the concerns and serve the needs of women, homosexuals, and other minority groups.

The 1960s saw the greatest expansion of the American theatre outside of New York since the nineteenth century. The first important impetus came in 1959 when the Ford Foundation made sizeable grants to a number of small companies that had managed to gain footholds in cities scattered throughout the country. This financial boost permitted such groups as the Alley Theatre in Houston, the Arena Stage in Washington, and the Actors' Workshop in San Francisco to become fully professional and relatively stable. The movement toward resident companies was further strengthened when Tyrone Guthrie announced his intention of founding a theatre in Minneapolis. When his theatre was opened in

1963 the favorable publicity motivated other cities to seek similar companies. By 1966 the regional theatres had so burgeoned (to about thirty-five) that for the first time in the twentieth century more actors were employed outside of than in New York. These troupes resembled European subsidized theatres in presenting a repertory of classics and recent successes and in relying little on new plays. But unlike their European counterparts they had no assured financial support from one year to the next.

A step toward acknowledging the government's responsibility to support the arts was taken in 1965 when federal legislation established the National Endowment for the Arts as an agency to make grants of appropriated funds to groups or projects with considerable potential for growth and audience appeal. Since then federal appropriations for the arts have steadily increased, although they are still woefully small in proportion to the country's population. The federal government has also encouraged each state to establish an arts council, and consequently most states now have an official body charged with assisting and encouraging the arts. Many of these groups now provide at least some subsidy to theatres. In addition, regional councils have linked member states in an effort to coordinate plans for assisting the arts. Despite these advances, few theatre groups have any assurance of continuing financial assistance (as do European companies) and consequently they seldom can make long-range plans. So, resident theatres have come and gone with some regularity. Still, in 1976 there were approximately fifty resident companies outside of New York.

Resident companies have become increasingly attractive to playwrights, since pressures there are considerably fewer than on Broadway. Resident groups usually are not concerned with long runs, nor do they expect to succeed or fail on the basis of a single production. Thus, they can afford to take more chances. Several resident companies—among them the Arena Stage in Washington, the Long Wharf Theatre in New Haven, and the Dallas Theatre Center—have been especially helpful to writers.

During the 1960s universities also increased their involvement with the theatre and a number of them established resident companies. The University Resident Theatre Association now includes about forty member groups ranging from those that are fully professional to those composed entirely of students.

The period since 1960 has been one of great innovation, experimentation, growth, and change for the

American theatre—a time of great vitality and of great anxiety. But with the early 1970s came uncertainty about almost every aspect of life—social, economic, political, educational, artistic—and a mood of hesitation and doubt, a state from which we have yet to recover.

POSTSCRIPT

What the future will bring for the theatre can only be a matter for speculation, for accurate prediction would require the ability to foresee the course of world events. Western theatre has always reflected changing views about man and his world. Thus, as conceptions about psychology, morality, sociology, and politics have altered, so too has the theatre. Many recent innovations which now seem important will in the future no doubt fade into oblivion because they were false starts, whereas others, perhaps unnoted in this book, will in retrospect be recognized as forerunners of major changes. History is constantly being rewritten because it is from present perspectives that we view the past, and as our values and interests change, so too does our estimate of the past. It is future conceptions of man—what sort of creature he is, what kinds of appeals must be made to his senses, what kinds of personal, moral, social, and political ideals he is capable of sustaining—that will determine the direction to be taken by theatre and drama. And that is history yet to be lived and written.

LOOKING AT THEATRE HISTORY

For the most part, history has been written from what is called the "consensus" point of view; that is, historians in each era have more or less consciously sought to agree on the significant issues and events and to focus on them. This does not mean there has always been unanimity among historians or that ideas about the appropriate focus have not changed from one generation to another, but it does mean that once a view or approach is accepted, it tends to become the norm for its age. For theatre history this point can best be illustrated in relation to the American situation, where the "melting pot" theory of culture has led to an almost total preoccupation with tracing the mainstream of the English-language stage. While that aspect of American theatre unquestionably is important, even primary, the "consensus" attitude has discouraged interest in the multicultural richness of the nation's theatrical history. As a result, most of us know little (or even care) about the theatrical traditions of Native Americans (the Indians), Mexican-Americans, Chinese-Americans, or the various foreign-language, religious and other groups that have contributed to the totality of our theatrical heritage. Since 1960 the consensus approach to history has come under strong attack, and increasingly there has been an attempt to broaden the scope of historical inquiry. These beginnings have yet to be fully implemented in theatre history. Until they are, the richness of our past will not be fully revealed to us.

Challenge to "consensus theatre" was also a hallmark of the 1960s. No group was more crucial in this role than the Living Theatre. Its challenge reached a climax in *Paradise Now* (1968), described by the company as "a vertical ascent toward Permanent Revolution." The production's most notorious feature, direct confrontation with audiences, was little understood, for in actuality the audience was cast as obstacles to successful revolution. Here is a passage from the printed version of the work:

> *The Confrontations are an attempt to define and thereby understand the characteristics of the stumbling block at each [phase], and of the form of action that can overcome it. Thus at the beginning the stumbling block is The Culture which is overcome by Aesthetic Assault; and at the end the stumbling block is Stasis which is overcome by Impetus. The Confrontations are guides to the relationship between the actor and the public at each stage of the trip. The Resistance to the Revolutionary Change is treated as the obstacle. The energy form designed is an appropriate strategy for the actor to use to transform the obstacle.*
>
> *Paradise Now, Collective Creation of the Living Theatre,* Written down by

Judith Malina and Julian Beck (New York: Vintage Books, 1971), pp. 11–12.

One major goal since 1960 has been to discover what is truly essential to "theatre." The search is probably best summed up in Grotowski's conception of "the poor theatre":

By gradually eliminating whatever proved superfluous, we found that theatre can exist without make-up, without autonomic costume and scenography, without a separate performance area (stage), without lighting and sound effects, etc. It cannot exist without the actor-spectator relationship of perceptual, direct, "live" communion. . . . when rigorously tested in practice it undermines most of our usual ideas about theatre. It challenges the notion of theatre as a synthesis of disparate creative disciplines. . . . This "synthetic theatre" is the contemporary theatre, which we readily call the "Rich Theatre"—rich in flaws.

JERZY GROTOWSKI, *Towards a Poor Theatre* (New York: Simon and Schuster, 1968), p. 19.

Simultaneously, all the technological means of the space age were being adapted to theatrical purposes, barriers between the arts were being broken down, and multimedia events of all sorts were flourishing. Josef Svoboda is probably the best known of those who sought to extend the theatre's range of expression through technological devices. Here are some excerpts from his statements about the production of Luigi Nonno's opera *Intoleranza* (produced in Boston in 1965):

Instead of film I used television techniques in such a way as to project a TV image onto many screens placed on the stage. . . . We were able to transmit parallel actions that were performed in adjoining studios, in fact in studios as far as three miles from the stage. All these studios were joined with each other by audio and visual monitors, so that the actors could see the conductor in relation to themselves, the actors in the studio could see what was being played on the stage, and . . . the actors on the stage see what was played in the studios. In this way, the conductor was absolute master of the rhythm of the performance. . . .

JARKA BURIAN, *The Scenography of Josef Svoboda* (Middletown, Conn.: Wesleyan University Press, 1971), p. 103.

By the 1970s the ferment of the 1960s had faded. Here are some of Margaret Croyden's comments on what went wrong:

As in the case of movements composed of all kinds of personalities, and especially where personality was itself supposed to be an artistic vehicle, some individuals lost sight of their original aim of building an authentic new theatre and got caught up in all sorts of fads and ego trips. . . . untried techniques were grafted onto undigested philosophies, the gestalt therapy theories mixed with R. D. Laing, confrontation politics with Artaud, consciousness expansion with Yoga, spontaneity with disciplined exercise, guruism with collective living, freakism with simplicity.

A serious problem . . . was the experimentalists' reliance on self-expression as a predominant aesthetic—the old romantic tenet. Self-expression became the answer to all arguments and served to hide a dearth of shallow ideas and unworkable theatrics. . . . it cultivated an intense and limited subjectivism and bred . . . a new anti-intellectualism. . . .

MARGARET CROYDEN, *Lunatics, Lovers and Poets: The Contemporary Experimental Theatre* (New York: McGraw-Hill Book Co., 1974), p. 289.

Of the dominant mood in the mid-1970s, Hilton Kramer writes:

The idea of the avant-garde, which commanded such immense prestige in the 60s, no longer inspires the same automatic assent. . . .

The appetite for outrage and innovation, for shock and squalor, for assaults on the audience and on the medium, has clearly diminished, where it has not completely disappeared. The taste now is for clarity and coherence, for the beautiful and the recognizable, for narrative, melody, pathos, glamour, romance, and the instantly comprehensible. . . . for art that is a pleasure rather than a moral contest.

Does this mean that the innovations of the 60s have disappeared without trace? Not at all, but where they survive . . . they have been . . . co-opted by the establishment, and put to eminently more benign use.

"A Yearning for 'Normalcy'—The Current Backlash in the Arts," *The New York Times*, May 23, 1976, Section 2, pp. 1, 25.

One of the ways of studying contemporary theatre history is by reading magazines and newspapers that report on current productions, experiments and theories. This is especially crucial for keeping up with the contemporary theatre, since it usually takes a year or more for a book to get into print. Some of the publications that are helpful in keeping abreast of current happenings in the theatre are listed at the end of this book's bibliography.

Perhaps even more important in the study of contemporary theatre history is regular attendance at theatrical performances, for what one sees on the stage tonight is a part of tomorrow's history. Few historical accounts of an event can ever be as vivid as personal participation in it.

Appendix

This book has not provided a systematic statement about the nature, scope, materials, and methods of historical study. For those interested, such a statement is given here in an article that I wrote for a Conference on Theatre Research held at Princeton University in 1966. A few alterations have been made in the original version, which may be found in Educational Theatre Journal, *XIX (June 1967), 267–275.*

I. NATURE AND SCOPE OF THEATRE HISTORY

The purpose of theatre history is to describe and explain the theatre as it has existed at specific times and places and to trace its successive changes. Like other branches of history, it seeks to provide a record of the past; in addition, it explores the causes and significance of events and seeks to set them in the appropriate artistic, intellectual, social, and economic context, and to relate them to the total development of the theatre.

Theatre history may appeal to many interests. First, and perhaps most fundamental, it may satisfy that basic human desire to understand more fully an important institution. Since the theatre is one of man's significant creations, its history is an important humanistic study. It may also serve more specialized needs. It aids in the understanding of the present theatre by showing the conditions out of which it has come, and may give insight and guidance for the future. It can also be a source of inspiration for practicing theatre artists by providing information and suggesting possibilities which may be adapted or transformed for modern audiences.

The scope of theatre history is extremely broad, for there is scarcely any aspect of human experience that is not at times relevant to it. Furthermore, the theatre itself is extremely complex, incorporating as it does so many elements from other areas: literature, the visual arts, music, and dance. Thus, a vast number of interests may be included under the general heading of theatre history: attempts to define the place of the theatre in various societies and cultures, to describe the theatre arts as they have been practiced in successive periods, to trace the major movements and styles and their interrelationships, to study individual artists and their contributions, to outline the artistic, social, intellectual, and economic milieu, and other similar topics. The scope may be further indicated by listing some of the typical areas of research: playwrights and plays, theatre architecture, theatrical management, directors and directing, actors and acting, scene designers and scenery, stage properties, machinery and special effects, costume designers and costumes, lighting, stage make-up, audiences, and theatrical criticism.

Theatre history should be extended as well to include such popular entertainments as variety and music halls, vaudeville and burlesque, and pantomime, since concentration upon the production of the "literary drama" has often obscured the importance of these activities to the history of the theatre. Studies of music (especially opera and musical comedy) and dance (especially ballet) also contribute much to our knowledge of the theatre.

Thus, the nature and scope of theatre history are such as to require both learning in the broadest sense and very specialized knowledge. As in other types of historical research, theatre history involves three basic steps: (1) the discovery and collection of pertinent evidence, (2) the criticism of evidence, and (3) the communication of results. Each is essential, and all require special skills.

II. MATERIALS FOR RESEARCH IN THEATRE HISTORY

The first task which faces the theatre historian after he has formulated a line of inquiry is the discovery of pertinent information. Unfortunately, a large share of the materials for theatre history is of unusually ephemeral nature. The theatrical performance exists briefly and then is gone forever; when we seek to define its quality or to reconstruct the process by which it came into being, we must depend principally upon accounts which are partial and personal.

As in other types of historical research, the materials for theatre history may be divided into primary and secondary sources. Primary sources are those which form a first-hand record of the original event: the prompt script, the stage upon which the play was performed, the scene and costume designs, photographs, engravings or other visual records of the production, reviews of the performance, and so on. It is such primary materials that the historian must seek out whenever possible. When he cannot find such records he may have to depend upon secondary sources, or accounts removed from the event itself: the playscript without any indications of how it may have been adapted for performance, descriptions of the stage and visual elements, second-hand reports of the performance, and so on.

The kinds of materials needed by the theatre historian are as diverse as theatre history is complex.

Some of those which must be available are:

1. *Scripts*
   Playscripts (especially as altered or adapted for a specific production)
   Promptbooks
   Actors' "sides"
2. *Music*
   Musical scores for theatrical pieces (operas, musical comedies, ballad operas, melodramas, etc.)
   Incidental music used for specific productions as indicated in play scripts, promptbooks, etc.
3. *Dance*
   Dance notations (or scores) for specific productions
   Other indications of dances (types, descriptions, etc.) found in scripts or in separate form
4. *Legal Documents Relating to the Theatre*
   Deeds of property or assignments of rights
   Contracts (relating to buildings, actors, designers, dramatists, etc.)
   Decrees, laws, or regulations promulgated by rulers or governing bodies designed to affect the theatre or theatrical personnel
   Probated wills
5. *Official Records*
   Records maintained by governments: didaskalic records of ancient contests; Office of Revels accounts; Lord Chamberlain's records; copyright and patent records; licenses for theatres and plays; records of payments or production arrangements by guilds, municipal governments, court officials, etc.
   Accounts and day books of theatrical companies and producers
   Correspondence of producing groups, government officials, etc.
6. *Advertisements and Playbills*
   Posters   Playbills
   Programs   Other forms of publicity
   Newspaper advertisements and announcements
7. *Original Designs, Sketches, Plans, Elevations*
   Buildings   Costumes
   Scenery   Lighting
   Machinery   Properties and special effects
8. *Other Pictorial Materials*
   Photographs of productions, actors, dancers, settings, costumes, buildings, etc.
   Engravings
   Easel and vase paintings
   Sculpture and bas reliefs
   Frescoes and other wall paintings
   Floor plans and diagrams for buildings, machinery, special effects, etc.
   Motion Pictures

9. *Artifacts*

Architectural remains of theatre buildings	Machinery
	Recordings and tapes
Costumes and masks	Promptbooks
Settings	Tickets
Lighting instruments	Programs
Properties	

10. *Personal Accounts*

Autobiographies	Memoirs
Interviews	Letters
Reviews	Diaries

Contemporary novels, plays, etc., which give details of contemporary life

11. *Theoretical Treatises*

Playwriting	Properties
Directing	Theatre music
Acting	Theatre architecture
Scenery	Theatrical dance
Lighting	Audience and audience psychology
Costume	Theatre aesthetics
Makeup	

12. *Historical, Biographical, and Critical Accounts*

Compilations of theatrical annals
Accounts of specific events, periods, and movements
Biographies of persons associated with the theatre
Critical evaluations of the work of playwrights, actors, directors, and other theatrical personnel
General histories of the theatre
Cultural and social histories

This summary of appropriate materials might be rearranged in a number of ways to indicate more specifically a relationship to each of the theatre arts, to particular periods, movements, countries, or personalities. The compilation as given, however, should be sufficient to indicate the wide range of materials required in theatre history and the difficulties likely to be involved in gathering evidence.

Although the kinds of materials needed by the historian for a specific project may be easily identified, it is no simple task to locate them. There are now a number of excellent theatre collections, but few have systematically acquired materials according to established standards of inclusiveness. As a result they often have extremely wide ranges with little depth of coverage, or may have excellent primary materials in a limited area without adequate supplementary items. Because of the haphazardness with which many collections have grown, it is extremely difficult for a scholar to determine the location of the materials he needs for his research, or even if the materials have been preserved. The size and rep-

utation of some collections make them obvious sources to consult; clues can also be gathered from the footnotes, bibliographies, and prefaces of scholarly works in the same general area of inquiry; much time can usually be saved by consulting such works as *Performing Arts Collections; An International Handbook;* and researchers through experience develop many short-cuts of their own. None of these methods is very precise, however, and sometimes scholars spend as much time in locating the appropriate collection as in using the materials after it is found.

Furthermore, the materials in theatre collections are often inadequately catalogued, in large part because so many of them are not in the form of books and periodicals, the typical content of libraries. Ephemeral items, such as programs, posters, engravings, designs, and scrapbooks, pose difficult and time-consuming problems for cataloguers. A single engraving, for example, may be pertinent to a specific author, director, a number of actors, a scene designer, and so on. Seldom, however, is it indexed under all of these. The researcher consequently cannot assume that the catalogue of a collection will guide him to all of the available evidence and thus he may need to undertake independent searches in order to uncover the material he is seeking.

Regardless of the difficulties, it is one of the scholar's responsibilities to judge when he has acquired sufficient evidence for his particular research. It is seldom possible to know with certainty when all of the pertinent evidence has been found, but it should be an article of the historian's faith not to be content until he is reasonably sure that his search is complete. If adequate evidence cannot be assembled, then either the historian must content himself with essaying tenative judgments or abandon his topic for another which can be answered more satisfactorily with the available information.

III. THE CRITICISM AND USE OF EVIDENCE

Although the discovery of evidence is indispensable, it is merely preliminary to the historian's principal task, the intelligent use of the evidence. At this stage, the scholar's critical faculties must be exercised in a number of ways.

First comes the task of authenticating the documents which have been discovered. Historians have often gone astray through the indiscriminate use of evidence without due regard for the possiblity that documents may have been forged, altered in some way, inaccurately dated, or that they may be faulty in some other way. The historian must establish as clearly as he can the authority of the materials he uses.

The authentication of documents often requires quite specialized skills or knowledge. As examples, the authentication of engravings depicting stage settings may require considerable knowledge of the history of engraving and the styles of various engravers, whereas the authentication of promptbooks may call for knowledge about particular prompters, their handwriting, and so on.

It is unlikely, however, that a single researcher will have all the skills or information required to meet every situation. Consequently, he must often depend upon others in this phase of his work. Most frequently he relies upon the curators of theatre collections to determine the provenance of the materials in the collections. The accuracy with which this task is done depends in large part upon the available personnel, and those collections which can offer trustworthy aid to the historian do much to simplify his task. It is important that the scholar receive reliable help, for the value of his research depends in large part upon the validity of the documents he uses.

Second, the historian must make some estimate of the reliability of the information contained in the documents, since even authentic materials may contain completely inaccurate information. In dealing with a written description of an event, the scholar needs to ascertain whether or not it is an eye-witness account, how much time elapsed between the event and its recording, whether the witness had any reason to distort what he saw; in looking at a painting of a theatrical scene, he needs to know whether or not the artist was setting down what he saw on the stage or merely creating from his own imagination; for a theatre building he needs to know whether the structure has been altered since it was built; and so on.

The processes involved in testing the reliability of evidence are too complex to describe here, but are outlined in a number of works on historical method. Nevertheless, it is pertinent to point out that they often lead the historian through mazes of biographical, economic, social, legal, political, philosophical, religious, and other materials and that he must be capable and willing to pursue the path wherever it leads. The degree of confidence with which the historian can speak and the reliability of what he has to say is largely dependent upon the care he has taken to verify the evidence he uses.

Third, the historian must interpret his evidence. Even if he is sure that he has authentic documents and reliable information, in most cases he must still seek to discover the significant patterns which lie behind the evidence. Occasionally a historian may merely record the facts he has uncovered, but ordinarily facts are merely the foundation of historical writing. The historian aims not only to describe a particular event but to explain its meaning in its own time and for theatre history in general. He is often concerned with causation and significance, the most difficult questions one can pose. Consequently, it is in the interpretation of evidence that the historian's personal qualities of mind and training are of maximum importance, for it is here that he enters the realm of value judgments.

The interpretation of evidence requires that it be placed in a relevant context. Unfortunately it is no small task to decide upon the relevant context, for in any period it may include the literary and artistic movements of the time, the social, political, and philosophical interest of the day, the psychological states of the participants, and so on through a multitude of possible determinants. Although one may say that all of the relevant factors should be considered, this is seldom possible in a single work and one or more of the elements are usually emphasized above other possible ones. No historian can treat every aspect of a question and his work would probably become an endless and repetitious treatise if he attempted to do so. The clear definition of the questions being asked is the safest guide in determining which aspects are essential and which merely peripheral.

Although the ideal of objectivity in historical writing is often stated, it is an extremely difficult, and perhaps impossible, one to achieve. Nevertheless the historian can learn to be aware of his own prejudices and to take them into account in his evaluations. While a degree of subjectivity may be inevitable, it cannot excuse the deliberate suppression or distortion of evidence in order to bolster a prejudice or to prove a thesis.

Good historical writing gives exciting and perceptive views of the past, but not even the best can recreate an event in its entirety. Consequently, no historical account is apt to satisfy all readers or to retain its admirers more than a generation or two, for history is a dynamic process in which the past is constantly being reexamined in light of present interests; its attraction lies in large part in its relevance to our own situation and as interests change so do the interpretations of past events.

Historical writing, therefore, depends as much upon the interpretation of events as upon the factual evidence which forms its basis, and it needs to be read with a critical eye both for the view which has shaped it and the evidence which is used to support that view. Although the interpretation of evidence differs somewhat with each historian, a few basic patterns are discernible.

First, the historian may place primary emphasis upon the theatre as a social and cultural institution and thus may concentrate upon the theatre as an expression and outgrowth of social, political, economic, philosophical, or psychological forces of a particular time and place. Other antecedents, such as myth and ritual or national and racial characteristics, may also enter into such accounts.

Second, the historian may emphasize that the theatre is a product of individual artists. Thus he may adopt a biographical approach and describe the lives and works of those persons who were most prominent in the theatrical activities of specific times and places.

Third, the historian may emphasize the process by which theatrical performances come into being. He may seek to describe how the various theatre arts have been practiced in different periods, concentrating upon the procedures followed from the origin to the completion of a theatrical production.

Fourth, the historian may seek to describe and analyze the product—the performance in the theatre as seen by an audience. Here the principal concern is with the art object, and consequently considerable attention may be paid to stylistic, formal, and aesthetic questions.

Obviously few historical accounts stay within the limits of any one of these approaches, for most incorporate elements from all. It is impossible to designate one approach as more fruitful than another since the value of each is determined by its usefulness in answering the particular questions being pursued.

Historical accounts may also be classified according to whether they concentrate upon a limited topic or attempt to cover a wide sweep of time and place. Both are important. The limited, specific study is essential to provide a firm basis for the broad, synthesizing study, and in turn the general study can supply background and perspective for the limited study.

In the use of evidence, then, the historian must bring all of his critical faculties to bear on the authentication of documents, the verification of their contents, and the search for significant patterns of meaning.

IV. COMMUNICATING THE RESULTS OF HISTORICAL RESEARCH

Although a scholar may undertake historical research merely for his own enlightenment, a much wider audience benefits when the results are put in a form which can be transmitted to others. Ordinarily we accord the title of theatre historian only to those researchers who have published accounts of their work. Thus, the ability to write well is one of the skills needed by every historian.

We have come to recognize that the emergence of the professional historian near the end of the nineteenth century was accompanied by a marked decline in the popularity of historical writing with the general public. History became, and to a large extent remains, the output of specialists intended for an audience of other specialists. It is perhaps inevitable that a large proportion of historical writing will appeal only to a limited group, but it should not be accepted as inevitable that historical accounts must necessarily be dull fare. The ability to write well should be considered as much a qualification for the historian as the other skills demanded of him.

Even the best of writing, however, will not make certain types of works interesting to the general reader. Some of the most useful of existing works and others which should be compiled cannot attract a large public for they are essentially reference works designed for specialized use. Nevertheless, we should still demand of them clarity, accuracy, and an efficient format.

Bibliography

This bibliography lists books that are either the most authoritative or the most representative of major points of view. Except in rare cases, they are in English.

GENERAL WORKS

ALTMAN, GEORGE. *Theatre Pictorial: A History of World Theatre as Recorded in Drawings, Paintings, Engravings, and Photographs.* Berkeley, 1953.

BERTHOLD, MARGOT. *A History of World Theatre.* New York, 1972.

BOWMAN, WALTER P., AND BALL, ROBERT H. *Theatre Language: A Dictionary of Terms in English of the Drama and Stage from Medieval to Modern Times.* New York, 1961.

CHENEY, SHELDON. *The Theater: Three Thousand Years of Drama, Acting and Stagecraft.* Rev. ed. New York, 1972.

CLARK, BARRETT H., ed. *European Theories of the Drama.* Newly revised by Henry Popkin. New York, 1965.

COLE, TOBY, and CHINOY, HELEN K., eds. *Actors on Acting.* New revised edition. New York, 1970.

DUERR, EDWIN. *The Length and Depth of Acting.* New York, 1962.

DUKORE, BERNARD F., ed. *Dramatic Theory and Criticism; Greeks to Grotowski.* New York, 1974.

FREEDLEY, GEORGE, and REEVES, J. A. *A History of the Theatre.* 3rd ed. rev. New York, 1968.

GASCIOGNE, BAMBER. *World Theatre: An Illustrated History.* Boston, 1968.

GASSNER, JOHN. *Masters of the Drama.* 3rd ed. New York, 1954.

GASSNER, JOHN, AND ALLEN, RALPH, eds. *Theatre and Drama in the Making.* 2 vols. Boston, 1964.

GASSNER, JOHN, AND QUINN, E., eds. *The Reader's Encyclopedia of World Drama.* New York, 1969.

HARTNOLL, PHYLLIS, ed. *The Oxford Companion to the Theatre.* 3rd ed. London, 1967.

KINDERMANN, HEINZ. *Theatergeschichte Europas.* 8 vols. Salzburg, 1957–1972.

LAVER, JAMES. *Drama, Its Costume and Decor.* London, 1951.

MACGOWAN, KENNETH, and MELNITZ, WILLIAM. *The Living Stage.* Englewood Cliffs, N.J., 1955.

MANTZIUS, KARL. *A History of Theatrical Art in Ancient and Modern Times.* 6 vols. London, 1903–1921.

MOLINARI, CESARE. *Theatre Through the Ages.* New York, 1975.

NAGLER, ALOIS M. *Sources of Theatrical History.* New York, 1952.

NICOLL, ALLARDYCE. *The Development of the Theatre.* 5th ed. London, 1966.

———. *World Drama.* Rev. ed. London, 1976.

ROBERTS, VERA M. *On Stage: A History of the Theatre.* 2nd ed. New York, 1974.

SOUTHERN, RICHARD. *The Seven Ages of the Theatre.* New York, 1961.

STUART, DONALD C. *The Development of Dramatic Art.* New York, 1928.

WIMSATT, WILLIAM K., and BROOKS, CLEANTH. *Literary Criticism: A Short History.* New York, 1957.

Chapter 1: The Origins of the Theatre

"Arts, Human Behavior, and Africa." *African Studies Bulletin,* 5 (May 1962), 1–70.

BREASTED, JAMES H. *The Development of Religion and Thought in Ancient Egypt.* New York, 1912.

BROWN, IVOR. *The First Player: The Origin of Drama.* New York, 1928.

BUDGE, E. A. W. *Osiris and the Egyptian Resurrection.* 2 vols. New York, 1911.

CAMPBELL, JOSEPH. *The Masks of God: Occidental Mythology.* New York, 1964.

——. *The Masks of God: Primitive Mythology.* New York, 1959.

FRANKFORT, HENRI. *Ancient Egyptian Religion.* New York, 1948.

FRAZER, J. G. *The Golden Bough.* 12 vols. London, 1913–1915.

FREUD, SIGMUND. *Totem and Tabu.* Vienna, 1913.

GASTER, THEODOR. *Thespis: Ritual, Myth and Drama in the Ancient Near East.* New York, 1950.

GRAHAM-WHITE, ANTHONY. "Ritual and Drama in Africa." *Educational Theater Journal,* 22 (1970), 339–349.

HAVEMEYER, LOOMIS. *The Drama of Savage Peoples.* New Haven, 1916.

HERSKOVITS, MELVILLE. "Dramatic Expression among Primitive Peoples." *Yale Review,* 33 (1944), 683–698.

HUNNINGHER, BEN. *The Origin of the Theater.* New York, 1961.

HUIZINGA, JOHANN. *Homo Ludens: A Study of the Play Element in Culture.* Boston, 1955.

KIRBY, E. T. *Ur-Drama: The Origins of Theatre.* New York, 1975.

LÉVI-STRAUSS, CLAUDE. *The Savage Mind.* Chicago, 1966.

RIDGEWAY, WILLIAM. *The Drama and Dramatic Dances of Non-European Races.* Cambridge, 1915.

Chapter 2:   Theatre and Drama in Ancient Greece

ALLEN, JAMES T. *Greek Acting in the Fifth Century.* Berkeley, 1916.

——. *The Greek Theatre of the Fifth Century before Christ.* Berkeley, 1920.

ARNOTT, PETER D. *Greek Scenic Conventions in the Fifth Century, B.C.* Oxford, 1962.

——. *The Ancient Greek and Roman Theatre.* New York, 1971.

BIEBER, MARGARETE. *The History of the Greek and Roman Theater.* 2nd ed. Princeton, N.J., 1961.

BUTLER, JAMES H. *The Theatre and Drama of Greece and Rome.* San Francisco, 1972.

CORNFORD, FRANCIS M. *The Origin of Attic Comedy.* London, 1914.

ELSE, GERALD F. *The Origin and Early Form of Greek Tragedy.* Cambridge, Mass., 1965.

FLICKINGER, ROY C. *The Greek Theatre and Its Drama.* 4th ed. enlarged. Chicago, 1936.

GREENE, WILLIAM C. *Moira: Fate, Good and Evil in Greek Thought.* Cambridge, Mass., 1944.

HAMILTON, EDITH. *The Greek Way.* New York, 1952.

HARSH, PHILIP W. *A Handbook of Classical Drama.* Stanford, Calif., 1944.

JAEGER, WERNER. *Paideia: The Ideals of Greek Culture.* Trans. by Gilbert Highet. 3 vols. New York, 1939–1944.

KITTO, H. D. F. *Greek Tragedy.* 2nd ed. London, 1950.

LAWLER, LILLIAN B. *The Dance of the Ancient Greek Theatre.* Iowa City, 1964.

LEVER, KATHERINE. *The Art of Greek Comedy.* London, 1956.

MURRAY, GILBERT. *Euripides and His Age.* New York, 1913.

NICOLL, ALLARDYCE. *Masks, Mimes, and Miracles.* New York, 1931.

O'CONNOR, JOHN B. *Chapters in the History of Actors and Acting in Ancient Greece.* Chicago, 1908.

PICKARD-CAMBRIDGE, A. W. *Dithyramb, Tragedy, and Comedy.* 2nd ed., revised by T. B. L. Webster. Oxford, 1962.

——. *The Dramatic Festivals of Athens.* 2nd ed. revised by John Gould and D. M. Lewis. Oxford, 1968.

——. *The Theatre of Dionysus in Athens.* Oxford, 1946.

REES, KELLEY. *The Rule of Three Actors in the Classical Greek Drama.* Chicago, 1908.

SIFASKIS, G. M. *Studies in the History of Hellenic Drama.* London, 1967.

VITRUVIUS. *Ten Books of Architecture.* Trans. by Morris H. Morgan. New York, 1960.

WEBSTER, T. B. L. *Greek Theatre Production.* 2nd ed. London, 1970.

Chapter 3:   Roman Theatre and Drama

ALLEN, JAMES T. *Stage Antiquities of the Greeks and Romans and Their Influence.* New York, 1927.

ARNOTT, PETER. See under chapter 2.

BEARE, WILLIAM. *The Roman Stage: A Short History of Latin Drama in the Time of the Republic.* 3rd ed. London, 1963.

BIEBER, MARGARETE. See under chapter 2.

BUTLER, JAMES H. See under chapter 2.

DUCKWORTH, GEORGE E. *The Nature of Roman Comedy.* Princeton, N.J., 1952.

FRIEDLANDER, LUDWIG. *Roman Life and Manners Under the Early Empire.* 3 vols. New York, 1910.

HAMILTON, EDITH. *The Roman Way.* New York, 1932.

HANSON, J. A. *Roman Theater-Temples.* Princeton, N.J., 1959.

HARSH, PHILIP W. See under chapter 2.

LUCAS, FRANK L. *Seneca and Elizabethan Tragedy.* Cambridge, 1922.

NICOLL, ALLARDYCE. See under chapter 2.

NORWOOD, GILBERT. *Plautus and Terence.* New York, 1932.

PALLOTTINI, MASSIMO. *The Etruscans.* Revised and enlarged edition. Bloomington, Ind., 1975.

SEGAL, ERICH. *Roman Laughter: The Comedy of Plautus.* Cambridge, Mass., 1968.

VITRUVIUS. See under chapter 2.

Chapter 4: East and West: Cross-Currents of 1000 Years

AND, M. *A History of Theatre and Popular Entertainment in Turkey.* Ankara, 1963.

ARLINGTON, L. C. *The Chinese Drama from the Earliest Times Until Today.* Shanghai, 1930.

BAYNES, N. H., and MOSS, H. eds. *Byzantium; An Introduction to East Roman Civilization.* Oxford, 1948.

BHARATA. *Natyasastra.* Trans. by M. Ghose. Bengal, 1950.

CHAMBERS, E. K. *The Mediaeval Stage.* 2 vols. Oxford, 1903.

CHEN, J. *The Chinese Theatre.* London, 1949.

COLLINS, FLETCHER. *The Production of Medieval Church Music-Drama.* Charlotte, Va., 1971.

DONOVAN, R. B. *Liturgical Drama in Medieval Spain.* Toronto, 1958.

GARGI, BALWANT. *Theatre in India.* New York, 1962.

HARDISON, O. B. *Christian Rite and Christian Drama in the Middle Ages: Essays in the Origin and Early History of Modern Drama.* Baltimore, 1965.

HUNNINGHER, BENJAMIN. See under chapter 1.

KEITH, A. B. *The Sanskrit Drama: Its Origin, Development, Theory and Practice.* Oxford, 1924.

LAPIANA, G. "The Byzantine Theatre." *Speculum,* 11 (1936), 171–211.

LIU, WU-CHI. *An Introduction to Chinese Literature.* Bloomington, Ind., 1966.

NICOLL, ALLARDYCE. See under chapter 2.

SCHUYLER, M. *A Bibliography of the Sanskrit Drama with an Introductory Sketch of the Dramatic Literature of India.* New York, 1906, 1965.

VOGT, A. "Le Théâtre à Byzance et dans l'Empire du IVe au XIIIe Siècle: Le Théâtre Profane." *Révue des Questions Historiques,* 115 (1931), 257–296.

WEINER, ALBERT B. *Phillippe de Mezieres' Description of the "Festum Praesentationis Beatae Mariae." Translated from the Latin and Introduced by an Essay on the Birth of Modern Acting.* New Haven, Conn., 1958.

WINSATT, G. *Chinese Shadow Shows.* Cambridge, Mass., 1936.

YOUNG, KARL. *The Drama of the Medieval Church.* 2 vols. Oxford, 1933.

Chapter 5: Theatre and Drama in the Late Middle Ages

CHAMBERS, E. K. See under Chapter 4.

COHEN, GUSTAVE. *Histoire de la Mise-en-scène dans le Théâtre Religieux Français du Moyen Age.* Paris, 1926.

———. *Le Livre de Conduite Du Régisseur et le Compte des Déspenses pour le Mystère de la Passion, joué a Mons en 1501. . . .* Paris, 1925.

CRAIG, HARDIN. *English Religious Drama of the Middle Ages.* Oxford, 1960.

CRAIK, THOMAS W. *The Tudor Interlude: Stage, Costume and Acting.* Leicester, 1958.

EVANS, MARSHALL B. *The Passion Play of Lucerne.* New York, 1943.

FARNHAM, WILLARD. *The Medieval Heritage of Elizabethan Tragedy.* Berkeley, 1936.

FRANK, GRACE. *The Medieval French Drama.* Oxford, 1954.

———. *The Medieval Drama.* Oxford, 1960.

GARDINER, HAROLD C. *Mysteries' End: An Investigation of the Last Days of the Medieval Religious Stage.* New Haven, Conn., 1946.

KOLVE, V. A. *The Play Called Corpus Christi.* Stanford, Calif., 1966.

NELSON, ALAN H. *The Medieval Pageants and Plays.* Chicago, 1974.

NICOLL, ALLARDYCE. See under Chapter 2.

POTTER, ROBERT A. *The English Morality Play: Origins, History and Influence of a Dramatic Tradition.* London, 1975.

SALTER, F. M. *Medieval Drama in Chester.* Toronto, 1955.

SHERGOLD, N. D. *A History of the Spanish Stage from Medieval Times until the End of the 17th Century.* Oxford, 1967.

SHOEMAKER, WILLIAM H. *The Multiple Stage in Spain during the Fifteenth and Sixteenth Centuries.* Princeton, N.J., 1935.

SOUTHERN, RICHARD. *The Medieval Theatre in the Round.* London, 1957.

STRATMAN, CARL J. *Bibliography of Medieval Drama.* Berkeley, 1954.

STUART, D. C. *Stage Decoration in France in the Middle Ages.* New York, 1910.

SUMBERG, S. *The Nuremberg Schembart Carnival.* New York, 1941.

WICKHAM, GLYNNE. *Early English Stages, 1300–1660.* 2 vols. New York, 1959–1972.

———. *The Medieval Theatre.* London, 1974.

WILLIAMS, ARNOLD. *The Drama of Medieval England.* East Lansing, Mich., 1961.

WOOLF, ROSEMARY. *The English Mystery Plays.* Berkeley, 1972.

Chapter 6:   The Italian Renaissance

BJURSTROM, PER. *Giacomo Torelli and Baroque Stage Design.* Stockholm, 1961.

BURCKHARDT, JAKOB C. *The Civilization of the Renaissance in Italy.* 3rd ed. New York, 1950.

CAMPBELL, LILY BESS. *Scenes and Machines on the English Stage during the Renaissance.* Cambridge, 1923.

DUCHARTRE, PIERRE L. *The Italian Comedy: The Improvisation, Scenarios, Lives, Attributes, Portraits and Masks of the Illustrious Characters of the Commedia dell' Arte.* Trans. by R. T. Weaver. London, 1929.

HATHAWAY, BAXTER. *The Age of Criticism: The Late Renaissance in Italy.* Ithaca, New York, 1962.

HERRICK, MARVIN. *Italian Comedy in the Renaissance.* Urbana, Ill., 1960.

———. *Italian Tragedy in the Renaissance.* Urbana, Ill., 1965.

———. *Tragicomedy: Its Origin and Development in Italy, France, and England.* Urbana, Ill., 1955.

HEWITT, BARNARD, ed. *The Renaissance Stage: Documents of Serlio, Sabbattini, and Furttenbach.* Coral Gables, Fla., 1958.

KENNARD, JOSEPH S. *The Italian Theatre.* 2 vols. New York, 1932.

KERNODLE, GEORGE. *From Art to Theatre: Form and Convention in the Renaissance.* Chicago, 1943.

LEA, KATHLEEN M. *Italian Popular Comedy: A Study of the Commedia dell' Arte, 1560–1620.* 2 vols. Oxford, 1934.

MULLIN, DANIEL C. *The Development of the Playhouse: A Survey of Architecture from the Renaissance to the Present.* Berkeley, 1970.

NAGLER, ALOIS M. *Theatre Festivals of the Medici, 1539–1637.* New Haven, Conn., 1968.

NICOLL, ALLARDYCE. See under chapter 2.

———. *Stuart Masques and the Renaissance Stage.* London, 1937.

OREGLIA, G. *The Commedia dell'Arte.* New York, 1968.

SCHWARTZ, ISIDORE A. *The Commedia dell' Arte and Its Influence on French Comedy in the Seventeenth Century.* Paris, 1933.

SMITH, WINIFRED. *The Commedia dell' Arte.* New York, 1912.

SPRINGARN, JOEL E. *A History of Literary Criticism in the Renaissance.* 2nd ed. New York, 1908.

STRONG, ROY. *Splendor at Court.* Boston, 1973.

SYMONDS, JOHN A. *The Renaissance in Italy.* 7 vols. London, 1909–1937.

VASARI, GIORGIO. *Vasari's Lives of the Artists.* Paris, 1927.

VITRUVIUS. See under Chapter 2.

WEINBERG, BERNARD. *A History of Literary Criticism in the Italian Renaissance.* 2 vols. Chicago, 1961.

WHITE, JOHN. *The Birth and Rebirth of Pictorial Space.* London, 1957.

WORSTHORNE, S. T. *Venetian Opera in the 17th Century.* Oxford, 1954.

Chapter 7:   The English Theatre from the Middle Ages to 1642

ADAMS, JOHN C. *The Globe Playhouse: Its Design and Equipment.* 2nd ed. New York, 1961.

ADAMS, JOSEPH Q. *Shakespearean Playhouses: A History of English Theatres from the Beginnings to the Restoration.* Boston, 1917.

BALDWIN, T. W. *The Organization and Personnel of the Shakespearean Company.* Princeton, N.J., 1927.

BECKERMAN, BERNARD. *Shakespeare at the Globe, 1599–1609.* New York, 1962.

BENTLEY, GERALD E. *The Jacobean and Caroline Stage.* 5 vols. Oxford, 1941–1956.

———. *The Profession of Dramatist in Shakespeare's Time, 1590–1642.* Princeton, N.J., 1971.

———. *Shakespeare: A Biographical Handbook.* New Haven, Conn., 1961.

BOAS, FREDERICK S. *An Introduction to Stuart Drama.* London, 1946.

———. *University Drama in the Tudor Age.* Oxford, 1914.

BROOKE, C. F. T. *The Tudor Drama: A History of English National Drama to the Retirement of Shakespeare.* Boston, 1911.

CAMPBELL, LILY BESS. See under chapter 6.

CHAMBERS, E. K. *The Elizabethan Stage.* 4 vols. London, 1923.

———. *A Short Life of Shakespeare.* Oxford, 1933.

DEBANK, CECILE. *Shakespearean Stage Production: Then and Now.* New York, 1953.

EBISCH, WALTHER and SCHUCKING, L. L. *A Shakespeare Bibliography.* Oxford, 1931. Supplement, 1935.

ELLIS-FERMOR, UNA. *The Jacobean Drama: An Interpretation.* 3rd ed. London, 1953.

GALLOWAY, DAVID, ed. *The Elizabethan Theatre.* Hamden, Conn., 1973.

GILDERSLEEVE, VIRGINIA. *Government Regulation of the Elizabethan Drama.* New York, 1908.

GURR, ANDREW. *The Shakespearean Stage, 1574–1642.* Cambridge, Eng., 1970.

HARBAGE, ALFRED. *Shakespeare's Audience.* New York, 1958.

HARRISON, GEORGE B. *Shakespeare's Tragedies.* London, 1951.

HODGES, C. W. *The Globe Restored.* 2nd ed. London, 1968.

———. *Shakespeare's Second Globe.* London, 1973.

HOTSON, LESLIE. *Shakespeare's Wooden O.* New York, 1960.

JOSEPH, BERTRAM. *Elizabethan Acting.* 2nd ed. London, 1962.

KING, T. J. *Shakespearean Staging, 1599–1642.* Cambridge, Mass., 1971.

LAWRENCE, W. J. *The Elizabethan Playhouse and Other Studies.* 2 vols. Stratford-on-Avon, 1912–1913.

———. *Pre-Restoration Stage Studies.* Cambridge, Mass., 1927.

NAGLER, A. M. *Shakespeare's Stage.* New Haven, Conn., 1958.

NICOLL, ALLARDYCE. See under chapter 6.

ORGEL, STEPHEN. *The Illusion of Power: Political Theatre in the English Renaissance.* Berkeley, 1975.

ORGEL, STEPHEN, and STRONG, ROY. *The Theatre of the Stuart Court; Including the Complete Designs . . . Together with Their Texts and Historical Documentation.* 2 vols. Berkeley, Cal., 1973.

PARROTT, THOMAS M. *Shakespearean Comedy.* New York, 1949.

———. and BALL, ROBERT H. *A Short View of Elizabethan Drama.* New York, 1958.

RALLI, A. J. *A History of Shakespearean Criticism.* 2 vols. London, 1932.

REYNOLDS, GEORGE F. *The Staging of Elizabethan Plays at the Red Bull Theatre, 1605–1625.* New York, 1940.

RIBNER, IRVING. *Jacobean Tragedy: The Quest for Moral Order.* New York, 1962.

ROSE, WILLIAM. *Shakespeare and the Craft of Tragedy.* Cambridge, Mass., 1960.

ROSSITER, A. P. *English Drama from Early Times to the Elizabethans: Its Background, Origins, and Developments.* New York, 1950.

"Shakespeare: An Annotated Bibliography." *Shakespeare Quarterly* (1924–present). [*SQ* was originally called *The Shakespeare Association Bulletin.*] Annual bibliography of writings about Shakespeare.

Shakespeare Survey: An Annual Survey of Shakespearean Study and Production. Cambridge, 1948–present.

SMITH, IRWIN. *Shakespeare's Blackfriars Playhouse: Its History and Its Design.* New York, 1964.

SOUTHERN, RICHARD. *The Staging of Plays Before Shakespeare.* New York, 1973.

SPRAGUE, A. C. *Shakespearean Players and Performances.* Cambridge, Mass., 1953.

STRONG, ROY. See under Chapter 6.

WELSFORD, ENID. *The Court Masque.* Cambridge, 1927.

WICKHAM, GLYNNE. See under chapter 5.

Chapter 8:   *The Spanish Theater to 1700*

BRENAN, GERALD. *The Literature of the Spanish People.* 2nd ed. New York, 1953.

CRAWFORD, J. P. W. *Spanish Drama before Lope de Vega.* Rev. ed. Philadephia, 1937.

RENNERT, HUGO A. *The Life of Lope de Vega.* Philadelphia, 1904.

———. *The Spanish Stage in the Time of Lope de Vega.* New York, 1909.

SHERGOLD, N. D. See under chapter 5.

SHOEMAKER, WILLIAM H. See under chapter 5.

WILLIAMS, RONALD B. *The Staging of Plays in the Spanish Peninsula Prior to 1555.* Iowa City, 1935.

WILSON, MARGARET. *Spanish Drama of the Golden Age.* New York, 1969.

Chapter 9:   *The Theatre in France, 1500–1700*

BJURSTROM, PER. See under chapter 6.

DEÏERKAUF-HOLSBOER, WILMA. *Histoire de la Mise-en-scène dans le Théâtre Français de 1600 à 1657.* Paris, 1933.

HUBERT, JUDD D. *Molière and the Comedy of Intellect.* Berkeley, 1962.

JACQUOT, J., ed. *Les Fêtes de la Renaissance.* 2 vols. Paris, 1956–1960.

———. *Le Lieu Théâtral à la Renaissance.* Paris, 1964.

JEFFERY, B. *French Renaissance Comedy, 1552–1630.* Oxford, 1969.

LANCASTER, H. C. *A History of French Dramatic Literature in the Seventeenth Century,* 5 vols. in 9. Baltimore, 1929–1942.

LAWRENSON, T. E. *The French Stage in the XVIIth Century: A Study in the Advent of the Italian Order.* Manchester, 1957.

LOCKERT, LACY. *Studies in French Classical Tragedy.* Nashville, 1958.

LOUGH, JOHN. *Paris Theatre Audiences in the Seventeenth and Eighteenth Centuries.* London, 1957.

MAHELOT, LAURENT. *La Memoire de Mahelot, Laurent et d'autres Décorateurs de l'Hôtel de Bourgogne et de la Comédie Française au XVIIe siècle.* Edited by H. C. Lancaster. Paris, 1920.

McGOWAN, M. *L'Art du Ballet de Cour en France.* Paris, 1963.

PALMER, JOHN. *Molière.* New York, 1930.

STRONG, ROY. See under Chapter 6.

TILLEY, A. A. *Molière.* Cambridge, 1936.

TURNELL, MARTIN. *The Classical Moment: Studies in Corneille, Molière, and Racine.* New York, 1948.

VINAVER, EUGENE. *Racine and Poetic Tragedy.* Trans. by P. M. Jones. Manchester, 1955.

WILEY, W. L. *The Early Public Theatre in France.* Cambridge, Mass., 1920.

Chapter 10: The Oriental Theatre

The Actor's Analects, edited, translated and with an Introduction and Notes by Charles J. Dunn and Bunzo Torigoe. Tokyo, 1969.

ALLEY, R. *Peking Opera.* Peking, 1957.

AMBROSE, K. *Classical Dances and Costumes of India.* London, 1950.

ANAND, M. R. *The Indian Theatre.* London, 1950.

ANDO, TSURUO. *Bunraku, the Puppet Theatre.* New York, 1970.

ARAKI, J. T. *The Ballad-Drama of Medieval Japan.* Berkeley, 1964.

ARLINGTON, LEWIS C. See under Chapter 4.

BOWERS, FAUBION. *Japanese Theatre.* New York, 1952.

BRANDON, J. R. *Theatre in Southeast Asia.* Cambridge, Mass., 1967.

CHEN, J. See under Chapter 4.

ERNST, EARLE. *The Kabuki Theatre.* New York, 1956.

GARGI, BALWANT. See under Chapter 4.

GUPTA, CHANDRA B. *The Indian Theatre.* Benares, 1954.

HAAR, FRANCIS. *Japanese Theatre in Highlight: A Pictorial Commentary.* Tokyo, 1952.

HIRONAGA, SHUZABURO. *Bunraku, Japan's Unique Puppet Theatre.* Tokyo, 1964.

IYER, K. B. *Kathakali: The sacred Dance-Drama of Malabar.* London, 1955.

KAWATAKE, SHIGETOSHI. *An Illustrated History of Japanese Theatre Arts.* Tokyo, 1956.

KEENE, DONALD. *Bunraku: The Art of the Japanese Puppet Theatre.* Tokyo, 1965.

KINCAID, ZOE. *Kabuki, the Popular Stage of Japan.* London, 1925.

LIU, WU-CHI. See under Chapter 4.

MACKERRAS, COLIN. *The Chinese Theatre in Modern Times.* Amherst, Mass., 1975.

MATHUR, JAGDESH. *Drama in Rural India.* New York, 1964.

MELLEMA, R. L. *Wayang Puppets: Carving, Colouring, Symbolism.* Amsterdam, 1954.

O'NEILL, P. G. *A Guide to Nō.* Tokyo, 1953.

————. *Early Nō Drama; Its Background, Character and Development, 1300–1450.* London, 1958.

POUND, EZRA, and FENOLLOSO, E. *The Classic Noh Theatre of Japan.* New York, 1959.

SAKANISHI, S. *Kyogen.* Boston, 1938.

SCOTT, A. C. *The Classical Theatre of China.* New York, 1957.

————. *The Kabuki Theatre of Japan.* London, 1955.

————. *Theatre in Asia.* New York, 1973.

TOITA, YASUJI. *Kabuki, the Popular Theatre.* New York, 1970.

WALEY, ARTHUR. *The Nō Plays of Japan.* London, 1921.

ZUCKER, ADOLF E. *The Chinese Theatre.* Boston, 1925.

Chapter 11: The English Theatre, 1642–1800

BERNBAUM, ERNEST. *The Drama of Sensibility: A Sketch of the History of Sentimental Comedy and Domestic Tragedy, 1696–1780.* Cambridge, Mass., 1915.

BOAS, FREDERICK. *An Introduction to Eighteenth Century Drama, 1700–1780.* New York, 1953.

BOOTH, MICHAEL et al. *The Revels History of Drama in English.* Vol. VI, 1750–1880. London, 1975.

BURNIM, KALMIN. *David Garrick, Director.* Pittsburgh, 1961.

CAMPBELL, LILY B. "A History of Costuming on the English Stage between 1660 and 1823." *University of Wisconsin Studies in Language and Literature,* II (1918), 187–223.

CIBBER, COLLEY. *An Apology for the Life of Mr. Colley Cibber.* London, 1740. Reprinted many times.

DOBRÉE, BONAMY. *Restoration Comedy, 1660–1720.* Oxford, 1924.

————. *Restoration Tragedy, 1660–1720.* Oxford, 1929.

DOWNER, ALAN S. "Nature to Advantage Dressed: Eighteenth Century Acting." *PMLA* (1943), 1002–1037.

DUNLAP, WILLIAM. *History of the American Theatre.* New York, 1832.

"English Literature, 1660–1800: A Current Bibliography." *Philological Quarterly* (1926–present). Annual list of publications.

FITZGERALD, PERCY H. *The Sheridans.* 2 vols. London, 1886.

HIGHFILL, PHILIP H., JR., BURNIM, KALMAN, and LANGHANS, EDWARD. *A Biographical Dictionary of Actors, Actresses,*

Musicians, Dancers, Managers, and Other Stage Personnel in London, 1660–1800. Carbondale, Ill., 1973–.

HOTSON, LESLIE. *The Commonwealth and Restoration Stage.* Cambridge, Mass., 1928.

JOSEPH, BERTRAM. *The Tragic Actor.* New York, 1959.

KRUTCH, JOSEPH W. *Comedy and Conscience after the Restoration.* New York, 1949.

LEACROFT, RICHARD. *The Development of the English Playhouse.* Ithaca, N.Y., 1973.

The London Stage, 1660–1800. 11 vols. Carbondale, Ill., 1960–1968.

LYNCH, JAMES J. *Box, Pit and Gallery: Stage and Society in Johnson's London.* Berkeley, 1953.

NICOLL, ALLARDYCE. *History of English Drama, 1660–1900.* 6 vols. London, 1955–1959.

ODELL, G. C. D. *Shakespeare from Betterton to Irving.* 2 vols. New York, 1920.

PALMER, J. L. *The Comedy of Manners.* London, 1913.

PEDICORD, HARRY W. *The Theatrical Public in the Time of Garrick.* New York, 1954.

PRICE, CECIL. *Theatre in the Age of Garrick.* Oxford, 1973.

RANKIN, HUGH F. *The Theater in Colonial Ameria.* Chapel Hill, N.C., 1965.

RICHARDS, K. R., ed. *Essays on the Eighteenth Century English Stage.* London, 1972.

ROSENFELD, SYBIL. *Strolling Players and Drama in the Provinces, 1660–1765.* Cambridge, 1939.

SEILHAMER, GEORGE O. *History of the American Theatre* [1749–1797]. 3 vols. Philadephia, 1888–1891.

SHERBO, A. *English Sentimental Drama.* East Lansing, Mich., 1957.

SOUTHERN, RICHARD. *The Georgian Playhouse.* London, 1948.

———. *Changeable Scenery: Its Origin and Development in the British Theatre.* London, 1952.

SUMMERS, MONTAGUE. *The Playhouse of Pepys.* London, 1935.

———. *The Restoration Theatre.* London, 1934.

THALER, ALWIN. *Shakespeare to Sheridan.* Cambridge, Mass., 1922.

WRIGHT, RICHARDSON. *Revels in Jamaica, 1682–1838.* New York, 1937.

Chapter 12: Italy, France, and Spain in the Eighteenth Century

BAUR-HEINHOLD, M. *Baroque Theater.* New York, 1967.

BJURSTROM, PER. See under chapter 6.

BORGERHOFF, ELBERT. *The Evolution of Liberal Theory and Practice in the French Theatre, 1680–1757.* Princeton, N.J., 1936.

BRENNER, C. D. *The Theatre Italien: Its Repertory, 1716–1793, with a Historical Introduction.* Berkeley, 1961.

COOK, JOHN A. *Neo-Classic Drama in Spain: Theory and Practice.* Dallas, 1959.

GOLDONI, CARLO. *Memoirs of Carlo Goldoni.* Trans. by John Black. New York, 1926.

GOZZI, CARLO. *The Memoirs of Count Carlo Gozzi.* Trans. by J. A. Symonds. 2 vols. London, 1890.

GREEN, FREDERICK C. *Minuet: Critical Survey of French and English Literary Ideas in the 18th Century.* New York, 1935.

HAWKINS, FREDERICK. *The French Stage in the Eighteenth Century.* 2 vols. London, 1888.

JOURDAIN, ELEANOR F. *Dramatic Theory and Practice in France, 1690–1808.* New York, 1921.

KENNARD, JOSEPH S. See under chapter 6.

LANCASTER, H. C. *French Tragedy in the Reign of Louis XVI and the Early Years of the French Revolution, 1774–1792.* Baltimore, 1953.

———. *French Tragedy in the Time of Louis XV and Voltaire, 1715–1774.* Baltimore, 1950.

———. *Sunset: A History of Parisian Drama in the Last Years of Louis XIV, 1701–1715.* Baltimore, 1945.

LOUGH, JOHN. See under chapter 9.

MAYOR, A. H. *The Bibiena Family.* New York, 1945.

———. *Giovanni Battista Piranesi.* New York, 1952.

MELCHER, EDITH. *Stage Realism in France Between Diderot and Antoine.* Bryn Mawr, Pa., 1928.

SCHOLZ, JANOS. *Baroque and Romantic Stage Design.* New York, 1950.

Theatrical Designs from the Baroque through Neo-Classicism. 3 vols. New York, 1940.

VIALE FERRERO, MERCEDES. *La Scenografia del '700 e i Fratelli Galliari.* Turin, 1963.

Chapter 13: Theatre in Northern and Eastern Europe During the Eighteenth Century

AIKIN-SNEATH, BETSY. *Comedy in Germany in the First Half of the 18th Century.* Oxford, 1936.

BAUER-HEINHOLD, M. See under chapter 10.

BEIJER, AGNE. *Court Theatres of Drottningholm and Gripsholm.* Trans. by G. L. Frolich. Malmo, 1944.

BREDSDORFF, ELIAS, et al. *An Introduction to Scandinavian Literature from the Earliest Time to Our Day.* Copenhagen, 1951.

BRUFORD, WALTER H. *Culture and Society in Classical Weimar, 1775–1806.* Cambridge, 1962.

———. *Germany in the Eighteenth Century: The Social Background of the Literary Revival.* Cambridge, 1935.

———. *Theatre, Drama and Audience in Goethe's Germany.* London, 1957.

GREGOR, JOSEPH. *The Russian Theatre.* London, 1930.

HEITNER, R. R. *German Tragedy in the Age of Enlightenment, 1724–1768.* Berkeley, 1963.

HILLESTROM, G. *Theatre and Ballet in Sweden.* Stockholm, 1953.

PASCAL, ROY. *The German Sturm und Drang.* Manchester, 1953.

PEACOCK, RONALD. *Goethe's Major Plays: An Essay.* New York, 1959.

PRUDHOE, JOHN. *The Theatre of Goethe and Schiller.* Oxford, 1973.

ROBERTSON, J. G. *The Life and Work of Goethe, 1749–1832.* London, 1932.

SLONIM, MARC. *Russian Theatre from the Empire to the Soviets.* Cleveland, 1961.

THOMAS, RICHARD R. *The Classical Ideal in German Literature, 1755–1805.* Cambridge, 1939.

VARNEKE, B. V. *History of the Russian Theatre: Seventeenth through Nineteenth Century.* Trans. by Boris Brasol. New York, 1951.

WILLOUGHBY, LEONARD A. *The Classical Age of German Literature, 1749–1832.* London, 1926.

Chapter 14: Theatre in Europe and America During the Early Nineteenth Century

ABRAMS, M. H. *The Mirror and the Lamp: Romantic Theory and the Critical Tradition.* New York, 1953.

ALLÉVY, MARIE ANTOINETTE. *La Mise-en-scène en France dans la première moitié du dix-neuvième siécle,* Paris, 1938.

APPLETON, WILLIAM W. *Madame Vestris and the London Stage.* New York, 1974.

ARVIN, NEIL E. *Eugène Scribe and the French Theatre, 1815–60.* Cambridge, Mass., 1924.

BOOTH, MICHAEL. *English Melodrama.* London, 1965.

BOOTH, MICHAEL et al. See under chapter 11.

CARLSON, MARVIN. *The French Stage in the Nineteenth Century.* Metuchen, N.J., 1972.

———. *The German Stage in the Nineteenth Century.* Metuchen, N.J., 1972.

———. *The Theatre of the French Revolution.* Ithaca, N.Y., 1966.

CARSON, W. G. B. *The Theatre on the Frontier.* Chicago, 1932.

———. *Managers in Distress.* St. Louis, 1949.

COAD, O. S., and MIMS, EDWIN, JR. *The American Stage* (Vol. XIV of *The Pageant of America*). New Haven, Conn., 1929.

DISHER, MAURICE. *Blood and Thunder: Mid-Victorian Melodrama and Its Origins.* London, 1949.

DOWNER, ALAN S. "Players and the Painted Stage: Nineteenth Century Acting." *PMLA,* 61 (1946), 522–576.

DUNLAP, WILLIAM. See under chapter 11.

GEORGE, A. J. *The Development of French Romanticism.* Syracuse, N.Y., 1955.

GREGOR, JOSEPH. See under chapter 13.

GRIMSTED, DAVID. *Melodrama Unveiled: American Theatre and Culture, 1800–1850.* Chicago, 1968.

HEWITT, BARNARD. *Theatre USA, 1668–1957.* New York, 1959.

HODGE, FRANCIS. *Yankee Theatre.* Austin, Texas, 1964.

JOSEPH, BERTRAM. See under chapter 11.

KAUFFMANN, F. W. *German Dramatists of the Nineteenth Century.* Los Angeles, 1940.

KENNARD, JOSEPH S. See under chapter 6.

KLENZE, CAMILLO VON. *From Goethe to Hauptmann.* New York, 1926.

LACEY, ALEXANDER. *Pixérécourt and the French Romantic Drama.* Toronto, 1928.

LEACROFT, RICHARD. See under chapter 11.

MACREADY, WILLIAM CHARLES. *Macready's Reminiscences.* New York, 1875.

MARSTERSTEIG, M. *Das Deutsches Theater im neunzehnten Jahrhundert.* 2nd ed. Leipzig, 1924.

MATTHEWS, BRANDER, and HUTTON, LAURENCE. *Actors and Actresses of Great Britain and the United States from the Days of David Garrick to the Present Time.* 5 vols. New York, 1886.

MELCHER, EDITH. See under chapter 12.

MOODY, RICHARD. *America Takes the Stage: Romanticism in American Drama and Theatre, 1750–1900.* Bloomington, Ind., 1955.

MOSES, MONTROSE J., and BROWN, JOHN M. *The American Theatre as Seen by Its Critics, 1752–1934.* New York, 1934.

NICOLL, ALLARDYCE. See under chapter 11.

ODELL, G. C. D. *Annals of the New York Stage.* 15 vols. New York, 1927–1949.

———. *Shakespeare from Betterton to Irving.* 2 vols. New York, 1920.

PEERS, E. A. *A History of the Romantic Movement in Spain.* 2 vols. Cambridge, 1940.

PLANCHÉ, J. R. *The Recollections and Reflections of James Robinson Planché.* 2 vols. London, 1872.

POLLAK, GUSTAV. *Franz Grillparzer and the Austrian Drama.* New York, 1907.

QUINN, ARTHUR H. *A History of the American Drama from the Beginning to the Civil War.* 2nd ed. New York, 1943.

ROWELL, GEORGE. *The Victorian Theatre.* 1st ed. Corr. London, 1967.

SAXON, ARTHUR H. *Enter Foot and Horse: A History of Hippodrama in England and France.* New Haven, Conn., 1968.

SHATTUCK, CHARLES H. *Shakespeare on the American Stage; From the Hallams to Edwin Booth.* Washington, 1976.

SLONIM, MARC. See under chapter 13.

SOUTHERN, RICHARD. See under chapter 11.

SPEAIGHT, ROBERT. *Shakespeare on the Stage: An Illustrated History of Shakespearean Performance.* London, 1972.

VARDAC, A. N. *Stage to Screen: Theatrical Method from Garrick to Griffith.* Cambridge, Mass., 1949.

VARNEKE, B. V. See under chapter 13.

WALZEL, OSKAR F. *German Romanticism.* New York, 1932.

WATSON, ERNEST B. *Sheridan to Robertson: A Study of the 19th Century London Stage.* Cambridge, 1926.

WELLEK, RENÉ. *A History of Modern Literary Criticism.* Vol. 2. New Haven, Conn., 1955.

WILLOUGHBY, LEONARD A. *The Romantic Movement in Germany.* New York, 1930.

WILSON, GARFF B. *A History of American Acting.* Bloomington, Ind., 1966.

——. *Three Hundred Years of American Theatre.* Englewood Cliffs, N.J., 1973.

WITOWSKI, GEORG. *The German Drama of the 19th Century.* New York, 1909.

WITTKE, CARL F. *Tambo and Bones: A History of the American Minstrel Stage.* Durham, N.C., 1930.

YOUNG, WILLIAM C. *Documents of American Theatre History: Famous American Playhouses.* 2 vols. Chicago, 1973.

——. *Documents of American Theatre History: Famous Actors and Actresses on the American Stage.* 2 vols. New York, 1975.

Chapter 15: Theatre and Drama in Europe and America During the Late Nineteenth Century

BANCROFT, MARIE EFFIE. *The Bancrofts.* New York, 1909.

BELASCO, DAVID. *Theatre Through Its Stage Door.* New York, 1919.

BERNHEIM, A. L. *The Business of the Theatre.* New York, 1932.

BOOTH, MICHAEL. See under chapter 14.

BOOTH, MICHAEL et al. See under chapter 11.

CARLSON, MARVIN. See under chapter 14.

COAD, O. S., and MIMS, EDWIN, JR. See under chapter 14.

COLE, J. W. *The Life and Theatrical Times of Charles Kean.* London, 1859.

COLEMAN, JOHN. *Memoirs of Samuel Phelps.* London, 1886.

DOWNER, ALAN S. See under chapter 14.

FELHEIM, MARVIN. *The Theatre of Augustin Daly: An Account of the Late Nineteenth Century Stage.* Cambridge, Mass., 1956.

FITZGERALD, PERCY. *The World Behind the Scenes.* London, 1881.

GLASSTONE, VICTOR. *Victorian and Edwardian Theatres.* Cambridge, Mass., 1975.

GREGOR, JOSEPH. See under chapter 13.

GRUBE, MAX. *The Story of the Meiningen.* Trans. by Ann Marie Koller. Coral Gables, Fla., 1963.

HENDERSON, MARY C. *The City and the Theatre: New York Playhouses from Bowling Green to Times Square.* Clifton, N.J., 1973.

HEWITT, BARNARD. See under chapter 14.

HOPKINS, ALBERT A. *Magic: Stage Illusions and Scientific Diversions.* New York, 1897.

IRVING, LAURENCE. *Henry Irving.* New York, 1952.

JOSEPH, BERTRAM. See under chapter 11.

KAUFFMANN, F. W. See under chapter 14.

KENNARD, JOSEPH S. See under chapter 6.

KLENZE, CAMILLO VON. See under chapter 14.

LEACROFT, RICHARD. See under chapter 11.

MAMMEN, EDWARD W. *The Old Stock Company School of Acting.* Boston, 1945.

MARSTERSTEIG, M. See under chapter 14.

MATTHEWS, BRANDER. *French Dramatists of the Nineteenth Century.* 5th ed. New York, 1914.

——. *The Theatres of Paris.* New York, 1880.

——, and HUTTON, LAURENCE. See under chapter 12.

MELCHER, EDITH. See under chapter 12.

MOODY, RICHARD. See under chapter 14.

MOSES, MONTROSE, and BROWN, J. M. See under chapter 14.

MOYNET, GEORGES. *La Machinerie Théâtrale: Trucs et Decors.* Paris, 1893.

MOYNET, JEAN-PIERRE. *French Theatrical Production in the Nineteenth Century (L'Envers du Théâtre).* Trans. and augmented by Allan S. Jackson with M. Glen Wilson. Binghamton, N.Y., 1976.

NICOLL, ALLARDYCE. See under chapter 11.

ODELL, G. C. D. See under chapters 11 and 14.

PLANCHÉ, J. R. See under chapter 14.

QUINN, ARTHUR H. *A History of the American Drama from the Civil War to the Present Day.* 2nd ed. New York, 1949.

ROWELL, GEORGE. See under chapter 14.

SACHS, EDWIN O., and WOODROW, E. A. E. *Modern Opera Houses and Theatres.* 3 vols. London, 1897–1898.

SHATTUCK, CHARLES H. See under chapter 14.

SLONIM, MARC. See under chapter 13.

SOUTHERN, RICHARD. See under chapter 11.

SPEAIGHT, ROBERT. See under chapter 14.

STEIN, JACK M. *Richard Wagner and the Synthesis of the Arts.* Detroit, 1960.

VARDAC, A. N. See under chapter 14.

VARNEKE, B. V. See under chapter 13.

WAGNER, RICHARD. *Opera and Drama.* Trans. by Edwin Evans. London, 1913.

WATSON, ERNEST B. See under chapter 14.

WEINBERG, BERNARD. *French Realism: The Critical Reaction, 1830–1870.* Chicago, 1937.

WELLEK, RENÉ. *A History of Modern Literary Criticism.* Vols. 3–4. New Haven, Conn., 1965.

WILSON, GARFF. See under chapter 14.

WITOWSKI, GEORG. See under chapter 14.

YOUNG, WILLIAM C. See under chapter 14.

Chapter 16: The Beginnings of The Modern European Theatre, 1875–1915

ANTOINE, ANDRÉ. *Memories of the Théâtre Libre.* Trans. by Marvin Carlson. Coral Gables, Fla., 1964.

APPIA, ADOLPHE. *The Work of Living Art and Man Is the Measure of All Things.* Coral Gables, Fla., 1960.

BABLET, DENIS. *Esthétique Générale du Décor de Théâtre de 1870 à 1914.* Paris, 1965.

———. *Edward Gordon Craig.* New York, 1967.

BENTLEY, ERIC. *The Playwright as Thinker: A Study of Drama in Modern Times.* New York, 1946.

BLOCK, HASKELL. *Mallarmé and the Symbolist Drama.* Detroit, 1963.

BOURGEOIS, MAURICE. *J. M. Synge and the Irish Theatre.* New York, 1965.

BRAUN, EDWARD. *Meyerhold on Theatre.* New York, 1969.

BROCKETT, OSCAR G., and FINDLAY, ROBERT R. *Century of Innovation: A History of European and American Theatre and Drama Since 1870.* Englewood Cliffs, N.J., 1973.

BRUSTEIN, ROBERT. *The Theatre of Revolt.* New York, 1964.

BYRNE, DAWSON. *The Story of Ireland's National Theatre: The Abbey.* Dublin, 1929.

CARTER, HUNTLY. *The Theatre of Max Reinhardt.* New York, 1914.

CARTER, LAWSON A. *Zola and the Theatre.* New Haven, Conn., 1963.

CHIARI, JOSEPH. *Symbolism from Poe to Mallarmé.* 2nd ed. New York, 1970.

COLE, TOBY, ed. *Playwrights on Playwriting: The Meaning and Making of Modern Drama from Ibsen to Ionesco.* New York, 1961.

COLE, TOBY, and CHINOY, HELEN K., eds. *Directors on Directing.* Indianapolis, 1963.

CORNELL, KENNETH. *The Symbolist Movement.* New Haven, Conn., 1951.

CRAIG, EDWARD GORDON. *On the Art of the Theatre.* 2nd ed. Boston, 1924.

DAHLSTROM, C. E. W. L. *Strindberg's Dramatic Expressionism.* Vol. VII of University of Michigan Publications, Language and Literature. Ann Arbor, 1930.

FROHMAN, DANIEL, and MACROSSON, I. T. *Charles Frohman, Manager and Man.* New York, 1916.

FUCHS, GEORG. *Revolution in the Theatre.* Trans. by C. C. Kuhn. Ithaca, N.Y., 1959.

FUERST, WALTER R., and HUME, SAMUEL J. *Twentieth Century Stage Decoration.* 2 vols. London, 1928.

GARTEN, H. F. *Modern German Drama.* New York, 1959.

GASSNER, JOHN. *Form and Idea in the Modern Theatre.* New York, 1956.

———. *The Theatre in Our Times: A Survey of the Men, Materials and Movements in the Modern Theatre.* New York, 1954.

GLASSTONE, VICTOR. See under chapter 15.

GORCHAKOV, NIKOLAI A. *The Theatre in Soviet Russia.* Trans. by Edgar Lehman. New York, 1957.

GORELIK, MORDECAI. *New Theatres for Old.* New York, 1940.

JASPER, GERTRUDE. *Adventure in the Theatre: Lugné-Poë and the Théâtre de l'Oeuvre to 1899.* New Brunswick, N.J., 1947.

KOCHNO, BORIS. *Diaghilev and the Ballets Russes.* New York, 1970.

KOHT, HALVDAN. *The Life of Ibsen.* 2 vols. New York, 1931.

LAMM, MARTIN. *August Strindberg.* New York, 1971.

LEHMANN, ANDREW G. *The Symbolist Aesthetic in France, 1885–1895.* Oxford, 1950.

LUMLEY, FREDERICK. *Trends in Twentieth Century Drama: A Survey Since Ibsen and Shaw.* 2nd ed. London, 1960.

MACCARTHY, DESMOND. *The Court Theatre, 1904–07.* London, 1907.

MARKER, LISE-LONE. *David Belasco; Naturalism in the American Theatre.* Princeton, N.J., 1975.

MATLAW, MYRON. *Modern World Drama: An Encyclopedia.* New York, 1972.

MILLER, ANNA IRENE. *The Independent Theatre in Europe, 1887 to the Present.* New York, 1931.

MODERWELL, HIRAM. *The Theatre of Today.* New York, 1914.

NEWMARK, MAXIM. *Otto Brahm: The Man and the Critic.* New York, 1938.

NORTHAM, JOHN. *Ibsen's Dramatic Method: A Study of the Prose Dramas.* London, 1953.

RISCHBEITER, HENNING. *Art and the Stage in the Twentieth Century.* Greenwich, Conn., 1968.

ROOSE-EVANS, JAMES. *Experimental Theatre: From Stanislavsky to Today.* New revised edition. London, 1973.

SAYLER, OLIVER M., ed. *Max Reinhardt and His Theatre.* New York, 1926.

SHATTUCK, ROGER. *The Banquet Years: The Arts in France, 1885–1918.* New York, 1961.

SLONIM, MARC. See under chapter 13.

SPEAIGHT, ROBERT. *William Poel and the Elizabethan Revival.* London, 1954.

STANISLAVSKI, KONSTANTIN. *An Actor Prepares.* Trans. by Elizabeth R. Hapgood. New York, 1936.

———. *Building a Character.* Trans. by E. R. Hapgood. New York, 1949.

———. *My Life in Art.* Trans. by J. J. Robbins. Boston, 1924.

———. *Creating a Role.* Trans. by E. R. Hapgood. New York, 1961.

TAIROV, ALEXANDER. *Notes of a Director.* Trans. by William Kuhlke. Coral Gables, Fla., 1969.

TREWIN, J. C., and KEMP, T. C. *The Shakespeare Festival: A History of the Shakespeare Memorial Theatre.* London, 1953.

VALENCY, MAURICE. *The Flower and the Castle: An Introduction to Modern Drama.* New York, 1963.

VOLBACH, WALTHER. *Adolphe Appia, Prophet of the Modern Theatre.* Middletown, Conn., 1968.

WAXMAN, S. M. *Antoine and the Théâtre Libre.* Cambridge, Mass., 1926.

WELLEK, RENÉ. *A History of Modern Criticism, 1750–1950.* Vols. 3 and 4. New York, 1965.

WILLIAMS, RAYMOND. *Drama from Ibsen to Eliot.* London, 1952.

ZUCKER, A. E. *Ibsen, the Master Builder.* New York, 1929.

Chapter 17: The Theatre in Europe and America Between the Wars

ARTAUD, ANTONIN. *The Theatre and Its Double.* Trans. by Mary C. Richards. New York, 1958.

BALAKIAN, ANNA E. *Surrealism.* New York, 1959.

BENTLEY, ERIC. See under chapter 16.

BISHOP, G. W. *Barry Jackson and the London Theatre.* London, 1933.

BOLESLAVSKY, RICHARD. *Acting: The First Six Lessons.* New York, 1933.

BRADSHAW, MARTHA. *Soviet Theatres, 1917–1941.* New York, 1954.

BRAUN, EDWARD. See under chapter 16.

BRECHT, BERTOLT. *Brecht on Theatre.* Trans. by John Willett. New York, 1964.

BRETON, ANDRÉ. *What Is Surrealism?* London, 1936.

BROCKETT, OSCAR G., and FINDLAY, ROBERT R. See under chapter 16.

BRUSTEIN, ROBERT. See under chapter 16.

CARTER, HUNTLY. *The New Spirit in the European Theatre, 1914–1924.* New York, 1926.

CHEKHOV, MICHAEL. *To the Actor on the Techinque of Acting.* New York, 1953.

CHENEY, SHELDON. *The New Movement in the Theatre.* New York, 1914.

———. *Stage Decoration.* New York, 1928.

CLURMAN, HAROLD. *The Fervent Years: The Story of the Group Theatre in the Thirties.* New York, 1957.

COLE, TOBY. See under chapter 16.

DAVIS, HALLIE FLANAGAN. *Arena.* New York, 1940.

DONOGHUE, DENIS. *The Third Voice: Modern British and American Verse Drama.* Princeton, N.J., 1959.

DOWNER, ALAN S. *Fifty Years of American Drama, 1900–1950.* Chicago, 1951.

ESSLIN, MARTIN. *Brecht: The Man and His Work.* Garden City, N.Y., 1960.

FOWLIE, WALLACE. *Age of Surrealism.* Bloomington, Ind., 1960.

FRANK, WALDO. *The Art of the Vieux-Colombier.* New York, 1918.

FUERST, WALTER R. and HUME, SAMUEL J. See under chapter 16.

GARTEN, H. F. See under chapter 16.

GIELGUD, JOHN. *Early Stages.* New York, 1939.

GORCHAKOV, NIKOLAI. See under chapter 16.

———. *The Vakhtangov School of Stage Art.* Moscow, n.d.

GORELIK, MORDECAI. See under chapter 16.

GREENE, NAOMI. *Antonin Artaud: Poet Without Words.* New York, 1970.

GROPIUS, WALTER, ed. *The Theater of the Bauhaus.* Middletown, Conn., 1961.

GUTHRIE, TYRONE. *A Life in the Theatre.* London, 1960.

HOGAN, ROBERT G. *After the Irish Renaissance.* Minneapolis, 1967.

HOOVER, MARJORIE L. *Meyerhold: The Art of Conscious Theatre.* Amherst, Mass., 1974.

HOUGHTON, NORRIS. *Moscow Rehearsals: An Account of Methods of Production in the Soviet Theatre.* New York, 1936.

ISSACS, EDITH J. R. *The Negro in the American Theatre.* New York, 1947.

KIRBY, MICHAEL. *Futurist Performance.* New York, 1971.

KNAPP, BETTINA. *Louis Jouvet, Man of the Theatre.* New York, 1958.

KNOWLES, DOROTHY. *French Drama of the Interwar Years, 1918–39.* New York, 1967.

KRUTCH, JOSEPH W. *The American Drama Since 1918.* Rev. ed. New York, 1957.

LEY-PISCATOR, MARIA. *The Piscator Experiment.* New York, 1967.

LUMLEY, FREDERICK. See under chapter 16.

MACCLINTOCK, LANDER. *The Age of Pirandello.* Bloomington, Ind., 1951.

MACGOWAN, KENNETH, and JONES, ROBERT E. *Continental Stagecraft.* New York, 1922.

MACKAY, CONSTANCE D. *The Little Theatre in the United States.* New York, 1917.

MARSHALL, NORMAN. *The Other Theatre.* London, 1947.

MATLAW, MYRON. See under chapter 16.

MODERWELL, HIRAM K. *The Theatre of Today.* New York, 1925.

MOUSSINAC, LEON. *The New Movement in the Theatre: A Survey of Recent Developments in Europe and America.* London, 1931.

QUINN, ARTHUR H. See under chapter 15.

RABKIN, GERALD. *Drama and Commitment: Politics in the American Theatre of the Thirties.* Bloomington, Ind., 1964.

RICHTER, HANS. *Dada: Art and Anti-Art.* New York, 1966.

RISCHBEITER, HENNING. See under chapter 16.

ROOSE-EVANS, JAMES. See under chapter 16.

SAINT-DENIS, MICHEL. *The Rediscovery of Style.* New York, 1960.

SAMUEL, RICHARD, and THOMAS, R. H. *Expressionism in German Life, Literature and the Theatre, 1910–1924.* Cambridge, 1939.

SIMONOV, REUBEN. *Stanislavsky's Protegé. Eugene Vakhtangov.* Trans. by Miriam Goldina. New York, 1969.

SLONIM, MARC. See under chapter 13.

SMITH, CECIL. *Musical Comedy in America.* New York, 1950.

SOKEL, WALTER H. *The Writer in Extremis: Expressionism in Twentieth Century German Literature.* Stanford, Calif., 1959.

STANISLAVSKI, KONSTANTIN. See under chapter 16.

SYMONS, JAMES. *Meyerhold's Theatre of the Grotesque: The Post-Revolutionary Productions, 1920–1932.* Coral Gables, Fla., 1971.

TAIROV, ALEXANDER. See under chapter 16.

Theatre Arts. 32 vols. Detroit and New York, 1916–1948.

TREWIN, J. C., and KEMP, T. C. See under chapter 16.

WELLEK, RENÉ. See under chapter 16.

WENGLER, HANS. *Bauhaus.* Cambridge, Mass., 1969.

WILLETT, JOHN. *Expressionism.* New York, 1970.

———. *The Theatre of Bertolt Brecht.* New York, 1959.

WILLIAMS, E. HARCOURT. *Old Vic Saga.* London, 1949.

WILLIAMS, RAYMOND. See under chapter 16.

Chapter 18: Theatre and Drama, 1940–1960

ALLSOP, KENNETH. *The Angry Decade: A Survey of the Cultural Revolt of the 1950s.* London, 1958.

BARRAULT, JEAN-LOUIS, *The Theatre of Jean-Louis Barrault.* Trans. by J. Chiari. New York, 1961.

BENTLEY, ERIC. *In Search of Theatre.* New York, 1953.

BOWERS, FAUBION. *Broadway, USSR: Theatre, Ballet and Entertainment in Russia Today.* New York, 1959.

BRECHT, BERTOLT. See under chapter 17.

BROCKETT, OSCAR G., and FINDLAY, ROBERT R. See under chapter 16.

BROWNE, TERRY. *Playwrights' Theatre: The English Stage Company at the Royal Court.* London, 1975.

BRUSTEIN, ROBERT. See under chapter 16.

CHIARI, JOSEPH. *The Contemporary French Theatre: The Flight from Naturalism.* London, 1958.

COLE, TOBY. See under chapter 16.

DONOGHUE, DENIS. See under chapter 17.

DOWNER, ALAN. *Recent American Drama.* Minneapolis. 1961.

ESSLIN, MARTIN. See under chapter 17.

———. *The Theatre of the Absurd.* Rev. ed. New York, 1969.

FOWLIE, WALLACE. *Dionysus in Paris: A Guide to Contemporary French Theatre.* 1960.

GARTEN, H. F. See under chapter 16.

GASSNER, JOHN. *Directions in Modern Theatre and Drama.* New York, 1965.

———. *Theatre at the Crossroads: Plays and Playwrights of Mid-Century American Stage.* New York, 1960.

GORCHAKOV, NIKOLAI. See under chapter 16.

GROSSVOGEL, DAVID I. *The Self-Conscious Stage in Modern French Drama.* New York, 1958.

GUICHARNAUD, JACQUES. *Modern French Theatre from Giraudoux to Beckett.* New Haven, Conn., 1961.

HAINAUX, RENÉ, ed., *Stage Design Throughout the World Since 1935.* New York, 1956.

———. *Stage Design Throughout the World Since 1950.* New York, 1964.

HOUGHTON, NORRIS. *Return Engagement: A Postscript to "Moscow Rehearsals."* New York, 1962.

KIENZLE, SIEGFRIED. *Modern World Theatre: A Guide to Productions in Europe and the United States Since 1945.* Trans. by A. and F. Henderson. New York, 1970.

KRUTCH, JOSEPH W. See under chapter 17.

LUMLEY, FREDERICK. See under chapter 16.

MATLAW, MYRON. See under chapter 16.

POPKIN, HENRY. *The New British Drama.* New York, 1964.

PRICE, JULIA. *The Off-Broadway Theatre.* New York, 1962.

RISCHBEITER, HENNING. See under chapter 16.

ROOSE-EVANS, JAMES. See under chapter 16.

SAINT-DENIS, MICHEL. See under chapter 17.

SHAW, LEROY R. *The German Theatre Today.* Austin, Texas, 1964.

SLONIM, MARC. See under chapter 13.

STRASBERG, LEE. *Strasberg at the Actors Studio.* New York, 1965.

STYAN, J. L. *The Dark Comedy: The Development of Modern Comic Tragedy.* Cambridge, 1962.

TAYLOR, JOHN R. *Anger and After: A Guide to the New British Drama.* London, 1962.

TREWIN, J. C., and KEMP, T. C. See under chapter 16.

WEALES, GERALD. *American Drama since World War II.* New York, 1962.

WELLWARTH, GEORGE E. *The Theatre of Protest and Paradox: Development in the Avant-Garde Drama.* New York, 1964.

WILLETT, JOHN. See under chapter 17.

Chapter 19: Theatre and Drama since 1960

ABRAMSON, DORIS E. *Negro Playwrights in the American Theatre.* New York, 1969.

ADDENBROOKE, DAVID. *The Royal Shakespeare Company: The Peter Hall Years.* London, 1974.

ANSORGE, PETER. *Disrupting the Spectacle: Five Years of Experimental and Fringe Theatre in Britain.* London, 1975.

BINER, PIERRE. *The Living Theatre.* 2nd ed. New York, 1972.

BROCKETT, OSCAR G. *Perspectives on Contemporary Theatre.* Baton Rouge, La., 1971.

————, and FINDLAY, ROBERT R. See under chapter 16.

BROOK, PETER. *The Empty Space.* New York, 1968.

BROWNE, TERRY. See under chapter 18.

BRUSTEIN, ROBERT. *Revolution as Theatre: Notes on the New Radical Style.* New York, 1971.

BURDICK, ELIZABETH B. et al., eds. *Contemporary Stage Design, USA.* Middletown, Conn., 1974.

BURIAN, JARKA. *The Scenography of Joseph Svoboda.* Middletown, Conn., 1971.

COOK, JUDITH. *The National Theatre.* London, 1976.

CROYDEN, MARGARET. *Lunatics, Lovers and Poets: The Contemporary Experimental Theatre.* New York, 1974.

ENGEL, LEHMAN. *The American Musical Theatre.* Rev. ed. New York, 1975.

ESSLIN, MARTIN. See under chapter 18.

————. *The Peopled Wound: The Work of Harold Pinter.* New York, 1970.

GROTOWSKI, JERZY. *Towards a Poor Theatre.* New York, 1968.

HAINAUX, RENÉ. *Stage Design Throughout the World.* New York, 1972.

————. *Stage Design Throughout the World, 1970–1975.* New York, 1976.

HINCHLIFFE, ARNOLD. *British Theatre, 1950–1970.* Totowa, N.J., 1975.

KIENZLE, SIEGFRIED. See under chapter 18.

KIRBY, MICHAEL. *Happenings.* New York, 1966.

KOSTELANETZ, RICHARD. *The Theatre of Mixed Means.* New York, 1968.

LESNICK, HENRY, ed. *Guerrilla Street Theatre.* New York, 1973.

LITTLE, STUART. *Enter Joseph Papp: In Search of a New American Theatre.* New York, 1974.

MAROWITZ, CHARLES, and TRUSSLER, SIMON. *Theatre at Work: Playwrights and Productions in the Modern British Theatre.* New York, 1968.

MATLAW, MYRON. See under chapter 16.

MITCHELL, LOFTEN. *Black Drama.* New York, 1967.

NEFF, RENFREU. *The Living Theatre USA.* Indianapolis, 1970.

NOVICK, JULIUS. *Beyond Broadway.* New York, 1968.

O'CONNOR, GARRY. *French Theatre Today.* London, 1975.

ORENSTEIN, GLORIA. *The Theatre of the Marvelous; Surrealism and the Contemporary Stage.* New York, 1976.

PASOLLI, ROBERT. *A Book on the Open Theatre.* New York, 1970.

PATTERSON, MICHAEL. *German Theatre Today.* London, 1976.

POGGI, JACK. *Theatre in America: The Impact of Economic Forces, 1870–1967.* Ithaca, N.Y., 1968.

RISCHBEITER, HENNING. See under chapter 16.

ROOSE-EVANS, JAMES. See under chapter 16.

SAINER, ARTHUR. *The Radical Theatre Notebook.* New York, 1975.

SCHECHNER, RICHARD. *Environmental Theatre.* New York, 1973.

————. *Public Domain: Essays on the Theatre.* Indianapolis, 1969.

SCHEVILL, JAMES. *Breakout! In Search of New Theatrical Environments.* Chicago, 1972.

TAYLOR, JOHN RUSSELL. *The Angry Theatre.* London, 1969.

————. *Second Wave: British Dramatists for the Seventies.* New York, 1971.

TAYLOR, KAREN M. *People's Street Theatre in Amerika.* New York, 1973.

TEMKINE, RAYMOND. *Grotowski.* New York, 1972.

TREWIN. J. C. *Peter Brook.* London, 1971.

WEALES, GERALD. *The Jumping Off Place: American Drama in the 1960s.* New York, 1969.

ZIEGLER, JOSEPH. *Regional Theatre: The Revolutionary Stage.* Minneapolis, 1973.

Information about recent developments must still be sought primarily in periodicals and newspapers. Some of the most helpful on the contemporary theatre are:

Alternative Theatre
Arts Reporting Service
Bühnentechnische Rundschau
Comparative Drama
Drama Survey
Educational Theatre Journal
Modern Drama
Modern International Drama
The New York Times
Performance
Plays and Players
The Drama Review (TDR)

Theater der Zeit
Theater Heute
Theatre Crafts
Theatre Design and Technology
Theatre in Poland
Theatre Quarterly
Theatrefacts
Travail Théâtral
Variety
The Village Voice
Westscene

Many of the periodicals listed above also publish articles about the theatre of the past. To these should be added:

Dance Perspectives
Nineteenth Century Theatre Research
Restoration and 18th Century Theatre Research
Revue d'Histoire du Théâtre

Shakespeare Quarterly
Theatre Notebook
Theatre Research International
Theatre Survey

Numerous other periodicals publish some articles on theatre history, though not as their primary concern. The list is too long to include here. Assistance in finding appropriate sources is available from the periodical or reference librarians in any major library.

INDEX

561,590

TM